The American Revolution in Drawings and Prints

The American Revolution

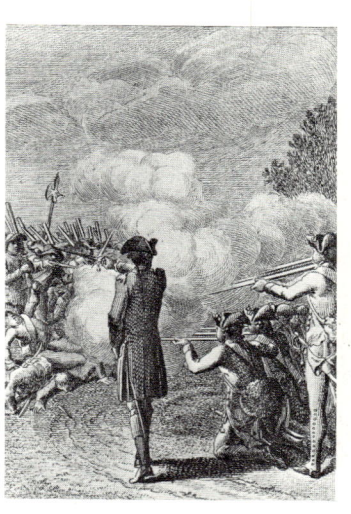
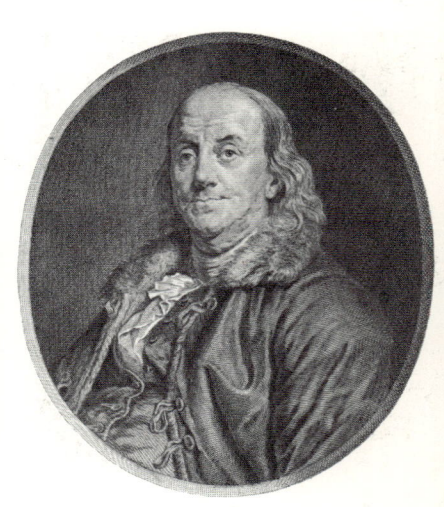

in Drawings and Prints

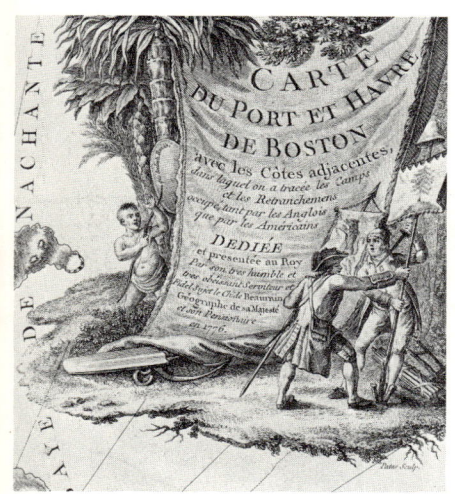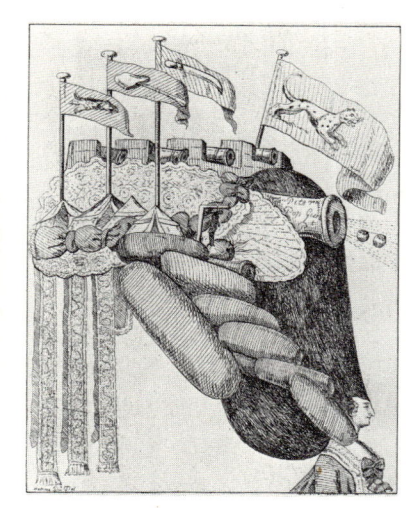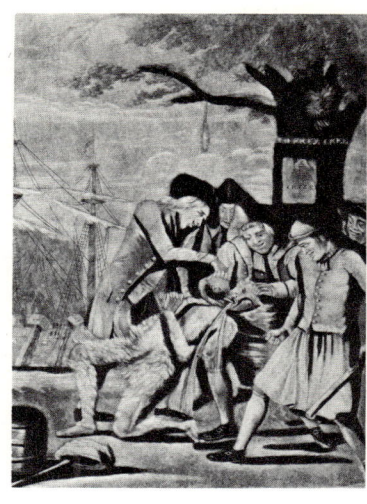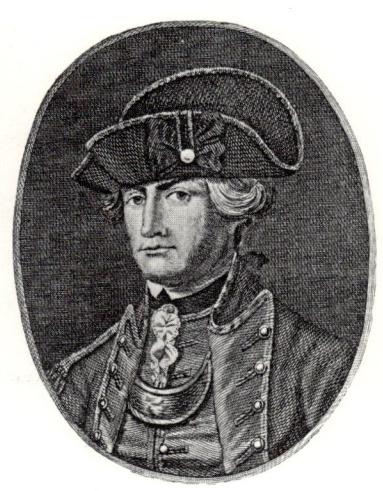

A Checklist of 1765-1790 Graphics in the Library of Congress

COMPILED BY Donald H. Cresswell WITH A FOREWORD BY Sinclair H. Hitchings

LIBRARY OF CONGRESS   WASHINGTON   1975

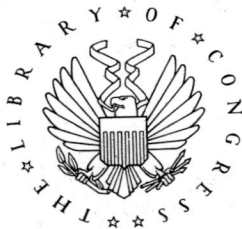

Library of Congress Cataloging in Publication Data

United States. Library of Congress.
   The American Revolution in drawings & prints.

   Bibliography: p. 000
   1. United States—History—Revolution—Pictorial works—Catalogs. 2. United States. Library of Congress. I. Cresswell, Donald H. II. Title.
E209.U54 1974 769'.4'99733 73-17405
ISBN 0-8444-0102-1

For sale by the Superintendent of Documents
U.S. Government Printing Office
Washington, D.C. 20402 - Price $14.35
Stock Number 3001-0050

Foreword

LOOKING BACK from the 20th century across 200 years to the American Revolution, a present-day student of history might see the struggle as a leisurely, spread-out, episodic affair. By the measurements of our congested age, the numbers of people engaged were small. The speed of events was the pace of ships sailing, men marching, a day's journey by a troop of cavalry. The pictorial record of the Revolution, as seen by all of us who live in the midst of photojournalism, halftone reproductions, and high-speed presses, producing a flood of images, seems meager.

Largely unknown, however, in the impatient age of the television producer and moviemaker, is a surprisingly extensive record in pictures. Scholars have worked on it persistently and with growing knowledge, ever since the centennial celebrations of 1876. In the realm of the scholar, however, rather than the reading and viewing public, it still largely remains. The maps and political caricatures which make up a large part of the record often must be reproduced in detail, rather than in the whole, and with accompanying analysis and explanation, to be made comprehensible to a modern viewer. Our historians and publishers, for the most part, have backed away from a task which is costly in both time and money.

Still, the maps and the caricatures exist as part of our pictorial legacy, and in addition there are a wealth of portraits (often of the great, seldom of the humble), a surprising number of reportorial views of places and events, a visual literature of allegories, emblems, and symbols, and an intriguing quantity of alleged representations drawn largely from imagination.

The scattering of fictitious renderings in the present book, though they are not always identified as such, can usually be easily recognized. When an Augsburg engraver, lacking accurate source material and knowing his audience's ignorance of faraway places, used familiar European architecture to create a scene labeled New York or Salem or Boston, he produced a picture European in concept and wondrously Baroque in detail to observers in our century. Lacking likenesses, English and European publishers on occasion were quite satisfied with imaginary portraits, too. *Commodore Hopkins* (Item 114) is not a factual portrait of Esek Hopkins, but the mezzotint does belong in the realm of the emblematic. (Many more of these pictures cross the boundaries of any categories which could be devised.) As a patriotic image and a piece of pro-American propaganda, the Commodore is spirited and appealing. One of the flags in the background shows a liberty tree, the other a rattlesnake with the words "Dont tread upon me." Hopkins at the time was 58, but the portrait shows a younger man, a dashing figure in his cocked hat and uniform.

The elements of symbolism and myth are important in a number of the portraits. A few people in every age become popular symbols. No man was more fully taken into the mind of humanity in this way than Benjamin Franklin, as a symbol of the culture which had developed in England's North American Colonies. His homely likeness, his scientific achievements, his simplicity, worldliness, industry, and charitable nature were known throughout Europe. As a symbol of common sense, practicality, inventiveness, and down-to-earth accomplishment, he also symbolized the aspirations of Americans.

The symbol of America most commonly found in these pages, however, in portraits, political caricatures, and the cartouches of maps, is the Indian. Mr. Cresswell's book could be the jumping-off place for a number of others, including a study of the Indians of North America as depicted occasionally by Americans and frequently by Europeans in the 18th century. The books which bring us the work of 19th-century painters and photographers of the American Indian have multiplied, making the record of the previous century seem neglected by comparison.

There are many ways to look at the pictorial legacy which has come down to us from the years of revolution in North America. Along with the pictures which symbolize, propagandize, and satirize, there are occasional genre or storytelling pictures and a great many others which express the natural desire to show people, places, and happenings as they really were. In portraiture, that Philadelphian-by-adoption, Pierre Eugene Du Simitière, put us deeply in his debt by drawing what seems to me to be a wholly convincing series of portraits from the Revolutionary years. They were engraved by Prévost in Paris and were copied in London. In retrospect we might wish that he had done many more, as St. Mémin was to do with equal care and conviction at the end of the century.

Mr. Cresswell's job has been like that of an archeologist patiently assembling a mosaic. He has gone from department to department in the far reaches of the Library of Congress in search of the pictures captured and exhibited in these pages. Multiply his undertaking many fold, substituting the numerous public and private collections here and abroad for the departments of a single great library, and a more accurate idea can be obtained of the pictorial material which is available. The single most important body of pictures which show us the war and its settings are the drawings (many maps, surprising numbers of topographical views, and not a few scenes of military movements and actions) by British and French Army and Navy personnel. Many of these men were military engineers, and most of them were officers. Often we know their work by engravings made when the designs were sent home. Many drawings were never engraved but survive in the original. They are represented here by a few frontline sketches, by many profiles, landscapes, and views engraved as part of Des Barres' supremely accurate and decorative charts in the *Atlantic Neptune* series, and by the designs by Pierre Ozanne, the official artist of the French fleet on duty in American waters in 1778–79. Of the books which could take their departure from the present survey, the most direct and attractive in summoning up the past would be a collection of the original drawings and watercolors by these civilized warriors who found time for their art not only in the line of duty but for their own pleasure as well. Des Barres, Montresor, Ozanne, Holland, Berthier, Davies, Robertson, Nicole, Pierrie, Dupré, Williams, Millar, Page, and many others left a record which today is to be found in the collections of the British Museum, Bibliothèque nationale, Library of Congress, New York Public Library, Clements Library, Huntington Library, and other repositories.

The pictorial record as made by Americans has a special eloquence and frequently the appeal of primitive art, but it is as limited as might be expected of a country in which the graphic arts were not to become an industry until well after 1800. We can be grateful for the artistic sophistication and skill that accompanied foreign military and naval forces to North America and for the very large production of pictures relating to America which came out of the graphic arts centers of London and Paris. However difficult it might be to bring even all the military drawings together, they constitute, for the handful of students who continue to list and survey the holdings of various institutions, a partial answer to the problem of building an authentic pictorial history of the Revolution.

Oil portraits and sculpture, which are part of the total pictorial record, do not appear in the present account of the Library of Congress collection, and maps are used only where they cease to be diagrammatic and show scenes and people in cartouches and inset views. Colonial and Continental currency is also omitted here but is cataloged and reproduced in other publications. It will have a place of interest in any broad survey of emblems of loyalty and liberty, still another of the books which might find its beginning in these pages.

In tiny woodcuts in newspapers, almanacs, and broadsides, on powder horns, in architectural carvings, in flags and coins and medals as well as single-sheet prints, the cartouches of maps, and paper currency, can be found the emblems of the Revolution. A small currency engraving by Paul Revere (Thirty-Six Shillings, December 7, 1775) shows a Continental soldier who holds a sword in one hand and Magna Carta in the other. Above his tricornered hat arch the words "Issued in defence of American Liberty." In Latin, curving from his right hand downward and under his feet, is the Massachusetts motto, which means "By the sword we seek peace, but peace only under liberty." There are surprisingly many such emblems to cheer the patriot after 200 years.

Mr. Cresswell's painstaking compilation is multiplied in value by the decision of the Library of Congress to illustrate it on a generous scale. Both the compiler and the publisher deserve congratulations for creating a pictorial sourcebook of the American Revolution. At best, only a few other volumes can qualify for the same usefulness in opening before us, in pictures, a decisive chapter of our past.

Sinclair H. Hitchings
Keeper of Prints
Boston Public Library

Preface

PICTURES OF THE REVOLUTIONARY PERIOD between 1765 and 1790 represent the immediate record of a major event in world history. Mostly European products from England, France, and Germany, they reflect propagandistic tones and hasty inaccuracies, but they also give a feeling of vital immediacy and show how men saw the Revolution while it was happening. We find few prints made in America during those years because type, steel, lead, paper, presses, and skilled manpower became scarce during the war, and only the most heroic printers continued their productions on a smaller scale.

A veritable flood of pictures concerning America had appeared in Europe during the French and Indian War. The Western World became aware that England had acquired a continent, and the glories of her military conquests in the Americas were celebrated by depicting portraits, cartoons, views, and historical events. When the Stamp Act was decreed in 1765, England's troubles were portrayed in prints that reflected the changing moods as well as the fortunes of a coming war between colonies and mother country. The number and urgency of the prints increased during the war until the defeat of Cornwallis at Yorktown in 1781, when the fighting died and Americans turned to farming and commerce. After 1781 the sources and subjects of the pictures changed. Britain ignored her former colonies due to contempt and a lively series of events elsewhere, and France was disappointed in the new nation for signing a separate treaty. After the Peace of Paris in 1783, attempts at political reform led to the adoption of the United States Constitution in 1789. At the same time the countries of Europe were swept into the French revolutionary whirlwind. With the founding of the new nation this checklist stops because new styles and ideas influenced drawings and prints of America. American engravers celebrated the American system and leaders with romantic portrayals which borrowed heavily from the Roman ideals found in French propagandistic art after 1789. These over-romanticized versions, which began with the stipple and steel engravings of the Federalist period and reached a climax in the extremely patriotic lithographs of the middle and late 19th century, have not been included here.

This checklist results from approximately two years of searching through bibliographies, cases, stacks, and the memories of librarians to uncover contemporary pictures of the American Revolution. An attempt was made to list all original pictures of this period which are in the collections of the Library of Congress. No photostats or restrikes after 1790 have been included, and each item has been inspected in the process of documentation. The list can never be complete because pictures in this category are found everywhere in the Library, and the insurmountable problems of documentation and control in the vast holdings of the Prints and Photographs Division, the Rare Book Division, the Manuscript Division, the Geography and Map Division, the Law Library, the Serial Division, and the general collections render omissions inevitable. The search for fugitive items might continue indefinitely, but time dictates that this book go to press so scholars can use it in connection with the Bicentennial celebration. The book, however, includes almost all the Library's pictorial holdings which are representative of America during the 25-year period.

The pictures are presented in five major divisions: portraits, events, views, cartoons and allegories, and weapons and implements. Each entry lists one picture plus any other "impressions"—pictures from the same plate—and "copies"—the same picture but reengraved. Only impressions and copies made between 1765 and 1790 are included. For each entry six basic pieces of information are supplied: title, artist's name, date, process, size, and annotation.

TITLE. All pertinent written explanation on each picture is exactly transcribed to give a basis for comparison between various prints of the same person or place. The wording is important because a print of "Genl. Washington," even with the same image, differs from one of "Gen. Washington," and a view of "Boston Harbor" differs from one of the "Harbour of Boston." If the entire title is of cumbersome length, part of it will be paraphrased in the annotation. Capitalization in the original title is followed, but no attempt is made to reproduce the various type faces used. Many of the more elaborate prints contain as many as eight different typefaces. Such markings as "Pl. 3" or "Vol. IX," which mean almost nothing when one is examining an isolated print, are noted because these prints were once parts of books, portfolios, or series, and the number can be used for identification of a particular print.

ARTIST AND ENGRAVER. Prints usually include the artist's name on the lower left and the engraver's name on the lower right. This information is transcribed verbatim after the title. When either or both of these are missing on the original, they have been identified, if possible, through reference to sources of information about each picture such as other impressions and copies, books and periodicals where the pictures appeared, artists' records of their works, and other catalogs of drawings and prints. When names or dates are supplied, they appear in brackets with all uncertainties noted.

PROCESS. In describing the mode of production for each picture the terminology from Louis A. Holman's *The Graphic Processes* (Boston, 1929) is used. The seven kinds of processes found in this checklist are: etching, aquatint, mixed method, stipple, line engraving, mezzotint, and woodcut. All aquatints listed are in shades of gray. All colored prints were hand colored after printing, and no attempt has been made to determine how or when they were colored. In many cases, labeling reflects a decision concerning which process predominates in the individual print. For instance, the mezzotint process usually dominates the etched lines which sharpen it, so prints of this kind are labeled "mezzotint." A print which has the freedom of execution derived from using a needle through a ground is designated "etching." Problems arise when, for example, the main lines are etched, the shading comes from stipple, and the border is of the heavy and straight quality of line engraving; then the picture has no predominant process, and it is designated "mixed method." Most of the prints so designated here are a combination of etching and stipple, line engraving and stipple, or all three techniques. Ultimately, many of these differences can be subjective, and it is not uncommon for print scholars to disagree about the process by which a single item was created.

SIZE. The dimensions of each drawing and print are given in inches, height first and width second. The measurements extend from the corners of the platemark unless there is none, as in the case of drawings, woodcuts, and trimmed impressions or when the platemark on a book illustration is sewn into the binding. Prints in these categories are measured from the extremes of the image, and the word "image" appears in parentheses after the measurements.

ANNOTATION. Additional pertinent information is given below the main entry. Essentially the annotation describes who or what appears where. If another checklist or reference book has already described a picture, then the annotation will be briefer, referring the reader to that source. Appendix B, "Secondary Sources Cited in the Text," gives the full bibliographic information on these books. The annotation sometimes explains other writing or marks on a print. It gives the full name or probable identity of some of the engravers or artists and, where pertinent, indicates what other pictures are companions or predecessors to the item examined. In addition, the annotation helps the researcher in the often considerable task of finding the picture within the Library of Congress. Unless otherwise stated, the pictures are in the Prints and Photographs Division. If the source is listed as part of a book, atlas, or special collection, then the picture may be found in the Rare Book Division, Geography and Map Division, Manuscript Division, Serial Division, or the general collections. Full bibliographical citations and locations of book illustrations are given in Appendix A, "List of Books and Atlases Containing Prints and Drawings." Items for which the Library of Congress has a negative include the number, beginning with LC–USZ, at the end of the annotation. Reproductions of these pictures can be ordered from the Library. Some negatives are in the Geography and Map Division in a separate file; they are noted as in G&M.

Each of the five major divisions of this work has a different organizing principle.

PORTRAITS. These are arranged alphabetically by name, and each individual's portraits are listed chronologically by date of imprint. All portraits of Americans which were produced during the Revolution are included because they reflect a personal image of the new nation. However, all the portraits of Europeans who had dealings with America could not be included because the number would be too large and often the connection would be tenuous. Those pictures of Europeans which contain specific pictured or written reference to the

American War and those portraits in books in which the text connects the portrait to the Revolution are included. This policy causes some arbitrary inclusions and unfortunate exclusions, as in a *London Magazine* series of pictures of British leaders, published from 1781 to 1782. The list records portraits of Camden, Thurlow, Macartney, and Hillsborough but excludes Temple and Dundas because their biographies do not mention their connections with America. Selections were also based on degrees of involvement with America. The question of whom to include from the quasi-fictitious "tete-a-tetes" in the *Town and Country Magazine* was determined by how much the story tells about the activity of the person in America. The stories of the American matron (*Town and Country*, August 1786) and the seduced soldier (*Town and Country*, March 1787) involve people who merely touched the shores of America during their lives; they are excluded. Other "tete-a-tetes" render stories of prominent political and military leaders whose private and sometimes secret lives influenced their public actions; they are included.

When examining portraits we must realize that essentially they are honors to a man who is seen as a hero—thus the resemblance of some to Greek and Roman bas-reliefs. These portraits celebrate the immediate heroes of the war, and the reader might be disconcerted to discover no pictures of Thomas Paine, Thomas Jefferson, or Benjamin Rush. On second thought, these absences should not surprise us. Paine, at the time of *Common Sense*, was infamous in England and popular with the Americans, but he was publishing anonymously. No frontispiece portraits of Paine appeared in any of the early editions of *Common Sense* examined. Paine did not become an identified celebrity until 1791, when he answered Burke's *Reflections on the Revolution in France* with *The Rights of Man*—then frontispieces and cartoons both celebrated him and vilified him as an advocate of the American and French Revolutions. To use a post-1790 picture of Paine to show an American Revolutionary hero would distort his image, because these later pictures show a dangerous, atheistic Jacobin and not an idealistic Son of Liberty. Neither Jefferson nor Rush had a public stature equal to Franklin's or Washington's during the war. Such interesting stipple portraits as Tiebout's *Jefferson* or Lemet's *Benjamin Rush* might have been included, but according to Stauffer, Tiebout did not learn stipple until 1794, and Lemet consciously copied St. Mémin, who began engraving in 1793. On the other hand, prints such as Leny's Schuyler and

Doolittle's Ezra Stiles are included because these engravers began working within the period.

Events. The arrangement—by date of the event pictured—separates the works of many of the engravers but provides an internal chronology for the historian. When an event is fictional, it is placed in sequence according to the time it was supposed to have happened; if this approach is impossible, it is placed in the year the picture was printed. Pictures of events are often difficult to distinguish from views of landscapes. If the picture of a battlefield has no activity portrayed, it is listed under views. Conversely, if a picture shows action but is entitled "View of . . .," then it is listed under events.

Views. The order follows a geographical sequence which begins in Canada with the upper part of the Saint Lawrence River and the Great Lakes, moves east to the Atlantic Ocean, and then proceeds south. The sequence of views goes up harbors and rivers and overland so that sometimes the direction will shift considerably, but essentially it is north to south.

    The basic purposes of these views were strategic, journalistic, and esthetic. Those found in *The Atlantic Neptune*, prepared by Des Barres and Company for the British Admiralty, were used by the British forces in America. They are accurate pictures of coasts and harbors. The views by Habermann, Leizalt, Vernet, and others, however, are artists' ideas of the appearance of places where great events were happening. The engravings by Canot and Nicole for Pownall and Montresor took data from strategic surveys and rendered beautiful pictures of the land and life in America. Although some pictures lend themselves more to one appeal than another, we must recognize that a large public was interested in an important war overseas, while a complacent and wealthy class loved to view sublime landscapes of many lands. These prints satiated both cravings.

Cartoons and Allegories. Another public diversion was the political cartoon and the somewhat more serious didactic allegory. These two forms are combined in one section because distinguishing between them is a matter of definition in theory but impossible in practice. Many of the "characters" or "caricatures," as they were interchangeably termed in those days, combined the elements of cartooning and allegory in one print. Often a cartoon satirized an allegory. The figures found in the most devastating cartoons were also seen as serious and ideal figures on the cartouche of a map or the frontispiece of a book.

Many of the allegorical figures such as Mercury or Fame are not unique or new to the American Revolution, but they conveyed a new message in a traditional form. Mapmakers' cartouches were the most conservative form of pictorial reporting; during the war we still find Indians and trees resembling those in the works of John White and Jacques LeMoyne portrayed on maps of New England, and America continued to be personified as the youngest daughter among the continents. Many of the cartouches listed were reprinted throughout the 18th century along with the maps. This trend shows that earlier European images of America survived strongly in those days; thus the scenes were not yet entirely out of character with the places mapped.

The cartoonists, on the other hand, used familiar emblems for their own propagandistic purposes. As the war progressed, America's image as a beautiful, mistaken daughter or a lovely, nude Indian woman was gradually replaced by one as a haggish Medusa figure stabbing Britannia in the back, or a rattlesnake. After the defeat of Cornwallis the cartoonists turned their attention to continental and internal political enemies with a vengeance while almost ignoring America. At the same time, commerce resumed in America, and we find an increase in printing accompanied by a spate of allegories showing America dressed as the goddess Liberty holding a staff with a liberty cap atop and enjoying the bounty of peace.

WEAPONS AND IMPLEMENTS. This book could have shown many pictures from European publications which illustrated weapons and implements used in the American war. Instead, only those weapons pictured in American books or in pictures which directly linked these implements to this one theater are shown.

A word should be added about categories of prints which have been excluded. One might argue that scientific and medical prints show part of a technological revolution that was happening in America. Admittedly, some of the best available workmanship contributed toward keeping Americans abreast of scientific knowledge during the war, but to include technological drawings of air pumps, flowers, beehives, and wheel ratios would portray part of a Newtonian revolution that had occurred in the larger Western World and not a phenomenon particular to America. Full pictures are preferred to diagrams. Thus, although John Norman engraved an interesting series of 27 plates for his edition of Muller's *Treatise of Artillery*, this list presents only the eight of these which show complete pictures of cannons, wagons, and other ordnance, rather than diagrams of parts. Among other forms of excluded technical pictures are diagrams of lines of march and doodles on maps and manuscripts. Another form of picture excluded consists of the many propagandistic illustrations of the French and Indian War in America, such as West's portrayals of Wolfe's death at Quebec and Bouquet's war on the Indians. These were often reprinted during the American Revolution and served to remind people that the British had fought for and won the continent which it was struggling to retain. But these pictures essentially show another war and have only an oblique interest for students of the Revolution.

This checklist contains 921 items. The reader may ask how well the collection at the Library of Congress represents the total contemporary pictorial output of the American Revolution. The answer is not simple, because it requires a comparison with such great depositories as the New York Public Library, the American Antiquarian Society, the British Museum, the Bibliothèque nationale, the Maritime Museum at Greenwich, the Mariner's Museum, the Clements Library, and the British Army Museum at Chelsea. Although the Library of Congress has a very large collection which adds considerably to knowledge of this field, it does lack some types of prints. For instance, the percentage of the known prints done by Americans and printed in America in the Library is not large when compared with those in the American Antiquarian Society, which has specialized in this native art. The Library has fewer foreign prints in French and German than the Bibliothèque nationale. The prints which show the French love of caricature through figures such as animals or allegorical personifications are sparsely represented by this collection. Also, most of the material in the Library of Congress shows the continental borders of the present-day United States of America. The British Museum and the National Maritime Museum contain a vast collection of prints on British heroes and battles in the West Indies, the Mediterranean Sea, the East Indies, and other places that Americans tend to ignore as a part of the Revolution. These shortcomings should not be viewed as errors because no one depository can have everything. Rather, we must realize that nationalistic attitudes have shaped all libraries and museums.

In order to interpret history properly through pictures, large collections such as the one at the Library of Congress must be presented to the professional and amateur historian. Retrieval of these media has been complicated by cataloging systems based on the printed book, but now the Library of Congress shows a small part of its pictorial collection with a surprisingly large number of contemporary drawings and prints of a great event in American history.

ACKNOWLEDGMENTS. Many devoted people at the Library of Congress assisted with this book. The staffs of the Prints and Photographs, Rare Book, Manuscript, and Geography and Map Divisions provided valuable guidance on what to examine in their collections. Research on annotations and editorial assistance were provided by the American Revolution Bicentennial Office and the Publications Office.

Much light was cast on the collection at the Library of Congress through examination of prints and reference materials at other depositories. I wish to thank Paul Hulton, Edward Croft-Murray, Helen Wallis, and Sarah Tyacke of the British Museum; Jean Adhémar, Michel Melot, and Nicole Villa at the Cabinet d'Estampes in the Bibliothèque nationale; Peter Ince, Allen Stimson, and Judy Claget at the Maritime Museum, Greenwich; Boris Mollo of the British Army Museum at Chelsea; John Lochhead and Albert Barnes at the Mariner's Museum; and Elizabeth Roth and Roberta Wong at the New York Public Library. Each of these people and their institutions have added much to this inquiry.

Donald H. Cresswell
Belmont Abbey College

List of Abbreviations

Locations:

　　LC　　Library of Congress
　　P&P　 Prints and Photographs Division
　　G&M　Geography and Map Division
　　RBC　Rare Book Collection

Primary and Secondary Sources; See Appendixes A and B under names of authors except for the following works published by institutions:

　　CPPS see under British Museum
　　LeGear ⎫
　　Phillips　　　⎬ see under U.S. Library of Congress
　　Phillips, *Maps* ⎭
　　Collection de Vinck see under Paris. Bibliothèque nationale

Orders for Reproductions

In the absence of copyright or other restrictions, photocopies may be obtained of illustrations belonging to the Library of Congress. Orders should be addressed to the Library of Congress, Photoduplication Service, Washington, D.C. 20540. A request should give the title or a brief description of the picture, the item number in this book, the location of the original (e.g., in G&M), and the photographic negative number as given in the annotation (e.g., LC–USZ62-19288). None of the color pictures can be reproduced inexpensively in color, but in many cases a black-and-white reproduction can be ordered. All orders must be prepaid; prices are available from the Photoduplication Service.

Contents

Foreword	*v*
Preface	*ix*
List of Abbreviations	*xviii*
Orders for Reproductions	*xviii*

CHAPTER I
PORTRAITS — 3
Portraits of Types — 76

CHAPTER II
EVENTS — 79

CHAPTER III
VIEWS
Saint Lawrence River and Gulf — 129
Maritime Provinces of Canada — 140
New England — 173
Middle Atlantic States — 195
Southern States — 227
The West Indies — 236

CHAPTER IV
CARTOONS AND ALLEGORIES — 239

CHAPTER V
WEAPONS, IMPLEMENTS, AND FORTIFICATIONS — 407

APPENDIX A
Books and Atlases Containing Contemporary Prints and Drawings — 414

APPENDIX B
Secondary Sources Cited in the Text — 421

Index of Titles — 423
Selective Subject Index — 435
Index of Artists — 444
Index of Publishers — 447
Index of Persons — 451

The American Revolution in Drawings and Prints

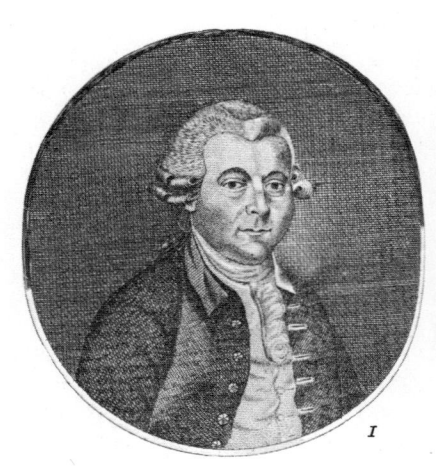

1

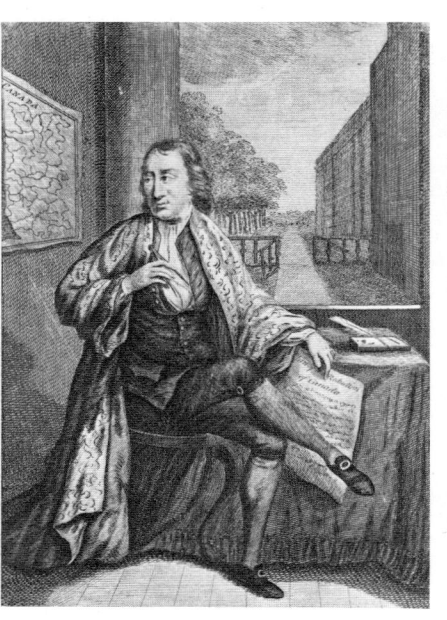

2

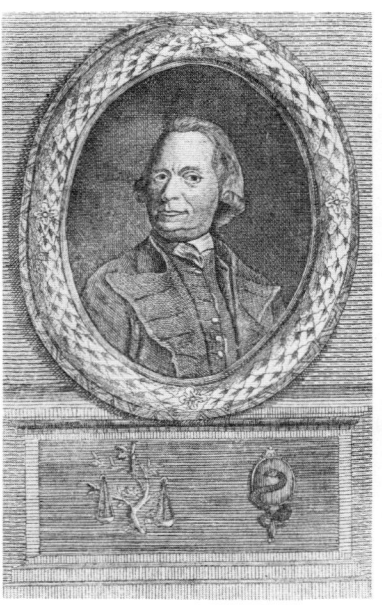

3

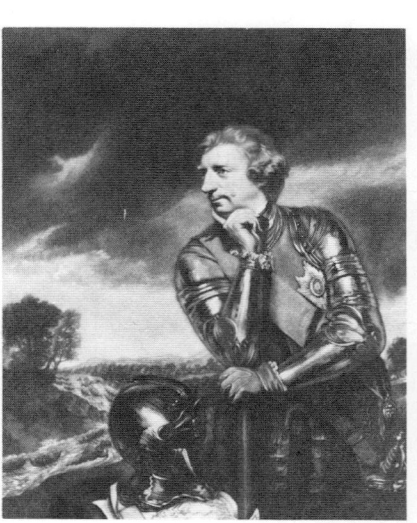

4

Chapter I

Portraits

John Adams, 1735–1826

1

His Excy. JOHN ADAMS, Esq. J. Norman Sc. [1784]
Mixed method 6 x 4 in.

A Massachusetts lawyer and delegate to the Continental Congress, Adams became Commissioner to France in November of 1777. During the war he helped to negotiate loans and treaties between the United States and her allies in Europe, and he joined Franklin and Jay in arranging the separate treaty with England in 1783. This frontispiece to *The Boston Magazine* of 1784 appeared when Adams left France to become the first American Ambassador to England. Stauffer, 2327. LC–USZ62–45280

Samuel Adams, 1722–1803

2

SAMUEL ADAMS Esq. One of the DELEGATES from the Province of MASSACHUSETTS-BAY to the General Continental CONGRESS of NORTH AMERICA. [1780]
Mixed method 6¾ x 4¾ in.

In September 1778, Adams, the foremost propagandist of the Revolution, served on a committee of Congress appointed to draw up a "Plan for Reducing the Province of Quebec." Later that year Congress approved a scheme submitted by this committee, but it was unable to raise the necessary men and supplies. This English portrait, published in *An Impartial History of the War in America* (London, 1780), p. 208, characterizes Adams as a principal formulator of the scheme.

——————Another impression. From *An Impartial History of the War in America* (London & Carlisle, 1780), p. 208. LC–USZ62–45248

3

The Honble. SAMUEL ADAMS, Esqr. First Delegate to Congress for Massachusetts. J. Norman Sc. [1781]
Mixed method 6¾ x 4 in.

The American engraver John Norman idealized Adams by using Copley's portrait for a model rather than the less flattering portrait of a political agitator found in the English edition of the same book. The scale hanging from an olive branch symbolizes justice in peace, and the rattlesnake gazing into a mirror represents Adams' ability to mirror the nature of America in his speeches and writings. The portrait appeared in *An Impartial History of the War in America*, v. 1 (Boston, 1781), copy 2, p. 325. Stauffer, 2328.

——————Another impression in copy 1, v. 1, p. 193. LC–USZ62–45237

Jeffery Amherst, 1717–1797

4

SIR JEFFREY AMHERST. Knight of the most honorable Order of the Bath, Governor of Virginia, Colonel of His Majesty's 15th. and 60th. Regiments of Foot, Lieutenant, and Commander in Chief of His Majesty's Forces in North America from 1758 to 1764. Sold by Ryland and Bryer at the King's Arms in Cornhill. J. Reynolds pinxt. J. Watson fecit. [1766]
Mezzotint 18 x 13 in.

This portrait celebrated Amherst's participation in the conquest of Canada during the Seven Years' War and reminded Englishmen that he, as well as the great hero Wolfe, had risked much to secure the North American continent. Although Amherst resigned his position as absentee Governor of Virginia in 1768 under pressure, he became reconciled to the King and, in his role as Commander in Chief of all British forces, supported the war against the Americans. Amherst, in armor, looks toward a river dotted with boatloads of troops. His helmet rests upon a map of Canada. A seal with chained Indians appears under the finished version of this engraving. Smith, 1488.

——————Another impression. The title and seal, as well as the writing on the map, are absent. The date 1766 appears next to Watson's name. LC–USZ62–45182

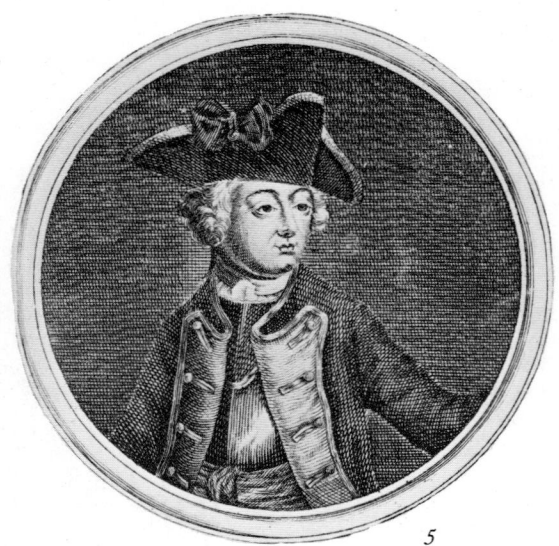
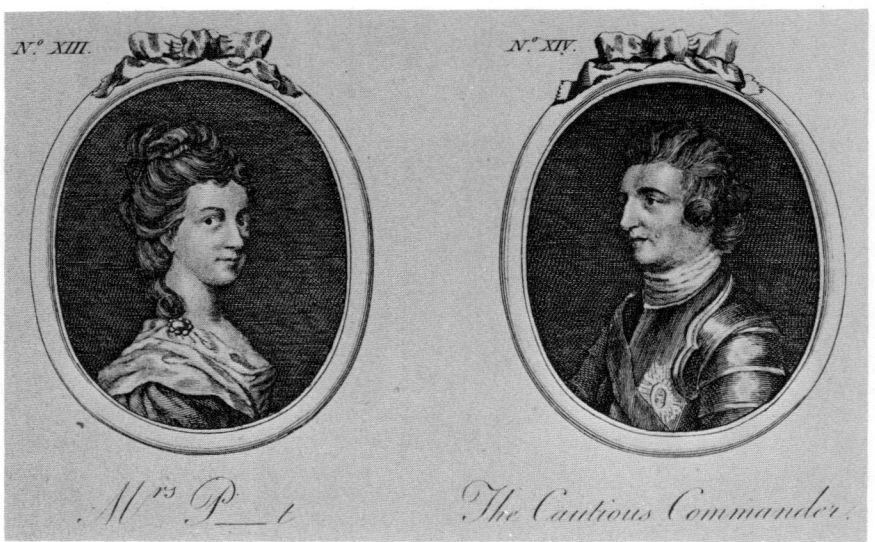

5

Mayjor General AMHERST. [1774]
  Line engraving 4⅛ x 3¾ in.

From *The Annual Register* (Dublin, 1774), p. 98. LC–USZ62–45203

6

Mrs. P_____t [and] The Cautious Commander. Published as the Act directs by A. Hamilton Junr. near St. John's Gate June 1, 1778.
  Mixed method 4¼ x 7 in.

In an accompanying article it is claimed that Lord Amherst obtained the wife of an officer who was on half pay in exchange for an appointment to a command with full pay outside England. The article is not entirely uncomplimentary to Amherst, however, and notes that:

at the breaking out of the present troubles in the Colonies, he was applied to and requested to take the command of the army there; he would willingly have accepted the honour proposed him, if his terms had been complied with; but he was too well acquainted with the country, and the temper and disposition of the inhabitants, to be misled by the erroneous opinions of those in power, who judged that a handful of men would be sufficient to bring the refractory colonists to reason: hence he has derived the title of the Cautious Commander. Had our hero's proposals been approved, most probably the unhappy war that now rages in that quarter of the world, would long since have been quelled, and all the fatal consequences that have ensued been prevented.

The name "Cautious Commander" had actually been applied to Amherst before the American Revolution because he had characteristically acted with precision and care, in contrast to his dashing and impetuous counterpart James Wolfe. As the Revolution became an increasingly unhappy affair for England, Amherst was among the Ministers who were criticized on the ground that they lacked military and diplomatic skills in dealing with the Americans. This simplified copy of Reynolds' popular portrait gives Amherst a youthful look which lends credibility to the personal and political satire of the tête-à-tête, which appeared in *The Town and Country Magazine*, May 1778, p. 233–236. CPPS 5503 LC–USZ62–45208

John André, 1751–1780

7

JOHN ANDRE, Esqr., late Adjutant General of the British Forces in America. [December 1780]

Mixed method 7 x 4¼ in.

Adjutant General to Sir Henry Clinton, André was involved in Benedict Arnold's plot to surrender West Point to the British. Sent behind the American lines to confer with Arnold, he was seized by American militiamen on the return trip, out of uniform and with condemning documents hidden in his boot. A military board convicted him of spying, and he was put to death by hanging. This engraving is from *The Hibernian Magazine*, December 1780, opposite p. 633.
LC–USZ62–45201

8

MAJOR JOHN ANDRE, Late Adjutant General to the British Army in North America. Dodd delin. Cook sculp. [1784]

Etching 10 x 6⅝ in.

André, whose military promise was shown by his rapid promotion and whose character, honor, and manners were praised by his contemporaries, impressed even his American captors. Pictures such as this (see also items 314–316), together with publication of his letters, diary, and sketches, led to a host of adulatory and sentimental ephemera, and he became a popular subject, especially among the ladies, on both sides of the Atlantic. The portrait is from Raymond, *History of England* (London, 1784), p. 591 LC–USZ62–45211

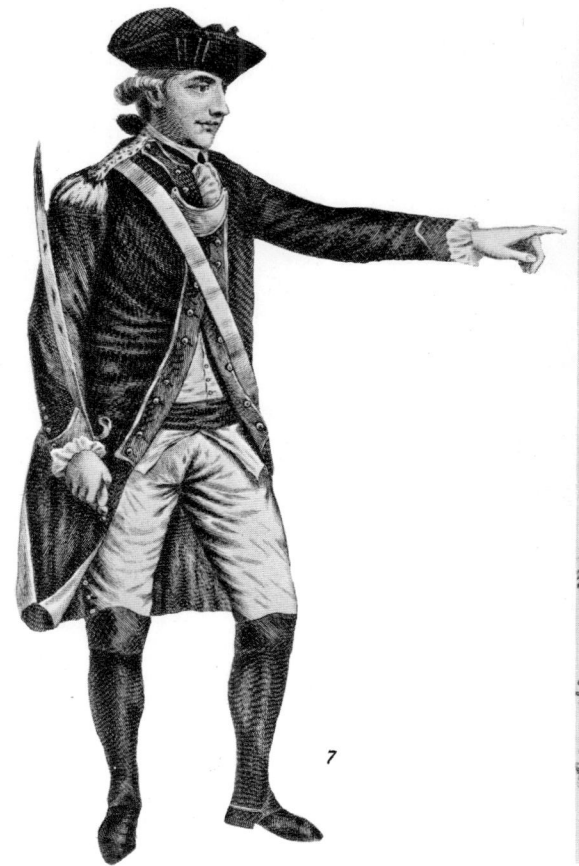

7

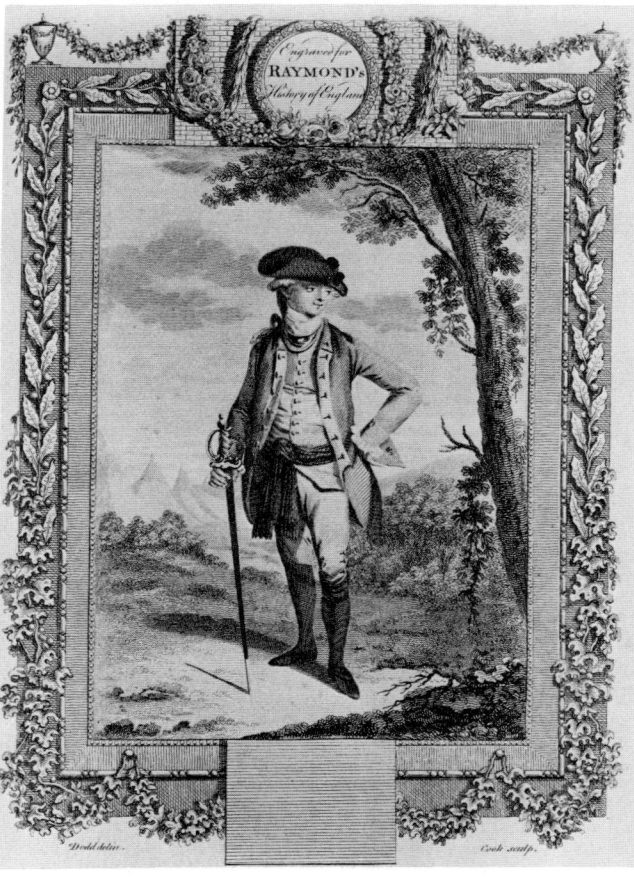

8

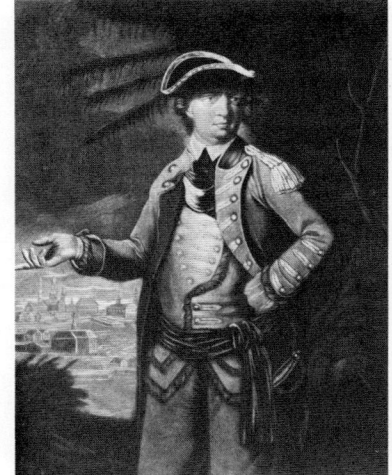

9

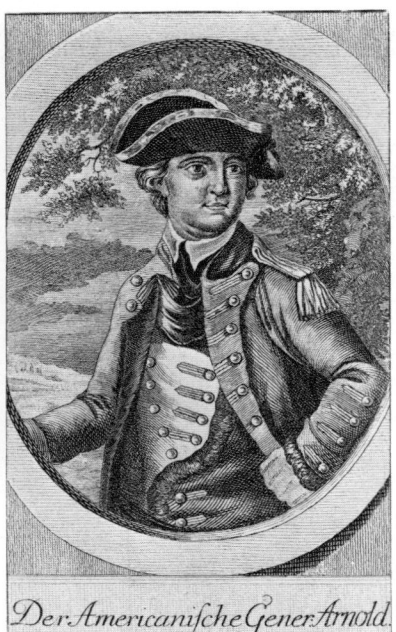

10

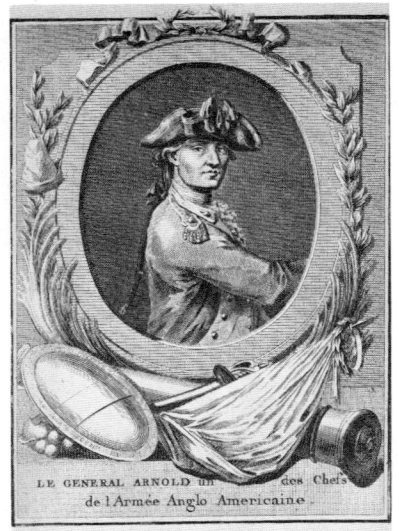

11

Benedict Arnold, 1741–1801

9

COLONEL ARNOLD. Who Commanded the *Provincial Troops* sent against QUEBEC, through the Wilderness of Canada, and was Wounded in Storming that City, under General Montgomery. Published as the Act directs, 26 March 1776, by Thos. Hart. London.
 Mezzotint 13¾ x 9¾ in.

This mezzotint is one of a series done in London by R. Purcell, under the pseudonym "C. Corbutt," in the early years of the American war. Arnold's aggressive attacks on Fort Ticonderoga, Quebec, and St. Johns had earned him a reputation as a leading figure in the war at this time. Although the title would indicate that Arnold is portrayed immediately before his attack on Quebec, December 31, 1775, his appearance is in sharp contrast to the harsh realities. The American troops had marched on a long overland route through forests and over mountains in order to surprise the British, and Arnold and his men were ragged and emaciated by the time they reached Quebec.
CPPS 5331A LC-USZ62-39570

——————Another copy. A series of these mezzotints was done soon afterwards by "Ioh Martin Will" in Augsburg. Other engravings after the mezzotints are items 10 and 13.

10

Der Americanische Gener: Arnold. [1778]
 Etching 6⅝ x 4 in.

From Korn, *Geschichte der Kriege* (Nürnberg, 1777–78), copy 2, p. 92.
LC-USZ62-45265

11

LE GENERAL ARNOLD un des Chefs de l Armée Anglo-Americaine. A Paris chez Esnauts et Rapilly, rue St. Jacques, a la Ville

de Coutances. A.P.D.R. [177–?]
Mixed method 7⅜ x 5 in.

This portrait was produced around 1778, at about the time of the French alliance with America. The house of Dupin produced a series of prints of American heroes, all of which feature an ornate border with ordnance, flags, olive branches, a laurel wreath, and a liberty cap. A comparison of this engraving with an English copy of the same portrait (item 14) will show the differences between French and English framing. LC-USZ62-45187

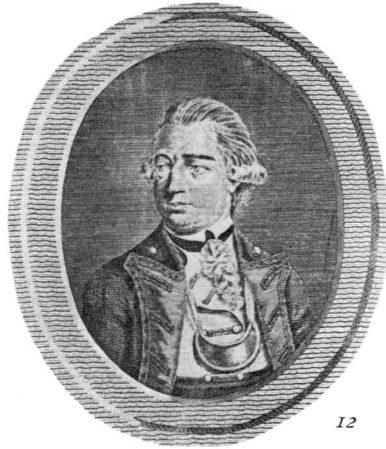

12

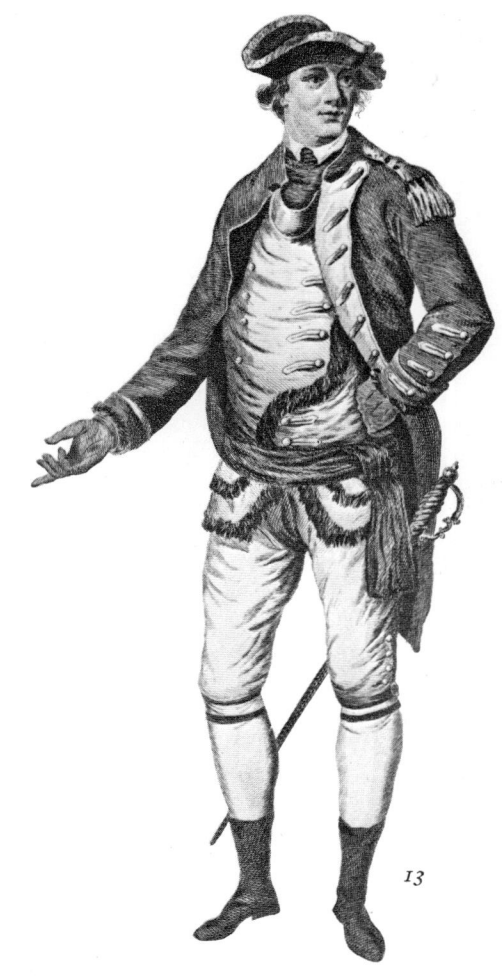

13

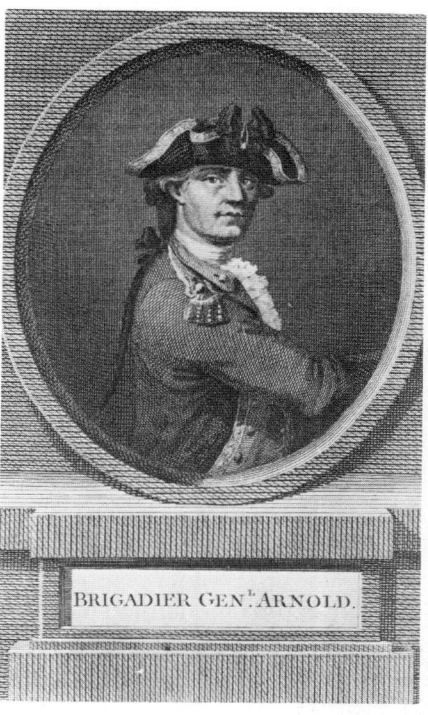

14

12
GENERAL ARNOLD. Printed for T. Robson, Newcastle, upon Tyne. [1778]
Mixed method 6¾ x 4¼ in.

From Murray, *An Impartial History of the Present War in America*, v. 2 (London, 1778), opposite p. 49.

———Another impression. From Murray, *An Impartial History of the War in America*, v. 1 (Newcastle Upon Tyne, 1782), opposite p. 544. LC-USZ62-45216

———Another impression. From *The Fall of Lucifer* (Hartford, 1781), frontispiece probably pasted in at a later date.

13
Major General Arnold Wounded Dec 31-1775 at the attack of Quebec. [1780]
Mixed method 7 x 4¾ in.

From *An Impartial History of the War in America* (London, 1780), p. 248.

———Another impression. From *An Impartial History of the War in America* (London & Carlisle, 1780), p. 249. LC-USZ62-45251

14
BRIGADIER GENL. ARNOLD. [July 1781]
Etching 7 x 4¼ in.

Benedict Arnold's exploits in Canada and at Ridgefield, Conn., and Saratoga, N. Y., brought him widespread fame as a patriot until 1780, when he gained even greater notoriety as a traitor. The title of this portrait includes the rank which Arnold demanded when he joined the British Army. A short accompanying biography dispassionately reports his collaboration with "the unfortunate Major Andre" and his subsequent flight to join Sir Henry Clinton in New York. From *The Universal Magazine*, July 1781, opposite p. 21. LC-USZ62-45217

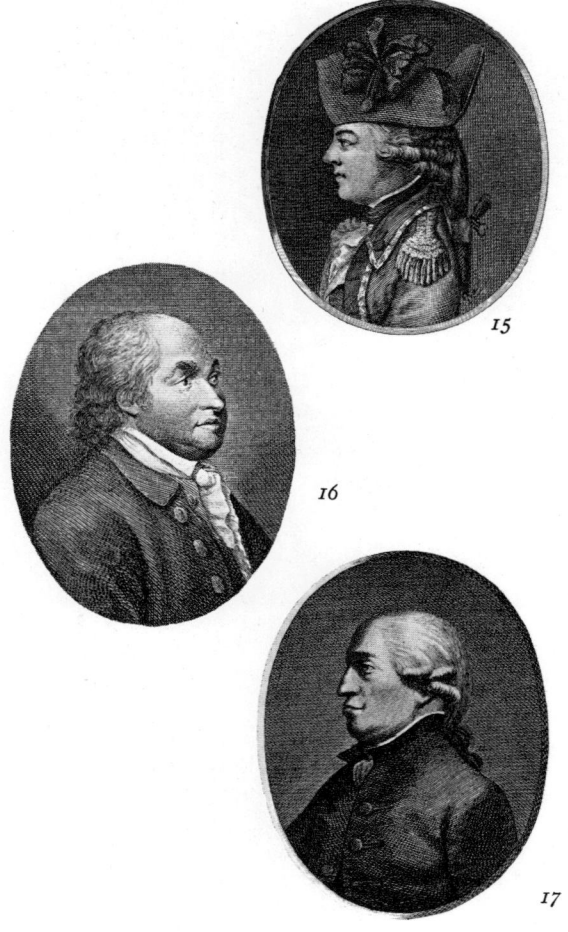

Charles Asgill, 1762 or 1763–1823

15

CAPTAIN ASGILL. Published April 1st. 1786. by J. Fielding Paternoster Row.
Mixed method 7 x 4⅜ in.

Asgill was taken prisoner by the American forces at Yorktown. When a British officer executed an American captain in retaliation for the death of a loyalist, and General Clinton declined to surrender the commanding officer responsible, Washington ordered that a British captain from among his prisoners be put to death in retaliation. The lot fell to Asgill. Clinton's intervention convinced Washington that a Tory court in New York held the blame and not the British Army. In the meantime, Asgill's mother appealed to the French Prime Minister, the Comte de Vergennes, who petitioned Louis XVI for the youth's release. The French King's appeal went through Washington to the American Congress, which then freed Asgill. The portrait is from Andrews, *History of the War with America, France, Spain, and Holland*, v. 4 (London, 1785), p. 416.
LC–USZ62–45219

Isaac Barré, 1726–1802

16

COLONEL BARRE. May 1780.
Mixed method 7¼ x 4½ in.

When James Wolfe fell at Quebec in 1759, Barré was at his side and received a wound which permanently disfigured his cheek. The scar (not visible in this portrait) later contributed to his effect as a vituperative opposition orator in Parliament, for he "paralyzed Charles Townshend and dismayed Wedderburn" (DNB) while offering spirited resistance to North's Ministry. He especially opposed the taxation of America as being inexpedient. A short biography that accompanies the portrait notes Barré's opposition to the war in America as well as his somewhat paradoxical support of the Boston Port Bill. The article also traces Barré's ancestry and his military career during the Seven Years' War. From *The London Magazine*, May 1780, p. 195–196.
LC–USZ62–45312

John Burgoyne, 1722–1792

17

GENERAL BURGOYNE. Pollard sc. Printed for T. Robson, Newcastle, upon Tyne. [1778]
Mixed method 7¼ x 4⅜ in.

"Gentleman John Burgoyne" is best known for his military activities but was also a politician, playwright, actor, and gambler. From a vessel off the Charlestown peninsula he observed some of the early engagements in Boston during 1775, and he later fought at the Battle of Lake Champlain. Execution of his plan for a three-column attack to divide and conquer the Colonies culminated in the defeat of his army at Saratoga. The portrait is from Murray, *An Impartial History of the Present War in America*, v. 2 (London, 1778), opposite p. 481. LC–USZ62–45354

18

The fair Virginian. [and] The devoted General. Published by A. Hamilton Junr. near St. John's Gate March 1, 1779.
Mixed method 4¼ x 6¾ in.

An accompanying article describes the love affair between General Burgoyne and the wife of a martyred Tory from Virginia. Rescued from the Continentals when Burgoyne captured Fort Ticonderoga, she stayed with him during the campaign which terminated at Saratoga and continued to support him when he subsequently faced charges in England. Burgoyne's defeat at Saratoga is portrayed as unavoidable bad luck and his mistress as a

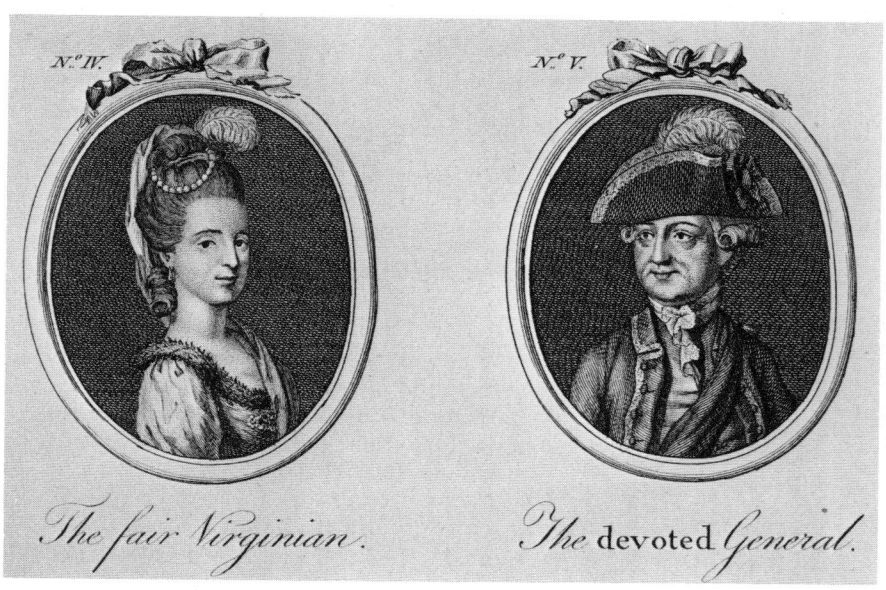

virtuous comfort in trying times. From *The Town and Country Magazine*, January 1779, p. 65–68. CPPS 5586 LC–USZ62–45318

❧Edmund Burke, 1729–1797

19
Edmund Burke Esqr [1778]
 Mixed method 3 ⅞ x 2¾ in. (image)

A consistent believer in adherence to the English Constitution, Burke also advocated that the rights of Englishmen be extended to the people of America and of Ireland. He opposed coercive measures against the Americans, and his efforts, together with those of Charles James Fox, finally brought down the Ministry of Lord North and helped terminate the American war in 1781. This engraving, after a painting by Joshua Reynolds, was pasted onto a leaf and inserted into Russell's *History of America* (London, 1778), copy 1, opposite p. 511. LC–USZ62–45224

20
EDMUND BURKE ESQR. [1778]
 Mixed method 7 x 4½ in.

From Russell, *History of America* (London, 1778), copy 2, opposite p. 511.
LC–USZ62–45260

❧John Byron, 1723–1786

21
ADMIRAL BYRON. Printed for T. Robson, Newcastle, upon Tyne. [1778]
 Mixed method 7 x 4½ in.

Byron, appointed admiral of the North American squadron in 1778, was given the task of intercepting the French fleet under Comte d'Estaing. He spent considerable time refitting his ships and training his crews in Nova Scotia and New England and in 1779 fought two inconclusive battles with the French in the West Indies. Owing to poor health, he

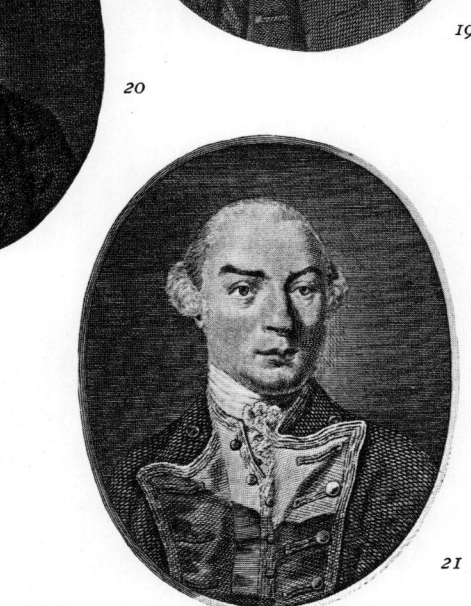

retired from active duty in October 1779. The portrait is from Murray, *An Impartial History of the Present War in America*, v. 2 (London, 1778), opposite p. 385.

——— Another impression. From Murray, *An Impartial History of the Present War in America*, v. 2 (Newcastle Upon Tyne, 1780), opposite p. 385. LC–USZ62–45226

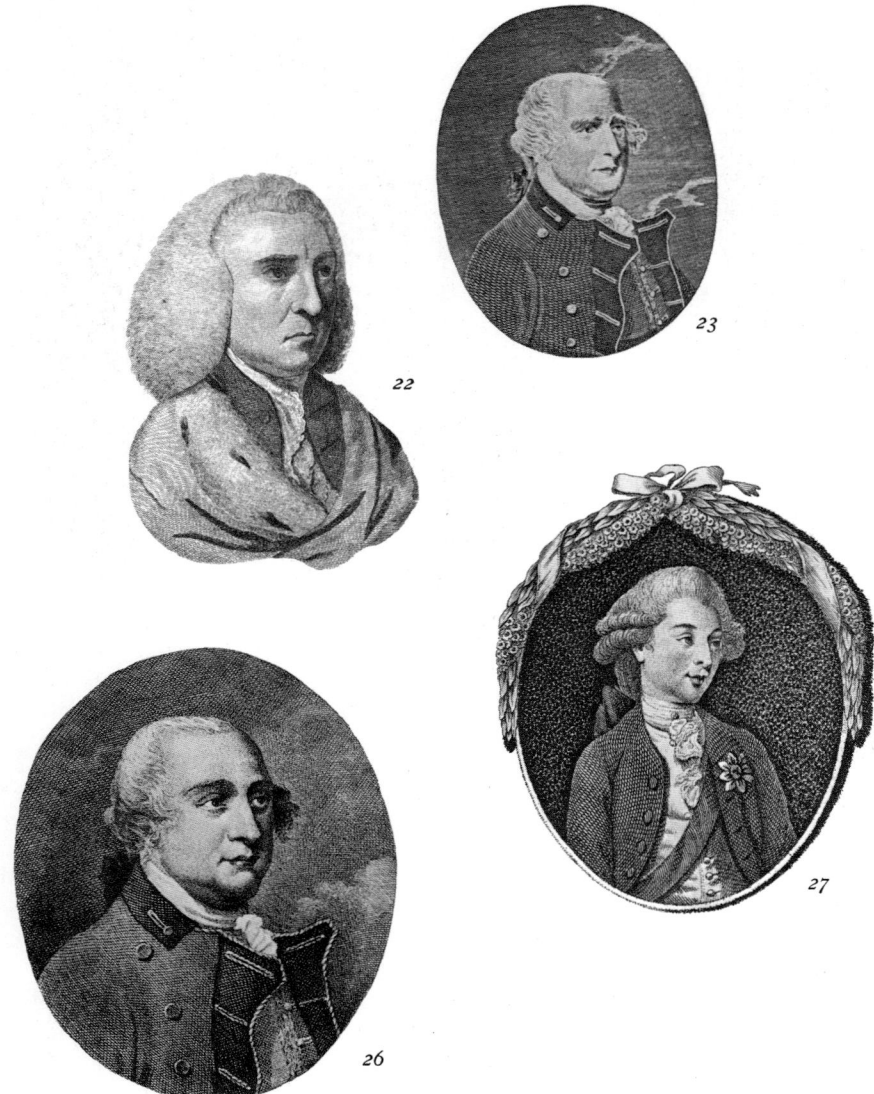

Charles Pratt
1st Earl Camden, 1714–1794

22

LORD CAMDEN. London Mage. Decr. 1781. Mixed method 7 x 4¼ in.

As Chief Justice of the Court of Common Pleas and a defender of constitutional rights, Camden became a popular figure comparable to Wilkes in the eyes of the English populace. Elected to Parliament in 1765, he was concerned about discontent in the American Colonies and denounced the Stamp Act for violating the English Constitution, maintaining that taxation without representation was tantamount to robbery. In 1775 he supported Chatham's attempt to avert the outbreak of war with America.

Camden wears a wig and a robe trimmed with ermine. A short biographical sketch accompanies the picture, describing him as a statesman who considered precedent before action and therefore opposed measures against the Colonies in America. From *The London Magazine*, December 1781, opposite p. 555. LC–USZ62–45317

Guy Carleton
1st Lord Dorchester, 1724–1808

23

GENERAL CARLETON. R. Pollard sct. Printed for T. Robson, Newcastle, upon Tyne [1778] Mixed method 7 x 4¼ in.

Carleton was appointed Governor of Quebec in 1758 and, when Gage was recalled in 1775, became commander of the army in Canada. In the winter of 1775–76 his troops held Canada against the invading American armies under Montgomery and Arnold. Reinforced in the spring, he and General Burgoyne pushed the Americans back to Crown Point. Carleton subsequently retired to England but returned to New York in the spring of 1782. He succeeded Sir Henry Clinton as Commander in Chief of British forces in America, assisted in making the peace, and evacuated New York in November of 1783. The portrait is from Murray, *An Impartial History of the Present War in America*, v. 2 (London, 1778), opposite p. 337.

———Another impression. From Murray, *An Impartial History of the War in America*, v. 1 (Newcastle Upon Tyne, 1782), opposite p. 420. LC–USZ62–45227

———Another impression. In P&P.

24
GENERAL SIR GUY CARLETON. London. Published by J. Bew Paternoster-Row 30 June 1782.
Mixed method 7 x 4¼ in.

Bust portrait facing partially left in oval. The engraved frame has ribbons on the top and foliage with crossed branches on the bottom. From *The Political Magazine*, June 1782, p. 350. Reverse copy similar to item 26.

25
Mrs. W____n. [and] The careful Commander. London, Publish'd by A. Hamilton Junr. Fleet Street, Sepr; 1; 1783.
Mixed method 4½ x 7 in.

The story accompanying this tête-à-tête describes Sir Guy Carleton as a careful and judicious commander of British troops in the Revolution. It explains that Mrs. W_____n's husband died soon after they arrived in New York and that she subsequently accepted the general's proposal of marriage. In reality, Carleton was married in May 1772 to Lady Maria, daughter of the second Earl of Effingham, who was to survive as his widow. Known as a severe disciplinarian but also as a man of humane and conciliatory nature, Carleton

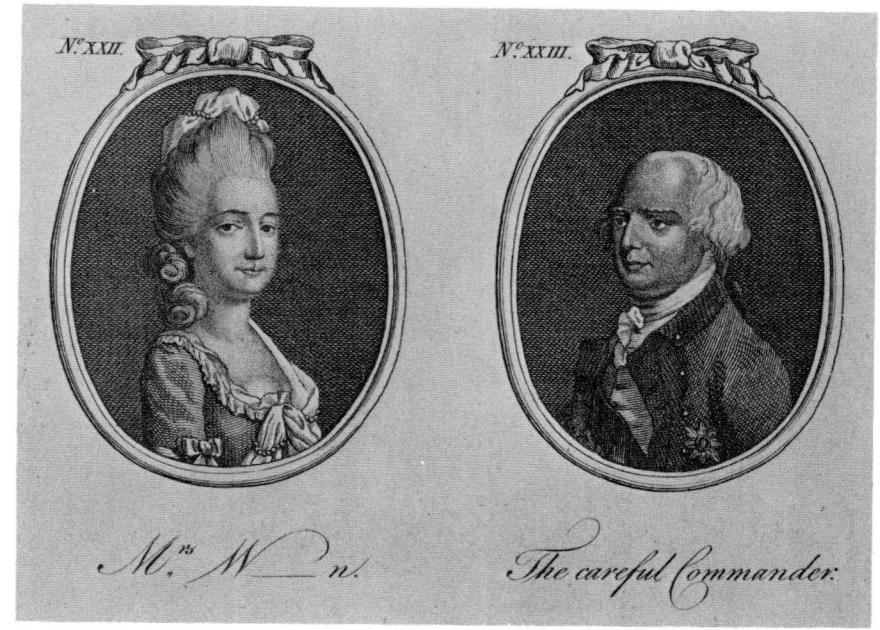

perhaps did not deserve the reputation which the article attempts to create for him. From *The Town and Country Magazine*, August 1783, p. 401–403. CPPS 6302
LC–USZ62–45494

26
SIR GUY CARLETON. Publish'd Octr. 31. 1783. by J. Walker.
Mixed method 6⅞ x 4 in.

An accompanying biography stresses Carleton's long, active, and exemplary military career in Germany, the West Indies, and Canada, apologizes for his inactivity during the American war, and suggests that he might have won victories if the war had continued in America. From *The Westminster Magazine*, October 1783, p. 507.

———Another impression. In P&P. LC–USZ62–7845

Frederick Howard
5th Earl of Carlisle, 1748–1825

27
The Right Honble. FREDK. EARL OF CARLISLE, Lord Lieutt. of the Kingdom of Ireland. Dec. 1780
Mixed method 7½ x 4½ in.

The short biographical sketch which accompanies this picture describes the young Carlisle's support of the administration on the coercion of the American Colonies and his duties with William Eden, 1st Baron Auckland (1744–1814), as an emissary to America in 1778. From *The London Magazine*, December 1780, p. 537–541. LC–USZ62–45277

———Another copy (reversed). From *The Hibernian Magazine*, January 1781, p. 1.

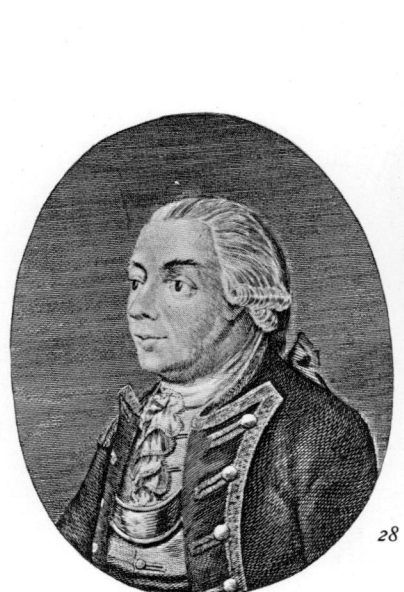
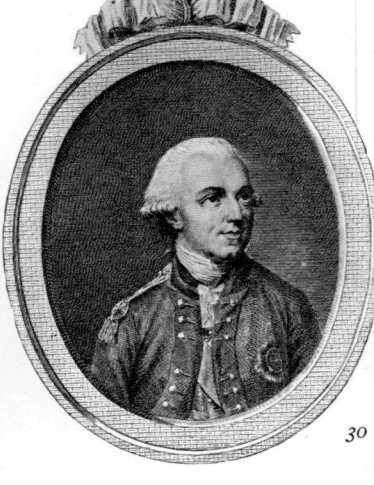
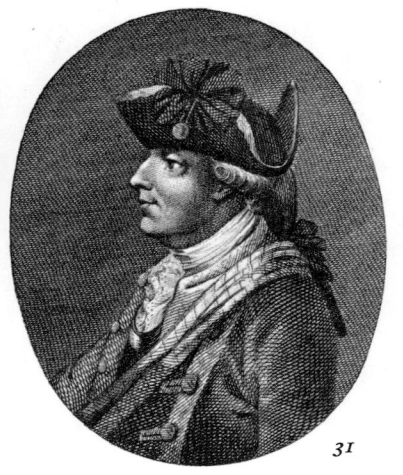
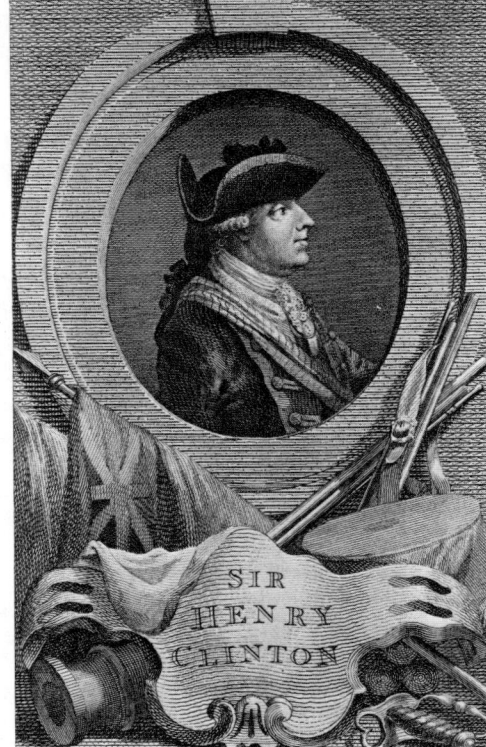

❧Sir Henry Clinton, 1738?–1795

28

GENERAL CLINTON. Printed for T. Robson, Newcastle, upon Tyne. [1778]
Mixed method 7 x 4¼ in.

Clinton succeeded General Howe as chief of British forces in May of 1778. He assumed a defensive strategy by evacuating Philadelphia and concentrating at New York. Attempting a southern campaign he took Charleston, S.C., in May 1780 but returned to New York, leaving Cornwallis in the south where the young general suffered the definitive defeat at Yorktown. From Murray, *An Impartial History of the Present War in America*, v. 1 (London, 1778), opposite p. 527.

———Another impression. From Murray, *An Impartial History of the War in America*, v. 2 (Newcastle Upon Tyne, 1782), opposite p. 186. LC–USZ62–45304

29

SIR HENRY CLINTON. Published 1st. Novr. 1778 by Fielding & Walker, Pater Noster Row.
Mixed method 6⅞ x 4½ in.

This portrait, decorated with British flags and other ordnance, is reversed in item 31. From Russell, *History of America* (London, 1778), opposite p. 574. LC–USZ62–45262

30

SIR HENRY CLINTON, K. B. Commandant en Chef les Troupes de Sa Majesté Britannique dans l'Amérique. Smart pinx. Dupin Sculp. A Paris chez Esnauts et Rapilly, rue St. Jacques. A.P.D.R. [177–?]
Mixed method 7½ x 5 3/16 in.

A French portrait. LC–USZ62–45188

31

SR. HENRY CLINTON. Cook sculp. Published May 21st. 1786. by J. Fielding Paternoster Row London.
Mixed method 7 x 4½ in.

From Andrews, *History of the War with America, France, Spain, and Holland*, v. 3 (London, 1785), opposite p. 150. LC–USZ62–45341

❧Samuel Cooper, 1725–1783

32

Revd. Samuel Cooper D.D. J. Norman Sc. [1784]
Mixed method 3⅛ x 3⅛ in. (image)

A native of Boston, Cooper graduated from

Harvard College in 1743 and became a pastor at the Brattle Square Church. As an active supporter of American independence, he was forced to flee Boston in April of 1775 to avoid being arrested by the British authorities. This portrait was accompanied by an obituary which praised Cooper as a divine, a political theorist, and a scientist. Several portraits of Cooper were printed by Copley, and a description of one of these in the DAB is equally applicable to Norman's engraving: "His portrait represents the typical clergyman of the period, in wig, gown, and bands. But the face indicates less austerity of character than is commonly associated with the eighteenth-century New England divines...." The engraving is from *The Boston Magazine*, March 1784, opposite p. 191. LC–USZ62–45281

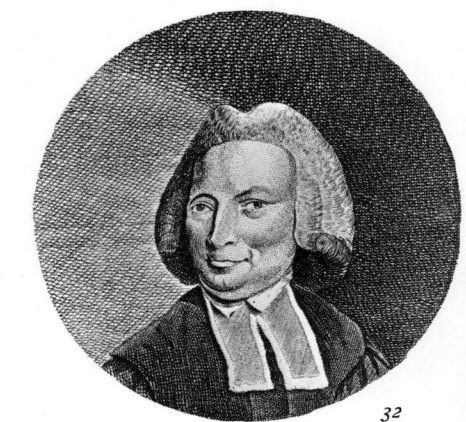

32

Charles Wolfran Cornwall
1735–1789

33

The Right Honble. CHAS. WOLFRAN CORNWALL ESQ. Speaker of the House of Commons. Nov. 1780.

Mixed method 7¼ x 4½ in.

Cornwall's marriage in 1765 to his cousin Elizabeth, sister of Secretary-at-War Charles Jenkinson, determined his political career by allowing him to rise in office through family influence. In Parliament Cornwall opposed the North Ministry on various domestic issues but not on the treatment of the American Colonies. The short biography which accompanies the portrait describes Cornwall's rise in Parliament and mentions his approval of the "coercive measures against America." In 1780 Cornwall became Speaker of the House of Commons, with Lord North's approval. From *The London Magazine*, November 1780, p. 491–492. LC–USZ62–45276

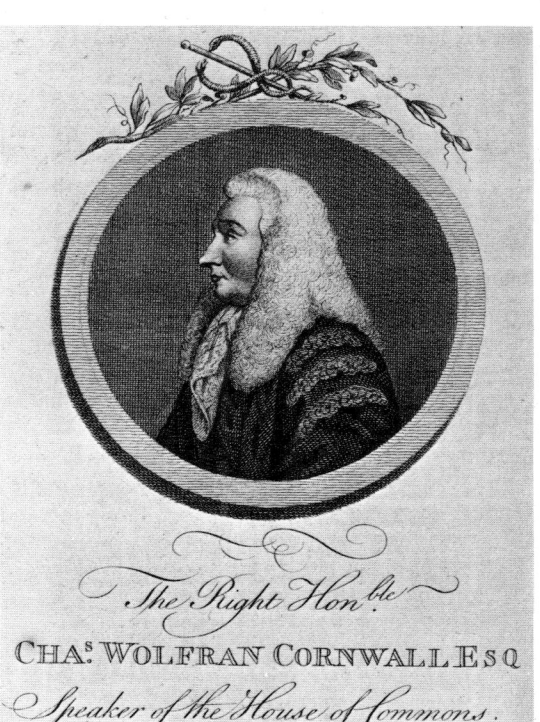

33

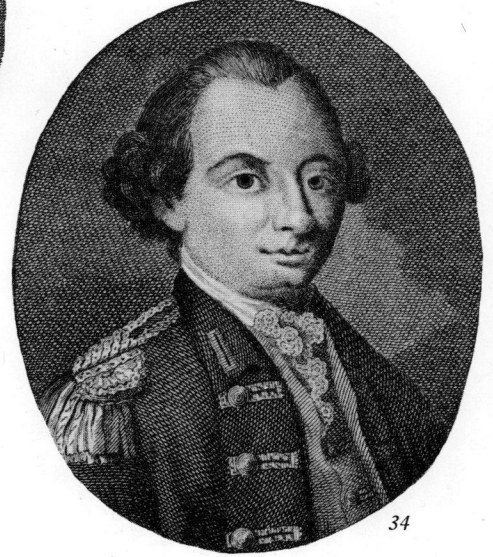

34

Charles Cornwallis
2d Earl Cornwallis, 1738–1805

34

LORD CORNWALLIS, Publish'd March 31st. 1786. by J. Fielding Paternoster Row London.
Mixed method 6⅞ x 4⅜ in.

Cornwallis, who was second in command to General Clinton from 1778 until his capture at Yorktown, drew considerable attention in the English press because of his postwar debate with Clinton over responsibility for the British defeat. The portrait is from Andrews, *History of the War with America, France, Spain, and Holland*, v. 2 (London, 1785), opposite p. 249. LC–USZ62–45340

Sir Roger Curtis, 1746–1816

35
Sir ROGER CURTIS. Drawn from the life by Miller & Engraved by Birrell. Published June 30, 1785 by J. Fielding, Pater-noster Row.
Mixed method 6⅞ x 4½ in.

When Captain Shuldham was appointed Commander in Chief of the North American station in 1775, Curtis became lieutenant of his flagship. In 1776, Curtis was promoted to commander of the *Senegal*, and soon thereafter he became commander of Lord Howe's flagship, the *Eagle*. He returned to England in 1778 with Howe. The portrait is from Andrews, *History of the War with America, France, Spain, and Holland*, v. 4 (London, 1785), opposite p. 301. LC–USZ62–45347

William Legge
2d Earl of Dartmouth, 1731–1801

36
The R. Honble EARL of DARTMOUTH. Oct. 1780.
Mixed method 7¼ x 4¼ in.

Dartmouth's hesitancy in making decisions is reflected in the biography accompanying this portrait, which states that he was not fit for the posts of President of the Board of Trade and Secretary for the Colonies because "his lordship's natural disposition was too timid, too cautious, and too humaine, for the active exertions of an offensive war against an unfortunate, deluded part of his fellow subjects." From *The London Magazine*, October 1780, p. 443–445. LC–USZ62–45313

Silas Deane, 1737–1789

37
S. Deane. Drawn from the life by Du Simitier

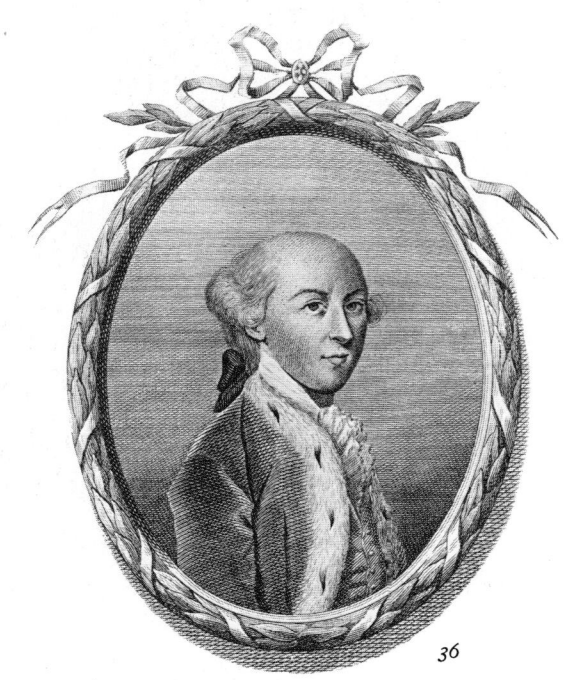

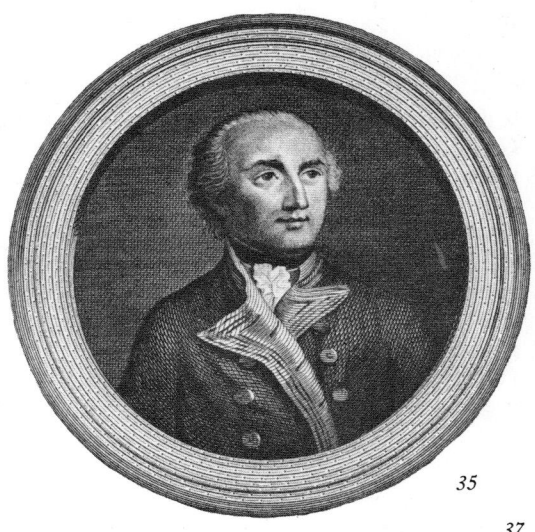

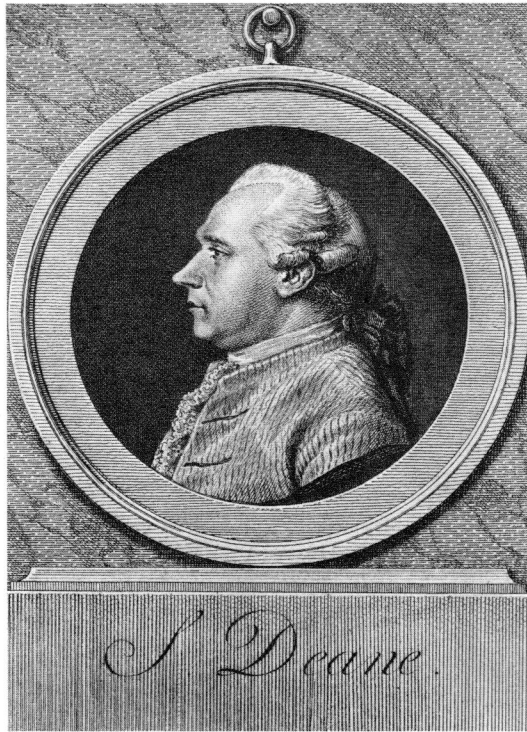

in Philadelphia. Engraved by B. L. Prevost at Paris. [178?]
Line engraving 7 x 5 in.

A Connecticut lawyer and a graduate of Yale College, Deane was one of three Connecticut delegates to the first Continental Congress in 1774 and the second Congress in 1775. All the portraits of Deane cited here (items 37–40) are after the drawings Du Simitière made in Philadelphia in 1779 after Deane's diplomatic mission to France. This particular engraving is from *Portraits des généraux* . . . (Paris, 1781), plate 9. Plates from this volume are in P&P. LC–USZ62–26779

38
SILAS DEANE ESQR. Commissioner from Congress in France. Pubd. May 15th 1783 by R. Wilkinson, No. 58 Cornhill, London. B.B.E.
Mixed method 5½ x 4¼ in.

Bust profile facing right. In Du Simitière, *Portraits of the Generals* . . . (London, 1783) plate 7. Similar to item 37.

39
SILAS DEAN, ESQ. Drawn from the Life by Dusimetiere, at Philadelphia. Publish'd Augt. 1 1783, by J. Fielding, No. 23, Pater noster Row. W: Angus Sculp.
Etching 7 x 4½ in.

In 1781 Deane returned to Europe as a private citizen in an attempt to recoup his financial losses. His belief in the cause of American independence waned, and his personal correspondence expressing a desire for an accommodation with Britain was published by Rivington's loyalist *New York Gazette*. Discredited, he lived the remainder of his life as an exile in Europe. This portrait accompanies a short biography which recounts Deane's life and explains his presence in England:

> We are inclined to think, that at the beginning of the unhappy contest between Great Britain and her American Colonies, Mr. Deane did not look forward to that species of independence which the Colonists have now established; but only aimed, with many other gentlemen of solid understanding, at independence in the articles of internal legislation and taxation; reserving to the Mother-country the right of exclusive commerce, in return for protection.

From *The European Magazine*, October 1783, p. 243. LC–USZ62–9931

40
The Captivating Miss B_____. [and] The American Negotiator. London, Publish'd by A. Hamilton Junr. Fleet Street, Octr. 1; 1783.
Mixed method 4½ x 7 in.

A scandalmongering text accompanying this tête-à-tête describes Deane as a well-educated American whose knowledge of statesmen and women in both America and Europe made him a successful negotiator for his country. Miss B_____ was identified as a "nominal widow" who was constantly being visited by Deane, and it was noted that he "seemed more enamoured with her than he was with the enchanting Mademoiselle Ro_____lle at Paris." From *The Town and Country Magazine*, September 1783, p. 457–459. CPPS 6303 LC–USZ62–45495

Louis de Berton des Balbes de Quiers duc de Crillon-Mahon, 1718–1796

41
DE CRILLON. Le Grand del. Birrell sc. Published Augt. 20, 1785, by J. Fielding, Pater-noster Row
Mixed method 7 x 4⅜ in.

An officer in the French Army, Crillon left France in 1782 to offer his services to the Spanish King. The portrait is from Andrews, *History of the War with America, France, Spain, and Holland*, v. 4 (London, 1785), p. 173. LC–USZ62–45221

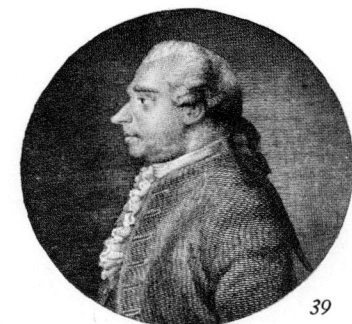
39

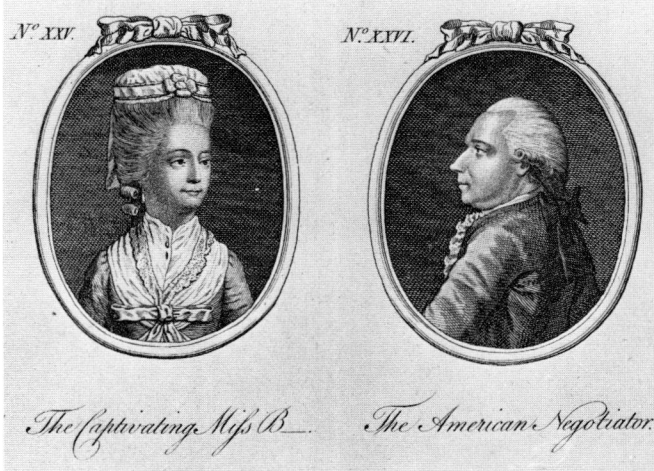
40

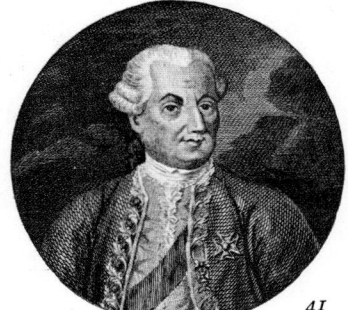
41

François Joseph Paul Comte de Grasse, 1722–1788

42
COUNT DE GRASSE. Augt. 1782.
Mixed method 7⅞ x 4½ in.

An admiral in the French Navy, de Grasse fought in the West Indies under de Guichen and d'Estaing and, during the Yorktown campaign, played a decisive role by blocking Chesapeake Bay from English vessels. He was defeated and captured in the West Indies in 1782. The "Anecdotes" which accompanied this picture described his visit to England as the prisoner of Admiral Peter Parker, who "treated him with every mark of respect and attention, which characterise the generous sons of Briton." From *The London Magazine*, August 1782, opposite p. 355.
LC–USZ62–45505

43
COUNT de GRASSE. Drawn from the life by Mr. Miller, on the 8th. & 9th. of Augt. at the Royal Hotel. Published Septr. 1, 1782, by J. Fielding, Pater-noster Row, J. Sewell, Cornhill, & J. Debrett, Piccadilly. Miller del. W Angus sculpt.
Mixed method 6⅞ x 4 in.

A prisoner of distinction in England, de Grasse eventually became the intermediary between Shelburne and the French Government in the preliminary peace negotiations. The portrait is from *The European Magazine*, August 1782, p. 83. LC–USZ62–45415

44
COUNT DeGRASSE. Miller del. Birrell Sc. Published Octr. 6 1785 by J. Fielding, Pater Noster Row.
Mixed method 6⅞ x 4½ in.

Bust portrait facing front in oval on pedestal. From Andrews, *History of the War with America, France, Spain, and Holland*, v. 4 (London, 1785), opposite p. 202. Similar to item 43.

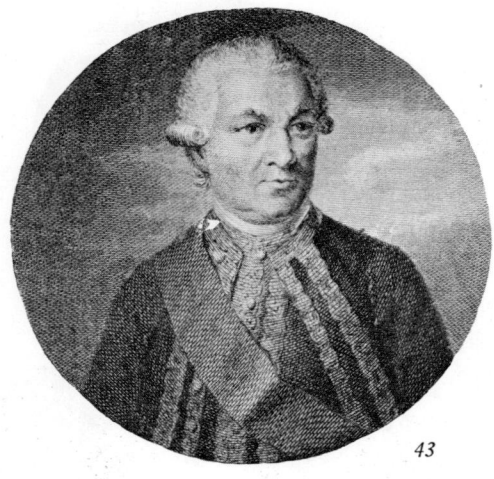

43

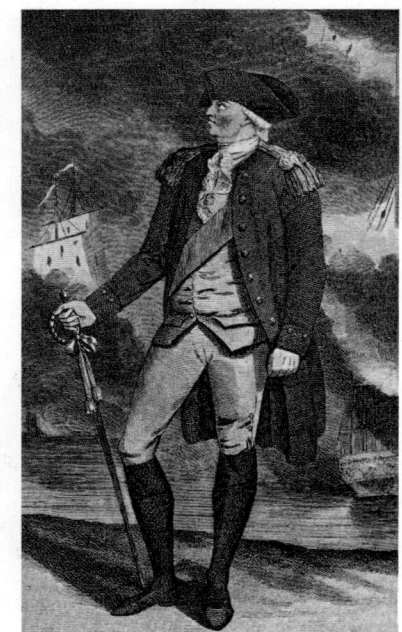

42

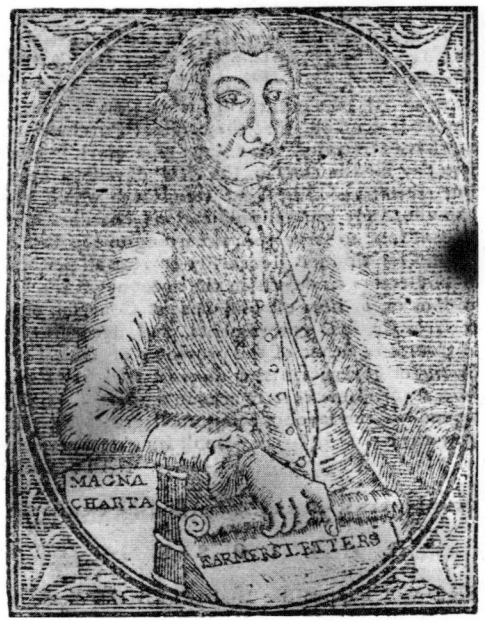

45

John Dickinson, 1732–1808

45
The PATRIOTIC AMERICAN FARMER. J____N D__K__NS__N, Esq; Barrister at Law. [1772]
Woodcut 3⅝ x 2⅞ in. (image)

Dickinson's elbow rests on a copy of the Magna Carta and he holds his "Farmer's Letters" in his right hand. The following lines appear below the picture:

Who with Attic Eloquence, and Roman Spirit, hath asserted the Liberties of the British Colonies in America.
'Tis nobly done to Stem Taxations Rage,
And raise the Thoughts of a degenerate Age,
For Happiness and Joy, from Freedom spring;
But Life in Bondage is a worthless Thing.

Dickinson practiced law in Maryland, Delaware, and Pennsylvania and, beginning in 1767,

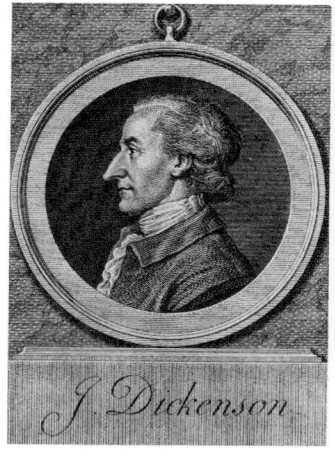
46

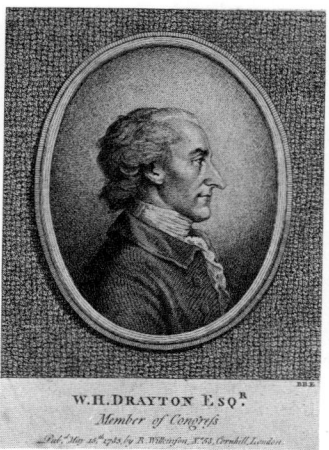
47

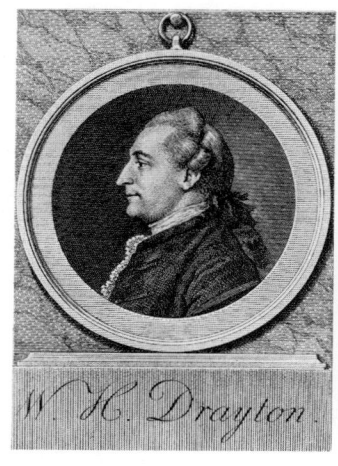
48

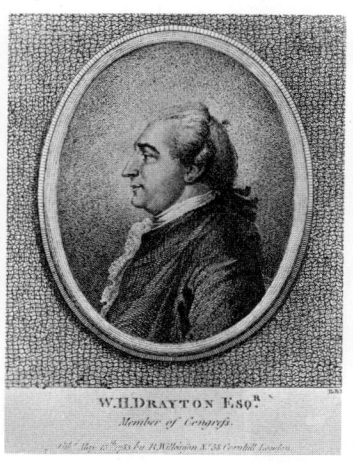
49

anonymously published a series of "letters" in the *Pennsylvania Chronicle*. Collected under the title *Letters From a Farmer in Pennsylvania to the Inhabitants of the British Colonies* (1768), these essays brought him fame in Europe as well as in America. Dickinson's knowledge of political theory and practical economics made him a leader in the early American Congresses. This picture is from Ames', *Astronomical Diary; or Almanack* (Boston, 1772). LC–USZ62–45528

————Another copy. 3⅝ x 2⅝ in. (image). Same title but imprint reads "Printed for and sold by Ezekial Russell, in Marlborough Street."

46
J. Dickenson. Drawn from the life by Du Simitier in Philadelphia. Engraved by B. L. Prevost at Paris. [178?]

Line engraving with etched border 7 x 5 in.

Although Dickinson was reluctant to advocate complete severance of relations with England, his writings appeared as outstanding defenses of the American cause and portraits of him were widely circulated. Du Simitière recognized Dickinson as a leading intellect among the Americans. This picture is from *Portraits des généraux . . .* (Paris, 1781), plate 11. Plates from this volume are in P&P. LC–USZ62–26777

47
J. Dickinson Esqr. Member of Congress & Author of Letters of a Farmer of Pennsylvania. Pubd. May 15th 1783 by R. Wilkinson No. 58 Cornhill, London. B.B.E.

Mixed method 5½ x 4¼ in.

————Another copy, with the same imprint and engraver, appears in Du Simitière's *Portraits of the Generals . . .* (London, 1783) but is designated "W. H. Drayton Esqr." (cf. entry no. 49). Dickinson is the younger, thinner man; he faces right, his hair is brushed back, and he has buttons on his coat. Ellis' engraving of Dickinson with the incorrect heading is shown here. LC–USZ62–45478

William Henry Drayton, 1742–1779

48
W. H. Drayton. Drawn from the life by Du Simitier in Philadelphia. Engraved by B. L. Prevost at Paris. [178?]

Line engraving with etched border 7 x 5 in.

Drayton was president of the South Carolina Provincial Congress, chief justice of the State during the war and a representative to the Continental Congress from March 1778 until his death in September 1779. From *Portraits des généraux . . .* (Paris, 1781), plate 10. Plates from this volume are in P&P. LC–USZ62–26776

49
W. H. Drayton Esqr. Member of Congress. Pubd. May 15th 1783 by R. Wilkinson, No. 58, Cornhill, London. B.B.E.

Mixed method 5½ x 4¼ in.

Copy in P&P. LC–USZ61–282

————Another copy, with the same imprint and engraver, appears in Du Simitière's *Portraits of the Generals . . .* (London, 1783) but is designated "J. Dickinson Esqr." (cf. entry no. 47). Drayton is the older, heavier man; he faces left and wears a wig with curls on the side and a ribbon in back. Not all the engravings by Ellis after Du Simitière have the titles and portraits reversed on these two men.

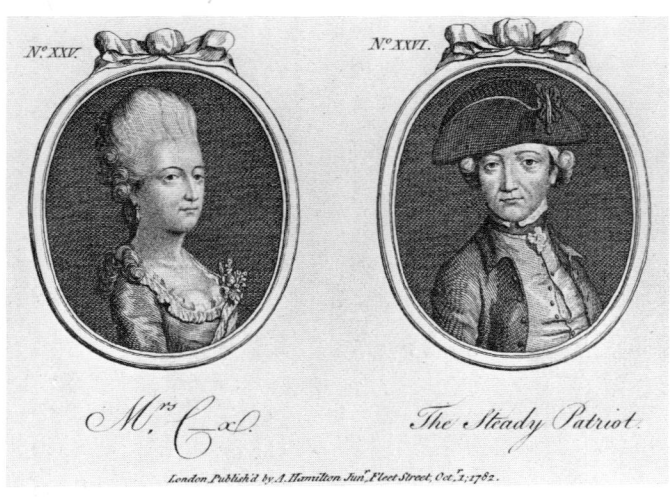 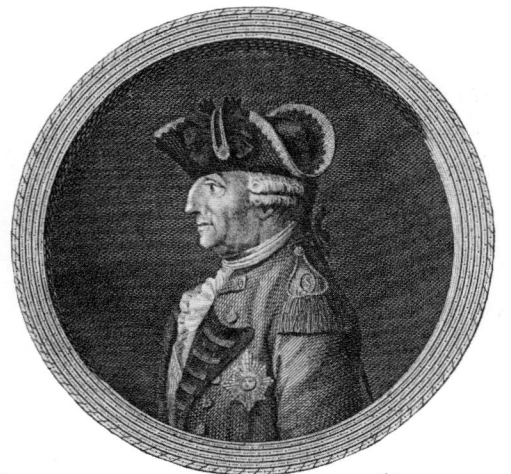 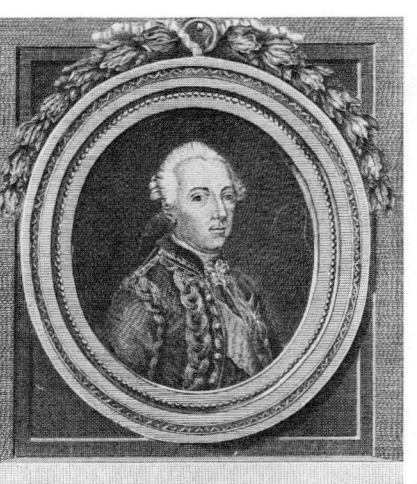

50   51   52

❧Thomas Howard
   3d Earl of Effingham, 1747–1791

50
Mrs. C____x. [and] The Steady Patriot. London, Publish'd by A. Hamilton Junr. Fleet Street, Octr. 1; 1782.
   Mixed method 4¼ x 7 in.

Lord Effingham entered the British Army in 1762 but resigned his commission because of his opposition to the use of force against the Colonies. An article accompanying this portrait explains the situation as follows:

When the fatal misunderstanding between Great Britain and her colonies commenced, he was a strenuous advocate for palliative measures, considering the colonists as fellow subjects, who might, by lenient operations, be brought to reason; but whom he judged would not submit to coercive measures, which he greatly condemned. Accordingly, we find, when his regiment was ordered for America he threw up his commission, saying, at such a period,

   "The post of honour was a private station."

In this opinion he continued to remain until very lately; when by the change of administration, his friends coming into power, he once more appeared upon the horizon of the political world, and offered to serve in a military capacity, as a volunteer at the siege of Gibraltar.

The article also includes a bit of gossip about Mrs. Amelia Cox, a lady he supposedly secretly married. The story is unconfirmed. From *The Town and Country Magazine*, September 1782, p. 457–459. CPPS 6087 LC–USZ62–45492

❧George Augustus Eliott
   1st Baron Heathfield, 1717–1790

51
GENERAL ELIOTT. G. Fredk Koehler delt. W: Angus Sculp. Published July 15, 1785, by J. Fielding, Pater Noster Row.
   Mixed method 6⅞ x 4⅝ in.

Eliott was appointed Governor of Gibraltar in 1777 and held out against the Spanish siege from 1779 until 1783, when Admiral Howe broke the blockade and relieved the garrison. In the face of the humiliations suffered in the American war, Eliott was a welcome hero for the British Government, and many portraits and battle views celebrated his victory. In contrast, very few prints about America appeared in England after 1781. From Andrews, *History of the War with America, France, Spain, and Holland*, v. 4 (London, 1785), p. 11. LC–USZ62–45222

❧Charles Hector
   Comte d'Estaing, 1729–1794

52
CHARLES HENRI COMTE DESTAING, Né le 24. Novembre 1729. [1782]
   Mixed method 6⅞ x 4¼ in.

A French admiral once captured by the British at the siege of Madras and later imprisoned at Portsmouth for violating his parole, d'Estaing had a strong hatred of England. In 1778 he sailed for America from Toulon but arrived too late to stop Howe at New York. In the West Indies he succeeded in taking St. Vincent and Grenada, staving off Admiral Byron, but his subsequent assault on Savannah failed. In 1780 he returned to France, where he recommended that the Government follow Lafayette's advice and send Rochambeau's expeditionary force to America. The portrait is from *Extrait du journal d'un officier de la marine de l'escadre de M. Le Comte D' Estaing* (1782), frontispiece. LC–USZ62–45349

53

D'Estaing. D'Haisnc Pinxt. Goldar Sculp. Published July 30, 1785, by J. Fielding Pater Noster Row.

Mixed method 6¾ x 4⅜ in.

Bust portrait facing partially left in oval. Decorative ribbon on top; pedestal on bottom. From Andrews, *History of the War with America, France, Spain, and Holland*, v. 3 (London, 1785), opposite p. 302. Similar to item 52.

Charles James Fox, 1749–1806

54

The Honble Chas. James Fox. Nov. 1779
Mixed method 7½ x 4½ in.

Fox, who entered Parliament at the age of 19, was well known not only for the great wealth of his father Lord Holland but also for his scholastic and social abilities. Opposing Wilkes and ignoring the people, he entered North's Ministry as one of the Lords of the Admiralty. Burke influenced him to break with North in 1772, and by supporting the Bostonians in 1773 he became a Rockingham Whig. The short biography accompanying his portrait emphasizes his opposition to North's conduct toward the American Colonies. From *The London Magazine*, November 1779, p. 483. LC-USZ62-45504

55

THE HONBLE. CHARLES JAMES FOX. [March 1781]
Mixed method 7¼ x 4½ in.

At the opening of Parliament on November 25, 1779, Fox defended the English Constitution, threatened George III by alluding to the punishments of Charles I and James II, and compared the reign of George III to that of Henry VI, under whom France was lost. The allegory below the portrait shows the destruction of the political state as the statue of the King based on the Magna Carta is destroyed. A man with the ears of an ass, representing Ignorance, chops at the statue with a pick. A satyr, probably representing Fox's vices—primarily gambling—breaks the King's sceptre over his knee. To the right a man with wild hair, usually representing Chaos, is about to club the statue while a haggish woman, Faction, disguised as Liberty, looks into a mirror. The short biography which accompanies this portrait stresses Fox's opposition to the North Ministry and accuses him of siding with the rebels in Ireland and America and of taking the position that these factions cry for "true constitutional interpretation while Britons do not." It includes the following quote from one of Fox's speeches:

The people must be the instruments of their own deliverence, and the road to it was open. Their brethren in America and their brethren in Ireland have taught them how to act....

The article concludes with the statement that Fox "is a strong advocate for the Americans, and often declared in Parliament 'that every victory we gain over the Americans is worse than a defeat.'" From *The Political Magazine*, 1781, p. 157–159. CPPS 5836 LC-USZ62-45423

56

The Honble. CHARLES JAMES FOX. Printed for S.A. Cumberlege, at the Kings Arms, in Pater-noster Row. [November 1781]
Etching 7 x 4½ in.

The short biography which accompanies this portrait outlines Fox's political career. From *The Universal Magazine*, November 1781, p. 225–228. LC-USZ62-45218

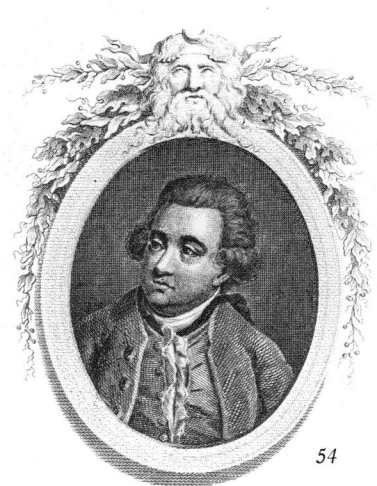

54

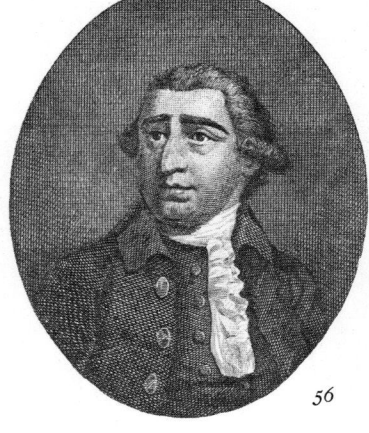

56

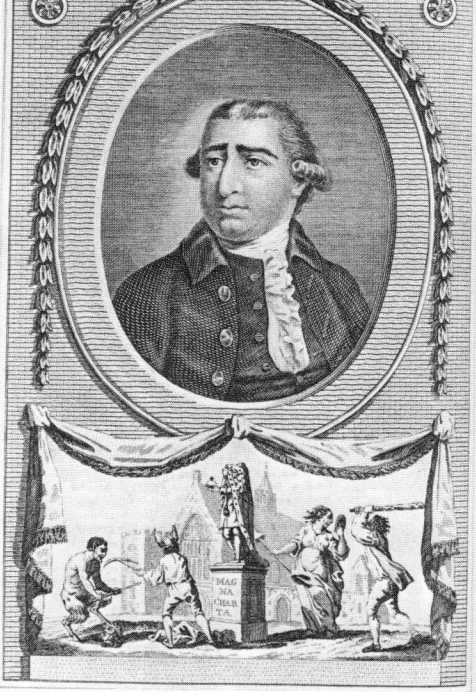

55

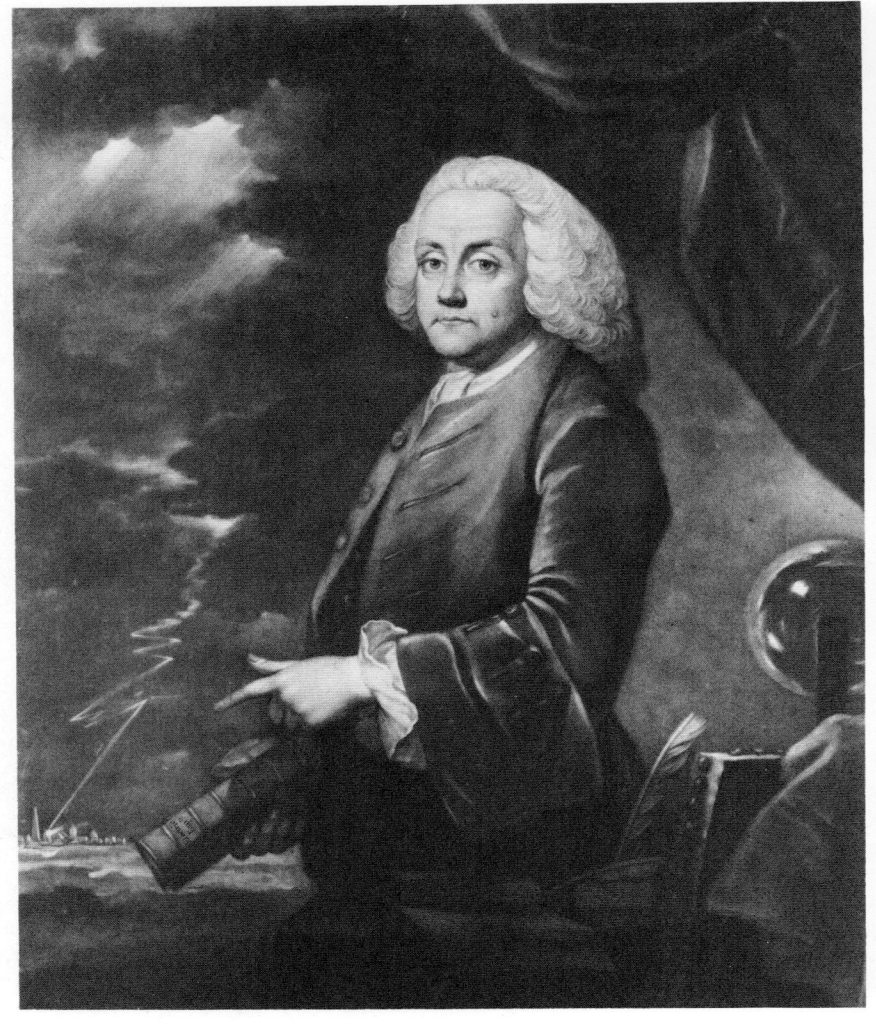

57

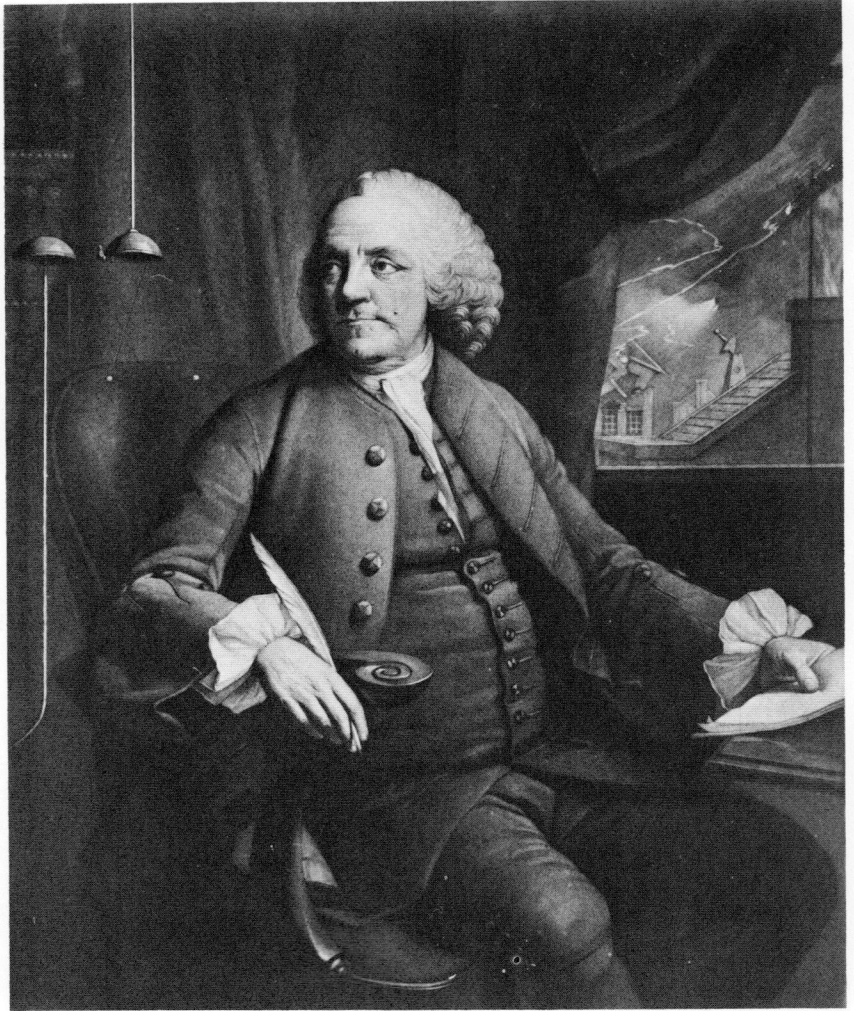

58

Benjamin Franklin, 1706–1790

57

B. Franklin of Philadelphia. L.L.D. F.R.S. 1761 B. Wilson pinxt. Js. McArdell fecit.
Mezzotint 12⅛ x 9¾ in. (image)

Before the American Revolution Franklin was internationally known as a philosopher and scientist. He was considered an example of the type of genius to be found in America, and his works provided the Colonies with a pride in the accomplishments of a native son. In this portrait Franklin holds a book entitled *Electric Expts.* In the foreground and to his left are scientific instruments and writing materials; in the background lightning strikes a town. Smith, p. 862. Sellers, p. 413. LC–USZ62–45191

58

B: Franklin of Philadelphia. L.L.D. F.R.S. M. Chamberlin pinxt. E. Fisher fecit. Sold by M. Chamberlin in Stewart Street, Old Artillery Ground, Spittalfields, Price 5s: [176?]
Mezzotint 14⅞ x 10⅛ in.

Scientific apparatus is at Franklin's right; outside the window to his left an electrical storm rages. This portrait is after a 1763 painting by Mason Chamberlin entitled "Portrait of a Gentleman: half length." It echoed the theme of Benjamin Wilson's painting, and the mezzotint version competed with the one by McArdell. Sellers, p. 218–222. Smith, p. 493. See also items 62 and 65 for other copies.

————Another impression. State before imprint and title. Scratching on the letter under his hand is absent. LC–USZ62–1434

59

Benjamin Franklin. Né à Boston, dans la nouvelle Angleterre le 17 Janvier 1706. Dessine par C.N. Cochin Chevalier de l'Ordre du Roi, en 1777, et Grave par Aug. de St. Aubin Graveur de la Bibliotheque du Roi. Se vend a Paris chez C.N. Cochin aux Galleries du Louvre: et chez Aug de St. Aubin, rue de Mathurins.
Etching 8⅛ x 6 in.

Bust portrait facing right. Franklin is wearing a fur hat and spectacles. The Cochin portrait and its variations (with or without spectacles, with or without book, fur hat shapeless or trimmed) was one of the most frequently reprinted engravings of Franklin. Its journalistic value derived from the fact that it showed the American genius as he appeared upon his arrival in France. From the J. Pierpont Morgan "Signers Collection" in the Manuscript Division. Sellers, p. 227. Items after the Cochin portrait are 60, 61, 64, 66, 67, 70, 72, and 76.

60

D. Beniamin Fraencklin. Grand Commissaire plenipotentiare du Congres d'Amerique en France né à Boston 1706, en 17. Janvier. Se vend a Londres chez Thom H desine par C. Cochin Chev. de l'Ordre du Roi a Paris 1777.
Mezzotint 7¾ x 6⅛ in. (image)

Half portrait facing left. Franklin wears a fur hat and spectacles and holds a paper in his left hand. From the J. Pierpont Morgan "Signers Collection" in the Manuscript Division. Reversed version of item 61.

61

Benjamin Franklin, L.L.D. F.R.S. J. Cook sc. [September 1777]
Mixed method 7 x 4¼ in.

Bust portrait facing left in oval. Franklin wears fur hat and glasses. The biographical sketch accompanying this picture stresses Franklin's work as a scientist and mentions his recent activities in England as a representative of the Colonies. While debating the patriotism of his motives, the article regrets that he has embarked for the French court, noting that this "man of austere manners" is "little suited to the pliability of courts, or the genius of the French nation." From *The Town and Country Magazine*, September 1777, p. 451–453. This portrait is after Cochin.

62

Dr. Franklin. [1778]
Mixed method 7⅛ x 4¾ in.

From Russell, *History of America* (1778), opposite p. 494. LC–USZ62–45259

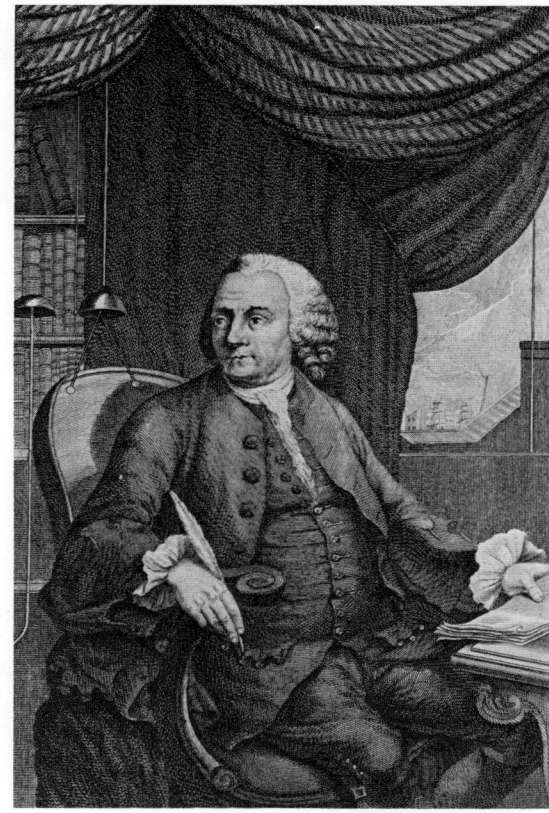

62

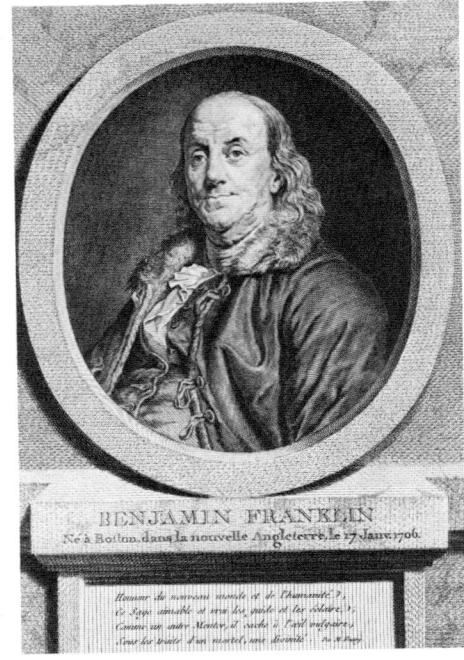

63

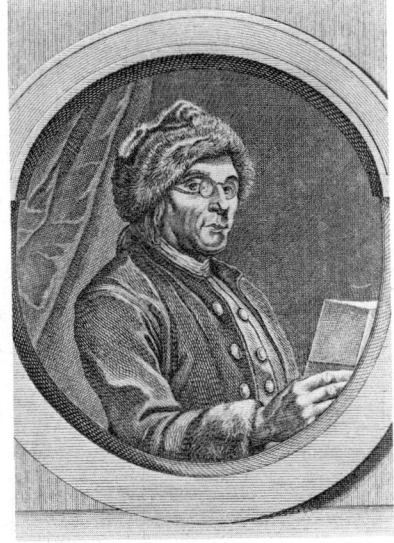

64

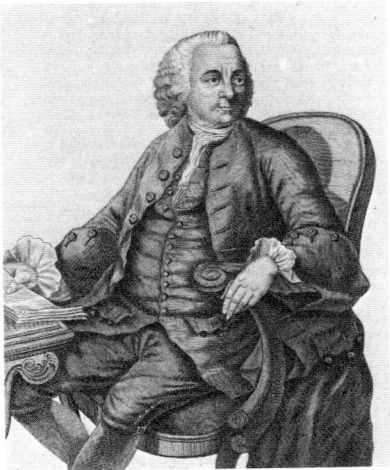

65

63
BENJAMIN FRANKLIN. Né à Boston, dans la nouvelle Angleterre, le 17 Janv. 1706. Duplessis Pinxit Parisiis 1778. Chevillet Sculpsit. Tiré du cabinet de M. Le Ray de Chaumont & ca.

Line engraving 11¾ x 8¼ in.

The following poem appears below the caption:

> Honneur du nouveau monde et de l'humanité,
> Ce Sage aimable et vrai les guide et les
>   éclaire;
> Comme un autre Mentor, il cache à l'oeil
>   vulgaire,
> Sous des traits d'un mortel, une divinité.
>   Par M. Feutry.

This is the finest of the Franklin portraits and probably the most often reproduced. It advertised Franklin's presence in France and was used in support of the alliance with America. Sellers, p. 249. LC–USZ62–45195

64
Dr. Beniamin Franklin. gebohrn zu Boston den 17. Janrü. 1706. [1778]

Etching 6⅞ x 4 in.

From Korn, *Geschichte der Kriege* (Nürnberg, 1777–78), copy 2, p. 92.
LC–USZ62–45264

65
Benjamin Franklin L.L.D. Envoy from the American Congress to the French Court. [1780]

Mixed method 6¾ x 4¼ in.

After the Chamberlin portrait, but without background or pen. By deleting the background of the original portrait, the engraver stresses Franklin the statesman and writer while deemphasizing his achievements in science. From *An Impartial History of the War in America* (London, 1780), p. 345.
LC–USZ62–45256

———Another impression. A later state with windows and curtains drawn in behind Franklin. From *An Impartial History of the War in America* (London & Carlisle, 1780), p. 345

66
D. BENJAMIN FRANKLIN, et vita inter Americanos acta, et magnis electricitatis periculis clarus. J. Elias Haid Sculp. 1780
  Mezzotint 8 x 5 in. (image)
  After the Cochin portrait.
LC–USZ62–45185

67
BENJAMIN FRANKLIN, L.L.D. F.R.S. One of the American Plenipotentiaries at the Court of France. Pollard sculp. Printed for T. Robson, Newcastle upon Tyne. [1780]
  Mixed method 6⅞ x 4¼ in.

  After the Cochin portrait, but without spectacles. From Murray, *An Impartial History of the Present War in America*, v. 1 (Newcastle Upon Tyne, 1780), opposite p. 49.
LC–USZ62–45298

68
B. Franklin, L.L.D. F.R.S. Ambassador from the Congress of America to the Court of France. J. Norman Sc. [1781]
  Etching 4¼ x 3½ in. (image)
  After the medal first done by the Manufacture Nationale de Sèvres in 1778. See item 71 for a German copy. From *An Impartial History of the War in America*, v. 2 (Boston, 1781), opposite p. 129. LC–USZ62–45241

69
BENJAMIN FRANKLIN J. Pelicier. Sculp. 1782.
  Etching 9⅞ x 6½ in.
  Bust portrait after Duplessis in an oval

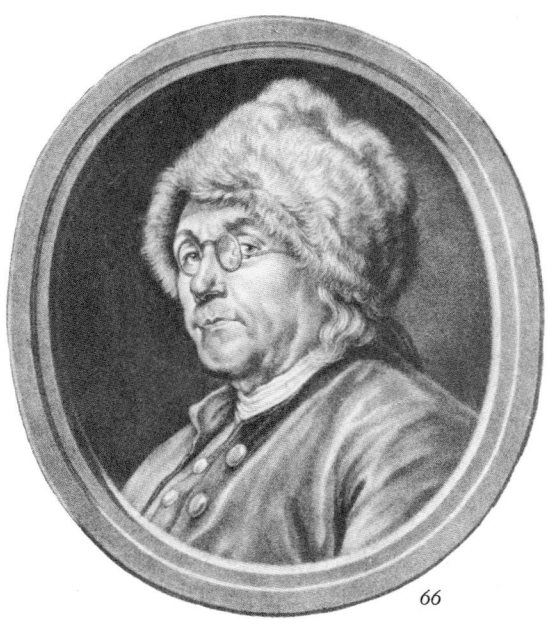
66

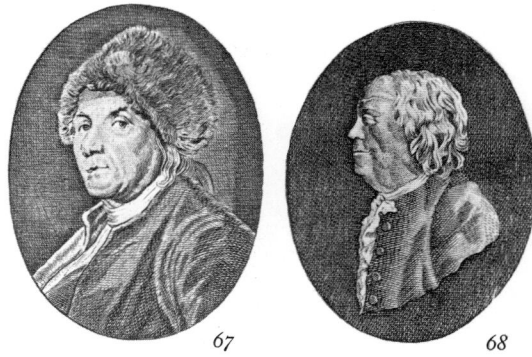
67 68

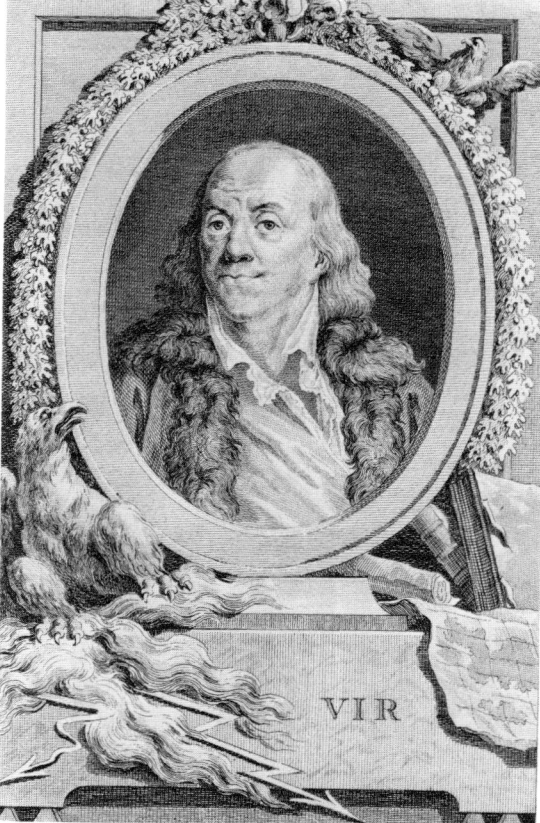
69

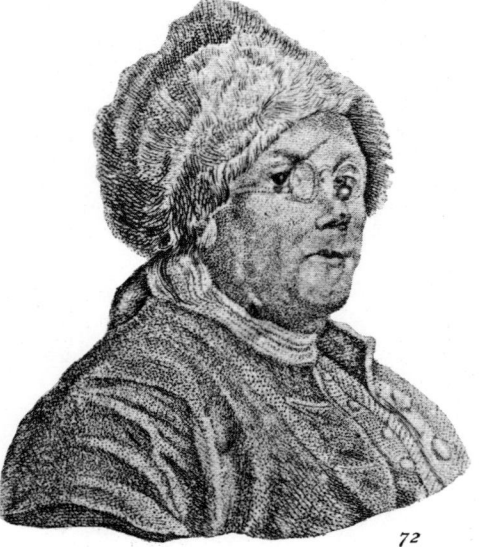
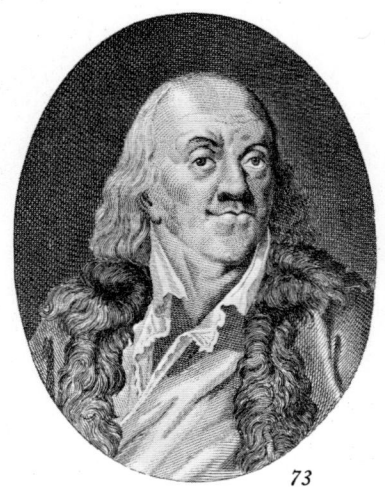
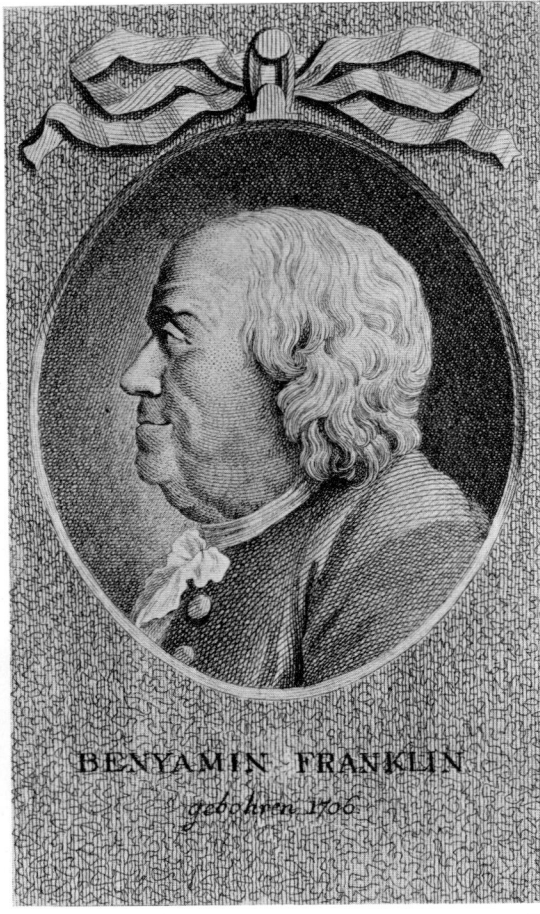

draped with foliage. Eagles on upper right and lower left, lightning and the letters "VIR" on base below, and books and a map on lower right. From Hilliard d'Auberteuil, *Essais historiques*, v. 3 (1782), p. [13]. Sellers, p. 284. LC–USZ62–45334

70
BENJAMIN FRANKLIN, L.L.D. F.R.S. J. Cook Scp. [1783]
   Mixed method 6¾ x 4¼ in.

The Cochin portrait of Franklin in fur cap and spectacles facing partially left in oval. From *The Constitutions of the Several Independent States of America* (Philadelphia, 1783), frontispiece.

71
BENYAMIN FRANKLIN. gebohren 1706. D. Berger Sculp. 1783.
   Mixed method 4⅝ x 2¾ in. (image)

See also item 68. Sellers, p. 369. LC–USZ62–45166

72
DR. FRANKLIN. COELIS ERIPUIT FULMEN SCEPTRUMQUE TYRANNIS. J. Norman Sc. [1784]
   Mixed method 2½ x 2 in. (image)

After the Cochin portrait. Frontispiece to *The Boston Magazine*, January 1784. Stauffer 2332.

———Another impression. In P&P. Stauffer, 2332. LC–USZ62–45168

73
BENJAMIN FRANKLIN. Goldar Sculpt. Published Sepr. 23d. 1785, by J. Fielding, Pater Noster Row.
   Mixed method 6¾ x 4½ in.

Portrait after Duplessis, with Franklin wearing fur collar. From Andrews, *History*

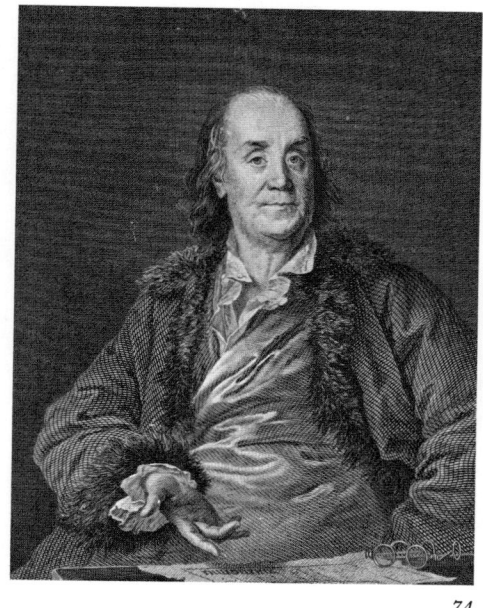

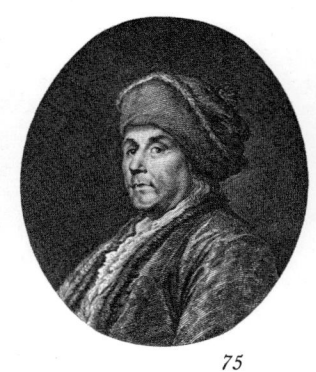

75

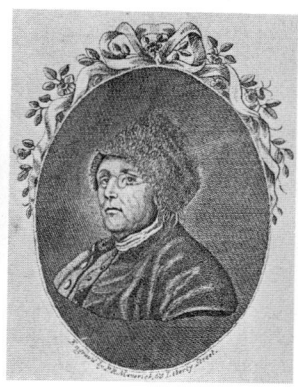

76

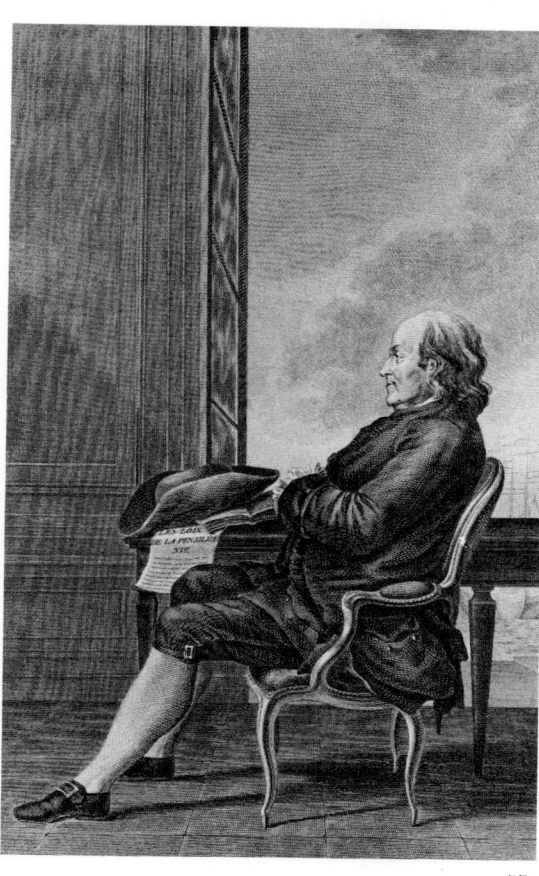

77

of the War with America, France, Spain, and Holland, v. 1 (London, 1785), p. 73. LC–USZ62–45305

———Another impression. In P&P.

74
BENJAMIN FRANKLIN. Né à Boston le 17. Janvier 1706. Eripuit coelo fulmen sceptrum que tyrannis. Peint par Madame Filleul. Gravé par Cathelin, Graveur du Roi. A Paris chez M. Boquet rüe Comtesse d'Artois vis-à-vis celle Mauconseil. [1779–178?]
Line engraving 14⅜ x 10 in.

Franklin seated at a table upon which are spectacles and a map of Philadelphia. By Louis-Jacques Cathelin after Anne Rosalie Filleul. Sellers, p. 282. LC–USZ62–45439

75
BENJAMIN FRANKLIN. Né à Boston dans la Nouvelle Angleterre, le 17 Janvier 1706. Desrayes del. le Beau scul. A Paris chés Esnauts et Rapilly, rue St. Jacques à la Ville de Coutances. A.P.D.R. [178?]
Mixed method 7¼ x 5 in.

Sellers states that Pierre Adrien LeBeau and Claude Louis Desrais revised the Cochin portrait "to accord with the dignity due the representative of a recognized power at the Court of France." p. 229. LC–USZ62–28230

76
Dr. BENJAMIN FRANKLIN. Engraved by P[eter] R. Maverick 65 Liberty Street. [1794]
Mixed method 3⅜ x 2½ in. (image)

After Cochin. Franklin in fur hat and glasses. LC–USZ62–45167

77
[Benjamin Franklin] On l'a vu désarmer les Tirans et les Dieux. L[ouis] C[arrogis] de Carmontelle, Del. [François Denis] Nee Sculp A Paris chez Née rue des Francs-Bourgeois. Porte St. Michel. A.P.D.R. [178?]
Line engraving 14¼ x 8½ in.

Paper on the table to Franklin's right reads "Les Loix de la Pensilvanie." Ships in background. Sellers, p. 215–216. LC–USZ62–21785

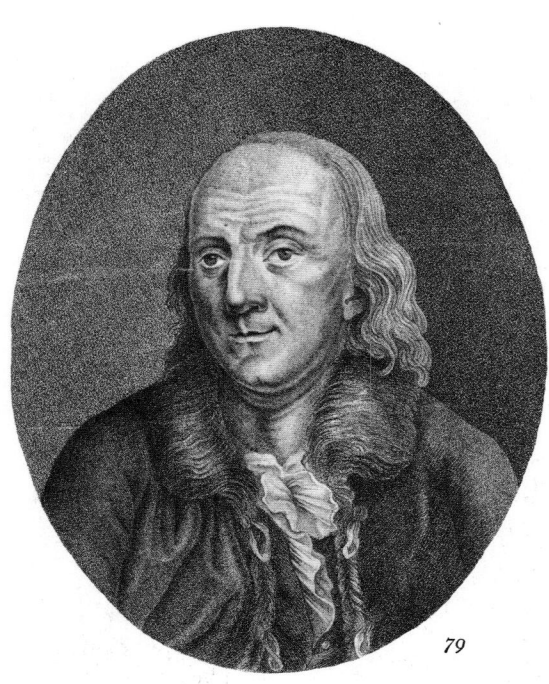

78

B. Franklin, L.L.D. F.R.S. Born at Boston in New England, Jan. 6th. 1706. Died at Philadelphia, April 17th 1790. Eripuit Caelo Fulmen; Sceptrumque Tyrannis.

Mixed method 3¾ x 3 in. (image)

Bust profile facing left in oval. After the Sèvres medal; see also items 68 and 71. From *The Massachusetts Magazine*, May 1790, frontispiece. LC–USZ62–31139

79

BENJAMIN FRANKLIN née a boston, le 17 janvier 1706 Imprimeur; Fondateur de la République des Etats unis de l'Amerique Septentrionale mort à Philadelphie en 1790. Dessiné par Desrais Gravé par la Cite. Montaland. A Paris, chez Basset Md. d'Estampes, rue

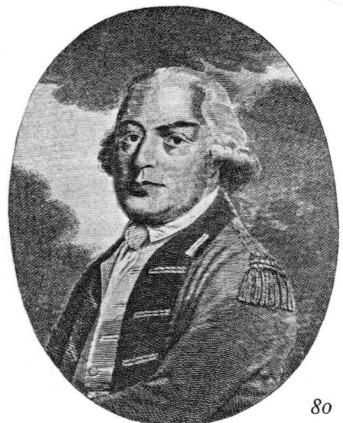

Jacques, au coin de celle des Mathurins. [1790?] Stipple 11 x 8⅝ in.

Sellers dates this engraving somewhat later than 1790, but it might have been produced in the year of Franklin's death (p. 229). LC–USZ62–45192

Thomas Gage, 1719?–1787

80

General Gage. R. Pollard sculp. Printed for T. Robson, Newcastle, upon Tyne. [1778]
Mixed method 6⅞ x 4⅜ in.

As Commander in Chief of the British Army in North America at the outbreak of the War of Independence, Gage was responsible for maintaining royal authority in the Colonies. His inability to check the spread of rebellion and his attitude toward the Americans, which many in England considered overly sympathetic, led to his replacement by Sir William Howe in October 1775. The portrait shown here supports contemporary descriptions of the general as a handsome man with regular features, large eyes, and a long, aristocratic nose. From Murray, *An Impartial History of the Present War in America*, v. 2 (London, 1778), opposite p. 145.

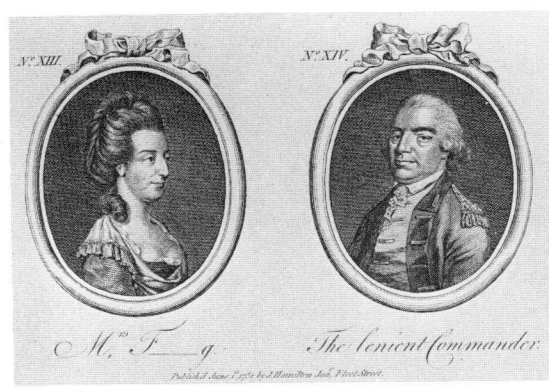

——Another impression. From Murray, *An Impartial History of the War in America*, v. 2 (Newcastle Upon Tyne, 1782), opposite p. 436. LC–USZ62–45229

81

Mrs. F____g. [and] The lenient Commander. Publish'd June 1st; 1781 by J. Hamilton Junr. Fleet Street.

Mixed method 4¼ x 7 in.

Following his return to England in 1776, Gage remained in disfavor with the Government as long as Germain was in authority. This tête-à-tête, from *The Town and Country Magazine*, May 1781, opposite p. 233, appearing one month after his appointment as commander of militia in Kent, was an attempt to perpetuate his image as a "lenient commander" and to further discredit him through allegations concerning an association with an unprincipled woman.

——Another copy. Publish'd as the Act directs by T: Walker No. 79 Dame Street. 4 x 7 in. From *The Hibernian Magazine*, July 1781, opposite p. 348.

Horatio Gates, 1728/29–1806

82

HORATIO GATES, ESQR. Major General of the American Forces. London: Publish'd as the Act directs, 2nd. Jany. 1778, by JOHN MORRIS.
Mezzotint 13⅞ x 9¾ in.

Gates points to a document upon which is written "Arti[cles] of Convention between Genl. Gates & Genl. Burgoyne." An American flag is in the left background. The gorget around Gates' neck designated an officer on duty. This mezzotint, one of a series of early portraits depicting American leaders in the War of Independence, probably by C. Corbutt, was later copied in Augsburg by J. M. Will and became the basis of many engravings throughout the decade following. See items 83 and 85 for prints after this one. CPPS 5469
LC–USZ62–3615

83

GENERAL GATES. Printed for T. Robson, Newcastle, upon Tyne. [1778]
Mixed method 7 x 4⅜ in.

Gates in uniform with gorget. From Murray, *An Impartial History of the Present War in America*, v. 2 (London, 1778), frontispiece.

——————Another impression. In Murray, *An Impartial History of the War in America*, v. 2 (Newcastle Upon Tyne, 1782), frontispiece.
LC–USZ62–45351

84

THE HONBLE. Horatio Gates. MAJOR GENERAL of the AMERICAN FORCES. [1780]
Mixed method 5⅞ x 3¾ in. (image)

Throughout the war Gates was known chiefly as the victor at the battle of Saratoga, although the wilderness, the lack of supplies for the British, and the Americans' superior numbers contributed more to the victory than

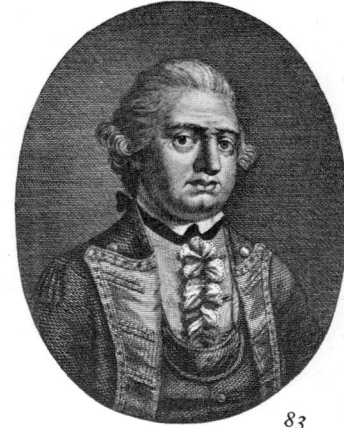

83

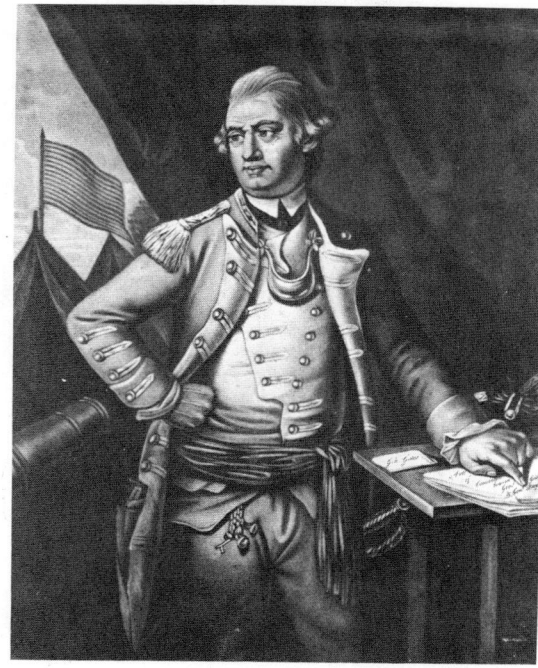

82

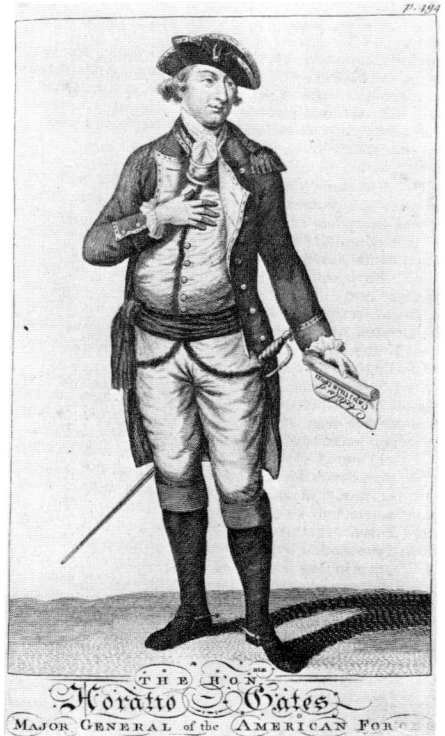

84

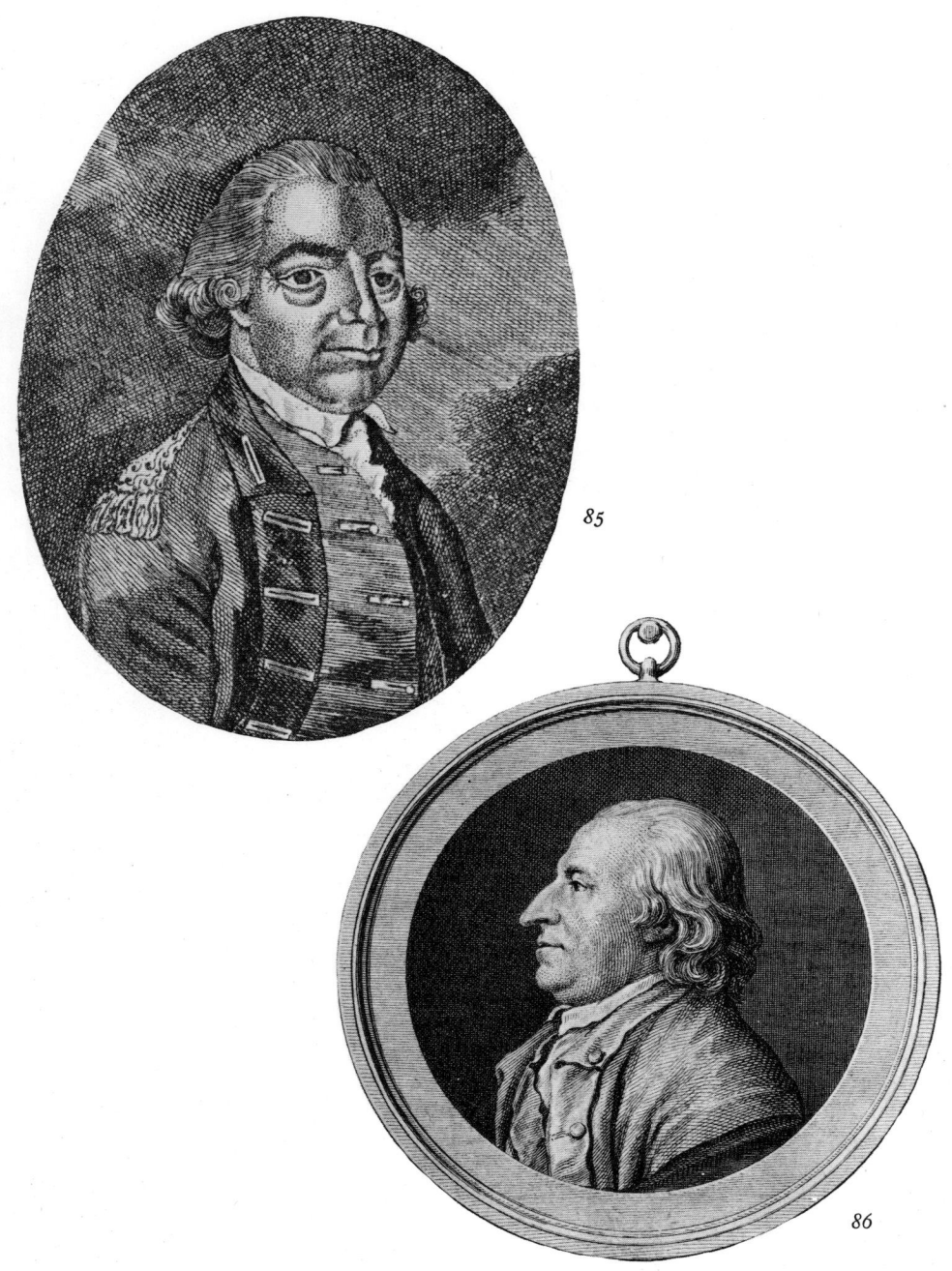

85

86

Gates' leadership. In this stylized portrait Gates holds a scroll reading "Articles of Capitulation." From *An Impartial History of the War in America* (London, 1780), p. 494.

———————Another impression. From *An Impartial History of the War in America* (London & Carlisle, 1780), p. 494. LC–USZ62–45258

85

The Honle. HORATIO GATES, ESQR. Major General in the American Army. J. Norman Sc. [1781]

Mixed method 4⅜ x 3½ in. (image)

The American engraver probably copied this portrait from the English edition of *An Impartial History* (item 83). Norman's shortcomings in skill and lack of materials become evident when this engraving is compared to the English illustration. From *An Impartial History of the War in America*, v. 2 (Boston, 1781), copy 1, p. 257. Stauffer, 2333. LC–USZ62–45243

———————Another impression. In v. 2, copy 2, frontispiece.

86

H. Gates. Drawn from the life by Du Simitier in Philadelphia. Engraved by B. L. Prevost at Paris. [1781]

Line engraving 7 x 5 in.

This portrait and the two following were drawn in the late 1770's and became very popular because the original sketch was the first "from the life." From *Portraits des généraux* . . . (Paris, 1781), plate 6. Plates from this volume are in P&P. LC–USZ62–26778

87

MAJOR GENERAL GATES. Pubd. 15th May 1783 by R. Wilkinson No. 58, Cornhill, London. B.B.E.

Mixed method 5½ x 4¼ in.

Bust profile to left. In Du Simitière, *Portraits of the Generals* ... (London, 1783), plate 12. Similar to item 86.

88

GENERAL GATES. Engraved for the Westminster Magazine. [November 1783]
Mixed method 7 x 4⅛ in.

Bust profile facing left in oval. The biography which accompanies this portrait explains that the valiant British troops were deserted by their Indian and Canadian allies at Saratoga and that Gates was a sympathetic and honorable victor. From *The Westminster Magazine*, November 1783, p. 163. After Du Simitière (see item 86).

George II, 1683–1760
George III, 1738–1820

89

K. GEORGE II. crowned June 11, 1727. K. GEORGE III. crowned Oct. 25, 1760. [1774]
Woodcuts, each 1¾ x 1¾ in. (image)

Bickerstaff wished to express his Tory sentiments by picture, poem, and genealogy. The two bust portraits, resembling Roman bas-reliefs, stress not only the Augustan nobility of George II and George III but also—by their physical resemblance—the virtues of succession. Between the portraits is a poem extolling the continuity of kingship:

> Happy the land to whom 'tis given
> T'enjoy that choicest boon of Heaven;
> Where, bound in one illustrious chain,
> The Monarch, and the People, reign.
> Hence is Britannia's weal maintain'd;
> Hence are the rights his Fathers gain'd
> To ev'ry freeborn subject known:
> Hence to the throne, in songs of praise,
> A grateful realm its tribute pays,
> And hails the King, whose int'rest is our own.

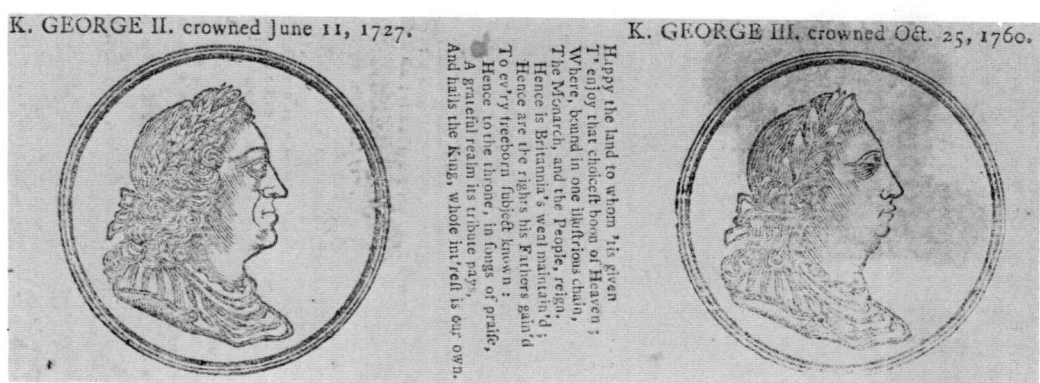

Another poem in an adjacent column praises George III:

> All hail! George renowned Prince of might,
> Our King by Providence, and lawful right,
> Rome's fatal foe, and protestant's delight,
> May peace and plenty all your days remain,
> And Nestor's years conclude your happy reign.
> Already round the globe your actions shine,
> Already you're acknowledg'd all divine,
> Whilst each succeeding year brings some new glory
> And adds a branch to your immortal story.

From Bickerstaff, *Boston Almanack* (Boston, 1774), p. 6. LC-USZ62-45320

90

His Majesty King George the III. Contemplating a Medal of King Alfred. [1774]
Mixed method 6⅜ x 3¾ in. (image)

The Hanoverian kings wished to strengthen their claim to the throne by showing descent from Alfred the Great. In this portrait the young King in his coronation robes holds up a medal of Alfred. The seal of England with the lion and the unicorn are over the doorway. From *The Annual Register* (Dublin, 1774), p. 383. LC-USZ62-45205

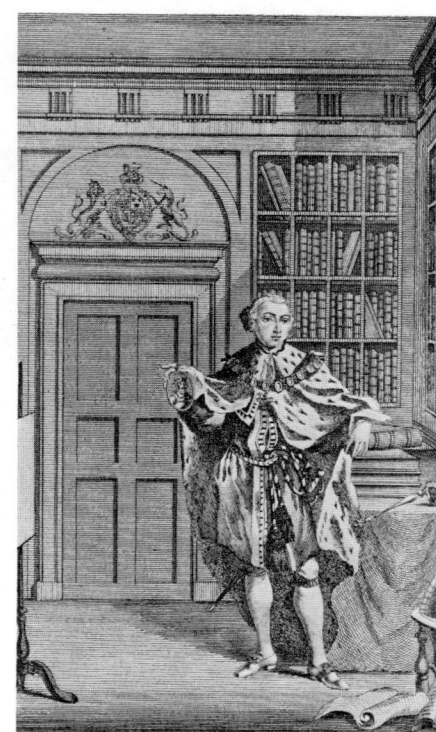

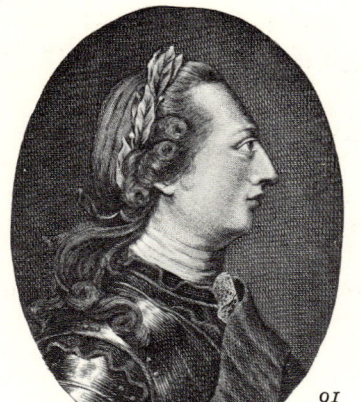

91

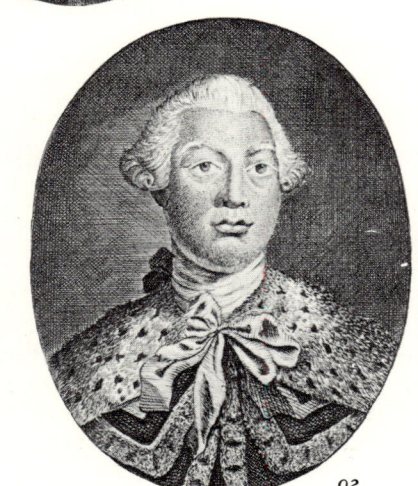

92

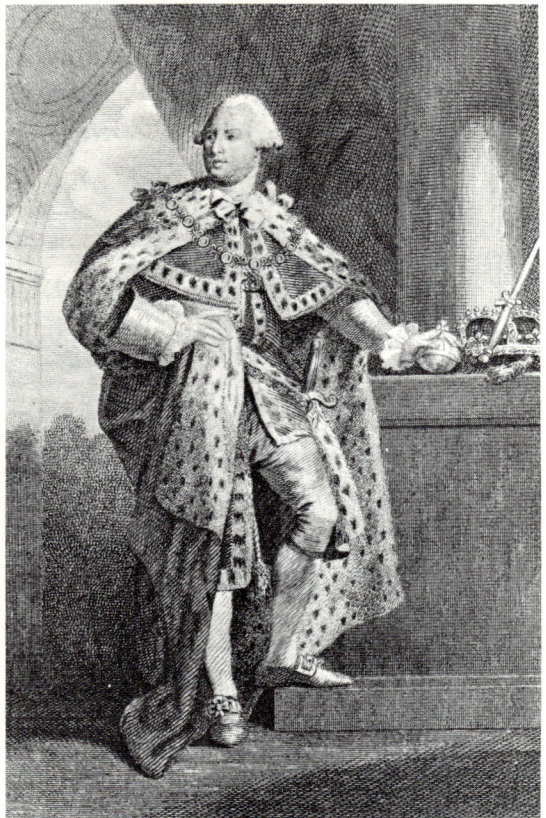

93

91
GEORGE the IIId. King of Great Britain, France and Ireland. Pollard sculpt. Printed for T. Robson, Newcastle upon Tyne. [1778]
Mixed method 7 x 4 in.

George III shown as a strong, young King in armor and wearing a laurel wreath. From Murray, *An Impartial History of the Present War in America*, v. 1 (London, 1778), frontispiece. LC–USZ62–45350

92
GEORGE III. King of Great Britain &c. Pollard sculp. Printed for T. Robson, Newcastle upon Tyne. [1780]
Mixed method 7 x 4⅜ in.

One of Reynold's coronation portraits, showing the King in white powdered wig and ermine stole. From Murray, *An Impartial History of the War in America*, v. 1 (Newcastle Upon Tyne, 1782), frontispiece. LC–USZ62–45228

———Another impression. From Murray, *An Impartial History of the Present War in America*, v. 1 (Newcastle Upon Tyne, 1780), frontispiece.

93
GEORGE the III. Reynolds del. Angus sculp. Published July 2, 1785, by J. Fielding Pater noster Row.
Mixed method 7 x 4¾ in.

Another coronation portrait after Reynolds. From Andrews, *History of the War with America, France, Spain, and Holland*, v. 1 (London, 1785). LC–USZ62–45307

George Sackville Germain, 1716–1785

94
LORD GEORGE GERMAINE. Apr. [1780]
Mixed method 7½ x 4½ in.

The accompanying biography refers to Germain's military errors, indicating that he "was always better calculated for the statesman, the man of letters, and the gentleman, than for an enterprising general." As Secretary of State for the Colonies, 1775–82, and Lord Commissioner of Trade and Plantations, 1775–79, he was an enthusiastic supporter of the policies of Lord North. When war broke out in America, Germain was placed in command of the British war effort by virtue of his civil post, in spite of the fact that he had been court-martialled earlier in his career. He was largely responsible for the military failures that resulted in the loss of the Colonies. From *The London Magazine*, April 1780, p. 147–148. LC–USZ62–45273

95

Lord George Germaine. Pollard sculp. Printed for T. Robson, Newcastle upon Tyne. [1782]

Mixed method 7¼ x 4⅜ in.

Bust portrait facing front in oval. From Murray, *An Impartial History of the War in America*, v. 2 (Newcastle Upon Tyne, 1782), opposite p. 297. Similar to item 94.

❧Lord George Gordon, 1751–1793

96

LORD GEORGE GORDON. Published by T: Walker No. 79 Dame Street. [July 1780]
Mixed method 6¾ x 4 in.

Gordon, the younger son of a duke, received a lieutenant's commission in the British Navy at the age of 21. He was eager to command his own ship in American waters and resigned when he was not promoted. He subsequently became a member of the opposition in Parliament. Gordon's political sympathies are discussed in a short biography accompanying the portrait. In 1780, the year of this engraving, he

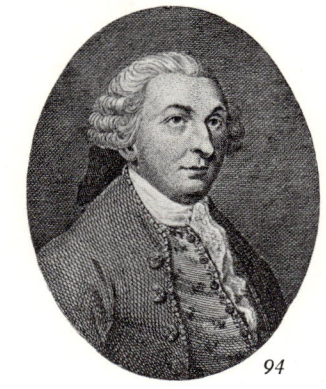
94

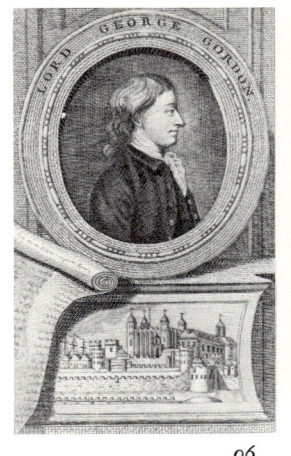
96

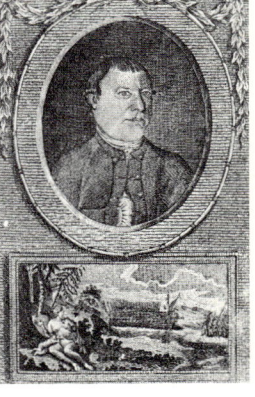
98

began to attract national attention because of his anti-Catholic agitation. The scroll beneath this bust profile, reading "Protestants Petition against Popery," refers to his role in the Gordon Riots. From *The Hibernian Magazine*, July 1780, p. 353–355. LC–USZ62–45202

97

Lord George Gordon. Publish'd 1st. July 1780 by Fielding & Walker. Pater Noster Row.
Mixed method 7 x 4½ in.

The biography accompanying this portrait implies that Gordon's disappointment at not receiving a much-deserved promotion influenced his decision to oppose the North Ministry and befriend the Americans. Similar to item 96. From *The Westminster Magazine*, June 1780, p. 295.

❧Nathanael Greene, 1742–1786

98

His Excy. Nathaniel Green Esq;—Major General of the American Army. J. Norman Sc. [1781]

Mixed method 5¾ x 3¾ in. (image)

Greene, who emerged from the Revolution with a military reputation second only to that of Washington, began his career as a militia private. He was chosen to serve as brigadier general of militia in 1775, became brigadier general in the Continental Army the same year, and was promoted to major general in 1776. He proved himself an able commander at Trenton and in 1778 reluctantly accepted an appointment as quartermaster general, a post in which he also excelled. His use of guerilla troops against Cornwallis in the Carolinas in 1780 and 1781 confirmed his reputation as a general of great ability. The allegory beneath Greene's portrait represents America nurturing the white and dark races. The feeding is interrupted by a military engagement of British and colonial troops; ships are in the background. From *An Impartial History of the War in America,* v. 1 (Boston, 1781), copy 2, p. 366.

———————Another impression. In v. 1, copy 1, p. 128. LC–USZ62–45236

99
GENERAL GREEN. Published Augt. 12, 1785, by J. Fielding, Pater-noster Row.

Mixed method 6¾ x 4⅜ in.

From Andrews, *History of the War with America, France, Spain, and Holland,* v. 1 (London, 1785), p. 356. LC–USZ62–45338

100
MAJR. GENL. GREENE. Trenchard Sculp. [1786]

Etching 6⅜ x 4⅜ in. (image)

Charles Willson Peale was designing plates for *The Columbian Magazine* in 1786, and Trenchard probably did this engraving after a Peale portrait. The work represents a memorial to Greene, and the items portrayed below the oval frame symbolize various aspects of his career. Frontispiece for *The Columbian Magazine,* September 1786. LC–USZ62–45507

Charles Grey
1st Earl Grey, 1729–1807

101
GENERAL GREY. Pollard sc. 1780 Printed for T. Robson, Newcastle upon Tyne.

Mixed method 7 x 4⅜ in.

Grey fought under Howe in 1776, was transferred to Clinton's command, and at the Battle of Brandywine led a surprise attack against General Anthony Wayne. A vigorous and able officer, he was critical of the management of the war by Germain and others in London. From Murray, *An Impartial History of the Present War in America,* v. 2 (Newcastle Upon Tyne, 1780), opposite p. 433. LC–USZ62–45232

———————Another impression. From Murray, *An Impartial History of the Present War in America,* v. 2 (London, 1778), opposite p. 433.

———————Another impression. From Murray, *An Impartial History of the War in America,* v. 2 (Newcastle Upon Tyne, 1782), opposite p. 271.

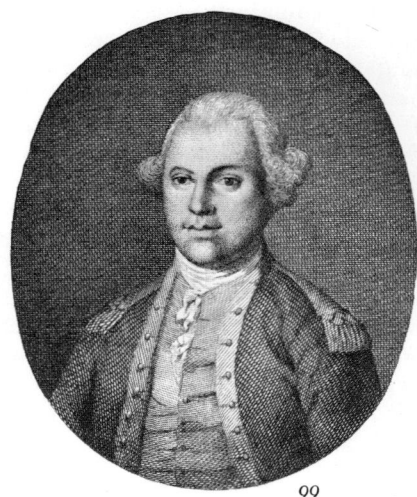

99

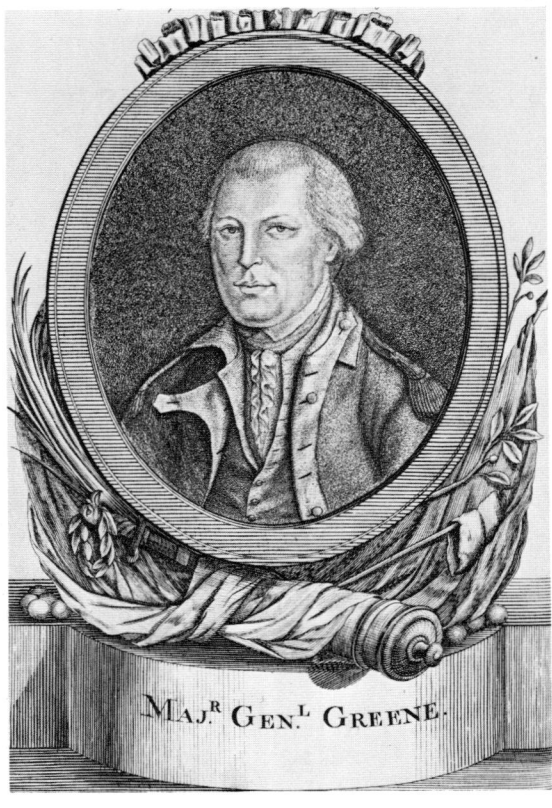

100

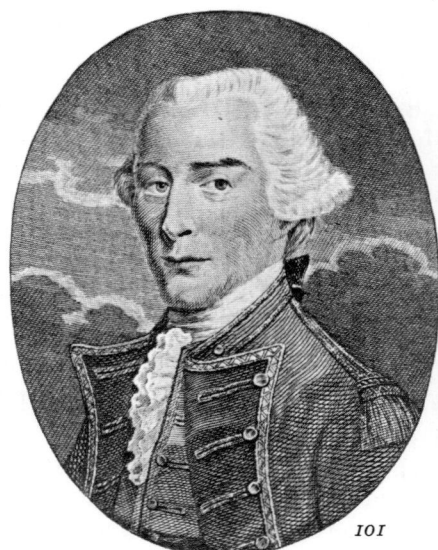

101

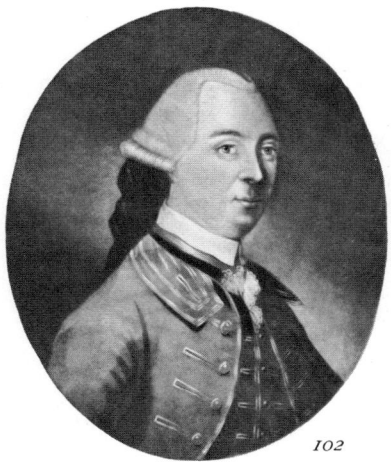 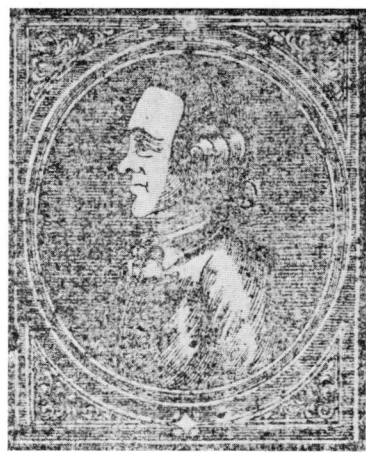 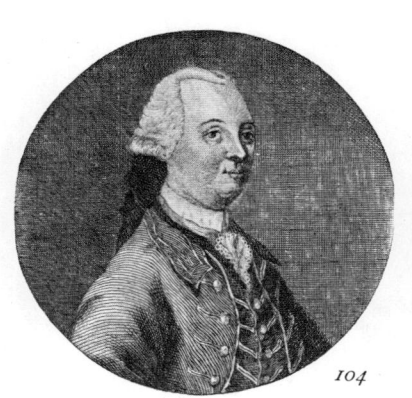 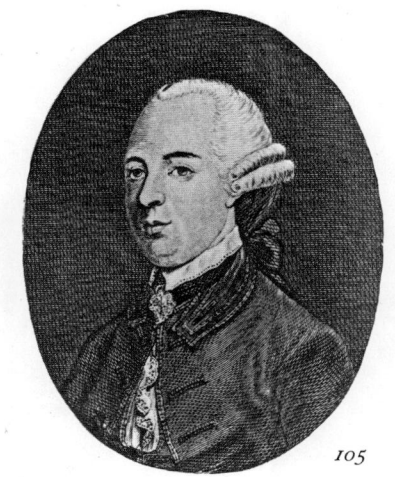

102 *103* *104* *105*

John Hancock, 1737–1793

102

The Honble John Hancock of Boston in New England; President of the American Congress. Done from an Original Picture Painted by Littleford. London, Published as the Acts directs 25 October 1775 by C. Shepherd.

Mezzotint 14 x 9⅞ in.

Hancock's involvement in the Revolution originated in his disagreements with Crown customs officials in connection with his thriving mercantile business in Boston. He was a leader among the militant patriots at the time of the Stamp Act crisis and the Boston Massacre and held elected offices in the Massachusetts Provincial Congress and the Continental Congress. As President of the Continental Congress he was the first to sign the Declaration of Independence, and he later served as president of the Massachusetts convention which ratified the Constitution. This portrait and items 104, 105, 108, and 109 are after a painting done by Copley in 1770–72. LC–USZ62–7340.

103

The Hon. JOHN HANCOCK, Esq; President of the Honourable the CONTINENTAL CONGRESS. [1777]

Woodcut 2⅝ x 2⅛ in.

From Bickerstaff, *Boston Almanack* (Boston, 1777), p. 3. LC–USZ62–45323

104

John Hankock. Praesident des Americane Congresses. [1777]

Etching 6⅝ x 4 in.

From Korn, *Geschichte der Kriege* (Nürnberg, 1777–78), copy 2, p. 120. LC–USZ62–45263

105

The Honble. John Hancock. Pollard sculp. Printed for T. Robson, Newcastle, upon Tyne. [1780]

Mixed method 7 x 4¼ in.

From Murray, *An Impartial History of the Present War in America*, v. 1 (Newcastle Upon Tyne, 1780), opposite p. 145. LC–USZ62–45300

——————Another impression. In the J. Pierpont Morgan "Signers Collection" in the Manuscript Division.

106

John Hancock, Esq: President of the American Congress. [1780]

Etching 6⅛ x 4¼ in. (image)

Hancock points his pen at a document entitled "To the People of Ireland," beside which are "Resolutions of the Continental Congress." The "Boston Port Bill," and a "Proclamation" are on the floor at his feet. On the wall behind him are three portraits. From *An Impartial History of the War in America*, v. 1 (London, 1780), p. 207. See also item 107.

——————Another impression. From *An Impartial History of the War in America*, v. 1 (London & Carlisle, 1780), p. 207.

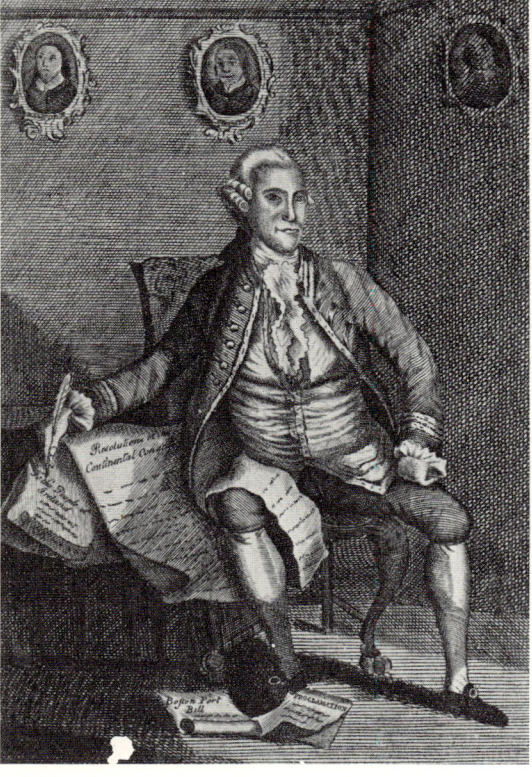

107

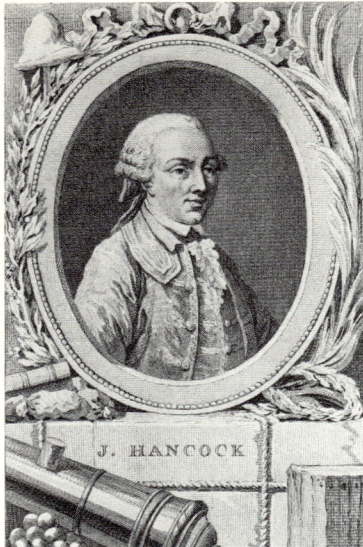

108

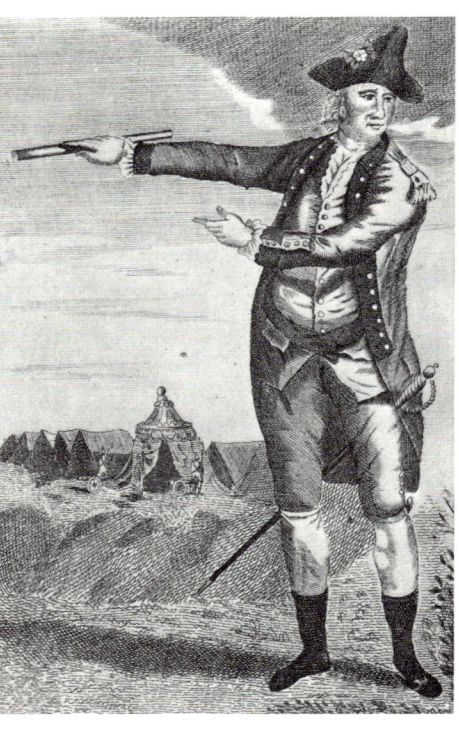

110

107

His Excy. JOHN HANCOCK, Esq:—LATE PRESIDENT of the AMERICAN CONGRESS. J. Norman, Sculp. [1781]
Etching 6 x 4 in. (image)

This picture is copied from item 106, with the exception that two of the pictures on the wall are identified as Hampden and Cromwell. From *An Impartial History of the War in America*, v. 1 (Boston, 1781), copy 1, frontispiece. Stauffer, 2335. LC–USZ62–45235

108

J. HANCOCK. J. Pelicier. Sculp. 1782.
Etching 6¼ x 3¾ in. (image)

The base below portrait resembles a shipping carton tied with rope. From Hilliard d'Auberteuil, *Essais historiques*, v. 3 (1782), p. [4]. LC–USZ62–45329

109

JOHN HANCOCK Esqr. Published Novr. 1, 1783 by J. Fielding, No. 23, Pater-noster Row.
Line engraving 5¾ x 3½ in. (image)

Bust portrait facing right in oval on pedestal with mask and ribbon on top. From the J. Pierpont Morgan "Signers Collection" in the Manuscript Division. Originally from *The European Magazine*, September 1783, p. 165. This print is similar to, and probably after, item 102.

William Heath, 1737–1814

110

His Excy. WILLIAM HEATH, Esq. Major General in the American Army. [1784]
Etching 6½ x 4 in. (image)

Heath's military abilities were limited and Washington assigned him primarily routine duties such as the handling of reserve troops and prisoners. His biographers agree that he was better suited to be a farmer and politician than a general. John Norman used the same background on this print and item 216. From *An Impartial History of the War in America*, v. 3 (Boston, 1784), copy 1, frontispiece. Stauffer 2336. LC–USZ62–45246

Hendrick, Tiyanoka the Great Sachem, ca. 1680–1755

111

The brave old [Tiyanoka] HENDRICK the great SACHEM or Chief of the Mohawk Indians, one of the Six Nations now in Alliance with, & Subject to the King of Great Britain. Sold by Eliz: Bakewell opposite Birchin Lane in Cornhill. [176?]|
Mixed method 14⅜ x 10¼ in.

Hendrick was killed in 1755 while fighting for the English at the battle of Lake George. Portraits of Hendrick and other Indians were widely reproduced in England during the last half of the 18th century and often showed the American Indian as an ally of Great Britain. Hendrick appears with painted face but in European dress and holding a European-made hatchet. LC–USZ62–45198

Wills Hill
1st Earl Hillsborough, 1718–1793

112

The Right Honble. The EARL of HILLSBOROUGH. [1781]
Mixed method 7 x 4½ in.

As Secretary of State for the Colonies from 1768 to 1772, Hillsborough consistently urged the House of Lords to condemn the colonist's efforts to resist taxation. Whether in office or out, he opposed all conciliatory actions toward the Americans until the end of the North administration in March 1782. The short

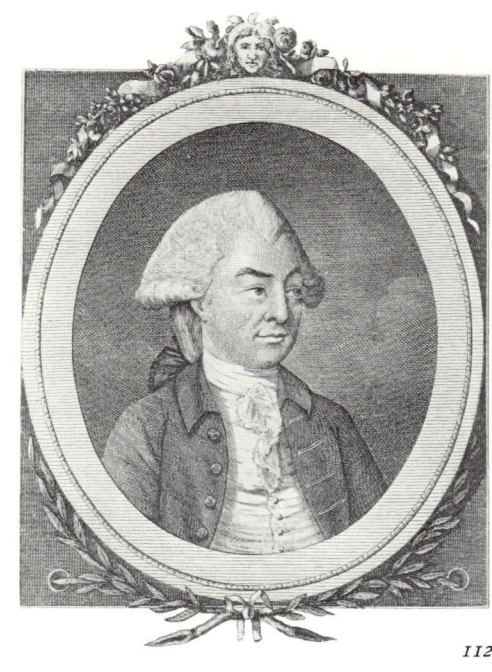

112

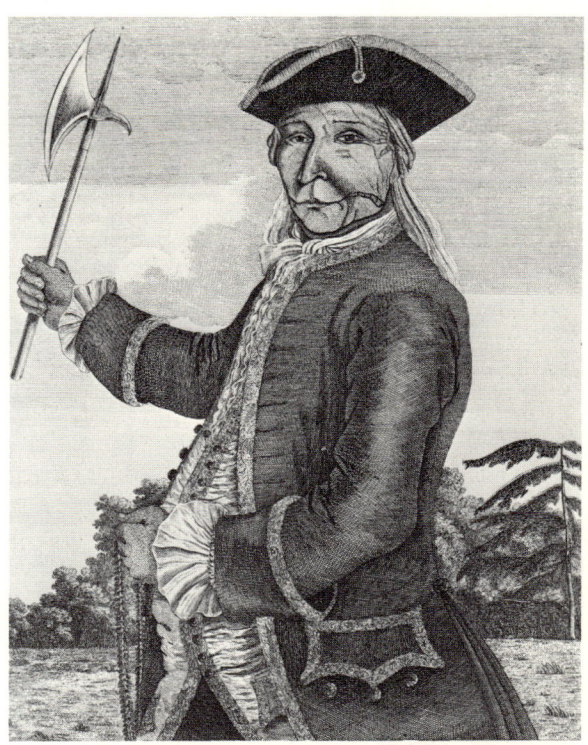

111

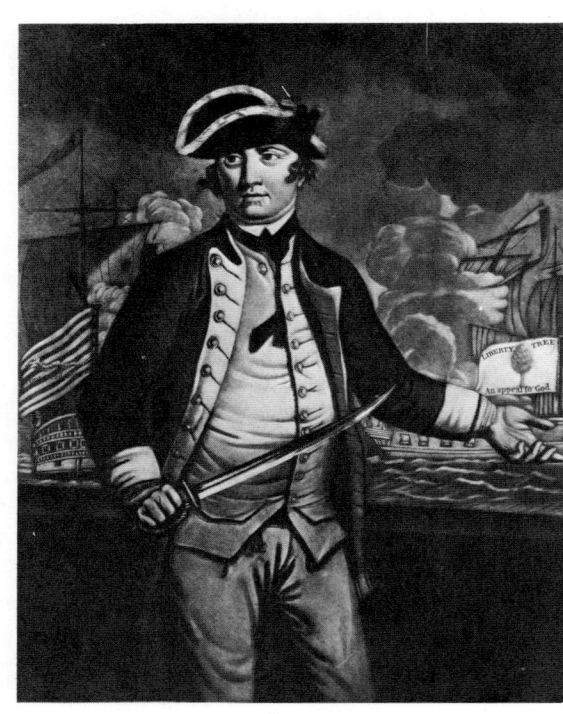

114

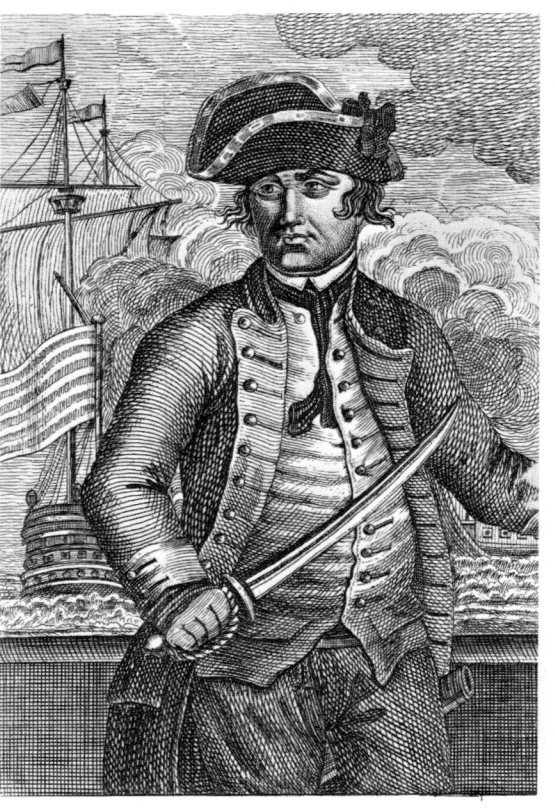

116

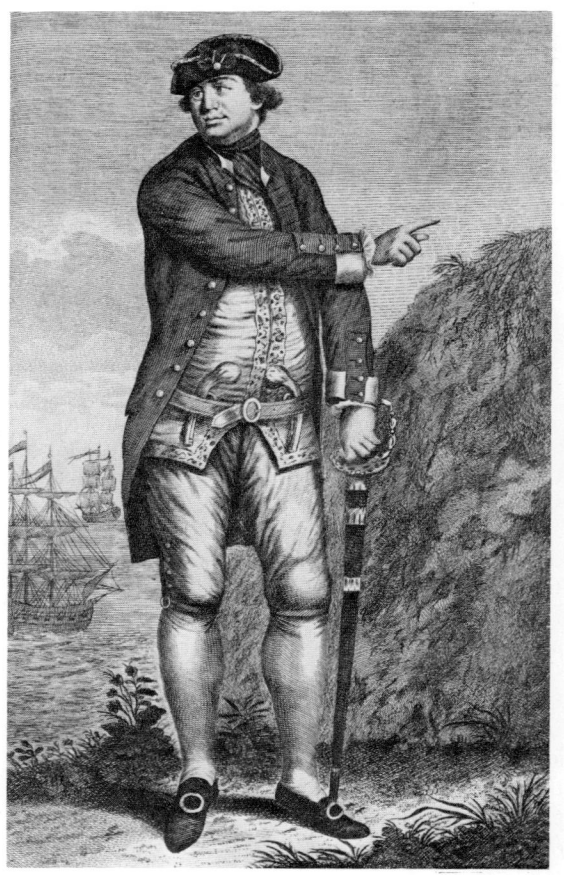

117

biography which accompanies this portrait suggests that although Hillsborough tried to coerce the Americans into acquiescence with the King's wishes, he received more than his share of blame for the ensuing fiascoes. From *The London Magazine*, August 1781, opposite p. 355. LC–USZ62–45315

———Another copy (reversed). From *The Hibernian Magazine*, September 1781, p. 449.

Samuel Hood
1st Viscount Hood, 1724–1816

113
LORD HOOD. Miller del. Birrell sculp. From a Painting by West in the Possession of Sir John Dick. Published June 21, 1785, by J. Fielding Pater-noster Row.
Mixed method 7 x 4¼ in.

Hood's service in North American waters began in 1763, and he was Commander in Chief in North America from 1767 to 1770. After two years of semiretirement as governor of the Naval Academy, 1778–80, he was sent to the West Indies, where he helped take St. Eustatius, blockaded Martinique, and assisted in holding off the superior forces of Comte de Grasse. Hood joined Graves off the Chesapeake Bay in a vain effort to relieve Cornwallis in 1781 at Yorktown, but having too small a force to be effectual, he returned to the West Indies to counter the French naval threat there. From Andrews, *History of the War with America, France, Spain, and Holland*, v. 4 (London, 1785), opposite p. 270. LC–USZ62–45344

Esek Hopkins, 1718–1802

114
COMMODORE HOPKINS, COMMANDER in CHIEF of the AMERICAN FLEET. Published as the Act directs 22 Augt. 1776 by Thos. Hart.
Mezzotint 13¾ x 10 in.

A successful sea captain before being appointed brigadier general in charge of Rhode Island's military forces, Hopkins met with reverses as a naval commander. He was dismissed from office by Congress in 1778 after the British blockaded his navy in Narragansett Bay in 1776 but remained a supporter of the American cause. This portrait shows him in uniform with ships in the background displaying a 1775 navy jack with the words "Dont tread upon me" and a "Liberty Tree" flag with the inscription "An appeal to God." The mezzotint pictured here was probably engraved by C. Corbutt, and it was later reproduced in Augsburg by J. M. Will. CPPS 5336 LC–USZ62–19219

115
COMMODORE HOPKINS. R. Pollard Sc. Printed for T. Robson, Newcastle, upon Tyne. [1778]
Mixed method 6⅞ x 4¼ in.

From Murray, *An Impartial History of the Present War in America*, v. 2 (London, 1778), opposite p. 289.

———Another impression. From Murray, *An Impartial History of the War in America*, v. 2 (Newcastle Upon Tyne, 1782), opposite p. 77. LC–USZ62–45353

116
Commodore Hopkins. Commandeur en Chef der Amerj: Flotte. [1778]
Etching 6⅝ x 3¾ in.

This German engraving is after the mezzotint by Corbutt (see item 114). The striped flag in the left background was often used to represent the American flag. From Korn, *Geschichte der Kriege* (Nürnberg, 1777–78), copy 2, p. 92. LC–USZ62–45266

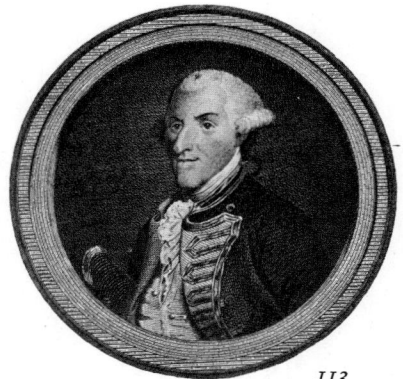

113

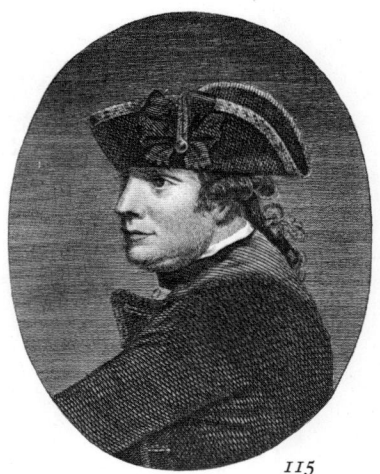

115

117
ROBERT HOPKINS. ESQR. Commodore of the AMERICAN Sea Forces. [1780]
Mixed method 7½ x 4½ in.

An idealized portrait. The engraver has used the wrong given name for Esek Hopkins. From *An Impartial History of the War in America*, v. 1 (London & Carlisle, 1780), p. 310. LC–USZ62–45252

———Another impression. From *An Impartial History of the War in America*, v. 1 (London, 1780), p. 310.

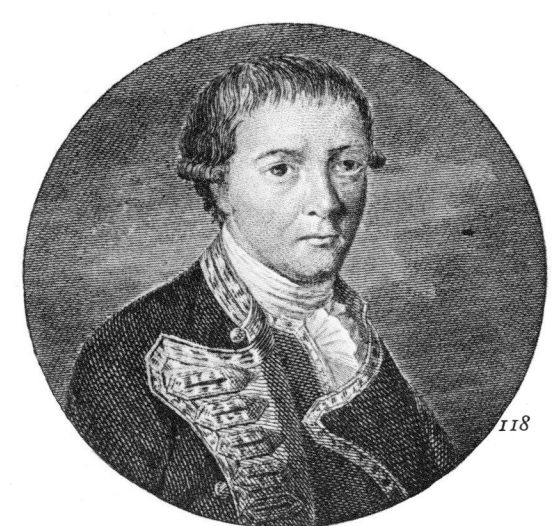

118

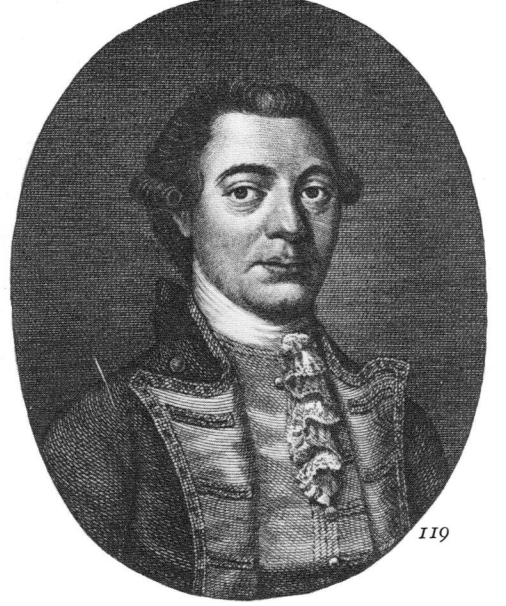

119

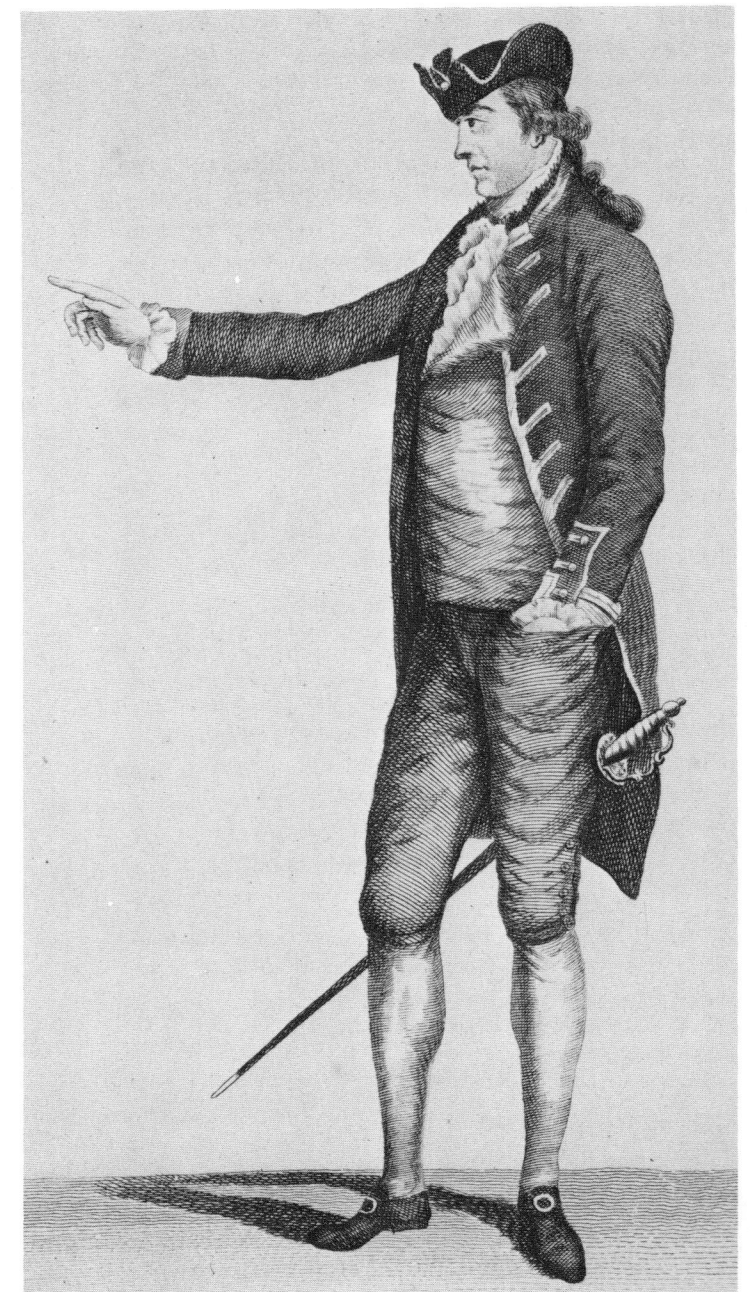

120

Richard Howe
Earl Howe, 1726–1799

118

LORD VISCOUNT HOWE. Angus Sculp. Published Novr. 1, 1782, by J. Fielding, Paternoster Row, J Sewell, Cornhill, & J Debrett, Piccadilly. European Magazine.

Mixed method 6¾ x 4 in.

An admiral in the British Navy, Howe served as Commander in Chief on the American station from 1776 to 1778 and as a member of the first peace commission. This portrait, made in 1782 when Howe was commanding naval forces in the English Channel, was inserted in a copy of *The Annual Register* (Dublin, 1774), opposite p. 119. LC–USZ62–45204

119

LORD HOWE. Printed for T. Robson, Newcastle, upon Tyne. [1778]

Mixed method 6⅞ x 4 in.

From Murray, *An Impartial History of the Present War in America*, v. 2 (London, 1778), opposite p. 97.

————Another impression. From Murray, *An Impartial History of the War in America*, v. 1 (Newcastle Upon Tyne, 1782), opposite p. 303. LC–USZ62–45352

120

Richd. Lord Viscount Howe REAR ADMIRAL of the WHITE and Commander in Chief of the Fleet in N. America. [1780]

Etching 6½ x 4¼ in. (image)

From *An Impartial History of the War in America*, v. 1 (London, 1780), p. 327.

————Another impression. From *An Impartial History of the War in America*, v. 1 (London & Carlisle, 1780), p. 327. LC–USZ62–45254

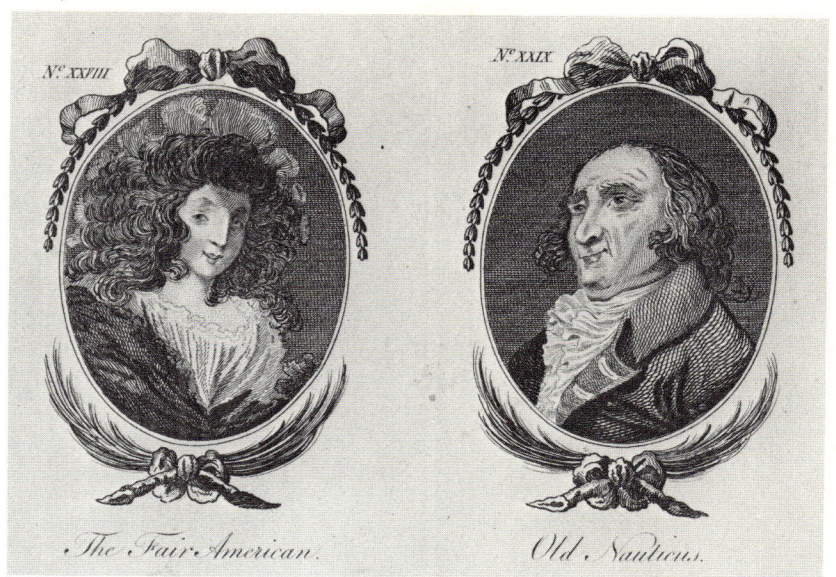

121

LORD HOWE. Publish'd March 25th. 1786. by J. Fielding Pater noster Row London.

Mixed method 6⅞ x 4⅜ in.

This portrait was made while Howe was First Lord of the Admiralty. Andrews, *History of the War with America, France, Spain, and Holland*, v. 1 (London, 1785), opposite p. 303. LC–USZ62–45337

122

The Fair American. [and] Old Nauticus. London, Publish'd by A. Hamilton, Junr. Fleet Street Novr. 1; 1788.

Mixed method 4½ x 6⅞ in.

Accompanying this tête-à-tête is a description of an affair between an American widow and an old sailor who seduces her. Dorothy George suspects that Lord Richard Howe is the old man, although the portrait does not resemble any likeness of him. See CPPS 7412. From *The Town and Country Magazine*, October 1788, p. 439–441. LC–USZ62–45420

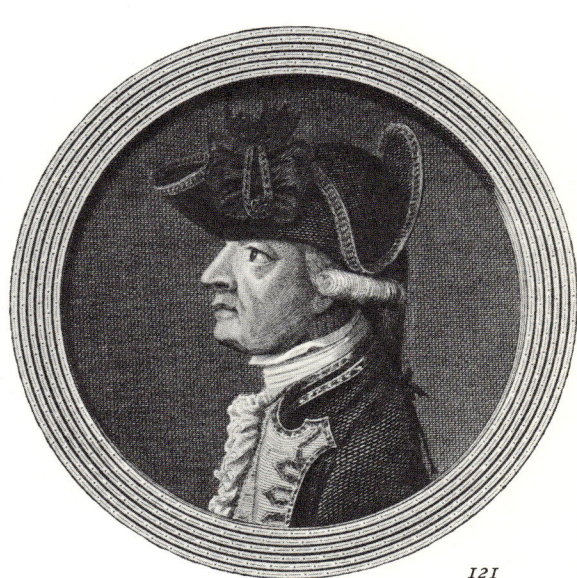

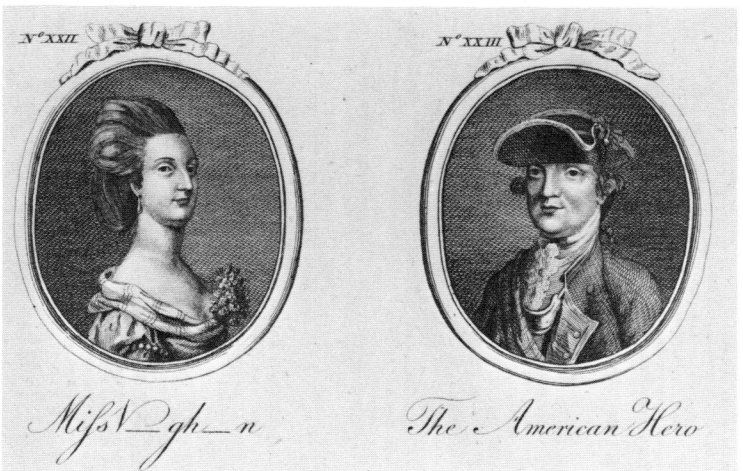

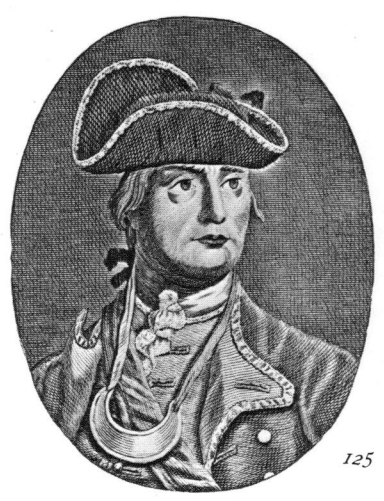

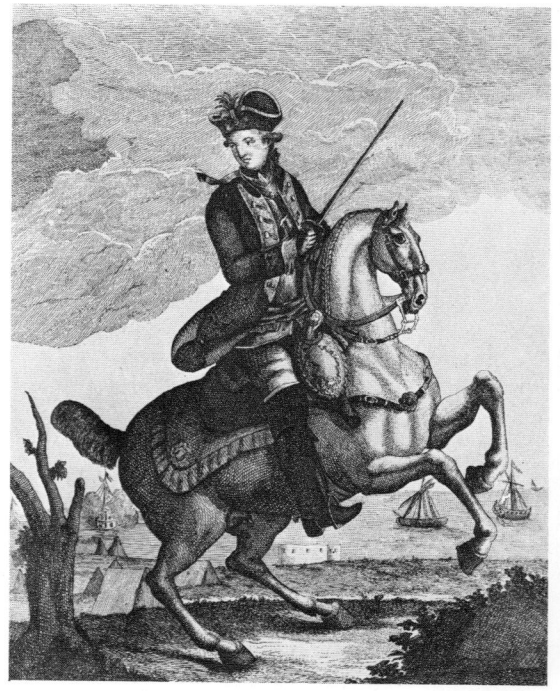

William Howe
5th Viscount Howe, 1729–1814

123

Miss V__gh__n. [and] The American Hero. Published as the Act directs by A. Hamilton Junr. near St. John's Gate. Sepr. 1. 1775.
Mixed method 4 x 7 in.

General William Howe, British Commander in Chief in the Colonies, 1776–78, earlier had sworn that he would never attempt to coerce the Americans, but many were skeptical about his strong pro-American feelings. This tête-à-tête appeared soon after the debacle at Bunker Hill, and the accompanying text is among the first to blame Howe for assuming a military post against an enemy for whom he had great sympathy. The article hints at the bond between Howe and the colonists with an irony typical of *The Town and Country Magazine*:

> The general's behavior on the 17th of June, in the action near Boston, has so perfectly established his character for coolness, fortitude, and bravery, that nothing can add to its lustre, except the esteem and veneration in which even his enemies held him, and who would not fire upon him when deserted by his own troops, before he could rally them.

The article next slanders Howe through a story of his fathering a child by Miss Vaughan, who was made a ward to Howe at the time of her father's death. From *The Town and Country Magazine*, August 1775, p. 401–403. CPPS 5308 LC–USZ62–45490

——————Another copy. Publish'd as the Act directs by T: Walker No. 79 Dame Street. From *The Hibernian Magazine*, September 1775, p. 514–516.

124

General Howe Esqr. of the Conecticut and comander Army in America. I.M. Probst. fc. Ioh. Mich: Probst. exc: A.V. [1776–178?]
Mixed method 10⅝ x 8 in.

A German representation of William Howe in America. LC–USZ62–45179

125

GENERAL HOWE. Printed for T. Robson, Newcastle, upon Tyne. [1778]
Mixed method 7 x 4¼ in.

A complimentary portrait, engraved while

Lieutenant General Howe was in possession of Philadelphia. Howe's large stature and handsome features were compared by some to those of Washington (cf. items 127 and 214). From Murray, *An Impartial History of the Present War in America*, v. 1 (London, 1778), opposite p. 287.

————Another impression. From Murray, *An Impartial History of the War in America*, v. 2 (Newcastle Upon Tyne, 1782), opposite p. 39. LC–USZ62–45303

126

The Hon; Sir Willm. Howe Kt. of the BATH. Commander in Chief of all his Majesty's Forces in America. [1780]
Mixed method 7½ x 4½ in.

Howe was made Knight of the Bath for his successful campaign in New York in 1776. From *An Impartial History of the War in America*, v. 1 (London & Carlisle, 1780), p. 205. LC–USZ62–45247

————Another impression. From *An Impartial History of the War in America*, v. 1 (London, 1780), p. 204.

127

GENERAL HOWE. Dodd del. Goldar sculp. Published May, 13, 1786, by J. Fielding Pater Noster Row.
Mixed method 6¾ x 4½ in.

From Andrews, *History of the War with America, France, Spain, and Holland*, v. 2 (London, 1785), copy 1, p. 226. LC–USZ62–45339

————Another impression. From Andrews, *History of the War with America, France, Spain, and Holland*, v. 1 (London, 1785), copy 3, p. 302.

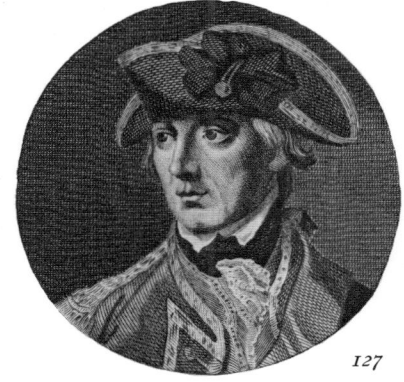
127

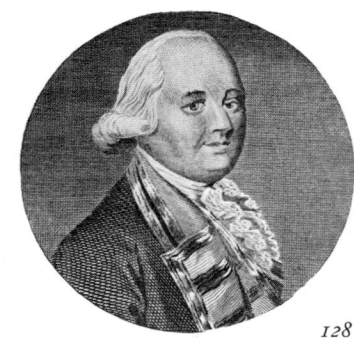
128

Edward Hughes, ca. 1720–1794

128

ADMIRAL HUGHES. Publish'd May 12, 1786, by John Fielding, Pater-noster Row.
Mixed method 6⅞ x 4¾ in.

Though Hughes did not fight in American waters, he did undertake expeditions against the principal Dutch settlements in the East Indies. From Andrews, *History of the War with America, France, Spain, and Holland*, v. 4 (London, 1785), p. 239. LC–USZ62–45220

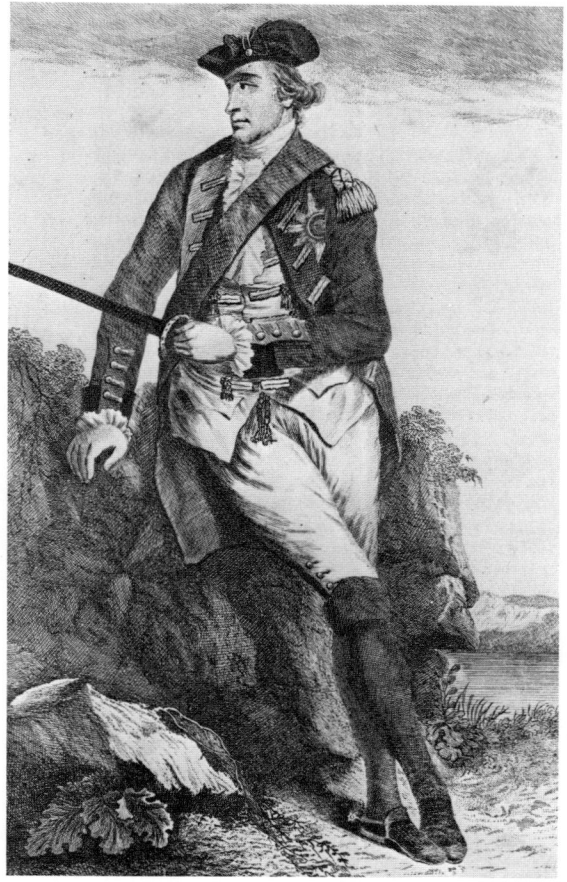
126

Samuel Huntington, 1731–1796

129

S. Huntingdon. Drawn from the life by Du Simitière in Philadelphia. Engraved by B. L. Prevost at Paris. [1781]

Line engraving with etched border 7 x 5 in.

Du Simitière probably drew the portrait from which this engraving was made in 1779, when Huntington was attending the Continental Congress as a delegate from Connecticut. From *Portraits des généraux*... (Paris, 1781), plate 8. Plates from this volume are in P&P. LC–USZ62–43020

130

His Excellency S. HUNTINGDON President of Congress. Pubd. May 15th 1783 by R. Wilkinson No. 58 Cornhill, London. B.B.E.

Mixed method 5½ x 4¼ in.

Bust profile facing left. In Du Simitière, *Portraits of the Generals*... (London, 1783), plate 4. Similar to item 129.

John Jay, 1745–1829

131

His Excellency JOHN JAY President of Congress & Minister Plenipotentiary from Congress at Madrid. Pubd. May 15th. 1783, by R. Wilkinson No. 58. Cornhill, London. B.B.E.

Mixed method 5½ x 4¼ in.

Engraved after Du Simitière's portrait of John Jay, drawn from life in Philadelphia in 1779. Jay was elected President of Congress in December 1778 and held that post until he was appointed Minister to Spain in September 1779. In Du Simitière, *Portraits of the Generals*... (London, 1783), plate 3. LC–USZ62–45481

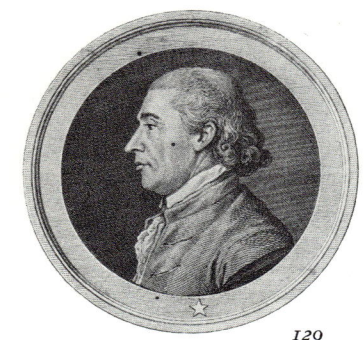
129

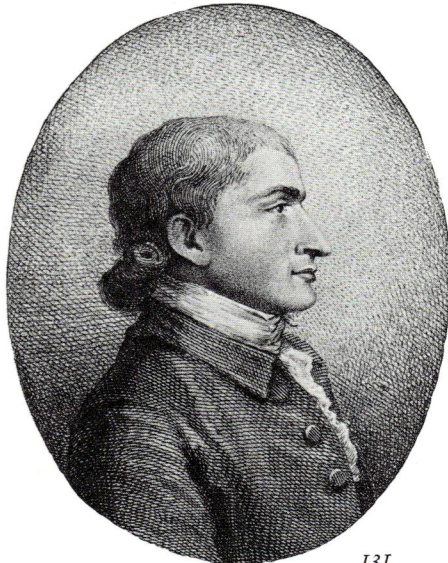
131

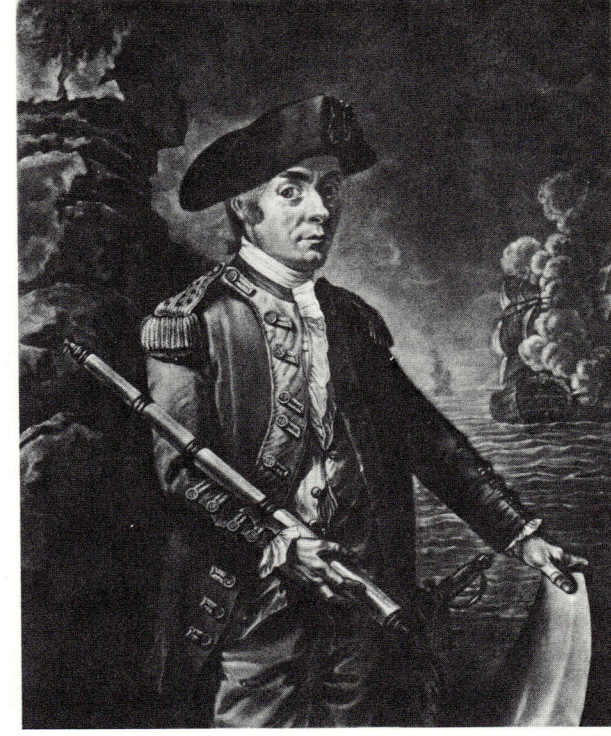
132

John Paul Jones, 1747–1792

132

JOHN PAUL JONES, Commander of a Squadron in the Service of THE THIRTEEN UNITED STATES OF NORTH AMERICA, 1779.

Mezzotint 13¾ x 9⅞ in.

Commissioned a lieutenant in the Continental Navy by Congress in 1775, John Paul Jones, a Scotsman by birth, soon proved himself exceptional in both seamanship and courage. The DAB describes Jones as "homely, small, thin, and active," but his size and stature never detracted from his proud bearing. LC–USZ62–19203

133

John Paul Jones. Dessiné par C. J. Notté. Gravé par Carl Guttenberg. A Paris chez Guttenberg rue St. Hyacinthe la 2me porte par la place St. Michel. [178?]

Line engraving 12½ x 9⅞ in.

The defeat of the British ship *Serapis* by the *Bonhomme Richard* (thus named by Jones in honor of Benjamin Franklin) was attributed solely to the courage of the stalwart commodore, who lashed his smaller vessel to the *Serapis* stem to stem so as to prevail through musketry in close action. The note appearing below the title describes the advantages held by the British and mentions that the *Richard* sank shortly after the battle:

Commodore au service des Etats-Unis de l'Amérique, tel qu'il était dans le combat du 23 7bre. 1779 contre le Commodore Pearson son Vaisseau le bon homme Richard montait 40. canons. le Vaisseau Anglais le Serapis 44. avait encore l'avantage du calibre, et la legèrté. le Commodore P. Jones, par sa maneuvre engagea le Beaupré de l'ennemi, et s'empara du Serapis en le combattant bord a bord pandant 2. heures ¾. l'Action dura 3. heures et ¼. Le bon homme Richard coula le lendemain.

LC–USZ62–45184

———A similar copy with no credits except, "A Paris chez Esnauts et Rapilly, rue St. Jacques."

7½ x 4⅞ in.

A note essentially identical to that quoted above appears below the title, together with the following anecdote describing the intrepid character of John Paul Jones, who it is said would rather have surrendered to the devil than to the British captain:

A la fin du Combat le Bon homme Richard se trouva être si désempare que le Capitaine du Sérapis cria à Paul Jones que s'il n'amenoit pas sur le champ, il alloit le couler bas: (coule-moi bas si tu peux, répondit l'intrépide Américain, lorsque le Diable voudra m'avoir, j'aime mieux me rendre à lui qu'à toi.)

LC–USZ62–2510

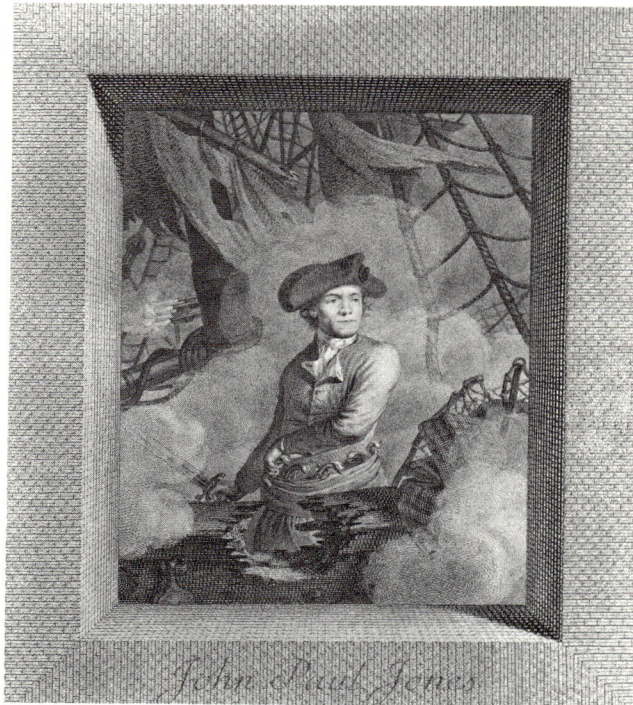

133a

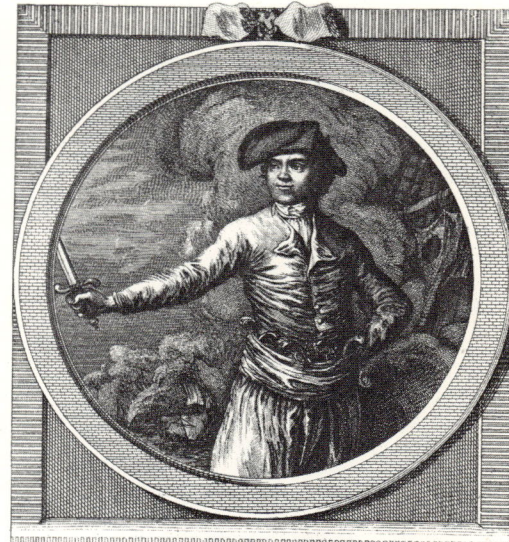

133b

43

134

John Paul Jones. A Paris chez l'Auteur rue du Cog St. Honoré, près le Louvre. Dessiné d'après nature au mois de May 1780 par J. M. Moreau le Jeune. Gravé a l'Eauforte par J. M. Moreau le Je. Terminé au burin par J. B. Fosseyeux, 1781.

Line engraving 8½ x 6½ in.

In April 1780 Jones went to France to negotiate the sale of his prize and was greeted as a popular hero of the American Revolution. The lines below the title of this portrait pay tribute to the rare genius of the naval officer:

> Tels hommes rarement se peuvent présenter,
> Et quand le Ciel les donne, il faut en profiter.

LC–USZ62–10884

Richard Kempenfelt, 1718–1782

135

ADML. KEMPENFELT. Publish'd April 27. 1786 by J. Fielding Pater Noster Row.

Mixed method 6⅞ x 4¼ in.

A rear admiral in the British Navy, Kempenfelt used a brilliant maneuver to disperse the French convoy of Admiral de Guichen which was bound for the West Indies in 1780. From Andrews, *History of the War with America, France, Spain, and Holland*, v. 4 (London, 1785), opposite p. 294. LC–USZ62–45346

Augustus Keppel Viscount Keppel, 1725–1786

136

ADMIRAL KEPPEL. [1778]

Mixed method 6½ x 4¼ in.

Keppel had performed well in the Seven Years' War but as the result of political intrigues was not offered a commission in the American war until January 1778, when the threat from France was acute. He needed six

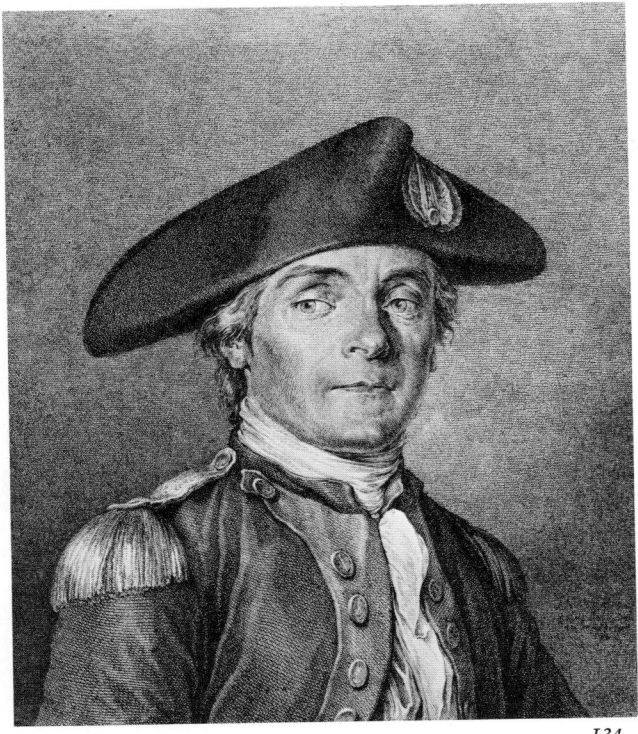
134

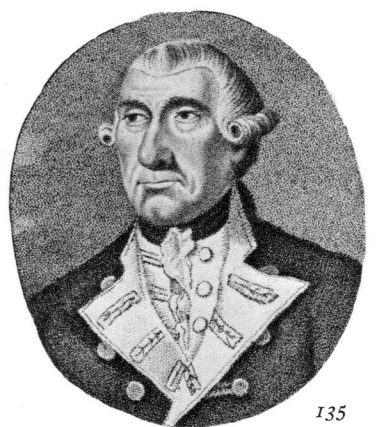
135

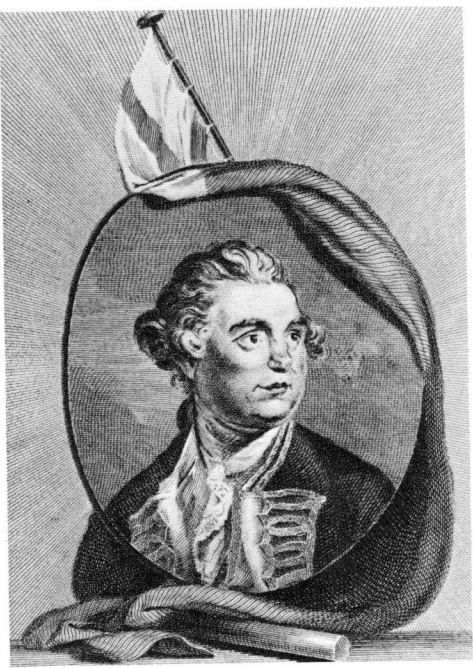
136

months to refit the fleet, and this portrait appeared before he sailed out for combat with the French and Spanish. In the short biography which accompanies this portrait, the hope is expressed that "Great Britain will still be enabled to preserve the empire of the seas, and to take ample vengeance on her perfidious neighbors for interfering in our unhappy quarrel with our American colonies." From *The London Magazine*, July 1778, p. 291.
LC–USZ62–45501

137
ADMIRAL KEPPEL. Printed for T. Robson, Newcastle, upon Tyne. [1778]
Mixed method 6⅞ x 4¼ in.

From Murray, *An Impartial History of the Present War in America*, v. 2 (London, 1778), opposite p. 529.

———Another impression. From Murray, *An Impartial History of the Present War in America*, v. 2 (Newcastle Upon Tyne, 1780), opposite p. 529. LC–USZ62–45233

138
LORD KEPPEL. Golder sculp. Publish'd March 18. 1786. by J. Fielding Pater noster Row.
Mixed method 6⅞ x 4½ in.

On February 11, 1779, Keppel was acquitted by a court martial trying him for inadequate performance. Since he had sailed judiciously and fought valiantly against the French, the people saw his acquittal as a victory over the Ministers who were responsible for the misconduct of the war. This portrait of Keppel, who was one of the few unscathed English heroes, appeared in Andrews, *History of the War with America, France, Spain, and Holland*, v. 3 (London, 1785), opposite p. 196.
LC–USZ62–45342

❧Henry Knox, 1750–1806

139
The Honle. HENRY KNOX, Esqr. Major General of the Artillery in the American ARMY. J. Norman Sc. [1782]
Etching 4¼ x 3⅜ in. (image)

Appointed brigadier general and subsequently major general of artillery, Knox developed this branch of the Continental Army into a viable fighting force. His command was particularly outstanding at Monmouth and Yorktown. From *An Impartial History of the War in America*, v. 2 (Boston, 1782), copy 1, p. 321. Stauffer, 2337. LC–USZ62–45244

❧Marie Joseph Paul Yves Roch Gilbert du Motier, Marquis de Lafayette, 1757–1834

140
The Honble. MARQUIS LAFAYETTE, Major General of the American Army. [1782]
Etching 4½ x 3¾ in. (image)

The dashing young marquis became the symbol of the French-American entente. He served Washington as a major general in the field and sparked enthusiasm for the American cause in France. Among the hundreds of Lafayette portraits engraved before 1790, relatively few connected him with the American Revolution, and he was generally portrayed as representing a hope for a new order emerging from the French Revolution. Americans continued to associate Lafayette with their own history, however, and the portraits by Norman and Hill (items 140 and 143) served to rekindle his popularity. From *An Impartial History of the War in America*, v. 2 (Boston, 1782), copy 1, p. 65. Stauffer, 2338.
LC–USZ62–45239

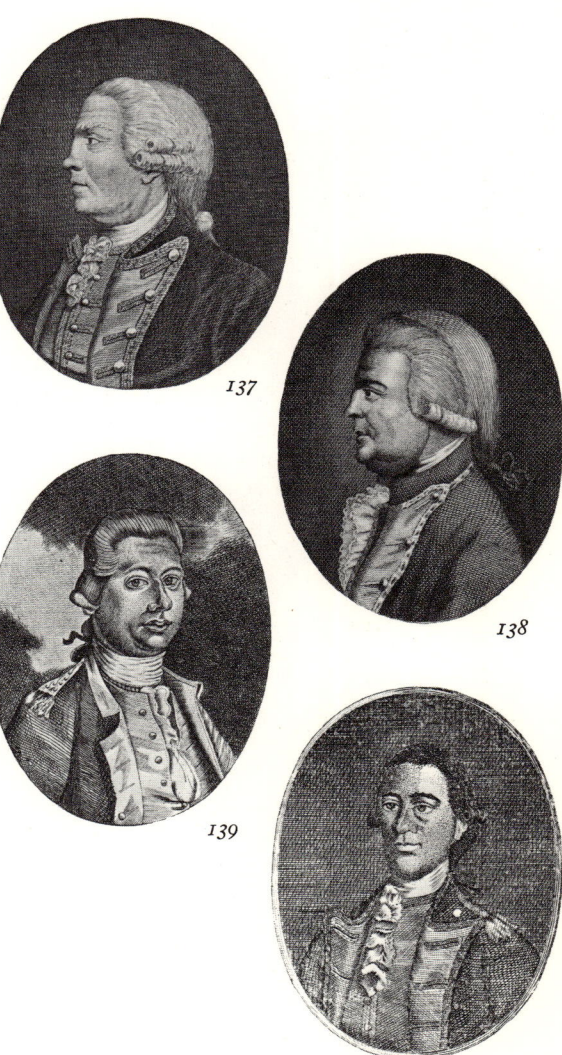

137
138
139
140

141

DE LA FAYETTE. Angus Sculp. Published Augt. 26, 1785, by J. Fielding, Pater-noster Row.

Mixed method 5¾ x 3¾ in. (image)

From Andrews, *History of the War with America, France, Spain, and Holland*, v. 2 (London, 1785), p. 422.
LC–USZ62–45308

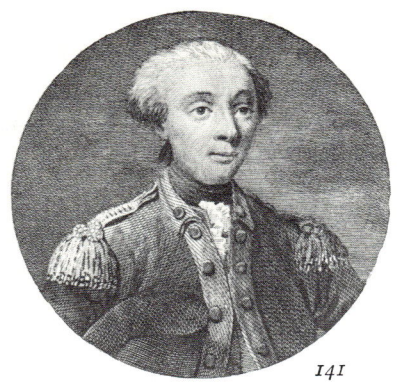
141

142

[LaFayette at Yorktown] Conclusion De La Campagne De 1781 en Virginie. To his excellancy General Washington this likeness of his friend, the Marquess de la Fayette, is humbly dedicated, by le Mire. [178?]

Line engraving 16½ x 12½ in. (image)

When Lafayette first joined the American Army, Congress appointed him a major general without command. After the Battle of Brandywine, he assumed command of various American troops and distinguished himself as strategist and leader. This French print, showing him directing troops against the British fortifications at Yorktown, was probably engraved soon after December 1781, when he returned to France to assist in the war against England. Probably by Noel le Mire. LC–USZ6–820

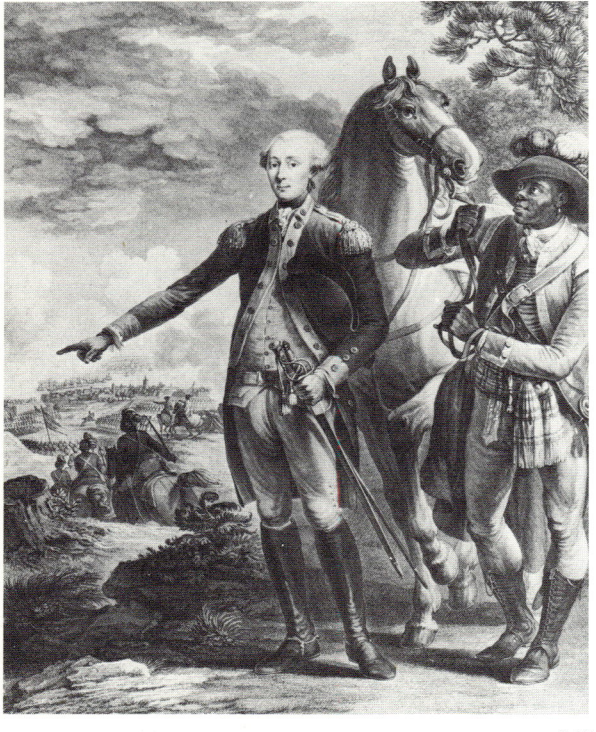
142

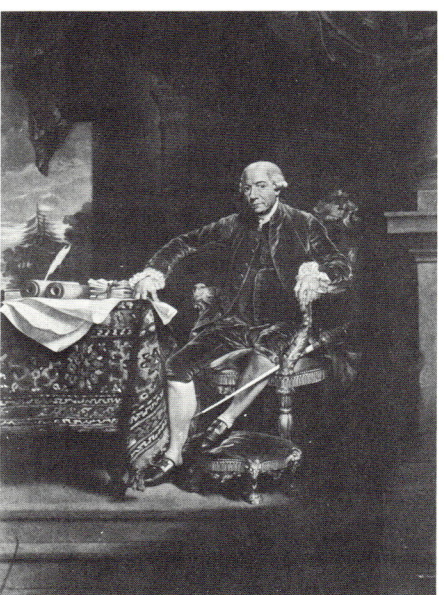
144

143

THE RIGHT HONOURABLE THE MARQUIS DE LA FAYETTE, Unanimously chosen Commandant of the National Guards. Engraved by S. Hill [1790]

Mixed method 4 x 3½ in. (image)

The verse below the portrait reads:

The brave FAYETTE, of late in foreign climes unfurl'd
The *Gallic* flag—and fought, to liberate a world:
Today, inspir'd by him, France breathes the godlike flame;
And millions, rang'd beneath his standard—FREEDOM claim.

Translated from the French of the Chev. P. de Berainville

From *The Massachusetts Magazine*, August 1790, frontispiece. Stauffer, 1370.
LC–USZ62–45525

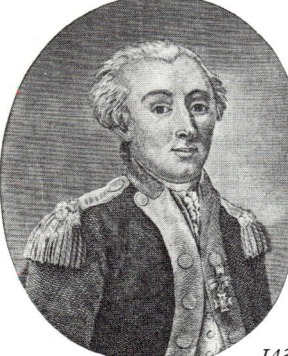
143

Henry Laurens, 1724–1792

144

HENRY LAURENS ESQR. PRESIDENT OF THE AMERICAN CONGRESS 1778. Painted by J. S. Copley, R. A. Elect. 1782. Engraved by V. Green Mezzotinto Engraver to his Majesty & to the Elector Palatine. Published Octr. 1st. 1782 by J. Stockdale Bookseller, No. 181, opposite Burlington House, Picadilly London.
Mezzotint 25½ x 16⅛ in.

Laurens had been President of the Continental Congress until December 1778, when he resigned due to a quarrel with Silas Deane. He continued to work for the cause of independence but was captured by the British while en route to Holland with a treaty from Congress. Charged with treason, he was placed in the Tower of London for over a year, until Franklin and Burke arranged his parole on December 31, 1781. He probably sat for this portrait shortly after his release. Copley pictures Laurens as an American aristocrat. On the table to his right are "Ratification Treaties . . . May 1778," a letter ending "We pray God very dear Friend and Wish to take You into his Holy Keeping. *Louis*," a paper signed "Carlisle, George Johnson, Wm. Eden" (the three peace commissioners), documents reading "Confederation 1778" and "Congress 22d April 1778," and a paper signed "H. Laurens, President." The columns surrounding the subject signify classic stability; the landscape in the background could represent his native South Carolina. LC–USZ62–5768

145

His Excellency HENRY LAURENS President of Congress, and Minister Plenipotentiary for treating of Peace with Grt. Britain. Pubd. May 15th. 1783, by R. Wilkinson No. 58, Cornhill London. B.B.E.
Mixed method 5½ x 4¼ in.

The artist drew this picture in the late 1770's, when Laurens was in Philadelphia. From Du Simitière, *Portraits of the Generals* . . . (London, 1783), plate 2. LC–USZ62–45480

146

HENY. LAURENS ESQR. J. Norman Sc. [1784]
Mixed method 3¼ x 2¼ in. (image)

Norman probably took this predominately stipple engraving from the mezzotint of the Copley portrait. From *The Boston Magazine*, September 1784, frontispiece. Stauffer, 2339. LC–USZ62–45284

Charles Lee, 1731–1782

147

CHARLES LEE, Esqr. MAJOR GENERAL of the CONTINENTAL-ARMY in AMERICA. Published as the Act directs, 31 Octr. 1775, by C. Shepherd. Thomlinson pinxt.
Mezzotint 14 x 10 in.

An idealized portrait with little resemblance to Lee, whom the DNB describes as "tall and remarkably thin with an ugly face and an aquiline nose of enormous size." This portrait was printed early in the war with the expectation that Lee would play a major role due to his past experience in the French and Indian conflict. The mezzotint was later copied by J. M. Will in Augsburg and became the basis for other portraits. Cannons and a flag with the motto "An Appeal to Heaven" are in the background. CPPS 5296 LC–USZ62–3617

148

Charles Lee. Esqr. Americanischer General-Major. [1778]
Etching 6½ x 4 in.

A German engraving after the mezzotint series cited in item 147. From Korn, *Geschichte der Kriege* (Nürnberg, 1777–78), copy 2, p. 92. LC–USZ62–45268

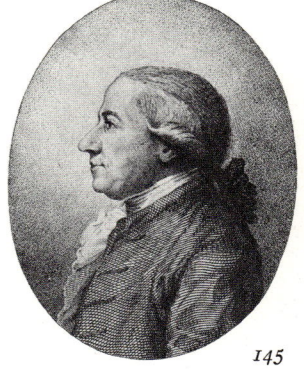

145

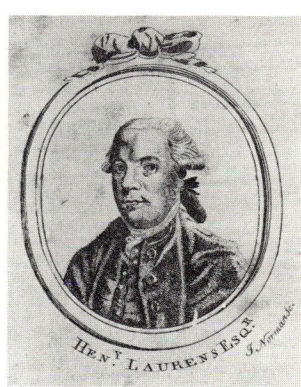

146

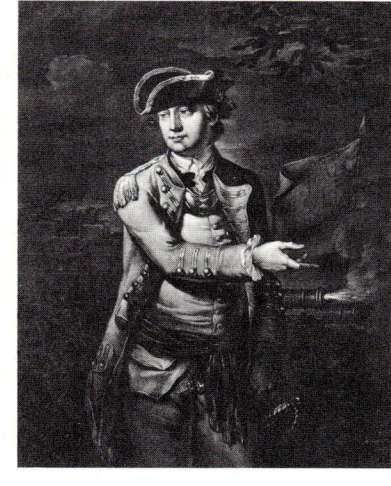

147

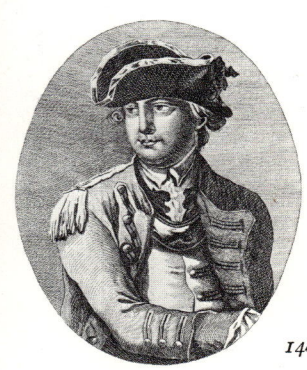

148

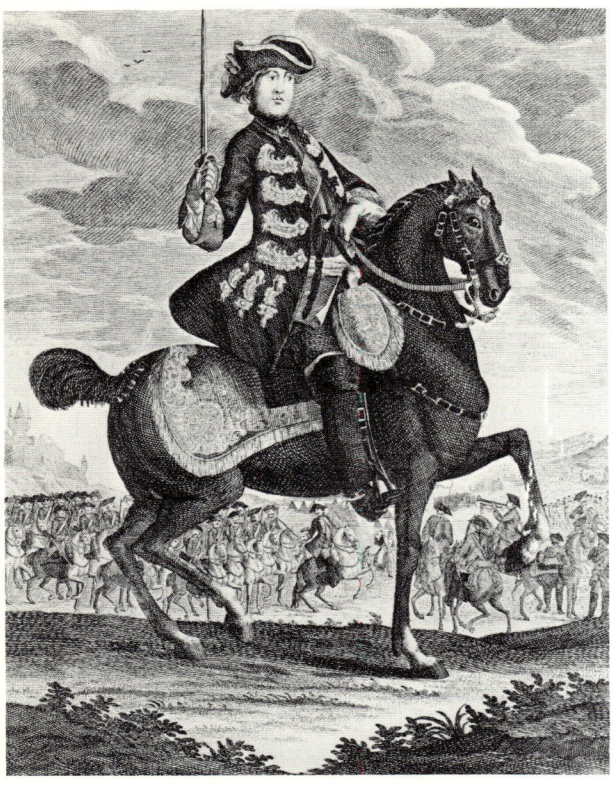

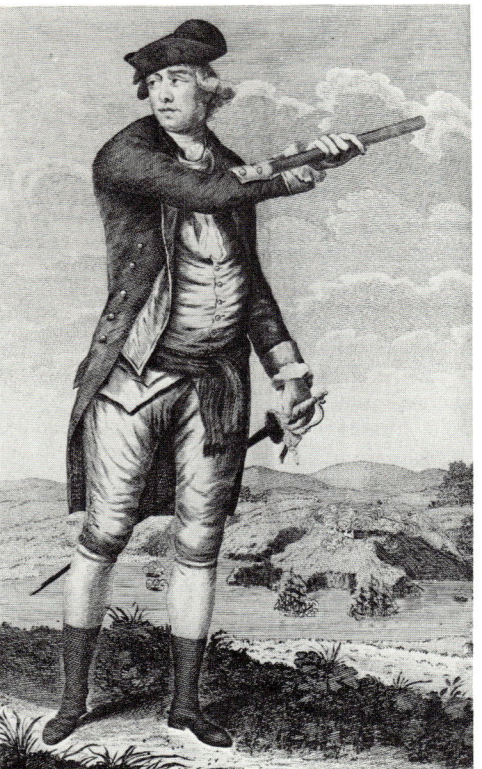

149

150

149

Charles Lee, Esqr. Major General of the Continental-Army in America. Ioh: Mich: Probst. jun. fc. Iohan Michael Probst: exc. A.V. [1776–178?]

Mixed method 11¾ x 8 in.

This engraving, which shows a European background complete with ancient castle, reflects a German view of Lee, probably based on his service in the Polish Army from 1769 to 1770. The poem below, in German and French, expresses Lee's love of liberty and his hatred of tyranny—the British Tory Government in this case:

Niu Sclaven schmigen sich ins Joch der Tyranney.
  Wir aber suchen uns die Freyheit zu erwerhen,
Und brechen mit Gewalt der Fesseln band entzwey;
  Denn unser Wahlsprach heist nur Siegen oder sterben.

Seulement les Esclaves se rendent volonterement à
  la Tyrannie,
  mais nous cherchons dàcquerir la libertè,
en rompent par force les sers què nous lient;
  parceque notre Symbole dit, victoriset ôu
  moûrir.

LC–USZ62–45180

150

Charles Lee Esqr. Major General of the American Forces. [1780]

Etching 7¾ x 4½ in.

This stylized portrait with ships bombarding a fort in the background, commemorates no specific place or incident. The awkward fitting of the head to the body suggests that it is a composite picture of head, body, and background. In item 204, an American engraver used this same background and body with a different head. From *An Impartial History of the War in America*, v. 1 (London, 1780), p. 319.

———Another impression. From *An Impartial History of the War in America*, v. 1 (London & Carlisle, 1780), p. 319.
LC–USZ62–45253

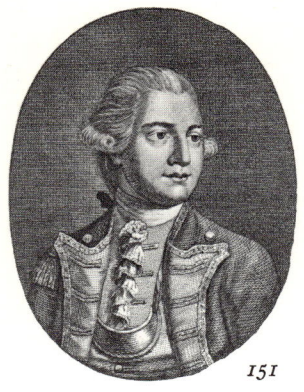 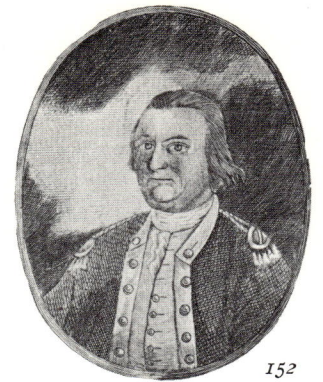 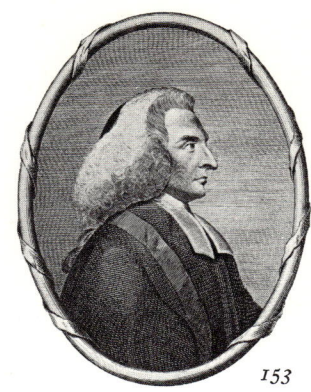 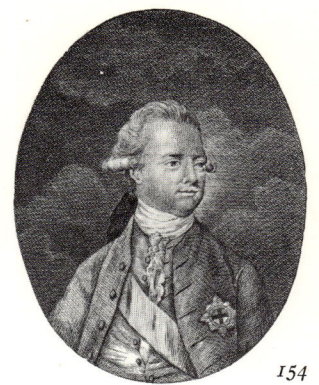 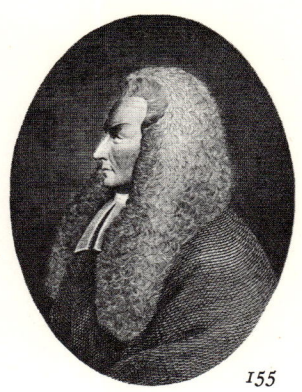

151 *152* *153* *154* *155*

151

GENERAL LEE. R. P[ollard] sc. Printed for T. Robson, Newcastle, upon Tyne. [1780]
Mixed method 7 x 4⅜ in.

Charles Lee in uniform with gorget. From Murray, *An Impartial History of the Present War in America*, v. 1 (Newcastle Upon Tyne, 1780), opposite p. 479. LC–USZ62–45302

———Another impression. From Murray, *An Impartial History of the War in America*, v. 2 (Newcastle Upon Tyne, 1782), opposite p. 202.

Benjamin Lincoln, 1733–1810

152

The Honle. B. LINCOLN, Esq. Major General in the American Army. J. NORMAN Sc [1782]
Etching 4⅛ x 3¼ in. (oval image)

A lieutenant colonel of New England militia in 1775, Lincoln had become one of Washington's leading major generals by 1777. John Norman shows a heavy-set, solid-looking officer in his engraving, reflecting the subject's reputation as a reliable leader. From *An Impartial History of the War in America*, v. 2 (Boston, 1782), copy 1, p. 385. Stauffer, 2340. LC–USZ62–45245

Alexander Wedderburn
1st Baron Loughborough, 1733–1805

153

Lord Loughborough. Aug. 1780.
Mixed method 7½ x 4½ in.

The short biography accompanying this picture stresses Loughborough's struggle to rise from the status of a Scottish provincial to that of a respected English peer. The ambitious Wedderburn moved from the opposition to embrace the cause of Lord North, and although he supported measures designed to ensure justice to the common man, he made "several warm speeches in favour of the coercive steps taken against the Americans." As a result, the opposition "styled him *turn-coat* and *weather-cock*; in short, every opprobrious epithet was freely bestowed upon him in every publication on that side of the question." From *The London Magazine*, August 1780, p. 347–348. LC–USZ62–45275

George Macartney
Earl Macartney, 1737–1806

154

The Right Honble. LORD MACARTNEY. February 1781.
Mixed method 7¼ x 4 in.

A short accompanying biography stresses Macartney's Irish background and his financial prowess. Regarding his appointment as Commander in Chief of Grenada, the Grenadines, and Tobago (known as the Caribee Islands), the article notes that he distinguished himself by making Grenada an important and profitable island and by resisting the forces under Comte d'Estaing, who attacked the island in 1779. From *The London Magazine*, February 1781, p. 51. LC–USZ62–45314

———Another copy (reversed). From *The Hibernian Magazine*, March 1781, p. 113.

William Murray
1st Earl of Mansfield, 1705–1793

155

Earl Mansfield. June 1780.
Mixed method 7¼ x 4½ in.

A lucid parliamentary debater, Mansfield steadily adhered to a policy of coercion toward the American Colonies. An accompanying biography stresses his role in British internal politics and mentions his opposition to the repeal of the Stamp Act. He maintained that the colonists enjoyed "virtual" representation in Parliament, and he drew up a protest against the repeal. From *The London Magazine*, June 1780, p. 243-245. LC–USZ62–45274

Richard Montgomery, 1738–1775

156

George Montgomery, Esqr Major General of the American Armies. Kill'd at Quebec Decr. 31st. 1775. [August 1777]
    Mixed method 7½ x 4½ in.

Having sold his commission in the British Army to emigrate to America in 1772, Richard Montgomery, represented here as George Montgomery, went on to become a delegate to the New York Provincial Congress and a general in the Continental Army. He was killed leading the attack on Quebec, December 31, 1775. From *The Hibernian Magazine*, August 1777, p. 513. LC–USZ62–45421

157

GENERAL MONTGOMERY. Printed for T. Robson, Newcastle, upon Tyne. [1778]
    Mixed method 6⅞ x 4⅜ in.

Montgomery's ability and courage as a soldier were praised in England after his death. From Murray, *An Impartial History of the Present War in America*, v. 2 (London, 1778), p. 193.

———— Another impression. In Murray, *An Impartial History of the War in America*, v. 1 (Newcastle Upon Tyne, 1782), p. 533. LC–USZ62–45231

158

MAJOR GENL. RICHD. MONTGOMERY Slain in Storming Quebec Decbr. 31st 1775 J. Norman Sc. [1781]
    Mixed method 5¾ x 3⅝ in. (image)

This portrait by John Norman in the American edition of this book is modeled on the portrait of Gates found in the English edition. Gates' scroll became a general's baton in the portrait of Montgomery. Cf. item 84. From *An Impartial History of the War in America*, v. 1 (Boston, 1781), copy 2, p. 396.

———— Another impression. In v. 1, copy 1, p. 383. Stauffer, 2340. LC–USZ62–45240

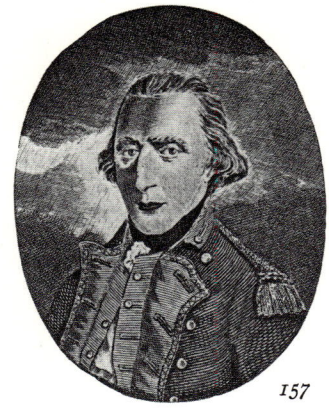

157

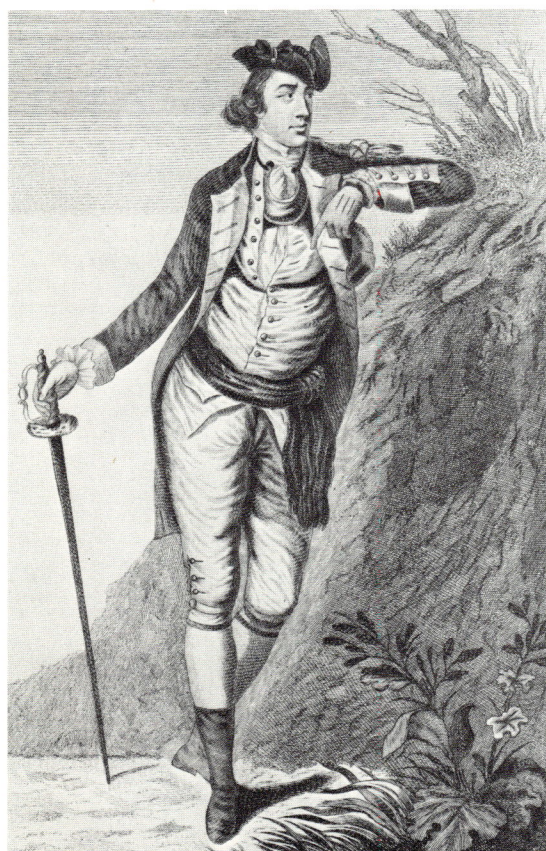

156

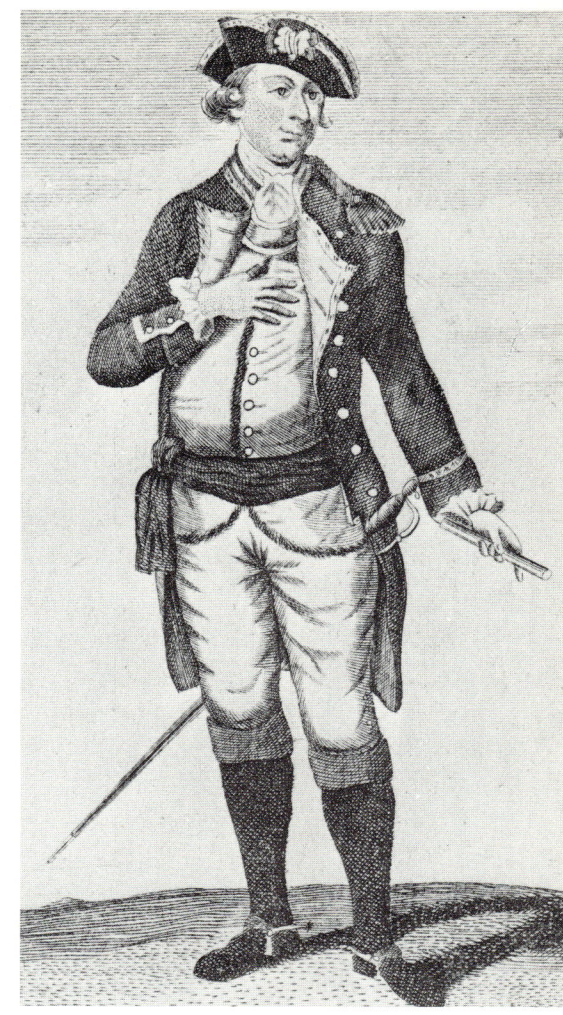

158

Gouverneur Morris, 1752–1816

159

GOVERNEER MORRIS ESQR. Member of Congress. Pubd 15th May 1783, by R. Wilkinson No. 58 Cornhill, London. B.B.E. [1783]
Mixed method 5½ x 4¼ in.

Although many aristocratic landholders in New York had loyalist tendencies, Morris was a wholehearted proponent of the American cause and served in the New York Provincial Congress, 1776–77, and the Continental Congress, 1778–79. Du Simitière drew the original sketch for this engraving in Philadelphia. In Du Simitière, *Portraits of the Generals* (London, 1783), plate 9.
LC–USZ62–45482

Frederick North
2d Earl of Guilford, 1732–1792

160

Miss Sp_c_r. [and] The Pliant Premier. Published as the Act directs by A. Hamilton Junr. near St. John's Gate, April 1st. 1778.
Mixed method 6¾ x 4¼ in.

The career of Lord North is described as a promising one until "a fatal misunderstanding arose between the Mother-Country and the Colonies." His affair with Charlotte Spencer is seen as the cause of his mishandling the war:

> Neither Putnam, Arnold, Gates, or Franklin, have once disturbed his repose, since the fair, or, as in his billets he calls her, the angelic S_____, has lulled our hero to slumber in her arms.

From *The Town and Country Magazine*, March 1778, p. 121–123. CPPS 5501
LC–USZ62–45209

————Another copy. Published as the Act directs by T: Walker No. 79 Dame Street. 1778. G: Byrne Sculpt. No. 43 Fishamble Street. 4 x 6¾ in. The accompanying article is the same as that in *The Town and Country Magazine*. From *The Hibernian Magazine*, May 1778, p. 260–262.

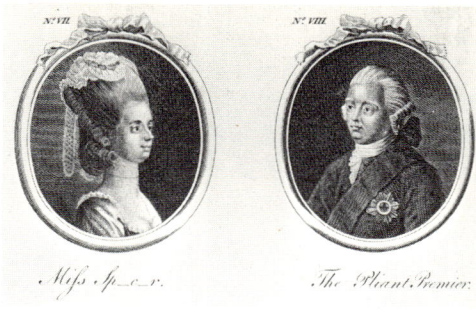

160

161

The Right Honble. Lord North. O Neale delint. Octr. [1779]
Mixed method 6½ x 4½ in.

A short biography accompanying this portrait describes North's loyal service to the King and observes

> ... he has involved the nation year after year, deeper and deeper in the fruitless and fatal American war; the whole blame of which must have lain at his door, if he had not eased himself very politically of part of the burthen by drawing in Lord George Germaine to be Secretary of State for the Colonies, who appears to have had the chief management of it since his appointment in 1775.

From *The London Magazine*, October 1779, p. 435. LC–USZ62–45503

162

FREDERICK lord NORTH. Pollard sculp. Printed for T. Robson, Newcastle, upon Tyne. [1780]
Mixed method 6⅞ x 4 in.

From Murray, *An Impartial History of the Present War in America*, v. 1 (Newcastle Upon Tyne, 1780), p. 97. LC–USZ62–45299

————Another impression. From Murray, *An Impartial History of the War in America*, v. 1 (Newcastle Upon Tyne, 1782), p. 212.

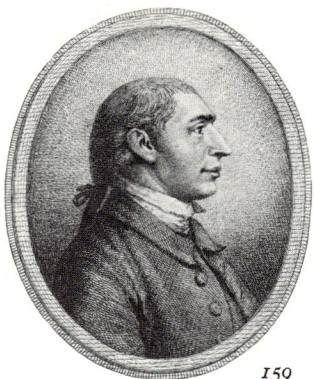

159

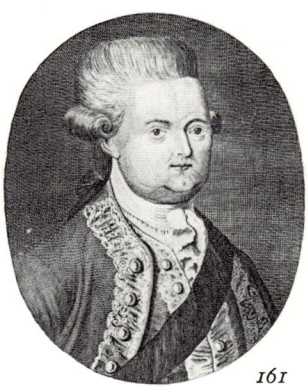

161

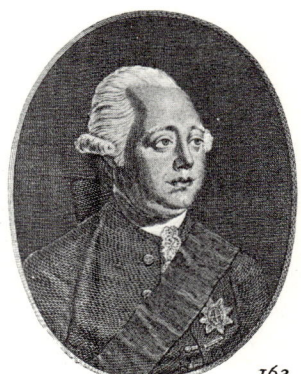

162

James Otis, Jr., 1725–1783

163
The Hon. JAMES OTIS, jun. Esq: [1770]
Woodcut 4½ x 3½ in. (image)

Otis, a leader in Massachusetts politics, expressed his belief in writings and speeches during the early 1760's that a law violating natural law was void. A few months before this portrait was published, he was wounded in a brawl with British officials. His wound drove him temporarily insane and ruined his political career. This portrait of the notoriously huge man is similar to the 1758 portrait by Copley and features Hercules on left crushing a serpent with his foot and Minerva on right holding a staff with a liberty cap. Cf. item 234. From Bickerstaff, *Boston Almanack* (Boston, 1770), title page. LC–USZ62–45327

Sir Peter Parker, 1721–1811

164
ADMIRAL PARKER. Birrell sculp. Published March. 10. 1786 by J. Fielding, Pater noster Row.
Mixed method 7 x 4¼ in.

An admiral in the British Fleet, Parker participated in the disastrous attack on Charleston in 1776 and was with Howe in the reduction of Long Island. He retained a command in the West Indies until 1782. From Andrews, *History of the War with America, France, Spain, and Holland*, v. 4 (London, 1785), p. 163. LC–USZ62–45343

Hugh Percy
2d Duke of Northumberland, 1742–1817

165
HUGH, Earl PERCY. [1778]
Mixed method 6¼ x 4 in.

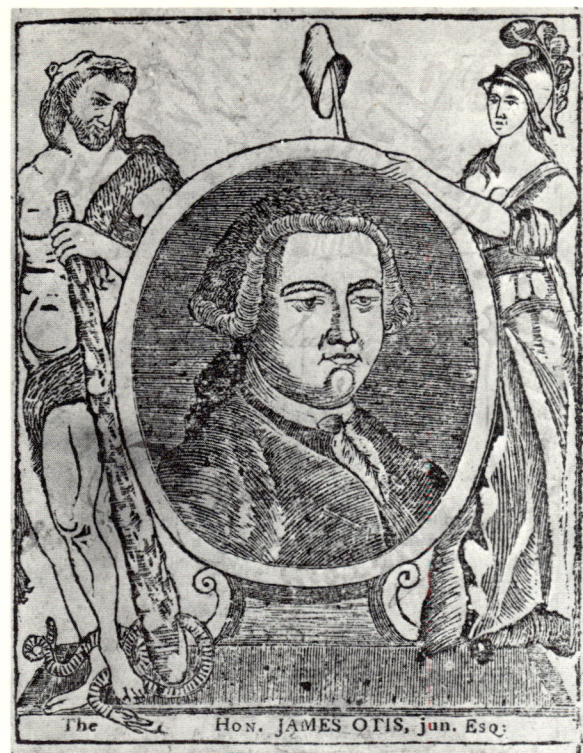
163

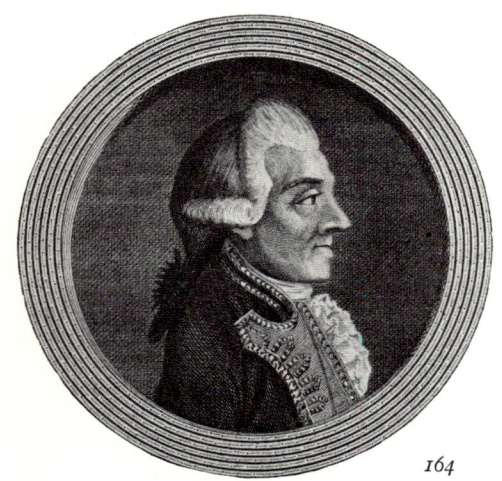
164

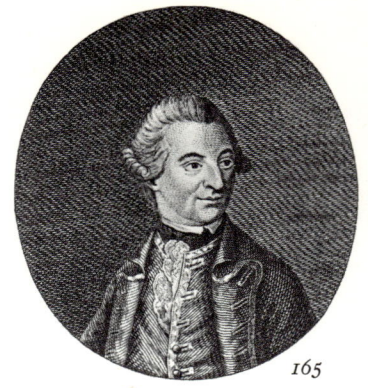
165

Despite his disapproval of the Crown's American policy, Percy joined Gage in Boston in 1774 and became the popular commander of the Northumberland Fusiliers. In April 1775 he covered the Army's retreat from Concord to Charlestown. After disputes with Howe, in 1777 Percy requested and obtained his recall from his post as general in America. From Russell, *History of America* (London, 1778), p. 574. LC–USZ62–45225

166
HUGH Earl PERCY. Pollard sc. Printed for T. Robson, Newcastle upon Tyne. [1780]
Mixed method 7 x 4¼ in.

Bust portrait facing partially right in oval. From Murray, *An Impartial History of the Present War in America*, v. 1 (Newcastle Upon Tyne, 1780), p. 383. Similar to item 165.

167
HUGH, Earl PERCY. Published Sepr. 30th 1785 by John Fielding, Pater Noster Row.
Mixed method 6½ x 4¼ in.

Bust portrait facing partially right in oval. Name on pedestal. From Andrews, *History of the War with America, France, Spain, and Holland*, v. 1 (London, 1785), p. 289. Same picture as item 165.

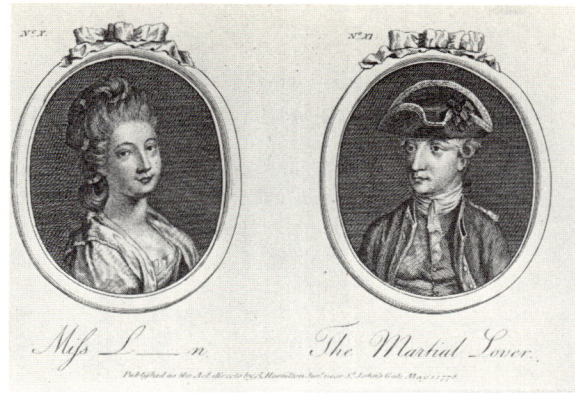

168

❧Charles (Stanhope), Viscount
Petersham
3d Earl Harrington, 1753–1829

168

Miss L_____n. [and] The Martial Lover. Published as the Act directs by A. Hamilton Junr. near St. John's Gate May 1, 1778.
Mixed method 4¼ x 7 in.

The text accompanying this tête-à-tête describes the military career of Viscount Petersham who was aide-de-camp to General Burgoyne at the time of the defeat at Saratoga. According to the article, Petersham returned to England a hero and helped defend Burgoyne's reputation. Miss L_____n met him after his tour of duty in America and became his mistress. From *The Town and Country Magazine*, April 1778, p. 177–179. CPPS 5502 LC-USZ62-45210

❧William Pitt
1st Earl of Chatham, 1708–1778

169

The Right Honourable WILLIAM PITT, Earl of Chatham. [1772]
Woodcut 1¾ x 1¾ in. (image)

169

Popularly known as "the Great Commoner," William Pitt is here celebrated for his leadership during the Seven Years' War and his constant defense of the English Constitution. In 1776 he opposed the Stamp Act in Parliament. Although he was retired because of illness at the time of this portrait, he continued to work for two favorite causes: he supported the dissenters against the Anglican Church and advocated a mutually profitable peace with the American Colonies. Benjamin West, the publisher of this almanac, must have wished for the return of a government with Pitt's ideals rather than the contemporary ministry. The poem below the picture reads,

Hail first of Patriots! whose extensive mind,
Revolves the vast concernments of mankind:
Contending realms accept controul from thee;
And BRITON's glory hangs on thy decree:
War, deals destruction, *Peace* her olive brings.
As thy supreme direction, governs Kings.
Where'er thou bid'st, the wreaths of conquest fall,
The guide, the friend, the guardian of us all.

This bust portrait is from a full-length portrait painted by Richard Brompton. J. K. Sherwin and Edward Fisher engraved a popular print which was probably the model for this woodcut. From Bickerstaff, *Boston Almanack* (Boston, 1772), title page. LC-USZ62-45326

170

The Rt. Hon. WILLIAM PITT, Chancellor of the Exchequer. [1774]
Mixed method 7 x 4¼ in.

Bust portrait facing partially right in oval set into an oblong frame. A ribbon tied in a bow is at top. From *The Annual Register* (Dublin, 1774), p. 414.

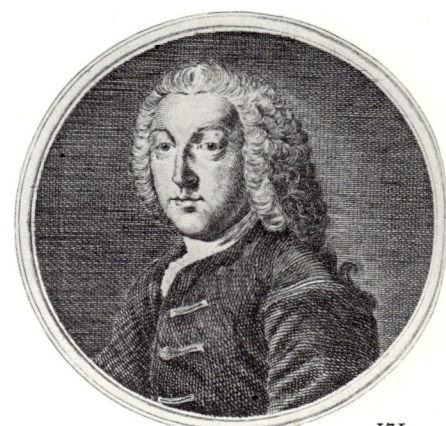

171

171

SECRETARY PITT. [1774]
Mixed method 4⅛ x 3½ in.

From *The Annual Register* (Dublin, 1774), p. 483. LC-USZ62-45206

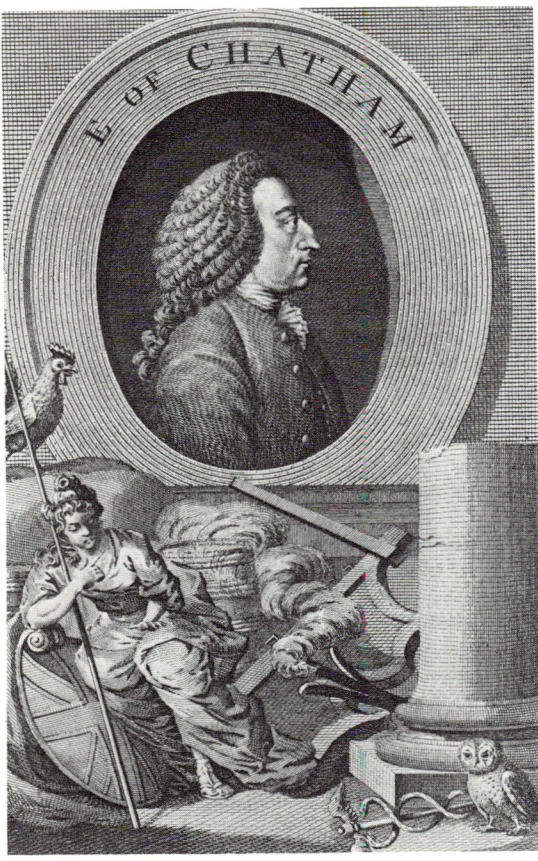

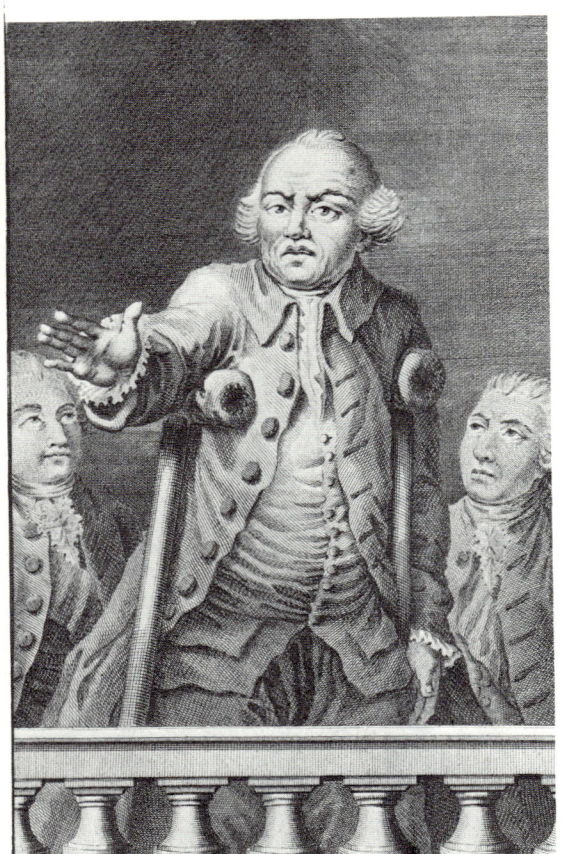

172

173

172
E OF CHATHAM. [1778]
  Mixed method 6⅞ x 4½ in.

The allegory accompanying this portrait shows a despondent Britannia sitting amid the symbols of commerce. The pillar has broken in half, and the owl of wisdom and the caduceus of Mercury are on the ground. Perhaps referring to Pitt's attempts to restore harmony with the Colonies and the decline of this hope with Pitt's death, the picture indicates that the outlook for the Empire in 1778 was gloomy. From Russell, *History of America* (London, 1778), opposite p. 492. LC–USZ62–45223

173
WILLIAM PITT. IL FAUT DÉCLARER LA GUERRE A LA FRANCE. L. Binet del. L. S. Berthet Sculp. [1782]
  Etching 7½ x 4¾ in.

This French print probably represents Pitt's last public appearance. In poor health and supported by crutches, he gave his last speech in Parliament in April 1778. Pitt had long advocated a more conciliatory attitude toward the Colonies but was vehemently opposed to making peace with the Americans under threat of war with France. From Hilliard d'Auberteuil, *Essais historiques*, v. 3 (1782), p. [14]. CPPS 5478 LC–USZ62–45335

Richard Price, 1723–1791

174
The Subtle Seducer. [and] The American Financier. London, Publish'd by A. Hamilton Junr. Fleet Street, Jany. 20, 1781.
  Mixed method 4¼ x 7 in.

Dr. Richard Price, a scholar in philology and antiquities, receives caviling treatment in the article accompanying this portrait. His theories on population, housing, and economics were debunked by the article, which implies that his ideas were welcomed by the Congress of the Independent American States. Price had intended to go to America but decided against it when he married a lady much his junior. The article states that she was desperate for any husband and that the affair must be platonic because of Price's age. From *The Town and Country Magazine*, 1780, Supplement, p. 689–691. CPPS 5864 LC–USZ62–45491

Israel Putnam, 1718–1790

175
ISRAEL PUTNAM Esqr. MAJOR GENERAL of the Connecticut Forces, and COMMANDER in CHIEF at the Engagement on BUNCKERS-HILL near BOSTON, 17 June 1775. Published as the Act directs by C. Shepherd. 9 Sepr. 1775. J. Wilkinson pinxt.

Mezzotint 14 x 9¾ in.

Putnam's reputation as a fighter and an explorer made him a popular figure before the war. When he left his plow to join the Americans at Lexington, he was expected to play a leading role in the fighting. Washington found his ability at independent command to be limited, and he was given fewer responsibilities as the war progressed. This portrait, probably by C. Corbutt, was printed when Putnam's fame was at its zenith. It states that Putnam commanded all the troops at Bunker Hill, but in reality he shared the command with William Prescott. Copies of the mezzotint were done in France and Germany, and all the Putnam engravings listed here are after the Corbutt work. CPPS 5292 LC–USZ62–3618

176
Israel Putnam. Esqr. General-Major der Americaner. [1778]

Etching 6½ x 3¾ in.

From Korn, *Geschichte der Kriege* (Nürnberg, 1777–78), copy 2, p. 92. LC–USZ62–45267

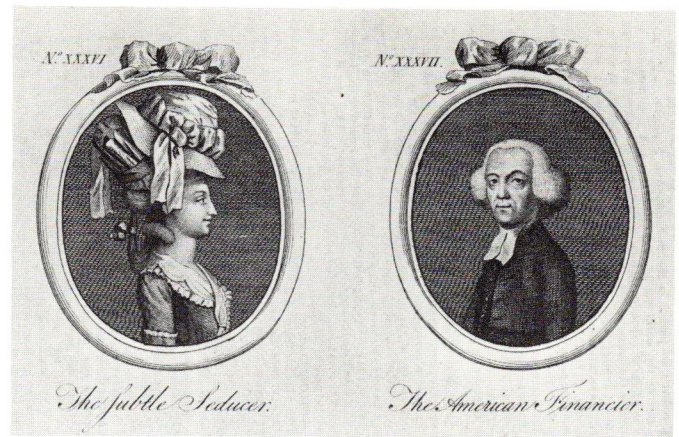
174

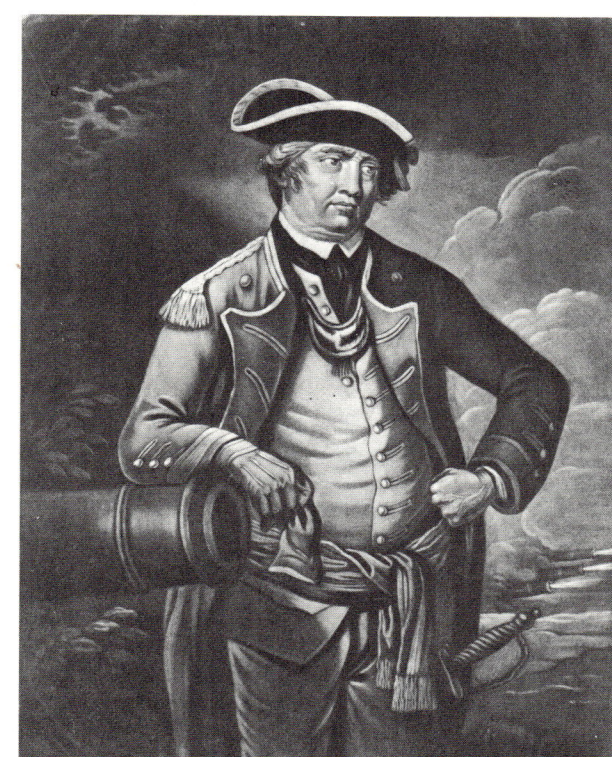
175

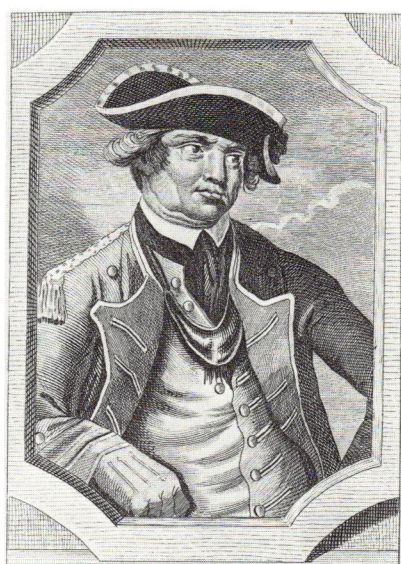
176

177
General PUTNAM. [1780]
  Mixed method 6⅜ x 4¼ in. (image)

Putnam wears a cap with skull and crossbones insignia and the words "or Liberty," signifying the slogan "Liberty or Death." From *An Impartial History of the War in America*, v. 1 (London, 1780), p. 336.

————Another impression. From *An Impartial History of the War in America*, v. 1 (London & Carlisle, 1780), p. 336. LC–USZ62–45255

178
GENERAL PUTNAM. Printed for T. Robson, Newcastle, upon Tyne. [1780]
  Mixed method 7 x 4¼ in.

From Murray, *An Impartial History of the Present War in America*, v. 1 (Newcastle Upon Tyne, 1780), opposite p. 335.

————Another impression. From Murray, *An Impartial History of the Present War in America*, v. 1 (Newcastle Upon Tyne, 1782), opposite p. 479. LC–USZ62–45230

179
ISRAEL PUTNAM, EQER. MAJOR Général des Troupes de Connecticut. Il commandoit en chef à l'affaire de Bunckeshill près Boston le 17 Juin 1775. A Paris chez Esnauts et Rapilly, rue St. Jacques a la Ville de Coutances. A.P.D.R. [178?]
  Mixed method 7¼ x 5⅛ in.

Probably by Dupin. LC–USZ62–45169

Joseph Reed, 1741–1785

180
J. Reed. Drawn from the life by Du Simitier in Philadelphia. Engraved by B. L. Prevost at Paris. [1781]
  Line engraving with etched border 7 x 5 in.

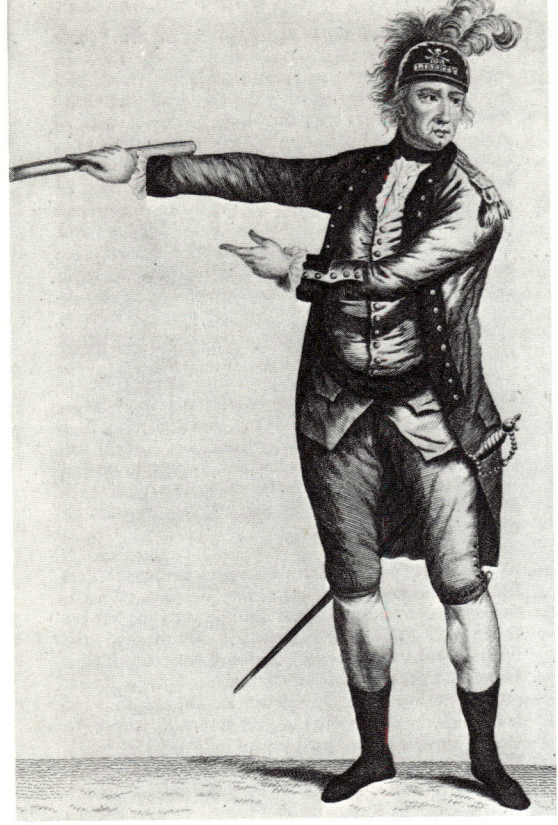

177

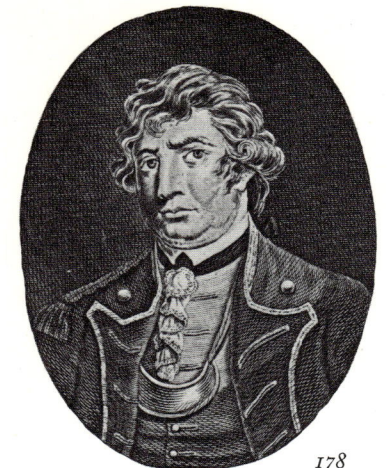

178

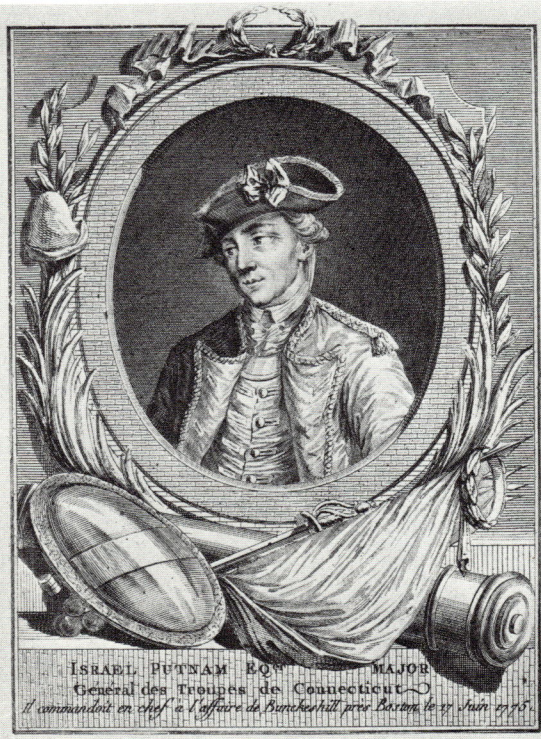

179

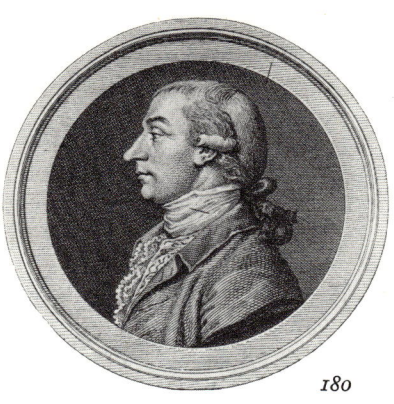

180

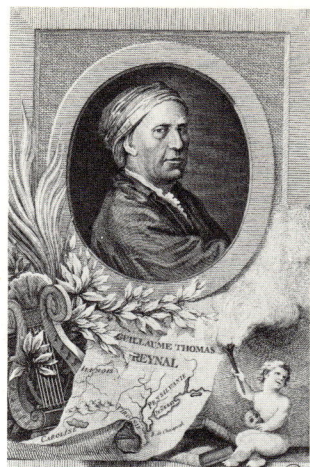

183

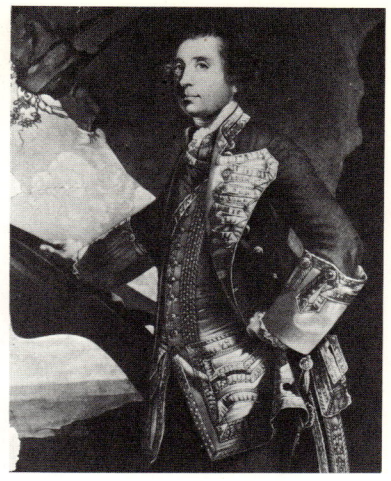

184

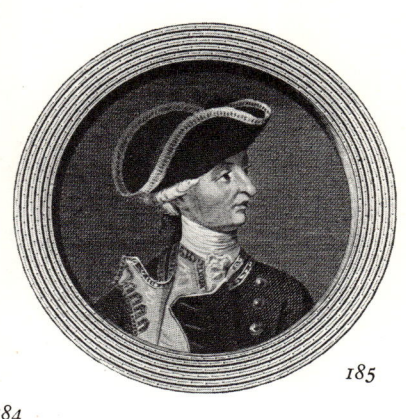

185

A Pennsylvania lawyer and statesman, Reed served on the State committee of correspondence and as president of the 2d Provincial Congress. An advocate of moderation, when hostilities began he espoused the cause of independence and served as Washington's military secretary and as adjutant general. In January 1777 he left the Army for a political career and was active in the Continental Congress and in Pennsylvania State politics. Du Simitière probably made the drawing from which this print is taken in 1779. From *Portraits des généraux* (Paris, 1781), plate 12. Plates from this volume are in P&P. LC–USZ62–45178

181

GENERAL REED. [December 1783]
Mixed method 7 x 4¼ in.

The title of general in this item and the next is derived from Reed's position as adjutant general while a colonel in the Continental Army. Bust profile facing left in oval, after Du Simitière. Similar to item 180. From *The Westminster Magazine*, December 1783, opposite p. 617.

182

GENERAL REED. Member of Congress, President & Commander in chief of the STATE of PENNSYLVANIA. Pubd. May 15th 1783 by R. Wilkinson No. 58, Cornhill, London. B.B.E. [1783]
Mixed method 5½ x 4¼ in.

Bust profile facing left. Similar to item 180. In Du Simitière, *Portraits of the Generals* (London, 1783), plate 8.

Guillaume-Thomas-François Raynal 1711–1796

183

GUILLAUME THOMAS REYNAL. [178?]
Line engraving 5⅝ x 3½ in.

The Abbé Raynal, a French natural philosopher whose fame did not survive the ages, is known today primarily for his *Histoire philosophique* (1770). His account of the American Revolution was criticized by Thomas Paine in *A Letter Addressed to the Abbé Raynal on the Affairs of North America* (1782). Probably by Dupin. LC–USZ62–45189

George Brydges Rodney, 1719–1792

184

SR. GEORGE BRIDGES RODNEY.... Admiral of the Blue & [Continental Fleet of his] Majesty's Ships sent to protect our Trade [in the] West Indies. [178?]
Mezzotint 12¾ x 9¾ in. (image)

Rodney's command in the West Indies was unimpressive until he captured Admiral de Grasse in the Battle of the Saints in April 1782. Although he was a skilled tactician, his unscrupulous attention to personal fortune after the capture of St. Eustatius deprived Admiral Hood of a sufficient fleet to relieve Cornwallis at Yorktown. LC–USZ62–45200

185

LORD RODNEY. Published 8 Decr. 1785, by John Fielding, Pater Noster Row.
Mixed method 6⅞ x 4⅜ in.

From Andrews, *History of the War with America, France, Spain, and Holland*, v. 4 (London, 1785), p. 277. LC–USZ62–45345

Robert Rogers, 1732–1795

186

Robert Rogers. Commandeur der Americaner. [1778]
Etching 6¼ x 3¾ in.

A noted Indian scout from the New Hampshire frontier and a colorful participant in the Seven Years' War, Rogers was romanticized in Europe and America. At the outbreak of the Revolution, he courted both the British and the Americans. His suspicions aroused, Washington had Rogers imprisoned in 1776. Escaping to the British lines, Rogers was given command of the Queen's American Rangers and when relieved of his command after a poor showing in a skirmish near White Plains, acted as a recruiter of loyalist troops. From Korn, *Geschichte der Kriege* (Nürnberg, 1777–78), copy 2, p. 92. LC–USZ62–45269. See CPPS 5339 for a description of the English and German mezzotint which preceded this engraving.

Philip John Schuyler, 1733–1804

187

PHILIP SCHUYLER ESQR. Majr. Genl. in the American Service. Leney sct. [179?]
Stipple 3⅜ x 2¾ in. (image)

One of the four major generals appointed by Washington in June 1775, Schuyler was assigned command of the Northern Department. His contributions to the American cause were considerable, but the loss of Fort Ticonderoga in 1777 enabled his opponents in Congress to remove him from command. Initially suspected of treason, he was finally charged with incompetence, and although acquitted by a court-martial, he resigned his commission. Schuyler was active in securing ratification of the Constitution and held public office continually from 1780 to 1798. Stauffer, 1848.
LC–USZ62–45170

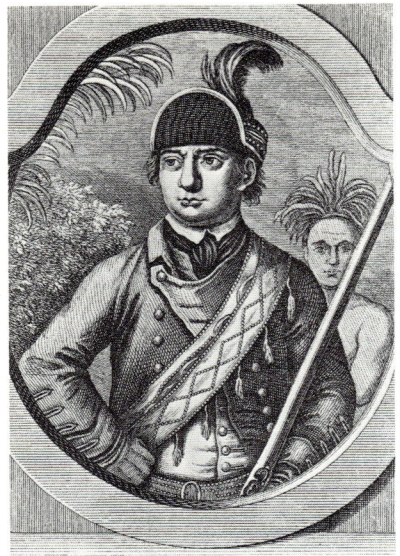
186

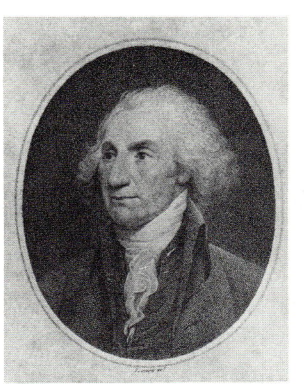
187

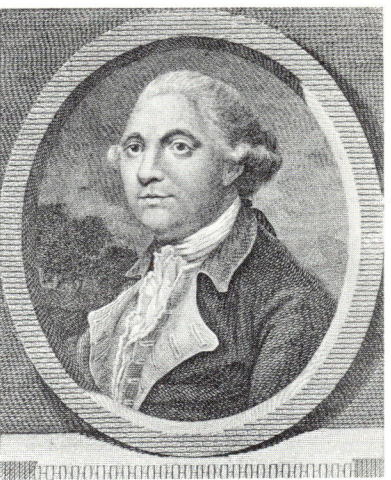
189

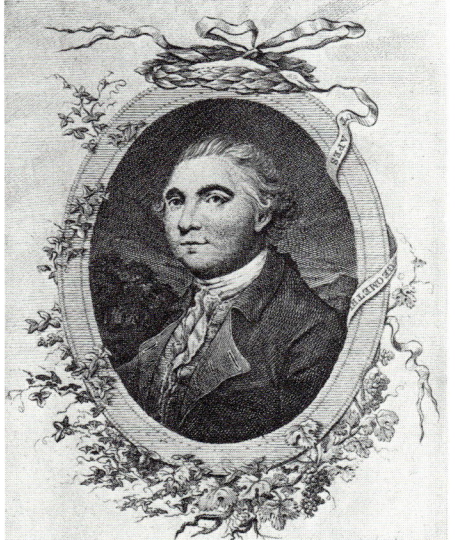
188

William Fitzmaurice Petty 2d Earl of Shelburne, 1732–1805

188

Lord Shelburne. March [1780]
Mixed method 7½ x 4½ in.

Shelburne attempted to improve Anglo-American relations and prevent American independence throughout his career. Opposed to the Stamp Act, he was active in its repeal. He favored the withdrawal of English troops from Boston in January 1775 and condemned other measures designed to coerce the Americans. From *The London Magazine*, March 1780, p. 99–100. LC–USZ62–45272

189

The EARL of SHELBURNE. [November 1782]
Mixed method 7 x 4¼ in.

An accompanying biography stresses his loyalty to the King and mentions his attention to the problems of colonial merchants. From *The Universal Magazine*, November 1782, p. 233–235. LC–USZ62–45422

Frederick William Augustus von Steuben, 1730–1794

190
MAJOR GENERAL BARON STEUBEN. Pubd May 15th. 1783, by R. Wilkinson No. 58 Cornhill, London. B.B.E. [1783]
Mixed method 5½ x 4¼ in.

Steuben, formerly an officer in the Prussian Army under Frederick the Great, arrived in America in 1777 to offer his services to the Continental Congress. As Washington's advisor, he was instrumental in the training of troops for the Continental Army. Steuben commanded one of the three divisions at Yorktown, helped Washington plan for the demobilization of the Army, and became an American citizen after the war. Du Simitière sketched this portrait in Philadelphia in 1779. From Du Simitière, *Portraits of the Generals* (London, 1783), plate 10. LC–USZ62–45483

Ezra Stiles, 1727–1795

191
EZRA STILES S.T.D. L.L.D. President of Yale College. Drawn, & Engraved by S. Hill, Boston. [1789–9?]
Stipple 6½ x 4⅜ in.

A prominent New England scholar, clergyman, and lawyer, Stiles became president of Yale College in 1778. His interests went beyond law and theology—he experimented with electricity, studied languages, and kept a detailed diary of the Revolutionary era. As president of Yale, he taught a variety of courses and enabled the institution to survive the difficult times. Stauffer, 1380. LC–USZ62–45171

192
EZRA STILES S.T.D. LL.D. President of

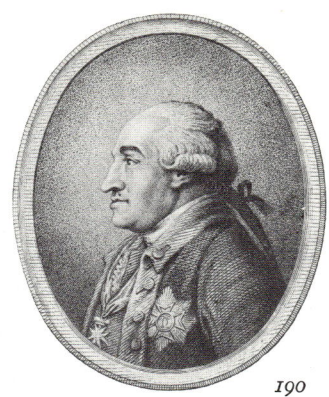
190

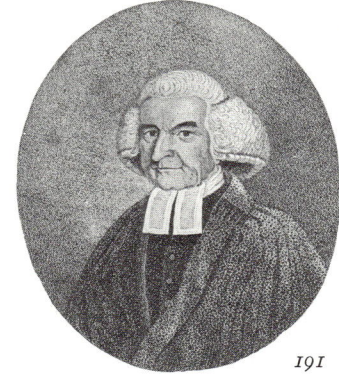
191

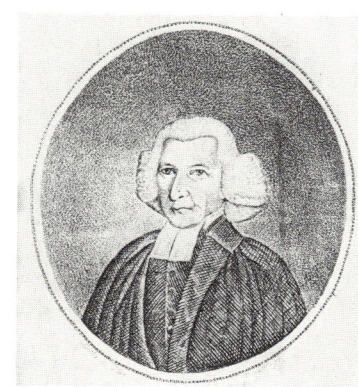
192

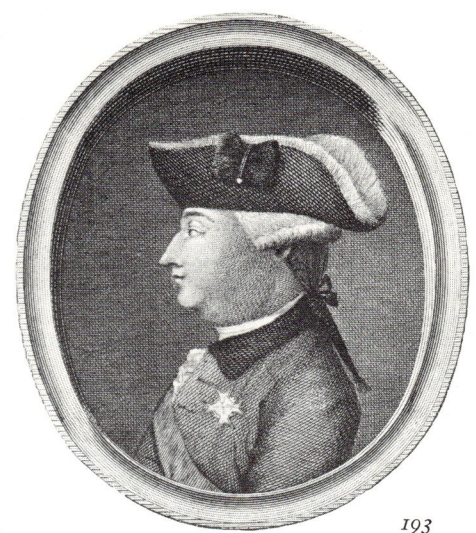
193

Yale College. R[euben] Molthrop pinxt [Amos] Doolittle sc. [178?]
Stipple 5¾ x 3⅜ in.
Stauffer, 516. LC–USZ62–45190

Pierre André de Suffren Saint-Tropez 1726–1788

193
SUFFREIN. Walker sculpt. Published July 20th. 1785, by J. Fielding, Pater-noster Row.
Mixed method 6⅞ x 4⅜ in.

Joining the French fleet of the Comte d'Estaing in American waters in 1778, Suffren engaged in successful battles against the British at Newport, Grenada, and Savannah. When England expanded the war to threaten Dutch colonies in the East Indies, Suffren distinguished himself in that theater of the war. From Andrews, *History of the Present War with America, France, Spain, and Holland*, v. 4 (London, 1785), p. 320. LC–USZ62–45348

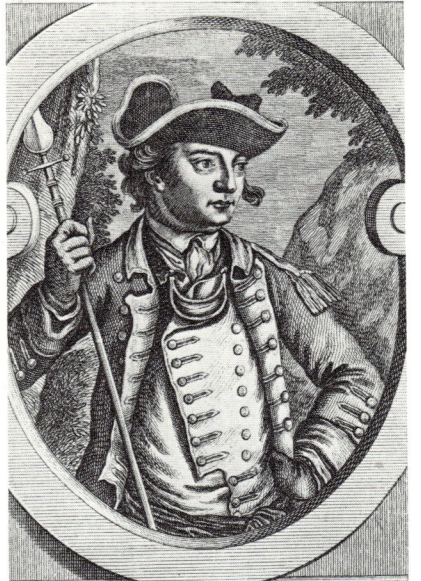

194

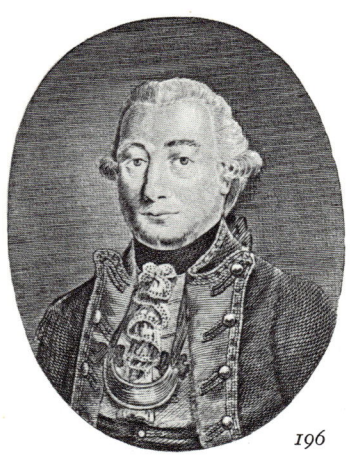

195

196

John Sullivan, 1740–1795

194

MAJOR GENERAL JOHN SULLIVAN, A distinguished OFFICER in the CONTINENTAL ARMY. Publish'd as the Act directs 22 Augt. 1776 by Thos. Hart.

Mezzotint 13¾ x 9⅞ in.

A delegate to the First and Second Continental Congresses, Sullivan participated in the invasion of Canada and was an important figure in the New York and New Jersey campaigns. In 1779 he led an expedition into the Iroquois country and routed Indian and loyalist forces near Elmira, N.Y. After resigning from the Army because of poor health, he returned to the Continental Congress. He attended the New Hampshire Constitutional Convention in 1782 and served as chairman of the New Hampshire convention which ratified the Federal Constitution in 1788. This portrait was engraved soon after the Quebec campaign by C. Corbutt in London. Other mezzotints after this one were done in Augsburg and Paris. See CPPS 5337, 5338. LC–USZ62–39567

195

Major-General John Sullivan. [1778]
Etching 6¼ x 3¾ in.

A German engraving after item 194. From Korn, *Geschichte der Kriege* (Nürnberg, 1777–78), copy 2, p. 104. LC–USZ62–45270

196

GENERAL SULLIVAN. Printed for T. Robson, Newcastle, upon Tyne. [1778]
Mixed method 6¾ x 4⅛ in.

From Murray, *An Impartial History of the Present War in America*, v. 2 (London, 1778), p. 241. LC–USZ62–45305

———————Another impression. From Murray, *An Impartial History of the War in America*, v. 2 (Newcastle Upon Tyne, 1782), p. 242.

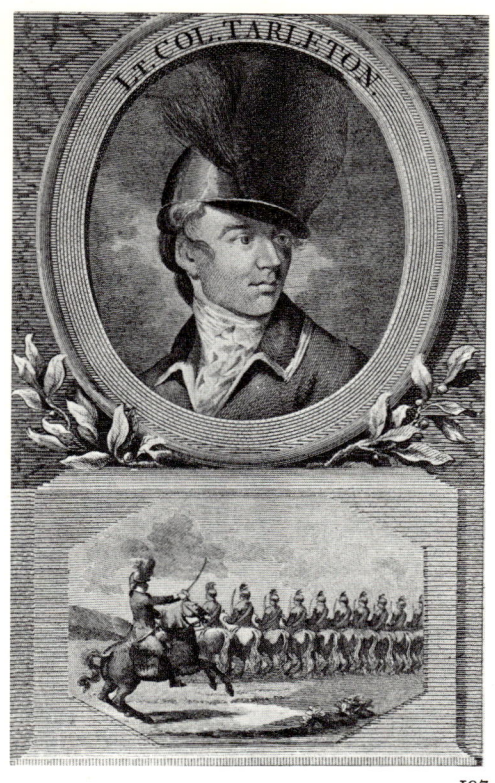

197

Banastre Tarleton, 1754–1833

197

LT. COL. TARLETON. Published April 1, 1782, by J. Walker, No. 20, Pater-noster Row.
Mixed method 6⅞ x 4½ in.

Tarleton accompanied Cornwallis to America early in 1776 and earned a reputation as a dashing cavalry officer in many theaters of the war. This portrait and a laudatory biography appeared about the time he returned to England on parole after being captured at Yorktown. A picture of cavalry maneuvers appears below the portrait. From *The Westminster Magazine*, March 1782, p. 115.
LC–USZ62–45487

198

The amiable Miss W_bb. [and] The intrepid Partizan. London, Publish'd by A. Hamilton Junr. Fleet Street Augt. 1, 1782.
Mixed method 4¼ x 7 in.

Tarleton was a highly popular figure in English society when this satirical portrait appeared. An article accompanying the tête-à-tête describes his career as having been successful until "Fortune chose to check his ambition," and he was taken prisoner at Yorktown. Miss Webb was apparently a fictitious person, who, according to the article, secretly eloped with Tarleton. From *The Town and Country Magazine*, July 1782, p. 345–348. CPPS 6085
LC–USZ62–45493

———————Another copy. Publish'd as the Act Directs by T: Walker No. 79 Dame Street. 4 x 6¾ in. From *The Hibernian Magazine*, September 1782, p. 461–463.

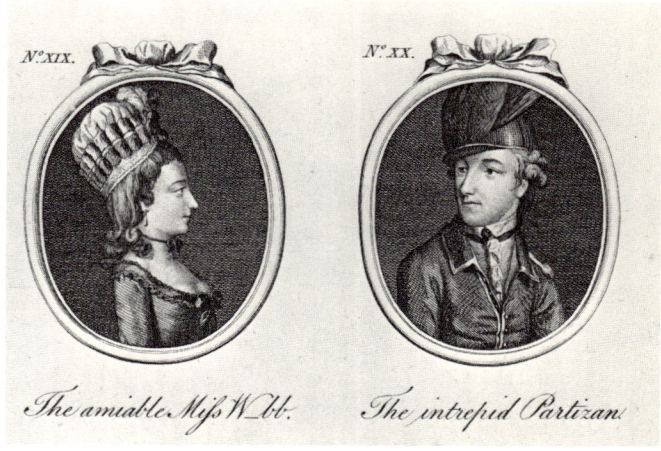

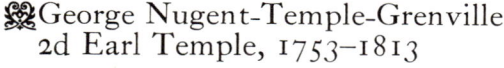

198

George Nugent-Temple-Grenville 2d Earl Temple, 1753–1813

199

EARL TEMPLE. Publish'd Septr 30, 1782 by J: Walker No. 44 Pater-noster Row.
Mixed method 6 x 4¼ in.

The accompanying article explains that George Nugent-Temple-Grenville was the son of George Grenville (1712–1770) and nephew of Richard Grenville, 1st Earl Temple (1711–1779). Upon marrying Lady Mary Nugent, daughter of Earl Nugent, and inheriting his uncle's estate and title, he assumed the additional names Nugent-Temple. As a member of Parliament he supported Lord North's policy of coercing the Colonies and was critical of the conduct of the war in America. The 2d Earl was appointed lord-lieutenant of Ireland and became a member of the English privy council in 1782, the date the portrait appeared as

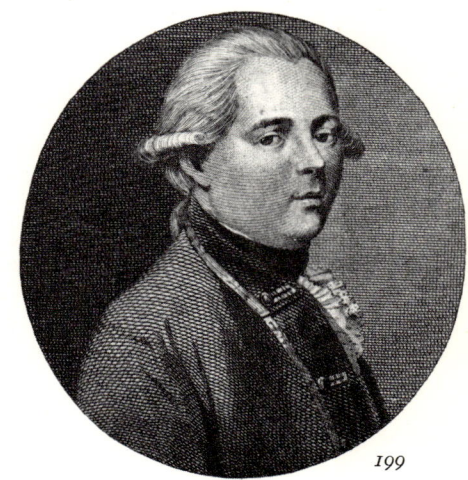

199

frontispiece of *The Westminster Magazine*, September 1782, opposite p. 449.
LC–USZ62–45488

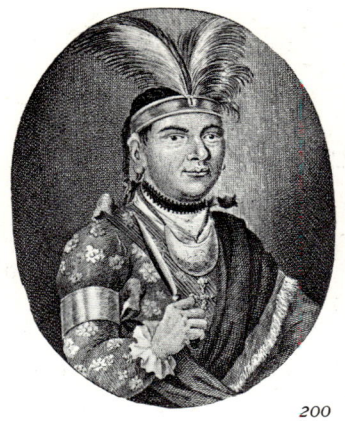
200

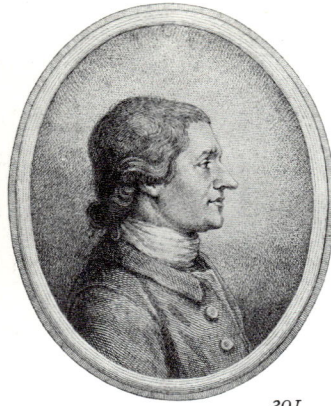
201

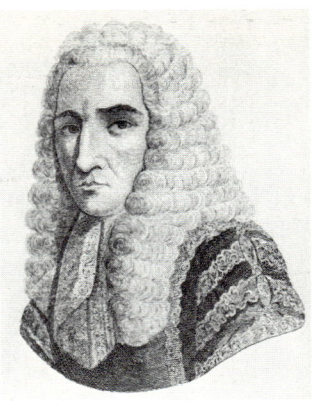
202

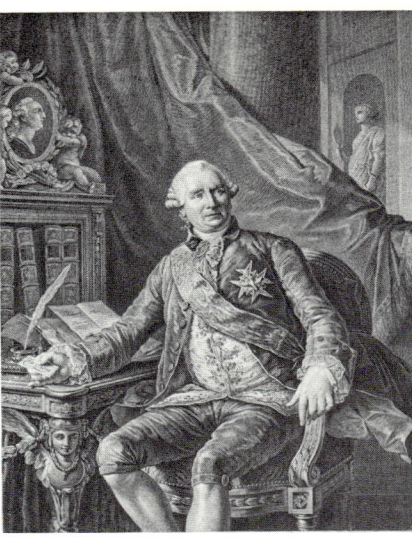
203

Thayendanegea (Joseph Brant) 1742–1807

200

JOSEPH THAYENDANEKEN The Mohawk Chief. From an Original Drawing in the Possession of James Boswell, Esqr: [1 July 1776]
Mixed method 6½ x 4¾ in. (image)

The Mohawk chief, popularly known as Joseph Brant, was commissioned a colonel in the British Army by Sir Guy Carleton and was an active participant in Canadian border fighting against the colonists. After the Revolution, Brant received a grant of land in Ontario. He wears a gorget with the British coat of arms, as well as an ornament cross. An article accompanying this portrait describes the peaceful and cooperative nature of his tribe and his visit to London in 1775. From *The London Magazine*, July 1776, p. 339. LC–USZ62–45500

Charles Thomson, 1729–1824

201

CHARLES THOMPSON ESQR. Secretary to Congress. Pubd. 15th. May 1783, by R. Wilkinson, No. 58 Cornhill, London. B.B.E. [1783]
Mixed method 5½ x 4¼ in.

Thomson was active in the Sons of Liberty, and John Adams called him "the Sam Adams of Philadelphia." He acted as secretary of the First Continental Congress until the Federal Constitution took effect. Du Simitière made the drawing for this print at Philadelphia in the late 1770's. In Du Simitière, *Portraits of the Generals* (London, 1783), plate 5.
LC–USZ62–44786

Edward Thurlow 1st Baron Thurlow, 1731–1806

202

LORD THURLOW.
Mixed method 7 x 4 in.

Thurlow, a British statesman, developed a reputation as a constitutionalist, defending the royal prerogative and supporting the ministry plan for the government of Quebec. He was inflexible on the American question and throughout the Revolution maintained the right of the mother country at the expense of the Colonies. His views made him popular with George III, who appointed him Lord Chancellor in 1778. From *The London Magazine*, November 1781, p. 507. LC–USZ62–45316

Charles Gravier Comte de Vergennes, 1717–1787

203

Charles Gravier Comte de Vergennes Conseiller d'Etat Ordinaire, Ministre et Secretaire d'Etat et Chef du Conseil Royal des Finances. Callet pinxt. Vangelisti sculp. Se vend à Paris à l'ancienne grande Poste Rue des Fossés St. Germain l'Auxerios. [1770–89?]
Steel engraving 17¼ x 13¼ in. (image)

Intense hatred of the English and the desire for revenge after the Seven Years' War led Vergennes to support the American Colonies in their struggle for independence. He secretly aided the cause before the ratification of the French Alliance in 1778 and was instrumental in France's entry into the conflict. Vergennes assumed the office of foreign minister in 1774 at the accession of Louis XVI. The portrait includes a picture of Louis and a note addressed to the King. The luxurious setting and attire reflect Vergennes' prestige in the French Government. *Collection de Vinck* 1228.
LC–USZ62–45183

Joseph Warren, 1741-1775

204

MAJOR GENL. JOSEPH WARREN. Slain at the Battle of Bunker's Hill June 17th 1775. J. Norman Sc [1781]

Mixed method 4 x 6⅝ in.

Warren, a physician, early identified himself with the revolutionary cause in Boston. He was a close associate of Samuel Adams, a member of the North End Caucus and the Massachusetts Committee of Safety, and the drafter of the Suffolk Resolves. A major general in the militia, he served under Israel Putnam at the Battle of Bunker Hill, where he died while attempting to rally the American troops. From *An Impartial History of the War in America*, v. 1 (Boston, 1781), copy 2, p. 349.

——————Another impression (partially colored). In P&P. LC-USZ62-27694

——————Another impression. In v. 1, copy 1, p. 321.

205

Major General Warren. J. Norman Sc [1784]

Mixed method 3⅛ x 3⅛ in. (image)

After the Copley portrait dating ca. 1765. From *The Boston Magazine*, April 1784, opposite p. 221. LC-USZ62-45282

George Washington, 1732-1799

206

GEORGE WASHINGTON, ESQR. GENERAL and COMMANDER in CHIEF of the CONTINENTAL ARMY in AMERICA. Published as the Act directs. 9. Sept 1775 by C. Shepherd London. Done from an Original, Drawn from the Life by Alexr. Campbell, of Williamsburgh in Virginia. Ioh. Martin Will excud. Aug. Vind.

Mezzotint 12¾ x 9¼ in. (image)

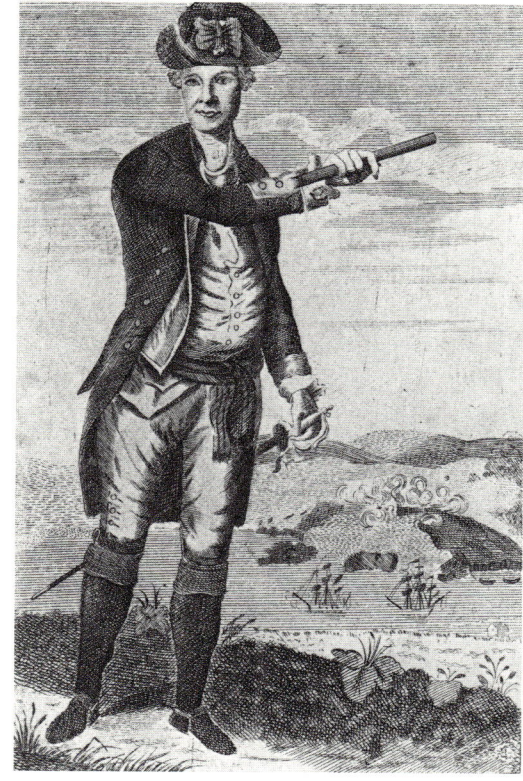
204

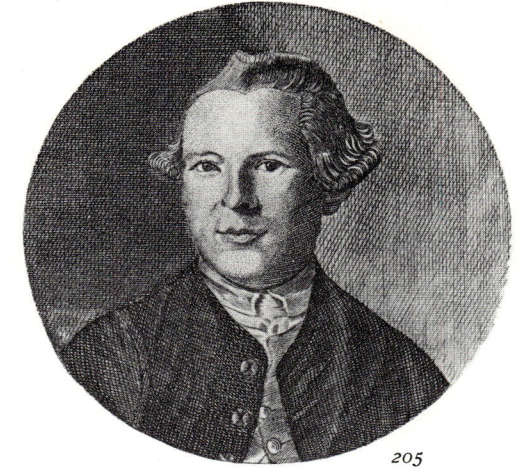
205

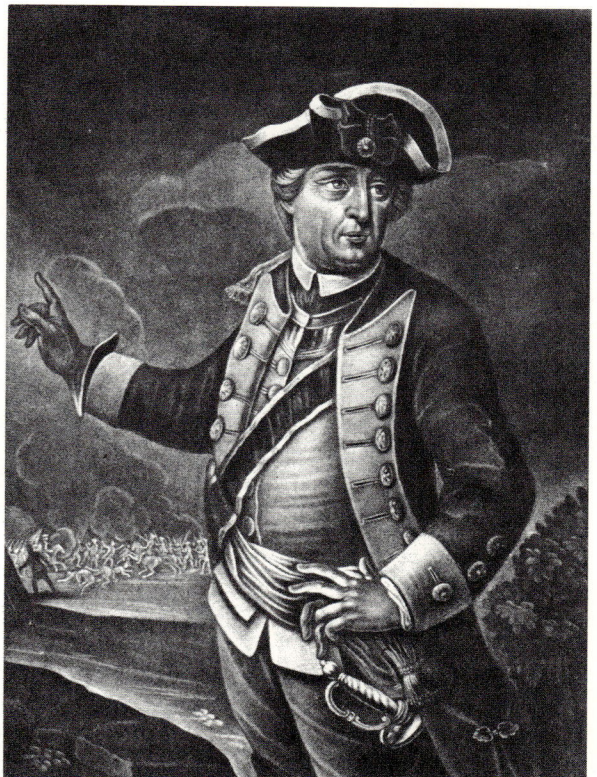
206

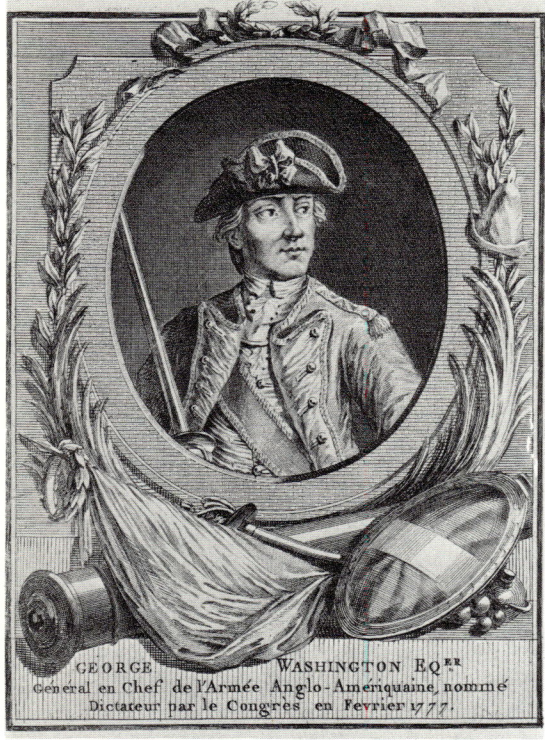

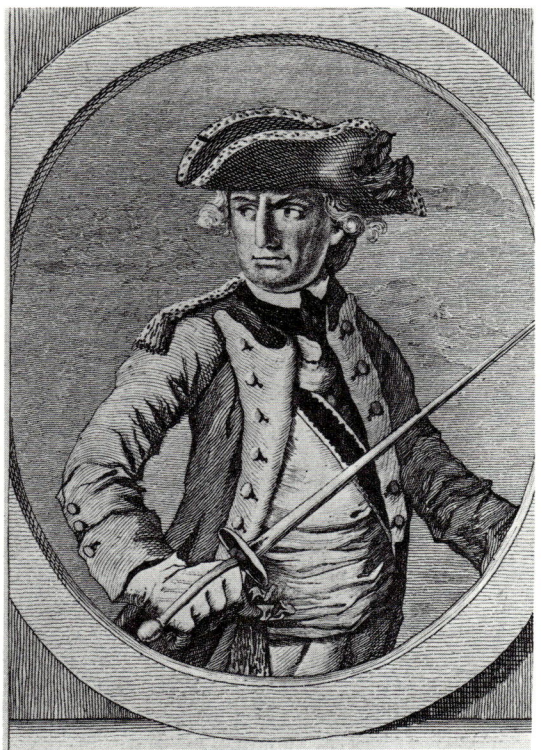

208

207

Alexander Campbell appears in no contemporary lists of artists, and Washington himself stated that he had never seen the man. This mezzotint and an equestrian portrait after Campbell survive in British and German editions. Many other engravings follow the lines of this early portrait for which Washington probably did not pose. Cf. items 207–208, 210, 212, 214, and perhaps 216. Baker, 49. CPPS 5290
LC–USZ62–3620

207

George Washington. Esqr. Americanischer Generalissimus.

Etching 6⅝ x 4 in.

German engraving after the equestrian portrait by Campbell. The horse and battle in the background have been deleted. From Korn, *Geschichte der Kriege* (Nürnberg, 1777–78), copy 2, p. 120. Baker, 48; Hart, 729.

——————Another impression. In P&P.
LC–USZ62–45175

208

George Washington Eqer. Général en Chef de l'Armée Anglo-Amériquaine, nommé Dictateur par le Congrès en Fevrier 1777. A Paris chez Esnauts et Rapilly, rue St. Jacques, à la Ville de Coutances. A.P.D.R.

Etching 7½ x 5¼ in.

A French engraving after Campbell and probably by Dupin. Baker, 58; Hart, 743.
LC–USZ62–45177

——————Another impression. In Sackville, *Correspondence du Lord G. Germain* (Berne, 1782), frontispiece.

209

The Glorious WASHINGTON and GATES. [1778] Woodcuts

Woodcuts, both are 2¾ x 1⅝ in. (image)

These portraits were published by Benjamin

West (1730–1813). He was an astronomer and almanac maker and should not be confused with the painter by this name, who was living in England at the time of this print. From Bickerstaff, *Boston Almanack* (Boston, 1778), title page. LC–USZ62–45321

210
GENL. GEORGE WASHINGTON. [1778]
Mixed method 6½ x 4¼ in.

After Alexander Campbell but without hat. From Russell, *History of America* (London, 1778), opposite p. 522. Baker, 54; Hart, 740. LC–USZ62–45261

211
GEORGE WASHINGTON. Commandant en Chef des Armées des Etats-unis de l'Amerique. N. Pruneau del. et Sculp. A Paris chez l'Auteur, rue St. Jacques vis à vis le College du Plessis. et chez Dennel graveur, rue du Pt. Bourbon attent la Foire St. Germain. [177?]
Etching 6⅛ x 4⅜ in. (image)

Pruneau's Washington, after Peale, was printed in the late 1770's. It and item 218 were used as illustrations in many books of the times. The portrait hangs from the staff of liberty with an American rattlesnake entwined near the liberty cap on top. Beneath are flags and ordnance. A bright sun shines from the upper right corner. Baker 29; Hart 94. LC–USZ62–45186

212
GEORGE WASHINGTON, EQER. Général en chef de l'Armée Anglo-Amériquaine nommé Dictateur par le Congrès en Fevrier 1777. Desrais del LeBeau Sculp a Paris chez Esnauts et Rapilly, rue St. Jacques à la ville de Coutances. [177?]
Line engraving 7⅝ x 4⅞ in.

Baker designates this engraving as a combination of the Peale and Campbell portraits. Baker, 19; Hart, 747. LC–USZ62–45199

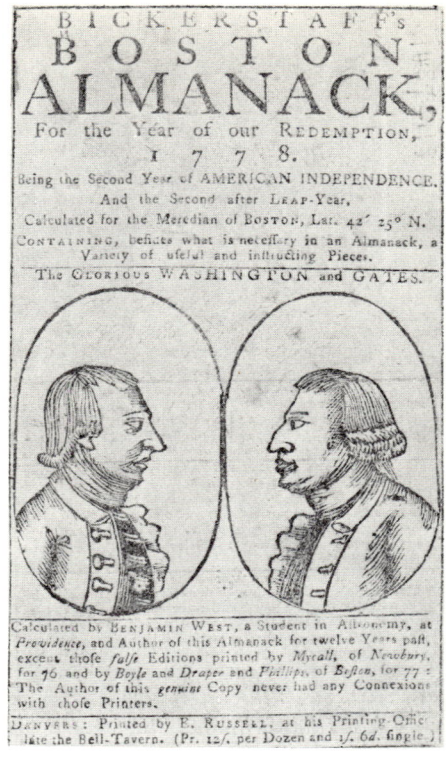
209

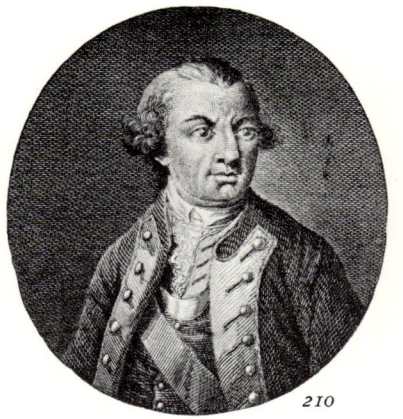
210

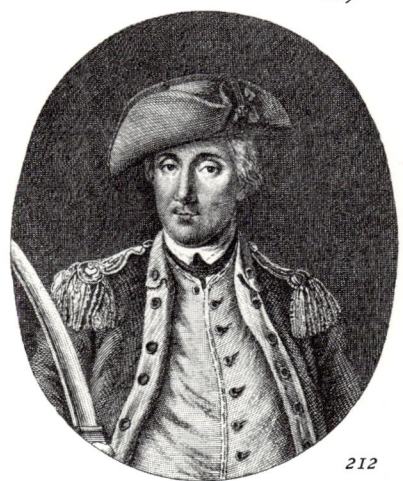
212

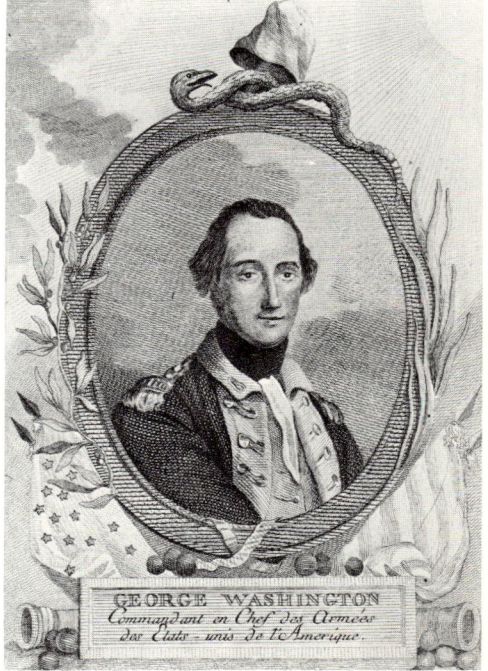
211

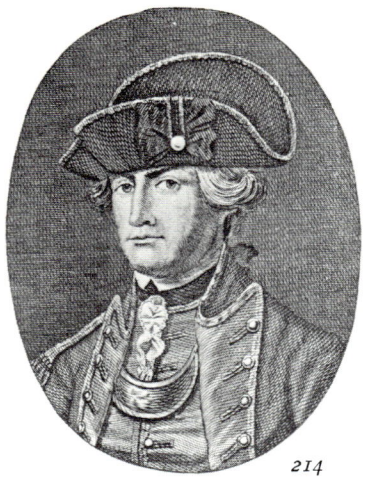
214

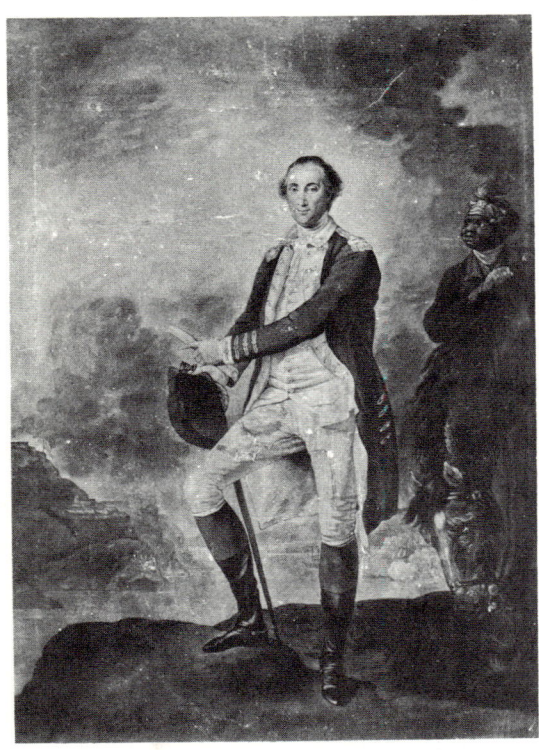
215

213

His Excellency George Washington Esqr. Captain General of all the American Forces. [1780]
Mixed method 4⅝ x 7⅝ in.

This fictitious portrait might be related to Peale's 1781 painting which also shows Washington leaning on a cannon. The pose, as well as the background, is stylized. The military camp also appears on item 110. From *An Impartial History of the War in America* (London, 1780), p. 221. Baker, 418; Hart, 760.

——————Another impression. In *An Impartial History of the War in America* (London & Carlisle, 1780), p. 221. LC–USZ62–45250

214

GENERAL WASHINGTON. Printed for T. Robson, Newcastle, upon Tyne. [1780]
Mixed method 7 x 4 in.

After the Campbell portrait. From Murray, *An Impartial History of the War in America*, v. 1 (Newcastle Upon Tyne, 1780), p. 239. Baker, 56; Hart, 742. LC–USZ62–45301

——————Another impression. In Murray, *An Impartial History of the Present War in America*, v. 2 (Newcastle Upon Tyne, 1782), p. 61.

——————Another impression. In P&P.

215

GENERAL WASHINGTON. Painted by J. Trumbull Esqr. of Connecticut 1780. Engraved by V. Green, Mezzotinto Engraver to his Majesty & to the Elector Palatine. Engraved from the Original Picture in the Possession of M. De Neufville of Amsterdam. Published by appointmt of M. De Neufville Janry 15th 1781, by V. Green, N29, Newman Street, Oxford Street, London.
Mezzotint 24½ x 15⅞ in.

John Trumbull was commissioned an aide-de-camp to Washington in 1775 and later served under other commanders. He received some art education and in 1780 went to Europe, where he painted his first full-length portrait of Washington. For the remainder of his life he pursued military, artistic, and political interests in Europe and America. Ships in the background bombard a fort, and beneath the picture an Indian holds the crest of Washington. Baker, 147; Hart, 84. LC–USZ62–45197

216

His Excy. George Washington Esqr. Captain General of all the American Forces. J. Norman [1781]
Mixed method 6 x 3¾ in. (image)

This portrait is by Norman after a similar one in the English editions of this book. The book, however, is markedly different and might be after a Peale portrait. Cf. item 213. From *An Impartial History of the War in America* (Boston, 1781). Copy in P&P. Baker, 419; Hart, 761. LC–USZ62–45172

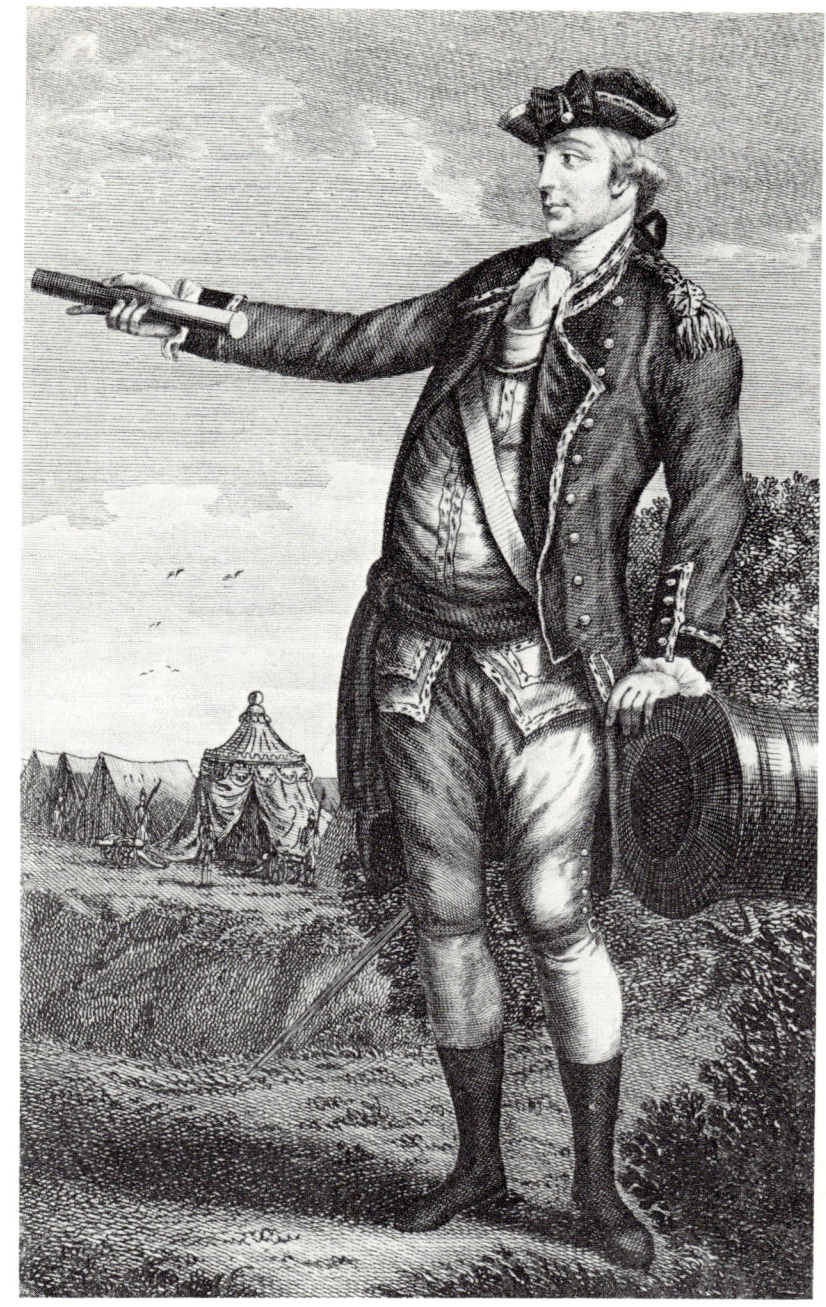

213

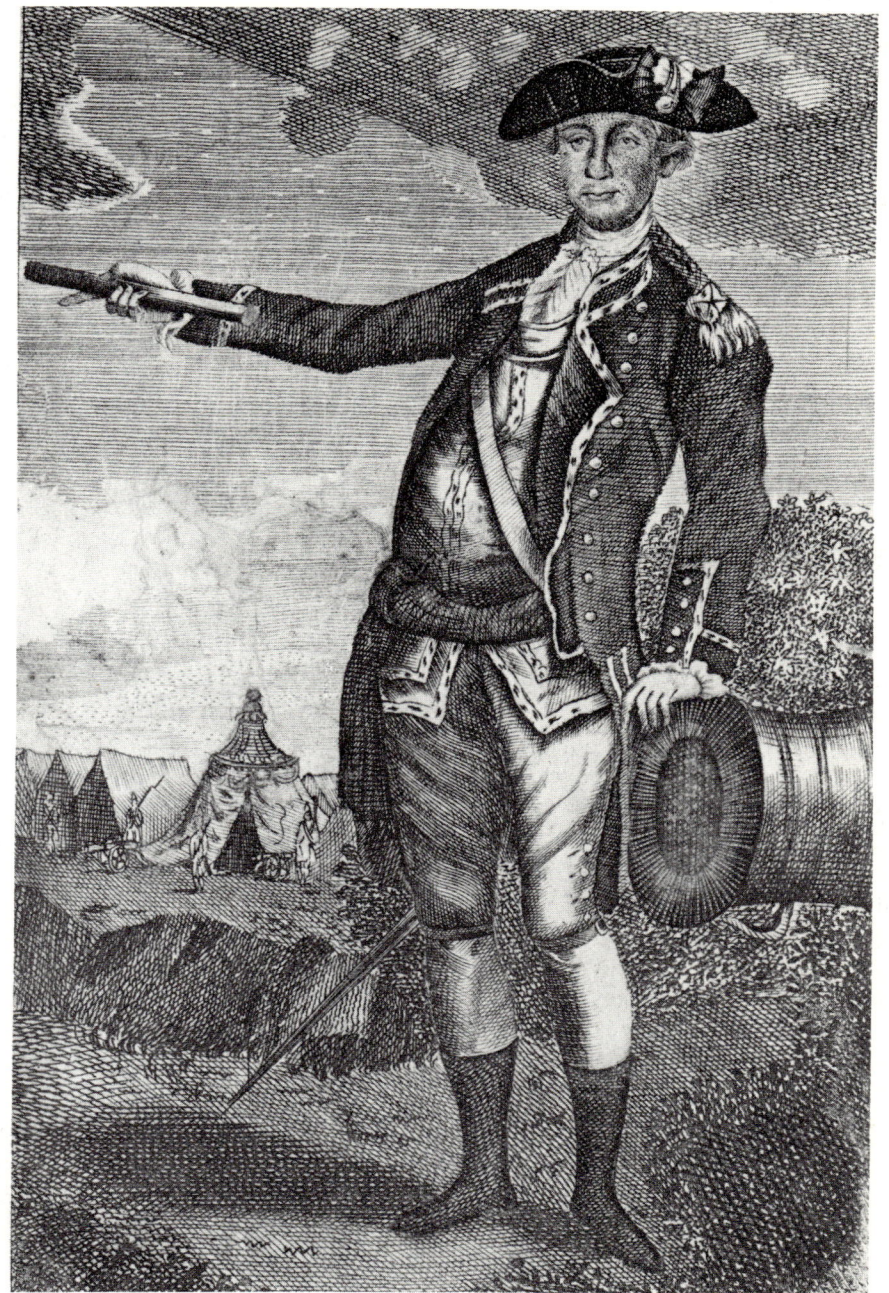

216

67

217

G. WASHINGTON. J. Trumbull Pinx. Ta. le Roy Sculp. [1782]

Etching 9¼ x 6¼ in.

After Trumbull. Cf. item 215. From Hilliard d'Auberteuil, *Essais historiques*, v. 3 (1782), p. [6]. Baker, 151; Hart, 85. LC–USZ62–45330

218

GEORGE WASHINGTON. Commander in Chief of ye Armies of ye UNITED STATES of AMERICA. Engrav'd by W. Sharp, from an Original Picture. London, Published according to Act of Parliament Feby. 22d. 1783 by J. Stockdale Piccadilly.

Mixed method 6⅛ x 4¼ in. (image)

This engraving is the reverse of item 211 with the addition of the words "Dont Tread On Me." From *The Constitutions of the Several Independent States of America* (London, 1783), frontispiece. Baker, 35; Hart, 92. CPPS 5641 LC–USZ62–45319

219

His Excellency GENERAL WASHINGTON Commander in Chief of the united States of North America &c. B.B.E. Pubd. May 15th. 1783 by R. Wilkinson, No. 58 Cornhill, London.

Mixed method 4⅜ x 3⅝ in. (image)

Du Simitière made the drawing for this portrait at Philadelphia in the late 1770's. Copy in P&P. Baker, 65; Hart, 75.

————Another impression. In Du Simitière, *Portraits of the Generals* (London, 1783), plate 1. 5½ x 4⅜ in. LC–USZ62–45479

220

[George Washington] J. Norman Sc [1784]

Mixed method 7 x 4⅛ in.

The explanation of the symbolism in this frontispiece to *The Boston Magazine* for April 1784 states:

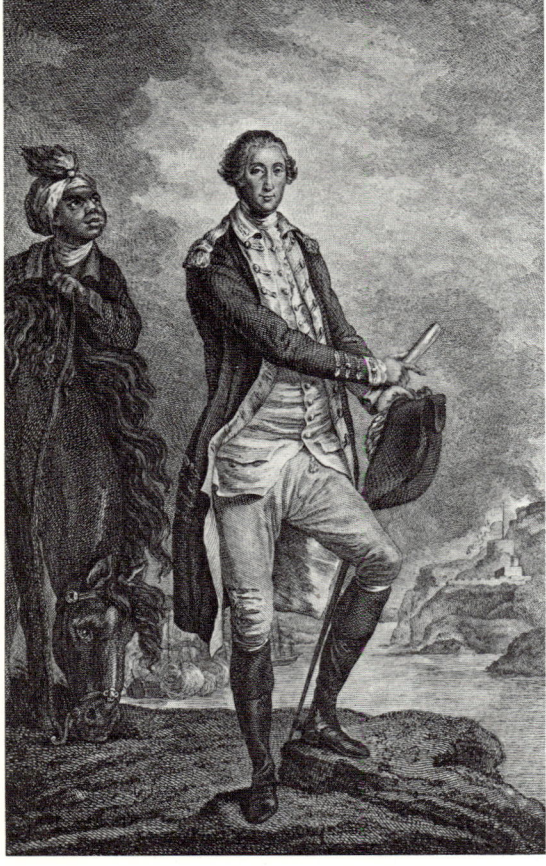

217

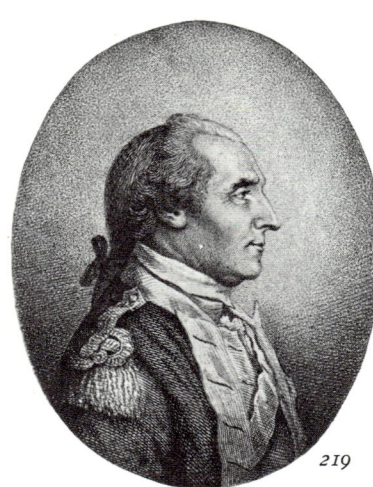

218

219

Nature stands ready to strike the Lyre, while the Genius of Liberty presents a medal of the illustrious man who hath defended her standard in this new World. Fame blows her trumpet, and Astrea finds a part of the earth where she may fix her residence.

In this portrait of Washington after Peale, 13 stars surround his head. Hart, 57; Stauffer, 2353. LC–USZ62–45278

221

1. General Washington. 2. General Gates. 3. Dr. Franklin. 4. Präsid Laurens. 5. Paul Jones. D. Berger Sculp. 1784.
Etching 4½ x 2¾ in.

The German engraver has portrayed Washington and Gates after Du Simitière, Franklin after Cochin, Laurens after Copley, and Jones after Notté. In Sprengel, *Allgemeines historisches Taschenbuch* (Berlin, 1784), p. 182 ff. Hart, 79. LC–USZ62–45517

222

GEN. WASHINGTON. Wm. Angus Sc. Published Sepr 23, 1785 by J. Fielding Pater Noster Row.
Mixed method 7 x 4⅜ in.

After Peale. From Andrews, *History of the War with America, France, Spain, and Holland*, v. 1 (London, 1785), opposite p. 354. Baker, 3; Hart, 38.

——————Another impression. In P&P.
LC–USZ62–45176

223

GENERAL WASHINGTON. J. Trenchard Scpt. [1787]
Etching 6⅛ x 3¾ in. (image)

Washington's seal surmounted by a crown appears below this portrait after Peale. A ribbon under the seal reads, "Exitus Acta Probat." From *The Columbian Magazine: or Monthly Miscellany*, January 1787, opposite p. 205. Baker, 37; Hart, 839. LC–USZ62–45510

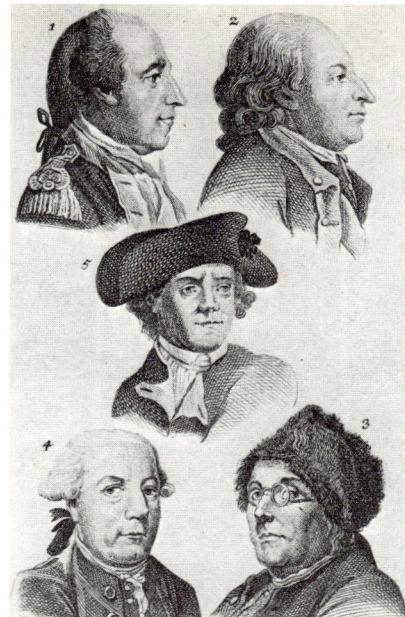
221

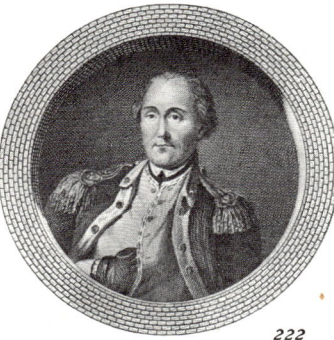
222

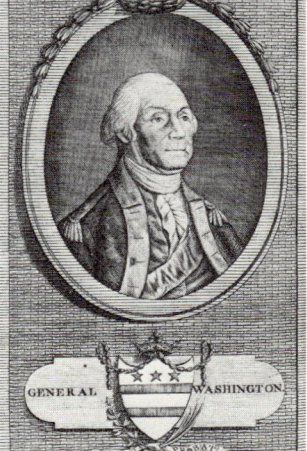
223

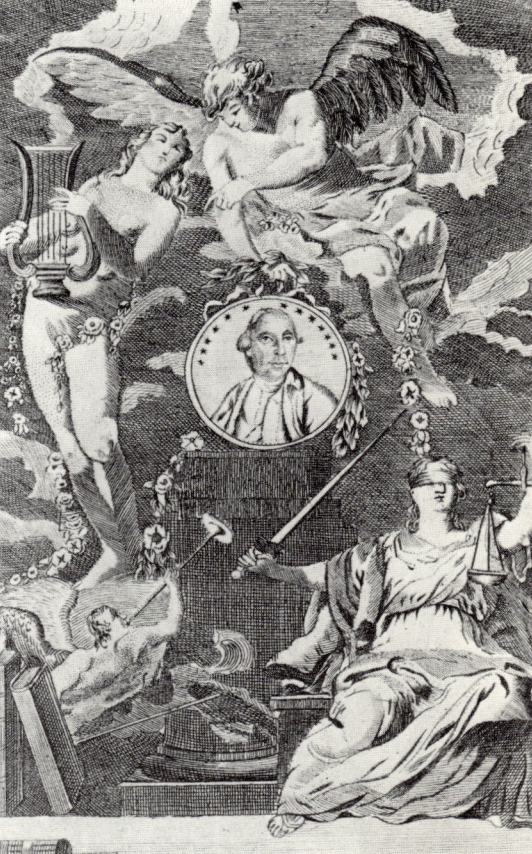
220

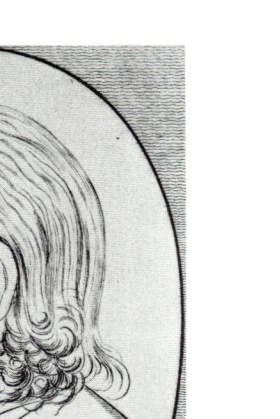

224

225

224

HIS EXCEL: G: WASHINGTON ESQ: L.L.D. LATE COMMANDER IN CHIEF OF THE ARMIES OF THE U.S. OF AMERICA & PRESIDENT OF THE CONVENTION OF 1787. Painted & Engrav'd by C. W. Peale. 1787.
Mezzotint 7¼ x 5¾ in.

Charles Willson Peale wished to express patriotic enthusiasm for his former commander and also show his approval of the Constitutional Convention, which was then sitting at Philadelphia. This mezzotint and others in the series by Peale were part of an attempt to rival the thriving print trade of London, but the scarcity of craftsmen and proper material made this difficult and unprofitable. See Richardson, p. 174. Baker, 1; Hart, 3b. LC-USZ62-45181

225

[Silhouette of George Washington and bust profile of Benjamin Franklin] 1788.
Etching 4⅜ x 7 in.

A letter to the editor of *The Columbian Magazine* called attention to Johann Lavater's *Essai sur physionomie*, probably the 1781-86 edition, in which he produced profiles resembling Washington and Franklin and analyzed their characteristics. The following selections are quoted from Lavater in the magazine:

> The first of these profiles [Washington], says Lavater, indicates a sound judgment; freedom from prejudices, and a heart that opens itself to truth, which it imbibes and cherishes. It designates, likewise, taste, or, if you please, a sense of beauty. The original must be distinguished by an indefatigable activity—a man who acts with prudence, and always with dignity.

> With respect to the second profile [Franklin], continues our author; it may be exhibited as the model of a *Thinker*, full of sagacity and penetration. This happy physiognomy characterizes, to a miracle, a mind which can elevate itself without the trouble of extraordinary exertions: it bespeaks a man who prosecutes his designs with a rational perseverance, but is, at the same time, exempt from a conceited obstinacy.

Lavater claimed that he never knew these men personally and had picked the portraits at random without an awareness of whom they portrayed. The writer of the letter to the editor notes a "strong likeness to two of the most distinguished citizens of America." From *The Columbian Magazine*, March 1788, p. 144-145. Hart, 810. LC-USZ62-45514

226
G. WASHINGTON, GENERAAL DER NOORD-AMERICAANEN. Reinr Vinkeles, sculp. naar een Origineel Schildery, by den Wel Ed. Heer P. van Winter, Nic:z. [178?]
Etching 6½ x 4⅜ in.
After Peale. Baker, 39; Hart, 56. LC-USZ62-45174

227
WASHINGTON. Généralissime des Americains, Libérateur des Etats-Unis. Contemporain et Ami du Général Lafayette. Dessiné par Bonnieu d'apres un Tableau fourni par M. le Marquis de la Fayette. Gravé par [Justus] Chevillet [178?]
Line engraving 14¾ x 11 in.
After Peale. Baker, 6; Hart, 29. LC-USZ62-45194

228
S.E. GEORGE WASHINGTON. Général en Chef des Armées des Etats unis de l'Amérique. Le B. Pinx. J.L. Sculp. [178?]
Line engraving 12 x 8 in.
After Peale. Baker, 18; Hart, 39. LC-USZ62-45193

229
LE GENERAL WASHINGTON. Ne Quid Detrimenti capiat Res publica. Gravé d'après le Tableau Original appartenant a Mr. Marquis de la Fayette. Cette Estampe ce Vend avec privilége du Roy à Paris chez le Mire Graveur rüe et porte St. Jacques. Maison de Mr. le

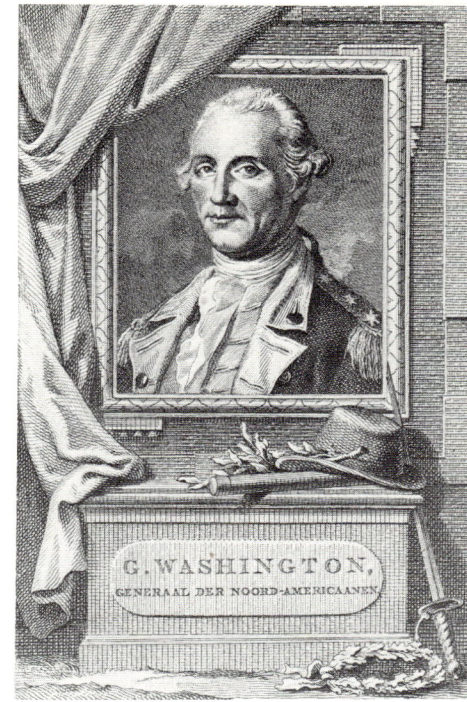
226

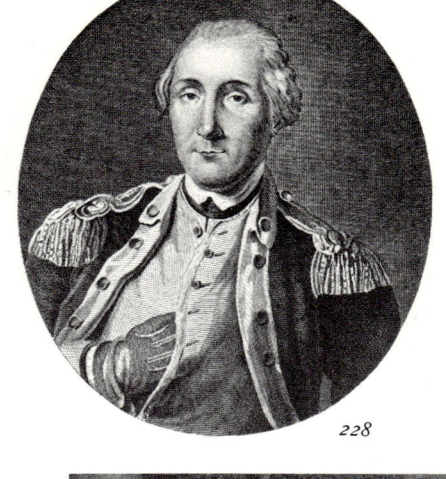
228

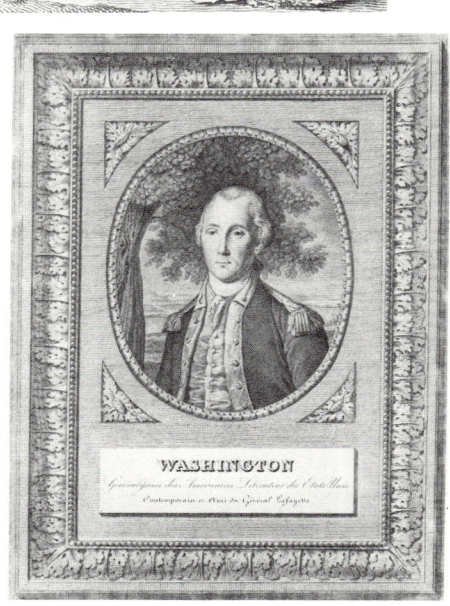
227

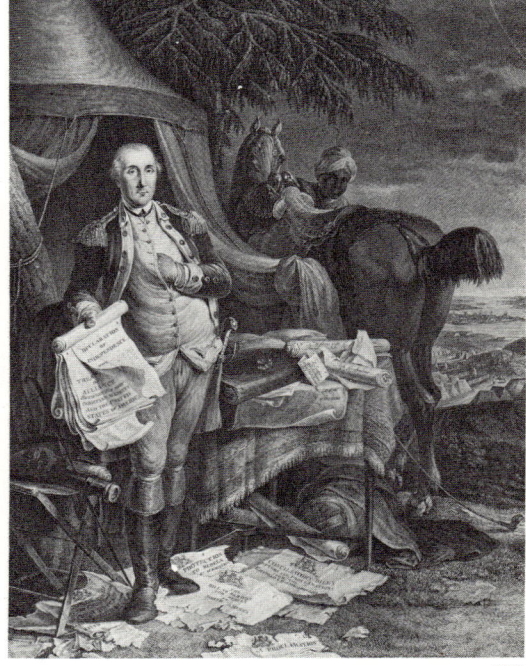
229

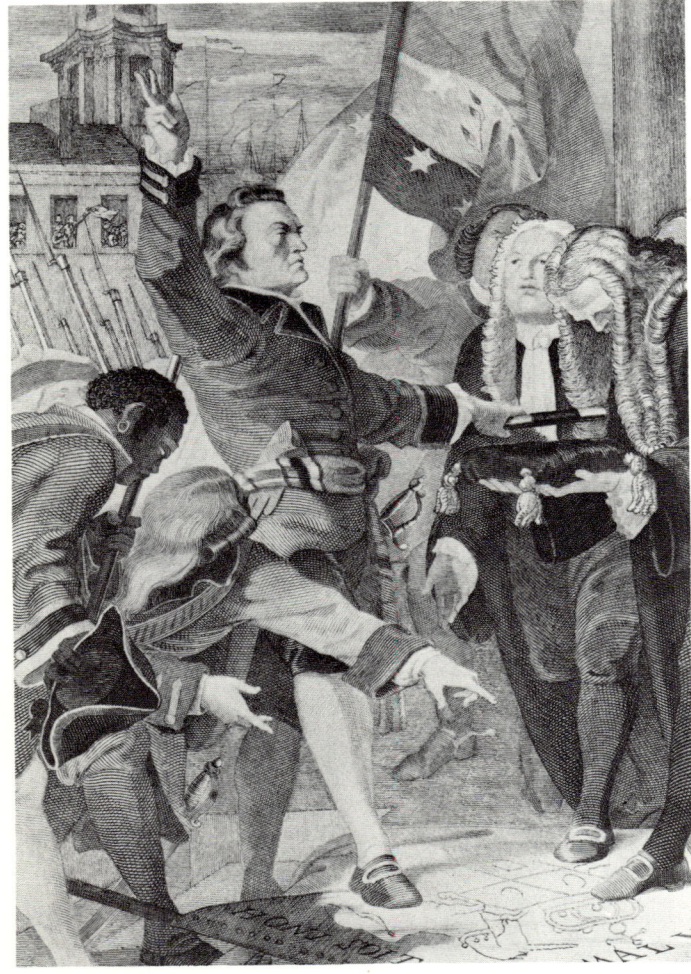

230

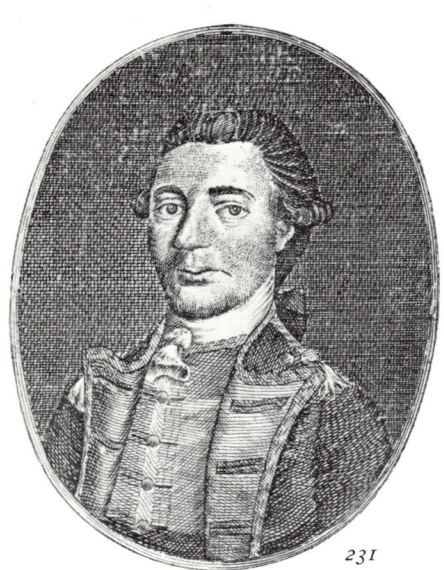

231

Camus Md. de Drap. prix 12 livres. Peint par L. le Paon Peintre de Bataille de S.A.S. Mgr. le Prince de Condé. Gravé par N[oel] le Mire des Academies Imperiales et Royales et de celle des Sciences et Arts de Rouen. [178?]

Line engraving 16¾ x 12¾ in. (image)

In this portrait after Peale, Washington holds the Declaration of Independence and the Treaty of Alliance with France. Documents relating to British attempts at reconciliation lie torn at his feet. A military camp is in the far background. Baker, 21; Hart, 31.
LC–USZ62–963

——————Three other impressions. In P&P. Two have imprint cropped.

230

Washington. [1790?]

Etching 5½ x 3¾ in. (image)

Washington and the magistrates step on a flag with the crest of England. In the background people cheer from windows, and ships' masts are visible in the distance. This engraving is probably by a German and contemporary with Washington's resignation from the Army.
LC–USZ62–45173

Anthony Wayne, 1745–1796

231

The Honle. ANTHONY WAYNE, Esqr. Major General in the American Army. J. Nor Sc. [1782]

Etching 4⅜ x 3½ in. (image in oval)

A brigadier general, Wayne was given command of the Pennsylvania Line in 1777, and although he was humiliated by the British at Paoli, his capture of the British garrison at Stony Point earned him a Congressional Medal. He participated in the battle of Yorktown and ended his Revolutionary career in the southern campaigns of Gen. Nathanael Greene. From

An Impartial History of the War in America, v. 2 (Boston, 1782), copy 1, p. 193. Stauffer, 2357. LC–USZ62–45242

George Whitefield, 1714–1770

232

GEORGE WHITEFIELD. M.A. Elisha Gallaudet Sculp. N. York. 1774
  Mixed method 5⅜ x 3⅜ in.

Whitefield, a noted evangelist in both England and America, showed remarkable preaching ability from the beginning of his illustrious career. Closely associated with the Colony of Georgia, where he founded an orphanage, he traveled throughout America, participating in and perpetuating the religious "Great Awakening." This posthumous depiction of Whitefield shows him preaching in a church; often, however, he spoke outdoors, drawing large crowds from all social classes. From Gillies, *Memoirs of the Life of the Reverend George Whitefield* (New York, 1774), frontispiece. Stauffer, 1025. LC–USZ62–45506

233

Parrawankaw. [and] Dr. Squintum. [1769]
  Mixed method 4 x 6⅞ in.

Whitefield made many enemies, particularly among religious conservatives. In 1760 Samuel Foote burlesqued Whitefield, who had a pronounced squint in one eye, as "Dr. Squintum." Numerous caricatures followed, attempting to discredit a man who seems to have been morally above reproach. The young Indian woman, reported in *The Town and Country Magazine* as the mother of numerous Whitefield offspring, was probably a figment of the editor's imagination. From *The Town and Country Magazine,* supplement, 1769, opposite p. 673. CPPS 4363 LC–USZ62–45489

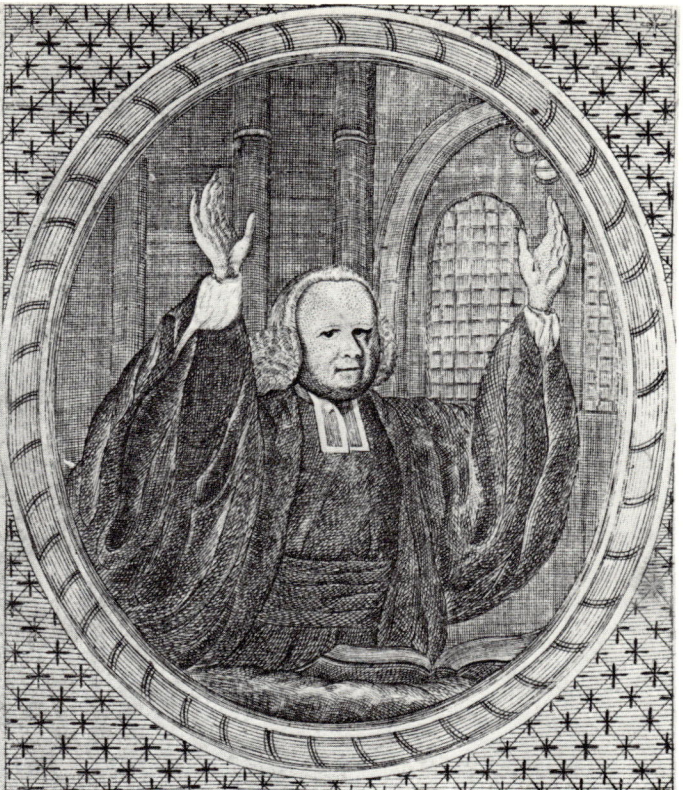
232

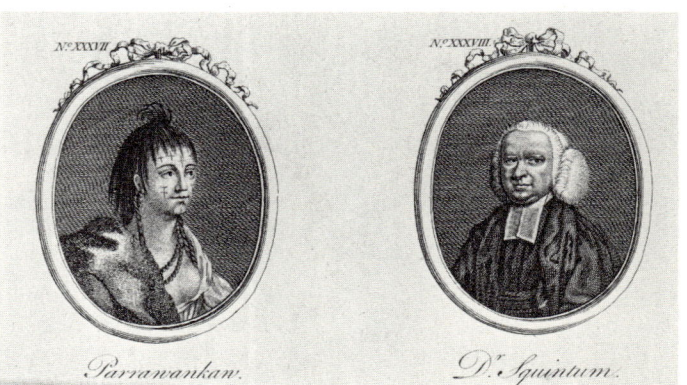
233

John Wilkes, 1727–1797

234
JOHN WILKES, Esq; [1769]
Woodcut (retouched with ink) 4⅞ x 3½ in.

The figures framing this portrait of Wilkes are also found on the title page of the *Boston Almanack* for the following year, framing a picture of James Otis. (Cf. item 163). On the next page of the 1769 volume, the printer explains that Wilkes is "crowned with Laurel" and "supported by Britannia in the dress of Minerva, the Goddess of Wisdom... and by Hercules, the God of Strength." Underneath is a serpent, "Emblem of Envy, which Hercules is treading under his feet... a Cupid, with the Cap of Liberty... A Shield with St. George's Cross, representing the arms of England..." and two books designated "Lockes Works" and "Sidney on Government." The description ends by explaining Wilkes' role as a defender of "Liberty" and "Republican Principles." At this time Wilkes was among the leaders of the opposition against the King's ministers in Parliament and supported the cause of the American colonists. From Bickerstaff, *Boston Almanack* (Boston, 1769), title page.
LC–USZ62–45322

David Wooster, 1711–1777

235
DAVID WOOSTER, Esqr. Commander in Chief of the Provincial Army against QUEBEC. London, Published as the Act directs 26, March 1776, by Thos. Hart.
Mezzotint 13⅞ x 9¾ in.

General Wooster, an elderly veteran of the French and Indian War, led Connecticut troops in 1775. He was found to be incompetent in the Canada invasion and returned to Connecticut, where he was killed opposing the Danbury Raid, 1777. This early mezzotint, probably by

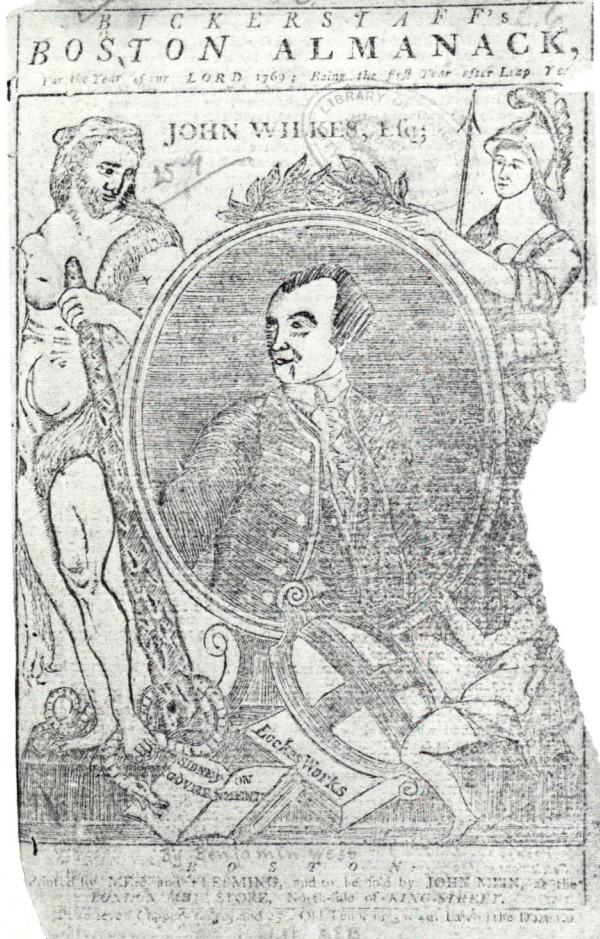

234

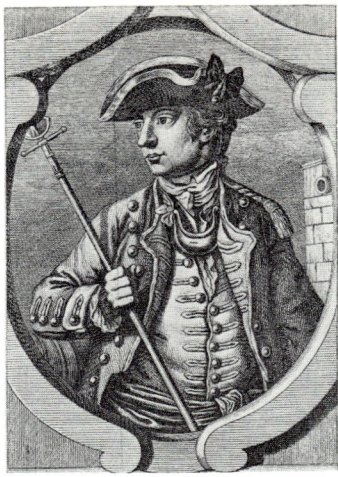

236

C. Corbutt, was copied by J. M. Will in Augsburg and is the model for the other portraits of Wooster in this list. CPPS 5332
LC–USZ62–3621

236
David Wooster, Esqr. Commander. bëy der Provincal. Armee in America. [1778]
Etching 6¼ x 3¾ in.

This German version is based on the preceding English portrait of Wooster. Neither picture reflects his true age at the time of the Revolution. From Korn, *Geschichte der Kriege* (Nürnberg, 1777–78), copy 2, p. 104.
LC–USZ62–45271

237
Major General David Wooster. [1780]
Etching 7½ x 4⅝ in.

From *An Impartial History of the War in America* (London & Carlisle, 1780), p. 400.
LC–USZ62–45257

———Another impression. In *An Impartial History of the War in America* (London, 1780), p. 400.

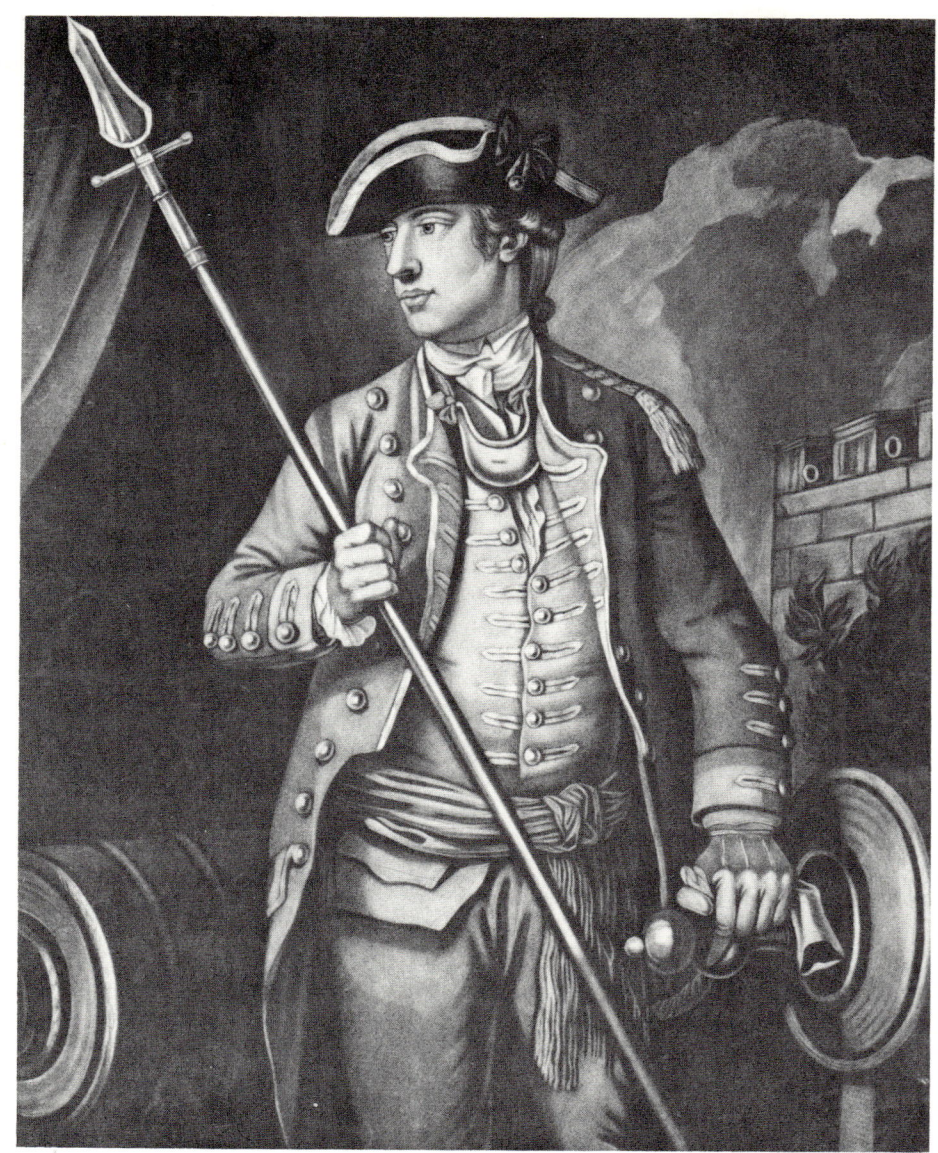

235

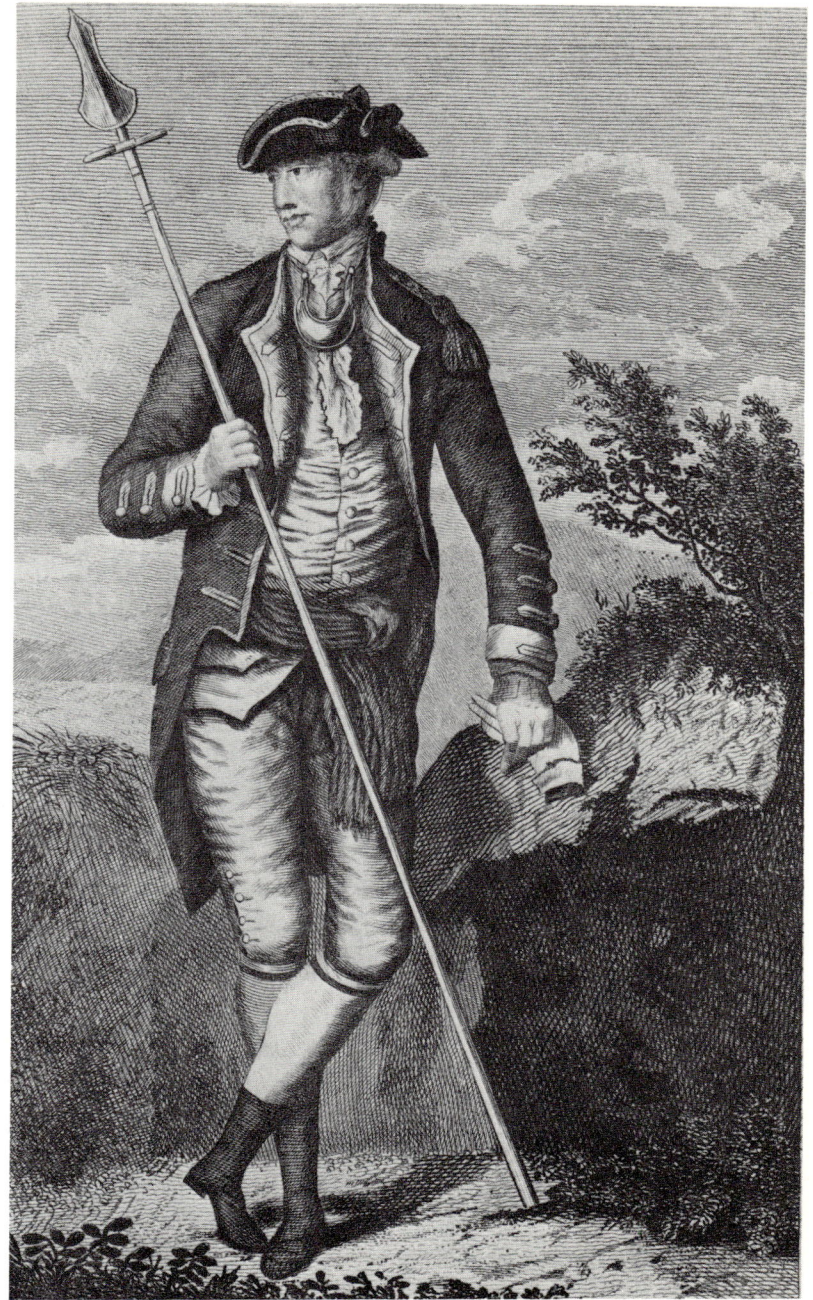

237

75

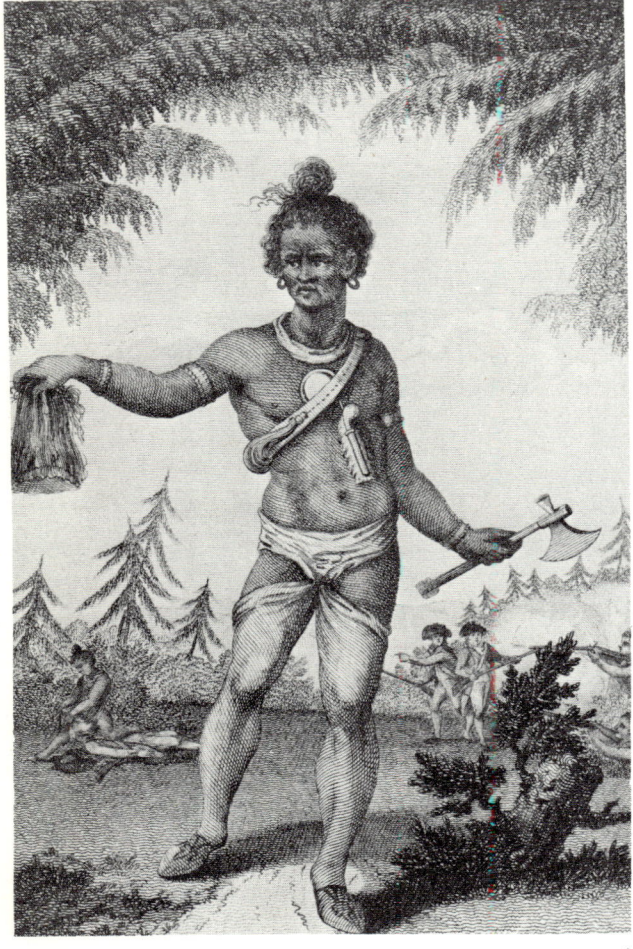

238

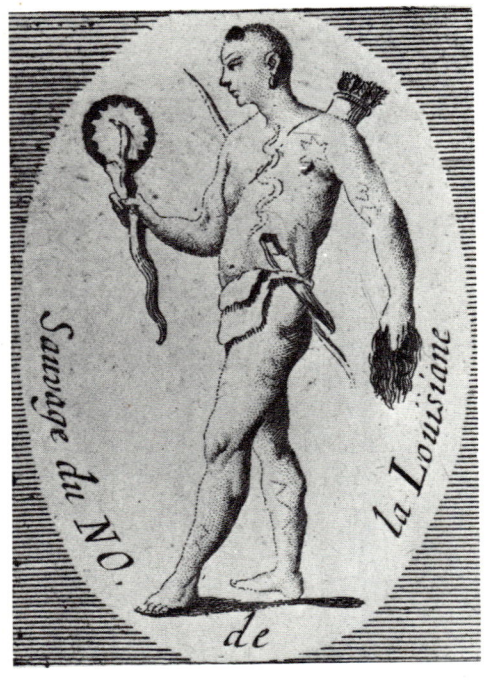

239

Portraits of Types

238
An Indian Warrior Entering his Wigwam with a Scalp. Barlow, Sc. [1789]
Etching 7 x 4¼ in.

In the background of this stylized portrait, an Indian scalps a fallen soldier and Indians fire from ambush at two startled soldiers. From Anburey, *Travels Through the Interior Parts of America*, v. 1 (London, 1789), opposite p. 291. LC–USZ62–45547

239
Sauvage du NO. de la Louisiane. [1750]
Etching 2½ x 1¾ in. (image)

Border ornament for a map entitled "Carte des Nouvelles Decouvertes au Nord de la Mer du Sud, tant a l'est de la Siberie et du Kamtchatka, qu'a l'ouest de la Nouvelle France." From P. Santini, *Atlas universal dressé sur les meilleures cartes modernes*, v. 2 (Venice, 1776–84), no. 44. LC–USZ62–45593

———Another impression with similar title. In Guillaume de L'Isle, *Atlas géographique et universal*, v. 2 (Paris, 1784), no. 115. Phillips 655.

240

A Real American Rifle Man. [1780]
Mixed method 6¾ x 4¼ in. (image)

British fascination with American riflemen is reflected in this conventional portrait. On the cap a skull and crossbones and the words "or liberty" portray one of the most popular slogans of the day, "Liberty or Death." The initials "CC" on the ammunition pouch designate a soldier in the service of the Continental Congress. From *An Impartial History of the War in America*, v. 1 (London & Carlisle, 1780), p. 212. LC–USZ62–45249

——————Another impression. From *An Impartial History of the War in America*, v. 1 (London, 1780), p. 212.

241

1. Americanischer Scharffschütz oder Jäger (Rifleman) 2. regulaire Infanterie von Pensylvanien. D. Chodowiecki Id. D. Berger Sc. [1784]
Etching (hand colored) 4½ x 2½ in.

A German portrayal of an American rifleman or "sharpshooter" and a regular soldier of the Pennsylvania Infantry. Found in Sprengel, *Allgemeines historisches Taschenbuch* (Berlin, 1784), p. 182 ff. LC–USZ62–45520

242

1. General Washington's reitende Leibgarde. 2. die independent Company, Chef General Washington. D. Chodowiecki Id. D. Berger Sc. [1784]
Etching (hand colored) 3½ x 2⅛ in.

Washington's lifeguard, officially known as the Commander in Chief's Guard, was organized on March 12, 1776. The second soldier, a member of an independent company under Washington's command, is dressed in the garb characteristic of Continental officers. Found in Sprengel, *Allgemeines historisches Taschenbuch* (Berlin, 1784), p. 182 ff. LC–USZ62–45519

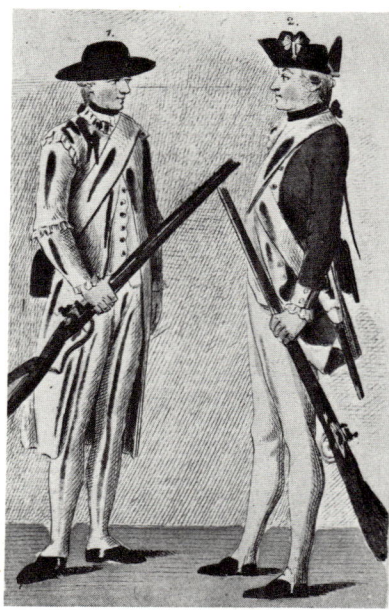
241

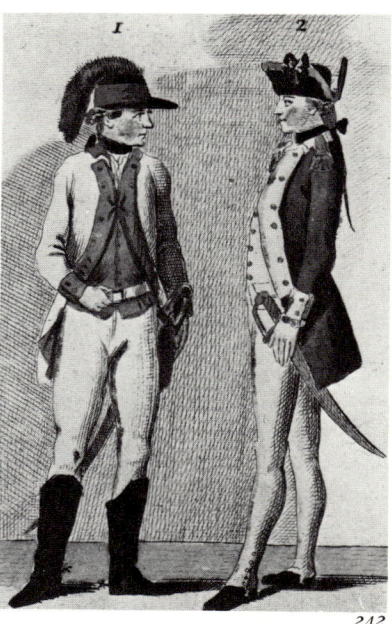
242

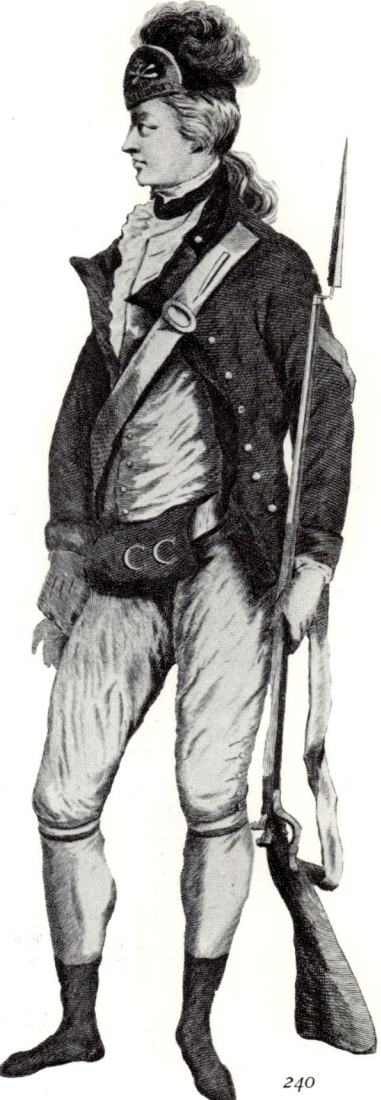
240

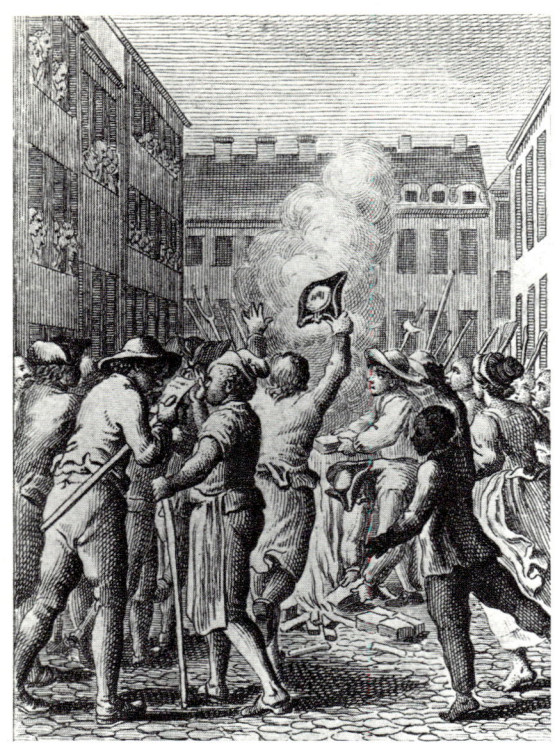

243

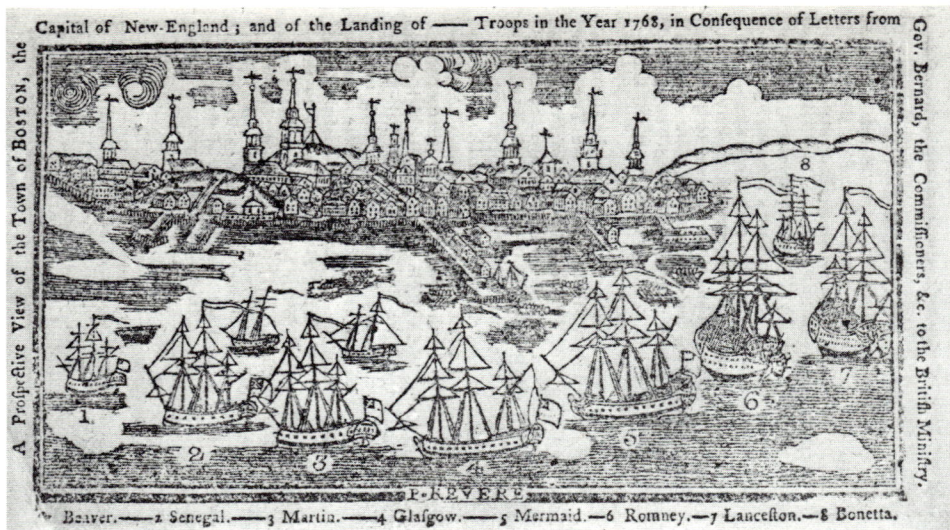

245

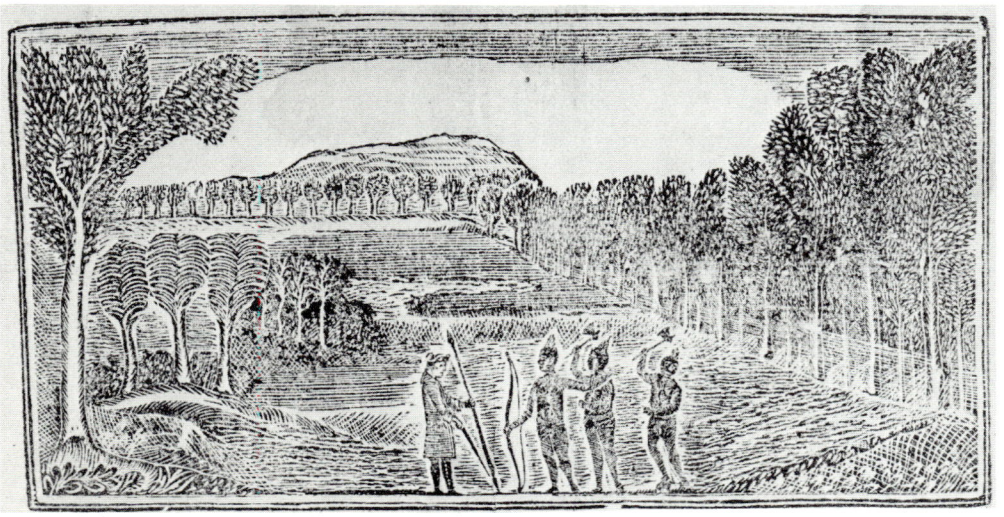

244

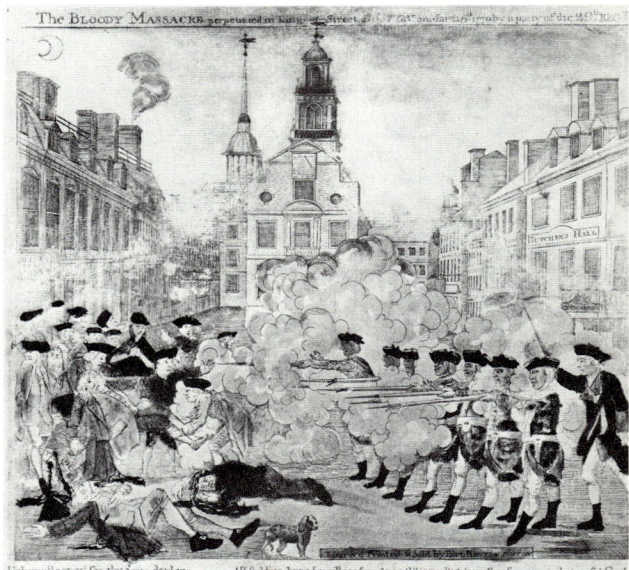

246

Chapter II

Events

243
Die Americaner wiedersetzen sich der Stempel-Acte, und verbrennen das aus England nach America gesandte Stempel-Papier zu Boston. im August 1764. D. Chodowiecki inv. et del. 1784

Etching 2⅞ x 2 in. (image)

Throughout August 1765 and during the months following, many kinds of protests against the Stamp Act flared up in America. Most of the people merely refused to handle the stamps, but militants in Boston burned the proclamations from England, destroyed Crown property, and frightened officials and their families. Number one in a series. The date 1764 in the caption is incorrect.

──────── Another copy. Engraved by D. Berger after Chodowiecki. LC–USZ61–449

──────── Another impression. In Sprengel, *Allgemeines historisches Taschenbuch* (Berlin, 1784).

244
A SACHEM of the Abenakee Nation, rescuing an ENGLISH Officer from the Indians. [1768]

Woodcut 2⅞ x 5¾ in. (image)

An Indian holds back two others who had intended to slay an Englishman. The story which accompanies this picture tells of a British officer who was held captive by the Indians for one winter and was returned to his own people by the old man who had saved him. The Abnaki, who once occupied parts of Maine, New Brunswick, and Quebec, were faithful allies of the French. They were almost annihilated in the French and Indian War. From Bickerstaff, *Boston Almanack* (Boston, 1768), p. E2. LC–USZ62–45552

245
A Prospective View of the Town of Boston, the Capital of New-England; and the Landing of—Troops in the Year 1768, in Consequence of Letters from Gov. Bernard, the Commissioners, &c. to the British Ministry. P. REVERE [1770]

Woodcut 3 x 5⅝ in. (image)

On October 1, 1768, two regiments of British regulars under General Gage disembarked at Boston to quell disorders caused by the Sons of Liberty. This print portrays the British ships *Beaver, Senegal, Martin, Glasgow, Mermaid, Romney, Lanceston,* and *Bonetta.* Boston is in the background. From *Edes & Gill's North–American Almanack, and Massachusetts Register* (Boston, 1770), frontispiece. LC–USZ62–45559

246
THE BLOODY MASSACRE perpetrated in King Street BOSTON on March 5th. 1770 by a party of the 29th. REGT. Engrav'd, Printed, & Sold by PAUL REVERE, BOSTON. [1770]

Etching (hand colored) 7¾ x 8¾ in. (image)

Revere's famous print of the "Boston Massacre" shows seven British soldiers firing their rifles into a patriot mob. This bloody scene made an effective propaganda piece and was widely circulated. An impassioned poem beneath the print reads as follows:

> Unhappy Boston! see thy Sons deplore,
> Thy hallow'd Walks besmear'd with guiltless Gore:
> While faithless P——n and his savage Bands
> With murd'rous Rancour stretch their bloody Hands;
> Like fierce Barbarians grinning o'er their Prey,
> Approve the Carnage, and enjoy the Day.
>
> If scalding drops from Rage from Anguish Wrung
> If speechless Sorrows lab'ring for a Tongue,
> Or if a weeping World can ought appease
> The plaintive Ghosts of Victims such as these
> The Patriots copious Tears for each are shed.
> A glorious Tribute which embalms the Dead.
>
> But know, Fate summons to that awful Goal,
> Where Justice strips the Murd'rer of his Soul:
> Should venal C——ts the scandal of the Land,
> Snatch the relentless Villain from her Hand.
> Keen Execrations on this Plate inscribed,
> Shall reach a Judge who never can be brib'd.

LC–USZ62–35522

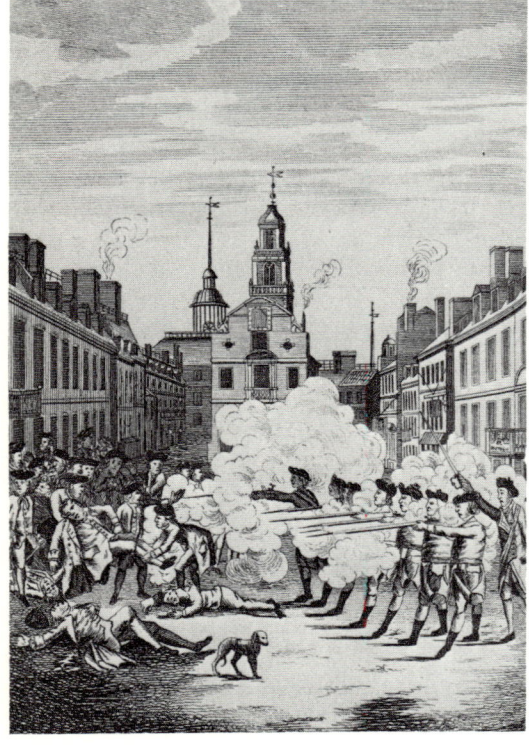

247

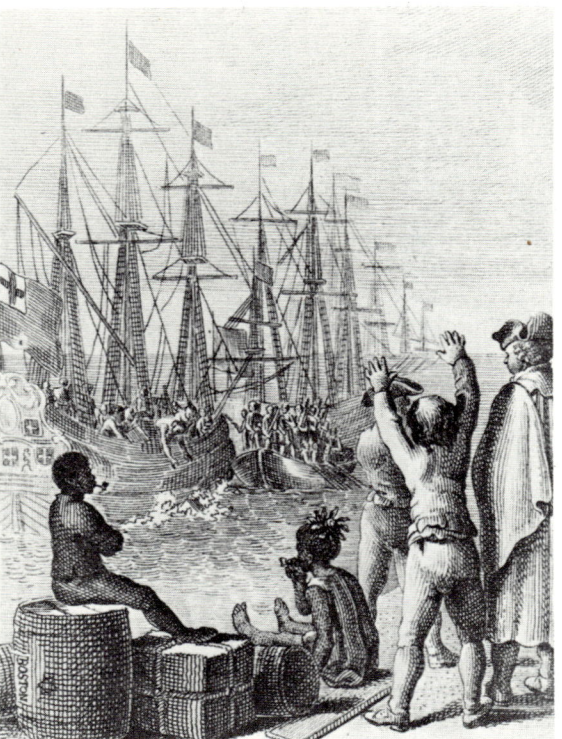

248

247
The Massacre perpetrated in King Street Boston on March 5th. 1770, in which Messrs Saml. Gray, Saml. Maverick, James Caldwell, Crispus Attucks, Patrick Carr were Killed, six others Wounded, two of them Mortally. [1770]

Mixed method 7⅜ x 4½ in.

A copy of the "Boston Massacre," based on the Pelham-Revere print. This picture appears as the frontispiece for *A Short Narrative of The Horrid Massacre in Boston, Perpetrated In the Evening of the Fifth Day of March 1770, by Soldiers of the XXIXth Regiment, Which, with the XIVth Regiment, were then Quartered There. With Some Observations on the State of Things Prior to that Catastrophe.* Printed by Order of the Town of Boston: London, Re-printed for E. and C. Dilly, in the Poultry; and J. Almon, in Piccadilly, M.DCC.LXX. LC–USZ62–45554

248
Die Einwohner von Boston wersen den englisch-ostindischen Thee ins Meer am 18. December 1773. [1784]

Etching 2⅞ x 2 in. (image)

Late in the evening of December 16, 1773, a group of Bostonians, disguised as Indians, swarmed onto ships in the harbor and dumped 342 chests of tea overboard. The date is wrong on this print. Number two in a series by "D[aniel N.] Chodowiecki inv. et del."

————Another copy. Engraved by D. Berger after Chodowiecki. LC–USZ61–450

————Another impression. In Sprengel, *Allgemeines historisches Taschenbuch* (Berlin, 1784).

249
JOHN MALCOM. Dessiné et Gravé par F. Godefroy de l'Académie Imple. et Rle. de

Vienne &c. A Paris chez Mr. Godefroy rue des Francs-bourgeois, Porte St. Michel. Et chez Mr. Ponce, rue St. Hiacinte, No. 19. A.P.D.R.

Etching 7½ x 8½ in.

John Malcolm, a customs officer in Boston, was tarred and feathered on January 27, 1774. The explanation below the picture describes the scene and identifies England's attempt to tax the Colonies as a cause of the Revolution. From Ponce, *Recueil d'estampes représentant* ... (Paris, 1784?), plate 2. *Collection de Vinck*, 1164. LC–USZ62–45556

——————Another impression, an earlier state, and a wash drawing of the same picture. In copy 3, in the Rare Book Division.

250

PREMIERE ASSEMBLÉE DU CONGRÈS. Dessiné par le Barbier Peintre du Roi. Gravé par Godefroy de l'Academie Imple. et Royale de Vienne &c. [1782]

Mixed method 6¼ x 3⅞ in. (image)

The First Continental Congress met on September 5, 1774, in Carpenter's Hall, Philadelphia. This stylized, French engraving distinguishes no recognizable individuals except, perhaps, Peyton Randolph, president, on the elevated chair and Charles Thomson, secretary, at the table. From Hilliard d'Auberteuil, *Essais historiques*, v. 3 (1782), p. [2]. LC–USZ62–45328

251

Das erste Bürger Blut, zu Gründung der Americanischen Freyheit, vergossen bey Lexington am 19ten April 1775. [1784]

Etching 2⅞ x 2 in. (image)

In this German print of the initial engagement of the Revolution, British soldiers fire on command into an undisciplined group of Massachusetts militiamen. Number three in a

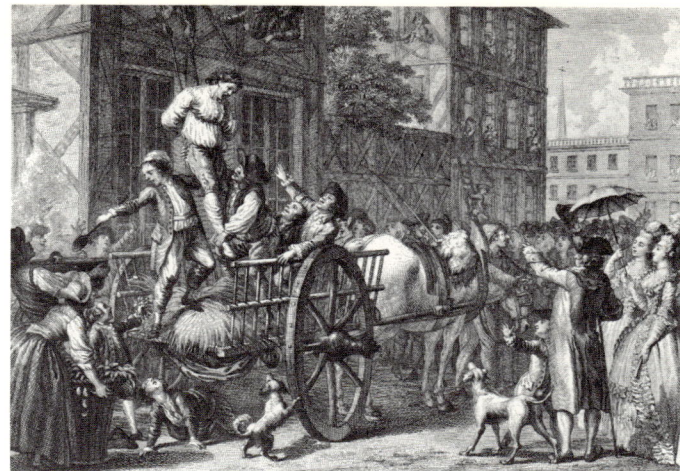
249

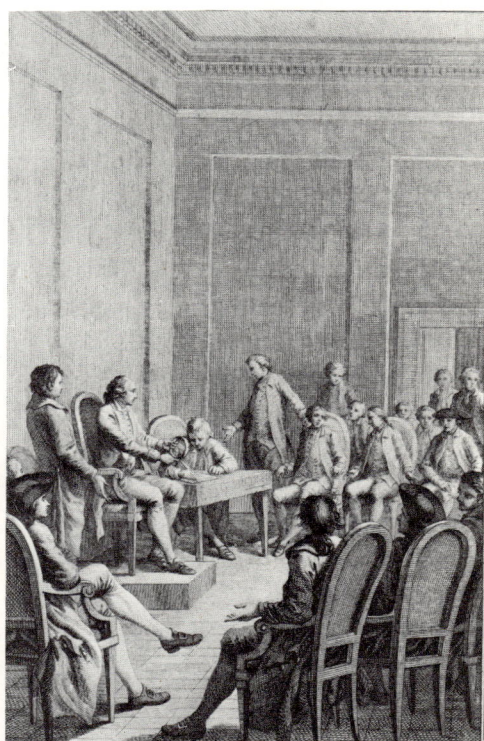
250

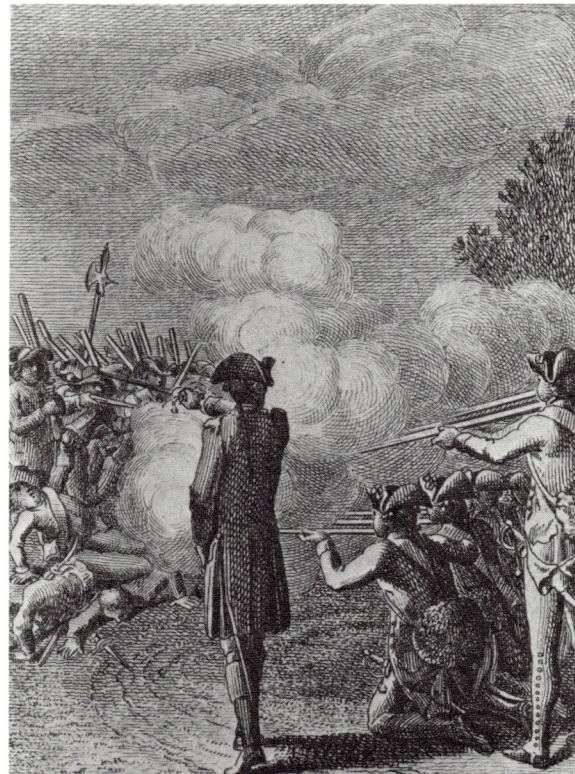
251

81

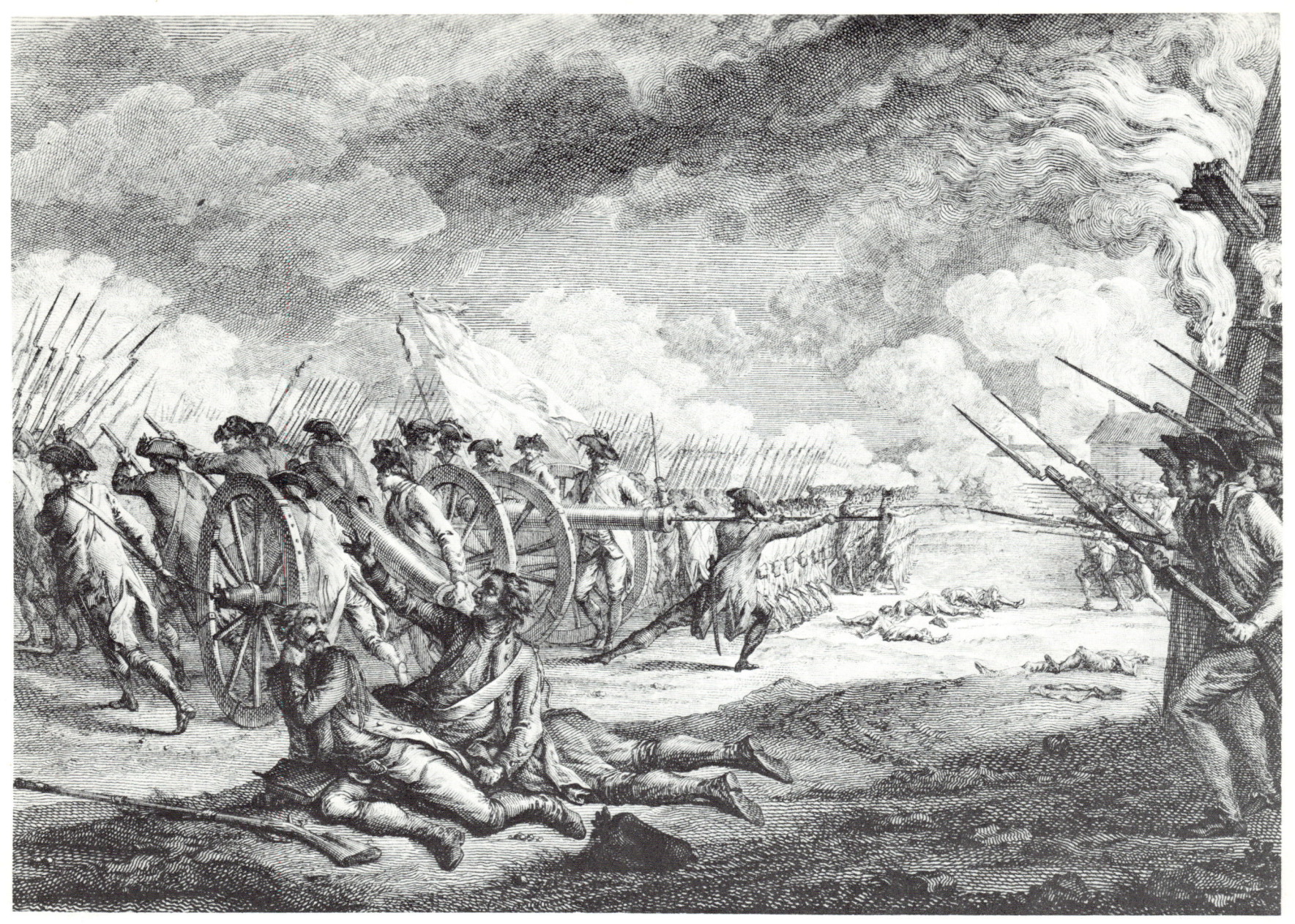

252 Engraving

series by "D[aniel N.] Chodowiecki inv. et del." The Battle of Lexington.
LC–USZ62–26669

————Another copy. Engraved by D. Berger after Chodowiecki.

————Another impression. In Sprengel, *Allgemeines historisches Taschenbuch* (Berlin, 1784).

252
JOURNÉE DE LEXINGTON. Dessiné et Gravé par F. Godefroy de l'Academie Imple. et Rle. de Vienne &c. A Paris chez Mr. Godefroy, rue des Francs Bourgeois, Porte St. Michel, et chez Mr. Ponce, rue St. Hyacinthe, au No. 19. A.P.D.R. [1784?]
  Etching 7½ x 8½ in.

An exaggerated view of the Battle of Lexington, with the British right wing retreating from charging militia. The standard above the troops in the center is the British Union Jack. The biased account below describes the attack as a coldblooded massacre. From Ponce, *Recueil d'estampes représentant . . .* (Paris, 1784?), plate 3.

————Two other impressions, an earlier state, and a wash drawing of the same picture done in reverse (four pictures) are in copy 3 in the Rare Book Division. The negative number for the engraving is LC–USZ62–39582; the number for the wash drawing is LC–USZ62–39583.

253
View of The ATTACK on BUNKER'S HILL, with the Burning of CHARLES TOWN, June 17. 1775. Drawn by Mr. Millar. Engraved by [John?] Lodge.
  Etching 8¼ x 11¾ in.

The patriot performance in the Battle of Bunker Hill, which was actually fought on Breed's Hill, rallied the Colonies, spurred the

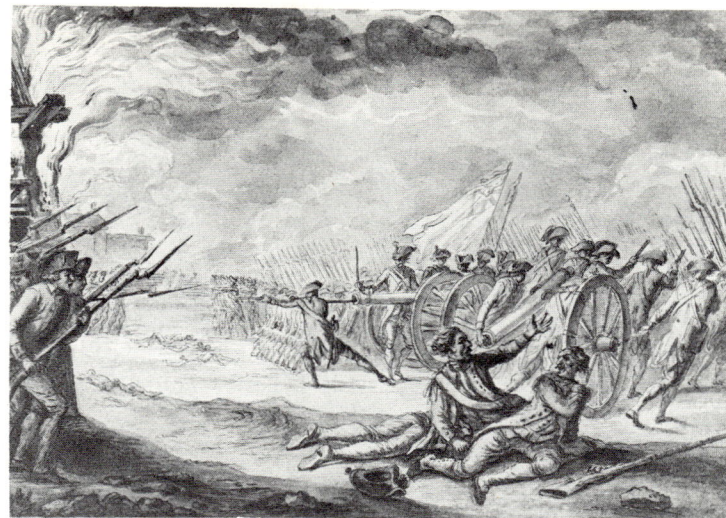
252
wash drawing

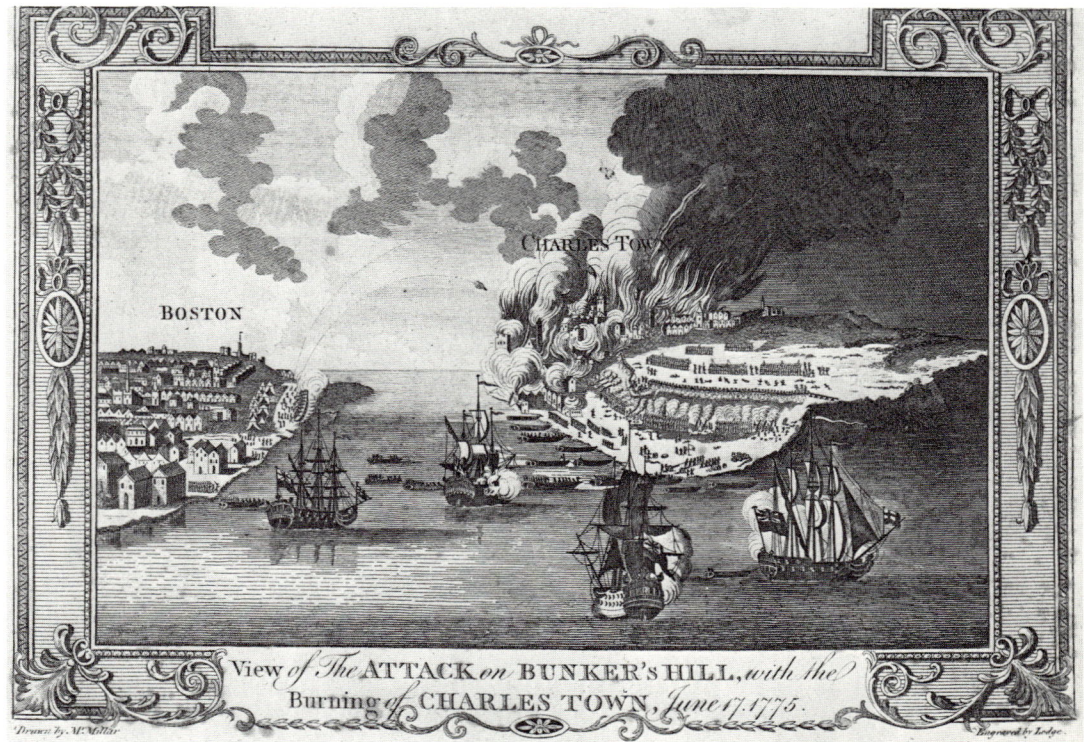
253

Continental Congress into action, and banished any real hope of reconciliation. The ships in the foreground supporting the landing are the *Falcon*, the *Lively*, the *Somerset*, and the *Glasgow*. A British battery on Copp's Hill in Boston is firing rockets into Charlestown. From Barnard, *History of England* (London, 1783), p. 687. Copy in P&P. LC–USZ62–8624

———Another copy. 4¾ x 8½ in. The print has no decorative border and includes the following notations: "A. Boston Battery," "B. Charles Town," "C. British Troops attacking," and "D. Provincial Lines." From Cockings, *The American War, A Poem* (London, 1781), frontispiece.

254
Die erste förmliche Action zwischen den Americanern und Engländern bey Bunkers Hill am 17ten. Junius 1775. [1784]
Etching 2⅞ x 2 in. (image)

Number four in a series by "D[aniel N.] Chodowiecki inv. et del." The Battle of Bunker Hill.

———Another copy. Engraved by D. Berger after Chodowiecki.

———Another impression. In Sprengel, *Allgemeines historisches Taschenbuch* (Berlin, 1784).

255
THE DEATH OF WARREN. M Inv. Norman Sc: [1776]
Etching 7½ x 4½ in.

Joseph Warren (1741–1775), a Boston physician and major general of the militia, was mortally wounded in the Battle of Bunker Hill. In the pre-Revolutionary period he distinguished himself as a political writer and orator. It was Warren who drafted the Suffolk Resolves, and in April 1775 he succeeded

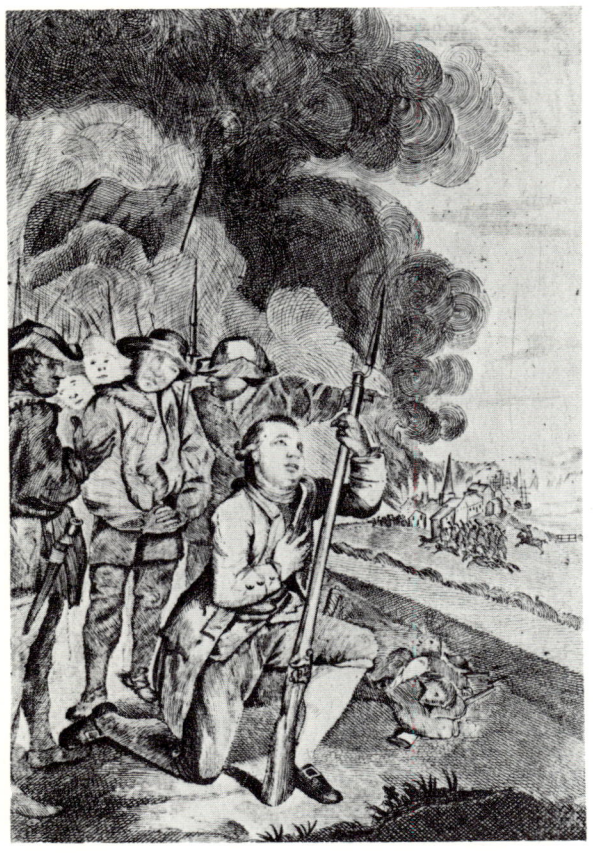

255

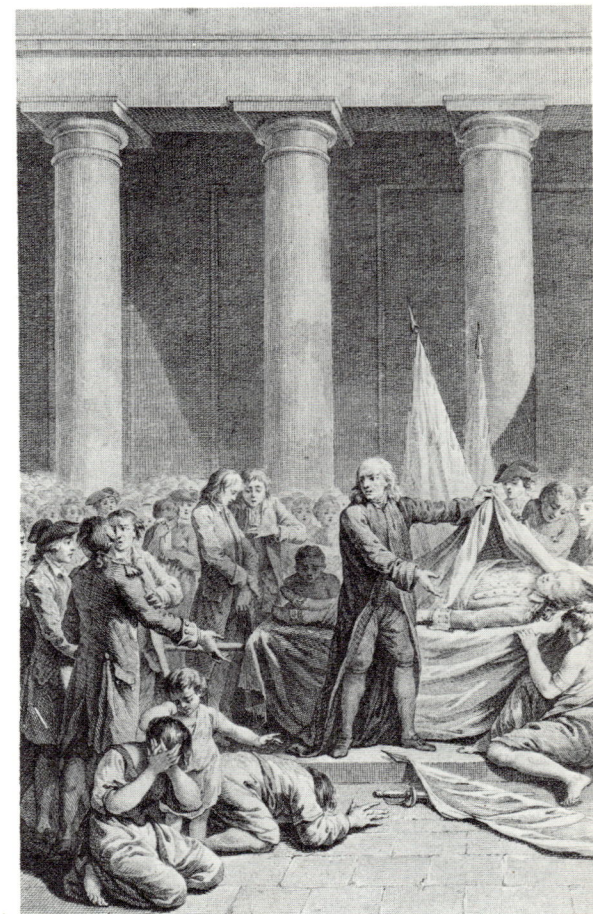

256

John Hancock as president of the Massachusetts Provincial Congress. From Brackenridge, *The Battle of Bunkers-Hill* (Philadelphia, 1776), frontispiece. LC–USZ62–45535

256

Contemplez l'ouvrage de pouvoir arbitraire. Le Barbier l'aîné inv. del. Patas sculp. [1781]
 Mixed method 6⅜ x 3¾ in. (image)

An imaginary depiction of a eulogy at the funeral of Dr. Joseph Warren by "Nelson" (Perez Morton?), who exhibits the body to his countrymen. From Hilliard d'Auberteuil, *Essais historiques* (1781–82), opposite p. 229.

————Another impression. From Hilliard d'Auberteuil, *Essais historiques*, v. 3 (1782), p. [7]. 9¼ x 6¼ in. LC–USZ62–45331

257

THE TOWN OF FALMOUTH, Burnt, by Captain MOET, Octbr. 18th 1775. [John Norman]
 Line engraving 5¼ x 11¼ in. (image)

The burning of Falmouth (now Portland), Maine, by Capt. Henry Mowat was a result of Adm. Samuel Graves' frustration over the activities of American privateers and his inability to support the British garrison at Boston. From *An Impartial History of the War in America*, v. 2 (Boston, 1782), copy 1, frontispiece. LC–USZ62–45238

258

Son mérite personnel l'emporte sur toutes les considérations. Le Barbier l'aîné del. N. Ponce sculp. [1782]
 Etching 6¼ x 3¾ in.

Idealized view of the funeral of Richard Montgomery (1738–1775), a Continental general killed in the abortive attack on Quebec on the night of December 31, 1775. Surveying the scene of battle the following day, the British

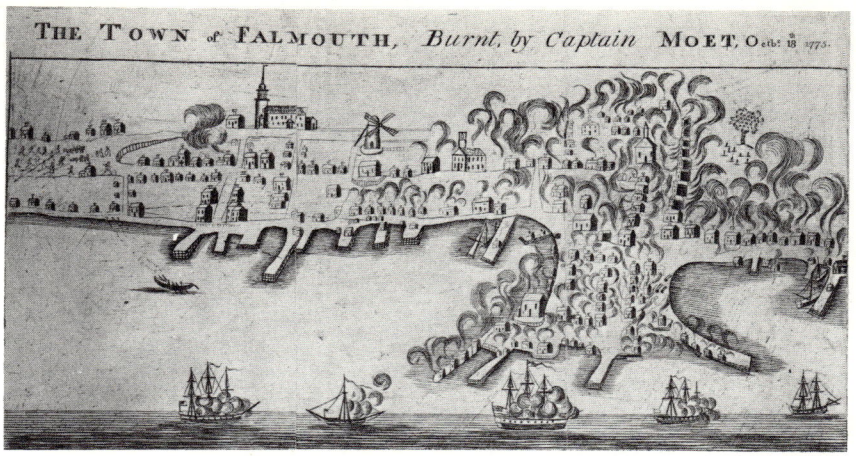
257

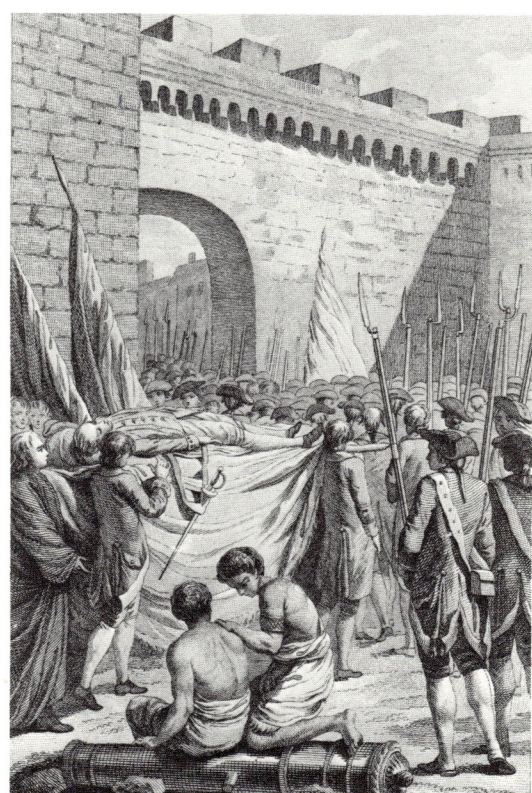
258

85

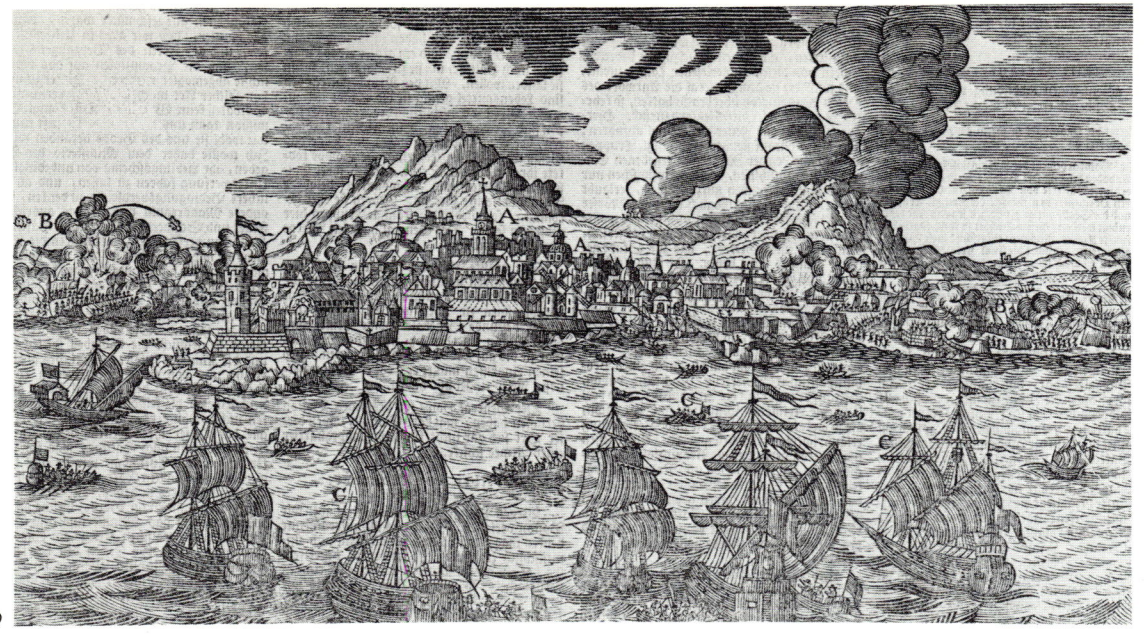

recognized Montgomery's body and gave it a decent burial. From Hilliard d'Auberteuil, *Essais historiques*, v. 3 (1782), p. [9]. LC–USZ62–45332

259

Richtige Abbildung der den Americanischen Probinzialisten belagerten und wiedereroberten Hauptstadt und Festung Boston in America, im Monat Merz 1776.

Woodcut 7 x 12½ in. (image)

German woodcut of the British evacuation of Boston, which took place on March 17, 1776. The evacuation was by tacit agreement, not under the kind of duress depicted here. On the back of the print is a description of the evacuation and a personal letter. LC–USZ62–45549

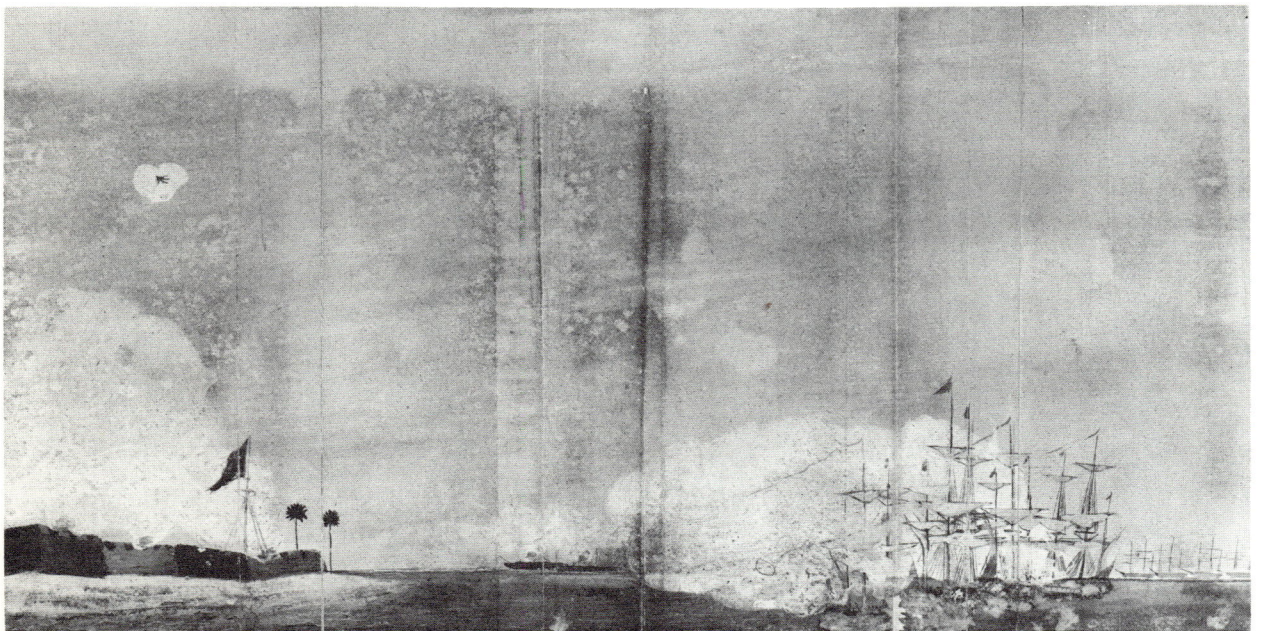

260

The attack of the Fort on Sulivan's Island the 28. June 1776. [1776?]

Water color drawing 7¾ x 15 in. (image)

On June 28, 1776, an American garrison stationed at a hastily constructed palmetto fort on the southern tip of Sullivan's Island in Charleston Harbor, S. C., prevented British ships under Adm. Sir Peter Parker from attacking the city. The fort, then known as Fort Sullivan, was later named after the officer who directed its defense, Col. William Moultrie. On the back of this drawing, a note reads "Painted by Henry Gray, who was a Lieutenant in the 2 Regiment which fought the battle of the 28th June 1776 against the British Fleet: and who was wounded in that engagement." Endpiece in Drayton, *Memoirs of the American Revolution . . . relating to the State of South-Carolina . . .* (Charleston, S.C., 1821). LC–USZ62–33995

261

Der Congress erklërt die 13 vereinigten Stäaten von Nord-America für independent. am 4ten July 1776 [1784]

Etching 2⅞ x 2 in. (image)

Number five in a series by "D[aniel N.] Chodowiecki inv. et del." The Continental Congress. LC–USZ62–26670

————Another copy. Engraved by D. Berger after Chodowiecki.

————Another impression. In Sprengel, *Allgemeines historisches Taschenbuch* (Berlin, 1784).

262

The Manner in which the American Colonies Declared themselves INDEPENDANT of the King of ENGLAND, throughout the different Provinces, on July 4, 1776. Hamilton delin. Noble sculp. [1783]

Mixed method 12½ x 8⅛ in. (image)

A horseman reads the Declaration of Independence to a cheering crowd. A sign reading "America Independant. 1776" is being posted on the wall at the left. From Barnard, *History of England* (London, 1783), p. 689. This copy in P&P. LC–USZ62–11336

263

LA DESTRUCTION DE LA STATUE ROYALE A NOUVELLE YORCK. Die Zerstorung der Koniglichen Bild Saule zu Neu Yorck. A Paris chez Basset Rue St. Jacques. [177?]

Etching (hand colored) 9 x 15⅛ in. (image)

On the evening of July 9, 1776, American troops in New York assembled to listen to the reading of the Declaration of Independence. In the excitement that followed, soldiers and civilians pulled down an equestrian statue of George III which stood on the Bowling Green

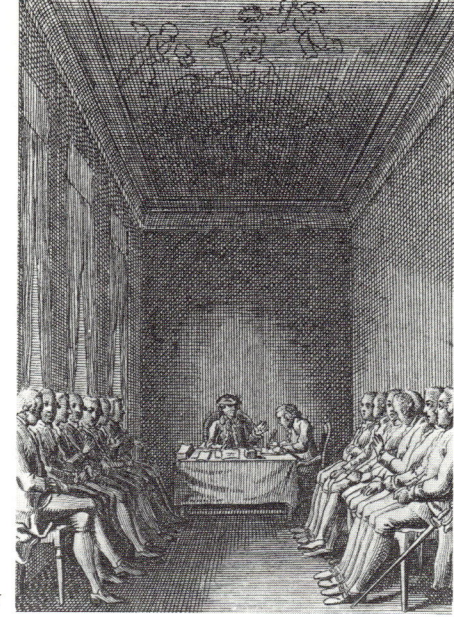
261

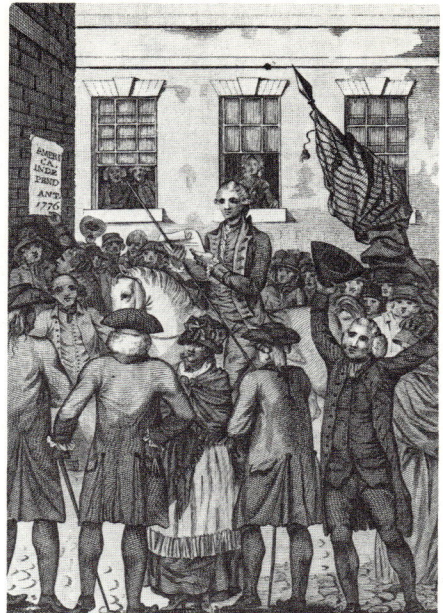
262

263

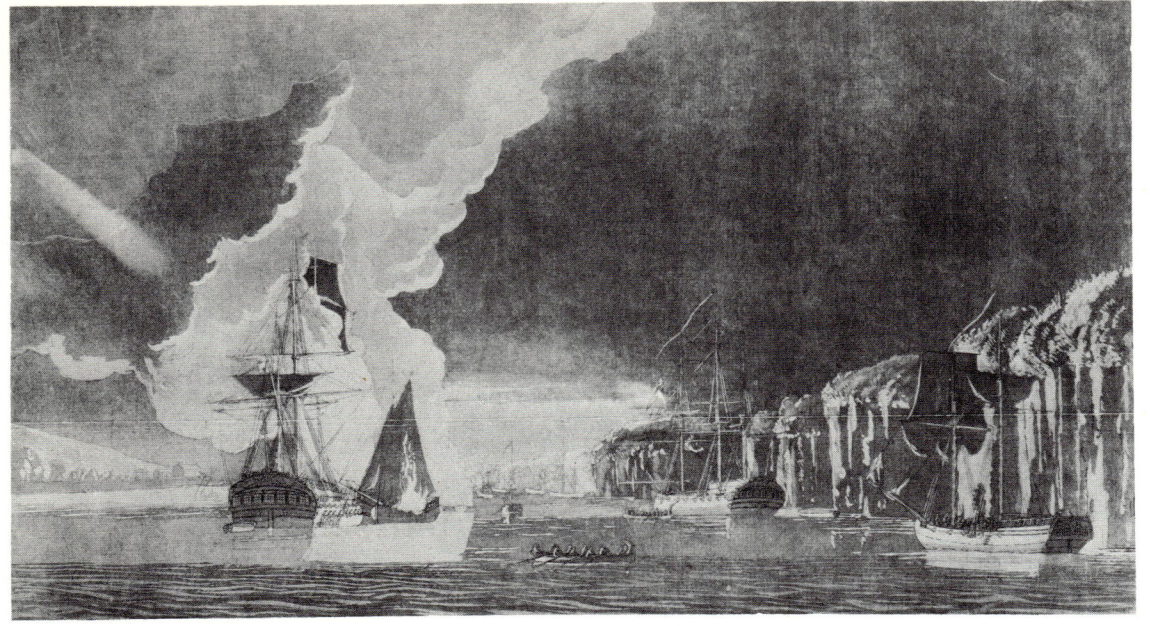

264

264

The PHOENIX and the ROSE Engaged by the ENEMY'S FIRE SHIPS and GALLEYS on the 16 Augst. 1776. Engrav'd from the Original Picture by D. Serres from a sketch of Sir James Wallace's. Publish'd according to Act of Parliament April 2, 1778 by J. F. W. Des Barres Esqr.

Aquatint with etching 14⅛ x 23½ in.

During the initial stages of the New York campaign, two British vessels, the 40-gun *Phoenix* and the 20-gun *Rose*, along with the schooner *Tryal* and two tenders, moved up the Hudson River to cut off patriot communications with New Jersey. On August 16 the Americans attacked the larger vessels with fire ships. The attack failed, but it so alarmed the British commander that he ordered his squadron to rejoin the main fleet in New York Harbor. *The Atlantic Neptune.* LeGear 10317, v. 2, no. 24. LC–USZ62–45594

at the foot of Broadway. This fictitious view of the affair, probably by André Basset l'ainé, was widely reprinted in Europe.
LC–USZ62–22023

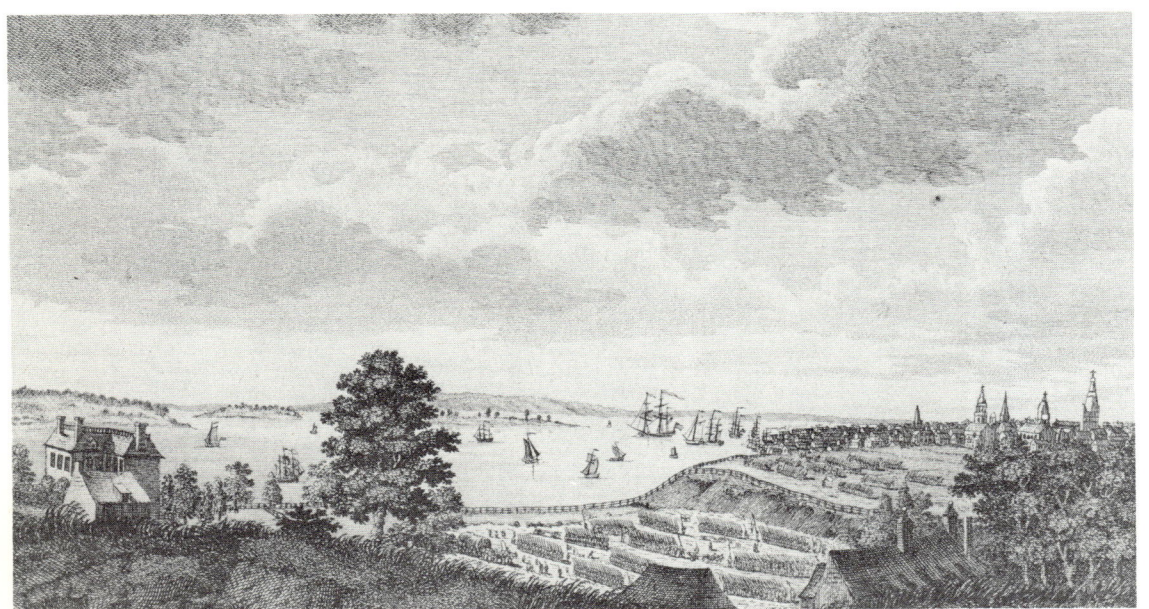

265

265

A View of New York, Governors Island, the River &c. from Long Island. Published as the Act directs by A. Hamilton Junr. near St. Johns Gate Novr. 1, 1776.

Etching 4½ x 7⅝ in.

A panoramic view of the Battle of Long Island, August 27, 1776. From *The Town and Country Magazine*, October 1776, p. 537. This picture is a copy of "A South West View of the City of New York" (item 552), drawn by Thomas Howdell and engraved by P. Canot for *Scenographia Americana* (London, 1768), with troops and more ships added.
LC–USZ62–45417

266

DEBARQUEMENT DES TROUPES ENGLOISES A NOUVELLE YORCK. Die Anländung der Englischen Trouppen zu Neu Yorck. Se vend à Augsbourg au Negoce commun de l'Academie Imperiale d'Empire des Arts libereaux avec Privilege de sa Majesté Imperiale et avec Defense ni d'en faire ni de vendre les copies. Gravé par Francois Xav. Habermann. [177?]

Etching (incompletely hand colored) 11⅜ x 16 in.

British troops disembark at New York following the patriot evacuation of the city, September 15, 1776. The caption above the picture (French only) is mirror image. From "Collection des prospects." LC–USZ62–45372

267

L'ENTRÉ TRIUMPHALE DE TROUPES ROYALES A NOUVELLE YORCK. Der Einzug der Königlichen Völcker in Neu Yorck. Se vend à Augsbourg au Negoce commun de l'Academie Imperiale d'Empire des Arts libereaux avec Privilege de Sa Majesté Imperiale et avec Defense ni d'en faire ni de vendre les Copies. Gravé par Francois Xav. Habermann. [177?]

Etching (hand colored) 9½ x 15⅝ in.

British troops march in triumph through the streets of New York. The caption above the picture (French only) is mirror image. From "Collection des prospects." LC–USZ62–26673.

———————A copy reversed and smaller. Line below titles reads: "A Paris chez J. Chereau rue St. Jacques au desous de la Fontaine St. Severin au 2 Colonnes. No. 257."

268

REPRESENTATION DU FEU TERRIBLE A NOUVELLE YORCK. Se vend á Augsburg au Negoce

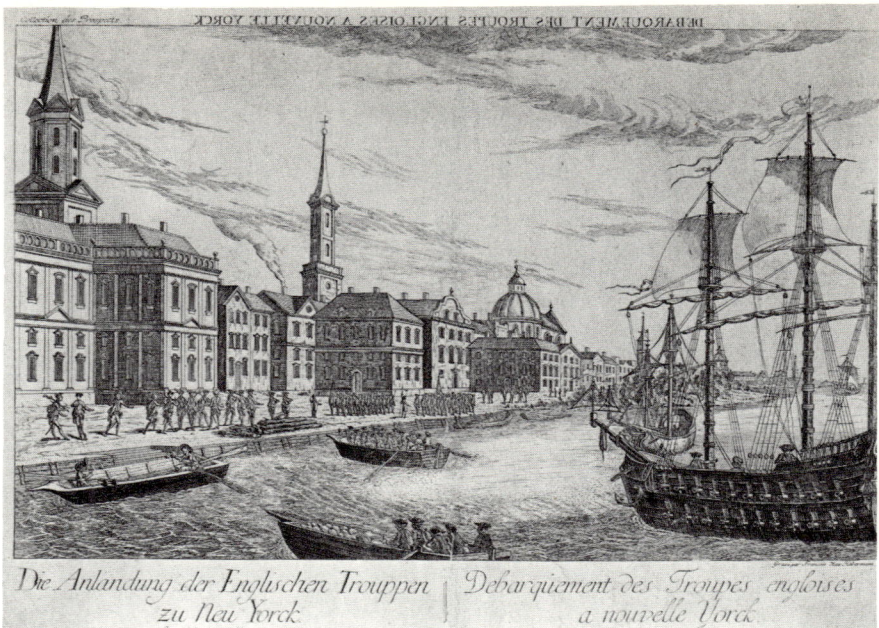

266

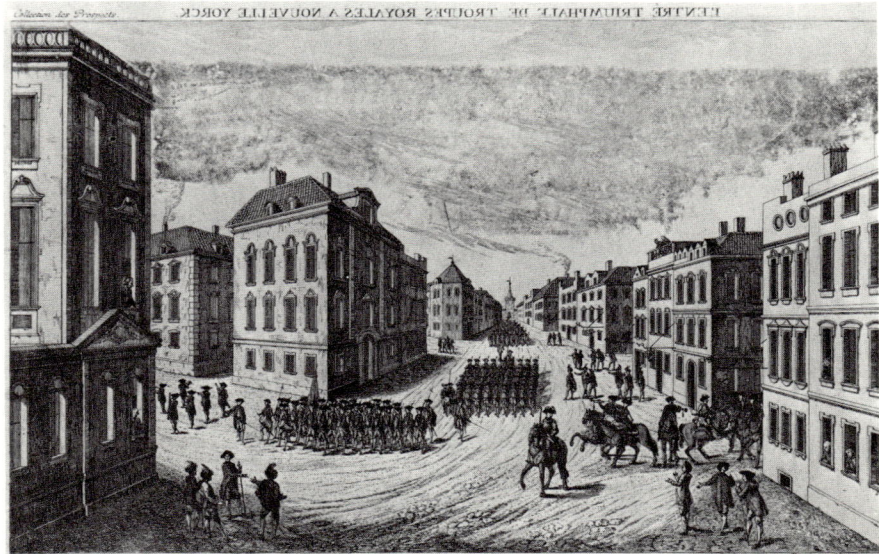

267

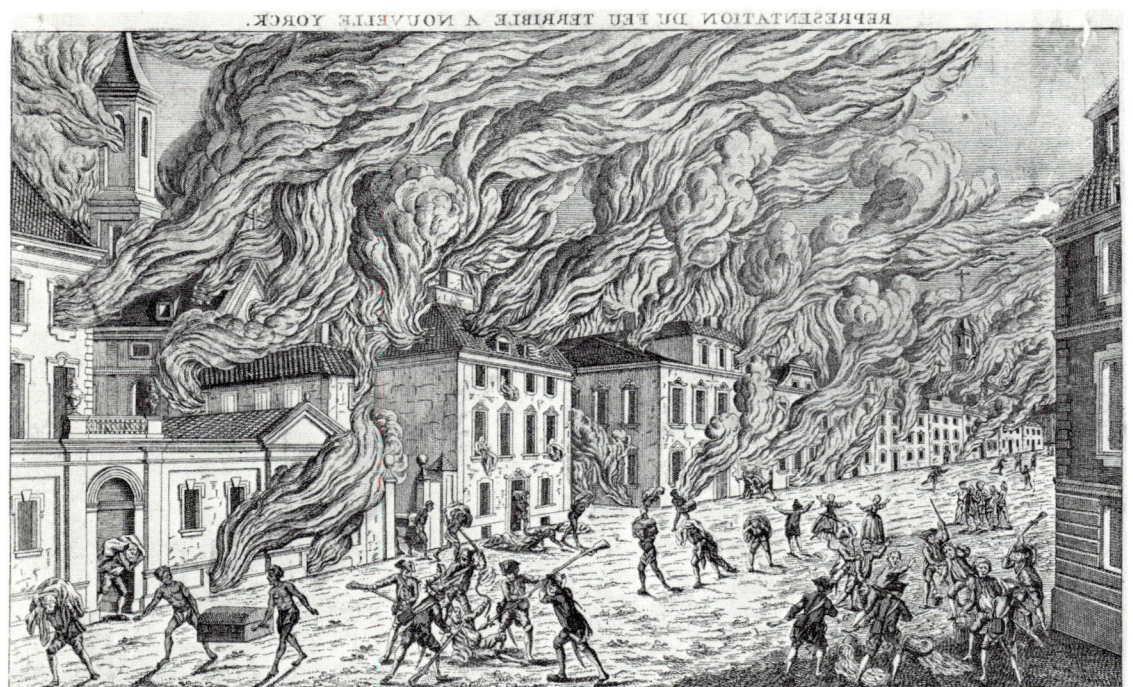

268

comun de l'Academie Imperiale d'Empire des Arts libereaux avec Privilege de Sa Majesté Imperiale et avec defense ni d'en faire ni de vendre les copies. Gravé par Francois Xav. Habermann. [177?]

Etching (hand colored) 11⅜ x 16⅛ in. (image)

New York burns, while people evacuate buildings and red-coated soldiers molest green-shirted citizens suspected of spreading the blaze. The following explanation, in German and French, appears below the picture:

Schröckenvolle Feuersbrunst welche zu Neu Yorck von denen Americanern in der Nacht vom 19 Harbst Monath 1776. angeleget worden, wodurch alle Gebäude aus der West Seite der neuer Börse langst der Broochstrent biss an das Könige Killegui mehr als 1600. Häusser, die Dreÿsaltigkeits Kirche, die Lutherische Kappelle u. die Armen Schule in Asche verwandelt worden.

Représentation du Feu terrible a Nouvelle Yorck, que les Americains ont allumé pendent la Nuit du 19 Septembre 1776 par le quel ont été brulés, tous les Batiments du Coté de Vest, a droite de Börse dans la Rue de Broock jusqu'au College du Roi et plus que 1600. maisons avec L'Eglise de la Ste Trinité la Chapelle Luthérienne et L'École des pauvres.

The account blames the Americans for the conflagration, which actually occurred on the night of September 20–21, but the true origin of the fire has never been determined. An estimated 493 houses were destroyed, causing untold suffering among British soldiers and Tories. This print was made for a vue d'optique.

—————Another impression. For a different viewing process; holes have been cut in the flaming sections and backed with red, transparent paper. No explanation printed.

—————Another copy. This print is a reverse of the previous two and is smaller in size. Title above picture is mirror image. Only the French legend appears at the bottom, with the notation: "A Paris chez Basset Rue S. Jacques au coin de la rue des Mathurins." Probably by André Basset l'ainé.
LC–USZ62-42

269
INCENDIE DE NEW-YORK. Dessiné par le Barbier, Peintre du Roi. Gravé par L. Halbou. 1782

Etching 6¼ x 3⅞ in. (image)

The burning of New York, September 20–21, 1776. From Hilliard d'Aubertueil, *Essais historiques*, v. 3 (1782), p. [12].
LC–USZ62–45333

270
The American General Lee taken Prisoner by Lieutenant Colonel Harcourt of the ENGLISH ARMY, in Morris Country, New Jersey, 1776. Hamilton delin. Hawkins sculp. [1783]

Mixed method 12¼ x 8¼ in.

Charles Lee, a major general in the Continental Army, was captured at Basking Ridge, N. J., December 13, 1776. Formerly an officer in the British Army, Lee was ordered returned to England to stand trial as a deserter, but Gen. William Howe was of the opinion that he had resigned his half pay before he joined the rebellion. Evidence available today suggests Lee committed treason against the Americans during his captivity. He was exchanged in April 1778. From Barnard, *History of England* (London, 1783), p. 690.
LC–USZ62–45309

271
Die Hessen, vom General Washington am 25ten Dec: 1776. zu Trenton überfallen, werden als Kriegsgefangne in Philadelphia eingebracht. [1784]

Etching 2⅞ x 2 in. (image)

Hessian soldiers captured in the Battle of Trenton being taken to Philadelphia. Number six in a series by "D[aniel N.] Chodowiecki inv. et del." LC–USZ62–19419

———Another copy. Engraved by D. Berger after Chodowiecki.

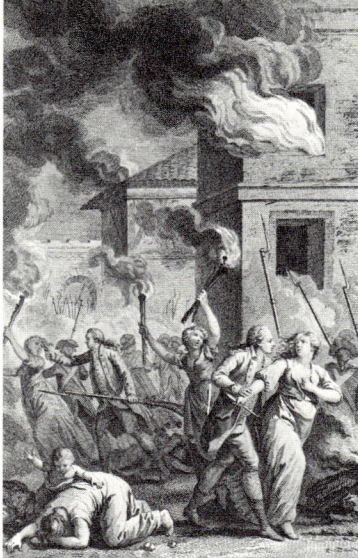
269

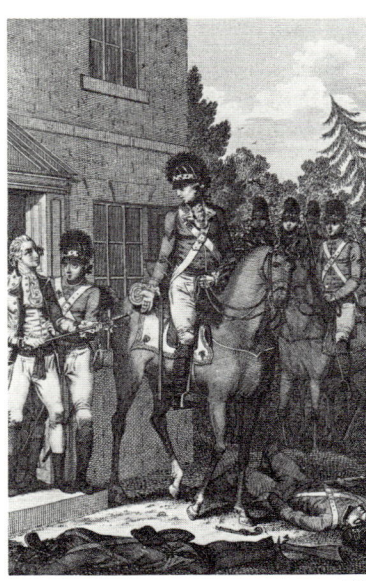
270

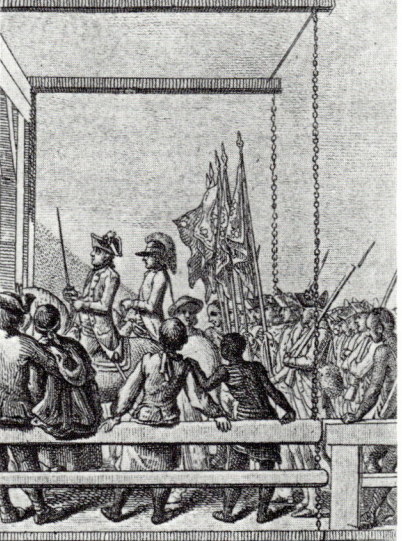
271

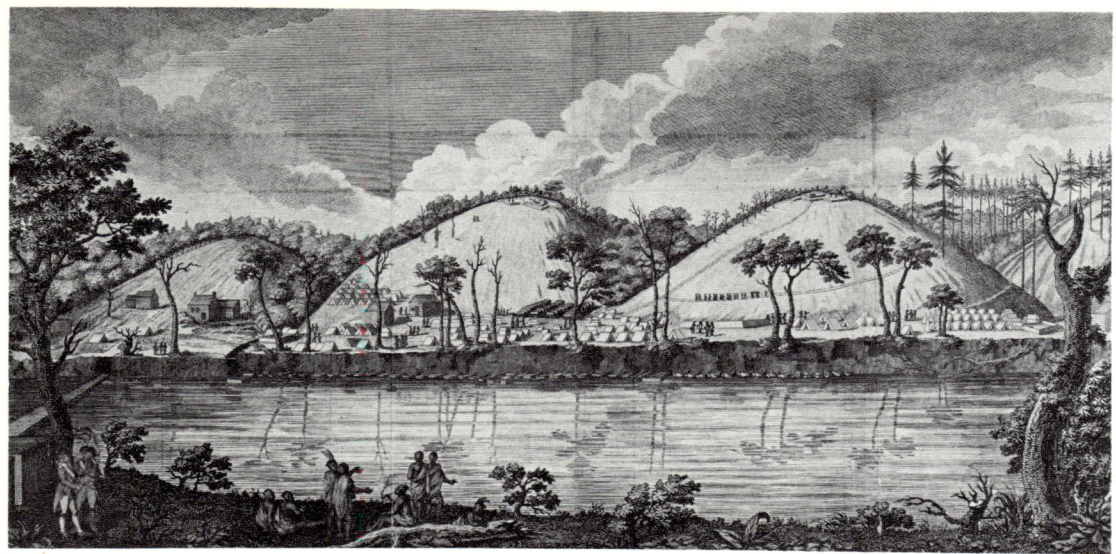

272

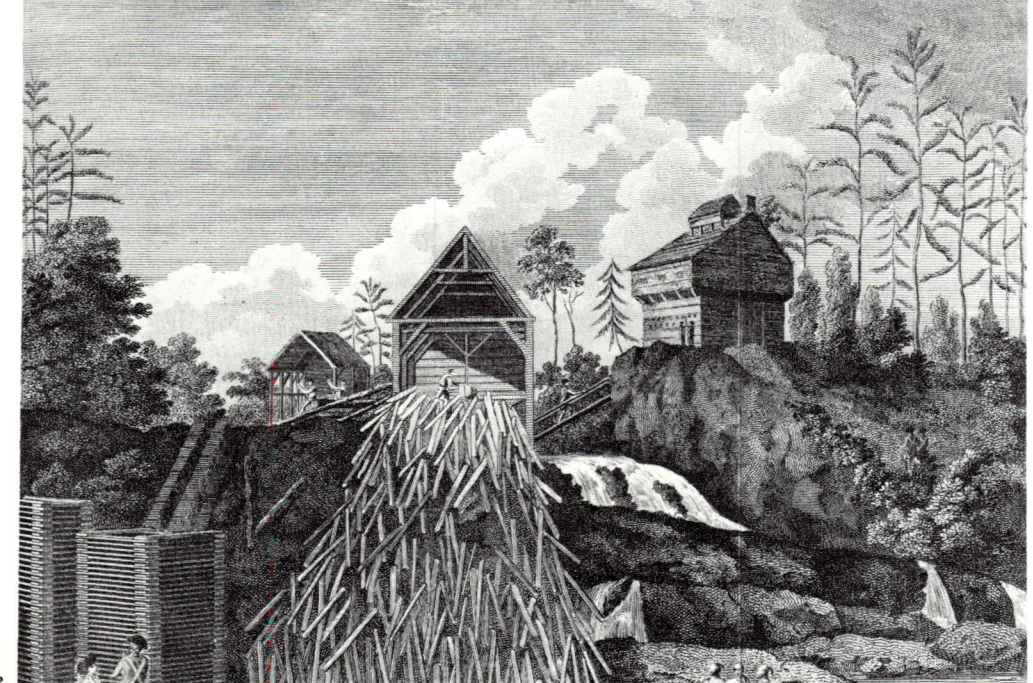

273

———— Another impression. In Sprengel, *Allgemeines historisches Taschenbuch* (Berlin, 1784).

272
View of the West Bank of the Hudson's River 3 Miles above Still Water, upon which the Army under the command of Lt. General Burgoyne, took post on the 20th. Sepr. 1777. (Shewing General Frazer's Funeral.) Publish'd as the Act directs, Jany. 1, 1789, by William Lane, Leadenhall Street, London. Barlow sculp.
Etching 9⅜ x 17 in.

Brig. Gen. Simon Fraser (1729–1777), who participated in General Burgoyne's invasion of New York, was mortally wounded in the action at Bemis Heights, popularly known as the Second Battle of Saratoga, October 7, 1777. Fraser was buried in one of the British redoubts, and during the funeral services, the Americans, unaware of what was taking place, directed a heavy fire against the work. From Anburey, *Travels Through the Interior Parts of America*, v. 1 (London, 1789), opposite p. 433. LC–USZ62–31881

273
A View of the Saw-Mill & Block House upon Fort Anne Creek, the property of Genl. Skeene, which on Genl. Burgoyne's Army advancing, was set fire to, by the Americans. Publish'd as the Act directs, 1 Jany. 1789 by W. Lane Leadenhall Street London.
Etching 7¾ x 9¾ in.

Philip Skene (1725–1810), a New York loyalist, land baron, and merchant, figured prominently in General Burgoyne's offensive. The destruction of his sawmill near Fort Anne by the patriots in their retreat before Burgoyne's advancing army was one of many financial reverses he suffered during the

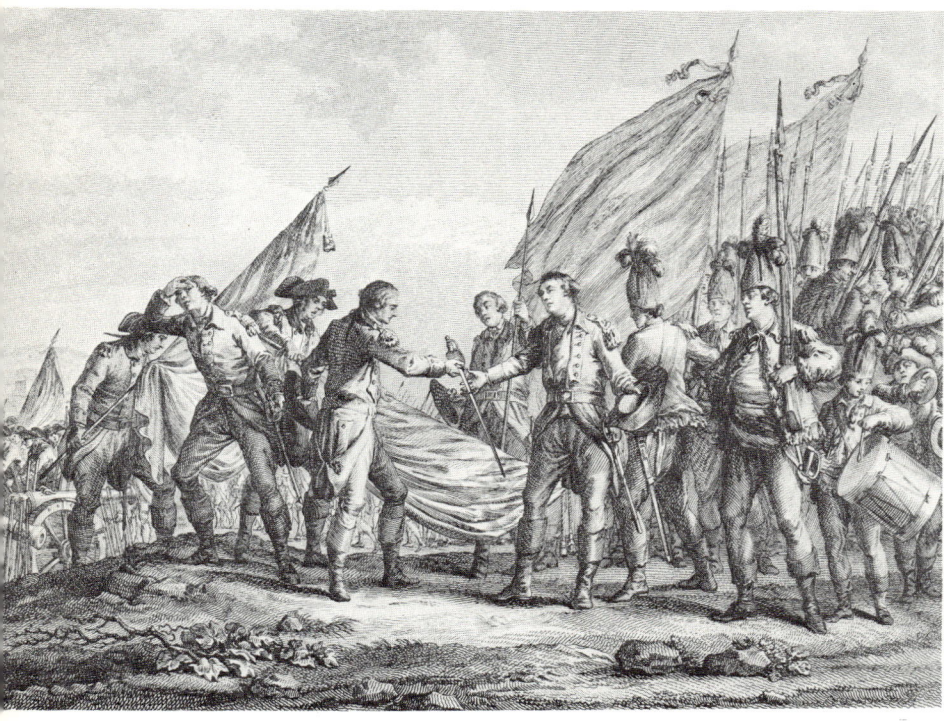
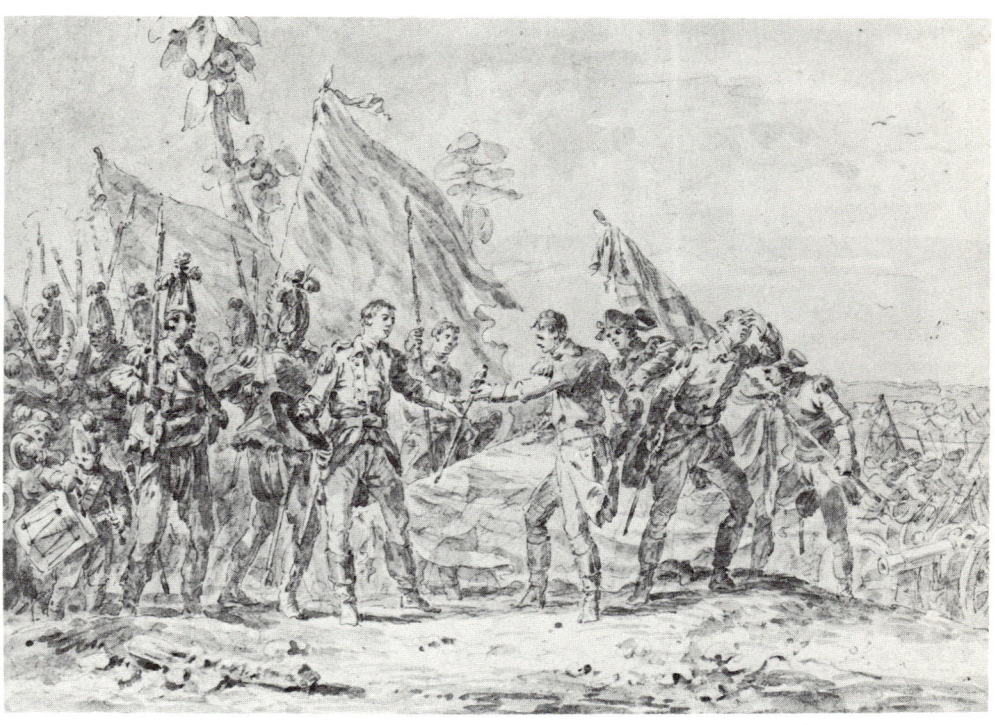

274 engraving *274 wash drawing*

Revolution. Eventually, Skene's entire wilderness empire, which included sawmills, foundries, and shipyards, was either destroyed or confiscated. From Anburey, *Travels Through the Interior Parts of America*, v. 1 (London, 1789), opposite p. 350. LC–USZ62–45548

274

SARRATOGA. Dessiné par Fauvel. Gravé par Godefroy de l'Academie Impériale et Royale de Vienne &c. [1784?]

Etching 7⅝ x 8½ in.

The surrender of Gen. John Burgoyne at Saratoga, October 17, 1777. The account below the picture treats the surrender as the climax of defeat for two British armies, and a footnote mentions Jane McCrea's death, which was a contributing factor in Burgoyne's defeat. Miss McCrea, the fiancée of a Tory soldier with Burgoyne, was slain by a Wyandot Indian escorting her to the main British camp. Skillful use of the incident by American propagandists produced an unusually large turnout of New England militia. From Ponce, *Recueil d'estampes représentant . . .* (Paris, 1784?), plate 4. *Collection de Vinck* 1167.

——————Another impression (LC–USZ62–39584), an earlier state, and a wash drawing (LC–USZ62–39585) of the same are in copy 3, in the Rare Book Division.

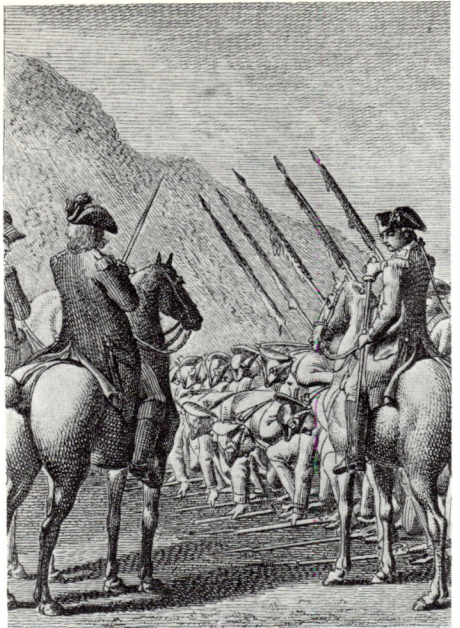

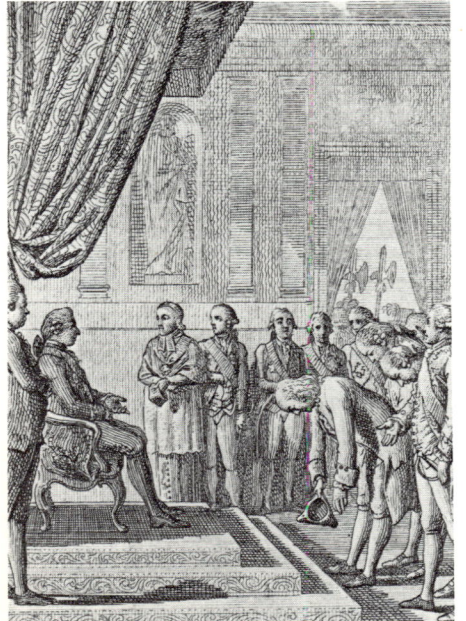

275

Die Americaner machen das Corps des General Bourgoyne zu Gefangnen, bey Saratoga. am 16ten. Octobr 1777. [1784]
    Etching 2⅞ x 2 in. (image)

German view of Burgoyne's surrender at Saratoga. Number seven in a series by "D[aniel N.] Chodowiecki inv. et del." LC–USZ62–39564

———————Another copy. Engraved by D. Berger after Chodowiecki.

———————Another impression. In Sprengel, *Allgemeines historisches Taschenbuch* (Berlin, 1784).

276

Lady Harriet Ackland. Drawn & Engraved by Robt. Pollard. London. Pubd. Novr. 15; 1784 by R. Pollard No. 7. Brayne's Row Spa Fields. Aquatinta by F. Jukes.
    Engraving and aquatint 15 x 20⅝ in. (image)

Lady Christian Henrietta Carolina Acland (1750–1815), wife of Maj. John Dyke Acland (d. 1778), a British politician and commander of grenadiers in Burgoyne's army. The following note appears below the picture:

> This amiable Lady accompanied her Husband to Canada in the year 1776, & during two campaigns under went such fatigue & distress as female fortitude was thought incapable of supporting, and once she narrowly escaped with her life from her Tent which was set on fire in the Night. The Event here commemorated deserves to be recorded in History. In the unfortunate action between G. Burgoyne and G: Gates Octr. 7; 1777, Major [John D.] Ackland [also Acland] was wounded & made Prisoner, when his Lady received the news she formed the heroic Resolution of delivering herself into the hands of the Enemy that she might attend him during his Captivity. For this purpose, with a Letter from G. Burgoyne to G. Gates, accompanied by the Rev. Mr. Brudinell who carried a Flag of Truce, one female servant, & her husband's Valet, she rowed down Hudson's River in an open boat towards the American Camp, but Night coming on before she reached their out posts the Guards on duty refused to receive her & threatened to fire upon her if she moved till morning. In this dreadful situation for 7 or 8 dark & cold hours, she was compelled to wait on the Water half dead with anxiety & terror. The morning put an end to her distress, she was received by Gen. Gates & restored to her husband with that politeness & humanity her sex, quality, & virtue so justly merit.

In early 1778 Lady Harriet returned to England with her husband, who had been placed on parole. Acland died later the same year from an illness brought on by exposure during a duel. LC–USZ62–45566

277

Dr. Franklin erhält, als Gesandter des Americanischen FreyStaats, seine erste Audienz in Frankreich, zu Versailles. am 20ten Märtz 1778. [1784]
    Etching 2⅞ x 2 in. (image)

German view of Benjamin Franklin's reception by the French Court. Number eight in a series by "D[aniel N.] Chodowiecki inv. et del." LC–USZ62–19420

———————Another copy. Engraved by D. Berger after Chodowiecki.

———————Another impression. In Sprengel, *Allgemeines historisches Taschenbuch* (Berlin, 1784).

278

L'Escadre françoise sortant de la Méditerranée le 16. Mai 1778. [Pierre Ozanne]
    Wash drawing 9 x 15½ in.

In this view the French fleet of Comte d'Estaing leaves the Mediterranean, May 16, 1778, 12 days after the ratification of the French Alliance by Congress, to encounter the British off the American coast. The following identifications are included in the legend below the title:

> A Le Mont Gibraltar. B Le Mont aux Singes.
> C Corvette Angloise mettant en panne dans la baye de Gibraltar en envoyant son canot a Terre.
> D Batiments hollandois sortant de la Méditeranée.

Ozanne Collection, no. 1. LC–USZ62–7698

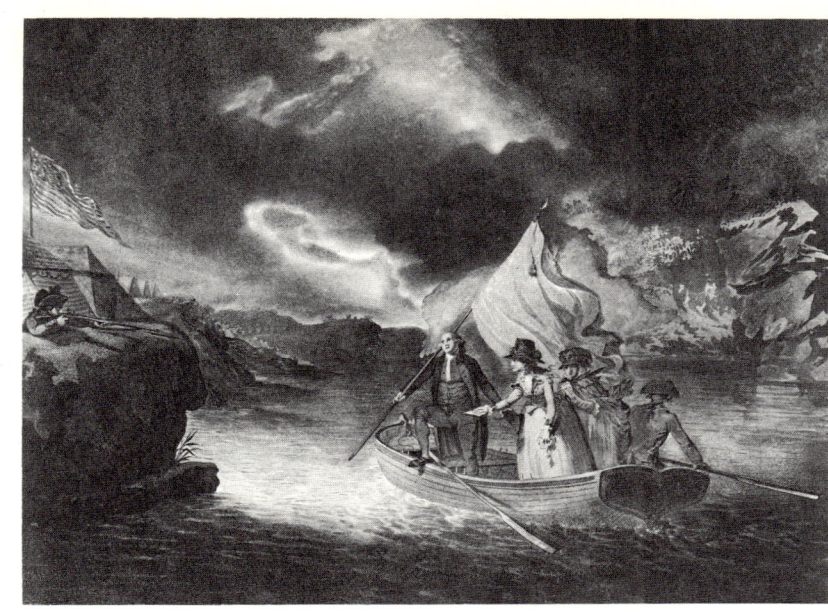

276

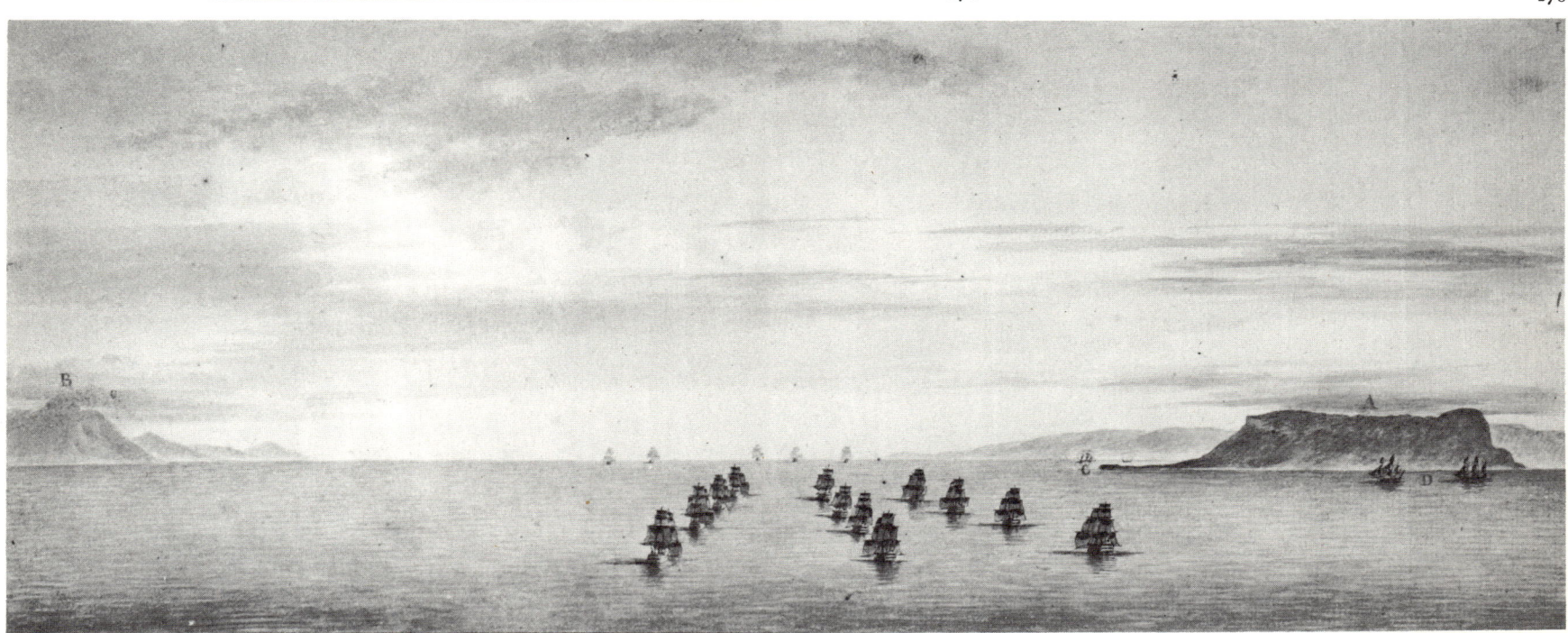

278

95

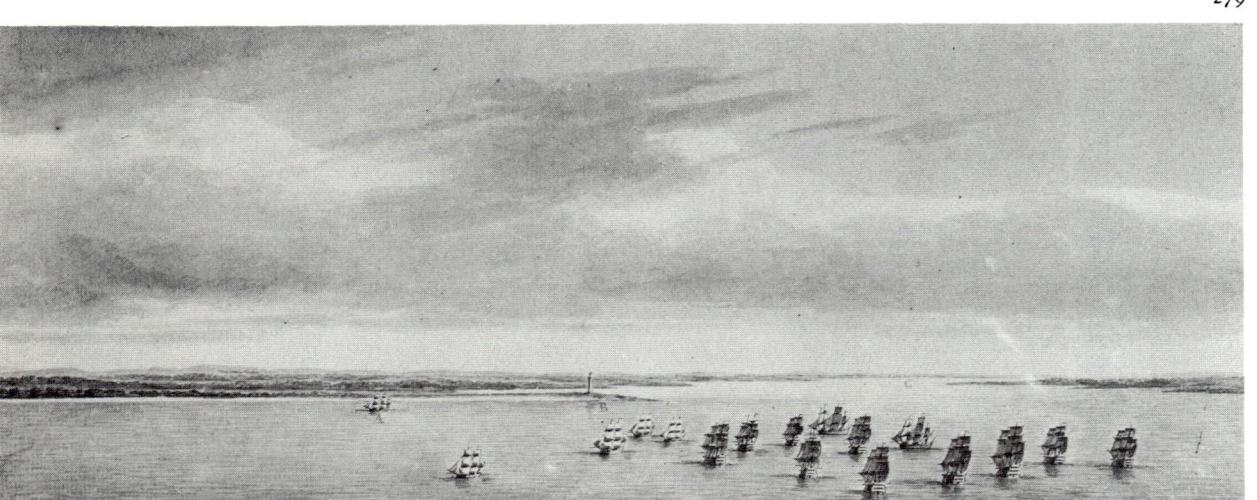

279

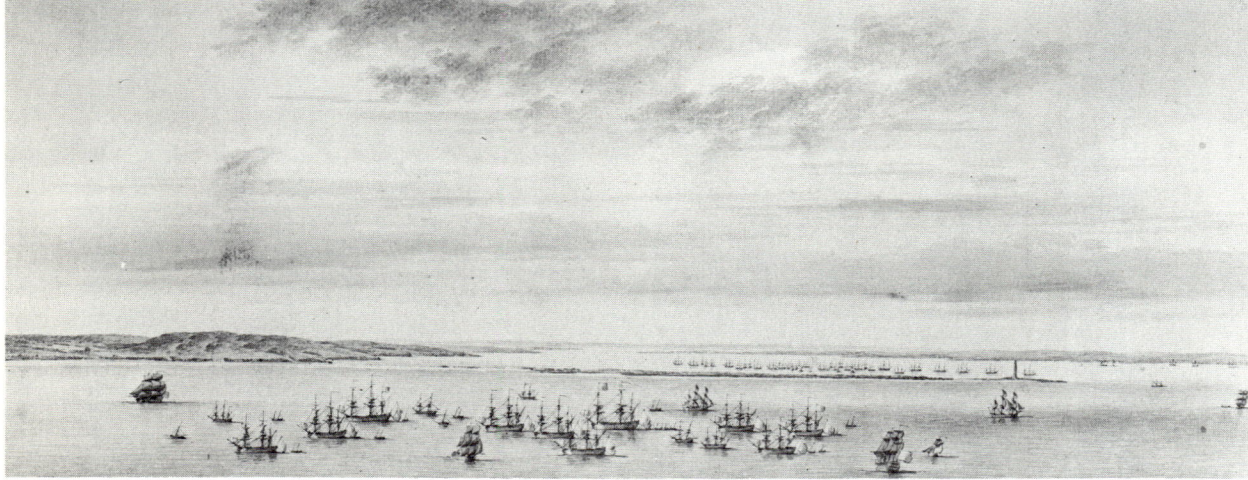

280

279

L'Escadre françoise entrant dans la Delaware et chassant la frégate la Mermaid. [1778?] [Pierre Ozanne]

Wash drawing 9 x 15½ in.

Four ships veer away from the French fleet to pursue the British ship *Mermaid*. Cape Henlopen lighthouse is in the center of the picture. Comte d'Estaing arrived at Delaware Bay on July 8, 1778, reconnoitered, and departed for New York. *Ozanne Collection*, no. 9. LC–USZ62–904

280

L'Escadre françoise mouillée devant Newyork, bloquant l'Escadre Angloise et interceptant les Batimens qui vouloient y entrer. Le 12 juillet 1778. [Pierre Ozanne]

Wash drawing 9⅛ x 15¾ in.

The French fleet is anchored outside New York in an attempt to blockade the British vessels in the harbor and prevent supply ships or reinforcements from entering. Identified are Sandy Hook with its signal light and the Shrewsbury shore where the legend says two French officers met a Quaker who delivered a letter from D'Estaing to General Washington. *Ozanne Collection*, no. 2. LC–USZ62–899

281

The SEA FIGHT between KEPPEL and D'ORVILLIERS. [1780]

Etching 9¾ x 6½ in.

In July of 1779, Admiral Keppel engaged the French fleet of the Count d'Orvilliers. Foggy weather and winds made the encounter difficult. The cautious D'Orvilliers passed ahead of the British, and Keppel, not pursuing them, was accused of "flying before the French." (DNB) From Cowley, *Ladies History of England* (London, 1780), opposite p. 677. LC–USZ62–45234

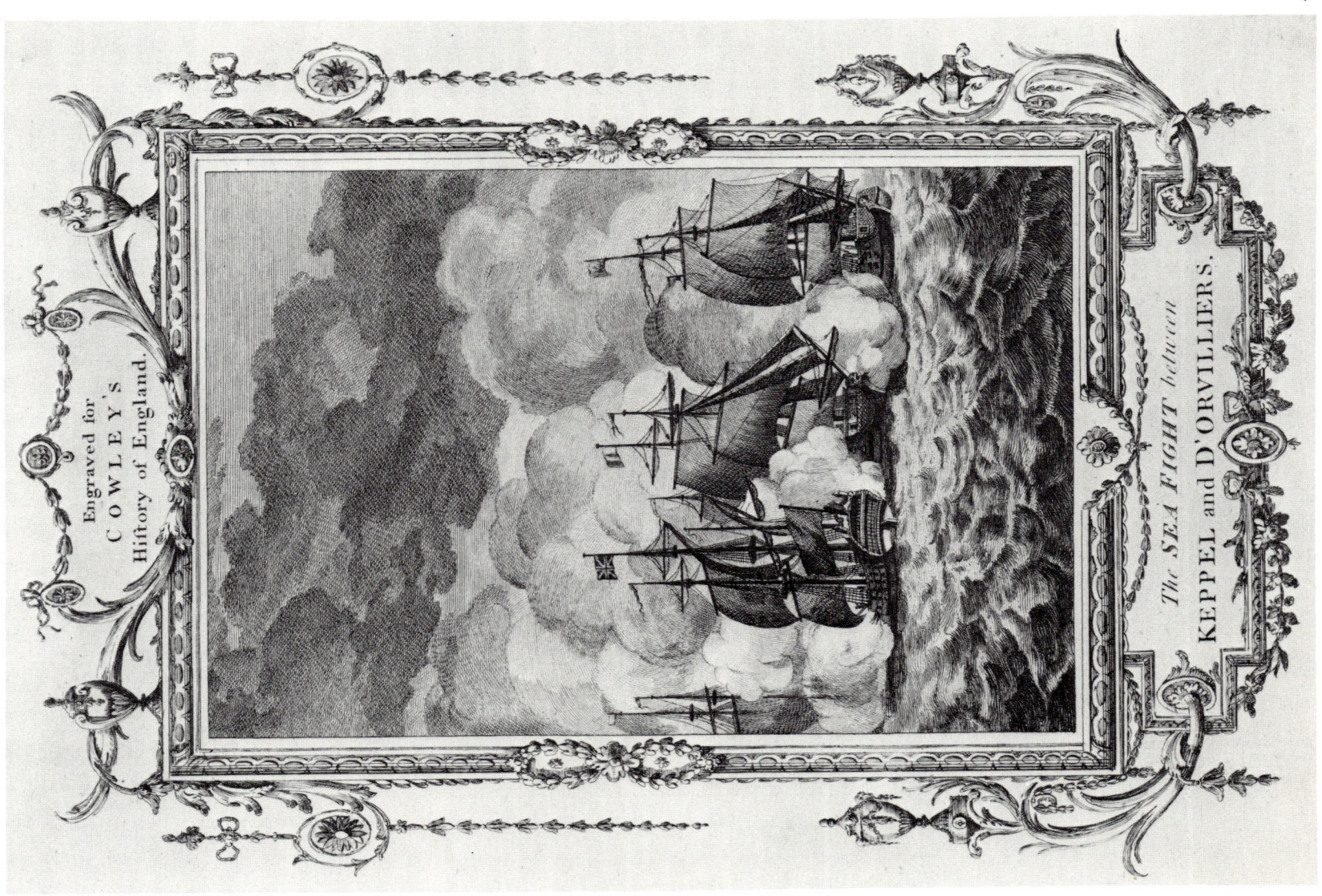

Engraved for COWLEY's History of England.

The SEA FIGHT between KEPPEL and D'ORVILLIERS.

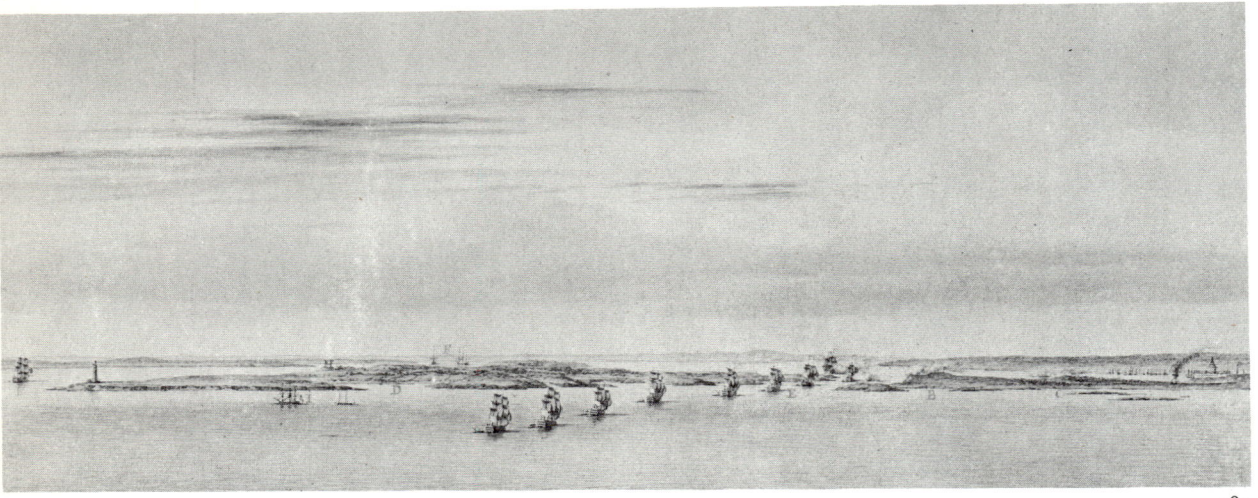

282

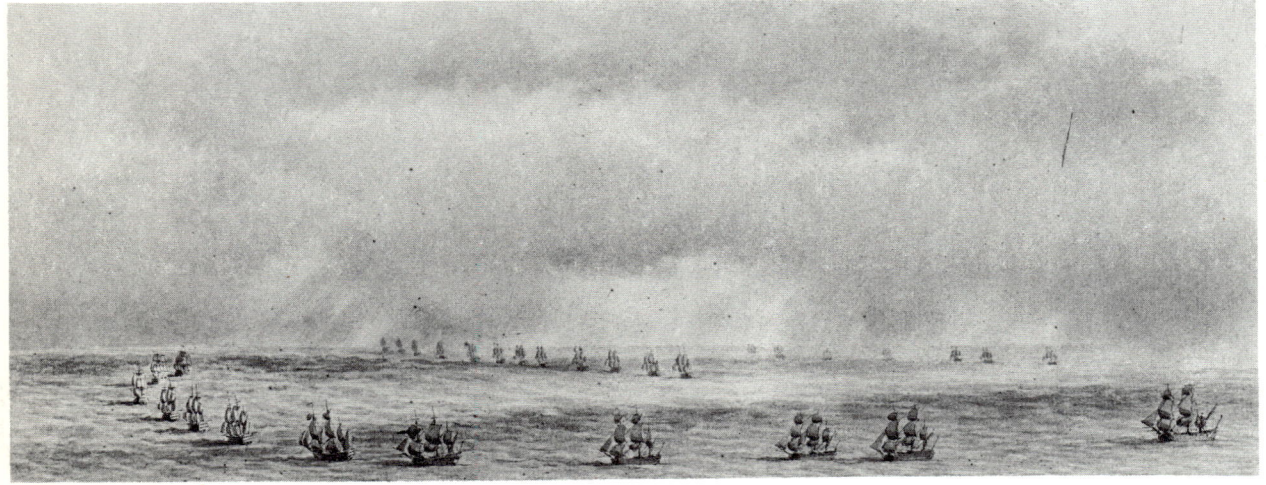

283

282
L'Escadre françoise entrant dans Newport sous le feu des Batteries et forcant le passage le 8 Aoust 1778. Jour que les Américains passerent sur l'Isle de Rode Island par le chemin d'howland's Ferry. [1778] [Pierre Ozanne]

Wash drawing 9½ x 15¾ in.

This print depicts the episode of August 8, 1778, when D'Estaing led his fleet up the Middle Passage at Newport, Rhode Island. The British ships burning in the background right, among them the *Cerberus*, *Juno*, *Orpheus*, *Lark*, and *Falcon*, had been destroyed when Admiral Suffren led two frigates up the east Sakonnet Passage. Sullivan's forces, meanwhile, had crossed over from Tiverton to land on Rhode Island. Also identified by the legend are Goat Island and Conanicut Island. After an auspicious start, however, the attack on Newport ended in a decided Franco-American failure upon the arrival of Lord Howe's fleet from New York. *Ozanne Collection*, no. 3. LC–USZ62–900

283
Moment de l'après midi du 11 Aoust 1778. Le coup de vent en se déclarant empêche le Combat; le signal de le commencemt. étoit viré. [1778] [Pierre Ozanne]

Wash drawing 9¼ x 15¾ in.

On August 11, 1778, D'Estaing's fleet reversed direction and left the Middle Passage to encounter the fleet of Lord Howe and Adm. John Byron arriving from New York, but a strong gale prevented any decisive action. D'Estaing left three frigates to defend the American land troops at Newport. *Ozanne Collection*, no. 4. LC–USZ62–901

284

Le Vaisseau le Languedoc démâté par le coup de vent dans la nuit du 12'. attaqué par un Vaisseau de Guerre Anglois l'après midy du 13 Aout 1778 [1778] [Pierre Ozanne]
Wash drawing 9 x 16 in.

The legend below this print describes how the French ship *Languedoc* lost her mast during the night when the winds also broke her rudder. Captain Dawson ordered the British warship the *Renown* to attack but ceased firing before nightfall: "Le Renown cessa de lui-même le combat contre le Languedoc, rien ne l'empechoit de le continuer; la soirée fut longue et la nuit très belle." *Osanne Collection*, no. 5.
LC–USZ62–902

285

Le Vaisseau le Languedoc remâté en pleine mer ainsi que le Marseillois avec des mats d'hunes rejoints par tous les Vaisseaux et les Frégates de l'Escadre, le Vaisseau le César excepté; et faisant route le 17 Aoust 1778. [1778] [Pierre Ozanne]
Wash drawing 9½ x 15¾ in.

On August 14 D'Estaing returned to Newport and Howe to New York. Most of the damage suffered was due to the weather, but the weaker British fleet had "thoroughly outgeneralled the stronger" French fleet (Mahan, *Sea Power*). The *Languedoc* (fifth from left) was provided with sails fashioned from the top masts of other vessels in the fleet. The *Marseillais* (fifth from right) also received new sails while on the high seas. A captured English vessel, the *Senegal*, appears third from the right. *Ozanne Collection*, no. 6.
LC–USZ62–903

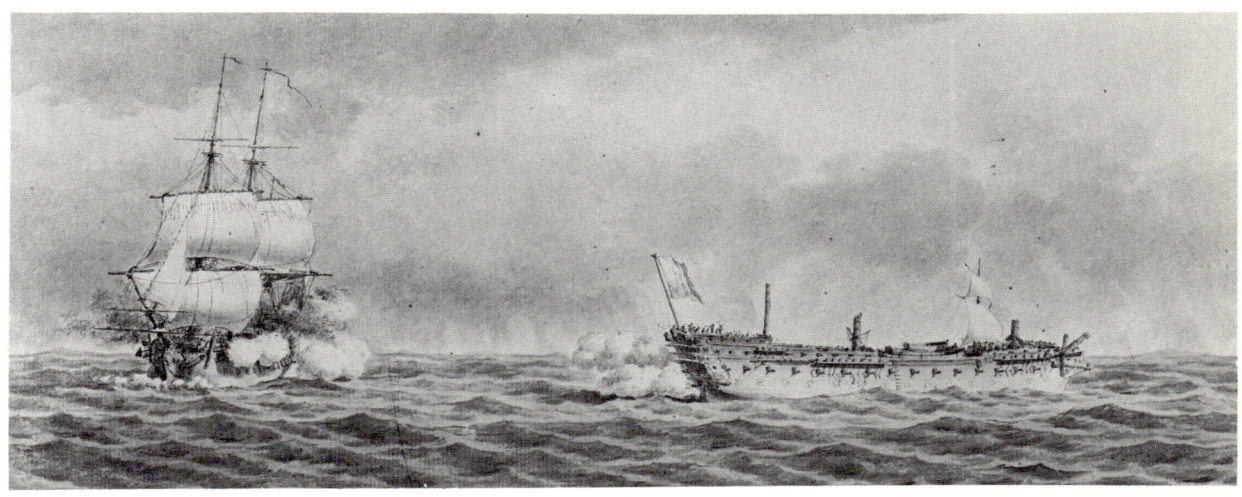

284

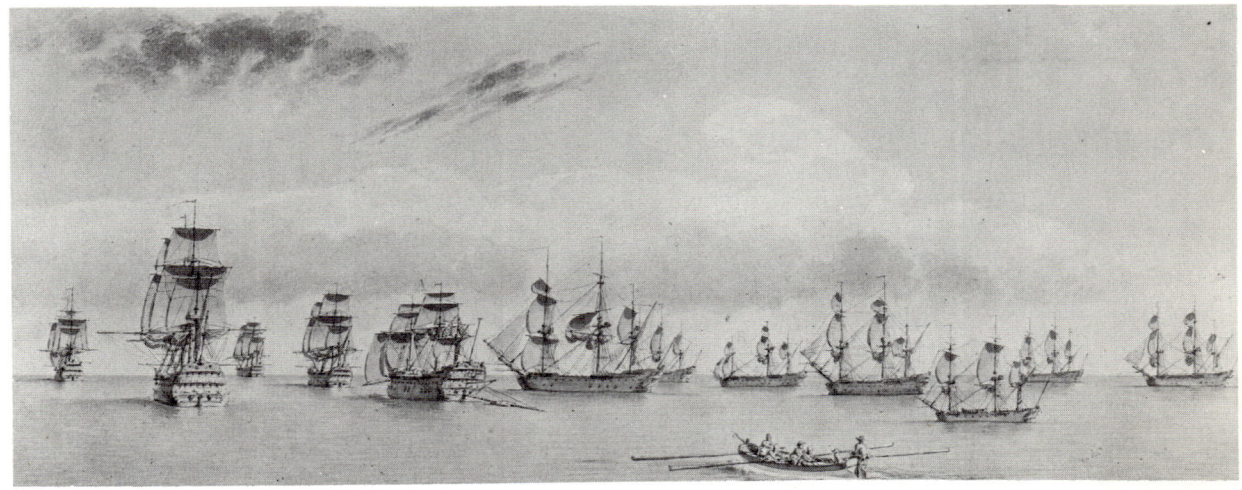

285

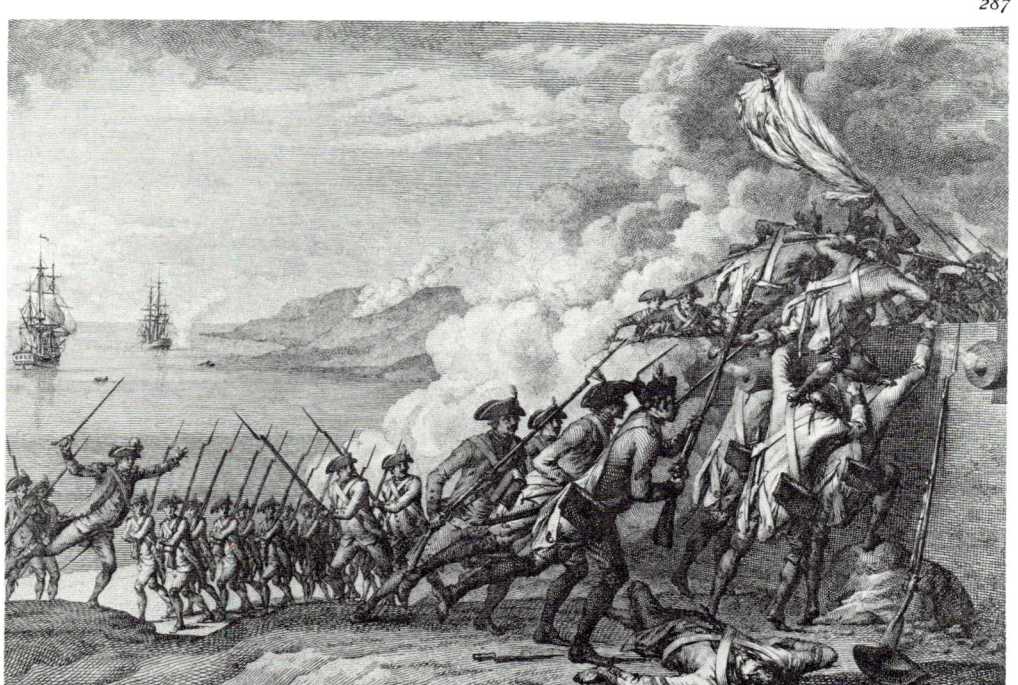

286

The SIEGE OF RHODE ISLAND, taken from Mr. Brindley's House, on the 25th. of August, 1778.
  Etching 6⅛ x 9 in.

  Washington directed Gen. John Sullivan to attack Gen. Robert Pigot's small force which was occupying Rhode Island. The French fleet under D'Estaing failed to blockade the harbor, and when the ships withdrew, the Americans ceased their atack. This picture shows Sullivan's forces advancing against Newport on August 25, 1778; three days later he began his retreat. This print is found in P&P and was originally from *The Gentleman's Magazine*, February 1779, p. 100–101. LC–USZ62–16834

287

PRISE DE LA DOMINIQUE. [Bertaux aqua forti] Gravé par Godefroy de l'Academie Imple. et Royale de Vienne &c. à Paris chés Godefroy rue des Francs-bourgeois Porte St. Michel et chés Ponce rue Hiacinte Avec Privilege du Roi. [1784?]
  Etching 7¼ x 8⅜ in.

  The French began their campaign in the West Indies with the seizure of the island of Dominica in the Leeward Islands. The Marquis de Bouillé, Governor of Martinique, landed with about 2,000 men and overcame the 500 British defenders of Dominica on September 7, 1778. Surrender was obtained by the French offer of generous terms, but the account below this view emphasizes the military success of zealous French troops. From Ponce, *Recueil d'estampes représentant* . . . (Paris, 1784?), plate 5. *Collection de Vinck* 1168.
LC–USZ62–45288

————Two earlier state impressions and a wash drawing of the same are in copy 3, in the Rare Book Division.

288

L'Escadre française mouillée à Boston remâtant les Vaisseaux. [1778] [Pierre Ozanne]
    Wash drawing 9¼ x 15⅞ in.

   Anchored at Boston in the fall of 1778, the French fleet was repaired. Visible is the *Languedoc*, foreground left, receiving a new mast from the *Protecteur*, foreground right. The *Vaillant*, first from right in the background, gave her masts to the *Protecteur* and sought native wood from the shore. Long Island, appearing in the center middleground, is the site of French workshops. The Comte d'Estaing left Boston on November 4, 1778. *Ozanne Collection*, no. 11. LC–USZ62–905

289

Vue de l'attaque de L'Isle de Ste. Lucie le 15. et le 17 Xbre 1778. [1778] [Pierre Ozanne]
    Wash drawing 9⅛ x 15⅝ in.

   The British captured the island of St. Lucia in the West Indies in December 1778. Although D'Estaing, coming from Boston, had 9,000 men, Admiral Barrington landed three detachments on the island before the arrival of the French and so skillfully positioned them as to be able to repulse the French attack. Shown on this picture is the Morne Fortuné on the left, the Morne de la Vigie on the right, and the town of Carénage between them. (Now called Castries, this port has an excellent landlocked harbor.) French troops are visible in the center foreground, but British troops occupy both bluffs. *Ozanne Collection*, no. 7. LC–USZ62–7702

290

St. Lucia in the West Indies taken Possession of by Admiral Barrington Monsieur de Micoud and the Inhabitants having Capitulated the 30th. of December, 1778, being the

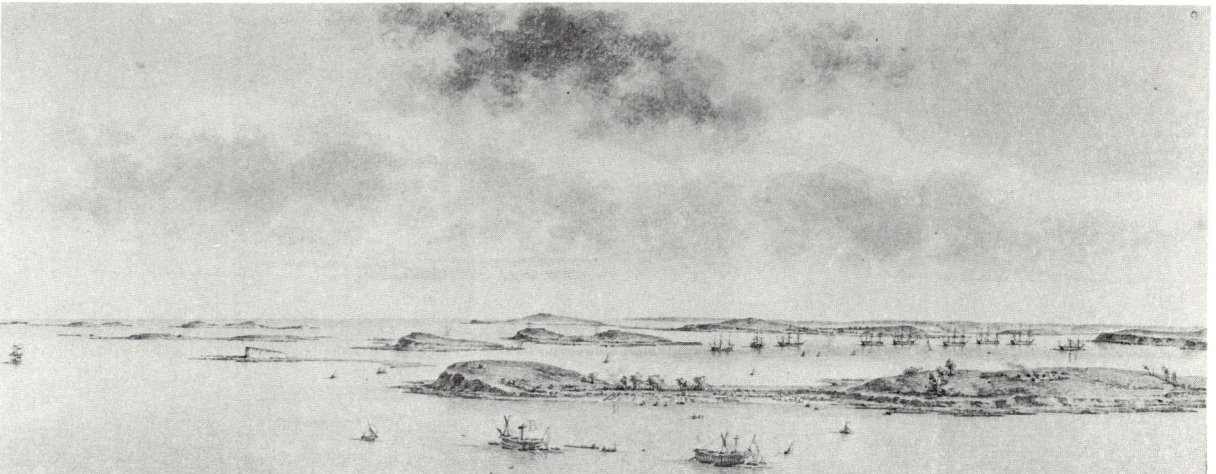
288

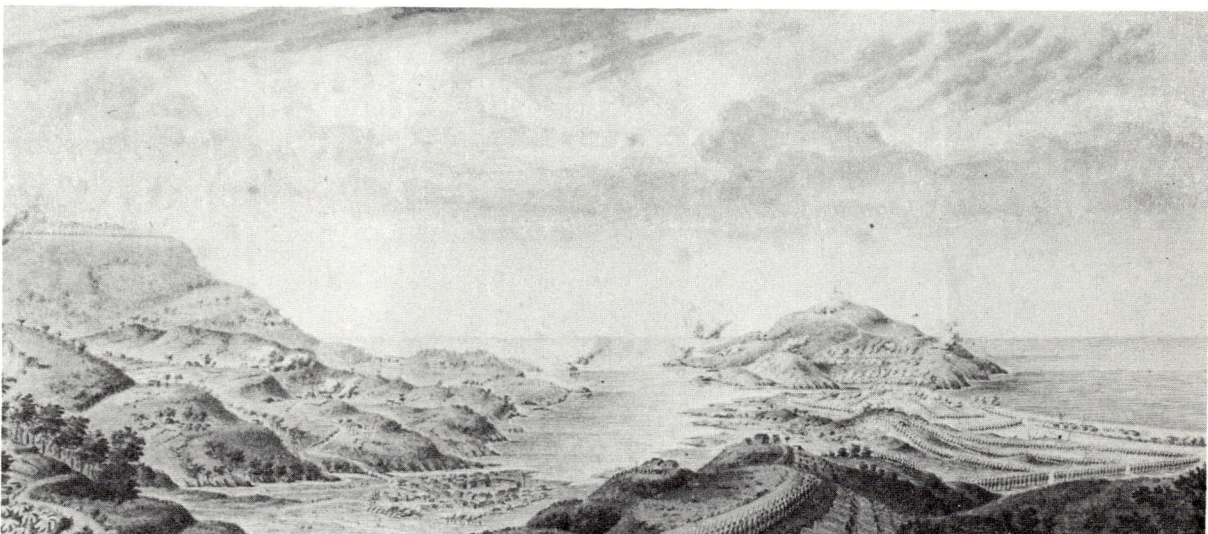
289

101

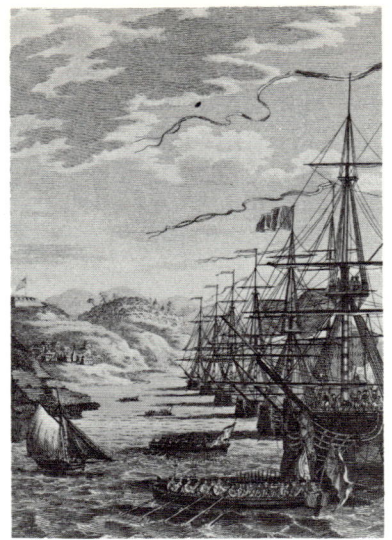

day after COUNT D'ESTAIGN left the Island much disconcerted. Engraved for BARNARD's New Complete & Authentic HISTORY of ENGLAND; A WORK Universally Acknowledged to be the Best Performance of the Kind,—on account of It's Impartiality, Accuracy, New Improvements, Superior Elegance, &c. Hamilton delin. Thornton sculp. [1783]

Etching 12¼ x 8½ in.

Troops being rowed ashore from six British ships anchored off Saint Lucia. The town in the background is probably Castries, and the French fort above it is newly occupied by the British. From Barnard, *History of England* (London, 1783), opposite p. 693. LC–USZ62–45310

291

Vue de la Baye de Kings-town, Isle de St. Vincent et de la prise de cette Isle par les francois sous les ordres de Mr. le Chevr. de Rumain lieutent. de Vaisseau chargé de cette expédition par Mr. d'Estaing le 16 juin 1779. [1779] [Pierre Ozanne]

Wash drawing 8¾ x 15½ in.

While Admiral Byron was occupied convoying British merchant ships, D'Estaing was easily able to take the island of St. Vincent in the Windward Islands on June 16, 1779. This view of Kingstown Bay shows the town of Kingstown, protected by British batteries at the mouth of the bay. Chevalier du Romain's troops are seen landing on the island, and the three sloops that transported them are identified as captured British vessels, the *Lively*, the *Weazle*, and the *Lilly*. *Ozanne Collection*, no. 19. LC–USZ62–7699

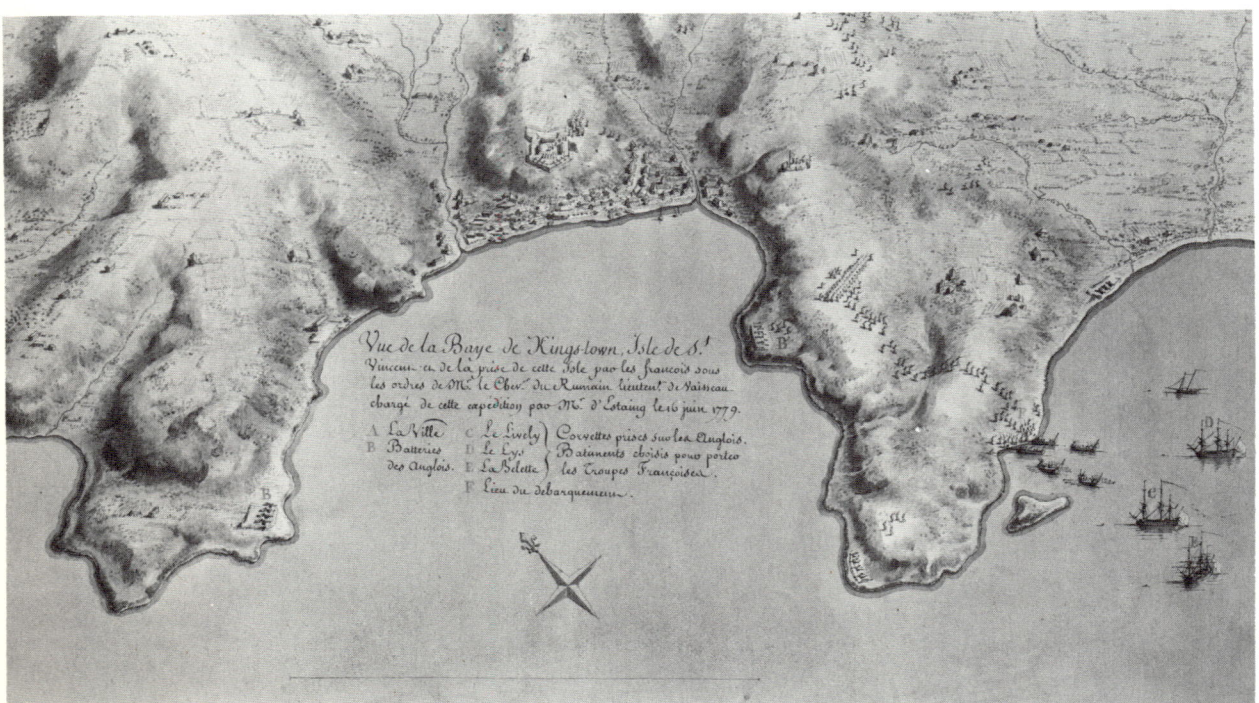

292

L'armée françoise Mouillée auprès de L'Ance Molenieu [Point] dans l'isle de la Grenade Et faisant le débarquement des Troupes le 2 Juillet 1779 [1779] [Pierre Ozanne]

Wash drawing 9 x 15½ in.

On July 4, 1779, D'Estaing took the island of Grenada. This picture portrays the landing of the French troops on July 2, and the point is identified as "L'Ance Molenieu." The town and fort of St. George are visible on the right. This is the first drawing in a series which depicts engagements between the French and British from July 2, 1779, to July 22, 1779. Their sequential numbers in the Ozanne Collection are: 15, 16, 8, 10, 12, 13, 14, and 17. *Ozanne Collection*, no. 15. LC–USZ62–7700

293
Vue du fort et Ville de St. George dans l'isle de la Grenade et du Morne de l'hopital emporté d'assaut par les troupes francoises aux ordres du vice-Amiral d'Estaing. le 4 Juillet 1779 [1779] [Pierre Ozanne]
 Wash drawing 9 x 15½ in.

 French troops under D'Estaing are pictured attacking the "Morne de l'hopital," the bluff in the foreground. A British battery on the bluff behind fires toward the sea to protect the channel against the French fleet. St. George and its fort are visible below the bluff to the left. *Ozanne Collection*, no. 16. LC–USZ62–7697

294
L'armée françoise Mouillée auprès de l'ance Molenieu dans L'isle de la Grenade le 6 Juillet 1779 Premiere Position Moment ou les frégates de découverte signalait L'armée Ennémie a 3 heures du matin [1779] [Pierre Ozanne]
 Wash drawing 9¼ x 15½ in.

 The French fleet appears in the center foreground, off the island of Grenada. The British fleet is barely visible on the horizon at the far left. Reconnaissance vessels precede the fleet. On the far right is St. George, also barely visible. *Ozanne Collection*, no. 8. LC–USZ62–7694

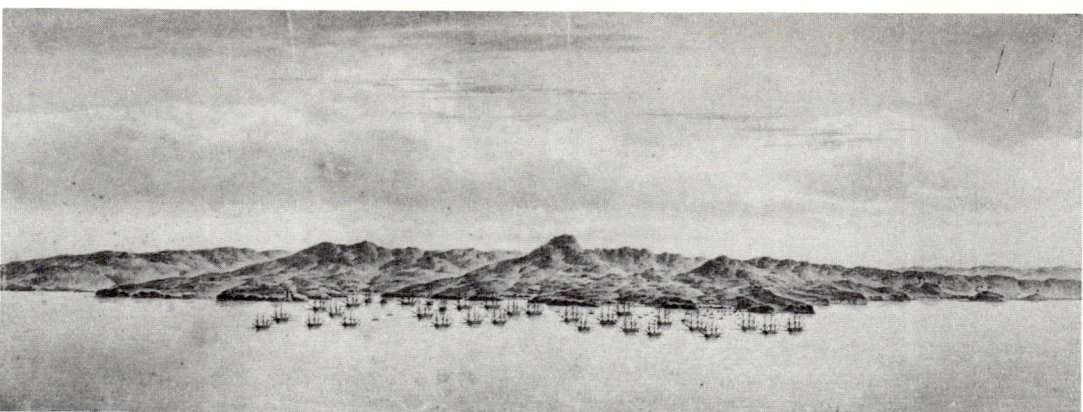

292

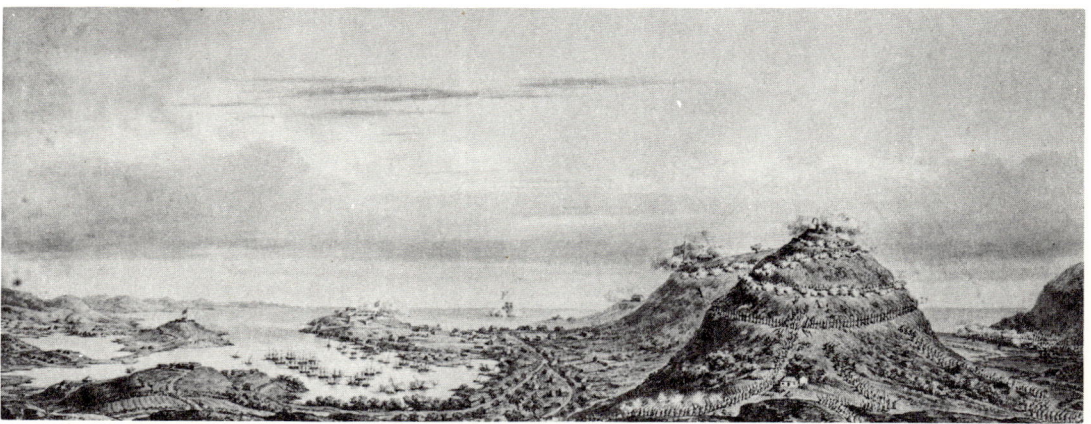

293

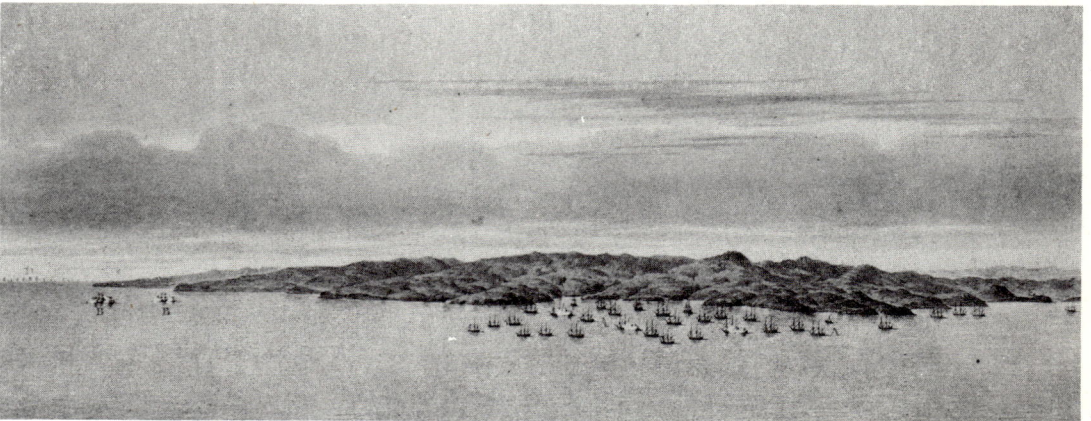

294

103

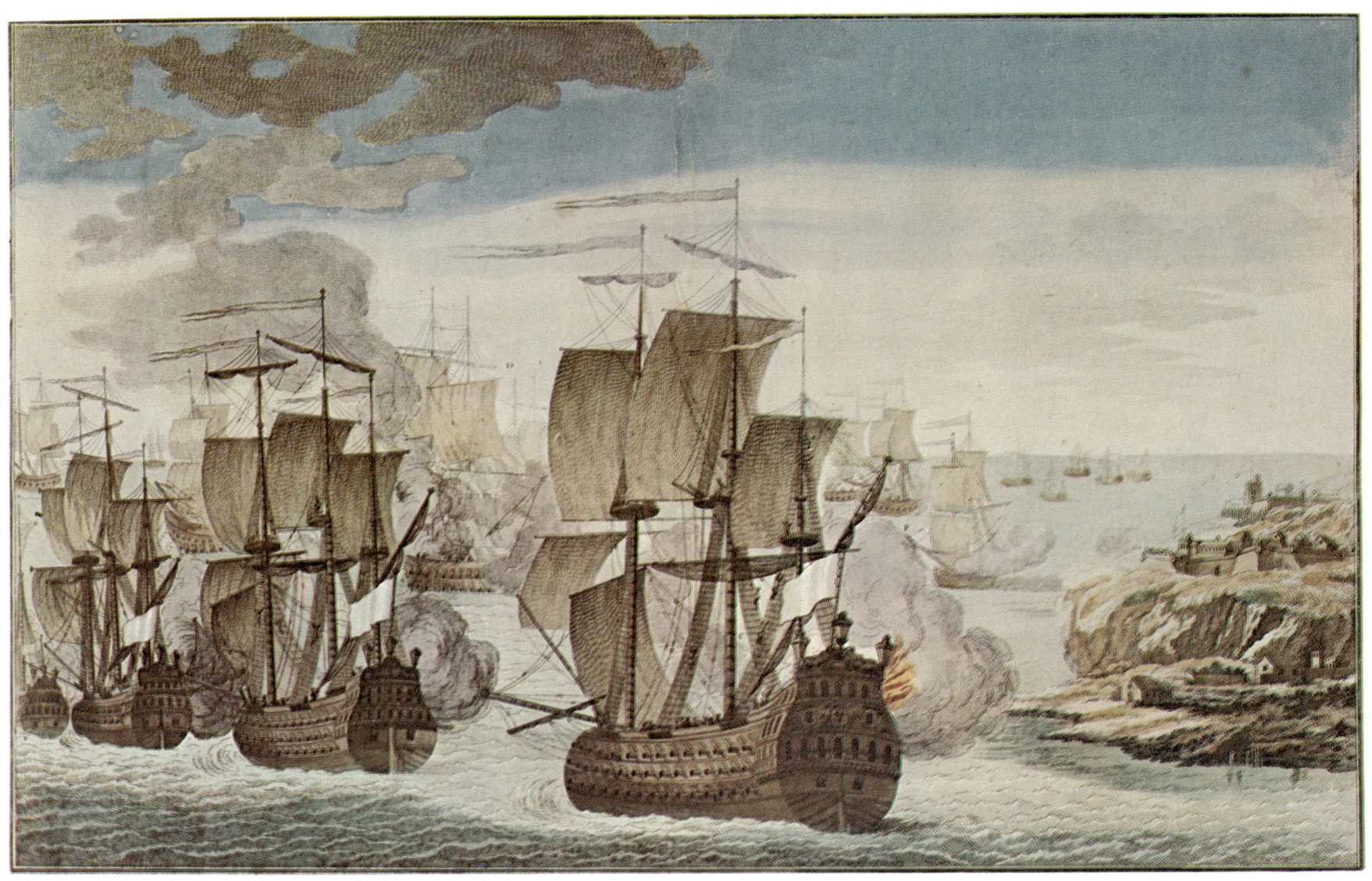

295

PLAN DU COMBAT DE LA GRENADE GAGNÉ PAR MR. LE CTE. D'ESTAING SUR L'AMIRAL BYRON LE 6. JUILLET 1779. A Paris chez Esnauts et Rapilly rue St. Jacques à la Ville de Coutances. [1779]

Etching (hand colored) 14½ x 20½ in.

On July 6 D'Estaing defeated Admiral Byron at Grenada. The batteries of Fort St. George fire upon the approaching English vessel. The French vessels in the foreground position themselves in a line while Admiral Byron's fleet arrives behind them and engages them in combat. Five English vessels in the background are retreating.

296

PRISE DE L'ISLE DE LA GRENADE. Dessiné par le Paon Peintre de S.A.S. Mgr. le Prince de Condé. Gravé par Godefroy de l'Académie Impèriale et Royale de Vienne &c. A Paris chez Mr. Godefroy, rue des Francs-Bourgeois, Porte S. Michel, et chez Mr. Ponce, rue St. Hyacinte, maison de M. Debure. A.P.D.R. [1784?]

Etching 7½ x 8⅜ in.

D'Estaing was victorious over Admiral Byron and took Grenada from the British. The scene depicts French officers cutting off their epaulets and affixing them to the shoulders of grenadiers who had behaved courageously during one of the battles. The account below the picture identifies the men involved in receiving honors and lists the wounded and dead officers. The report of the battle stresses the valor of the French and the heroism of D'Estaing who "triompha sur terre et sur mer en moins de 60 heures." From Ponce, *Recueil d'estampes représentant* . . . (Paris, 1784?), plate 7. *Collection de Vinck* 1170.
LC–USZ62–45290

————Another impression, two earlier states, and a wash drawing of the same picture are in copy 3, in the Rare Book Division.

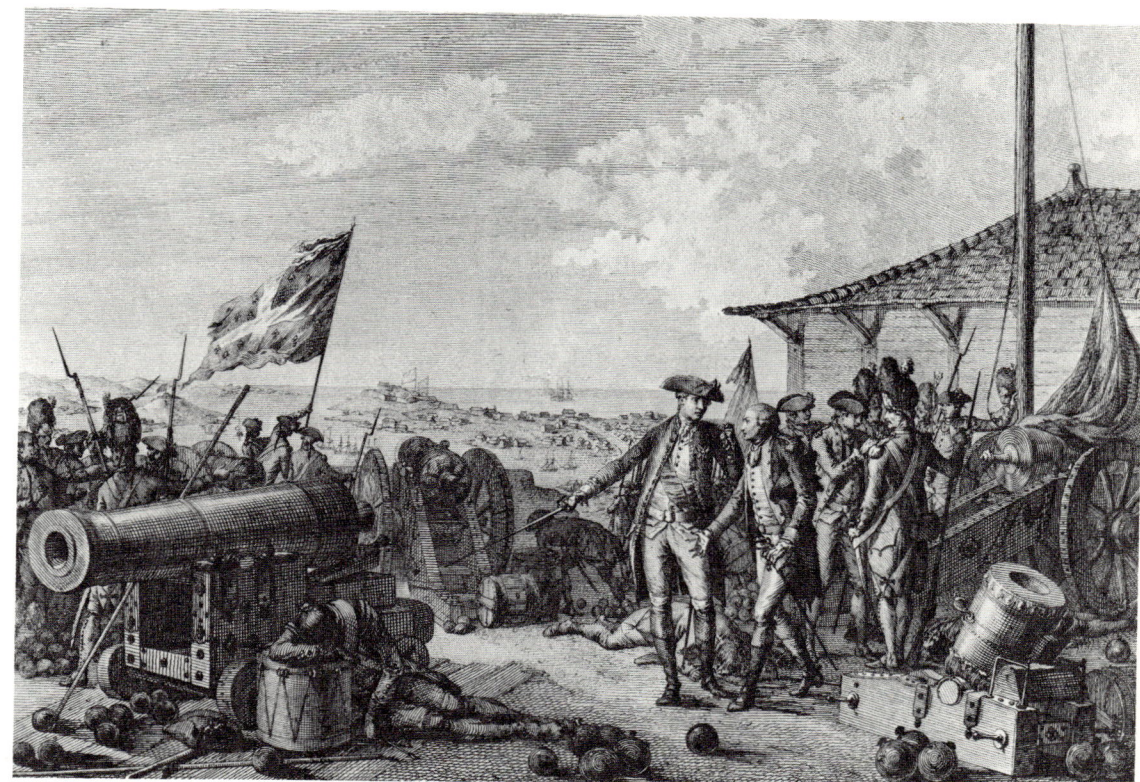

296

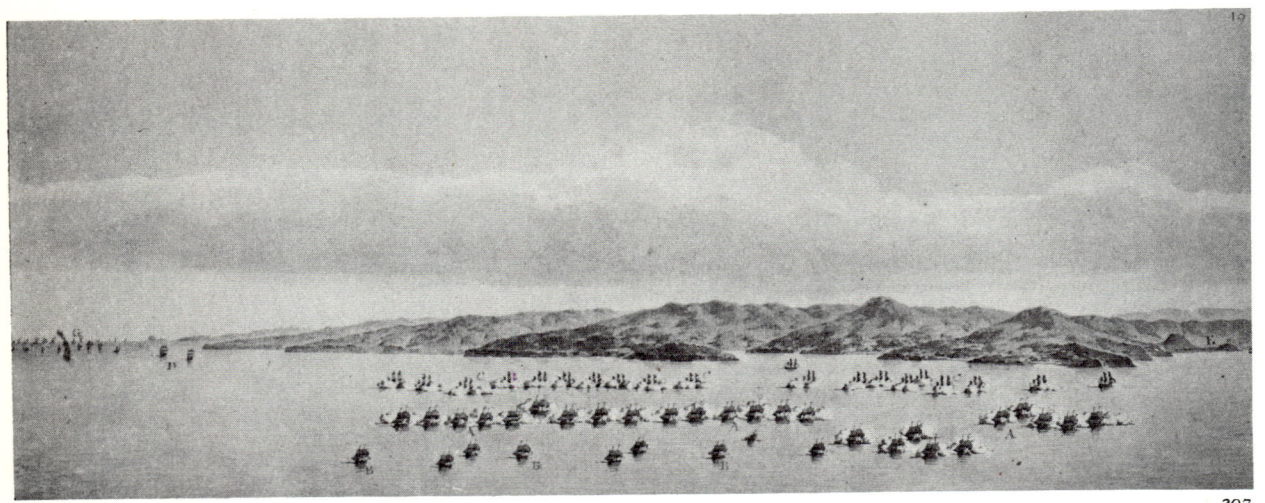

297

297
L'Armée françoise Combattant L'Armée Angloise à bord opposé Troisieme Position. [1779] [Pierre Ozanne]

Wash drawing 9⅛ x 15½ in.

The battle for Grenada continues as the British fleet, in line closest to the island, encounters the French fleet, advancing from the foreground. In the background left is a British convoy; two vessels from the convoy are on their way to join the fleet in battle. St. George is barely visible in the background right. *Ozanne Collection*, no. 10.
LC-USZ62-7693

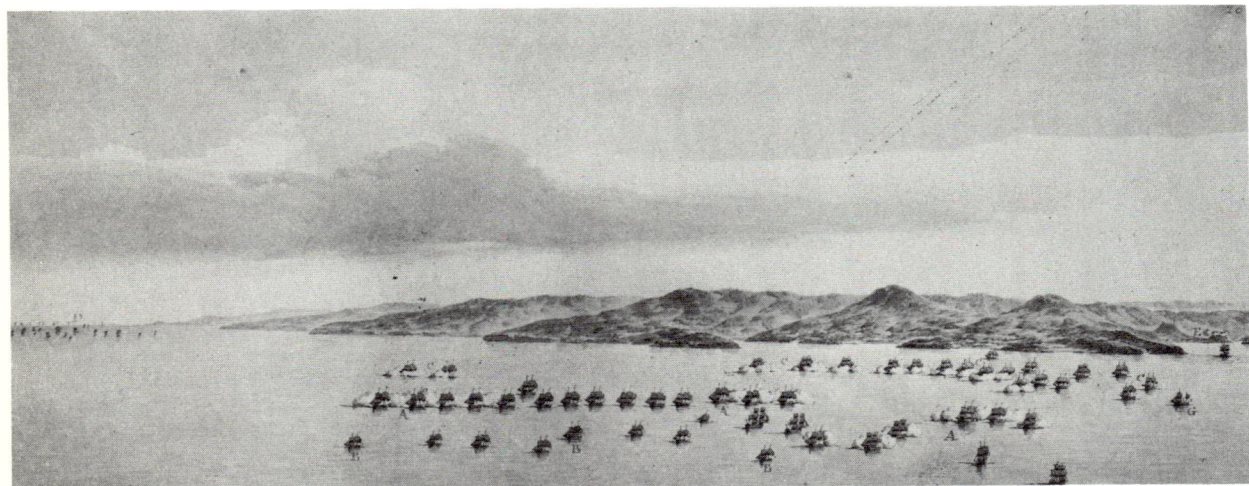

298

298
L'Armée françoise faisant signal aux Vaux. sous le Vent de Virer de bord pour se mettre en ligne Et attendre l'Armée Angloise à petites Voiles pour la Combattre au même Bord. Quatrieme Position. [1779] [Pierre Ozanne]

Wash drawing 9¼ x 15½ in.

The British fleet is obliged to put about and attack the rear guard of the French fleet in the foreground. The French ships are signalling the vessels to leeward to tack about to form a line and wait for the British so as to attack from the same side at once. The British convoy remains in the background left. Fort St. George, background right, is firing on a British ship. *Ozanne Collection*, no. 12.
LC-USZ62-7706

299

L'Armée françoise courant en Echiquier pour Rejoindre L'Armée Angloise Et tâcher de couper les trois Vaisseaux désemparés restés de l'arrière qui réjoignait leur Armée. Sixieme Position [1779] [Pierre Ozanne]
Wash drawing 9⅛ x 15½ in.

The legend explains that the British fleet, avoiding combat, has left Grenada far in the right background. The French fleet here sails in bow and quarter line to catch up with the British and to cut off the three disabled ships seeking to rejoin the other vessels of the fleet.
Ozanne Collection, no. 13. LC–USZ62–7696

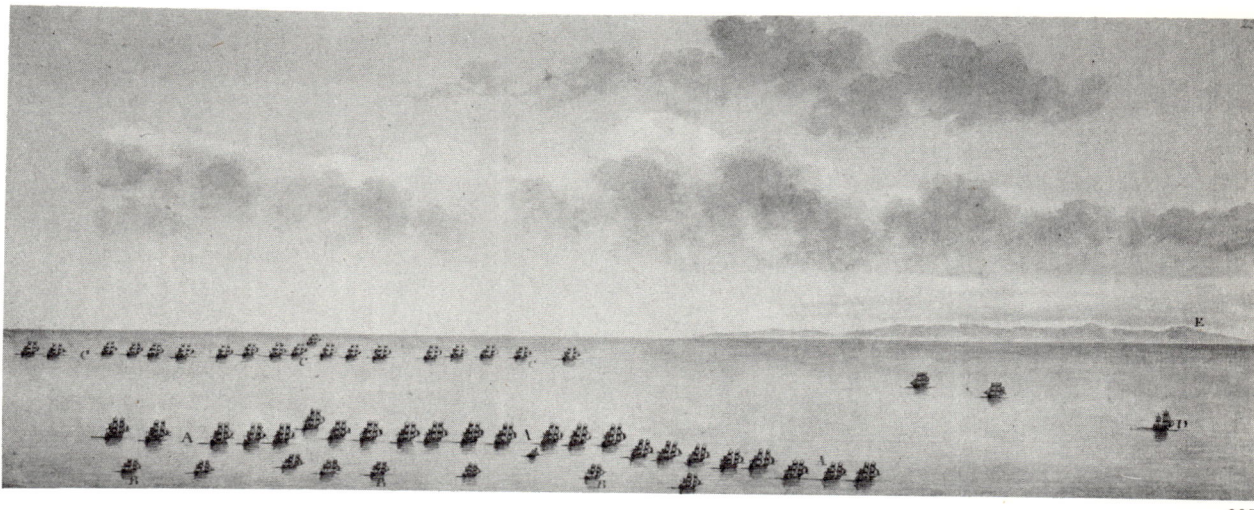

299

300

L'Armée française courant en Echiquier et Combattant les Vaisseaux desemparés restés de l'arrière qui Rejoignait leur Armée. Septieme Position. [1779] [Pierre Ozanne]
Wash drawing 9¼ x 15½ in.

The French fleet continues in pursuit of the British vessels and fires upon the disabled English ships. Grenada is in the background.
Ozanne Collection, no. 14. LC–USZ62–7701

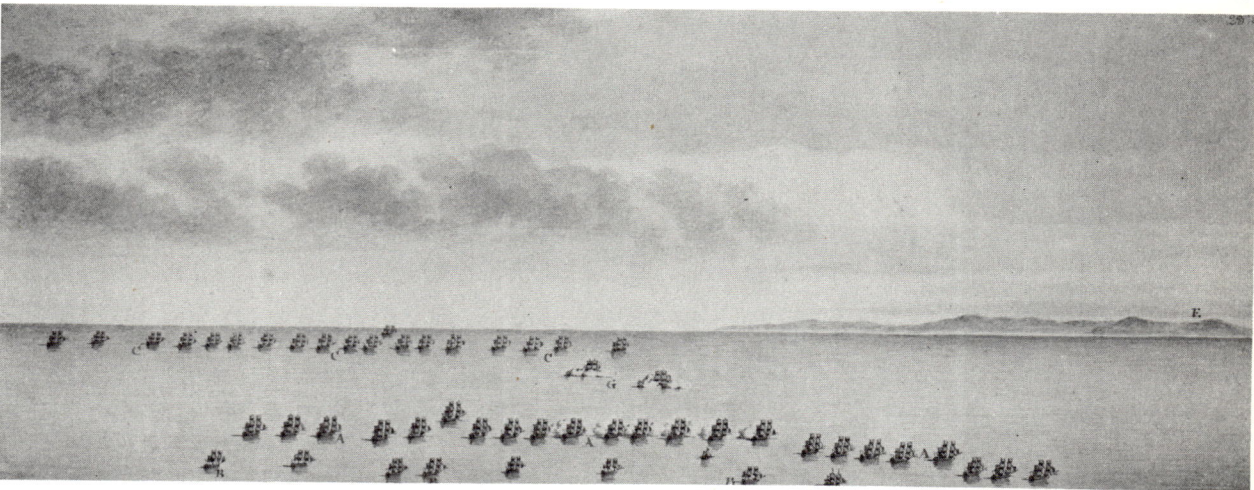

300

107

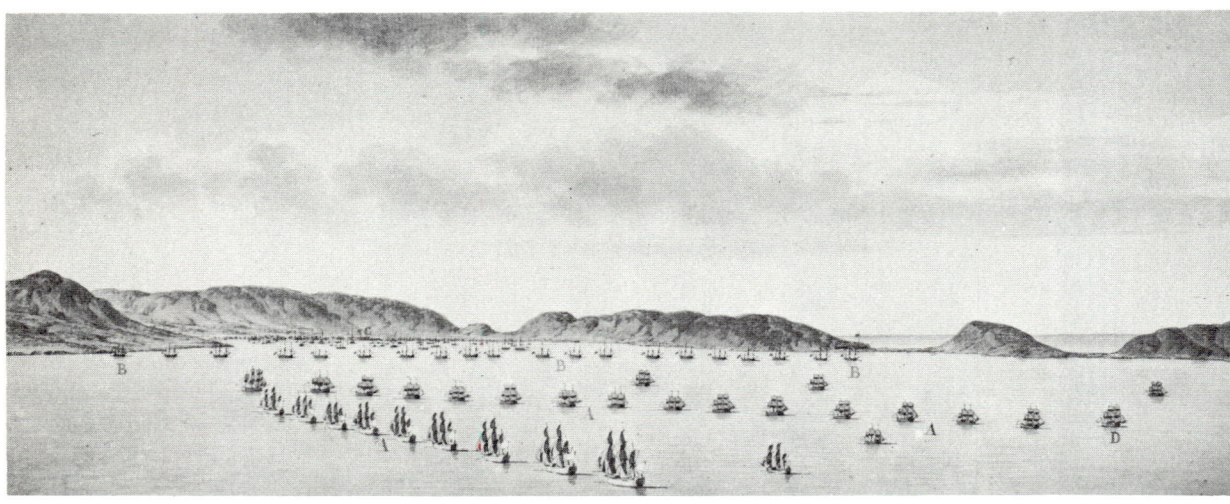

301

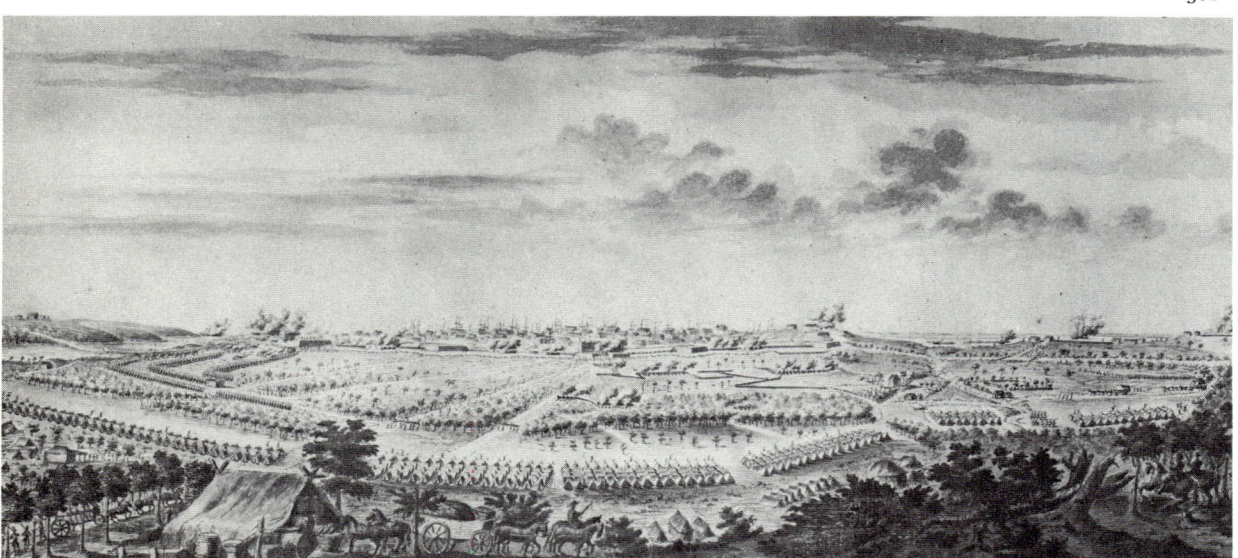

302

301

L'Armée françoise allant reconnoitre à St. Cristophe, l'Armée Angloise, s'assurant du mauvais etat ou l'a réduit le combat de la Grenade, avant de quitter les Iles du vent, présentant le combat et observant si les Vaisseaux désemparés peuvent être attaqués le 22. juillet 1779. [1779] [Pierre Ozanne]
Wash drawing 9¼ x 15¾ in.

The British fleet here is in the harbor of St. Kitts (or St. Christopher) in the Leeward Islands, where they are under fire from the fort of Basseterre, the port in the background. The French fleet is shown tacking in the foreground. The legend also identifies the *Robuste*, the vessel second from right. *Ozanne Collection*, no. 17. LC–USZ62–7703

302

Vue de la Ville de Savannah, du Camp, des Tranchées et de L'attaque Octobre 1779. [1779] [Pierre Ozanne]
Wash drawing 9⅛ x 15 in.

A view of Savannah looking north from the French camp during the Franco-American catastrophe of October 9, 1779. The Savannah River is visible in the background with French ships to the east and Germain's vessels to the west. Gen. Benjamin Lincoln had appealed to D'Estaing for aid to oust the British from the city. The French commander demanded the surrender of Savannah before Lincoln had time to join him there, but the British general Augustine Prevost asked for and received a short delay during which time he was reinforced by the arrival of Gen. John Maitland. The British withstood a three-week siege by the Americans. The French navy, plagued by scurvy and fearing the upcoming hurricane season, then decided to attack. D'Estaing's assault was a resounding failure, however, and Savannah remained in the hands of the British. *Ozanne Collection*, no. 18. LC–USZ62–11898

303-307

PRÉCIS DE CETTE GUERRE. A Paris chez M. Ponce, Graveur de Mgr. Comte d'Artois, Rue Ste. Hyacinthe, No. 19. et chez M. Godefroy, Graveur de Sa Majesté Imperiale, Rue des Francs-Bourgeois, Porte St. Michel. M. Niquet, Scrip. A.P.D.R. [1784?]

Etching 7½ x 8⅛ in.

Five small pictures frame a précis of the war, which begins with Boston and Lexington and continues the story of the Revolution through to the peace of 1783. Various theaters of combat are depicted. The first, chronologically, is Ushant where D'Orvilliers fought Admiral Keppel on July 27, 1778; 27 smaller French vessels opposed 30 British ships of the line. The second, dated March 14, 1780, shows the Spanish general Gálvez taking the fort at Mobile after having chased the English from Louisiana. In the third picture, the Dutch Admiral Zoutman encounters Admiral Parker on the Dogger Bank in the North Sea and proves his ability and courage in engaging the superior British force. The fourth picture shows how the Dutch colonies of Demerara, Essequibo, and Berbice (now united to form British Guiana) were retaken by De Kersaint and D'Alais. The fifth episode depicted takes place off the Coromandel Coast of India where De Suffren fought four English commanders and succeeded in taking one ship of the line plus more than 100 vessels from the British. From Ponce, *Recueil d'estampes représentant . . .* (Paris, 1784?), frontispiece, plate 1. *Collection de Vinck* 1163. LC–USZ62–46094

———Another impression, two earlier states, and a wash drawing of the same are in copy 3 in the Rare Book Division.

308

ENCAMPMENT of the CONVENTION ARMY. At Charlotte Ville in Virginia after they had

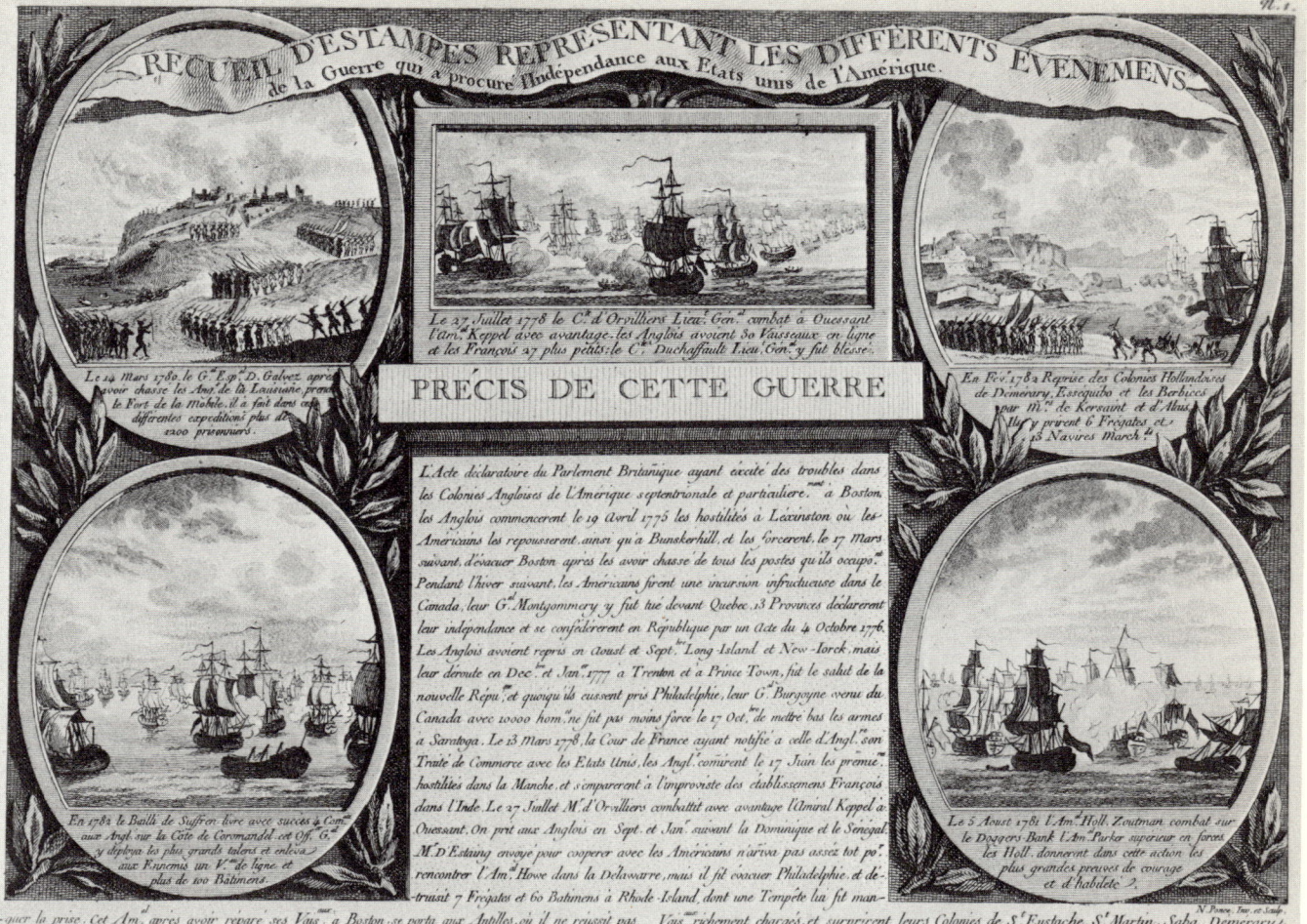

109

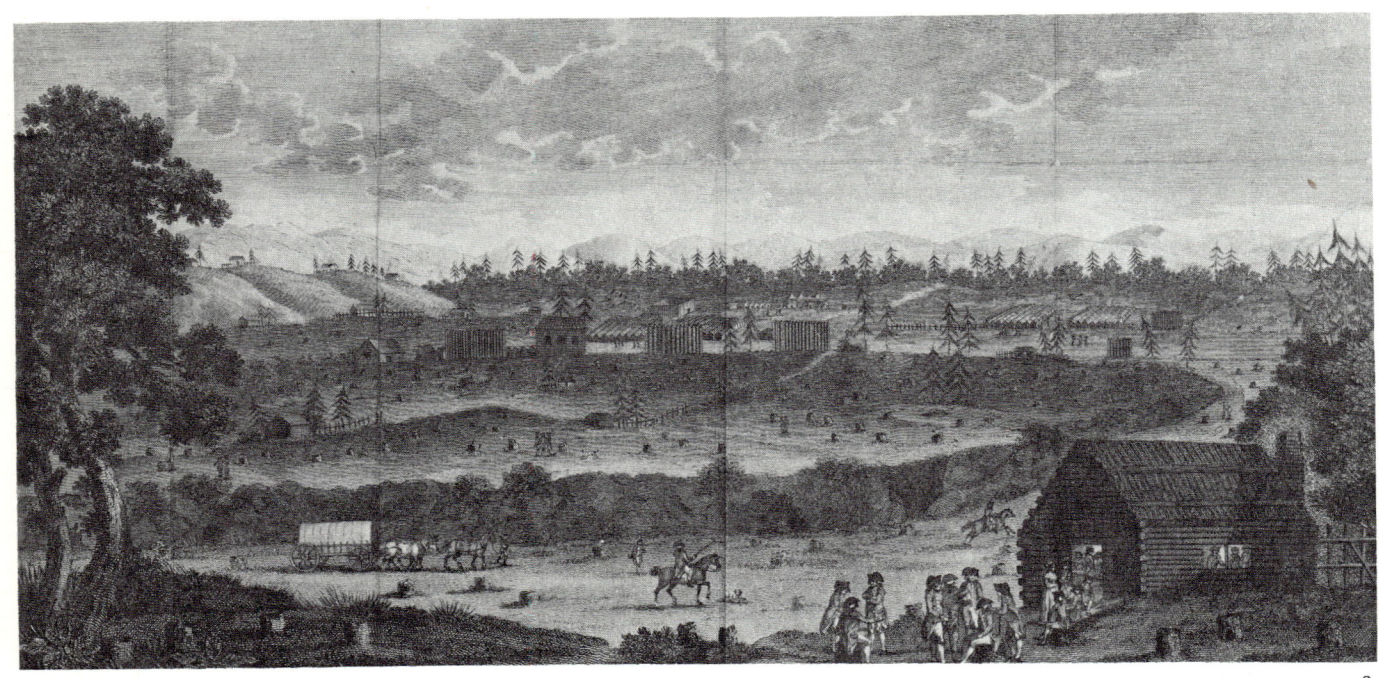

308

309

surrendered to the Americans Publish'd as the Act directs, Jany 1, 1789, by William Lane, Leadenhall Street, London.
Etching 9½ x 16½ in.

Since Burgoyne's surrender at Saratoga was by convention, the army under his command was popularly designated the "Convention Army." After it became clear that neither Congress nor Washington would abide by the terms of the Saratoga Convention, these troops were marched southward to the Charlottesville, Va., area, where they were allowed to build cabins and engage in subsistence farming. During the invasions of Virginia they were moved to Winchester, Va., Frederick, Md., and parts of Pennsylvania. From Anburey, *Travels Through the Interior Parts of America*, v. 2 (London, 1789), opposite p. 443. LC–USZ62–31960

309
VIEW of the British Fortress at Stoney-Point, stormed and carried by a party of the Light Corps of the American Army, under the command of Gen. WAYNE, on the Morning of the 16th of July last. [1780]
Woodcut 3 x 3¾ in. (image)

Brig. Gen. Anthony Wayne's surprise attack on the garrison at Stony Point, overlooking the Hudson, avenged the "Paoli Massacre." The operation was of little strategic value, but its masterful execution had a pronounced effect on patriot morale. This rough sketch shows the fort, the abatis, the reserve, and the detachment leading the attack. From Bickerstaff, *Boston Almanack* (Boston, 1780), verso of title page. LC–USZ62–45553

310

COMBAT MEMORABLE ENTRE LE PEARSON ET PAUL JONES. Richard Paton pinxit. Gravé par Balth. Frederic Leizalt. Se vend à Augsbourg au Negoce commun de l'Academie Imperiale d'Empire des Arts liberaux avec Privilege de sa Majesté Imperiale et avec Defense ni d'en faire ni de vendre les Copies. [178?]

Etching (hand colored) 9¾ x 14¾ in. (image)

View of the famous engagement between the converted merchantman, *Bonhomme Richard*, commanded by John Paul Jones, and the *Serapis*, under British captain Pearson. The action took place in the English Channel off Flamborough Head, September 23, 1779. The vessel firing at the left is the *Alliance*, commanded by Pierre Landais, a half-mad French naval officer assigned to Jones' squadron. Taken from a drawing by Richard Paton and probably copied from Lerpiniere and Fittler's engraving, which was published by John Boydell in 1781. Title above picture is mirror image. From "Collection des prospects." The following notes appear below the picture:

Das merckwurdige See Gefecht zwischen Capitain Pearson und Paul Jones welches 1779 den 22 September sich eraugnet wo der Cap: das Schiff den Serapis, und der Paul Jones, den guten Mann Richard genannt Commandirte.

Combat memorable entre le Pearson et Paul Jones donné le 22 7bre 1779. le Capitaine Pearson commendant le SERAPIS et Paul Jones commandant le Bon homme Richart et son Escadre.

———————Another impression (not colored).
LC–USZ62–112

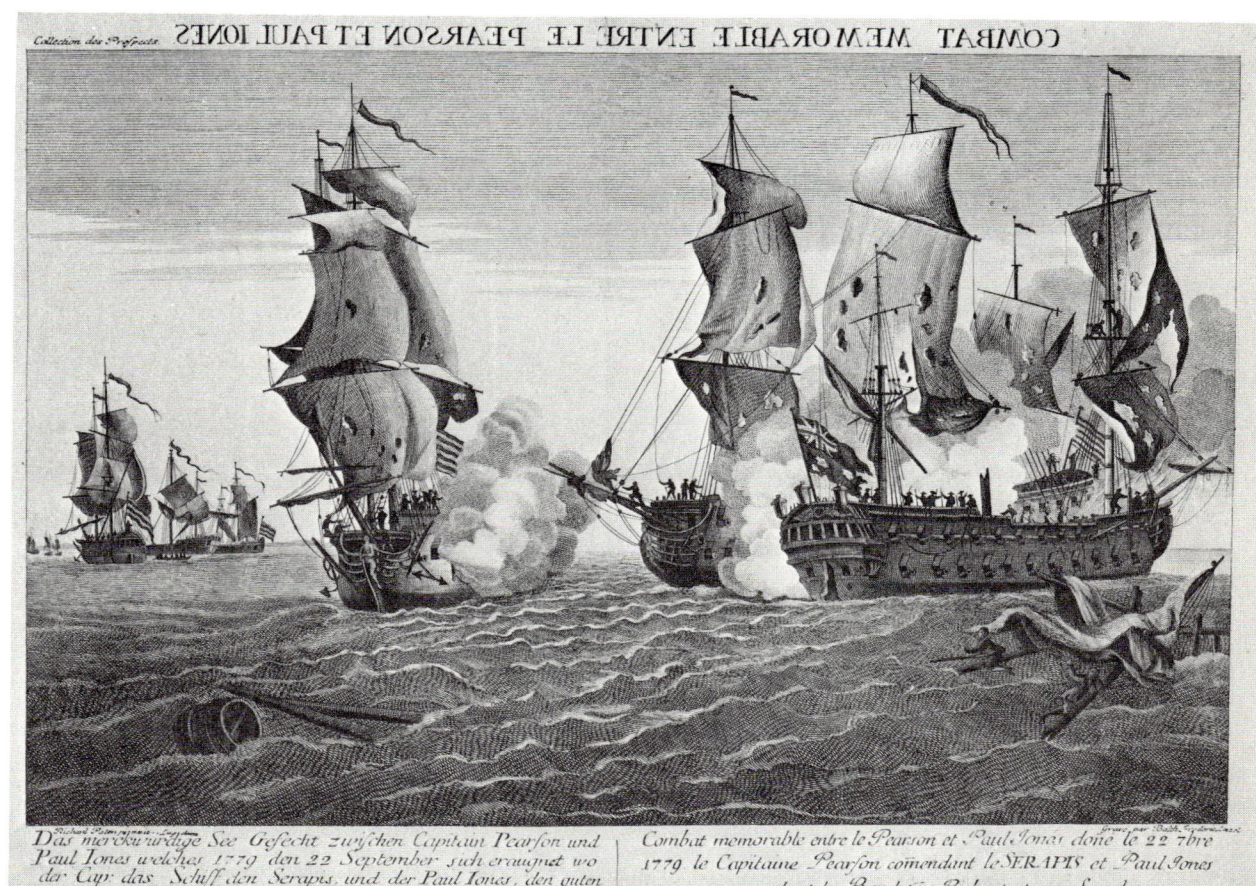

310

311

A BRITISH SAILOR offering a Sword to an Unarmed SPANISH OFFICER to defend himself, at the Attack of FORT OMOA, which was taken by Escalade, on the 20 of Octr. 1779, under the Command of Captn. Dalrymple and Commodore Lutterell. Engraved for BARNARD's New Complete & Authentic HISTORY OF ENGLAND; A WORK Universally Acknowledged to be the Best Performance of the Kind,—on account of It's Impartiality, Accuracy, New Improvements, Superior Elegance, &c. Hamilton delin. Thornton sculp.

Mixed method 12¼ x 8½ in.

Omoa, a key Spanish fort in the Bay of Honduras, was captured by the British in October 1779 in a daring maneuver led by Maj. John Dalrymple (1749–1821). Although Dalrymple was outnumbered more than two to one and was attacking a strong work, he did not lose a single man. Spanish losses totaled 365 prisoners and $3,000,000 in gold, ships, and supplies. From Barnard, *History of England* (London, 1783), p. 694. LC–USZ62–45311

312

Gallant behavior of an ENGLISH SAILOR in offering a SWORD to an unarmed SPANIARD to defend himself, at the taking of FORT OMOA, in the Bay of Honduras, October 20th. 1779. Metz delin. Record sculp. [1784]

Mixed method 10⅜ x 6¾ in.

In this version of the capture of Fort Omoa, a Spanish officer, with a look of fear, refuses the offer of a sword. From Raymond, *History of England* (London, 1784), p. 591. LC–USZ62–45212

———— ——Another impression (hand colored).

313

The Defeat of the Spanish Fleet under Don Juan de Langara, by Sir George Brydges

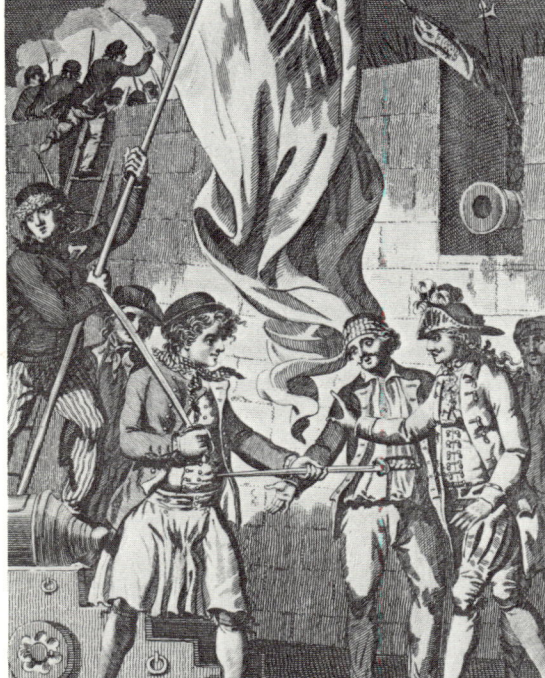
311

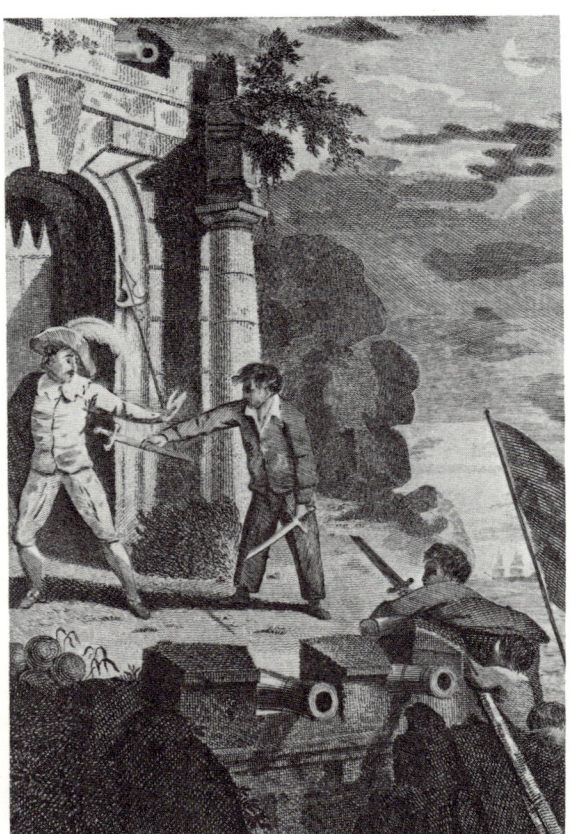
312

Rodney, Decr. 16th. 1779; off Cape St. Vincent. Most humbly Inscribed to Prince William Henry. [March 1780]

Etching 4¾ x 6⅜ in.

Admiral Rodney's defeat of the Spanish fleet under Don Juan de Langara, which actually took place on January 16, 1780, won him great applause in England. Since his fleet was twice the size of Langara's, the outcome of the battle was never in doubt, but Rodney displayed unusual skill in positioning his ships between the Spanish fleet and the rock-bound cape in a tempestuous sea and with darkness fast approaching. The victory contributed to the relief of Gibraltar, which at that time was under heavy siege by the Spanish. The portrait inset at the top is probably Prince William Henry. From *The Town and Country Magazine*, March 1780, p. 153. LC–USZ62–45418

314

Lieutenant Moody. This Officer during the American War distinguish'd himself as one of the most gallant Partizans in the British Service, & by the number of Mails that he seized made himself the terror of the Rebels. . . . Drawn & Engraved by Robt. Pollard. London, Pubd. Feby. 19; 1785, by R. Pollard No. 7 Braynes Row Spa Fields.

Aquatint with engraving 15 x 20½ in. (image)

Lt. James Moody (d. 1809), an officer in the 1st battalion of New Jersey Volunteers, is said to have struck terror into the hearts of New Jersey Whigs. Moody is shown here freeing a prisoner held by the Americans in a jail about 70 miles from New York City. Not long after the event, which occurred in May 1780, Moody was himself captured by troops under the command of Gen. Anthony Wayne and placed in irons in a rock dungeon at West Point. LC–USZ62–16969

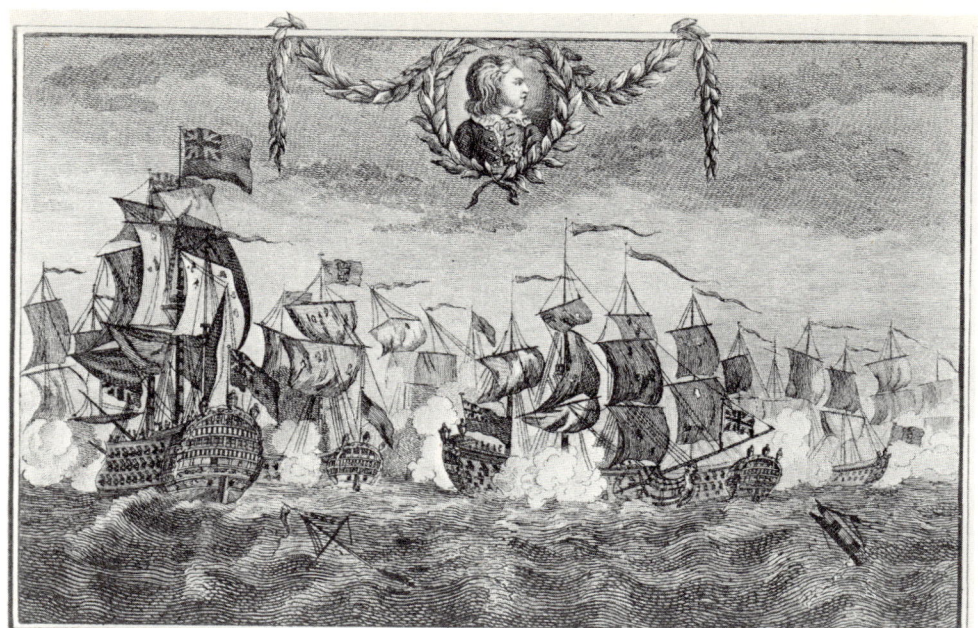

313

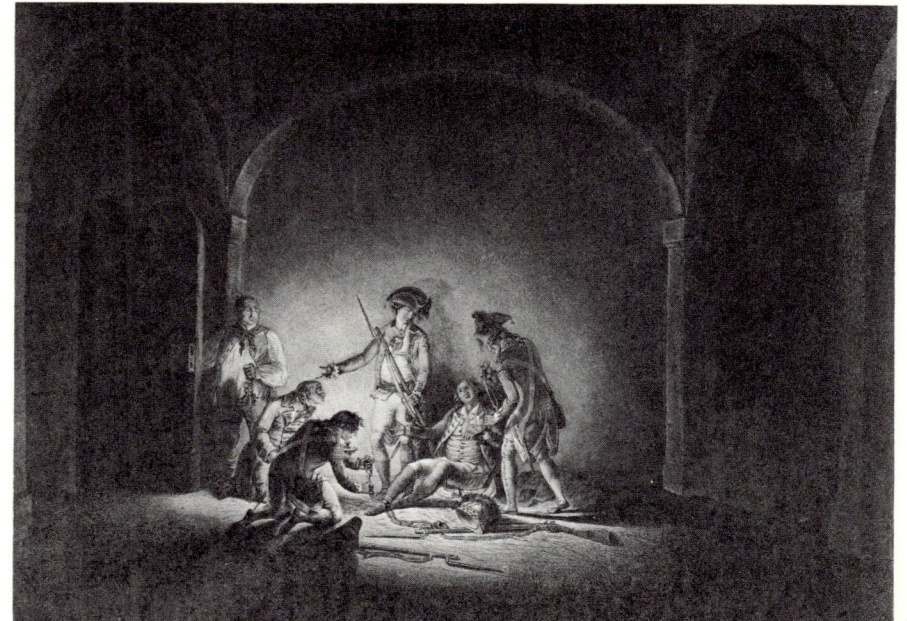

314

113

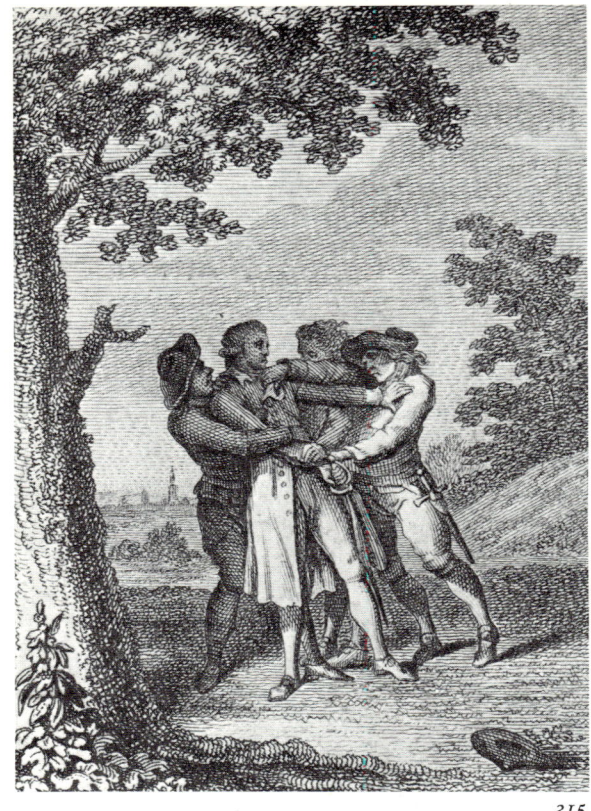
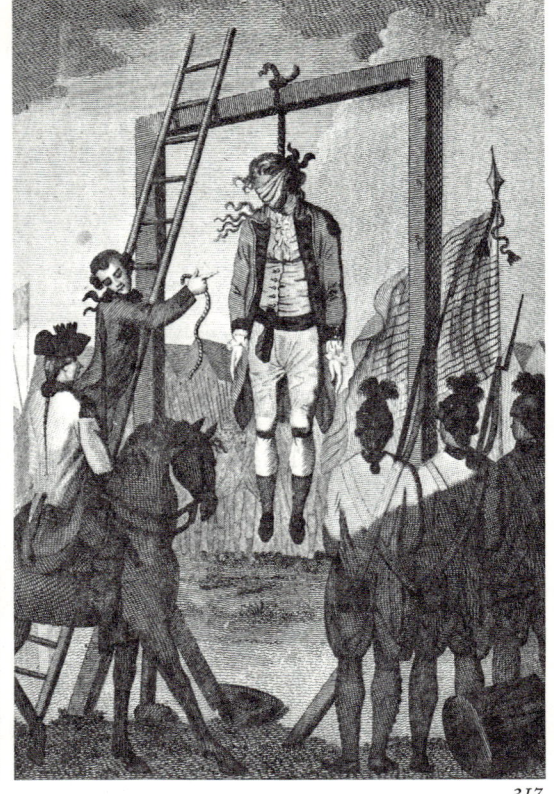
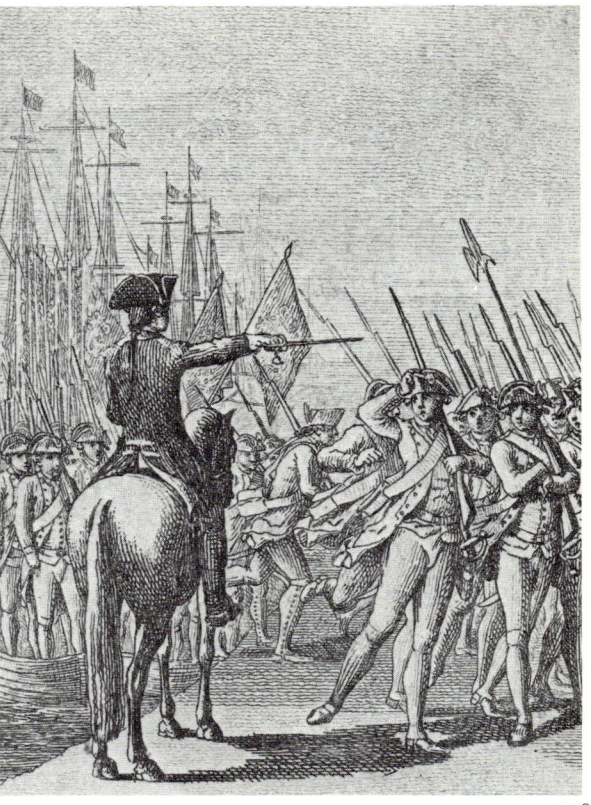

315

Major André, von drey Americanern angehalten zu Tarrytown am 23ten Septembr 1780. [1784]

Etching 2⅞ x 2 in. (image)

German impression of the arrest of Maj. John André near Tarrytown, N. Y. The three "volunteer militiamen" making the arrest, John Paulding, Isaac Van Wart, and David Williams, probably were operating under a New York act which permitted anyone apprehending an enemy to claim any valuables he had in his possession. André's being out of uniform and behind the American lines weighed heavily against him at his trial. Number 10 in a series by "D[aniel N.] Chodowiecki inv. et del." LC–USZ62–39565

——————Another copy. Engraved by D. Berger after Chodowiecki.

——————Another impression. In Sprengel, *Allgemeines historisches Taschenbuch* (Berlin, 1784).

316

The unfortunate Major Andre offering his watch to procure his release. [1780?]

Etching 8½ x 12½ in. (image)

André attempts to bribe two American soldiers.

317

The Unfortunate DEATH of MAJOR ANDRE (Adjutant General of the English Army) at Head Quarters in New York, Octr. 2. 1780, who was found within the American Lines in the character of a Spy. Hamilton delin. Goldar sculp. [1783]

Mixed method 11½ x 7½ in. (image)

His request to be shot by a firing squad denied, André hangs from a gibbet. The execution took place near Tappan, N. Y., on the above date. From Barnard, *History of England* (London, 1783), p. 694. This copy in P&P. LC–USZ62–52

318

Landung einer Frauzösischen Hülfs-Armee in America, zu Rhode Island. am 11ten. Julius 1780. [1784]

Etching 2⅞ x 2 in. (image)

German view of the landing of Comte de Rochambeau's 5,500-man army at Newport, R. I., July 11, 1780. Number nine in a series by "D[aniel N.] Chodowiecki inv. et del." LC–USZ62–19422

——————Another copy. Engraved by D. Berger after Chodowiecki.

——————Another impression. In Sprengel, *Allgemeines historisches Taschenbuch* (Berlin, 1784).

319

PRISE DE PENSACOLA. Dessiné par Lausan. Berteaux, Aqua. Gravé par N. Ponce, Graveur de Mgr. Comte d'Artois. Paris chez Mr. Ponce, Graveur de Mgr. Comte d'Artois, Rue St. Hyacinthe, No. 19, et chez Mr. Godefroy, Graveur de Sa Majeste Imperiale, Rue des Francs-Bourgeois. A.P.D.R. [1784?]

Etching 7⅛ x 8 in.

A chance shot fired by Spanish troops in the siege of Pensacola exploded the principal British magazine. Over 100 British soldiers were killed or disabled by the blast, and one of their main redoubts destroyed. Taking advantage of the opening, the Spanish fought their way to the ruined fortification and forced the surrender of the entire garrison, May 9, 1781. The officer represented on horseback is probably Bernardo de Gálvez, the Spanish commander. From Ponce, *Recueil d'estampes représentant . . .* (Paris, 1784?), plate 8. *Collection de Vinck* 1182.

——————Another impression (LC–USZ62–39588), two earlier states, and a wash drawing (LC–USZ62–39589) of the same are in copy 3, in the Rare Book Division.

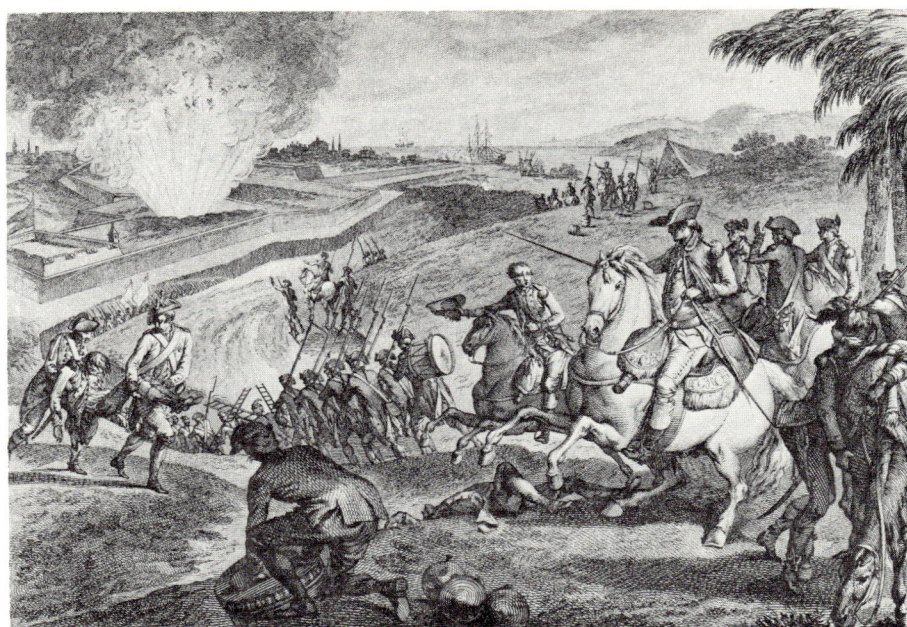

319 engraving

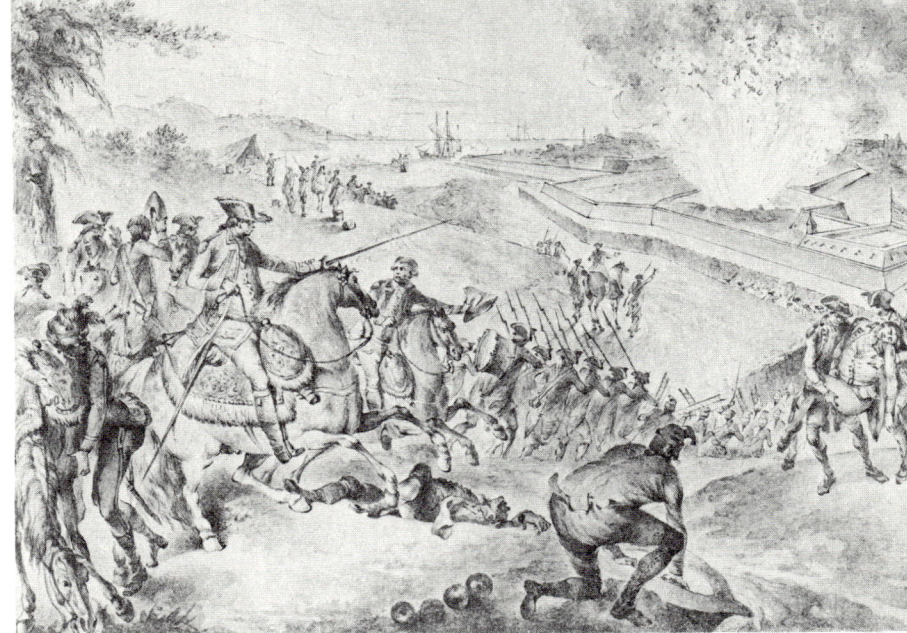

319 wash drawing

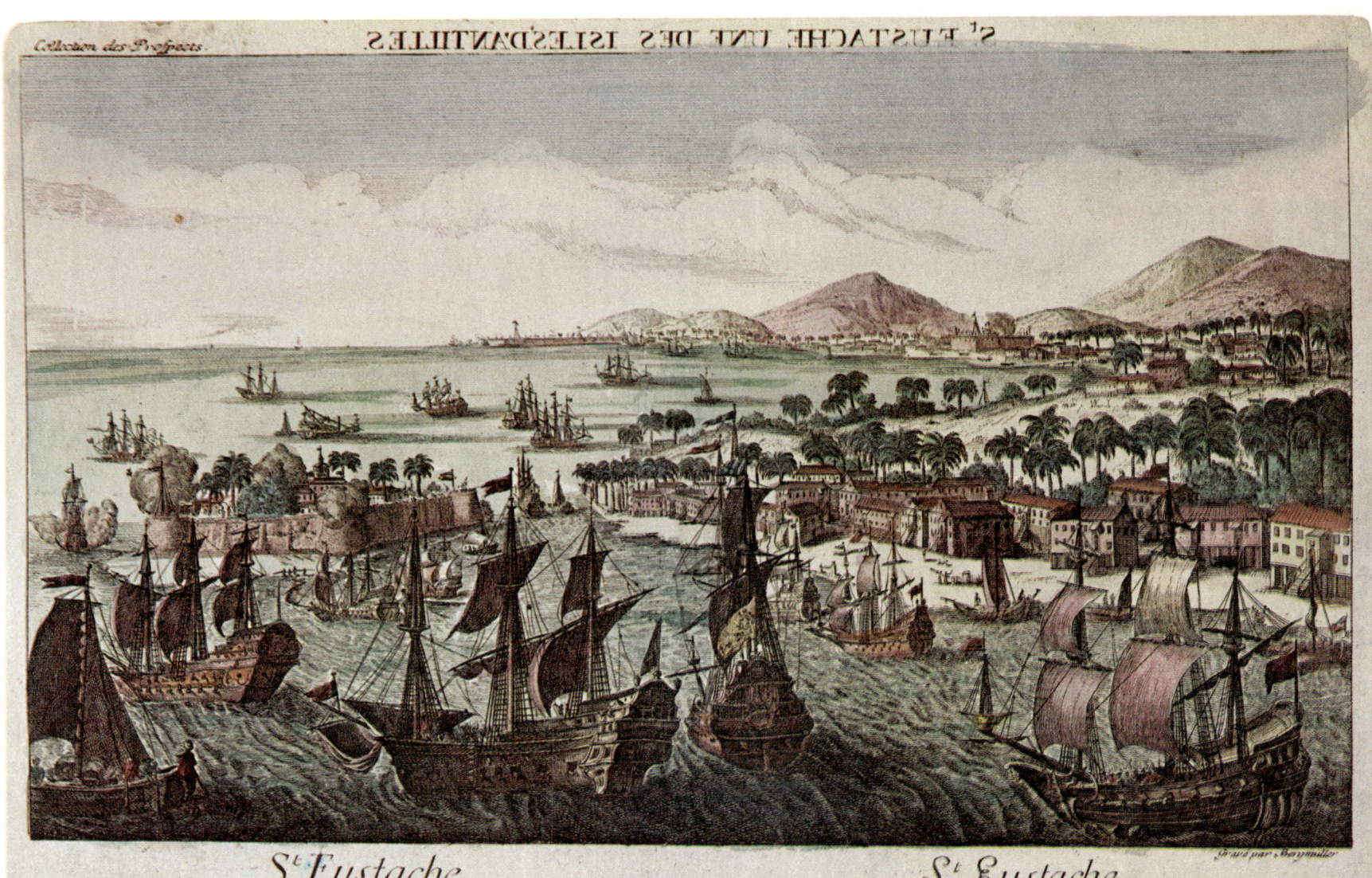

St. Eustache, eine der Antillischen Inseln in Nord-America welche 1781 von den Engelländern erobert und denen Holländern abgenomen worden.

St. Eustache, une des Isles d'Antilles dans L'Amerique du Nord, la quelle fut prise aux Hollandois en 1781 par les Anglois.

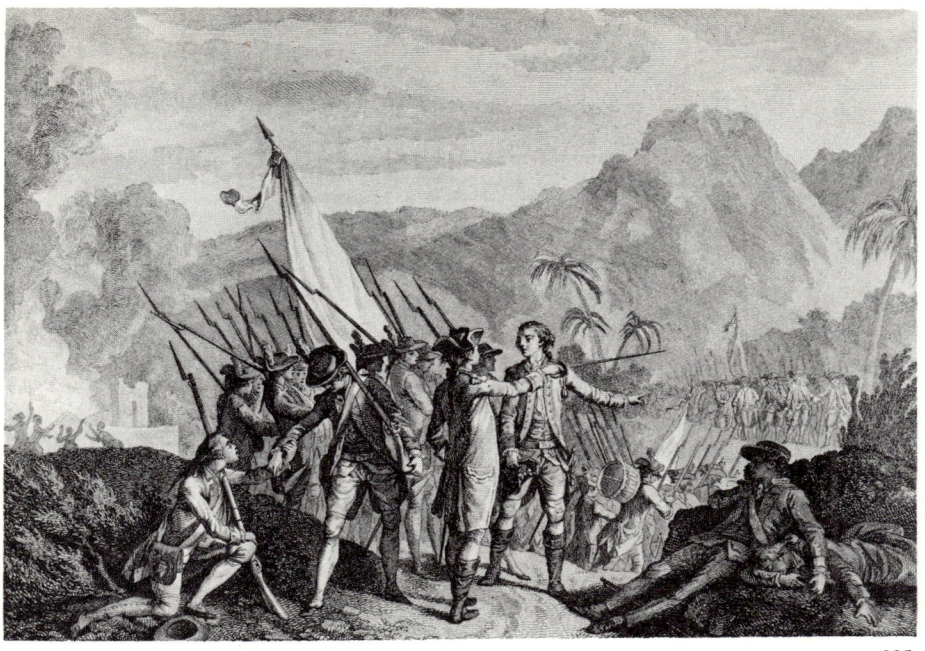

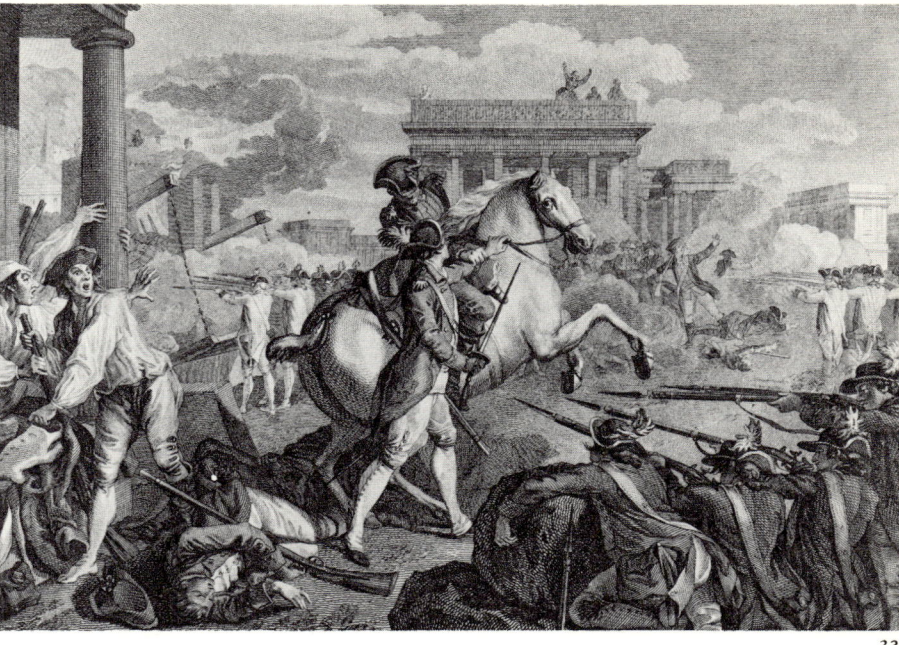

320

ST. EUSTACHE UNE DES ISLES D'ANTILLES. St. Eustache eine der Antillischen Insuln in Nord-America welche 1781 von den Engelländern erobert und denen Holländern abgenommen worden. St. Eustache une des Isles d'Antilles dans l'Amerique du Nord laquelle fut prise aux Hollandois en 1781 par les Anglois. Gravé par Bergmuller. Se vend a Augsbourg au Negoce: commun de l'Academie Imperiale d'Empire des Arts libereaux avec Privilege de Sa Majesté Imperiale et avec Defense ni d'en faire ni de vendre les Copies. [178?]

Etching 11½ x 16¼ in.

View of Admiral Rodney's attack on the Dutch possession of St. Eustatius, a center of contraband trade with the Americans. Rodney captured the island on February 3, 1781, but it was recaptured by the French in November 1781.

321

PRISE DE TABAGO. Dessiné par William. Gravé par N. Ponce, Graveur de Mgr. Comte d'Artois. A Paris chez Ponce, rue St. Hyacinte, maison de M. Debure Et chez Godefroy, rue des Francs Bourgeois, Porte S. Michel. A.P. D.R. [1784?]

Etching 7 x 8 in.

The Comte de Grasse, who had sailed from Brest in March 1781 with the French Navy, left Fort Royal on Martinique in May to take Tobago. The description under this print recounts the landing of the French troops and capture of 900 enemy troops. De Grasse was joined by the Marquis de Bouillé, and the British capitulated on June 2, 1781. The description ends with a list of the virtues of the island, which remained a French colony after the peace of 1783. From Ponce, *Recueil d'estampes représentant . . .* (Paris, 1784?), plate 9. *Collection de Vinck* 1183. LC–USZ62–45292

———Another impression, two earlier states, and a wash drawing of the same are in copy 3, in the Rare Book Division.

322

SURPRISE DE ST. EUSTACE. Dessiné par P. C. Marillier. Gravé par N. Ponce Graveur de Mgr. le Comte d'Artois. A Paris chez Ponce, rue St. Hyacinte, maison de M. Debure. Et chez Godefroy, rue des Francs Bourgeois, Porte S. Michel. A.P.D.R. [1784?]

Etching 7¼ x 8¼ in.

In a surprise attack on November 25, 1781, the Marquis de Bouillé recaptured St. Eustatius from the British. The Dutch islands had been taken by Admiral Rodney in February 1781, when Holland declared war on England. After capturing St. Eustatius, De Bouillé went on to take back Saba and St. Martin. From Ponce, *Recueil d'estampes représentant* . . . (Paris, 1784?), plate 11. *Collection de Vinck* 1186. LC–USZ62–45294

──────── Another impression, two earlier states, and a wash drawing of the same are in copy 3, in the Rare Book Division.

323
LA BALLE A FRAPPÉ SON AMANTE. Dessiné par le Barbier, Peintre du Roi. Gravé par. L. Halbou. 1782.

Mixed method 6⅛ x 3¾ in. (image)

The brief narrative "Histoire de Seymour & de Molly" tells of an American boy who joined the Continental Army to seek his fortune. When on leave, he and Molly were wed amid the bucolic loveliness of the American wilderness in the company of their rustic, virtuous friends. Just as the ceremony ended and the wedding feast was about to begin, a troop of British soldiers marched into the settlement and fired a volley into the fleeing patriots. The one person who fell dead was Molly, pierced through the heart by a rifle ball. This fiction is a splendid example of sentimental propaganda. From Hilliard d'Auberteuil, *Essais historiques*, v. 3 (1782), p. [17]. LC–USZ62–45336

324
REDDITION DE L'ARMÉE DU LORD CORNWALLIS. Dessiné par le Berbier Peintre du Roi. Gravé par Godefroy de l'Academie Imple. et Royale de Vienne &c. à Paris, chéz Mr. Godefroy, rue de Francs bourgeois Porte St. Michel; et chéz Mr. Ponce, Graveur de Mgr. le Comte. d'Artois, rue Hiacinte. A.P.D.R. [1784?]

Etching 7¼ x 8 in.

This print of the surrender of the army of Lord Cornwallis possibly portrays Rochambeau

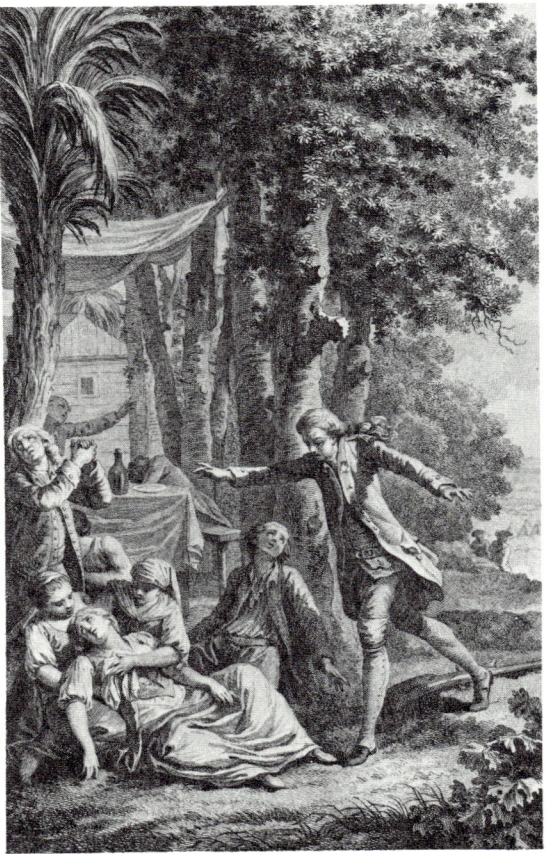

323

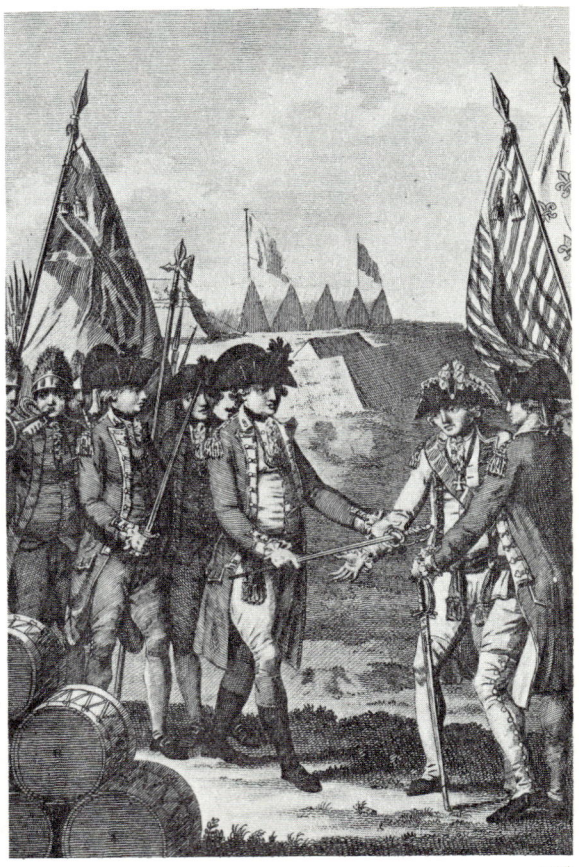

325

118

motioning to Cornwallis' deputy, Gen. Charles O'Hara of the Guards, to present his sword to the American Commander in Chief. The narrative below this picture provides a summary of particulars regarding the siege of Yorktown, including lists of arms and equipment rendered, participating French and American officers, and officers who distinguished themselves as well as those killed or wounded. From Ponce, *Recueil d'estampes représentant* . . . (Paris, 1784?), plate 10. Collection de Vinck 1184.

————Another impression (LC–USZ62–39586), two earlier states, and a wash drawing (LC–USZ62–39587) of the same are in copy 3, in the Rare Book Division.

————Another impression. In P&P.

325
The SURRENDER OF EARL CORNWALLIS (Lieutenant-General of the British Army in North America) to GENERAL WASHINGTON & COUNT DE ROCHAMBEAU, on the 19th. of Octr. 1781— whereby the Posts of York-Town & Gloucester in Virginia, were then given up to the combined Forces of America & France. Engraved for BARNARD'S New Complete & Authentic HISTORY OF ENGLAND; A WORK Universally Acknowledged to be the Best Performance of the Kind,—on account of It's Impartiality, Accuracy, New Improvements, Superior Elegance, &c. Hamilton delin. Thornton sculp.
Mixed method 12¼ x 8½ in.

Gen. Charles O'Hara, commander of the 2d Battalion of Guards, represented Cornwallis in the surrender at Yorktown. In a final gesture of British defiance toward the Americans, O'Hara first offered his sword to Rochambeau, but the French officer quickly directed him to General Washington. Maj. Gen. Benjamin Lincoln actually received the weapon. Barnard, *History of England* (London, 1783), opposite p. 696. LC–USZ62–22034

————Another copy. In P&P.

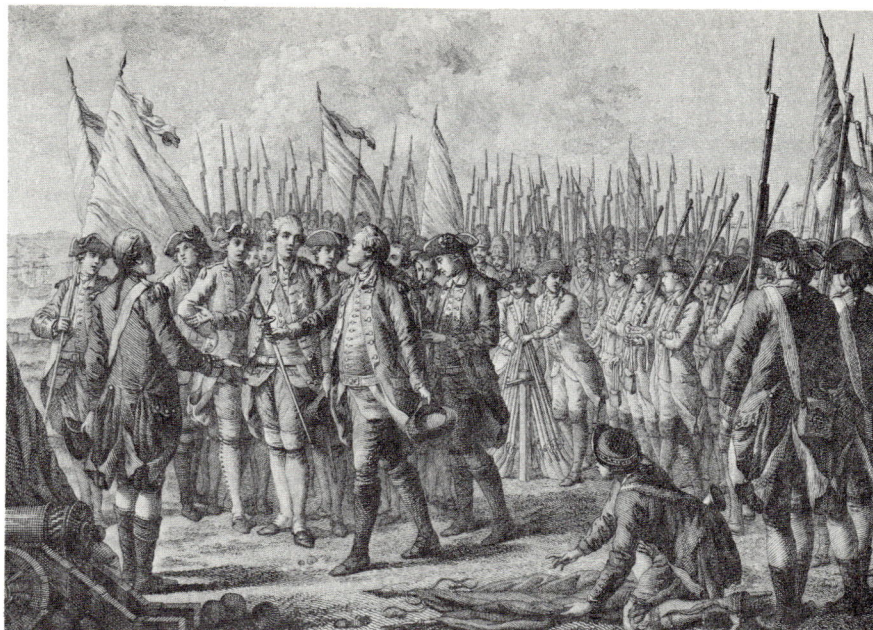

324
engraving

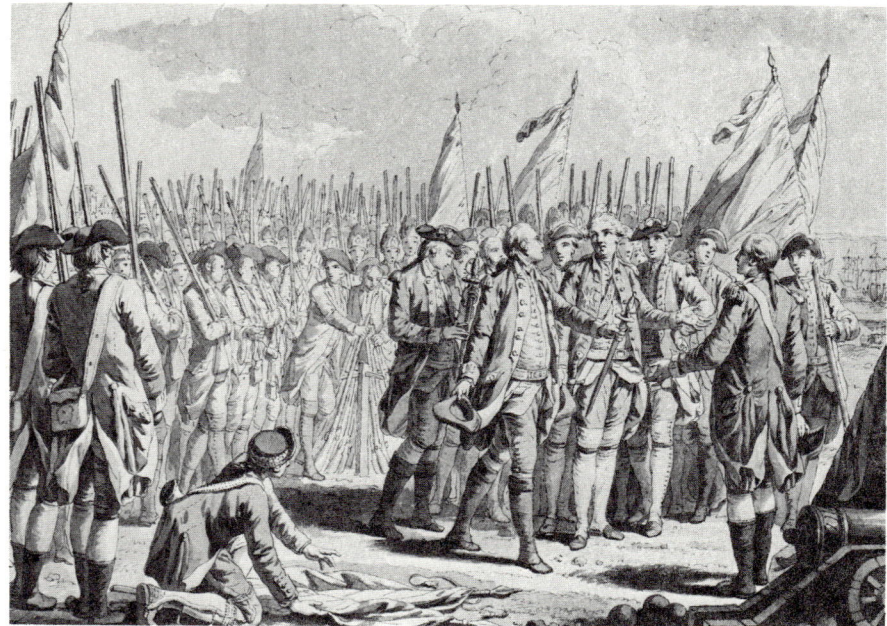

324
wash drawing

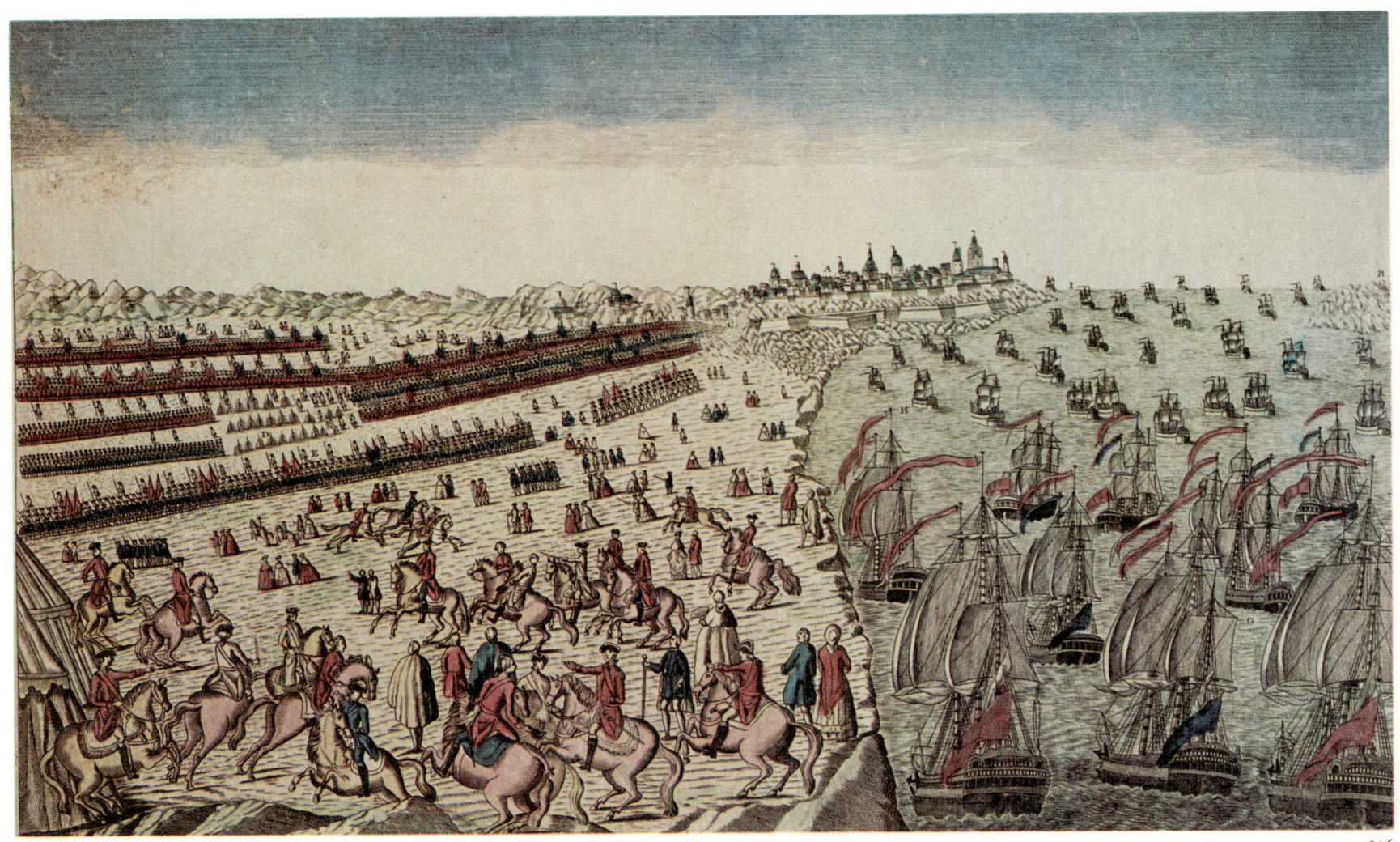

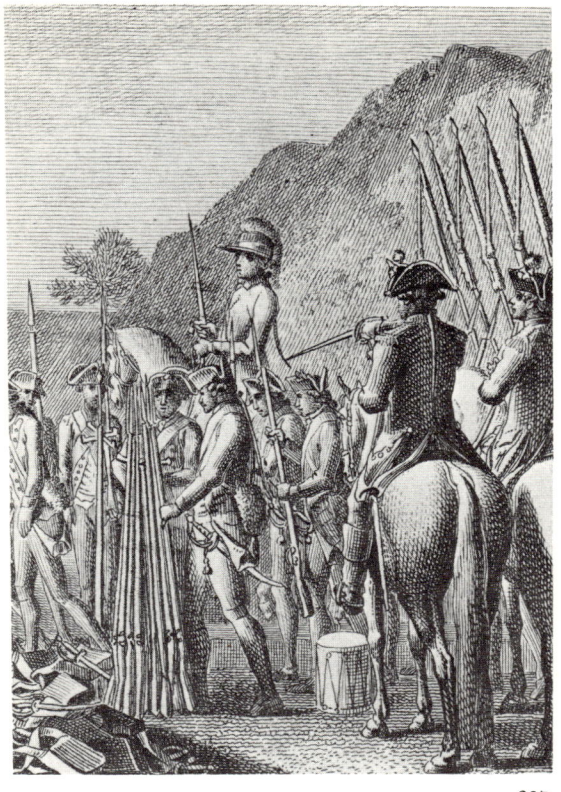

327

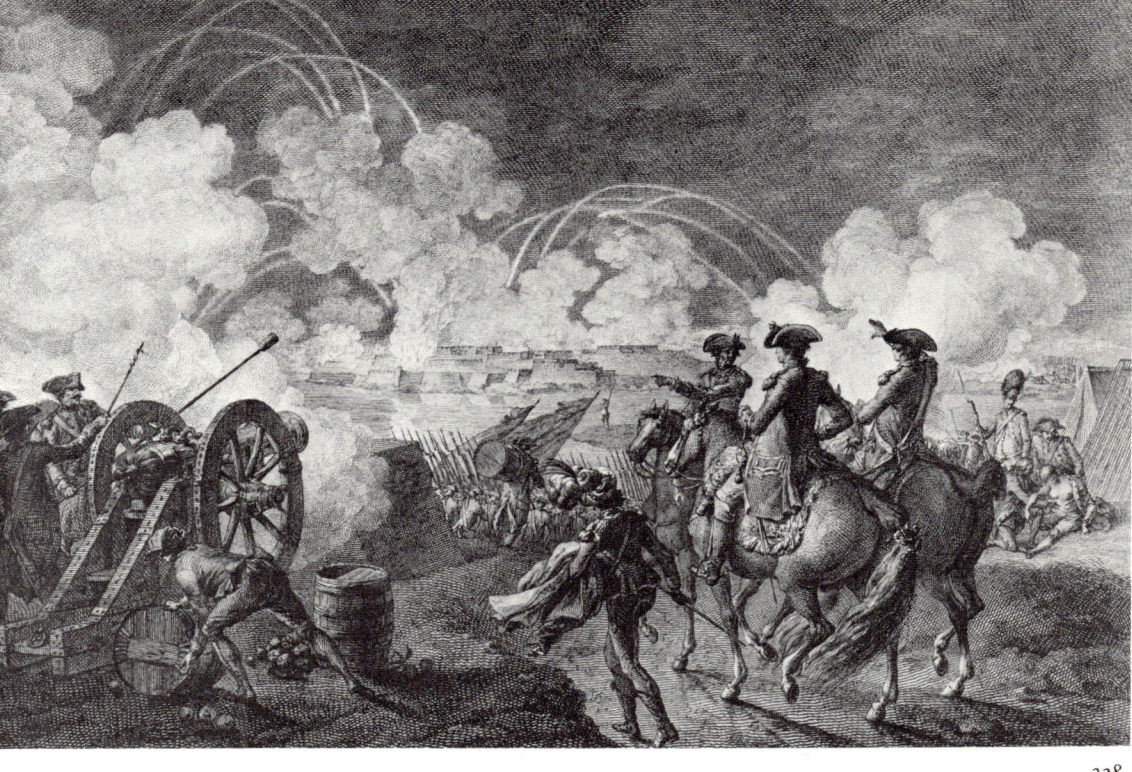

328

326
Reddition de l'Armée Angloises Commandée par Mylord Comte de Cornwallis aux Armees Combinées des Etats unis de l'Amerique et de France aux ordres des Generaux Washington et de Rochambeau a Yorck touwn et Glocester dans la Virginie. le 19 Octobr 1781. A Paris chez Mondhare rue St. Jean de Beauvais pres celle des Noyers. [1781?]

Etching (hand colored) 12½ x 20¼ in. (image)

This view of the surrender of the British to the combined American and French armies shows Yorktown in the background, with Gloucester on the point of land to the right of it. In the Chesapeake Bay sail the ships of the French Navy commanded by De Grasse. The American Army stands in columns to the left, and in front of them the British Army is seen marching out of Yorktown. The enemy's arms are stacked in bundles. Closer to the foreground is the French Army. The accompanying explanation describes the memorable event: "Ce jour à jamais memorables pour les Etats unis en ce qu'il assura definitivement leurs independances." This print was intended for use in a vue d'optique. From G&M.

327
Die Americaner machen den Lord Cornwallis mit seiner Armee zu Gefangnen, bey Yorktown den 19ten Octobr 1781. [1784]

Etching 2⅞ x 2 in. (image)

Number eleven in a series by "D[aniel N.] Chodowiecki inv. et del." German view of the surrender at Yorktown. LC–USZ62–39563

————Another copy. Engraved by D. Berger after Chodowiecki.

————Another impression. In Sprengel, *Allgemeines historisches Taschenbuch* (Berlin, 1784).

328
SIEGE DU FORT S. PHILIPPE. Dessiné par le Paon Peintre de S.A.S. Mgr. le Prince de Conde. Gravé par Godefroy de l'Academie Imperiale et Royale de Vienne, &c. A Paris

121

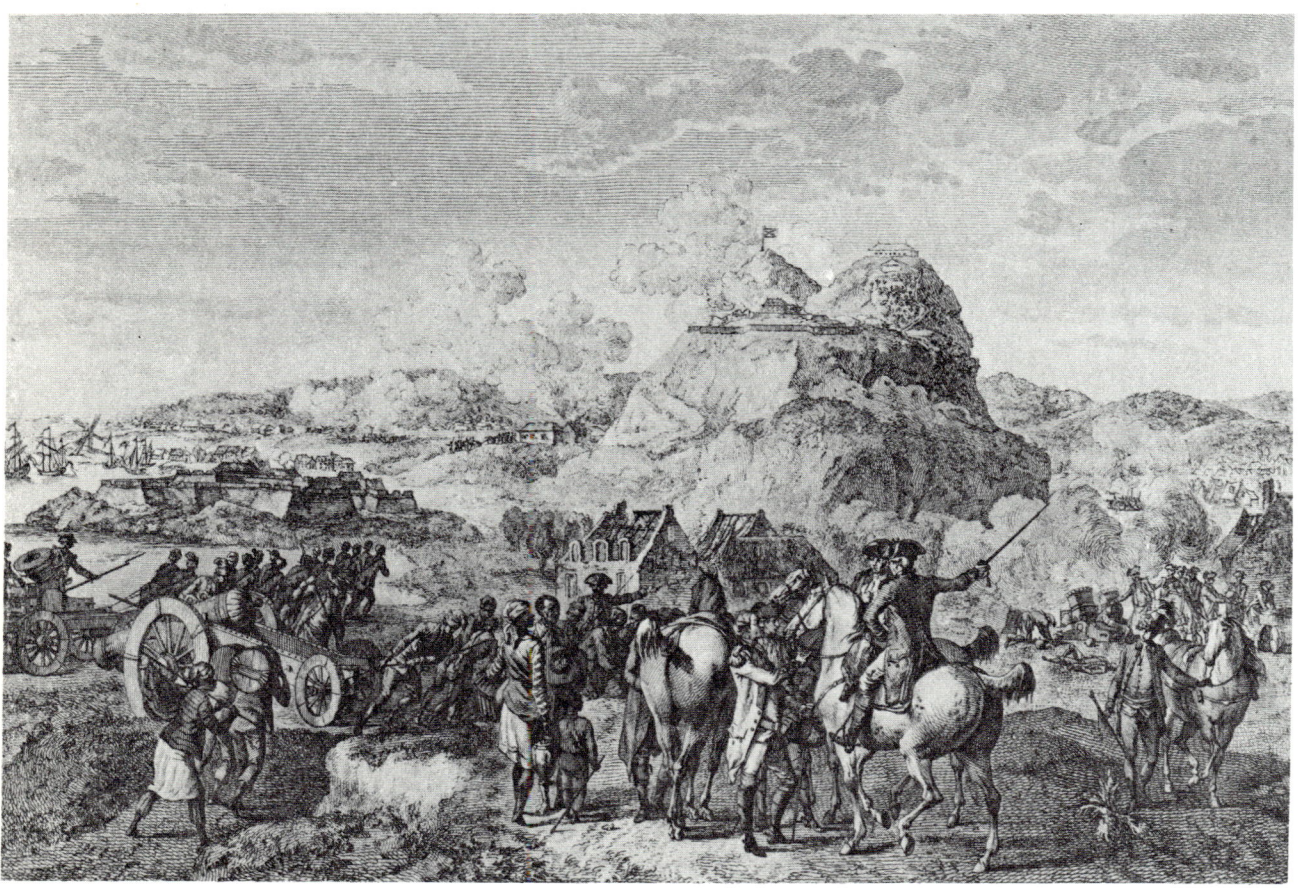

chez Mr. Godefroy, rue des Francs-bourgeois Porte St. Michel et chez Mr. Ponce Graveur de Mgr. le Comte d'Artois, rue Hiacinthe. A.P.D.R. [1784?]
Etching 7⅜ x 8⅛ in.

This picture shows the French Lt. Gen. Duc de Crillon watching the bombardment of Ft. St. Philip on the island of Minorca on the night of January 15, 1782. The British Gen. James Murray (1719–1794) had shut himself into the fort with a few men on August 20, 1781, and he successfully concealed his small, weak garrison behind massive fortifications. The French and Spanish forces never realized the English weakness until five months later on February 4, 1782, when 600 decrepit soldiers and sailors and about 100 Corsicans, Greeks, Turks, Moors, and Jews marched out and surrendered to 14,000 well-equipped men. The island remained under Spanish control by the peace treaty of 1783. From Ponce, *Recueil d'estampes représentant . . .* (Paris, 1784?), plate 12. *Collection de Vinck* 1187. LC–USZ62–45295

——————Another impression, two earlier states, and a wash drawing of the same picture are in copy 3, in the Rare Book Division.

329
ATTAQUE DE BRIMSTOMHILL. en l'Île St. Christophe, Vue prise entre le Fort Charles, et le Ravin de Molener. Dessiné par le Paon Peintre de S. a S Mgr. le Prince de Condé. Gravé par N. Ponce Graveur de Mgr. Comte d'Artois. A Paris chez Mr. Ponce, rue St. Hyacinte, maison de M. Debure. Et chez Mr. Godefroy, rue des Francs Bourgeois, Porte S. Michel. A.P.D.R. [1784?]
Etching 7 x 8¼ in.

The explanation below this print describes how the Marquis de Bouillé landed at Basseterre on January 11, 1782, to besiege the fortress of Brimstone Hill on St. Kitts.

Inside the fort were 1,442 British soldiers under the command of Sir Thomas Shirley and Gen. Simon Fraser. They gave themselves up as prisoners of war on February 12, 1782. The islands of St. Kitts and Nevis thereby came into the hands of the French. From Ponce, *Recueil d'estampes représentant ...* (Paris, 1784?) plate 13. *Collection de Vinck* 1188. LC–USZ62–45296

————Another impression, two earlier states, and a pen-and-ink drawing of the same are in copy 3, in the Rare Book Division.

330
The Gallant and Right Hon. Captain Lord Robert Manners Mortally Wounded, on board the Resolution, in the Glorious Victory obtained over the French Fleet, the 12th of April 1782, in the West Indies. Engraved for Barnard's New Complete & Authentic History of England. Hamilton delin. Pollard sculp.

Mixed method 12¼ x 8½ in.

Lord Robert Manners (1758–1782), captain of the *Resolution*, took part in the action off Cape Henry, September 4, 1781, and was with Admiral Hood at St. Kitts in January 1782. In the battle off Saints Passage, April 9–12, 1782, the 74-gun *Resolution* was in the center of the British line. Beneath the frame is the statement: "A more Exact Representation of An Affecting Event (which deprived this Country of a brave Officer) than is given in any other History of England whatever—." Barnard, *History of England* (London, 1783), opposite p. 697.

————Another copy with the title reading, "Lord Robert Manners Mortally Wounded, on board the Resolution, in the memorable Engagement between Admiral Rodney & Count de Grasse, in the West Indies, the 12th. of April 1782. Metz delin. Grignion sculp." Mixed method 10 x 6½ in.

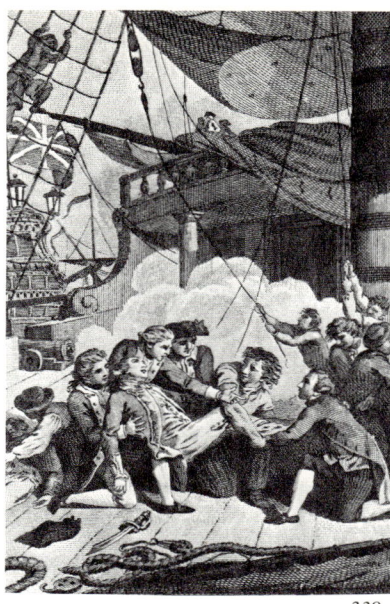
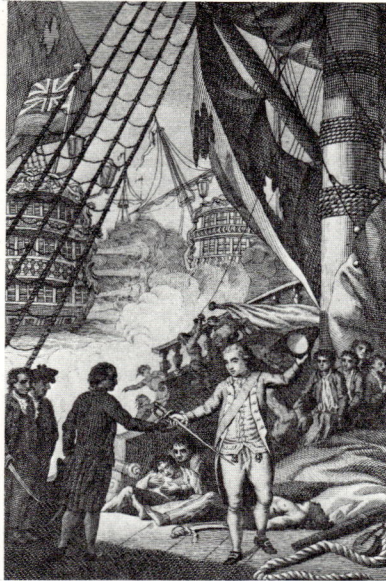
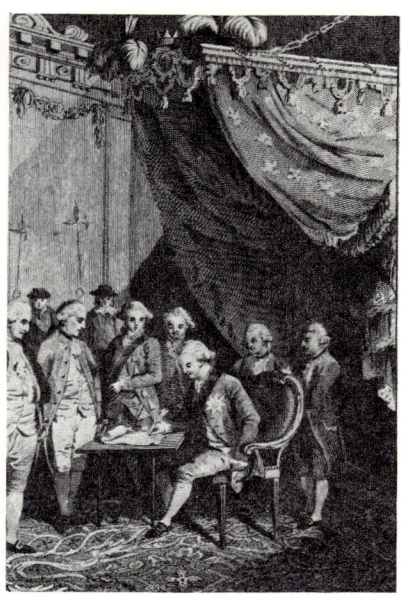

330 *331* *332*

From Raymond, *History of England* (London, 1784), p. 597. LC–USZ62–45214

————Another impression (hand colored).

331
Count de Grasse, the French Admiral, resigning his Sword to Admiral Rodney, after being defeated by that gallant Commander in the West Indies, on April 12th. 1782. Metz delin. Fiegl sculp. [1784]

Mixed method 10⅛ x 6⅞ in.

Comte de Grasse, the hero of the Yorktown capitulation, was captured aboard the battered *Ville de Paris* in the Battle off Saints Passage, April 12, 1782. Released on parole the following August, he served as an intermediary between the Governments of England and France during the preliminary stages of the peace negotiations. From Raymond, *History of England* (London, 1784), p. 595. LC–USZ62–45213

332
Mr. Fitzherbert the British Minister Plenipotentiary, with Gravier de Vergennes, and Le Compte d'Aranda Ministers Plenipotentiary of the Courts of France & Spain, Signing the Preliminary Articles of Peace at Versailles (on Jany. the 20th. 1783) previous to their final Ratification. Metz delin. Cook sculp. [1784]

Etching 9⅞ x 6½ in.

Alleyne Fitzherbert (1753–1839) replaced Grenville as minister plenipotentiary at Paris, August 1782. Raymond, *History of England* (London, 1784), p. 601. LC–USZ62–45215

————Another copy, with title reading, "The Preliminary Articles of Peace between Great Britain & France and Great Britain and Spain, Signed at Versailles Jany 20. 1783, by Mr. Fitzherbert his Britannic

Majesty's Ambassador & Minister Plenipotentiary, and the Minister's Plenipotentiary of the Courts of France & Spain—Which were RATIFIED in FORM on Feby the 3d. & 9th. 1783, the Exchanges being then made by and with the said Ambassadors. Engraved for BARNARD's New Complete & Authentic HISTORY of ENGLAND. Hamilton delin. Pollard sculp." [1783] Etching 12½ x 8½ in. From Barnard, *History of England* (London, 1783), opposite p. 699.

333–342
PRÉCIS DU TRAITÉ DE PAIX, Signé à Versailles le 3 Septembre 1783. N. Ponce, inv. et Sculpsit. A Paris chez Mr. Ponce, Graveur de Mgr. Comte d'Artois, Rue Ste. Hyacinthe, No. 19. et chez Mr. Godefroy, Graveur de Sa Majesté Imperiale, Rue des Francs-Bourgeois. A.P.D.R. [1784?]
Etching 7⅜ x 8¼ in.

Ten small pictures of Revolutionary War battles frame a pedestal upon which the names of French, American, Dutch, and Spanish officers killed or wounded are inscribed. Fame blows a trumpet from which hangs a flag listing in the left column the names of Louis XVI, De Vergennes, Montgomery, Warren, D'Estaing, Duchaffault, La Motte Piquet, D. Gálvez, and LaFayette. The right column lists Charles III, De Castries, De Ségur, Washington, Gates, Franklin, De Crillon, De Rochambeau, De Bouillé, D'Orvilliers, and De Suffren. The ten pictures represent various victories for the American side. The first in chronological order is the Battle of Trenton, won by Washington, December 26, 1776, (top row, second picture, 1¼ x 1 in. image). June 28, 1778, General Washington defeated Clinton at Monmouth, N. J., (top row, fourth picture, 1⅜ x 1 in. image). The Comte d'Estaing took the island of St. Vincent June 18, 1779, (bottom row, right 1¼ x 1¼ in. image). John Paul Jones' battle with the *Serapis* on September 23, 1779, is also commemorated (middle row, third picture, 1⅜ x 1 in. image), as is the blowing up of the British frigate *Quebec* on October 7, 1779, (middle row, second picture, 1⅜ x 1⅛ in. image). La Motte Piquet is pictured fighting off Martinique in the lee of Fort Royal in December of 1779 (top row, first picture, 1⅜ x 1 in. image). Also pictured is the capture of 57 ships by the combined French and American fleet on August 8, 1789, (middle row, first picture, 1⅛ x ¾ in. image). In the next picture, De Suffren's troops are seen storming the fort of Trincomalee; the French took this important port in the Indian Ocean from Sir Edward Hughes in late September 1782 (top row, third picture, 1¼ x ¾ in. image). In August 1782 La Perouse chased the British from Hudson Bay (middle row, fourth picture, 1⅜ x 1 in. image). The last picture celebrates the courage and ability of the Comte de Grimouard (1743–1794), who commanded the *Scipion* in the West Indies and engaged two British vessels, one with 98 cannons, in November of 1782 (bottom row, first picture, 1¼ x 1¼ in. image). From Ponce, *Recueil d'estampes représentant* ... (Paris, 1784?), plate 16. LC-USZ62-45297

——————Another impression, two earlier states, and a wash drawing of the same are in copy 3, in the Rare Book Division.

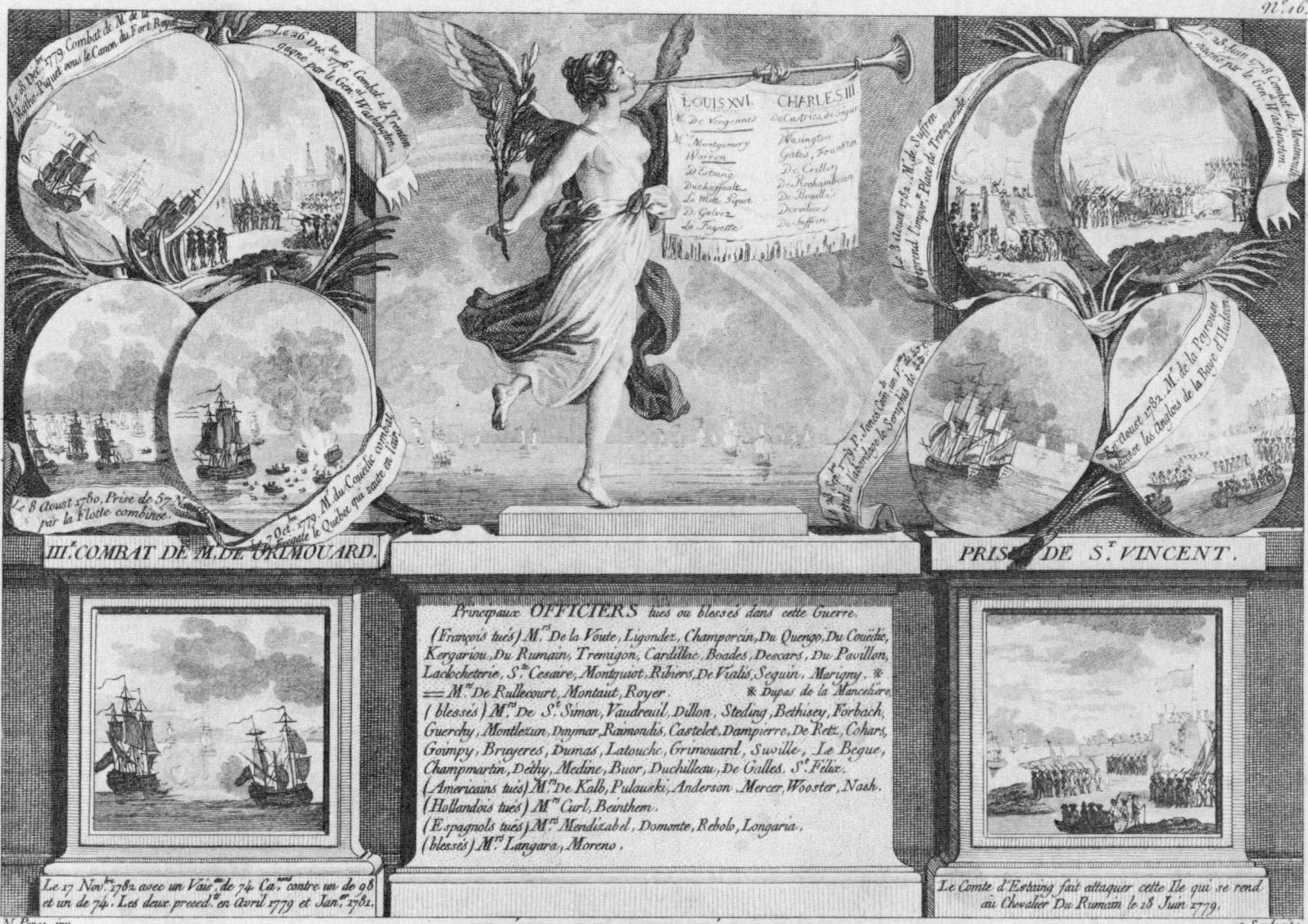

PRÉCIS DU TRAITÉ DE PAIX,
Signé à Versailles le 3 Septembre 1783.

Les Provinces de Massachusset, Connecticut, Hampshire, Plantations de Providence, Rhode-Island, New-Iork, New-Jersey, Delawarre, Pensilvanie, Maryland, Virginie, Caroline Sept.le, Caroline Merid.le et de la Géorgie sont reconnues Etats libres et indépendants. S. M. Britanique renonce pour elle et ses successeurs à toute espece de souveraineté sur ces Pays, et sur les Iles qui bordent leurs Côtes jusqu'à la distance de 20 Lieues. Les bornes de cette nouvelle République sont fixées, au Nord, par la Riviere S.te Croix et par une ligne tirée à travers les Lacs jusqu'à celui des Bois, à l'Ouest, par le Fleuve Missisipi; au Sud par les Florides aux-quelles on donne pour limites la Riviere Marys, et le 31.me degré de Latitude; et à l'Est par la Mer.

L'Angleterre cede à l'Espagne l'Ile Minorque, la Floride Orien.le et la Floride Occid.le Elle conserve la liberté de la Coupe du bois de Campêche, mais cette liberté est circonscrite entre les Rivieres Belise et Rio-Hondo.

L'Angleterre cede à la France l'Ile de Tabago, le Sénégal et ses dépendances, les Forts de S.t Louis, Podor, Galam, d'Arguin, et Portendic; une étendue plus considérable à Terreneuve pour y Pêcher et sécher la Morue, les Districts de Bahour et Velanour aux environs de Pondichery, et les quatres Magans qui avoisinent Karikal &c. Elle annulle les clauses des derniers Traités relatives aux Ouvrages du Port de Dunkerque, aux Fortifications et aux Garnisons des Iles S.t Pierre et Miquelon.

La Hollande cede à l'Angleterre la Ville de Négapatnam sur la Côte de Coromandel, ou un equivalent. Restitution mutuelle entre les Puissances belligérantes, des autres Conquêtes faites pendant la Guerre.

TABLE DES ESTAMPES QUI COMPOSENT CETTE SUITE.

- N.os 1. Frontispice et Précis de la Guerre.
- 2. Origine de la Revolution.
- 3. Journée de Lexington.
- 4. Reddition de l'Armée du Gén.l Burgoyne.
- N.os 5. Prise de la Dominique.
- 6. Prise du Sénégal.
- 7. Prise de la Grenade.
- 8. Prise de Pensacola.
- N.os 9. Prise de Tabago.
- 10. Reddition de l'Armée de Cornowallis.
- 11. Surprise de S.t Eustache.
- 12. Siege du Fort S.t Philippe.
- N.os 13. Attaque de Brimstomhill.
- 14. Carte des Etats unis.
- 15. Cartes particulieres.
- 16. Précis du Traité de Paix.

A.P.D.R.

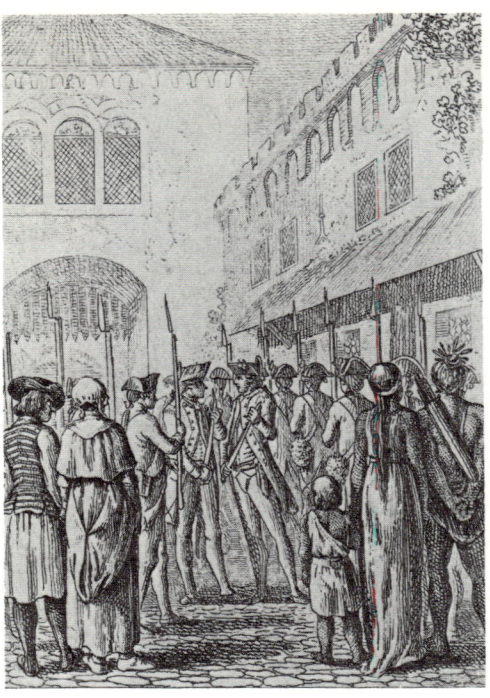

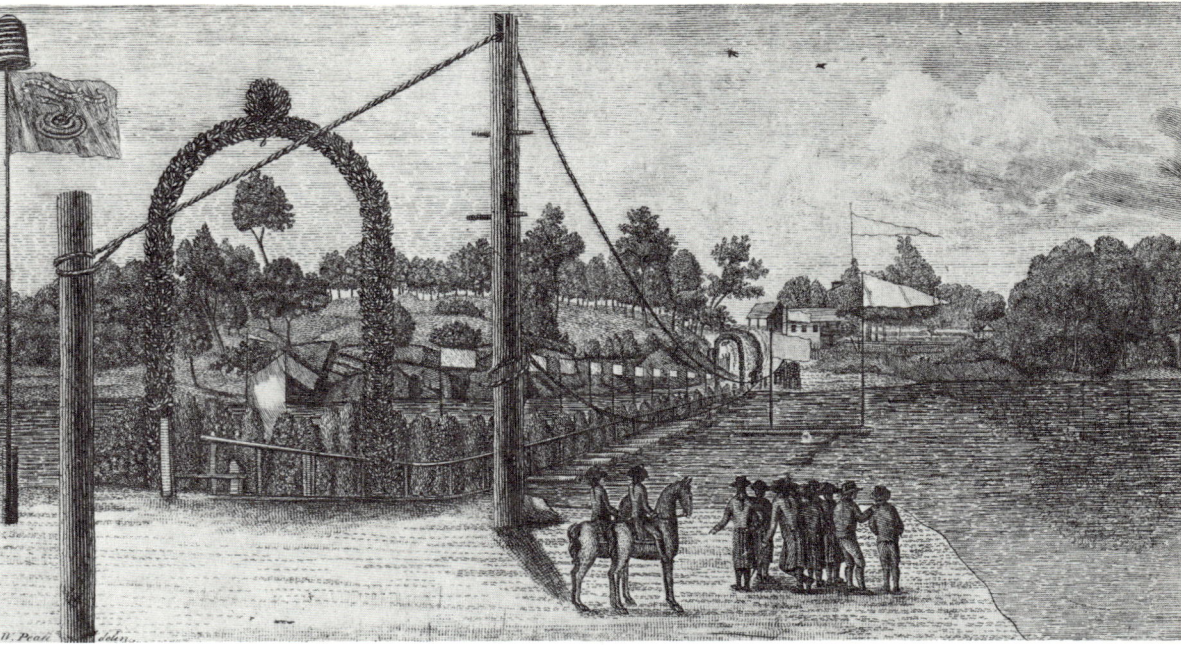

343

344

345

343
Ende der Feindseeligkeiten. Die Engländer räumen den Americanern Neu-Yorck ein—1783. [1784]

Etching 2⅞ x 2 in. (image)

Number 12 in a series by "D[aniel N] Chodowiecki inv. et del." Germain view of the evacuation of New York on November 25, 1782. LC–USZ62–19421

───────Another copy. Engraved by D. Berger after Chodowiecki.

───────Another impression. In Sprengel, *Allgemeines historisches Taschenbuch* (Berlin, 1784).

344
Amelia: or the faithless Briton. J. Trenchard Delineate & Sculpst. [1787]

Etching 5 x 3⅜ in. (image)

Depicts a scene from a novel serialized in *The Columbian Magazine*. Amelia, a virtuous girl from a farm in New York, has been seduced by a British officer named Doliscus. When she has a child by him, he tries to escape to London, but the girl follows him. He spirits her away from his London estate and leaves her in a distant slum. The picture shows Amelia about to take her own life with a cup of laudanum when her father, Horatio Blyfield, enters the door. "(*To be continued*)!" *The Columbian Magazine*, October 1787, frontispiece.

345
An East View of GRAY'S FERRY, near Philadelphia, with the TRIUMPHAL ARCHES, &c. erected for the Reception of General Washington, April 20th. 1789. C. W. Peale delin. J[ames] Trenchard Sculp.

Etching 4¼ x 7 in.

With the help of Charles Willson Peale, the owners of the bridge at Gray's Ferry, Pa., prepared to receive Washington during his trip to New York in 1789. They adorned the structure with laurel, cedar, banners, and flags. Flags of the 11 States that had ratified the Constitution were strung across the length of the bridge, and four other flags proclaimed "The New Era," "May Commerce Flourish," "Don't Tread on Me," and the rising sun empire. The pole from which the familiar rattlesnake flag is flying holds a large liberty

cap on top. The flag on the barge anchored in midstream to the right of the bridge was the American Union Flag. From *The Columbian Magazine*, May 1789. Stauffer, 3290.
LC–USZ62–342

346
View of the TRIUMPHAL ARCH, and the manner of receiving General Washington at Trenton, on his Route to New-York, April 21st. 1789.

Etching 3¾ x 6¾ in. (image)

The bridge over Assunpink Creek at Trenton, N. J., was decorated in honor of Washington's repulse of an attacking British column at that site on January 2, 1777. The arch depicted here was built at the time of his triumphal journey from Mount Vernon to New York for his inauguration. It measured about 12 feet in length and 20 feet in height and was an ediface of greenery. Probably engraved by James Trenchard. From *The Columbian Magazine*, May 1789. Stauffer, 3291.
LC–USZ62–338

347
View of the triumphal ARCH and COLONNADE, erected in BOSTON, [in honour of the PRESIDENT of the UNITED STATES.] Engrav'd by S. Hill. [1790]

Etching 4⅛ x 6⅝ in. (image)

This arch, erected in Boston for Washington's visit to that city in October 1779, reached across the street in front of the statehouse. The inscription visible here reads: "TO THE MAN WHO UNITES ALL HEARTS." On the opposite side were the words: "TO COLUMBIA'S FAVORITE SON." The panel to the right shows the arms of the United States, the State of Massachusetts, and France. Washington reported the inscription in the wreath of laurel as: "BOSTON RELIEVED, MARCH 17th, 1776." *The Massachusetts Magazine*, January 1790, frontispiece. Stauffer, 1392. LC–USZ62–31137

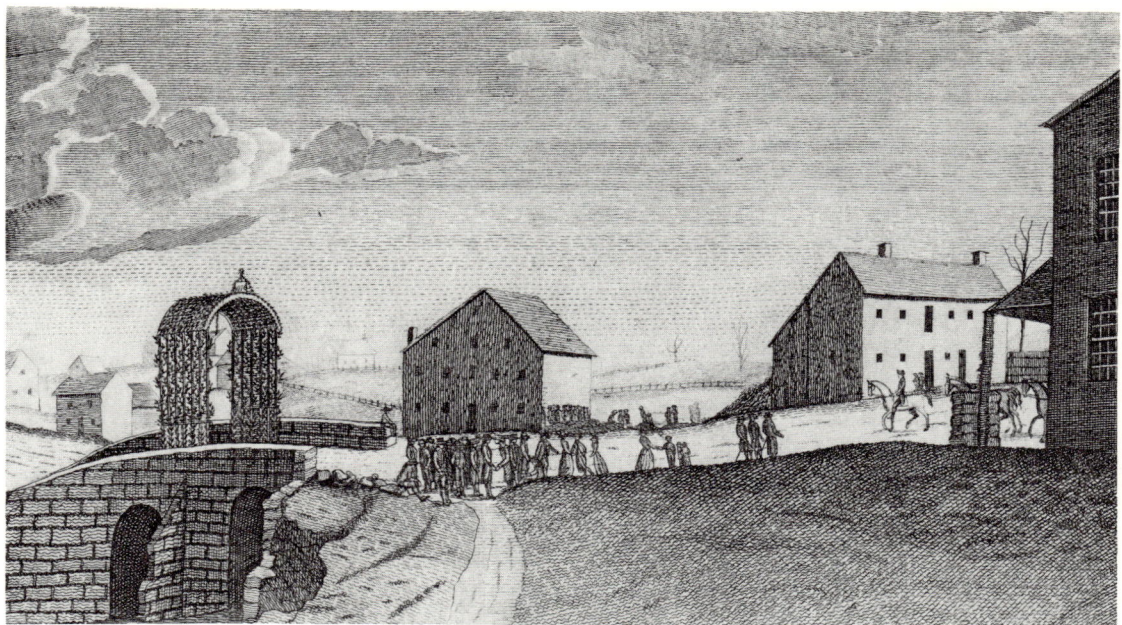
346

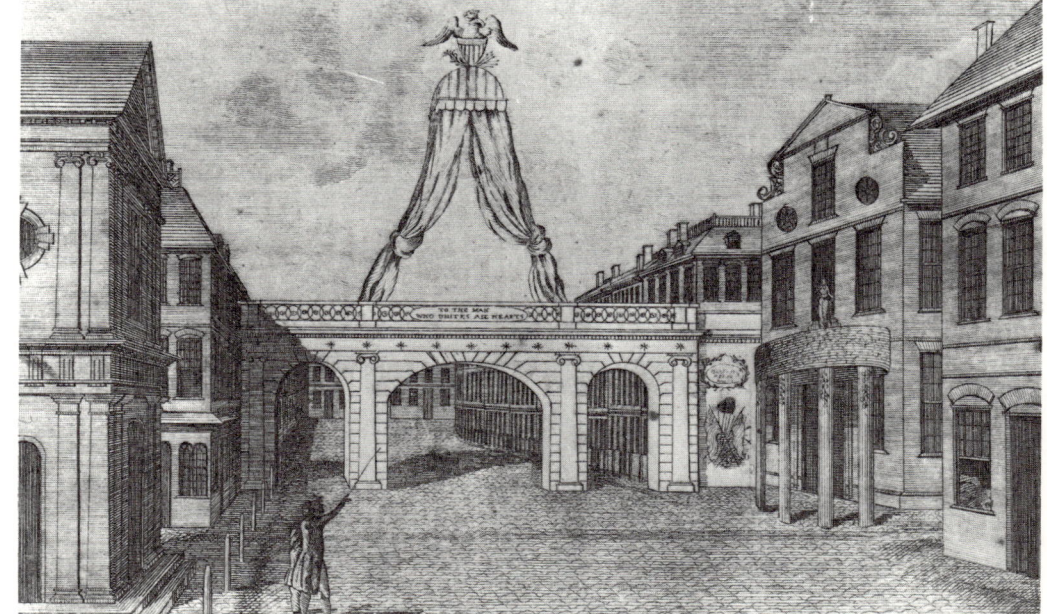
347

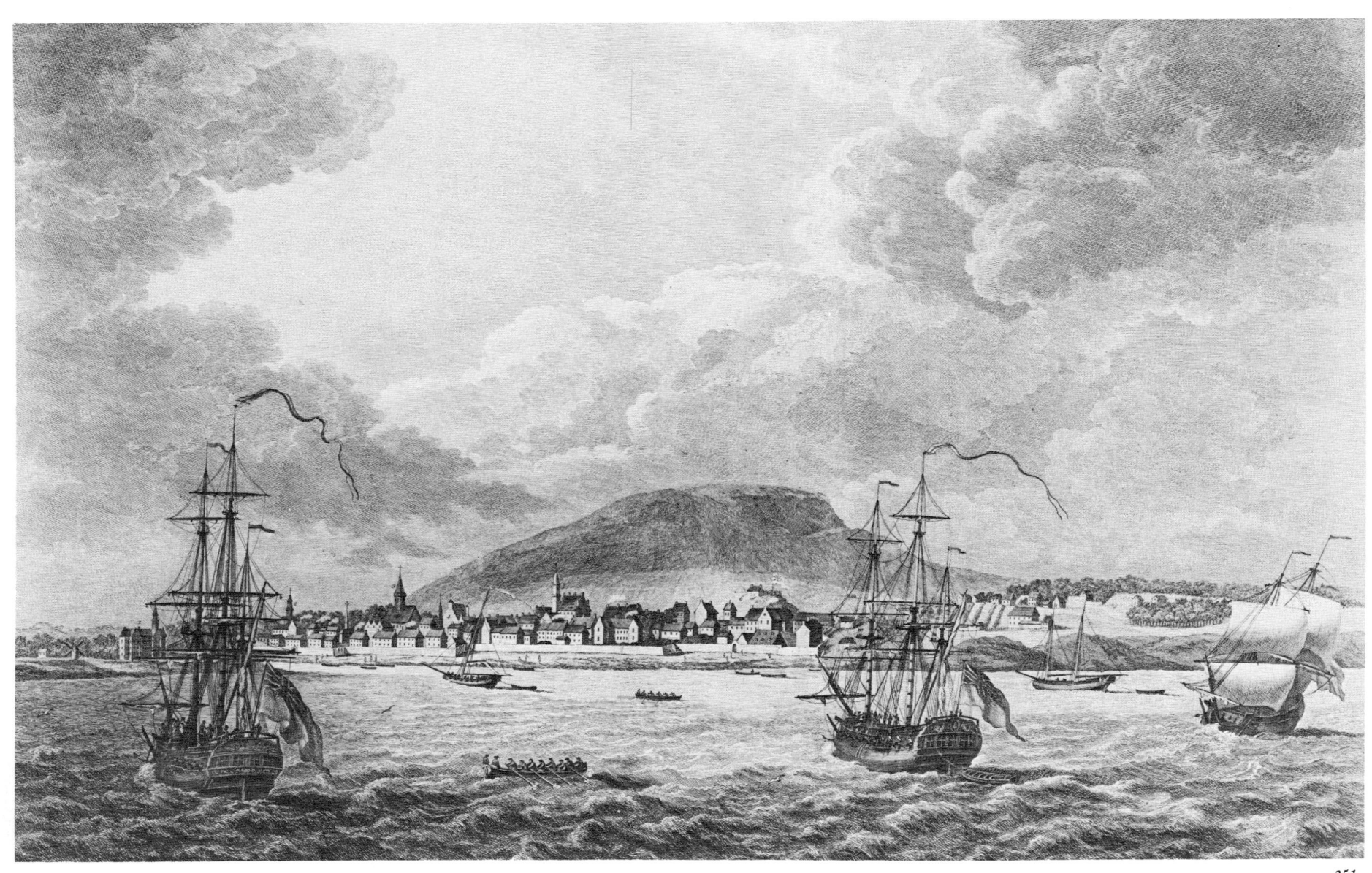

(See next page for additional views)

Chapter III

Views

SAINT LAWRENCE RIVER AND GULF

Upper Regions and Montreal

348

[Englishmen trade with Indians in a wilderness—a cartouche] LONDON, Published as the Act directs Feby. 25. 1777. by WM. FADEN, Corner of St. Martin's Lane, Charing-Cross.

Etching 7½ x 11 in. (image)

Englishmen barter with Indians for furs in the foreground. In the background to the right is a fort flying the British flag. From "A Map of the Inhabited Part of Canada ... with the Frontiers of New York and New England ... By Claude Joseph Sauthier," in Faden, *North American Atlas* (London, 1777), no. 4. LC–USZ62–45595

349

A View of ST. JOHN'S, upon the RIVER SORELL, in CANADA, with the Redoubts, Works, &c. Taken in the Year 1776, during the late War in America. Publish'd as the Acts direct, Jany. 1st. 1789, by William Lane Leadenhall Street, London.

Etching 9¼ x 16¾ in.

Strategically located on the Richelieu or Sorel River between Lake Champlain and the St. Lawrence River, St. John was a settlement consisting primarily of fortifications. The British built ships there for use on Lake Champlain. Brig. Gen. Richard Montgomery led an attack on the fort, capturing it in November 1775, but the British retook St. John the following year. From Anburey, *Travels Through the Interior Parts of America*, v. 1 (London, 1789), opposite p. 136. LC–USZ62–45545

350

A Perspective View of MONTREAL in Canada. [1765]

Etching 6⅜ x 10½ in.

The capture of St. John left Montreal vulnerable to American attack. The low lying city, located on an island, was captured November 13, 1775, two days after Brig. Gen. Richard Montgomery landed there with about 1,200 men, but the Americans held Montreal for only a few months. Having failed in their efforts to take Quebec, the British were able to bring up reinforcements and drive their attackers out of Canada. From *The Universal Magazine*, 1765, p. 361. LC–USZ62–46311

351

An East View of MONTREAL, in Canada. Vue Orientale de Montréal, en Canada. Drawn on the SPOT by Thomas Patten Engraved by P. Canot. London Printed for John Bowles at No. 13 in Cornhill, Robert Sayer at No. 53 in Fleet Street, Thos. Jefferys the corner of St. Martins Lane in the Strand, Carington Bowles at No. 69 in St. Pauls Church Yard, and Henry Parker at No. 82 in Cornhill. [1768]

Etching 14¼ x 21 in.

A legend below the picture identifies the General Hospital, the "Recollects," St. Sulpicius, the nunnery, the Jesuit's Church, and the fort. *Scenographia Americana* (1768). LC–USZ62–45324

352

A Perspective View of the Town and Fortifications of Montreal in Canada. D. Pomarede Sculp. [1774]

Etching 5¾ x 8⅜ in.

The St. Lawrence River is in the foreground. From *The Annual Register* (Dublin, 1774), p. 407. LC–USZ62–45207

353

View of the Town &c of Montreal. Aitkin Sc. [1775]

Etching 2½ x 4 in. (image)

Insert on a map entitled "Plan of the Town & Fortifications of Montreal, or Ville Marie in Canada." Engraved for *The Pennsylvania Magazine*, 1775, p. 517. Stauffer, 7. LC–USZ62–45558

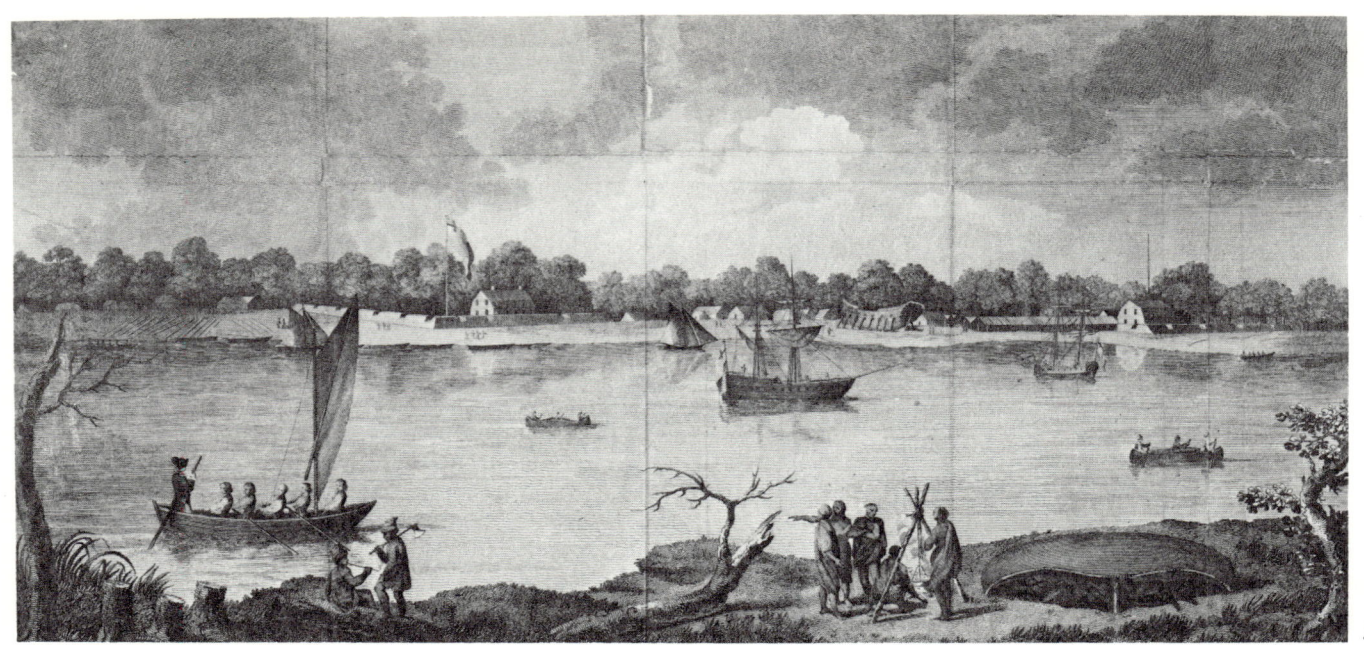

349

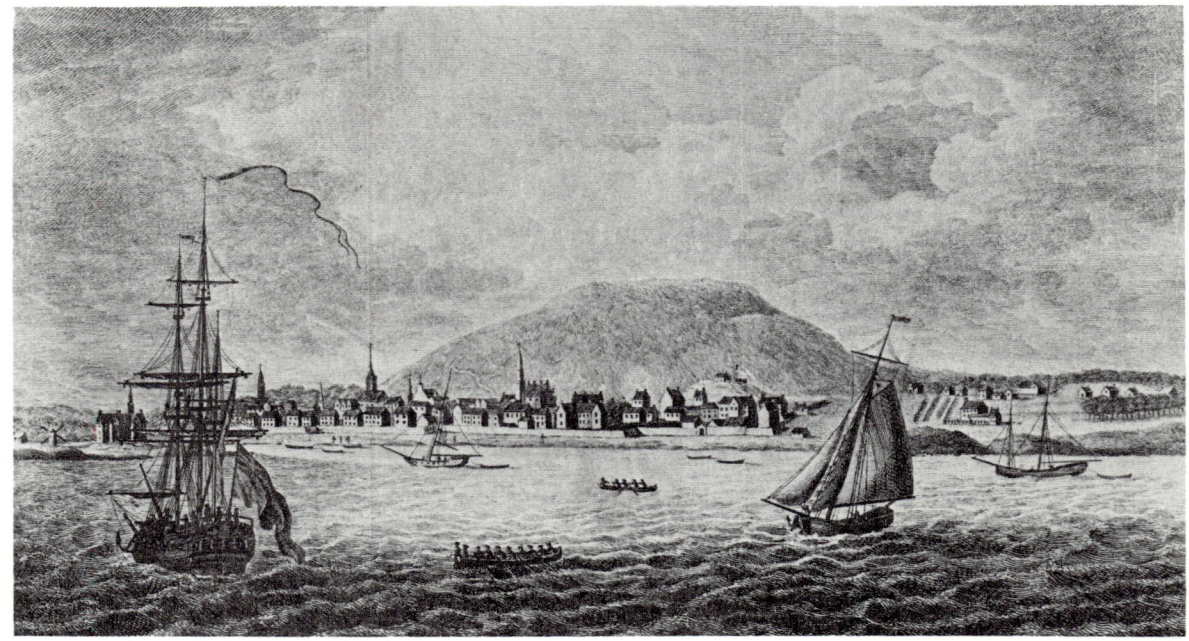

350

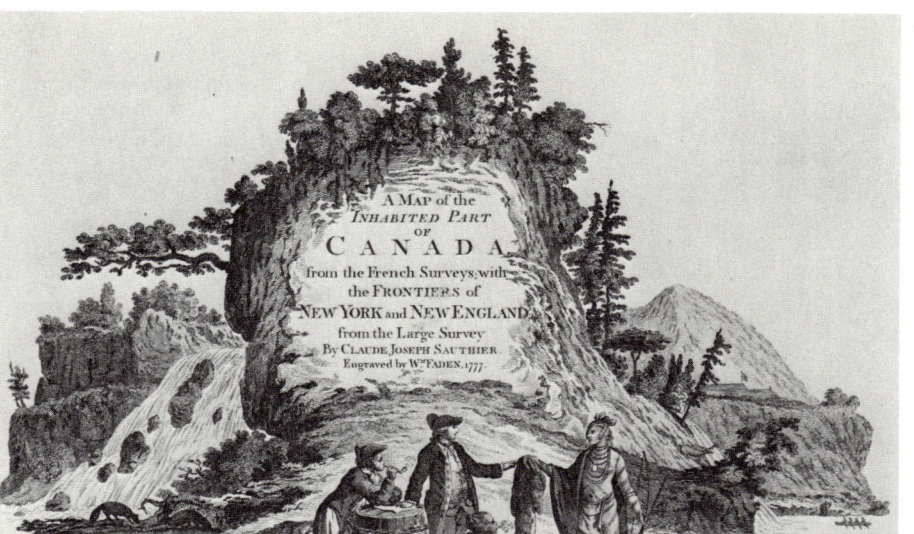

348

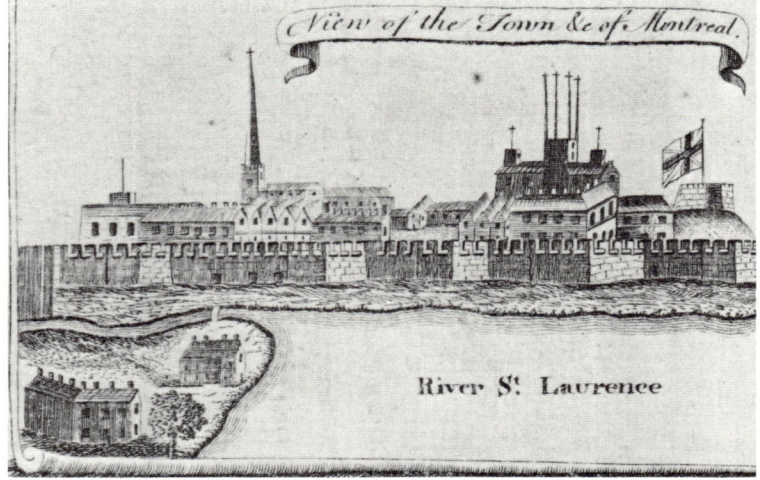

353

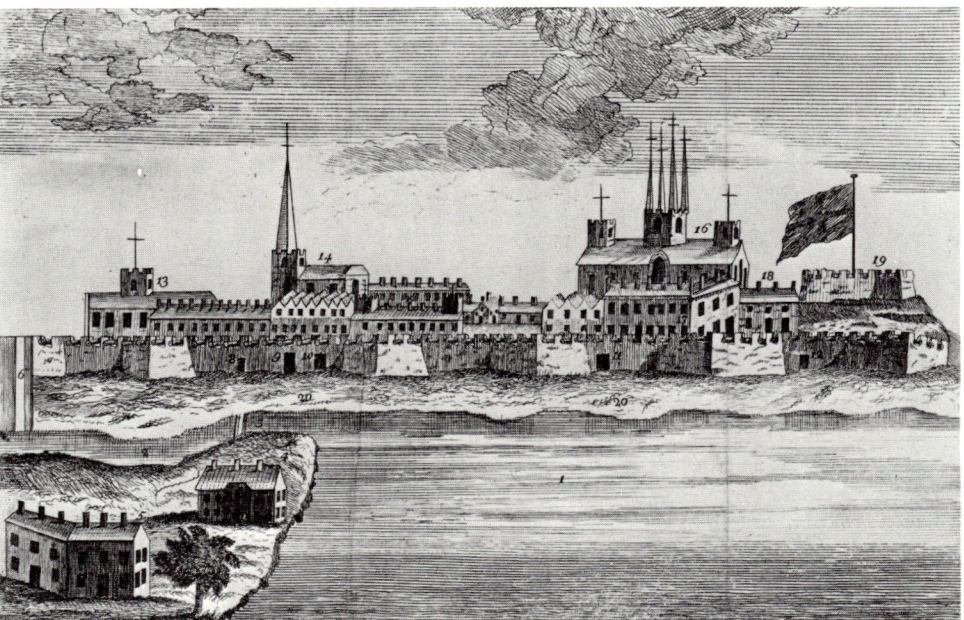

352

131

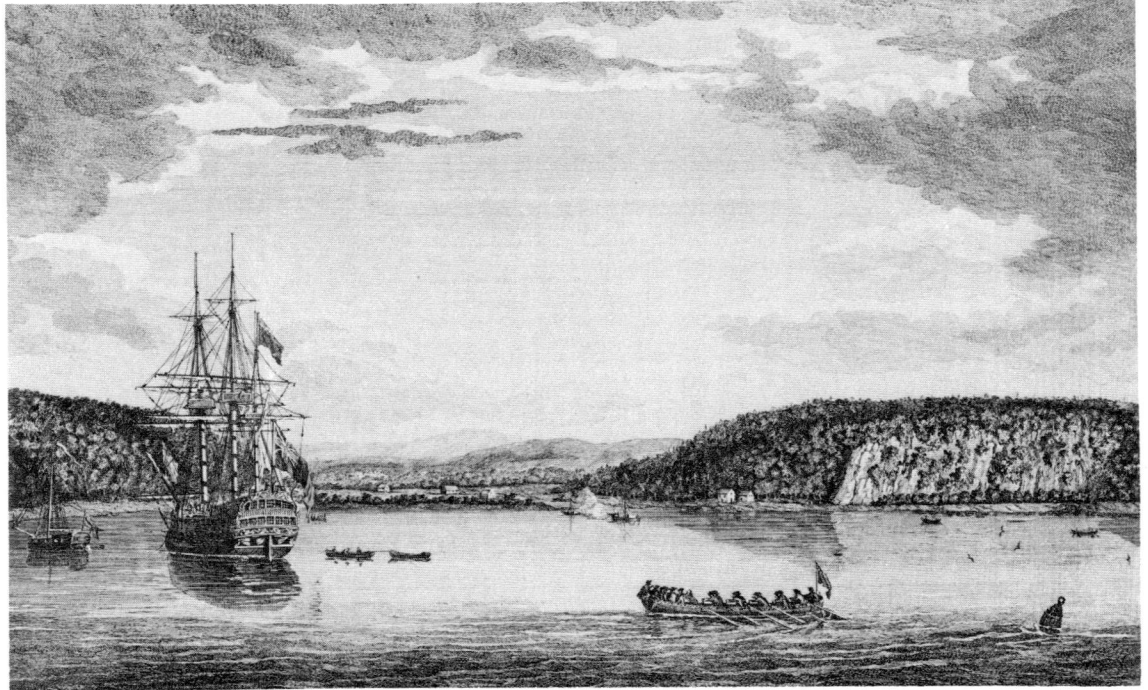

354

354

A View of Cape Rouge or Carouge, Nine Miles above the City of Quebec on the North Shore of the River ST. LAURENCE. From this place 1500 chosen Troops at the break of Day fell down the River on the Ebb of Tide to the place of Landing 13 Sept. 1759. Vue de Cap Rouge vulgairement Carouge, a 9 Miles au dessus de la Ville de Québec. Sur le bord septentrional de la RIVIERE de ST. LAURENT. C'est de Carouge que 1500 Hommes de Troupes choisies descendirent avec La Marée au Lieu de debarquement 13 Sept. 1759. Drawn on the spot by Capt. Hervey Smyth. Engraved by Peter Mazell. London Printed for John Bowles at No. 13 in Cornhill, Robert Sayer at No. 53 in Fleet Street, Thos. Jefferys the corner of St. Martins Lane in the Strand, Carington Bowles at No. 69 in St. Pauls Church Yard, and Henry Parker at No. 82 in Cornhill. [1768]

Etching 14¼ x 21 in.

From *Scenographia Americana* (1768). LC–USZ62–45581

Quebec

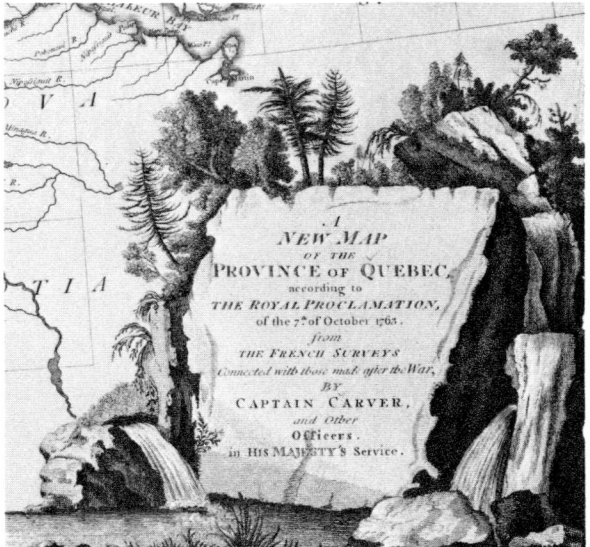

355

355

[A view of the countryside near Quebec—a cartouche] BY CAPTAIN CARVER. London, Printed for Robt. Sayer and John Bennett, Map and Print sellers, No 53 in Fleet Street, as the Act directs 16th February 1776.

Etching 7¼ x 8 in. (image)

A rocky, woodland scene represents Canada. From "A New Map of the Province of Quebec" in Jefferys, *The American Atlas* (London, 1776), no. 19. This cartouche also appears in the 1778 and 1782 editions. Negative in G&M.

——————Another impression. In Faden, *North American Atlas* (London, 1777), no. 3.

356

[A mountain landscape in Quebec—a cartouche]
1777
   Etching 3¾ x 6¾ in.

A wilderness scene set into a map entitled "Nouvelle Carte de la Province de Quebec." In Le Rouge, *Atlas Ameriquain Septentrional* (Paris, 1778–92), no. 7. LC–USZ62–45600

357

A View of the City of QUEBEC, the Capital of Canada, taken partly from Pointe des Peres, and partly on Board the Vanguard Man of War, by Captain Hervey Smyth. Vue de la Ville de QUÉBEC, Capitale du Canada. Prise en partie de la Pointe des Peres, et en partie àbord de l'Avantgarde Vaisseau de Guerre, par le Cape. Hervey Smyth P. Benazech Sculp. London Printed for John Bowles at No. 13 in Cornhill, Robert Sayer at No. 53 in Fleet Street, Thos. Jefferys the corner of St. Martins Lane in the Strand, Carrington Bowles at No. 69 in St. Pauls Church Yard, and Henry Parker at No. 82 in Cornhill. [1768]
   Etching 14½ x 21 in.

This view and many others of Quebec drawn at the time of the French and Indian War reappeared during the American Revolution as British artists attempted to celebrate the repulse of an American attacking force before the city on December 31, 1775. It contains the following dedication:

To the Right Honourable William Pitt One of his Majesties most Honourable Privy Council & Principal Secretary of State. These SIX VIEWS of the most remarkable places in the Gulf and River of St. Laurence are most humbly Inscribed by his most Obedient humble servant Hervey Smith. Aid du Camp to the late GENL. WOLFE.

From *Scenographia Americana* (1768).
LC–USZ62–45579

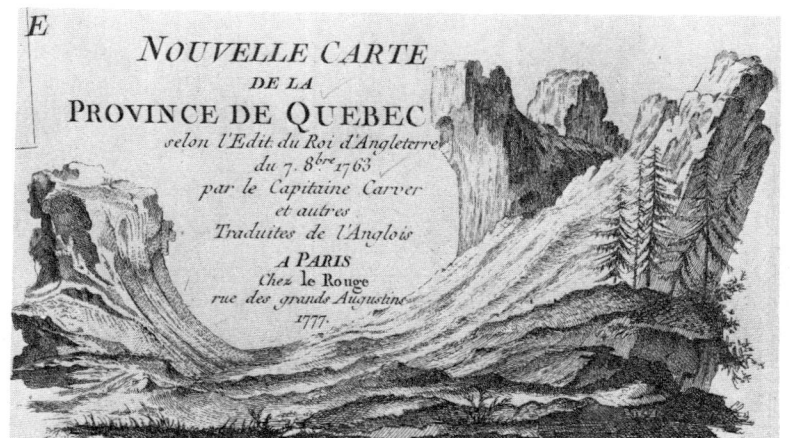
356

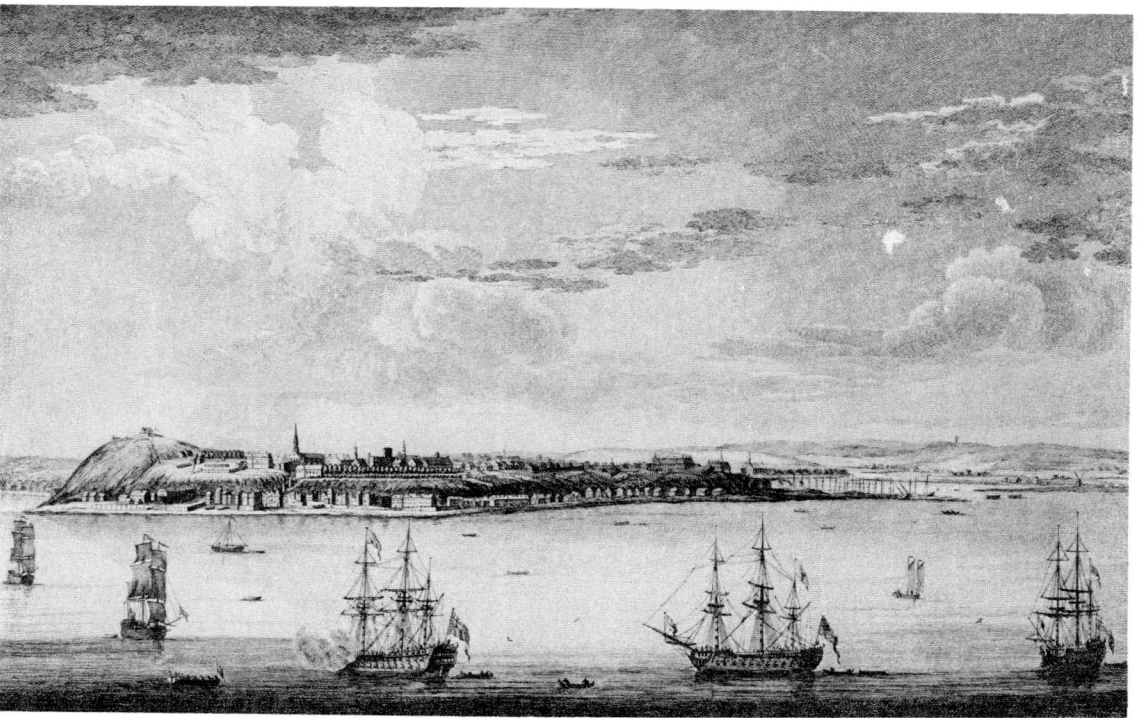
357

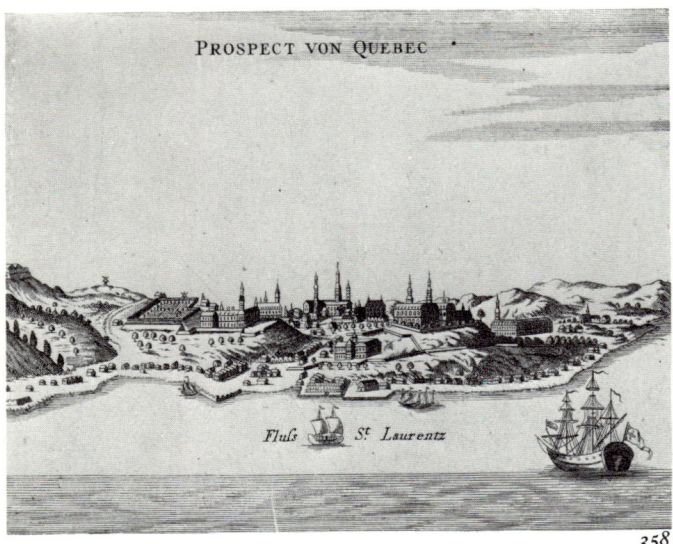

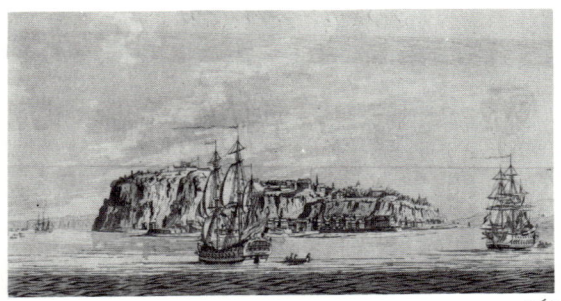

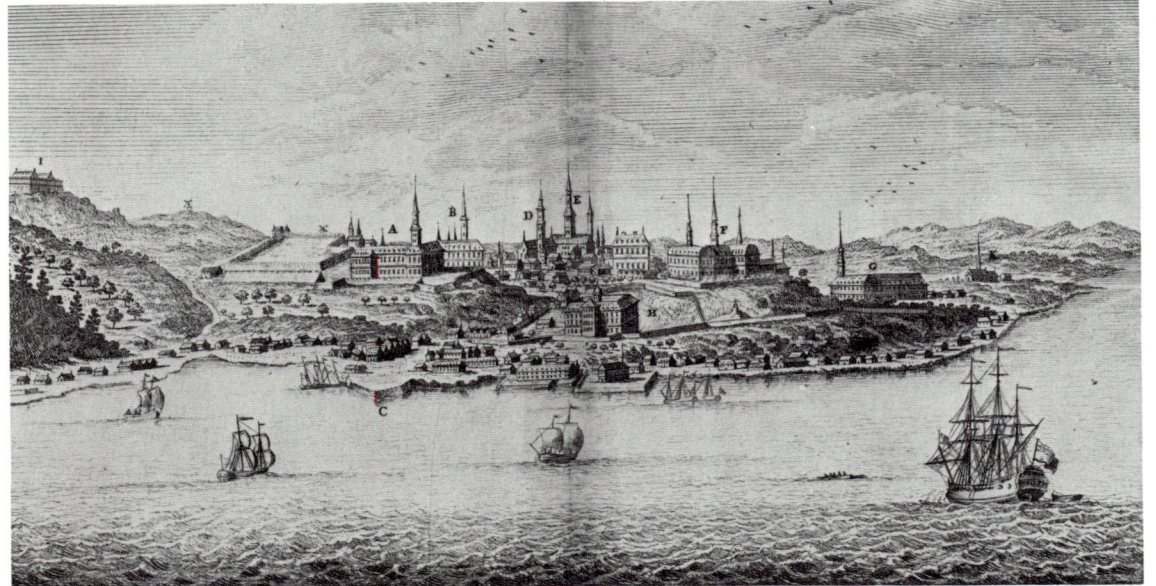

358

359

362

358
PROSPECT VON QUEBEC. [1776]
Etching 5⅝ x 7 in. (image)

From Korn, *Geschichte der Kriege* (Nürnberg, 1776), frontispiece. LC–USZ62–45375

————Another impression. In P&P under "Anonymous—Q." LC–USZ62–45375

359
QUEBEC [1777]
Etching 7⅜ x 10¾ in.

A legend at the top of the picture reads as follows:

    A. Il Forte B. I Recolletti C. La Piattaforma
    D. I Gesuiti E. La Cattedrale F. Il Seminario
    G. L'Hotel Dieu H. Il Palazzo del Vescovo
    I. Il Ridotto K. La Spedale

From *Atlante dell' America* ... (Livorno, 1777), no. 7½. LC–USZ62–46020

360
QUEBEC. [1777]
Etching 4¾ x 6½ in. (image)

View of the city and fortifications of Quebec from across the St. Lawrence River. In the foreground left is a large ship flying the British flag; the city is to the right. From Fenning, *Neue Erdbeschreibung von Amerika* (Gottingen und Leipzig, 1777), p. 76. Similar to item 367.

361
A View of QUEBEC from the Bason. Royce Sc. [1778]
Etching 6¾ x 9½ in.

A large British ship appears in the left foreground. Panoramic view from Russell, *History of America* (London, 1778), opposite p. 365. Similar to item no. 367 but a closer view.

362

A View of Quebec from the South East. [From surveys taken by Samuel Holland, engraved by J. F. W. Des Barres, 177?]

Aquatint with etching 15 x 23¾ in. (image)

Barges carrying soldiers are at the extreme left. *The Atlantic Neptune.* Phillips 1198, v. 2, no. 6. LC–USZ62–46047

———Another impression. LeGear 10323, v. 2, no. 3a.

363

Vue de la basse Ville à Quebec vers le fleuve St. Laurent. Gravé par François Xav. Habermann [177?]

Etching (hand colored) 12½ x 16¾ in.

German view of the city of Quebec. Probably taken from a European print. LC–USZ62–15753

364

VUË DE LA RUE DES RECOLETS DE QUEBECK Prospect der Strasse, gegen der Kirche der Recolecten in der obern Stadt zu Quebec. Vuë de la Rue des Recolets dans la haute Ville de Quebec. Se vend à Augsbourg au Negoce commun de l'Academie Imperiale d'Empire des Arts libereaux avec Privilege de Sa Majesté Imperiale et avec Defense ni d'en faire ni de vendre les Copies. Gravé par Francois Xav. Habermann. [177?]

Etching (hand colored) 12½ x 16½ in.

Title above picture is mirror image. From "Collection des prospects." LC–USZ62–45385

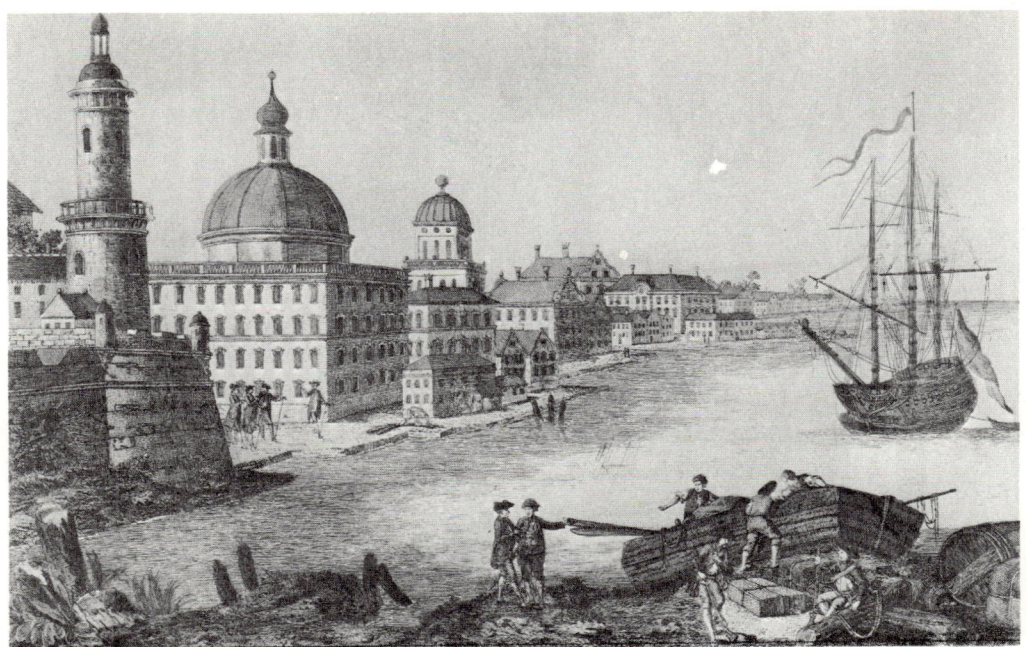

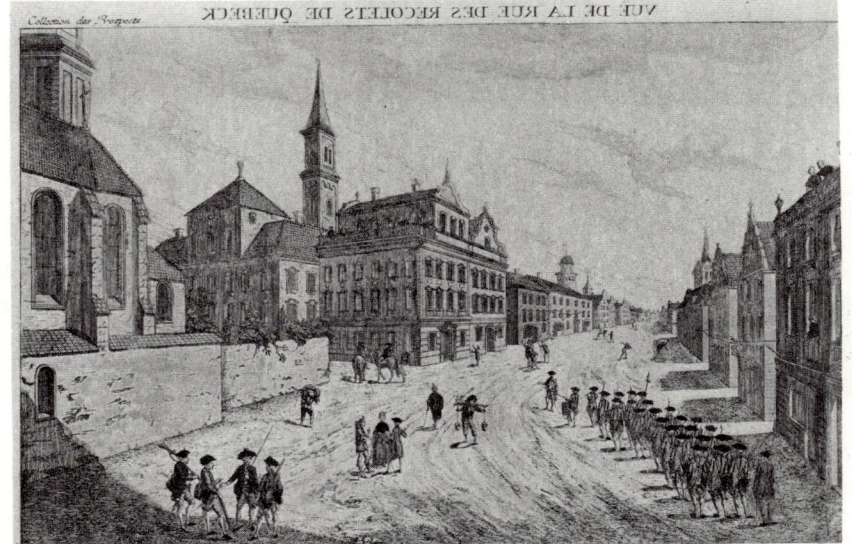

135

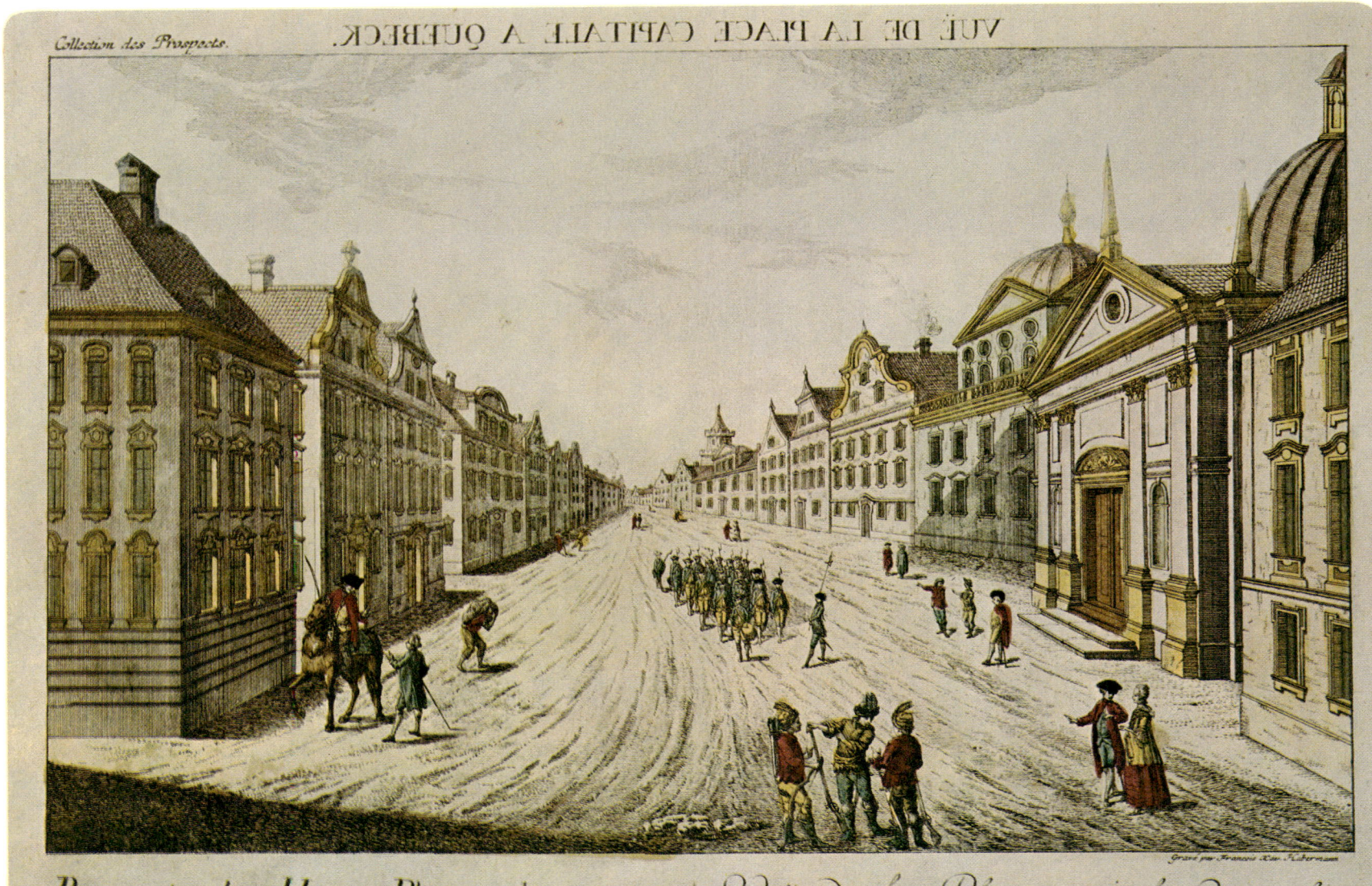

136

365

VUË DE LA PLACE CAPITALE A QUEBECK. Prospect des Haupt Plazes der untern Stadt zu Quebec. Vuë de la Place capitale dans la Ville basse a Quebec. Se vend à Augsbourg au Negoce commun de l'Academie Imperiale d'Empire des Arts libereaux avec Privilage de Sa Majesté Imperiale et avec Defense ni d'en faire ni de vendre les Copies. Gravé par Francois Xav. Habermann. [177?]

Etching (hand colored) 12½ x 16¾ in.

Title above picture is a mirror image. From "Collection des prospects."

366

Quebeck. Se vend à Augsbourg au Negoce commun de l'Academie Imperiale d'Empire des Arts libereaux avec Privilege de Sa Majesté Imperiale et avec Defense ni d'en faire ni de vendre les Copies. Gravé par Balth. Frederic Leizelt. [177?]

Etching (hand colored) 9¾ x 15¾ in. (image)

Captions below the picture read:

Eine Stadt in Nord-America, in Canada, an den lincken Ufer des Fluses St. Laurenz, sie ware die Haupt Stadt in Neu Franckreich, wurde aber 1759 von den Engelländern erobert, und in dem darauf erfolgten Frieden nebst ganz Canada an die Crone Engelland abgetretten. Une Ville de Canada dans l'Amerique Septentrionale auprès du rivage gauche du fleuve St. Laurent, elle etoit la Capitale de la nouvelle France, mais les Anglois la prirent en 1759 et par la Paix suivante elle fut cédée à la Couronne d'Angleterre avec Canada en entier.

LC-USZ62-45387

367

A View of QUEBEC the Capital of Canada, in North America. Roberts sculp. [1780?]

Etching 8 x 12 in. (image)

Probably from Cowley, *Ladies History of England* (London, 1780). This copy in P&P. LC-USZ62-45373

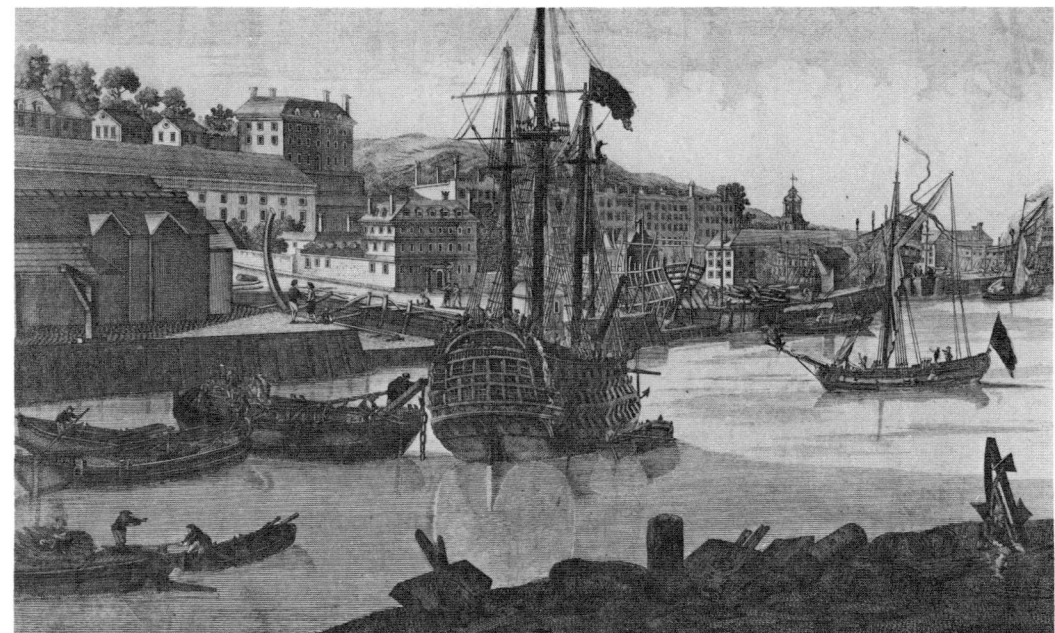

366

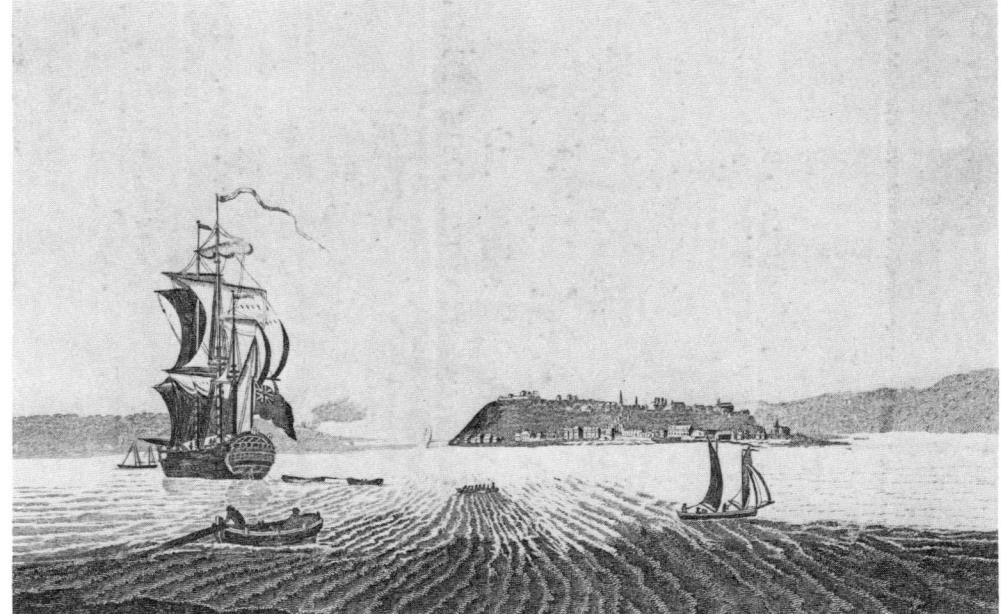

367

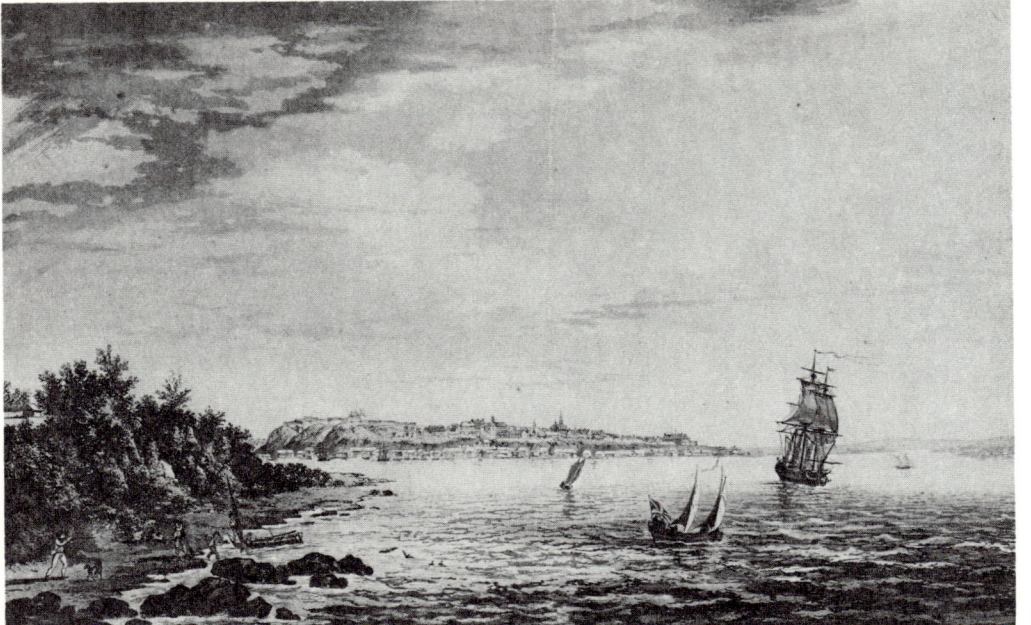

368

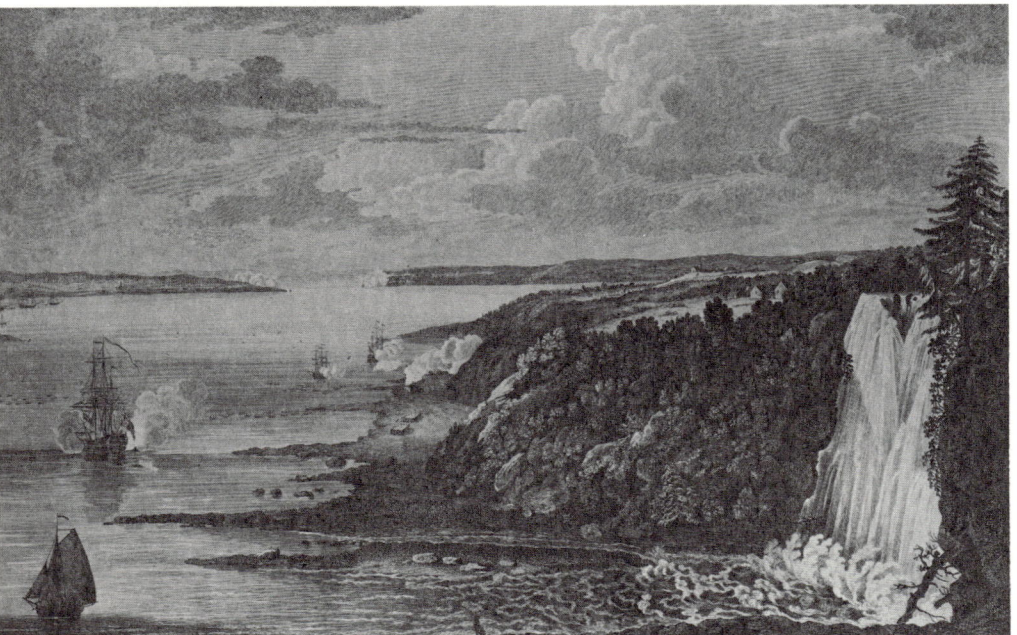

369

368
A View of the City of QUEBEC, the Capital of CANADA, taken from the Rock on Point Levi, by Wm. Peachy, Octr. 23d. 1784. London. Publish'd Nov.r 1st. 1786 by R. Pollard, Engraver, No. 15 Braynes Row, Spa Fields. Engraved by J. Wells.

Aquatint with etching 14 x 20½ in.

LC–USZ62–45383

369
A View of the Fall of Montmorenci and the Attack made by General Wolfe, on the French Intrenchments near Beauport, with the Grenadiers of the Army, July 31. 1759. Vue de la Chûte ou Saût de Montmorenci et de l'Attaque des Retrenchments Francois près de Beauport, par le Général Wolfe avec le Grenadiers de l'Armée le 31 Juillet 1759. Drawn on the SPOT by Capt. Hervey Smyth. Engraved by Wm. Elliot. London Printed for John Bowles at No. 13 in Cornhill, Robert Sayer at No. 53 in Fleet Street, Thos. Jefferys the corner of St. Martins Lane in the Strand, Carington Bowles at No. 69 in St. Pauls Church Yard, and Henry Parker at No. 82 in Cornhill. [1768]

Etching 14¼ x 21 in.

British ships discharge troops which land in small boats, form ranks, and climb the cliffs to the Plains of Abraham. In the foreground a hugh waterfall crashes into the St. Lawrence River, and in the background smoke rises from another battle. *Scenographia Americana* (1768). LC–USZ62–45580

Gulf of Saint Lawrence

370
A View of the Pierced Island, a remarkable Rock in the Gulf of St. Laurence. Two Leagues to the Southward of Gaspée Bay. Vüe de l'Isle Percée, Rocher remarquable dans le

Golfe St. Laurent a 2 Lieues au Sud de la Baye de Gaspe. Drawn on the SPOT by Capt. Hery. Smyth. Engraved by P. Canot. London Printed for John Bowles at No. 13 in Cornhill, Robert Sayer at No. 53 in Fleet Street, Thos. Jeffreys the corner of St. Martins Lane in the Strand, Carington Bowles at No. 69 in St. Pauls Church Yard, and Henry Parker at No. 82 in Cornhill. [1768]

Etching 14¼ x 21 in.

Scenographia Americana (1768).
LC–USZ62–45583

371
A View of Miramichi, a French Settlement in the Gulf of St. Laurence, destroyed by Brigadier Murray detached by General Wolfe for that purpose, from the Bay of Gaspe. Vue de Miramichi Etablissement Francois dans le Golfe de St. Laurent, détruit par le Brigadier Murray, détaché a cet effet de la Baye de Gaspé, par le Général Wolfe. Drawn on the Spot by Capt. Hervey Smyth, Etch'd by Paul Sandby, Retouched by P. Benazech. London Printed for John Bowles at No. 13 in Cornhill, Robert Sayer at No. 53 in Fleet Street, Thos. Jefferys the corner of St. Martins Lane in the Strand, Carington Bowles at No. 69 in St. Pauls Church Yard, and Henry Parker at No. 82 in Cornhill. [1768]

Etching 14¼ x 20¾ in.

British soldiers row into a small settlement.
Scenographia Americana (1768).
LC–USZ62–45582

372
A View of Gaspe Bay, in the Gulf of St. Laurence. Vue de la Baye de Gaspé dans le Golfe de St. Laurent. Drawn on the SPOT by Capt. Hervey Smyth. Engraved by Peter Mazell. London Printed for John Bowles at No. 13 in Cornhill, Robert Sayer at No. 53 in Fleet Street, Thos. Jefferys the Corner of

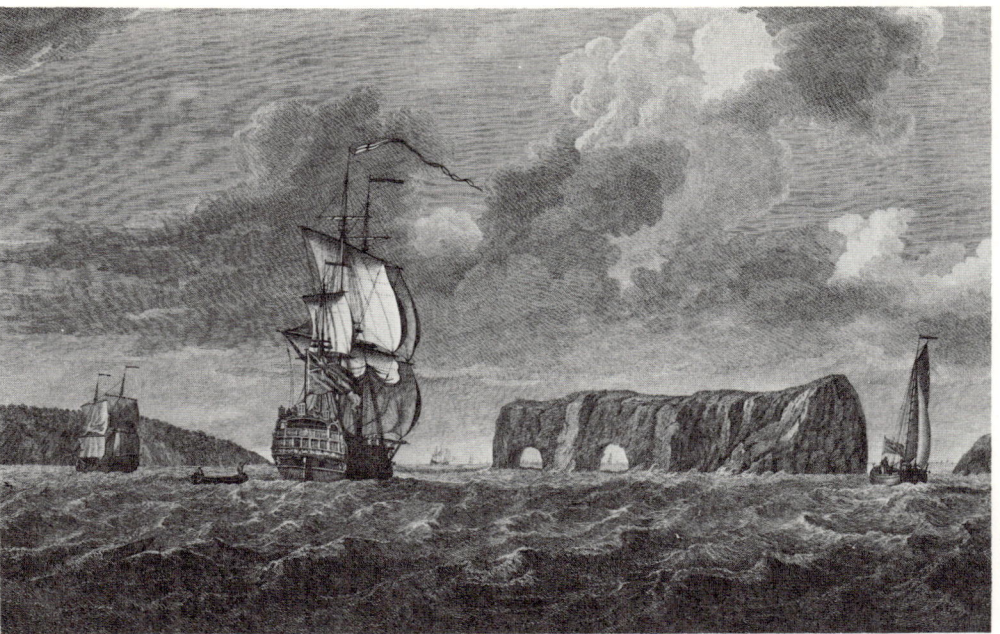

370

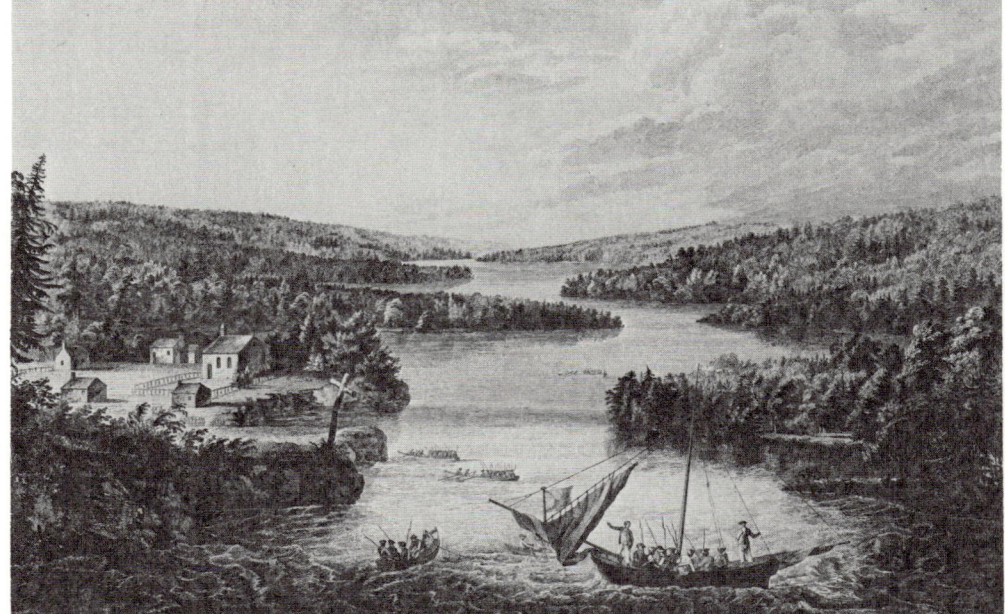

371

139

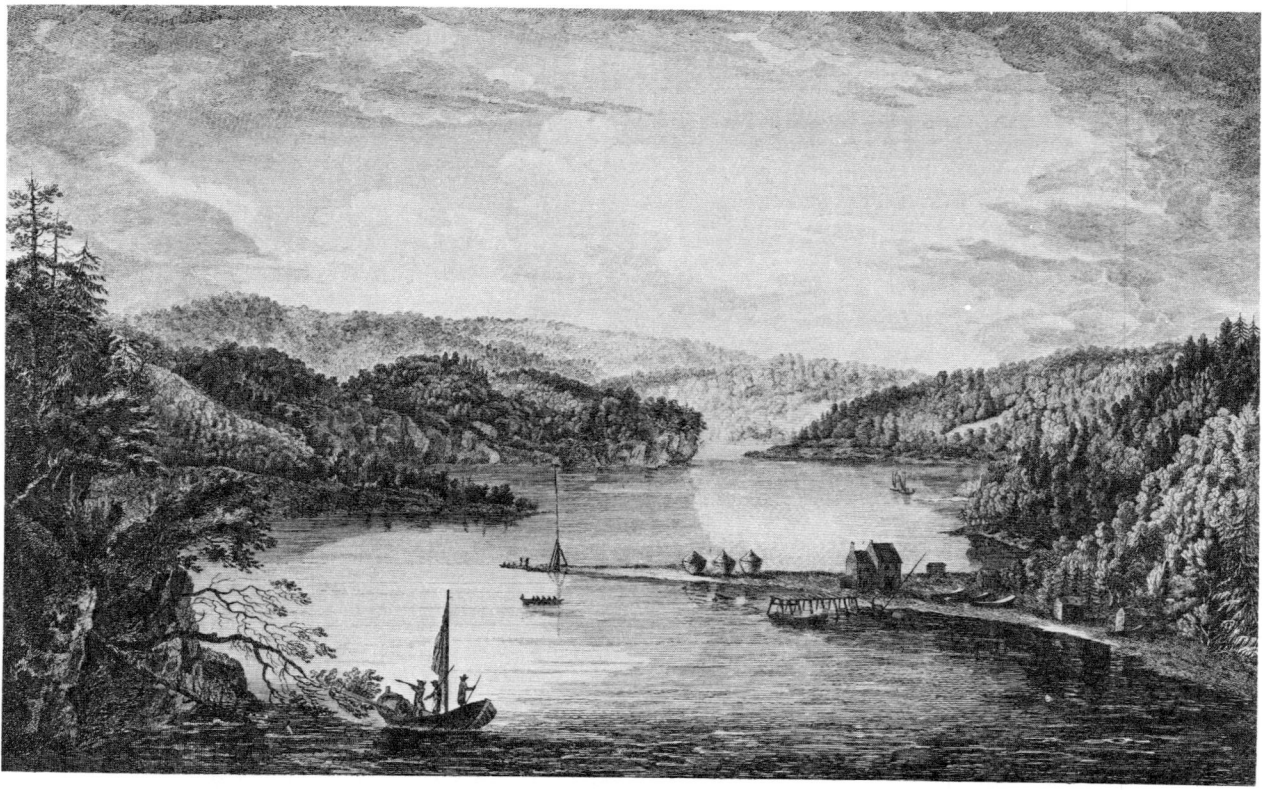

372

St. Martins Lane in the Strand, Carington Bowles at No. 69 in St. Pauls Church Yard, and Henry Parker at No. 82 in Cornhill. [1768]
Etching 14¼ x 20¾ in.

Captions below the picture read:

This French Settlement used to supply Quebec with Fish till it was destroyed by General Wolfe after the surrender of Louisburg in 1758. During the stay of the British Fleet in 1759, General Wolfe resided at the House on the Beach. Cet Établissement Francois fournissoit Québec de poisson jusqu'a ce qu'il fut détruit par le Général Wolfe, aprés la reddition de Louisbourg en 1758. Pendant le séjour de la Flotte Angloise en 1759 le Général Wolfe fit sa résidence dans la Maison sur la Grève.

Scenographia Americana (1768).
LC–USZ62–43543

MARITIME PROVINCES OF CANADA

Newfoundland

373
Cape St. Mary N:E: one Mile. [J.F.W. Des Barres, 1777]
Etching (hand colored) 8 x 17½ in. (image)

A single boat sails toward the cliffs to the right. *The Atlantic Neptune*. Phillips 3657, v. 1, no. 17.

——————Other impressions: LeGear 10323, v. 1, no. 8b; LeGear 10317, v. 1, no. 10a (Publish'd according to Act of Parliament July 26, 1777, by J.F.W. Des Barres Esqr.); LeGear 10320, v. 1, no. 20.

——————Another copy with same title, but imprint reads, "Publishd as the Act directs Feb 1st 1781 by J.F.W. Des Barres Esqr." Aquatint with etching 7¼ x 17¼ in. (image). The cape to the right of the picture. Many boats sail on the passage to the left. *The Atlantic Neptune*. Phillips 1198, v. 1, no. 13.

The negative number for this picture and the next two is LC–USZ62–46030

———Another impression. Phillips 3658, pt. 1, no. 24a.

374
South Entrance of Grand Passage. [J.F.W. Des Barres, 1777]
Etching (hand colored) 6½ x 17½ in. (image)
The bay in the center. *The Atlantic Neptune.* Phillips 3657, v. 1, no. 17.

———Other impressions: LeGear 10323, v. 1, no. 8b; LeGear 10317, v. 1, no. 10a (Publish'd according to Act of Parliament July 26, 1777, by J.F.W. Des Barres Esqr.); LeGear 10320, v. 1, no. 20.

———Another copy with same title, but imprint reads, "Publishd as the Act directs Feb 1st 1781 by J.F.W. Des Barres Esqr." Aquatint with etching 6½ x 17¼ in. (image). *The Atlantic Neptune.* Phillips 1198, v. 1, no. 13.

———Another impression. Phillips 3658, pt. 1, no. 24a.

375
St. Mary's Bay. [J.F.W. Des Barres, 1777]
Etching (hand colored) 9 x 17⅜ in. (image)
A single boat sails past the cliffs on the left, proceeding toward the bay on the right. *The Atlantic Neptune.* Phillips 3657, v. 1, no. 17.

———Other impressions: LeGear 10323, v. 1, no. 8b; LeGear 10317, v. 1, no. 10a (Publish'd according to Act of Parliament July 26, 1777, by J.F.W. Des Barres Esqr.); LeGear 10320, v. 1, no. 20.

———Another copy with same title, but imprint reads, "Publishd as the Act directs Feb 1st 1781 by J.F.W. Des Barres Esqr." Aquatint with etching 8⅞ x 17¼ in. (image). The bay to the right. Many boats are present.

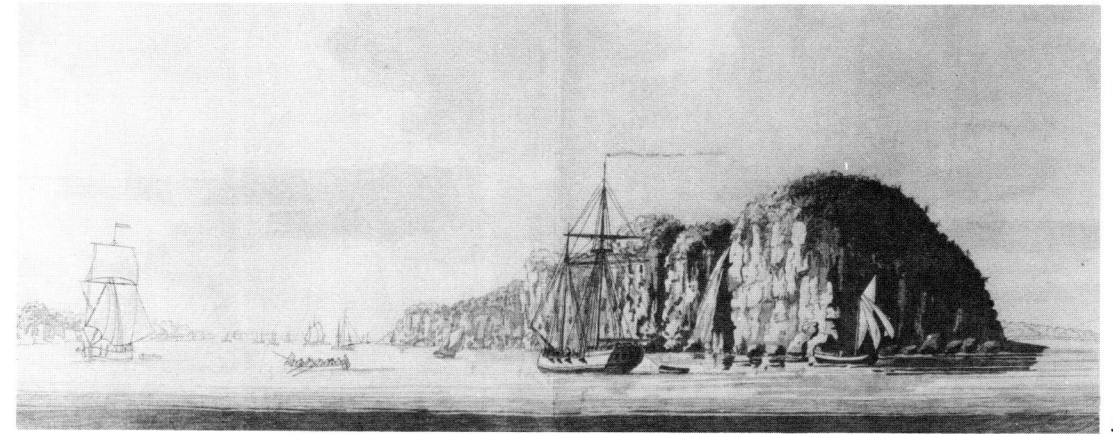

373

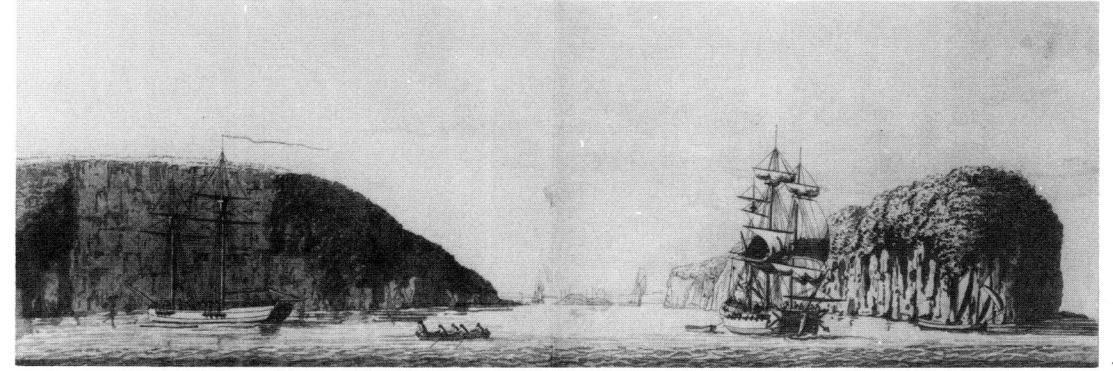

374

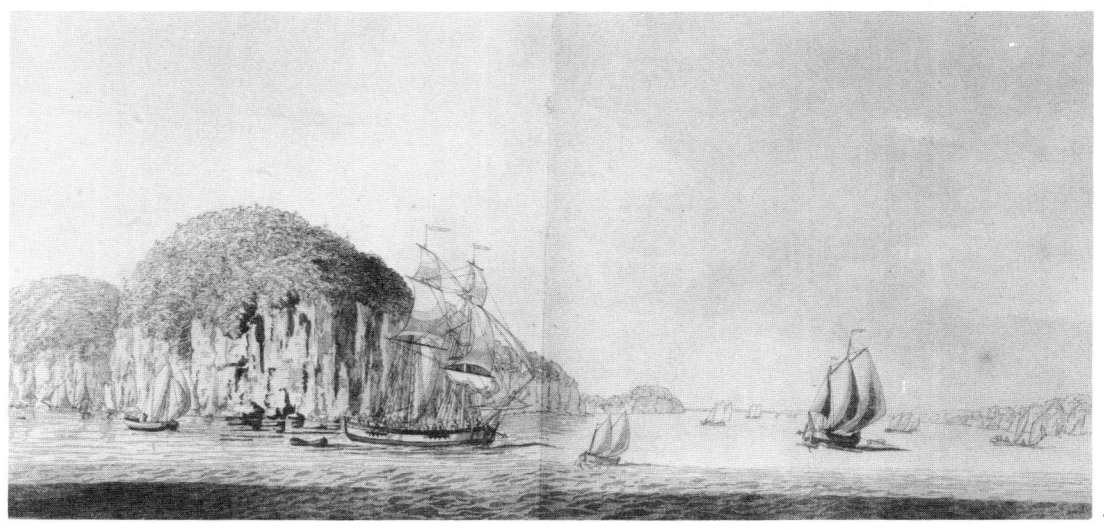

375

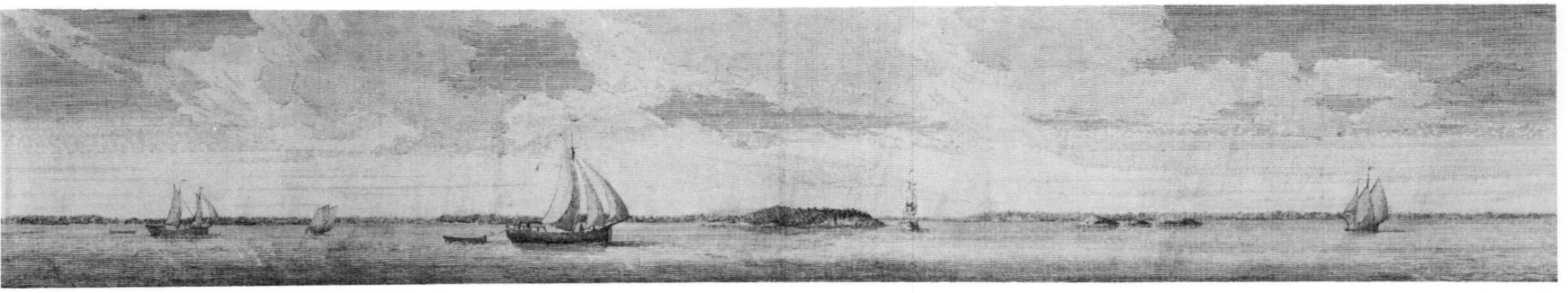

376

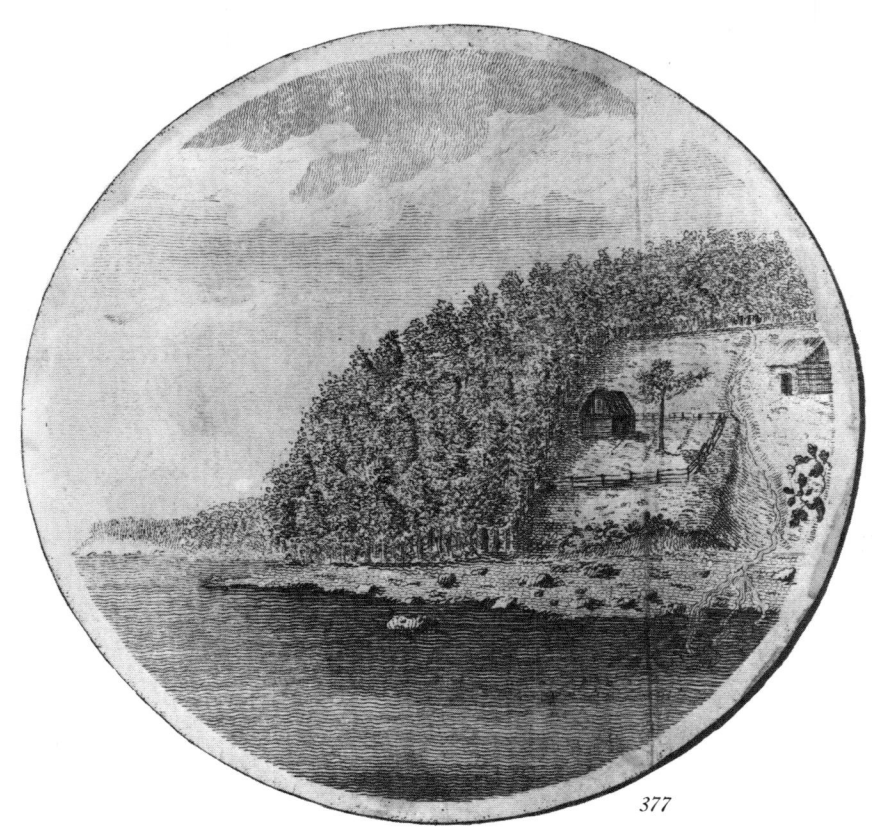

377

The Atlantic Neptune. Phillips 1198, v. 1, no. 13.

———Another impression. Phillips 3658, pt. 1, no. 24a.

Prince Edward Island

376
[Egmont Harbor—a distant view] Survey'd & Published according to Act of Parliament by J.F.W. Des Barres. April 1st. 1779.
Etching 3¼ x 17¼ in. (image)

The entrance to the harbor is to the right center. Egmont Harbor had limited facilities for refitting and supplying ships of His Majesty's Navy. *The Atlantic Neptune.* Phillips 1198, v. 1, no. 37. LC–USZ62–46037

———Other impressions: Phillips 1199, v. 1, no. 25; Phillips 1200, v. 1, no. 25; Phillips 1201, v. 1, no. 25; Phillips 1202, v. 1, no. 25; Phillips 1203, v. 1, no. 25; Phillips 1205, v. 1, no. 28; Phillips 1250, v. 2, no. 14; Phillips 3658, pt. 1, no. 21; Phillips 3655, v. 1, no. 21; Phillips 3656, v. 1, no. 21; Phillips 4473, v. 1, no. 20; LeGear 10323, v. 1, no. 21; LeGear 10320, v. 2, no. 40.

377
[A farm at Egmont Harbor] Survey'd and Published according to Act of Parliament by

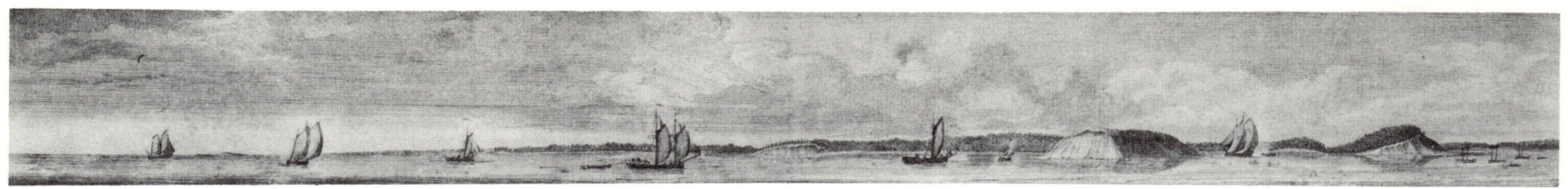

378

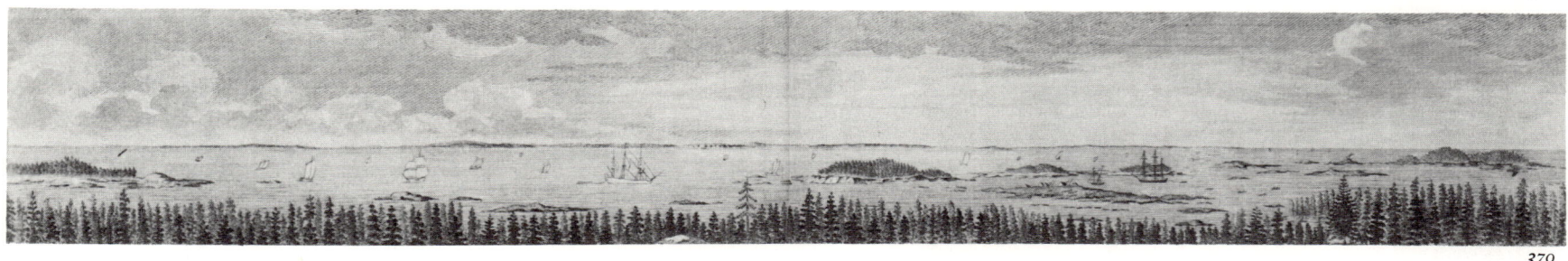

379

J.F.W. Des Barres. April 1st. 1779.
Etching 4¼ x 4¼ in. (circular image)

The Atlantic Neptune. Phillips 1198, v. 1, no. 37. LC–USZ62–46038

————Other impressions: Phillips 1199, v. 1, no. 25; Phillips 1200, v. 1, no. 25; Phillips 1201, v. 1, no. 25; Phillips 1202, v. 1, no. 25; Phillips 1203, v. 1, no. 25; Phillips 1205, v. 1, no. 28; Phillips 1250, v. 2, no. 14; Phillips 3658, pt. 1, no. 21; Phillips 3655, v. 1, no. 21; Phillips 3656, v. 1, no. 21; Phillips 4473, v. 1, no. 20; LeGear 10323, v. 1, no. 21; LeGear 10320, v. 2, no. 40.

378
VIEW of Cape Round bearing West distant ¾ of a Mile. Publish'd according to Act of Parliament by Joseph Frederick Wallet DesBarres Esqr. April 2, 1775.
Etching 2½ x 20¾ in. (image)

Ornamental view beneath a map of St. Peter's Bay. *The Atlantic Neptune.* Phillips 1199, v. 1, no. 36.

————Other impressions: Phillips 1200, v. 1, no. 35; Phillips 1201, v. 1, no. 35; Phillips 1202, v. 1, no. 35; Phillips 1203, v. 1, no. 35; Phillips 1250, v. 2, no. 23; Phillips 3658, pt. 1, no. 31; Phillips 3655, v. 1, no. 31; Phillips 3656, v. 1, no. 31; Phillips 4473, v. 1, no. 33; LeGear 10323, v. 1, no. 29.

————Other copies with imprint reading "Survey'd and Publish'd according to Act of Parliament by Joseph Frederick Wallet DesBarres Esqr. April 2, 1779." In Phillips 1205, v. 1, no. 38, and LeGear 10320, v. 2, no. 50.

————Another copy with imprint reading "Survey'd & Publish'd . . . May 1st 1781." In Phillips 1198, v. 1, no. 48. LC–USZ62–46042

Nova Scotia and the Isle of Sable

379
View of PORT GEORGE taken from the Top of Binney Isle. Survey'd & Publish'd according to Act of Parliament by Joseph Frederick Wallet Des Barres Esqr. May 1st 1781.
Etching 3 x 18¾ in.

Ornamental border beneath a map of Canso Harbor. *The Atlantic Neptune.* Phillips 1198, v. 1, no. 45. LC–USZ62–46041

————Other impressions: Phillips 1199, v. 1, no. 32; Phillips 1200, v. 1, no. 32; Phillips 1201, v. 1, no. 32; Phillips 1202, v. 1, no. 32; Phillips 1203, v. 1, no. 32; Phillips 1205, v. 1, no. 35; Phillips 1250, v. 2, no. 21; Phillips 3658, pt. 1, no. 28; Phillips 3655, v. 1, no. 28; Phillips 3656, v. 1, no. 28; Phillips 4473, v. 1, no. 27; LeGear 10323, v. 1, no. 28; LeGear 10320, v. 2, no. 48.

380
A View of Port Hood, sailing into the Harbor. [J.F.W. Des Barres, 1776–77?]
Etching (hand colored) 9 x 18¾ in. (image)

The harbor to the right. *The Atlantic Neptune.* Phillips 3657, v. 1, no. 19.

————Another copy (closer view), entitled, "A View of the Entrance of PORT HOOD. Pubd. According to Act of Parliament June 1, 1781 by J.F.W. DesBarres Esqr." Aquatint with etching 20⅞ x 29½ in. High cliffs are to the right and islands to the left. *The Atlantic Neptune.* LeGear 10323, v. 1, no. 33a.

381

A View of the Plaister Cliffs, in George's Bay. [J.F.W. Des Barres, 1776–77?]

Etching (hand colored) 12¼ x 15¾ in. (image)

The chalk cliffs are on both sides of the bay. *The Atlantic Neptune.* Phillips 3657, v. 1, no. 19.

————————Another copy, entitled, "A View of the Plaister Cliffs, on the West Shore of Georges Bay." [Des Barres, 1774–81?] Aquatint with etching 16¾ x 21⅛ in. *The Atlantic Neptune.* Phillips 1198, v. 1, no. 58. LC–USZ62–46044

————————Other impressions: Phillips 3658, pt. 1, no. 28a; LeGear 10323, v. 1, no. 33b (hand colored).

382

A View of Louisburg in North America, taken near the Light House when that City was besieged in 1758. Vue de Louisburg, dans L' Amerique Septentrionale, prise du fanal durant le dernier Siege en 1758. Drawn on the Spot by Capt. Ince of the 35t. Regt. Engraved by P. Canot. London Printed for John Bowles at No. 53 in Fleet Street, Thos. Jefferys the corner of St. Martins Lane in the Strand, Carington Bowles at No. 69 in St. Pauls Church Yard, and Henry Parker at No. 82 in Cornhill. [1768]

Etching 14¼ x 20¾ in.

Legend at bottom indicates locations of the city, Garbarus Bay, The English camp, the French fleet, an island battery, and a lighthouse. *Scenographia Americana* (1768). LC–USZ62–2771 is the negative number for the 1762 edition.

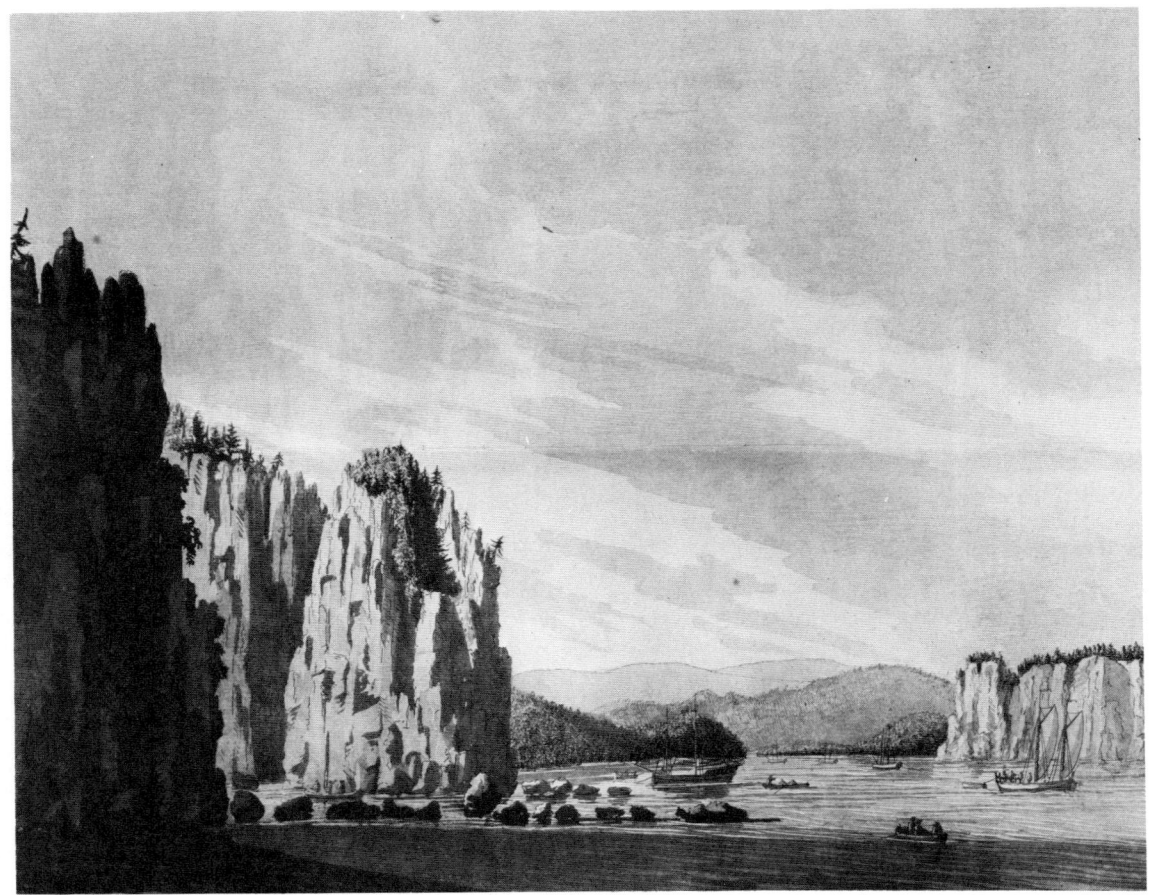

381

383

A View of Louisbourg Harbor, on the South Coast of the Island of Cape Breton, the Lighthouse bearing N.N.E. [J.F.W. Des Barres, 1777?]

Etching (hand colored) 4¼ x 29⅝ in. (image)

The town is in the left part of the picture; the lighthouse is to the right. No ships are shown. *The Atlantic Neptune.* Phillips 3657, v. 1, no. 18.

——————Other impressions: LeGear 10323, v. 2, no. 21a; LeGear 10320, v. 2, no. 55a (Publish'd according to Act of Parliament July 26, 1777 by J.F.W. Des Barres Esqr.).

——————Another copy with same title, but imprint reads, "Publish'd according to Act of Parliament July 26, 1777 by J.F.W. DesBarres Esqr." Aquatint with etching 4¼ x 29½ in. (image). The town is in the left part of the picture; the lighthouse is to the right. Various ships are shown. *The Atlantic Neptune.* Phillips 1198, v. 2, no. 25.

384

A View of the Shore to the Westward of Gabbarrus Bay on the South Coast of Cape Breton Island. [J.F.W. Des Barres, 1777?]

Etching (hand colored) 3¼ x 19¼ in. (image)

No ships are shown. *The Atlantic Neptune.* Phillips 3657, v. 1, no. 18.

——————Other impressions: LeGear 10323, v. 2, no. 21a; LeGear 10320, v. 2, no. 55a (Publish'd according to Act of Parliament July 26, 1777 by J.F.W. DesBarres Esqr.).

——————Another copy with same title, but imprint reads, "Publish'd according to Act of Parliament July 26, 1777 by J.F.W. DesBarres Esqr." Aquatint with etching 3½ x 19 in. (image). Various ships are shown. *The Atlantic Neptune.* Phillips 1198, v. 2, no. 25.

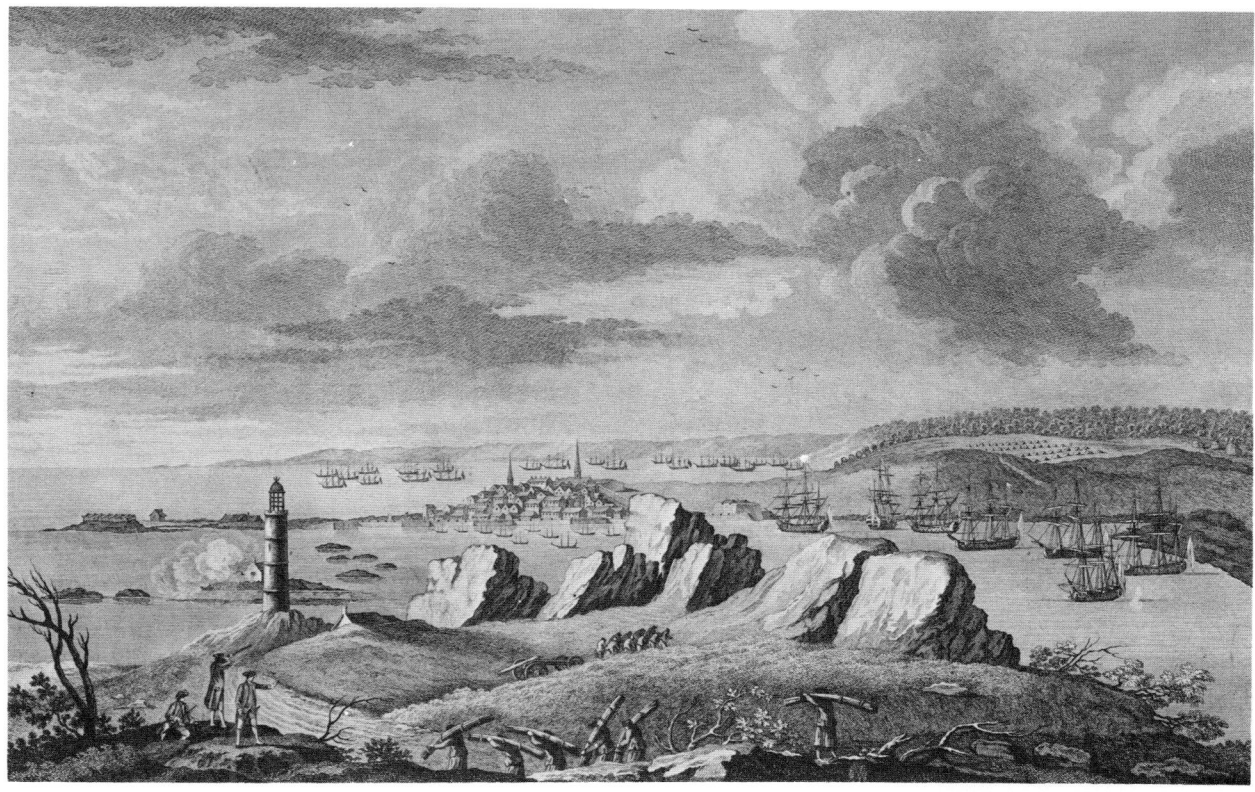

382

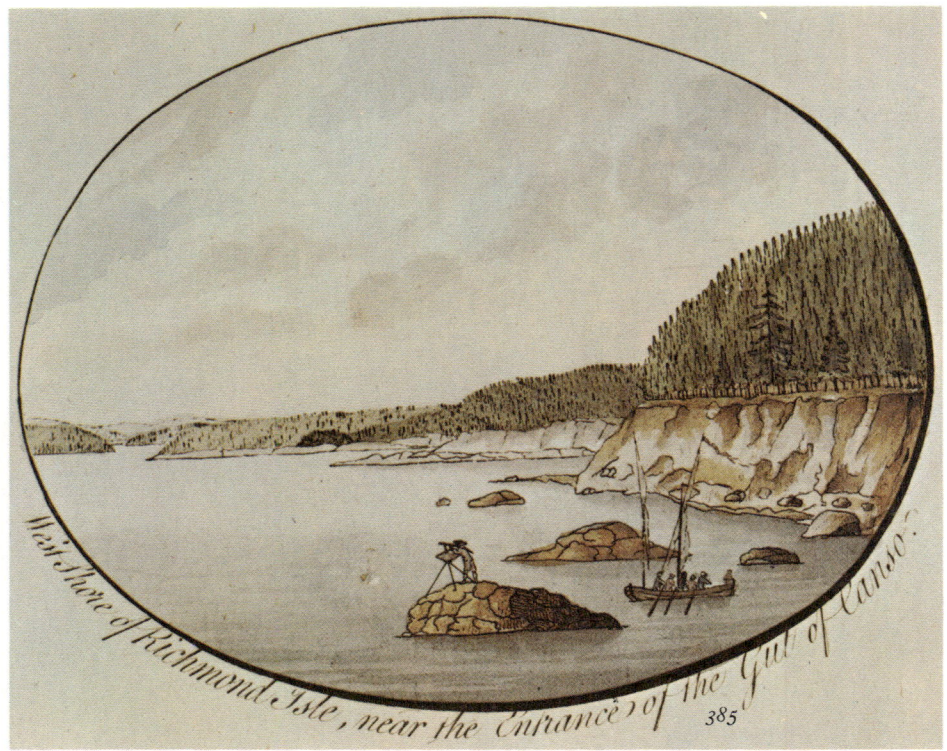

385
West Shore of Richmond Isle, near the Entrance of the Gut of Canso. [Publishd according to Act of Parliament July 26, 1777 by J.F.W. DesBarres Esqr.]

Aquatint with etching 3¾ x 4¾ in. (oval image)

The Atlantic Neptune. Phillips 1198, v. 2, no. 25.

──────Other impressions: Phillips 3657, v. 1, no. 18 (hand colored); LeGear 10323, v. 2, no. 21a (hand colored); LeGear 10320, v. 2, no. 55a (hand colored).

386
A View of the S.W. Shore of Cape Breton Island, from St. Peter's Bay Eastward. [J.F.W. Des Barres, 1777?]

Etching (hand colored) 2⅞ x 25¼ in. (image)

The shore of the island is to the left. No ships are shown. *The Atlantic Neptune.* Phillips 3657, v. 1, no. 18.

──────Other impressions: LeGear 10323, v. 2, no. 21a; LeGear 10320, v. 2, no. 55a (Publish'd according to Act of Parliament July 26, 1777 by J.F.W. DesBarres Esqr.).

──────Another copy with same title, but imprint reads, "Publish'd according to Act of Parliament July 26, 1777 by J.F.W. DesBarres Esqr." Aquatint with etching 2⅞ x 25⅛ in. (image). The shore of the island is in the left part of the picture. Various ships are shown. *The Atlantic Neptune.* Phillips 1198, v. 2, no. 25.

387
Ramea Isles on the S.W. Coast of Newfoundland, bearing N.N.W. 4 Miles distant. [J.F.W. Des Barres, 1777]

Etching (hand colored) 7⅝ x 12¼ in. (image)

No ships are shown. *The Atlantic Neptune.* Phillips 3657, v. 1, no. 18.

———Other impressions: LeGear 10323, v. 2, no. 21a; LeGear 10320, v. 2, no. 55a (Publish'd according to Act of Parliament July 26, 1777 by J.F.W. DesBarres Esqr.).

———Another copy reading, "Ramea Isles on the S:W: Coast of Newfoundland, bearing N.N.W. 4 Miles distant. Publish'd according to Act of Parliament July 26, 1777 by J.F.W. DesBarres Esqr." Aquatint with etching 7⅝ x 12¼ in. (image). Various ships are shown. *The Atlantic Neptune*. Phillips 1198, v. 2, no. 25.

388

Sta. Maria Island the Southernmost of the Western Isles, bearing N.b.E. 9 Leagues distant. [J.F.W. Des Barres, 1777]

Etching (hand colored) 7⅝ x 12 in. (image)

No ships are shown. *The Atlantic Neptune*. Phillips 3657, v. 1, no. 18.

———Other impressions: LeGear 10323, v. 2, no 21a; LeGear 10320, v. 2, no. 55a (Publish'd according to Act of Parliament July 26, 1777 by J.F.W. DesBarres Esqr.).

———Another copy with same title, but imprint reads, "Publish'd according to Act of Parliament July 26, 1777 by J.F.W. DesBarres Esqr." Aquatint with etching 7⅝ x 12 in. (image). Various ships are shown. *The Atlantic Neptune*. Phillips 1198, v. 2, no. 25.

389

A View of Louisbourg from the North East. [Publish'd according to Act of Parliament July 26, 1777 by J.F.W. Des Barres Esqr.]

Aquatint with etching 15 x 26¼ in.

The town and principal fort are visible on the horizon at the center of the picture. *The Atlantic Neptune*. Phillips 1198, v. 2, no. 26. LC–USZ62–46048

———Another impression. Phillips 3658, pt. 2, no. 7a.

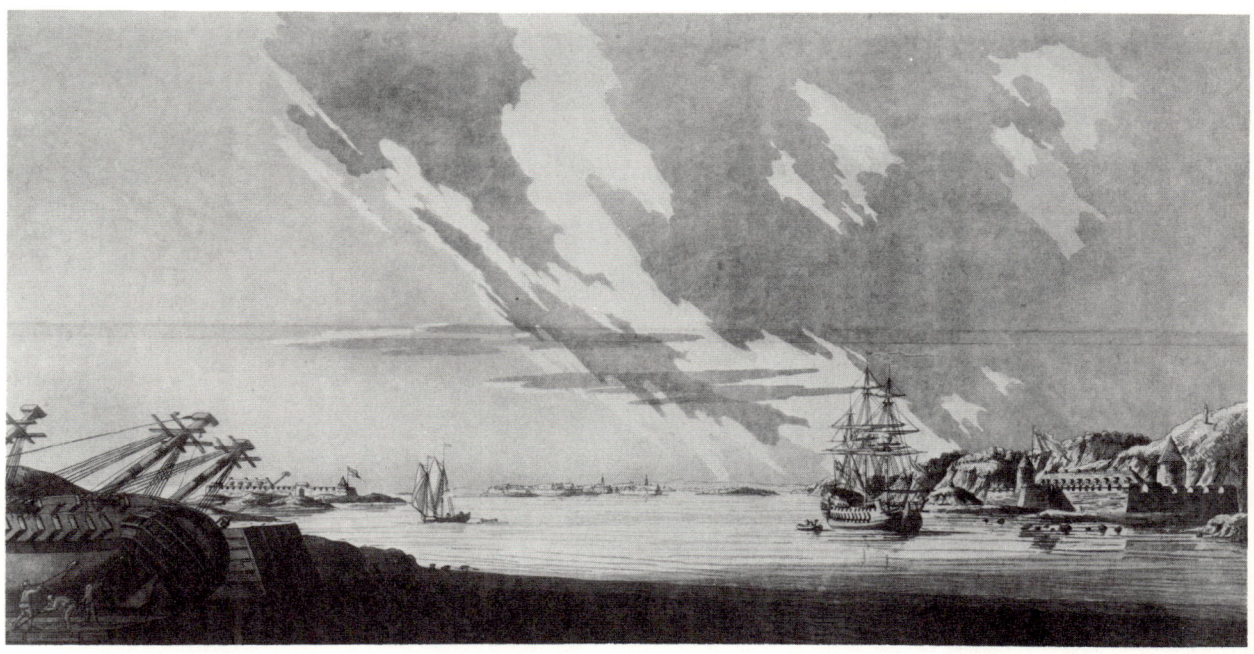

389

390

A View of LOUISBURG. Publish'd according to Act of Parliament Octr. 4. 1777, by J.F.W. DesBarres Esqr.

Etching (hand colored) 15¾ x 21¼ in.

The walled town is to the left, an island redoubt in the center, and a lighthouse to the right. In the foreground two barges filled with troops are being rowed toward the lighthouse, and in the inner harbor four ships are anchored. *The Atlantic Neptune.* LeGear 10323, v. 2, no. 20a.

391

A VIEW taken from the Entrance of LOUISBOURG HARBOUR. Publish'd according to Act of Parliament, Jany. 29, 1778, by J.F.W. DesBarres Esqr.

Etching (hand colored) 14½ x 22¾ in. (image)

The fortress is in the background at the left. *The Atlantic Neptune.* LeGear 10317, v. 1, no. 7. LC–USZ62–46065

——————Another impression. LeGear 10320, v. 2, no. 55.

392

[A View of Milford Haven. J.F.W. Des Barres, 1774–81]

Etching 3¼ x 18¼ in. (image)

Forest scene in the left foreground, Hadley beach in center, Bay of Chedabucto to the right. *The Atlantic Neptune.* Phillips 1199, v. 1, no. 35.

——————Other impressions: Phillips 1200, v. 1, no. 34; Phillips 1201, v. 1, no. 34; Phillips 1202, v. 1, no. 34; Phillips 1203, v. 1, no. 34; Phillips 3655, v. 1, no. 30; Phillips 3656, v. 1, no. 30; Phillips 4473, v. 1, no. 30; LeGear 10323, v. 1, no. 30.

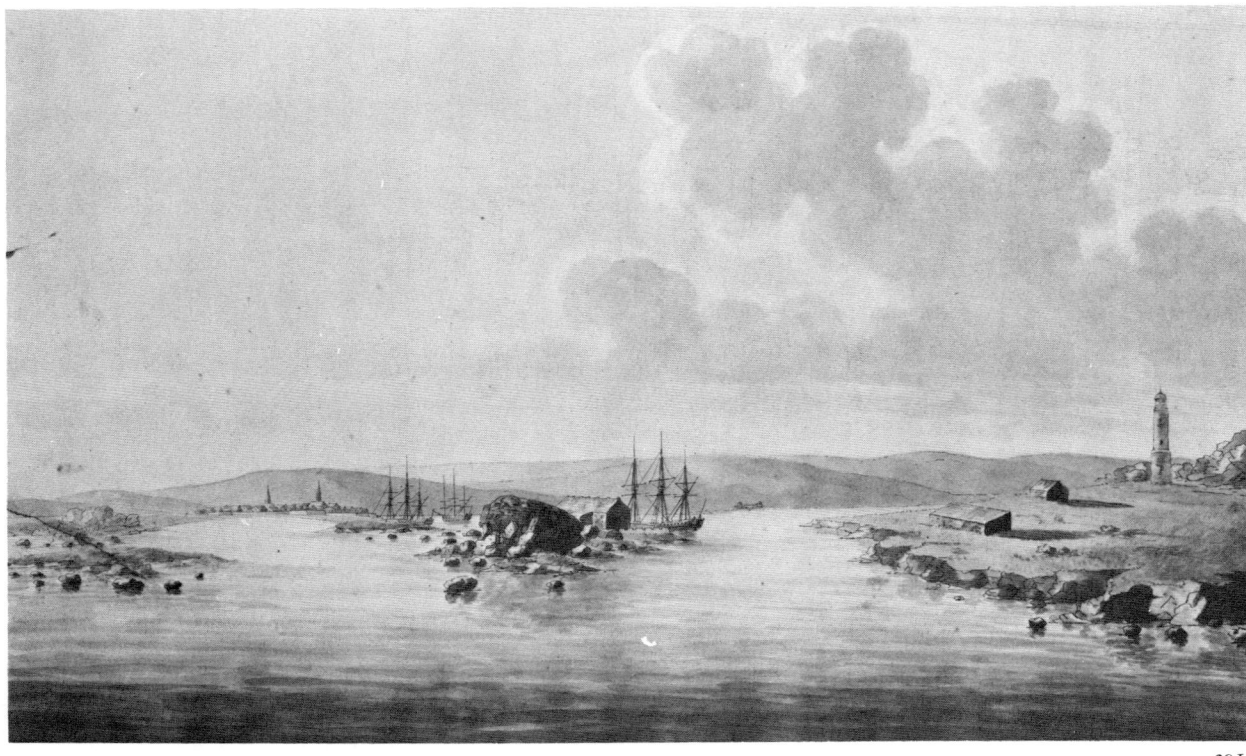

391

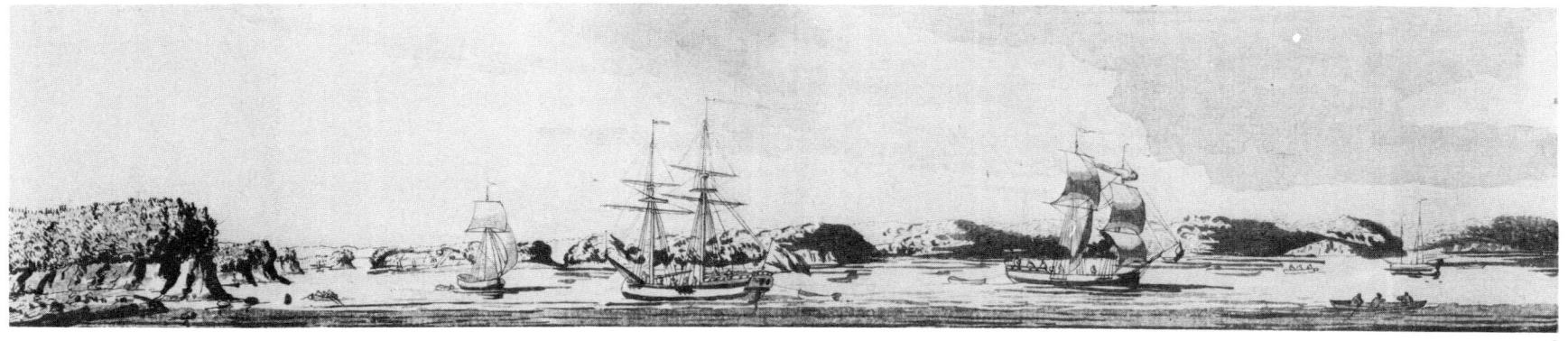

393

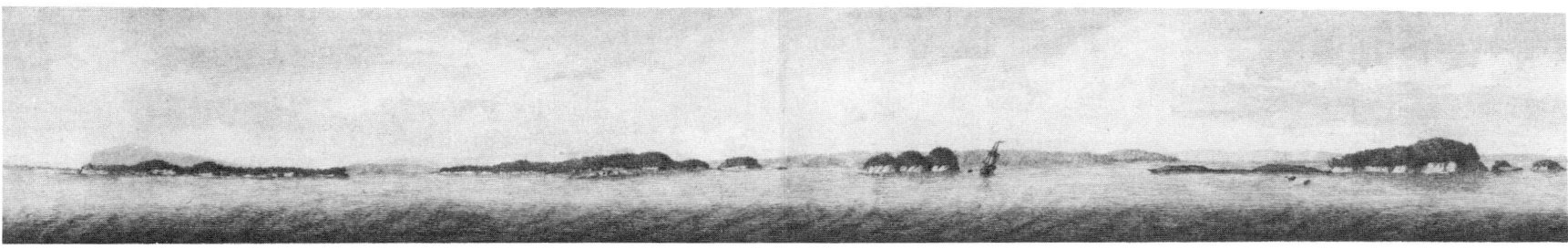

395

393

[Milford Haven. The Head of the Bay of Chedabucto] Survey'd and Publish'd according to Act of Parliament July 1, 1777 by J.F.W. DesBarres Esqr.

Etching (hand colored) 3⅜ x 15⅜ in. (image)

The entrance to Milford Haven is to the left. Phillips 1250, v. 1, no. 37.

─────── Another impression. LeGear 10320, v. 2, no. 51.

─────── Another copy. "Survey'd and Publish'd according to Act of Parliament Feb. 1, 1779 by J.F.W. DesBarres Esqr." Phillips 1205, v. 1, no. 37.

─────── Another copy. "Survey'd and Publish'd according to Act of Parliament May 1st: 1781 by J.F.W. DesBarres Esqr." Aquatint with etching. Phillips 1198, v. 1, no. 49. LC–USZ62–46043

394

CROW HARBOR, on the South Shore of Chedabuctou Bay. W.N.W. four Leagues from Canso. Published according to Act of Parliament by J.F.W. DesBarres, April 1, 1779.

Etching 1½ x 7¾ in. (image)

The entrance to the harbor is to the right, Philip inlet to the left. *The Atlantic Neptune.* Phillips 1198, v. 1, no. 45.

─────── Other impressions: Phillips 1199, v. 1., no. 34; Phillips 1200, v. 1, no. 33; Phillips 1201, v. 1, no. 33; Phillips 1202, v. 1, no. 33; Phillips 1203, v. 1, no. 33; Phillips 1205, v. 1, no. 36; Phillips 1250, v. 2, no. 22; Phillips 3658, pt. 1, no. 29; Phillips 3655, v. 1, no. 29; Phillips 3656, v. 1, no. 29; Phillips 4473, v. 1, no 29; LeGear 10323, v. 1, no. 29; LeGear 10320, v. 2, no. 49.

395

[View of the entrance to White Haven] Publish'd according to Act of Parliament, by J.F.W. Des Barres, March 20th, 1774.

Etching 2⅞ x 18½ in. (image)

View set into a map entitled "White Haven" and "Port Howe." Identifies three islands which surround White Haven: Cape Martingo, Three Top Island, and Whitehead Island. *The Atlantic Neptune.* Phillips 1198, v. 1, no. 45. LC–USZ62–46040

─────── Other impressions: Phillips 1199, v. 1, no. 31; Phillips 1200, v. 1, no. 31; Phillips 1201, v. 1, no. 31; Phillips 1202, v. 1, no. 31; Phillips 1203, v. 1, no. 31; Phillips 1205, v. 1, no. 34; Phillips 1250, v. 2, no. 20; Phillips 3658, pt. 1, no. 27; Phillips 3655, v. 1, no. 27; Phillips 3656, v. 1, no. 27; Phillips 4473, v. 1, no. 28; LeGear 10323, v. 1, no. 27; LeGear 10320, v. 2, no. 47.

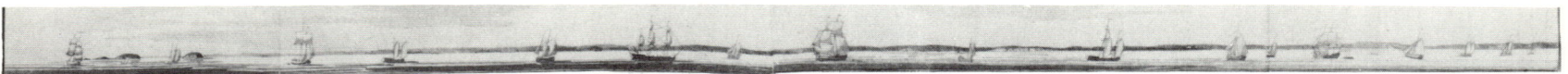

397

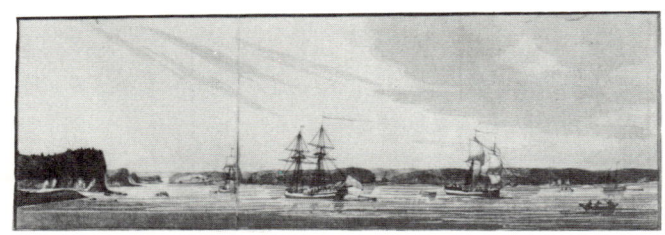

398

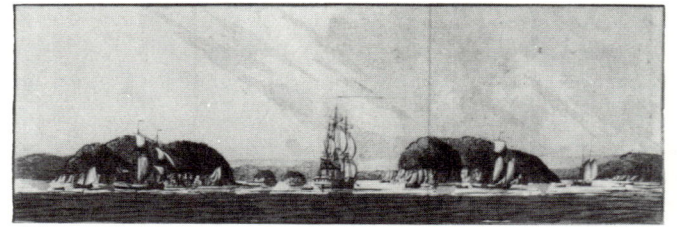

399

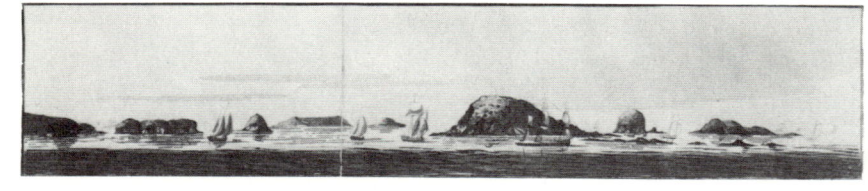

400

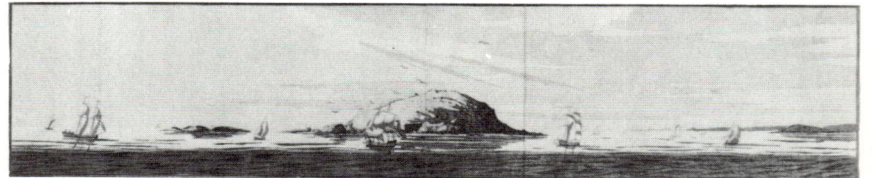

401

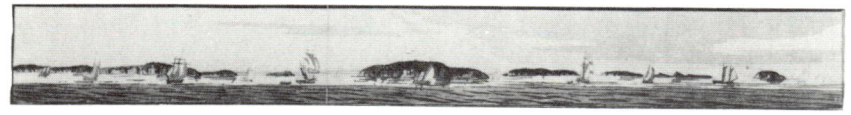

402

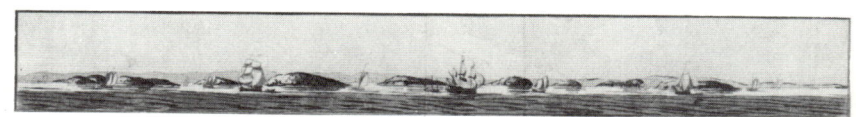

403

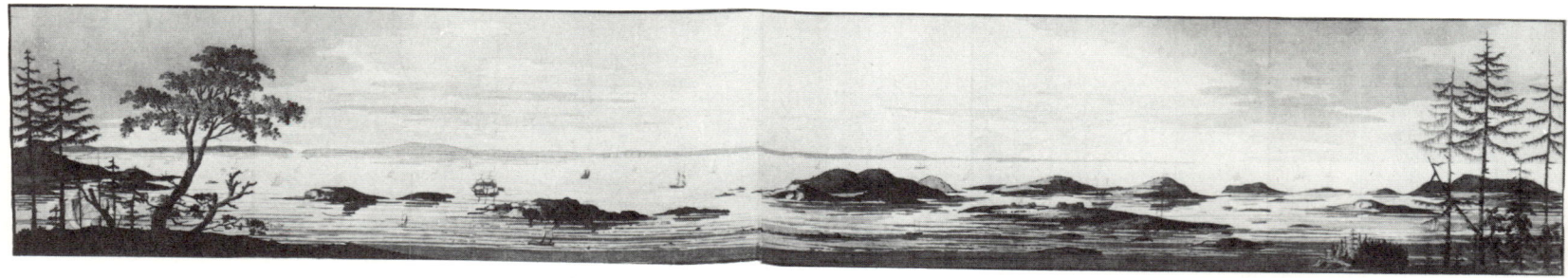

404

396

BERRY HEAD bearing North 21° East Distant 6 Miles & WHITE HEAD ISLAND North 63° East Distant 11 Miles. Survey'd & Publish'd according to Act of Parliament by Joseph Frederick Wallet DesBarres Esqr. May 1st, 1781.

Etching 2½ x 25 in. (image)

The Atlantic Neptune. Phillips 1198, v. 1, no. 44.

——————Other impressions: Phillips 1199, v. 1, no. 30; Phillips 1201, v. 1, no. 30; Phillips 1202, v. 1, no. 30; Phillips 1205, v. 1, no. 33; Phillips 1250, v. 2, no. 19; Phillips 3658, pt. 1, no. 26; Phillips 3655, v. 1, no. 26; Phillips 3656, v. 1, no. 26; Phillips 4473, v. 1, no. 26; LeGear 10323, v. 1, no. 26; LeGear 10320, v. 2, no. 46.

397

Appearance of the Land from the White Islands to St. Marys River taken two Leagues off Shore. Published according to Act of Parliament July the 30th. 1777. by J.F.W. DesBarres Esq.

Etching (hand colored) 2 x 40 in. (image)

No ships are shown. *The Atlantic Neptune.* LeGear 10323, v. 1, no. 29a.

——————Another impression. LeGear 10320, v. 2, no. 52.

——————Another copy with same title, but imprint reads, "Published according to Act of Parliament May the 1st 1781 by J.F.W. DesBarres Esq." Aquatint with etching 2 x 39¾ in. (image). *The Atlantic Neptune.* Phillips 1198, v. 1, no. 41. The negative number for this picture and the next seven is LC-USZ62-46039.

398

The Entrance of MILFORD HAVEN at the Head of Chedabucto Bay. Published according to Act of Parliament July the 30th. 1777. by J.F.W. DesBarres Esq.

Etching (hand colored) 5 x 15¼ in. (image)

The entrance to the bay is to the left. *The Atlantic Neptune.* LeGear 10323, v. 1, no. 29a.

——————Another impression. LeGear 10320, v. 2, no. 52.

——————Another copy with same title, but imprint reads, "Published according to Act of Parliament May the 1st 1781 by J.F.W. DesBarres Esq." Aquatint with etching 5¼ x 15¼ in. (image). *The Atlantic Neptune.* Phillips 1198, v. 1, no. 41.

399

The Entrance of PORT BICKERTON bearing N.W. Published according to Act of Parliament July the 30th. 1777. by J.F.W. DesBarres Esq.

Etching (hand colored) 5¼ x 15¼ in. (image)

The Atlantic Neptune. LeGear 10323, v. 1, no. 29a.

——————Another impression. LeGear 10320, v. 1, no. 52.

——————Another copy with same title, but imprint reads, "Published according to Act of Parliament May the 1st 1781 by J.F.W. DesBarres Esq." Aquatint with etching 5¼ x 15¼ in. (image). *The Atlantic Neptune.* Phillips 1198, v. 1, no. 41.

400

A View taken off the Entrance of Beaver Harbor Bald Isle bearing E. 150 N. Published according to Act of Parliament July the 30th. 1777. by J.F.W. DesBarres Esq.

Etching (hand colored) 4 x 20 in (image)

The island is to right of center. No ships are shown. *The Atlantic Neptune.* LeGear 10323, v. 1, no. 29a.

——————Another impression. LeGear 10320, v. 2, no. 52.

——————Another copy with same title, but imprint reads, "Published according to Act of Parliament May the 1st 1781 by J.F.W. DesBarres Esq." Aquatint with etching 4 x 19¾ in. (image). *The Atlantic Neptune.* Phillips 1198, v. 1, no. 41.

401

A View taken in the Offing of Beaver Harbor Bald Isle bearing W. by S. ¾ S. distant ¾ of a Mile. Published according to Act of Parliament July the 30th. 1777. by J.F.W. DesBarres Esq.

Etching (hand colored) 4 x 19¾ in. (image)

The island is in the center, and the entrance to the harbor is to the right. No ships are shown. *The Atlantic Neptune.* LeGear 10323, v. 1, no. 29a.

——————Another impression. LeGear 10320, v. 2, no. 52.

——————Another copy with same title, but imprint reads, "Published according to Act of Parliament May the 1st 1781 by J.F.W. DesBarres Esq." Aquatint with etching 4 x 19¾ in. (image). *The Atlantic Neptune.* Phillips 1198, v. 1, no. 41.

402

Appearance of the Shore to the Westward of Canso Cranberry Isle bearing N. by E. ½ E. distant 4 Miles. Published according to Act of Parliament July the 30th. 1777. by J.F.W. DesBarres Esq.

Etching (hand colored) 2¼ x 19¾ in. (image)

The Atlantic Neptune. LeGear 10323, v. 1, no. 29a.

——————Another impression. LeGear 10320, v. 2, no. 52.

———————Another copy with same title, but imprint reads, "Published according to Act of Parliament May the 1st 1781 by J.F.W. DesBarres Esq." Aquatint with etching 2¼ x 19¾ in. (image). *The Atlantic Neptune.* Phillips 1198, v. 1, no. 41.

403

The Beaver Islands. C. Bald Isle N. ½ E. Published according to Act of Parliament July the 30th. 1777. by J.F.W. DesBarres Esq.

Etching (hand colored) 2¼ x 19½ in. (image)

No ships are shown. *The Atlantic Neptune.* LeGear 10323, v. 1, no. 29a.

The Atlantic Neptune. LeGezr 10323, v. 1, no. 29a.

———————Another impression. LeGear 10320, v. 2, no. 52.

———————Another copy with same title, but imprint reads, "Published according to Act of Parliament May the 1st 1781 by J.F.W. DesBarres Esq." Aquatint with etching 2¼ x 19½ in. (image). *The Atlantic Neptune.* Phillips 1198, v. 1, no. 41.

404

Appearance of the S:E: Point of NOVA SCOTIA taken from CANSO ISLAND Shewing the distant Land of Richmond Isles the GUT of CANSO &c. Published according to Act of Parliament July the 30th. 1777. by J.F.W. DesBarres Esq.

Etching (hand colored) 6¼ x 38¾ in. (image)

A small village is on an island in the right foreground; a few ships are near the village. *The Atlantic Neptune.* LeGear 10323, v. 1, no. 29a.

———————Another impression. LeGear 10320, v. 2, no. 52.

———————Another copy with same title, but imprint reads, "Published according to Act of Parliament May the 1st 1781 by J.F.W. DesBarres Esq." Aquatint with etching 6¼ x 38¾ in. (image). *The Atlantic Neptune.* Phillips 1198, v. 1, no. 41.

405

Cape Southampton West 1 Mile & ½ distant. Survey'd and Publish'd according to Act of Parliament Feby 7, 1779, by J.F.W. DesBarres Esqr.

Etching 3 x 18¼ in. (oval image)

The cape is on the right. *The Atlantic Neptune.* Phillips 1198, v. 1, no. 38.

———————Other impressions: Phillips 1199, v. 1, no. 26; Phillips 1200, v. 1, no. 26; Phillips 1201, v. 1, no. 26; Phillips 1202, v. 1, no 26; Phillips 1203, v. 1, no. 26; Phillips 1205, v. 1, no. 29; Phillips 1250, v. 2, no. 15; Phillips 3658, pt. 1, no. 22; Phillips 3655, v. 1, no. 22; Phillips 3656, v. 1, no. 23; Phillips 4473, v. 1, no. 22; LeGear 10323, v. 1, no. 22; LeGear 10320, v. 2, no. 41.

406

Entrance of Keppel Harbour North by West 4½ Miles distant. Survey'd and Publish'd according to Act of Parliament Feby 7, 1779, by J.F.W. DesBarres.

Etching 3 x 18¼ in. (oval image)

Entrance to the harbor is on the right. *The Atlantic Neptune.* Phillips 1198, v. 1, no. 38.

———————Other impressions: Phillips 1199, v. 1, no. 26; Phillips 1200, v. 1, no. 26; Phillips 1201, v. 1, no. 26; Phillips 1202, v. 1, no. 26; Phillips 1203, v. 1, no. 26; Phillips 1205, v. 1, no. 29; Phillips 1250, v. 2, no. 15; Phillips 3658, pt. 1, no. 22; Phillips 3655, v. 1, no. 22; Phillips 3656, v. 1, no. 23; Phillips 4473, v. 1, no. 22; LeGear 10323, v. 1, no. 22; LeGear 10320, v. 2, no. 41.

407

Hopsons Nose bearing N:N:W: two Miles. Survey'd & Publish'd according to Act of Parliament by J.F.W. DesBarres Esqr. March 1st 1781.

Etching 3½ x 13¾ in. (image)

Hopsons Nose (island) to the left. *The Atlantic Neptune.* Phillips 1198, v. 1, no. 30.

———————Other impressions: Phillips 1199, v. 1, no. 23; Phillips 1200, v. 1, no. 23; Phillips 1201, v. 1, no. 23; Phillips 1202, v. 1, no. 23; Phillips 1203, v. 1, no. 23; Phillips 1205, v. 1, no. 26; Phillips 1250, v. 2, no. 12; Phillips 3658, v. 1, no. 19; Phillips 3654, v. 1, no. 19; Phillips 3656, v. 1, no. 19; Phillips 4473, v. 1, no. 17; LeGear 10323, v. 1, no. 19; LeGear 10317, v. 1, no. 20; LeGear 10320, v. 1, no. 34.

408

Cape Spry N:N:E 1 Mile and ¼ distant. Beaver Isles E. by N. 10 Miles distant. Westermost Ledge of Pegasus Wing East 5 Miles distant. Publish'd according to Act of Parliament, by J.F.W. DesBarres, Esqr. March 11th, 1779.

Etching 3¾ x 29½ in. (image in oval)

The caption identifies the landforms from left to right. *The Atlantic Neptune.* Phillips 1198, v. 1, no. 40.

————Other impressions: Phillips 1199, v. 1, no. 27; Phillips 1200, v. 1, no. 27; Phillips 1201, v. 1, no. 27; Phillips 1202, v. 1, no. 27; Phillips 1203, v. 1, no. 27; Phillips 1205, v. 1, no. 30; Phillips 1250, v. 2, no. 16; Phillips 3658, pt. 1, no. 23; Phillips 3655, v. 1, no. 23; Phillips 3656, v. 1, no. 23; Phillips 4473, v. 1, no. 23; LeGear 10323, v. 1, no. 23; LeGear 13020, v. 2, no. 43.

409
View of Cape Egmont and Winter Rock from the Eastward. [J.F.W. Des Barres, 1777?]

Etching (hand colored) 4¼ x 18¼ in. (image)

The cape is to the left and the bluffs of Winter Rock to the right. *The Atlantic Neptune.* Phillips 3657, v. 1, no. 22.

————Other impressions: LeGear 10323, v. 1, no. 21a; LeGear 10320, v. 2, no. 42.

————Another copy with same title, but imprint reads, "Publishd according to Act of Parliament April 1st 1781, by J.F.W. Des Barres Esqr." Aquatint with etching 4⅜ x 18⅛ in. (image). Ships in the foreground. *The Atlantic Neptune.* Phillips 1198, v. 1, no. 39.

————Other impressions: Phillips 3658, pt. 1, no. 21a; Phillips 4473, v. 1, no. 21.

410
Entrance of Egmont Harbor. [J.F.W. Des Barres, 1777?]

Etching (hand colored) 3⅛ x 18⅝ in. (image)

Entrance in right, center of picture. *The Atlantic Neptune.* Phillips 3657, v. 1, no. 22.

————Other impressions: LeGear 10323, v. 1, no. 21a; LeGear 10320, v. 2, no. 42.

————Another copy with same title, but imprint reads, "Publishd according to Act of Parliament April 1st 1781, by J.F.W. Des Barres Esqr." Aquatint with etching 3⅛ x 18½ in. (image). Entrance in right center of picture. Ships in the foreground. *The Atlantic Neptune.* Phillips 1198, v. 1, no. 39.

————Other impressions: Phillips 3658, pt. 1, no. 21a; Phillips 4473, v. 1, no. 21.

411
The Entrance of Keppel Harbor; 10 Leagues to the Eastward of Halifax. [J.F.W. Des Barres, 1777?]

Etching (hand colored) 2½ x 16¾ in. (image)

Depicts "A. Owls Head." *The Atlantic Neptune.* Phillips 3657, v. 1, no. 22.

————Other impressions: LeGear 10323, v. 1, no. 21a; LeGear 10320, v. 2, no. 42.

————Another copy with same title, but imprint reads, "Publishd according to Act of Parliament April 1st 1781, by J.F.W. DesBarres Esqr." Aquatint with etching 2½ x 16¾ in. (image). Ships in the foreground. *The Atlantic Neptune.* Phillips 1198, v. 1, no. 39.

————Other impressions: Phillips 3658, pt. 1, no. 21a; Phillips 4473, v. 1, no. 21.

412
Falls of Hinchinbroke River, the North East Branch of Sandwich Bay. [J.F.W. Des Barres, 1777?]

Etching (hand colored) 4 x 4⅛ in. (circular image)

A woodland scene. *The Atlantic Neptune.* Phillips 3657, v. 1, no. 22.

————Other impressions: LeGear 10323, v. 1, no. 21a; LeGear 10320, v. 2, no. 42.

————Another copy with same title, but imprint reads, "Publishd according to Act of Parliament April 1st 1781, by J.F.W. DesBarres Esqr." Aquatint with etching 4 x 4 in. (circular image). *The Atlantic Neptune.* Phillips 1198, v. 1, no. 39.

————Other impressions: Phillips 3658, pt. 1, no. 21a; Phillips 4473, v. 1, no. 21.

413
The Entrance into Chisetcook Inlet 4 Leagues Eastward of Halifax. [J.F.W. Des Barres, 1777?]

Etching (hand colored) 3⅜ x 16¾ in. (image)

The entrance is in the right center. No ships are shown. *The Atlantic Neptune.* Phillips 3657, v. 1, no. 22.

————Other impressions: LeGear 10323, v. 1, no. 21a; LeGear 10320, v. 2, no. 42.

————Another copy with same title, but imprint reads, "Publishd according to Act of Parliament April 1st 1781, by J.F.W. DesBarres Esqr." Aquatint with etching 3⅜ x

414

16¾ in (image). Ships in the foreground. *The Atlantic Neptune*. Phillips 1198, v. 1, no. 39.

————Other impressions: Phillips 3658, pt. 1, no. 21a; Phillips 4473, v. 1, no. 21.

414
Dartmouth Shore in the Harbor of Halifax. [J.F.W. Des Barres, 1777?]

Etching (hand colored) 6 x 16¾ in. (image)

Founded in 1749 to strengthen the English claim to Nova Scotia, Halifax was the location of the Vice Admiralty Court established by George Grenville in 1764. Part of the plan to enforce the trade laws more stringently in North America, the Vice Admiralty Court was protested as a threat to colonial liberties as it deprived the colonists of local justice in customs cases. Halifax was also a major depot for supplies during the Revolutionary War. *The Atlantic Neptune*. Phillips 3657, v. 1, no. 22.

————Other impressions: LeGear 10323, v. 1, no. 21a; LeGear 10320, v. 2, no. 42.

————Another copy with same title, but imprint reads, "Publishd according to Act of Parliament April 1st 1781, by J.F.W. DesBarres Esqr." Aquatint with etching 6 x 16¾ in. (image). *The Atlantic Neptune*. Phillips 1198, v. 1, no. 39.

————Other impressions: Phillips 3658, pt. 1, no. 21a; Phillips 4473, v. 1, no. 21.

415
Light House S.W.b.S. 1. Mile distant. Survey'd and Published according to Act of Parliament by J.F.W. DesBarres Esqr. April 1st, 1781.

Etching 5⅜ x 13½ in. (circular image)

Coastal view set into a map of Halifax Harbor. *The Atlantic Neptune*. Phillips 1198, v. 1, no. 33. LC-USZ62-46036

————Other impressions: Phillips 1202, v. 1, no. 24; Phillips 1205, v. 1, no. 27; Phillips 3658, v. 1, no. 20; Phillips 3655, v. 1, no. 20; Phillips 3656, v. 1, no. 20; LeGear 10323, v. 1, no. 20; LeGear 10320, v. 2, no. 37.

————Other copies: Title reads, "Light House S.E. 1 Mile distant." Etching. Ships absent. Phillips 1199, v. 1, no. 24; Phillips 1200, v. 1, no. 24; Phillips 1201, v. 1, no. 24; Phillips 1203, v. 1, no. 24; Phillips 1250, v. 2, no. 13; Phillips 4473, v. 1, no. 19.

416
(a) Light House West 3° South 2½ Miles distant (b) Chebucto Head North 4° West distant 2 Miles (c) Citadel Hill Survey'd and Published according to Act of Parliament by J.F.W. DesBarres Esqr. April 1st, 1781.

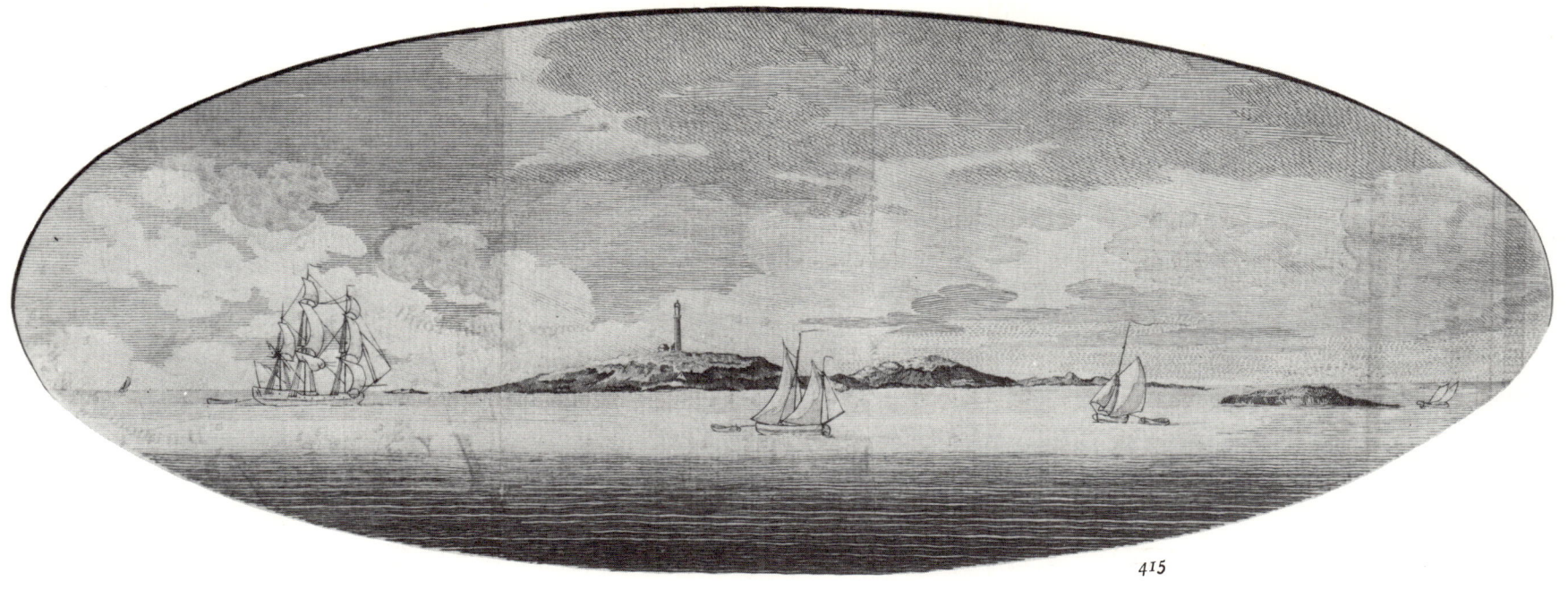

415

Etching (hand colored) 4⅛ x 53⅝ in. (image)

Coastal view set below a map of Halifax Harbor. *The Atlantic Neptune*. Phillips 1198, v. 1, no. 33.

——————Other impressions: Phillips 1202, v. 1, no. 24; Phillips 1205, v. 1, no. 27; Phillips 3658, v. 1, no. 20; Phillips 3655, v. 1, no. 20; Phillips 3656, v. 1, no. 20; LeGear 10323, v. 1, no. 20; LeGear 10320, v. 2, no. 37.

——————Other copies. These are farther views in oval with no hand coloring and no letters to designate points. Etching. Phillips 1199, v. 1, no. 24; Phillips 1200, v. 1, no. 24; Phillips 1201, v. 1, no. 24; Phillips 1203, v. 1, no. 24; Phillips 1250, v. 2, no. 13; Phillips 4473, v. 1, no. 19.

417
A View from the South Eastward of Halifax Harbor. [J.F.W. Des Barres, 177?]

Etching (hand colored) 2⅜ x 25¼ in. (image)

This picture identifies "The High-lands of Jeddore, bearing N.E.b.E. 3 leagues distant." *The Atlantic Neptune*. Phillips 3657, v. 1, no. 21.

——————Other impressions: Phillips 4473, v. 1, no. 18; LeGear 10320, v. 1, no. 39a; LeGear 10323, v. 1, no. 20a.

——————Another copy with same title, but imprint reads, "Publish'd according to Act of Parliament, July 26, 1777 by J.F.W. DesBarres Esqr." Aquatint with etching. Phillips 1198, v. 1, no. 36.

——————Another impression. Phillips 3658, pt. 1, no. 20a.

418
Appearance of the Shore (at three Miles off) four or five leagues to the Eastward of Halifax Harbor. [J.F.W. Des Barres, 177?]

Etching (hand colored) 2½ x 25¼ in. (image)

The Atlantic Neptune. Phillips 3657, v. 1, no. 21.

——————Other impressions: Phillips 4473, v. 1, no. 18; LeGear 10320, v. 1, no. 39a; LeGear 10323, v. 1, no. 20a.

——————Another copy with same title, but imprint reads, "Publish'd according to Act of Parliament, July 26, 1777 by J.F.W. DesBarres Esqr." Aquatint with etching. Phillips 1198, v. 1, no. 36.

——————Another impression. Phillips 3658, pt. 1, no. 20a.

419

A View taken 4 Miles off Shore, Halifax Harbor bearing North. [J.F.W. Des Barres, 177?]
Etching (hand colored) 2½ x 23⅛ in. (image)

The picture indicates "A. Sambro Lighthouse, B. Halifax harbor, and C. Rocky Bay." *The Atlantic Neptune.* Phillips 3657, v. 1, no. 21.

————Other impressions: Phillips 4473, v. 1, no. 18; LeGear 10320, v. 1, no. 39a; and LeGear 10323, v. 1, no. 20a.

————Another copy with same title, but imprint reads, "Publish'd according to Act of Parliament, July 26, 1777 by J.F.W. DesBarres Esqr." Aquatint with etching. Phillips 1198, v. 1, no. 36.

————Another impression. Phillips 3658, pt. 1, no. 20a.

420

Sambro Light-house, bearing west 1½ Miles distant. [J.F.W. Des Barres, 177?]
Etching (hand colored) 2¾ x 22 in. (image)

The Atlantic Neptune. Phillips 3657, v. 1, no. 21.

————Other impressions: Phillips 4473, v. 1, no. 18; LeGear 10320, v. 1, no. 39a; LeGear 10323, v. 1, no. 20a.

————Another copy with same title, but imprint reads, "Publish'd according to Act of Parliament, July 26, 1777 by J.F.W. DesBarres Esqr." Aquatint with etching. Phillips 1198, v. 1, no. 36.

————Another impression. Phillips 3658, pt. 1, no. 20a.

421

Sambro Light-house, south-east distant 1 Mile. [J.F.W. Des Barres, 177?]
Etching (hand colored) 3½ x 12⅞ in. (image)

The lighthouse is right of center. *The Atlantic Neptune.* Phillips 3657, v. 1, no. 21.

————Other impressions: Phillips 4473, v. 1, no. 18; LeGear 10320, v. 1, no. 39a; LeGear 10323, v. 1, no. 20a.

————Another copy with same title, but imprint reads, "Publish'd according to Act of Parliament, July 26, 1777 by J.F.W. DesBarres Esqr." Aquatint with etching. Phillips 1198, v. 1, no. 36.

————Another impression. Phillips 3658, pt. 1, no. 20a.

422

Chebucto Head, bearing North 6° East, distant 2 Miles. [J.F.W. Des Barres, 177?]
Etching (hand colored) 2⅞ x 25¾ in. (image)

The Head is in the right part of the picture; also identified are Sambro lighthouse and Halifax Harbor. *The Atlantic Neptune.* Phillips 3657, v. 1, no. 21.

————Other impressions: Phillips 4473, v. 1, no. 18; LeGear 10320, v. 1, no. 39a; LeGear 10323, v. 1, no. 20a.

————Another copy with same title, but imprint reads, "Publish'd according to Act of Parliament, July 26, 1777 by J.F.W. DesBarres Esqr." Aquatint with etching. Phillips 1198, v. 1, no. 36.

————Another impression. Phillips 3658, pt. 1, no. 20a.

423

Halifax in Nova Scotia. Publish'd according to Act of Parliament, Octr. 14, 1777 by J.F.W. DesBarres Esqr.
Etching (hand colored) 15½ x 21⅛ in.

Two boys in foreground, one holding a dog. A man launches a small boat into the harbor. The view looks out over the harbor and city of Halifax to the sea. *The Atlantic Neptune*, LeGear 10320, v. 2, no. 39.

424

A View of the Town & Harbour of Halifax, from Dartmouth Shore. Pubd. as the Act Directs by J.F.W. DesBarres Esqr. March 1st, 1781.
Aquatint with etching 20 x 28½ in.

The town and fortress are to the right. *The Atlantic Neptune.* Phillips 1198, v. 1, no. 35. LC–USZ62–34798

————Another impression. LeGear 10323, v. 1, no. 19a.

425

A View of the East End of the Isle Sable, bearing S:2°W: distant 4 Miles, Naked Sand Hills appearing over the Land, Rams Head S:57°W: distant 17 Miles. [J.F.W. Des Barres, 1777?]
Etching (hand colored) 2¾ x 23¼ in. (image)

The Atlantic Neptune. Phillips 3657, v. 1, no. 16.

————Other impressions: Phillips 4473, v. 1, no. 4; LeGear 10323, v. 1, no. 38; LeGear 10320, v. 2, no. 64.

————Another copy with same title, but imprint reads, "Publish'd according to Act of Parliament June 1, 1779. by J.F.W. DesBarres Esqr." Aquatint with etching 2¾ x 23¼ in. (image). Ships in the waters. *The Atlantic Neptune.* Phillips 1198, v. 1, no. 64. The negative number for this picture and the next four is LC–USZ62–46045.

————Other impressions: Phillips 1205, v. 1, no. 3; Phillips 3658, pt. 1, 2a.

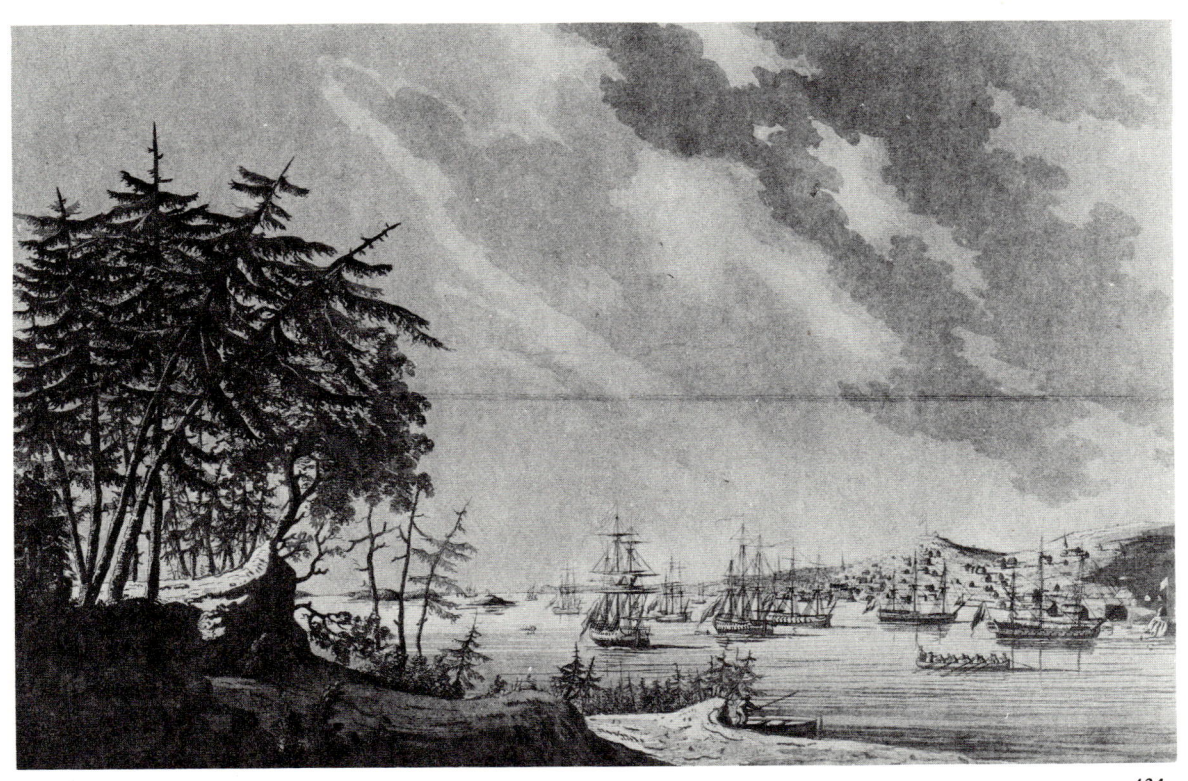

424

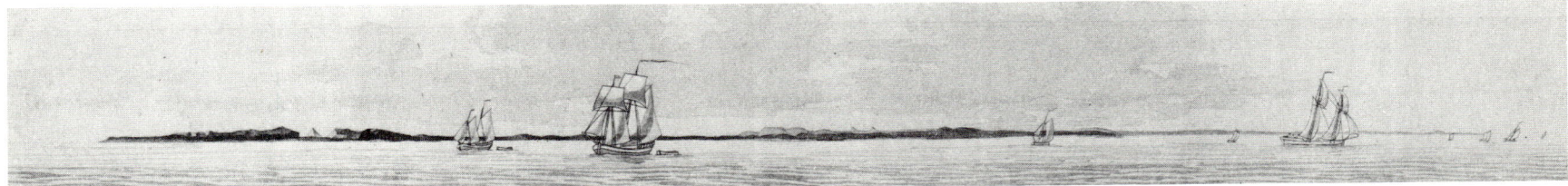

425

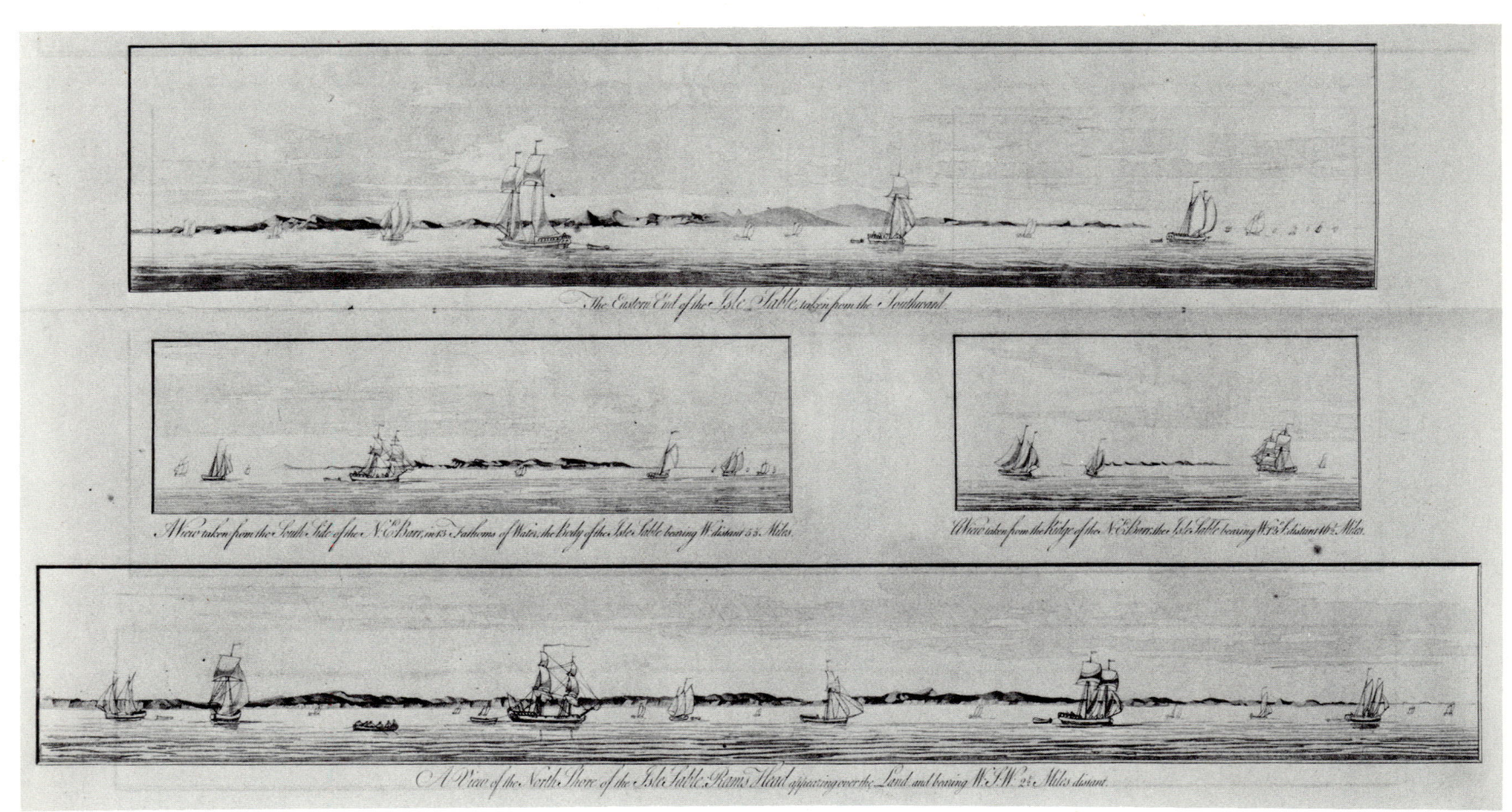

426, 427, 428, 429

426

The Eastern End of the Isle Sable, taken from the Southward. [J.F.W. Des Barres, 1777?]

Etching (hand colored) 4½ x 23¾ in. (image)

The Atlantic Neptune. Phillips 3657, v. 1, no. 16.

——————Other impressions: Phillips 4473, v. 1, no. 4; LeGear 10323, v. 1, no. 38; LeGear 10320, v. 2, no. 64.

——————Another copy with same title, but imprint reads, "Publish'd according to Act of Parliament June 1, 1779. by J.F.W. DesBarres Esqr." Aquatint with etching 4½ x 23¾ in. (image). Ships in the waters. *The Atlantic Neptune.* Phillips 1198, v. 1, no. 64.

——————Other impressions: Phillips 1205, v. 1, no. 3; Phillips 3658, pt. 1, no. 2a.

427

A View taken from the South Side of the N:E: Barr, in 13 Fathoms of Water; the Body of the Isle Sable bearing W: distant 5⅓ Miles. [J.F.W. Des Barres, 1777?]

Etching (hand colored) 3¼ x 11⅝ in. (image)

The Atlantic Neptune. Phillips 3657, v. 1, no. 16.

——————Other impressions: Phillips 4473, v. 1, no. 4; LeGear 10323, v. 1, no. 38; LeGear 10320, v. 2, no. 64.

——————Another copy with same title, but imprint reads, "Publish'd according to Act of Parliament June 1, 1779. by J.F.W. DesBarres Esqr." Aquatint with etching 3¼ x 11⅝ in. (image). Ships in the waters. *The Atlantic Neptune.* Phillips 1198, v. 1, no. 64.

——————Other impressions: Phillips 1205, v. 1, no. 3; Phillips 3658, pt. 1, no. 2a.

428

A View taken from the Ridge of the N:E:Barr, the Isle Sable bearing W:12°S: distant 16½ Miles. [J.F.W. Des Barres, 1777?]

Etching (hand colored) 3¼ x 7¼ in. (image)

The Atlantic Neptune. Phillips 3657, v. 1, no. 16.

——————Other impressions: Phillips 4473, v. 1, no. 4; LeGear 10323, v. 1, no. 38; LeGear 10320, v. 2, no. 64.

——————Another copy with same title, but imprint reads, "Publish'd according to Act of Parliament June 1, 1779. by J.F.W. DesBarres Esqr." Aquatint with etching 3¼ x 7¼ in. (image). Ships in the waters. *The Atlantic Neptune.* Phillips 1198, v. 1, no. 64.

——————Other impressions: Phillips 1205, v. 1, no. 3; Phillips 3658, pt. 1, no. 2a.

429

A View of the North Shore of the Isle Sable; Rams Head appearing over the Land, and bearing W:S:W: 2½ Miles distant. [J.F.W. Des Barres, 1777?]

Etching (hand colored) 3½ x 26⅕ in. (image)

The Atlantic Neptune. Phillips 3657, v. 1, no. 16.

——————Other impressions: Phillips 4473, v. 1, no. 4; LeGear 10323, v. 1, no. 38; LeGear 10320, v. 2, no. 64.

——————Another copy with same title, but imprint reads, "Publish'd according to Act of Parliament June 1, 1779 by J.F.W. DesBarres Esqr." Aquatint with etching 3½ x 26⅕ in. (image). Ships in the waters. *The Atlantic Neptune.* Phillips 1198, v. 1, no. 64.

——————Other impressions: Phillips 1205, v. 1, no. 3; Phillips 3658, pt. 1, no. 2a.

430

West End of the Isle of Sable from the Northward, 2 Miles distant. Entrance of the Pond. [J.F.W. Des Barres, 1776–77?]

Etching (hand colored) 3⅞ x 30⅛ in. (image)

Entrance of the pond to the left; west end of the island to the right. *The Atlantic Neptune.* Phillips 3657, v. 1, no. 20.

——————Other impressions: LeGear 10323, v. 1, no. 36a; LeGear 10320, v. 2, no. 65.

431

Wreckers Den near the Pond on the Isle of Sable. [J.F.W. Des Barres, 1776–77?]

Etching (hand colored) 6 x 12¼ in. (image)

In the foreground three men work around a cabin which is built into a sand dune. In the background men chase horses, and on top of a large dune a surveyor is at work. The sea is to the right. *The Atlantic Neptune.* Phillips 3657, v. 1, no. 20.

——————Other impressions: LeGear 10323, v. 1, no. 36a; LeGear 10320, v. 2, no. 65.

432

North Shore. [J.F.W. Des Barres, 1776–77?]

Etching (hand colored) 6⅛ x 8⅛ in. (image)

The picture shows large sand dunes with grass on top. *The Atlantic Neptune.* Phillips 3657, v. 1, no. 20.

——————Other impressions: LeGear 10323, v. 1, no. 36a; LeGear 10320, v. 2, no. 65.

433

North Shore of Isle Sable, 2 Miles distant. [J.F.W. Des Barres, 1776–77?]

Etching (hand colored) 4 x 39¾ in. (image)

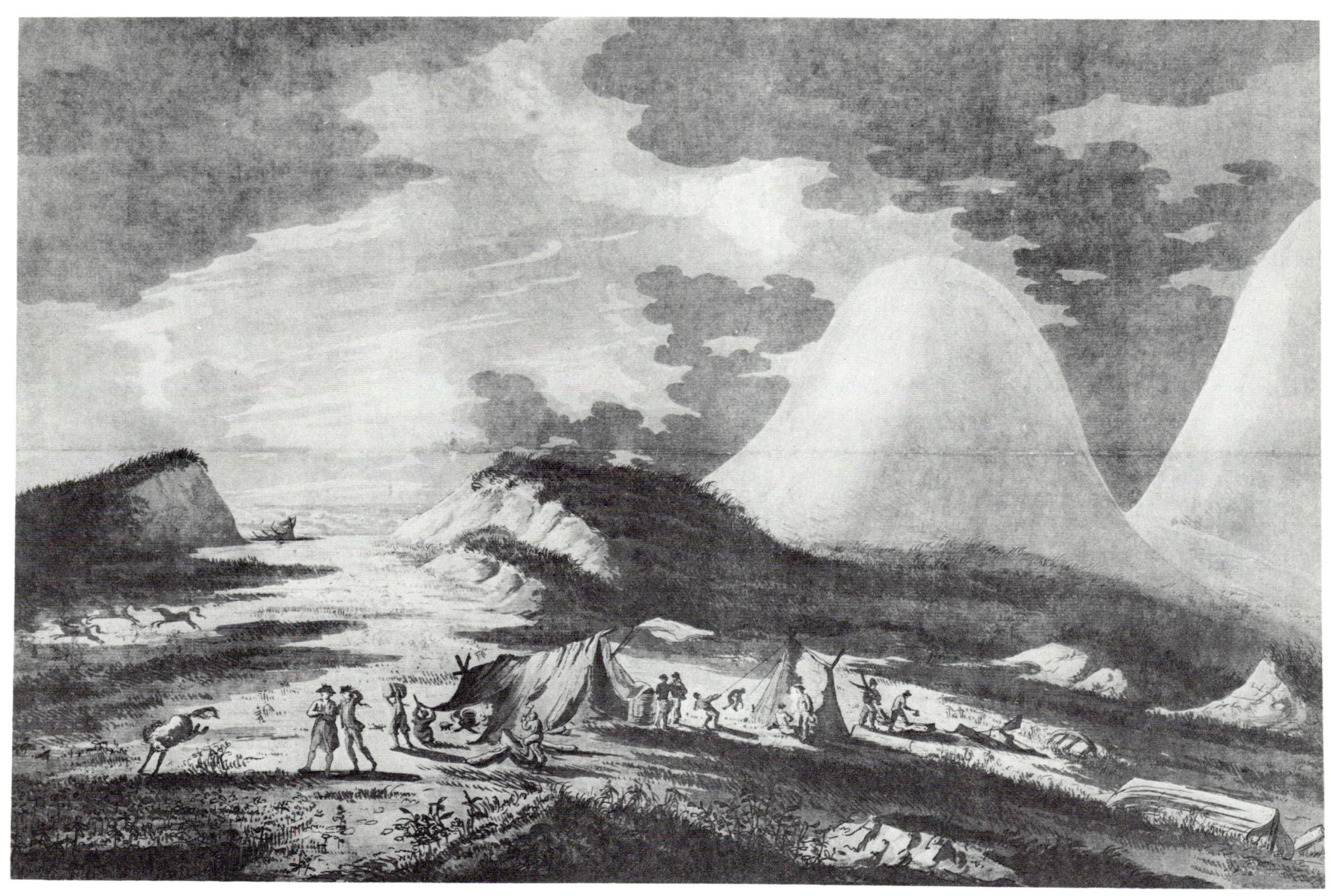

434

The Atlantic Neptune. Phillips 3657, v. 1, no. 20.

———Other impressions: LeGear 10323, v. 1, no. 36a; LeGear 10320, v. 2, no. 65.

434
A View from the Camp at the East End of the Naked Sand Hills, on the South East Shore of the Isle of Sable. Pub According to Act of Parliament June 1, 1781 by J.F.W. DesBarres Esqr.

Aquatint with etching 21⅗ x 30¾ in. (image)

The Atlantic Neptune. Phillips 1198, v. 1, no. 65. LC–USZ62–46046

———Other impressions: Phillips 1205, v. 1, no. 5; LeGear 10232, v. 1, no. 37; LeGear 10230, v. 2, no. 67.

435
A. Cape Prospect bearing N: by E: distant 10½ Miles. B. Cape Sambro N:N:E: ¾ E: 14 Miles. [J.F.W. Des Barres, 1777?]

Etching (hand colored) 2⅜ x 13¾ in. (image)

Landforms in the far background. No ships are shown. *The Atlantic Neptune.* LeGear 10323, v. 1, no. 16a.

———Other impressions: LeGear 10317, v. 1, no. 10d; LeGear 10320, v. 1, no. 35.

———Another copy with same title, but imprint reads, "Pub. as the Act Directs by J.F.W. DesBarres Esqr. March 1st 1779." Aquatint with etching 2⅜ x 13¾ in. (image). Landforms in the far background. Ships in the water. *The Atlantic Neptune.* Phillips 1198, v. 1, no. 19.

———Other impressions: Phillips 3658, v. 1, no. 3a; Phillips 4473, v. 1, no. 14.

436
C. The High Lands of Haspotagoen bearing N: W: ½ N being three Leagues off Shore. [J.F.W. Des Barres, 1777?]

Etching (hand colored) 2⅛ x 17½ in. (image)

The landform in the far background. *The Atlantic Neptune.* LeGear 10323, v. 1, no. 16a.

———Other impressions: LeGear 10317, v. 1, no. 10d; LeGear 10320, v. 1, no. 35.

———Another copy with same title, but imprint reads, "Pub as the Act Directs by J.F.W. DesBarres Esqr. March 1st 1779." Aquatint with etching 2⅛ x 17½ in. (image). The landform in the far background. Ships in the water. *The Atlantic Neptune.* Phillips 1198, v. 1, no. 19.

———Other impressions: Phillips 3658, v. 1, no. 3a; Phillips 4473, v. 1, no. 14.

437
The Ovens at the Entrance of Lunenburg Bay. [J.F.W. Des Barres, 1777?]

Etching (hand colored) 4¾ x 6¼ in. (image)

The bluffs to the left. This image is set into an oval. *The Atlantic Neptune.* LeGear 10323, v. 1, no. 16a.

———Other impressions: LeGear 10317, v. 1, no. 10d; LeGear 10320, v. 1, no. 35.

———Another copy with same title, but imprint reads, "Pub as the Act Directs by J.F.W. DesBarres Esqr. March 1st 1779." Aquatint with etching 4¾ x 6¼ in. (image). The bluffs to the left. Ships in the water. This image is set into an oval. *The Atlantic Neptune.* Phillips 1198, v. 1, no. 19.

———Other impressions: Phillips 3658, v. 1, no. 3a; Phillips 4473, v. 1, no. 14.

438
D. Cape Sable bearing N.N.W. distant 2 Leagues. E. The Entrance of Barrington Bay N: by E: [J.F.W. Des Barres, 1777?]

Etching (hand colored) 2½ x 20½ in. (image)

Cape Sable to the left and the bay to the right. No ships are shown. *The Atlantic Neptune.* LeGear 10323, v. 1, no. 16a.

———Other impressions: LeGear 10317, v. 1, no. 10d; LeGear 10320, v. 1, no. 35.

———Another copy with same title, but imprint reads, "Pub as the Act Directs by J.F.W. DesBarres Esqr. March 1st 1779." Aquatint with etching 2½ x 20½ in. (image). Cape Sable to the left and the bay to the right. Ships in the water. *The Atlantic Neptune.* Phillips 1198, v. 1, no. 19.

———Other impressions: Phillips 3658, v. 1, no. 3a; Phillips 4473, v. 1, no. 14.

439
F. Cape Sable bearing N. E: by N: distant 4 Miles. [J.F.W. Des Barres, 1777?]

Etching (hand colored) 3¼ x 20½ in. (image)

The cape to the right. No ships are shown. *The Atlantic Neptune.* LeGear 10323, v. 1, no. 16a.

———Other impressions: LeGear 10317, v. 1, no. 10d; LeGear 10320, v. 1, no. 35.

———Another copy with same title, but imprint reads, "Pub as the Act Directs by J.F.W. DesBarres Esqr. March 1st 1779." Aquatint with etching 3⅜ x 20¼ in. (image). The cape to the right. Ships in the water. *The Atlantic Neptune.* Phillips 1198, v. 1, no. 19.

———Other impressions: Phillips 3658, v. 1, no. 3a; Phillips 4473, v. 1, no. 14.

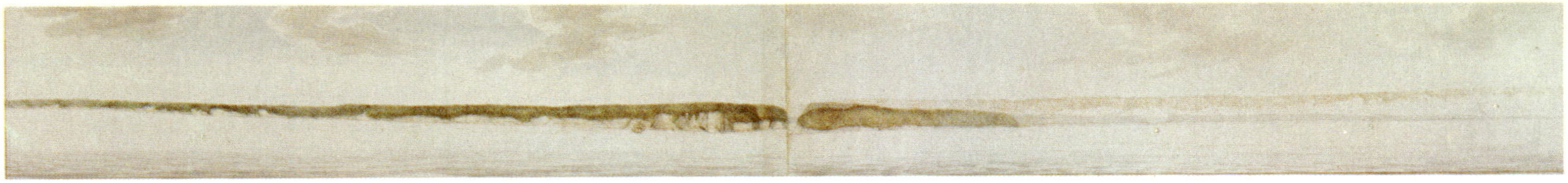

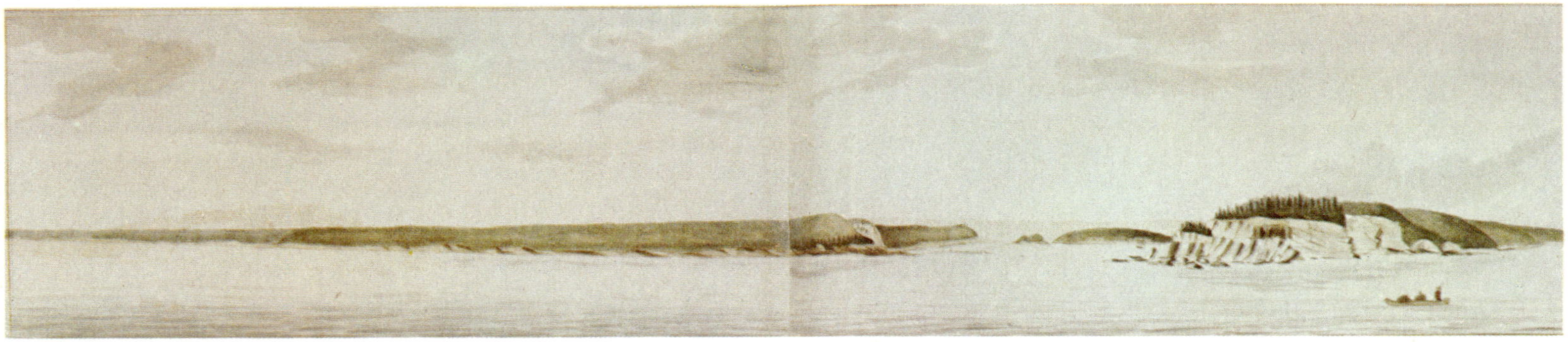

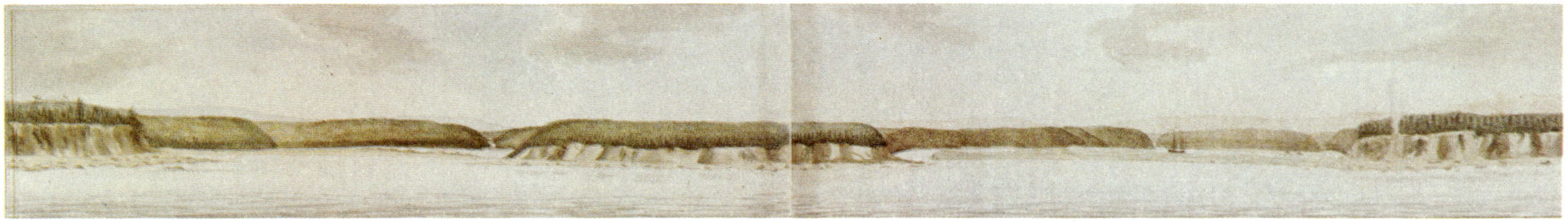

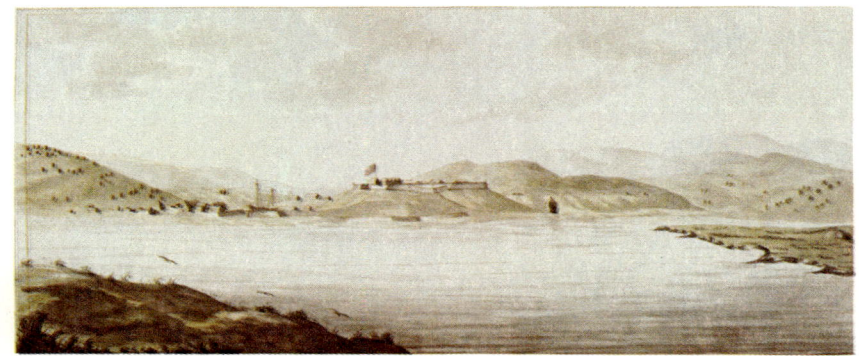
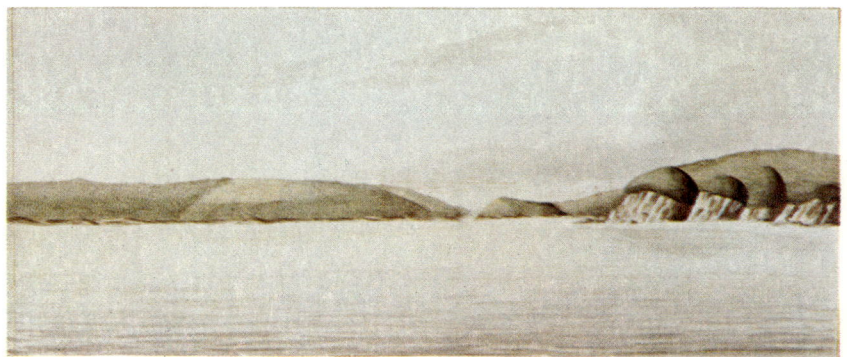

445, 446, 449, 450, 451

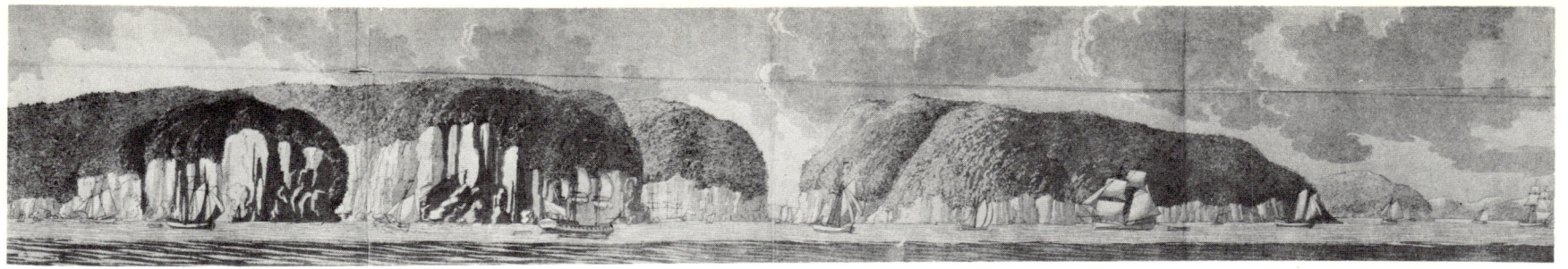

445a

440
The South West Coast of Nova Scotia the Brazil Sunken Rock bearing E.b.S. ½ Mile. [J.F.W. Des Barres, 1776–77?]

Etching (hand colored) 3 x 38 in. (image)

Legend reads: "a. Cape Sable W.N.W.; b. Cape Negro N.N.E." *The Atlantic Neptune.* Phillips 3657, v. 1, no. 23.

———————Other impressions: LeGear 10317, v. 1, no. 10b; LeGear 10320, v. 1, no. 27.

441
Cape Sable. [J.F.W. Des Barres, 1776–77?]

Etching (hand colored) 5¼ x 41½ in. (image)

The Atlantic Neptune. Phillips 3657, v. 1, no. 23.

———————Other impressions: LeGear 10317, v. 1, no. 10b; LeGear 10320, v. 1, no. 27.

442
The South West Coast of Nova Scotia. [J.F.W. Des Barres, 1776–77?]

Etching (hand colored) 3⅞ x 41¾ in. (image)

Legend reads: "a. Cape Negro, N.W.b.W. 2 Miles b. Argyle Head in the Entrance of Port Campbell." *The Atlantic Neptune.* Phillips 3657, v. 1, no. 24.

———————Other impressions: LeGear 10317, v. 1, no. 23; LeGear 10320, v. 1, no. 26.

443
The South West Coast of Nova Scotia. [J.F.W. Des Barres, 1776–77?]

Etching (hand colored) 4⅜ x 33¼ in. (image)

Legend reads: "a. Cape Sable W.S.W. 4 Leagues; b. Port Haldimand." *The Atlantic Neptune.* Phillips 3657, v. 1, no. 24.

———————Other impressions: LeGear 10317, v. 1, no. 23; LeGear 10320, v. 1, no. 26.

444
The Southern Seal Isle, N.N.W. 2 Leagues distant. [J.F.W. Des Barres, 1776–77?]

Etching (hand colored) 2½ x 7¼ in. (image)

The Atlantic Neptune. Phillips 3657, v. 1, no. 24.

———————Other impressions: LeGear 10317, v. 1, no. 23; LeGear 10320, v. 1, no. 26.

445
View of the Entrance into Annapolis Bason. [J.F.W. Des Barres, 1776–77?]

Etching (hand colored) 4¾ x 36¾ in. (image)

The caption identifies: "A. Gulliver's Hole B. Sandy Cove." *The Atlantic Neptune.* Phillips 3657, v. 1, no. 14. Items 445, 446, and 449–451 are illustrated in color.

———————Another impression. LeGear 10320, v. 1, no. 19.

———————Another copy entitled, "A View of the Entrance of the Gut of Annapolis Royal." [J.F.W. Des Barres, 178?]. Aquatint with etching 6¼ x 35¼ in. (image). A closer view than the previous copy with many ships added. *The Atlantic Neptune.* LeGear 10317, v. 1, no. 9a. LC–USZ62–46064

446
View of the North Entrance of Grand Passage. [J.F.W. Des Barres, 1776–77?]

Etching (hand colored) 8 x 36¾ in. (image)

The entrance is to the right. *The Atlantic Neptune.* Phillips 3657, v. 1, no. 14.

———————Another impression. LeGear 10320, v. 1, no. 19.

447
A View of the Entrance of Petit Passage. Publishd as the Act directs 1st Jany 1780. [J.F.W. Des Barres]

Aquatint with etching 14 x 17 in.

The Atlantic Neptune. Phillips 1198, v. 1, no. 12. LC–USZ62–46034

———————Another impression. LeGear 10317, v. 1, no. 9a (trimmed to image 10 x 16 in.).

448
Grand Passage in the Bay Fundy, on the Western Shore of Nova Scotia. Publishd as the Act

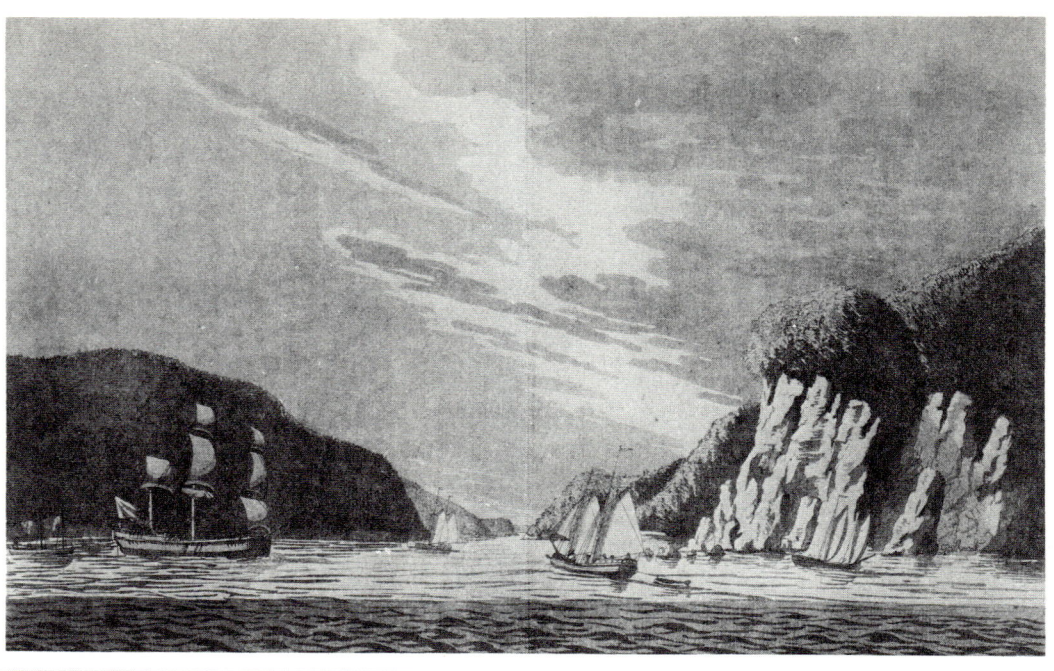

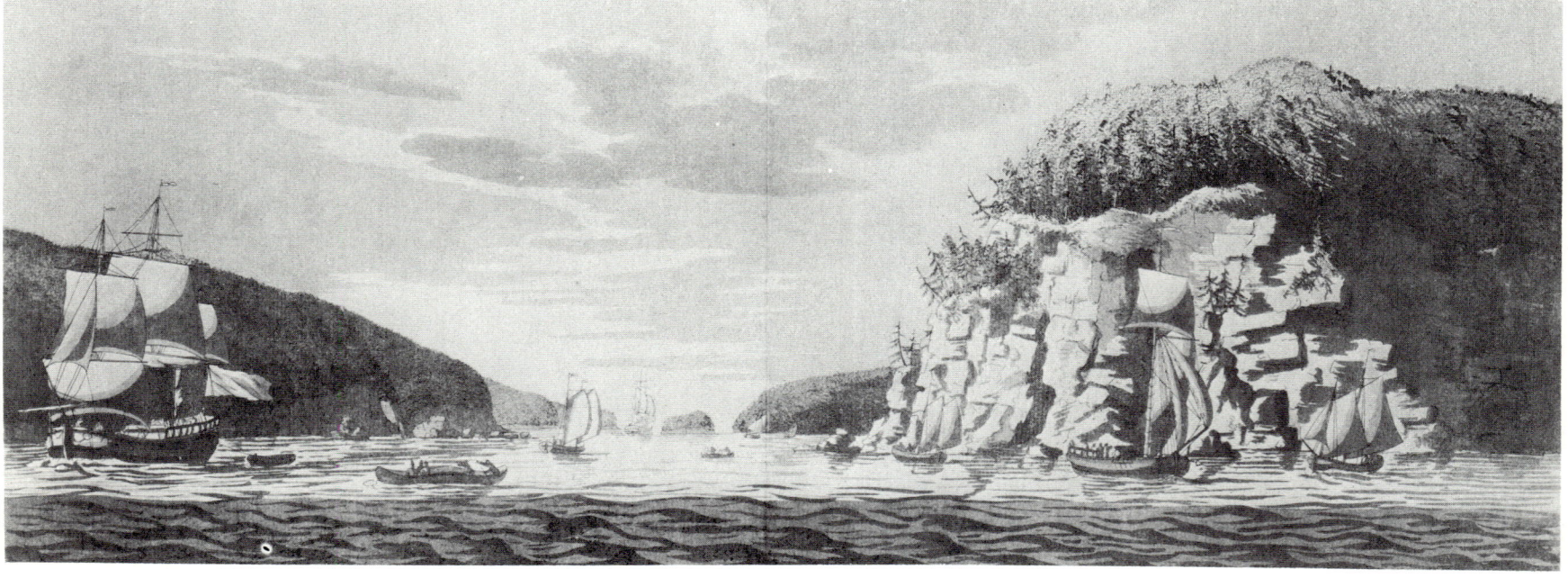

447 448

164

directs 1st Jany 1780. [J.F.W. Des Barres]
Aquatint with etching 12 x 23¼ in.

The Atlantic Neptune. Phillips 1198, v. 1, no. 12. LC–USZ62–46035

449
View of Eden and Gascoyne Rivers, at the Entrance of the Basin of Mines. [J.F.W. Des Barres, 1776–77?]
Etching (hand colored) 5⅜ x 36¾ in. (image)

Eden River to the left; Gascoyne River to the right with a ship anchored in its channel. Five Indians dance around a fire on cliffs to the right. *The Atlantic Neptune.* Phillips 3657, v. 1, no. 14.

——————Another impression. LeGear 10320, v. 1, no. 19.

450
View of Annapolis Royal. [J.F.W. Des Barres, 1776–77?]
Etching (hand colored) 8¼ x 19⅜ in. (image)

The Atlantic Neptune. Phillips 3657, v. 1, no. 14.
——————Another impression. LeGear 10320, v. 1, no. 19.

451
View of the North Entrance of Petit Passage. [J.F.W. Des Barres, 1776–77?]
Etching (hand colored) 8¼ x 19⅜ in. (image)

Passage to the right of center. *The Atlantic Neptune.* Phillips 3657, v. 1, no. 14.

——————Another impression. LeGear 10320, v. 1, no. 19.

452
View of Gulliver's Hole. Published According to Act of Parliament, by J.F.W. DesBarres, Esqr. January 1st, 1781.

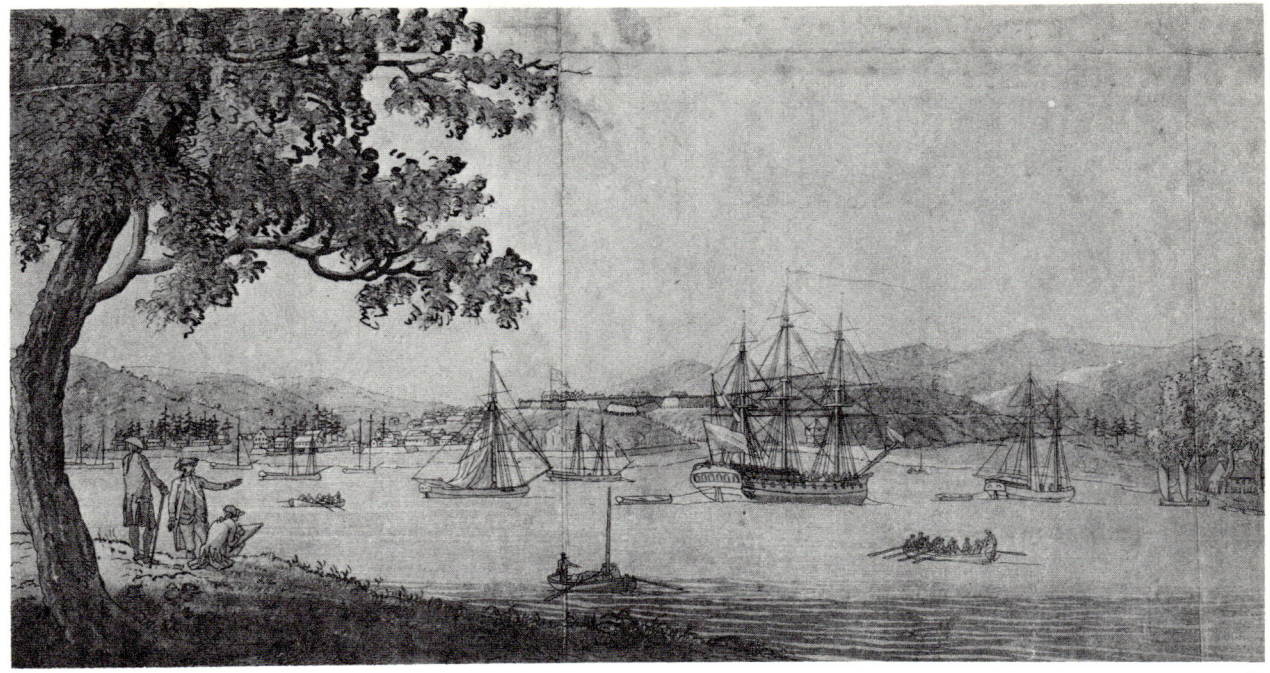

Etching 7½ x 19 in. (image)

This view is an inset into a map of Annapolis Royal and St. Mary's Bay. *The Atlantic Neptune.* Phillips 1198, v. 1, no. 10.

——————Other impressions: Phillips 1199, v. 1, no. 10; Phillips 1200, v. 1, no. 10; Phillips 1201, v. 1, no. 10; Phillips 1202, v. 1, no. 10; Phillips 1203, v. 1, no. 10; Phillips 1205, v. 1, no. 13; Phillips 1250, v. 1, no. 7; Phillips 3658, pt. 1, no. 8; Phillips 3655, v. 1, no. 8; Phillips 3656, v. 1, no. 8; Phillips 3657, v. 1, no. 5; Phillips 4473, v. 1, no. 46; LeGear 10323, v. 1, no. 8; LeGear 10317, v. 1, no. 10; LeGear 10320, v. 1, no. 18.

453
ANNAPOLIS ROYAL. Published as the Act directs by J.F.W. DesBarres Esqr. Jany. 1st 1781.

Aquatint with etching 15½ x 23½ in.

View across the bay; the city on bluffs, mountains in the background. *The Atlantic Neptune.* Phillips 1198, v. 1, no. 11.

——————Other impressions: Phillips 3658, pt. 1, no. 8a; and LeGear 10323, v. 1, no. 8a.

——————Another copy, smaller and trimmed to image, entitled, "A View of Annapolis Royal" 10 x 18¾ in. LeGear 10317, v. 1, no. 9a. LC–USZ62–46063

454
The ISLE HAUT, bearing N.b.W. distant 4 Miles and CAPE CHIGNECTO, N.N.E. 3 Leagues. [J.F.W. DesBarres, 1777?]
Etching (hand colored) 3⅞ x 19¼ in. (image)

The isle set to left and the cape to right. No ships are shown. A farther view than that

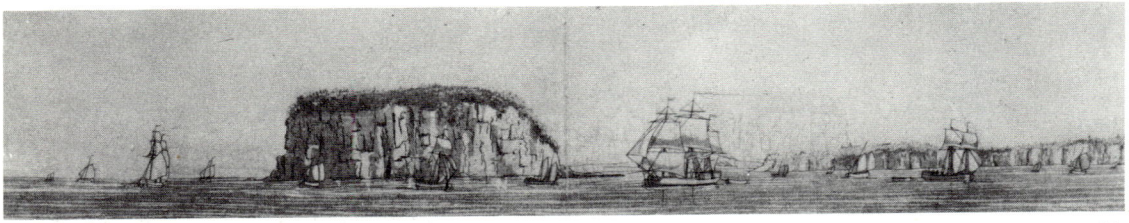

454

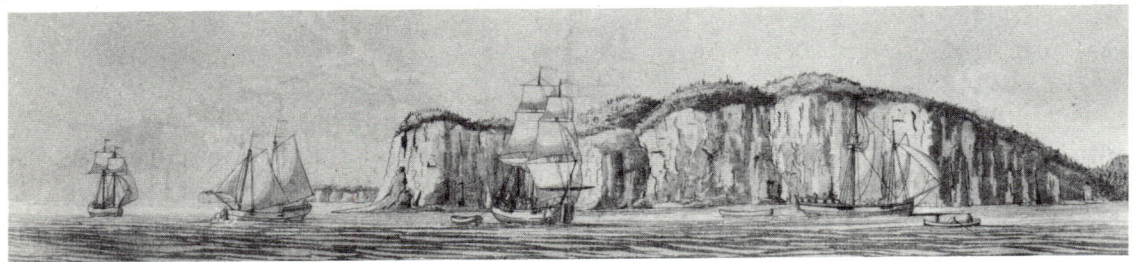

455

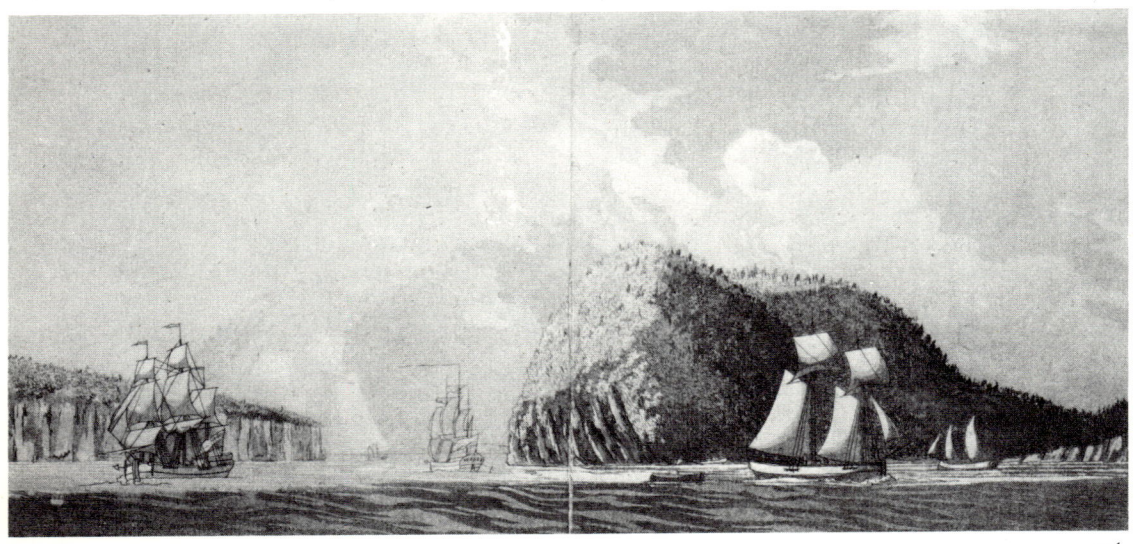

456

illustrated. *The Atlantic Neptune.* LeGear 10317, v. 1, no. 9c.

———— Another impression. LeGear 10320, v. 1, no. 16.

———— Another copy with same title but of a later date. [178?] Aquatint with etching 3⅞ x 19¼ in. (image). *The Atlantic Neptune.* Phillips 1198, v. 1, no. 6. The negative number for this picture and the next five is LC–USZ62–46032.

———— Other impressions: Phillips 3658, pt. 1, no. 7b; LeGear 10323, v. 1, no. 6b.

455

The Western Cliffs of CAPE DORE. [J.F.W. Des Barres, 1777?]

Etching (hand colored) 4½ x 14½ in. (image)

Cliffs are set to center and right of the picture. A single rowboat is in the foreground. A farther view than that illustrated. *The Atlantic Neptune.* LeGear 10317, v. 1, no. 9c.

———— Another impression. LeGear 10320, v. 1, no. 16.

———— Another copy with same title but of a later date. [178?] Aquatint with etching 4¾ x 18½ in. (image). *The Atlantic Neptune.* Phillips 1198, v. 1, no. 6.

———— Other impressions: Phillips 3658, pt. 1, no. 7b; LeGear 10323, v. 1, no. 6b.

456

A View of CAPE BAPTIST in the Entrance in the BASON of MINES, bearing W.b.N. 2 Miles distant. [J.F.W. Des Barres, 1777?]

Etching (hand colored) 7¼ x 14½ in. (image)

A single ship sails into the entrance of the basin in left center. A farther view than that

166

illustrated. *The Atlantic Neptune.* LeGear 10317, v. 1, no. 9c.

——————Another impression. LeGear 10320, v. 1, no. 16.

——————Another copy with same title but of a later date. [178?] Aquatint with etching 7¼ x 14½ in. (image). *The Atlantic Neptune.* Phillips 1198, v. 1, no. 6.

——————Other impressions: Phillips 3658, pt. 1, no. 7b; LeGear 10323, v. 1, no. 6b.

457
A View of the ENTRANCE into the BASON of MINES, bearing East distant 4 Leagues. [J.F.W. Des Barres, 1777?]

Etching (hand colored) 2⅞ x 14½ in. (image)

The entrance to the basin in left center of the picture. A farther view than that illustrated. *The Atlantic Neptune.* LeGear 10317, v. 1, no. 9c.

——————Another impression. LeGear 10320, v. 1, no. 16.

——————Another copy with same title but of a later date. [178?] Aquatint with etching 3 x 14½ in. (image). *The Atlantic Neptune.* Phillips 1198, v. 1, no. 6.

——————Other impressions: Phillips 3658, pt. 1, no. 7b; LeGear 10323, v. 1, no. 6b.

458
The ISLE HAUTE, bearing W.N.W. distant 2 Miles. [J.F.W. Des Barres, 1777?]

Etching (hand colored) 4¼ x 8½ in. (image)

The island to the right. A farther view than that illustrated. *The Atlantic Neptune.* LeGear 10317, v. 1, no. 9c.

——————Another impression. LeGear 10320, v. 1, no. 16.

——————Another copy with same title but of a later date. [178?] Aquatint with etching 4½ x 8⅝ in. (image). *The Atlantic Neptune.* Phillips 1198, v. 1, no. 6.

——————Other impressions: Phillips 3658, pt. 1, no. 7b; LeGear 10323, v. 1, no. 6b.

459
CAPE BLOWMEDOWN, open with CAPE SPLIT, bearing E.N.E. 1 League distant. [J.F.W. Des Barres, 1777?]

Etching (hand colored) 4¼ x 8½ in. (image)

The cape is on the right. A farther view than that illustrated. *The Atlantic Neptune.* LeGear 10317, v. 1, no. 9c.

——————Another impression. LeGear 10320, v. 1, no. 16.

——————Another copy with same title but of a later date. [178?] Aquatint with etching 4½ x 8⅝ in. (image). *The Atlantic Neptune.* Phillips 1198, v. 1, no. 6.

——————Other impressions: Phillips 3658, pt. 1, no. 7b; LeGear 10323, v. 1, no. 6b.

460
A View of PARTRIDGE ISLAND, from the West. Publish'd according to Act of Parliament July 26, 1777, by J.F.W. DesBarres Esqr.

Aquatint with etching 21 x 30⅝ in.

Distinguishes "A. The Harbor" and "B. Cape Blowmedown, S.b.W. 4 Miles distant." One ship at anchor in the left foreground; another sailing to the right of the island in the right foreground. *The Atlantic Neptune.* Phillips 1198, v. 1, no. 4.

——————Other impressions: Phillips 3657, v. 1, no. 15 (hand colored); LeGear 10323, v. 1, no. 5a; LeGear 10317, v. 1, no. 9b; LeGear 10320, v. 1, no. 17.

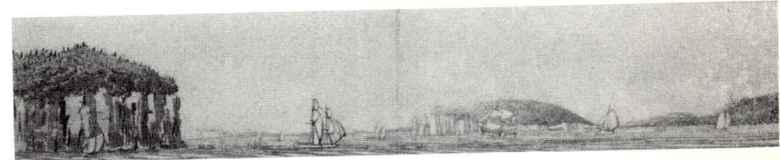

457

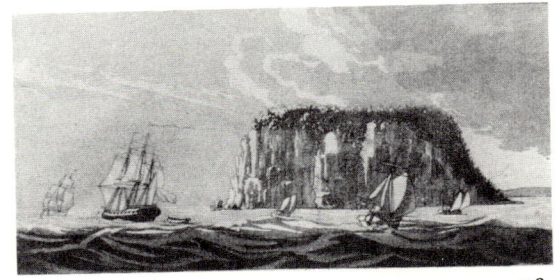

458

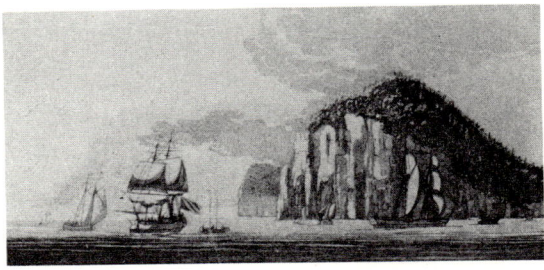

459

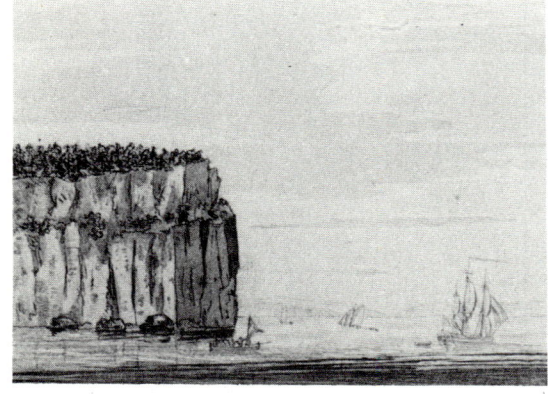
461

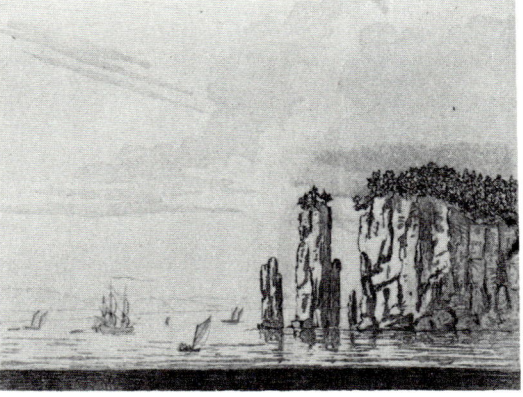
462

461

Cape Blowmedown. Published according to Act of Parliament, July 26, 1777, by J.F.W. DesBarres Esqr.

Etching (hand colored) 5⅝ x 7½ in. (image)

No ships are shown. *The Atlantic Neptune.* Phillips 3657, v. 1, no. 13.

——————Other impressions: LeGear 10323, v. 1, no. 6c; LeGear 10317, v. 1, no. 10c; LeGear 10320, v. 1, no. 14.

——————Another copy with same title, but imprints reads, "Publish'd as the Act directs Jany 1st 1779 by J.F.W. DesBarres Esqr." Aquatint with etching 5¾ x 7⅜ in. (image). *The Atlantic Neptune.* Phillips 1198, v. 1, no. 7. The negative number for this picture and the next three is LC–USZ62–46033.

——————Another impression. Phillips 3658, pt. 1, no. 7a.

462

Cape Split. Published according to Act of Parliament, July 26, 1777, by J.F.W. DesBarres Esqr.

Etching (hand colored) 5⅝ x 7⅜ in. (image)

The Atlantic Neptune. Phillips 3657, v. 1, no. 13.

——————Other impressions: LeGear 10323, v. 1, no. 6c; LeGear 10317, v. 1, no. 10c; LeGear 10320, v. 1, no. 14.

——————Another copy with same title, but imprint reads, "Publish'd as the Act directs Jany 1st 1779 by J.F.W. DesBarres Esqr." Aquatint with etching 5¾ x 7¼ in. (image). *The Atlantic Neptune.* Phillips 1198, v. 1, no. 7.

——————Another impression. Phillips 3658, pt. 1, no. 7a.

463

Spencers Island and the Entrance of Mines Bason. Published according to Act of Parliament, July 26, 1777, by J.F.W. DesBarres Esqr.

Etching (hand colored) 6⅝ x 16⅝ in. (image)

The entrance is to the right, and the island is in the center. In the left foreground a man plays a flute in a small boat, while three men row and another fishes. *The Atlantic Neptune.* Phillips 3657, v. 1, no. 13.

——————Other impressions: LeGear 10323, v. 1, no. 6c; LeGear 10317, v. 1, no. 10c; LeGear 10320, v. 1, no. 14.

——————Another copy with different title and imprint. "The Entrance of Mines Bason. Publish'd as the Act directs Jany 1st 1779 by J.F.W. DesBarres Esqr." Aquatint with etching 7⅞ x 16½ in. (image). The entrance in the center and Spencer's Island to the right of the picture. *The Atlantic Neptune.* Phillips 1198, v. 1, no. 7.

——————Another impression. Phillips 3658, pt. 1, no. 7a.

464

Isle Haut and Cape Chegnecto. Published according to Act of Parliament, July 26, 1777, by J.F.W. DesBarres Esqr.

Etching (hand colored) 8¾ x 16½ in. (image)

Three boats sail around the island in the center; the cape is to the right. A farther view than that illustrated. No ships are shown. *The Atlantic Neptune.* Phillips 3657, v. 1, no. 13.

——————Other impressions: LeGear 10323, v. 1, no. 6c; LeGear 10317, v. 1, no. 10c; LeGear 10320, v. 1, no. 14.

——————Another copy with same title, but imprint reads, "Publish'd as the Act directs Jany 1st 1779 by J.F.W. DesBarres Esqr."

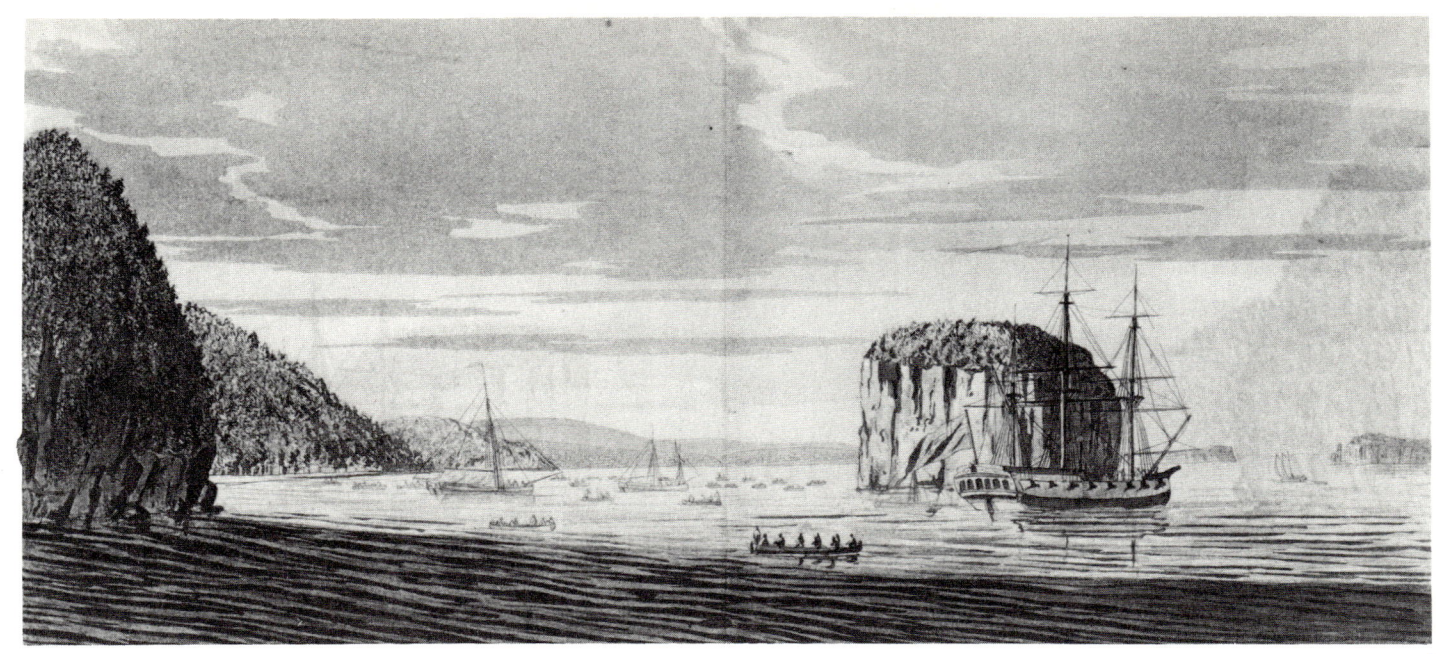

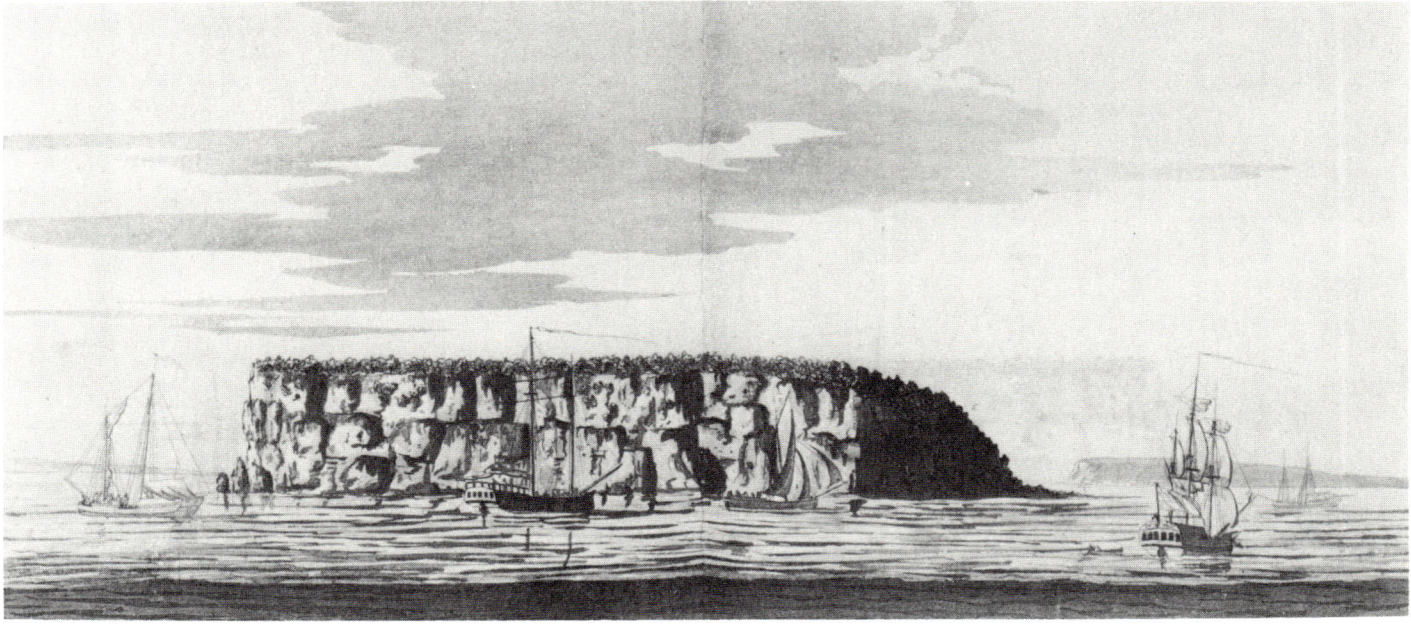

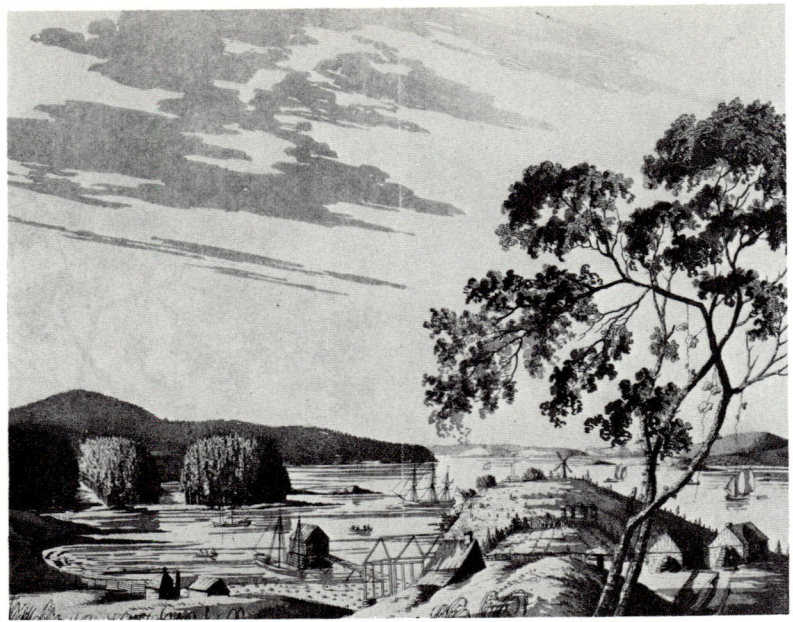

465

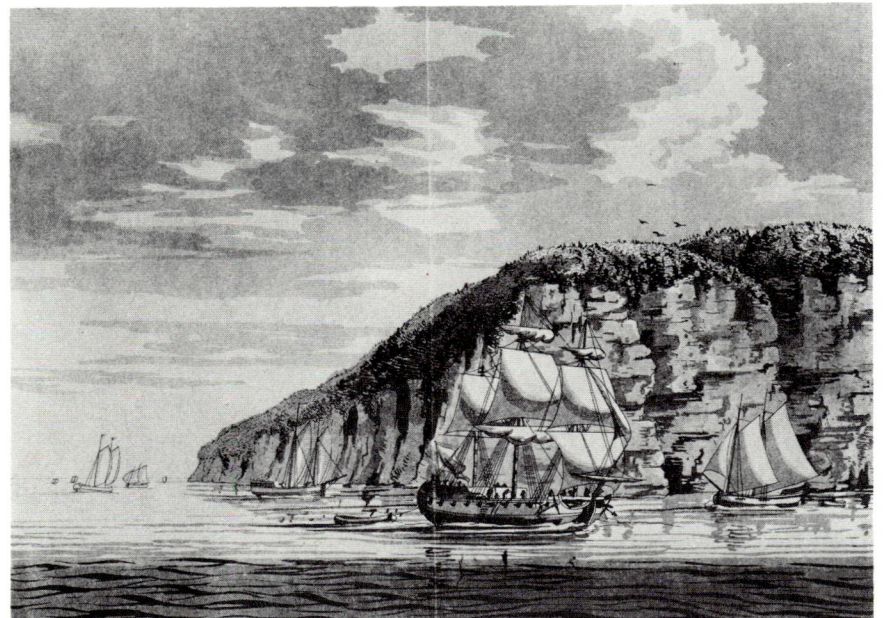

466

Aquatint with etching 7⅞ x 16½ in. (image). *The Atlantic Neptune.* Phillips 1198, v. 1, no. 7.

————Another impression. Phillips 3658, pt. 1, no. 7a.

465
A View of CAMPO BELLO at the Entrance of Passamaquady Bay. [J.F.W. Des Barres, 1780]
Aquatint with etching 12 x 14½ in. (image)

The Atlantic Neptune. Phillips 1198, v. 3, no. 5. LC–USZ62–31951

————Another impression. LeGear 10323, v. 2, no. 26c.

————Another copy with minor variations. LeGear 10320, v. 1, no. 9 (hand colored).

466
The NORTH POINT of GRANDMANAN ISLAND in the Bay Fundy bearing E.N.E. distant two Leagues. [J.F.W. Des Barres, 1779–80?]
Etching (hand colored) 11 x 15 in. (image)

The cliffs of the point are in the right two-thirds of the picture. A farther view than that illustrated. No ships are shown. *The Atlantic Neptune.* LeGear 10320, v. 1, no. 9.

————Another copy with same title but of a later date [J.F.W. Des Barres, 1780]. Aquatint with etching 11⅜ x 15 in. (image). *The Atlantic Neptune.* Phillips 1198, v. 3, no. 5. LC–USZ62–46054

————Another impression. LeGear 10323, v. 2, no. 26c.

New Brunswick

467
The WOLVES, a Cluster of Isles lying S.E. near 3 Leagues from Pasamaquady Bay, the bald Point of the Southernmost bearing S.E.b E.½ E. 1 League distant. Published according to

Act of Parliament July 26, 1777, by J.F.W. DesBarres Esqr.

Etching (hand colored) 2½ x 14¼ in. (image)

Legend reads: "1.2. Bald Isles, the Point of Eastern Isle E.½S. 1 League." No ships are shown. *The Atlantic Neptune.* LeGear 10323, v. 2, no. 26a.

————Other impressions: LeGear 10317, v. 1, no. 10c; LeGear 10320, v. 1, no. 12.

————Another copy with similar title, of a later date. "The Wolves, (a cluster of Isles) lying SE off the Entrance of Passamaquadi Bay" [J.F.W. Des Barres, 1780]. Aquatint with etching 2⅝ x 14⅛ in. (image). *The Atlantic Neptune.* Phillips 1198, v. 3, no. 4. The negative number for this picture and the next two is LC–USZ62–46053.

————Other impressions: Phillips 3658, pt. 1, no. 6a; Phillips 4473, v. 1, no. 49; LeGear 10323, v. 1, no. 6a (hand colored).

468

GRAND MANAN ISLAND, bearing from S.b.E. to S.W.b.S. eight Miles distant. Published according to Act of Parliament July 26, 1777, by J.F.W. DesBarres Esqr.

Etching (hand colored) 2½ x 13¾ in. (image)

Legend reads: "3. The South Point of Campo Bello Island, S.W. two Leagues." No ships are shown. *The Atlantic Neptune.* LeGear 10323, v. 2, no. 26a.

————Other impressions: LeGear 10317, v. 1, no. 10c; LeGear 10320, v. 1, no. 12.

————Another copy with similar title, of a later date. "Grand-Manan Island, bearing from S b E to S W b S, distant eight Miles and the South Point of Campobello Island S W distant two Leagues" [J.F.W. Des Barres, 1780]. Aquatint with etching 2⅝ x 13¾ in. (image). *The Atlantic Neptune.* Phillips 1198, v. 3, no. 4.

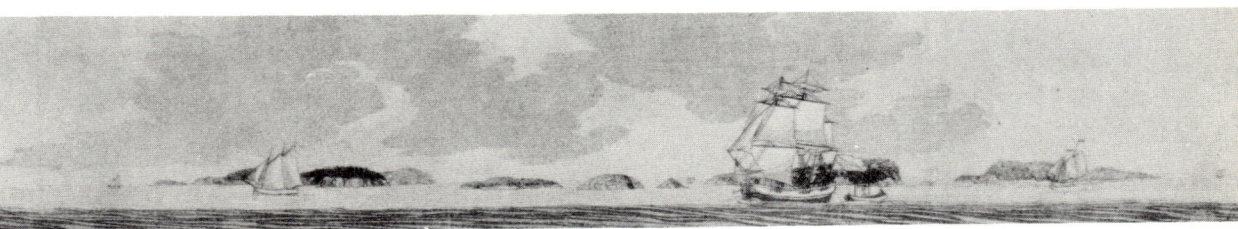

467

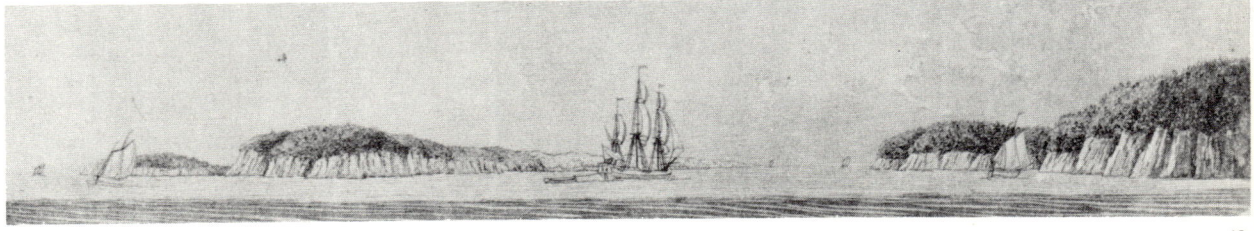

468

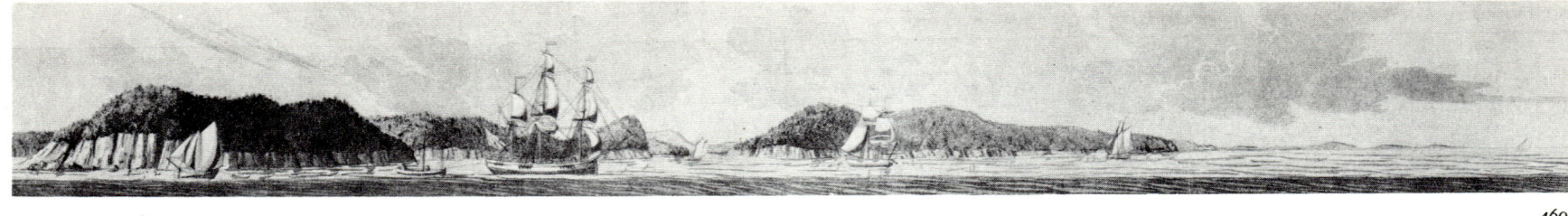

469

———Other impressions: Phillips 3658, pt. 1, no. 6a; Phillips 4473, v. 1, no. 49; LeGear 10323, v. 1, no. 6a (hand colored).

469
A VIEW of the SHORE Westward of the RIVER ST. JOHN. Published according to Act of Parliament July 26, 1777, by J.F.W. DesBarres Esqr.

Etching (hand colored) 3½ x 27¾ in. (image)

Legend reads: "4. Greville Cove bearing N.N.E. distant four Miles 5. The Entrance of the River St. John N.E.b E.½E. four Leagues." No ships are shown. *The Atlantic Neptune.* LeGear 10323, v. 2, no. 26a.

———Other impressions: LeGear 10317, v. 1, no. 10c; LeGear 10320, v. 1, no. 12.

———Another copy with similar title but no imprint. "View of the Shore Westward of St. John's River, the Entrance bearing N E b E ½ E, distant four Leagues [J.F.W. Des Barres, 178?]." Aquatint with etching 3⅝ x 27⅜ in. (image). *The Atlantic Neptune.* Phillips 1198, v. 3, no. 4.

———Other impressions: Phillips 3658, pt. 1, no. 6a; Phillips 4473, v. 1, no. 49; LeGear 10323, v. 1, no. 6a (hand colored).

470
A VIEW of the COAST at the ENTRANCE of the RIVER ST. JOHN, in the Bay of Fundy. Published according to Act of Parliament July 26, 1777, by J.F.W. Des Barres Esqr.

Etching (hand colored) 4⅛ x 28 in. (image)

Legend reads: "6. Partridge Isle bearing N.E.b.N. seven Miles distant." *The Atlantic Neptune.* LeGear 10323, v. 2, no. 26a.

———Other impressions: LeGear 10317, v. 1, no. 10c; LeGear 10320, v. 1, no. 12.

471
A VIEW of the ENTRANCE of PASAMAQUADY BAY. Published according to Act of Parliament July 26, 1777, by J.F.W. DesBarres Esqr.

Etching (hand colored) 3⅝ x 28½ in. (image)

Legend reads: "7. The West Entrance into Head Harbor. 8. The East Entrance into Head Harbor. 9. The Channel leading to Campo Bello Harbor. 10. A Bill with a steep rocky face very descernable from the Offing. 11. The White Horse, a remarkable white rocky Isle, bearing North 1 League distant." *The Atlantic Neptune.* LeGear 10323, v. 2, no. 26a.

———Other impressions: LeGear 10317, v. 1, no. 10c; LeGear 10320, v. 1, no. 12.

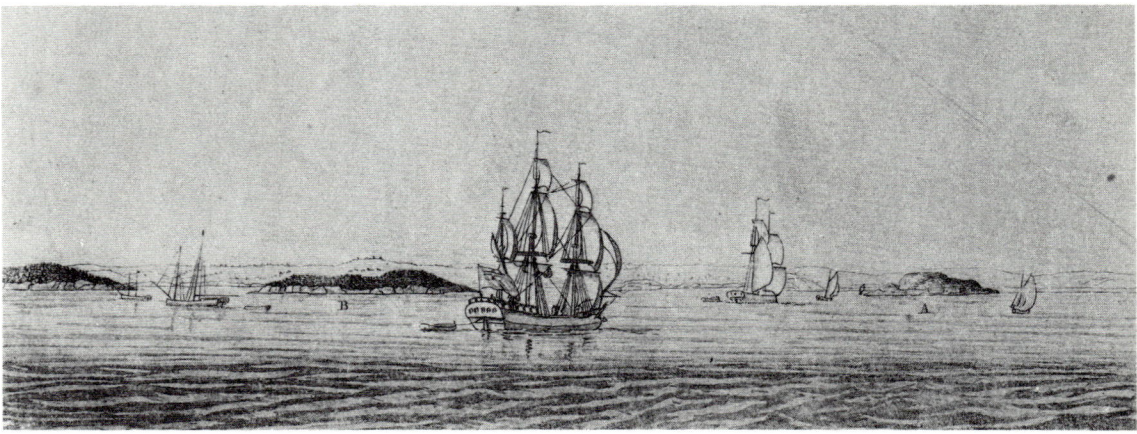

472

472
The Entrance of the River St. John. Published according to Act of Parliament Novr. 14, 1776, by J.F.W. DesBarres Esqr.

Etching 4½ x 8¾ in. (image)

Legend reads: "A. Partridge Island N.E.b.N. 7 Leagues distant B. Meogenes Island." *The Atlantic Neptune.* Phillips 1199, v. 1, no. 7. LC–USZ62–46031

——————Other impressions: Phillips 1199, v. 1, no. 7; Phillips 1201, v. 1, no. 7 (hand colored); Phillips 1202, v. 1, no. 7; Phillips 1203, v. 1, no. 7; Phillips 1205, v. 1, no. 10; Phillips 1250, v. 2, no. 1; Phillips 3658, v. 1, no. 6; Phillips 3655, v. 1, no. 6; Phillips 3656, v. 1, no. 6; Phillips 4473, v. 1, no. 48; LeGear 10323, v. 1, no. 6 (hand colored); LeGear 10317, v. 1, no. 21; LeGear 10320, v. 1, no. 11 (hand colored).

NEW ENGLAND

Maine and New Hampshire

473
[A small cottage by the sea with barrels for merchandise stacked about it—a cartouche] 1766

Etching 6 x 7½ in. (image)

Part of cartouche for map entitled "A New and Accurate Map of the British Dominions in America, according to the Treaty of 1763; Divided into the Several Provinces and Jurisdictions. By Thos. Kitchin Geographer." From *An Universal History, The Maps and Charts to the Modern Part . . .* (London, 1766), no. 39.

474
MECHIOS RIVER near the MILLS. Publish'd according to Act of Parliament, July 31, 1777, by J.F.W. DesBarres Esqr.

Aquatint with etching 9¼ x 9¼ in. (circular image)

View of the Machias River along the upper coast of Maine. The entrance to Machias Harbor was the scene of the first naval engagement of the war, sometimes referred to as "The Lexington of the Sea." The incident occurred on May 10–11, 1775, one week after the British schooner *Margaretta*, accompanied by the sloops *Polly* and *Unity*, entered the port to load lumber for British troops in Boston. *The Atlantic Neptune.* Phillips 1198, v. 1, no. 24. LC–USZ62–46063 is the negative number for this picture and the next one.

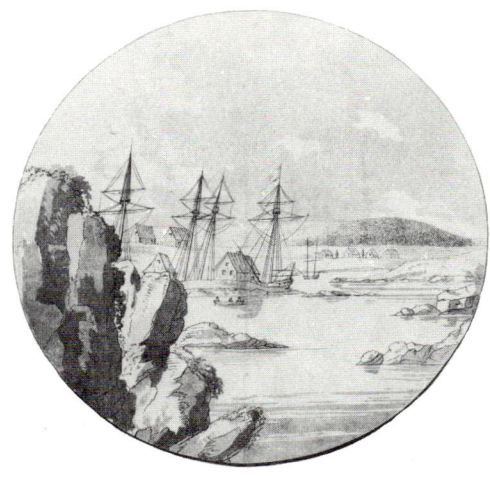

474

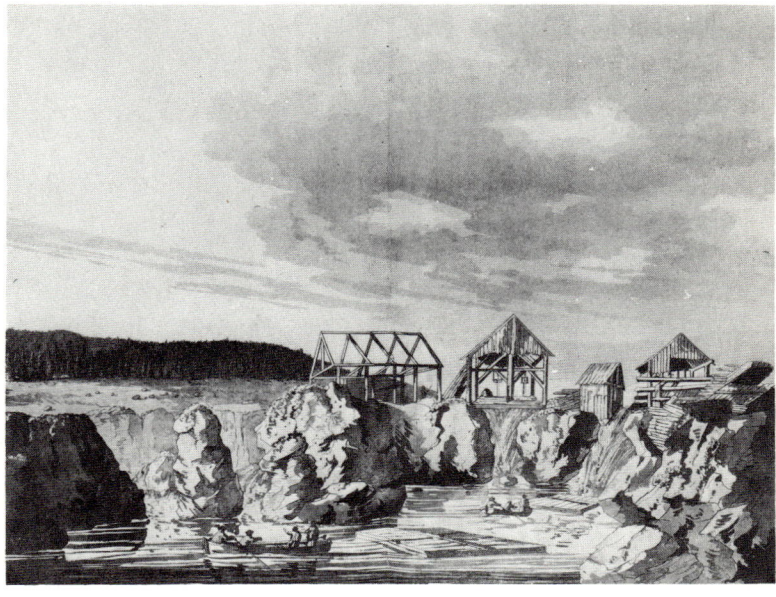

475

——————Other impressions: LeGear 10323, v. 2, no. 26b (hand colored); LeGear 10317, v. 1, no. 6 (hand colored); LeGear 10320, v. 1, no. 10 (hand colored).

475
A SKETCH of MECHIOS MILLS. Publish'd according to Act of Parliament, July 31, 1777, by J.F.W. DesBarres Esqr.

Aquatint with etching 14½ x 18¼ in. (image)

The Atlantic Neptune. Phillips 1198, v. 1, no. 24.

——————Other impressions: LeGear 10323, v. 2, no. 26b (hand colored); LeGear 10317, v. 1, no. 6 (hand colored); LeGear 10320, v. 1, no. 10 (hand colored).

476
A View of the Coast of New-Hampshire to the Eastward of Mount Desart. [J.F.W. DesBarres, 1776–77?]

Etching (hand colored) 6 x 42 in. (image)

Legend reads: "a. Mount Desart, bearing West, distant 4 Leagues; b. Petit Manan Isle W.b.N. 1 League; c. Distant Mountains at the Head of Frenchman's Bay; d. A Hill on the Eastern Shore of Gouldsborough Harbor; e. A Remarkable Isle off Pleasant River, called Ships Stern." *The Atlantic Neptune.* Phillips 3657, v. 1, no. 23.

173

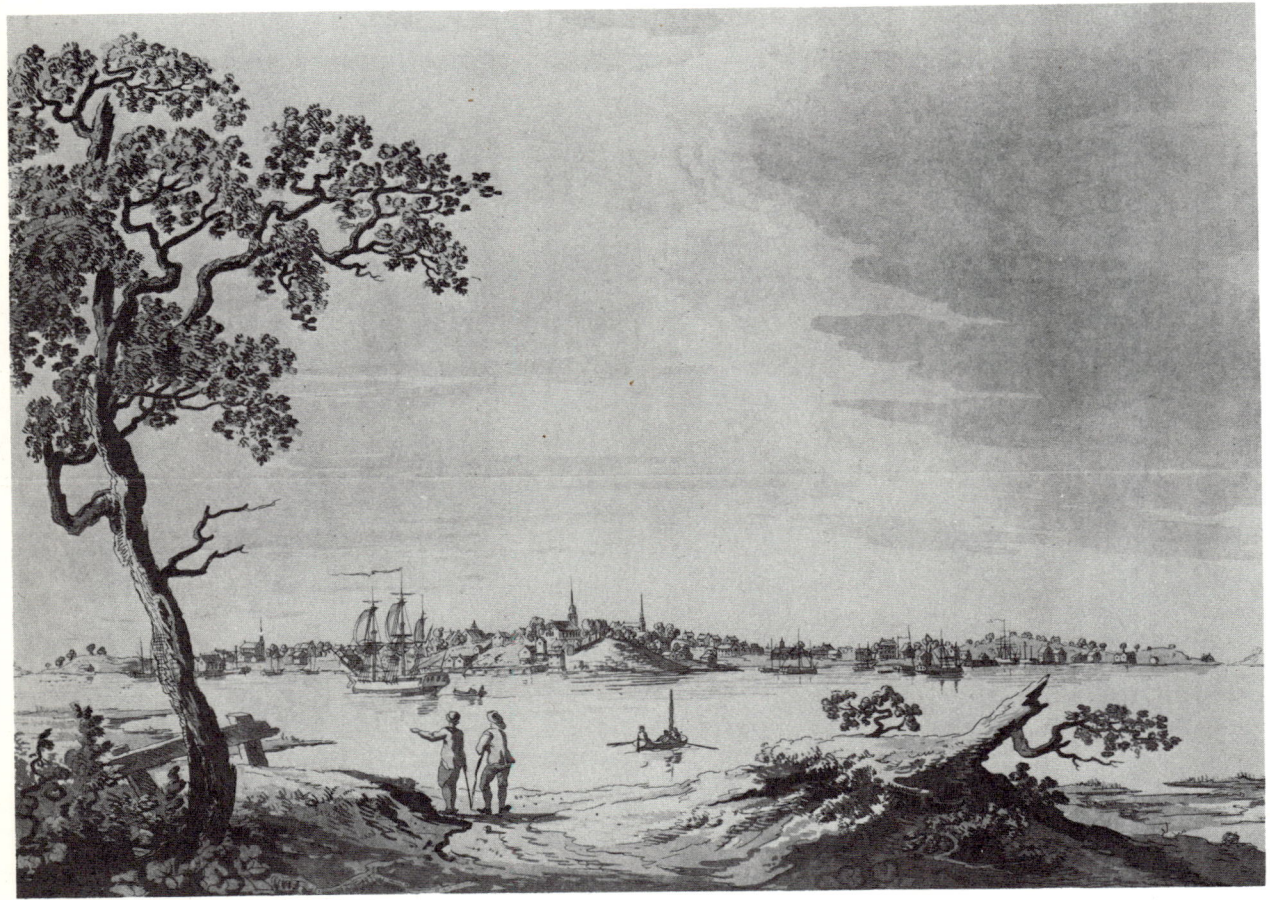

479

477
A View of New Castle with the Fort and Light House on the Entrance of Pisquataqua River. [J.F.W. Des Barres, 1780]

Etching 7½ x 11½ in.

Small farms and fields in the foreground; in the background the fort on the left and the town to the right. *The Atlantic Neptune.* Phillips 1198, v. 3, no. 5.

————Other impressions: Phillips 3657, v. 3, no. 29 (hand colored); LeGear 10323, v. 2, no. 36a (hand colored); LeGear 10320, v. 3, no. 22.

478
A View of Portsmouth, in New Hampshire, taken from the East Shore. [J.F.W. Des Barres, 1776–77?]

Etching (hand colored) 12 x 25½ in. (image)

An artist sketches in the left foreground beside two cows. Portsmouth is across the water. *The Atlantic Neptune.* Phillips 3657, v. 3, no. 30.

————Another impression. LeGear 10323, v. 2, no. 36b.

479
[View of Portsmouth, N. H. J.F.W. Des Barres, 1780]

Aquatint with etching 18 x 23½ in.

The colonial capital and only seaport of New Hampshire, Portsmouth was active in the export trade in the late 18th century. In addition to supplying lumber, masts, and fish to the West Indies and Europe, the port became a center for ship construction about the time of the Revolution. The North Meetinghouse, built in 1714 and a prominent feature of the skyline of the town, had a belfry and steeple

————Other impressions: LeGear 10317, v. 1, no. 10b; LeGear 10320, v. 1, no. 27.

similar to those appearing in the background of this print. *The Atlantic Neptune.* Phillips 1198, v. 3, no. 18. LC–USZ62–46055

480

[Portsmouth. J.F.W. Des Barres, 1776–77?]
Etching (hand colored) 19 x 27¾ in.

A man and woman with a dog stroll in the foreground; the harbor and town are in the background. *The Atlantic Neptune.* Phillips 3657, v. 3, no. 32.

———————Another impression. LeGear 10320, v. 3, no. 21.

Massachusetts

481

VUË DE SALEM. Salem. Eine Stadt im Engelländischen America, in der Grafschafft Essex, welche von den Engelländern 1629. erbauet worden, und 2. Häfen hat einen für den Sommer, und einen für den Winter. Salem. Une Ville de l'Amerique angloise dans le Comté d'Essex, elle fut bâttie par les Anglois en 1629. et a deux Ports, l'un pour l'Eté et l'autre pour l'Hyver. Se vend à Augsbourg au Negoce commun de l'Academie Imperiale d' Empire des Arts libereaux avec Privilege de Sa Majesté Imperiale et avec Defense ni d'en faire ni de vendre les Copies. Gravé par Balth. Frederic Leizelt. [177?]
Etching (hand colored) 9¾ x 15½ in. (image)

The port of Salem was declared closed by the town meeting to show sympathy with Boston following the Port Bill. Salem's action was significant because of the profits which could have been made while Boston was prevented from trading. The town continued to participate actively in the events leading up to the Revolution, and the port was an important privateering base during the war. Title above picture is mirror image. From "Collection des prospects." LC–USZ62–41172

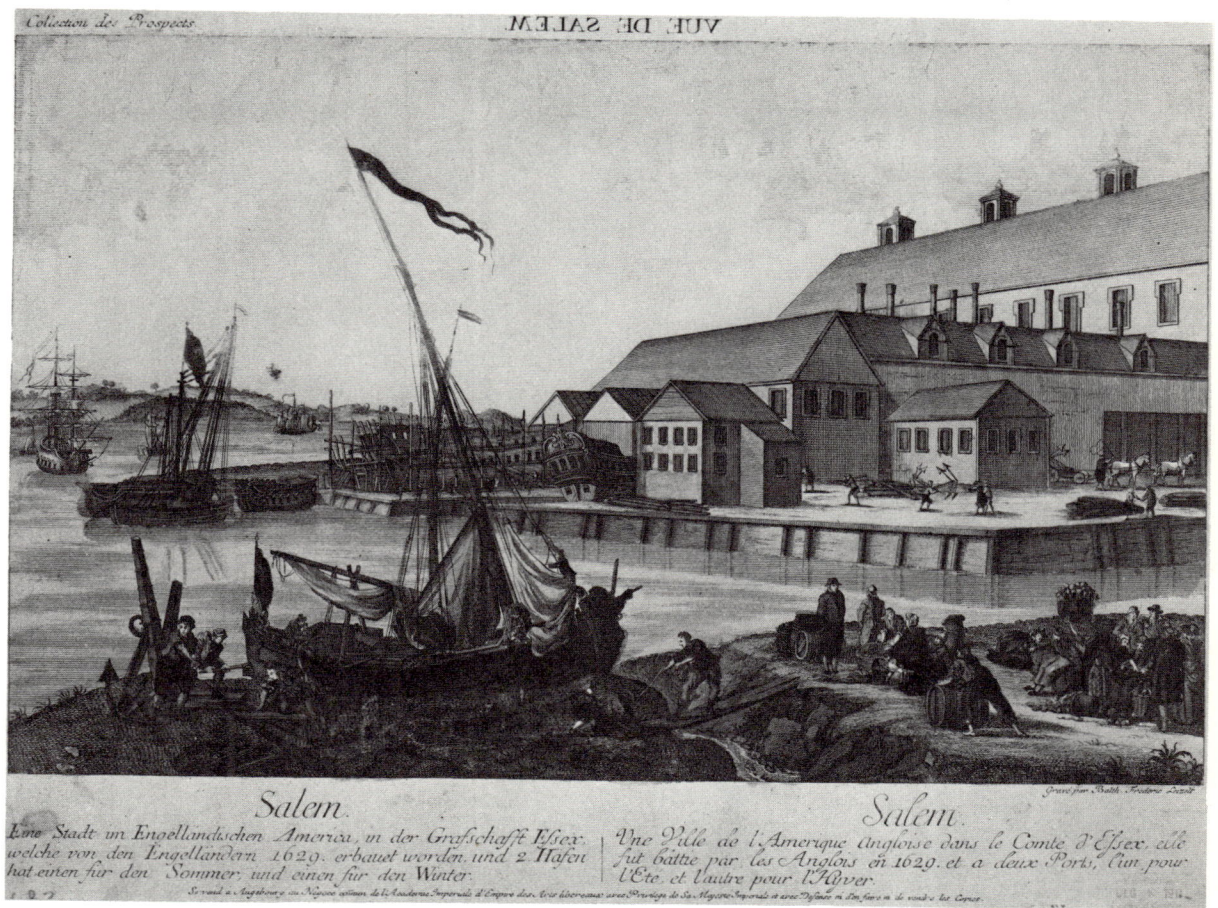

481

175

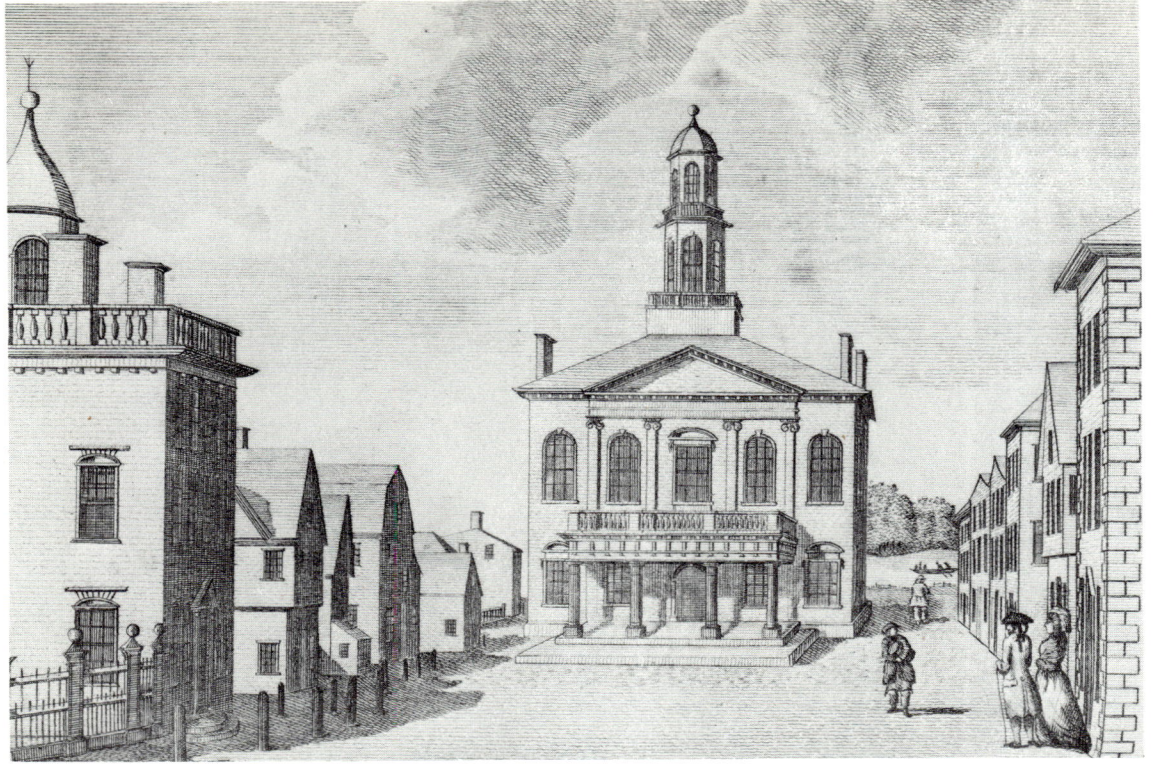

482

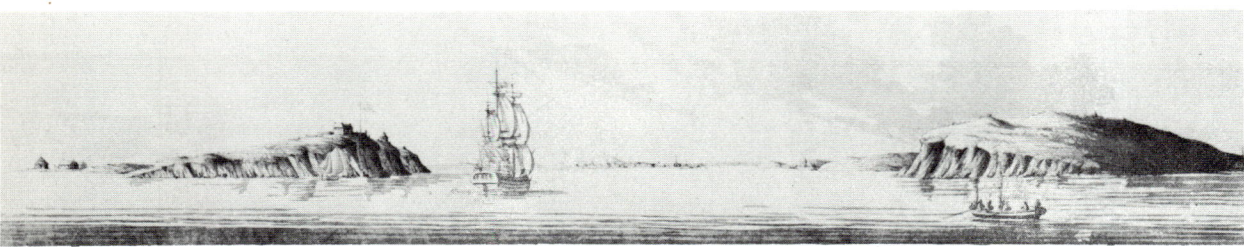

484

482
View of the COURT HOUSE in Salem Massachusetts. W. Gray, del. Engraved by S. Hill.
Etching 4 x 5¾ in. (image)

In the wake of the Boston Port Bill, the military governor Thomas Gage ordered the Massachusetts General Court moved from Boston to Salem. The courthouse was the site of the meeting in October 1774 at which the members declared themselves a Provincial Assembly, separate from Gage and the authority of Parliament. Frontispiece for *The Massachusetts Magazine*, March 1790.
LC–USZ62–31140

483
Boston Bay. [J.F.W. Des Barres, 1776–77?]
Etching (hand colored) 4¼ x 45½ in. (image)

Legend reads: "a. The Garnet Head, S.b.E. 3 to 4 Leagues distant; b. Monument Land on the South Shore of Plymouth Harbor; c. Cohasset Point, bearing N.W. about 2 Leagues." *The Atlantic Neptune*. Phillips 3657, v. 1, no. 24.

———Other impressions: LeGear 10317, v. 1, no. 23; LeGear 10320, v. 1, no. 26.

484
BOSTON, seen between Castle Williams and Governors Island, distant 4 Miles. Publish'd according to Act of Parliament Oct 7, 1777, by J.F.W. DesBarres Esqr.
Aquatint with etching 4⅝ x 29 in.

The main water entrance to Boston is between Castle Island and Governor's Island, the two most prominent islands in Boston Harbor. They lie 2½ miles east of the city and divide the inner and outer harbors. *The Atlantic Neptune*. Phillips 1198, v. 3, no. 24. The negative number for this picture and the next three is LC–USZ62–46056.

———Other impressions: Phillips 3658, pt. 3, no. 6a; Phillips 4473, v. 1, no. 56; LeGear

10323, v. 2, no. 40a (hand colored); LeGear 10320, v. 3, no. 25 (hand colored).

485
Appearance of the HIGH LANDS of AGAMETICUS, N.E. with PENOBSCOT HILLS, to the Eastwards, at 3 to 4 Leagues off Shore. Publish'd according to Act of Parliament Oct 7, 1777, by J.F.W. DesBarres Esqr.

Aquatint with etching 3¼ x 15½ in. (image)

The Atlantic Neptune. Phillips 1198, v. 3, no. 24.

————Other impressions: Phillips 3658, pt. 3, no. 6a; Phillips 4473, v. 1, no. 56; LeGear 10323, v. 2, no. 40a (hand colored); LeGear 10320, v. 3, no. 25.

486
BOSTON BAY, the Light House bearing N.W. b.W. distant one League. Publish'd according to Act of Parliament Oct 7, 1777, by J.F.W. DesBarres Esqr.

Aquatint with etching 2¾ x 18¼ in. (image)

The lighthouse is to the right. *The Atlantic Neptune.* Phillips 1198, v. 3, no. 24.

————Other impressions: Phillips 3658, pt. 3, no. 6a; Phillips 4473, v. 1, no. 56; LeGear 10323, v. 2, no. 40a (hand colored); LeGear 10320, v. 3, no. 25.

487
The Entrance of BOSTON HARBOR. Publish'd according to Act of Parliament Oct 7, 1777, by J.F.W. DesBarres Esqr.

Aquatint with etching 4⅝ x 29 in. (image)

The lighthouse is to the right. *The Atlantic Neptune.* Phillips 1198, v. 3, no. 24.

————Other impressions: Phillips 3658, pt. 3, no. 6a; Phillips 4473, v. 1, no. 56 (hand colored); LeGear 10323, v. 2, no. 40a (hand colored); LeGear 10320, v. 3, no. 25 (hand colored).

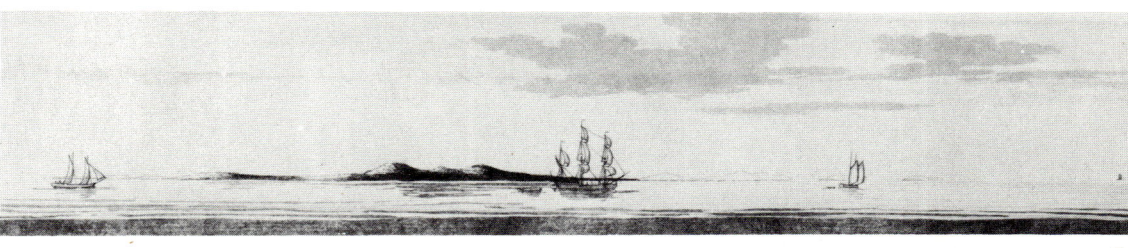
485

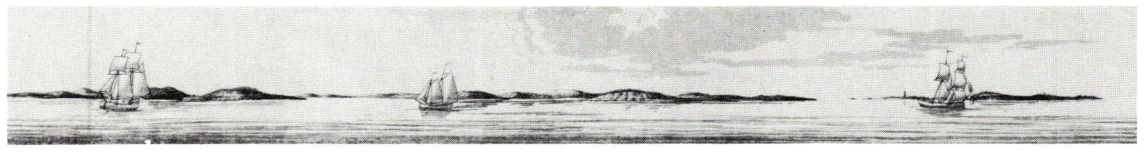
486

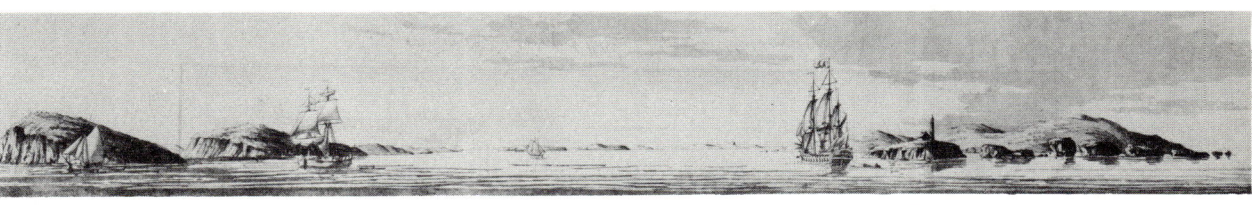
487

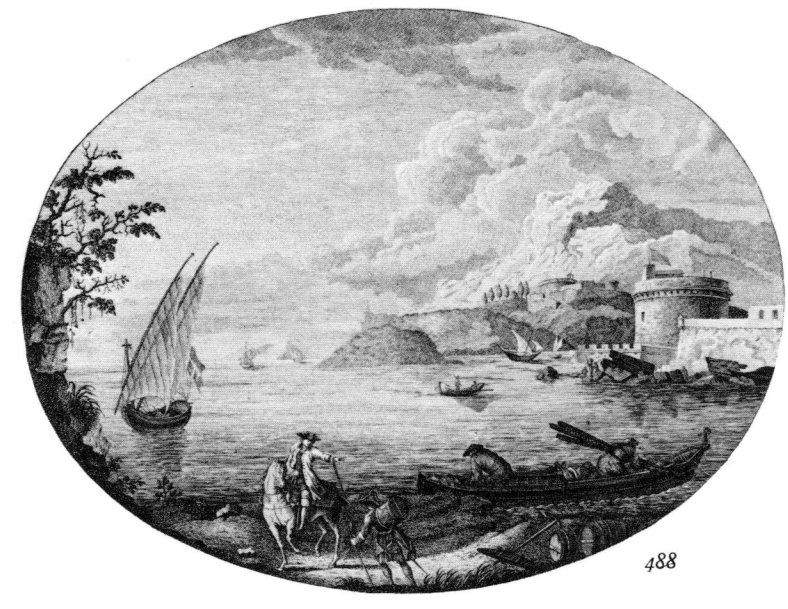
488

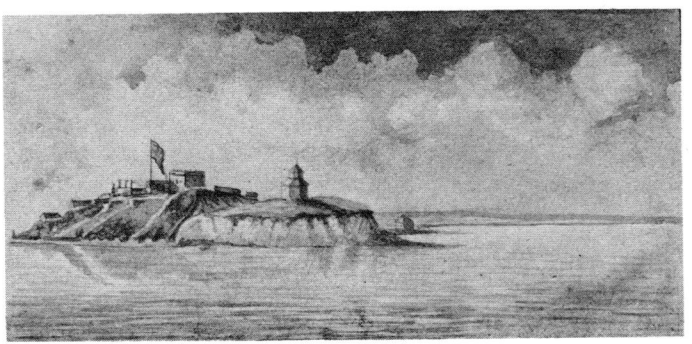
490

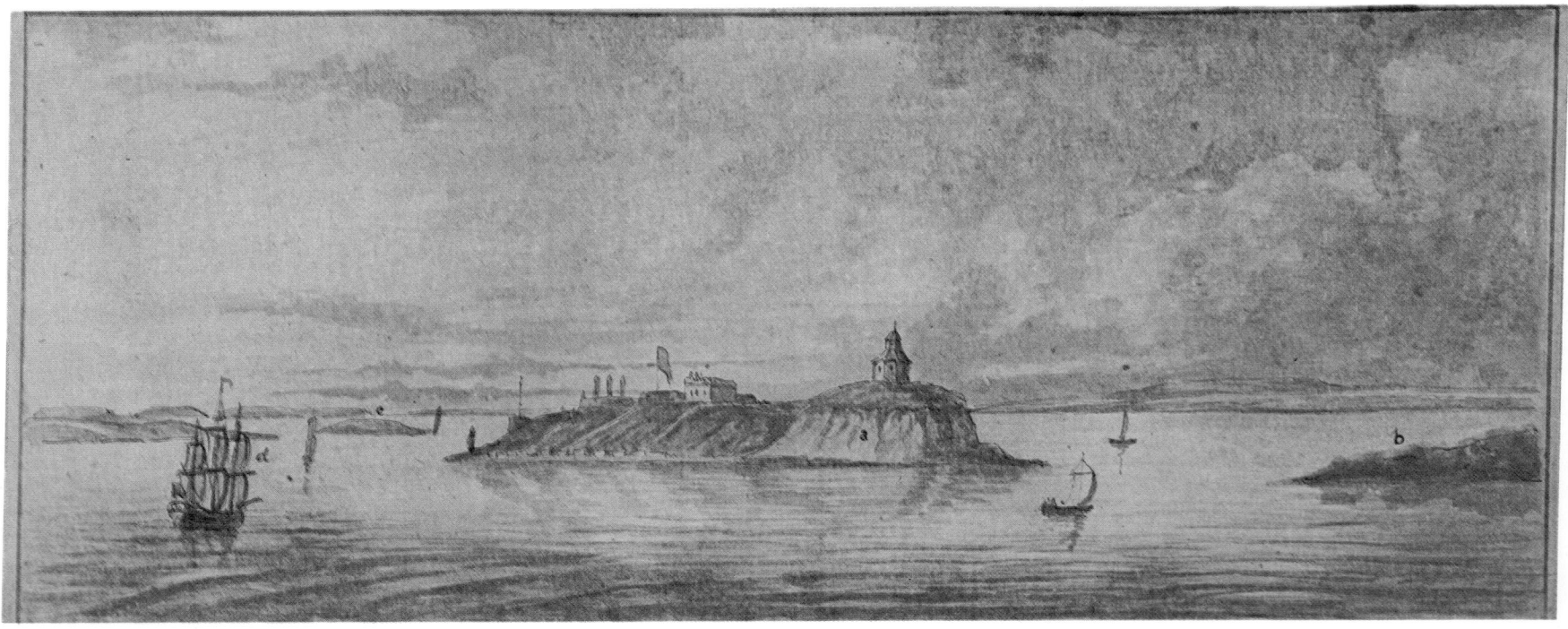
489

488
L'ENTRÉE AU PORT DE BOSTON DANS L'AMÉRIQUE. Vernet pinxit. F A Annert sc: [177?]

Etching 5¾ x 8⅛ in. (image)

The building at the entrance to the harbor, drawn after a European model, probably represents Castle William, a fortress on Castle Island. LC-USZ62-45537

———Another copy. "L'Entree au Port de Boston. Dans l'Amerique. Gravee d'apres le Tableau de Vernet. Vernet pinxit."

489
View of Fort William a The Neck b Lighthouse c Sailing out of harbour d 1770.

Ink and water color drawing 4¾ x 11½ in. (image)

Fort William was renamed Castle William in 1705 in honor of the late King William III.

490
Castle William. 1773.

Ink and water color drawing 4 x 8 in. (image)

Before the first British soldiers landed at Boston in October 1768, repairs were made at Castle William so that troops could be stationed there if quarters were difficult to obtain in Boston. Part of the two regiments from Ireland were quartered in the barracks there upon their arrival with the remainder of the troops stationed in Boston. After the Boston Massacre, on demand of the rebels, all of the redcoats were withdrawn from the city and sent to Castle William. LC-USZ62-45381

491
A North View of CASTLE WILLIAM in the HARBOUR of BOSTON. May 1789. [S. Hill?]

Etching 4½ x 7⅛ in.

When the British troops evacuated Boston in March 1776, the fortifications on Castle Island were destroyed by the departing army. This view shows the rebuilt fort under the stars and stripes. Frontispiece for *The Massachusetts Magazine*, May 1789. LC-USZ62-31790

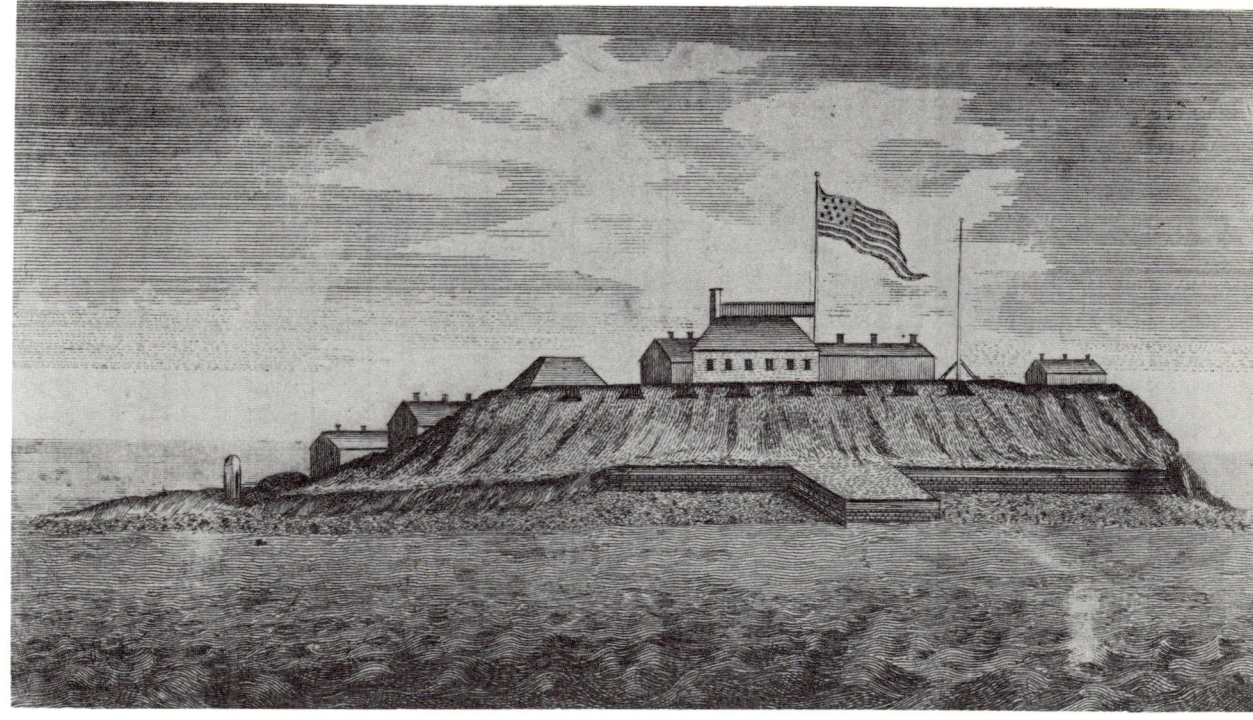
491

———Other impressions: Phillips 3657, v. 3, no. 29; LeGear 10323, v. 2, no. 36a (hand colored); LeGear 10320, v. 3, no. 22.

492
Castle William. [J.F.W. Des Barres, 1780]

Etching 6¾ x 10⅛ in.

The fort, with large flag, stands atop a series of bluffs by the water. *The Atlantic Neptune*. Phillips 1198, v. 3, no. 17.

493
[A view of Castle William. J.F.W. Des Barres, 1776-77?]

Etching (hand colored) 15¾ x 23½ in.

In the foreground a man with a cane walks toward a gate and turnstile. To the left is a house surrounded by a picket fence. The harbor and Castle William are in the background. *The Atlantic Neptune.* Phillips 3657, v. 3, no. 28.

494
[A view of Boston] 1 Mistic River 2 Charles-Town Point where the British Troops landed the 17 June 3 Redout of the Rebels 4 Noodles Island 5 Hog Island 6 Boston Harbour 7 The Dykes 8 Boston North 9 Kops Hill and Battery which played on the Rebels Redout on Bunkers Hill the 17 of June 10 Beacon Hill 11 The Somerset [177?]

Ink and water color drawing 5 x 12 in.

On June 17, 1775, British troops landed at Charlestown in readiness for the Battle of Bunker Hill. Noodle's Island is now called East Boston. LC–USZ62–19362

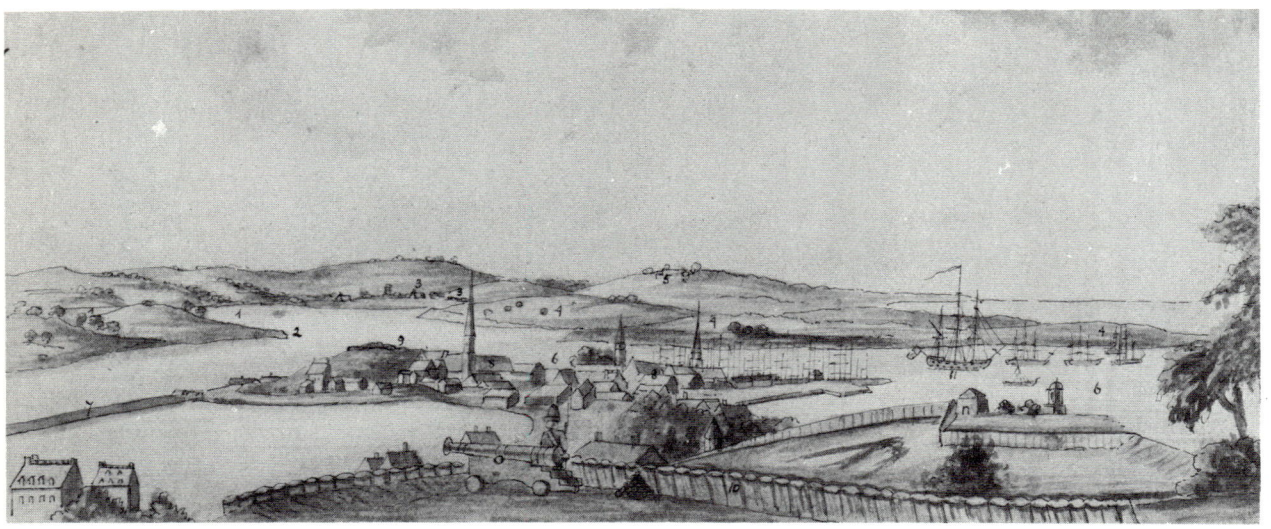
494

495
View from Charlestown 1773.
Ink and water color drawing 4 x 8 in.

View of Boston from the north side of the city. LC–USZ62–45379

496
A South East View of the Great Town of BOSTON in New England in America. Printed for Carington Bowles Map and Printseller at No. 69 in St. Pauls Church Yard, London. I Carwitham sculp. [1760–80?]

Etching (hand colored) 10¾ x 17¼ in. (image)

The print shows Fort Hill on the left, Long Wharf in the center, and Hancock's Wharf to the right. Copied from the 1743 print by William Price, but with fewer ships and less detail. LC–USZ62–46312

497
A View of Boston taken on the Road to Dorchester. Publish'd according to Act of Parliament May 30th. 1776 by J.F.W. DesBarres

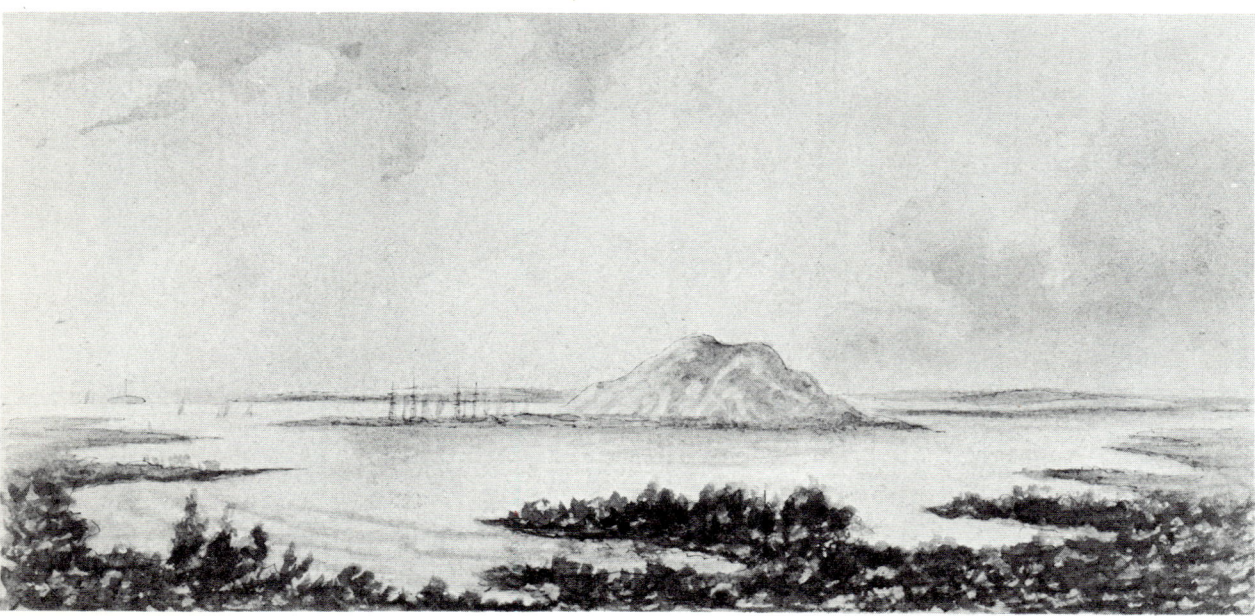
495

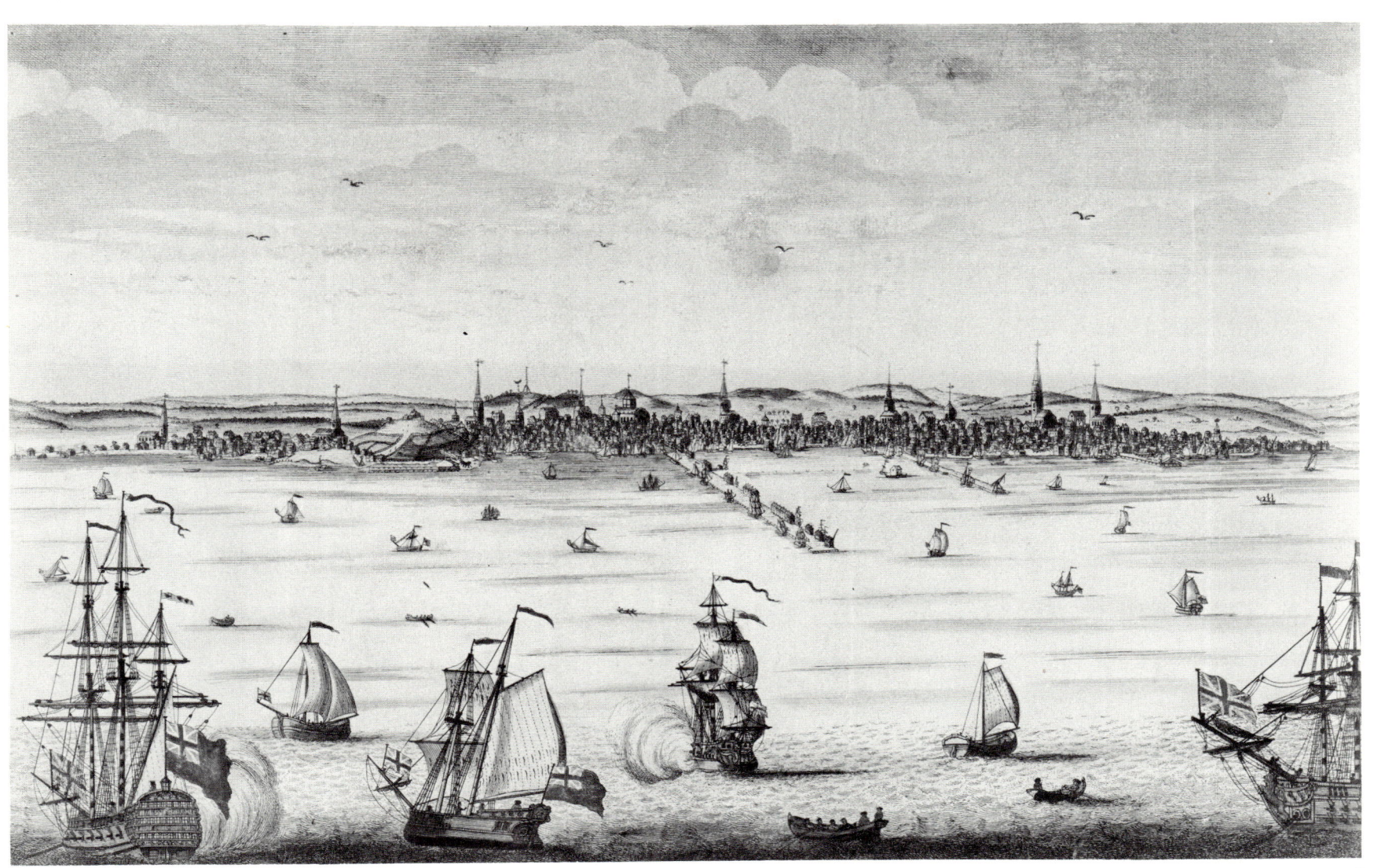

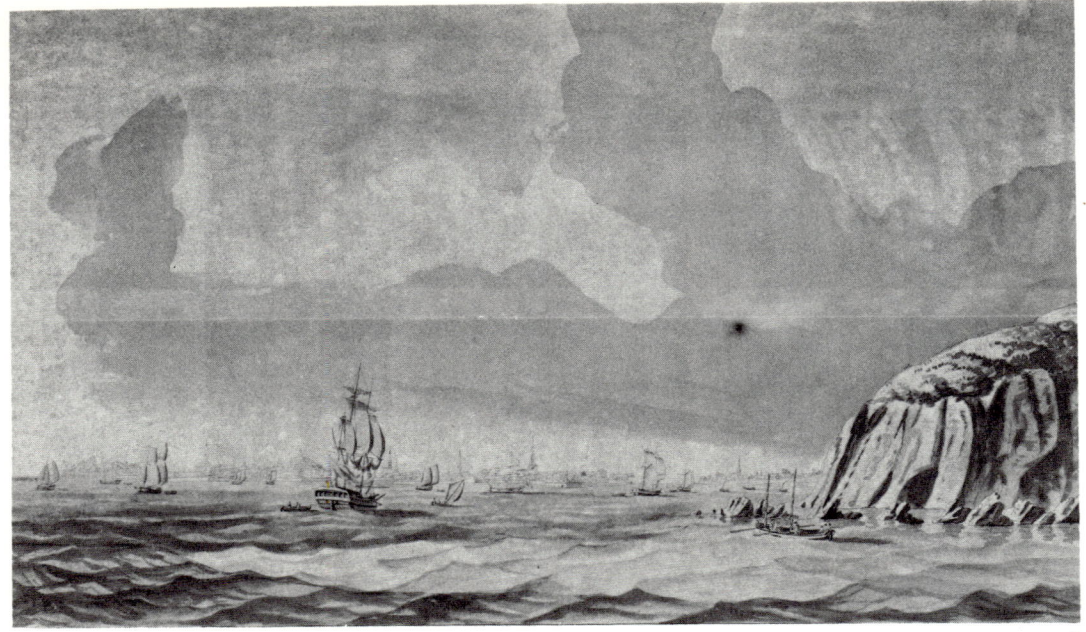

498

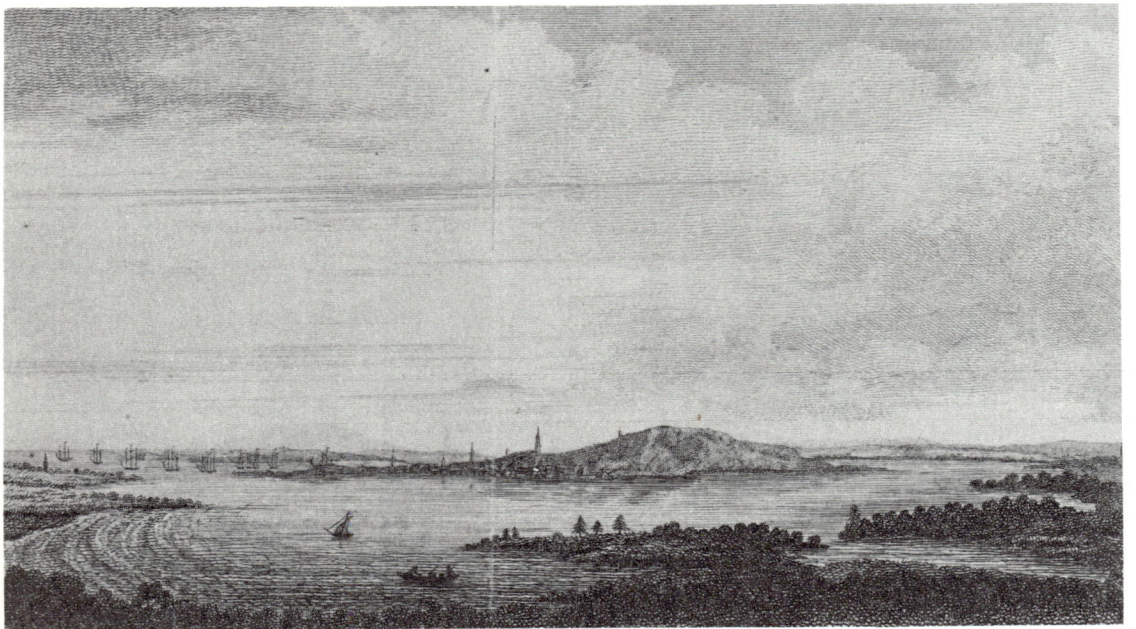

500

Esqr. Drawn by W. Pierre. Engraved by James Newton.

Etching 18¾ x 25¾ in.

In the foreground two shepherds sit in a bucolic setting. The town is in the right background across the bay, and to the left is a large house surrounded by orchards and fields. *The Atlantic Neptune.* LeGear 10320, v. 3, no. 26.

498

A View of Boston. Published by J.F.W. Des-Barres Esqr. May 19th 1779.

Aquatint with etching 21½ x 30½ in.

The Atlantic Neptune. Phillips 1198, v. 3, no. 27. LC–USZ62–46062

——————Another impression: LeGear 10320, v. 3, no. 27.

499

[Boston. J.F.W. Des Barres, 1776–77?]

Etching (hand colored) 12¾ x 31 in. (image)

A panoramic view of the city with much vivid detail: ships in the foreground, landform to the right, town and hills in the background. *The Atlantic Neptune.* Phillips 3657, v. 3, no. 26.

500

Boston from Willis Creek. Wm. Pierrie delin. Publish'd according to Act of Parliament Septr. 16, 1775, by J.F.W. DesBarres Esq.

Etching 6½ x 10 in.

Willis' Creek, later known as the Miller River, separated Cambridge from Somerville. *The Atlantic Neptune.* Phillips 1198, v. 3, no. 25. LC–USZ62–46058

——————Other impressions: Phillips 3657, v. 3, no. 27; LeGear 10323, v. 2, no. 41a (hand colored); LeGear 10320, v. 3, no. 24.

501

Long Island open on the North Side of Nicks Mate Island. [J.F.W. Des Barres, September 16, 1775]

Etching 6½ x 10 in.

Long Island stands in the outer Boston Harbor. Between Long Island Head and Gallop Island is Nix's Mate, an irregular, rocky island which is almost covered by water at high tide. The town of Boston is in the right background. *The Atlantic Neptune.* Phillips 1198, v. 3, no. 25. LC–USZ62–46057

————Other impressions: LeGear 10323, v. 2, no. 41a (hand colored); LeGear 10320, v. 3, no. 23.

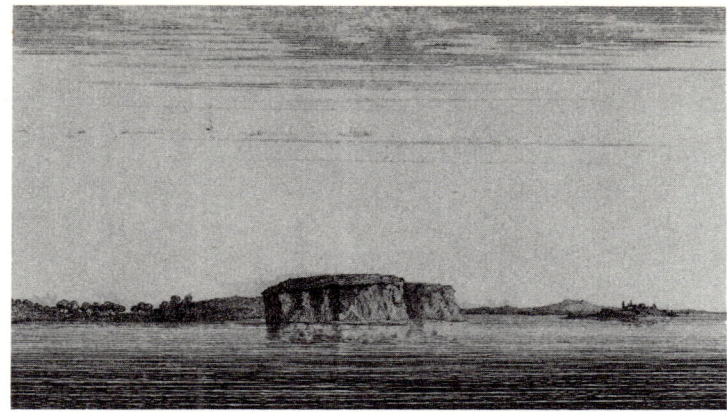

502

A View of the Country towards Dorchester, taken from the advanced works on Boston Neck. [J.F.W. Des Barres, 1775?]

Etching 6½ x 10 in.

Soldiers stand guard in a redoubt on the left. *The Atlantic Neptune.* Phillips 1198, v. 3, no. 26. LC–USZ62–46061

————Other impressions: Phillips 3657, v. 3, no. 27; LeGear 10323, v. 2, no. 40b (hand colored); LeGear 10320, v. 3, no. 23.

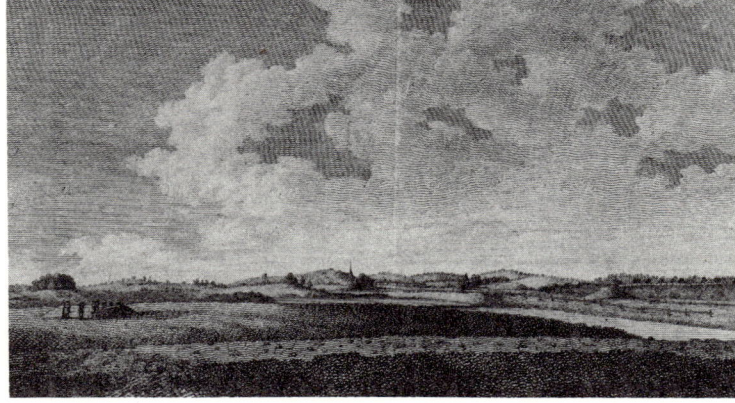

503

A View of Boston from Dorchester Neck Wm. Pierrie delin Publish'd according to Act of Parliament Septr. 16, 1775, by J.F.W. Des-Barres Esq.

Etching 6½ x 10 in.

Boston on the right. *The Atlantic Neptune.* Phillips 1198, v. 3, no. 25. LC–USZ62–33035

————Other impressions: LeGear 10323, v. 2, no. 41a (hand colored); LeGear 10320, v. 3, no. 24; LeGear 10321, v. 1, no. 12.

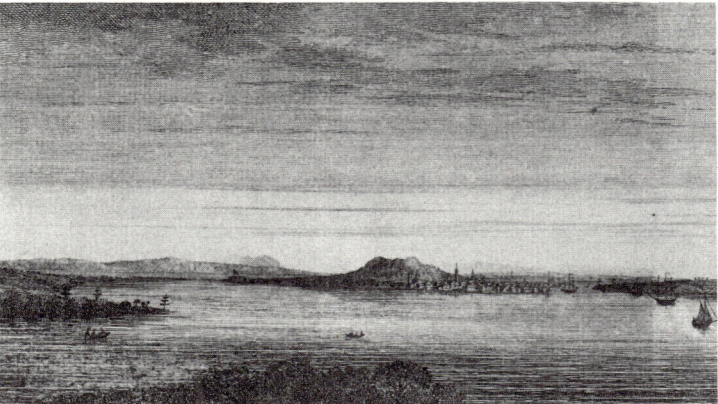

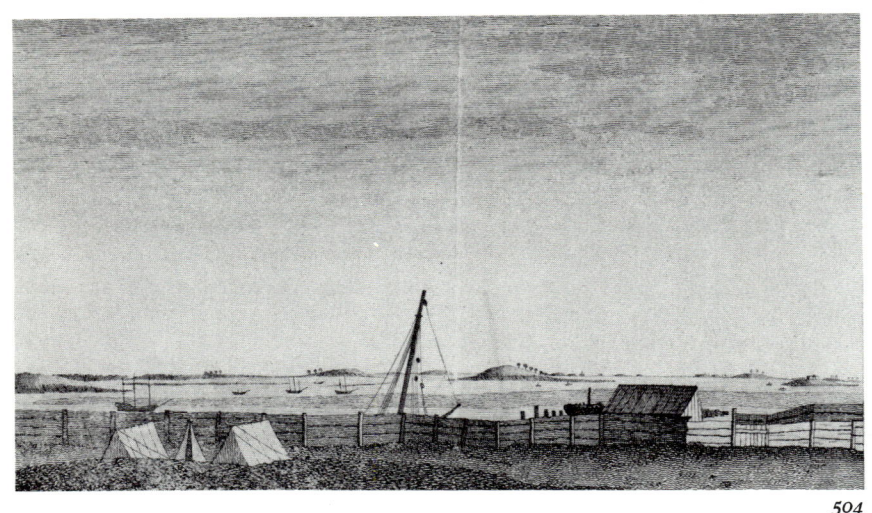

504

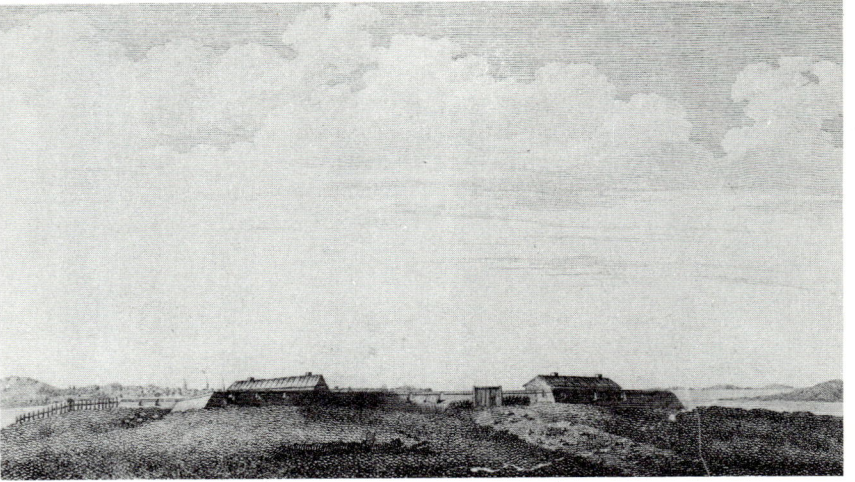

505

References
1. Boston
2. Mr Hancocks House
3. Enemys Camp on Mt Hill
4. Blockhouse
5.5 Guard Houses
6. Gate & Draw Bridge
7. Beacon Hill

A view of the Lines thrown upon BOSTON NECK; by the Ministerial Army

506

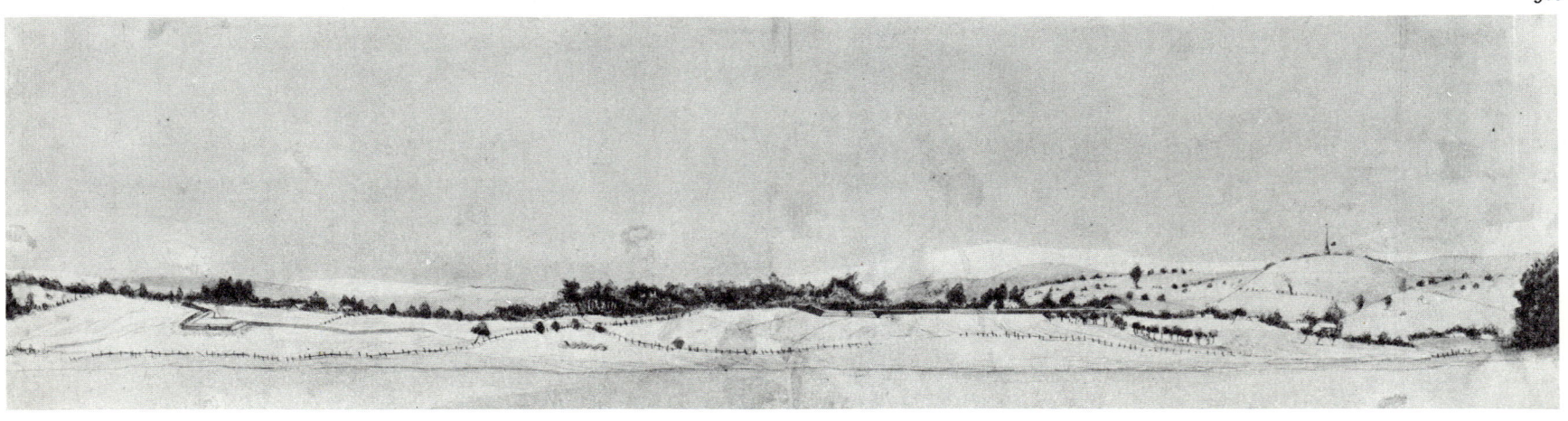

507

504

A View of the Harbour of Boston taken from Fort Hill. [J.F.W. Des Barres, 1775?]

Etching 6¼ x 9¾ in.

Fort Hill was on the south side of the city and faced the harbor. Its strategic value was considerable. *The Atlantic Neptune.* Phillips 1198, v. 3, no. 26. LC–USZ62–46060

———Other impressions: Phillips 3657, v. 3, no. 27; LeGear 10323, v. 2, no. 40b (hand colored); LeGear 10320, v. 3, no. 24.

505

A Front View of the Lines taken from the advanced Post near Browns House. [J.F.W. Des Barres, 1775?]

Etching 6½ x 10 in.

Two chevaux-de-frise are beside the gate to the fort. Boston is in the far background. *The Atlantic Neptune.* Phillips 1198, v. 3, no. 26. LC–USZ62–46059

———Other impressions: LeGear 10323, v. 2, no. 40b (hand colored); LeGear 10320, v. 3, no. 23.

506

A View of the Lines thrown upon BOSTON NECK, by the Ministerial Army. 1774 B. Romans

Etching (hand colored) 1 x 7½ in. (image)

In June and July of 1775, the British constructed defenses on Boston Neck where many of their troops were stationed. The neck was the site of minor skirmishes from July 1775 until the British Army left Massachusetts in March 1776. The legend reads: "1 Boston 2 Mr. Hancocks House 3 Enemy's Camp on McHill 4 Blockhouse 5 5 Guard Houses 6 Gate & Draw Bridge 7 Beacon Hill." With a map entitled "Plan of Boston and its Environs 1775" in G&M vault. LC–USZ62–46324

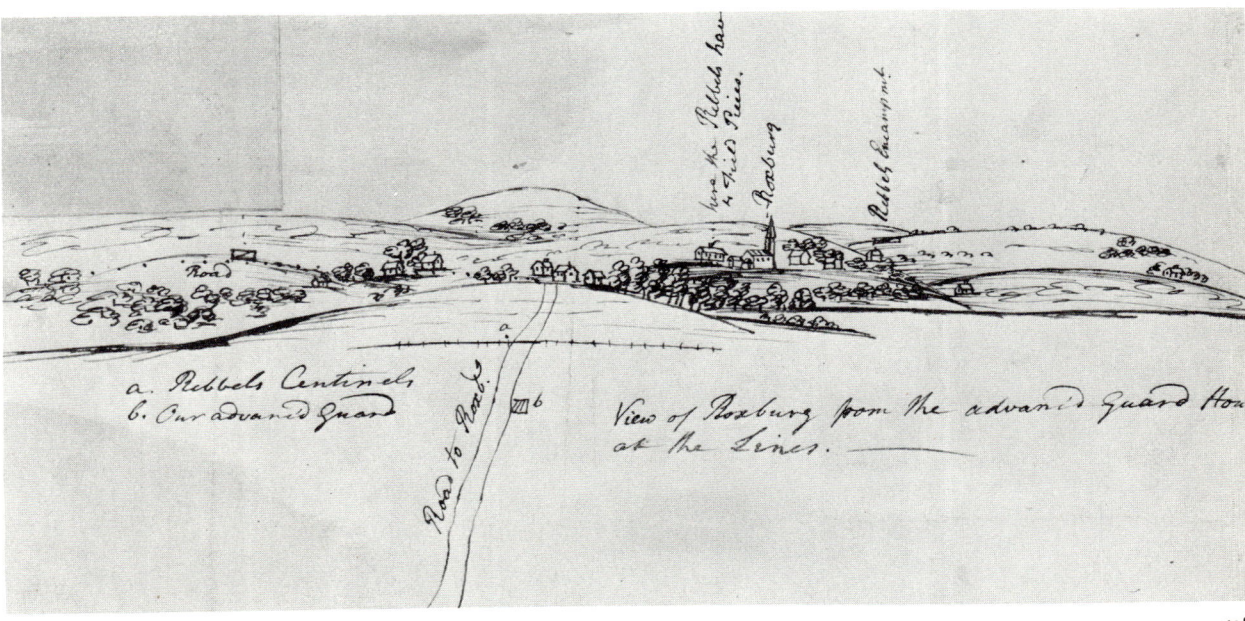

507

[View of fortifications around Dorchester, 1776?]

Pen and water color drawing 6 x 19¼ in.

Washington decided to break the stalemate of the siege of Boston in March 1776 by fortifying the last unoccupied heights around the city. The Dorchester Heights works were constructed in a single night, despite frozen ground, in an amazing feat of military planning and execution. The British cannons in the harbor were unable to adjust their fire high enough to threaten the fortifications, and instead of attempting a frontal assault, the British decided to evacuate the city. Dorchester steeple, the only landmark identified in this print, is on the hill to the right. LC–USZ62–45538

508

View of Roxbury from the advanc'd Guard Hous[e] at the Lines. [177?]

Ink sketch 6⅜ x 13¼ in. (image)

The right wing of the American Army was at Roxbury under the command of Maj. Gen. Artemas Ward during the siege of Boston. This sketch made behind British lines identifies "a. Rebbels Centinels" "b. Our advanc'd Guard" "Road to Roxby." "Here the Rebbels have 4 Field Pieces" "Roxbury" "Rebbels Encampmt." LC–USZ62–45378

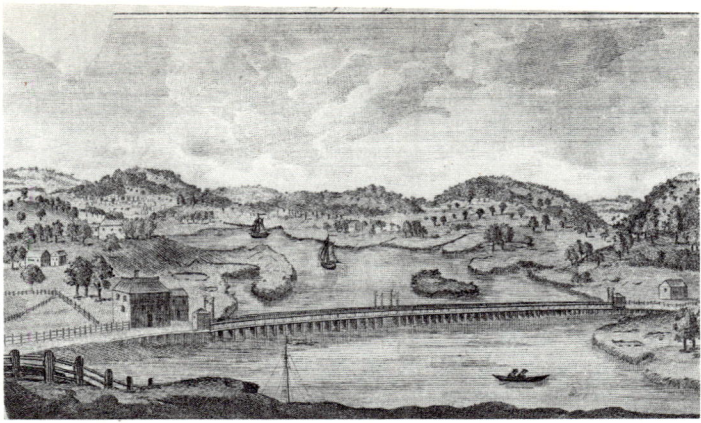

509

509
View of the Bridge over Mystic River & the Country adjacent from Bunker's Hill. Engraved by S. Hill. [1790]

Etching 4 x 6¼ in.

Malden Bridge in Middlesex County was built in 1787 at the cost of approximately £5,300. This view is from Bunker Hill; Medford township is in the background. Frontispiece for *The Massachusetts Magazine*, September 1790, opposite p. 515. Stauffer, 1408. LC–USZ62–45526

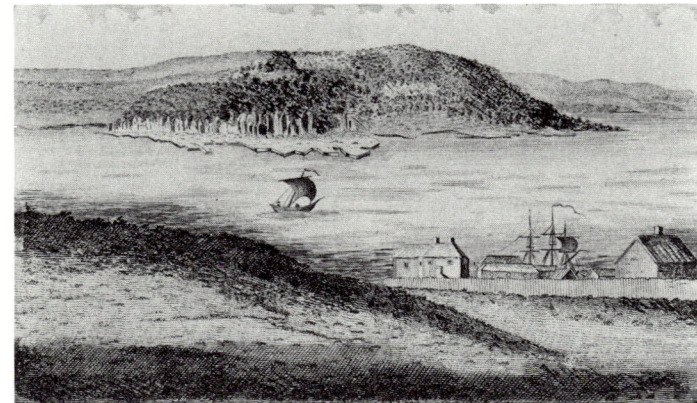

510

510
View of Bunker's Hill. From a Drawing in Possession of the Revd. Mr. Elderton. Feby. 1790.

Etching 4½ x 6¾ in. (image)

On the night of June 16, 1775, the American troops built a redoubt on Breed's Hill, adjacent to Bunker Hill. The redoubt was discovered at daybreak, and the Battle of Bunker Hill began. The British captured the hill at enormous cost in casualties, and the War for Independence began. From the *Gentleman's Magazine*, February 1790, opposite p. 140. LC–USZ62–46023

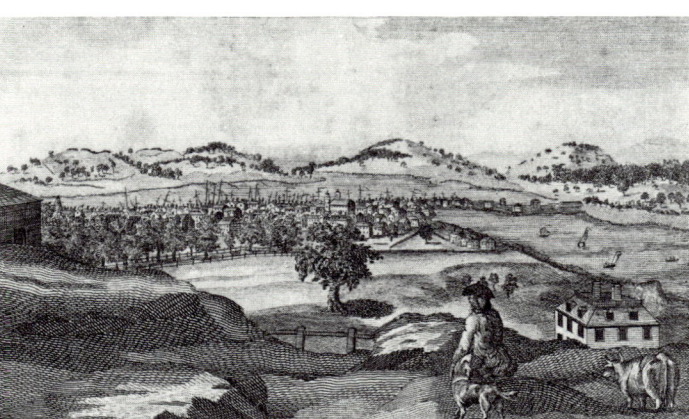

511

511
S.E. Prospect from an Eminence near the Common, Boston. Del. & Engrav'd by S. Hill. [1790]

Etching 4½ x 7 in.

This view is of southeast Boston from a rise of land near the Hancock mansion. Dorchester Heights is in the background. An accompanying article describes the engraving:

The great variety of objects, that croud [sic] upon the point of vision, are too numerous for detail.—Suffice it to observe, that the busy din of the town, and the quiet stillness of the rural hamlet, appear in striking contrast, and furnish a luxuriant feast, to the contemplative and philosophick mind.

Frontispiece for *The Massachusetts Magazine*, November 1790.

512

View of the ancient Buildings belonging to Harvard-College, Cambridge, New England. [1788]

Etching 4¼ x 7 in.

Frontispiece for *The Columbian Magazine*, December 1788. This view shows fewer buildings than item 513, and they appear older and less substantial. Fielding, 1819.

513

View of the Colleges at Cambridge, Massachusetts. Delineated & Engraved by S. Hill. [1790]

Etching 3¾ x 6¼ in. (image)

The accompanying article describes the engraving as "a prospective view of the buildings belonging to the University of Cambridge, the most ancient seminary of literature in the United States." The buildings on the campus of Harvard College from left to right are: Holden Chapel, erected in 1745 in memory of Samuel Holden, a director of the Bank of England; Hollis Hall, built in 1762; Harvard Hall, the building with the cupola; and Massachusetts Hall. Massachusetts Hall, the oldest building on the campus, was built in 1720; Hollis Hall was rebuilt after the fire of 1764. *The Massachusetts Magazine*, June 1790, frontispiece. Stauffer, 1396. LC–USZ62–45523

514

View of Faneuil-Hall in BOSTON, Massachusetts March 1789. W. Pierpont Del. S. Hill Sculp.

Etching 4¼ x 7 in.

The original building was constructed in 1740, the gift of merchant Peter Faneuil (1700–1743) to the city of Boston for a market place and town hall. The roof and interior were burned in 1761 and reconstructed in 1763.

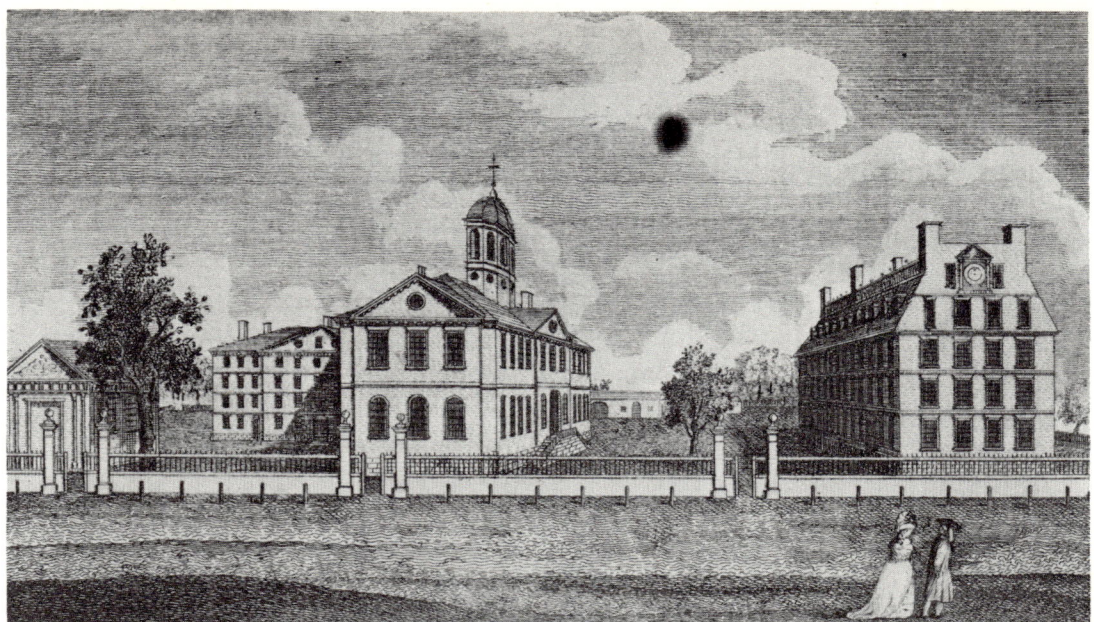

513

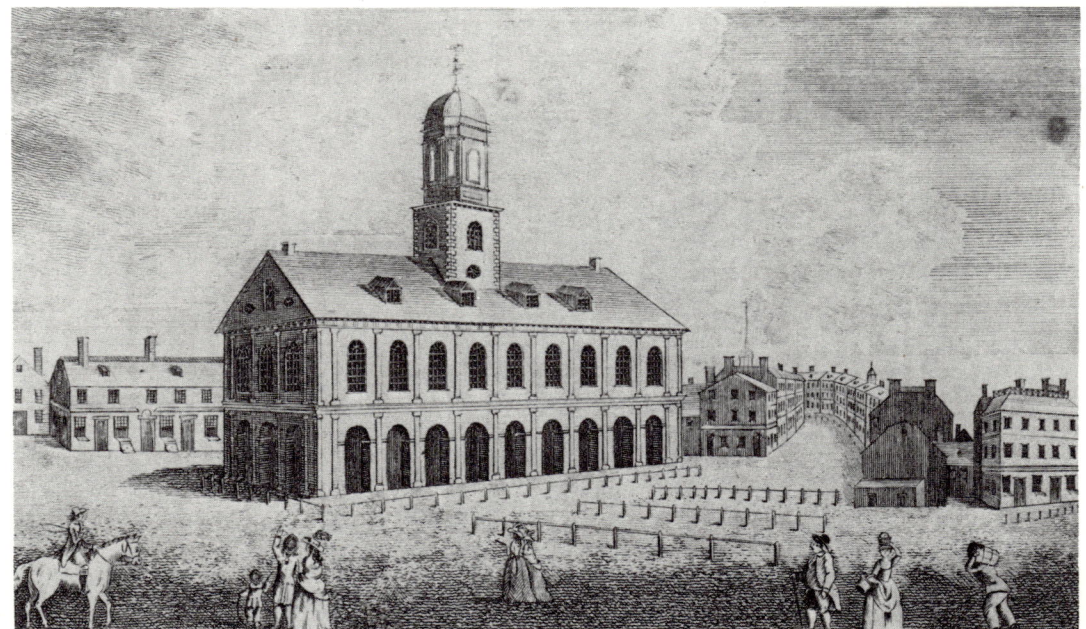

514

187

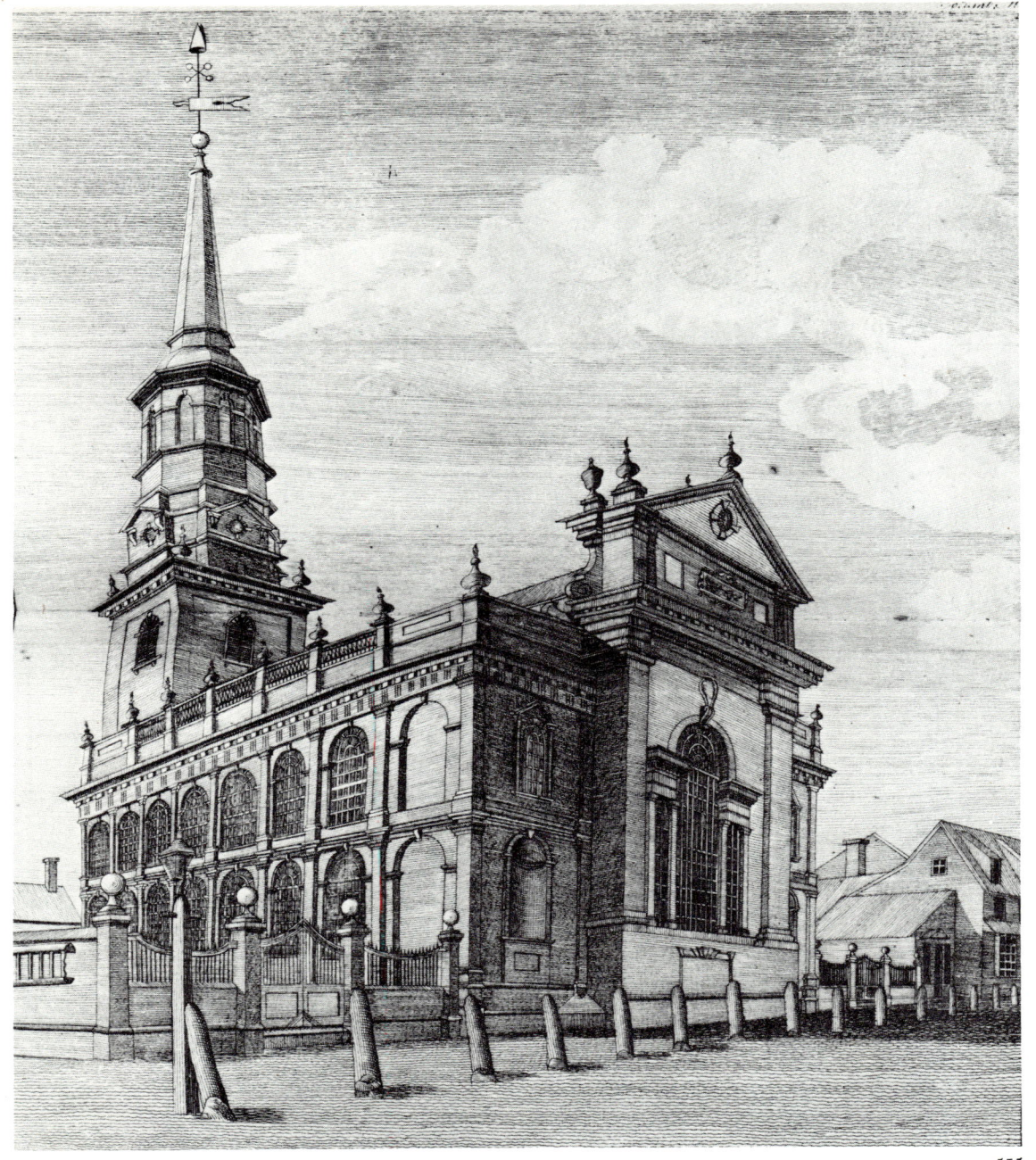

515

Called the "Cradle of Liberty," Faneuil Hall was the scene of many patriot meetings. During the siege of Boston, the British soldiers used it as a theater. This is a northeast view of the building, taken from the town dock. Frontispiece for *The Massachusetts Magazine*, March 1789. Stauffer, 1402. LC–USZ62–45571

515

A South East View of Christ's Church. [1787]
Etching 7⅞ x 6¾ in.

Christ Church, founded by Anglicans in 1723, was located on Salem Street. Its steeple was 175 feet high and, at the time of the Revolution, contained the only church bells in Boston. E. P. Richardson credits Charles Willson Peale with the design of this plate. *The Columbian Magazine*, 1787, opposite p. 839.
LC–USZ62–46025

516

View of the BRIDGE over CHARLES RIVER. Sept. 1789. [Samuel Hill?]
Etching 4¼ x 6⅞ in.

Built in 1786 by a private group of investors, which included John Hancock, this bridge was the first in the Boston area. It was 1,503 feet long, connecting the city with Charlestown. The view is from Atkins Wharf. *The Massachusetts Magazine*, September 1789, frontispiece. Stauffer, 1398. LC–USZ62–24045

517

An East View of the Meeting House in Hollis Street, BOSTON; now erecting on the ruins of one lately destroyed by fire. C: BULFINCH DELIN Vallance Sc. [1788]
Etching 6⅛ x 6¾ in.

This church, designed by Charles Bulfinch (1763–1844) the prominent Bostonian architect, was constructed on the site of the old Hollis Street Church, which burned in 1787. It

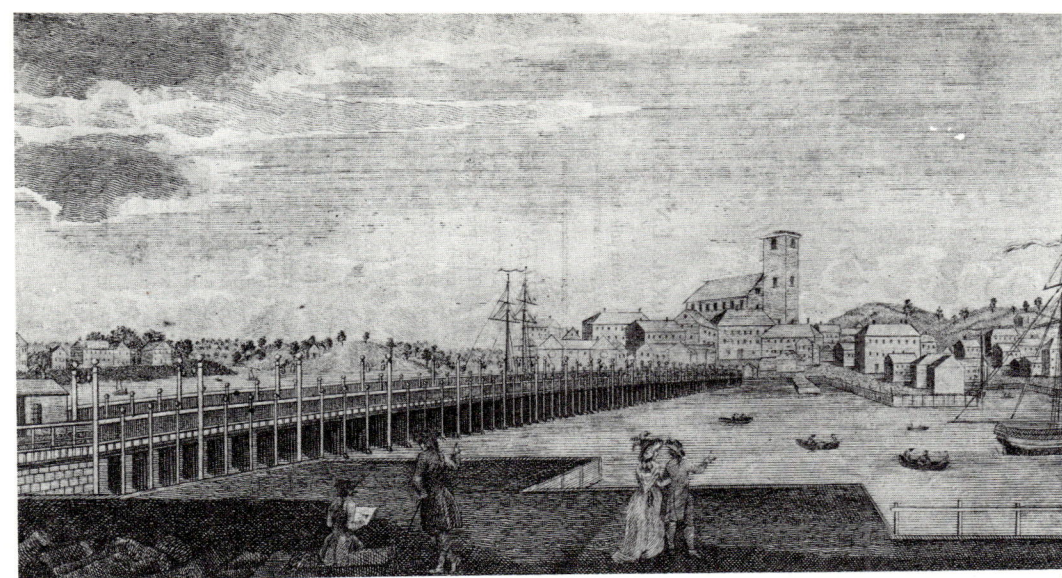

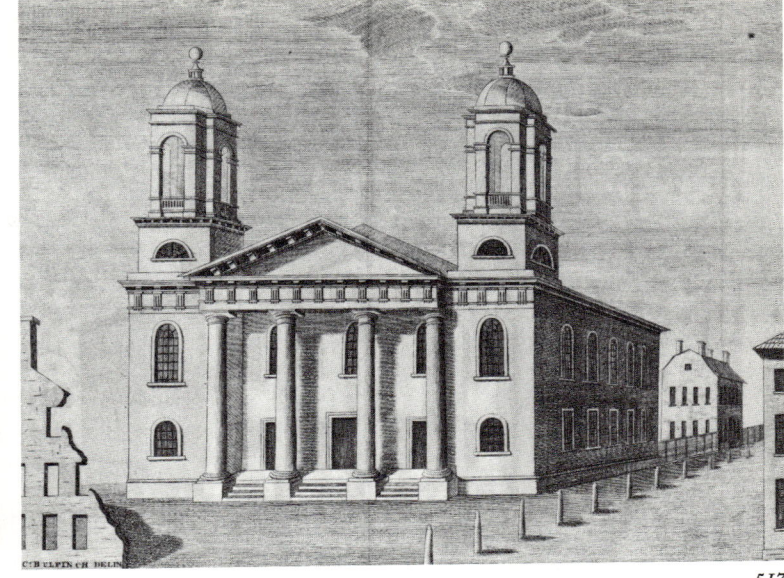

was Bulfinch's first building, and it reflected his fondness for European styles. The square structure had a domed interior, and twin cupolas flanked the Tuscan portico. See Whitehill, *Boston, A Topographical History*, p. 50. Frontispiece for *The Columbian Magazine*, April 1788, opposite p. 175. Stauffer, 3341.
LC–USZ62–46027

518
View of the SEAT of his Excellency JOHN HANCOCK ESQR. BOSTON July 1789. Hill, del. et Sculp:
  Mixed method 3¾ x 6¼ in. (image)

  The Hancock house, built in 1737, stood on Beacon Street. The handsome stone building faced south and commanded a wide view of the city on all sides. While John Hancock (1737–1793), the wealthy merchant, President of Congress, and Governor of Massachusetts, inhabited the house, the east wing contained a spacious hall for entertaining. Frontispiece for *The Massachusetts Magazine*, July 1789. Stauffer, 1406. LC–USZ62–45572

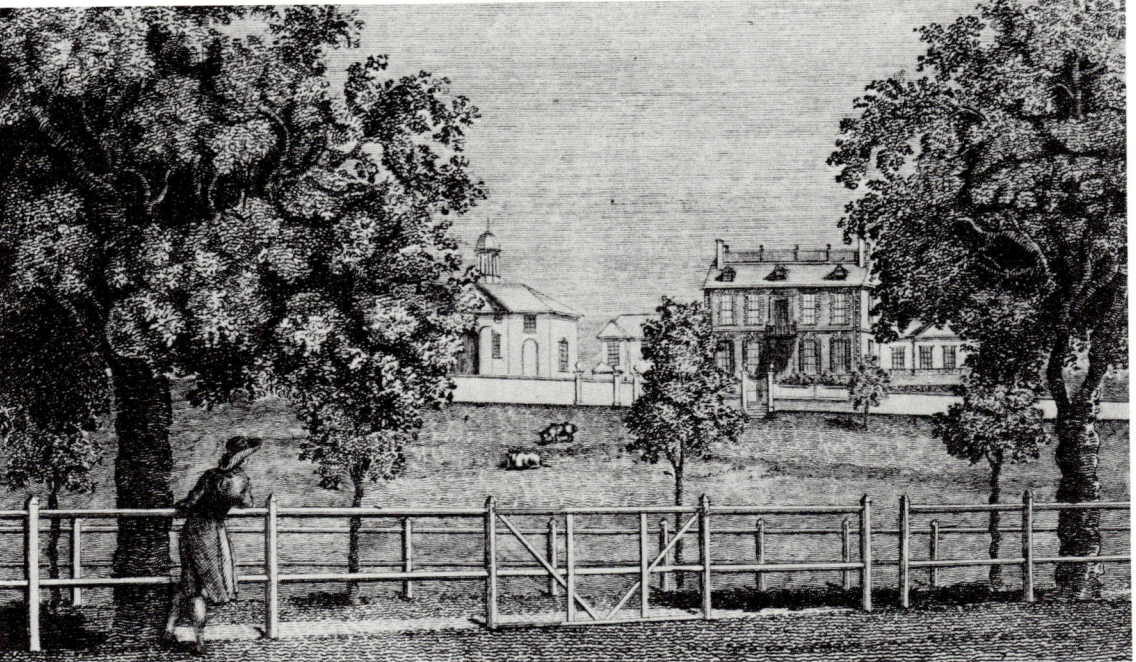

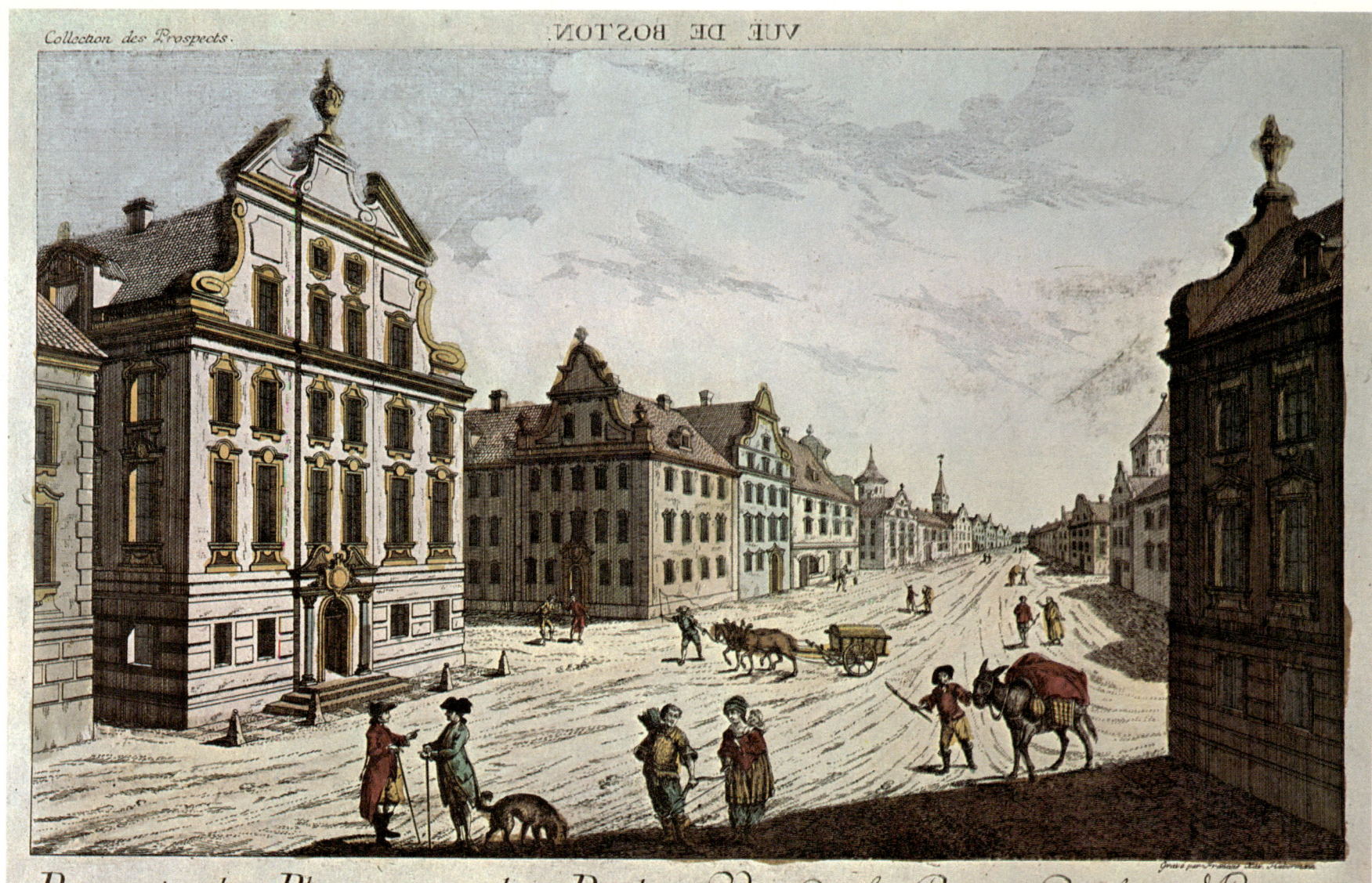

Prospect des Plazes vor dem Rath Haus zu Boston. | Vuë de la Rue et de la Maison de Ville à Boston.

519

VUË DE BOSTON. Prospect von Boston gegen der Bucht am Hasen. Vue de Boston vers le Cale du Port. Se vend a Augsbourg au Negoce commun de l'Academie Imperiale d'Empire des Arts libereaux avec Privilege de Sa Majeste Imperiale et avec Defense ni d'en faire ni de vendre les Copies. Gravé par Francois Xav. Habermann. [177?]

Etching (hand colored) 12½ x 16⅜ in. (image)

A stylized view of the port of Boston, the center of New England shipping in the colonial period. The closing of the port after the Boston Tea Party, led to the calling of the First Continental Congress. From "Collection des prospects." LC–USZ62–15353 is the negative number for the black-and-white print.

————————Another copy entitled, "Vue de Boston vers le Cale du Port." The details are less clear, and the colors are darker. 12½ x 16¾ in.

520

VUË DE BOSTON. Prospect des Plazes vor dem Rath Haus zu Boston. Vuë de la rue et de la Maison de Ville à Boston. Se vend à Augsbourg au Negoce commun de l'Academie Imperiale d'Empire des Arts libereaux avec Privilege de sa Majesté Imperiale et avec Defense ni d'en faire ni de vendre les Copies. Gravé par Francois Xav. Habermann. [177?]

Etching (hand colored) 12½ x 16½ in.

The old statehouse, built in 1657, was the center of government of both the Colony and Boston, as well as the public market place. When Faneuil Hall became the site for town meetings, this building continued to be used by the provincial legislature and courts. A more accurate representation can be seen in the Paul Revere engraving of the Boston Massacre, which took place a short distance away. The title at the top of the picture is a mirror image. From "Collection des prospects."

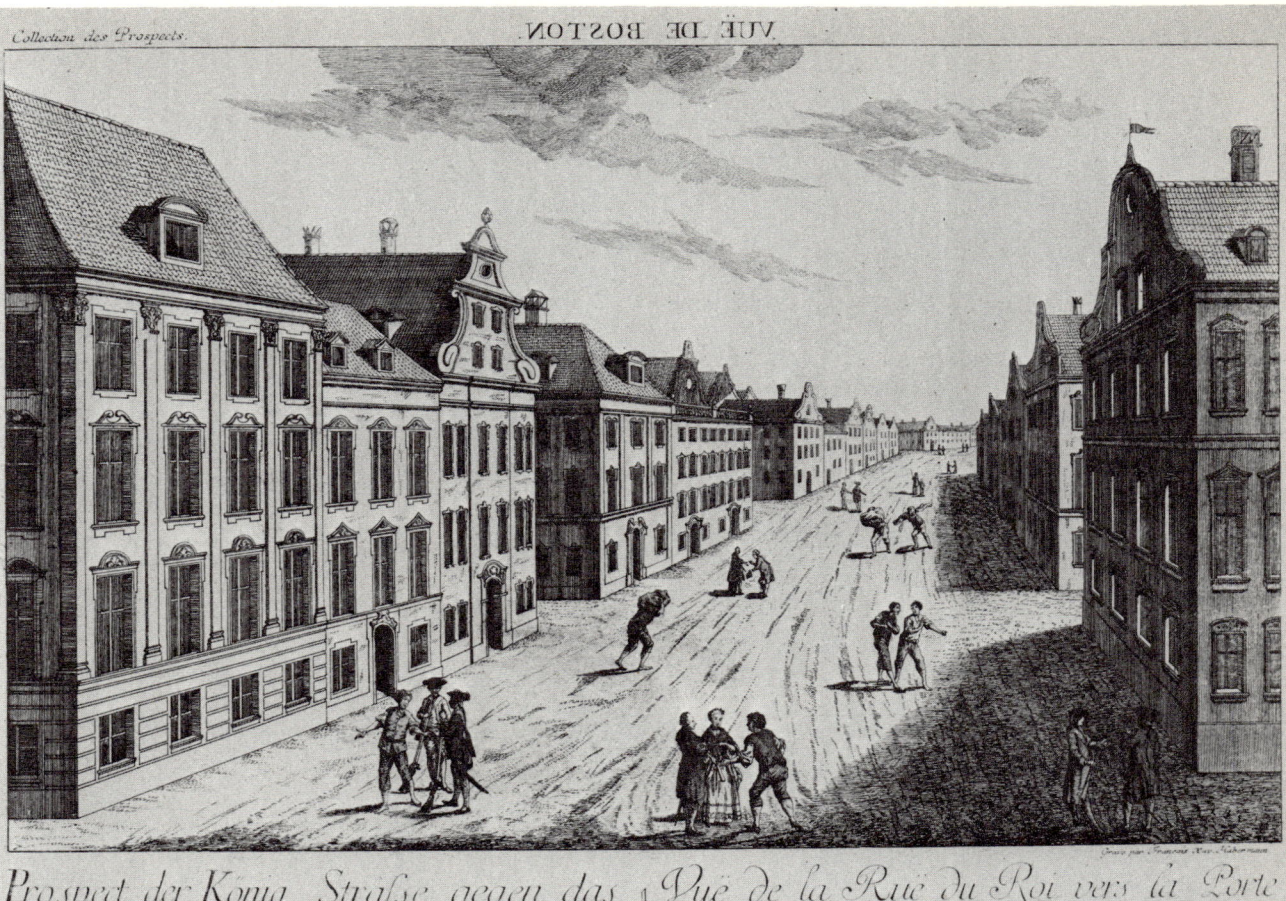

521

521

VUË DE BOSTON. Prospect der König Strasse gegen das Land Thor zu Boston. Vuë de la Ruë du Roi vers la Porte de la Campagne a Boston. Se vend à Augsbourg au Negoce commun de l'Academie Imperiale d'Empire des Arts libereaux avec Privilege de Sa Majesté Imperiale et avec Defense ni d'en faire ni de vendre les Copies. Gravé par Francois Xav. Habermann. [177?]

Etching (hand colored) 9⅞ x 15½ in. (image)

Stylized view of King Street. Title at top of picture is mirror image. From "Collection des prospects." LC–USZ62–45388

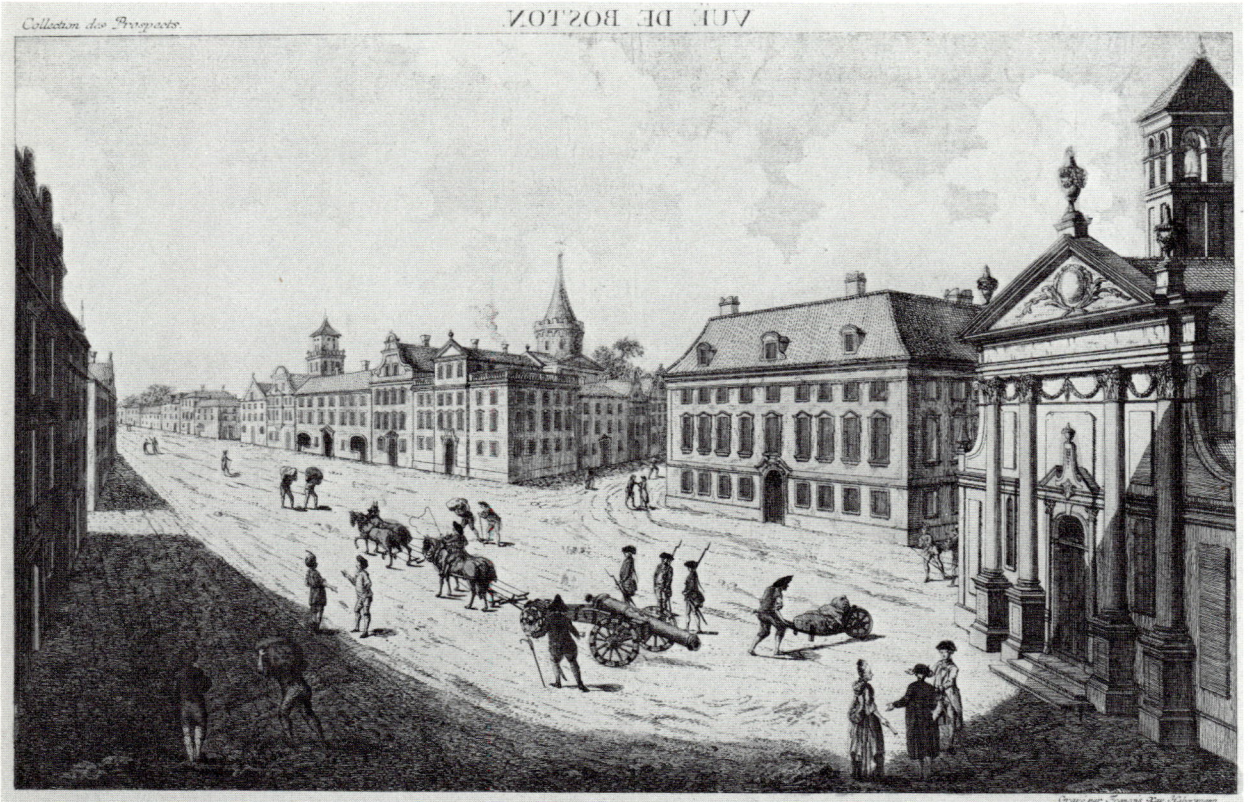

522

522

VUË DE BOSTON. Prospect des grossen Plazes gegen der alten Sud Kirche der Presbiterianer zu Boston. Vuë de la Ruë grande vers l'Eglise du Sud des Presbiteriennes a Boston. Se vend à Augsbourg au Negoce commun de l'Academie d'Empire des Arts libereaux avec Privilege de Sa Majesté Imperiale et avec Defense ni d'en faire ni de vendre les Copies. Gravé par Francois Xav. Habermann. [177?]

Etching (hand colored) 10 x 15¾ in. (image)

Old South Congregational Church was the third church to be built in Boston. It was the scene of many patriotic meetings in the years immediately preceding the War for Independence. Unlike the church pictured, Old South had a tall steeple. The title at the top of the picture is a mirror image. From "Collection des Prospects." LC–USZ62–45389

523

A View of the City of Boston the Capital of NEW ENGLAND, in North America. Vue de la Ville de Boston, Capitale de la NOUVELLE ANGLETERRE, dans l'Amérique Septentrionale. Drawn on the Spot by his Excellency, Governor Pownal; Painted by Mr. Pugh, & Engraved by P. C. Canot. London, Printed for John Bowles, at No. 13 in Cornhill; Robert Sayer, at No. 53 in Fleet Street; Thos. Jeffreys, the Corner of St. Martins Lane in the Strand; Carington Bowles, at No. 69 in St. Pauls Church Yard; & Heny. Parker, at No. 82 in Cornhill. [1768]

Etching 14½ x 20¾ in.

The view is from Cambridge across the Charles River to the Boston Common. Thomas Pownall (1722–1805), the artist, was the Governor of Massachusetts, 1757–59. From *Scenographia Americana* (1768). LC–USZ62–45584

─────── Another copy entitled, "A View of the Town of Boston the Capital of New England." [Trenchard?] Reduced (5¾ x 9 in.) and reproduced as the frontispiece for *The Columbian Magazine*, December 1787. The American flag has been substituted for the Union Jack, and ships have been removed from the harbor and fortifications from the shore. Stauffer, 3285. LC–USZ62–16685

524

CAPE POGE bearing S 52° E, distant two Miles. [J.F.W. Des Barres, 1781?]

Aquatint with etching 2⅛ x 16¼ in. (image)

The cape is on the extreme left. *The Atlantic Neptune*. Phillips 1198, v. 3, no. 33.

———Other impressions: Phillips 3658, pt. 3, no. 24a; Phillips 4473, v. 1, no. 60; LeGear 10323, v. 2, no. 43a (hand colored); LeGear 10320, v. 3, no. 28.

525

SANDY POINT bearing W S W distant four Miles. [J.F.W. Des Barres, 1781?]

Aquatint with etching 2 x 12¾ in. (image)

The point is to the right. *The Atlantic Neptune*. Phillips 1198, v. 3, no. 33.

———Other impressions: Phillips 3658, pt. 3, no. 24a; Phillips 4473, v. 1, no. 60; LeGear 10323, v. 2, no. 43a (hand colored); LeGear 10320, v. 3, no. 28.

526

GAY HEAD bearing N E ¼ E and NOMANSLAND E ¼ S. [J.F.W. Des Barres, 1781?]

Aquatint with etching 2¾ x 28 in. (image)

The Atlantic Neptune. Phillips 1198, v. 3, no. 33.

———Other impressions: Phillips 3658, pt. 3, no. 24a; Phillips 4473, v. 1, no. 60 (hand colored); LeGear 10323, v. 2, no. 43a (hand colored); LeGear 10320, v. 3, no. 28.

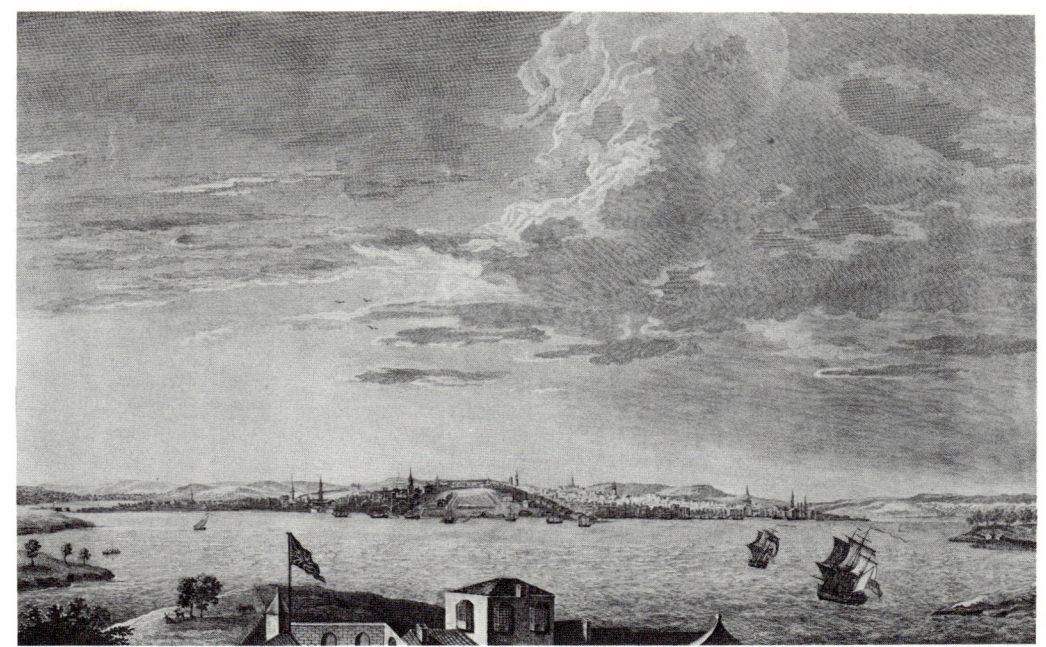

523

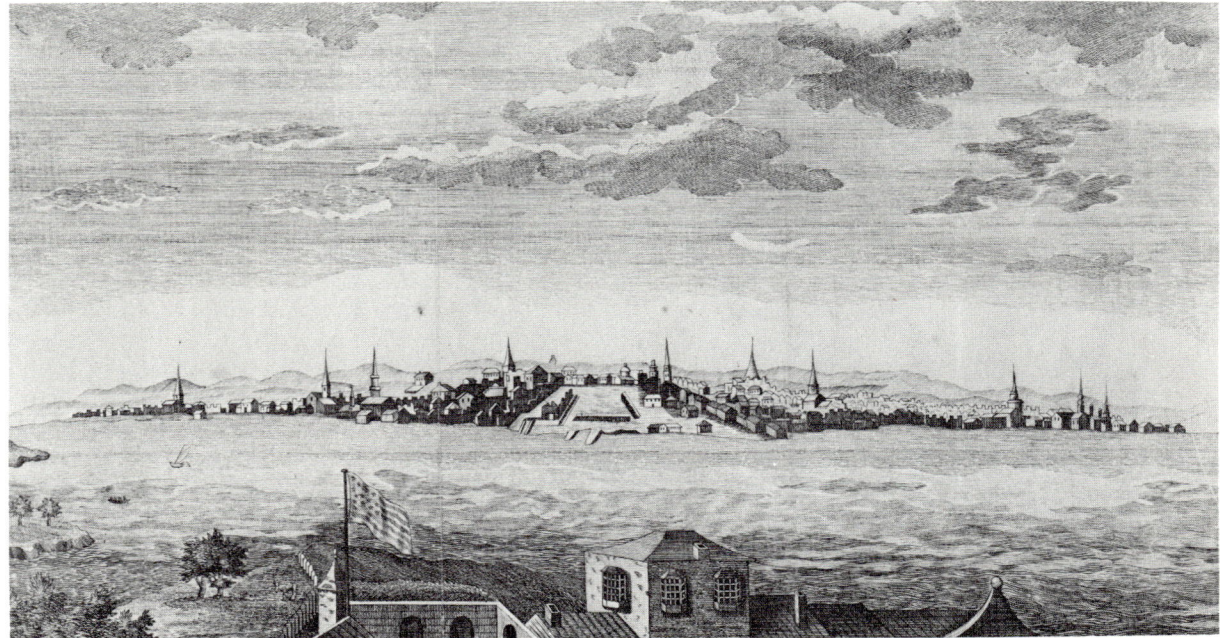

523a

193

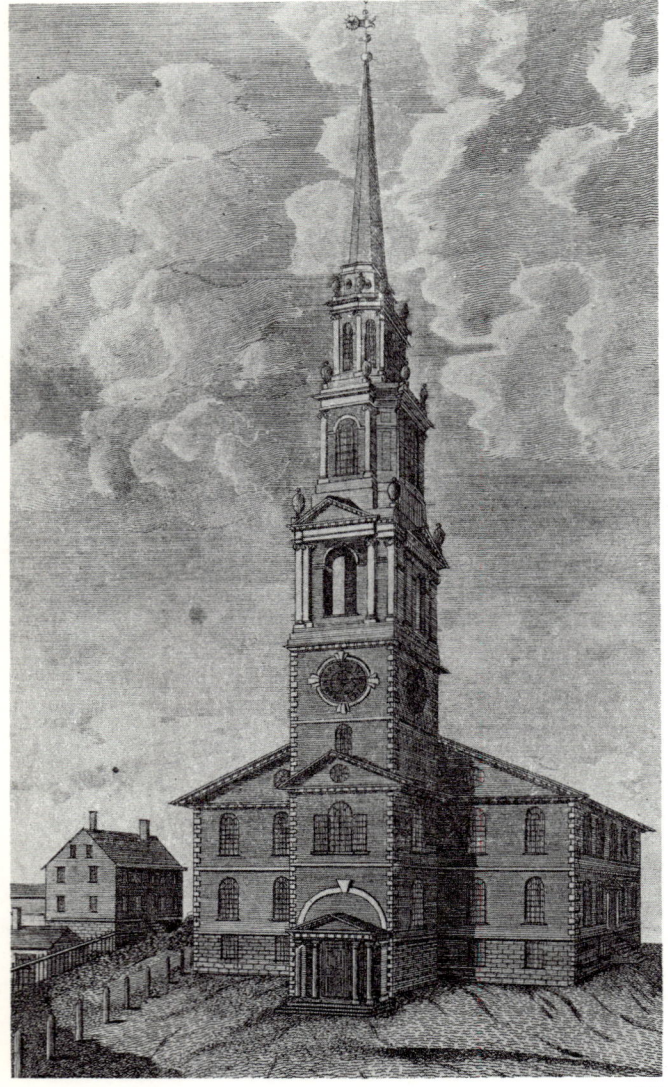

532

527
GAY HEAD bearing SE distant one Mile. [J.F.W. Des Barres, 1781?]

Aquatint with etching 2⅞ x 22⅜ in. (image)

The head is to the left. *The Atlantic Neptune.* Phillips 1198, v. 3, no. 33.

———————Other impressions: Phillips 3658, pt. 3, no. 24a; Phillips 4473, v. 1, no. 60; LeGear 10323, v. 2, no. 43a (hand colored); LeGear 10320, v. 3, no. 28.

528
SANKOTY HEAD, bearing S b W, distant 10 Miles. [J.F.W. Des Barres, 1781?]

Aquatint with etching 2¼ x 6¾ in. (image)

The head is to the left. *The Atlantic Neptune.* Phillips 1198, v. 3, no. 33.

———————Other impressions: Phillips 3658, pt. 3, no. 24a; Phillips 4473, v. 1, no. 60; LeGear 10323, v. 2, no. 43a (hand colored); LeGear 10320, v. 3, no. 28.

529
SANKOTY HEAD bearing SW when clear of the Shoals distant 4 Leagues. [J.F.W. Des Barres, 1781?]

Etching (hand colored) ¾ x 7⅞ in.

A single boat and the head are to the left. *The Atlantic Neptune.* Phillips 1198, v. 3, no. 33.

———————Other impressions: Phillips 3658, pt. 3, no. 24a; Phillips 4473, v. 1, no. 60 (hand colored); LeGear 10323, v. 2, no. 43a (hand colored); LeGear 10320, v. 3, no. 28 (hand colored).

530
[A View of Cape Cod, J.F.W. Des Barres, 1776–77?]

Etching (hand colored) 11¾ x 20 in. (image)

The view shows a large area of white cliffs with the open sea to the right. *The Atlantic Neptune.* Phillips 3657, v. 3, no. 25.

531
[Shirley Point open with Deer Island, Sailing into Boston Harbor, J.F.W. Des Barres, 1776–77?]

Etching (hand colored) 11 x 20½ in. (image)

A small village is to the left. *The Atlantic Neptune.* Phillips 3657, v. 3, no. 25.

Rhode Island and Connecticut

532
A S.W. View of the BAPTIST MEETING HOUSE, Providence, R.I. S. Hill Sculp. August, 1789.

Etching 7⅜ x 4½ in.

Sometimes called the "Mother Church of American Baptists," this church, founded by Roger Williams in 1639, was the first of its denomination in the New World. The building was designed by James Gibbs after the church of St. Martin's-in-the-Fields in London and was built in 1774. From *The Massachusetts Magazine*, August 1789, frontispiece. Stauffer, 1412. LC–USZ62–31789

533
BRISTOL NECK Rhode Island 1765.

Ink and water color drawing 6¾ x 12 in.

A similar view in the British Museum has the title "View of Bristol Neck from Trips's in Rhode Island September 1765." LC–USZ62–45382

534
A View of the GUARD-HOUSE and SIMSBURY-MINES, now called Newgate. A Prison for the Confinement of Loyalists in Connecticut. Pub. by J. Bew, Pater-Noster-Row Nov 1st 1781 London.

Etching 6 x 4¾ in. (image)

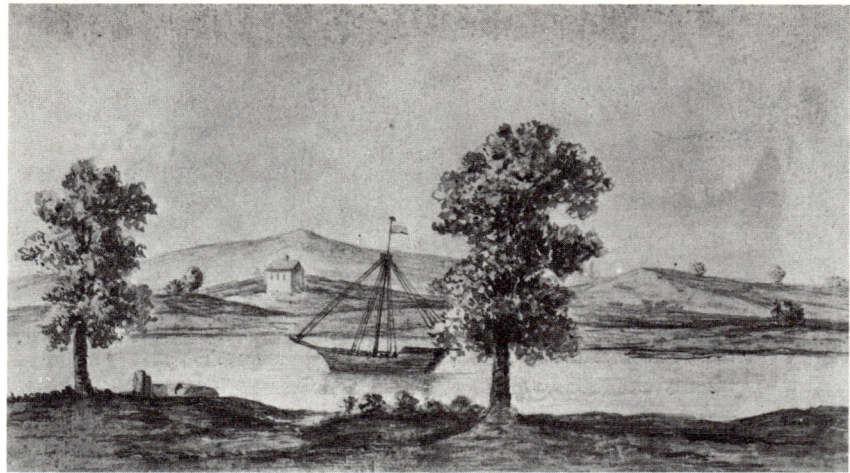

533

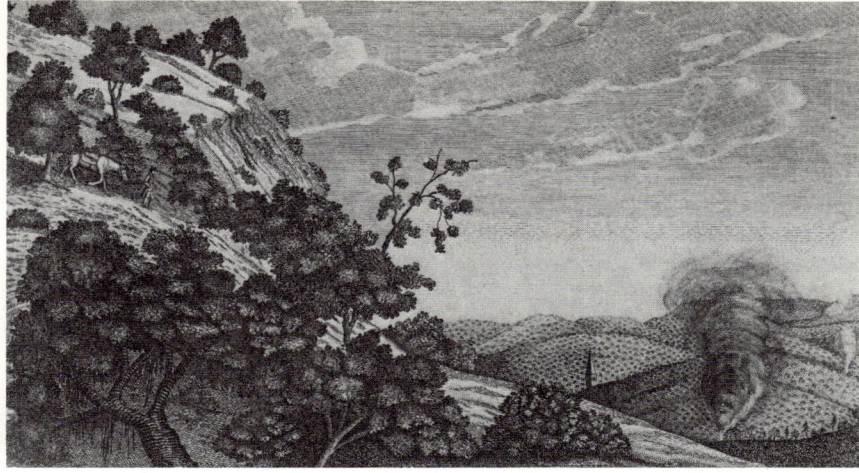

535

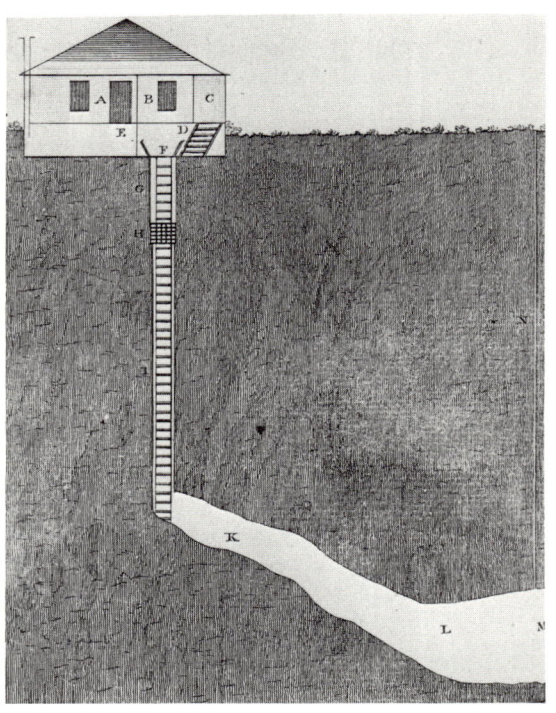

534

The accompanying article in the British publication *The Political Magazine*, October 1781, p. 597, describes the "Symsbury Mines, The Rebel Prison for the King's Loyal Subjects." Newgate, or Hell, as it was sometimes called, was a former copper mine, and the cells were 120 feet below the surface. The British complained that conditions there were inhumane, that loyalists were denied visits by the clergy, and that prisoners frequently died.

The legend identifies the following:

A. Gaurd [sic] room. B. Lodging room for the officer of the guard. C. A closet from which the stair leads down. D. The stairs. E. A kitchen, divided off by a partition, the door of which is locked when a prisoner is let up to cook. F. A strong trap door opening the descent to Hell. G. A step ladder descending eight feet to an iron grate. H. An iron grate. I. A ladder descending through a shaft in the rock, about forty feet. K. A descent through the broken cavities of the rock about forty feet. L., M. The prison commonly called Hell. N. A hole bored through the rock, seventy feet in depth, about an inch and an half in diameter, the only passage by which the prisoners are furnished with air.

CPPS 5853 LC–USZ62–50390

535
View from THE GREEN WOODS towards Canaan and Salisbury, in Connecticut. [1789, ascribed to Trenchard]

Etching 4½ x 7⅜ in.

The Green Woods in Connecticut were so named because of the green-bearded moss which grew on the pine trees. Located between Hartford and Canaan, they were very hilly and were 20 to 30 miles in length. In this view; a horseman walks his mount down a steep hill to the right toward a valley where a steeple and columns of smoke are visible. From *The Columbian Magazine, or Monthly Miscellany*, June 1789, opposite p. 366. Stauffer, 3292.

LC–USZ62–45576

MIDDLE ATLANTIC STATES

New York

New York City and Vicinity

536
Bond Hollow bearing S.bE. Publish'd by J.F.W. DesBarres Esqr. May 19th. 1779.

Etching (hand colored) 2¼ x 8⅛ in. (image)

View set into "A Chart of New York Harbor...." *The Atlantic Neptune*. Phillips 1198, v. 3, no. 39.

——————Other impressions: Phillips 1199, v. 3, no. 25; Phillips 1200, v. 3, no. 26; Phillips 1205, v. 3, no. 27; Phillips 3658, pt. 3, no. 13; Phillips 3655, v. 3, no. 13; Phillips 3656, v. 3, no. 13; Phillips 3659, v. 3, no. 13; Phillips 4473, v. 1, no. 63; LeGear 10323, v. 2, no. 50; LeGear 10320, v. 3, no. 31. Negative in G&M.

537

Mount Pleasant half way between the Cedars on the Hook & the Light House. Publish'd by J.F.W. DesBarres Esqr. May 19th. 1779.

Etching (hand colored) 2⅝ x 9 in. (image)

View set into "A Chart of New York Harbor...." *The Atlantic Neptune*. Phillips 1198, v. 3, no. 39.

——————Other impressions: Phillips 1199, v. 3, no. 25; Phillips 1200, v. 3, no. 26; Phillips 1205, v. 3, no. 27; Phillips 3658, pt. 3, no. 13; Phillips 3655, v. 3, no. 13; Phillips 3656, v. 3, no. 13; Phillips 3659, v. 3, no. 13; Phillips 4473, v. 1, no. 64; LeGear 10323, v. 2, no. 50; LeGear 10320, v. 3, no. 31. Negative in G&M.

538

[View of Hell Gate, J.F.W. Des Barres, 1776–77?]

Etching (hand colored) 15½ x 21 in.

A ship passes through the narrow part of the East River near New York City. *The Atlantic Neptune*. Phillips 3657, v. 3, no. 31.

539

A View of the HIGHLAND of NEVERSUNK, N.W.b.W. four Miles distant, with the Light House, on Sandy Hook. N.W. Note. This Highland is very remarkable as the Coast Southward of it is low with Sand Beaches, and from its Northern End a low Sandy Beach extends with Clumps of Shrub Pines, at the

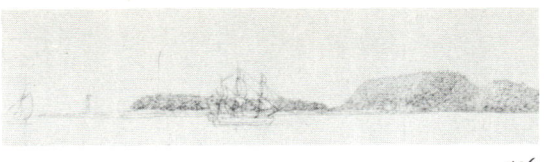

536

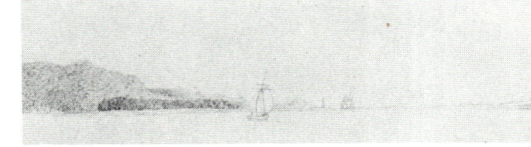

537

extremity of which stands the Light House of Sandy Hook. Publish'd according to Act of Parliament Octr. 4, 1777, by J.F.W. DesBarres Esqr.

Aquatint with etching 3¾ x 19¼ in. (image)

Gen. Henry Clinton withdrew his troops to Sandy Hook after the Battle of Monmouth in July 1778. From there the British fleet ferried the troops to New York. The lighthouse is barely visible to the right. *The Atlantic Neptune*. Phillips 1198, v. 3, no. 41. The negative number for this picture and the next four is LC–USZ62–46049.

——————Other impressions: Phillips 3658, pt. 3, no. 13a (hand colored); Phillips 4473, v. 1, no. 64; LeGear 10323, v. 2, no. 50c (hand colored); LeGear 10317, v. 2, no. 14 (hand colored).

540

The SOUTH SHORE of LONG ISLAND, ten leagues Eastward of Sandy Hook, four Miles distant. Publish'd according to Act of Parliament Octr 4, 1777, by J.F.W. DesBarres Esqr.

Aquatint with etching 2¾ x 18¾ in. (image)

The Atlantic Neptune. Phillips 1198, v. 3, no. 41.

——————Other impressions: Phillips 3658, pt. 3, no. 13a (hand colored); Phillips 4473, v. 1, no. 64; LeGear 10323, v. 2, no. 50c (hand colored); LeGear 10317, v. 2, no. 14 (hand colored).

541

NEW YORK, with the ENTRANCE of the NORTH and EAST RIVERS. Publish'd according to Act of Parliament Octr 4, 1777, by J.F.W. DesBarres Esqr.

Aquatint with etching 4¼ x 18½ in. (image)

New York is in the center, with the North River to the left and the East River to the right. The North River, or Hudson, bounds Manhattan Island to the west. The East River connects New York's Upper Bay and Long Island Sound. British control of the waterways around New York prevented the patriots from attacking the city. *The Atlantic Neptune*. Phillips 1198, v. 3, no. 41. Also available separately on negative number LC–USZ62–46050.

——————Other impressions: Phillips 3658, pt. 3, no. 13a (hand colored); Phillips 4473, v. 1, no. 64 (hand colored); LeGear 10323, v. 2, no. 50c (hand colored); LeGear 10317, v. 2, no. 14 (hand colored).

542

The LIGHT HOUSE on SANDY HOOK, S.E. one Mile. Publish'd according to Act of Parliament Octr 4, 1777, by J.F.W. DesBarres Esqr.

Aquatint with etching 4⅛ x 18¼ in. (image)

The Atlantic Neptune. Phillips 1198, v. 3, no. 41.

——————Other impressions: Phillips 3658, pt. 3, no. 13a (hand colored); Phillips 4473, v. 1, no. 64 (hand colored); LeGear 10323, v. 2, no. 50c (hand colored); LeGear 10317, v. 2, no. 14 (hand colored).

543

The NARROWS, (between Red and Yellow Hook, on Long Island, & the East Bluff of

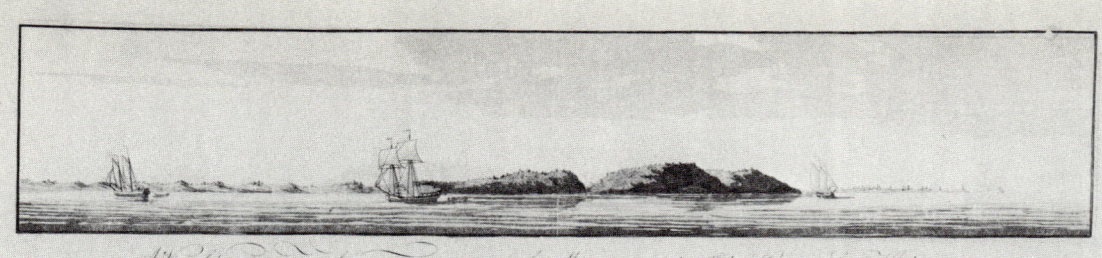

A View of the HIGHLAND *of* NEVERSUNK, *N.W.b.W. four Miles distant, with the Light House on Sandy Hook. N.W.*

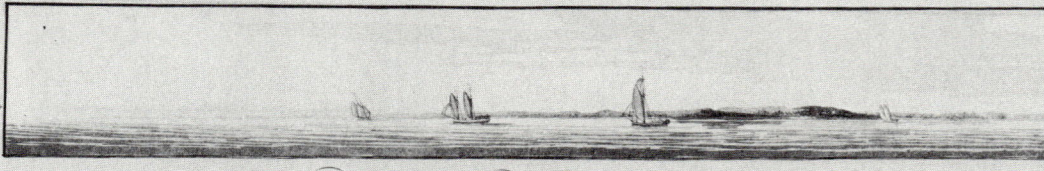

The SOUTH SHORE *of* LONG ISLAND, *ten leagues Eastward of Sandy Hook, four Miles distant.*

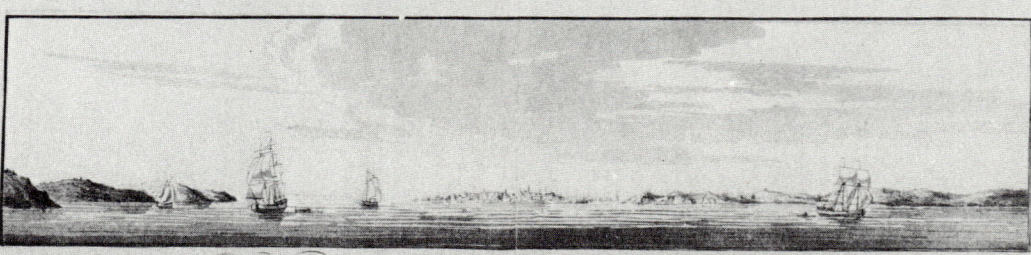

NEW YORK, *with the* ENTRANCE *of the* NORTH *and* EAST RIVERS.

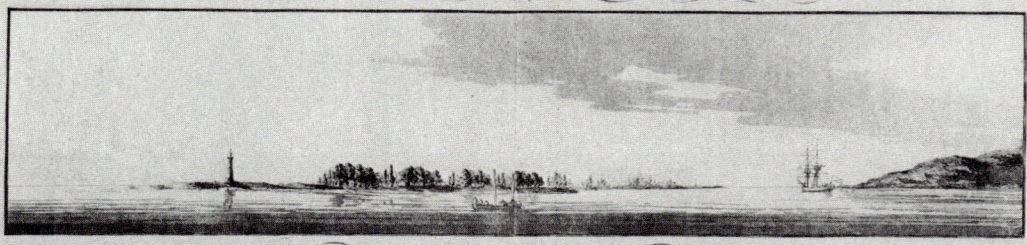

The LIGHT HOUSE *on* SANDY HOOK, S.E. one Mile.

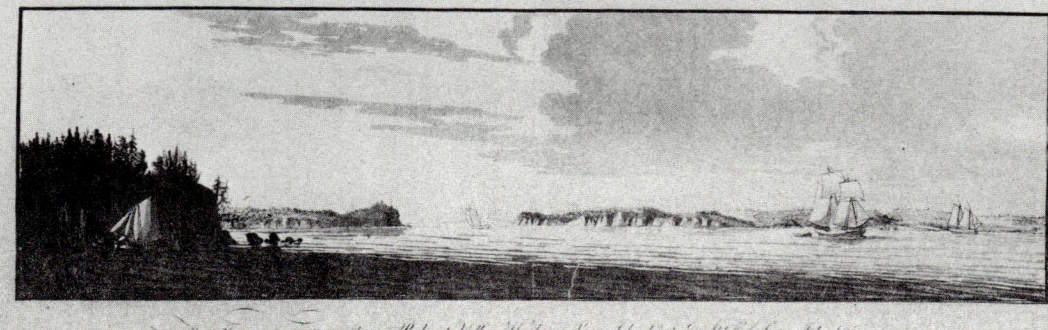

The NARROWS *between Red and Yellow Hook on Long Island, & the East Bluff of Staten Island, bearing S.b.W.*

Staten Island,) bearing S.b.W. Publish'd according to Act of Parliament Octr 4, 1777, by J.F.W. Des Barres Esqr.

Aquatint with etching 5⅜ x 18½ in. (image)

The Atlantic Neptune. Phillips 1198, v. 3, no. 41.

————Other impressions: Phillips 3658, pt. 3, no. 13a (hand colored); Phillips 4473, v. 1, no. 64 (hand colored); LeGear 10323, v. 2, no. 50c (hand colored); LeGear 10317, v. 2, no. 14 (hand colored).

544

East View of Hell Gate in the Province of New York. W A Williams del. 1775.

Etching 5 x 8 in.

Hell Gate was a dangerous waterway between New York and Connecticut, Rhode Island, and Massachusetts. Ships frequently crashed on the rocks there on their way to New England. The route's one advantage was that it bypassed the Atlantic. Pictured is the location at which Harlem Creek, the East River, and Flushing Sound meet. This view and a map accompany a glowing description of New York City and its environs. From *The London Magazine*, April 1778, p. 147. LC-USZ62-46095

545

S View of the City of New York [1776?]

Pen and ink drawing 4¼ x 15¼ in. (image)

This view, probably from a point on Long Island near Red Hook, shows the skyline of New York City sometime before the fire of September 20–21, 1776. The steeple of Trinity Church is on the far left. Stokes, *Iconograpy of Manhattan Island*, v. 1 (New York, 1915), p. 361. LC-USZ62-45539

539, 540, 541, 542, 543

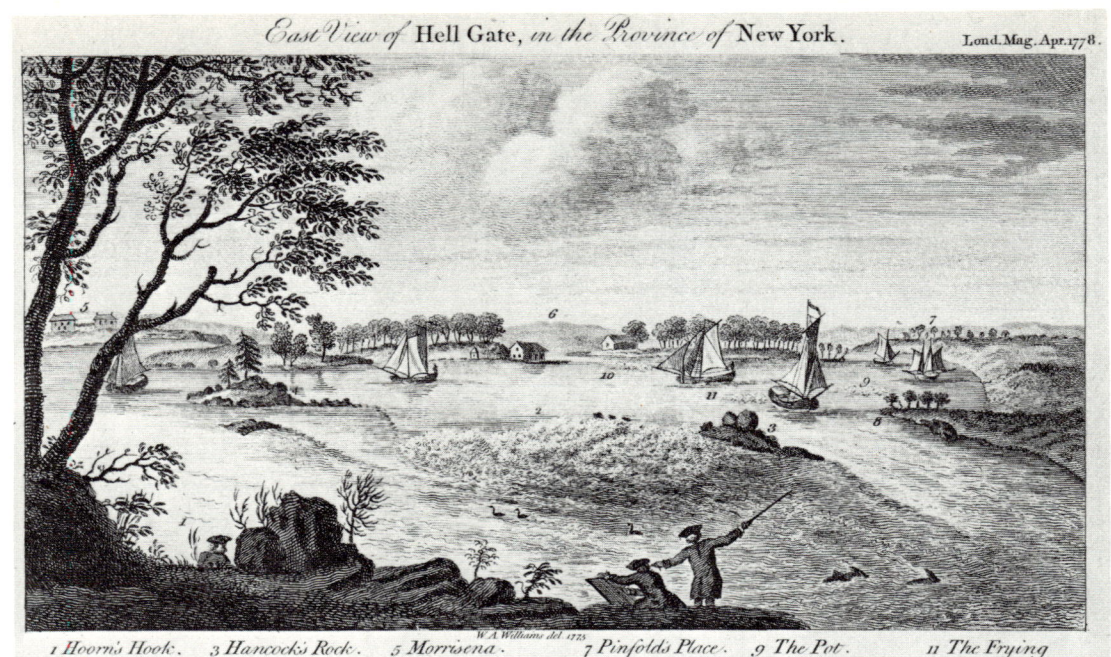

544

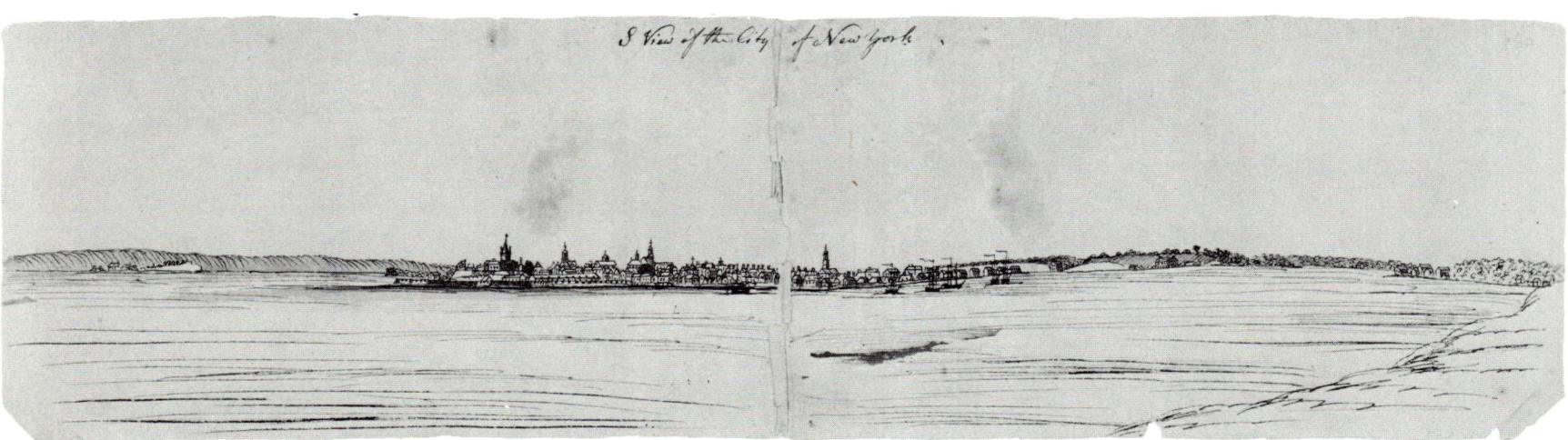

545

546

E View of the City of New York. er: 41. [1776?]
  Ink drawing 4¼ x 15¼ in. (image)

This view was also drawn before the New York City fire. In the foreground is the Rutgers House, and Trinity Church steeple is visible in the background. The ships in the harbor may represent the fleet under Adm. Richard Howe, which anchored there in early September 1776. Stokes, *Iconography of Manhattan Island*, v. 1 (New York, 1915), p. 361. LC-USZ62-45540

547

A View of the City of New York from Long Island [Montresor? 177?]
  Ink and water color drawing 9⅞ x 17⅛ in.

This view shows Trinity Church without its steeple, dating the drawing sometime between the fire of 1776, when the steeple was destroyed, and 1784, when the remainder of the tower was removed. Other buildings on the skyline include St. Paul's Chapel, New Dutch Church, Middle Dutch Church, the French Church, Federal Hall, Wall Street Presbyterian Church, and St. George's Chapel. Stokes, *Iconography of Manhattan Island*, v. 1 (New York, 1915), p. 361-362. LC-USZ62-20492

548

Bunker's Hill on N. York Island [177?]
  Ink sketch 6¾ x 19¾ in.

Bunker's Hill, the highest point on the southern side of the island, was fortified by the Americans during the Revolution. The hill was also known as Mount Pleasant and as Bayard's Mount. The name "Montresor" appears on the reverse, probably indicating that at one time the picture was in John Montresor's possession. Stokes, *Iconography of Manhattan Island*, v. 1 (New York, 1915), p. 362, and v. 3 (New York, 1918), p. 867. LC-USZ62-45377

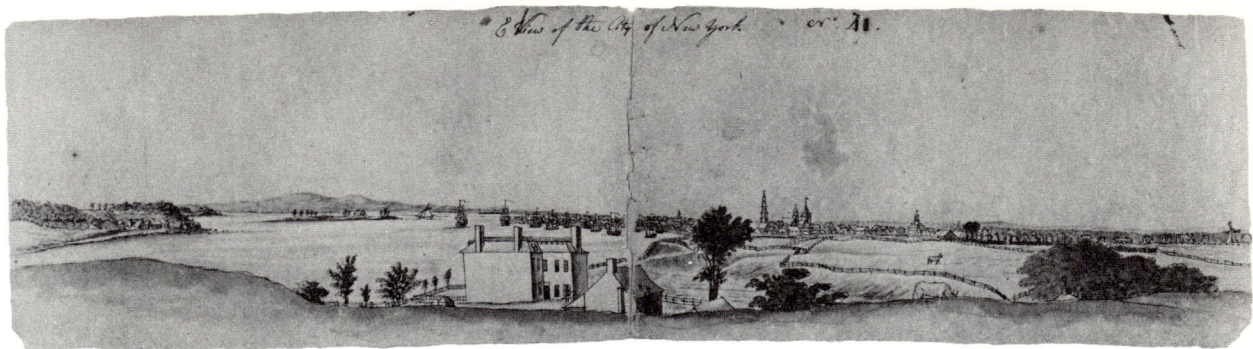

546

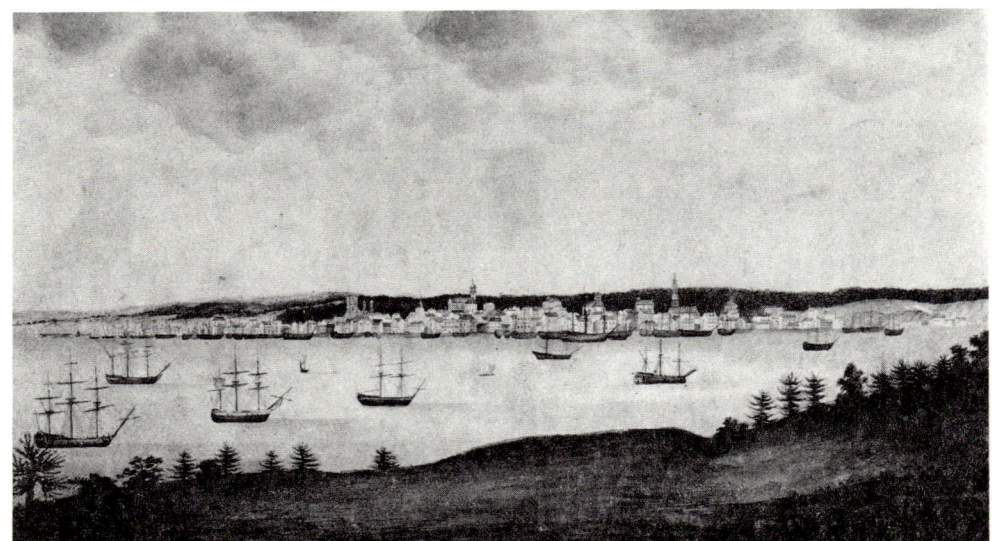

547

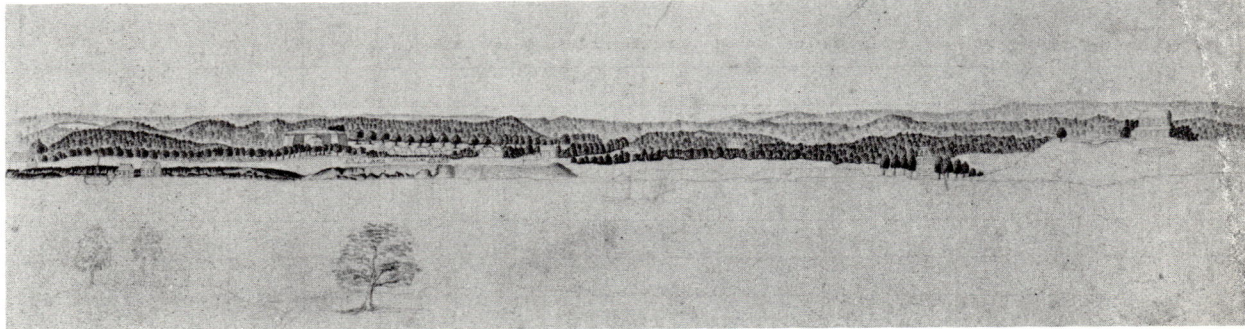

548

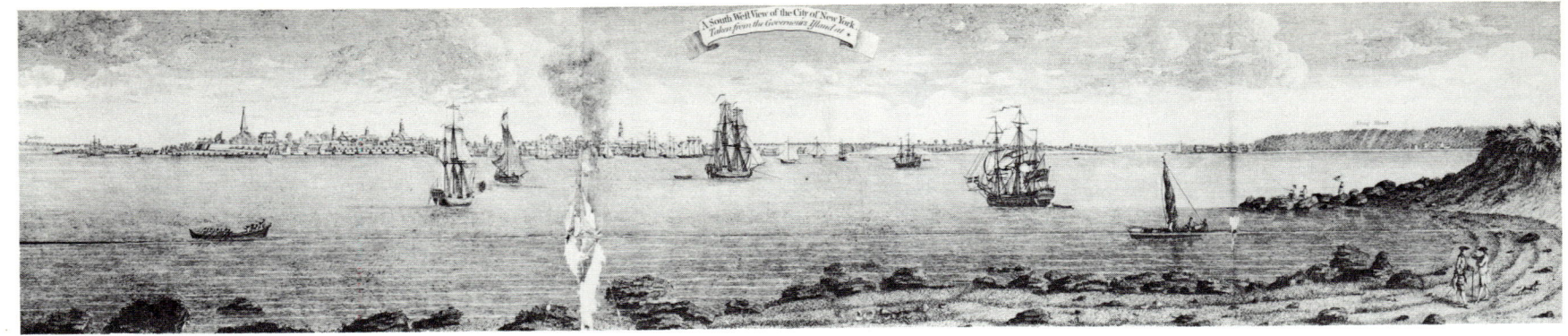

549

549
A South West View of the City of New York, Taken from the Governours Island at* [NW tip of island—designated on map] London, Published according to Act of Parliament, Jany 12, 1776, by Jefferys and Faden, Corner of St. Martins Lane, Charing Cross. [After B. Ratzer and engraved by Thos. Kitchin]

Etching 7½ x 34 in. (image)

This view accompanies the map "Plan of the City of New York in North America: Surveyed in the Year 1766 & 1767" from Faden, *North American Atlas* (London, 1777), no. 20–21. The cloud of smoke near St. George's Chapel could not represent the great fire of September 1776, as earlier editions of the map with copies of this view were offered for sale in 1770. It has been suggested that the smoke is from a kettle of tar being used for ship repairs. See Stokes, *Iconography of Manhattan Island*, v. 1 (New York, 1915), p. 341. See also item 694.
LC-USZ62-45598

550
Neu Jorck sive Neu Amsterdam. Tob. Conr. Lotteri [1778]

Etching 2¾ x 14¾ in. (image of an irregular pentagon)

This view of 17th-century New York was reprinted into the late 18th century and was part of the ornamentation on the map "Recens Edita totius Novi Belgii, in America Septentrionali" in Lotter, *Atlas Géographique* (Nürnberg, 1778), no. 92. The captions, in Latin, identify several buildings including the Dutch Reformed Church, the Lutheran Church, the public scales and granary, the governor's house, the prison, and a windmill. Smoke billows from a recently fired cannon, and in the foreground six additional cannon guard the waterfront. Among the inaccuracies in this view, which may have been drawn in Holland from verbal descriptions or rough sketches, is the size of the harbor's fortifications. Stokes, *Iconography of Manhattan Island*, v. 1 (New York, 1915), p. 223. See also item 742.
LC-USZ62-46068

551
A South East View of the City of New York,

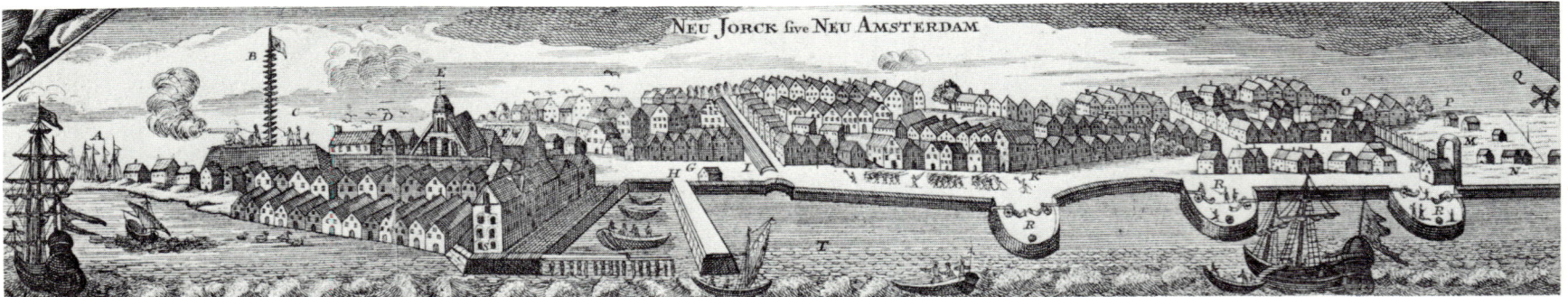

550

in NORTH AMERICA. Vue de Sud Est de la Ville de New York, dans L'AMERIQUE SEPTENTRIONALE. Drawn on the SPOT by Capt. Thomas Howdell, of the Royal Artillery. Engraved by P. Canot. London Printed for John Bowles at No. 13 in Cornhill, Robert Sayer at No. 53 in Fleet Street, Thos. Jefferys the corner of St. Martins Lane in the Strand, Carington Bowles at No. 69 in St. Pauls Church Yard, and Henry Parker at No. 82 in Cornhill. [1768]

Etching 14¼ x 20¾ in.

The large building in the center is "New College," the King's College building which opened in 1760. The college was founded in 1754 to prevent the exposure of New York youths to radical political ideas at either Yale or Princeton. King's supposedly taught submission to the English Crown, but ironically both Alexander Hamilton and Gouverneur Morris were students there. Also identified in the legend are "Old English Church," "City Hall," "French Church," "North River," "Staten Island," and "The Prison." The palm tree was probably added by the engraver. See *Scenographia Americana* (1768).
LC-USZ62-43544

552
A South West View of the City of New York, in NORTH AMERICA. Vue de Sud Ouest de la Ville de New York, dans L'AMERIQUE SEPTENTRIONALE. Drawn on the SPOT by Capt. Thomas Howdell, of the Royal Artillery. Engraved by P. Canot. London Printed for John Bowles at No. 13 in Cornhill, Robert Sayer at No. 53 in Fleet Street, Thos. Jefferys the corner of St. Martins Lane in the Strand, Carington Bowles at No. 69 in St. Pauls Church Yard, and Henry Parker at No. 82 in Cornhill. [1768]

Etching 14¼ x 20¾ in.

This view shows New York City with its many steeples in the background. Among

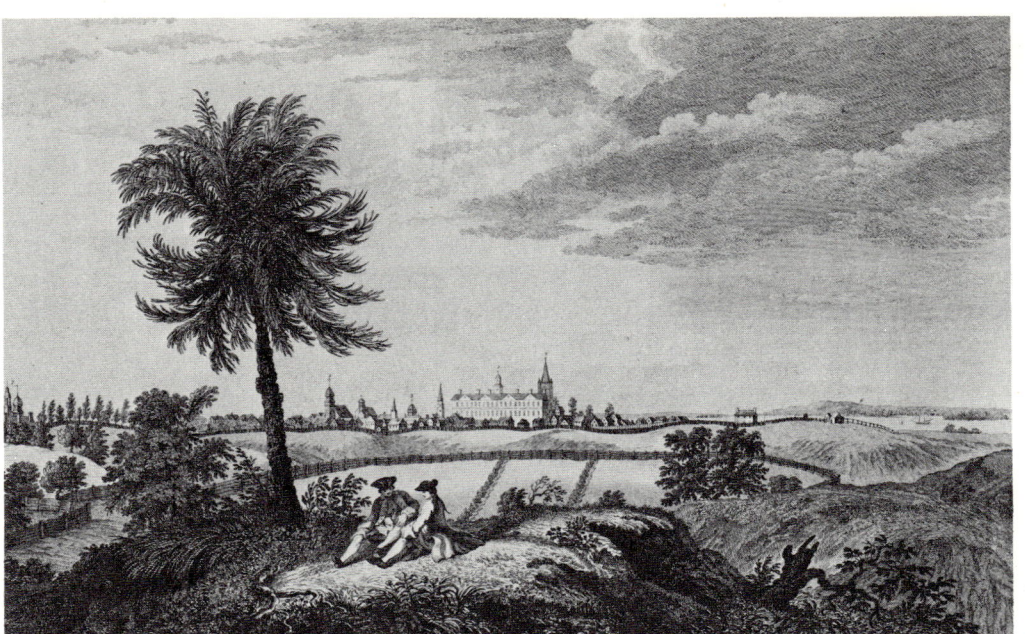
551

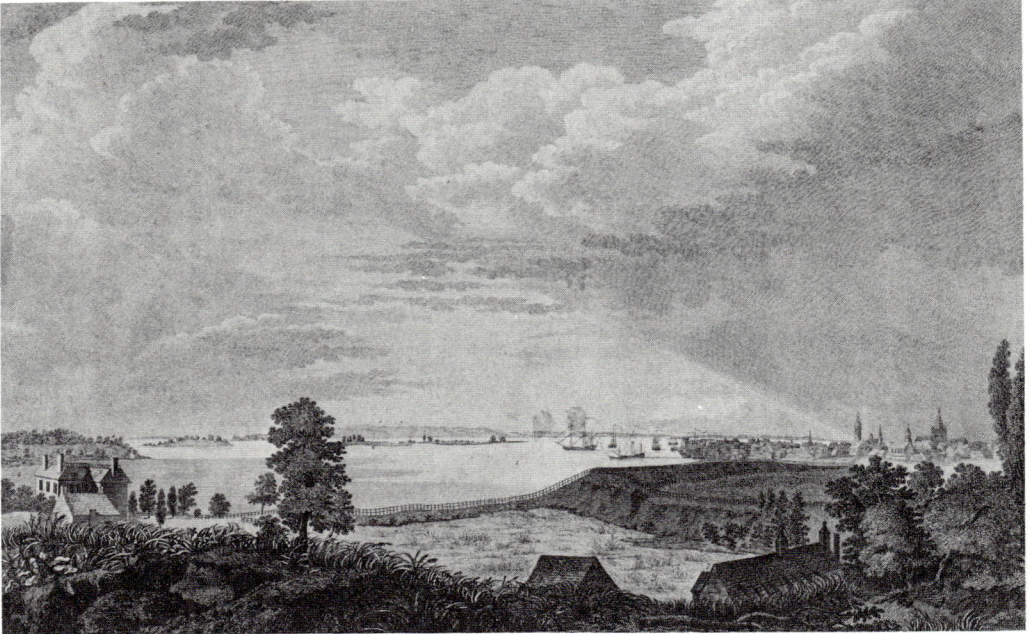
552

201

those shown is Trinity Church on the far right. Staten Island is on the horizon, and Long Island is shown directly in front of it in the harbor. In the left foreground is the Rutgers House with the South River flowing behind it. On the other side of the river is Nutting Island. On the right is a building identified in the legend as "Brew House." See *Scenographia Americana* (1768).

———Another impression. In P&P (trimmed edges). Imprint reads; "Published according to Act of Parliament by Thos. Jefferys at Charing Cross." LC–USZ62–19363

553

VUE DE LA NOUVELLE YORCK. Neu Yorck. Eine Stadt in Nord-America auf einer Insul Manahattan genannt an der Mündung des Hudsons Flusses welche 1615 von der Holländern zu erst zu bauen angesangen und neu Amsterdam genennet, hernach aber 1666 von den Engelländern ihnen abgenommen und neu Yorck um getauft worden. La nouvelle Yorck. Une Ville dans l'Amerique Septentrionale sur une Isle, dite Manahatan, près de l'orifice du fleuve Hudson, les Hollandois commencérent a la battir en l'anée 1615 et l'appellerent nouvelle Amsterdam, mais en 1666 ils en fierent privés par les Anglois qui la nommérent nouvelle Yorck. Se vend à Augsbourg au Negoce commun de l'Academie Imperiale d'Empire des Arts libereaux avec Privilege de Sa Majesté Imperiale et avec Defense ni d'en faire ni de vendre les Copies. Gravé par Balth Frederic Leizelt. [177?]

Etching (hand colored) 12½ x 17 in.

This view from "Collection des prospects" was engraved by Leizelt whose stylized versions of North American sites rarely reflected reality. LC–USZ62–41170

———Another copy entitled "La Nouvelle Yorck," with the explanation same as above but in French only. "Présentement chez Basset

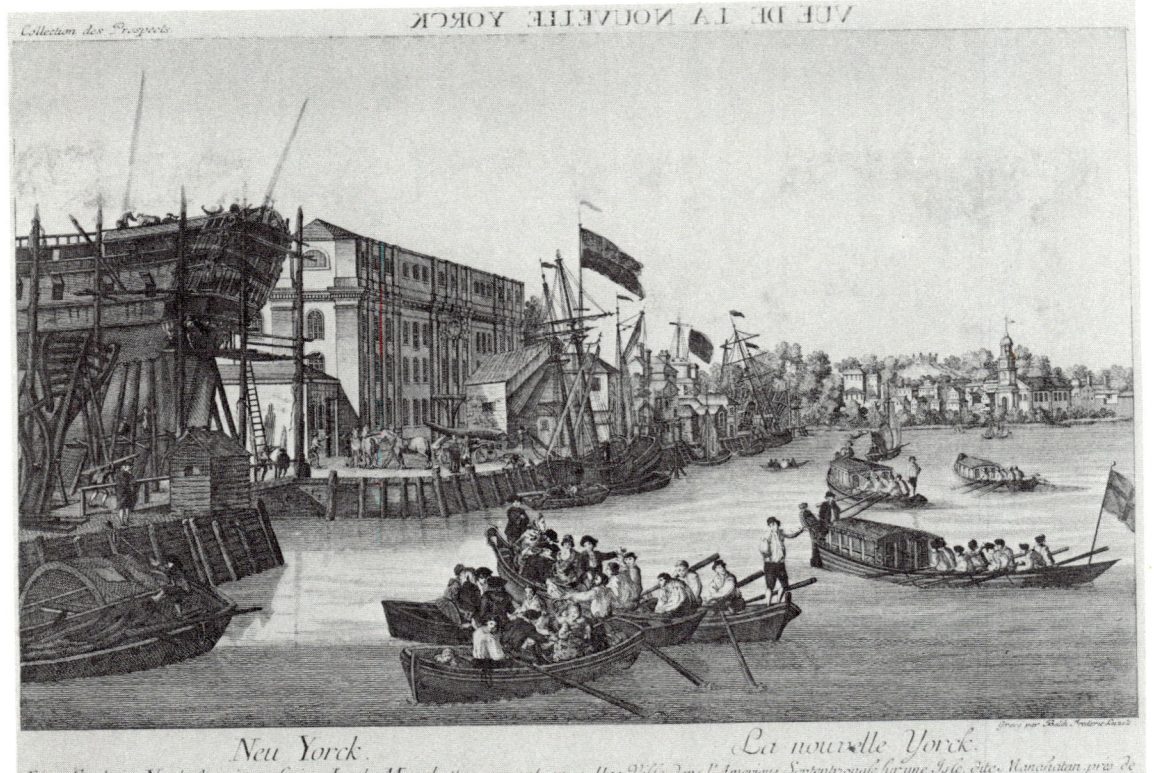

553

rue St. Jacques au coin de celle de Mathurins, Tient Fabrique de Papiers." Probably by André Basset l'aîne. 13½ x 17½ in.

554
View of the FEDERAL EDIFACE in NEW YORK. [1789]
Etching 8¾ x 8 in.

On September 13, 1788, Congress chose New York as the site of the New Government. New York City, hoping to become the permanent seat, enlarged and repaired the city hall and renamed it Federal Hall. Washington's inauguration was held on the balcony of Federal Hall, and the first inaugural address was delivered in its Senate Chamber. An accompanying article describes the interior of the building in detail and says of its external appearance:

This building is situated at the end of Broad Street, where its front appears to great advantage. The basement story is Tuscan, and is pierced with seven openings; four massy pillars in the center support four doric columns and a pediment. The frieze is ingeniously divided to admit thirteen stars in the metopes; these, with the American Eagle and other insignia in the pediment, and the tablets over the windows, filled with the thirteen arrows and the olive branch united, mark it as a building set aside for national purposes.

From *The Columbian Magazine*, August 1789, opposite p. 473. LC–USZ62–45577

Hudson River Valley and Upper New York

555
[A View of an American River—a cartouche] Printed for Robt. Sayer in Fleet Street, and T. Jefferys in the Strand. Published as the Act directs 16 June 1775.
Etching 8½ x 13 in. (image)

A spacious scene of a river, probably the Hudson, with the map's title engraved on the side of a tall cliff. This cartouche fits into the lower right-hand corner of a map entitled "The Provinces of New York, and New Jersey; with

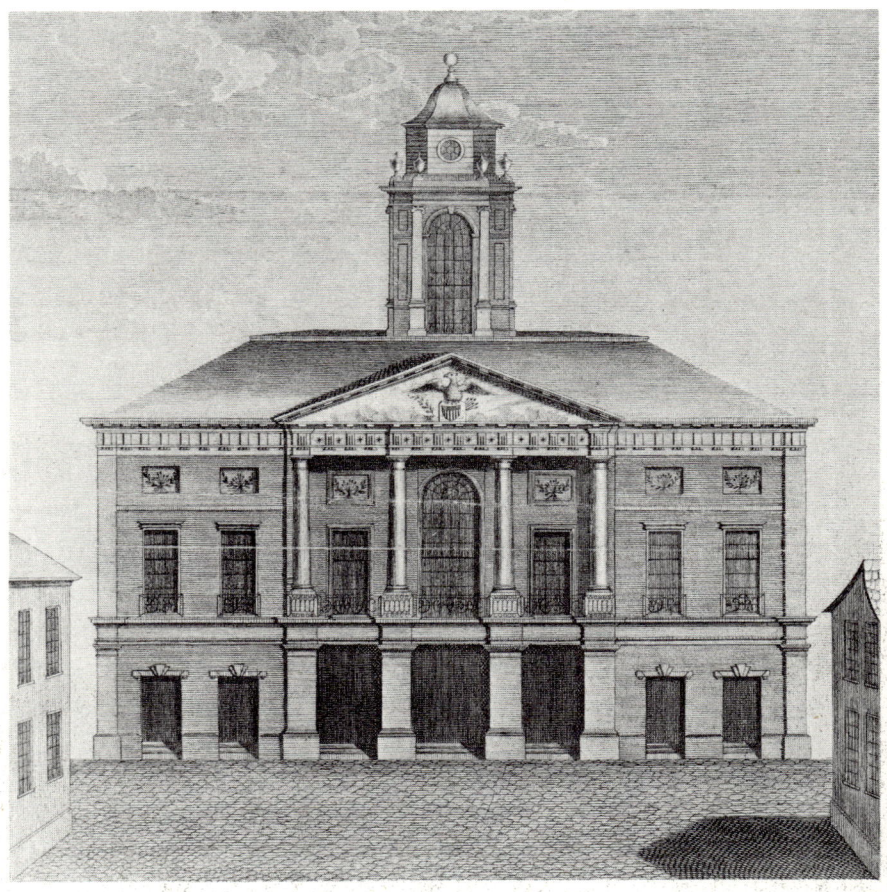

554

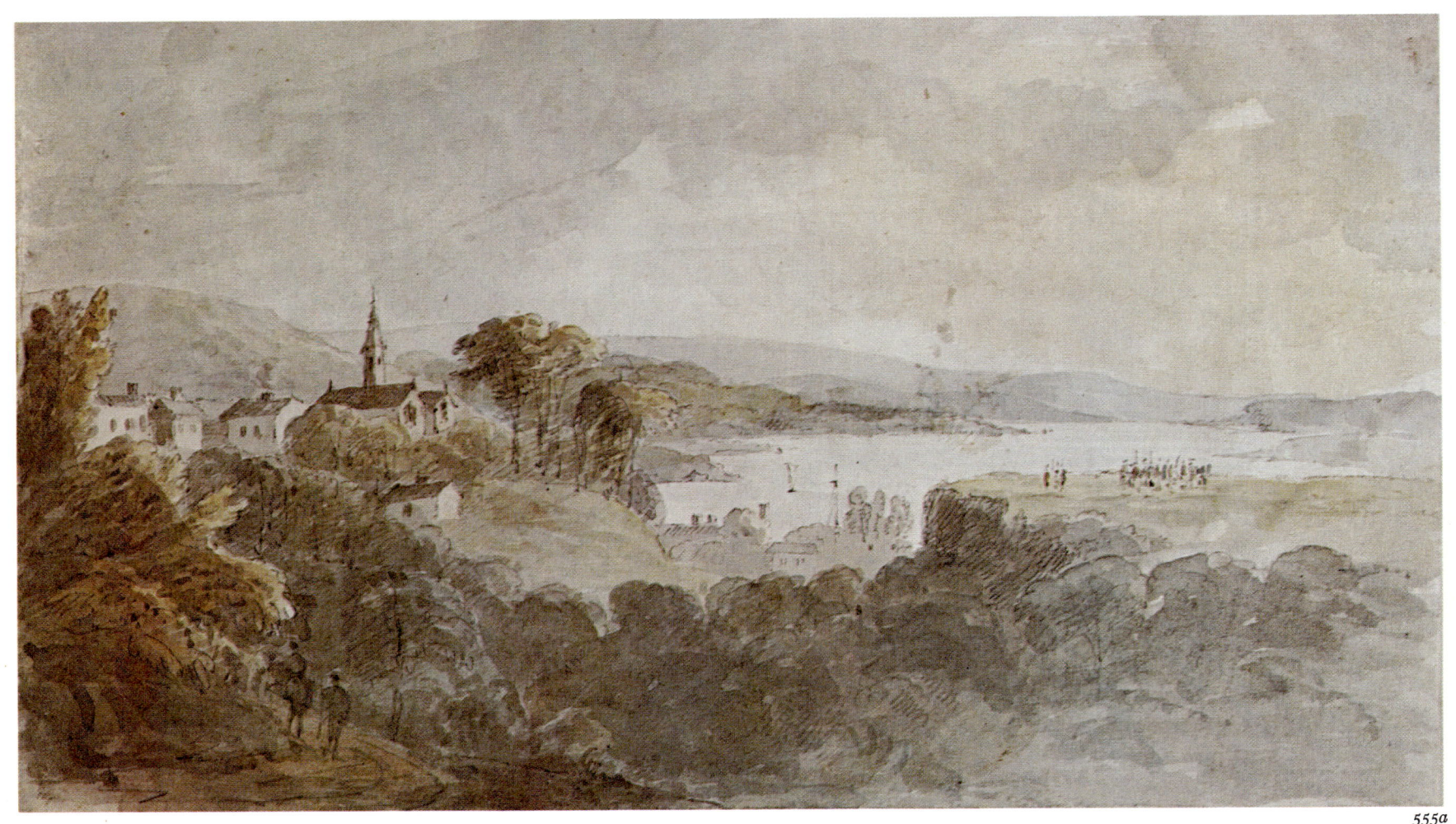

555a

part of Pensilvania, and the Governments of Trois Rivieres, and Montreal: Drawn by Capt. Holland. Engraved by Thomas Jefferys, Geographer to His Majesty." From Jefferys, *The American Atlas* (London, 1775), no. 18. The cartouche also appears in the editions for 1776, 1778, and 1782; they all carry the 1776 date.

————Another copy with no date. In Jefferys, *A General Topography of North America* (London, 1768), no. 34.

555a
[Kings Bridge, New York, August 1778?]
Watercolor 6⅝ x 10⅛ in.

This view looks past the town, over Harlem Creek, toward the Hudson River. From Simcoe, *A Journal of the Operations of the Queen's Rangers* (Exeter, [1787]), opposite p. 68.

556
A View in Hudson's River of the Entrance of what is called the Topan Sea. Vue sur la Riviere d'Hudson, de l'entree counue sous le nom de Mer de Topan. Sketch'd on the Spot by his Excellency Governor Pownal. Painted by Paul Sandby, Engraved by Peter Benazech. London, Printed for Jn. Bowles at No. 13 in Cornhill, Robert Sayer at No. 53 in Fleet Street, Thos. Jefferys the Corner of St. Martins Lane in the Strand, Carington Bowles at No. 69 in St. Pauls Church Yard, and Henry Parker at No. 82 in Cornhill. [1768]
Etching 14¼ x 20¾ in.

Thomas Pownall (1722–1805), who served in America as lieutenant governor of New Jersey and as governor of Massachusetts, visited Tappan Sea, N.Y., in October 1755. Pownall's description of the area, published in Lois Mulkearn, ed., *A Topographical Description of the Dominions of the United States of America* (Pittsburgh, 1949), p. 39, was written a decade later from notes kept in a journal:

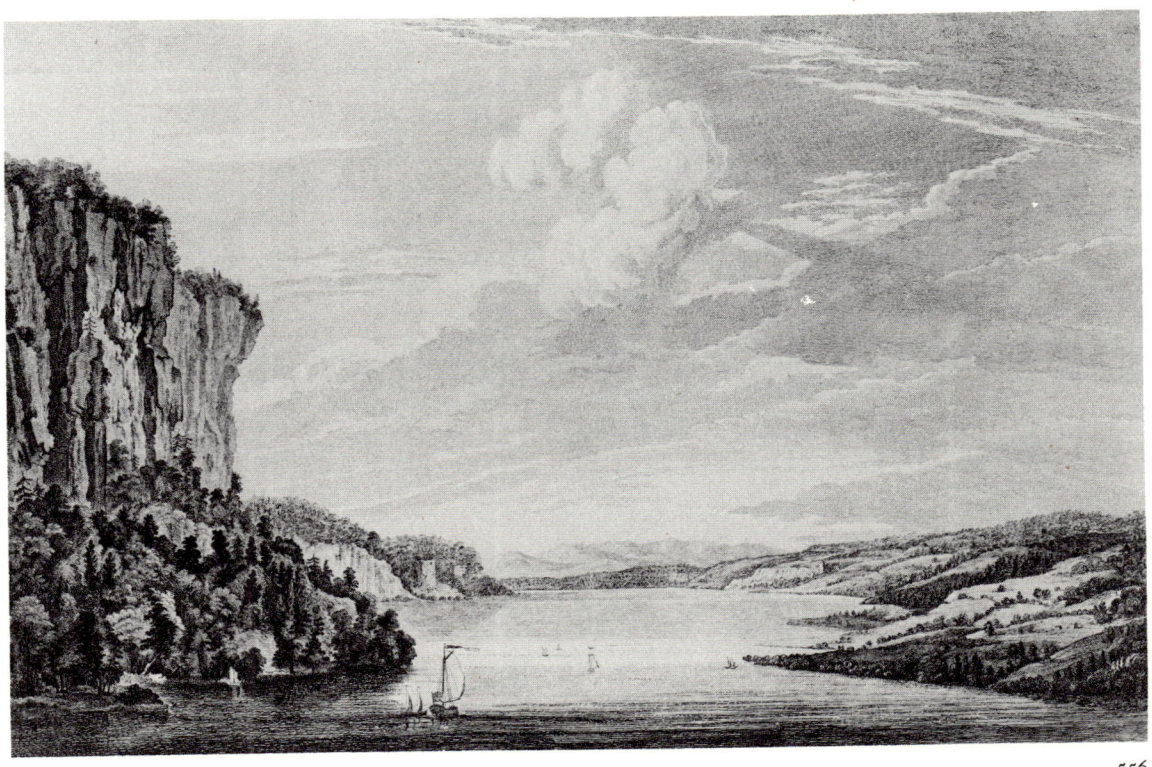

556

After emerging out of this Pass, it [the Hudson River] spreads itself in the Form of a great Lake 15 Miles in Length by one Way of reckoning, and by another 20, and about Four Miles broad, and is called the Topang Sea: The western Banks are perpendicular rocky Cliffs of an immense Height, Covered with Woods at the Top, which from the great Height of the Cliff seem like Shrubs. The Eastern Coasts are formed by a gently rising Country, Hill behind a Hill, of fruitful Vegetation at the back of which lye the White-plains: It then again for 20 Miles more or thereabouts takes the Form of a River, but above a Mile and Half broad, and passes by New York.

During the Revolution, Tappan Sea was the scene of a small engagement with a small British flotilla that had run past American batteries near the entrance to the river. See item 264. From *Scenographia Americana* (1768). LC–USZ62–43548

————Another impression. In P&P (trimmed edges). Imprint reads, "London, Published according to Act of Parliament, May 20, 1761 by Thos. Jefferys the Corner of St. Martin's Lane."

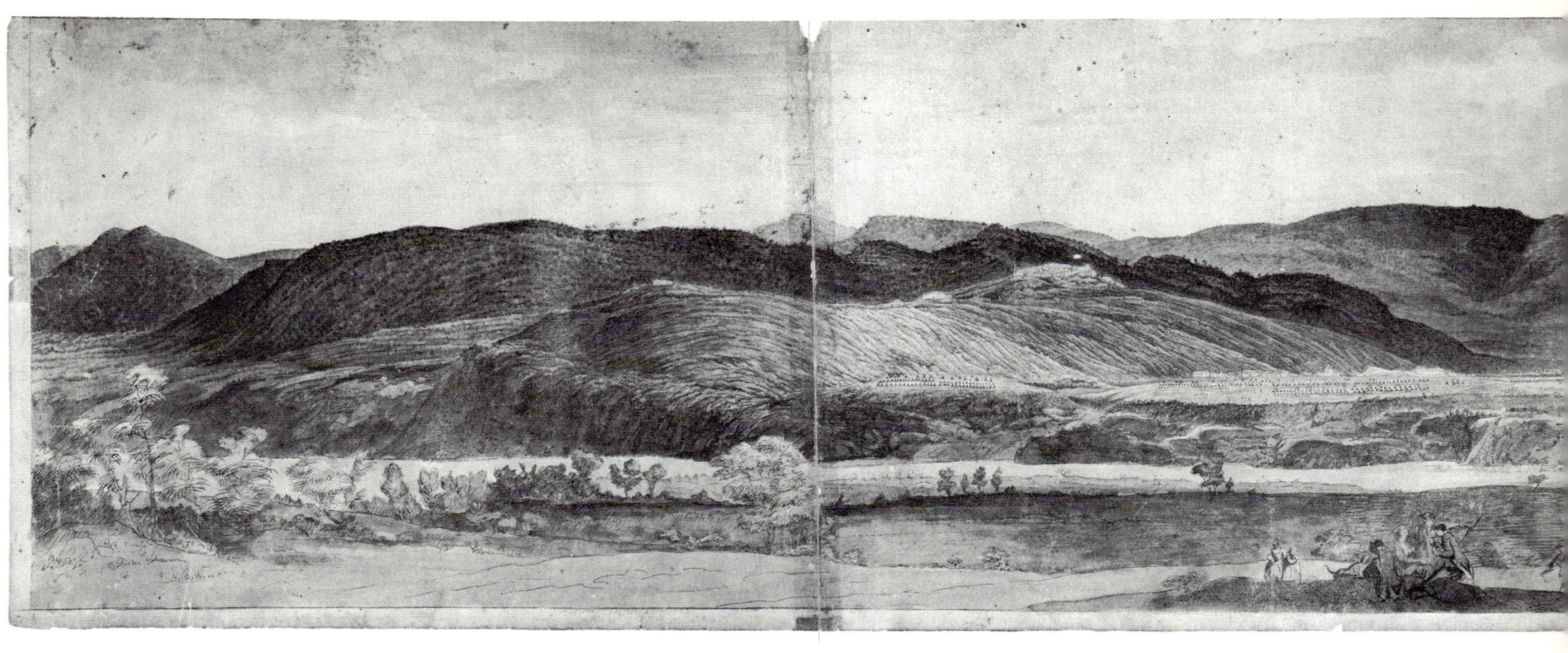

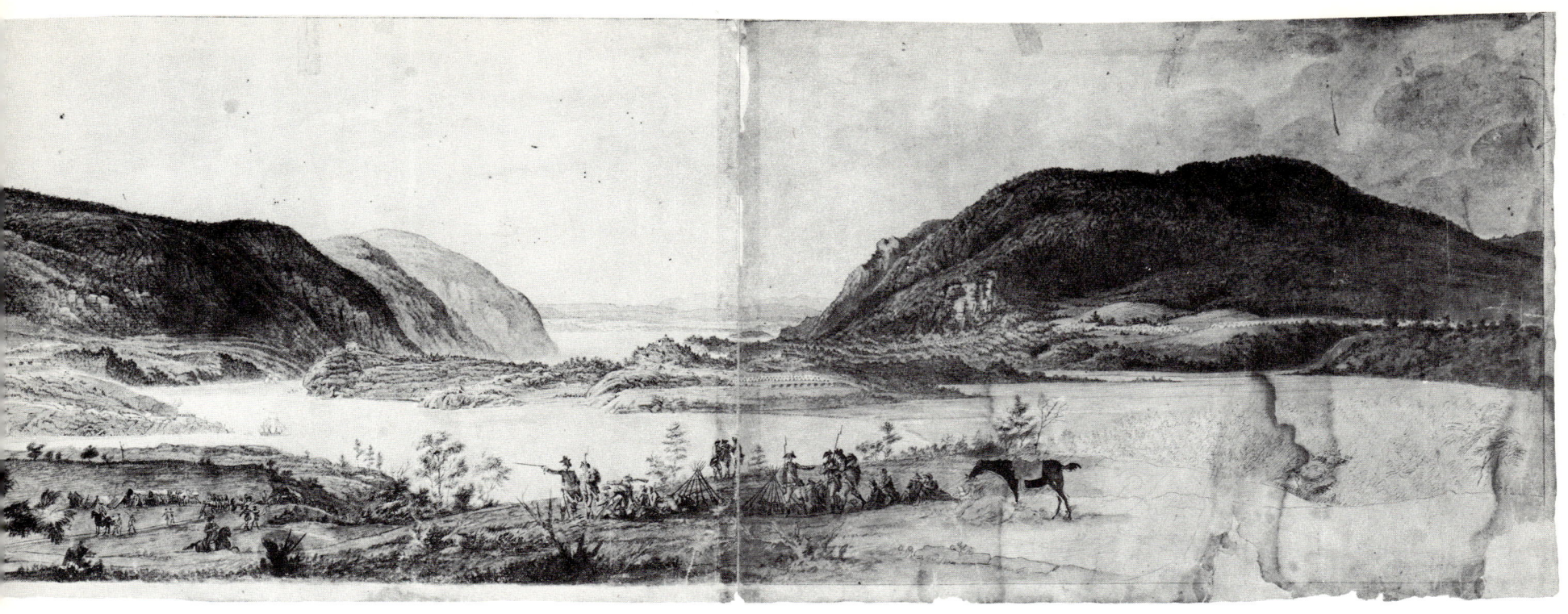

557

557
[West Point, New York, painted by Pierre L'Enfant 1778?]
Watercolor 10¼ x 55½ in.

These panoramic views of the encampments of American troops near the Hudson River at West Point may have been drawn in late summer 1778 while L'Enfant was attached to the staff of General Baron von Steuben.
LC–USZ62–40974, LC–USZ62–40975, LC–USZ62–40976, LC–USZ62–40977

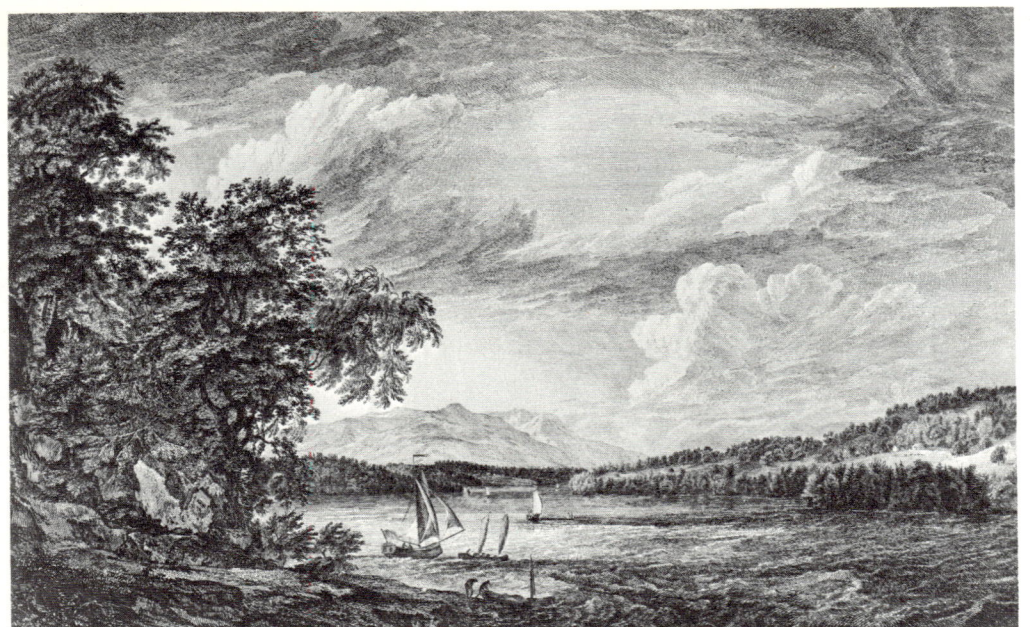

558

558
A View in Hudson's River of Pakepsey & the Catts-Kill Mountains, From Sopos Island in Hudson's River. Vue sur la Riviere d'Hudson dans Pakepsey et des Montagnes de Catts-Kill. Prise de l'Isle de Sopos, Situee dans cette Riviere. Sketch'd on the SPOT by his Excellency Governor Pownal. Painted and Engraved by Paul Sandby. London, Printed for John Bowles at No. 13 in Cornhill, Robert Sayer at No. 53. in Fleet Street. Thos. Jefferys the Corner of St. Martins Lane in the Strand, Carington Bowles at No. 69 in St. Pauls Church Yard, and Henry Parker at No. 82 in Cornhill. [1768]
Etching 14¼ x 20¾ in.

Governor Pownall probably drew the original sketch from which this view of early Poughkeepsie was made in 1755. Esopus Island in the Hudson River is about halfway between Hyde Park and Staatsburg. From *Scenographia Americana* (1768). LC–USZ62–43545

―――――Another impression. In P&P (trimmed edges). Imprint reads, "London, Publish'd according to Act of Parliament 20 May 1761 by Thos. Jefferys the Corner of St. Martin's Lane."

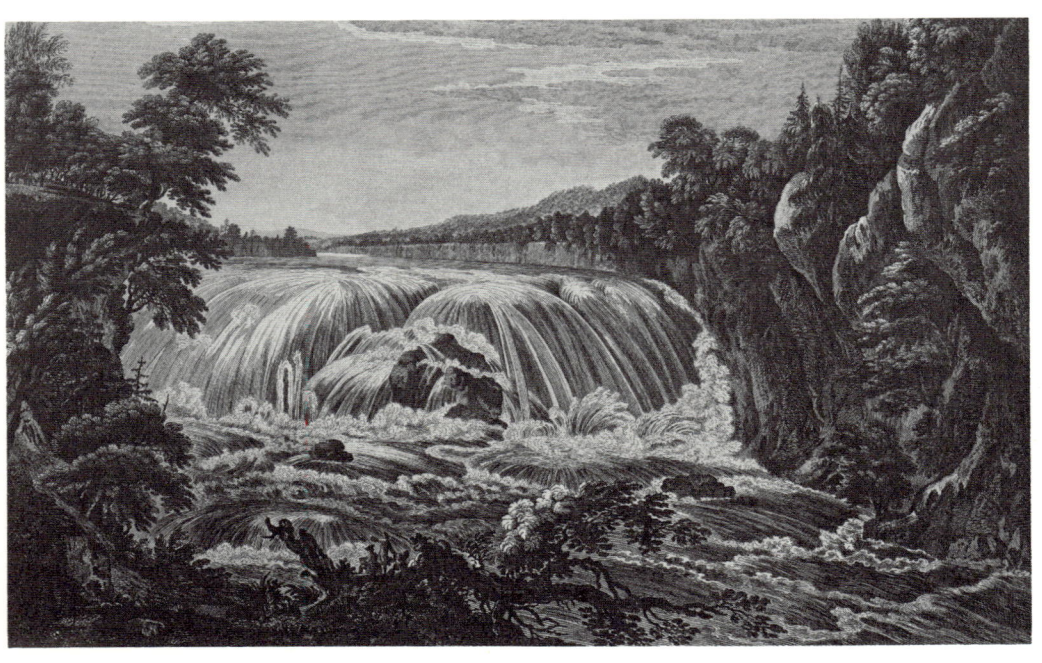

559

559
A View of the Great Cohoes Falls, on the Mohawk River; The Fall about Seventy Feet; the River near a Quarter of a Mile broad. Vue de la Grande Cataracte de Cohoes, sur la Riviere des Mohawks; La Hateur est l'environ 70 pieds; 1 sa Riviere a pres l'un quart de Mile de large. Sketch'd on the SPOT by his Excellency Governor Pownal. Painted by Paul Sandby, & Engraved by Wm. Elliot. London, Printed for John Bowles at No. 13, in Cornhill, Robert Sayer at No. 53, in Fleet Street, Thos. Jefferys the Corner of St. Martins Lane in the Strand, Carington Bowles at No. 69 in St. Pauls Church Yard, and Henry Parker at No. 82 in Cornhill. [1768]
Etching 14¼ x 20¾ in.

Pownall observed the Cohoes Falls on June 25, 1754, while the river was at flood level. His description of the falls is published in Mulkearn, ed., *Topographical Description of the United States*, p. 35-36. From *Scenographia Americana* (1768). LC–USZ62–43549

———Another impression. In P&P (trimmed edges). Imprint reads, "London, Publish'd according to Act of Parliament 20 May 1761 by Thos. Jefferys the Corner of St. Martins Lane."

560
A View of the Cohoes or Great Falls of the Mohawk River taken from below. [Verso] A View of the Cohoes or Great Falls of the Mohawk River taken from above. [1754]
Pencil sketch 7½ x 9¾ in.

Some authorities speculate that these drawings are also the work of Pownall. See Mulkearn, ed., *Topographical Description of the United States*, p. 37n. LC–USZ62–45550, LC–USZ62–45551

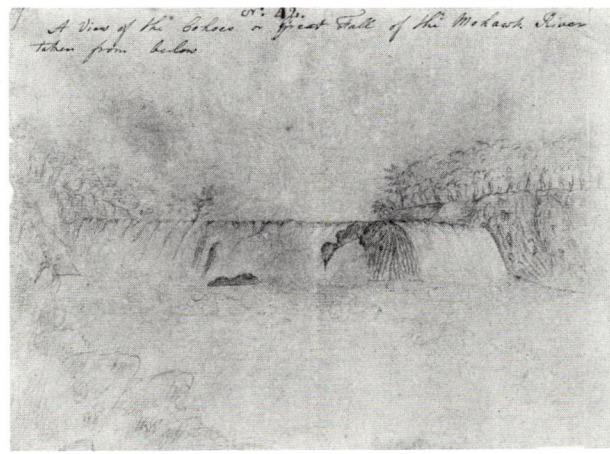 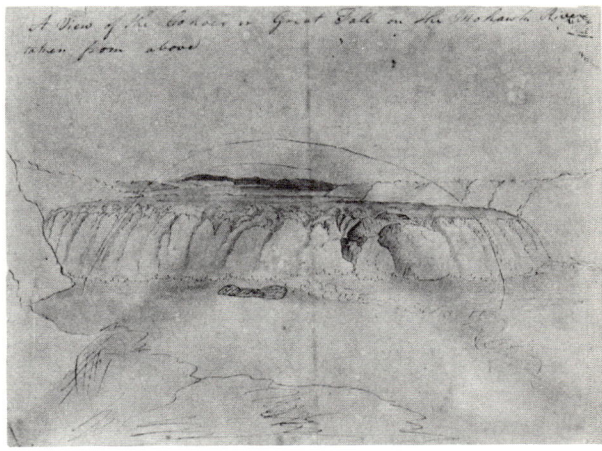

560   560

561
A View of Houses in the City of Albany. [1789]
Etching 3½ x 6 in. (image)

The view is accompanied by an essay, "Description of the City of Albany." The city's architecture was predominately Dutch. The article explains the markings on the exterior of the houses in the view:

> The walls of the houses are clamped with iron, in the form of letters, numerical figures, arrows, and other devices; the letters generally designating the proprietor of the house, by the initials of his name, and the figures denoting the year in which it was built.

From *The Columbian Magazine*, December 1789, frontispiece. LC–USZ62–31154

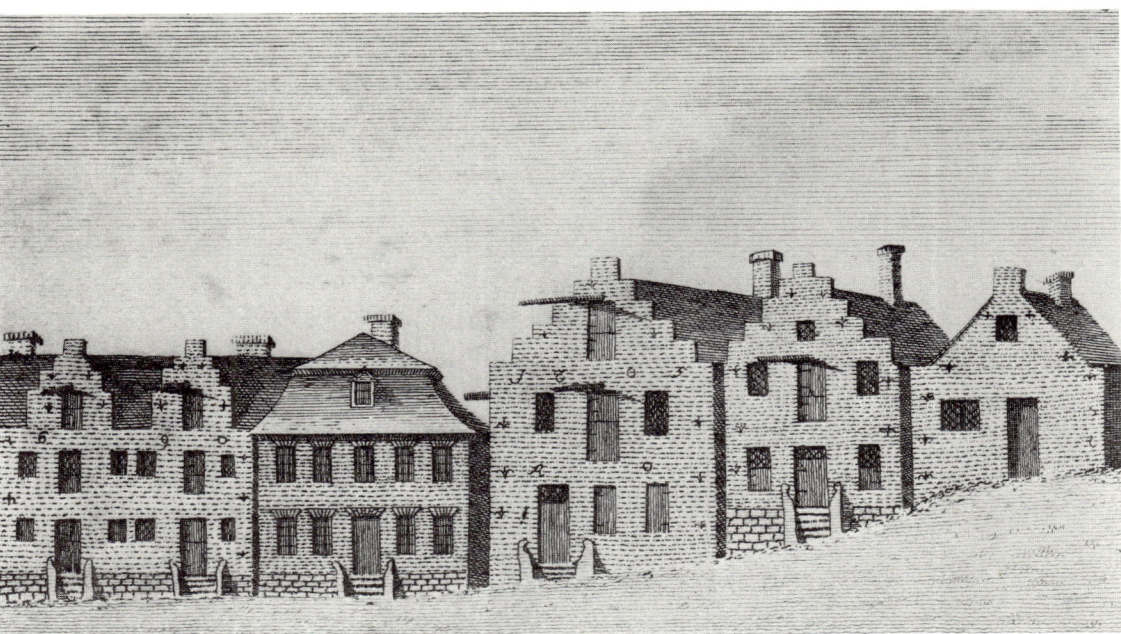

561

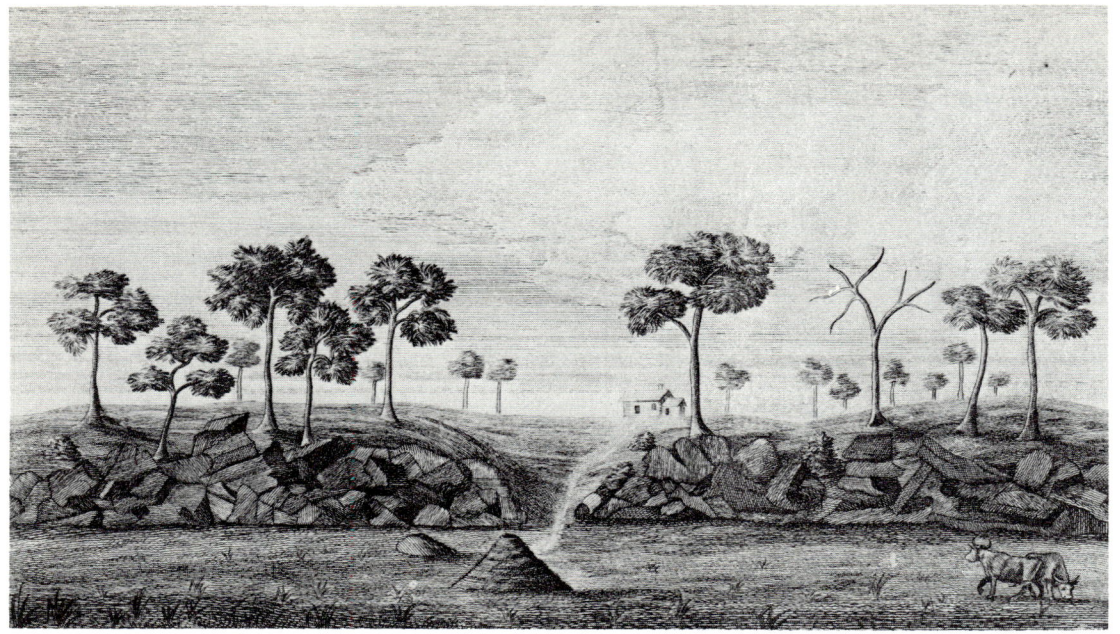

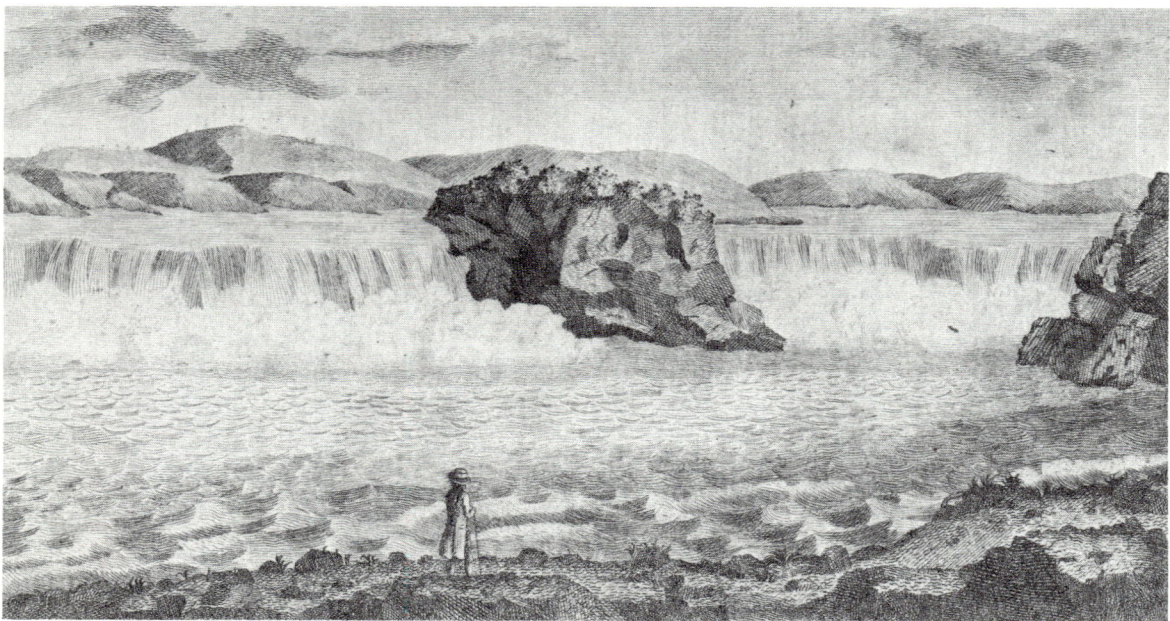

562
CHALBEATE SPRING near Saratoga. JT Sc. [1787]
 Etching 4½ x 7 in.

Chalbeate Springs, eight or ten in number, are located about 11 miles west of Saratoga. This view was used to illustrate an article on the springs in *The Columbian Magazine*, March 1789. Stauffer, 3298. LC–USZ62–50391

563
CADUTA DI NIAGARA. G.M.T. fc: 1777
 Etching 9⅞ x 7¼ in.

At the time of the Revolution, the region around Niagara Falls was in British hands as a result of the Seven Years' War. The British attempted to colonize the area, but on September 14, 1763, 25 wagons of settlers were ambushed while making portage around the falls, and only eight of more than 300 survived. Maj. Gen. John Sullivan's expedition into the area in 1779 was intended to terminate Indian and loyalist attacks in the area, but although the Iroquois civilization was annihilated, skirmishes continued there until 1782. From *Atlante dell' America* . . . (Livorno, 1777), no. 6. LC–USZ62–46019

563a
SAULTE DU NIAGARA. 1777
 Etching 1⅛ x 2¼ in. (image)

A panoramic view similar to "Caduta di Niagara." This picture appears on a map entitled "Theatre de la Guerre en Amerique" in Le Rouge, *Atlas Ameriquain Septentrional* (Paris, 1778–92), no. 4a.

564
VIEW of the FALLS of NIAGARA. Del. 1790 Engrav'd by S. Hill.
 Etching 7 x 3¾ in. (image)

Andrew Ellicott, visiting Niagara Falls in December 1789, wrote to Benjamin Rush of

Philadelphia describing the magnificence of the falls. He mentioned the roar that could be heard at a distance of 20 miles and the heavy fog over the falls which contained rainbows when the sun was shining. The mist, settling on the trees in freezing weather, created a glistening winter scene. The letter and this illustration were published in *The Massachusetts Magazine*, July 1790, the view opposite p. 387. Stauffer, 1410. LC–USZ62–45524

New Jersey

565
[A New Jersey scene—a cartouche] Engraved & Published by Wm. Faden, Charing Cross, December 1st. 1777.
   Etching 8 x 7½ in. (image)

Depicts a small, prosperous farm with large haystacks and a wheatfield. In the foreground are racoons, a snake, and a squirrel. From a map entitled "The Province of New Jersey, Divided into East and West commonly called The Jerseys." In Faden, *North American Atlas* (London, 1777), no. 22. LC–USZ62–45599

566
Appearance of the leading Mark over the bar [of Sandy Hook, with the lighthouse]
   Drawing (hand colored) 2½ x 4¼ in. (image)

This picture shows the lighthouse to the right and the Cedars to the left. An inset view from a map entitled "Soundings of the Bar of Sandy Hook at Low Water . . ." in G&M Manuscript Map Collection.

567
A View from Paulushook of Horsimus on the Jersey shore and part of York Island [1777?]
   Ink and water color drawing 9⅞ x 16¾ in.

During the Revolutionary War the British established an outpost on Paulus Hook.

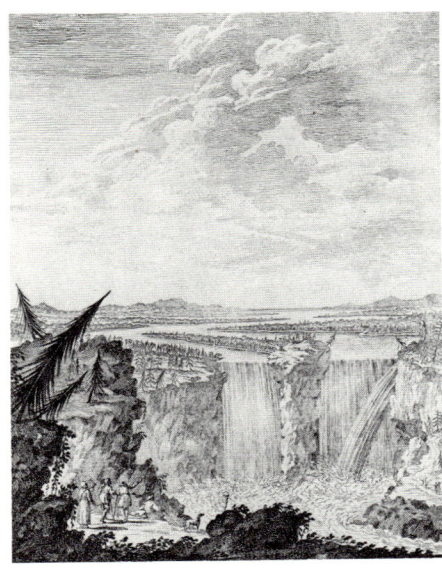
563

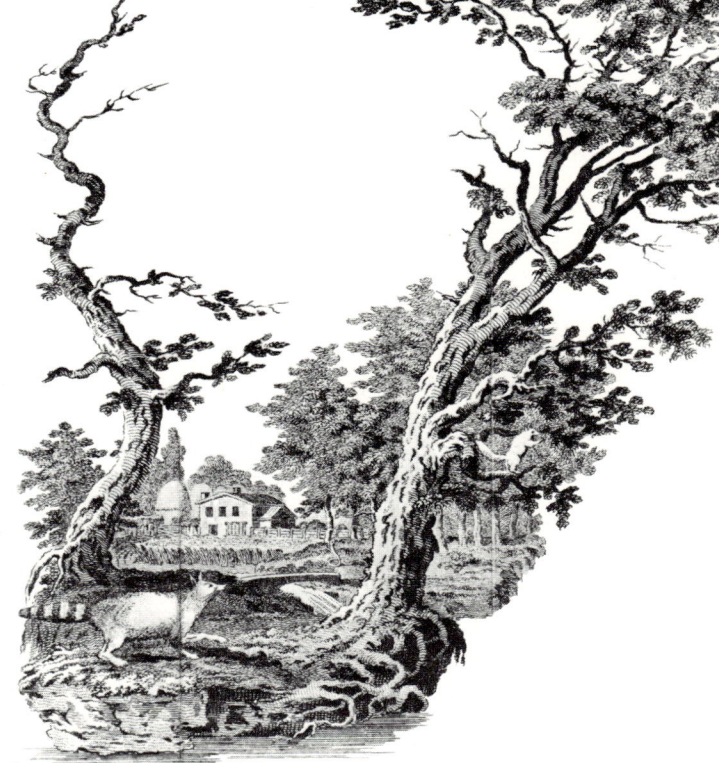
565

211

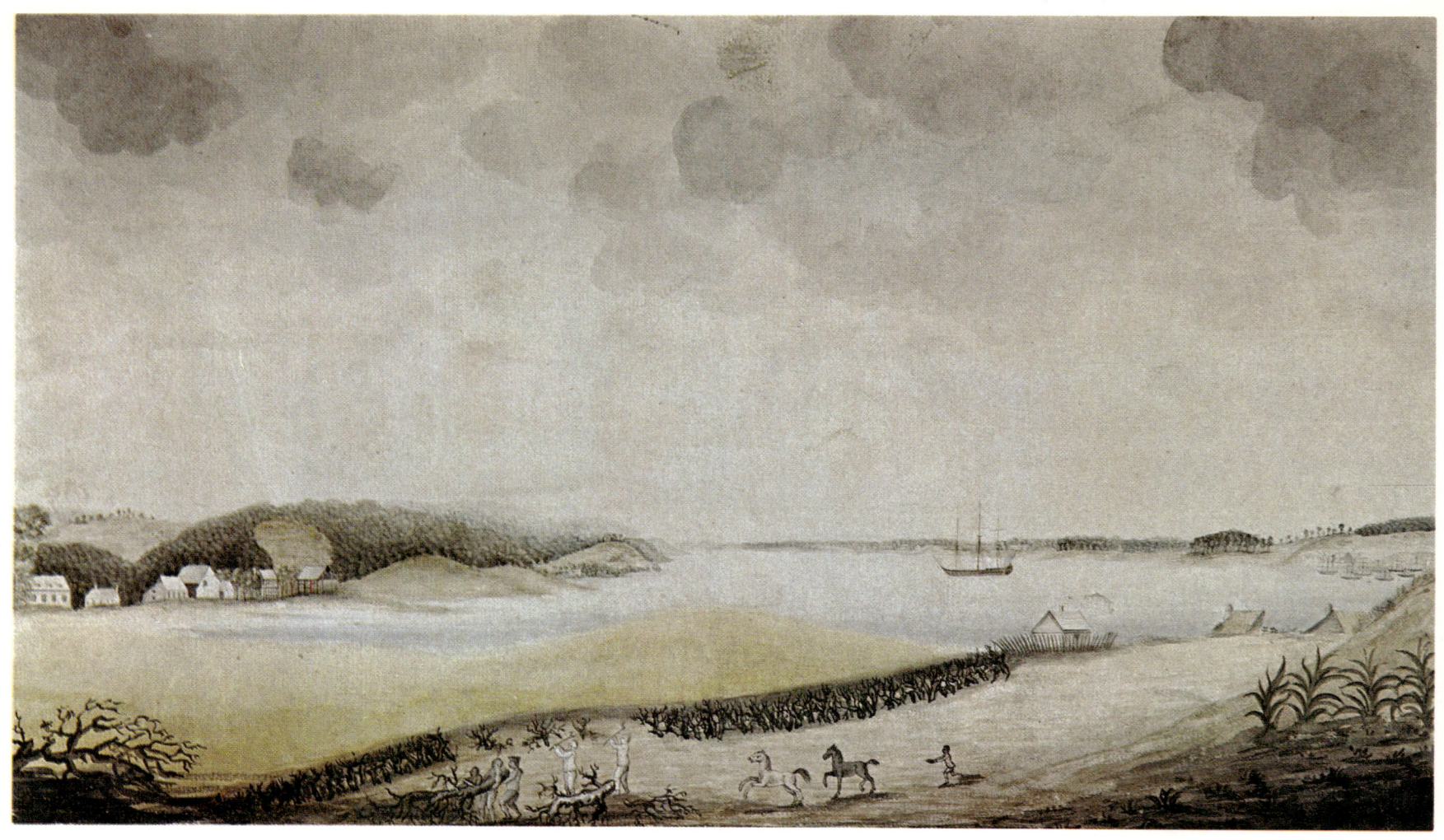

Patriot troops led by Col. Henry Lee attacked the post in August 1779 but withdrew when they failed to take one of three redoubts. In the foreground of this view a group of men cut branches for wood while making a stump fence. The bay is in the background. Stokes, *Iconography of Manhattan Island*, v. 1 (New York, 1915), p. 362, and v. 3 (New York, 1918), p. 867.

568

A View of the Falls on the Passaick, or second River, in the Province of New Jersey, The height of the Fall between Eighty and Ninety feet; the River about Eighty Yards broad. Vue de l'Cataracte de Passaick, ou seconde Riviere, dans la province du Nouveau Jersey, La Hauteur de cette Chute est de 80 à 90 pieds, et la Largeur de la Riviere d'environ 40 Foises. Sketch'd on the Spot by his Excellency Governor Pownal. Painted and Engraved by Paul Sandby. London, Printed for John Bowles at No. 13 in Cornhill, Robert Sayer at No. 53 in Fleet Street, Thos. Jefferys the Corner of St. Martins Lane in the Strand, Carington Bowles at No. 69 in St. Pauls Church Yard, and Henry Parker at No. 82 in Cornhill. [1768]

Etching 14⅜ x 21 in.

Pownall described the falls on the Passaic River in New Jersey as:

> ... a very curious natural Phenomenon. The River running round the Back of a Rocky Cliff, which by some Accident has been shattered & riven Top to Bottom about 90 feet, turns short & Tumbles head long with an Inconceivable force & Velocity down this horrid chasm foaming with its hoarse stunning roar at its base more like something combustible than Water.

See Mulkearn, ed., *Topographical Description of the United States*, p. 98–99. From *Scenographia Americana* (1768). LC–USZ62–43550

——————Another impression. In P&P (trimmed edges). Imprint reads, "London, Publish'd according to Act of Parliament 20 May 1761 by Thos. Jefferys the Corner of St. Martins Lane."

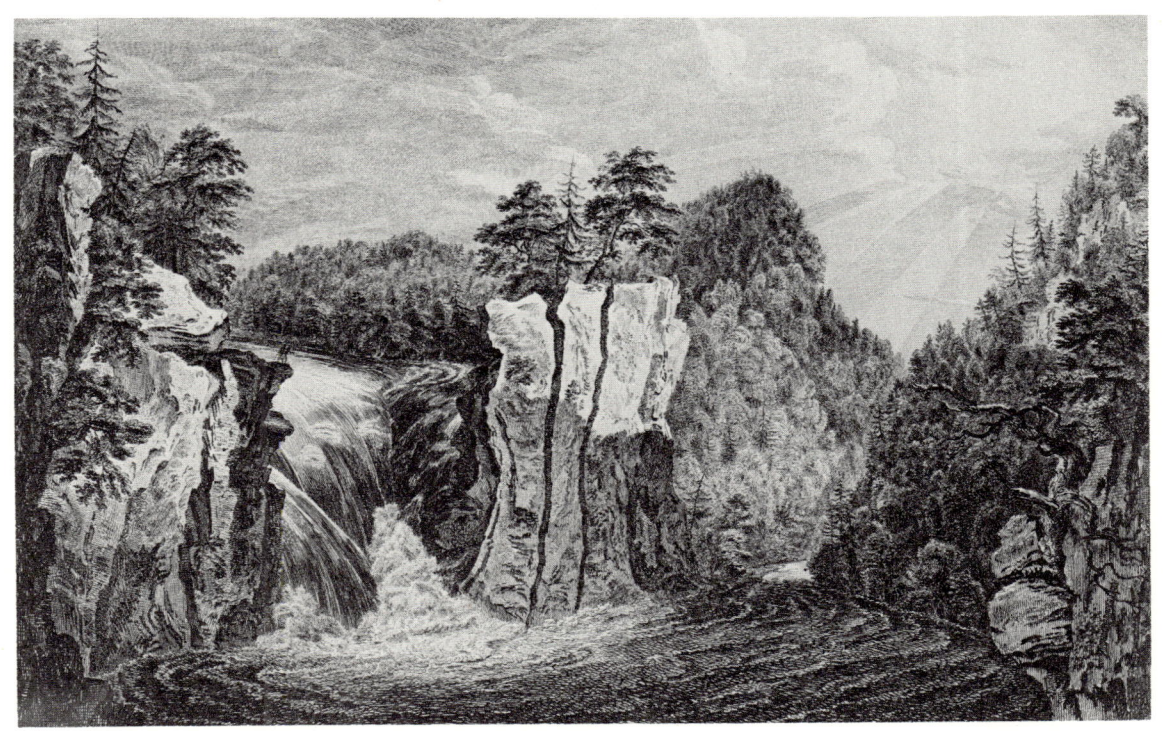

568

569
Prospect of the Paysaick Falls in New-Jersey. [1789]
Etching 3¾ x 6½ in. (image)

An accompanying article describes the falls located 23 miles from Elizabeth, N.J., (called Elizabethtown until 1740), on the Second or Passaic River. From *The Columbian Magazine*, supplement 1789, opposite p. 766.

570
View upon the Road from New-Windsor, towards, Morris Town, JERSEY. [1789]
Etching 4⅜ x 7⅜ in.

The road from New Windsor, N.Y., to Morristown, N.J., linked the site of George Clinton's (1739–1812) home and the location of Washington's winter headquarters, 1776–77 and 1779–80. Morristown produced iron during the Revolution as well as serving as a military headquarters. From *The Columbian Magazine*, October 1789, opposite p. 600. Fielding, 1847. LC–USZ62–45578

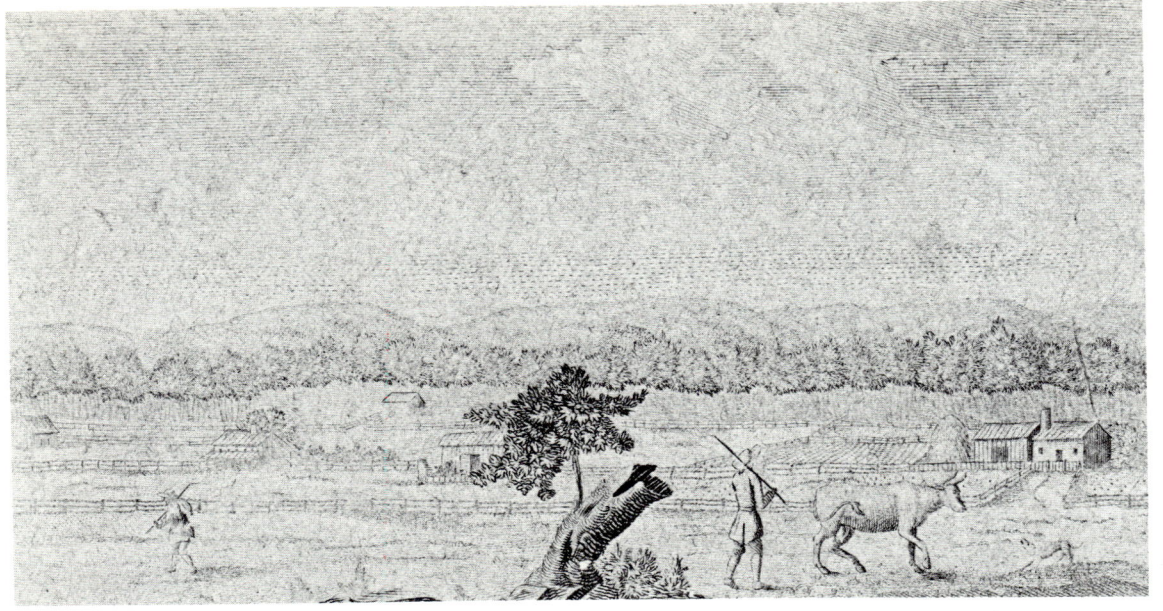
570

Pennsylvania

Interior

571
A View of the Pulpit Rocks, between Huntingdon & Bald Eagle Valley, State of Pennsylvania. [1788]
Etching 3¾ x 7 in.

This frontispiece for *The Columbian Magazine*, September 1788, opposite p. 475, was used to illustrate an article describing Bald Eagle Valley, commonly called Sinking Spring Valley, about 200 miles west of Philadelphia. The article describes its peculiar rock formations:

There is a set of sandy hills, high masses of which are in places left bare, and from the lowness of their nature, and the washing of the storms, have assumed different forms, some of which the country people have likened to

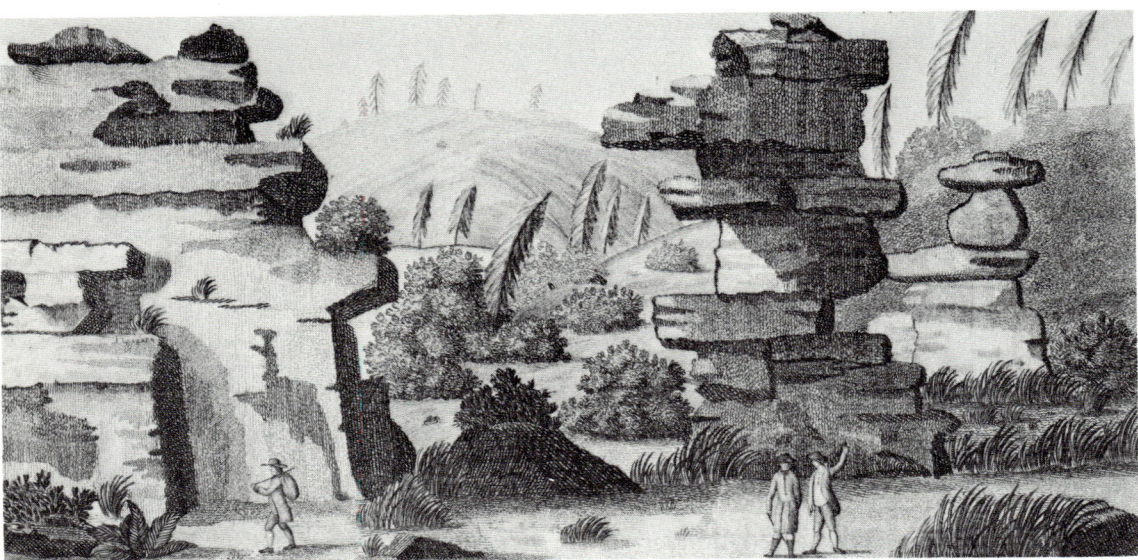
571

pulpits, bowls, teapots, &c. In general, it is known by the name of Pulpit-Rocks, of which the annexed plate will communicate an accurate idea.

LC–USZ62–46029

572

A View of a Swallow, or Pit, at Sinking Spring Valley, State of Pennsylvania. [1788]
  Etching 3¾ x 6¼ in. (image)

The peculiar geology of Sinking Spring Valley produced the pits or swallows for which the valley was named. The floor of the valley was limestone, and when several streams converged, they eroded the soft stone and became underground rivers. Thus the waters flowed only a short distance before "sinking" of disappearing. Frontispiece for *The Columbian Magazine*, October 1788, opposite p. 547.

573

A View of Fort Robertdeau, in Sinking-Spring Valley, State of Pennsylvania. [1788]
  Etching 4⅜ x 7¾ in.

In 1779 about 60 families moved to Sinking Spring Valley to mine lead which was badly needed by the Continental Army. Fort Robertdeau was built to protect the miners from attack by the Indians, but continuing difficulties finally resulted in the abandonment of the project. By 1788 when the view and article were printed, all that remained in the valley were a few mine shafts and the fort. From *The Columbian Magazine*, December 1788, opposite p. 703. LC–USZ62–31155

574

A View of OHIOPYLE FALLS, in Pennsylvania. [1787]
  Etching 4⅜ x 7 in. (image)

An accompanying article describes the falls:

The Falls of Yochiogeny, called in the maps, Ohiopyle Falls, are by far the most magnificent, of any thing of this kind, in the state of Pennsylvania. The several branches of

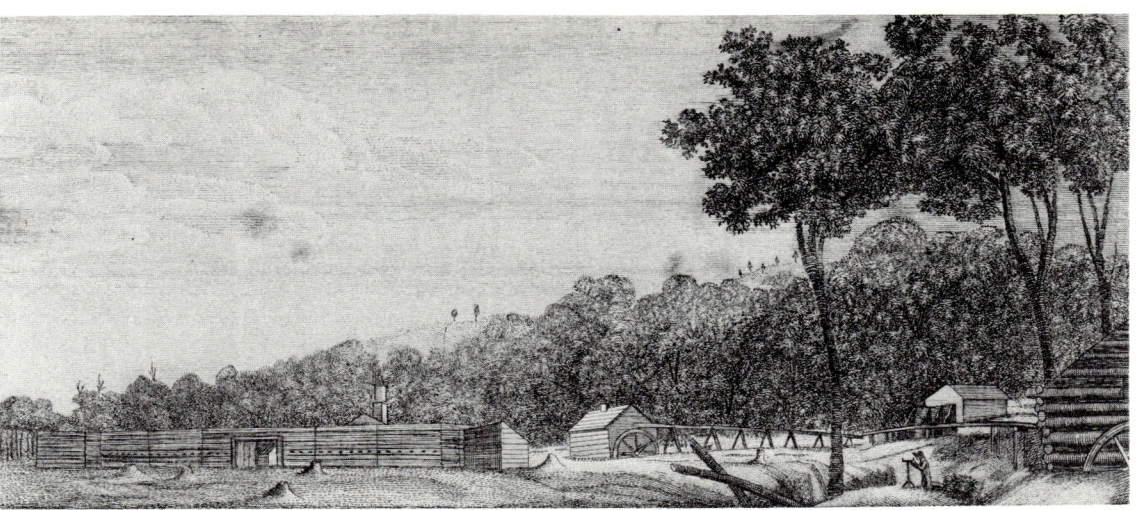
573

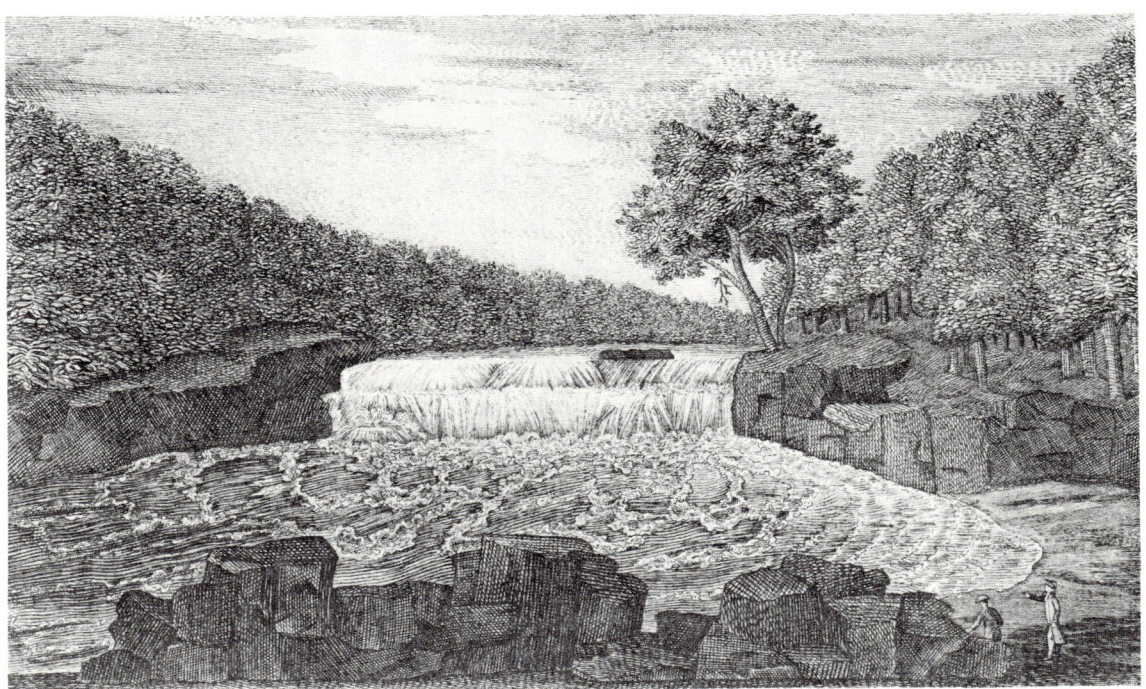
574

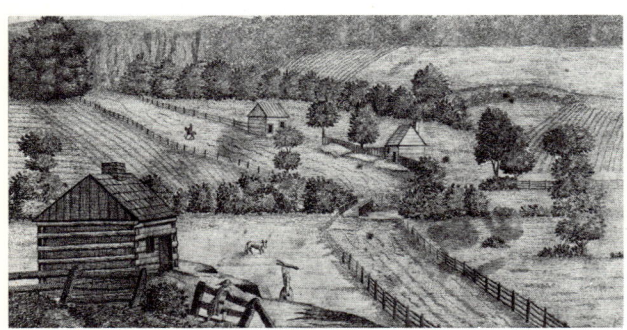
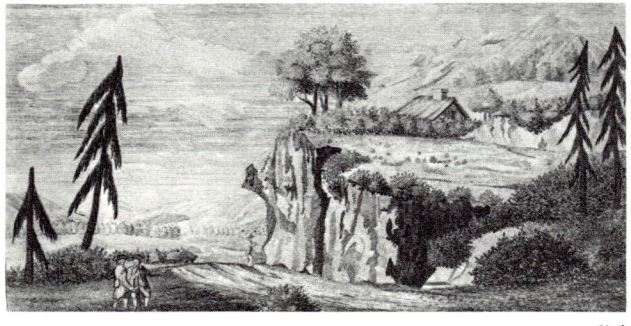
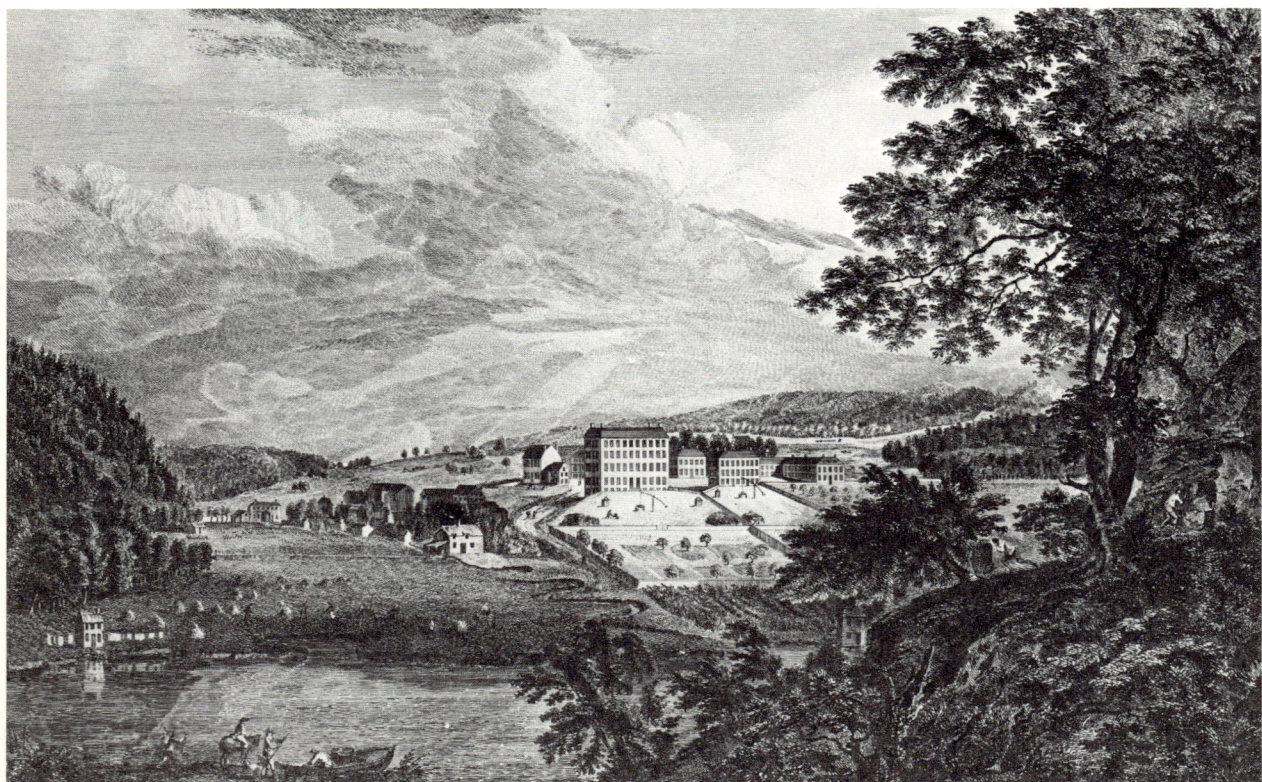

Yochiogeny river . . . form a large and beautiful river, which, in passing through the most western ridges of the mountains, precipitates itself over a level ledge of rocks, lying nearly at right angles to the course of the river. The falls are, by estimation, about 20 feet in perpendicular height, and the river is perhaps 80 yards wide. For a considerable distance below the falls, the water is very rapid; and boils and foams vehemently, occasioning a continual mist to rise from it, even at noon-day, and in fair weather.

Frontispiece for *The Columbian Magazine*, February 1787, opposite p. 253. Fielding, 1860. LC–USZ62–46022

575
View of a pass over the South Mountain from York Town to Carlisle. Bedwell delt. [Thackera Sc., 1788]
Etching 4 x 7⅛ in.

York Town is the old name for York, Pa., where the Continental Congress met for nine months during 1777–78 while the British held Philadelphia. The Articles of Confederation were drawn up while the Congress was sitting at York. Frontispiece for *The Columbian Magazine*, May 1788, opposite p. 236. Fielding, 1570. LC–USZ62–46028

576
View from Bushongo Tavern 5 miles from York Town on the Baltimore Road. [1788]
Etching 3¾ x 7⅛ in.

Frontispiece for *The Columbian Magazine*, July 1788. Stauffer, 3283, credits James Trenchard with this engraving. LC–USZ62–31149

577
A View of Bethlem, the Great Moravian Settlement in the Province of PENNSYLVANIA. Vue de Bethlem, principal Etablissement des Freres Moraves dans la Province de PENNSYLVANIA. Sketch'd on the SPOT by his Excellency Governor Pownal, Painted and Engraved by Paul Sandby. London, Printed for John Bowles at No. 13 in Cornhill, Robert Sayer at No. 53 in Fleet Street, Thos. Jefferys the Corner of

St. Martins Lane in the Strand, Carington Bowles at No. 69 in St. Pauls Church Yard, and Henry Parker at No. 82 in Cornhill. [1768]

Etching 14⅜ x 21 in.

Pownall's keen delight at his first sight of the village of Bethlehem is evident in the following account:

Coming out from amidst a wilderness of woods through which I had been travelling some daies all at once at the top of a hill & viewing hence this cultivated populous settlement & its cluster of College like buildings large & spacious all of stone; with the grounds all around planted with orchards; & varied with tillage in all its forms of culture; & border'd on the banks of the river on which it lyes & of the rivulet which runns thro' it which rich & green meadows My Eye was struck with unexpected pleasure.

See Mulkearn, ed., *Topographical Description of the United States*, p. 102. During the winter at Valley Forge, the Americans established their principal hospital at Bethlehem. From *Scenographia Americana* (1768). LC–USZ62–43546

————Another impression. In P&P (trimmed edges). Imprint reads, "London, Published according to Act of Parliament, May 20, 1761 by Thos. Jefferys the Corner of St. Martin's Lane."

578
A Design to represent the beginning and completion of an American SETTLEMENT or FARM. Dessein qui represente la maniere d'etablir et de parachever une Habitation ou FERME AMERICAINE. Painted by Paul Sandby, from a Design made by his Excellency Governor Pownal. Engraved by James Peake. London, Printed for John Bowles at No. 13 in Cornhill, Robert Sayer at No. 53 Fleet Street, Thos. Jefferys the Corner of St. Martins Lane in the Strand, Carington Bowles at No. 69 in St. Pauls Church Yard, and Henry Parker at No. 82 in Cornhill. [1768]

Etching 14¼ x 20⅞ in.

From *Scenographia Americana* (1768). LC–USZ62–31185

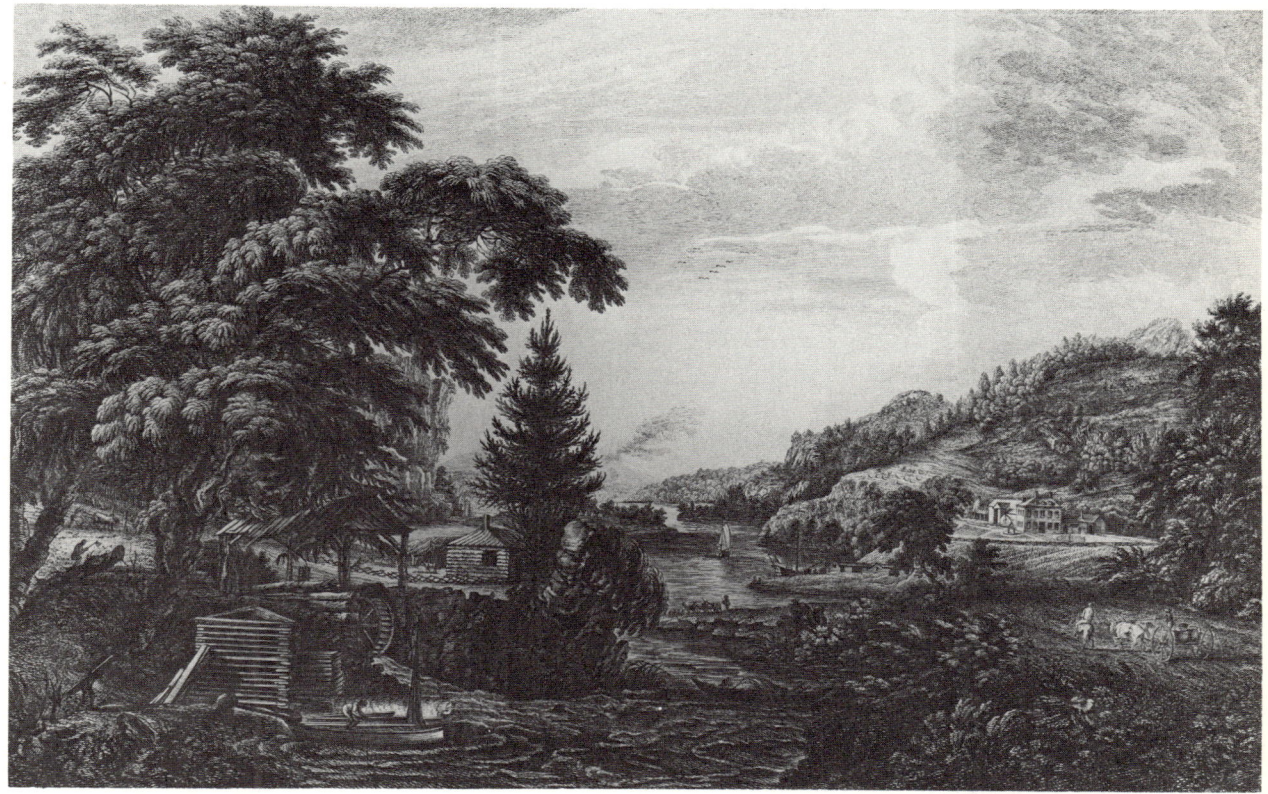

578

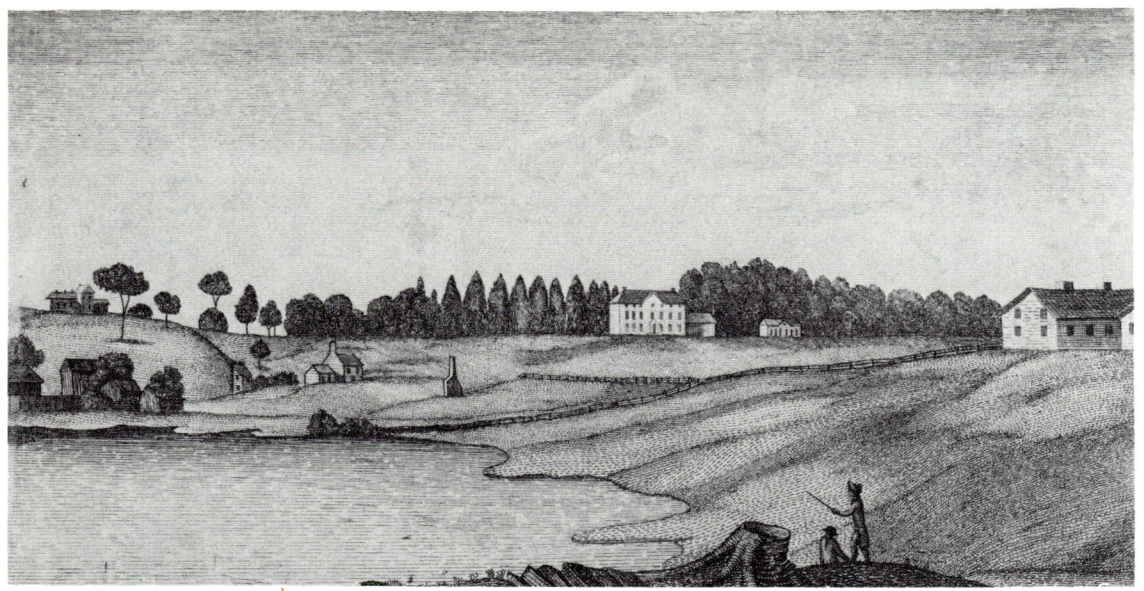

581

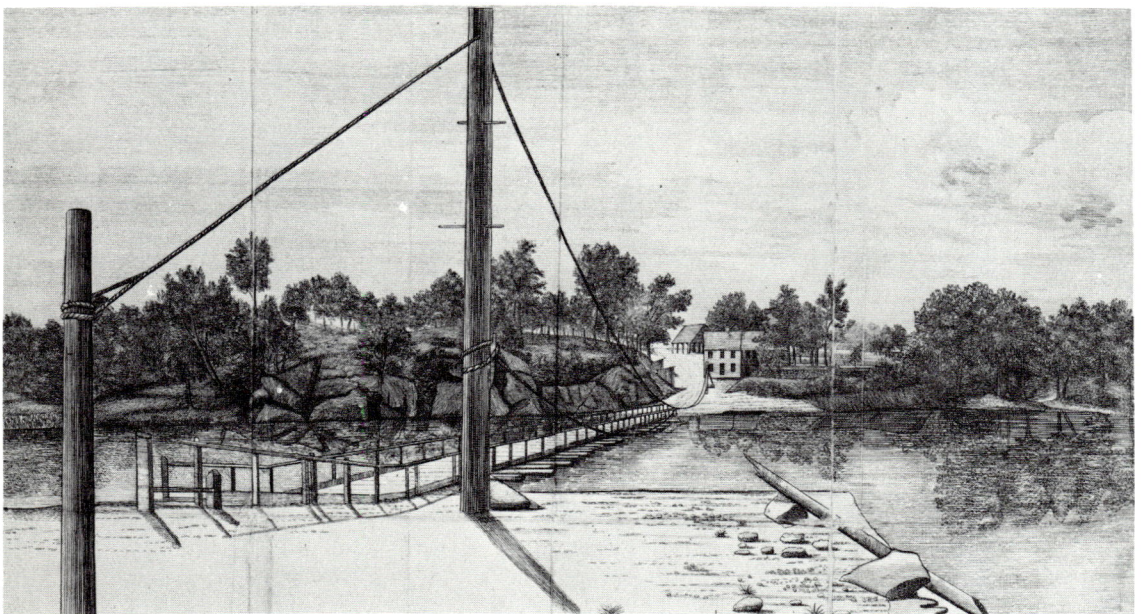

582

———— Another impression. In P&P (trimmed edges). Imprint reads, "London, Published according to Act of Parliament, May 20, 1761 by Thos. Jefferys the Corner of St. Martin's Lane."

579
Elevation of Campus Martius at A.B. [1788]
Etching 1⅛ x 5¾ in. (image)

Campus Martius, a fort built on the public square in Marietta, Ohio, is described in the article which accompanies the view published in *The Columbian Magazine*, November 1788, opposite p. 646. "This fortification is all of hewn timber, and, for appearance, convenience, and defence, [is] of superior excellence." This view is part of "A Plan of Campus Martius at the City of Marietta Territory of the United States, N.W. of River Ohio." Designated on the plan are "Block Houses of Hewed Logs," "Gate ways," "well," "Dwelling Houses," "Watch Tower," and "Belfry."

🙵 *Philadelphia and Vicinity*

580
A View on Schuylkill, near Philadelphia. [1789]
Etching 4¼ x 7⅛ in.

A sailboat in the right foreground and rowboat to its left. Behind the rowboat and to its left is a farmhouse, and in the far distance are fields, woods, and mountains. From *The Columbian Magazine*, November 1789, opposite p. 625.

581
A View on the Schuylkill; with a SW. Prospect of Bush-Hill, one of the Seats of William Hamilton, Esq; [1789]
Etching 4¼ x 7⅜ in.

From *The Columbian Magazine*, February 1789, opposite p. 116. LC–USZ62–45575

582

AN EAST VIEW of GRAY'S FERRY, on the RIVER SCHUYLKILL. C. W. Peale delin. J. T. Sculp. [1787]

Etching 7⅞ x 13¼ in.

Land travelers reached Philadelphia by crossing Gray's Ferry Bridge over the Schuylkill River. George Gray was the proprietor of this floating bridge during the Revolutionary era. Frontispiece for *The Columbian Magazine*, August 1787, opposite p. 565. Stauffer, 3291. LC–USZ62–46024

583

VUE DU PORT PHILADELPHIE DANS L'AMÉRIQUE. Gravée d'aprés le Tableau de Vernet. Vernet pinxit. [177?]

Etching (hand colored) 5⅞ x 8¼ in. (image)

Joseph Vernet (1714–1789), who recorded many details of 18th-century life in a series called "Ports of France," presents an imaginary representation of the commercial activity of America's busiest port. Through the shrewdness and drive of Quaker businessmen, Philadelphia was for a time the third most important commercial city in the British Empire. Wheat and flour, pelts and furs supplied by the Indians, and barrels and staves were sent to the West Indies where they were traded for sugar and other products to be exchanged for British manufactures. LC–USZ62–1417

584

VUE DE PHILADELPHIA. Philadelphia. Die Haupt Stadt in der Nord-Americanischen Provinz Pensylvanien, sie ist vom William Penn (dem Caroll II König in Engelland, die ganze Provinz geschencket hatte) im Jahr 1682, zwischen 2. Schiffreichen Flüssen angelegt und desswegen Philadelphia genen, net wordē, weil die Einivohner in Brüderlicher Einigkeit daselbst lebesollen. Philadelphie. La Ville Capitale de Pensylvanie, Province Nord-Americaine, William Penn à qui Charles II Roi

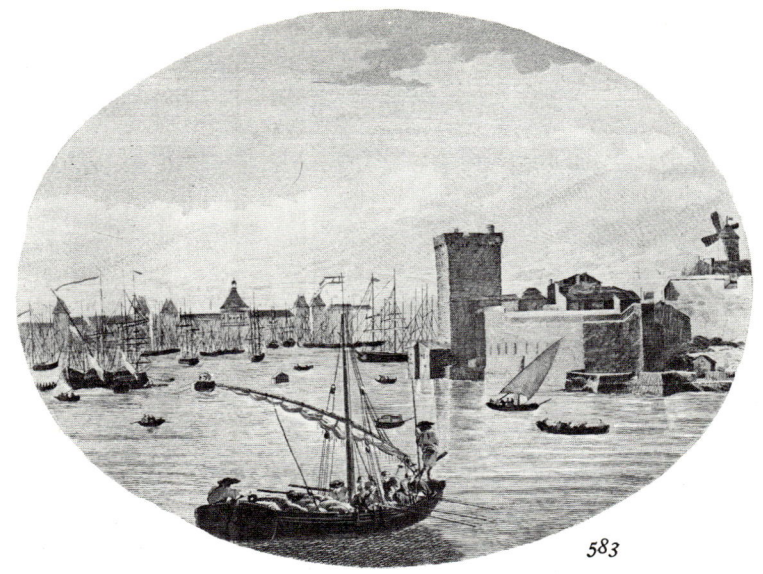

583

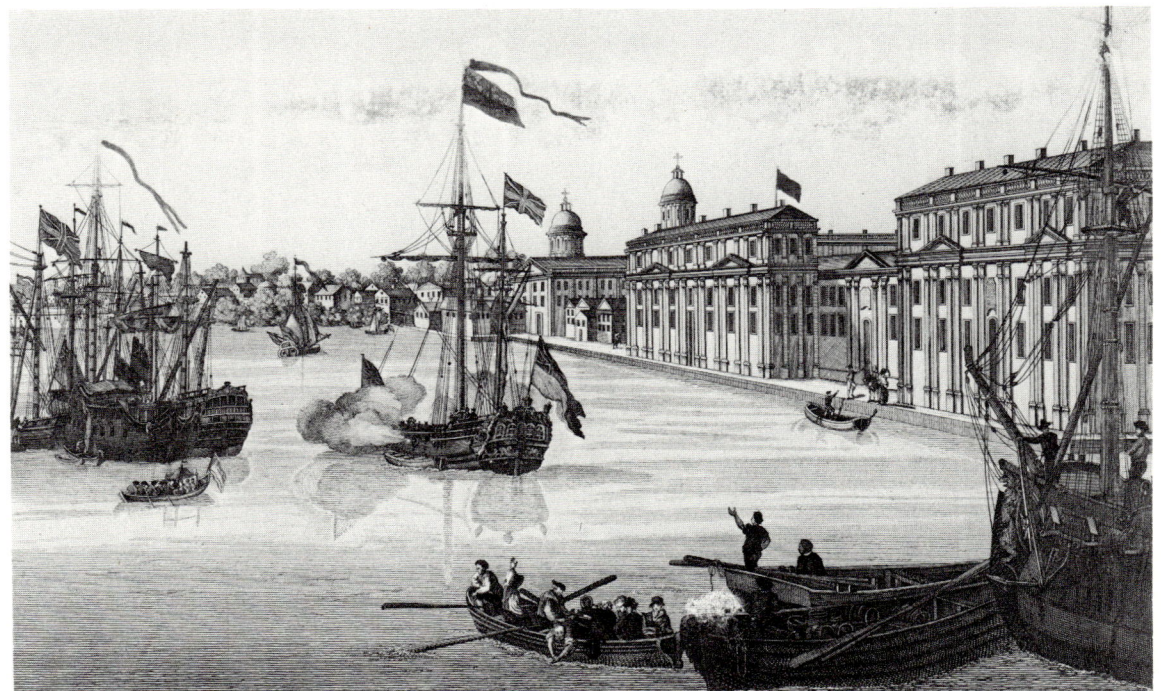

584

219

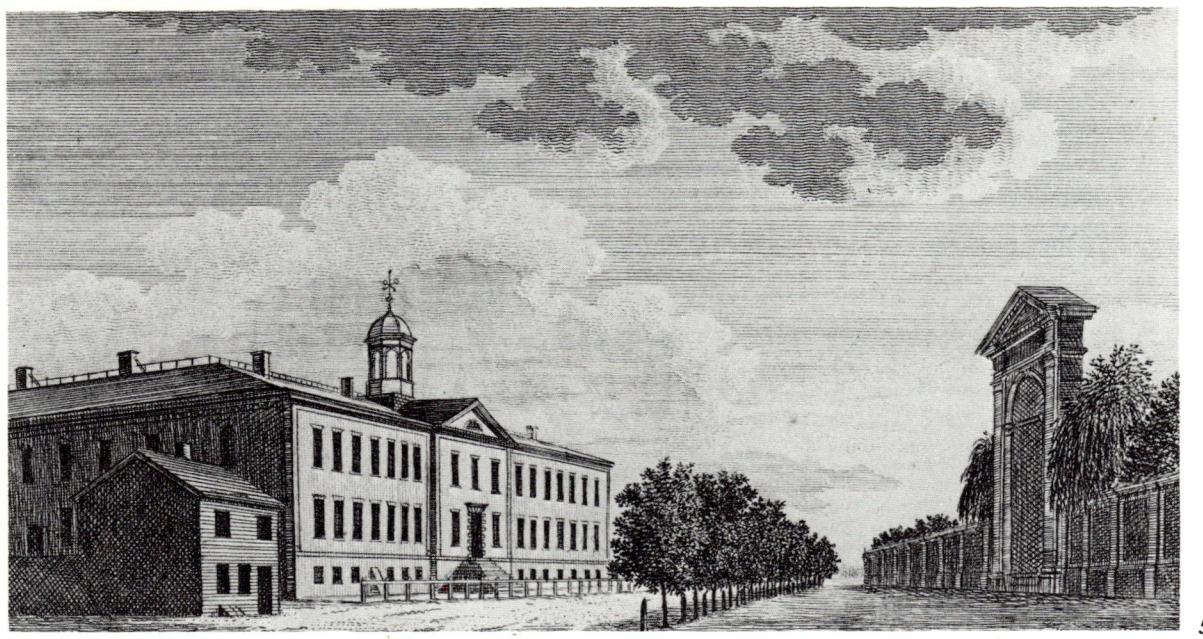

d'Angleterre donna cette Province entiére la planta en 1682 entre deux fleuves navigables et l'appella Philadelphie, parceque les habitans y vivoient dans une Harmonie fraternelle. Se vend à Augsbourg au Negoce commun de l'Academie Imperiale d'Empire des Arts libereaux avec Privilege de Sa Majesté Imperiale et avec Defense ni d'en faire ni de vendre les Copies. Gravé par Balth Frederic Leizelt [177?]
Etching (hand colored) 12½ x 17 in.

Another imaginary view of America's major port laid out between the Delaware and Schuylkill Rivers in 1682 by the surveyor general Thomas Holme and named by William Penn the "city of brotherly love." From "Collection des prospects." LC–USZ62–41172

——————Another copy entitled "Philadelphie," with the explanation same as above but in French only. "Présentement chez Basset rue St. Jacques au coin ce celle de Mathurins, Tient Fabrique de Papiers." Probably by André Basset l'aîné. 13½ x 17¼ in. (hand colored).

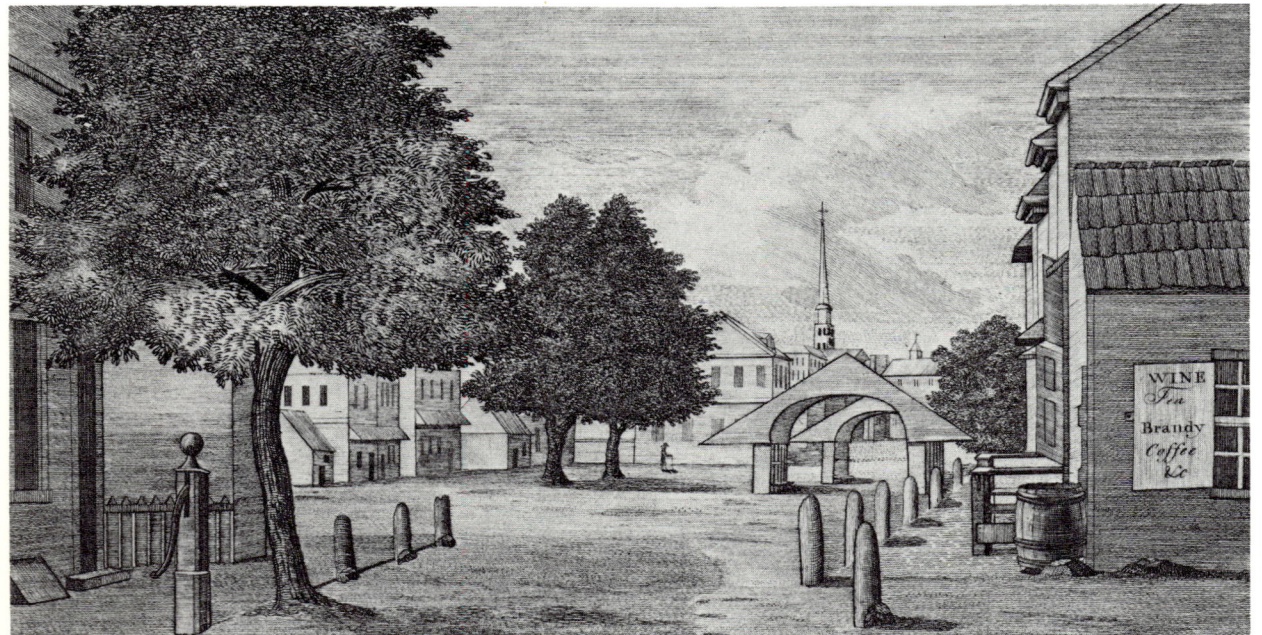

585
The Jail. Philada. Malcom delt. et sc. [1789]
Etching 3¾ x 6 in.

The Walnut Street Jail, located between Walnut and Spruce Streets at the corner of Sixth Street, was built shortly after 1770. In 1789 and 1790 legislation was passed changing the institution from a jail for Philadelphia County to a State prison where reforms such as the segregation of the sexes, the introduction of prison industries and educational opportunities, and sound health and sanitation practices were carried out. In the background of this view, a ship is barely visible on the Delaware River. From *The Universal Magazine*, July 1789, p. 17. LC–USZ62–45561

586

A View of the New Market from the Corner of Shippen & Second-Streets Philada. 1787. Thackara Sc.
Etching 4½ x 7¼ in.

Philadelphia's markets were celebrated for their provisions of beef, mutton, excellent butter and melons, peaches, and pears obtained from nearby New Jersey gardens. The South Second Street Market was the city's second oldest and second largest, stretching south from Pine Street along Second Street. *The Columbian Magazine*, February 1788, opposite p. 53. Fielding, 1569. LC–USZ62–46026

587

The ACCIDENT in LOMBARD-STREET PHILADA. 1787 design'd & engrav'd by C. W. Peale. No. 1
Etching 7¾ x 11¾ in.

This view of Lombard Street, six blocks south of Market Street, pictures everyday life in Philadelphia. Below the picture is a poem:

> The pye from Bake-house she had brought
> But let it fall for want of thought
> And laughing Sweeps collect around
> The pye that's scatter'd on the ground.

E. P. Richardson credits this print as "the earliest etching done by an American painter and the earliest genre street scene of an American city." It was intended to be the first in a series depicting the principal streets in the city. Charles Willson Peale's house is in the foreground, and the little girl is probably his daughter Angelica. LC–USZ72–213

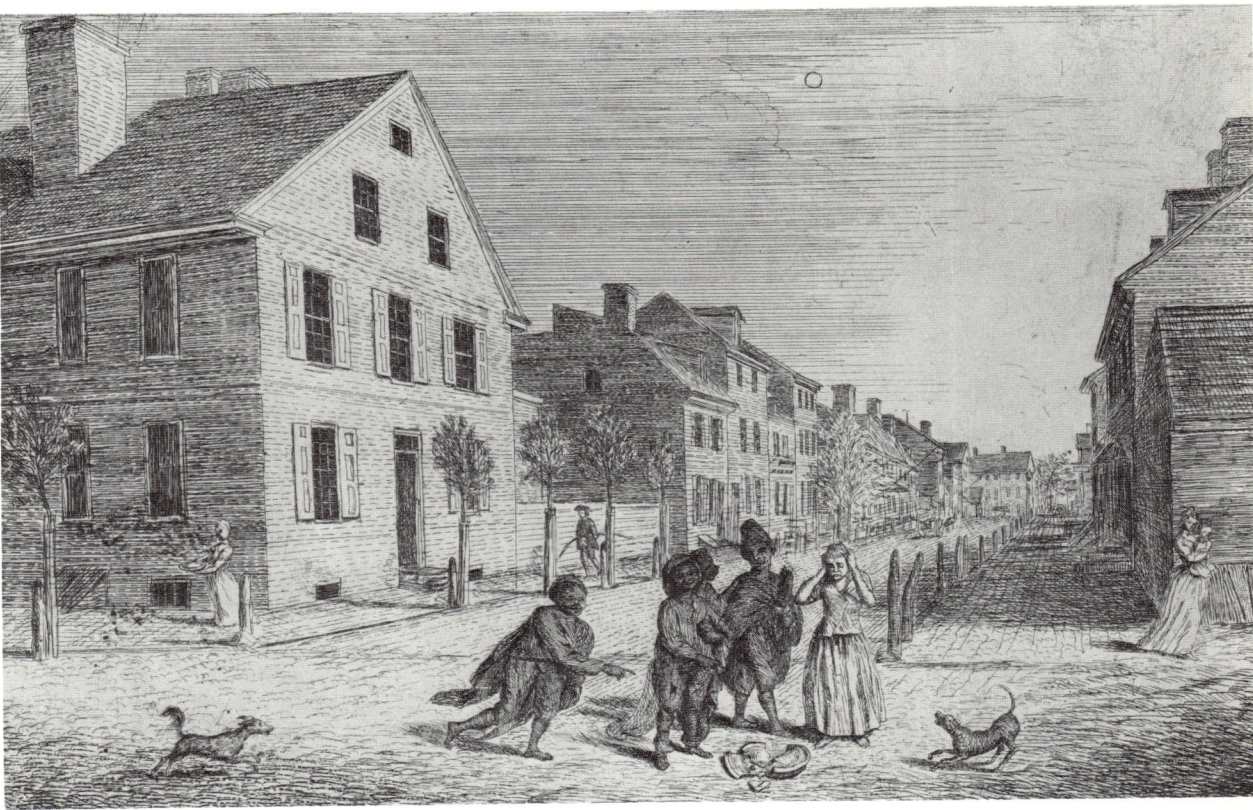
587

588

An EAST PROSPECT of the CITY of PHILADELPHIA: taken by GEORGE HEAP from the JERSEY SHORE, under the Direction of NICHOLAS SCULL Surveyor General of the PROVINCE of PENNSYLVANIA. Engrav'd & Publish'd according to Act of Parliament, by

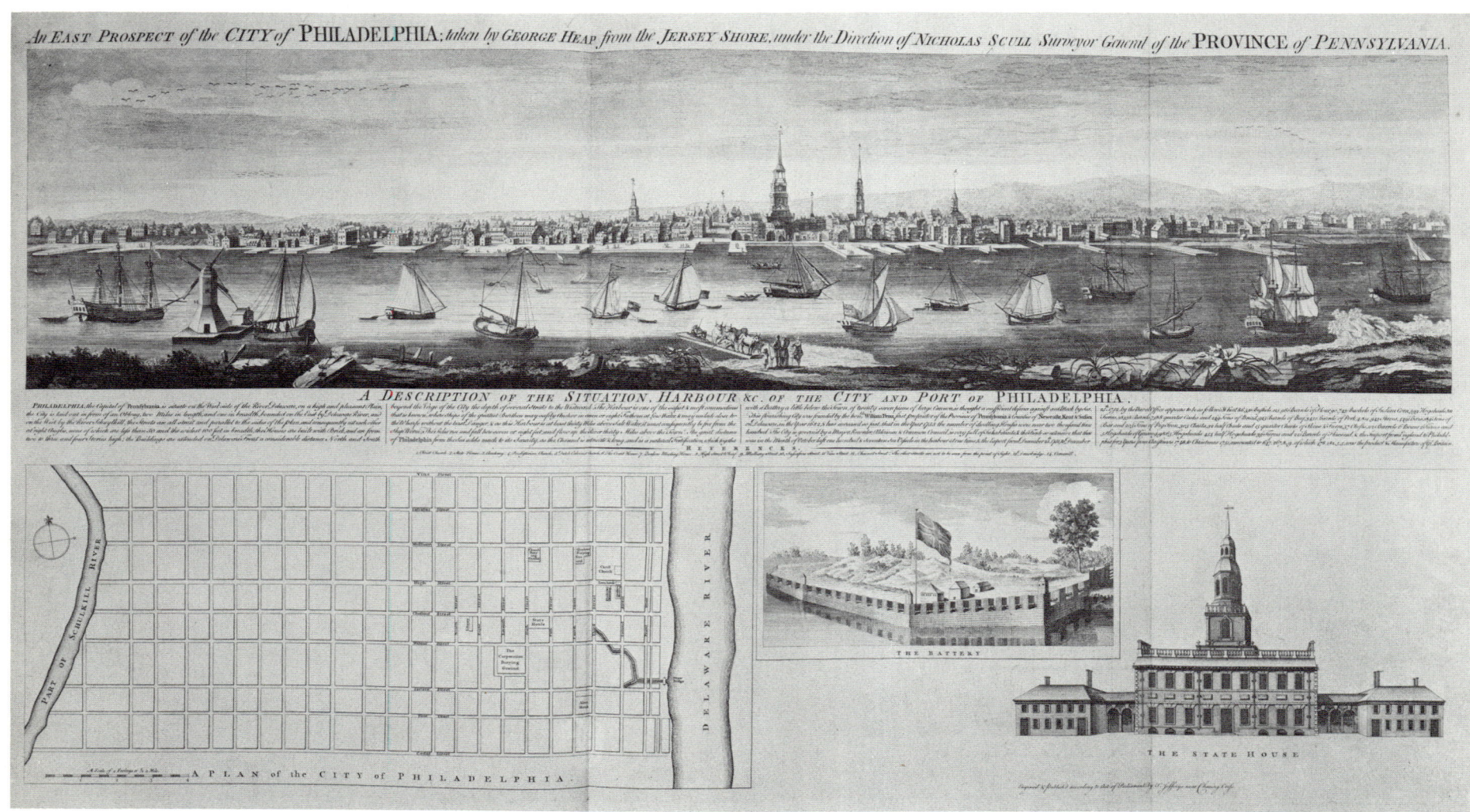

T. Jeffereys near Charing Cross. [1768]
Etching 18¾ x 36 in. (image)

Three pictures and a map on one print. LC–USZ62–3282

a. A DESCRIPTION OF THE SITUATION, HARBOUR &c. OF THE CITY AND PORT OF PHILADELPHIA. 8⅝ x 36 in. (image)

Beneath this picture is the following description of the city. "Philadelphia, the Capital of Pennsylvania, is situate on the West side of the River Delaware, on a high and pleasant Plain, the City is laid out in form of an Oblong, two Miles in length, and one in breadth, bounded on the East by Delaware River, and on the West by the River Schuylkill, the streets are all strait and parallel to the sides of the plan, and consequently cut each other at right angles, none of which are less than 50 and the widest 100 feet in breadth, the Houses are built with Brick and are from two to three and four Stories high; the Buildings are extended on Delaware Front a considerable distance North and South beyond the Verge of the City the depth of several Streets to the Westward. The Harbour is one of the safest and most commodius that is known, where Ships of the greatest Burthen may safely Anchor in seven or eight Fathom at Low Water, and may unload close to the Warfs without the least Danger, and as this Harbour is at least thirty Miles above Salt Water, it must consequently be free from Ship Worms; The Tides rise and fall here seven or eight feet, and flow up the River thirty Miles above the Town. The great distance of Philadelphia from the sea adds much to its Security, as the channel is intricate and long and is a natural fortification which together with a Battery a little below the Town of twenty seven pieces of large Cannon, is thought a sufficient defense against an attack by Sea. This flourishing City was founded by the honble. William Penn first proprietor of the Province of Pennsylvania & Counties of Newcastle, Kent and Sussex in Delaware, in the Year 1682, and has increased so fast, that in the Year 1753 the number of dwelling Houses were near two thousand three hundred. The City is governed by a Mayor, Recorder, Alderman, and Common Council, is very full of inhabitants, and the Trade so extensive that there was in the month of October last one hundred and seventeen Sea Vessels in the harbour at one time, and the export from December 25th 1751 to December 25th 1752, by the Naval Office appears to be as follows. Wheat 86,550 Bushels, 125,960 Barrels of Flour, 90,743 Bushels of Indian Corn, 599 Hogsheads, 812 Tierces, 28,338 Barrels, 7,588 quarter Casks and 249 Tons of Bread, 925 Barrels of Beef, 3,431 Barrels of Pork, 4,812,943 Staves, 4,491 Bars, 189 Tons of Bar and 205 Tons of Pig Iron, 305 Chests, 32 Half Chests and 15 Quarter Chests of Skins and Furs, 57 Chests, 112 Barrels 6 Boxes 2 Tierces and 5 Hogsheads of Ginseng. 9,865 Hogsheads, 454 half Hogsheads, 39 Tierces and 221 Barrels of Flaxseed, and the import from England to Philadelphia for 3 Years from Christmas 1748 to Christmas 1751, amounted to £647,267„8„9, of which £478,282„5„5, was the product and Manufacture of Grt. Britain." The picture identifies: "1. Christ Church. 2. State House. 3. Academy. 4. Presbyterian Church. 5. Dutch Calvinist Church. 6. The Court House. 7. Quakers Meeting House. 8. High Street Warf. 9. Mulberry Street. 10. Sasafras Street. 11. Vine Street. The Other Streets are not to be seen from the point of Sight. 13. Drawbridge. 14. Cornmill."

b. THE BATTERY [Philadelphia] 4⅜ x 8⅞ in. (image). A redoubt with 27 cannons, a Union Jack, and auxiliary buildings.

c. THE STATE HOUSE [Philadelphia] 5⅞ x 11 in. (image)

———————Another copy. In Jefferys, *A General Topography of North America* (London, 1768), no. 44.

589
A N.W. VIEW OF THE STATE HOUSE IN PHILADELPHIA taken 1778. C. W. Peale delin. J. T. Sculp. [1787]
Etching 4½ x 7¼ in.

The account which accompanies this view describes the statehouse as "a building which will, perhaps, become more interesting in the history of the world, than any of the celebrated fabrics of Greece or Rome." Located on Chestnut Street between Fifth and Sixth, the building was ornamented with two clocks and a steeple which was removed soon after the British evacuation of Philadelphia. From *The Columbian Magazine*, July 1787, opposite p. 516. Fielding, 1710. LC–USZ62–9486

590
ELEVATIONS OF THE STATE HOUSE [Philadelphia] London Publish'd according to Act of Parliament March 12th. 1777 by W. Faden Successor to the late Mr. Jefferys Geographer to the King Charing Cross
Etching (hand colored) 25⅜ x 18½ in. (entire map)

The statehouse, or Independence Hall, housed both the Continental Congress and the Constitutional Convention. This picture is an ornament on a map entitled "A Plan of the City and Environs of Philadelphia Survey'd by N: Scull and G: Heap Engraved by Willm. Faden 1777" from Faden, *North American Atlas* (London, 1777), no. 19. Similar to item 588c.

———————Another copy "engraved and published by Matthew Albert Lotter. 1777." In Lotter, *Atlas Géographique* (Nürnberg, 1778), no. 99.

591
PENNSYLVANIA HOSPITAL [Philadelphia]. James Smither Sculp. Printed by Tho. Man. [1774]
Etching 2½ x 5 in. (image)

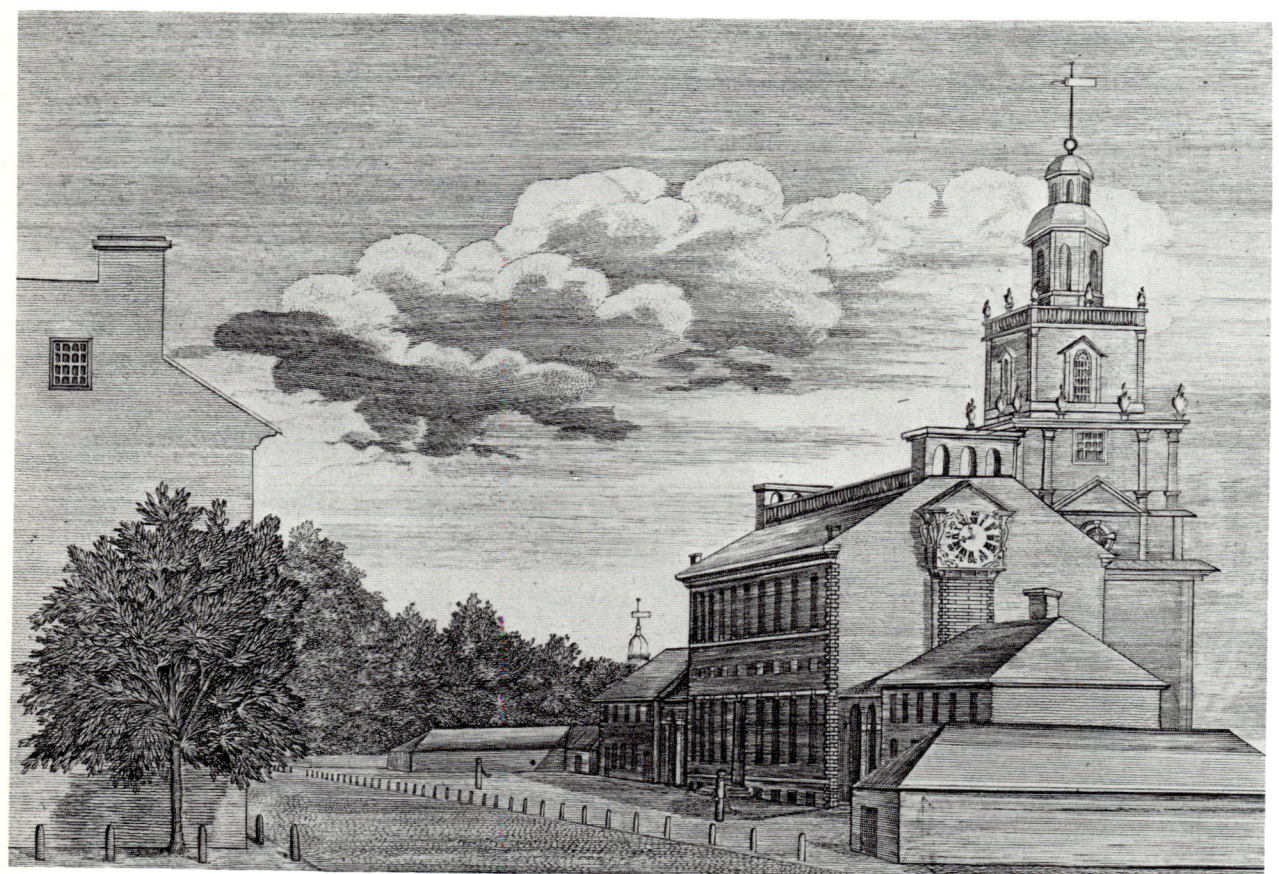

589

The Pennsylvania Hospital for the Insane admitted its first patients in 1756. During the Revolution, the British Army took over the buildings and used them as a dispensary. An inset view on the John Reed "Map of Philadelphia" (Philadelphia, 1774). Stauffer, 2986, enters items 591–593 as one number.

592

THE STATE HOUSE [Philadelphia]. James Smither Sculp. Printed by Tho. Man. [1774]
Etching 5½ x 9½ in. (image)

An inset view on the John Reed "Map of Philadelphia" (Philadelphia, 1774).

593

THE HOUSE OF EMPLOYMENT & ALMS HOUSE [Philadelphia]. James Smither Sculp. Printed by Tho. Man. [1774]
Etching 2¼ x 6½ in. (image)

Completed in 1767, the Philadelphia Almshouse shared the grounds on Spruce Street with the House of Employment and the Philadelphia Hospital, which was an infirmary for the city's poor. An inset view on the John Reed "Map of Philadelphia" (Philadelphia, 1774).

Delaware River and Bay

594

Perspective View of the Country between Wilmington and the Delaware. Taken from the Hill S.W. of the Academy.
Etching 7¼ x 13½ in. (image)

E. P. Richardson credits Peale with the design of this large panoramic view which unfolds to exhibit farms, woods, and the river in the background. The Academy is probably the Academy of Newark, Del., moved to that site from Philadelphia (via Elkton, Md.) in 1767. From *The Columbian Magazine*, October 1789, opposite p. 600. Stauffer, 3301.
LC-USZ62-45578

595

MUD FORTE [from] Province Island. [1777?]
Drawing (hand colored) 4⅝ x 6½ in.

This view is inset on a map entitled "Plan of Part of the River Delaware, from Chester to Philadelphia, in which is mark'd the position of His Majs: Ships on the 15th of November 1777." A redoubt is in the left foreground, ships are anchored in the river to right of center, and the fort is in the background. Howe Collection, no. 14. Negative in G&M.

596

VIEW of the Rebel Fort and Works, on Mud Island comprehending Red-Bank on the Jersey shore; taken from* [southeast shore of Carpenter's Island] in front of the 6 Gun Battery. [Pierre Nicole] 1777

Drawing (hand colored) 2½ x 27½ in. (side and bottom measurement of irregular pentagon)

A view produced from the surveys of John Montresor, this picture is found at the base of a map entitled "A Survey of the City of Philadelphia and its Environs Shewing the Several Works constructed by his Majesty's Troops, under the Command of Sir William Howe, since their possession of that City 26th: September 1777, comprehending likewise the Attacks against Fort Mifflin on Mud Island and until its Reduction, 16th November 1777." It differs slightly from the drawing "View of Mud Island . . ." since it is a slightly nearer view, the middle blockhouse has a roof, and there are no designations. In Manuscript Maps in G&M. LC–USZ62–44848 is the negative number for a black-and-white print.

597

Elevation of the Commanding Officer's House [on Mud Island, Pierre Nicole] 1777
Drawing (colored) 2¾ x 4½ in.

A view of the house inset on a map entitled

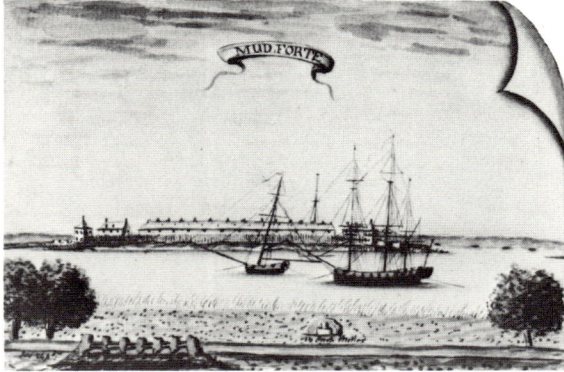
595

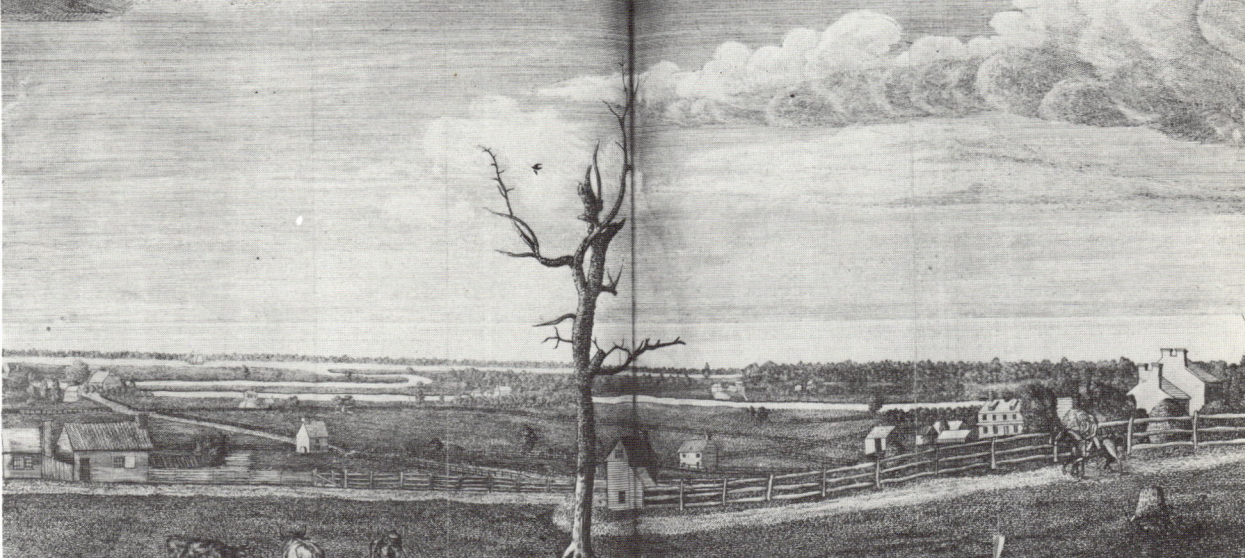
594

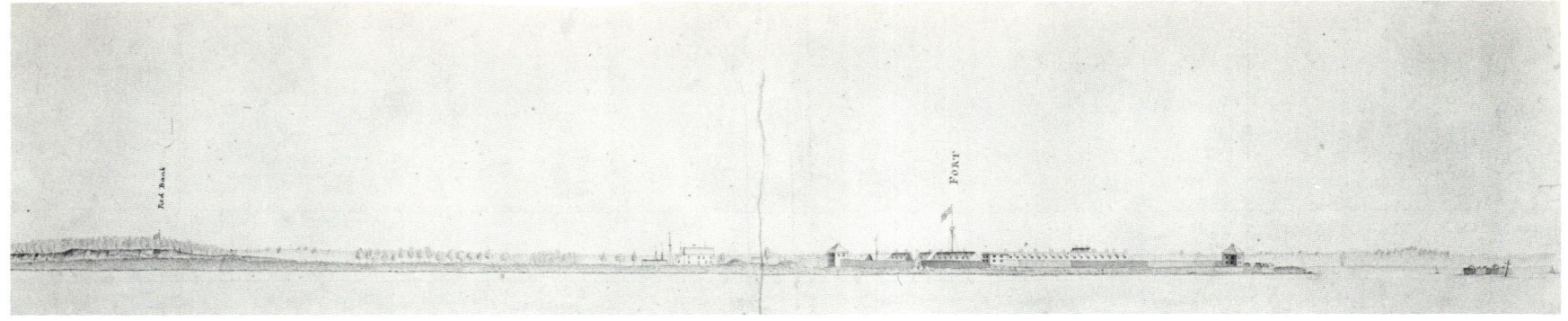

599

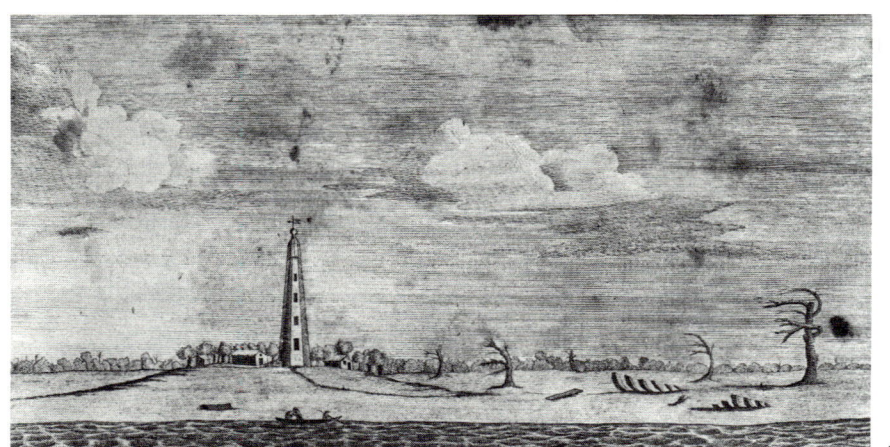

600

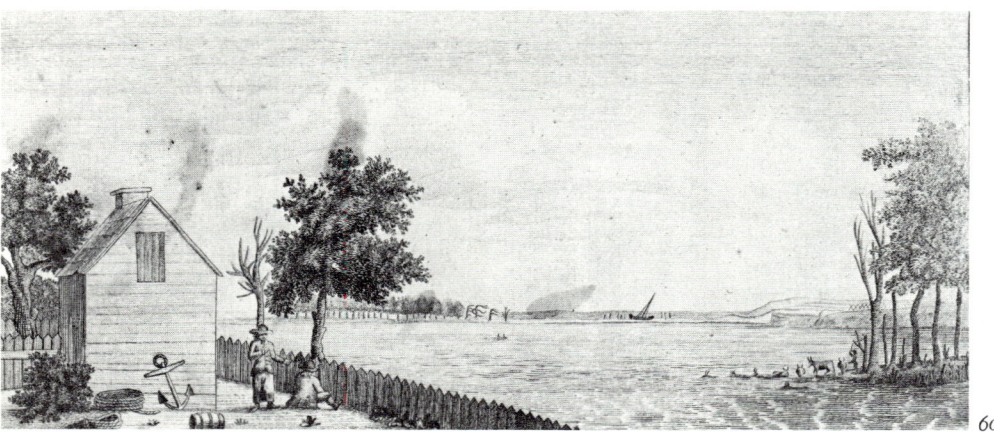

601

"A survey of the City of Philadelphia . . . 1777." In Manuscript Maps in G&M.

598
[Interior view of the Fort on Mud Island (Fort Mifflin)] Section through A: B. [Pierre Nicole] 1777
Drawing (colored) 2¾ x 18¾ in.

A cutaway view of the fort's construction inset on a map entitled "A Survey of the City of Philadelphia . . . 1777." In Manuscript Maps in G&M.

599
View of Mud Island before it's Reduction 16th Novr. 1777 under the Direction of John Montresor Esqr. Chief Engineer in America taken from the Dyke in the Front of the Six Gun Battery on Carpenter's Island. no. 15 [1777]
Ink and pencil with water color 11¼ x 29½ in. (image)

John Montresor (1736–1799), the chief British military engineer in America, designed the defenses on Mud Island and was with the forces of William Howe when the British took Fort Mifflin in November 1777. Montresor returned to England in 1778. The reduction of the Delaware River forts marked the end of the successful British Philadelphia Campaign. LC–USZ62–94

600

A View of the Lighthouse on Cape Henlopen; taken at Sea, August 1780. [1788]
Mixed method 3½ x 6⅜ in. (image)

The Cape Henlopen lighthouse was built of stone on the south cape of the Delaware River in 1765. Nearby salt works are visible. An accompanying article states that "the wrecks that lie plentifully scattered over the beach, affort a melancholy proof of the great necessity for this lighthouse . . ." From *The Columbian Magazine*, February 1788, opposite p. 108. Stauffer, 3293. LC–USZ62–31786

601

A View of the Sea & Beach, from Mr. James Newbolds Plantation, near Indian River. Trenchard Sculp. [1788]
Etching 3¾ x 7 in.

The Indian River of southeast Delaware flows into Indian River Bay south of Rehoboth. The Newbold plantation beach is on a fresh water pond protected from the Atlantic by a narrow isthmus. The contemporary account of this view describes the Indian corn, cider, iron ore, yellow ocher, and seaweed useful in glass manufacture available in the area and remarks:

Many other valuable articles of trade and manufacture might be obtained here with proper attention and encouragement. But without the industry of man, the best shores of nature must lie useless and unexplored.

Frontispiece for *The Columbian Magazine*, June 1788. Stauffer, 3296.
LC–USZ62–31796

SOUTHERN STATES

Virginia

602

[A Port Scene in the South—a cartouche] Drawn by Joshua Fry & Peter Jefferson in 1775.

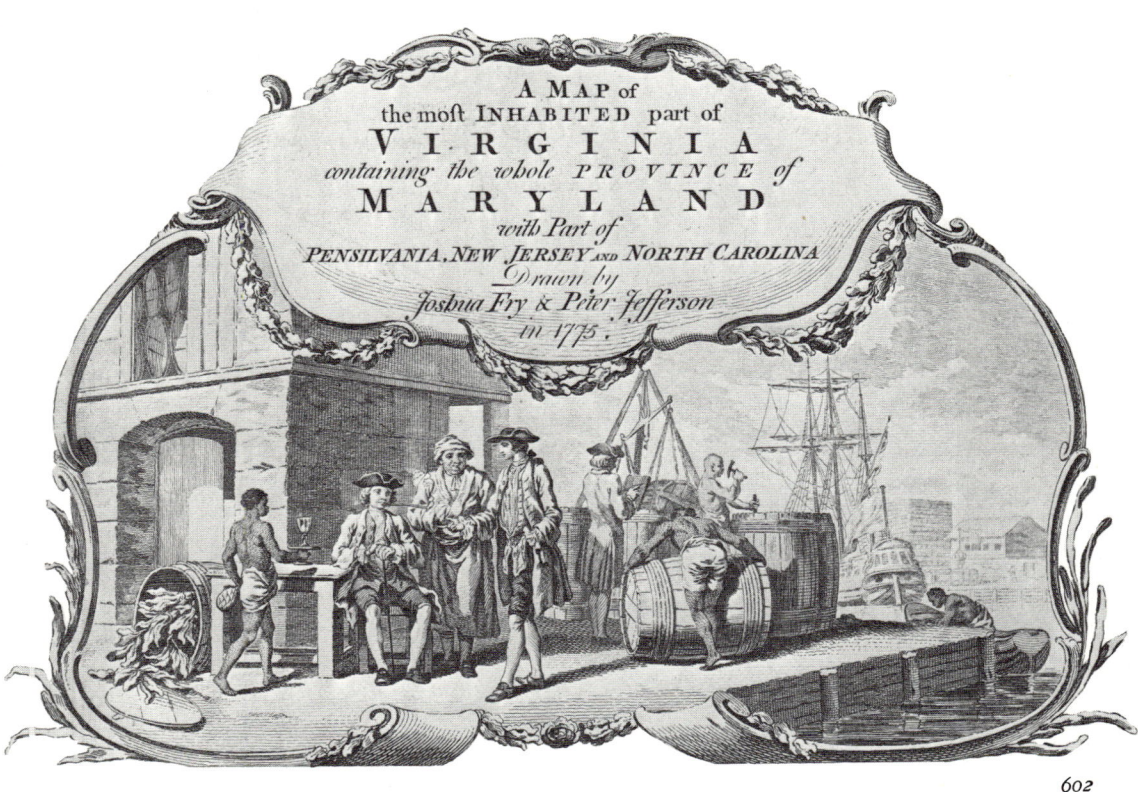

602

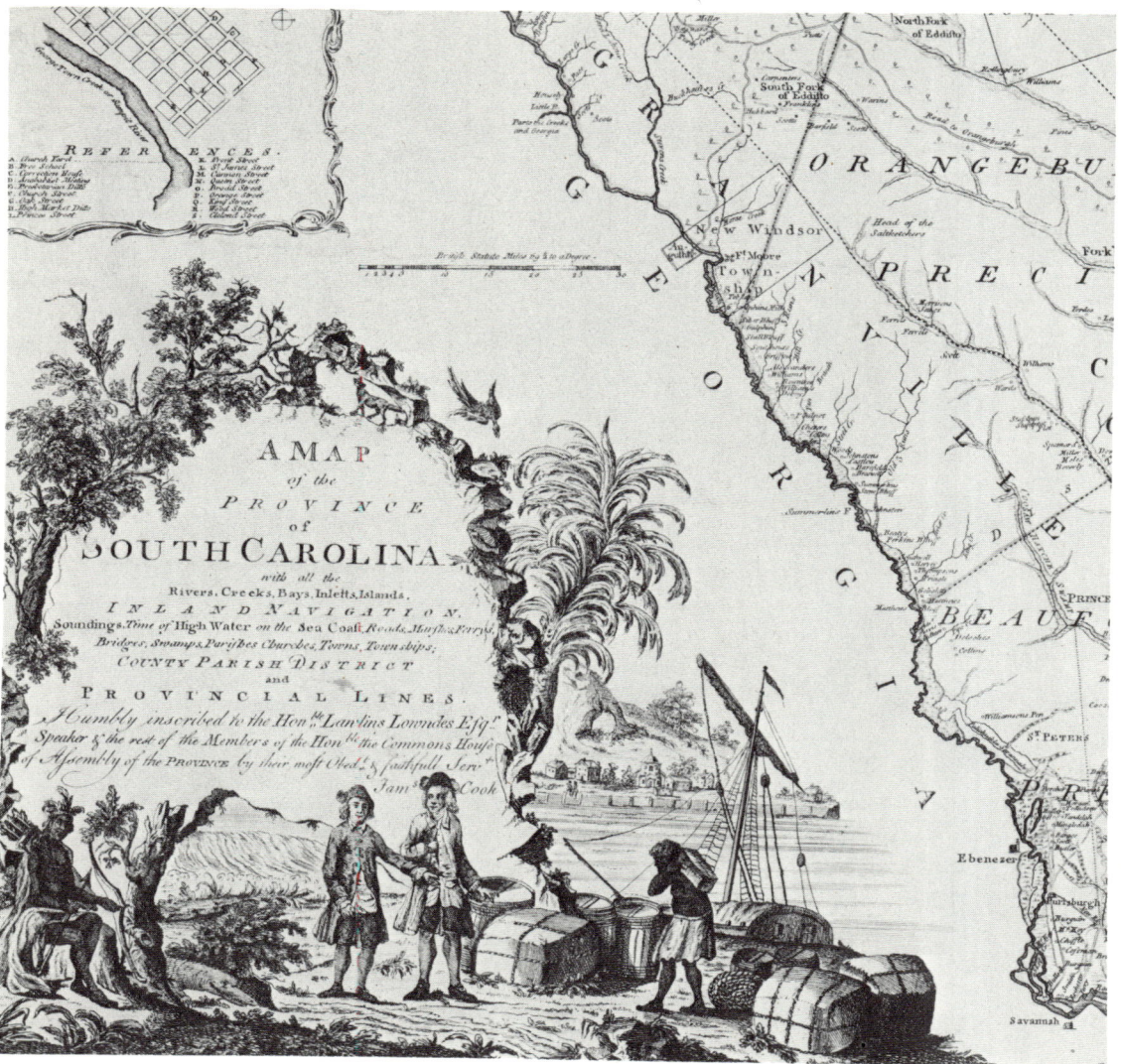

604

Etching 8¾ x 10¾ in. (image)

This cartouche for the well-known Fry-Jefferson map of Virginia, Maryland, and parts of Pennsylvania, New Jersey and North Carolina, represents the tobacco trade, which was the economic lifeline of the Chesapeake area. From Jefferys, *The American Atlas* (London, 1775), no. 20-21. The cartouche, first printed in 1751, also appears in the editions for 1776, 1778, and 1782. Negative in G&M.

―――――Another impression. In Faden, *North American Atlas* (London, 1777), no. 27-28.

―――――Another impression. In Jefferys, *A General Topography of North America* (London, 1768), no. 57.

603

A View of the Natural Bridge in Virginia. [1787]

Etching 5⅜ x 7⅞ in. (image)

Frontispiece for *The Columbian Magazine*, September 1787, opposite p. 617. Stauffer, 3294.

The Carolinas

604

[A Port Scene in South Carolina—a cartouche] Publish'd according to Act of Parliament July 7th. 1773 and Sold By. H. Parker in Cornhill. Thos. Bowen sculpt.

Etching 10½ x 13 in. (image)

Two white men direct the unloading of parcels and barrels from a ship tied to the dock. A Negro carries a box from the wharf, and an Indian watches from the woods. Across the river is another wharf and a town. From "A Map of the Province of South Carolina with all the Rivers, Creeks, Bays, Inletts, Islands . . . by . . . Jams Cook" in G&M Vault.
LC–USZ62–46100

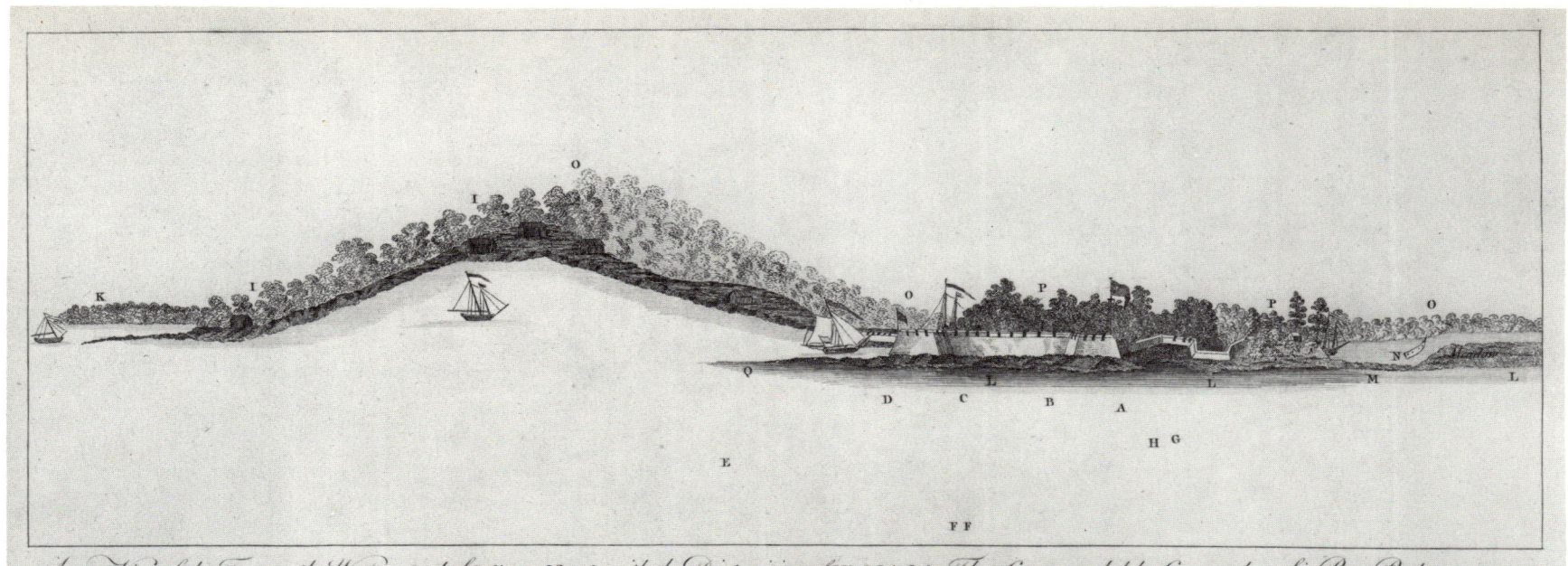

605

A Birds Eye View from part of Mount Pleasant A. to the Eastern point of Long Island B____C. The Lady William an Armed Schooner, and Sloop D. The Fort on Sulivans Island E. Sulivans Island. F. The Rebels Tents, Huts and Redoubt. G. Green Island. H. The British Camp on Long Island. I. The Ranger Snow of War. K. The Anchorage of the Commodore Sir Petr. Parker Knt. &c. &c. LONDON, Engraved & Publish'd according to Act of Parliament Augt. 10th 1776 by Wm. Faden Corner of St. Martins Lane Charing Cross.

Etching 7⅝ x 23½ in.

This view was dedicated to Sir Peter Parker by Col. Thomas James. From Faden, *Atlas of Battles of the American Revolution* (London, 1770–93), no. 27.

606

A N.b.E. View of the Fort on the Western end of Sulivan's Island with the Disposition of His Majesty's Fleet Commanded by Commodore Sir Peter Parker Knt. &c. &c. &c. during the Attack on the 28th. of June 1776, which lasted 9 hours and 40 minutes. London. Engraved & Publish'd according to Act of Parliament Augt. 10th. 1776 by Wm. Faden Corner of St. Martin's Lane Charing Cross.

Etching 7¾ x 16½ in.

View of Sullivan's Island at the north side of the entrance to Charleston Harbor, S.C. In June 1776 the British tried to attack Fort Sullivan (renamed Fort Moultrie) by land and sea, but an unfavorable wind prevented the tide from going out enough to allow land forces on Long Island to ford the Breach, a narrow channel separating the two islands. Three frigates ran aground attempting to approach the fort from the side here visible. The positions of the attacking vessels are indicated on the key below the print. The ship *Acteon* was burned to prevent the Americans from seizing her where she was stuck on the shoals. From Faden, *Atlas of Battles of the American Revolution* (London, 1770–93), no. 26.
LC-USZ62-28131

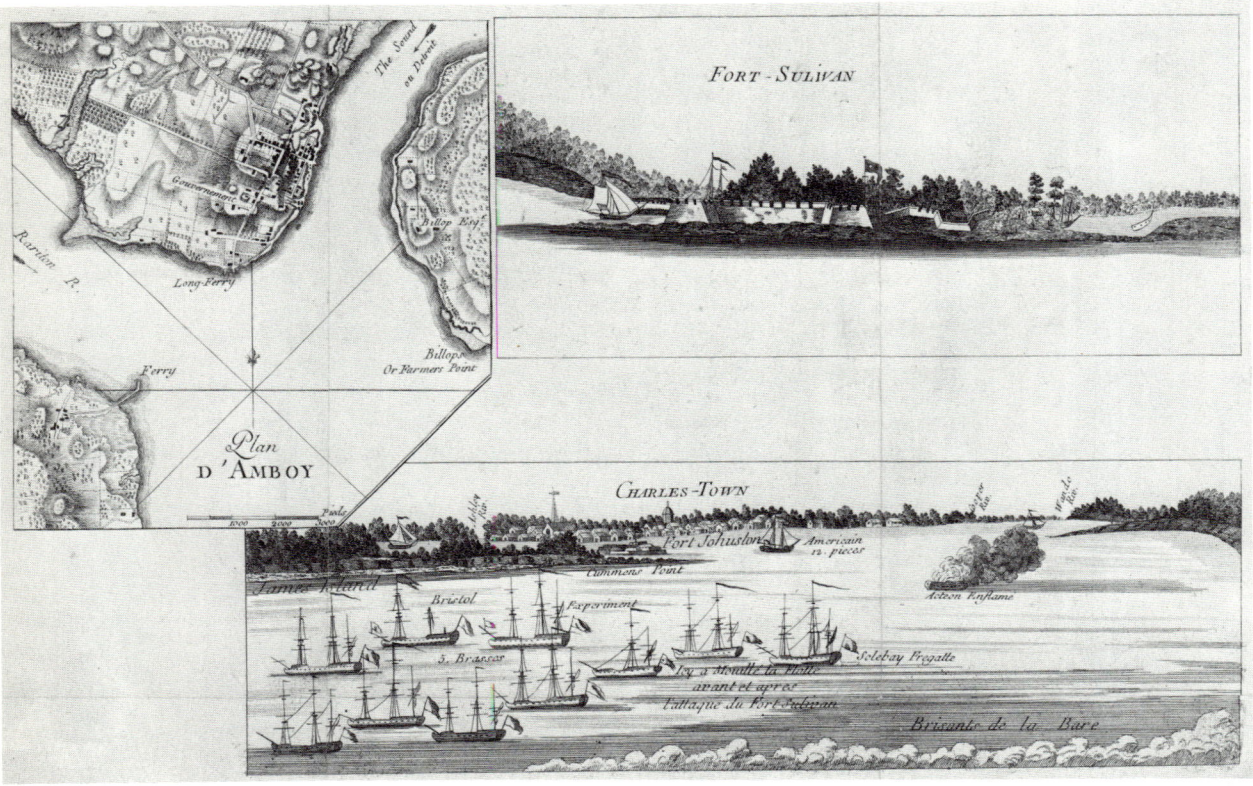

607

607

Charles-Town [and] Fort-Sulivan. [1780]
Etching 9½ x 14⅞ in.

The top view shows Fort Sullivan with the harbor behind it. The view of Charleston shows the position of the British fleet before and after the attack on Fort Sullivan. It distinguishes the ships *Bristol, Experiment, Solebay,* and *Acteon,* which is in flames. In the background from left to right are the Ashley River, Fort Johnson, an American ship, and the entrances to the Cooper and Wando Rivers. The view of Charleston is similar to the English view in item 611. From the Rochambeau Collection, no. 19 in G&M. LC–USZ62–46298

608

[A View of the Town of Charles Town in South-Carolina from the South Shore of Ashley River] Published according to Act of Parliament Nov. 1st 1777 by J.F.W. DesBarres Esqr.
Aquatint with etching 6¼ x 14⅛ in. (image)

Inset for a map entitled "The Harbour of Charles Town in South-Carolina, from the Surveys of Sr. Jas. Wallace Captn in his Majestys Navy & Others." Two men are fishing in the foreground. Across the river is the town surrounded by crenellated walls. *The Atlantic Neptune.* Phillips 1198, v. 3, no. 51.

———Other impressions: Phillips 1199, v. 3, no. 33; Phillips 1200, v. 3, no. 34; Phillips 1205, v. 3, no. 35; Phillips 3658, pt. 3, no. 18; Phillips 3655, v. 3, no. 18; Phillips 3656, v. 3, no. 18; Phillips 3659, v. 3, no. 18; Phillips 4473, v. 1, no. 68; LeGear 10323, v. 1, no. 64; LeGear 10317, v. 1, no. 15.

———Other copies: Same title and imprint. Etching (hand colored) 7⅛ x 15 in. (image). A man and a woman with cows lounge in the foreground. In the background is the walled city. Phillips 1202, v. 3, no. 31;

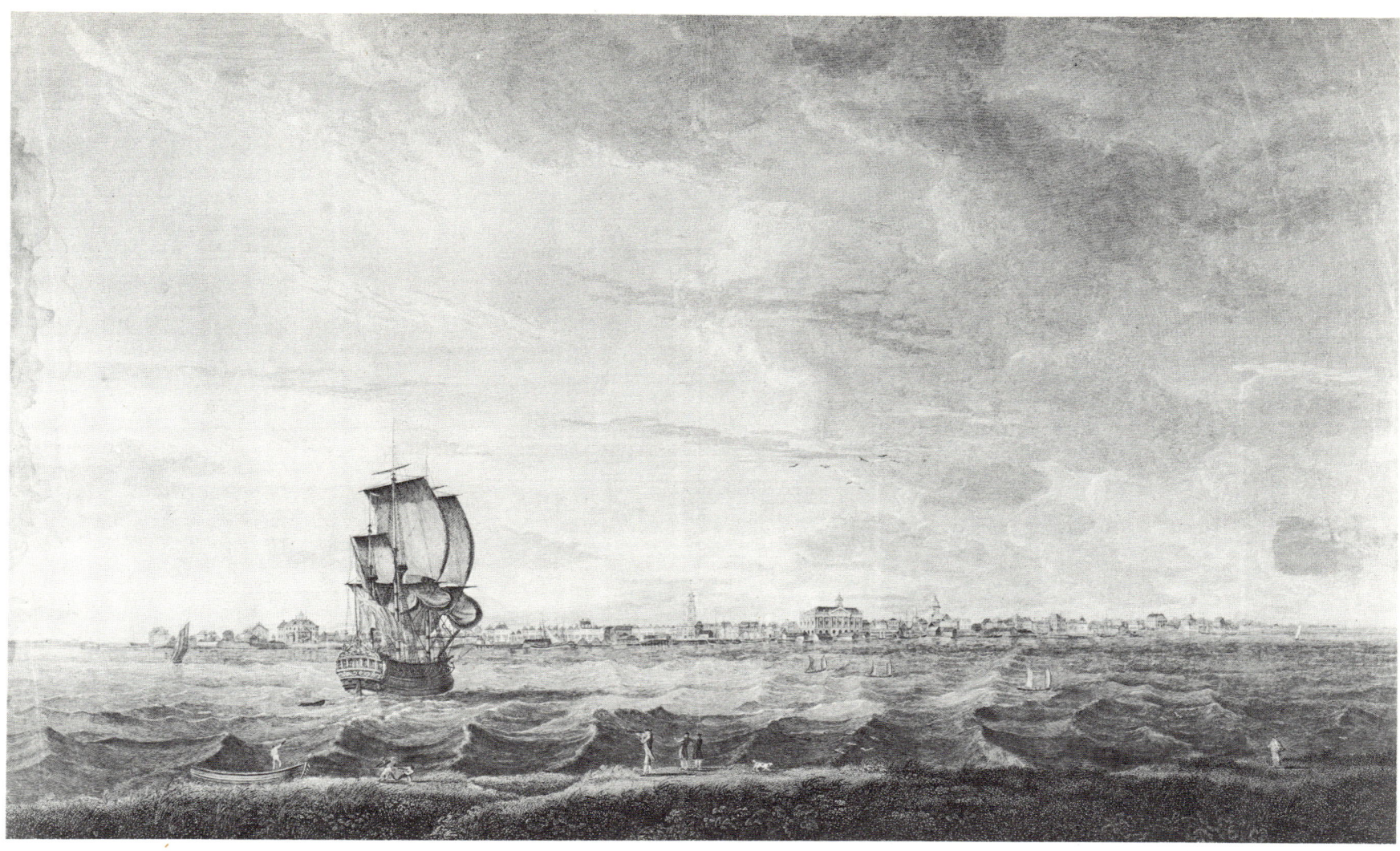

609

Phillips 1203, v. 3, no. 31; Phillips 4474, v. 3, no. 30.

609

A View of CHARLES-TOWN, the Capital of SOUTH CAROLINA. From an Original Picture painted at Charles Town, in the Year 1774. Painted by Thos. Leitch. Engraved by Saml. Smith. Published as the act directs 3d June 1776 by S. Smith, Green Street, Leicester Fields, London.

Etching 16¾ x 28⅞ in. (image)

View of Charleston, probably from Shutes Folly. LC–USZ62–14865

610

A View of CHARLES TOWN the Capital of South Carolina in North America. Vue de CHARLES TOWN Capitale de la Carolina du Sud dans l'Amérique Septentrionale. Engraved by C. Canot from an Original Painting of T. Mellish, in the Collection of Mr. John Bowles. LONDON.

231

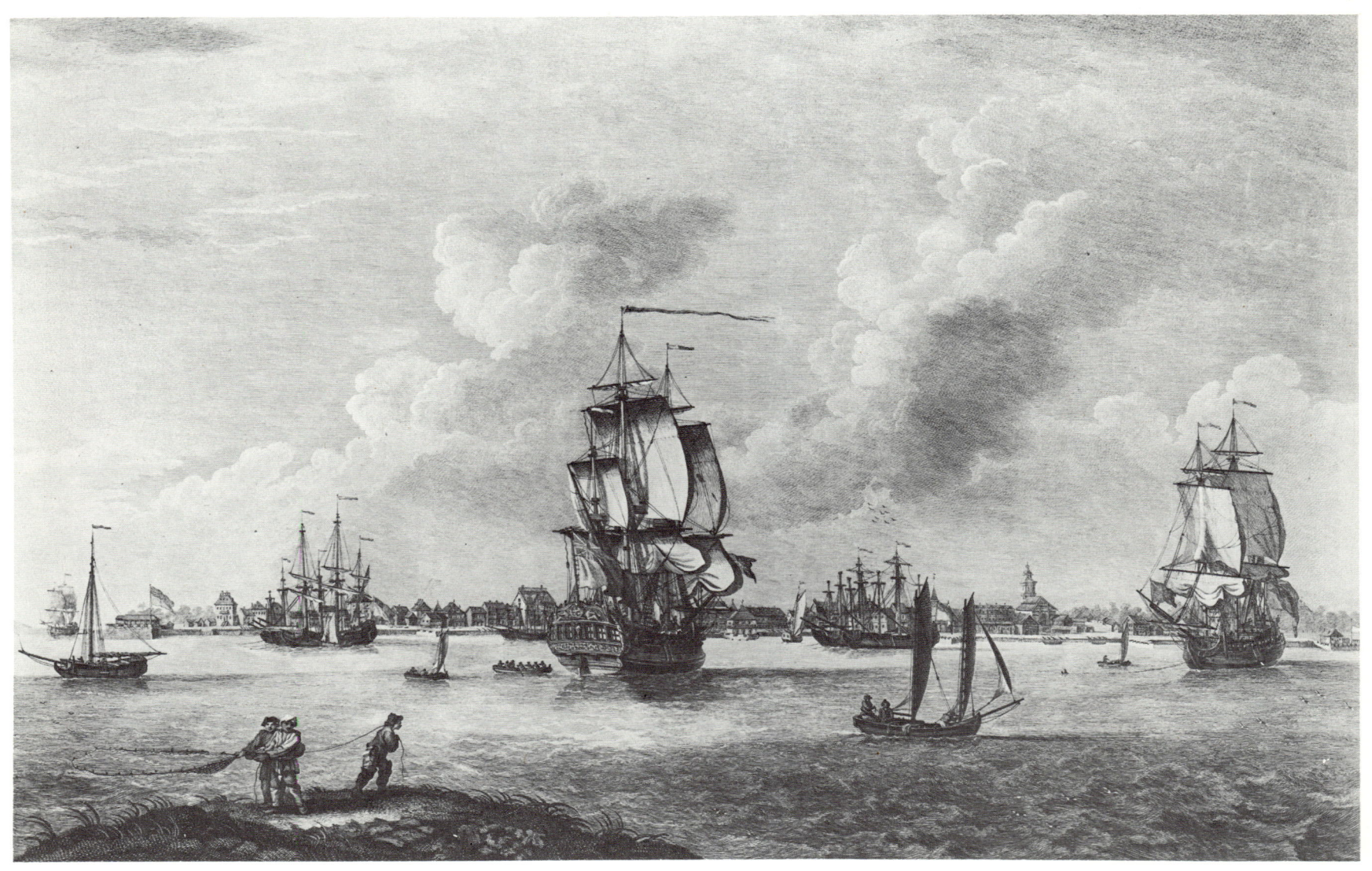

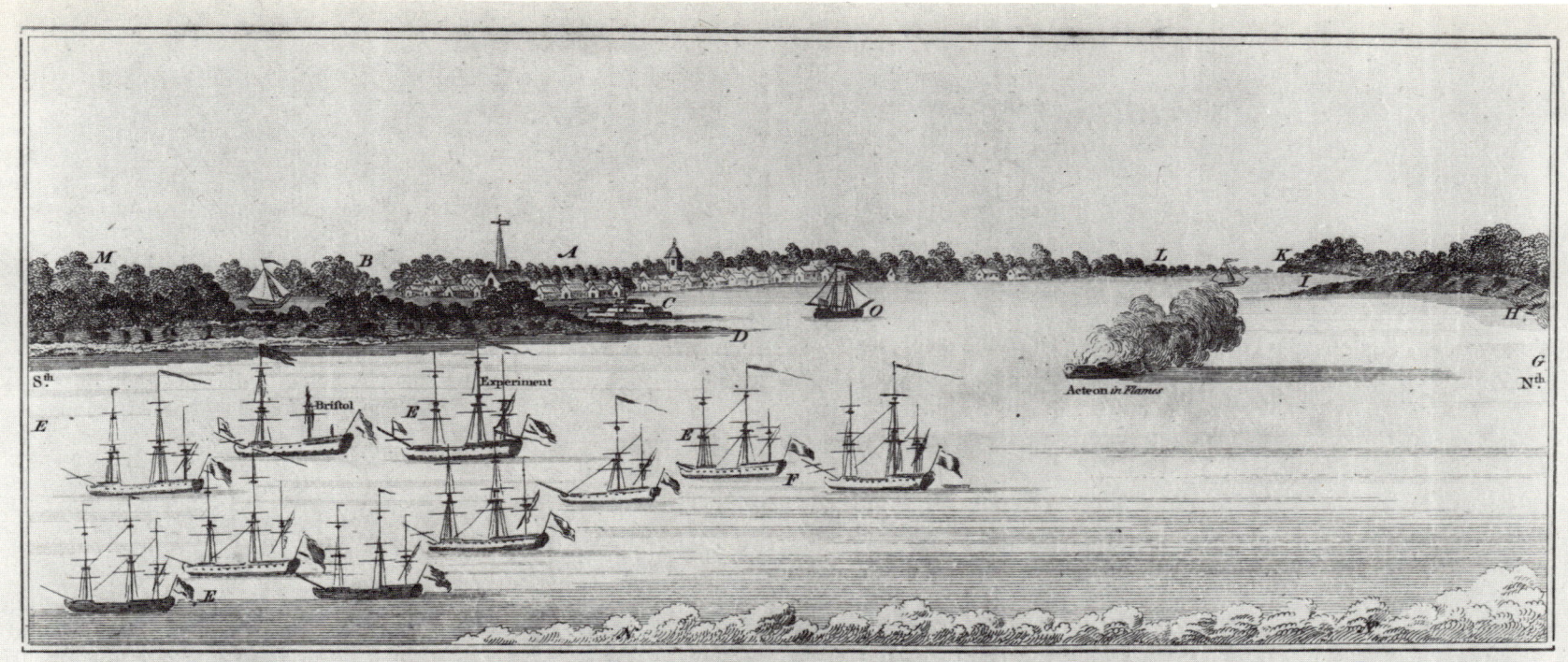

Printed for John Bowles at No. 13 in Cornhill, Robt. Sayer at No. 53 in Fleet Street, Thos. Jefferys at the Corner of St. Martins Lane in the Strand, & Carington Bowles at No. 69 in St. Pauls Church Yard. [1768]

Etching 14½ x 20¾ in.

Another view of the flourishing commercial city of Charleston in the 18th century. Called a true city state, the town represented a close association of urban and rural life. Its merchants and businessmen tended to invest in land, and many planters chose to maintain townhouses in the city. See *Scenographia Americana* (1768). LC–USZ62–45325

611

A N.W.b.N. View of CHARLES TOWN from on board the Bristol ... taken in Five Fathom Hole the day after the Attack upon Fort Sulivan by the Commodore & his Squadron, which Action continued 9 hours & 40 minutes. LONDON, Engrav'd & Publish'd according to Act of Parliament Augt. 10th 1776 by Wm. Faden Corner of St. Martins Lane Charing Cross.

Etching 8½ x 12¼ in.

This view, also dedicated to Sir Peter

Parker by Col. Thomas James, depicts Charleston Harbor the day after the battle of Sullivan's Island. Identified in the picture are the Ashley, Cooper, and Wando Rivers, James Island, Fort Johnson, Hog Island, Mount Pleasant, Cummins' Point, Five Fatham Hole, and the breakers on Charleston Bar. Also identified are the British ships *Bristol*, *Experiment*, and *Acteon*, the latter in flames. An American vessel is visible in the center background. From Faden, *Atlas of Battles of the American Revolution* (London, 1770–93), no. 28. LC–USZ62–46097

Georgia and Florida

612

A View of the Entrance into St. Mary's River. Published 26 March 1770 according to Act of Parliament by Thomas Jefferys Geographer to the King, in the Strand.

Mixed method 1¾ x 6¾ in. (image)

This view designates the inner points of Amelia and Cumberland Islands. St. Mary's River, which rises in Okefenokee Swamp, Georgia, forms part of the border between that State and Florida. This inset is for a map entitled "A Chart of the Entrance into St. Mary's River taken by Capt. W. Fuller in November 1769" from Faden, *North American Atlas* (London, 1777a), no. 26.

————————Another copy entitled "Vue de l'entre de la Riviere de St. Mary Tiree de la carte de W: Fuller." In France, Depot des cartes et plans de la marine, *Neptune Americo-Septentrional* (Paris, 1778–80), no. 26.

613

A North View of Pensacola, on the Island of Santa Rosa, Drawn by Dom. Serres. [1768]

Etching 6⅜ x 10½ in.

In 1722 when Pensacola was restored to the Spanish by the French, the town, originally established in 1696, was rebuilt on Santa Rosa Island where it was believed to be safer from Indian attacks. This island very nearly encloses Pensacola Bay, called by the early explorers Santa Maria Bay. The key to this view identifies the fort, the church, the Governor's house, the commandant's house, a well, and a small craft called a "Bungo." From Jefferys, *A General Topography of North America* (London, 1768), no. 68a. LC–USZ62–46099

Possibly derived from a 1743 source. An earlier Dutch copy in the New York Public Library has caption: "Gezigt Van't Spaansche Hek Pensacola. . . . Naar een Tekening, die op de Plaats zelre, in't jaar 1743, is gamaakt." Another impression in *Hedendaagsche Historie, of Tegenwoordige Staat van Amerika*, v. 3 (Amsterdam, Isaak Tirion, 1766), p. 314.

614

A View of Pensacola in West Florida. Vue de Pensacola dans le Florida Occidentale. To the Honourable Sr. William Burnaby Rear Admiral of the Red, & Commander in Chief of His Majesty's Ships at Jamaica, & in the Gulf of Mexico, &c. This View of Pensacola is Dedicated by his most Obedt. humble Servt. Geo. Gauld. Publish'd according to Act of Parliament by G. Gauld & Sold by T. Jefferys in the Strand, London. [177?]

Etching 14½ x 21 in.

View of Pensacola, the capital of West Florida, after the city was moved from Santa Rosa Island to a regularly laid out area on the north side of the bay. The ships in the foreground are British. The crest of William Burnaby beneath the picture shows a lion standing over two horizontal bars with a star between them and a banner reading "Pro Rege." LC–USZ62–45384

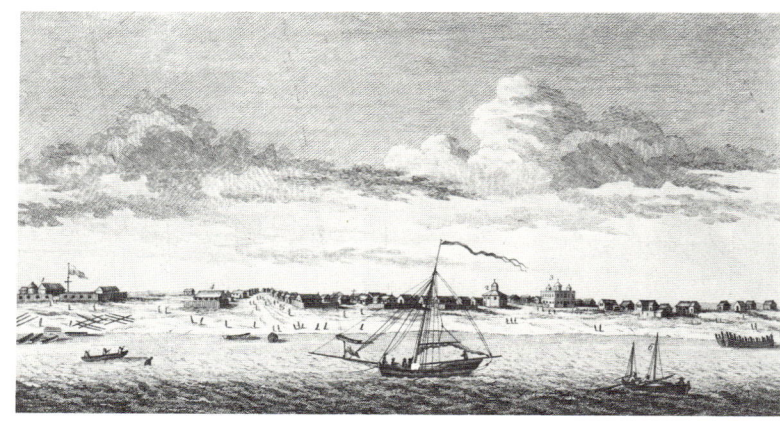

613

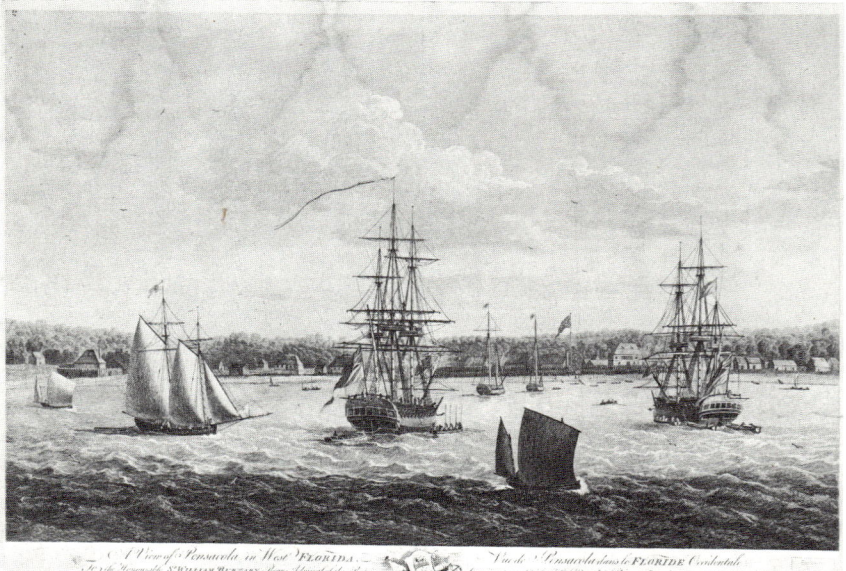

614

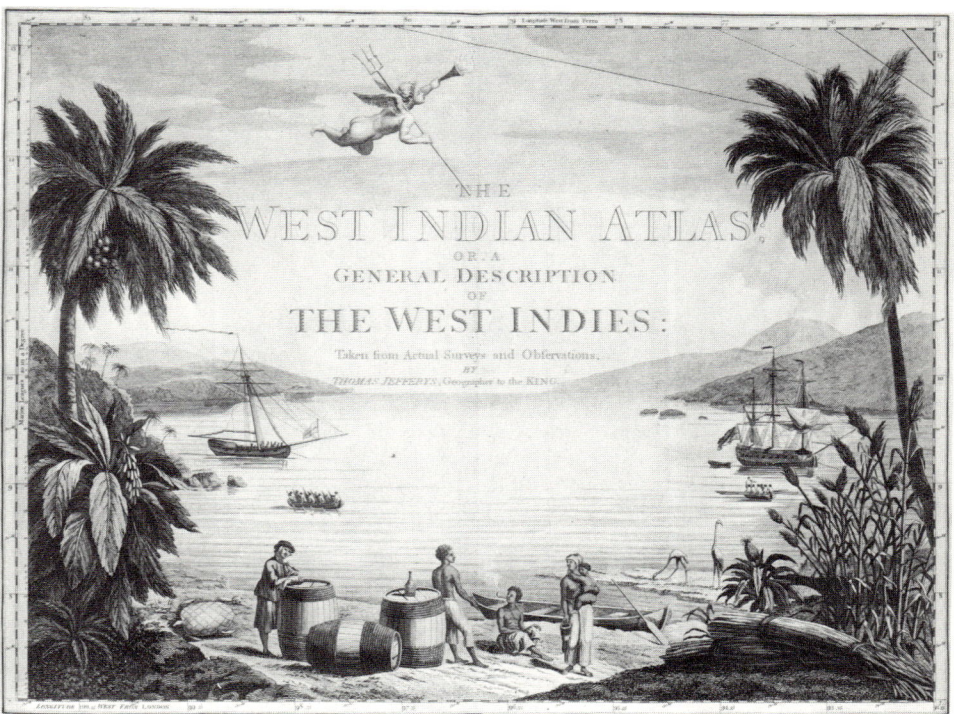

615

THE WEST INDIES

615
[A Scene in the West Indies] London. Printed for Robt. Sayer & John Bennett. Map and Print sellers No. 53 in Fleet Street, as the Act directs 20 Feby. 1775.
Etching 20 x 25¼ in.

Ornamentation for title page to Jefferys, *The West-India Atlas* (London, 1775). The scene depicts a tropical harbor with two small ships flying the British flag. In the foreground a British sailor leans against a hogshead. Lush foliage of bananas, coconuts, pineapples, and sugar cane frames the scene. Fame flies over the entire scene carrying a torch and trident.
LC–USZ62–46098

———Other impressions: In the 1777, the 1780, and the 1787 editions of this atlas. Another impression is in the French edition entitled *Atlas des Indes Occidentales* (Londres, 1777).

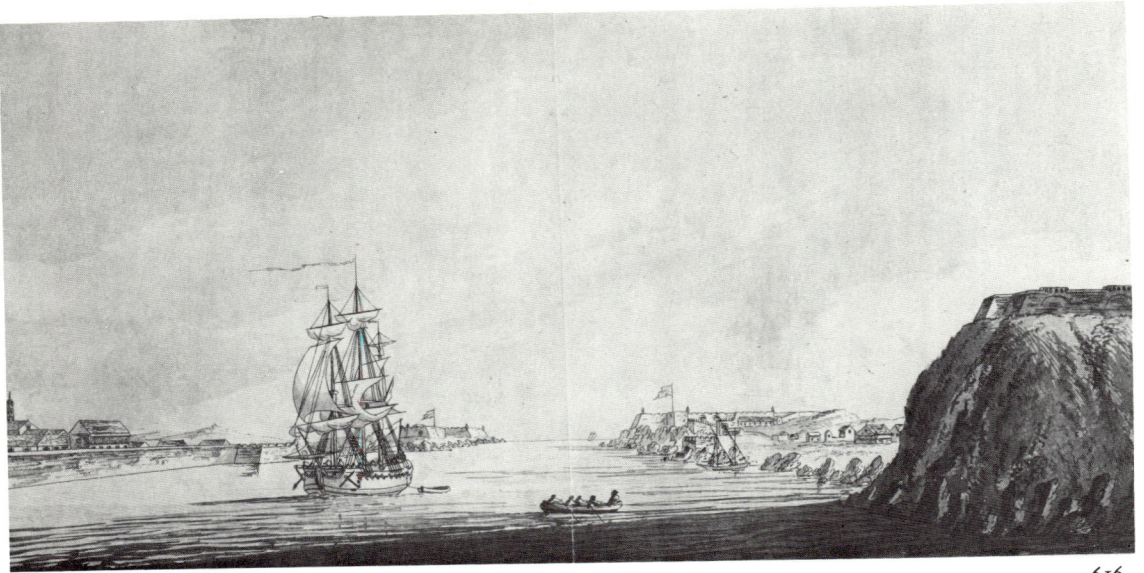
616

616
The Entrance of HAVANNAH, from within the Harbour. [J.F.W. Des Barres, 1774–81]
Aquatint with etching 9¾ x 17¾ in.

One of the finest harbors in the Northern Hemisphere, Havana (or Habana) is pictured here with its channel guarded by forts; the city itself is surrounded by a wall. At one time the most fortified city in Spanish America (its largest fort, La Cabaña, was completed in 1774), Havana was captured by the British in 1762 and held for one year. *The Atlantic Neptune*. Phillips 1198, v. 3, no. 67.
LC–USZ62–46051

616a
The HARBOUR and part of the TOWN of HAVANNAH. [J.F.W. Des Barres, 1774–81]
Aquatint with etching 9¼ x 18 in.

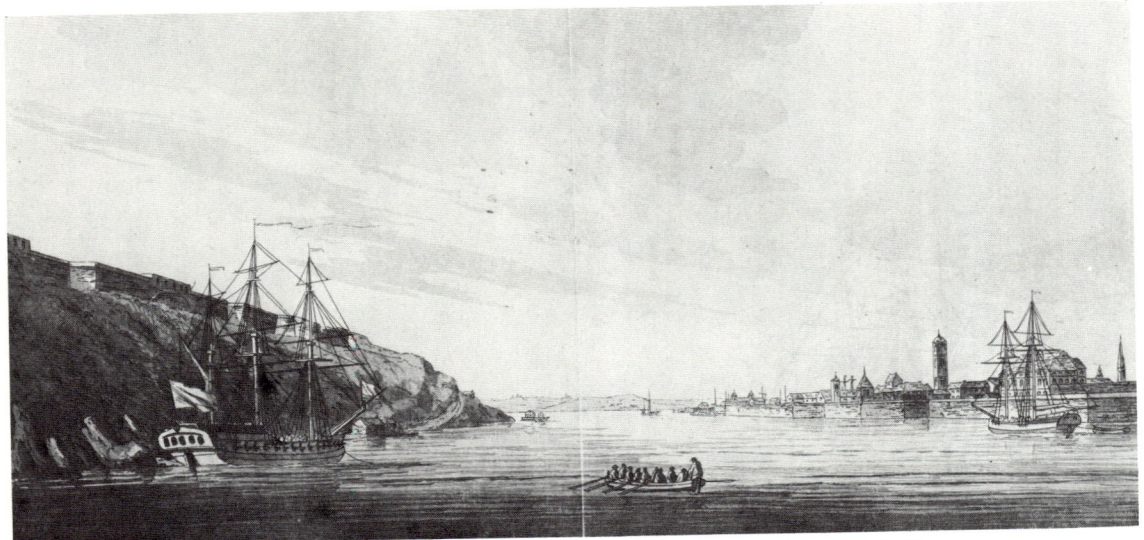
616a

From *The Atlantic Neptune*. Phillips 1198, v. 3, no. 67. LC–USZ62–46052

617

LE MOLE ST. NICOLAS DANS L'ISLE DE ST. DOMINGUE, Vu du Mouillage Tiré d'un Recueil de differens Ports des Isles Antilles dessinés en 1780. Reunis à la Collection des Ports de France, gravés par le Sr. Gouaz. N. Ozanne del. Jeanne Fa Ozanne sculp. [178?]

Line engraving 5⅞ x 12¾ in. (image)

This pier on the island of Dominica in the Windward Islands is identified as St. Nicolas Mole. The view of ships anchored in the port was done by Nicolas Ozanne (1728–1811), elder brother of Pierre (1737–1786), and by Jeanne-Françoise, their older sister. This family of French artists did different views of the French colonies at the time of the American Revolution. The younger sister, Marie-Jeanne, was the wife of Yves-Marie le Gouaz, engraver and author of a collection of more than 60 views of ports of France and the Antilles after the designs of Nicolas Ozanne. LC–USZ62–45374

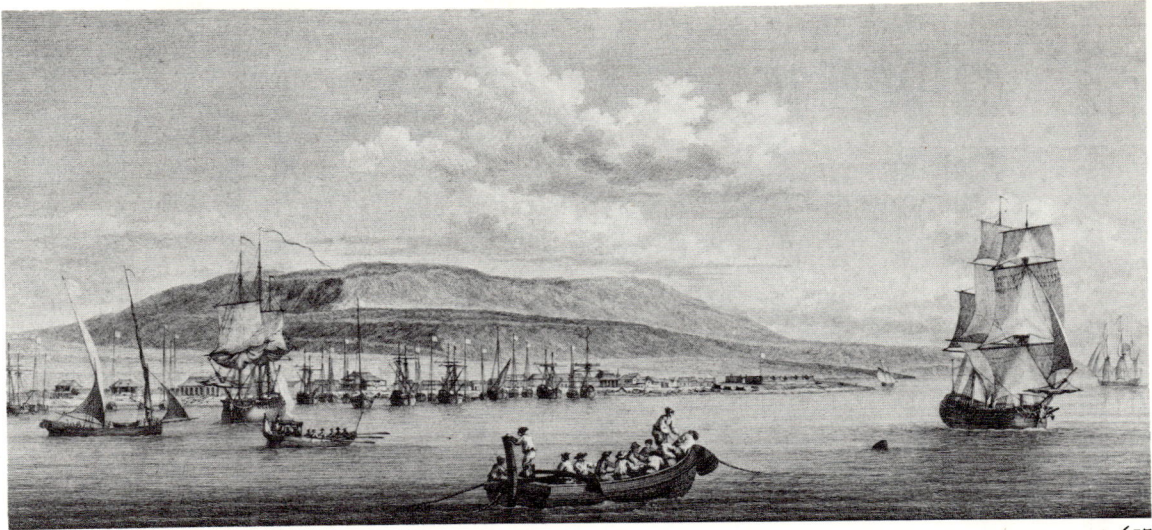
617

618

VEDUTA DI S. EUSTACHIO. N. Matraini del. J Ottaviani inc. [1777]

Etching 8¼ x 14 in.

View of St. Eustatius, an islet in the Leeward Islands belonging to the Dutch West Indies. Shown here is the principal settlement of Oranjestad, located between the island's two volcanic peaks. The legend identifies a fissure of a lake on the volcano at the right, the Dutch church, the fort, the English church, the wharf for unloading merchandise, the piazza of the customhouse, the town, the governor's residence, and the private Roman church. The island prospered during the American Revolution when it served as a supply base for the Colonies, but it declined with the British occupation in 1781. From *Atlante dell' America...* (Livorno, 1777), no. 22. LC–USZ62–46021

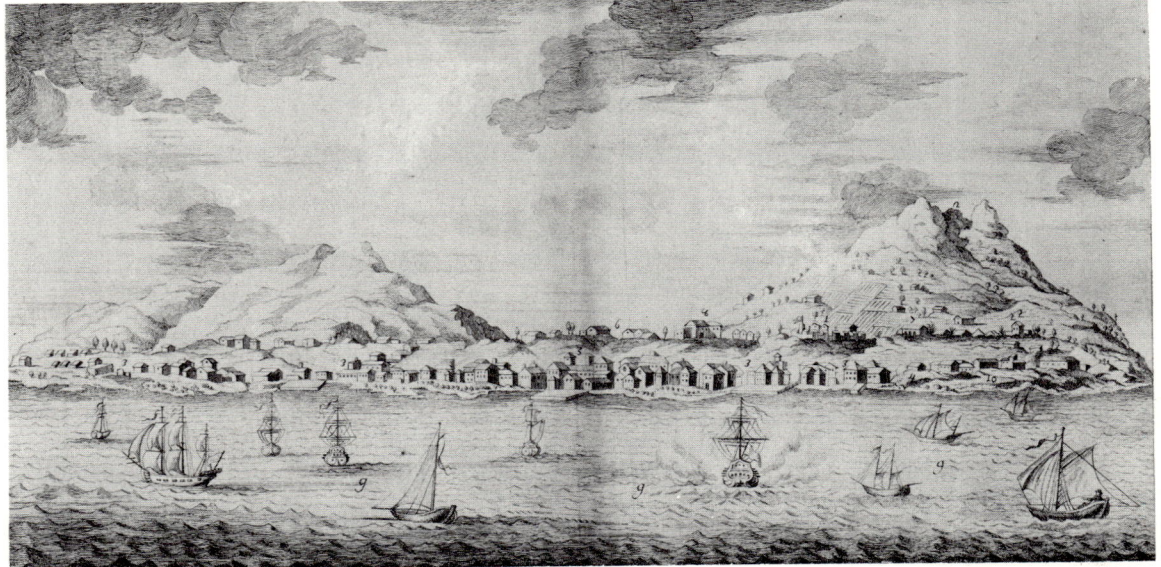
618

The TIMES are
𝔇𝔯𝔢𝔞𝔡𝔣𝔲𝔩,
𝔇𝔦𝔰𝔪𝔞𝔩
𝔇𝔬𝔩𝔢𝔣𝔲𝔩
𝔇𝔬𝔩𝔬𝔯𝔬𝔲𝔰, and
DOLLAR-LESS.

An Emblem of the Effects of the STAMP
Of the fatal Stamp

Thurfday, October 31, 1765.   THE   NUMB. 1195.

PENNSYLVANIA JOURNAL;
AND
WEEKLY ADVERTISER.

EXPIRING: In Hopes of a Refurrection to LIFE again.

I AM forry to be obliged to acquaint my Readers, that as The STAMP-ACT, is fear'd to be obligatory upon us after the *Firft of November* enfuing, (the *fatal To-morrow*) the Publifher of this Paper unable to bear the Burthen, has thought it expedient TO STOP awhile, in order to deliberate, whether any Methods can be found to elude the Chains forged for us, and efcape the infupportable Slavery, which it is hoped, from the laft Reprefentations now made againft that Act, may be effected. Mean while, I muft earneftly Requeft every Individual of my Subfcribers, many of whom have been long behind Hand, that they would immediately Difcharge their refpective Arrears that I may be able, not only to fupport myfelf during the Interval, but be better prepared to proceed again with this Paper, whenever an opening for that Purpofe appears, which I hope will be foon.   WILLIAM BRADFORD

Chapter IV

Cartoons and Allegories

619

This is the Place to affix the STAMP. [October 24, 1765]
Woodcut 1⅜ x 1⅜ in. (image)

A skull and crossbones placed at the bottom right corner of *The Pennsylvania Journal and Weekly Advertiser* for October 24, 1765. The articles and letters on this page expressed shock and anger at news of the Stamp Act.
LC–USZ62–242.

———For the skull and crossbones motif, see also the masthead for *The Pennsylvania Journal and Weekly Advertiser* for October 31, 1765. William Bradford reiterates his earlier woodcut with a funereal masthead and a black border around the page.
LC–USZ62–21637

———Another skull and crossbones with the caption, "Hereabouts will be the Place to affix the STAMP." In the lower right corner of *The Boston Gazette and Country Journal* for October 7, 1765.

620

THE TOMB-STONE. Here lieth the Body of WILLIAM DUKE OF CUMBERLAND &c. lamented by his Country, which he twice Sav'd. First by overcoming the joint forces of France and S———d, at the Battle of CULLODEN; and after by selecting a MINISTRY, out of those

619-1

virtuous few, who gloriously withstood GENERAL WARRANTS, AMERICAN STAMPS, EXTENSION OF EXCISE.———&c. &c. &c. Printed for Mr. Smith and Sold at the Woolpack in Long Acre, near Drury Lane, London. [October 1765]
Etching 17⅛ x 9¾ in.

In the foreground is a sarcophagus adorned with bas-reliefs of Britannia and America. On the top are George Grenville, Lord Bute, and the Duke of Bedford. Dr. W. Scott, portrayed as a small dog labeled "AntiSejanus" is on a leash, signifying control of his anti-Bute activities. On the ground from left to right are Lord Sandwich (Jemmy Twitcher), the Earl of Halifax, Earl Temple, the Devil, and two churchmen. One of the churchmen is probably Warburton. This cartoon satirizes the joy among corrupt elements over the death of the Duke of Cumberland who helped repeal the American Stamp Act. CPPS 4124
LC–USZ62–45397

621

ANTISEJANUS. Drink deep, or taste not the Portereal Spring [1765]
Etching 10½ x 7¼ in.

This cartoon criticizes the Rev. Dr. W. Scott who supported repeal of the Stamp Act. He is dressed in a slovenly manner and surrounded by articles of ridicule: an empty tankard, an owl sitting on a keg of spirits, and a donkey pegasus. The aphorism below adds to the sentiment:

A Parson in Politics is like a Monkey in a Toyship—
He may do much Mischief, but cannot possibly do any Good.
    Witness (being first duly STAMPT)

CPPS 4127 LC–USZ62–45398

622

The Great Financier, or British Economy for the Years 1763, 1764, 1765. Publd. according to Law. [1765]
Etching 12½ x 8½ in. (image)

Pictured is George Grenville trying to balance the budget with Pitt, a Frenchman,

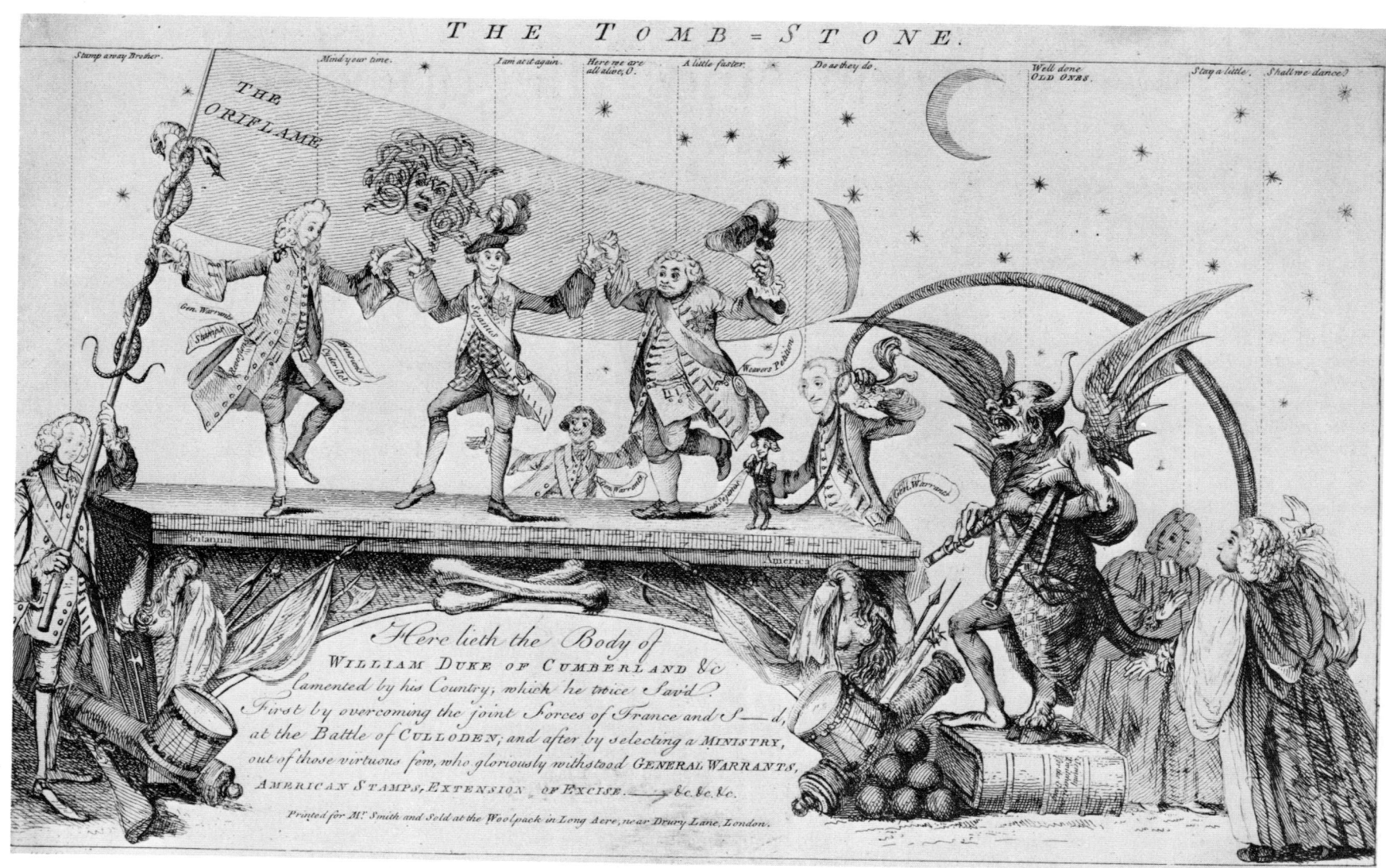

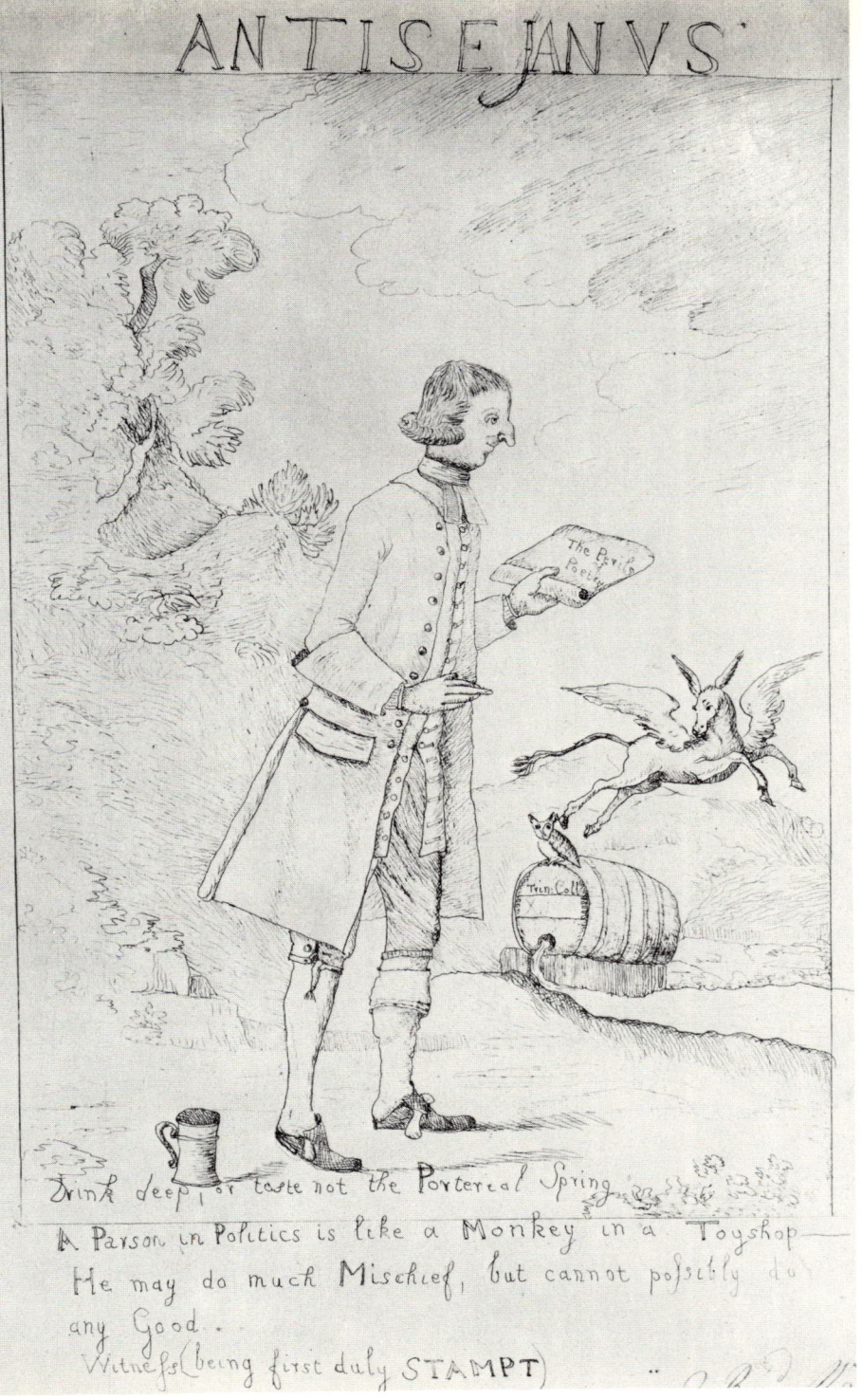

a Spaniard, Britannia, and a figure representing economy. The American Indian plays a prominent role by wearing a yoke designated "Taxed without Representation" and kneeling before the English Ministers. He holds a large sack of dollars and tells the Englishmen, "Commerce will outweigh it [the deficit]. The song at the bottom reads:

1
Our Budget is empty, & upwards it flies,
But our Debt is too unweildy & sullen to rise;
Such Wonders our Grand Financier can dispense,
That he'll pay off ten Millions by saving ten Pence.
　　　　　　　　　　Derry down.

2
For Conquests, or Commerce he cares not a Straw,
Nor if French, Dutch or Spaniards, in Trade give us Law;
Oeconomy only shall cure every Evil,
Pitt, Merchants & Soldiers may go to the Devil.
　　　　　　　　　　Derry down.

3
Sea Captains that once fill'd the World with Alarms,
Chang'd to pilfring Tide Waiters dishonour their Arms;
But let not rash Critics his measures upbraid,
He discharges our Debts by destroying our Trade.
　　　　　　　　　　Derry down.

4
America groans & petitions in vain,
Her grief is his Toy, & her Loss is his Gain;
For ways and means curious his Brain he ne'er racks,
He stops all her wealth & then lays on his Tax.
　　　　　　　　　　Derry down.

5
See the Mimick of Business sap Britain's proud Throne,
How her Spear broken lies & Her Honours are flown;
But Oeconomy quickly will set all to rights,
Such Legerdemain is ye bravest of Sights.
　　　　　　　　　　Derry down.

6
His wonderful Budget will ruin our Foes
While his saveall most sweetly perfumes Britains Nose
Oh! may he like his Budget triumphant arise
Whilst a Lord helps his nearer Approach to the Skies.
　　　　　　　　　　Derry down.

CPPS 4128 LC-USZ62-45399

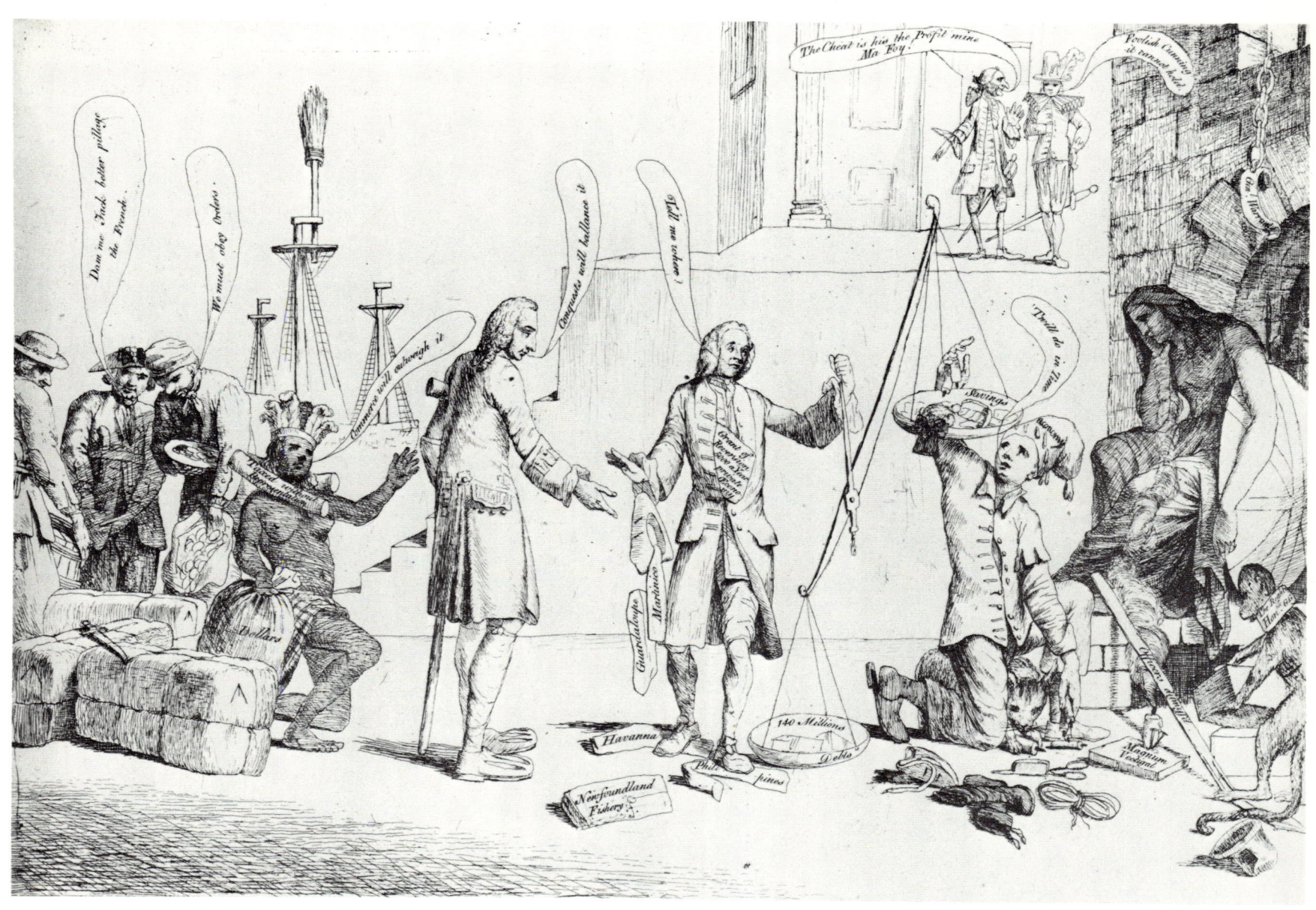

622

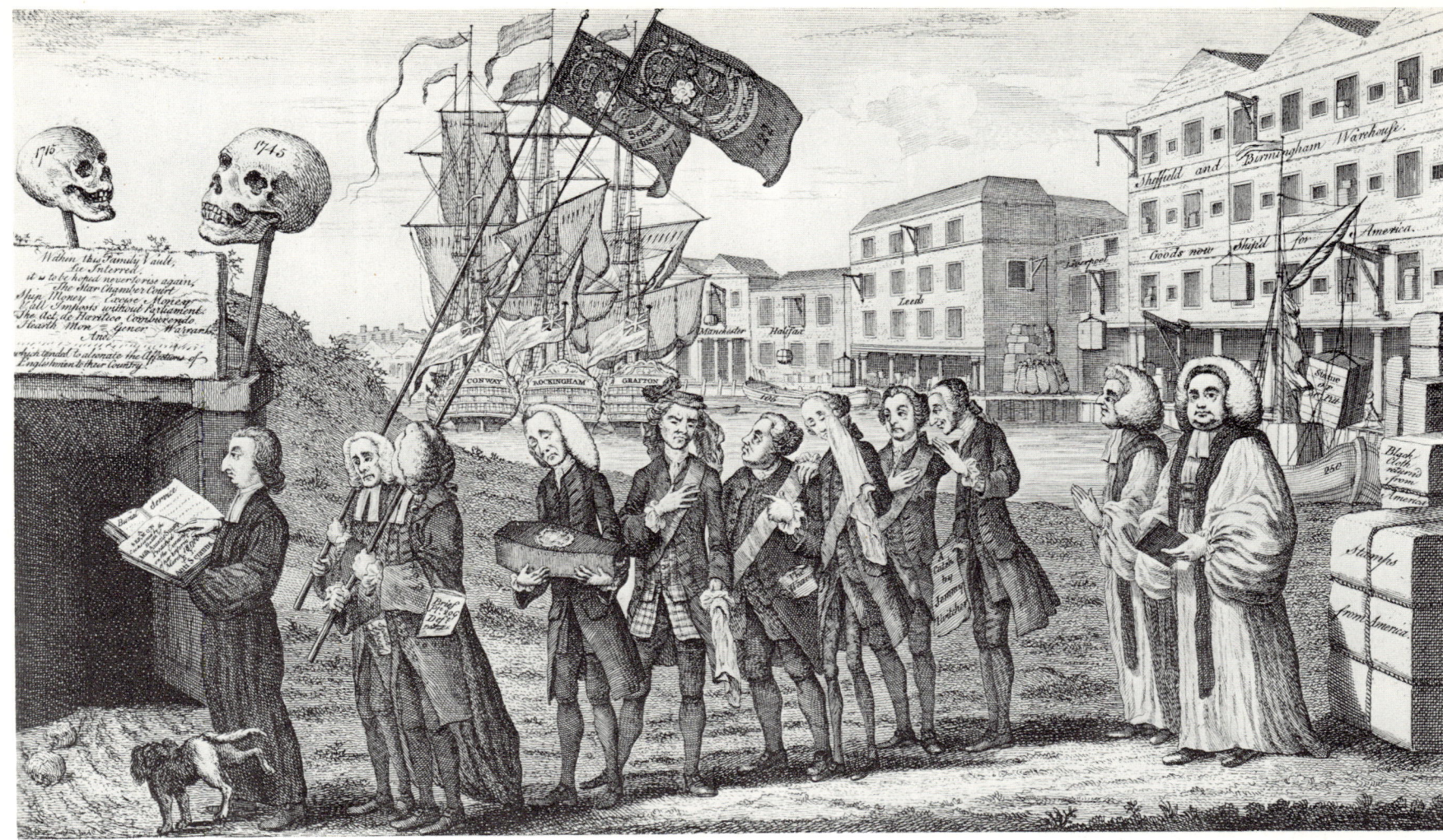

623

THE REPEAL. or the Funeral Procession, of
MISS AMERIC-STAMP. [March 18, 1766]
Mixed method 10 x 14 in.

This cartoon predicts the flourishing of English commerce with the repeal of the Stamp Act. The print provides the following explication of the complicated allegory:

Over the Vault are placed two Skeleton Heads, Their elevation on poles, and the dates of the two Rebellion Years [1715 and 1745] sufficiently shew what party they espoused, and in what cause they suffered an ignominious Exit.

The reverend Mr. Anti-Sejanus [Rev. Dr. W. Scott] (who under that signature hackney'd his pen in support of the Stamps) leads the procession as officiating Priest, with the burial service and funeral sermon in his hands.

Next follow two eminent Pillars of the Law, [Alexander Wedderburn and Fletcher Norton] supporting two black flags, on which are delineated the Stamps with the White Rose and Thistle interwoved an expressive design, supposed to have been originally contrived on the 10 of June. The significative motto Semper Eadem is preserved, but the Price of the Stamp is changed to three farthings, an important sum taken from the Budget. The numbers 122 and 71 declare the minority which fought under these Banners.

Next appears the honourable Mr. George Stamp, [George Grenville] full of Grief and dispair, carrying his favourite Childs Coffin Miss Americ Stamp, who was born in 1765, and died hard in 1766.

Immediately after, follows the chief Mourner Sejanus [Lord Bute].

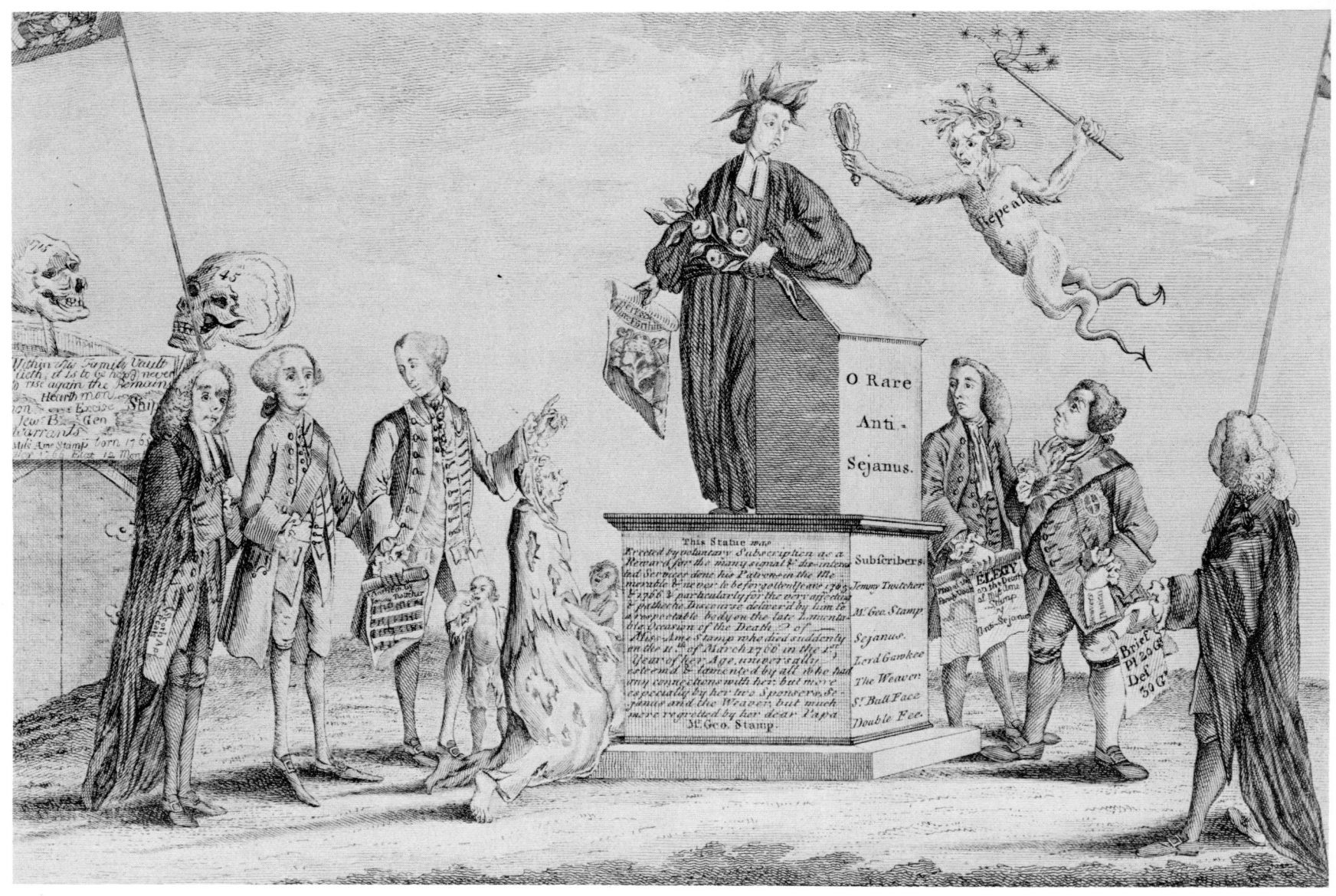

Then his Grace of Spital Fields, [Duke of Bedford] and Lord Gawkee [Earl Temple].

After these Jemmy Twitcher, [Earl of Sandwich] with a Catch, by way of funeral anthem, & by his side his friend and partner Mr. Falconer Donaldson of Halifax [Lord Halifax].

The rear is brought up by two right reverend Fathers of the Church [Warburton holding a book].

These few mourners are seperated from the joyful scene which appears on the River Thames, where three first rate ships are riding. Viz. the Conway, Rockingham, and Grafton [names of ministers who supported the repeal]. Along the opposite shore, stand open Warehouses for the several goods of different manufactoring towns from which Cargoes are now shipping for America. Among these is a large Case containing the Statue of Mr. Pitt, which is heaving on board a Boat No. 250, there is another boat taking in goods nearer the first Rates, which is No. 105. These Numbers will ever be held in esteem by the true Sons of Liberty.

See CPPS 4140 LC–USZ62–1505

———————Another impression in the Peter Force Collection in the Manuscript Division.

624

THE REPEAL, OR THE FUNERAL OF MISS AME-STAMP. [March 18, 1766]
Etching 8¼ x 13 in.

A cartoon similar to item 623. Described in CPPS 4140. LC–USZ62–21264

———————Another impression. In the Peter Force Collection in the Manuscript Division.

———————Another copy. Same as above except with no explanation and the designation: "Printed for & sold by Carington Bowles, No. 69 in St. Pauls Church Yard, London."

625

THE STATUE, or the ADORATION of the WISE-MEN of the—WEST, Sold by Mr. Smith No. 45 Long Acre, and Mr. Clagget Junr. in Sugar Loaf Court, Fanchurch Buildings London. Publish'd April 21st 1766
Mixed method 12 x 8¼ in.

A sequel to "The Repeal," item 624. Dr. W. Scott stands on a pedestal holding a picture of the stamp which would no longer be used in America and an apple tree branch representing the cider tax. A wife and two children of a weaver kneel before Scott, and members of the Ministry look on. From left to right the members are Wedderburn, the Earl of Halifax, Lord Sandwich (Jemmy Twitcher), George Grenville, Duke of Bedford, and Fletcher Norton. A Fury flies up with a hand mirror for Dr. Scott to examine himself. CPPS 4141 LC–USZ62–45400

626

A VIEW of the OBELISK erected under LIBERTY-TREE in BOSTON on the Rejoicings for the Repeal of the—Stamp-Act 1766. To every Lover of LIBERTY, this Plate is humbly dedicated, by her true born SONS, in BOSTON New England. Paul Revere sculp
Etching 9⅜ x 13⅛ in. (image)

Shows the four sides of the monument: 1) America in distress, anticipating the total loss of liberty, 2) she implores the aid of her patrons, 3) she endures the conflict for a short season, 4) she has her liberty restored by the royal hand of George III. Some of the 16 people depicted at the top of the monument are Duke of York, Marquis of Rockingham, Queen Charlotte, King George III, Gen. H. S. Conway, Colonel Barré, William Pitt, Lord Dartmouth, Alderman Beckford, Charles Townshend, Lord George Sackville, Dennis De Berdt, John Wilkes, and Lord Camden. Most of the figures have little resemblance to the real people. See Brigham, *Paul Revere's Engravings* (Worcester, Mass., 1954). This print is probably a restrike done after 1839. LC–USZ62–22385

627

THE NEW COUNTRY DANCE, as DANCED at C****. July the 30th. 1766. Sold by J. Pridden in Fleet Street. Price 6ᵈ. [July 30, 1766]
Etching 13 x 8¼ in.

Characterizations of John Wilkes, the Earl of Bute, the Prince of Wales, William Pitt, America (a half-naked Indian woman), the devil, Henry Fox (Lord Holland), Charles Townshend, the Earl of Northington, George III, the Earl of Rockingham, the Duke of Newcastle, Earl Temple, Frank Hayman, and Lord Winchelsea, engaged in a political dance. A song at the bottom:

> Here You see de Country Dance, Sir,
> See each Couple how dey Prance, Sir,
> First of all dat Foot to Foot a
> Is de _____ and Lord Boot a.
>   Doodle doodle doo

> 2
> Next You see Lord Cheat'em come a
> With America and Rum a,
> His ambition's Pow'r & Pelf, Sir,
> He serv'd You, to serve Himself, Sir.
>   Doodle &c.

> 3
> There C__rl__s T__th__d cuts a Caper,
> Weather-cock like turn'd by Vapour;
> While Britannia's fill'd with Dread, Sir,
> Topsy turvey on Her Head Sir.
>   Doodle &c.

> 4
> Next to Him is N__th__n a,
> With his Miss, and full of Fun a;
> He can __and Crack his Jest, Sir,
> Ther's his Bumper, to the Best, Sir,
>   Doodle &c.

> 5
> Fox is to Old Nick attach'd a,
> Ne'er were Partners better match'd a,
> Frenchman, Spaniard's very merry;
> Laughing at such Hey down derry.
>   Doodle &c.

> 6
> But whose Fiddler to these Dancers?
> These great patriotic Financers?
> Why the__, or He's bely'd Sir,
> With a Sawney at each Side, Sir.
>   Doodle &c.

> 7
> See to Paris, to be free a,
> Wilkes retreat for Liberty a;
> Why the Devil's all this Fuss, Sir,
> He's bewitch'd as well as us, Sir.
>   Doodle &c.

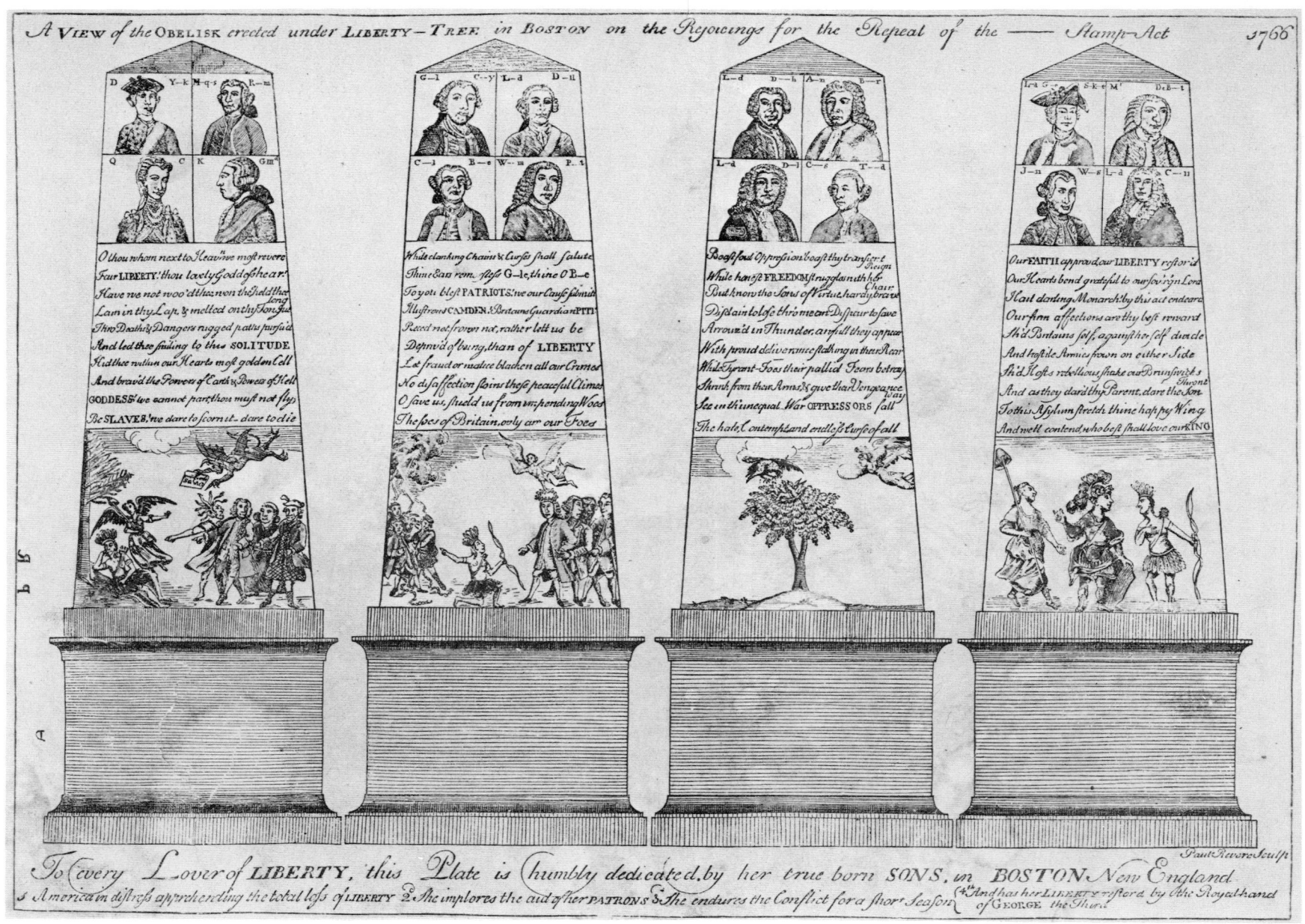

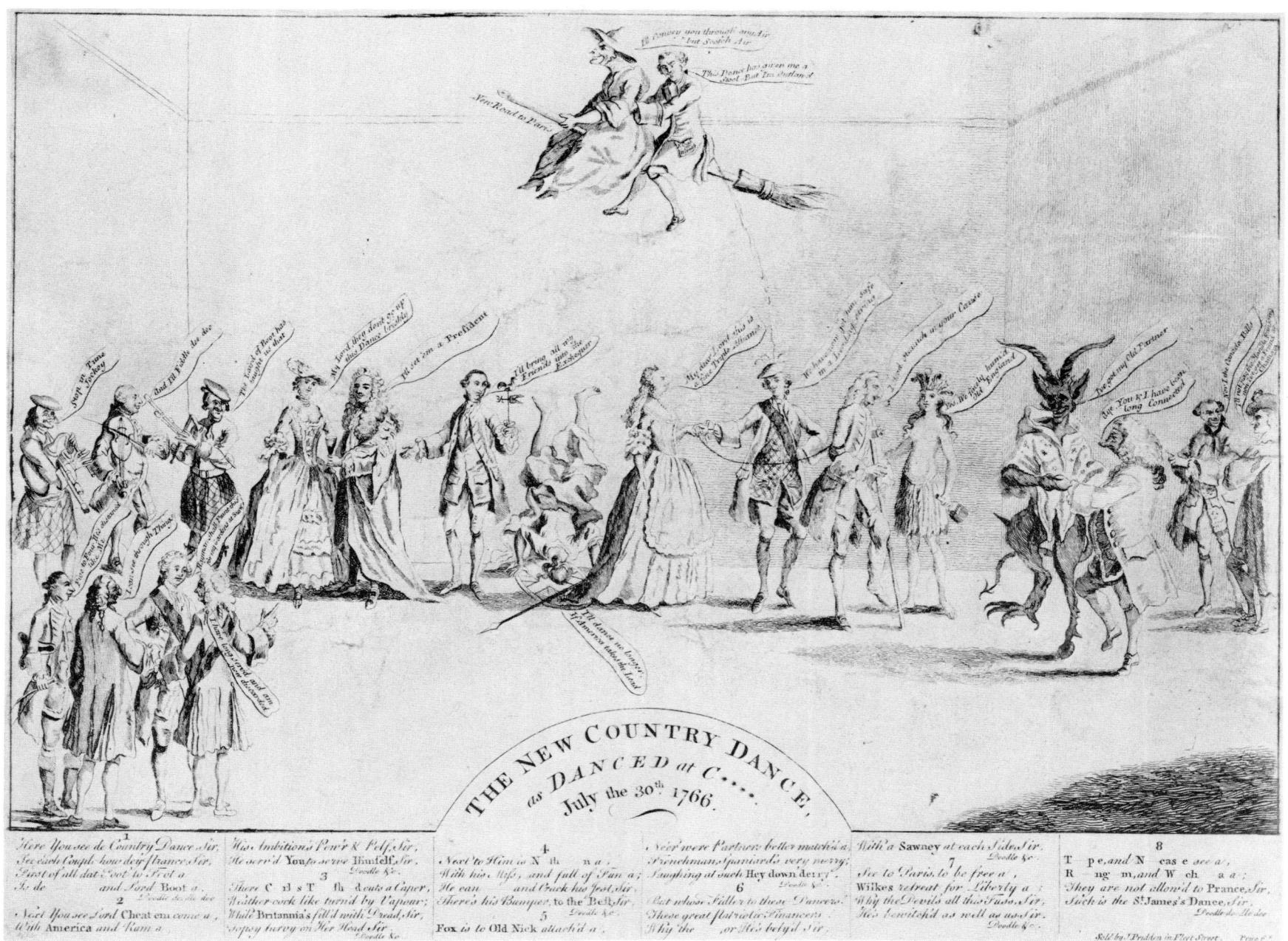

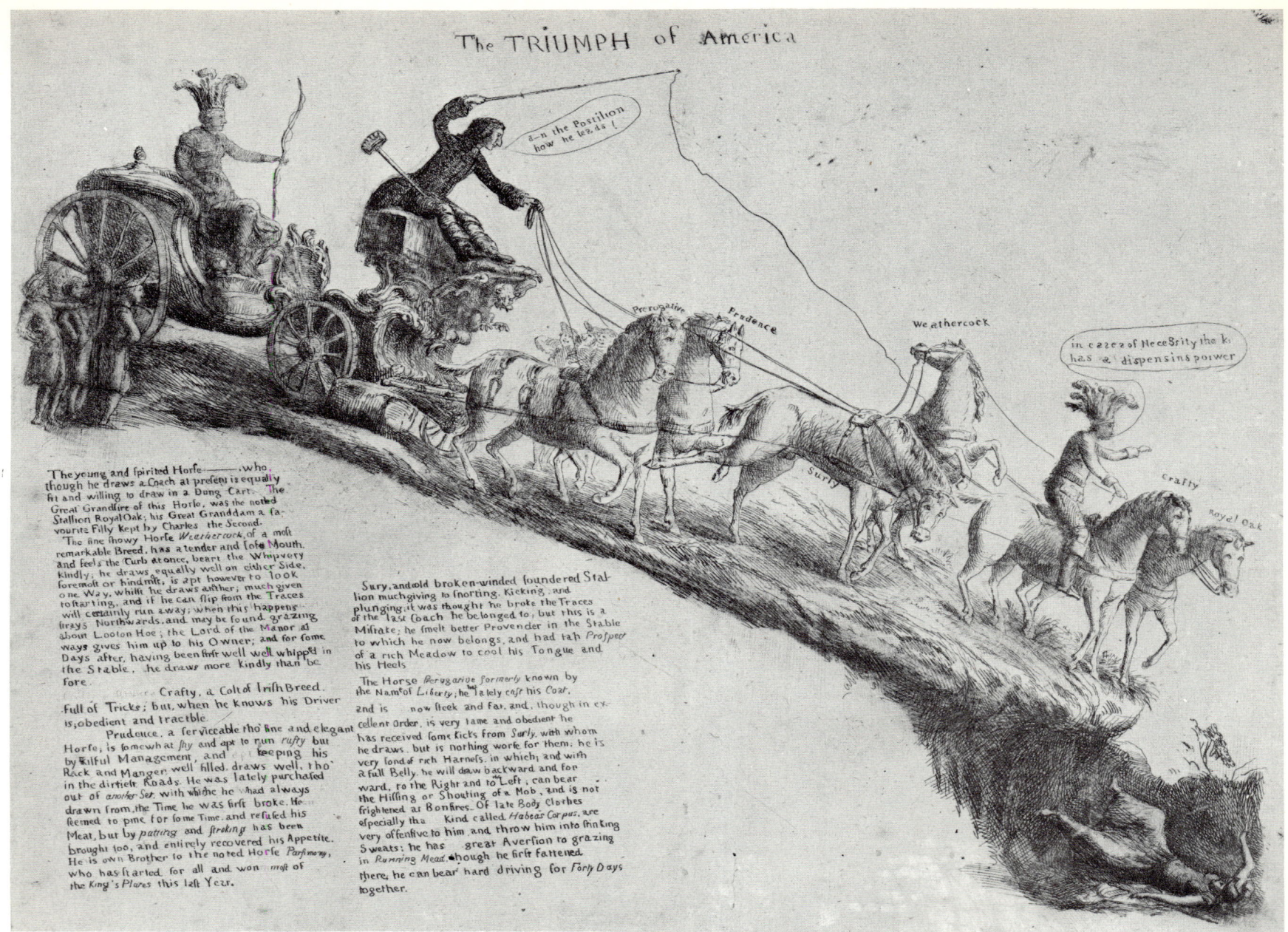

T____pe, and N____cas e see a,⁸
R____ng__m, and W__ch__a a;
They are not allow'd to Prance, Sir,
Such is the St James's Dance, Sir.
                    Doodle doodle doo

CPPS 4147 LC-USZ62-45401

628

The TRIUMPH of America. [August 1766]
Etching 8 x 10 in.

America is represented as an Indian seated in a landau with William Pitt as the driver. The horses represent the Duke of Grafton, Charles Townshend, the Earl of Shelburne, H.S. Conway, Robert Henley (Earl of Northington), and Lord Camden. The ministers hold the carriage back from falling off the cliff, and another Indian, the postilion, states that the King has a "dispensing power" when necessary. Britannia lies at the bottom of the cliff; she will be crushed if the carriage continues. Pitt had recently formed a new Ministry designed to eliminate dissension, but his choice of ministers from disparate factions stalled government processes, and his acceptance of a peerage made him unpopular. Burke's description of this Ministry might well describe this cartoon:

a tesselated pavement without cement; here a bit of blackstone, and there a bit of white; patriots and courtiers, king's friends and republicans; whigs and tories; treacherous friends and open enemies . . . a very curious show, but utterly unsafe to touch and unsure to stand on.

Works of Edmund Burke (1815), ii, 420. CPPS 4152 LC-USZ62-17241

629

A POLITICAL, ANATOMICAL, SATIRICAL, LECTURE on HEADS and No HEADS; as Exhibited at St. J———s's 1766.
Mixed method 5⅞ x 9¼ in. (image)

The Earl of Bute holds up a bust of Pitt showing the features to a devil and a group of courtesans. The text below identifies the bust:

This is the Head of one of those celebrated Personages called Patriots; it is taken from the Statue now carving, to be sent to America; he was formerly stiled the G____t C_____r, he gained the Name of GREAT from the Great Number of People he had deceived; he made them believe that he had nothing so much at Heart as their Interest; that his Country was more dear to him than himself, or his Wife, that Gold and Titles could never seduce him to act contrary to the Interest of his Country; but on touching his Temples with an Earl's Coronet, the Mask fell off, and instead of the candid, placid, true Patriot, he appeared the corrupted, selfwill'd conceited, avaricious, and superserviceable Courtier, on his Brows were written in large Characters, PEERAGE.

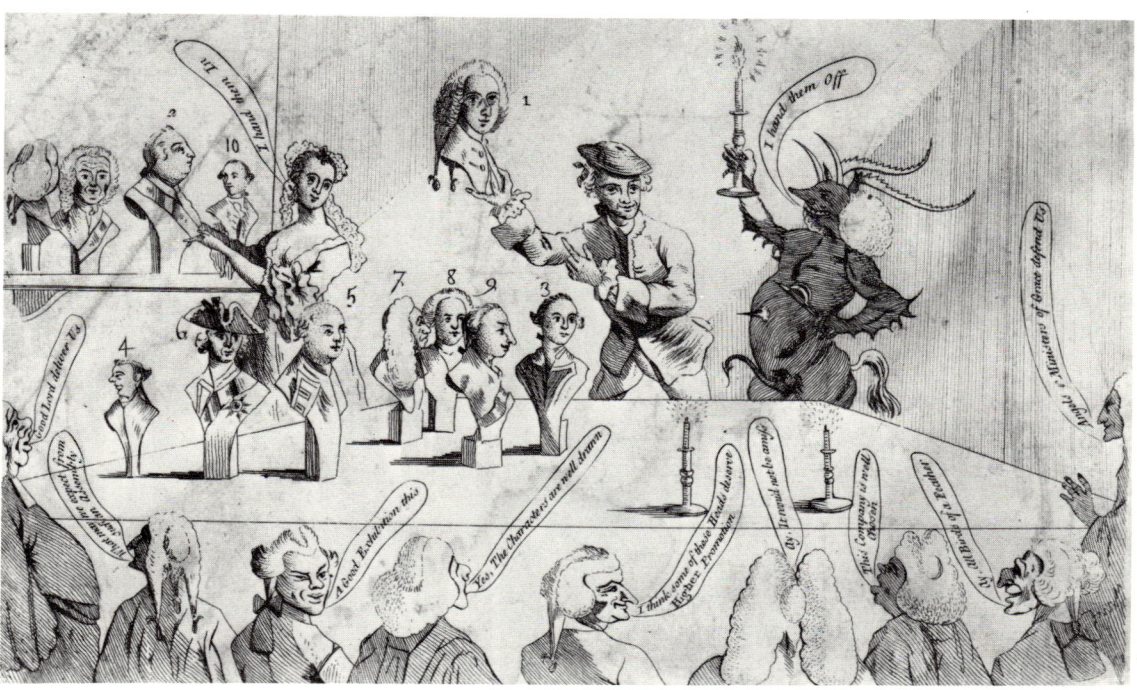

629

William Pitt, known as the Great Commoner, is here condemned because he assumed a title and re-entered the Government. This broadside indicates the ironic situation of a man's statue being sent to America to celebrate his repeal of the Stamp Act while he was under the influence of corrupt officials. Cf. item 623 for reference to Pitt's statue sent to America. Another bust represents George III, who is described as lacking the power of action. Other ministers have charges against them.
LC-USZ62-46658

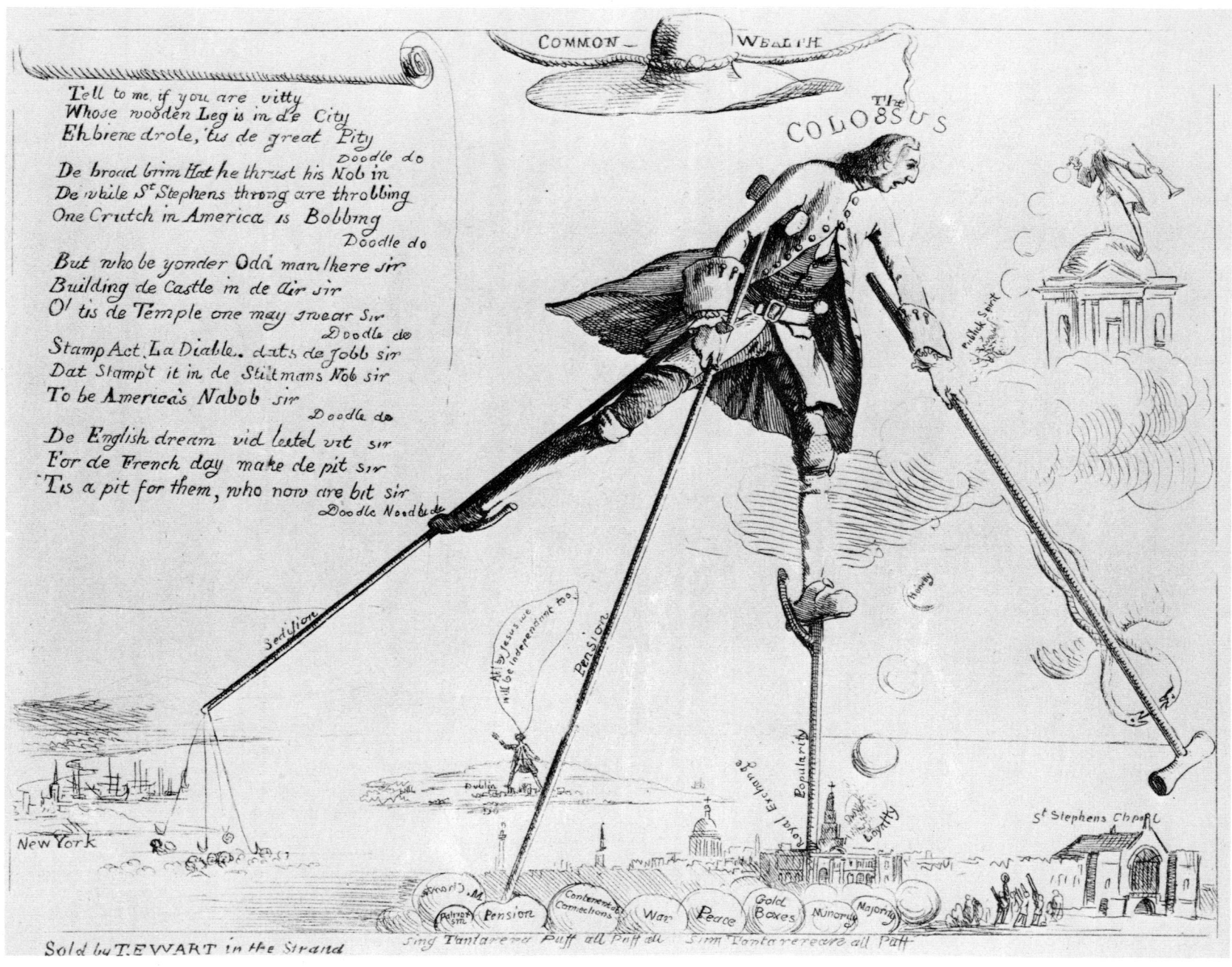

630

COMMON-WEALTH. THE COLO8SUS. Sold by T. EWART in the Strand. [1766]

Etching 7 x 9 in.

William Pitt straddles the world on two stilts. The one designated sedition dangles hooks before a group of people near New York; the other labeled popularity rests in London. He is supported by a crutch designated pension which rests among bubbles entitled "M. Charta," "Patriotism," "Pension," "Continental Connections," "War," "Peace," "Gold Boxes," "Minority," "Majority." The bubbles "loyalty" and "publick spirit" break in their fall from a temple in the sky where Earl Temple is blowing them. A song to the left reads:

> Tell to me if you are vitty
> Whose wooden Leg is in de City
> Eh biene, tis de great Pity
>   Doodle do
>
> De broad brim Hat he thrust his Nob in
> De while St Stephens throng are throbbing
> One Crutch in America is Bobbing
>   Doodle do
>
> But who be yonder Odd man there sir
> Building de Castle in de Air sir
> O'tis de Temple one may swear Sir
>   Doodle do
>
> Stamp Act, La Diable. dats de Jobb sir
> Dat Stamp't it in de Stiltmans Nob sir
> To be America's Nabob sir
>   Doodle do
>
> De English dream vid leetel vit sir
> For de French day make de pit sir
> Tis a pit for them, who now are bit sir.
>   Doodle Noodle do

CPPS 4162 LC–USZ62–45402

———————Another copy without imprint and with fewer details.

631

AMERIQUE. [1766]

Etching 2¾ x 2¼ in. (image)

America pictured as a woman with a skirt

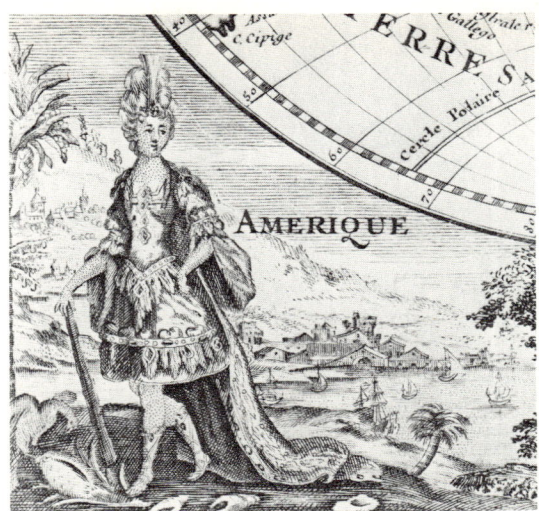

631

made of feathers. Tropical port in the background. Border ornament for a map entitled "Mappe-monde Dresse ... en 1741, par Mrs. Tchirikcow et de l'Isle ... par le Chr. de Beaurain. ..." From Brion de la Tour, *Atlas Ecclesiastique* (Paris, 1766), no. 1.
LC–USZ62–46089

632

The Colonies Reduced. Its Companion. Design'd and Engrav'd for the Political Register. [1767]

Mixed method 2⅜ x 3⅞ in. and 3½ x 3⅞ in. (image)

Two pictures printed on a single sheet. Britannia seen dismembered of limbs designated Virginia, Pennsylvania, New York, and New England. Inactive ships are in the background; a broken tree and olive branch are in the foreground. The second picture shows Britannia attacked by the Earl of Bute who holds up her skirt so that Spain and France can attack her buttocks. France, meanwhile, steals away America dressed as an Indian, a Dutchman steals a ship, and a serpent attacks

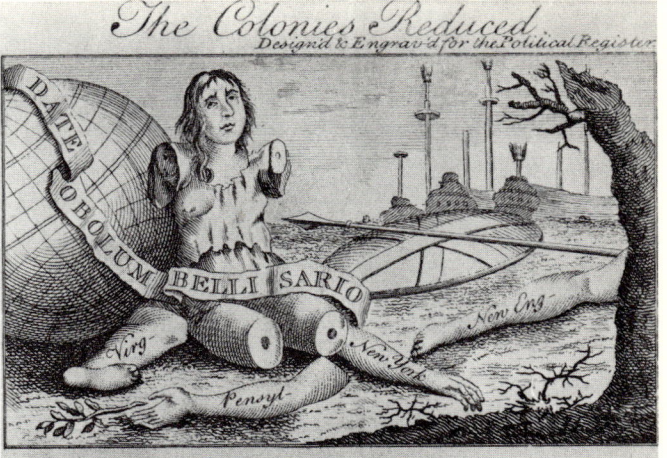
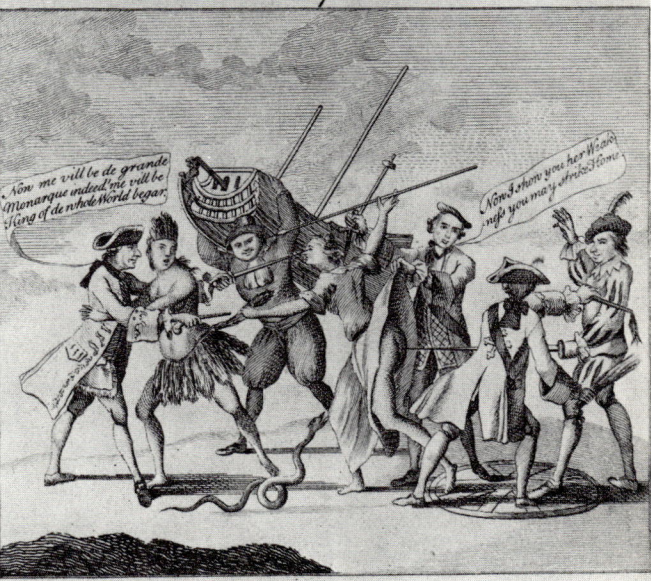

632

Britannia. These pictures show that the dismemberment of the Colonies from the body of England will result in the loss of trade and, thus, the eventual destruction of the British Empire. CPPS 4183 LC–USZ62–34866

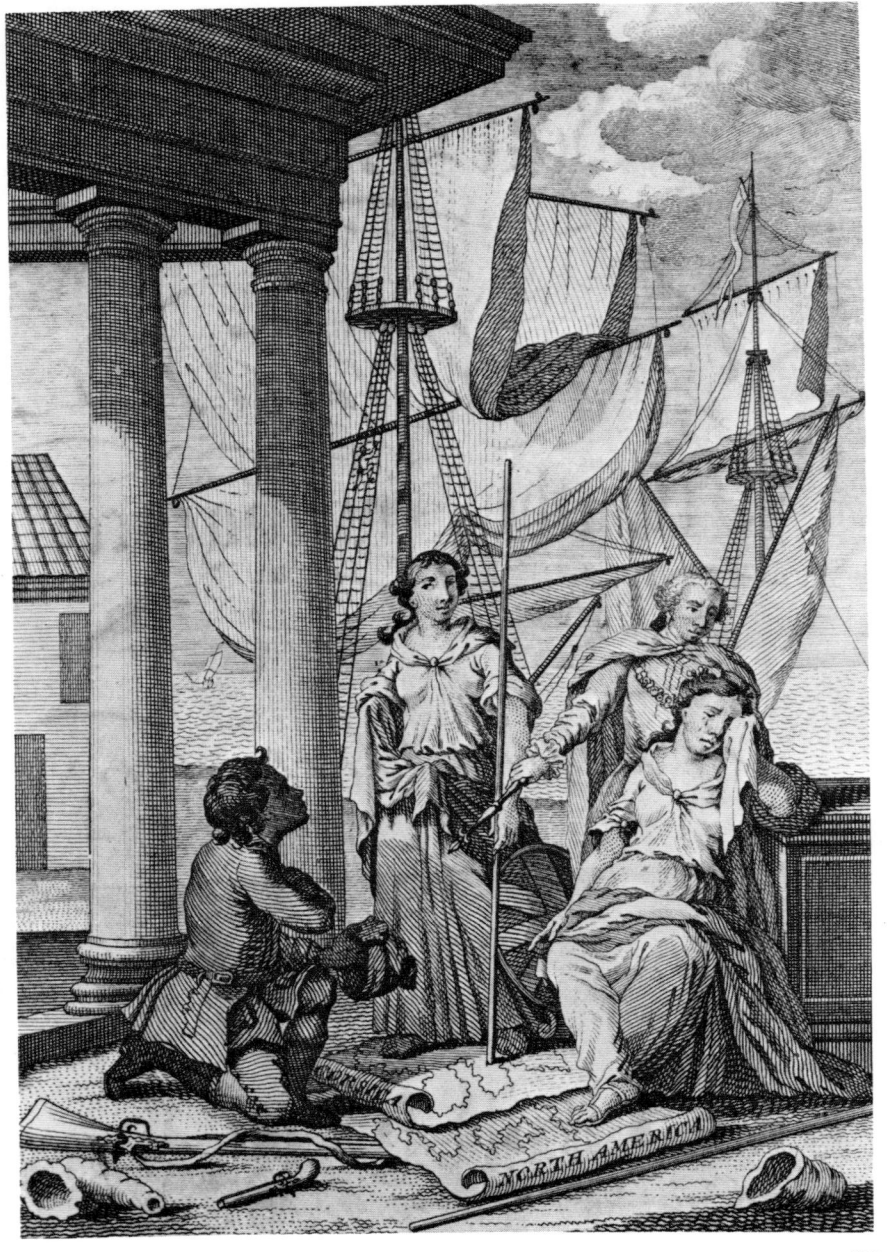

635

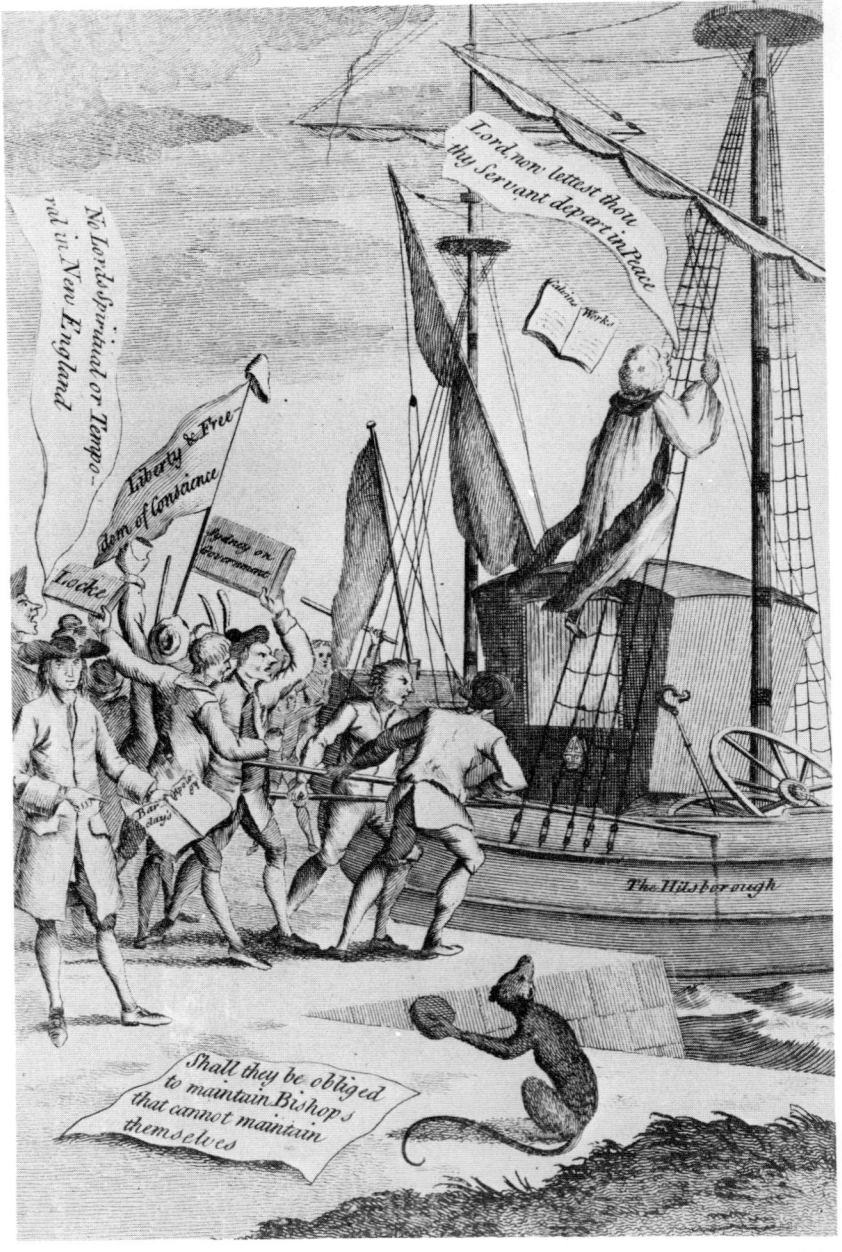

636

633

[A Christian figure appears to an Indian—a cartouche, 1767]

Etching 5¾ x 6¼ in. (image)

An Indian in a skirt made of feathers or leaves sees a woman in the sky holding a cross. Wild animals are around the Indian on the ground. These figures form the top and the bottom of a cartouche on a map entitled "L'Amérique Septentrionale et Méridionale ... par le sr. Robert" from Julien, *Le Théatre du Monde* (Paris, 1768), no. 54.

634

[America and two children—a cartouche, 1768?]

Etching 8½ x 7½ in. (image)

America is a beautiful, naked woman; her children are playing and working among the animals and foliage. From a map entitled "Amerique Septentrionale ... Par le Sr. d'Anville" in Julien, *Le Théatre du Monde* (Paris, 1768), no. 56.

————Another copy. "London Printed for John Bowles at the Black Horse in Cornhill, & Carington Bowles next the Chapter House in St. Pauls Church Yard." [1755–71?] 6 x 6½ in. (image). This cartouche is on a map entitled "A Map on the Whole Continent of America" in Palairet, [*Collection of Maps*] (London, 1755–71), no. 2.

635

Avaunt ye troublers of a World's repose. [1768]

Mixed method 7⅛ x 3¾ in.

Liberty weeps for the cause of a commoner who kneels before her. Maps of Corsica and North America are at her feet. With her are George III and Britannia supporting the cause of the commoners. The verse below the picture reads:

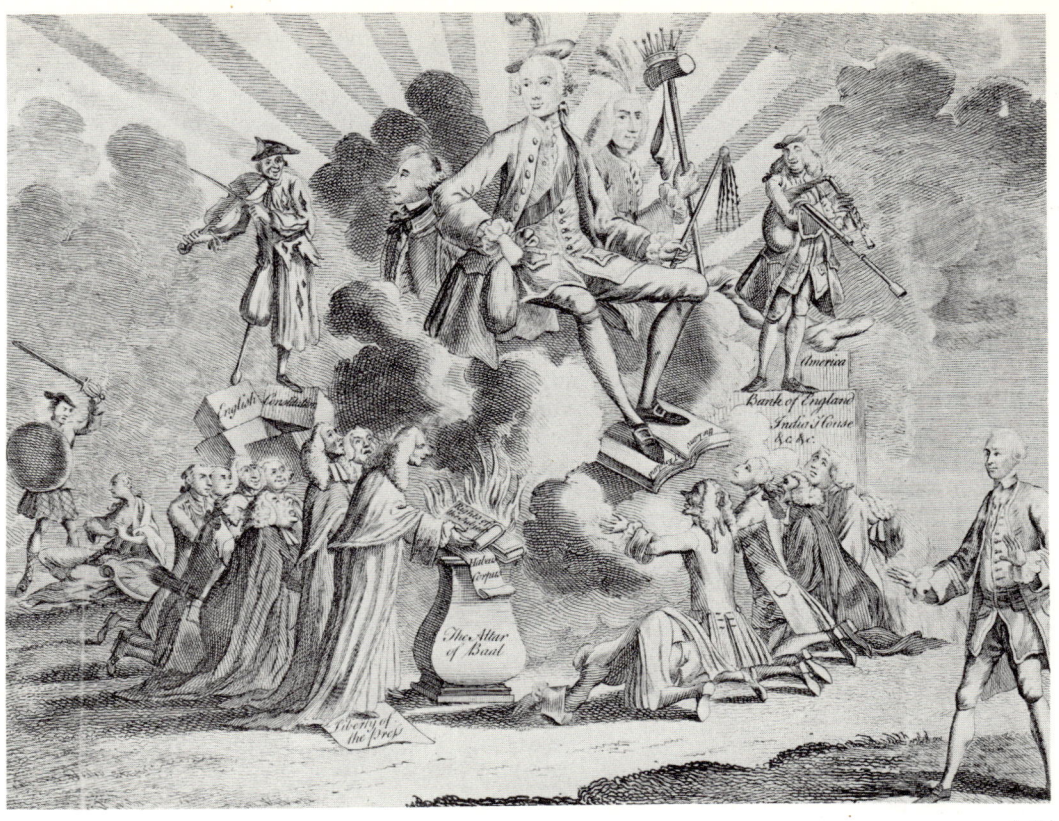

637

Avaunt ye troublers of a World's repose.
No more your base destructive schemes disclose:
For GEORGE shall yet support the fainting Fair,
Restore her Peace, & shield her from Despair.

From *The London Magazine*, 1768, frontispiece. LC–USZ62–45496

636

[An Attempt to Land a Bishop in America, 1768]

Mixed method 6 x 3¾ in.

American colonists chase an Anglican bishop onto a ship named the *Hilsborough*. They wave books entitled "Locke" and "Sydney on Government" and throw a copy of "Calvin's Works" after him. After being appointed Secretary of State for the Colonies in 1768, Lord Hillsborough supported Archbishop Secker's plan to send a bishop to North America. The bishop was never sent, but this cartoon shows what might have happened if he had come to America at this time. CPPS 4227 LC–USZ61–78

637

The North Star. [1768]

Mixed method 7½ x 5¾ in. (image)

Lord Bute sits on a cloud with a whip and money bag. To his left sits William Pitt, the

Earl of Chatham, with Indian feathers in his hair and a gouty foot resting on a pillar designated "America." Other figures participating in the destruction of English liberties resemble Grafton, Warburton, Mansfield, the Earl of Hertford, Northington, Fletcher Norton, Rochford, and Granby. A ragged English sailor fiddles, and the English Constitution crumbles beneath him. Wilkes looks on in horror. This cartoon reflects the grave concern of Englishmen for the nation's problems, which many saw as caused by the Scottish influences of Bute and others. This is shown explicitly by the figure of a Scotsman martyring Britannia with a broadsword. Chatham was one of the main hopes for such people as Wilkes, but he is preceded here by Bute. Pitt's gouty foot and crutch symbolize his illness, and a beggar's pouch and coronet show his subservience to the King due to his title and pension. CPPS 4229 LC–USZ62–45403

638

[Britannia] G. B. Cipriani inv. F. Bartolozzi sculp. [1768]

Etching 9¼ x 8 in. (image)

This national figure of strength and beauty, holding peace and liberty, reflects the Roman ideal of all Englishmen and the aspirations expressed in Bollan's book. From Bollan, *Continued Corruption, Standing Armies, and Popular Discontents Considered* (London, 1768), frontispiece. LC–USZ62–45529

639

[The products of Nova Scotia—a cartouche] J. Caldnall sculp. 1768

Etching 8 x 12 in. (image)

A pole supports a sail which has an inscribed message reading, "To the most Noble John Manners, Marquis of Granby ... this map ... is most humbly inscribed by ... John Montresor, Engineer." Surrounding this dedication are fish, wheat, rope, an anchor, a tiller, a small boat, nets, a boat fender, a float, a gaff, and an English flag. From a map entitled "A Map of Nova Scotia ... by Captain Montresor ... 1768" in Faden, *North American Atlas* (London, 1777), no. 6–7.

640

[America—a cartouche, 1756–82]

Etching 12 x 8 in. (image)

America is a lovely, half-naked Indian woman who sits above a male figure. They are surrounded by symbols of America: corn, lumber, fish nets, a beaver, a coconut tree, and in the background is a port with ships at anchor and merchandise on the shore. Above the scene, two cherubs lift a quartered crest with symbols of France and England. This cartouche is from the famous "A Map of the British Colonies in North America ..." by John Mitchell. From 1755 to 1782 the map was published about 21 times in English, French, Dutch, and Italian editions. For a discussion and compilation of the variant editions see the articles by Walter W. Ristow and Richard W. Stephenson in *A La Carte; Selected Papers on Maps and Atlases* (Washington, 1972) p. 102–113. Negatives in G&M.

641

[An allegory of Boston, 1769—a cartouche, William Price]

Etching 6¾ x 6 in. (image)

This cartouche was printed on previous editions of this map (see Wheat and Brun, p. 50–53). From "A New Plan of ye Great Town of Boston in New England in America with the many Additionall Buildings, & New Streets, to the Year, 1769" in G&M Vault. Negative in G&M.

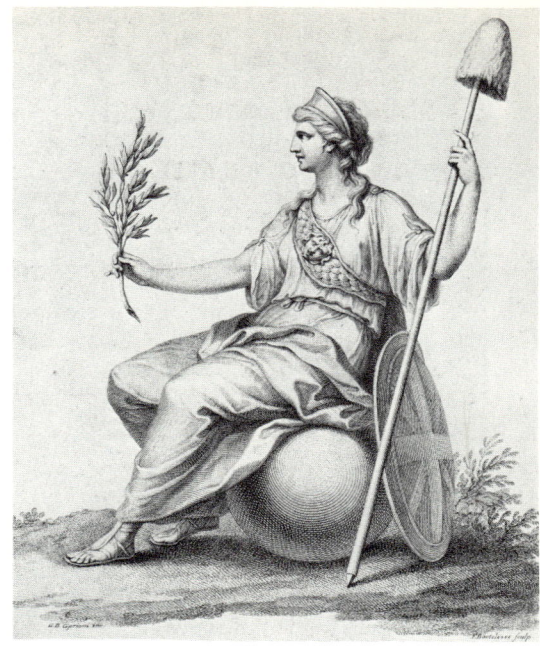

638

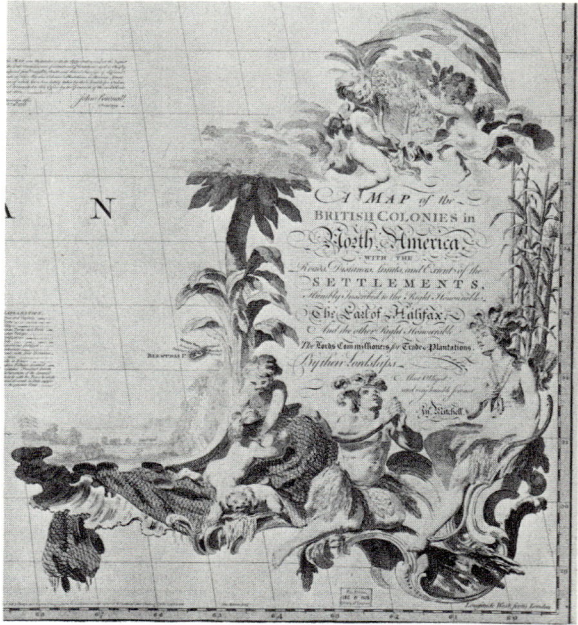

640

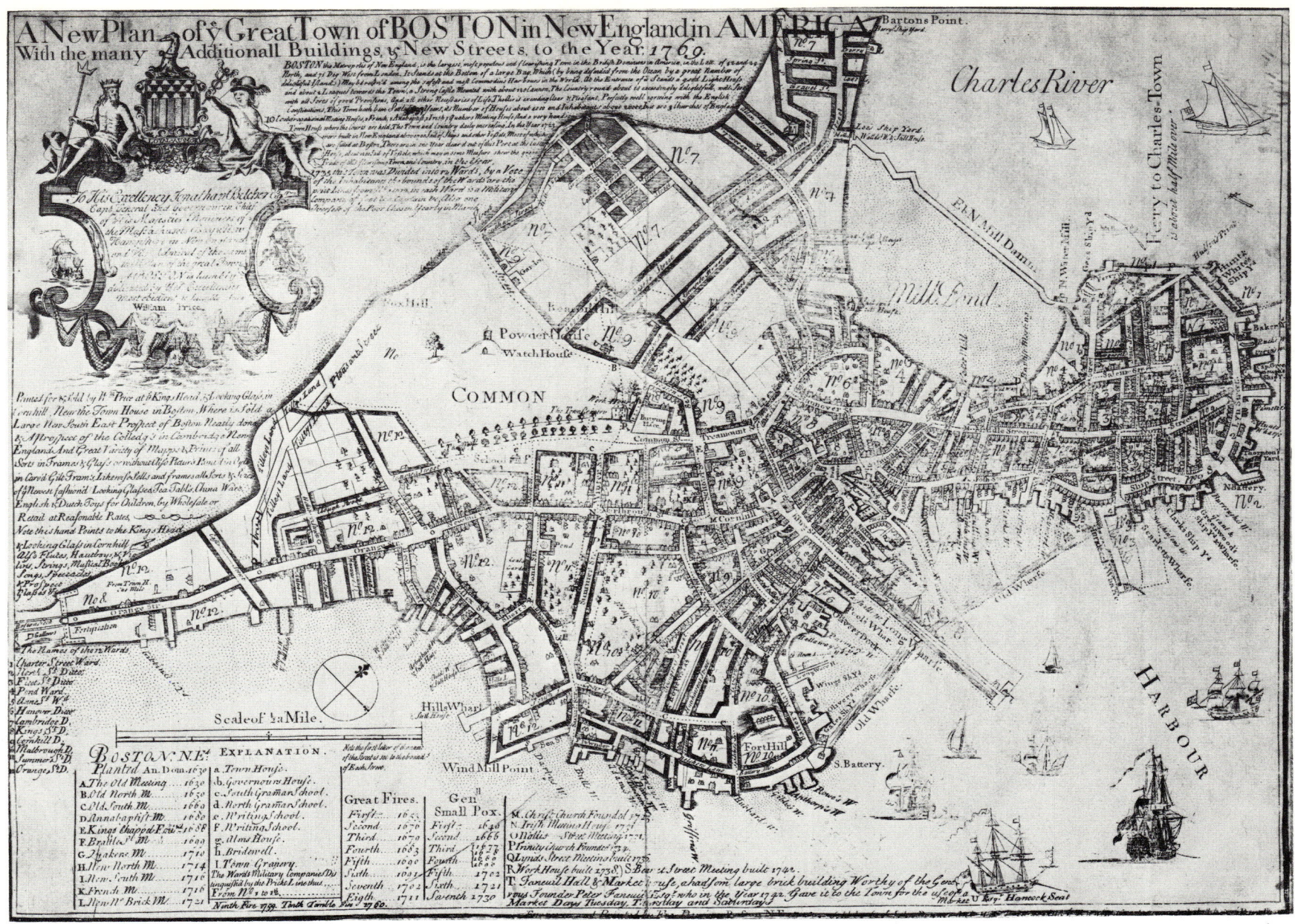

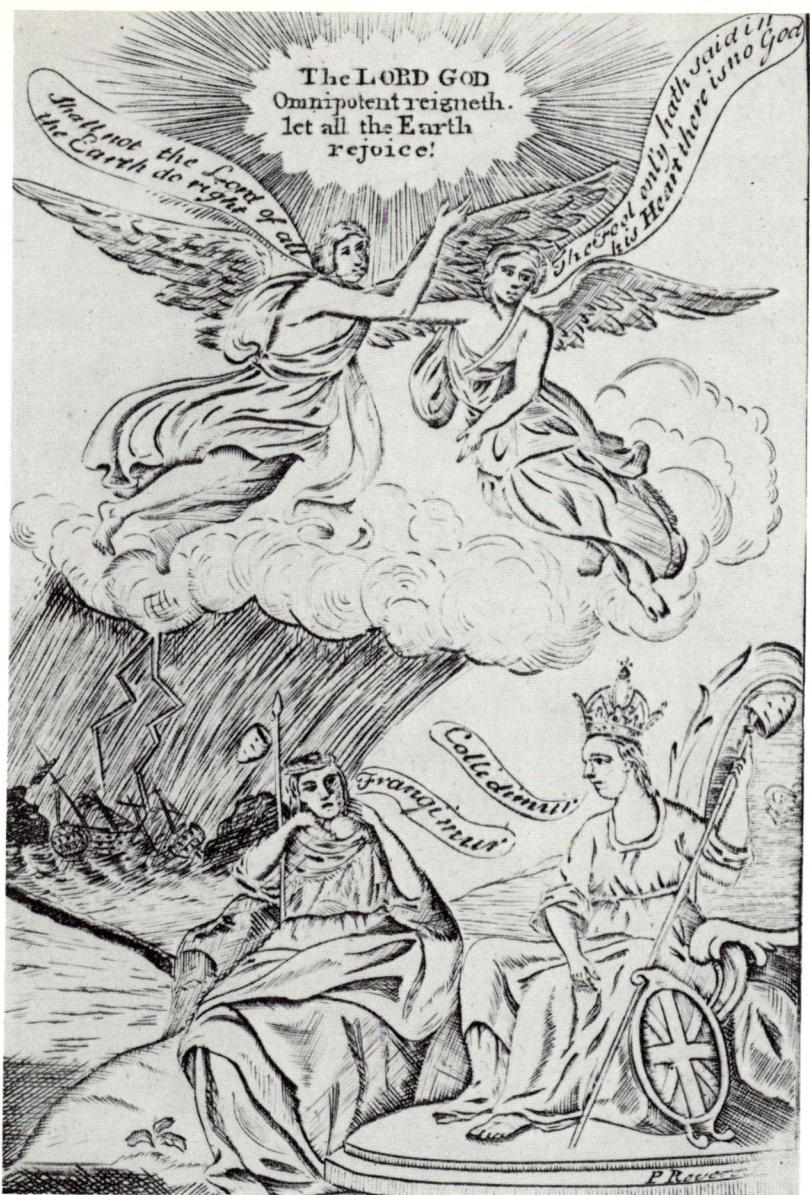

642

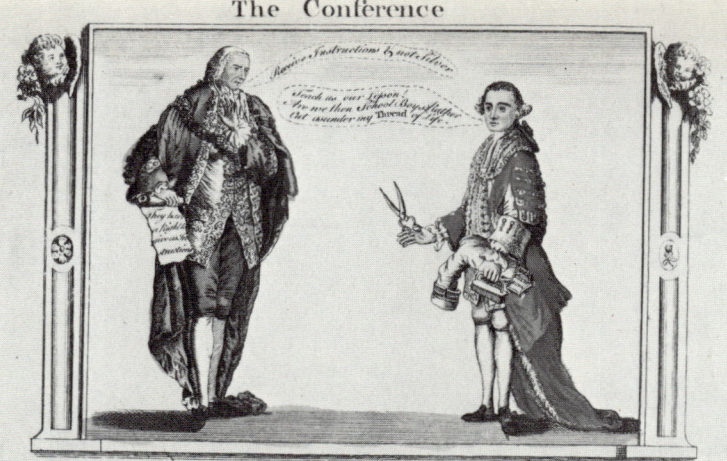

The Conference

INSTRUCTIONS

Given to Sir ROBERT LADBROOKE, Knt. WILLIAM BECKFORD, Esq; the Right Hon. THOMAS HARLEY, Esq; and BARLOW TRECOTHICK, Esq; REPRESENTATIVES of the City of LONDON: By their CONSTITUENTS.

GENTLEMEN,

WE your Constituents, assembled in the Guildhall of London, fully sensible of the Value of the Laws and Constitution, transmitted to us by our Ancestors, and firmly resolved to preserve this Inheritance entire, as we have received it, think it our indispensible Duty at this Time, as well as our undoubted Right to instruct you, our Representatives in Parliament, as follows:

I. We recommend, that you exert your utmost Endeavours, that the Proceedings in the Case of Libels, and all other Criminal Matters, may be confined to the known Rules of Law, and not rendered dangerous to the Subject, by forced Constructions, new Modes of Enquiry, unconstitutional Tribunals, or new and unusual Punishments, tending to take away or diminish the Benefit of Tryal by Juries.

II. That you carefully watch over the great Bulwark of our Liberties, the Habeas Corpus Act; and that you enquire into, and Censure any Attempt to elude, or enervate the Force of that Law.

III. That you preserve equally inviolate the Privilege of Parliament, and the Rights of the Electors in the Choice of their Representatives.

IV. That you do not discourage Petitions, by selecting such Parts thereof as may tend not to relieve, but to criminate the Petitioner, so as to prevent all Approach to your House, by which means the most essential Article of the Declaration of Rights may be eluded, or rendered of the less Effect.

V. That you Endeavour to prevent all Applications of the public Money to influence Elections of Members to serve in Parliament.

VI. That you give no Countenance to the dangerous Doctrine of constructive Treasons, or to the Application of doubtful or uncertain Laws to this interesting Object, nor suffer Ministers to be invested with a vague and discretionary Power of judging on, or prosecuting this Offence, and that you will vigorously oppose any Measures tending to introduce Modes and Circumstances of Tryal, which may render it difficult or impossible for the Party accused to obtain full and equal Justice.

VII. That you will, as the Representatives of this great commercial City, be particularly attentive to the Interest of the Manufactures, and the Trade of this Kingdom in all Parts of the World, and more especially in the British American Colonies, the only profitable Trade this Kingdom enjoys unrivaled by other Nations; for which Purpose we recommend your utmost Endeavours to reconcile the unhappy Differences subsisting between the Mother Country and the Colonies, the fatal Effects of which have, in part been, severely felt by the Manufacturer, and the commercial Part of this Kingdom.

VIII. That you will, at this Time particularly, attend to the Preservation of public Faith, the sole Foundation of public Credit; and that you do not, upon any Pretence of public Good whatsoever, concur in any Measure that shall tend to weaken or destroy that Faith.

IX. That you use your utmost Endeavours that the Civil Magistracy of this Kingdom be put on a respectable Footing, and thereby remove the Pretence of calling in a Military Force, and preserve this Nation, from a Calamity which has already been fatal to the Liberties of every Kingdom round us, and which we at this Day are beginning to feel.

X. That you promote a strict Enquiry into the Use which has lately been made of Military Power, whether any Encouragement has been given to premature or injudicious Military Alacrity, and whether any undue Measures have been taken, to prevent or elude the Course of public justice on such an Occasion.

XI. That you use your best Endeavours for having a Standing Committee appointed, from Time to Time, to examine and to state the public Accounts.

XII. That if any Demand should come before Parliament for Payment of the Debts of the Civil List, you will diligently enquire how those Debts have been incurred, to the Prejudice of the Subject, and the Dignity of the Crown.

XIII. That you will promote a Bill for limiting the Number of Placemen and Pensioners in the House of Commons, for preventing the Peers of Great Britain from interfering in Elections for Members of Parliament, and that an Oath to prevent Bribery and Corruption be taken not only by the Electors, but also by the Candidates, at the Opening of the Poll.

XIV. That you use your utmost Endeavours to obtain an Act to shorten the Duration of Parliaments; and lastly, we submit it to your Consideration, whether a Change in the present Mode of Election, to that of Ballot, would not be the most likely Method of procuring a Return of Members on the genuine and uncorrupt Sense of the People.

(Signed)   CHARLES CLAVEY.
Chairman of the Common Hall.

Guildhall, Feb. 10, 1769.

642

The LORD GOD Omnipotent reigneth. let all the Earth rejoice! P. Revere [1768]

Line engraving 5¼ x 3¾ in.

This plate was engraved about the time the British troops landed at Boston in September 1768. The title page contains an explanation:

> Two Female Figures. The principal [Britannia] richly decorated, is seated on a Throne with an Imperial Diadem on her Head, and a Spear in her left Hand. The other figure [America or Liberty?] exhibits a Virgin with a Civic Crown, in the utmost Agonies of Distress and Horror. The Cap of Liberty falling from the Spear of one [America], and tottering to fall from the other. The Label of one [Britannia], is saying Collidimur [to collide]; of the other, Frangimur [to shatter]. Two Ships are represented to View in a Tempest in the Instant of dashing to Pieces against one another, and sinking between the Rocks of Sylla and Caribdis. In the Interim are seen two Arch-Angels, flying as "on the Wings of the Wind." The Label of one is, "Shall not the Lord of all the Earth do Right." The other is, "The Fool" only "hath said in his Heart there is no God." Above all, in a Glory, is inscribed these Words, "The Lord God Omnipotent reigneth, let the Earth Rejoice!"

From *Edes and Gill's North American Almanack* (Boston, 1769), frontispiece. See under *Massachusetts Register*, 1769. LC–USZ62–45568

643

The Conference. INSTRUCTIONS Given to Sir ROBERT LADBROOKE, Knt. WILLIAM BECKFORD, Esq; the Right Hon. THOMAS HARLEY, Esq; and BARLOW TRECOTHICK, Esq; REPRESENTATIVES of the City of London: by their CONSTITUENTS. Guildhall, Feb. 10, 1769.

Etching (hand colored) 5¼ x 3½ in.

This broadside is a petition from the people of London giving instructions to their representatives pictured above. Beckford, a friend of Pitt and champion of liberty, rebukes Harley who is subservient to Bute. In the cartoon Beckford says, "Receive instructions & not silver." Item VII of the instructions reads:

> That you will, as the Representatives of this great commercial City, be particularly attentive to the Interest of the Manufactures, and the Trade of this Kingdom in all Parts of the World, and more especially in the British American Colonies, the only profitable Trade this Kingdom enjoys unrivaled by other Nations; for which Purpose we recommend your utmost endeavors to reconcile the unhappy Differences subsisting between the Mother Country and the Colonies, the fatal Effects of which have, in part been, severely felt by the Manufacturer, and the commercial Part of this Kingdom.

CPPS 4269 LC–USZ62–45404

———— Another impression. Uncolored.

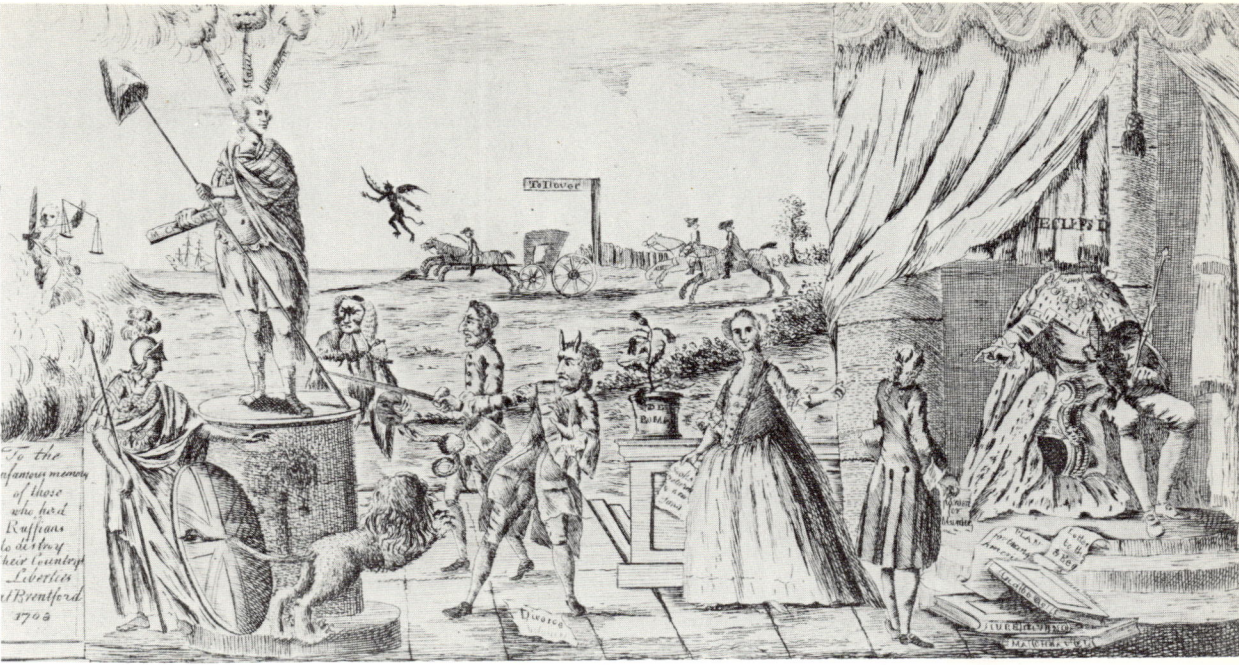

644

644

THE PATRIOT. DEDICATED to the Freeholders of Middlesex. [1769]

Etching 5 x 9¼ in.

Depicts the struggle for election between John Wilkes and Henry Luttrell in Middlesex County. While Wilkes, representing liberty, is endangered, George III sits on his throne with a curtain hiding his face. At his feet are many plans, including one for taxing America. The verse below reads:

> Sons of freedom view this Sketch,
> View it too each sordid wretch.
> Some oppressions dagger draw,
> Others dare corrupt the Law,
> Some their Princes heart betray.
> Tear his Peoples rights away.
>
> Each considers only self.
> Vernal wretches, cursed pelf.
> Brandishing corruptions arms,
> Hireling Ruffians raise alarms,
> Murder in the Devils cause,
> Then defy the Nations laws.
>
> Yet free from guilt untouched with blame
> Some there are who grasp at fame.
> Some there are corruption checks,
> Chiefly thee, O Middlesex.
> Shall thy labours be in vain?
> Shall thy Wilks opprest remain?
>
> No. The British Lion roars.
> Bribers, Bravo's, quit our shores.
> Still theres hope determind stand:

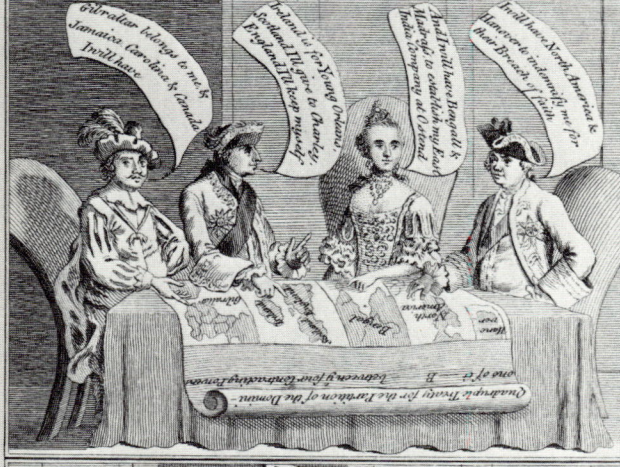

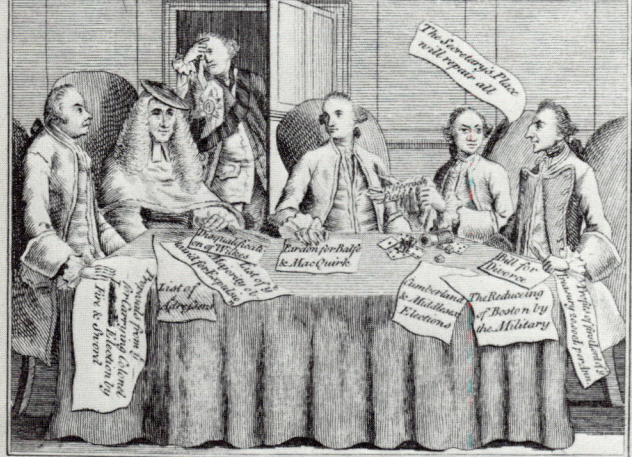

645

Still support the sinking land:
Future ages then shall join
To bless the year of sixty nine.

CPPS 4284 gives a description of the political background of this print. P&P lists it as 4284B. LC–USZ62–45405

645

What may be done Abroad. What is doing at Home. Design'd & Engrav'd for the Political Register. [April 16, 1769]
Mixed method 3¼ x 4 in. (image) and 3¼ x 4 in. (image)

On the continent four monarchs divide the world among themselves. The King of Spain claims Gibraltar, Jamaica, Carolina, and Canada; the King of France wants England, Scotland, and Ireland; Queen Maria Theresa points to India; the King of Prussia wants North America and Hanover. Below members of the Duke of Grafton's administration—the Duke of Bedford, Lord Mansfield, Viscount Rochford, Viscount Weymouth, and Grafton—handle internal disputes, while George III weeps at the doorway. Among these disputes is a plan for "The Reducing of Boston by the Ministry." The moral of the contrasting pictures is that while the Ministry schemed at home, foreign enemies plotted their conquest over the British Empire. CPPS 4287 LC–USZ62–45406

———Another impression. From *The Political Register*, May 1769, opposite p. 257.

646

The HUMBLE PETITION of the FREEHOLDERS of the COUNTY of MIDDLESEX. [May 24, 1769]
Etching 3 x 5½ in. (image)

This petition protesting evils of the day charges the King's ministers with corruption and the abuse of such civil liberties as habeas corpus, freedom of the press, right to private property; military power over civil; mob rule; mismanagement of money; and immorality. It adds, "The same descretion has been extended by the same evil counsellors to your Majesty's dominions in America, and has produced to our suffering fellow-subjects in that part of the world, grievances and apprehensions similar to those of which we complain at home." CPPS 4289 LC–USZ62–45407

647

THE CITY CARRIERS. [July 5, 1769]
Etching 4 x 7 in. (image)

Officials of the City of London present many petitions to the King. Samuel Turner, Lord Mayor of London, and Liberty lead the procession. They are followed by a mule bearing a beautiful, naked personification of truth. Next come William Beckford, Barlow Trecothick, and Robert Ladbroke. Harley is represented by an effigy on a pole. Among the many written and spoken grievances is Ladbroke's, "I feel for the Wrongs of America." The procession is in front of St. James Palace where Lord Holland, caricatured as a Fox, points to a fool's cap. From *The London Magazine*, 1769, opposite p. 393. CPPS 4296 LC–USZ62–45408

648

The ever-memorable Peace-Makers Settling their Accounts. [July 5, 1769]
Mixed method 6⅛ x 3¾ in.

The Duke of Bedford, the Earl of Bute, and Lord Holland (in caricature) sit at table with plans for West Indies, North America, Manillas, and Neg. 150,000. The devil looks on, holding an inkwell for them. CPPS 4300 LC–USZ62–45409

———Another impression. In *Town and Country Magazine*, December 1769, p. 641.

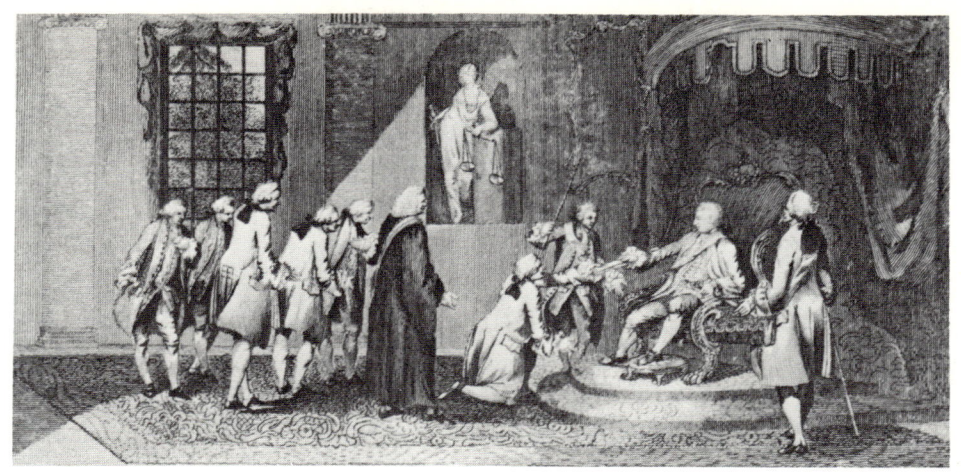

646

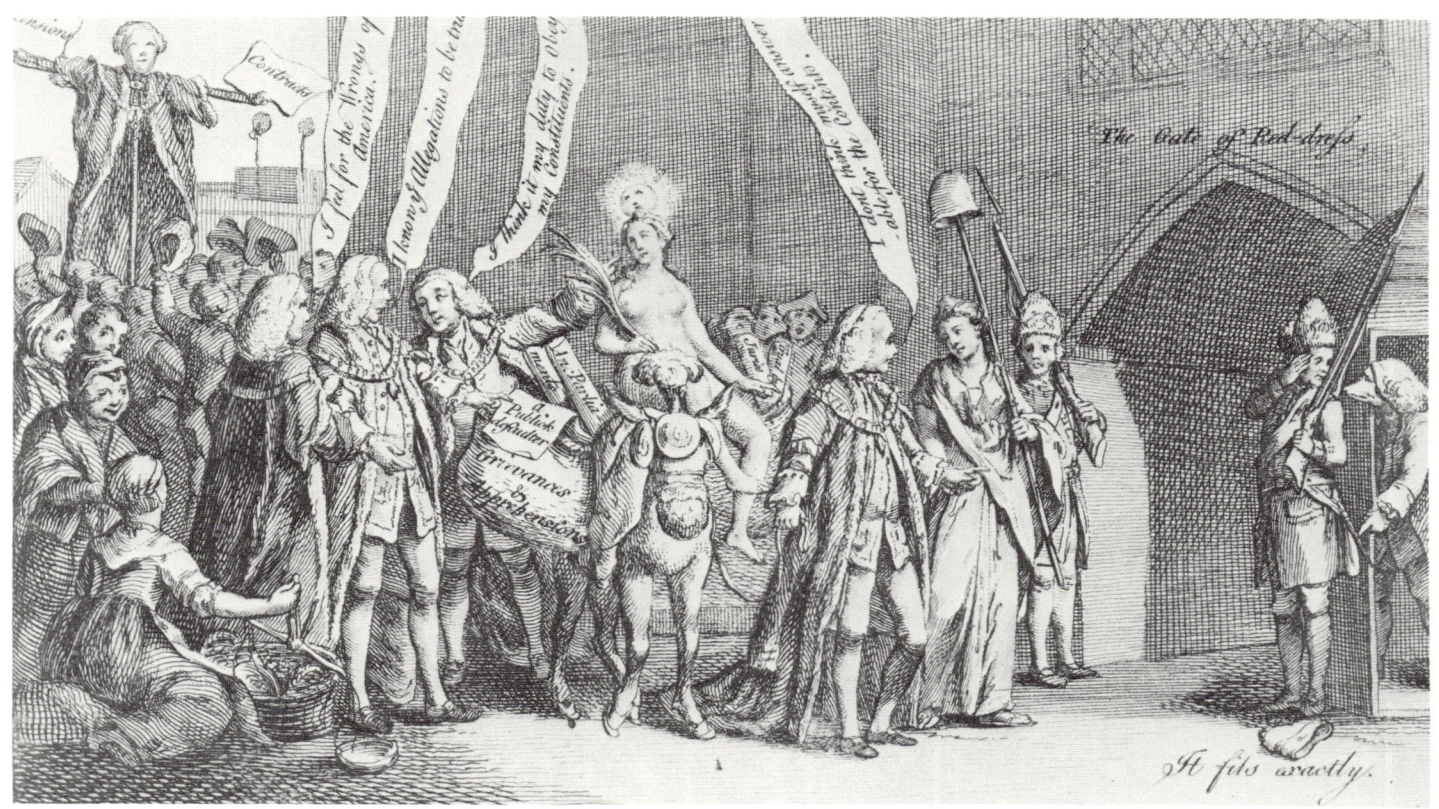

647

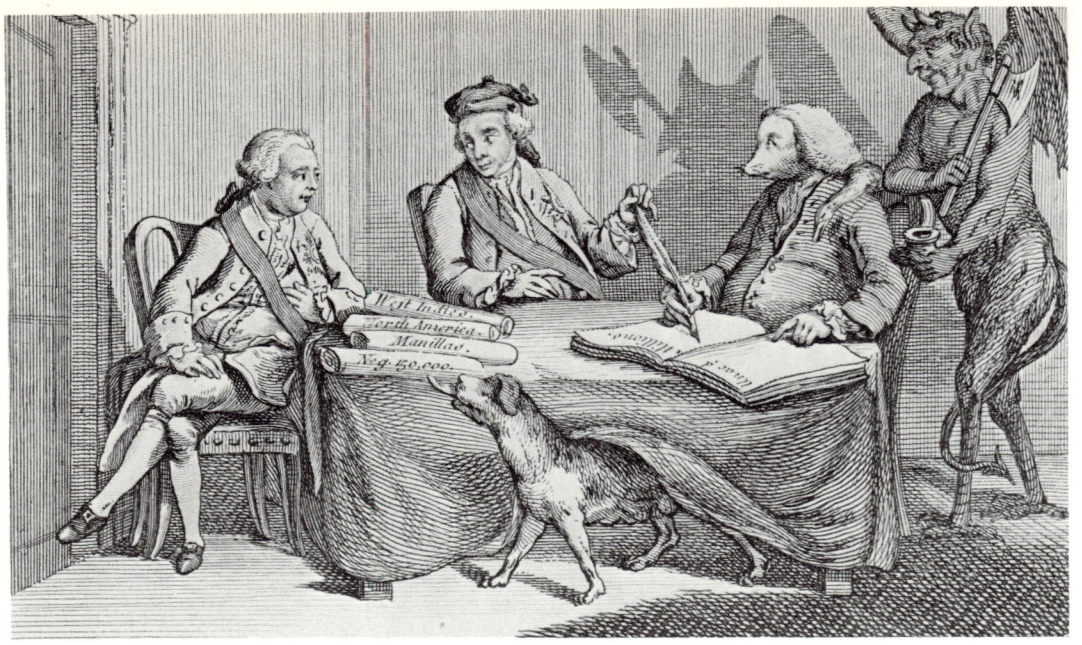

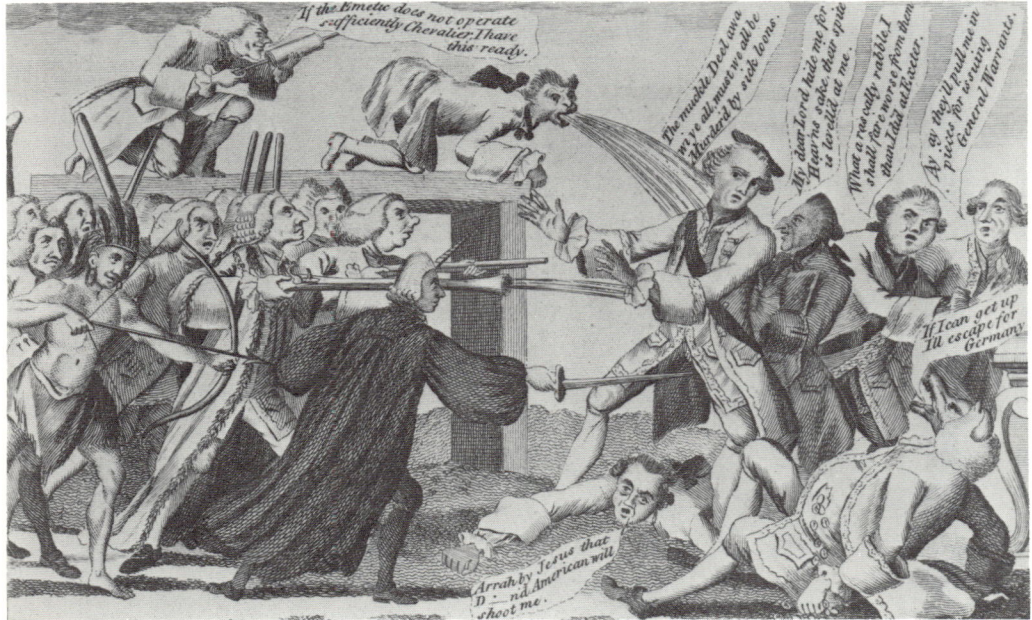

649

The Chevalier D'____n producing his Evidence against certain Persons. [August 12, 1769]
Mixed method 6⅜ x 4 in. (image)

The Chevalier D'Eon with Dr. Samuel Musgrave, John Horne Tooke, William Beckford, and an American Indian attack Bute, Hillsborough, Holland, the Duke of Grafton, Bedford, and the Earl of Halifax. This cartoon was published at a time when D'Eon was expected to produce startling evidence against members of the Grafton administration. Thus his allies were interpreted as opposing the present Ministry. Hillsborough, Secretary of State for the North American Colonies, grovels on the ground crying, "Arrah by Jesus that D____n'd American will shoot me." Originally from *The Oxford Magazine*, 1769, opposite p. 184. This copy in P&P. CPPS 4308 LC–USZ62–45410

650

The Times. Taken from an Original Character which appear'd at the Masquerade at Lincoln. Decr. the 21st. 1769 Publish'd as the Act directs by J. Marks on the pav'd Stones St. Martin's Lane. 21 December 1769
Mixed method 10 x 12 in.

A man draped in ribbons and scrolls which list the issues of the times. One ribbon on the left leg states "NO AMERIC: ST: ACT."
CPPS 4315

————Another copy. Publish'd as the Act directs by W. Holland. LC–USZ62–45425

651

The Machine to go without Asses. Design'd & Engraved for the Political Register. [1769]
Mixed method 4¾ x 7⅜ in.

George III and Britannia ride over Grafton, Bute, Holland, and the Earl of Mansfield in a carriage entitled "Magna Charta." The wheels

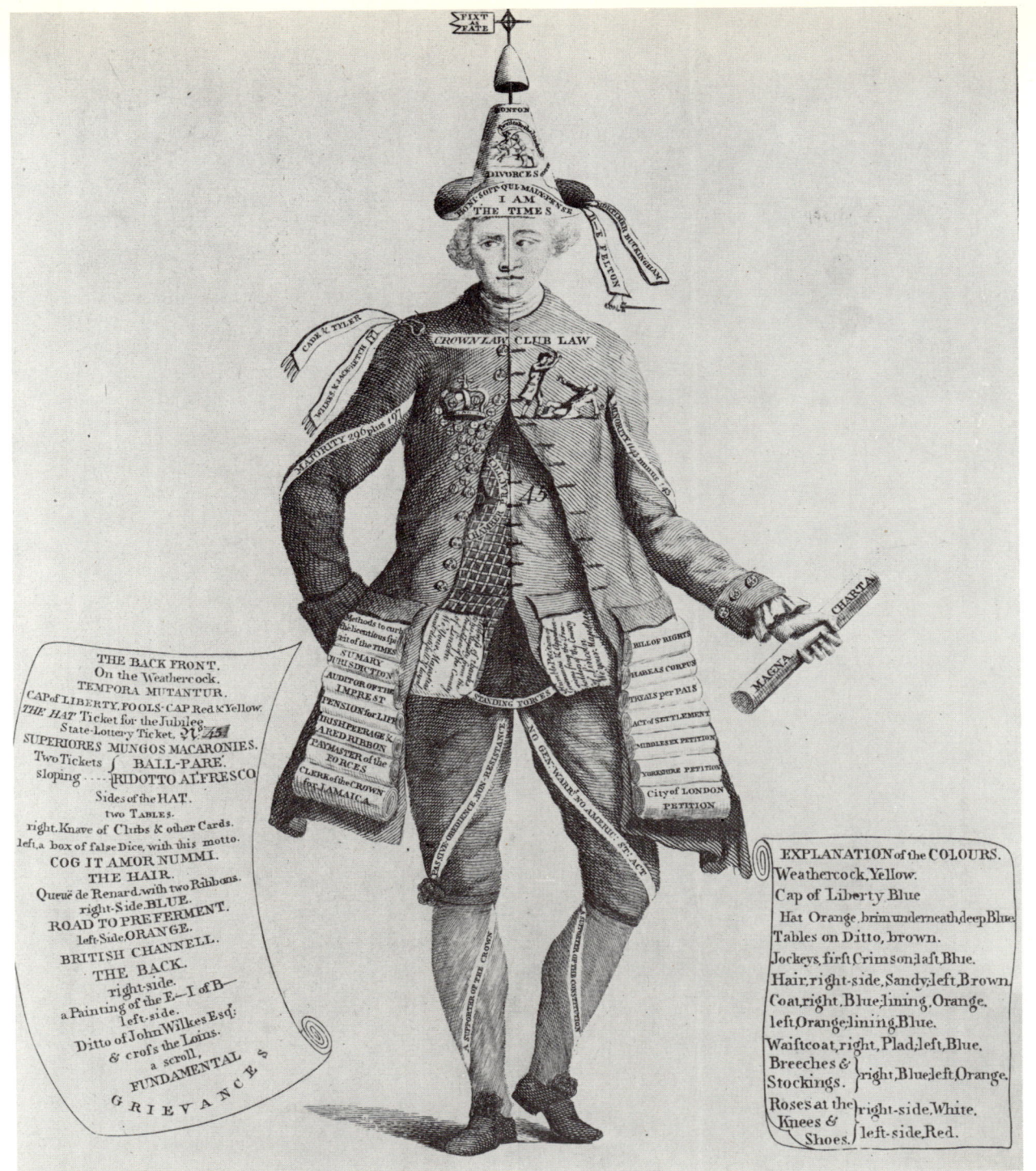

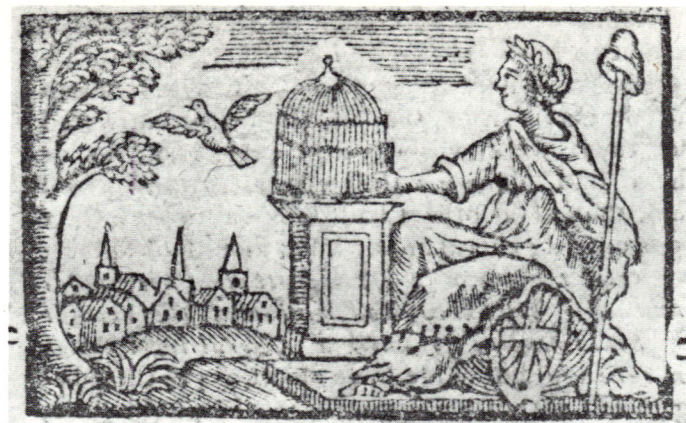

652

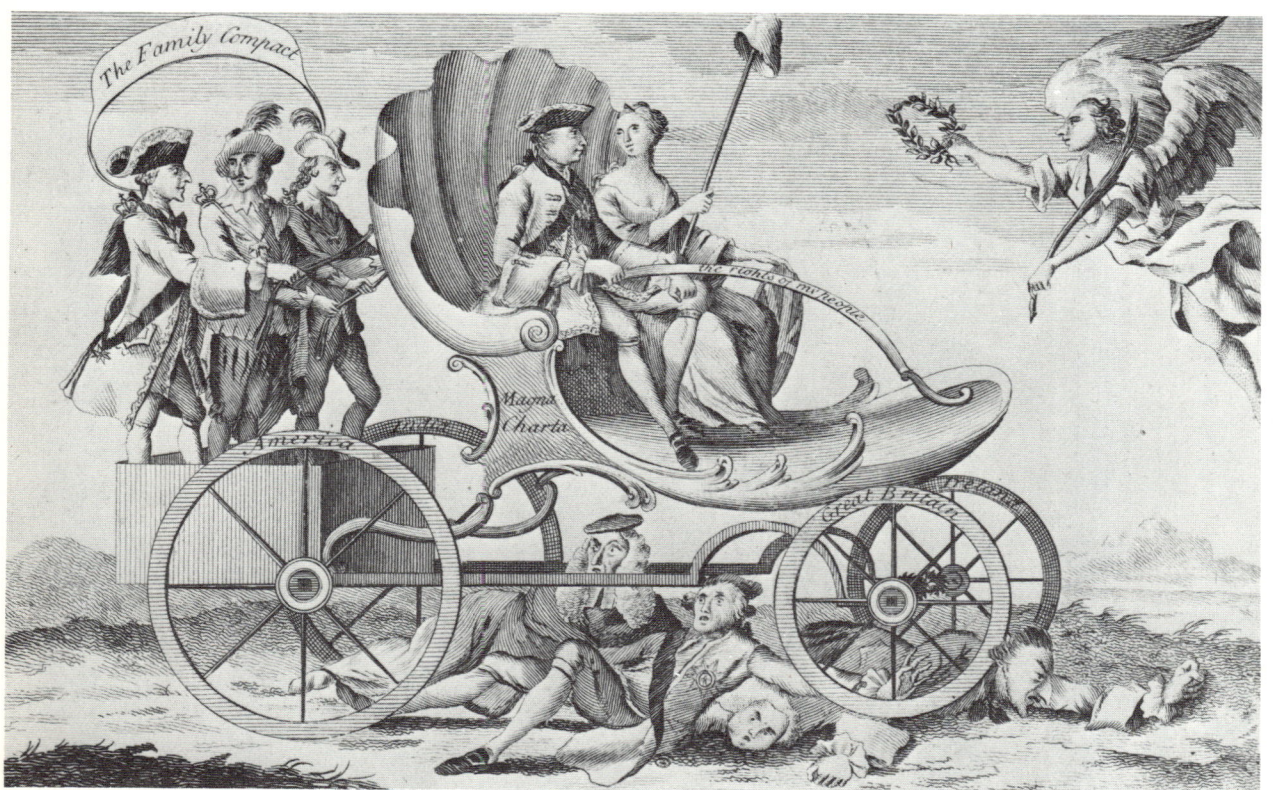

651

of the carriage are designated "America," "India," "Ireland," and "Great Britain." From *The Political Register For* 1769, facing p. 247. CPPS 4318

———Another impression. In P&P, 4 x 6½ in. (image). LC–USZ62–45424

652

[Britannia frees the dove of peace] January 1, 1770 [Paul Revere]

Woodcut 2¼ x 3½ in.

Britannia opens a bird cage to let a dove fly out. A town, probably Boston, is in the background. From the masthead of *The Boston Gazette, and Country Journal* beginning with the issue of January 1, 1770. LC–USZ62–45585

653

Wide o'er the Ocean while Britannia reigns. Bonnor, del. et sculp. [January 1770]

Mixed method 7½ x 4¾ in.

Britannia, led by a soldier (probably Mars) and Cupid, steps over the crests of Spain and France to go to the temple. A poem beneath the picture reads:

> Wide o'er the Ocean while Britannia reigns.
> She bears no Insult and she dreads no Chains.
> And Spanish Pow'r shall mourn her Thunder hurld.
> Thro' all it's Insolence in either World.

The English often blamed their colonial troubles on France's desire for revenge and Spain's desire for land. From *The London Magazine*, January 1770, frontispiece. LC–USZ62–45497

654

[Four coffins of men killed in the Boston Massacre, March 12, 1770, Paul Revere]

Woodcut. Each coffin is 1½ x ⅝ in.

The four coffins with skulls and crossbones represent the dead men: Samuel Gray, Samuel

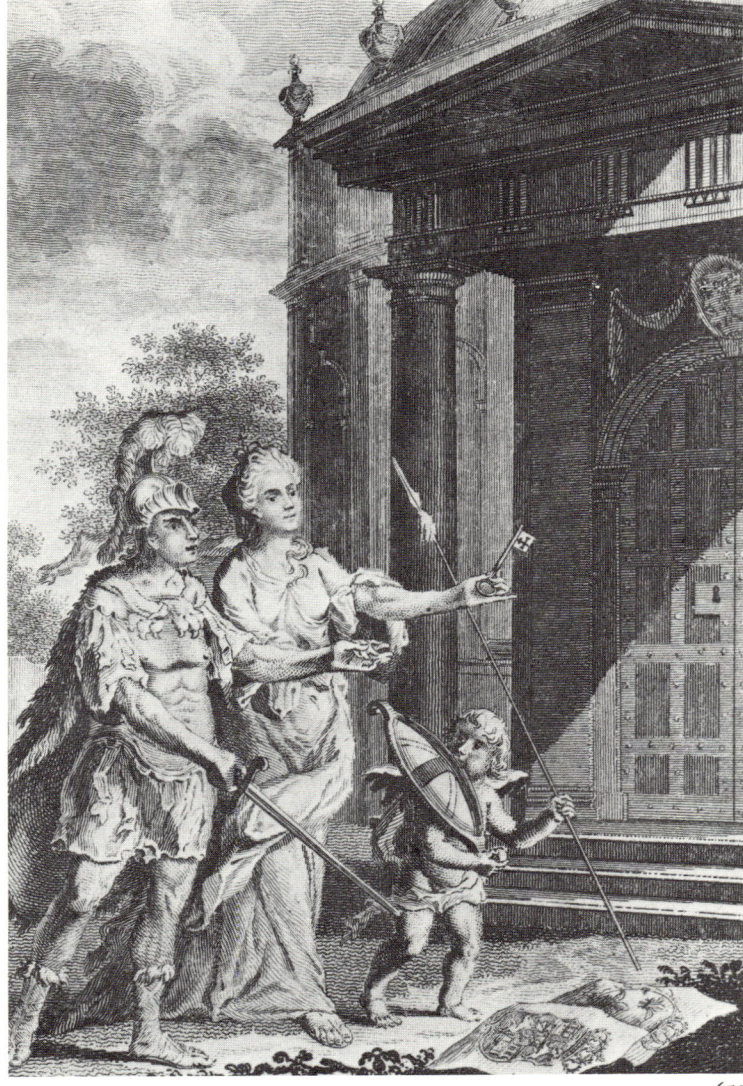

653

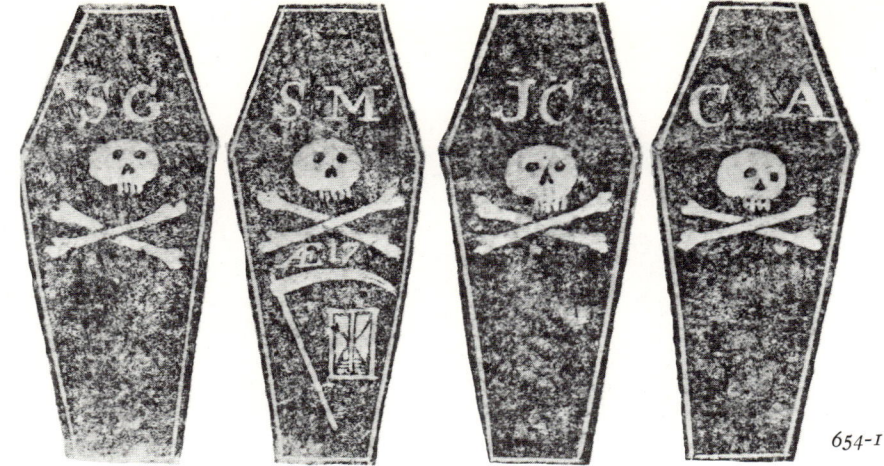

654-1

Last Wednesday Night died, *Patrick Carr*, an Inhabitant of this Town, of the Wound he received in King-Street on the bloody and execrable Night of the 5th Instant——— He had just before left his Home, and upon his coming into the Street received the fatal Ball in his Hip which passed out at the opposite Side; this is the fifth Life that has been sacrificed by the Rage of the Soldiery, but it is feared it will not be the last, as several others are dangerously languishing of their Wounds. His Remains were attended on Saturday last from Faneuil-Hall by a numerous and respectable Train of Mourners, to the *same* Grave, in which those who fell by the *same* Hands of Violence were interred the last Week.

654-2

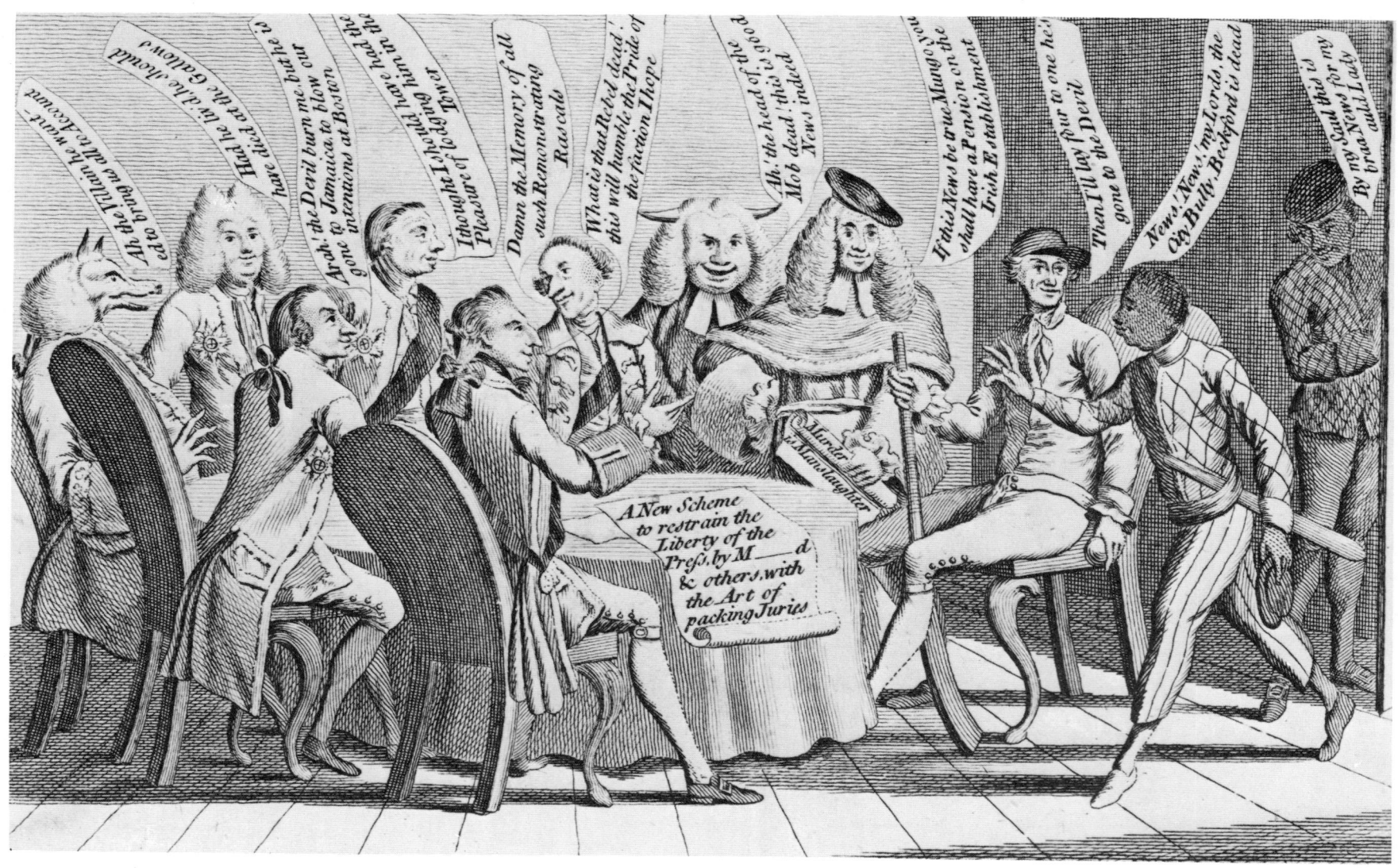

Maverick, James Caldwell, and Crispus Attucks. From *The Boston Gazette*, March 12, 1770. LC–USZ62–45586

[The coffin of Patrick Carr, March 19, 1770]
 Woodcut 1½ x ⅝ in.

The article which accompanies this woodcut describes the death of Patrick Carr who was critically wounded in the Boston Massacre. From *The Boston Gazette*, March 19, 1770. LC–USZ62–45587

655

The Courtiers Assembled, on hearing the News of the Death of the Rt. Honble. Wm. Beckford [June 21, 1770]
 Etching 3¾ x 6 in.

On the death of William Beckford, Lord Mayor of London, many courtiers had cause for joy. Among those pictured are Jeremiah Dyson, Earl of Sandwich, Mansfield, Fletcher Norton, Grafton, Weymouth, Bedford, Winchelsea, Holland, and Bute. Lord Hillsborough, Secretary of State for the Colonies, says, "Arah! the Devil burn me, but he is gone to Jamaica, to blow our intentions in Boston." CPPS 4393 LC–USZ62–45426

See also: "The Citizens of London lamenting the Death of Beckford." [June 21, 1770] etching 4 x 6¼ in. This is a companion piece showing John Horne Tooke, Pitt, Temple Wilkes, Britannia, and citizens weeping. CPPS 4394

656

Political Electricity; or, An Historical & Prophetical Print in the Year 1770. [The date of this copy is penned over to read "1776." Bute and Wilkes invent. Veridicus & Junius fect. [1770]
 Mixed method 15¾ x 22¾ in.

Most of the scenes depict political and social problems in England. One shows Franklin

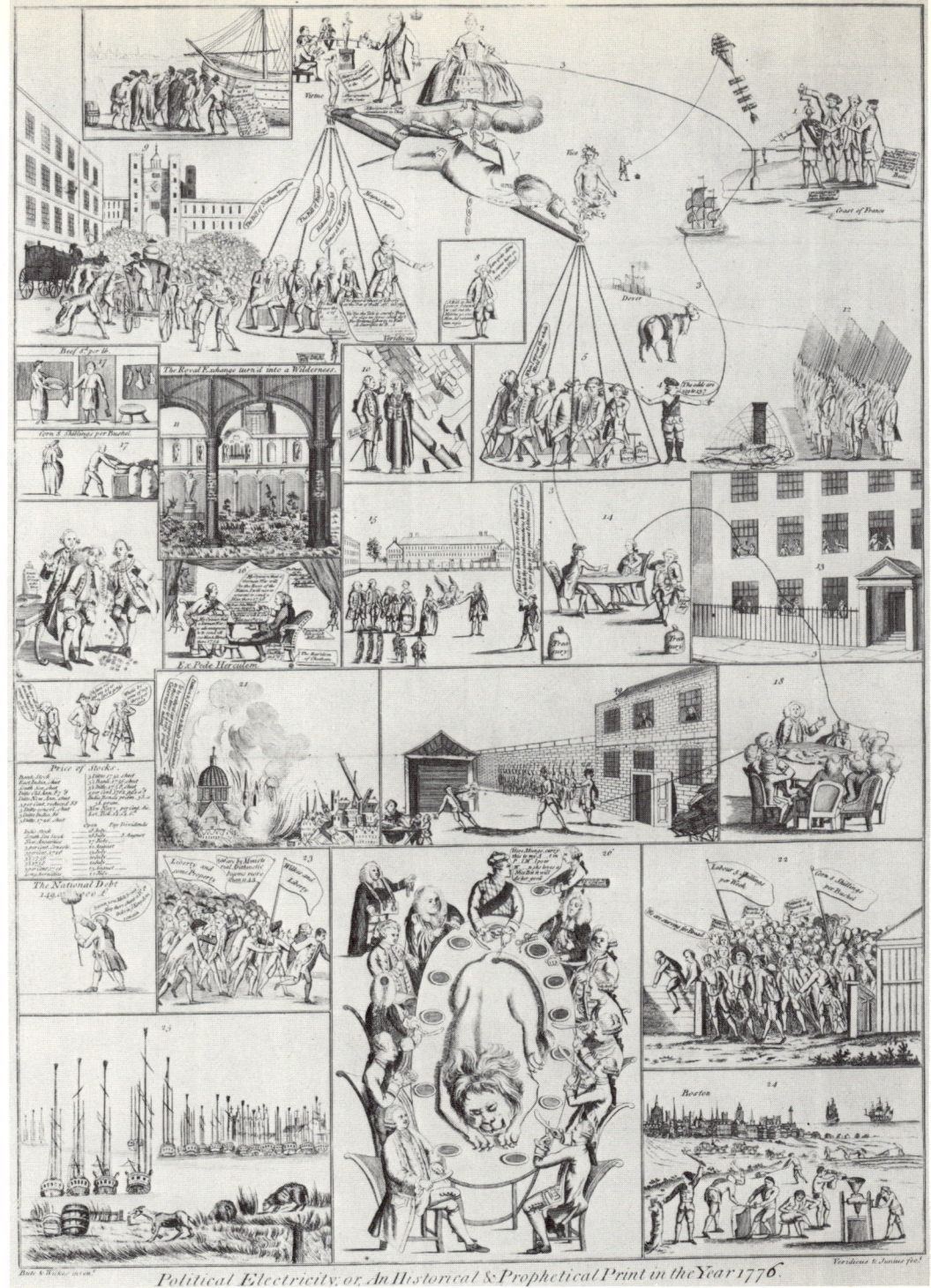

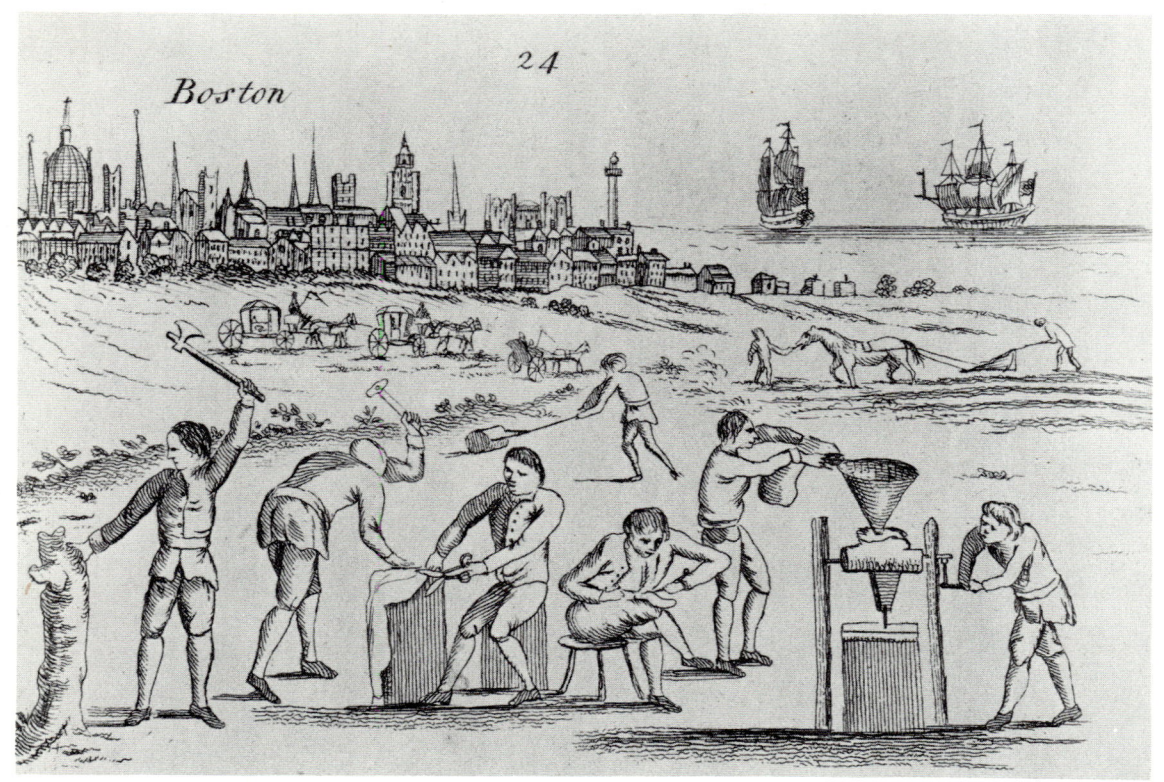

656-1

flying a kite with various petitions on its tail. The combination of petitions with electricity seems to produce the idea of Bute as an electrical generator drawing power from the royal family and creating a chain of events throughout the world. The 24th section depicts Boston resembling London, with the implication that the hard working citizens in the foreground will make their city the leader of the world through honest industry, while Britain sinks due to political corruption. The Library of Congress has a negative of this section (LC–USZ62–1504) and one for the entire print (LC–USZ62–45564). CPPS 4422

——————Another copy. A second state of the plate in which the signature is altered to read, "Mercurius & Apelles fect."

657

[Masthead for *The Massachusetts Spy*, Paul Revere, 1771–84]

Woodcut 1¾ x 1⅝ in. (image) 3⅞ x 10 in. (image)

On the left Liberty sits leaning her right elbow on a copy of *The Massachusetts Spy*, and her left hand holds a staff with a liberty cap on top. The figure to the right is an allegory on American commerce in which two cherubs sort flowers. Underneath the picture is the motto "They Cull The Choices." Both woodcuts adorned the masthead of Isaiah Thomas' *The Massachusetts Spy* from July 17, 1770, until he escaped from the British to Worcester after his edition of April 6, 1775. When Thomas re-established the paper at Worcester, he used only the woodcut on the left. On July 7, 1774, he began using the symbol of the rattlesnake attacking the griffon as part of the masthead. The snake is in pieces designated G, SC, NC, V, M, P, NJ, NY, and NE, and above the pieces is the motto "Join or Die." A similar snake device, first used in 1754, was designed by Benjamin Franklin to promote a united defense against the French and Indians. See

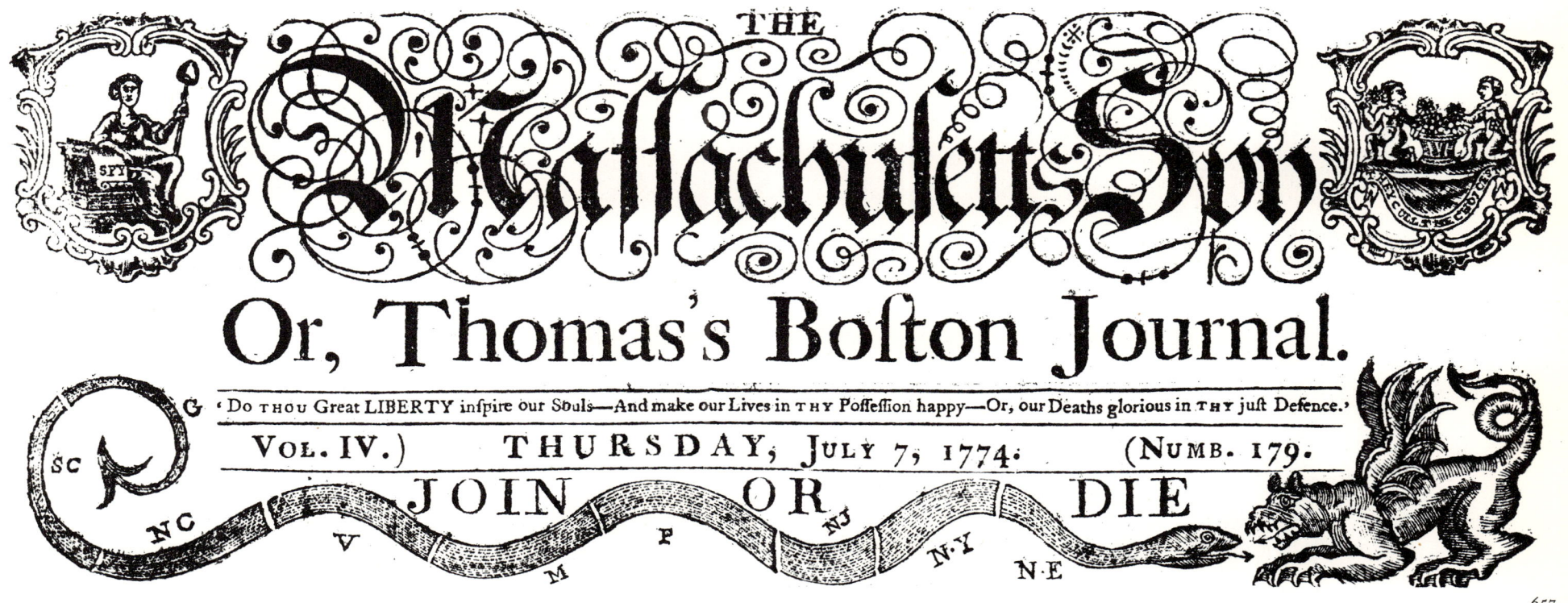

Sinclair Hamilton, "The Earliest Device of the Colonies," *The Princeton University Library Chronicle*, X:117 (April 1949). All three woodcuts are included on one negative. LC–USZ62–7984

658
[America, 1771]
 Etching 3½ x 3 in. (image)

America is pictured as a half-naked Indian woman wearing a skirt made of feathers and holding a bow and quiver. A lizard or alligator stands behind her and in the background is a tropical scene. See item 716 for a similar image. One of four pictures ornamenting the title page of Andrews, *A Collection of Plans of the Capital Cities . . .* (London, 1771). LC–USZ62–46091

659
[An American Indian points to a map of America—ornament from a title page] Iacob Christoph Weÿerman inv. et delin. Martin Gottfried Cophius, sculps. [1772?]
 Etching 5 x 4 in. (image)

Part of an elaborate title page which depicts the four continents personified. From Lotter, *Atlas Novus Sive Tabulae Geographicae* (Augsburg, 1772?), title page. LC–USZ62–46066

660
[The Four Continents—a cartouche, 1772?]
 Etching 6½ x 15 in.

America pictured as an Indian with feathered headdress, skirt, and garters. From Lotter, *Atlas Novus Sive Tabulae Geographicae* (Augsburg, 1772?), no. 1.

———Another impression with statement "Matthaeus Albrecht Lotter Sculpsit Aug. V." In Lotter, *Atlas Géographique* (Nürnberg, 1778), no. 3. LC–USZ62–46067

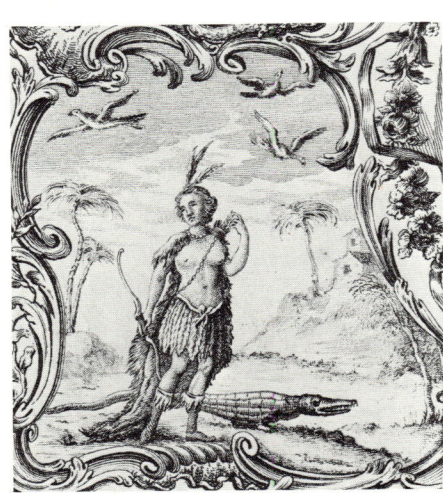
658

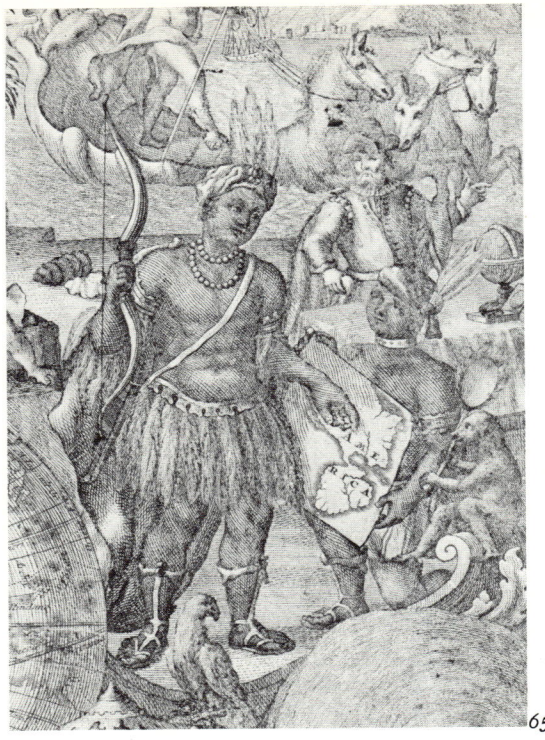
659

660

661

[An allegory on America during the 1770's—a cartouche] G. F. Lotter Sculps. [1772?]
Etching 7 x 6½ in. (image)

An Indian offers food to a sleeping lion which lies amid seafood, a piece of ivory, silver plate, and what might be a liberty cap. From the right side an English merchant views the scene. On a map entitled "America Septentrionalis . . . per G. de L'Isle . . ." in Lotter, *Atlas Novus Sive Tabulae Geographicae* (Augsburg, 1772?), no. 6. LC–USZ62–45596

———Another impression. In Lotter, *Atlas Géographique* (Nürnberg, 1778), no. 90.

662

Britain, America, at length be Friends, [January 1774]
Mixed method 7¾ x 4½ in.

Britannia with shield and spear takes the hand of America dressed as an Indian with a gorget around her neck. Between them stands Concord holding a globe in her right hand and an olive branch in her left. In the foreground at Britannia's feet sit a lion and a lamb, and at the feet of America lies a cornucopia. In the background are ships loading at a dock and a church. Beneath the picture a poem:

> Britain, America, at length be Friends,
> Accept the terms which Concord, recommends!
> Be ye but steady to each others Cause,
> Protect, defend, and not infringe the Laws;
> Ye may together—come the World in Arms,
> Bear the brunt Shock of hostile, dire alarms.
> Tis Peace, Trade, Navigation, will support
> The poor with bread—in Dignity the Court.
> Rush to each others Arms, be firm and true;
> One Faith, one Fame, one intrest, makes the two.
>   E.T.

From *The London Magazine*, 1774, frontispiece. LC–USZ62–45498

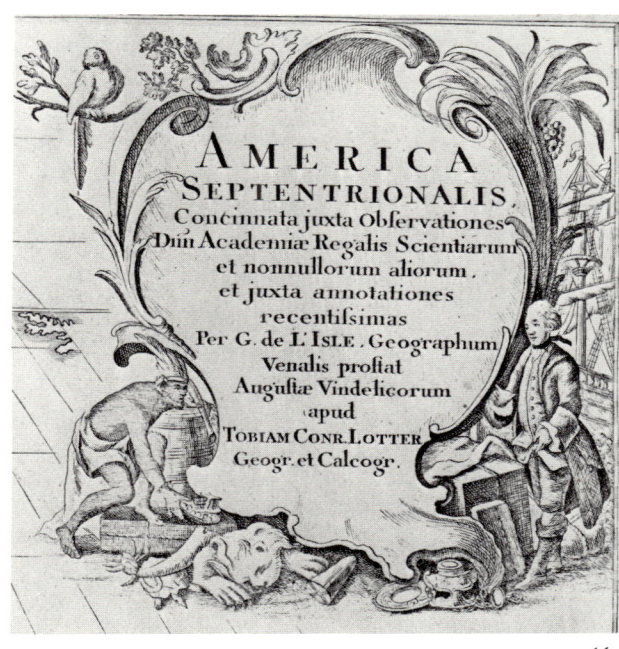

661

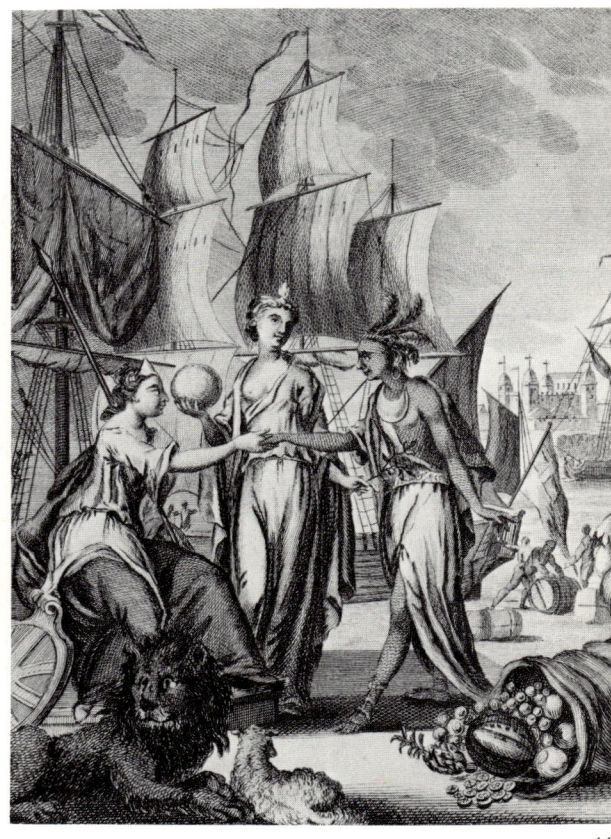

662

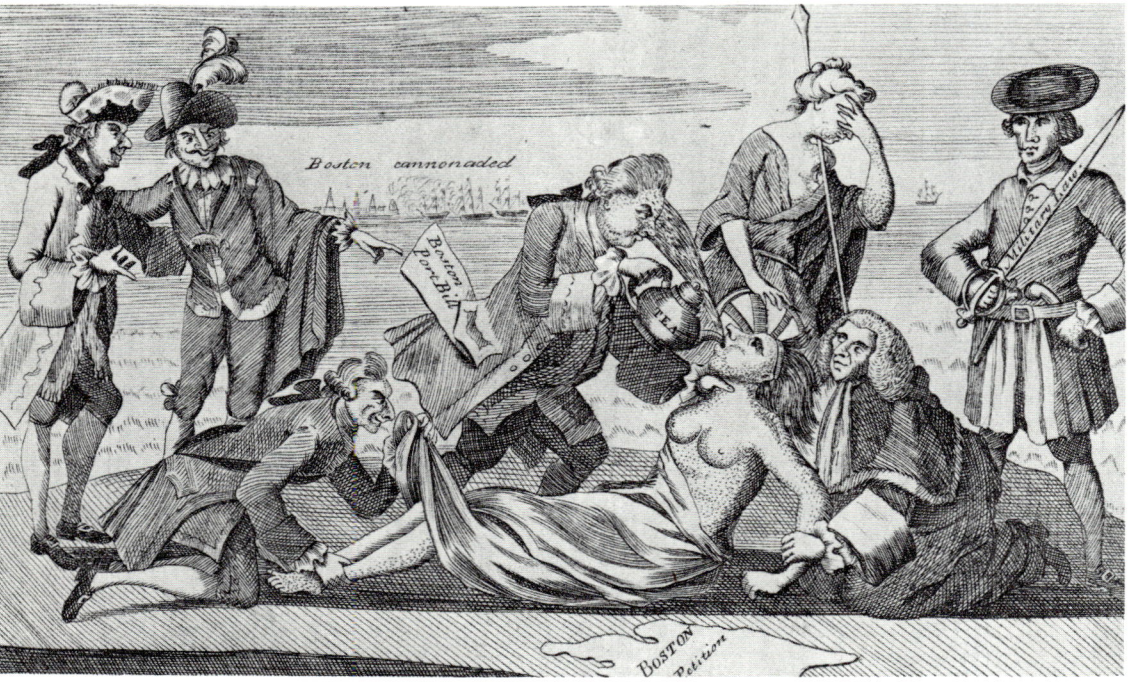

664

663

[The oracle representing, Britannia, Hibernia, Scotia, & America, as assembled to consult the oracle, on the present situation of public affairs, time acting as priest. Dedicated to Concord.] Invt. Drawn & Engrav'd by J. Dixon. Published According to Act of Parliament March 30, 1774.

Mezzotint 20 x 23⅛ in.

Father Time uses a magic lantern to show a picture of the triumph of Concord over Discord. His audience is Britannia, Hibernia, Scotia, and America (an Indian woman). Prints similar to this one are listed as items 738, 739, and 851. CPPS 5225. See also CPPS 5491, 6190.

664

The able Doctor, or America Swallowing the Bitter Draught. [May 1, 1774]

Mixed method 3¾ x 5⅞ in. (image)

America, a half-clad Indian woman, is attacked by Mansfield, North (who is pouring the tea down her throat and has a copy of "Boston Port Bill" in his pocket), Bute, and the Earl of Sandwich. A Frenchman and Spaniard look on, while Britannia weeps. In the foreground a "Boston Petition" lies torn on the ground, and in the background the British fleet is bombarding Boston. CPPS 5226 LC-USZ61-77

—————Another impression. This cartoon originally appeared to illustrate a text describing the debate on the Boston Port Bill. A retaliation for the Boston Tea Party, the bill was passed on March 31, 1774. No bombardment occurred at this time, but with Gage closing the port, military force was imminent. From *The London Magazine*, April 1774, p. 184.

—————A reverse copy. In *The Hibernian Magazine*, May 1774, p. 251.

—————Another copy. Signed "P. Revere Sculp" published in *The Royal American Magazine*, June 1774. LC-USZ62-39592

665

The Whitehall Pump. [May 1, 1774]
  Mixed method 6⅜ x 4¾ in.

The tea torture in item 664 is echoed in this print. Lord North pumps water from a fountain into the mouth of Britannia lying on top of America, represented as an Indian. The fountain is surmounted with the head of George III, and ministers such as Apsley, Mansfield, Sandwich, Bute, and Holland (with fox's head) approve the action, while Wilkes and Camden (?) protest. The Ministry is using the King's resources to torture England as well as America. This copy in P&P is originally from *The Westminster Magazine*, 1774, opposite p. 168. CPPS 5227 LC–USZ62–45371

666

The Mitred Minuet. [May 1, 1774]
  Line engraving 6⅜ x 3¾ in. (image)

Four bishops cross hands over a copy of the Quebec Bill. Three ministers, two of whom are Bute and North, and the devil stand by smiling. In England as well as America the Quebec Act (May 20, 1774) was viewed with suspicion. Englishmen feared that the Anglican Church and the North administration were leaning toward reconciliation with the Roman Catholic Church. In the Colonies the acceptance of Catholicism for French Canadians and the land concessions in the interior revived the antagonisms of the French and Indian War. Stauffer, 2688. CPPS 5228 LC–USZ62–45376

————Another impression. In *The London Magazine*, July 1774, p. 312.

————Another copy. In *The Hibernian Magazine*, August 1774, p. 416.

————Another copy by Paul Revere. In *The Royal American Magazine*, October 1774.

667

A Political Lesson. J. Dixon invenit et fecit.

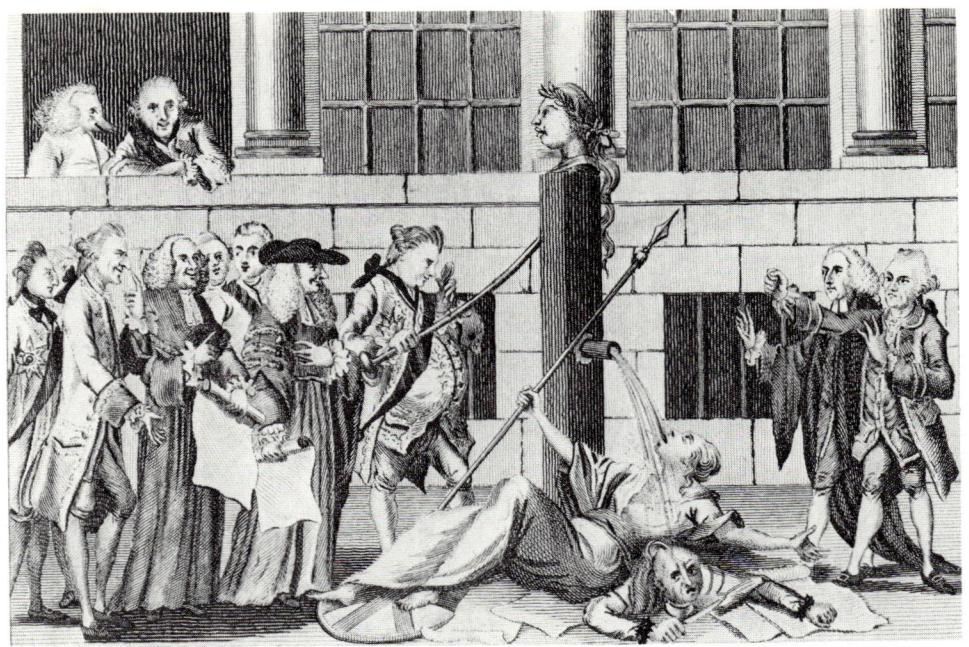

665

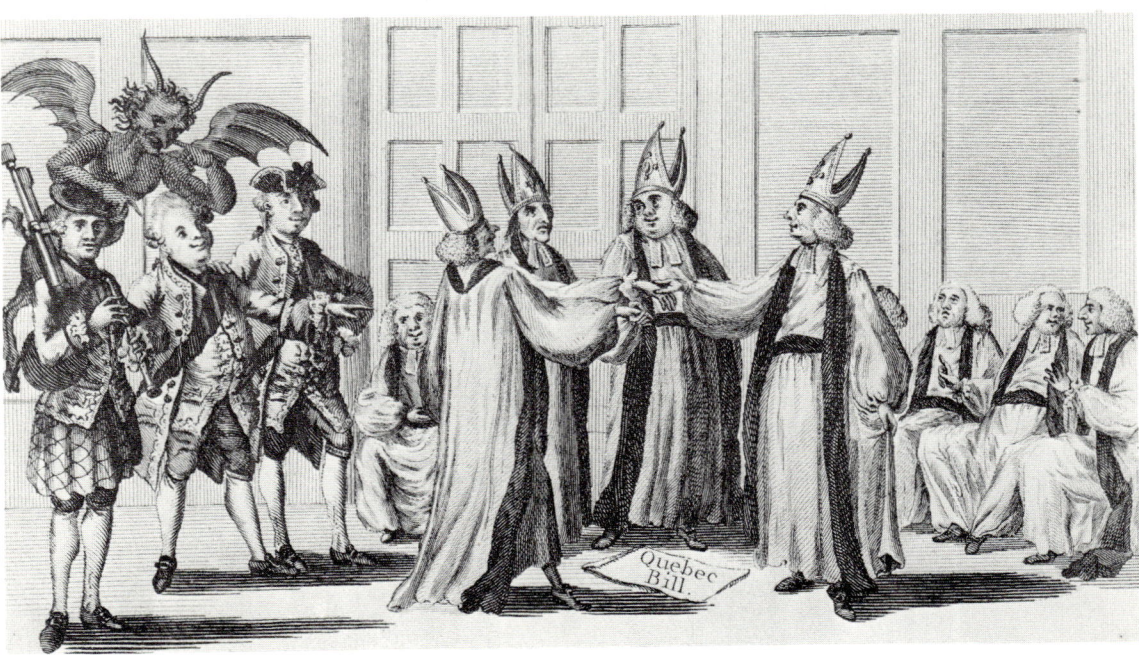

666

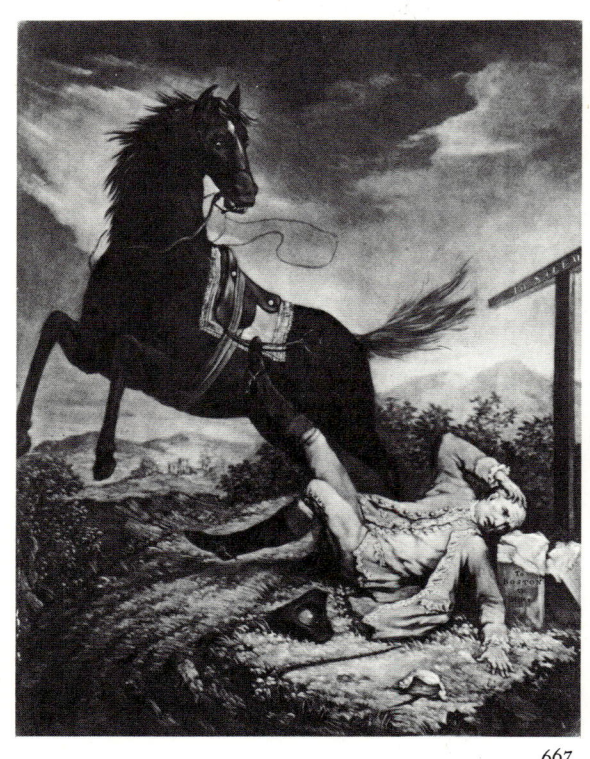

667

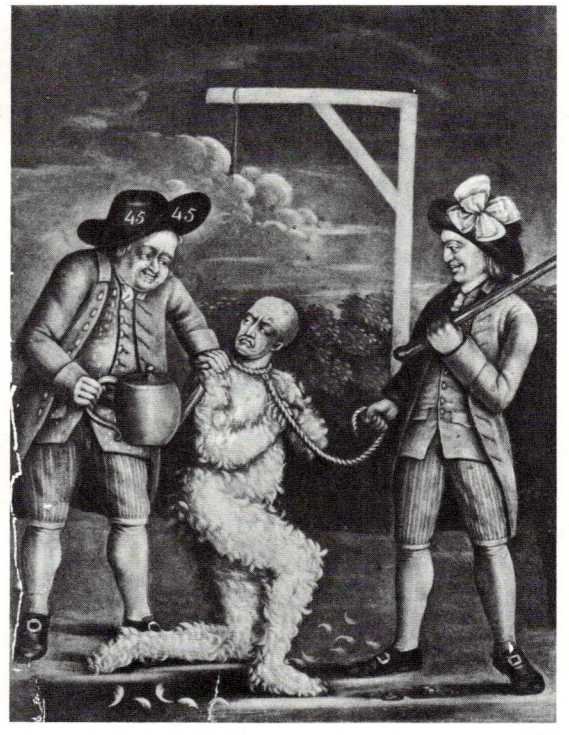

668

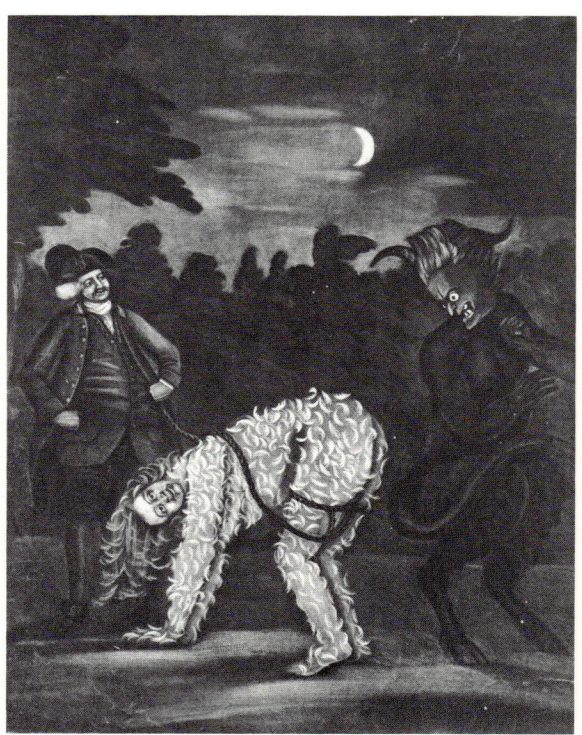

699

Published 7 Sepr. 1774. [Printed for John Bowles, at No 13 in Cornhill.]
Mezzotint 9¾ x 14 in.

A rider representing England falls off a horse on the road between Boston and Salem. He has broken a milestone with his head; the stone reads "to Boston VI Miles." At this time the port of Boston was closed, and Salem was the nearest port. CPPS 5230
LC–USZ62–45380

668

A New Method of MACARONY MAKING, as practised at BOSTON. [Printed for Carington Bowles, No. 69 in St. Pauls Church Yard, London. Published 12 Octr 1774.]
Mezzotint 9⅜ x 12¾ in. (image)

Depicts two Bostonians preparing to pour tea down the throat of a customs officer who has been tarred and feathered. A gallows stands in the background. Probably refers to a riot in Boston involving John Malcom who was tarred and feathered and threatened with hanging. See CPPS 5232 for a description of a miniature version of this print.
LC–USZ62–45386

669

[Tarring and feathering, 177?]
Mezzotint 10 x 12½ in.

Possibly another version of the John Malcom incident. See CPPS 5232 for possible connection. LC–USZ62–45390

670

The BOSTONIAN'S Paying the EXCISE-MAN, or TARRING & FEATHERING [Dawe?] London Printed for Robt. Sayer & J. Bennett, Map & Printseller No. 53, Fleet Street as the Act directs 31 Octr. 1774
Mezzotint 14 x 9½ in.

Another version of the John Malcom inci-

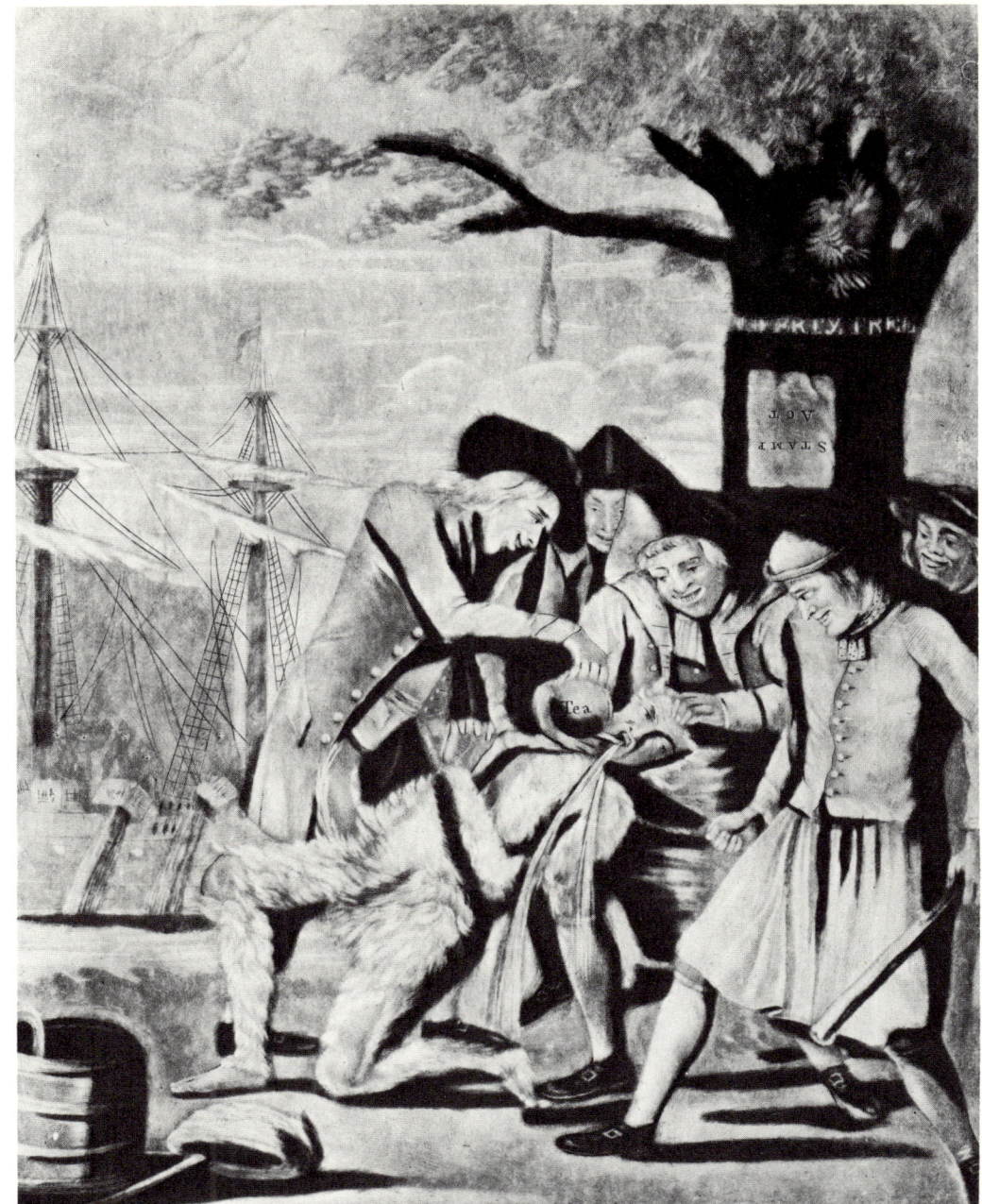

670

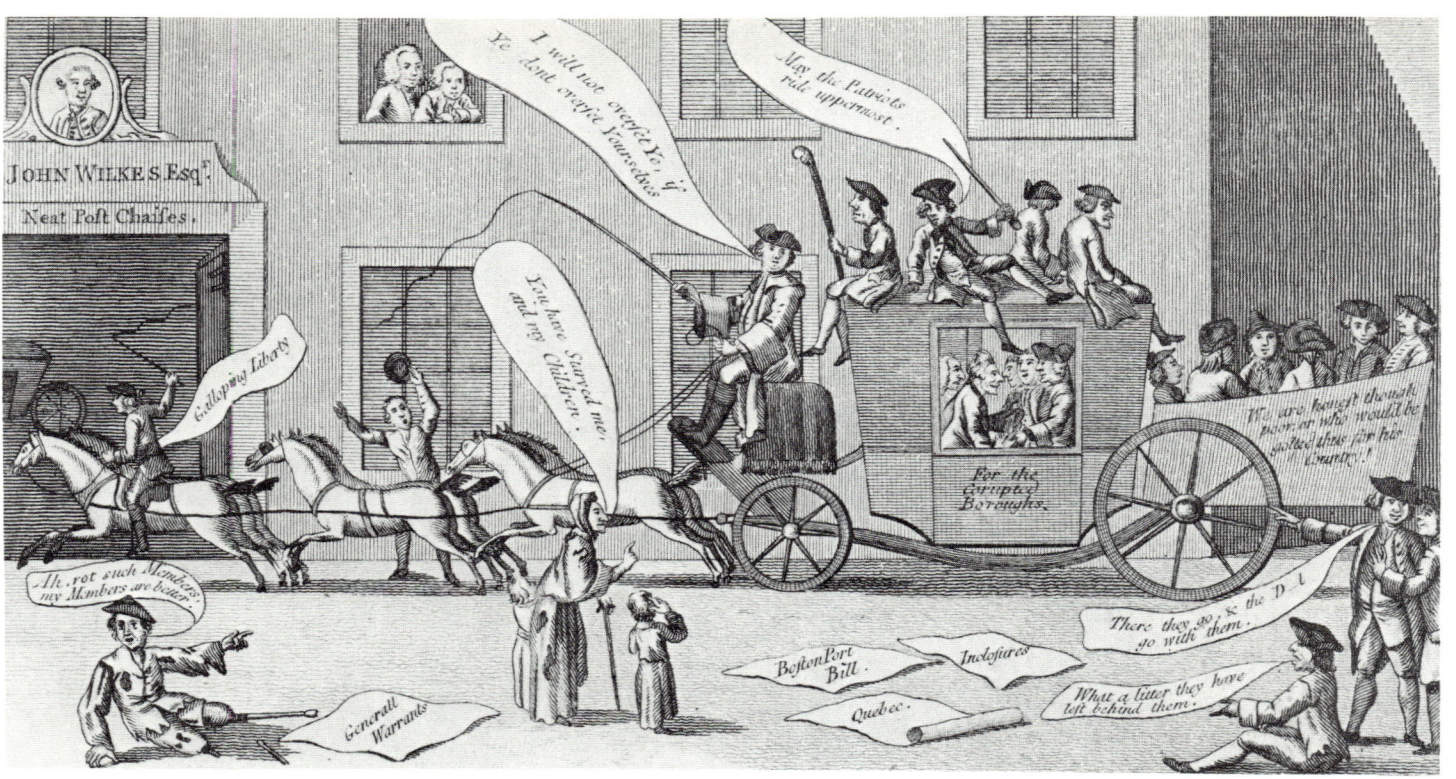

dent. Five Bostonians pour tea down the throat of a tarred and feathered excise man. In the background tea is poured from a ship, the Liberty Tree has a noose hanging from a branch, and a sign reading "stamp act" hangs upside down. Probably by Philip Dawe. See R. T. H. Halsey, *The Boston Port Bill as Pictured by a Contemporary London Cartoonist* (New York, 1904) for a full study of this cartoon and others by Dawe, who was a pupil of Hogarth. CPPS 5232 LC–USZ62–9487

671
The Dissolution of P_____t. [November 1, 1774]
Mixed method 7½ x 4 in. (image)

Parliament was dissolved on September 30, 1774. This scene shows MP's in a carriage driving past a building which commemorates Wilkes. Scattered on the ground are documents which contributed to the dissolution: "Inclosures," "Generall Warrants," "Quebec" [Act], and the "Boston Port Bill." North prematurely closed the session ("the most fateful in the history of the British Parliament" according to Namier and Brooke in *History of Parliament*, v. 1, p. 73) because his ministry had recently passed acts coercing the Bostonians while mollifying the Canadians, and "it was better for the Government to face the next stage of the American dispute with a new Parliament, rather than be caught by it in the middle of preparations for a general election."

(ibid., p. 74) The next entry and items 675 and 676 deal with this event. CPPS 5236 LC–USZ62–45427

————Another impression. In *The London Magazine*, November 1774, opposite p. 464.

672
The Parlmt. dissolved, or, The DEVIL turn'd FORTUNE TELLER. Design'd & Engrav'd by G. Terry, Paternoster Row. [1774?]
Mixed method 9¾ x 6¼ in. (image)

The Devil conjures up an American Indian who steps on the neck of a British soldier and taps a model of the Parliament building causing bodies to fall out. Lord North and another minister look on in horror. This

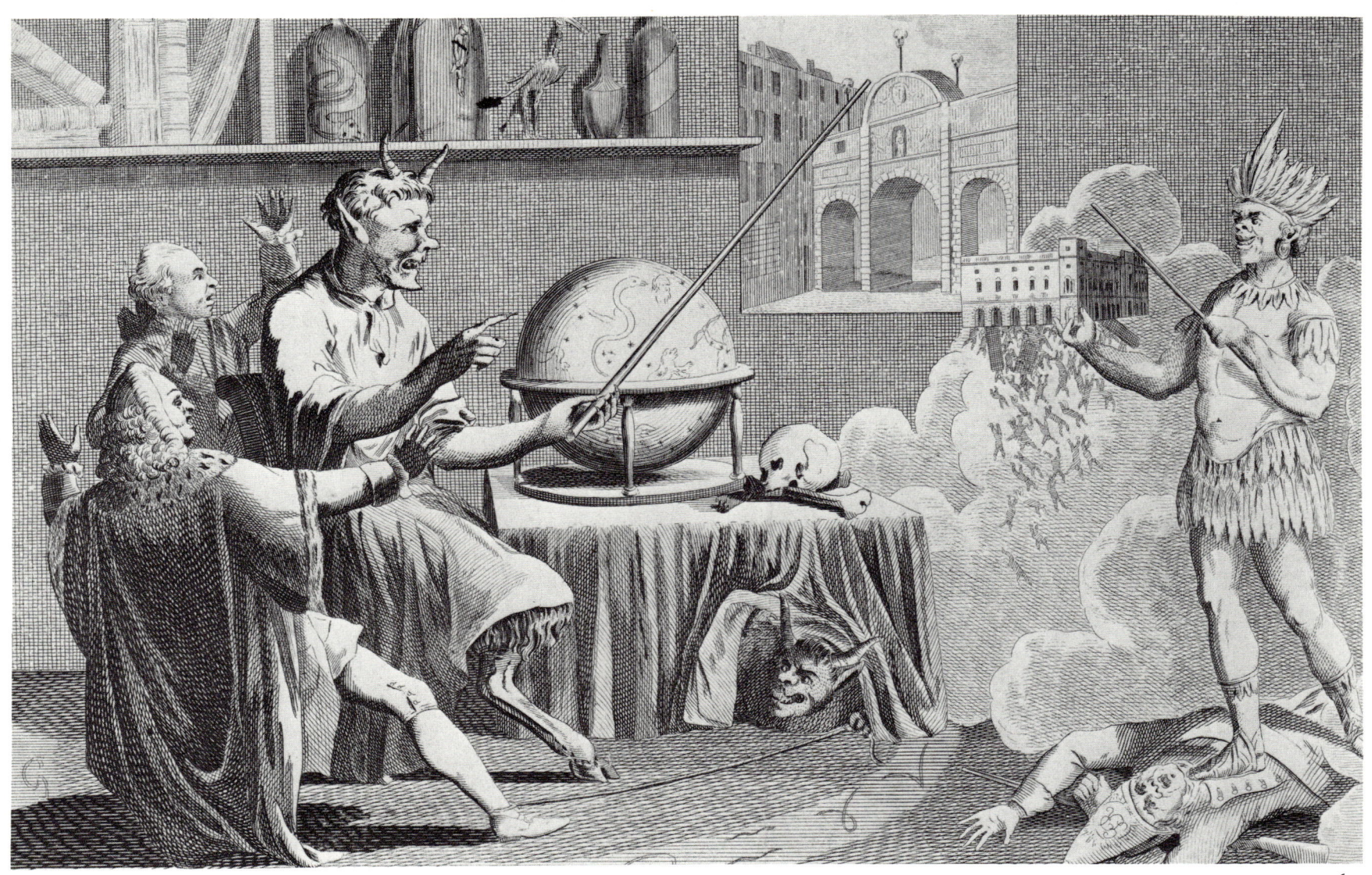

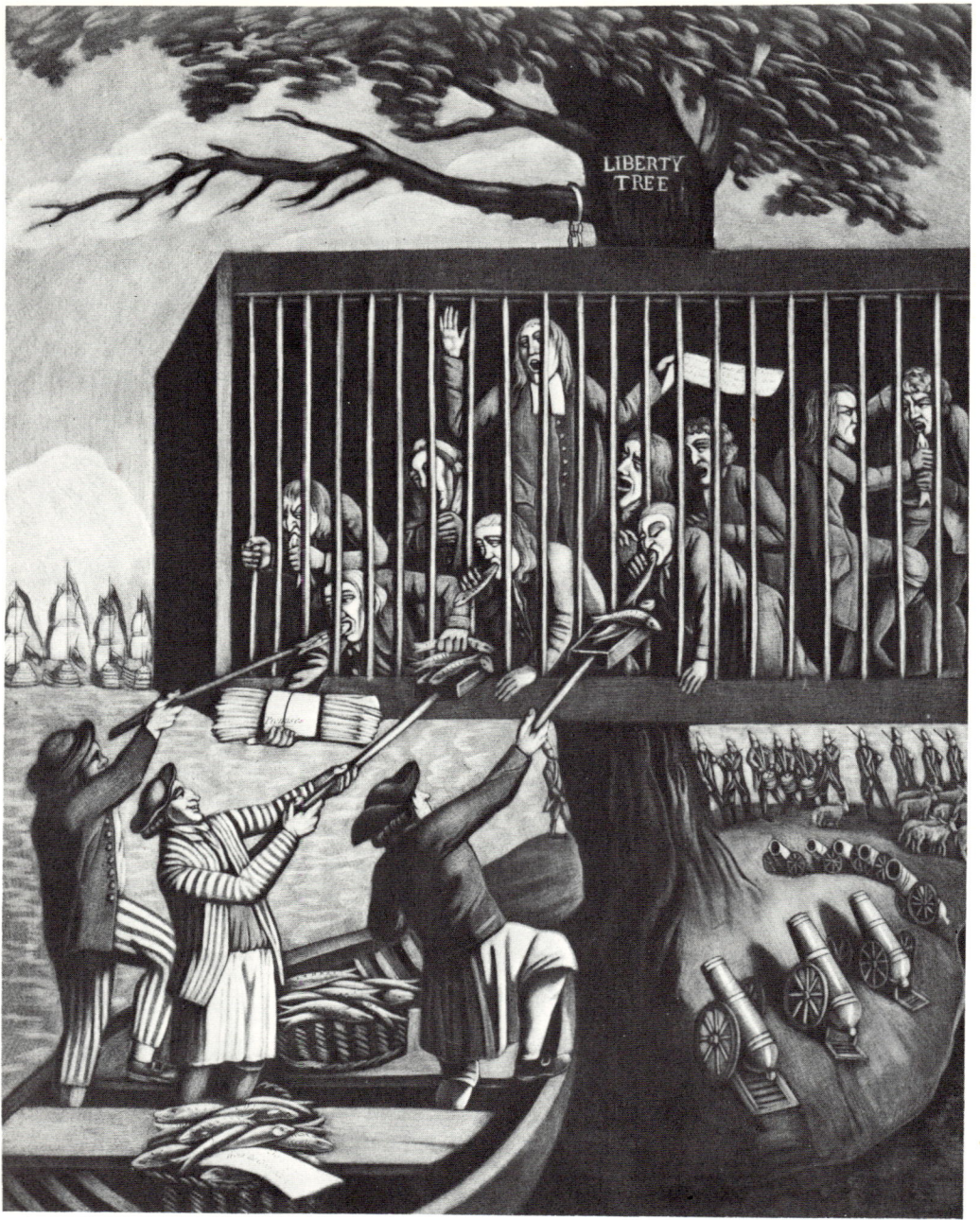

673

cartoon predicts the consequences of North's dissolution. The King and North were determined to hold their American policy at this point, and the colonists had to accept it or fight. CPPS 5238 LC–USZ62–45428

673

The BOSTONIANS in DISTRESS. London. Printed for R. Sayer and J. Bennett. Map & Printsellers, No. 53 Fleet Street, as the Act directs, 19 Novr. 1774

Mezzotint 14 x 9¾ in.

Ten Bostonians trapped in a cage hanging from the Liberty Tree exchange fish and promises with three British seamen. Cages like this were used for punishing slaves. In the foreground the British troops and cannons guard the caged colonists. At that time Boston had been closed by the Boston Port Bill. Probably by Philip Dawe. CPPS 5241 LC–USZ62–11139

———Another copy reversed.

674

PLYMOUTH MDCXX [a cartouche celebrating the landing of the Pilgrims] November 29th. 1774. Published according to Act by Thos. Jefferys Geographer to His Royal Highness the Prince of Wales near Charing Cross.

Mixed method 8¼ x 11¼ in. (image)

A group of four Englishmen, a woman, and two boys are ushered into the New World by a goddess who carries a liberty cap on top of a staff. This picture is from a map entitled "A Map of the most Inhabited part of New England containing the Provinces of Massachusetts Bay and New Hampshire, with the Colonies of Connecticut and Rhode Island, divided into Counties and Townships . . . ." From Thomas Jefferys, *The American Atlas* (London, 1775), no. 15–16. This cartouche also appears in the editions for 1776, 1778, and 1782. Negative in G&M.

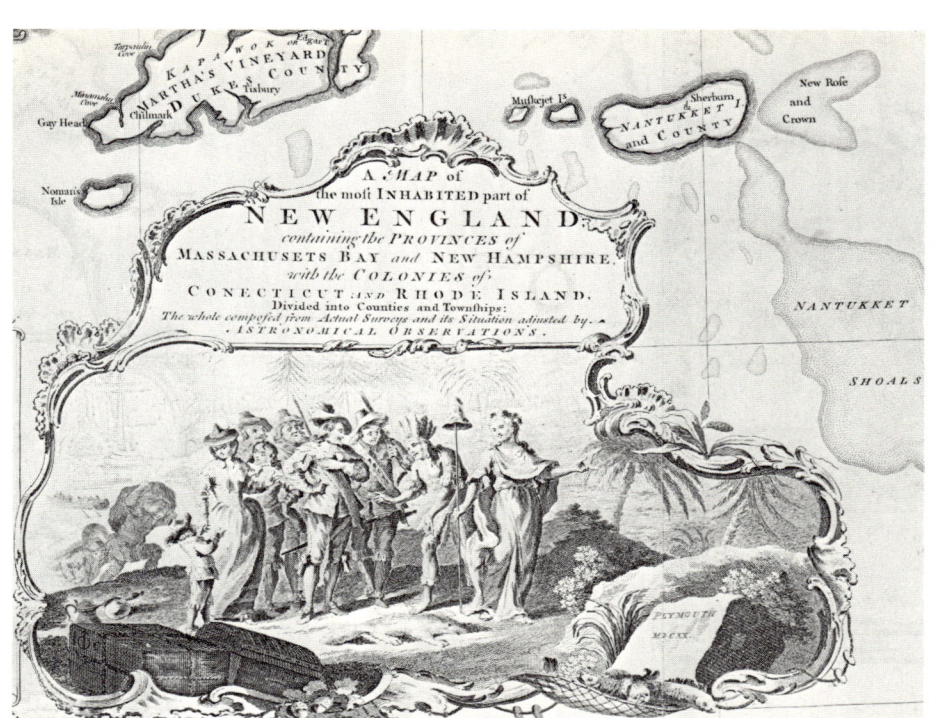

674

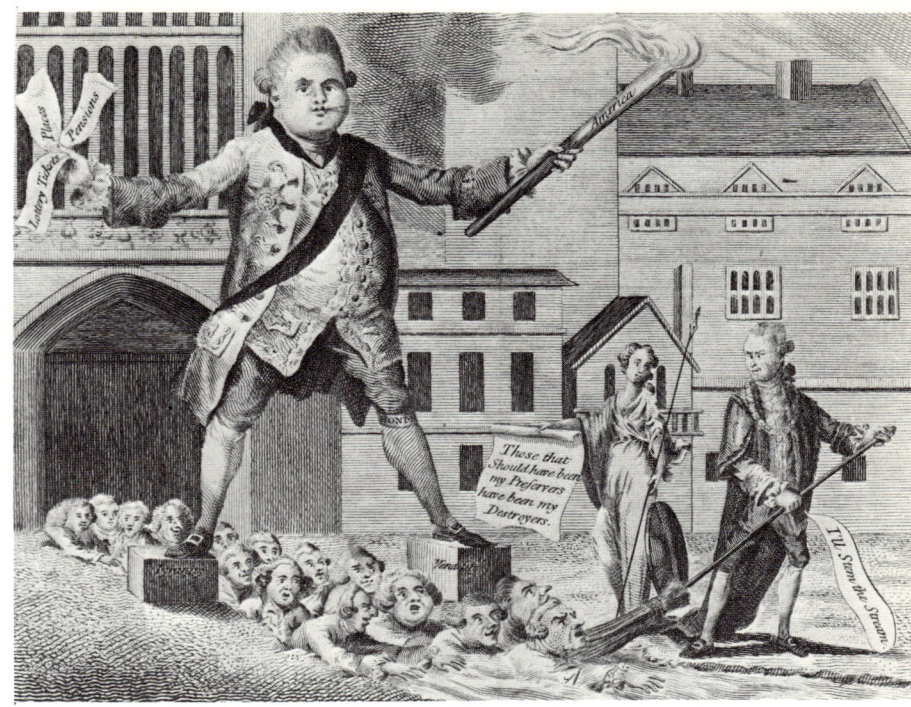

675

———Another copy (reversed). In Le Rouge, *Atlas Ameriquain Septentrional* (Paris, 1778–92), no. 10.

———Another impression. In Faden, *North American Atlas* (London, 1777), no. 8–9.

———Another impression. In Jefferys, *A General Topography of North America* (London, 1768), no. 29.

———Another copy "published by Tobias Conrad Lotter, in Augsburg." In Lotter, *Atlas Géographique* (Nürnberg, 1778), no. 101.

675

The Colossus of the North; or The Striding Boreas. [December 1, 1774]

Mixed method 6¾ x 5 in.

Lord North astride a stream full of members of Parliament flowing from Westminster. He holds papers reading "Lottery Tickets," "Pensions," and "Places" in one hand and a burning torch labelled "America" in the other. Wilkes and Britannia try to "Stem the Stream." The radical elements interpreted North's dissolution as an attempt to secure more members and thus strengthen the King's hold on Parliament. This intention is doubtful. North must have known that Wilkes' popularity was increasing, and although the radicals gained members, they never had enough votes to defeat all of North's policies. This cartoon expresses the hope that Wilkes, a man of the people, will change the course of the stream. CPPS 5242 LC–USZ62–34869

———Another impression (hand colored).

———Another impression. In *The London Magazine*, November 1774, opposite p. 520 (folding plate).

———Another copy. In *The Hibernian Magazine*, December 1774.

676

The Council of the Rulers, & the Elders against the Tribe of ye Americanites. Sold by W. Gillman Rochester. [January 1, 1775]

Etching 4 x 5¾ in.

After the election of 1774, Wilkes returned to Parliament with no trouble and with more supporters from Middlesex. He points at Lord North who is slipping bank notes into the pockets of an MP. In the background members argue around a table, and on the wall a map

277

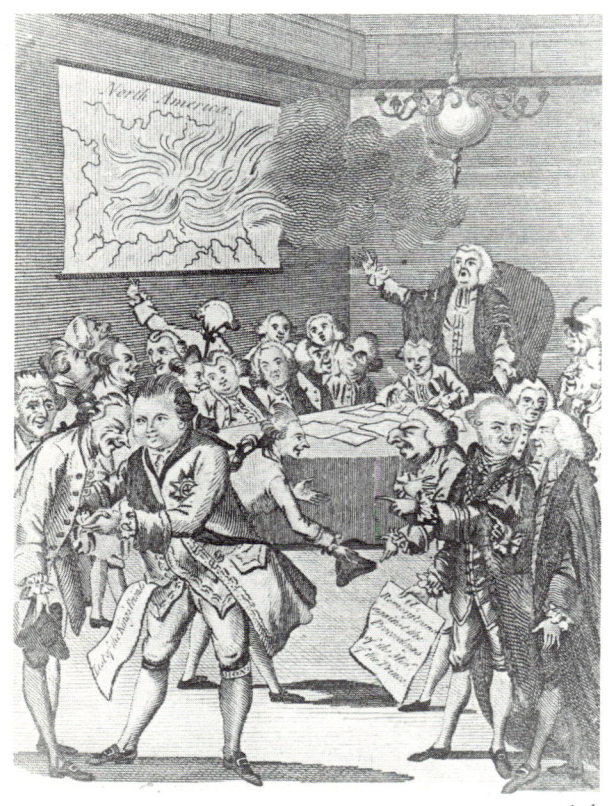

676

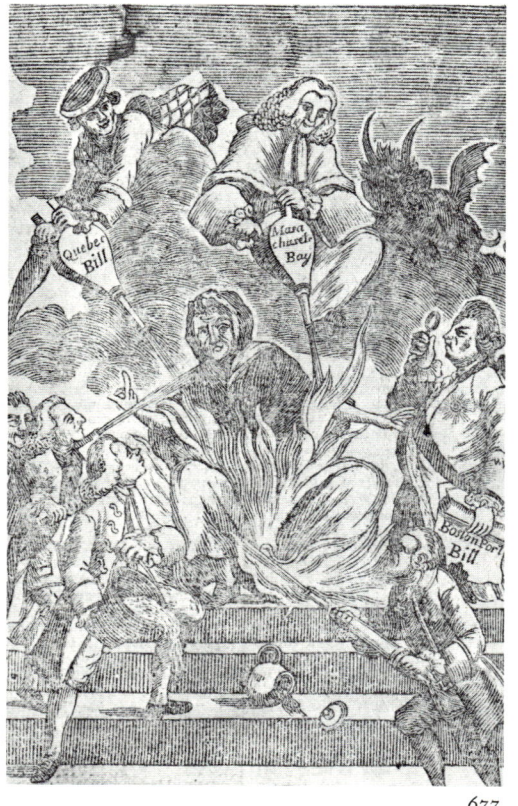

677

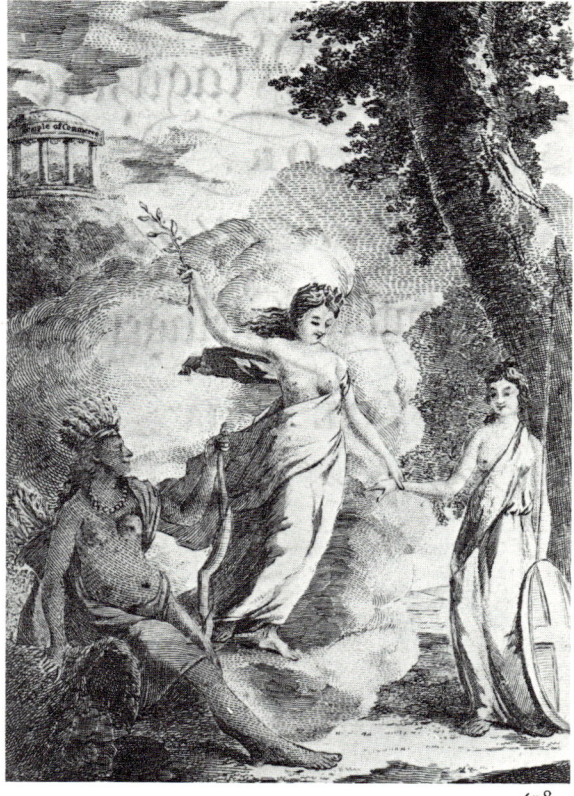

678

of America bursts into flames. CPPS 5281
LC–USZ61–79

677

AMERICA IN FLAMES. [December 1, 1774]
Woodcut 5¾ x 3⅝ in.

America is pictured as an old lady seated on flames. Bute blows a bellows designated "Quebec Bill," and Mansfield works a bellows marked "Masachusets Bay." The Devil and Lord North look on. At the bottom four patriots, possibly including Wilkes and John Horne Tooke, try to extinguish the flame. The same letter of explanation accompanies the two copies of this picture in *The Town and Country Magazine* and *The Hibernian Magazine*:

> Sir,
> I have sent the inclosed drawing, which you may lay before your readers in a wooden block, as it will lead to point out the chief actors in the American tragedy which is upon the point of being represented in that quarter of the globe. The three most elevated characters consist of a well known trio, who constantly act in conjunction, and may be considered as the first movers of the late American acts that have given the Bostonians and the other colonists so much disquietude. The gentleman on the right hand side with his glass, and one of the bills in his hand [Boston Port Bill], is considered as the ostensible agent of the trio. America is represented under the figure of a venerable lady, whose critical situation requires the aid and assistance of all the patriotic band, who are exerting their utmost endeavor, to quench the flames that threaten the existence of our colonies, for little more than the demolition of an old tea-pot. In the patriotic group are some well known faces, that may be often seen in and near the Mansion-house, and among the members of the society of the Bill of Rights. How far their endeavors may prove successful, time only can determine, as we see the chief engines on the opposite side keep in constant play to blow the flames of discord.
> As an impartial by-stander, I have endeavoured to represent the conduct of both parties, leaving your readers to determine upon the rectitude of their measures.

From *The Town and Country Magazine*, December 1774, p. 659. CPPS 5282 LC–USZ62–34864

———Another copy. 5¾ x 3½ in. From *The Hibernian Magazine*, January 1775, p. 52–53.

678

When fell Debate & civil Wars shall cease. [January 1775]
Mixed method 7½ x 4¾ in.

Peace descends on a cloud from the "Temple of Commerce" and is joined by America and Britannia. The verse below reads:

> When fell Debate & civil Wars shall cease,
> Commerce shall spread her Sails o'er all the Seas.
> ENGLAND unrivall'd in the liberal Arts,
> Shall bear her Genius to remotest Parts,
> Take to thy Breast, AMERICA again,
> Thou may'st defy imperious FRANCE & SPAIN.

From *The London Magazine*, 1775, frontispiece. CPPS 5283 LC–USZ62–45499

679

The PATRIOTICK BARBER of NEW YORK, or the CAPTAIN in the SUDS. [Dawe?] London, Printed for R. Sayer, and J. Bennett, No. 53 Fleet Street, as the Act directs 14 Feb. 1775.
Mezzotint 12¾ x 9¾ in.

The scene is a New York barbershop where Jacob Vredenburgh refused to finish shaving an English seaman when the latter's identity was revealed as Capt. John Crozer. The London cartoonist portrayed a patriotic barber's shop with prints of Pitt and Camden, both favored for their resistance to the Stamp Act, on the wall. The names of prominent patriots on wig boxes list regular customers: Cornelius Low, Abraham Livingston, Alexander McDougall (the American Wilkes), John Lamb, Isaac Sears, John Blagge, William Lugg, Antony Griffiths, Francis Van-Dyke, Broome, Jacobus Van Zandt, and Welle (Walter) Franklin. A verse below the title exhorts other patriots to follow the barber's example.

> Then Patriot grand maintain thy stand,
> And whilst thou sav'st America's Land,
> Preserve the Golden Rule;
> Forbid the Captain there to roam,
> Half shave them first, then send 'em home
> Objects of ridicule.

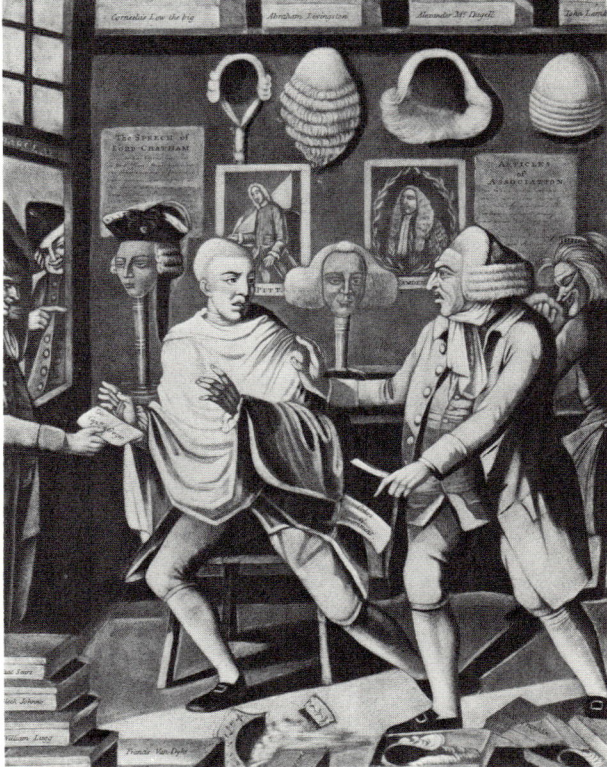

679

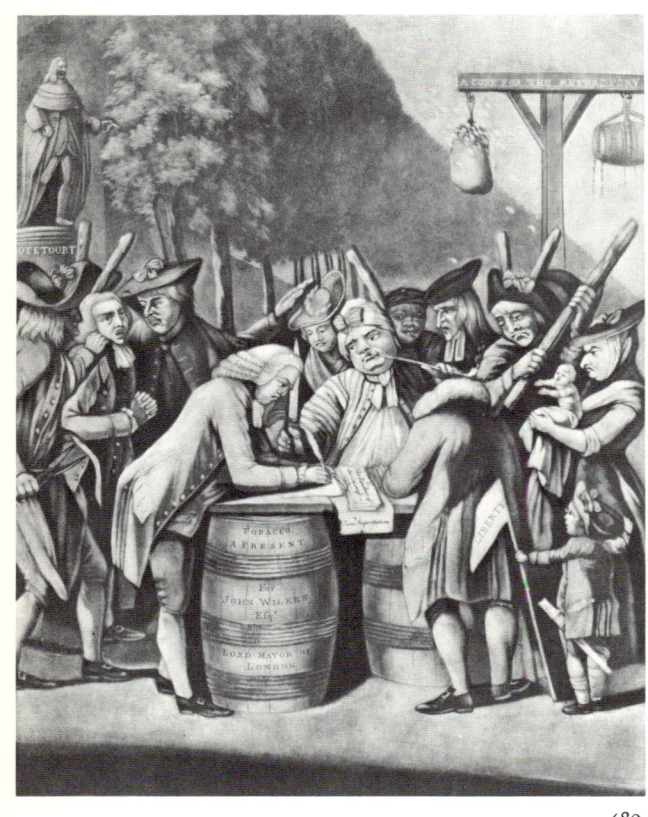

680

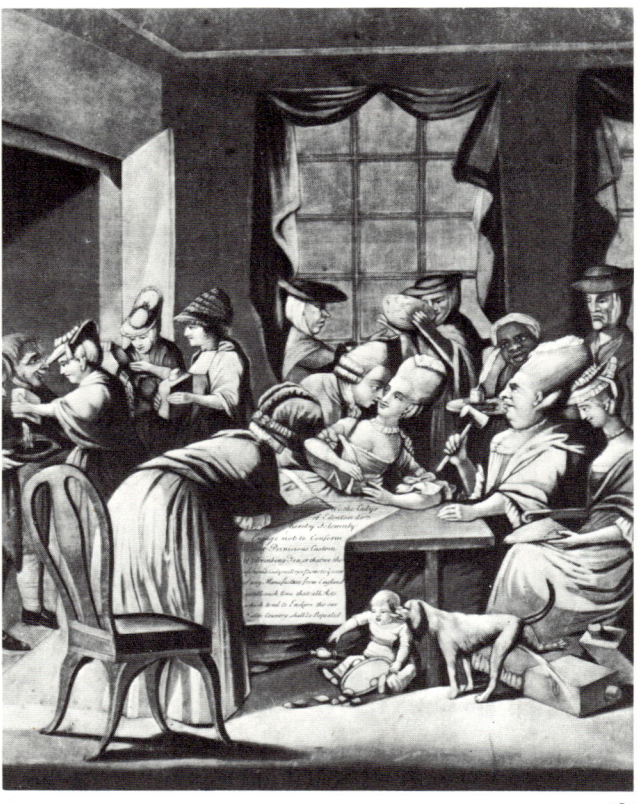

681

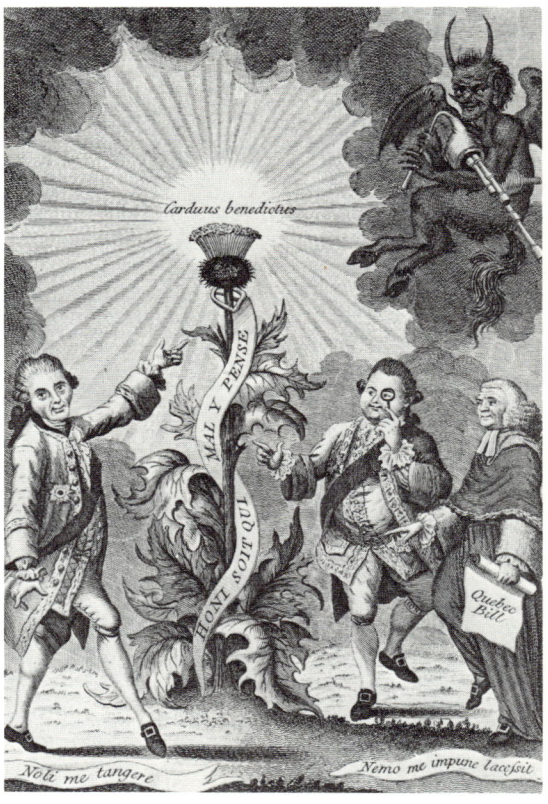

682

See Halsey, *The Boston Port Bill* (New York, 1904), p. 217–222. CPPS 5284
LC-USZ62-17658

680

THE ALTERNATIVE OF WILLIAMS-BURG [Dawe?] London. Printed for R. Sayer, & J. Bennett, No. 53 Fleet Street, as the Act directs, 16 Feb. 1775.

Mezzotint 10 x 12¾ in.

In Virginia the Sons of Liberty forced loyalists to sign either the Associations or the Resolutions of the Williamsburg Convention of 1774. The patriots ran up a barrel of tar and a sack of feathers on a gibbet, and the threat produced many signatures. To the left a loyalist is dragged toward the gibbet in the background. A statue of Lord Botetourt, the former governor, overlooks the scene of threatened violence. In this print the colonists are writing on a barrel marked, "Tobacco, A Present For John Wilkes Esqr. Lord Mayor of London." CPPS 5284, Pl. IV LC-USZ62-9488

681

A SOCIETY OF PATRIOTIC LADIES, at EDENTON in NORTH CAROLINA. [Dawe?] London. Printed for R. Sayer & J. Bennett, No. 53 Fleet Street, as the Act directs 25 March 1775.

Mezzotint 13¾ x 10 in.

North Carolina ladies sign an agreement not to drink tea. The document reads:

We the Ladys of Edenton do hereby Solemnly Engage not to Conform to that Pernicious Custom of Drinking Tea, or that we the aforesaid Ladys will not promote ye wear of any Manufacture from England untill such time that all Acts which tend to Enslave this our Native Country shall be Repealed.

CPPS 5284, Pl. V LC-USZ62-12711

682

The Thistle Reel. [March 1, 1775]
Etching 6¼ x 4¼ in. (image)

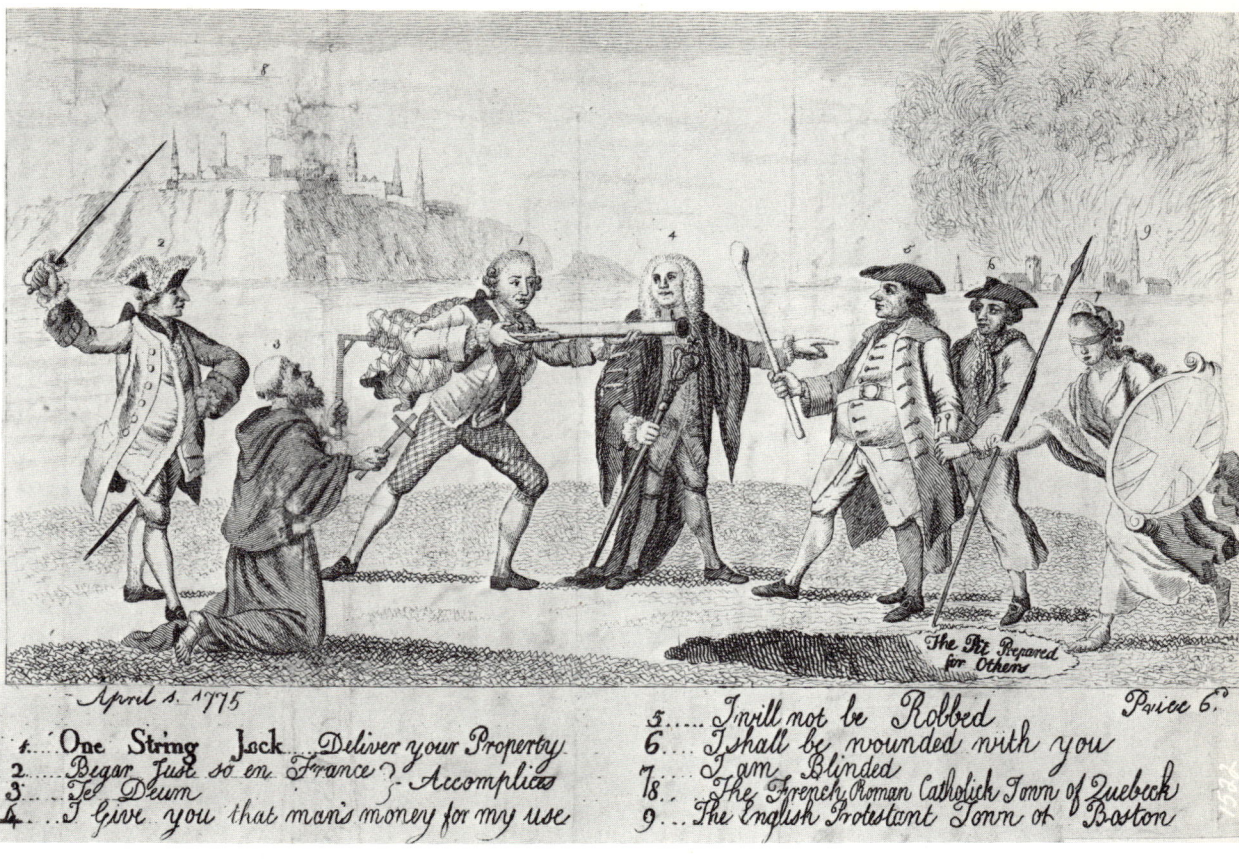

683

The cartoon attacks British policy in America as inspired by Bute, Mansfield, North, and other Scottish influences. The devil plays a bagpipe. Mansfield holds a copy of the Quebec Bill, while they all dance a reel. CPPS 5285 LC-USZ62-45429

——————Another impression. In *The London Magazine*, February 1775, p. 56.

683

VIRTUAL REPRESENTATION. 1775. April 1. 1775 Price 6d.

Mixed method 6½ x 11⅛ in. (image)

Lord Bute aims a blunderbuss at a stout American who threatens him with a club and says, "I will not be Robbed." An English sailor supports the American saying, "I shall be wounded with you," and Britannia blindfolded steps towards a hole designated "The Pit Prepared for Others." A Frenchman and a Catholic priest look on. In the background, "The French Roman Catholick Town of Quebeck" stands serenely above the water, and on the right side, "The English Protestant Town of Boston" is enveloped in flames. The irony of favoring Quebec over Boston prompted this cartoon which accuses Bute of allying

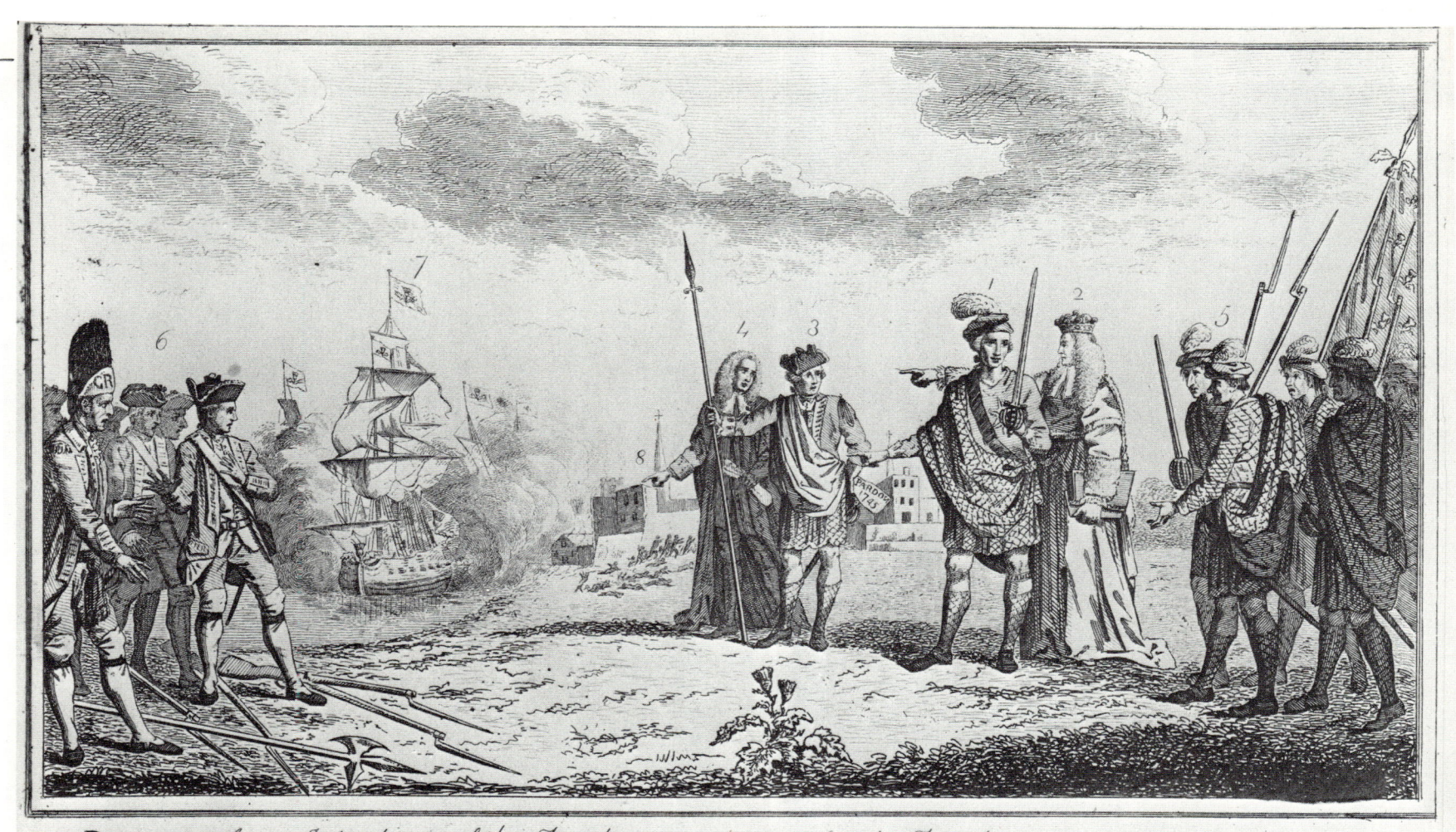

himself with France. CPPS 5286 LC–USZ62–1522

684

The Scotch Butchery, Boston, 1775. Pubsd: According to Act of Parlnt 1775

Etching 6¾ x 12 in. (image)

While British ships under the ensign of a thistle bombard Boston, Bute, Mansfield, Simon Fraser, and Alexander Wedderburn direct Scottish soldiers to attack. English soldiers, struck with horror, drop their arms. CPPS 5287 LC–USZ62–1512

685

The Political Cartoon, for the Year 1775. [May 1, 1775]

Mixed method 7 x 4⅛ in. (image)

Mansfield drives an open coach carrying George III and Lord Bute toward a ravine. A group of Scotsmen make plans at a table, and a group of fat Anglican clergymen, North among them, looks on with approval. A member of Parliament offers bribes to a crowd, while Chatham and Camden try in vain to stop the coach. America, pictured as a city across the sea, burns. This cartoon from P&P was originally from *The Westminster Magazine*, May 1775, opposite p. 209. CPPS 5288 LC–USZ62–12302

686

[An Indian Bows to Europe] R. R. inv & fect [1775]

Etching 5½ x 3¼ in. (image)

A kneeling Indian presents a map of his lands to Europe. At her feet a cherub plays, and Neptune sits between two jugs, one marked Mississippi, pouring water into the ocean. From Romans, *A Concise Natural History of East and West Florida* (New York, 1775), frontispiece. Stauffer, 2734. LC–USZ62–45536

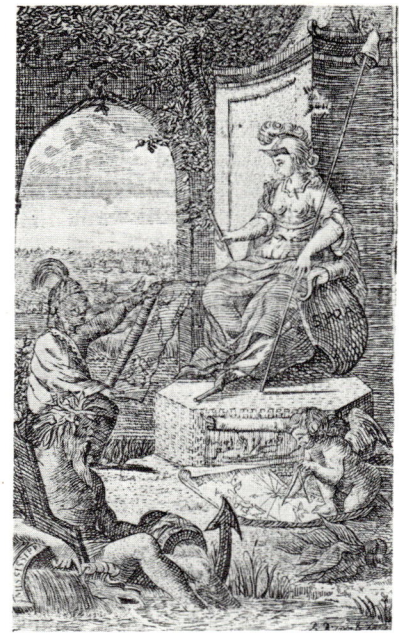

686

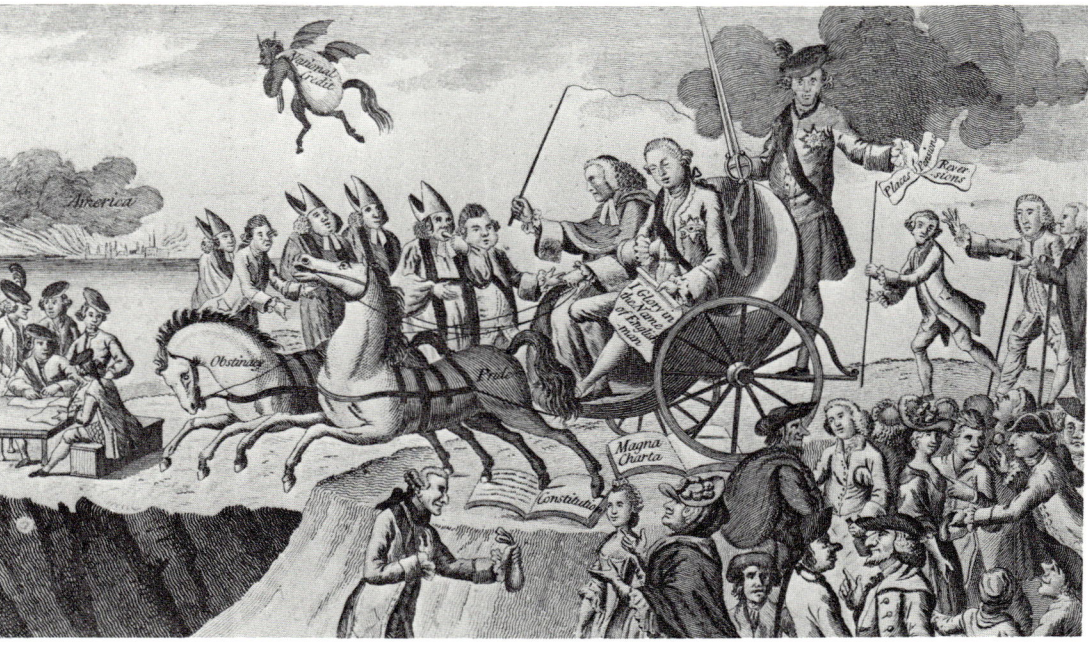

685

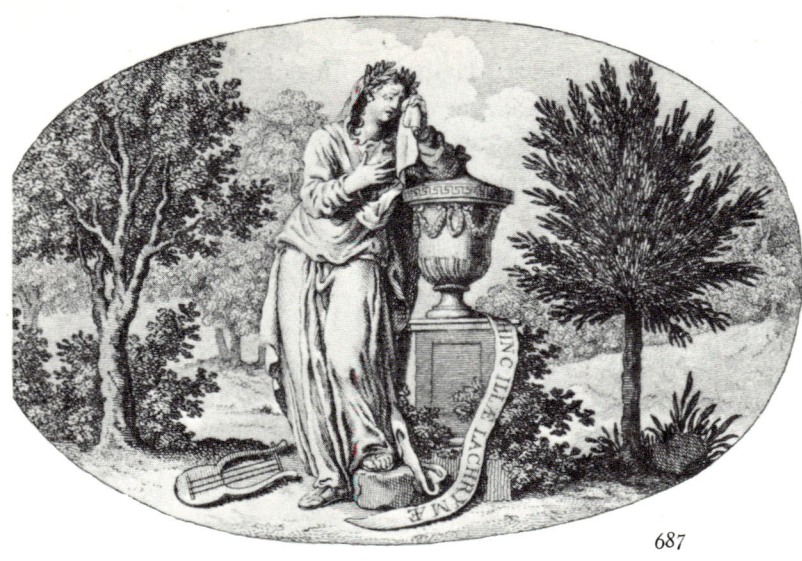

687

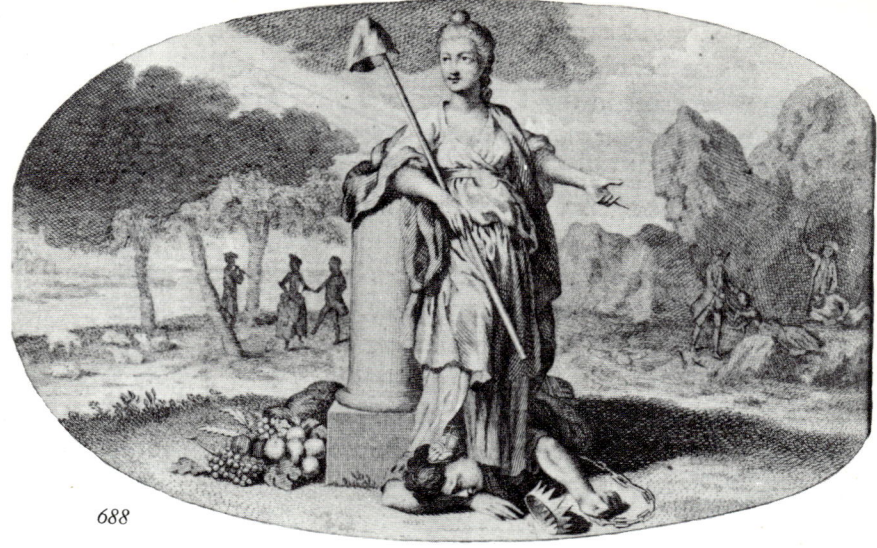

688

687

[Harmony Weeps for the Present Situation of American Affairs.] Isc. Taylor sc. J. C. invt. [1775]

Mixed method 2½ x 3¾ in. (image)

The goddess Harmony leans on an urn weeping. A ribbon draped on the pedestal reads, "HINC ILLAE LACHRYMAE." From William Smith, *Sermon on the Present Situation of American Affairs* (London, 1775), title page. LC–USZ62–45533

688

[Liberty Conquers Tyranny] Isaac Taylor del et sculp. [1775]

Etching 2⅞ x 4¼ in. (image)

Liberty leans on a pillar with her right foot on the neck of a man whose crown and chain is lying beside him on the ground. From William Smith, *Sermon on the Present Situation of American Affairs* (London, 1775), p. 32, tailpiece. LC–USZ62–45534

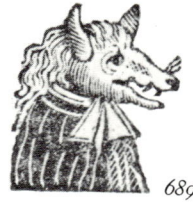

689

689

[A fox in preacher's clothes—a caricature of John Wesley 1775]

Woodcut ¾ x ⅝ in. (image)

In his early years, John Wesley (1703–1791) would have sympathized with the dissenters and the colonists—he spent almost two years (1735–36) as a missionary in Georgia. In 1775, however, he published *A Calm Address to our American Colonies* which stated that taxation was not tyranny. Wesley had become content to settle into quieter preaching and the protection of the Toleration Act. The clash between Wesley and Toplady began in 1758 over the latter's extreme Calvinism. In the work in which this caricature appears, Toplady accused Wesley of plagiarizing from Samuel Johnson's *Taxation No Tyranny* (1775). From Toplady, *An Old Fox Tarr'd and Feather'd* (London, 1775), title page. LC–USZ62–50392

690

A Map of the Present Seat of War on the Borders of Canada [Cartouche] Aitken Sculp [1775]

Mixed method 3 x 4½ in. (image)

An Indian and a frontiersman stand beside the title. On top a cherub sits with staff and liberty cap amid implements of war. In the foreground is a beaver. From *The Pennsylvania Magazine: or, American Monthly Museum*, 1775, opposite p. 463.

691

[Frontispiece for *The Pennsylvania Magazine*] P.E.D. inv. & delin. R. Aitken. Sculp. [1775]

Mixed method 3½ x 4½ in. (image)

The goddess America sits on the ground with

a shield bearing the emblem of the Penn family and a staff with liberty cap on top. Surrounding her are implements of war. The artist used the Greek goddess figure, which often represented America, but portrayed her in a contemporary style. This print was designed by Pierre Eugene Du Simitière and found on the title page of *The Pennsylvania Magazine: or, American Monthly Museum,* 1775. Stauffer, 10. LC–USZ62–45557

692

The CONGRESS or The NECESSARY POLITICIANS. [1775?]

Etching 8 x 6½ in.

Two men in a privy or "necessary house." One sits reading a book entitled "Answer to a P[amphlet En]titled Taxation [No] Tir[anny]," and the other wipes himself with paper from "Resolution[s] of the [C]ongress." This cartoon shows that Englishmen had great interest in American affairs, although some did not think highly of the statements of the colonists. On the wall are a partial portrait of John Wilkes and a picture of a man tarred and feathered. When the colonists chastised John Malcom with tar and feathers, they symbolically chastised Pitt's government. CPPS 5297 LC–USZ62–1511

693

Der Siegende Engeländer und der Streitende Americaner Welches sich den 19. Sept: Anno. 1777, zugetragen das General Howe die Americaner unter Wasshington gänzlich geschlagen habe der Verlust wird aus 600, Tode und blessirte und 200, Krigs-Gefangene geschäzet. J.M.P. sc. J.M. Probst exc. A.P. [177?]

Line engraving 6¼ x 11 in.

This battle scene is more an allegory than a depiction of a particular event. In the foreground, a white man, probably Gen. William

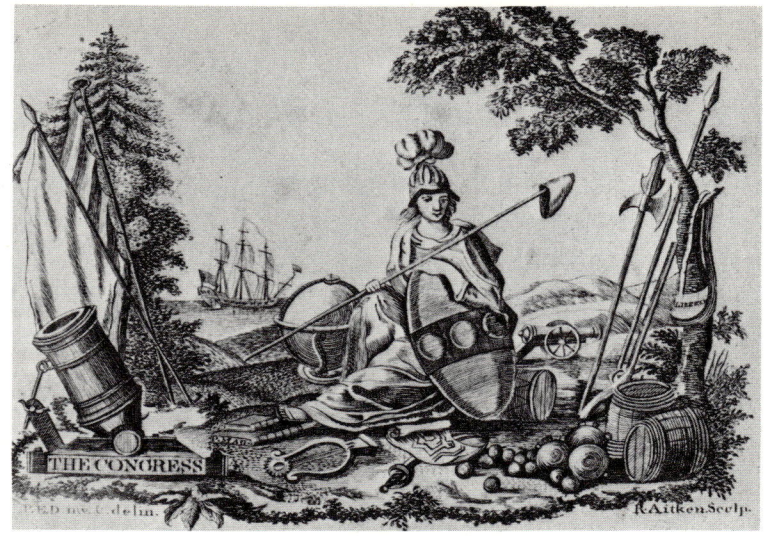
691

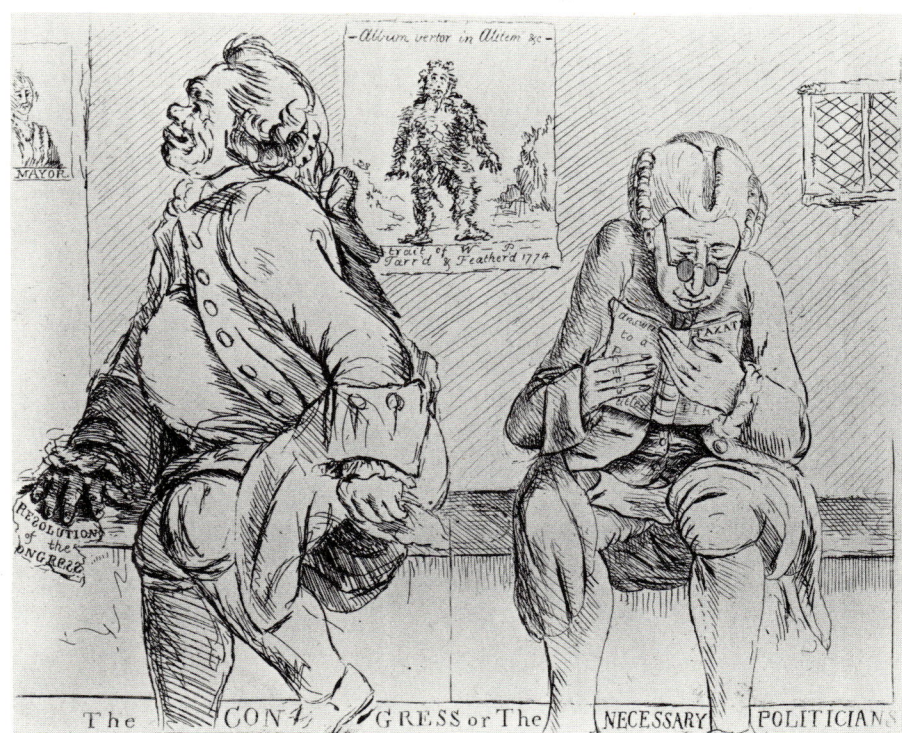
692

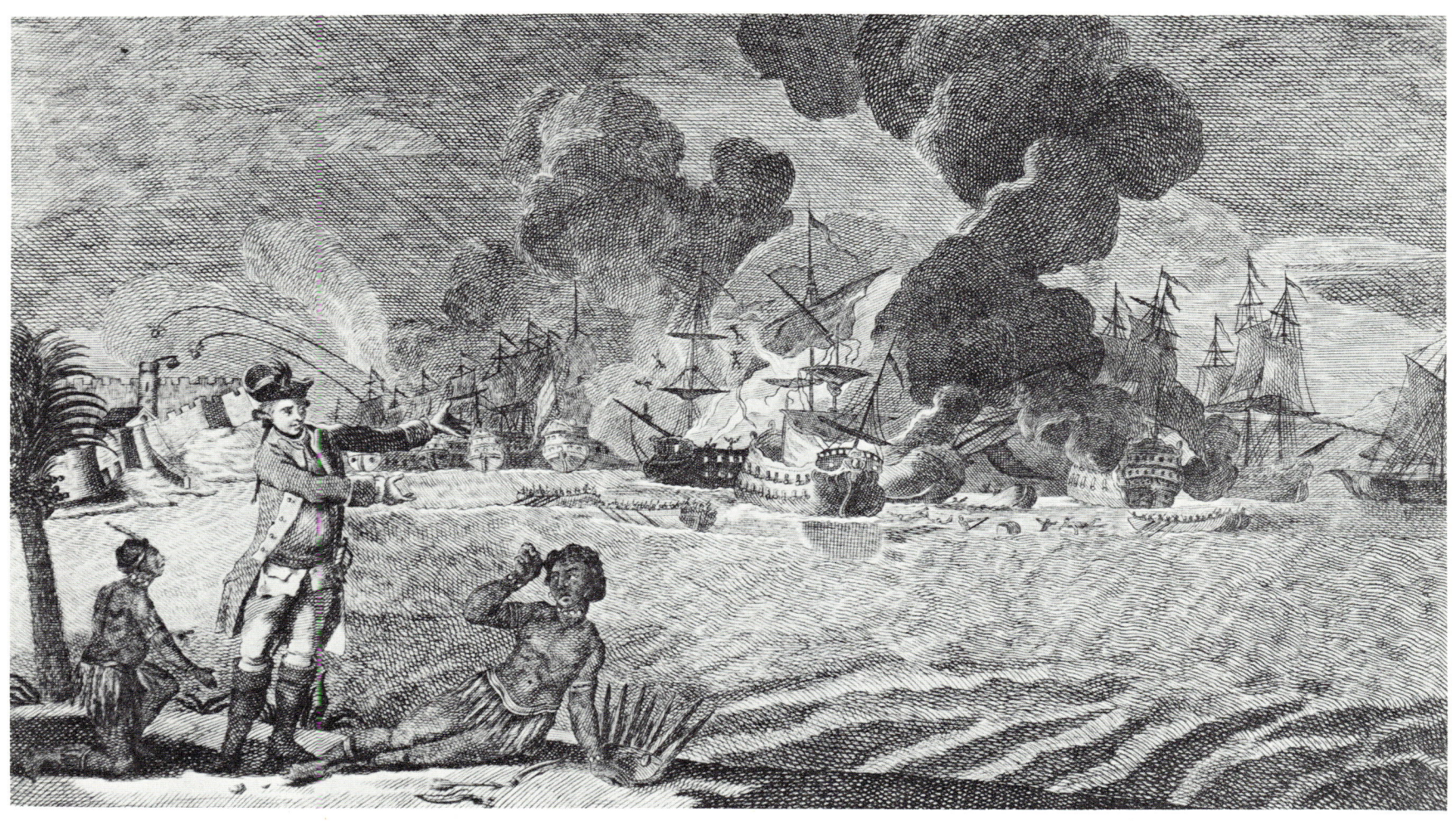

Howe but maybe General Washington, shows the battle of Philadelphia to dark-skinned natives who represent America. In the background a furious sea battle rages, and to the left cannon balls are lobbed into a fortress with crenellated walls. Howe's campaign lasted from July to December 1777. Since no specific date in the campaign correlated with the action shown here, the portrayal is probably imaginary, representing either the British occupation of Philadelphia on the 26th of September or the fall of Forts Mifflin or Mercer between the 15th and 21st of November.
LC-USZ62-5219

694

[An allegory on New York—a cartouche] London, Publishd according to Act of Parliament, Jany 12, 1776: by Jefferys & Faden, Corner of St. Martins Lane Charing Cross.

Etching 8½ x 6¾ in. (image)

The cartouche is entitled "Plan of the City of New York in North America: Surveyed in the Years 1766 & 1767." From Faden, *North American Atlas* (London, 1777), no. 20–21. LC-USZ62-45597. See also item 549.

695

THE WISE MEN OF GOTHAM and their GOOSE. Pubd. 16th. Feby. 1776, by W. Humphrey, Gerrard Street Soho.

Mezzotint 10 x 13 in. (image)

Bute and other ministers slaughter the goose (the American Colonies) that laid the golden egg. A dog urinates on a map of North America in the foreground, and in the background is a picture of the British lion asleep. A poem in the two upper corners:

> In Gotham once the Story goes
> A lot of Wise-acres arose
> Skill'd in the great Politic Wheel
> Could pound a Magpie, drown an Eel,
> With many Things of worthy Note
> At present much too long to quote,
> Their district was both far and wide

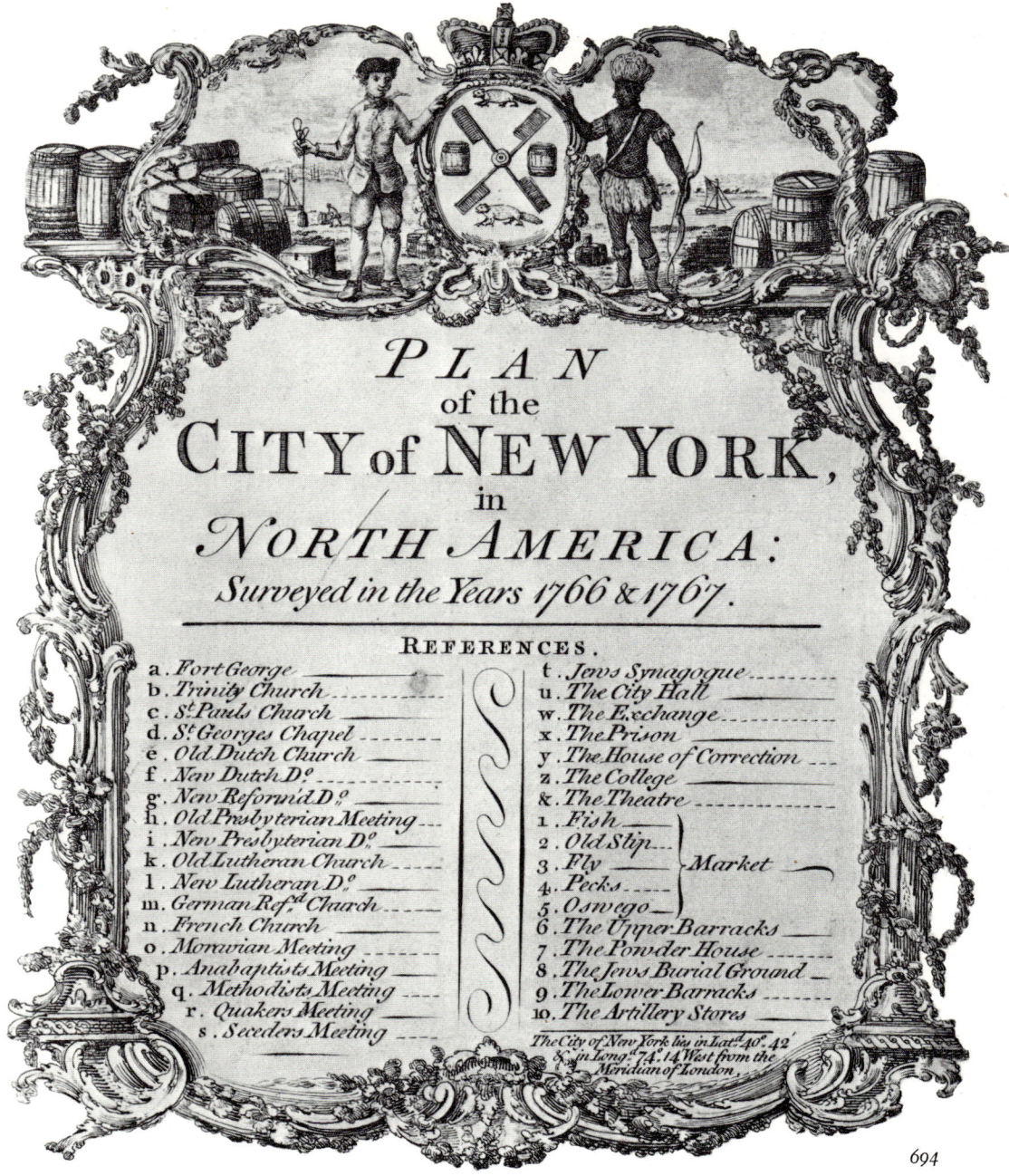

694

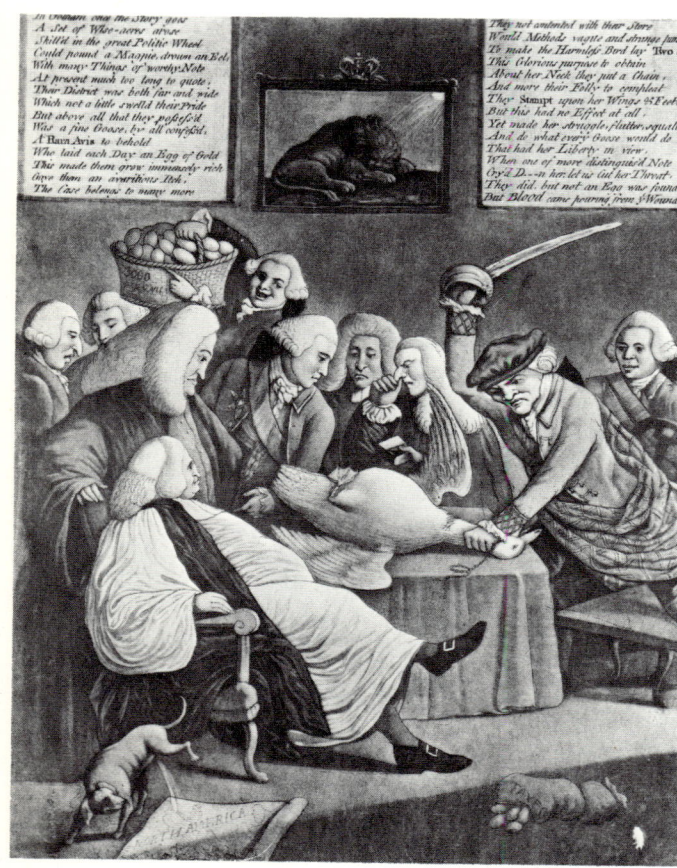

Which not a little swelld their Pride
But above all that they possess'd
Was a fine Goose, by all confess'd,
A Rara Avis to behold
Who laid each Day an Egg of Gold
This made them grow immensely rich
Gave them an avaritious Itch,
The Case belongs to many more
They not contented with their Store
Would Methods vague and strange pursue
To make the Harmless Bird lay Two,
This Glorious purpose to obtain
About her Neck they put a Chain,
And more their Folly to compleat
They Stampt upon her Wings and Feet,
But this had no Effect at all,
Yet made her struggle, flutter, squall,
And do what every Goose would do
That had her Liberty in view,
When one of more distinguis'd Note
Cry'd D____n her, let us Cut her Throat,
They did, but not an Egg was found
But Blood come pouring from ye Wound.

CPPS Vol. 5 p. 216 LC–USZ62–1514

696

THE STATE BLACKSMITHS Forging fetters for the Americans. Published according to Act of Parliament 1st March 1776. Engrav'd for the General Magazine.
  Mixed method 7⅝ x 4⅜ in.

North, Bute, Sandwich, Mansfield, and other ministers work in a blacksmith's shop, while George III smiles his approval through an open window to the left. North's Ministry had blockaded ports and seized American shipping in recent months, and the cartoonist depicted a confident English Government busy making the tools to enslave the Americans. This print originally appeared in *The General Magazine* in 1776; it was inserted into LC's copy of Clarke, *An Impartial and Authentic Narrative of the Battle ... on Bunker's Hill ... in New England* (London, 1775), frontispiece.
CPPS 5328 LC–USZ62–45532

697

BUNKERS HILL or America's Head Dress. Pubd. April 19 by M. Darly 39 Strand. [1776]
  Etching 9¾ x 7 in.

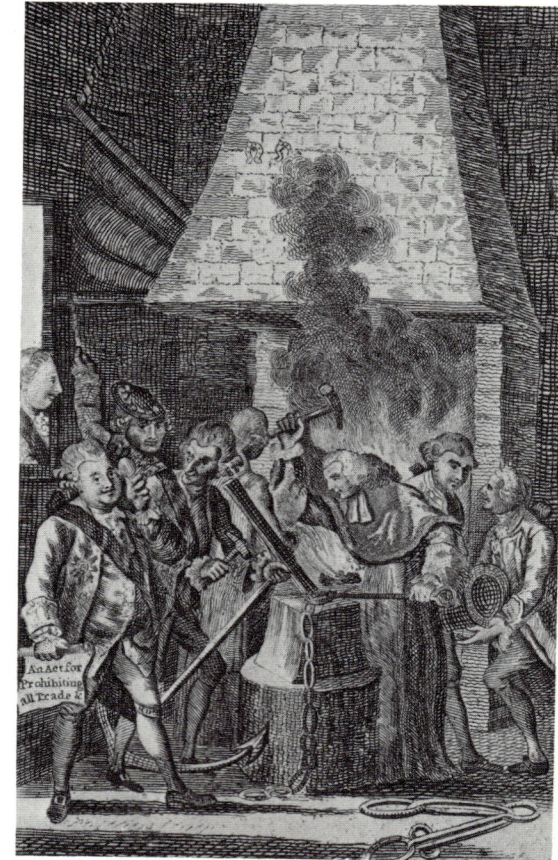

Within a huge coiffure, the battle of Bunker Hill rages with ships, tents, infantry, and flags. This cartoon simultaneously ridicules a contemporary fashion in vogue with the London ladies and the English attempts to coerce the colonists. By placing the battle within a hairpiece, the cartoonist belittles the military efforts at the battle fought on June 17, 1775. A companion print in the British Museum shows the British evacuation of Boston on March 17, 1776 (CPPS 5335). These two cartoons probably were issued at the same time. They reflected popular sentiment that England was not doing enough to control the rebellion. For a similar cartoon cf. item 701. CPPS 5330 LC–USZ62–54

698
The BLESSED EFFECTS of VENALITY. Pubd. as ye Act directs, May 1, 1776.
Mixed method 4¾ x 6½ in.

An English statesman chops at a bench with three legs marked "Commons," "Privy Council," and "Lords." To the left Britannia sits exhausted with her shield resting and staff with liberty cap drooping. In the foreground are caricatures of a Dutchman, a Spaniard, and a Frenchman. The absence of America is explained by the article on the next page.

The increase of taxes, the decline of trade, and Britain's present distressing situation is chiefly to be imputed to that *diabolical corruption*, which bids fair for the ruin of our lately flourishing empire, and the aggrandizement of the proud Spaniard, the ambitious Frenchman, and the avaritious Dutchman. The present contest between ministry and America, affords them fine sport, and rather than parliamentary corruption should decline, they would each furnish some purses to support it.

From *The London Magazine*, April 1776, p. 171. CPPS 5333 LC–USZ62–45430

699
[An allegory on the British Empire in North America—a cartouche] By Samuel Dunn ...

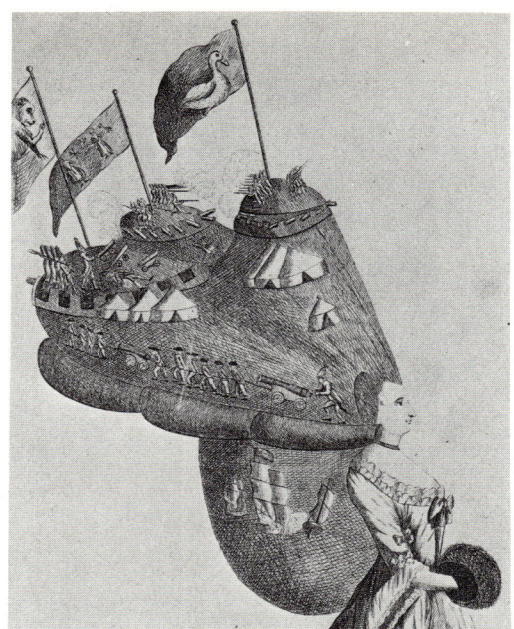
697

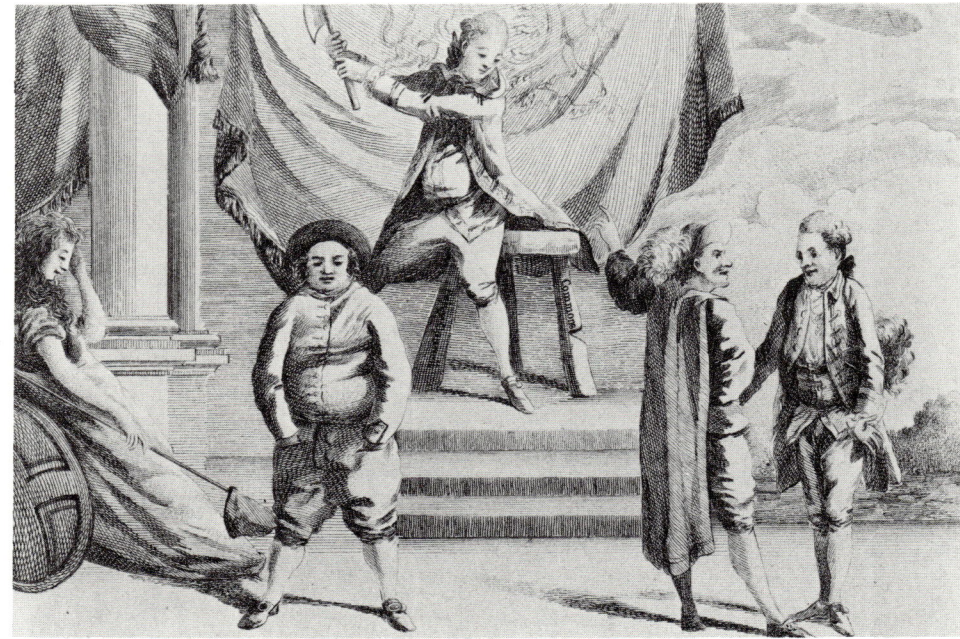
698

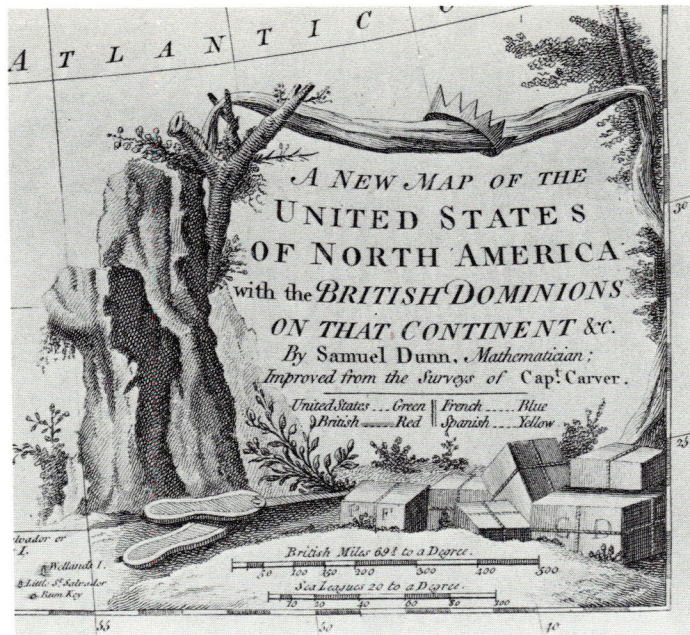

699

from the Surveys of Capt. Carver. London. Published for R. Sayer & J. Bennett, Map and Sea Chartsellers, No. 53, Fleet Street, as the Act directs Augst. 17th. 1776.

Etching 4¾ x 5 in. (image)

A crown hanging over a forest scene with packages and a gourd, representing commerce and agriculture, symbolizes the rule of the King of England over North America. From "A Map of the British Empire in North America" in Jefferys, *The American Atlas* (London, 1776), no. 8. This cartouche also appears in the 1778 and 1782 editions.

——————Another impression. In Samuel Dunn, *A New Atlas of the Mundane System* (London, 1778–[83]), no. 40. LC-USZ62-46085

700

The Parricide. A Sketch of Modern Patriotism. [May 1, 1776]

Mixed method 3¾ x 6⅛ in.

America dressed as an Indian woman proceeds to stab a half-clothed Britannia who is also attacked by the British lion. Wilkes directs America, while Camden guides the lion. The Duke of Grafton and George Hayley hold Britannia, and Charles James Fox, the Earl of Chatham, and other patriots watch the killing. To the far left a figure of Discord with hydra hair raises two torches in victory. One of the earliest vicious satires, it lacks the humor found in most British cartoons of the time. This cartoon is a frontispiece for an article which shows a reaction against those ministers who supported America. As the war became longer and deadlier, more cartoons were issued in a spirit of anger. This print in P&P was originally from *The Westminster Magazine*, 1776, p. 216–219. CPPS 5334
LC-USZ62-34868

——————Another impression (cropped at top).

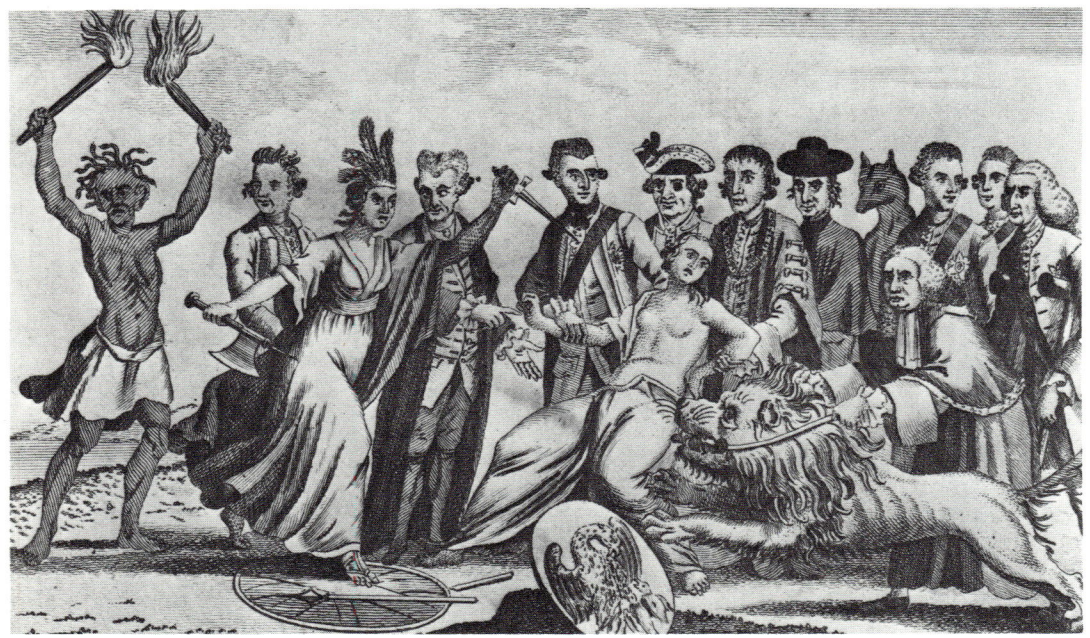

700

701

Miss Carolina Sulivan one of the obstinate daughters of America 1776 Pub Sepr 1: 1776 by Mary Darly 39 Strand.
Etching 9¾ x 7 in.

A young woman, with a nose resembling William Pitt's, wears a huge wig which has cannons, fortifications, flags, tents, and a gallows protruding from it. A large cannon, inscribed, "To Peter Pop Gun P__t, "shoots balls designated red and hot. The cartoonist ridicules contemporary fashions and the defeat of the British at Sullivan's Island in South Carolina on June 28, 1776. Cf. item 697. By drawing Miss Carolina Sullivan to resemble Pitt, she uses the theme of America as a misdirected daughter who now hangs tax collectors, makes military preparations, and fires cannons in defiance of England. LC–USZ62–46309

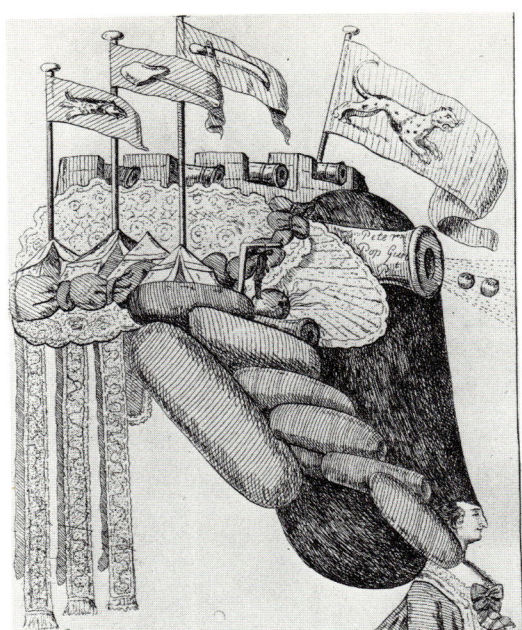

702

Take Your Choice. Publish'd by I. Almon in Picadilly, Octr. 14: 1776 as the Act Directs.
Etching 6⅛ x 9⅜ in. (image)

Alternative leviathans presented in the form of two pyramids. The first is solid, surrounded by a fortified wall, built on "Natural and Civil Liberty" of the people who support the crown through "Representation Equal & Annual." Beneath this pyramid is a quotation from Blackstone, "It is this ascending & contracting proportion that adds stability to any government &c." The other pyramid is built in a flimsy manner around a single central pillar designated "Despotism." From the crown on top four wires support two platforms. The wires are designated "Places and Pensions," "Douceurs," "Expectation," and "Influence." The top platform, "Little Theatre Royal," has a pair of dice and a shaker with a prince's crown on top. There is also a bishop, designated "Quebec," who bows to a hand offering him three crowns (a tiara). The other platform,

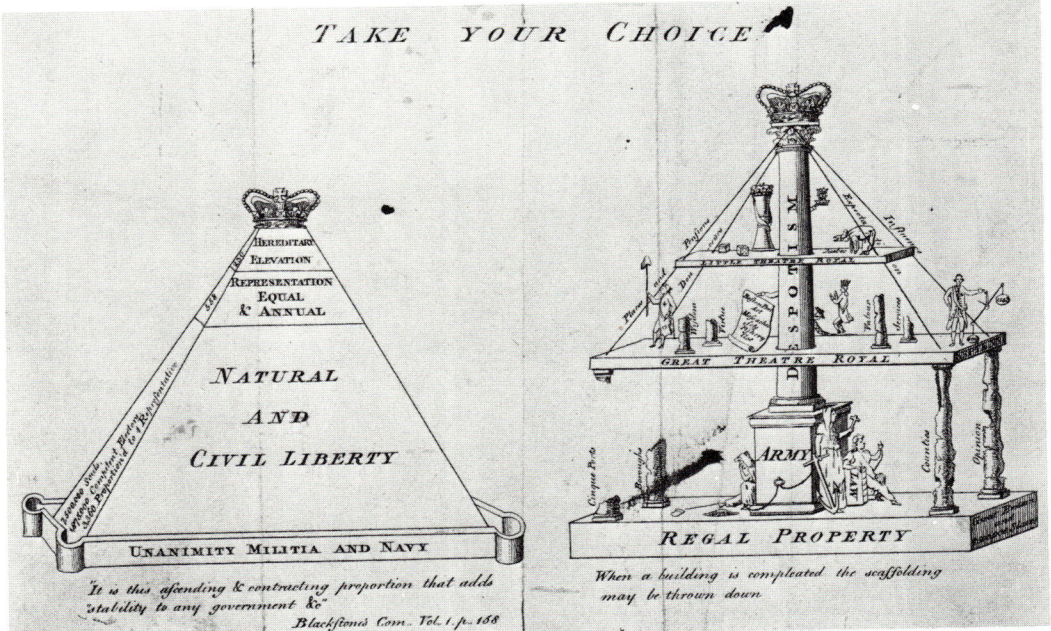

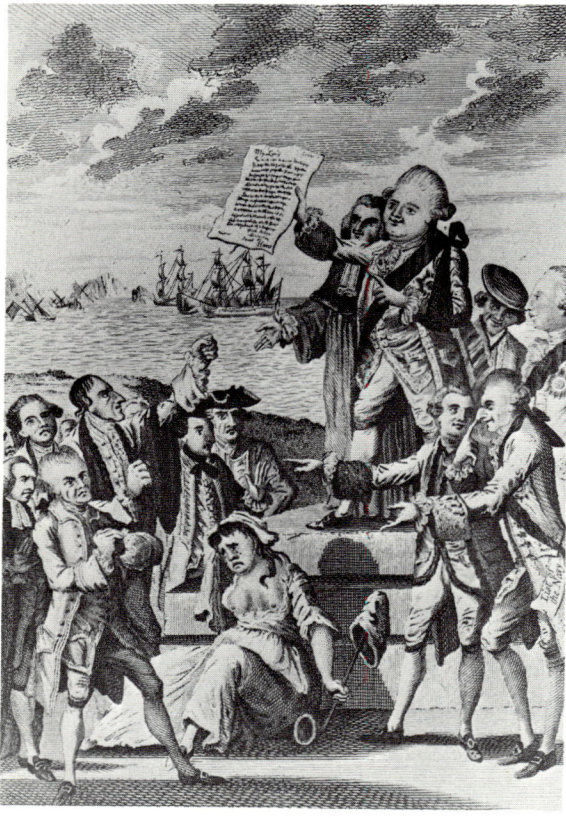

703

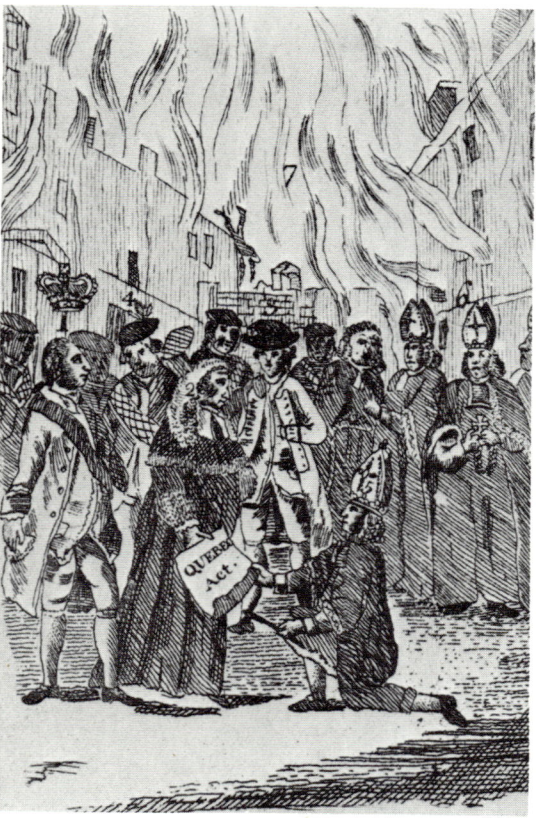

704

"Great Theatre Royal," supports four crumbling pillars marked "Wisdom," "Virtue," "Valour," and "Services." On one extreme of the platform a figure wearing the star of the garter, probably North, holds a liberty cap atop a pole, and at the other side Henry Luttrell holds a scale in which 296 outweighs 1,143. These figures allude to his displacement of Wilkes in the Westminster election. From the pillar Lord Bute bows to the King, and an arm presents a scroll listing "Boston Port Act" and "Massachusetts Fishery Act." The base of the pillar is the "Army" with figures representing justice, Christianity, and war leaning against it in a despondent manner. Four crumbling pillars once supported the above platform—"Cinque Ports" and "Buroughs" are already broken while "Counties" and "Opinion" are badly deteriorated. The entire structure rests on "Regal Property." LC–USZ62–46310

703
[News from America, or the Patriots in the Dumps. Nov. 1776.]
  Mixed method 6¾ x 4¼ in.

  North and Mansfield show a letter from the victorious General Howe. Bute, George III, Sandwich, and probably Germain are pleased, and a group of commoners led by Wilkes scowl. A tawdry, bare-breasted woman with a liberty cap on a staff falls down weeping. Howe's dispatch announcing the British victory at Long Island was published in London on October 10, 1776. CPPS 5340 LC–USZ61–80

——————Another impression. In *The London Magazine*, November 1776, p. 599.

704
Protestants, remember the Massacre of St. Bartholemews in Paris, & the burning of Martyrs in Smithfield. [1776]
  Etching 5¼ x 3½ in. (image)

  A minister of state, possibly Mansfield but

more fittingly Dartmouth, hands the Quebec Act to a kneeling bishop. Behind the minister stands George III with a crown suspended over his head, and behind him stands Bute. Other gentlemen and bishops are not identified, and in the far background a town burns, while a man falls from a flaming building. The message below the picture exhorts Protestants to remember the slaughter of Huguenots at Paris in 1572 and the executions in Smithfield, England, during the Reformation and Counter-reformation. This cartoon warns Protestants that by legitimizing Catholicism in Canada, the English Government was empowering the Catholics to persecute their countrymen and fellow Protestants. Numbers designate the main characters, but no explanation is given in the book for which it is a frontispiece. This cartoon might not be the original frontispiece for the book. From *The Rise, Progress, and Present State of the Dispute between the People of America and the Administration* (London, 1776), frontispiece. LC–USZ62–45531

705
[America pois'd in the balance of justice 1776]
Mixed method 8 x 6½ in.

An "elegiace frontispiece" shows two despondent women on a cliff, while in the background a fleet sails by a burning town. Mercury and another god, probably Abundance since he carries a cornucopia, fly away. The identity of Britannia or America is unclear in this print. Below the cliff a single ship emerges with the word "Burn" written beside it. The print shows the belligerents in despair, while the gods of fortune leave the scene of warfare. From P-oplicola H-istoricus, *America pois'd in the Balance of Justice* (London, 1776), frontispiece. A "reconciliatory Tail-Piece" on p. 37 shows birds flying peacefully in a quiet and beautiful land. LC–USZ62–45530

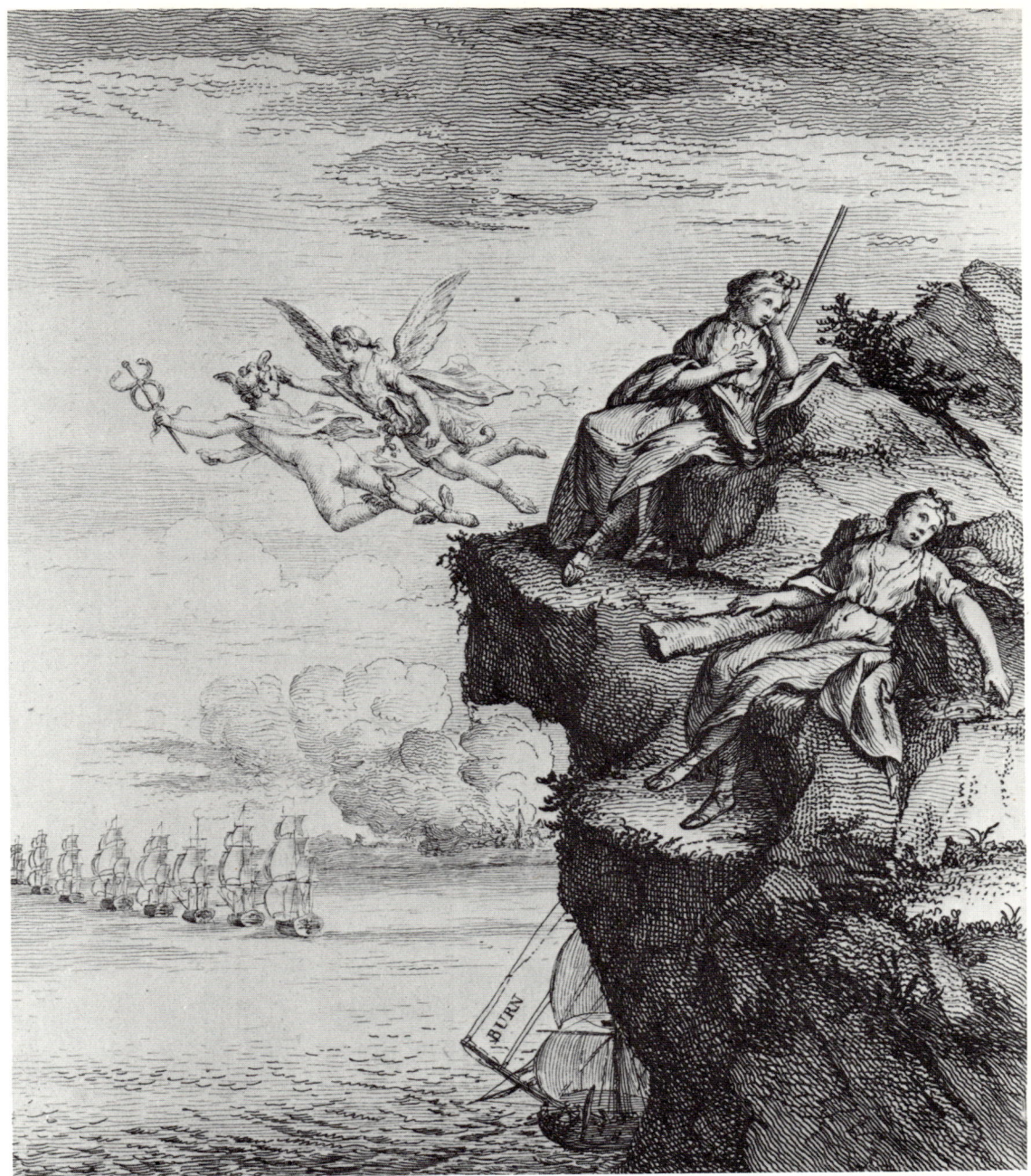

705

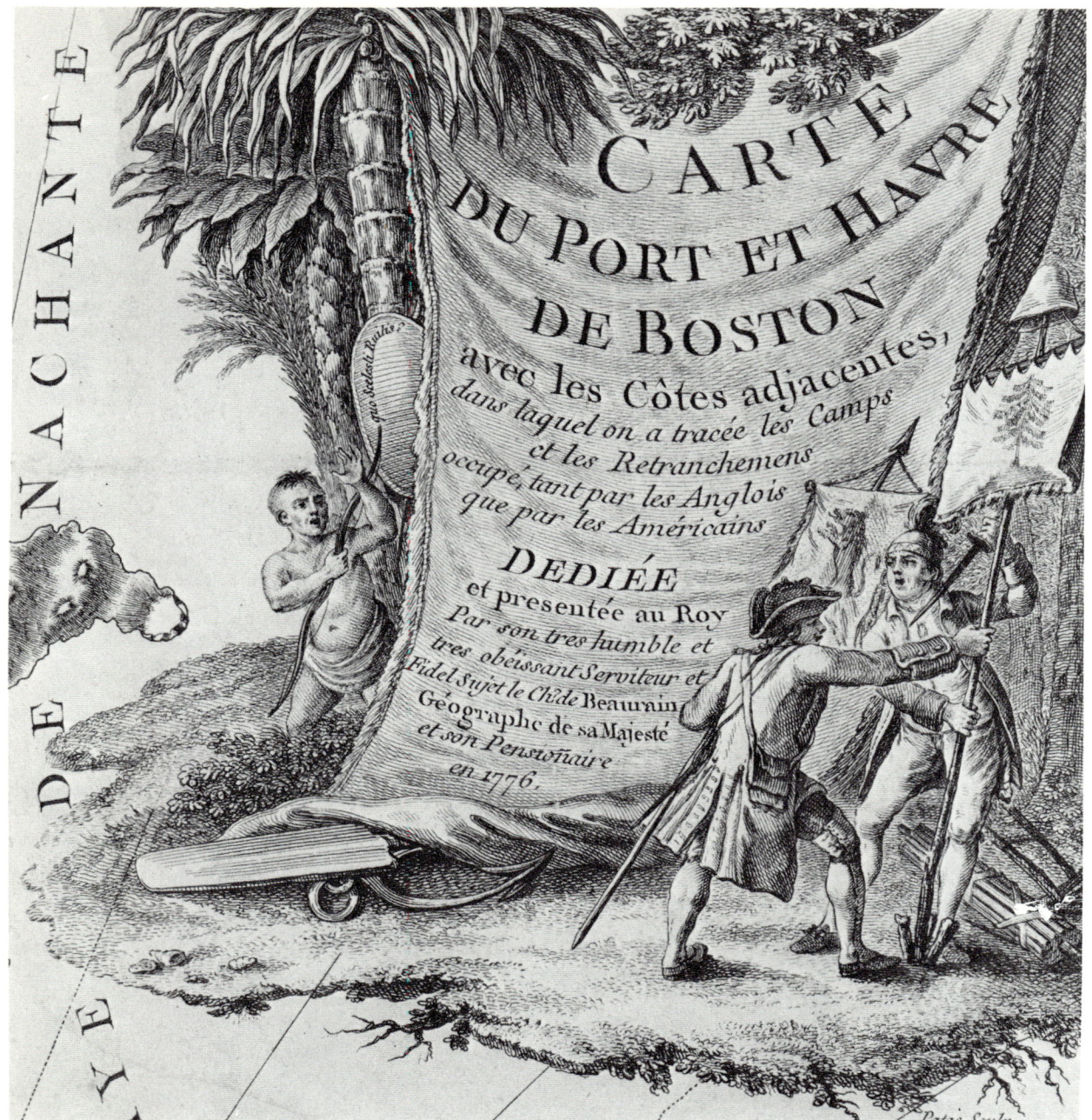

706

[A Patriot and a Tory wrestle for a pine tree flag—a cartouche] G.F.J. Frentzel Sculps: 1776

Mixed method 7 x 4½ in. (image)

The patriot holds a banner with a pine tree on it and a liberty cap on top. With a knife he lunges at a Tory who tries to grab the banner with his left hand while carrying a banner with the English lion in his right. Behind the two men a plow and fasces lay idle. From a map entitled "Carte von dem Hafen und der Stadt Boston mit den um liegenden Gegenden und den Lagernsowohl der Americaner als such der Englander von dem Cheval de Beaurin nach dem Pariser Original von 1776" in G&M Vault.

707

[A Patriot and a Tory wrestle for a pine tree flag while an Indian watches—a cartouche] Patas Sculp. 1776

Mixed method 7 x 6½ in. (image)

This cartouche is similar to item 706 with the addition of an anxious Indian watching the struggle from behind an anchor and oar. Today's scholar can see an allegorical message that was not intended by the artist—the one group who lost from the Revolution was the American Indian. From a map entitled "Carte du Port et Havre de Boston avec les Cotes adjacentes, dans laquel on a tracée les Camps et les Retranchemens occupé, tant par les Anglois que par les Américains Dediée et presentée au Roy par son tres humble et tres obéissant Serviteur et Fidel Sujet le Ch de Beaurain Géographe de sa Majesté et son Pensionaire en 1776" in G&M Vault.
LC–USZ62–46076

708

[An Allegory on the British Colonies in North America—a cartouche] Engraved for the

Universal Magazine 1776

Etching 2¾ x 3¼ in. (image)

Symbols of America are in the foreground: a pine tree, a flowering plant, an alligator, and a barrel. The themes of the great lizard (Cf. item 716), agriculture, and commerce were used by Europeans to represent America throughout the 18th century. From a map entitled "An accurate Map of the present Seat of War, between Great Britain and her Colonies in North America." In G&M Vault.

———— Another impression.

709
Poor old England endeavoring to reclaim his wicked American Children. Pub Apr 1777 by M Darly 39 Strand.

Etching 13¾ x 9¾ in.

England as an old man with crutch and peg leg has hooks through the noses of five Americans across the ocean, but they resist him; two shoot pellets at him, two shout, and one exposes his backside. Below the title is a quotation: "And therefore is England maimed & forc'd to go with a Staff. shakespeare" CPPS 5397 LC-USZ62-34862

710
QUALIFYING for a CAMPAIN. Verney delint. London, Printed for R. Sayer & J. Bennett Map & Printsellers No. 53 Fleet Street, as the Act directs 4 June 1777.

Etching (hand colored) 10 x 14½ in.

British soldiers in red coats play with pistols and cats, shoot down a stack of playing cards, duel with blunt rapiers, and sit around amusing themselves. On the back wall a vague map, designated "Seat of War in North America," identifies Boston and New York. Throughout the American Revolution, criticism of the British Army grew constantly. This cartoon is one of many to link misfortunes in America with an inadequate Army. LC-USZ62-1515

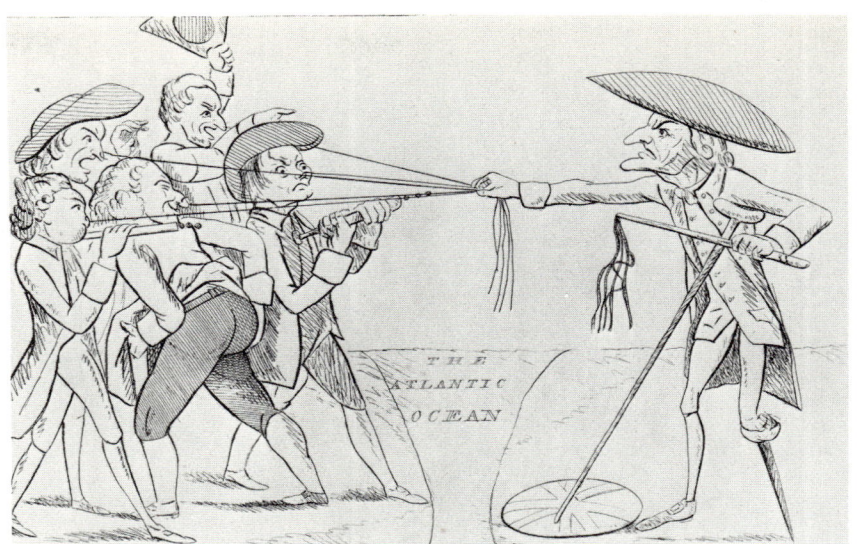

709

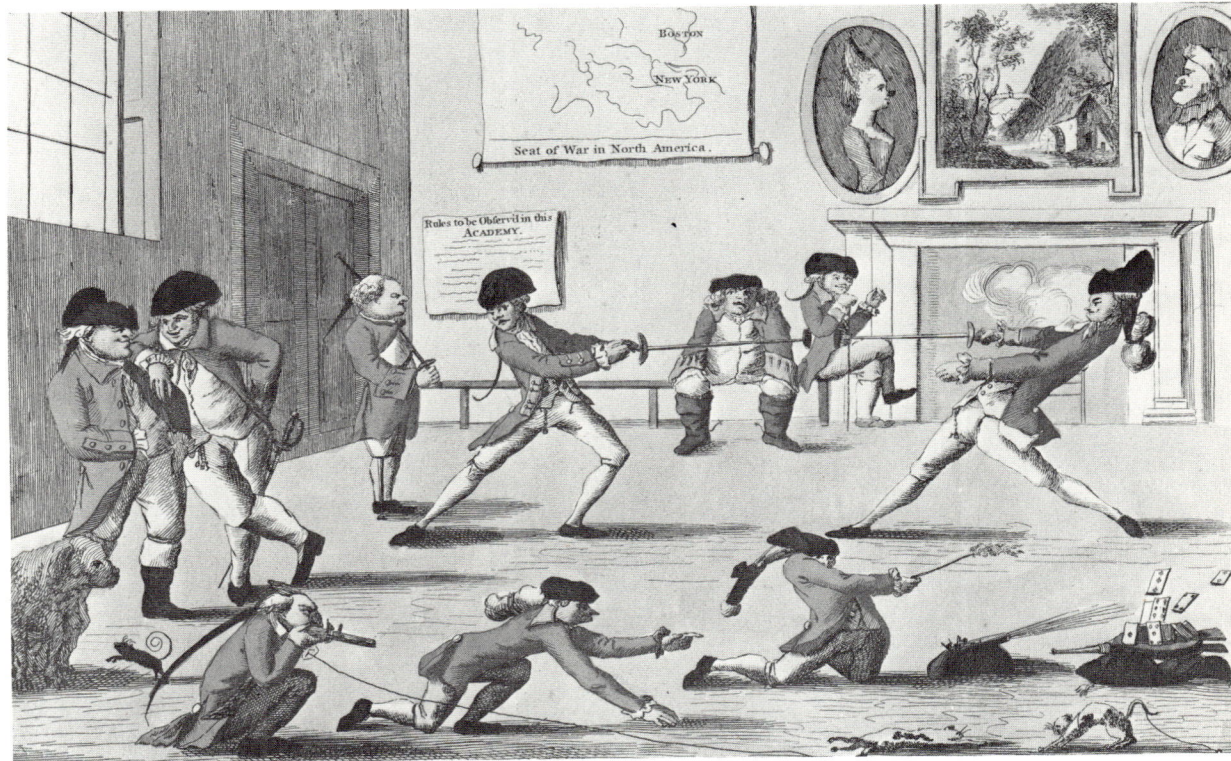

710

295

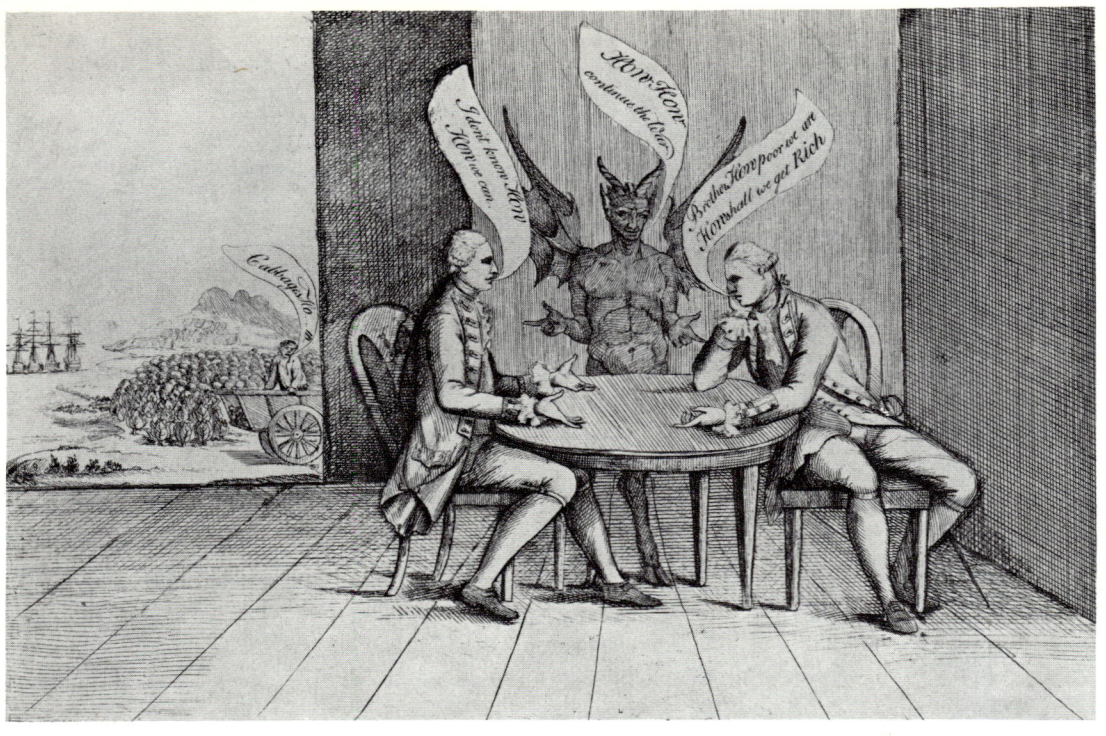
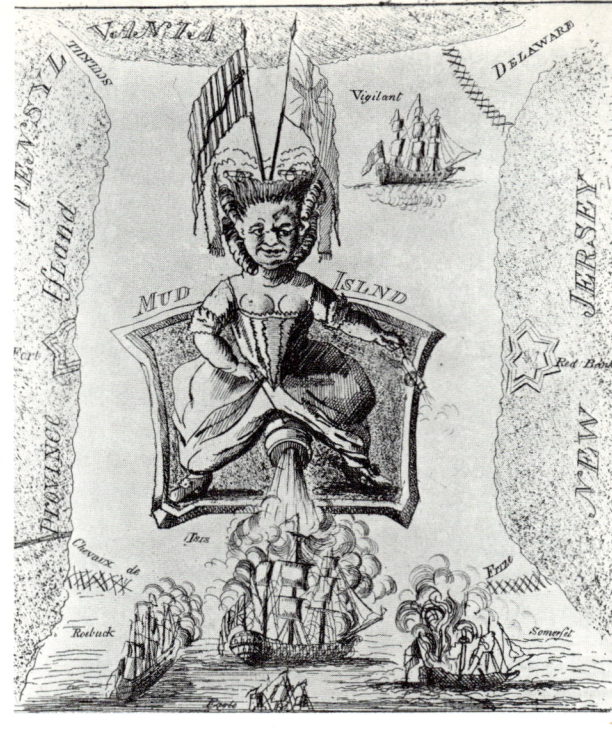

711

711
The Conference between the Brothers How to get Rich. Publish'd by W Williams Fleet Street as the Act directs Oct: 10, 1777.

Etching 8⅜ x 12½ in. (image)

Adm. Lord Richard Howe and Gen. Sir William Howe sit at a table with a devil standing between them pointing to each saying, "How, How, continue the war." The one says, "I don't know How How we can," and the other says, "Brother How poor we are How shall we get Rich." In the far background to the left is a fleet at anchor, and in the near background a man loads cabbages on a cart saying, "Cabbages Ho ... w." The implication here is that the Howe brothers were more interested in profiteering and improving their positions than in ending the war. William Howe had been appointed Commander in Chief of all forces in America in October 1775, but the command in Canada was split off and given to Guy Carleton. Four months later his brother received command of all naval forces. The two had powers to treat with the Americans or attack them, and when neither strategy succeeded, the Howes were criticized in London. This cartoon appeared when the Howes were in Philadelphia after inconclusive campaigns in New York, New Jersey, and Pennsylvania. Cf. items 726, 748, 781, 782. CPPS 5399 LC-USZ62-41467

712
THE TAKEING OF MISS MUD I'LAND. Sold by W Humphrey 227 Strand London [December 1777?]

Mixed method 10 x 7¾ in.

Celebrates the victory of Howe's fleet over Fort Mifflin, Pa., at Mud Island near the mouth of the Schuylkill River on October 25, 1777. This battle opened Philadelphia to him. The satire shows a woman with an American flag with stripes and rattlesnake and a Union flag sitting on a cannon firing at the warship *Isis*. Also in the fleet are the ships *Somerset*, *Roebuck*, *Eagle* (Howe's flagship), and *Vigilant*. The land on the left is designated Pennsylvania and on the right New Jersey. CPPS 5402 LC-USZ62-1509

713
[Two American Indians—a cartouche, 1768-83?]

Etching 16 x 12½ in. (image)

This cartouche represents an idealized personification of the British Colonies. The Indian figures are noble savages surrounded by an abundance of animals and fish nets. The man pets a lion cub, perhaps representing the offspring of the English lion; the traditional large lizard (cf. item 716), a beaver, a parrot, and two monkeys are also in the picture. The man and woman sit beneath the title "A New and Correct Map of North America with the West India Islands Divided According to the last Treaty of Peace Concluded at Paris. 10th Feby. 1763 wherein are particularly distinguished the Several Provinces and Colonies which compose the British Empire." From Thomas Kitchin, *General Atlas* (London, 1773), no. 7.

——————Other copies are on the map entitled, "An Accurate Map of North America, describing . . . the British and Spanish Dominions . . . according to the . . . treaty concluded at Paris 10th Feby. 1763 . . . By Eman Bowen . . . and John Gibson." This map appears in Thomas Jefferys, *The American Atlas* (London, 1775), no. 5–6, and also in the edition for 1776.

——————Other copies are on a map entitled "A New and Correct Map of North America with the West India Islands divided according to the Preliminary Articles of Peace . . . 1763, wherein are particularly distinguished the United States, & the Several Provinces and Colonies which compose the British Empire, laid down according to the latest surveys and corrected from the Original Materials of Governor Pownall . . . 1777." This map appears in Thomas Jefferys, *The American Atlas* (London, 1778), no. 5–6, and also in the edition for 1783. Negative in G&M.

——————Another copy. In Faden, *North American Atlas* (London, 1777), no. 1.

——————Another copy. In Jefferys, *A General Topography of North America* (London, 1768), no. 9.

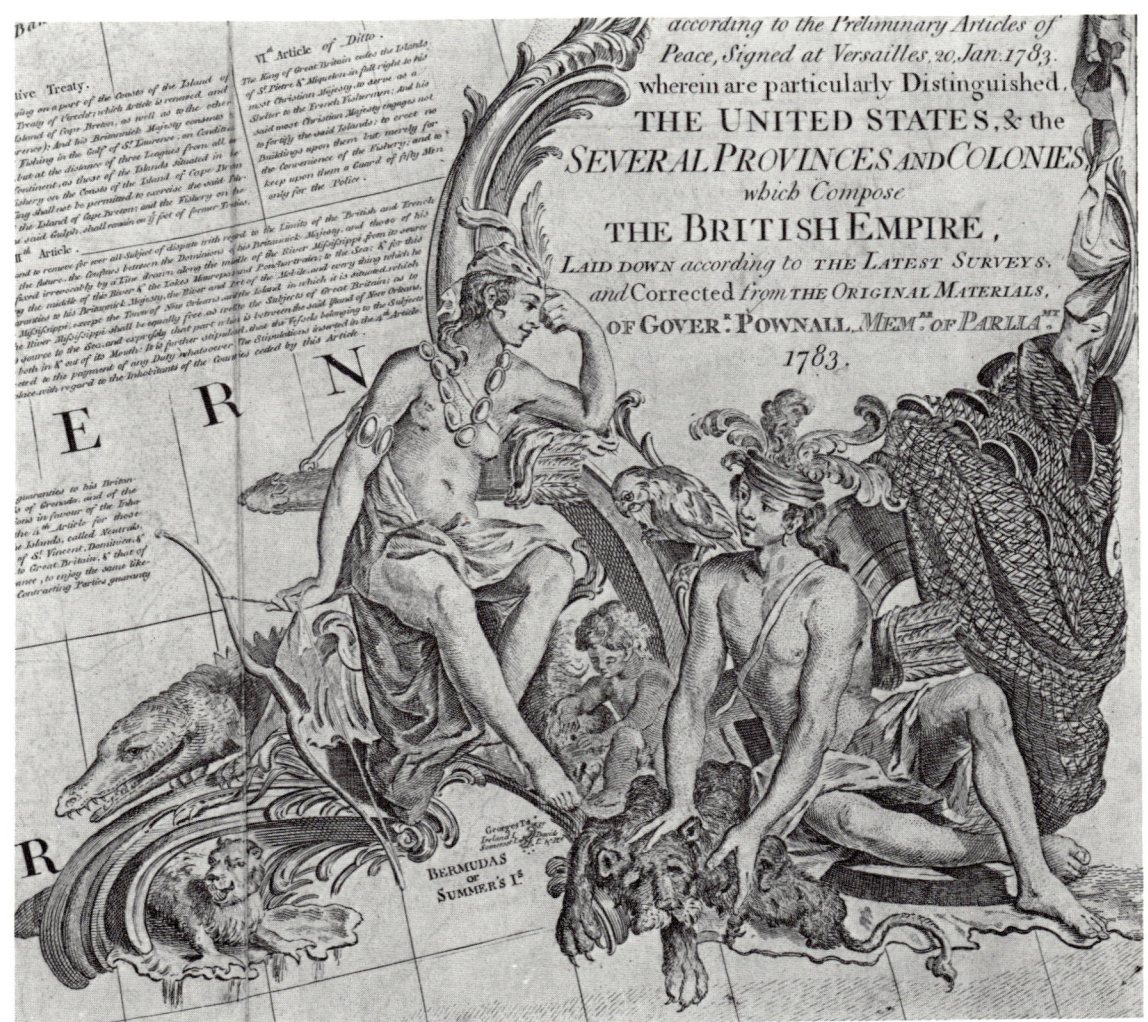

713

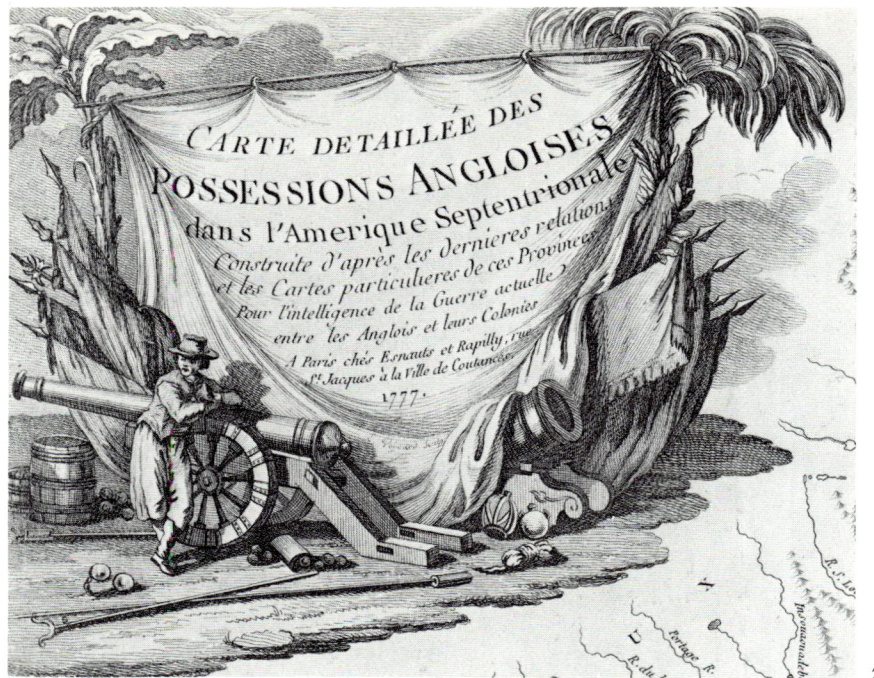

714

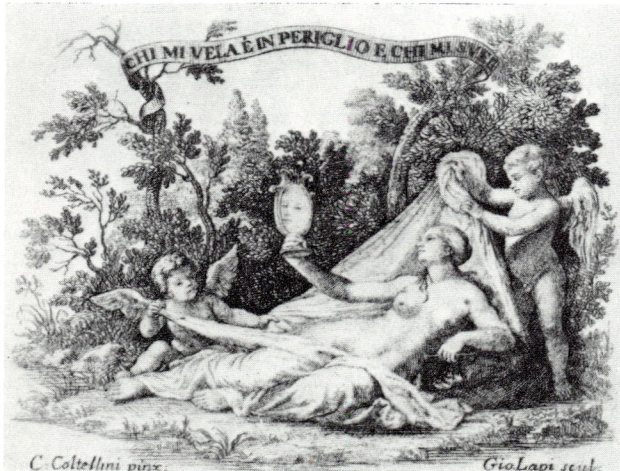

715

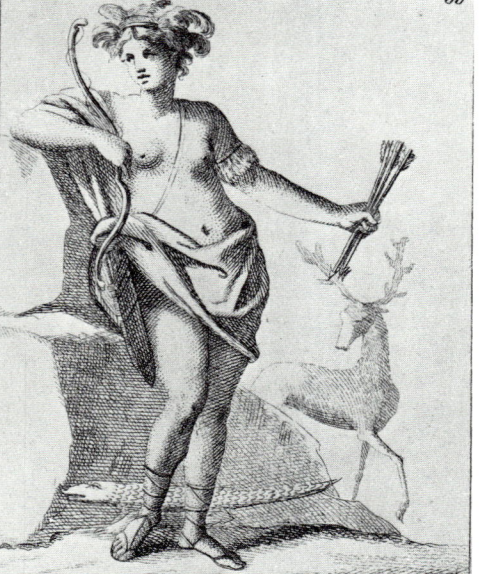

716

714

[The war in America—a cartouche] E. Voysard sc. A Paris chez Esnauts et Rapilly, rue St. Jacques à la Ville de Coutances. 1777

Etching 5¾ x 7 in. (image)

A seaman leans on a cannon, and flags and ordnance surround the title, "Carte Detaillée des Possessions Angloises dans l'Amerique Septentrionale Construite d'après les dernieres relations et les Cartes particulieres de ces Provinces Pour l'intelligence de la Guerre actuelle entre les Anglois et leurs Colonies." In G&M Vault. LC–USZ62–46079

715

CHI MI VELA É IN PERIGLIO E CHI MI SVEL. C: Coltellini pinx. Gio. Lapi scul: [1777]

Mixed method 3 x 3¾ in.

During the 18th century artists were praised for holding up a mirror to nature. No more fitting ornament could adorn this Italian atlas than a picture of America, a beautiful, naked goddess surrounded by cherubs, looking into a mirror. From *Atlante dell' America* . . . (Livorno, 1777), title page. LC–USZ62–46018

716

AMERICA. [W. Hamilton del.] E. M[alpas] Published as the Act directs Novr. 23d. 1776.

Mixed method 4 x 3⅛ in. (image)

America is pictured and described in this work in a manner characteristic of many cartoons and cartouches.

The fourth and last part of the world is represented almost naked, of a tawny complexion, and a fierce aspect; has her head and other parts of the body adorned with various coloured feathers, according to the custom of the country. In the left hand she holds a bow, and in the right a bunch of arrows, these being the arms of both men and women in many of the provinces. The lizard which abounds in that country, is of such an enormous size, and of such fierceness, that it not only devours other animals, but frequently attacks the inhabitants. The moose deer is also a notable animal in that part of the world, and may with propriety be introduced.

This figure is one among 423 allegories in Richardson's edition of Ripa, *A Collection of Emblematical Figures* (London, 1777), figure 60. LC–USZ62–46532

717
[A Continental soldier stands by broken pillars —a map ornament] by Nicos. Scull . . Engraved by L. Jackson [1777]

Etching 3¼ x 3½ in. (image)

A soldier points to the map with a baton in his left hand. The style and pose are similar to the engraved portraits of American leaders found in the various editions of *An Impartial History of the War in America* and *The Hibernian Magazine*. From "A Map of that part of Pensylvania now the Principle seat of War in America wherein may be seen the Situation of Philadelphia, Red Bank, Mud Island, & Germantown . . ." in G&M Vault. LC–USZ62–46075

————Another picture. The cartouche shows products of America—a bee hive, barrels, bundles, wheat, a goat, and shipping at sea.

718
[An American Indian Warrior rests from the war—a cartouche] A Paris Chez Esnauts et Rapilly, rue St. Jacques à la Ville de Coutances. 1777

Etching 7 x 10¼ in. (image)

From a map entitled "Carte du Théatre de la Guerre entre les Anglais et les Américains: dressée d'après les Cartes Anglaises les plus modernes, par M. Brion de la Tour, Ingénieur-Géographe du Roi 1777." In G&M Vault.

————Another copy. 1778.

————Another copy. 1779.
LC–USZ62–46071

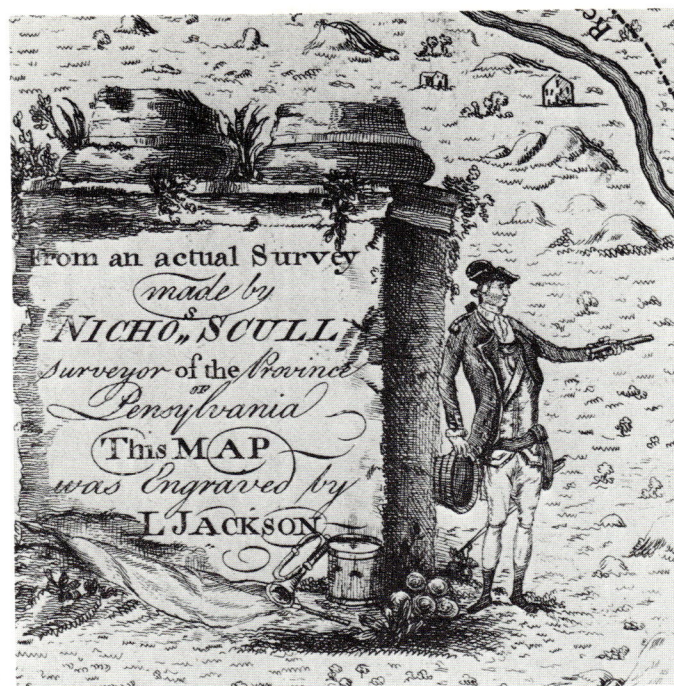
717

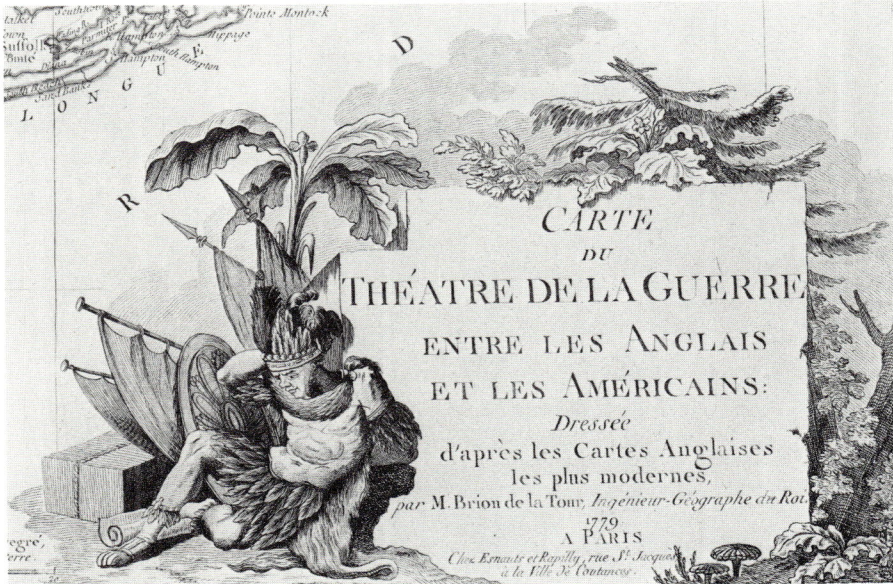
718

299

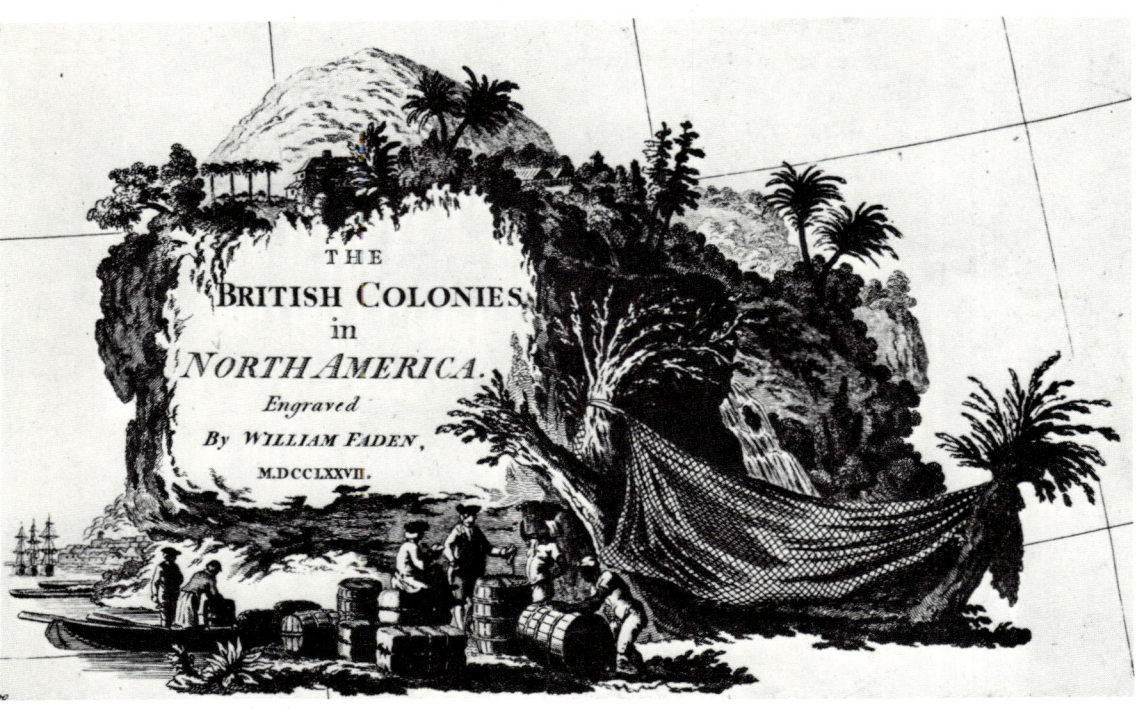

719

719
[A Scene in the British Colonies in North America—a cartouche, 1777?]
Etching 5½ x 9 in. (image)

Idealized view of trading, shipping, and fishing. From a map entitled "The British Colonies in North America. Engraved by William Faden, MDCCLXVII" in Faden, *North American Atlas* (London, 1777a), no. 1. Negative in G&M.

720
[The god Mars watches the goddess Fame unfurl a detailed map of New York and Pennsylvania—map ornament] Beaurain 1777
Mixed method 11½ x 12 in. (image)

Mars, dressed as a Roman soldier, looks up to Fame who proclaims the new country. This ornament could represent the attention given to the American war by the "gods of war" in Europe. Many French maps of North America appeared in the late 1770's, and they indicate the growing interest which developed into the French alliance of 1778. Cf. items 714 and 718. From a map entitled "Carte de l'Amérique Septle. pour servir à l'intelligence de la Guerre entre les Anglois et les Insurgents dédiée a Mgr De Sartine Ministre de la Marine par M. le Chr. de Beautain Géographe du Roi et son Pensionnaire 1777" in G&M Vault. LC-USZ62-46078

721
[A Scene on the Island of St. John—a cartouche, 1777?]
Etching 5 x 6 in. (image)

Implements of farming, fishing, and shipping surround the cartouche which reads "A Plan of the Island of St. John with the divisions of the Counties, Parishes, & the Lots as granted by Government... Survey'd by Capt. Holland 1775" in Faden, *North American Atlas* (London, 1777a), no. 6.

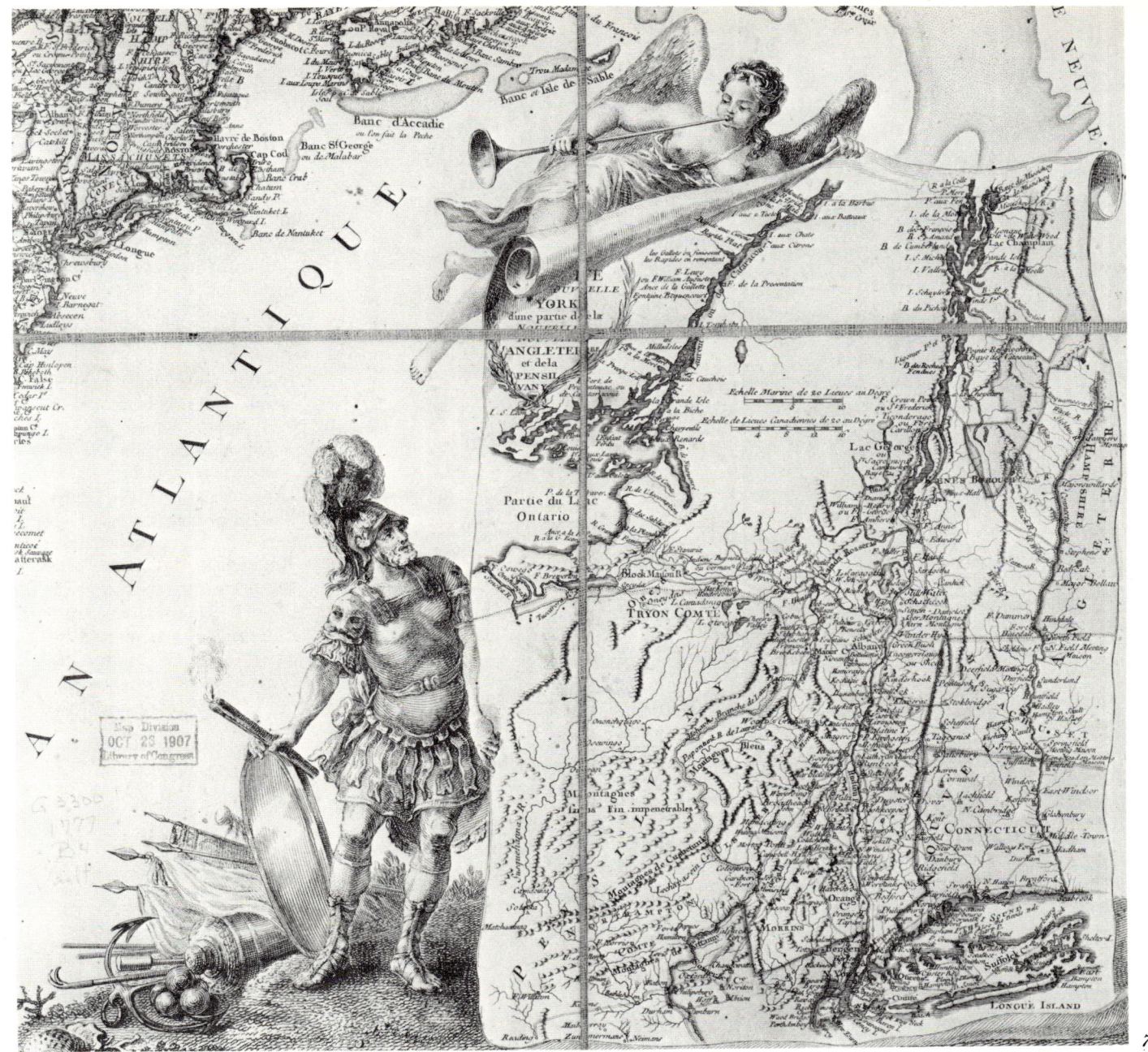

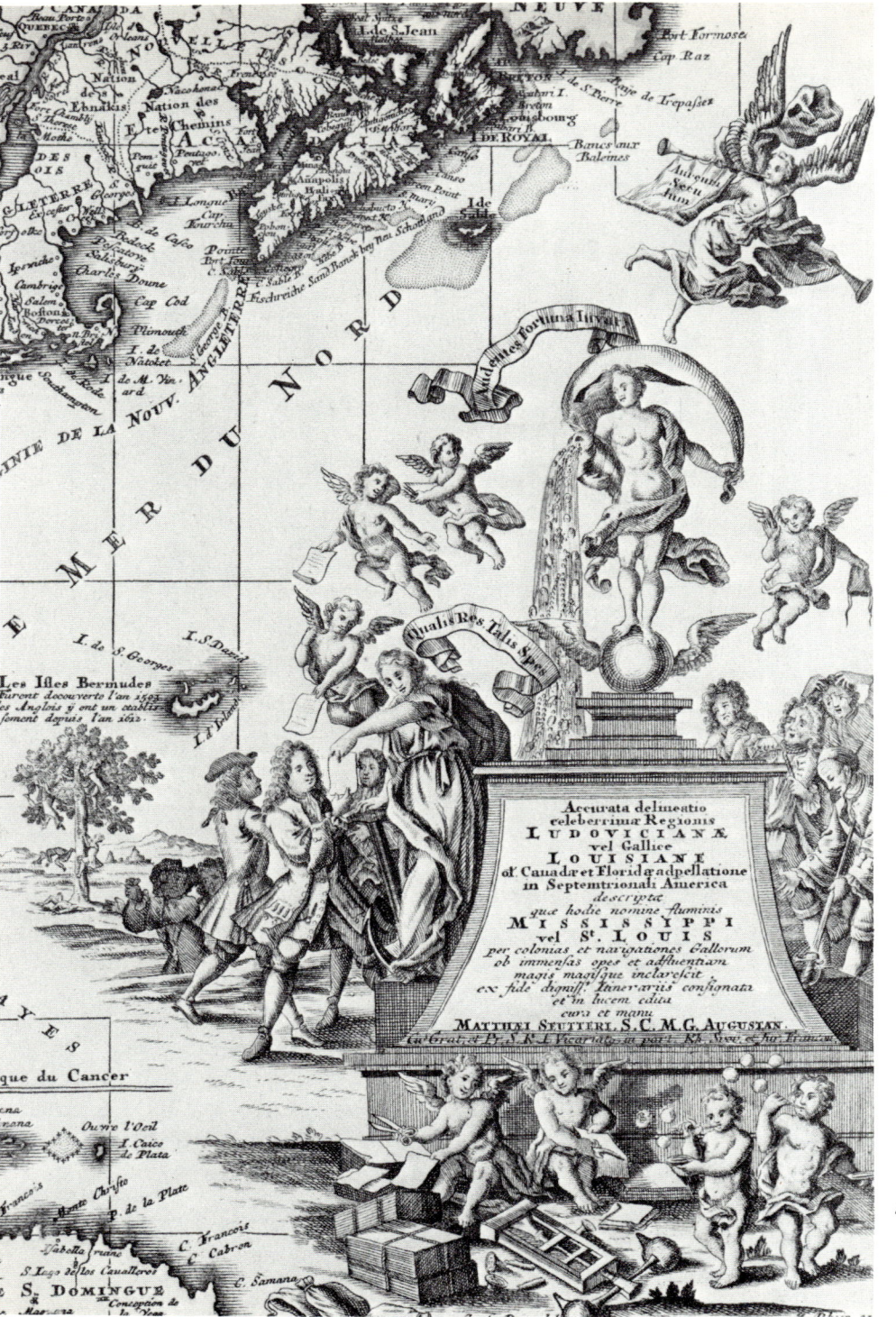
722

722

[An allegory on the Mississippi Bubble—a cartouche] Gottfri Rogg del M. Rhein sc. [before 1778]

Etching 11¾ x 7¾ in. (image)

Although this cartouche is in a 1778 atlas, it probably was designed soon after the collapse of the Mississippi Bubble in 1720. Many old maps and cartouches were used repeatedly throughout the century, and although much of the information became anachronistic, they continued to reflect common attitudes about the New World. The theme of speculation for riches conveyed by this cartouche was far from obsolete in 1778. This picture shows a god pouring coins and jewels from a cornucopia, often a symbol for the Mississippi River in early maps, while men on the left side receive riches, and men on the right commit suicide in despair. To the left background men fall out of a tree, and in the center foreground cherubs blow bubbles and cut papers. From a map entitled "Accurata delineatio Celeberrimae Regionis Ludovicianae vel Gallice Louisiane ol. Canadae et Floridae adpellatione in Septemtrionali America descriptae quae hodie nomine fluminis Mississippi vel St. Louis . . . in lucem edita cura et manu Matthaei Seutteri" in Lotter, *Atlas Géographique* (Nürnberg, 1778), no. 95. LC–USZ62–46070

723

[Minerva, the goddess of wisdom and war, 1778]

Mixed method 7 x 4¼ in.

An "Explanation of the Frontispiece" is on page 4.

The Frontispiece shows Minerva, the Goddess of Wisdom and of War, that she has laid down her Shield, hung up her Arms, and, in the dress becoming her Sex, nurses an Infant, whilst Mentor holds the Olive-Branch, and teaches two Children the advantages of Peace. ——— May our American Brethren view this Scene, and, after hanging up their Arms, present the Olive-Branch to the Commissioners empowered to make Peace!

This allegory expresses the hopes of peace-loving elements for a cessation of hostilities with the arrival of a civilian peace commission in America on June 6, 1778. It also shows how idealized pictures were intended to inspire men. From *The Westminster Magazine*, 1778, frontispiece. LC–USZ62–45486

724

EUROPE, ASIA, AFRICA and AMERICA bringing Intelligence to the GENIUS of the LONDON MAGAZINE. Desd. Drawn and Engraved by Bonnor. [January 1778]

Mixed method 5⅞ x 4⅛ in. (image)

An angelic woman with large wings writes in the "London Magazine 1778," and a cherub at her feet looks into a book marked "London Magazine Continued from the Year 1731." The four continents approach her. Cherubs add Baroque richness to an Augustan setting. From *The London Magazine*, 1778, frontispiece. LC–USZ62–45502

725

The CLOSET. No. 1 Price 1s. Bute Invt. Germaine Ext. Mansfield Sculpt. Publish'd as the Act directs Jany. 28th 1778. by I. Williams No. 39 Fleet Street.

Aquatint with etching 8¾ x 14 in.

Scenes showing America and England are separated by pictures of ships taking troops to Quebec and Boston and cripples back to England's Chelsea Hospital. The picture in the King's closet shows George III, the devil, Bute, Mansfield, and Germain discussing the problems of the war. Below them, Charles Yorke, Lord Chancellor, commits suicide. On the left side are four panels showing (1) the death of Jane McCrea, (2) seven savages roasting a white man on a spit, (3) Burgoyne and his captive army marching past Gates and the victorious Americans, and (4) German and Scottish mercenaries fleeing the Americans. CPPS 5470 LC–USZ62–45431

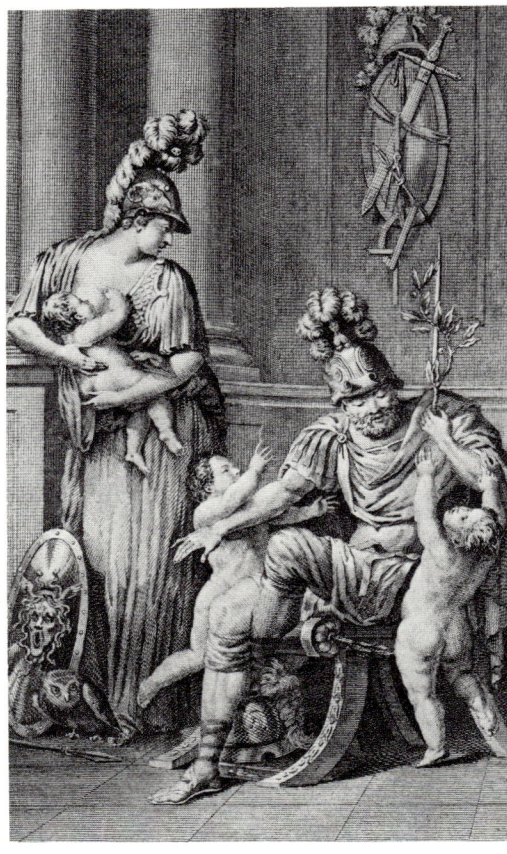

723

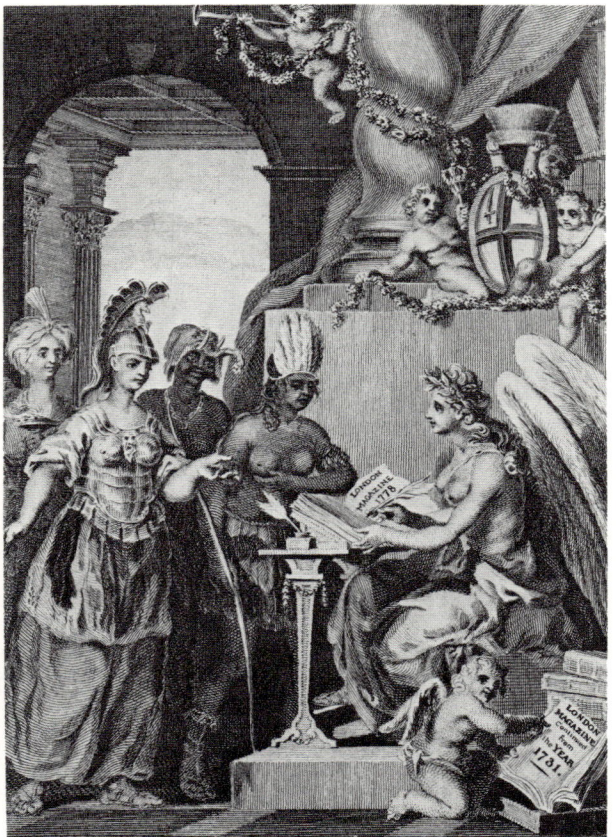

724

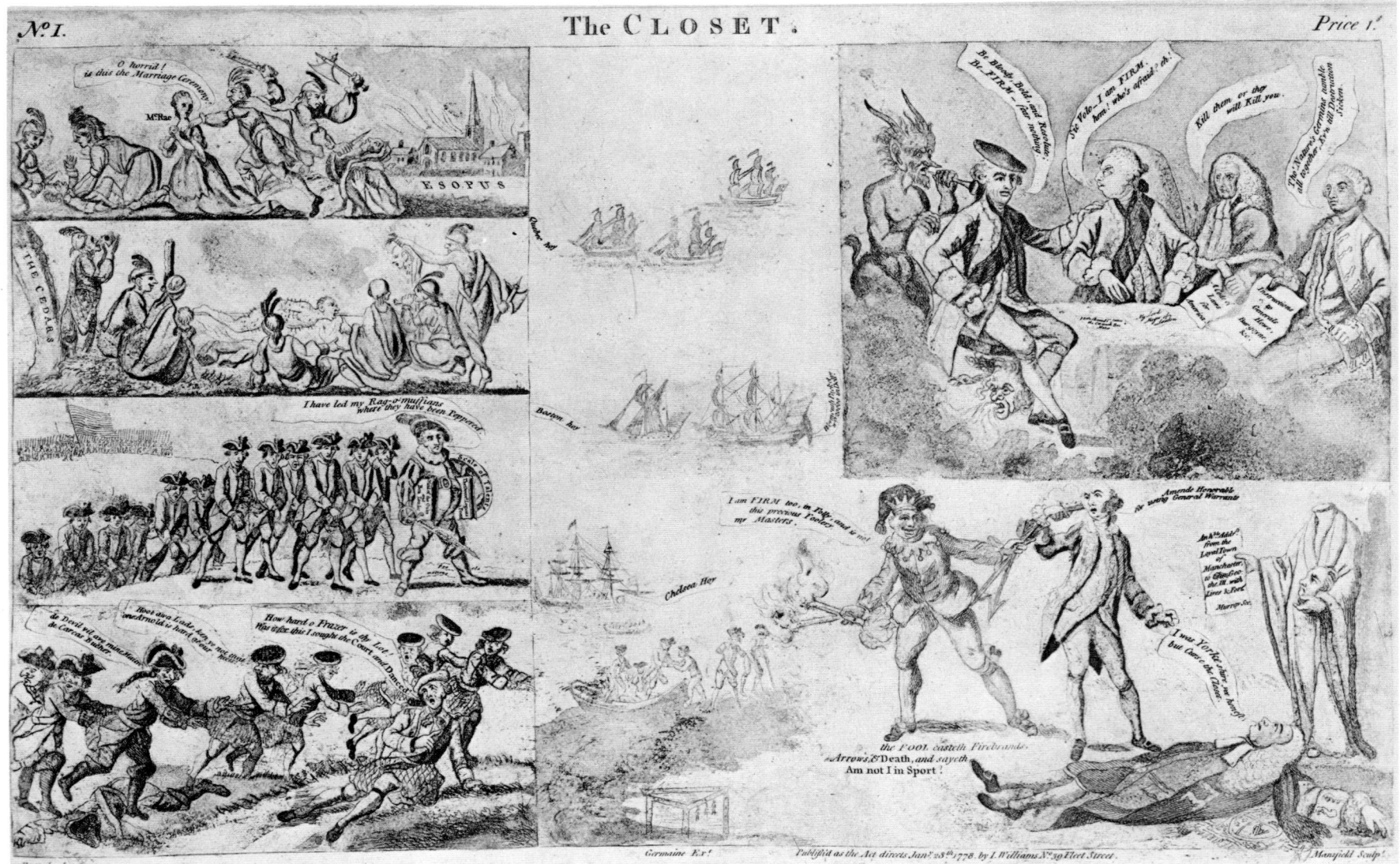

726

A Picturesque View of the State of the Nation for February 1778.

Mixed method 3⅞ x 6¼ in.

An explanation in *The Westminster Magazine* states: "I. The commerce of Great Britain, represented in the figure of a Milch-Cow. II. The American Congress sawing off her horns, which are her natural strength and defense: one being already gone, the other just a-going. III. The jolly, plump Dutchman milking the poor tame Cow with great glee. IV and V. The Frenchman and Spaniard, each catching at their respective shares of the produce, and running away with bowls full ... VI. The good ship Eagle laid up, and moved at some distance from Philadelphia ... VII. The two brothers [Richard and William Howe] napping it, one against the other, in the City of Philadelphia, out of sight of fleet and army. VIII. The British Lion lying on the ground fast asleep, so that a pug-dog tramples upon him [the pug urinates on the lion] ... IX. A Free Englishman in mourning stands by him [the British lion]...." While showing the threat which the allies present to English commerce, this cartoon also contributes to the great pamphlet war over the conduct of the Howe brothers in America. The controversy began in January of 1778 when Fox asked for an investigation by Parliament. From *The Westminster Magazine*, February 1778, p. 66. CPPS 5472 LC–USZ62–39591

727

DÉDIÉ AUX MILORDS DE L'AMIRAUTÉ ANGLAISE PAR UN MEMBRE DU CONGRÈS AMÉRICAIN. Dessiné d'apres nature à Boston par Corbut en 1778 et gravé a Philadelphie par Va de bon coeur. 1778

Mixed method 6⅜ x 10⅛ in.

An English admiral, with the appendages of an eagle, is tied to a tree. His claws and wings are clipped by Frenchmen, Dutchmen, and an American. A short poem accompanies the picture:

> Tel qu'un âpre Vautour dévorant l'Amerique,
> Anglais, impunément tu crus la mettre à sac.
> Mais pour la bien venger d un traitement inique
> Il ne l'y reste pas une once de Tabac.

Collection de Vinck 1209. CPPS 5472a

728

THE COMMISSIONERS. M DARLY Pubd April 1. 1778 by M DARLY 39 Strand. 1778

Etching (hand colored) 8¼ x 12¼ in. (image)

Five obeisant British peace commissioners, the Howe brothers, the Earl of Carlisle, William Eden, and George Johnstone, kneel before America dressed as an Indian woman, contemplating a liberty cap. She sits on containers marked "Tobacco for Germany," "Tobacco for France," "Tobacco for Holland," "Rice for France," "Indigo for Spain," and "Indigo for the Mediterannean Ports." This cartoon telescopes time by showing two sets of peace commissioners. William Howe left Philadelphia on May 25, 1778, and the three commissioners arrived on June 6, 1778. It recognizes the commercial losses which England was suffering because of the opening of American trade with continental powers. CPPS 5473

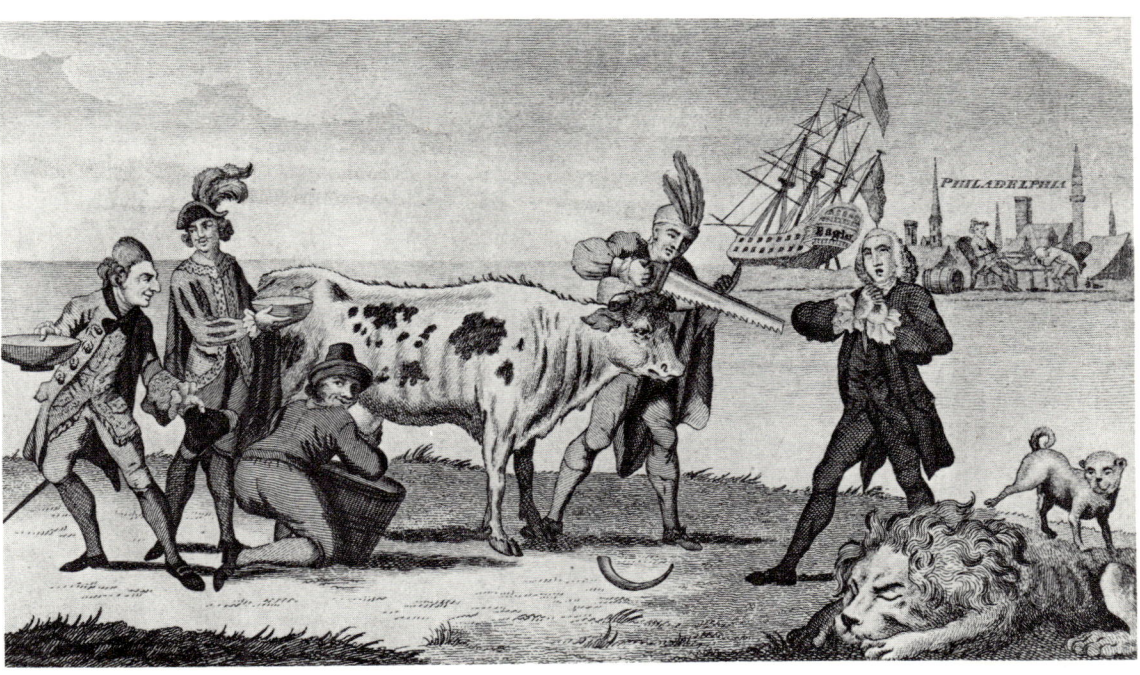

726

729

The Commissioner's Interview with CONGRESS. Pub'd by M Darly 39 Strand April 1 1778.
Etching 8½ x 12¾ in.

Three congressmen in long robes seem to have the better part of an argument with Carlisle, Eden, and Johnstone. The Earl of Bute looks on sadly. Although the peace commission was given broader powers than the Howe brothers, it still could not meet the increased demands of the colonists for full recognition as an independent country. This cartoonist and many other Englishmen saw the commission as hopeless from the beginning, as witnessed by this cartoon and the previous item which are dated before the commissioners' departure from England on April 16, 1778.
CPPS 5474 LC–USZ62–45432

730

[Britannia toe] Amer[eye]ca. Pubd by M Darly May 6 1778 Strand.
Etching 13¾ x 9¾ in.

A rebus satirizing England's appointing commissioners to settle the differences with the "colonists" after France had already acknowledged America as an independant country. Translated, it reads:

My dear Daughter I cannot behold without great pain your headstrong backwardness to return to you Duty in not opposing all the good I long intended for your sole Happiness & being told that you have giv'n your hand to a base & two-faced Frenchman I have sent you over five wise men the greatest of all my children to put you to rights & hope you will listen to them & mind what they say to you they have instructions to give you those things you formerly required so be a good girl discharge you soldiers and ships of war & do not rebel against your mother rely upon me & do not trust to what that french rascal shall tell you I see he wants to bring on an enmity to all unity between you & I but listen not to him all the world takes notice of his two faces. I'll send him such Messages from my great cannons as shall make his heart repent & know that one good or ill turn merits another. NB let not hate take too much hold of your heart.
I am your friend & mother.

CPPS 5474a LC–USZ62–45411

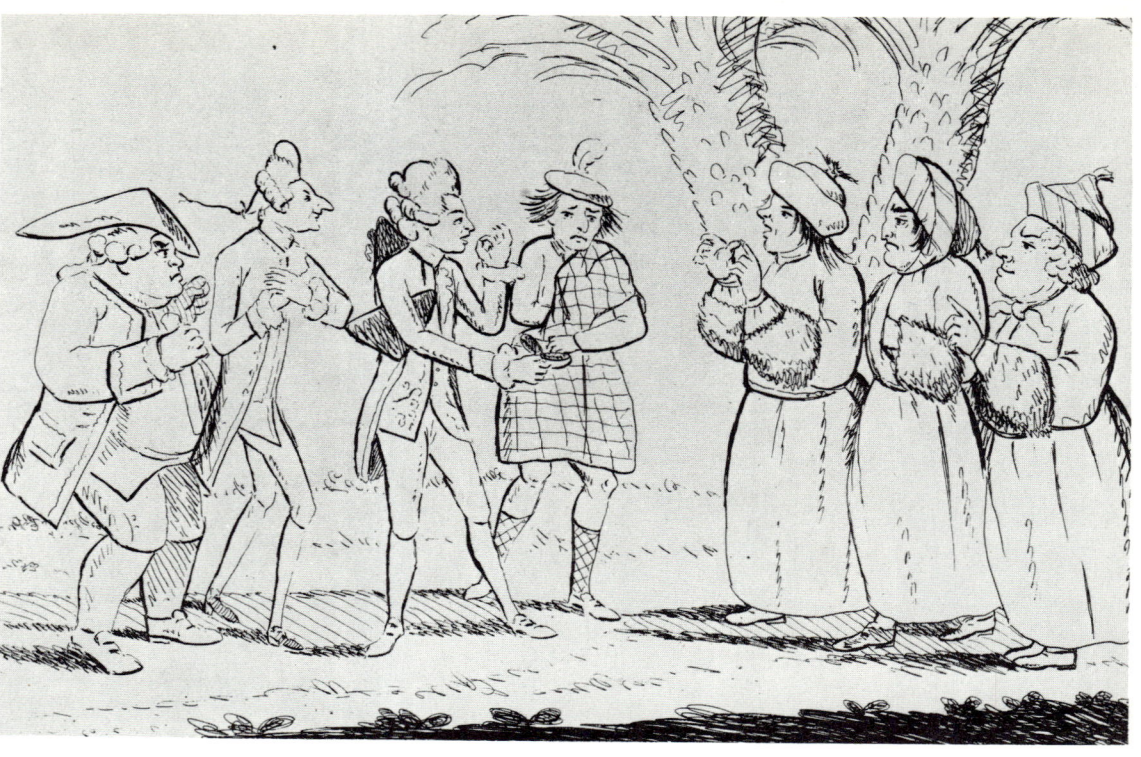

729

731

[America toe] her [Miss]taken [Moth]er. Pubd by M Darly. May 11 1778 Strand.
Etching 13¾ x 9¾ in.

America as an Indian woman holds an American flag. This rebus answers the previous one "Britannia to America."

You silly old woman that you have sent a dove to us is very plain to draw our attention from our real interests but we are determin'd to abide by our own ways of thinking your five children you have sent to us shall be treated as Visitors, & safely sent home again you may trust them & admire them, but you must not expect one of your puppets will come home to you as sweet as you sent him, twas cruel to send so pretty a man so many thousand miles & to have the fatigue of returning back after bobbing his coat and dirtying those red heel shoes if you are wise follow your own advice you gave to me take home your ships [and] soldiers guard well you own trifling & leave me to my self as I am at age to know my own interests. without your foolish advice & know that I shall always regard you & my Brothers as relations but not as friends.
I am your greatly injured
Daughter America.

CPPS 5475 LC–USZ62–45412

——————Another impression (hand colored).

732

THE OLIVE REJECTD. OR THE YANKEES REVENGE. Pubds. as the act Directs may 4 1778. LE LORD BURTHE COURONNÉ SUR UN ANE Infortunéz Anglois, a quoi vos Bills Conciliatoire ont-ils servis? [1778]
Mixed method 9¼ x 12¾ in.

Lord North, mounted on an ass, tries to jump the Atlantic Ocean. Although he has an

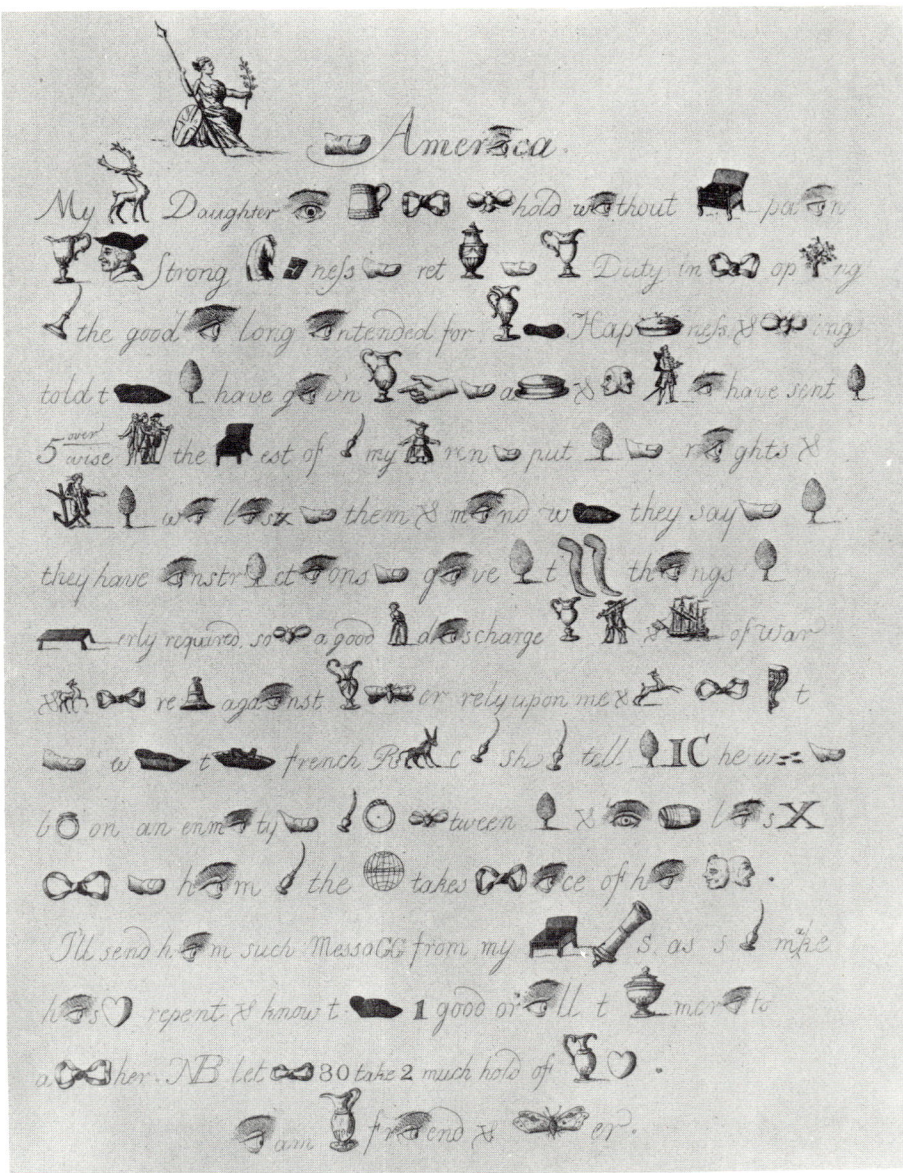
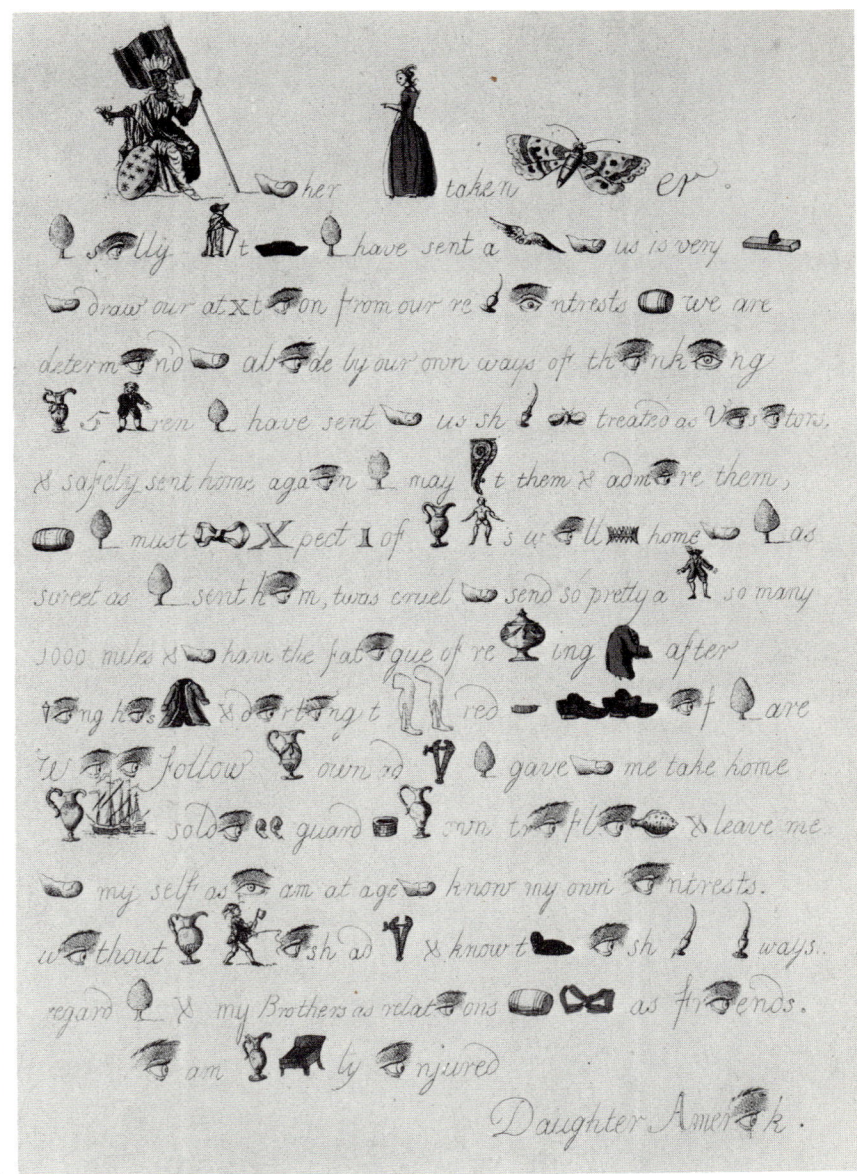

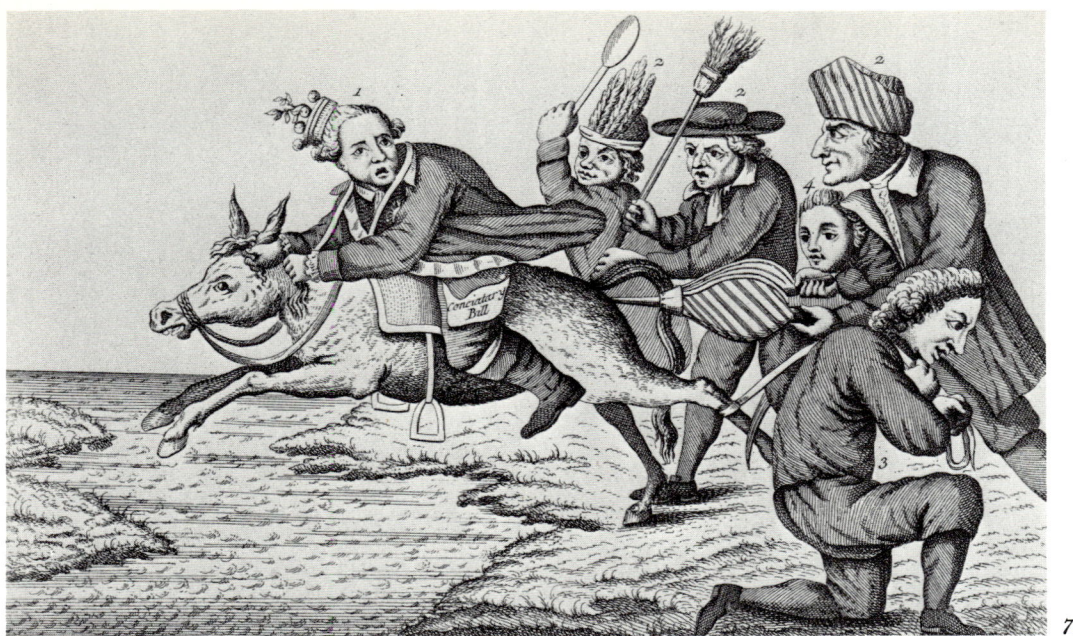

olive branch in his hat and the "Conciatary Bill" in his pocket, the Americans drive him away with paddle, broom, bellows, and a trip rope. An explanation below the picture distinguishes each character:

1 Le representant de la Grande Bretagne pressé de fuir l'Amérique monté sur un Coursier a longues oreilles ne pouvant regagner l'Angleterre qu'à la nage, sa Flotte étant dispersé ou deffaite et ne pouvant lui donner du secour en ayant besoin elle meme par les Signaux de détresse qu'elle fait entendre de tous cotez. 2 plusieurs Américains faisant treve a leur moderation naturelle que leurs ennemis ont gratuitement qualiffies de poltronnerie, chassent honteusement l'agent qui sous un voile honete vouloit ebranler leur liberté en semant la division parmi eux. 3 un Anglois faisant partie du petit nombre de ceux qu'on souffre encor en Amerique fait les plus pour y retenir l'amiral. 4 Un Francois representant son Pays digne soutien et allié du plus beau de l'Univers sempresse de couper le foible lien dont vainement l'anglois vouloit se servir.

CPPS Vol. V, p. 289. *Collection de Vinck* 1215
LC–USZ62–45392

733

THE ENGLISHMAN IN PARIS. Sold by C. Sheppard, Lambeth Hill, Doctors Commons. [1777-78]

Etching 8⅝ x 13⅛ in.

An Englishman begins to eat a goose representing America at a Frenchman's dinner. Verse below reads:

> An American goose came hot from the spit
> Egad says the Englishman I'll have a bit
> His jaws he applies with wond'rous speed
> To devour the viands on which others shou'd feed.
> Fie, fie, Monsr. La Anglois cries the frenchman;—forebear,
> Why the limbs of your brother thus furiously tear?
> Think you we'll tamely look on and starve?
> No, no, Monsr. Anglois, we wait for to carve.

This cartoon and verse express the English suspicion that France was preparing to enter the war to reclaim her lost land in North America. Many Americans, Patriots as well as Tories, held this opinion. CPPS 5477
LC–USZ62–45433

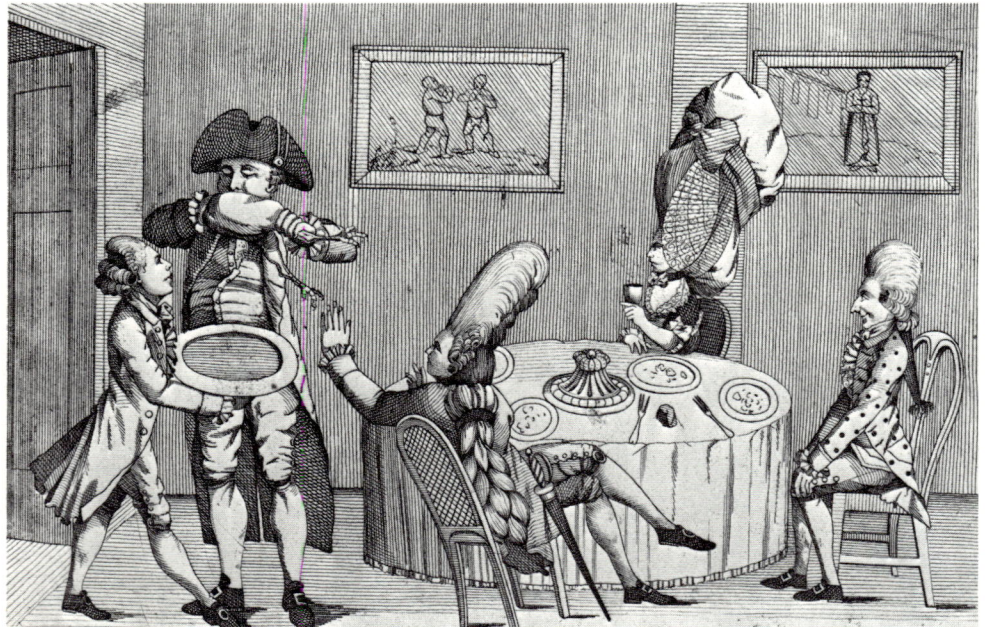

734

A VIEW IN AMERICA in 1778. Pub by M Darly Augt. 1 1778

Etching 8⅞ x 12 9/16 in.

Two men, one in military uniform and one dressed as a congressman in Darly's "The Commissioners' Interview with Congress," stand over a prostrate Negro and beside some wretched soldiers. In the background a war goes on. This print probably satirizes the poor conditions of slaves and soldiers in a land dedicated to liberty. LC–USZ62–46659

735

AN EXTRAORDINARY GAZETTE or the DISAPPOINTED POLITICIANS. [1778?]

Etching and mezzotint 4⅝ x 6 in.

Englishmen receive news of Clinton's evacuation of Philadelphia in June of 1778. Two maps are on the wall: one shows English possessions in 1762, and a smaller one with serpents crawling throughout represents the possessions in 1778. The shrinking map indicates a pessimistic view of the war's direction even though Clinton wrote that battles at Freehold and Monmouth were victories. CPPS 5485 LC–USZ62–1516

736

[Emblematical Print Adapted to the Times.] London Mag: [Augustus Keppel?] August 1778.

Mixed method 3⅞ x 6⅜ in.

Neptune and Britannia laugh at America sitting on the opposite shore. America is a young man with an American flag and a cock (representing France) on his shoulder. In the background the English fleet under Keppel and the French fleet under D'Orvilliers out of Brest are battling. This plate and an accompanying explanation defend the recent action of Admiral Keppel who fought the French in the Channel that summer. In August

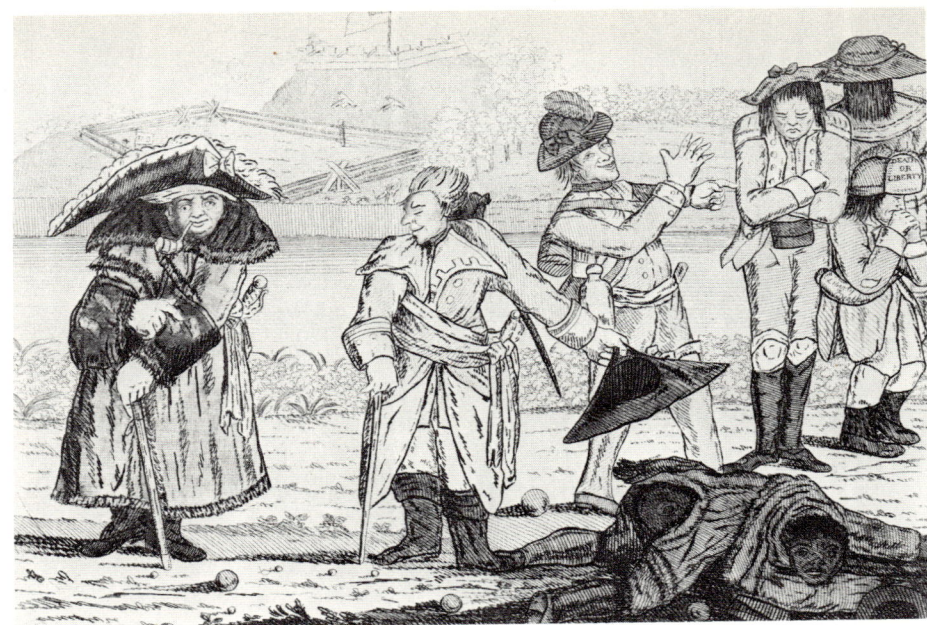
734

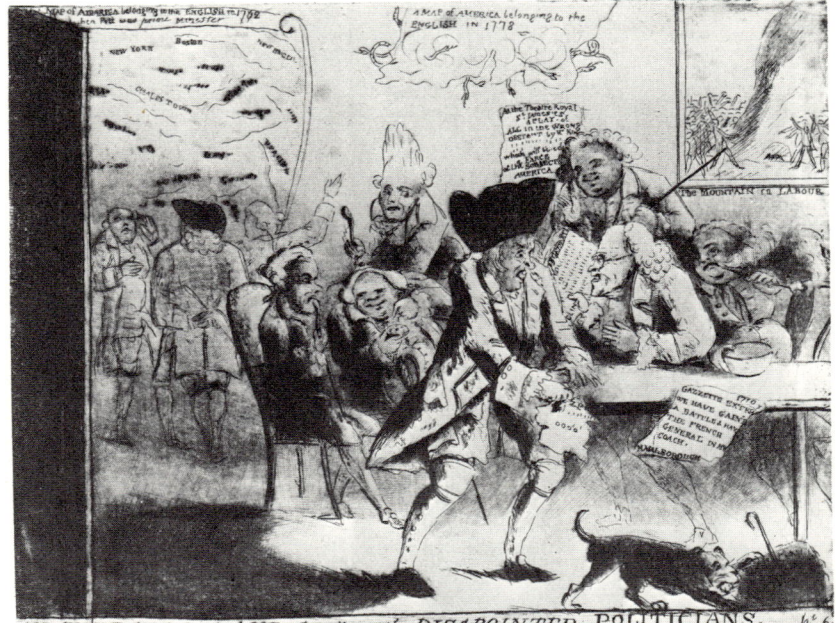
735

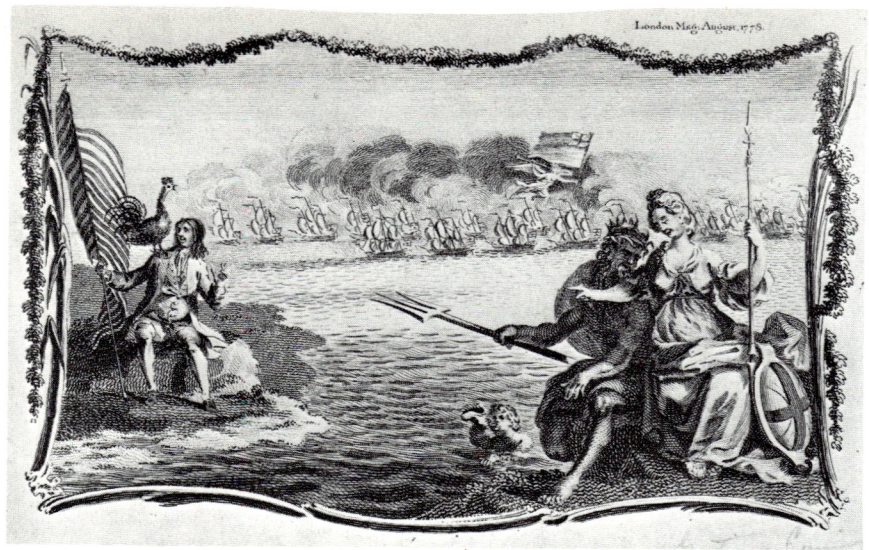

736

of 1778 Keppel was brought before a court-martial and charged with lack of aggressiveness. The explanation states that he won the greater victory by containing the French and saving the English Navy to fight another day. It also says that Keppel drew this cartoon to show how his victory over the French paved the way to ultimate victory over the Americans.

> ... he [Keppel] ventures to prophesy that Great-Britain, if she understands her own interest by augmenting her navy, at all events, (though she considerably diminish her land forces) will be enabled to break this unnatural alliance, and to make the Americans, if not the French, sorely repent the impolitic and unjust measure.

This copy in P&P is originally from *The London Magazine*, August 1778, opposite p. 339. CPPS 5486 LC–USZ62–45434

737

THE CURIOUS ZEBRA. alive from America! walk in Gem'men and Ladies, walk in. London, printed for G. Johnson as the Act directs 3 Sepr. 1778, and Sold at all the Printshops in London & Westminster. 1778

Mixed method 6¾ x 10 1/16 in.

America, represented by a zebra with each stripe designated a Colony, has a saddle marked "Stamp Act" put on it by George Grenville. North holds the reins and George Washington and a Frenchman pull on the tail. The three peace commissioners, Carlisle, Eden, and Johnstone, stand behind North and explain that America will settle for independence alone. CPPS 5487 LC–USZ62–1517

738

The Tea-Tax-Tempest, or the Anglo-American Revolution. Angewitter entstanden durch die Auslage aus den Thee in Amerika. Orage causé par l'Impôt sur le thé en Amerique. [Carl Guttenberg of Nuremberg] 1778

Mixed method 13 x 17 in.

Father Time uses a magic lantern to show a picture of a tea pot exploding in the midst of

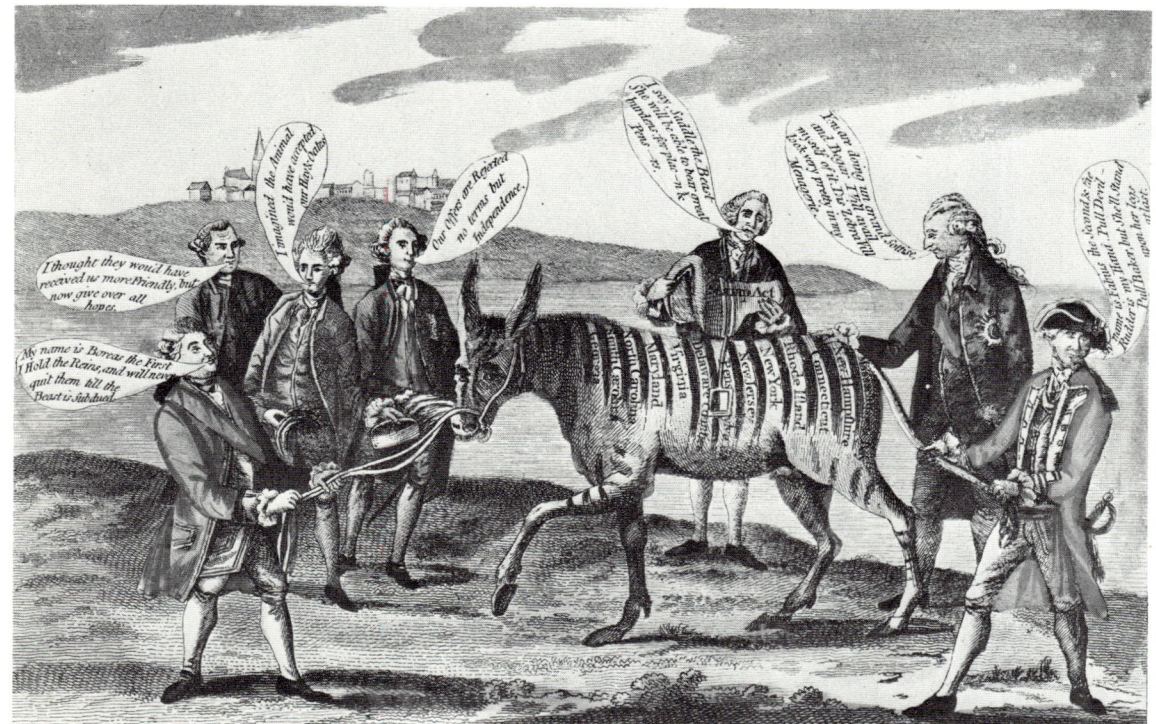

737

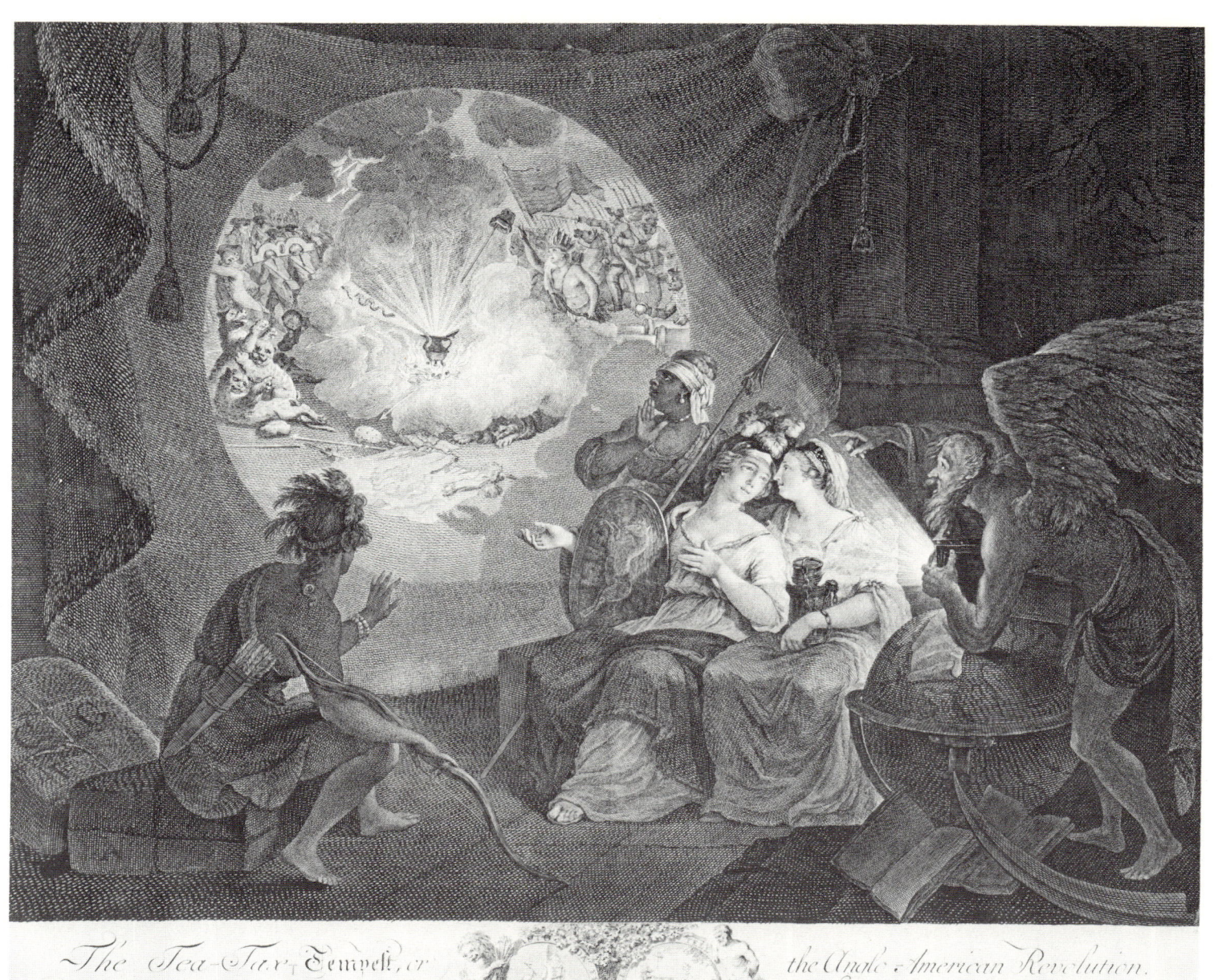

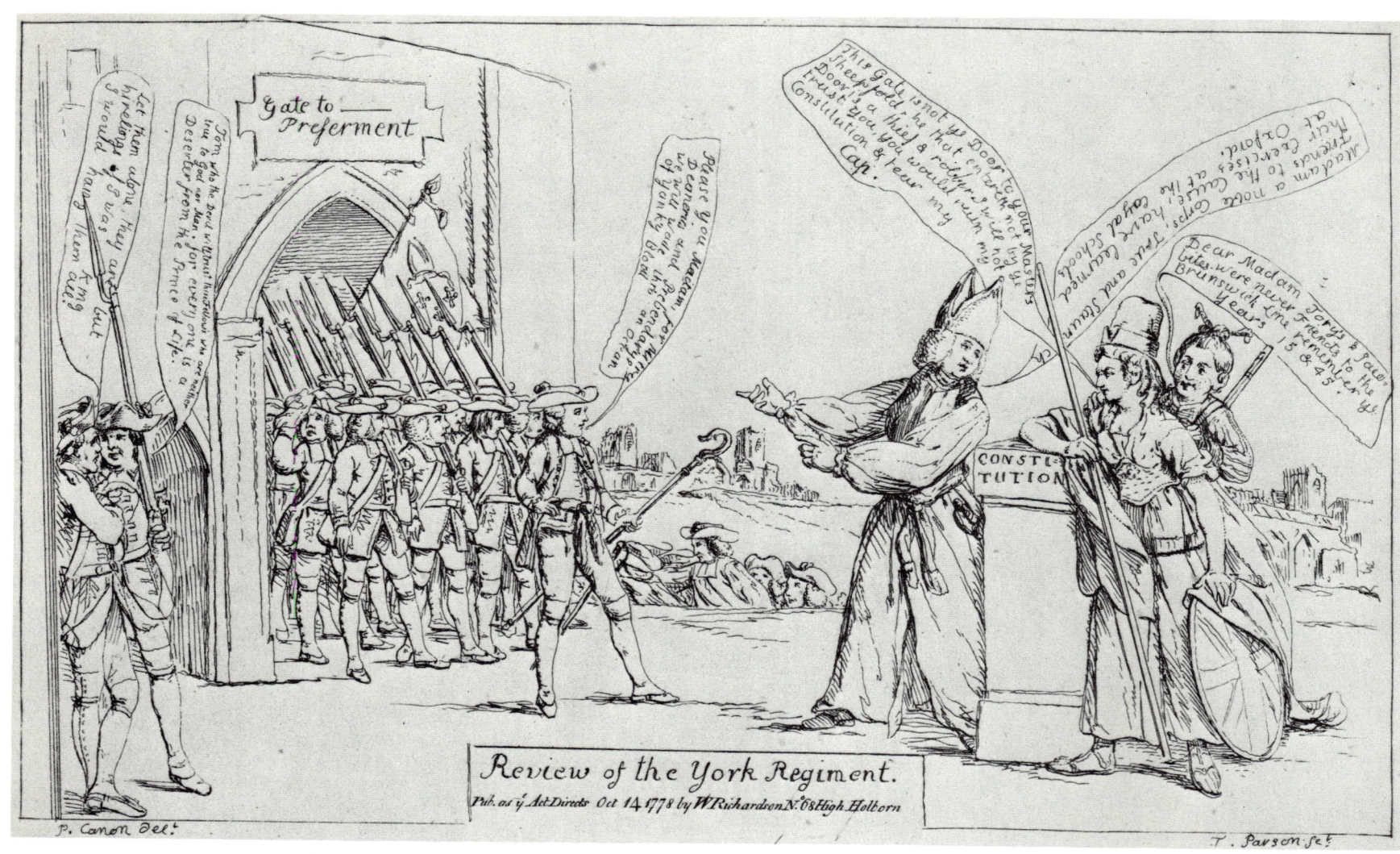

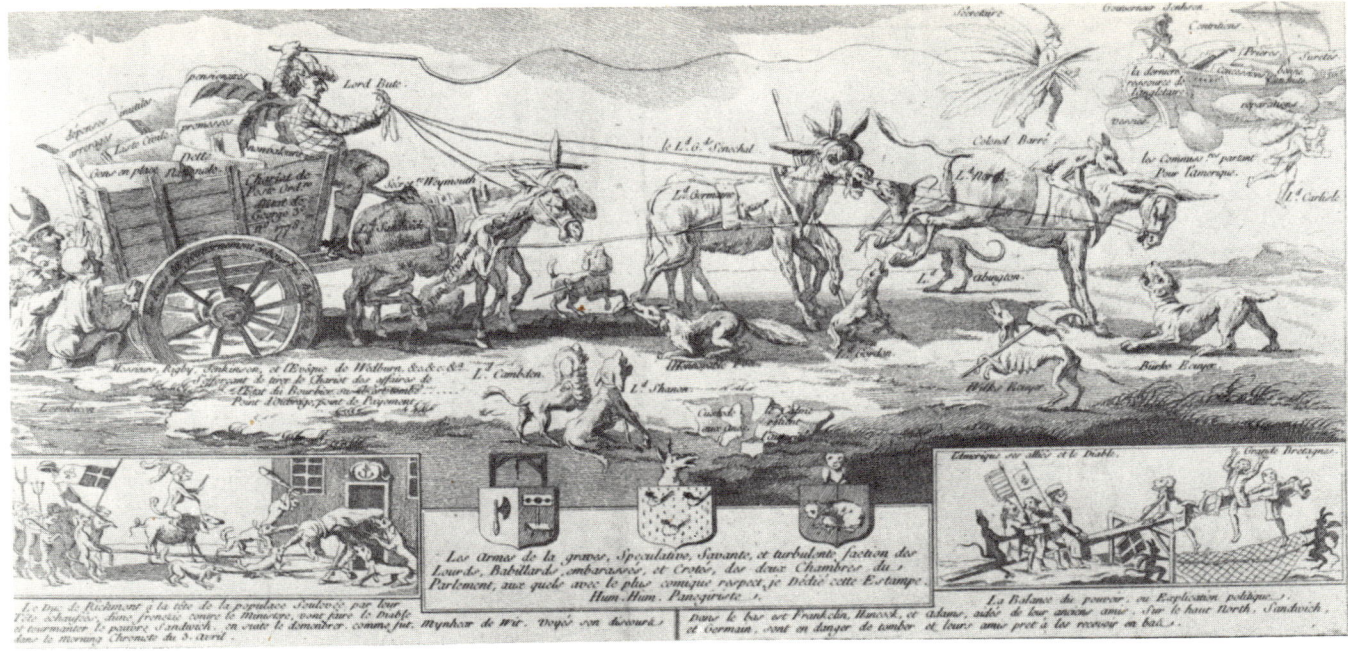

an American army composed of colonists and an Indian. They chase a fleeing British army of yoked soldiers and lion cubs. Four people watch the show: an Indian (America), a Negro woman (Africa), a woman holding a lantern (Asia), and a white woman holding shield and spear (Europe). At the base of the print are two pictures in ovals comparing the American Revolution to Holland's auto da fé (1560) and Switzerland's William Tell (1200). CPPS 5490 LC–USZ62–1523

739

Orage causé par l'Impôt sur le Thé en Amérique. [1778?]

Mixed method 5¼ x 6⅞ in.

A reduced and reversed version of item 738. Below is engraved:

Le temps fait voir avec sa Lanterne Magique aux quatre parties du Monde, que cet Orage que les Anglois ont excité, les foudroye eux-memes, et va donner à l'Amérique les moyens de se saisir du bonnet de la Liberté.

CPPS 5491; see also 5225, 5490, 6190.

740

Review of the York Regiment. P. Canon delt. T. Parson sct Pub. as ye Act Directs Oct 14, 1778 by W. Richardson No. 68 High Holborn [177?]

Etching 6¼ x 10⅞ in.

Archbishop Markham of York points to a regiment of his soldiers and praises them to Britannia. The leader of the soldiers claims they "will wade thro an Ocean of Yank'y Blood." This cartoon satirizes the support given to the war by the Church of England. CPPS 5492 LC–USZ62–45435

——————Another impression.

741

LA FOLIE DES DEUX PARTIS, OÙ VUE POLITIQUE DE L'ETAT ET DE LA NATION ANGLAISE, AVEC LES SENATEURS EN PERSONNES. [1778?]

Etching 5½ x 12 in. (image)

Three pictures showing the contemporary condition of England. Lord Bute drives a wagon designated "Chariot de Poste Ordre L'Etat de George 3e. no. 1778" carrying bags marked "dépenses," "inutiles," "arrerages," "promesses," "Liste Civile," "Gens en place," "Dette Nationale," and "nonvaleurs." The wagon is pushed by a mob led by an Anglican bishop and pulled by animals designated as Weymouth, Richmond, Senechal, Germain, and North. Dogs chase around the stuck livery. The dogs are Effingham, Fox, Gordon, Abingdon, Burke, Wilkes, Shanon, and Camden; C. J. Fox is a fox. An airship designated "La derniere resource de l'angleterre" carrying

313

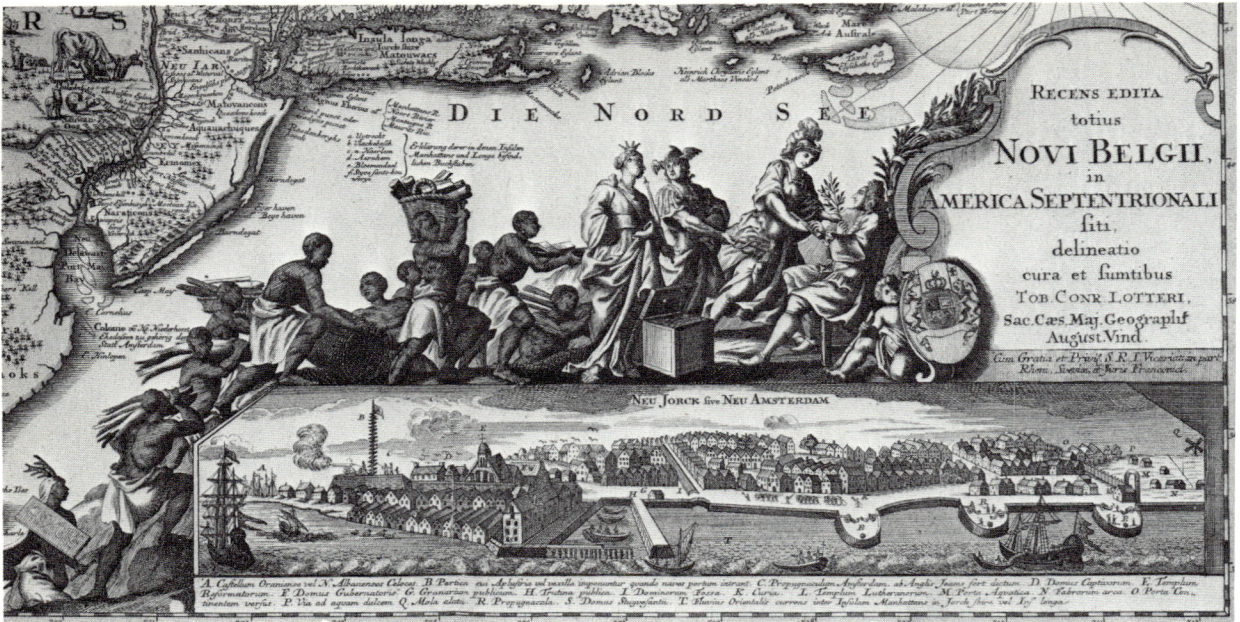

742

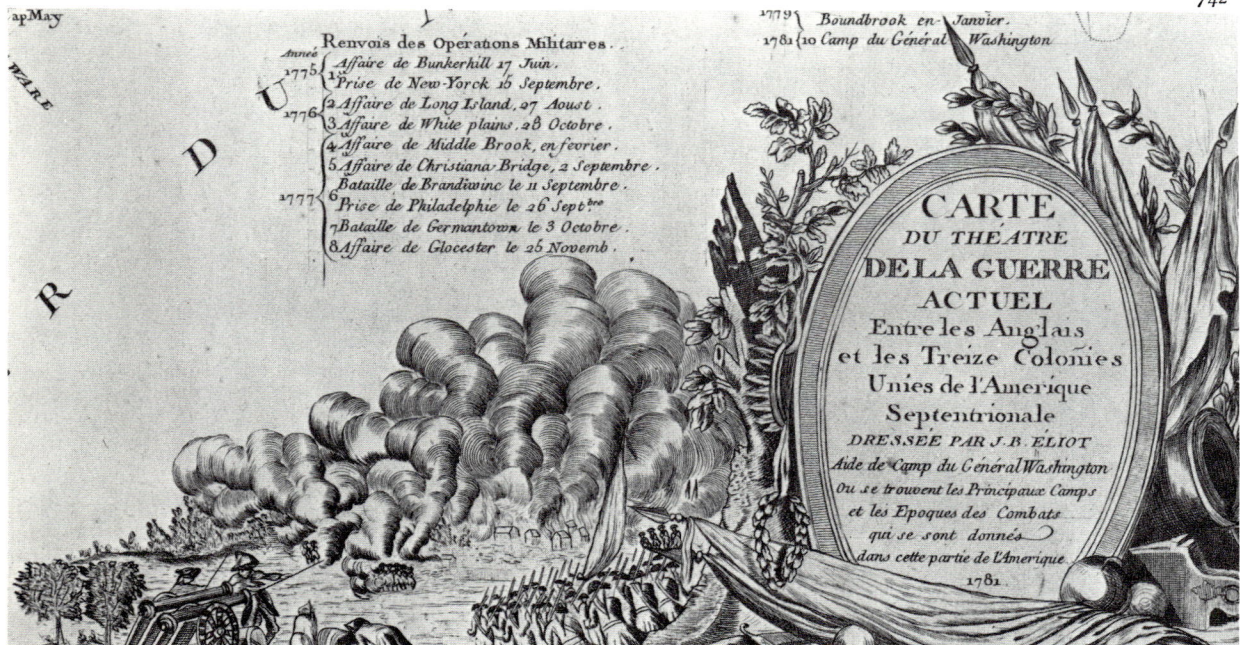

744

"reparations" in the form of "Suretés," "Concessions," "Prieres," and "bonne conduite" flies off to America with "Ld. Carlisle" and "Gouverneur Jenhson." Beneath the central picture are two smaller pictures and three satirical crests. LC-USZ61-808

741a

La Balance du pouvoir, ou Explication politique. Dans le bas est Frankclin, Hancock, et Adams, aidés de leur anciens amis. Sur le haut North, Sandwich et Germain sont en danger de tomber et leurs amis pret à les recevoir en bas.

Etching 1¼ x 3⅝ in.

An American, probably Franklin, with fur hat and spectacles, a Frenchman, a Spaniard, and a devil outweight three Englishmen on a seesaw. The Englishmen fall off into a net held by two devils. This cartoon is an inset in the lower right corner of "La folie des deux partis," item 741.

742

[Cartouche and ornament from a map of New York] Tob. Conr. Lotteri, Sac. Caes, Maj. Geographi, August. Vind. [1778?]

Etching (hand colored) 20 x 23¼ in. (entire map)

A view of New York forms the base of the cartouche, which features the dark natives of America carrying produce to a seated figure, probably the King of England. The god Mercury and two goddesses also bring favors to the King. On the map are pictures of many animals and two Indian villages, which show the John White influence. From a map entitled "Recens Edita totius Novi Belgii, in America Septentrionali ..." in Lotter, *Atlas Géographique* (Nürnberg, 1778), no. 92. See Stokes, *Iconography of Manhattan Island*, v. 1 (New York, 1915), p. 223. See also item 550.
LC–USZ62–46068

743

[A European directs two Indians where to place their goods for barter—a cartouche]
Tob. Conr. Lotter, sculps Aug V: [1778]
   Etching 11¼ x 6¾ in. (image)

Indians bring fish and skins to the European who has bundles and barrels stacked nearby. In the background another Indian is smoking in the woods, and the rest of the cartouche is filled with many wild animals. The entire design is surmounted by a crown resting on an escutcheon showing English lions and French fleur-de-lis. The traditional theme here is of commerce amid great abundance in the colonies of England and France. From a map entitled "Pensylvania, Nova Jersey et Nova York cum Regionibus ad Fluvium Delaware in America . . . per Tob. Conr. Lotter Geographum Aug. Vind." in Lotter, *Atlas Géographique* (Nürnberg, 1778), no. 94. LC–USZ62–46069

744

[Representation of a battle—a cartouche]
A Paris chez Mondhare Rue St. Jacques A la Ville de Caen. 1778
   Etching 7¼ x 13½ in. (image)

Troops march toward a burning town, while others load a cannon. To the right is a cartouche with flags and ordnance framing the title "Carte du Théatre dela Guerra Actuel entre les Anglais et les Treize Colonies Unies de l'Amerique Septentrionale dressée par J. B. Éliot Ingénieurs des Etats Unis 1778." In G&M Vault.

———Another impression.

———Another impression.

———Another copy which describes J.B. Eliot as "Aide de Camp du Général Washington ou se trouvent les Principaux Camps et les Epoques des Combats qui se sont donnés dans cette partie de l'Amerique 1781."
LC–USZ62–46077

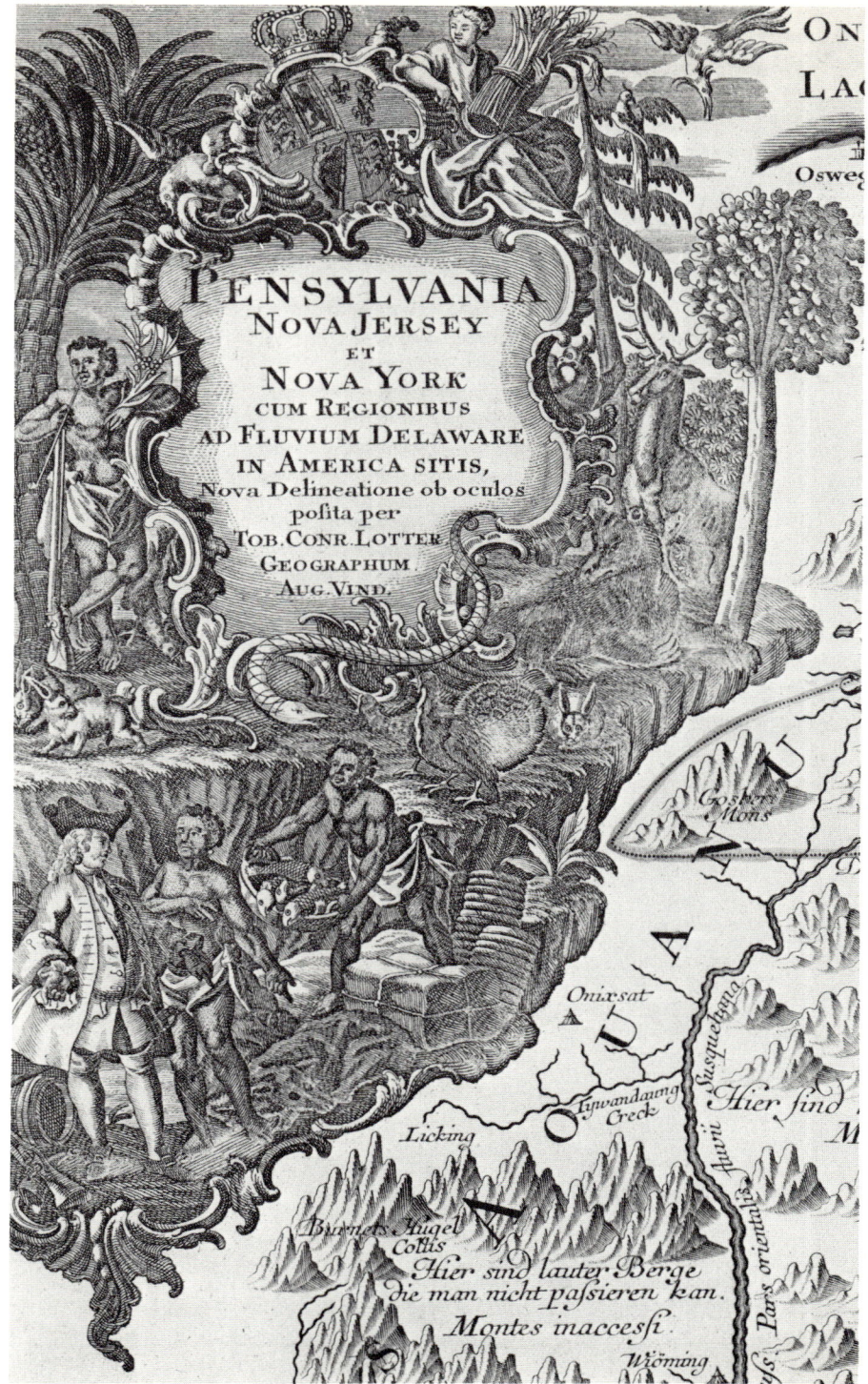

743

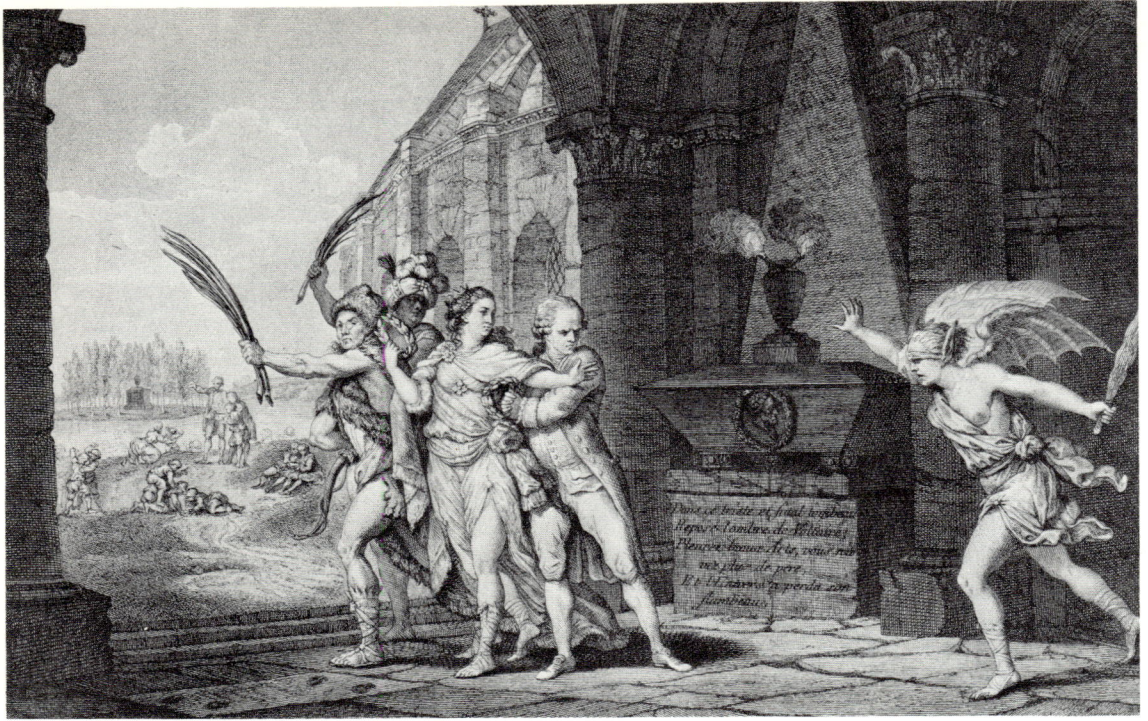

745

745

LE TOMBEAU DE VOLTAIRE. Dédié à Madame la Marquise de Villette, Dame de Ferney. L.V. inv. C.M. sculp. Se vend à Paris chez Alibert Md. d'Estampes, au Palais Royal. Et chez le Noir Mo. du Cabinet des Estampes du Roi, au Louvre. [1778?]

Mixed method 10 x 14 in.

The explanation beneath this print describes the allegorical tableau. Preparing to deck the tomb of the bard Voltaire are the four continents personified: Europe by d'Alembert, Asia by Catherine II, Africa by the Prince Oronoco, and America by the scholar and liberator, Benjamin Franklin. Suddenly, however, the rash and ruthless Prejudice of Ignorance interrupts the ceremony. In the distance is the contrasting calm of another monument, this one to the Swiss philosopher Rousseau who is buried there in the poplar grove consecrated by friendship. The group of people of all ages demonstrate by their actions the philosophy expressed by Rousseau in *Emile*. The portrait of Franklin is the famous head, after Cochin, on the body of a muscular youth. LC–USZ62–45436

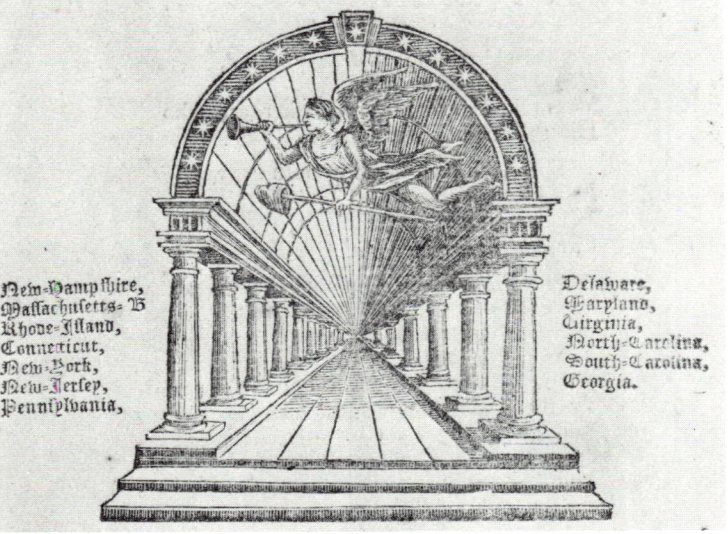

746

746

THE UNITED STATES MAGAZINE FOR JANUARY 1779. [title page]

Woodcut 2¾ x 2¾ in. (image)

Fame flies through an archway with trumpet in one hand and staff with liberty cap in the other. Stars representing the 13 Colonies adorn the top of the arch; the pillars also represent the original and new States. A poem on the next two pages of *The United States Magazine* for January 1779 explains the picture.

> A Bold triumphal Arch you see,
> Such as by antiquity
> Was raised to Rome's great heroes, who
> Did the rage of war subdue.

The Arch high bending doth convey,
In a hieroglyphic way,
What in noble stile like this,
Our United Empire is.

The Pillars which support the weight,
Are each of them a mighty State:
Thirteen and more the vista shews,
As to vaster length it grows:
For new states shall added be,
To the great Confederacy.
And the mighty arch shall rise,
From the cold Canadian skies,
And shall bend through heaven's broad way,
To the noble Mexic bay.

In the lofty arch are seen,
Stars of lucid ray—Thirteen:
And when other states shall rise,
Other stars shall deck these skies;
There in wakeful light to burn,
O'er the hemisphere of morn.

Fame before the vista flies,
Rising to the western skies:
A golden trumpet still she bears;
Sounding through the coming years:
Sounding o'er the west-way plain;
Where but solitude doth reign;
But where new states shall yet have place,
Founded on an equal base;
Founded far beyond the groves,
Where the Yochagany roves;
Or where Cochnawage fills
Her urn, at the Shanduski hills.

Here in gilded roofs and halls,
At city feasts and festivals,
The wise and brave shall reckon o'er
The story of the years before;
And with delighted fancy tell,
How the first heroes fought and fell—
The heroes who, in early day,
Opposed Britannia's ruthless sway,
And her mad monarch, o'er whose mind,
Rolled angry vengeance to mankind.

O! heavenly-winged cherub, Fame,
Bear aloft each noble name
Of those whose comprehensive mind,
The fabric of the states design'd;
Or those who to support it, fought,
Warm with the advent'rous thought;
Bear aloft the names which we
Guard with popularity:
If they deserve it may they bloom,
Through ev'ry age and year to come;
And no malignant breath profane,
Imprint upon their worth a stain:
And even those who yet may lie,
Prest with present obloquy;
If they are injured may they rise,

And wing their way through placid skies;
The impartial voice of future days,
Ascribing to their acts just praise.

O! Thou, who on the circle high
Dost sit, of vast eternity;
At whose command the spinning ball
Rolls on, and empires rise and fall:
May this our empire built by thee,
Remain with great stability,
And while the east or western wave,
The margin of the land shall lave;
Or angry winds from Hudson's bay,
Shall drive the southern clouds away;
May the Confederate Arch prevail
Above the tyrants that assail:
And parallel with that on high,
The heav'ns and starry canopy,
Exist a Structure of renown,
And but with Time's great ARCH go down.

LC–USZ62–45570

747

THE BIRTH-DAY ODE.* As it was preformed before his M_____, on the 4th of JUNE, BY THE ROYAL BAND. [June 1779]
Etching 6 x 7¾ in. (image)

Three musicians, Sandwich on kettle drums, North a violinist, and Germain a flutist, and four vocalists perform the music entitled "The Distresses of the Nation: an Ode Performed in honor of his Majesty's Birth Day." At the bottom of the print is a note corresponding to the asterisk in the title which reads: "As several spurious copies of the Birth-Day Ode made their appearance in the Newspapers, that the Public may be no longer deceived, they are here presented with the

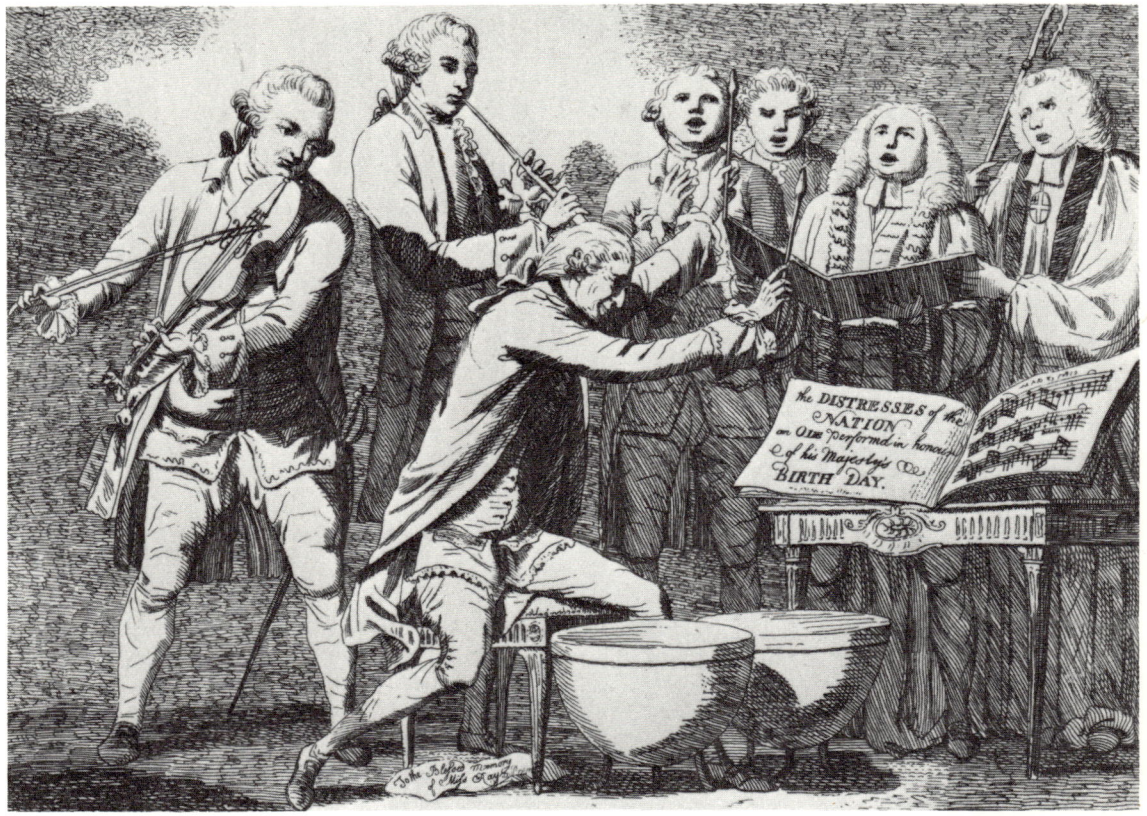

747

genuine Ode, as it was actually performed on the 4th of June."

I. STROPHE.

Now Caesar sits on Throne sublime,
To snuff the Laureat's drousy Rhime,
And take his annual Sleep in state,
To please the Slaves that round him wait;
Swift, from the starry Courts above,
Descend some Dream, (for Dreams descend from Jove)
And to the Monarch's mental Ear,
The wonders of his Reign declare:
While a grateful People's Voice,
Shall in choral Peals rejoice,
And to the Nations round proclaim,
Caesar, Virtue, and Wisdom are the same.

I. ANTISTROPHE.

Swift from the starry Courts above
Descends the Dream divine, from Jove___
Mark! o'er the Monarch's slumbring Head,
A raven Gloom his Pinions spread!
And hark, the Spectre speaks! ___G___E
Attend, and N___h, and all your pliant Train,
Attend! and while celestial Lays
Sweetly warble Caesar's praise,
Rouse your boldest Minstrelsy,
And swell the joyful Symphony:
To you her blessings Britain owes,
And yours the high Applause approving Heaven bestows.

I. EPODE.

Hark, he sings the Caribb-War!
Brightest Ray of Britain's Fame!
"Caesar! that Year some partial star
"Shed unopposed its splendour on thy name!
"O'er Nations long in Arms renown'd,
"Britain had been with Conquest Crown'd,
"While Justice urg'd their righteous Rage;
"But never gainst a naked Foe
"Had dared her veteran Sword to draw,
"Dishonest War to wage;
"This Caesar did and triumph'd!"—join the Song
M_____! to thee the Laurel does belong!

II. STROPHE.

"Beyond the vast Atlantic Main
"What Myriads bless thy gracious Reign;
"To Jove their Prayers ascend, for thee,
"The Father of their Liberty!
"For thee their Prayers—Ah! why, that Groan?
"Why trembles mighty Caesar on his Throne?
"I come to chase these generous Fears—
"For thee their Prayers Saturnius hears,
"And, by the ninefold Stream below,
"Swears they never shall forgoe
"Thy Gift—The Thunder's awful Sound
"Confirm'd the Oath, and shook Creation's ample round.

II. ANTISTROPHE.

"Hibernia, Britain's Sister-Isle,
"With equal Freedom soon shall smile;
"Taught by thy prudent Sway to know
"No Blessing rivals this below.—
"And lo! their worth in Luxury drown'd)
"While Caledonia's Chieftains kiss the Ground,
"Her humbler Sons, an untam'd Race,
"Instinctive feel the Fire of Grace;
"And, in the name of Jove, demand
"Like good from Caesar's liberal Hand,
"Religion never asks too late,
"So pious S—— Swears, and what he Swears is Fate.

II. EPODE.

"Gallia, hide thy recreant Head,
"Vain thy Arms, thy Craft as vain;
"Spight of the Snares, by treachery spread,
"Britain preserves her Empire o'er the Main!
"But ah how long!—in awful Gloom
"The Fates involve Britannia's Doom——
"Yet, ye who Counsel Caesar, hear!
"Perchance the Hour is nigh——Pursue
"Your Schemes, perchance 'tis fix'd that you
"The glorious wreath shall wear:
"His worth's the same in Jove's impartial Eyes,
"Who saves a sinking Empire or destroys."

FULL CHORUS.

Yes——we will our Schemes pursue,
We will the Wreath of Glory wear;
His Worth's the same in Jove's impartial Eyes,
Who saves a sinking Empire, or destroys.

CPPS 5540 LC–USZ62–45437

748

The POLITICAL RAREE-SHOW: or a Picture of PARTIES and POLITICS, during and at the close of the Last Session of Parliament. June 1779. For the Westminster Magazine June 1779. Published 1st of July by Fielding & Walker Pater-Noster-Row.

Mixed method (hand colored) 8 x 13 in. (image)

A youth looks into a peepshow to see a series of 12 pictures of happenings in the British Empire. The top middle picture shows Sir William Howe sleeping outside a tent, while in the background General Burgoyne surrenders at Saratoga. CPPS 5548.

LC–USZ62–1519 is the negative number of a black-and-white print.

749

THE HORSE AMERICA, throwing his Master. Pubd. as the Act directs, Augst. 1st, 1779 by Wm. White, Angel Court, Westminster.

Mixed method 7½ x 11½ in.

George III is thrown from a horse which he has beaten with a lash made of swords, bayonets, and other cutting tools. In the background a Frenchman carries a flag decorated with fleur-de-lis. CPPS 5549 LC–USZ62–1521

750

THE EUROPEAN DILIGENCE. sold by W Humphrey No. 227 Strand. [October 5, 1779]

Mixed method 7 x 9½ in.

A Dutchman rolls a wheelbarrow over Britannia who says, "Ah Cruil Neighbours thus to assist Rebellious Children." In the wheelbarrow is France dressed as a gentleman saying, "O Madame tis de fine Politique," and behind him America dressed as an Indian woman says, "My Good & Great Ally Strike Home." Also in the vehicle, a Spaniard says to a dark-visaged person, "Now Brother of Portugal join the Confaderacy and agrandize our Family." A Russian soldier blocks the progress of the wheelbarrow, saying, "My Mistress is determined to Chastise yr. HOGEN MOGEN for yr. Ingratitude & Duplicity & Oblige you to assist that Power that first assisted you." This cartoon satirizes Holland, which was using its colony at St. Eustatius for a shipping center to send war materials to America. At this time Britain hoped that Catherine of Russia would join her against the continental powers, but Russia later joined

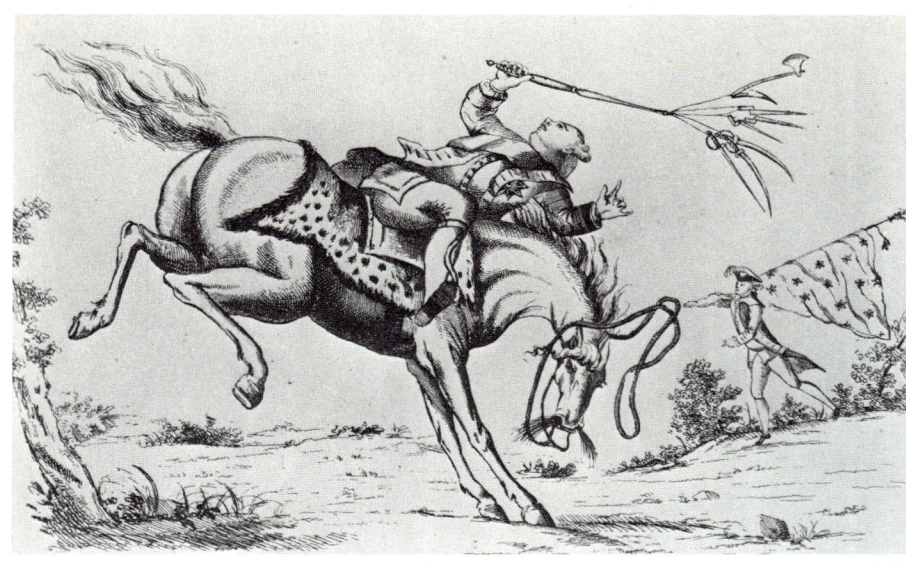

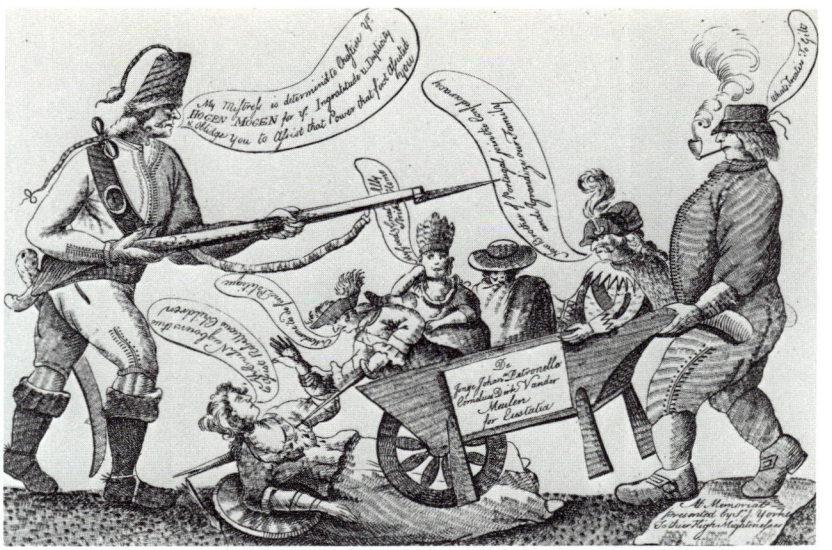

749

750

Denmark and Sweden in the Armed Neutrality agreement of February 29, 1780. CPPS 5557
LC–USZ62–45438

751
A PRIVY COUNCIL. Published Novr 24 1779 by M.S. Dareny Opposite to the Kings Head Strand.

Etching 7⅛ x 9½ in. (image)

A group of animals around a table exhibit extreme moods of boredom and excitement. An ass with ermine cloak represents George III, and to his left a figure in tartan plaid representing Bute whispers in his ear. To the King's right sits a sleeping bear; he is probably Lord North. To North's right are a boar, a bull, and a goat. On the floor lies a muzzled bull dog designated "Jon Bull." Behind them on the wall is a map showing a jagged split between England and America. CPPS 5569
LC–USZ62–45440

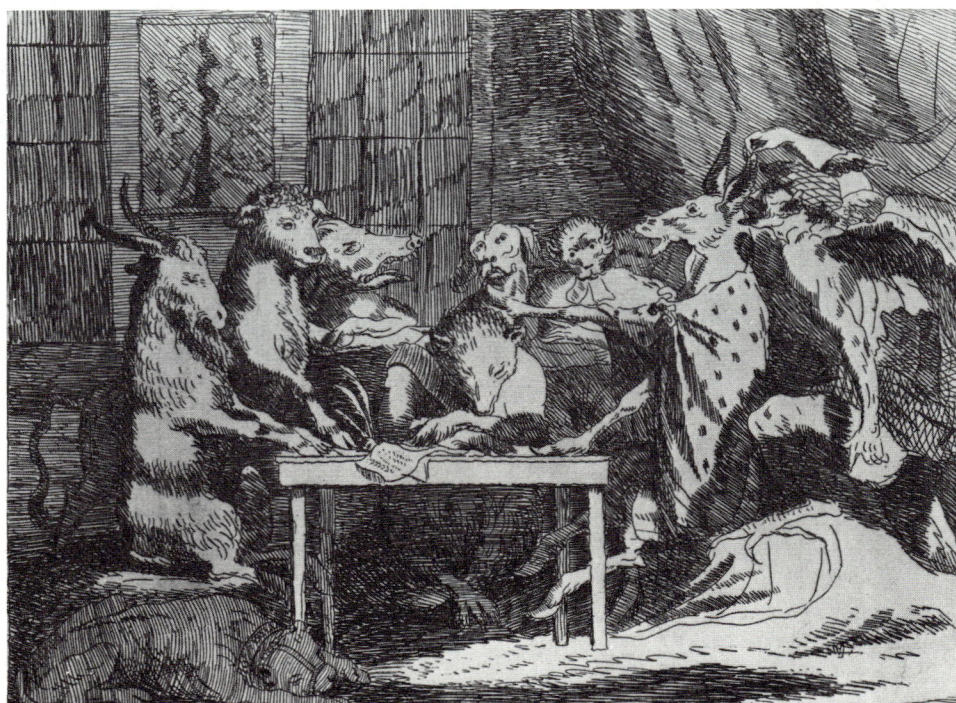

751

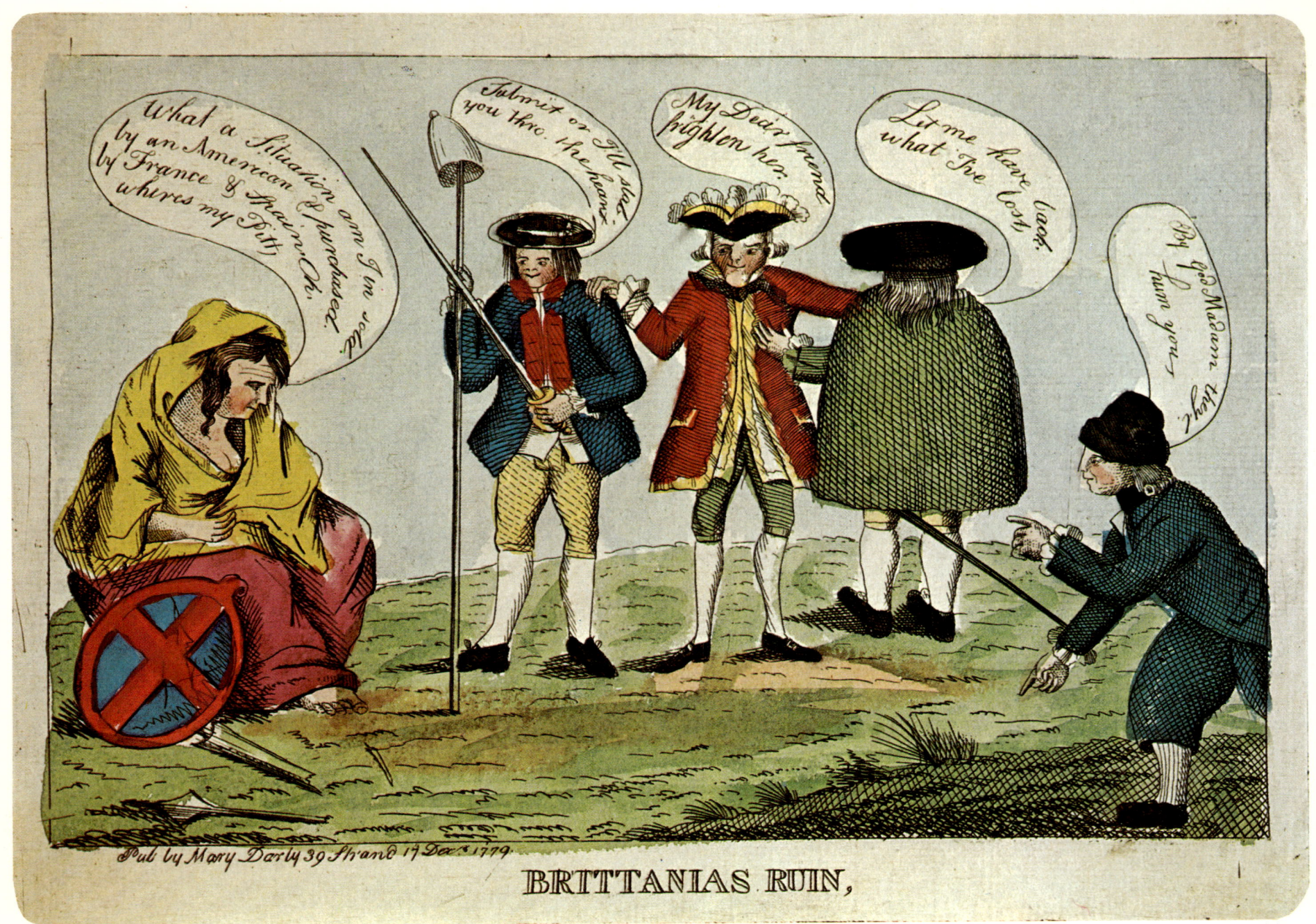

752

BRITTANIAS RUIN. Pub by Mary Darly 39 Strand 17 Dec 1779.

Etching (hand colored) 7 x 9¾ in.

Britannia dressed as an old beggar woman sits with her shield and broken spear on the ground. An American dressed as a commoner holding a staff with liberty cap atop in his right hand and a sword in the left hand says, "Submit or I'll slash you thro the heart." Three men, probably representing France, Spain, and Holland, look on. The Frenchman with his hand on the American's shoulder says, 'My Dear friend frighten her." The Spaniard, with his back turned, says, "Let me have back what I've lost." The Dutchman stands apart saying, "By God Madam they'l hum you." This cartoon depicts the foreign threat to Britain's security. France had been an ally to America since February 1778, the Dutch were continually capitalizing on the situation to improve their own trade, and in June of 1779 Spain formally entered the war.

753

MR. TRADE & Family or the State of ye NATION. TO HIS EXCELY. GENL. WASHINGTON PAT. PATAE. This Plate is humbly Address'd by His obedient Servt. Thos. Tradeless. St___t, B___rn___d, & Co. Origt. G___rm___e, N___h & Co. Excr. Publish'd by Virtue of Parliament not this day in particular—Dec. 1779.

Mixed method 9¾ x 13½ in.

An English tradesman and his family turned to beggary blame their problem on George Washington and the war. In the background Norfolk and Aesopus burn, and George III goes hunting with his hounds. Norfolk, Va., had been bombarded by Lord Dunmore on January 1, 1776, and later burned by the colonists. Aesopus, N.Y. (also called Kingston and Wiltwyck) was burned by Gen. John Vaughn in October 1777. Although George III frivolously hunts deer while his people starve, the poem below the picture blames Washington for the troubles of Englishmen.

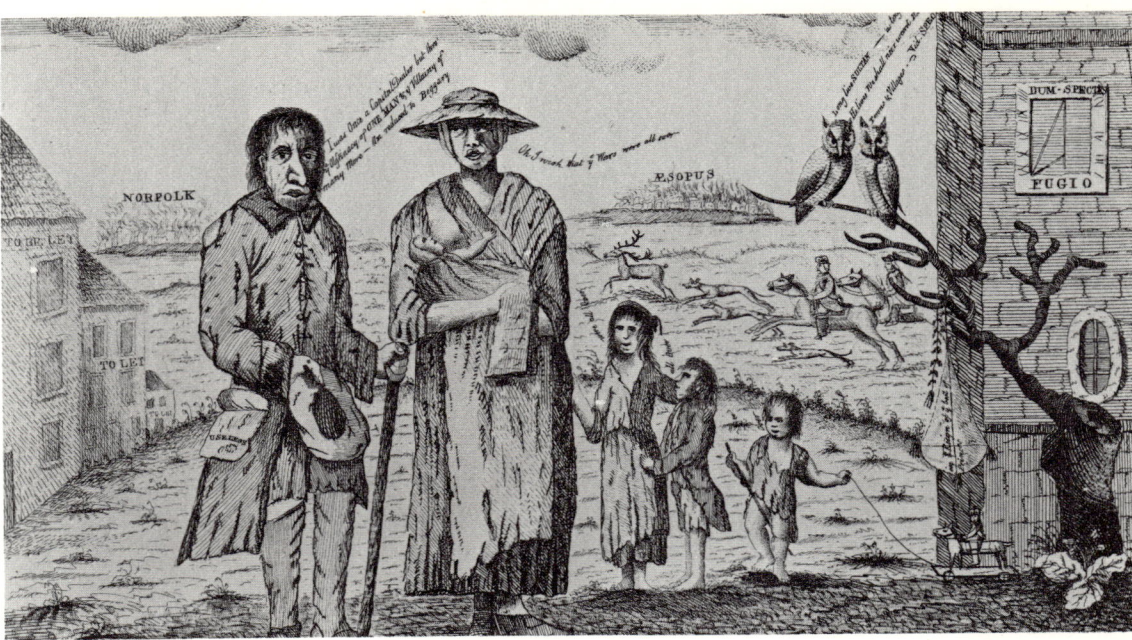

753

> Oh Wash'gton is there not some Chosen Curse
> Some Hidden Thunder; in the Stores of Heav'n,
> Red with uncommon Wrath, to Blast those Men,
> Who owe their Greatness to their Country's Ruin?
> Addiss. Cato.

Risqué or libelous cartoons often concealed the artist and engraver by listing famous people as the originator and the executor. This cartoon lists St[uar]t (Earl of Bute), B[e]rn[ar]d (former governor of Massachusetts), G[e]rm[ain]e, and N[ort]h as the creators. CPPS 5574 LC–USZ62–1520

754

THE BOTCHING TAYLOR Cutting his Cloth to cover a Button. John Simpson Aqua forti. Publish'd by James Tomlinson Oxford Street Decr 27th 1779.

Etching and mezzotint 9⅞ x 11⅞ in. (image)

George III sits like a tailor on a table while Bute shows him how to cut cloth. On his lap is a length marked "Ireland Great Britain Hanover." Lord North holds severed pieces of cloth marked "North America," "West Indies," and "Africa." Behind North stand Sandwich, Mansfield, and Germain. On the floor lie strips designated "Magna Charta," "Bill of Rights," "Protestants," "Petitions," "Intelligence," "Expresses," "Memorials," "Remonstrances," and "Dispatches." In the right corner the Pope embraces Charles Edward the Pretender, while they both watch the King. This cartoon satirizes George III's hobby of button making. The American problem is one of many which the poor mad King is botching. CPPS 5573 LC–USZ62–45441

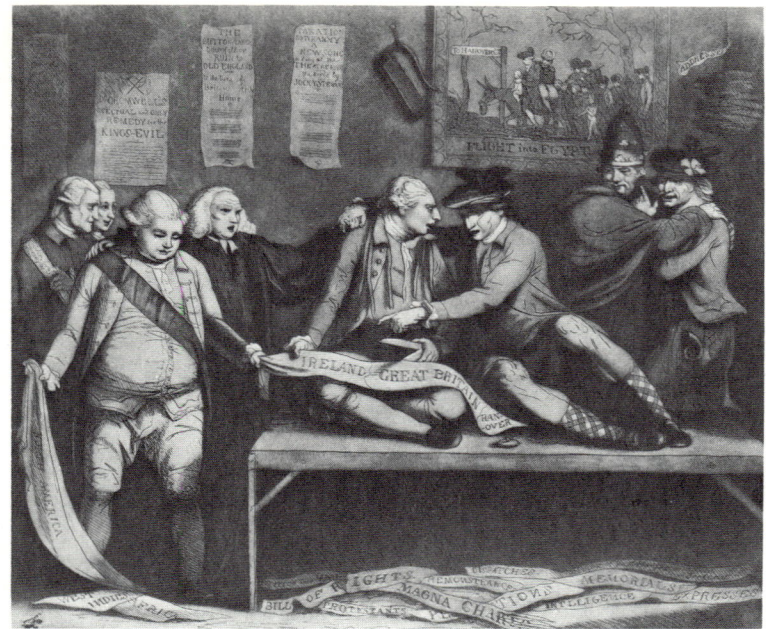

754

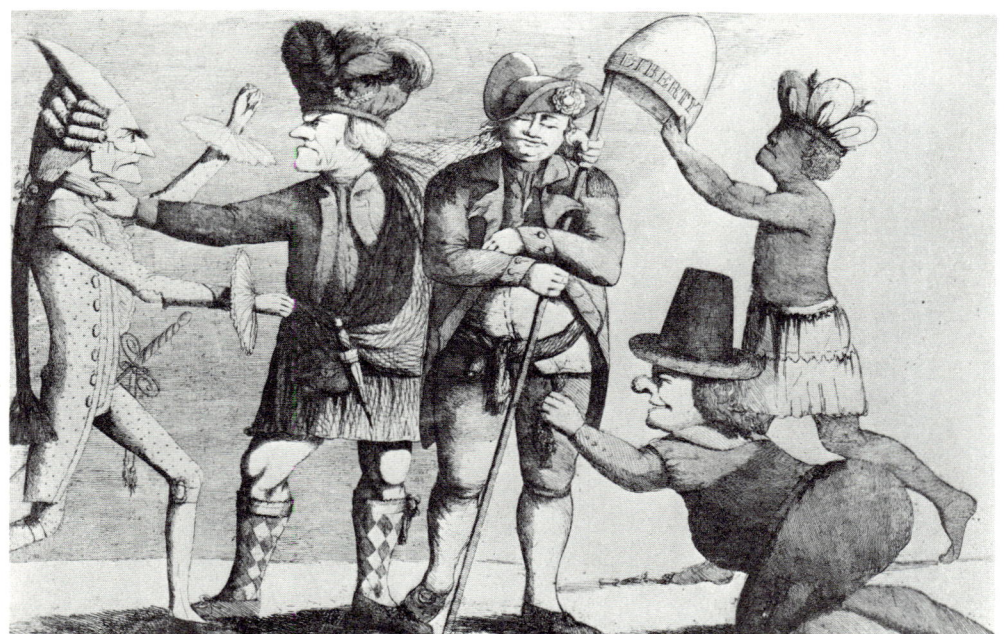

755

755
THE PRESENT STATE OF GREAT BRITAIN. Pubd by W. Humphrey. No. 227 Strand. J. Phillips Fecit. [1779]

Etching 10½ x 16 in.

England pictured as a stout man protected by a Scot. The Scotsman fends off a Frenchman, while a Dutchman picks a purse from the Englishman's pocket, and an American Indian lifts a liberty cap off a pole held by the two Britons. CPPS 5579 LC–USZ62–45442

756
LES ANGLOIS MOLESTES ET CHATIEES. 1. Le Soleil de la France eclairant l'Amerique et Foudroiant la Grande Bretagne, 2. Un Anglois Americain fustigeant ses anciens Freres devenus ses esclaves, 3. Un Anglois, 4. Un Ecossoise, 5. Un Irlandois. [1779?]

Etching (hand colored) 8¾ x 12¼ in. (image)

An American soldier with a hat designated "Congress" and "Washington" lashes three representatives of Britain who are in chains. From his whip lightning bolts strike the English fleet in a storm. A bright sun representing France with fleur-de-lis shines on the entire scene.

757
LE DESTIN MOLESTANT LES ANGLOIS. [1779?]

Mixed method 8¼ x 12¼ in. (image)

The Comte d'Estaing in armor presents a palm to America who is dressed as an Indian holding a liberty cap on a staff. The Indian sits on boxes and leans on barrels marked "Ris pour la France," "Indigo pour le Repos de la Mediteranée," "Tabac pour la Hollande," "Tabac pour la France 1780," "Tabac pour la Russie," "Tabac pour l'Allemagne," and "Indigo pour la France." D'Estaing holds three muzzled animals on a leash; they represent the people of England. A winged figure representing Fame crowns America while blowing a trumpet reading, "Vive Destaing." "Destin" in the title is a pun on the admiral's name. French enthusiasm for D'Estaing is evident in this allegory, as opposed to the contemporary American reaction which was suspicious and critical of him. See CPPS 5581 *Collection de Vinck* 1176 LC–USZ62–34859

758
Ô QU'EL D'ESTAIN. Tu la voulu. Du sein de la tyrannie naquit l'Independance. M.A. Voltaire. [1779?]
Etching 9⅜ x 6⅞ in.

A rattlesnake (L'Amerique), a cock (La France), and a lion (L'Espagne) attack a cat-like animal (L'Angleterre). CPPS 5581

759
[Representation of the American war—a cartouche] A Paris chez Basset Rue St. Jacques au coin de celle des Mathurins a Ste. Genevieve. 1779
Mixed method 8¾ x 11½ in. (image)

America leans on a bale of goods and holds a staff with liberty cap on top. Rich tropical fruit and corn grow around her, and she watches a battle raging behind her. From a map entitled "Carte Theatre de la Guerre Presente en Amerique dresée d'après les Nouvelles Cartes Anglaises par L. Denis Geographe et Auteur de Conducteur Francais dediée et presentée a Monsieur le Noir Conseiller d'Etàt, Lieutenant général de Police &c. Par son très humble Serviteur [André] Basset en 1779" in G&M vault.
LC–USZ62–46080

——————Another impression.

760
PRATTLE. [Gillray?] Pub by M Darly 39 Strand Augt. 12 1779.
Etching 5⅜ x 7 in. (hand colored)

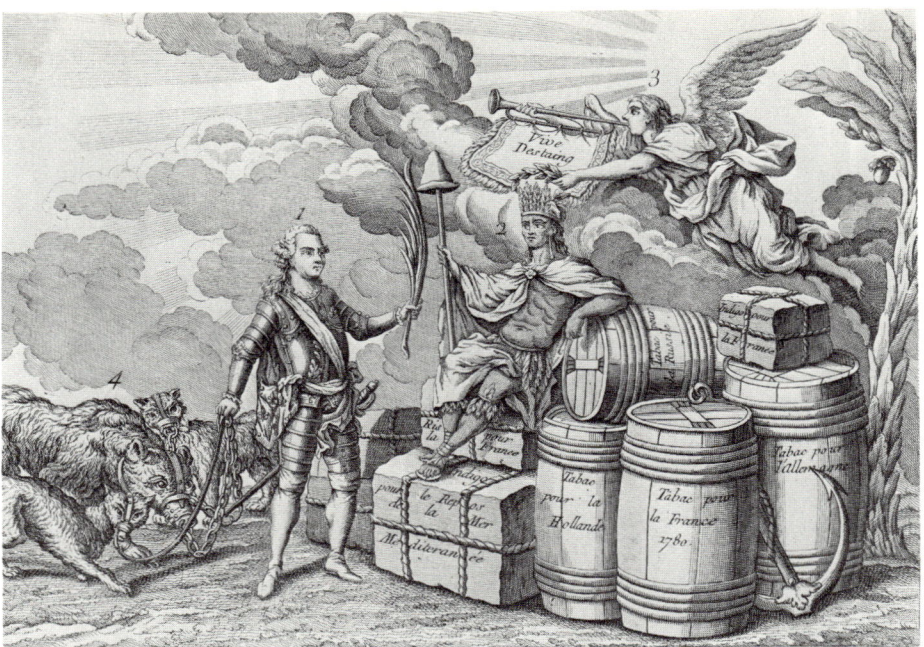
757

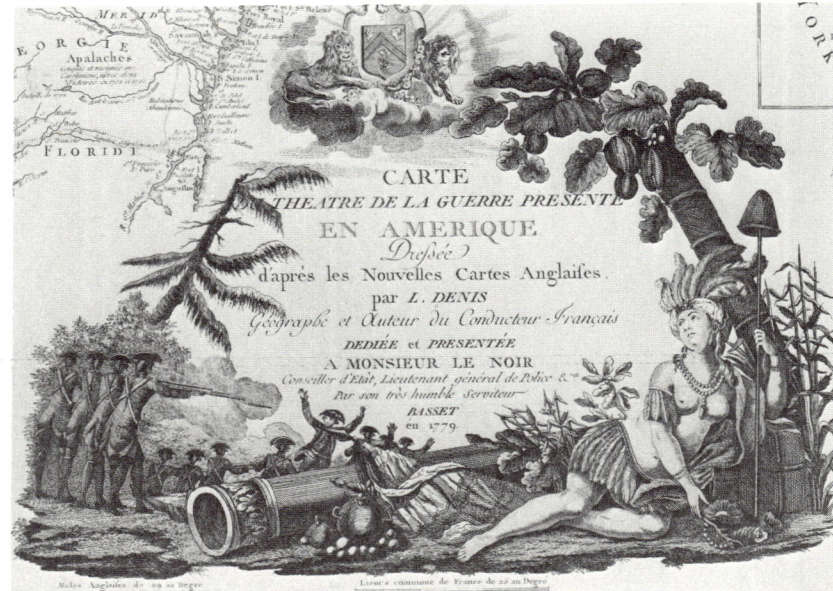
759

323

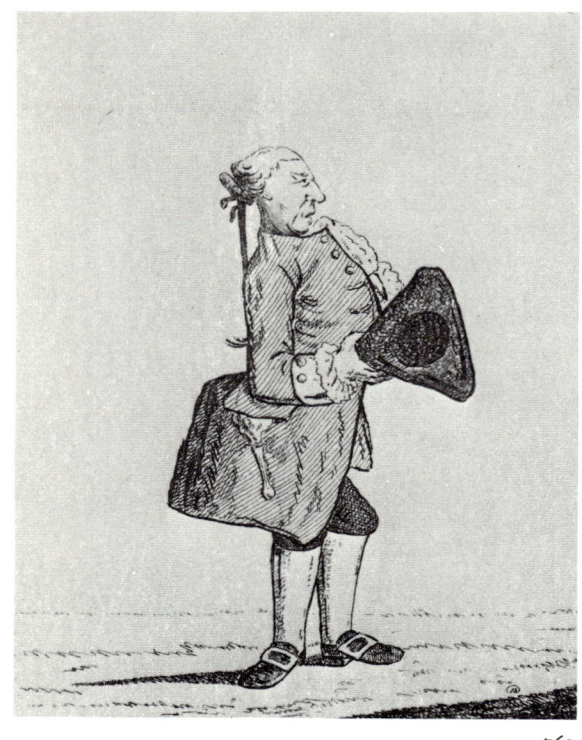

760

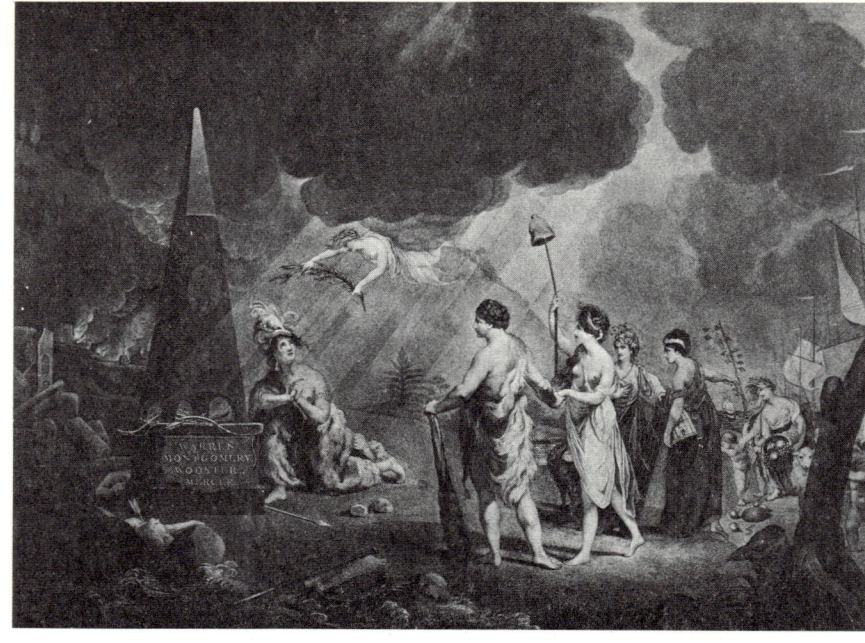

761

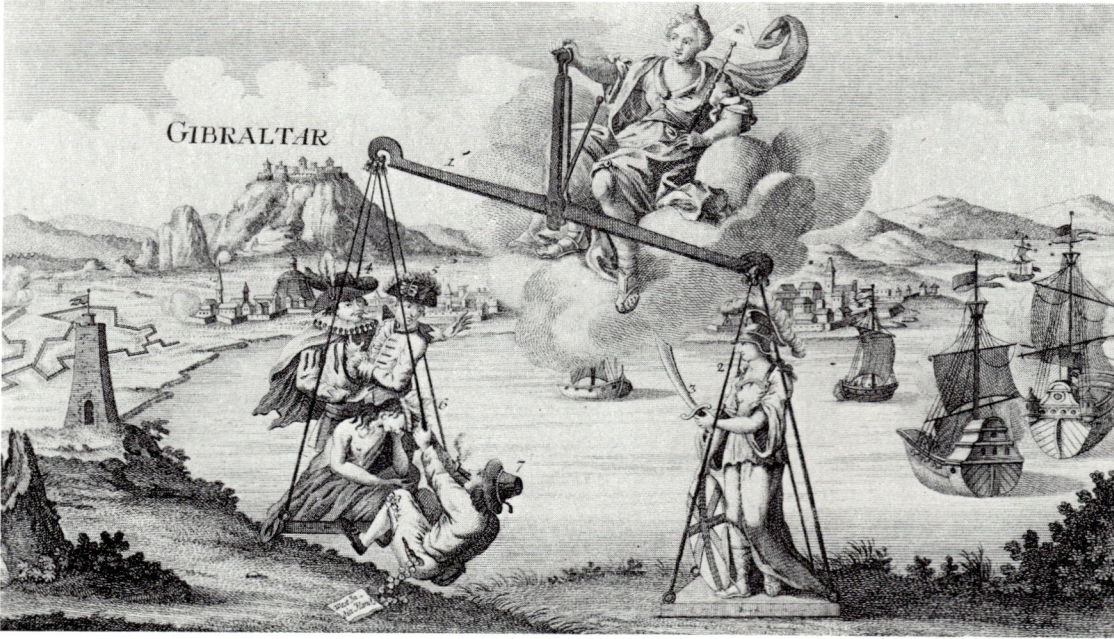

762

An apothecary comments on the war. "Beg your pardon my Dear Sir—had it from my Lud Fiddle faddle—nothing to do but cut 'em off pass the Susquhanna and proceed to Boston possess himself of Crown point then Philadelphia would have fallen of course—& a communication opend with the Northern Army as easyly as I'd open a Vein." CPPS 5603 LC–USZ62–45444

————Another impression. "Prattle the political apotecary. Pubd. by H Humphrey No 18 New Bond Street."

761

AMERICA. To Perpetuate to Posterity the Memory of those Patriotic Heroes, who Fought, Bled & Died in Establishing Peace, Liberty, and Tranquility to their Country. Doolittle sculp. Newhaven [177?]

Stipple engraving printed in red 17½ x 23¼ in. (image)

America kneels beside an obelisk which commemorates the war. The names Warren, Montgomery, Wooster, and Mercer (leaders who died in battle) are engraved on the monument, and in the background is a burning city, fences and walls in ruins, and two corpses. One corpse has an Indian arrow protruding from his breast. A female figure, probably Peace, brings an olive branch from the sky. Heroic Virtue, a noble savage clothed in skins, comes to America presenting Liberty, carrying a liberty cap on a staff; Virtue, carrying a club; and Concord, wearing flowers in her hair. Industry holds a bundle of wood and a bee hive. Plenty carries a cornucopia and is surrounded by children and animals. A fleet of ships docks in the background.

————Another copy. AMERICA. To THOSE who wish to SHEATHE the DESOLATING SWORD of WAR. And, to RESTORE the BLESSINGS of PEACE and AMITY, to a divided PEOPLE. R.E. Pine pinxt. Joseph Strutt sculp.

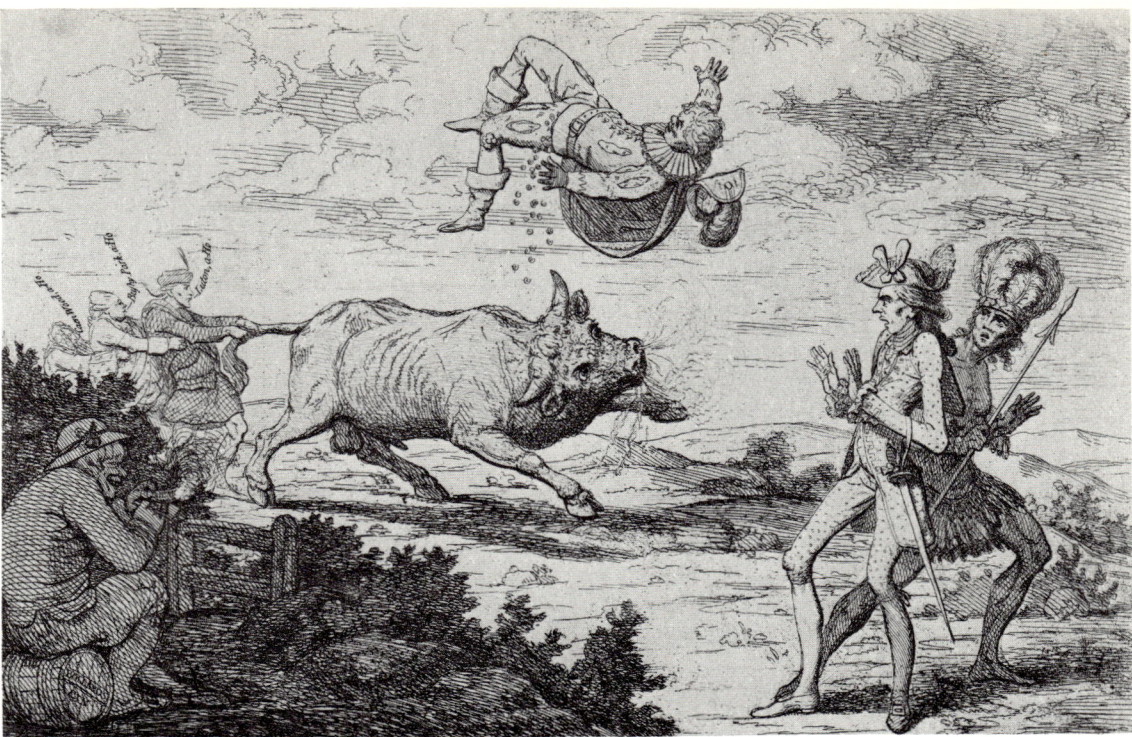
763

1778 Stipple engraving printed in red 17½ x 23½ in. (image). This copy is the same picture as Amos Doolittle's, but this print is clearer and in better condition. LC–USZ62–15366

762

1. Die Wage der Mache. 2. Niemand beleidiges mich ohngesfraft. 3. Das Schwerd der Gerechtigkeit 4. Rodneÿ has unsre Flotte zu Grund gerichtet. 5. Mein Herr Stehet uns beis oder mir sind verloren. 6. Mein Undank wird mit allem Recht bestruft. 7. Ich will etwas thun furs Geld. [or] 1. La balance de la puissance. 2. ne personne m'offense sans puni. 3. l'Epee de la jiustice. 4. Rodney a ruine notre Flotte. 5. Monsieu aidez a nous ou nous sommes perdu. 6. Mon ingratitude est puni comm tous raison. 7. Je ferai quelque chose pour l'argent. A Augsbourg chez I. Mart. Will Fauxbourg S. Jacques. [178?]

Mixed method 8½ x 13¼ in.

A German cartoon favoring the British. The goddess Justice holds a scale on which Britannia outweighs a Spaniard (4), a Frenchman (5), an American Indian (6), and a Dutchman (7)—all despairing. In the background is Gibraltar. Similar to item 786. LC–USZ62–45393

763

JOHN BULL TRIUMPHANT. Publish'd Jany. 4th 1780, by W. Humphrey No. 227 Strand.

Etching 14 x 9¾ in.

A bull, representing Britain's John Bull, tosses a Spaniard into the air. France, dressed

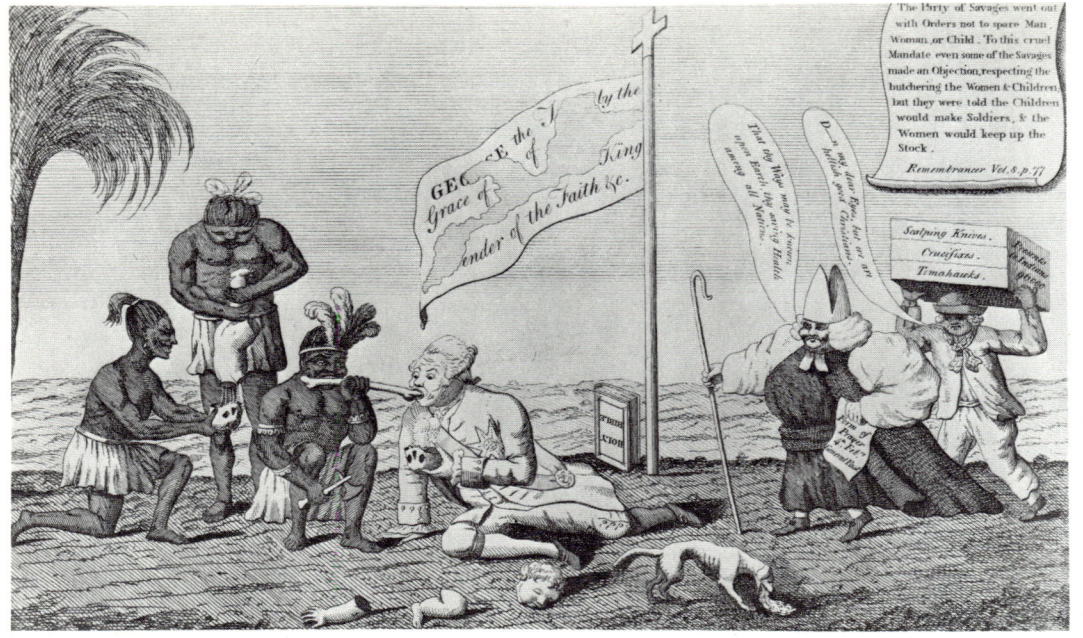

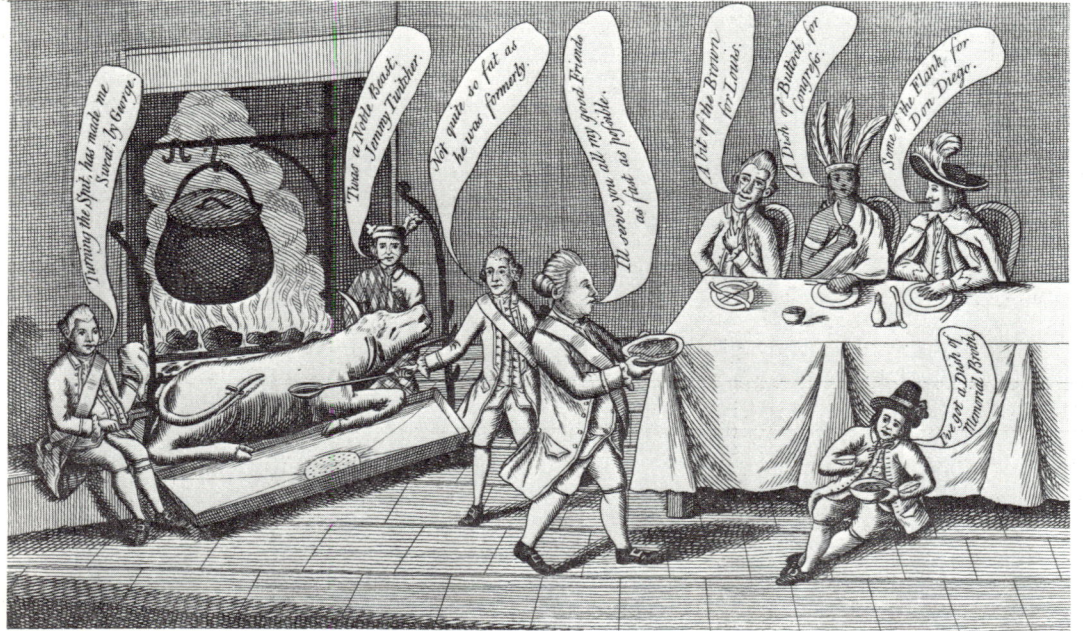

as a dandy, and America, dressed as an Indian, show fear. Bute, North, and Mansfield pull the bull's tail, while a laughing Dutchman sits on a keg of gin representing trade. A poem at bottom reads:

> The Bull see enrag'd, has the Spaniard engag'd,
>   And gave him a Terrible Toss,
> As he mounts up on high, the Dollars see fly,
>   To make the bold Britton rejoice.
>
> The Yankee & Monsieur, at this look quite queer,
>   For they see that his Strength will prevail,
> If they'd give him his way, and not with foul play,
>   Still lug the poor Beast by the Tail.

CPPS 5624 LC–USZ62–1524

764

THE ALLIES.—Par nobile Fratrum! Indignatio fecit Pubd. as the Act Directs Febry. 3, 1780 by I. Almon Piccadilly.
Etching 14 x 8½ in. (image)

George III feasts on human meat with a savage. Two other savages wring blood from the corpse of a white baby and drink from a skull. A sailor unloads boxes of scalping knives, crucifixes, and tomahawks at the bidding of a bishop. This print supports Jefferson's charge that the King incited the Indians to attack the colonists. CPPS 5631 LC–USZ62–34860

765

THE BULL ROASTED: or the POLITICAL COOKS Serving their CUSTOMERS. Publish'd as the Act directs Feby. 12, 1780 by I Harris, Sweetings Alley. Cornhill, London.
Line engraving 9¾ x 13¾ in.

George III turns the spit on which the British bull roasts. Bute sits behind the bull watching, while North serves portions at a table where a Frenchman, a Spaniard, and an American sit. America is an Indian woman who says, "A Dish of Buttock for Congress." A Dutchman eats on the floor. Below a poem:

Behold the poor Bull! once Britania's chief boast.
Is kill'd by State Cooks, and laid down for a Roast!
While his Master, who should all his Honours maintain,
Turns the Spit tho' he should such an Office disdain.

Monsieur licks his gills at a bit of the Brown,
And the other two wish for to gobble him down.
But may ill digestion attend on the treat,
And the Cooks every one soon be roasted & Eat.

CPPS 5636 LC–USZ62–45445

766

BRITANIA AND HER DAUGHTER. A Song. Publish'd as the Act directs, March 8th, 1780, by I. Mills No. 1 Ratcliff Row near the French Hospital Old Street.

Etching 6⅜ x 9 in. (image)

Britannia in Roman garb approaches Spain, America (dressed as an Indian woman), and France; they prepare to fight for America. Below a song:

Miss America North, so News-paper records;
With her Mother Britania one day had some words,
When behold Monsieur Louis, advanc'd a new whim,
That she should leave her Mother for to live with him.
          Derry Down.

The Damsel consented but quickly found out,
That her Paramour was not sufficiently stout;
Besides he was poor, and she wanted fine things,
So he sent to Don Carlos for Cash and Gold-rings.
          Derry Down.

Says Monsieur to the Don, if you take my advice,
Then you of young Miss may come in for a slice;
The Don being am'rous was easy brought o're,
And he Cuddled, and Kiss'd as Monsieur did before.
          Derry Down.

Britania beheld her with tears in her eyes,
O! Daughter return to your duty she cries,
But she replies no I'm a Woman full grown,
And long for to keep a good house of my own.
          Derry Down.

If you'd used me kind when I was in your power,
I then had lived with you at this very hour,
But now on my Lovers so much do I doat,
That we'r Arm'd and I'll help 'em to cut your old throat.
          Derry Down.

Then with Hatchet, and Scalping-knife, Miss did advance,
On one side of her Spain on the other side France;
Britania thus threatned does all three oppose,
And how it will end the Lord above knows.
          Derry Down.

Britania of late sent out one of her*sons,
Who has given Don Carlos, a thump o'the Munns,
Knock'd out Five of his Teeth, all double ones too,
And keeps 'em to help Old Britania to chew.
          Derry Down.

Now for the Old Lady let all of us pray,
May Monsieur, and the Don for their perfidy pay,
May young Miss, return to her duty agen,
And may Britons be Free in despight of Base Men.
          Derry Down.
    *Rodney

CPPS 5647 LC–USZ62–1525

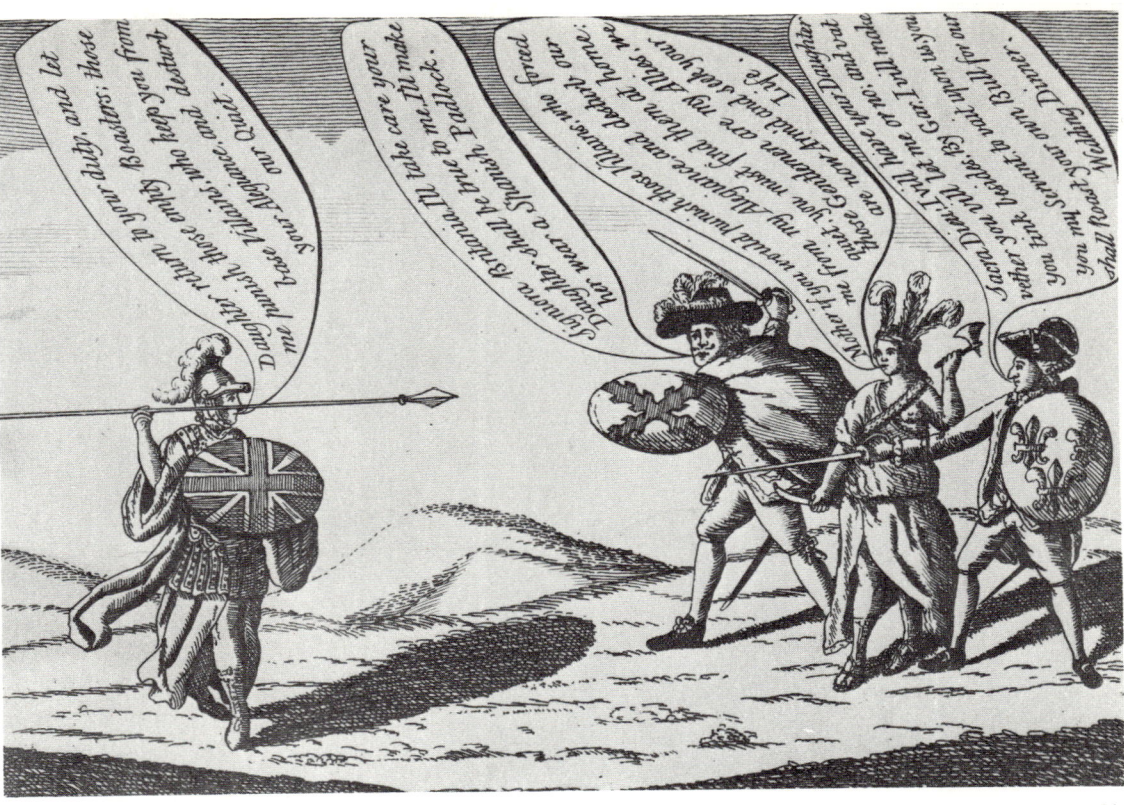

766

767

THE ENGLISH LION DISMEMBER'D Or the Voice of the Public for an Enquiry into the Public Expenditure. [T. Colley?] Pub by E. Hedges No 2, Under the Royal Exchange Cornhill March 12th, 1780.

Line engraving 9⅛ x 13⅜ in.

Lord North carries a large sack designated BUDGET, attached by a chain to the British lion. An American Indian has cut off one paw and says, "This Lion belongs to me in spite of fate." A Spaniard and a Frenchman want parts, and three Englishmen representing Associations pursue the Lion. The intransigence of the North Ministry on many issues created a new force in English politics. Due to pleas by

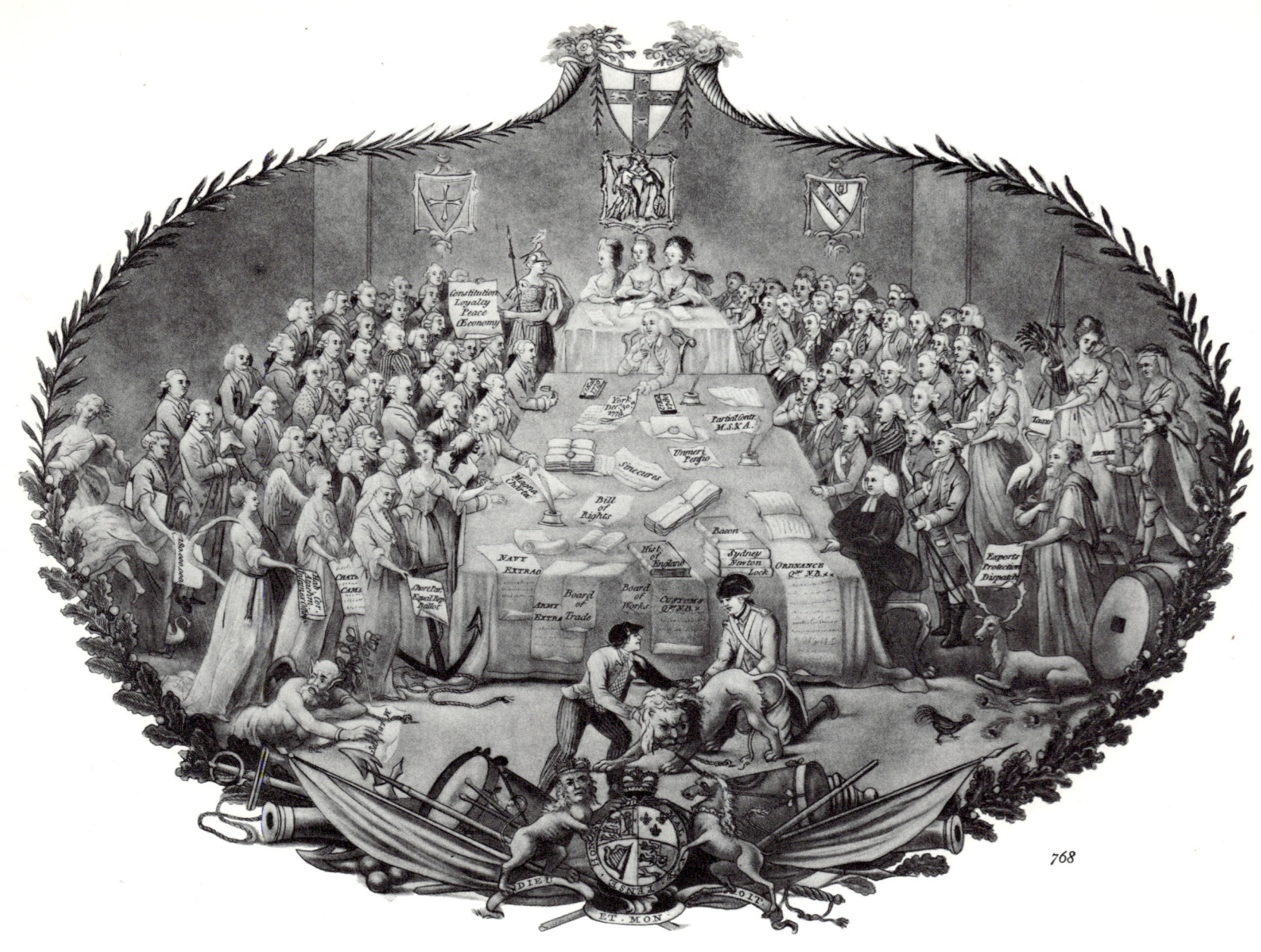

Burke and other reformers, a great meeting was held at York on December 30, 1779, to list grievances and circulate petitions on issues of the day. This cartoon shows members of the Association ready to intervene in the government's handling of the war with America, France, and Spain. CPPS 5649 LC–USZ62–1526

768

[Association meeting at York] London, Publish'd as the Act directs. April 6th 1780 by Robt. Laurie, No 17, Rosomonds Row. Clerkenwell. Price 2S

Mezzotint 13¼ x 9 in.

An allegorical representation of the December 30, 1779, meeting of the Association of York. The wall in the back of the room holds a picture of Britannia and America embracing. The lesson here is that if all civil disputes could be settled as amicably as those settled by this Association, the war with America would be unnecessary. CPPS 5657 LC–USZ62–45446

769

AN HIEROGLYPHYCAL EPISTLE FROM [Britannia] [toe] ADMIRAL [Rodney]. Sold by W. Humphrey 227 Strand London. [1780]

Line engraving 6¾ x 11½ in.

A rebus letter praising Rodney. Translated it reads:

To you my Darling Child I Deign to Write
Who Dar'd the Haughty Spanish Dons to Fight
The Cause like others you did not betray
Who faintly Fought and almost Ran away
Like a Bold man you used Britannia's Power
And Scorn'd that Dreaded circumstance—Lee Shore
Close on their Coast you did Attack the Foe.
And Gave their ships a total Overthrow.
My Thunders roar'd to Awe the Subject world
The Prince beheld with Rapture and Surprise
While the true Hero, Sparkl'd in his eyes
To you the Wreath of victory I Send
Thy Countrys Guardian and my trusty Friend
Go on Brave Rodney in thy Bold career
And let thy Vengeance, Burst on False Monsieur

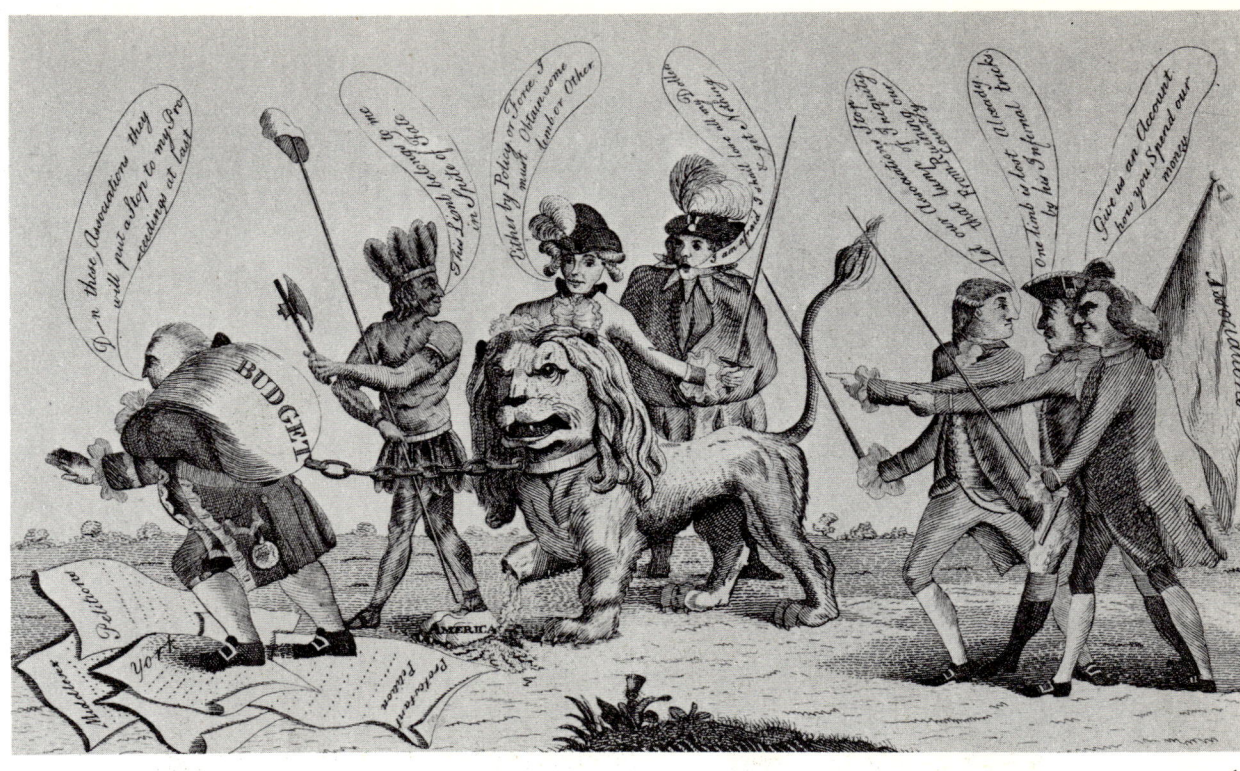

767

Then lost America no more shall Roam
But find with me true greatness is at Home
Peace shall again her Olive branch expand
And Smiling plenty crown the Happy Land
       Brittania

CPPS 5658 LC–USZ62–45447

770

PREROGATIVES DEFEAT or LIBERTIES TRIUMPH. Publisd Aprill 20, 1780 by E. Darchery St Js' Street.

Etching (hand colored) 9¼ x 11⅝ in. (image)

Bute and North lie on the ground, while Fox helps Lord John Dunning (1731–1783) walk over them. A Scot, probably William Fullarton, attacks Dunning. An American and an Irishman watch the action; the first says, "Now we will treat with them," and the second says, "We are loyal but we will be free." This cartoon celebrates Dunning's long opposition to the prerogatives of the King and his ministers. In the previous February, Dunning led the House of Commons in the vote to abolish the Board of Trade and to publicize a list of all pensions granted by the Crown. On April 6, 1780, he moved that

the influence of the crown has increased, is increasing, and ought to be diminished, [and] it is competent to this house to examine into and correct abuses in the expenditure of the civil list revenues, as well as in every other branch of the public revenue, whenever it shall appear expedient to the wisdom of the house so to do.

Dunning's movement was the beginning of

329

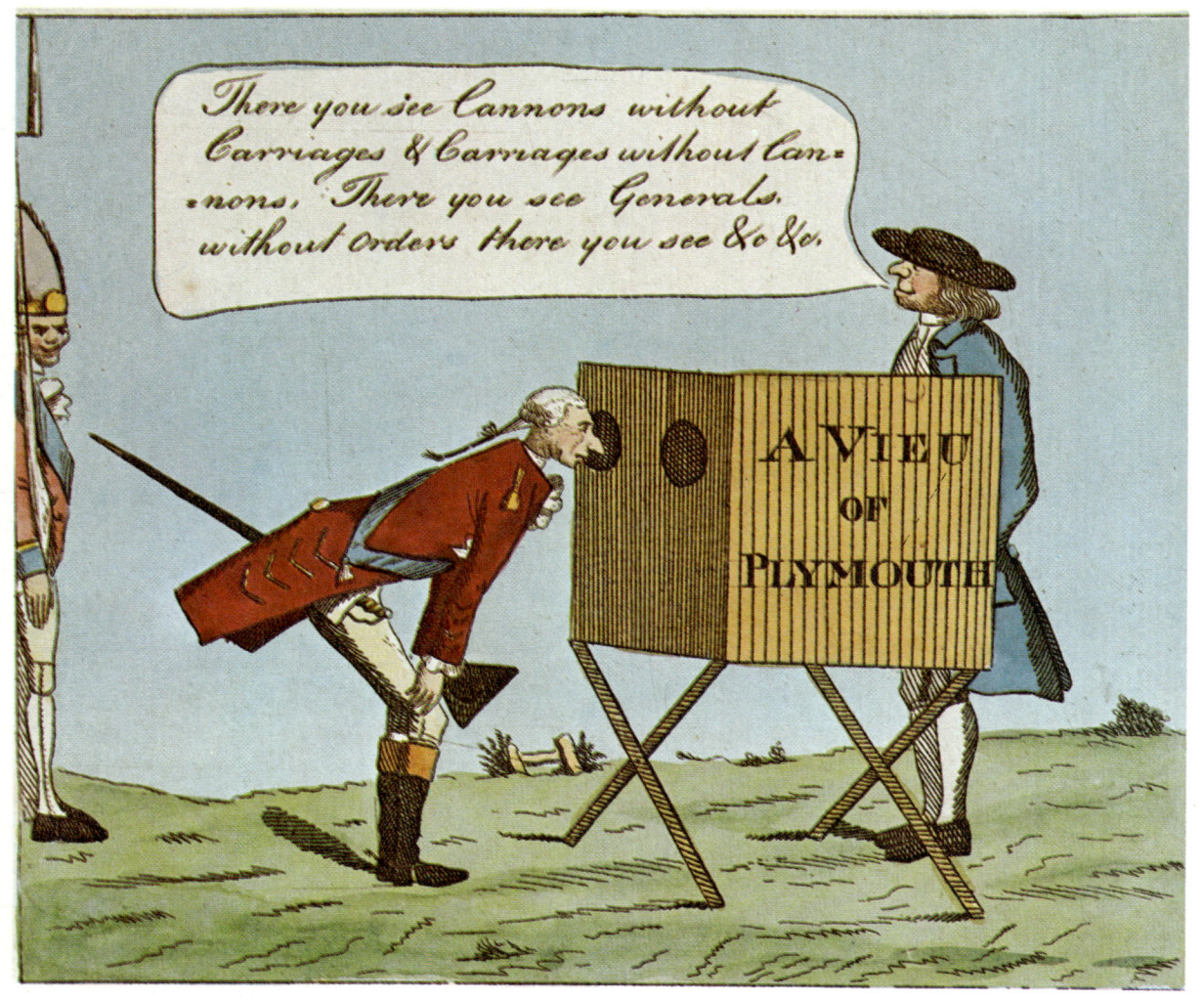

771

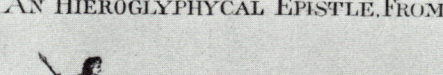
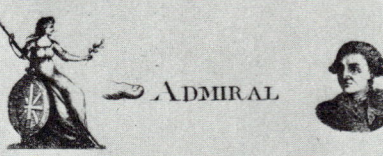

769

330

the end for the North Ministry and, ultimately, the war in America. CPPS 5659
LC–USZ62–45448

771

A VIEU OF PLYMOUTH. Pub by H Humphrey. No. 18 New Bond Street. [1780]

Etching (hand colored) 6½ x 5½ in. (image)

Amherst looks into a raree show to see the progress of the war in America. The explanation below reads, "Col. Mushroom Compts. to Lord Am_____t recommends this cheap but Satisfactory mode of viewing distant Garrisons hopes his Lordship has received the Golden Pippins a few of them are for his Secretary." The vendor says, "There you see Cannons without Carriages & Carriages without Cannons. There you see Generals without orders . . . ." This cartoon criticizes Amherst who handled ordnance and was nominal Commander in Chief because he was the highest ranking advisor to the King for the American War. His viewing of the war from a distance is satirized by his use of a vue d'optique. For examples of the kind of view seen in a vue d'optique see items 263, 266–268, 310, 320, 326, 364–366, 748, and 771. CPPS 5662

772

ARGUS. [Gillray] Pubd. May 15th. 1780. by W. Renegal.

Etching 13¾ x 9¾ in.

George III sleeps, while Bute and Mansfield try to decide what to do with his crown. America, in the dress of an Indian, looks on from behind the bushes and says, "We in America have no crown to fight for or lose." Around this group a British merchant stands in his rags, an Irishman goes his own way, a Dutchman steals honey from some hives, and Britannia weeps while her lion sleeps. CPPS 5667

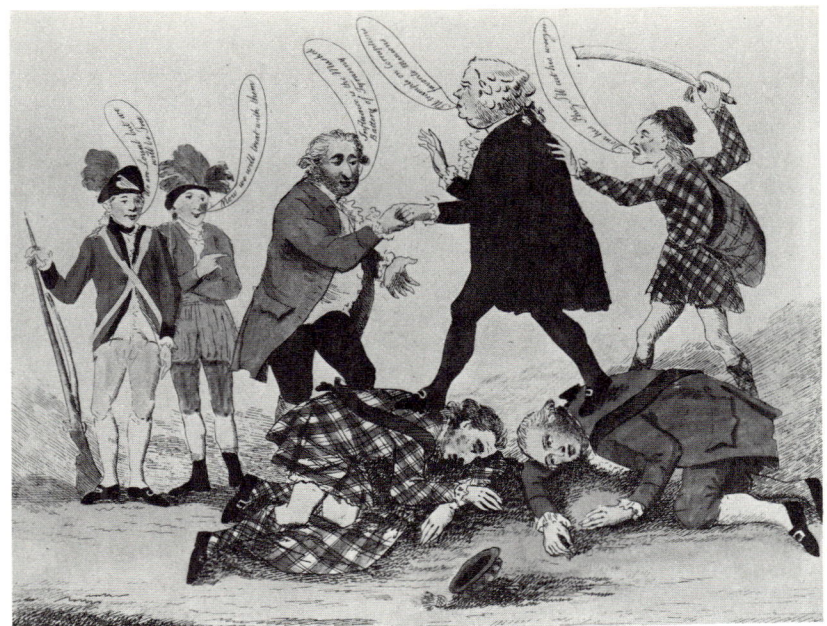

770

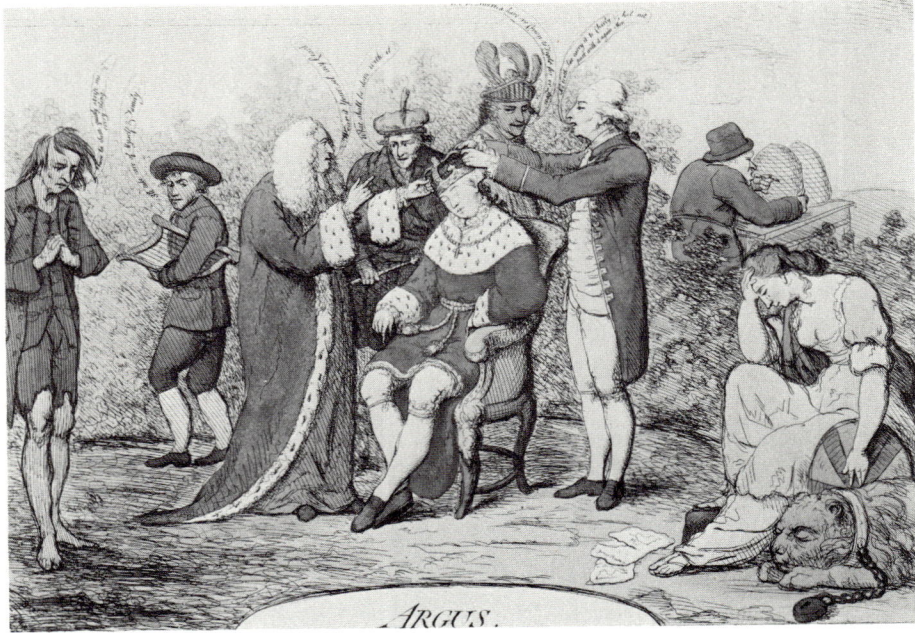

772

331

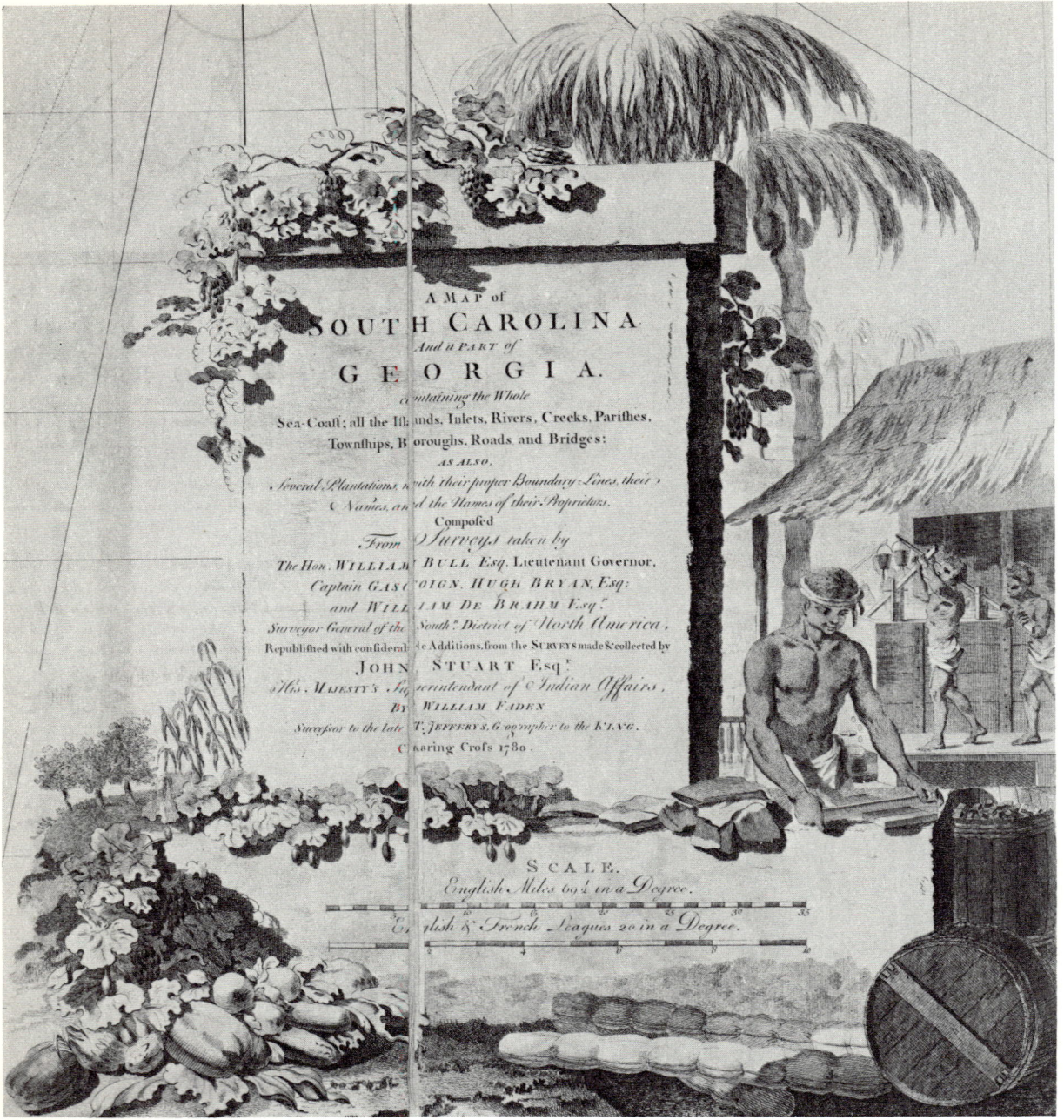

773

———Another impression (hand colored).
LC–USZ62–45562

———Another impression.

773

[Slave workers in South Carolina and Georgia—a cartouche] London Published as the Act directs by Wm. Faden, Charing Cross. June 1st 1780.

Etching 17½ x 16½ in. (image)

In a tropical scene including melons, grapes, bread, and other products, Negro slaves work near a thatched hut. The themes of abundance, industry, and commerce are reiterated in this cartouche of America. The picture also shows the presence of slaves in the area mapped. From "A Map of South Carolina and a part of Georgia" in Jeffreys, *The American Atlas* (London, 1776), no. 24a.

———Another copy. On William Gerard DeBrahm's map of the same title published by Jefferys in 1757.

———Another copy. In Faden, *North American Atlas* (London, 1777), no. 34. Negative in G&M.

———Another copy. In Thomas Jefferys, *A General Topography of North America* (London, 1768), no. 60.

774

THE F—X and H—D or RIVAL CANDIDATES. Humbly Address'd to the Worthy Electors of W———r. Pubd. as the Act directs Septr. 18, 1780.

Etching (hand colored) 9½ x 7 in. (image)

Fox with the head of a fox and Lord Lincoln (Thomas P. Clinton, 1752–1795) with the head of a dog offer their platforms. Fox's reads, "On the Freedom of Elections"; Lincoln's reads, "Services done in America." In the 1780 Westminster election Fox represented the opposition to Government, calling himself the candidate of the people. Among his opposition measures was one to end the war in America. Lord Lincoln was a war hero who brought Sir Henry Clinton's dispatches after the victory at Charleston, S.C. Loyal to the Ministry, he wished to continue the war in America. Fox's defeat in this election would have been a setback to the Whig ascendency. CPPS 5698 LC–USZ62–45449

775

WESTMINSTER ELECTION. 1780. Publish'd as the Act directs Septr 25. 1780 by P Mitchell North Audly St Grosr Sqr & J. Harris, Sweething Alley, Cornhill.

Etching 10½ x 16 in. (image)

This cartoon features the three candidates of the election with a huge mob of Hogarth-type characters. The vast majority of the singing, eating, drinking, and playing crowd is for Fox who stands with Britannia and the English lion in the center of St. Paul's portico holding a copy of the "Magna Charta." To Fox's left stands Lord Lincoln holding a sword and a paper reading "4257 Votes purchas'd. I brought the News from America of the taking of Charles Town." Above him flies a demon figure, probably representing discord. To Fox's right stands Adm. James Young (d. 1789), proxy for Rodney. Neptune is beside him, and he holds a sign reading "5298 the Spanish Fleet totally defeated off Gibraltar Jany. 16 1780." The vote was 4,878 for Fox, 5,298 for Rodney, and 4,257 for Lincoln. On September 23, the crowd chaired Fox. CPPS 5699 LC–USZ62–45450

776

COUNT DE ROCHAMBEAU French General of the Land Forces in America reviewing the French Troops. [1780]

Etching 9¾ x 13¾ in.

A satire on Rochambeau and his army using

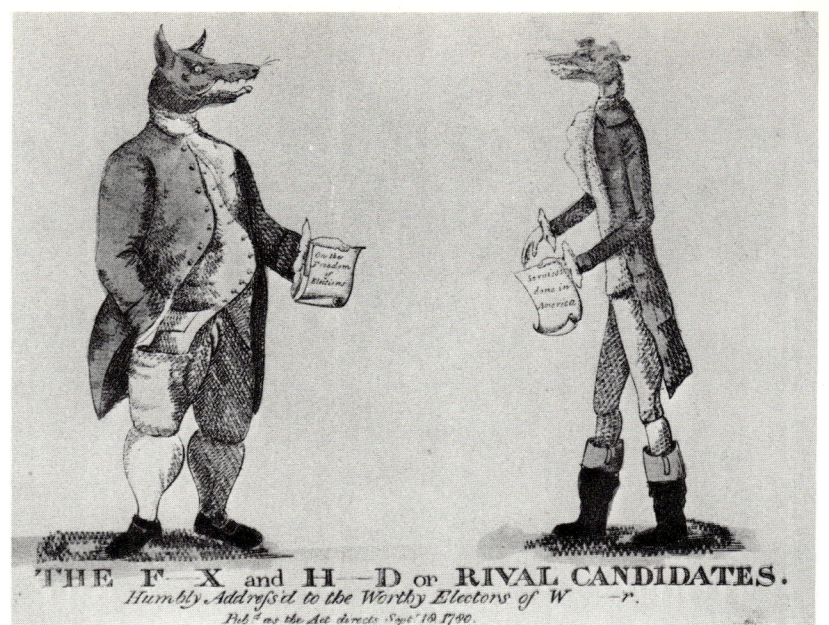

774

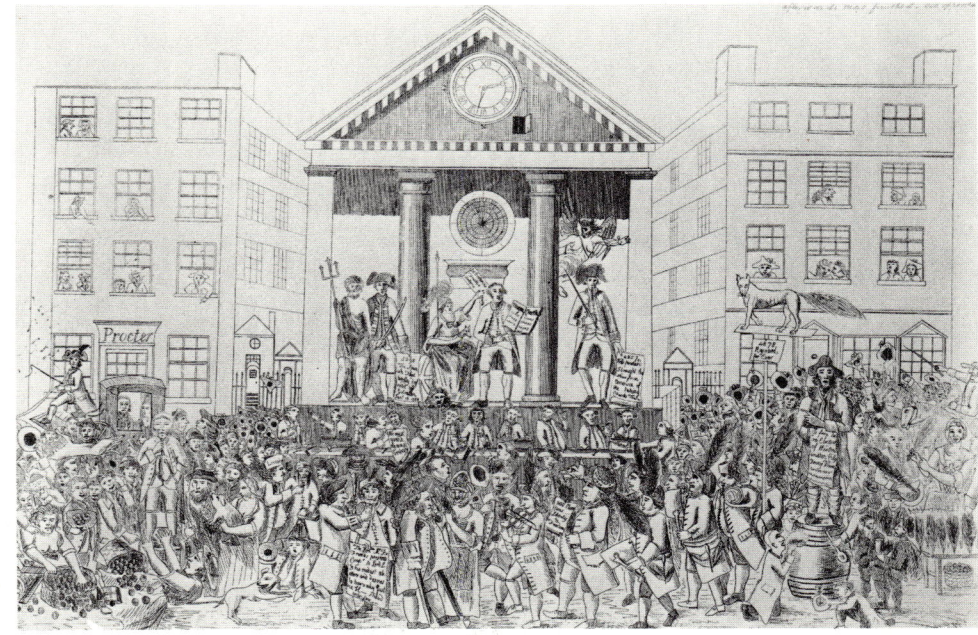

775

333

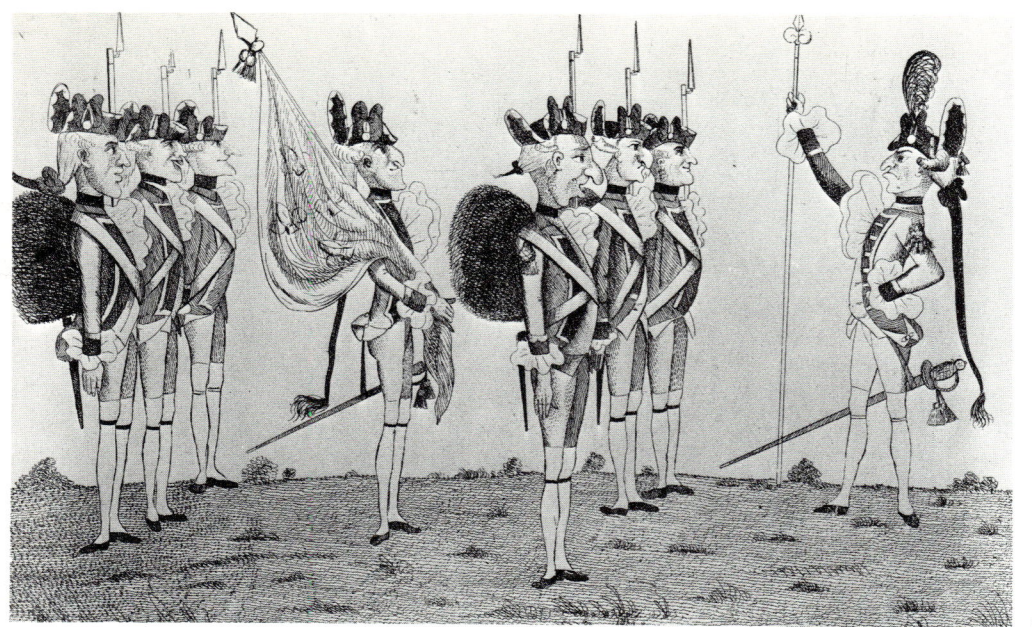

776

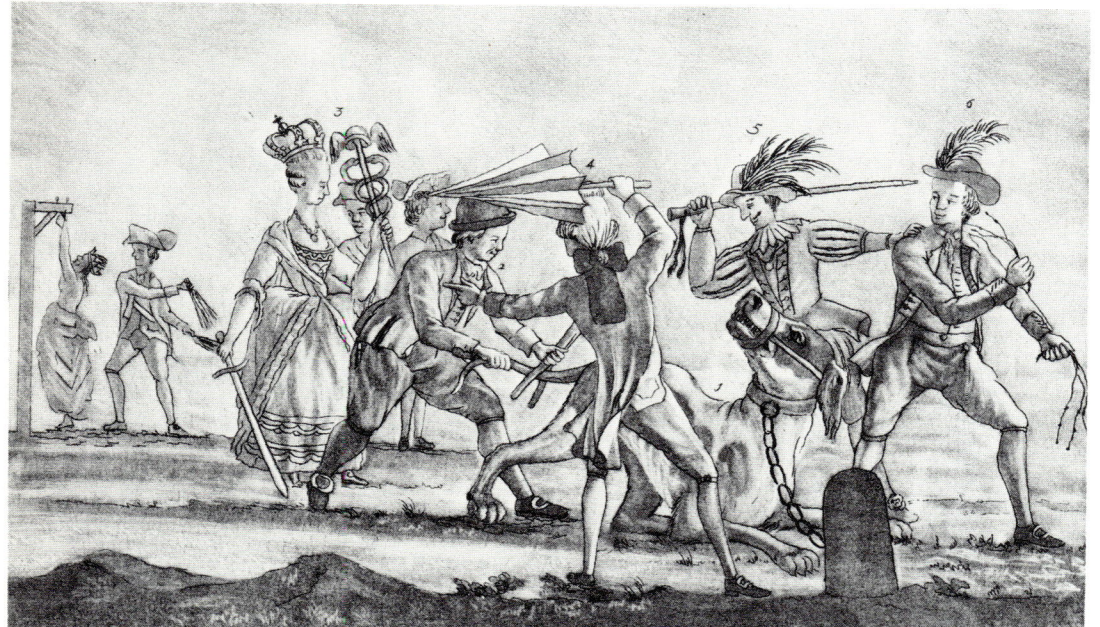

778

exaggerated features to ridicule. CPPS 5706
LC–USZ62–1518

777
[America with gods and continents watches the activities of Geography—title page]
Berthalt S. 1780
  Mixed method 12½ x 11¼ in. (full page)

  The Muses discuss the sciences, and Geography exhibits a map of the world. Four figures, probably the continents, sit on the right. America, dressed as an Indian, and Europe, dressed as a queen, take more interest in the activities than do the other two. Cherubs play in the foreground, and two of them fly with a banner bearing the title of Clouet's *Géographie Moderne avec Introduction* (Paris, 1780).

778
LOON NA WERK 1780. [A Due Reward 1780] No 1 Verbeelt Een Engelse Dogge, geketent aan een Ronde Onzydige Paal No 2 Een Hollander alvorens door hem int been gebeten zynde set hem een Knip op de Staart Geadsisteerdt Door de Neutraliteyt No 3 aan t Hooftderzebve Een Gekroonde Vorstin Edelmoedig den Vryjen Handel Beschermende No. 4 een Frans man den Hont afrossende Couragerende den Hollander hem wÿsende op Zyn Vrienden No 5 Ein Spanjaart Met Zÿn Rotting den Rekel Deftig Strelende en den Amerikaan No 6 Aanmoedigt die den Menscheplaag Dapper voor Zyn brutale Muÿl Slaadt. In T Verchiet ziet Men de Hoogmoedige Koningin der Zee Werdende gegeeselt door J: poül Jones. De piris is 8 stuyvers. 1780
  Mezzotint in brown 8¼ x 10¾ in.

  England, represented by a big, chained and muzzled dog, is attacked by figures representing the countries of the armed neutrality league: Catherine of Russia, a Swede, and a Dane (cf. item 750); and the allies: a Frenchman, a Dutchman, a Spaniard, and an American. In the background John Paul Jones whips a crowned woman who is designated "Queen of the Sea." CPPS 5715 LC–USZ62–45394

779

DE MAN IN'T HEMBD, OF DE GEFNUIKTE HOOGMOED. [The Man in the Shirt or Pride Brought Low.] VERKLARING. I. EEN MAN IN'T HEMBD, IN VOLLE RAZERNY. 2. EEN AMERIKAAN, DIE LACHENCE ZYN BEURS EN KLEDEREN WEGDRAAGT. 3. EEN MUSKOVIETER DREIGENDE HEM TE SLAAN. 4. EN 5. EEN DEEN EN ZWEED HEM DE ARMEN VASTHOUIENDE. 6. EEN HOLLANDER DIE HEM AAN DE KETTING LEGT. 7. EEN FRANSCHMAN HEM EEN ZOTSKAP OPZETTENDE. 8. EENIGE AFGETAKELDE KAPERS. 9. EEN VLOOT KOOPVAARDY-SCHEPEN ONGESTOORD VARENDE. 10. EEN MAN DIE DIT STAMPVOETENDE AANZIET. 11. EENIGE VERSCHEURDE TRAKTATEN. [178?]
Etching 6¾ x 8¾ in.

England in a nightshirt is held by Denmark and Sweden, while France places a dunce cap on his head, and Holland shackles him. Russia is about to hit him with a club, and America runs away with his clothes. In the background is a merchant fleet sailing out to sea, and some privateers are grounded on the beach; in the foreground are torn treaties. The cartoon satirizes the unabashed opportunism of the Armed Neutrality League. By securing protection for their trade with the belligerents, the League inflicted considerable damage on England, which was the largest mercantile power. CPPS 5716 LC–USZ62–45395

———Another impression of an earlier state shows the outline. This state was possibly used for coloring.

780

Freedom, Peace, Plenty, all in vain advance, [1780]
Mixed method 5⅜ x 3⅝ in. (image)

Britannia carries her spear with a liberty

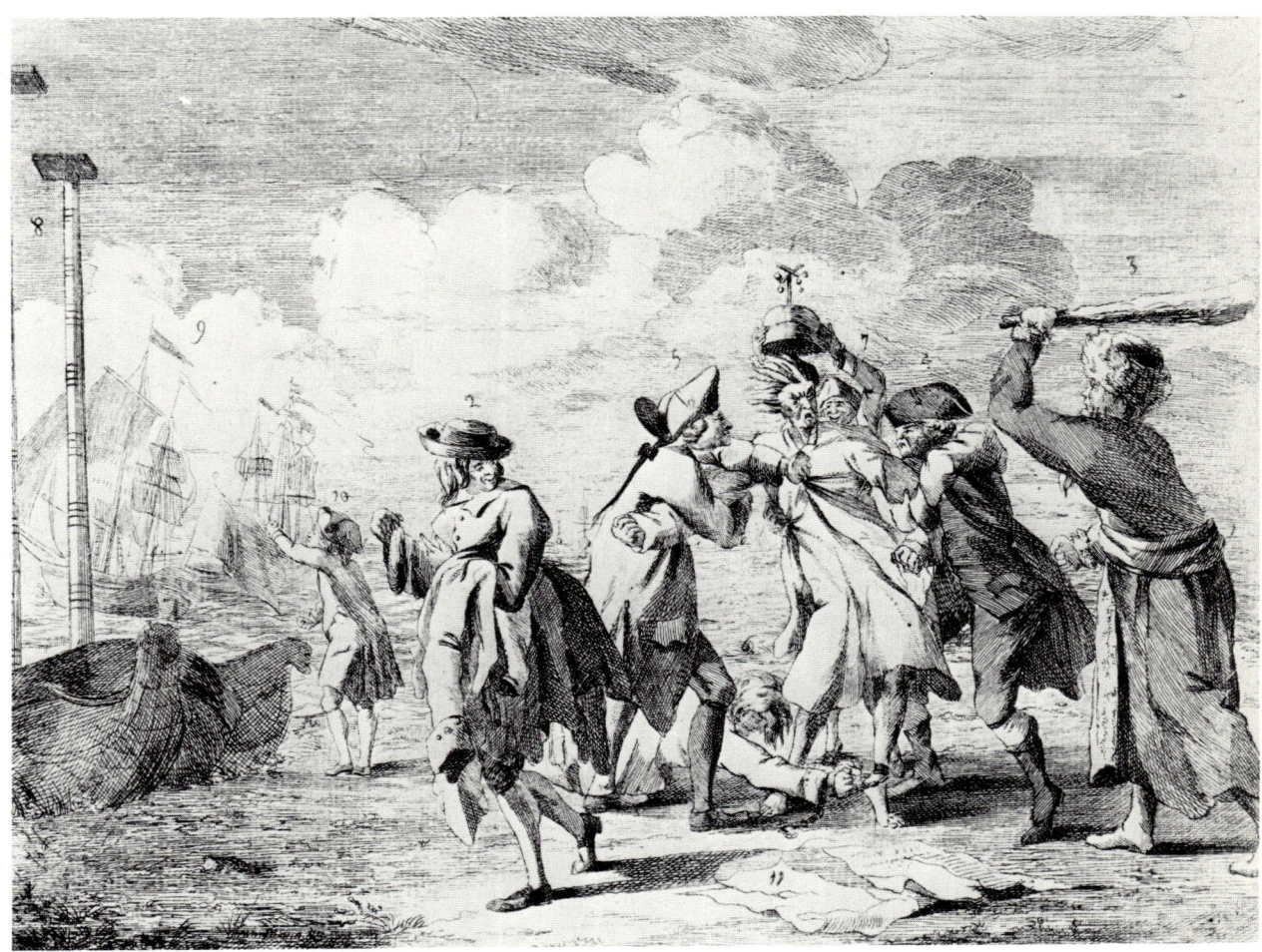

779

cap on top as she advances over a shield with fleur-de-lis, weapons, and a paper designated "Treaty of Alliance with France." In the left background, soldiers with the American flag are fighting a battle, and one aims his rifle at Britannia. An accompanying lyric explains the scene.

> Freedom, Peace, Plenty, all in vain advance,
> Spurn'd by Brittannia's Children, dupes to France:
> Aspring Chiefs in congress, scourge the land,
> All Laws subverting to usurp command:
>
> Tyrants they prove, while Patriots they appear,
> And Popish Leagues mark their absurd career,
> May Heav'n in timely mercy make them wise,
> Ere French and Spanish Chains their crimes chastize.

From *The Universal Magazine*, 1780, frontispiece. LC–USZ62–29192

781

Wegens de Staat der Engelsche Natie, in't Jaar 1778. [1780]
Mixed method 6¾ x 10½ in. (image)

A larger version of item 726. An Englishman wrings his hands over the state of English commerce which is represented by a cow. An American has sawed off one horn and is proceeding to cut off the second. A Dutchman, a Frenchman, and a Spaniard milk the cow. In the foreground a small dog urinates on the sleeping British lion, and in the background is the city of Philadelphia with Howe's flagship the *Eagle* aground and the drunk Howe brothers at a table. This continental print, later than the British version, was often reprinted because in continued to represent the state of the American War until about 1782. CPPS 5726A

———Another version, numbered and with an explanation in French. The Englishman has tears in his eyes in this print. CPPS 5726B LC–USZ62–15755

782

MAL LUI VEUT MAL LUI TOURNE DIT LE BON HOMME RICHARD [1780]
Mixed method 6¾ x 10¼ in. (image)

Print similar to item 781, but reversed, with more objects identified. The explanation accompanying this print is entitled "Le Commerce de la Grande Britagne sous la Forme d'une Vache." CPPS 5727 *Collection de Vinck* 1212 LC–USZ62–28229

783

DEN ENGELSMAN OP ZYN UITERSTE. L'ANGLOIS A TOUTE EXTREMITEZ. A Lyon, chez Nicolas Ciseau, a L'Ensigne des Armes de Bourges. [1780]
Etching 6½ x 10 in.

An Englishman vomits into a pan held by a Dutchman, while a Frenchman and a Spaniard hold back a crowd waving enema syringes. Others would like to relieve England of her treasures. Behind the Englishman stand two Americans ready to give him an enema. On this copy the names Franklin and Paul Jones are penned beside the Americans. The occasion of this cartoon was probably England's declaration of war against Holland on December 20, 1780. CPPS 5731 LC–USZ62–34861

784

BY HIS MAJESTYS ROYAL LETTERS PATENT. THE NEW INVENTED METHOD OF PUNISHING STATE CRIMINALS. [Publish'd as the Act directs Octr 12th 1780 & sold by J. Russell No 7 Blewets Buildings Fetter Lane, London. 1780]
Etching 7¾ x 10½ in. (image)

Britannia about to be torn apart by three horses racing in different directions: "Tyranny" on a road to America, "Venality" to Spain, and "Ignorance" to France. A fourth rope leads to a stake designated "court influence" on a road marked "Despotism." A courtesan holds this stake. Behind the main action on a stone pedestal is George III smiling, and Bute

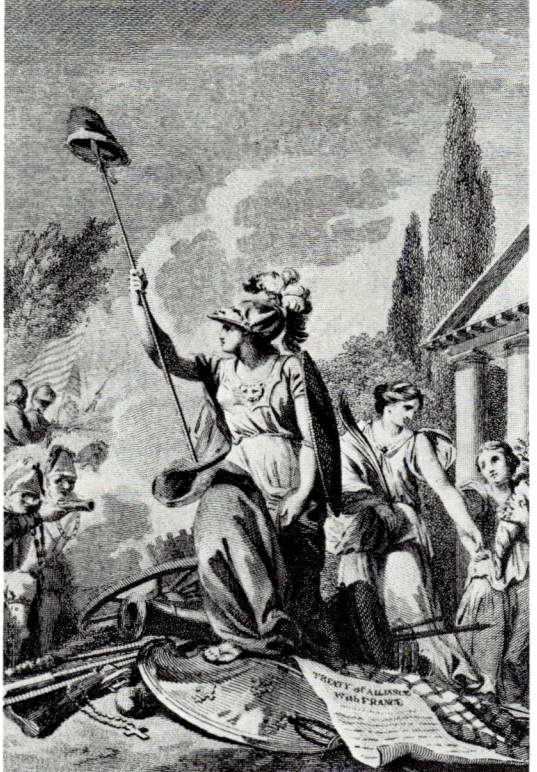

780

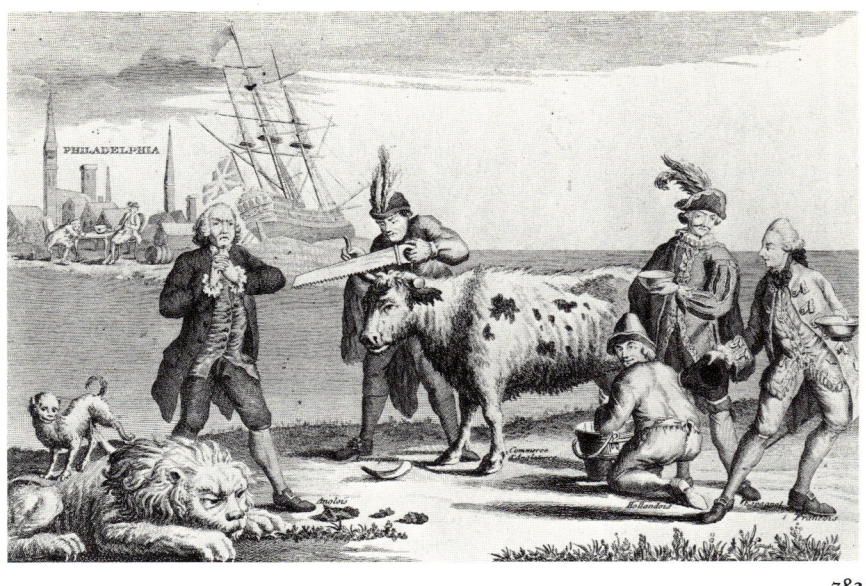

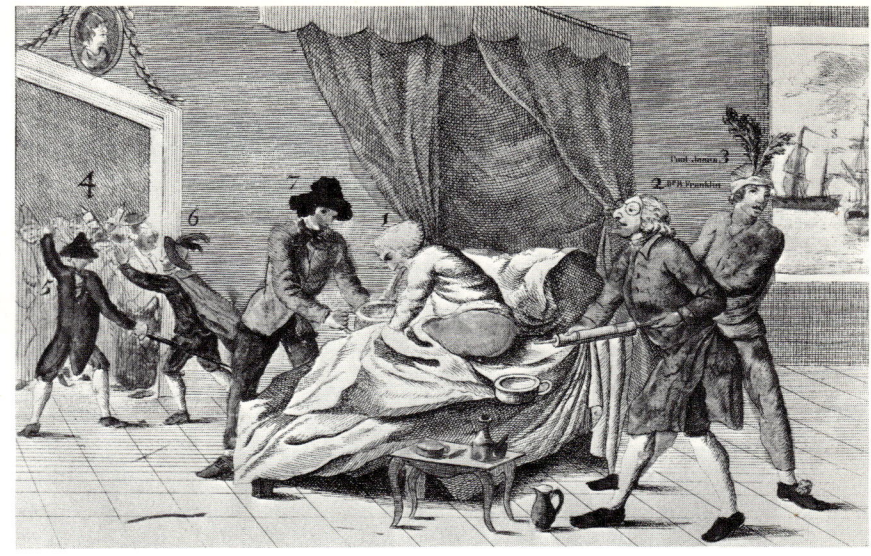

782

783

stands lashing the four horses. In the sky winged Liberty flies sadly away toward America. CPPS 5580 LC–USZ62–45443

785

The desponding HERO of the COLDSTREAM. A MILITARY MADRIGAL. LONDON: Published by TOMMY COLDSTREAM. PETTYFRANCE. [178?]

Etching (hand colored) 10¼ x 13¼ in. (image)

Five members of the Coldstream Guard deplore their fate around a banquet table as they think of their coming assignments. One refers to a possible assignment in America by saying, "Tis a shmeful thing to puzzle a man in this manner—yes, yes, we'll be food for the Indians to a certainty." Below is a song:

Air____"Despairing beside a clear Stream."

O'er Parsloe's most sumptuous board,
A Colonel, desponding, was laid;
Neglected lay gorget and sword,
And a magnum supported his head:

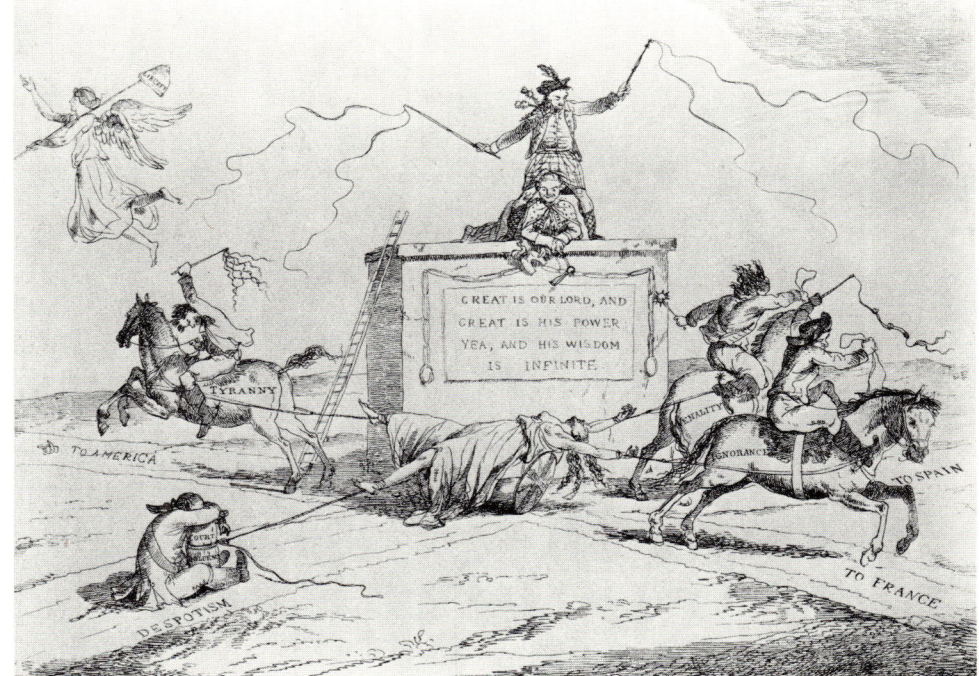

784

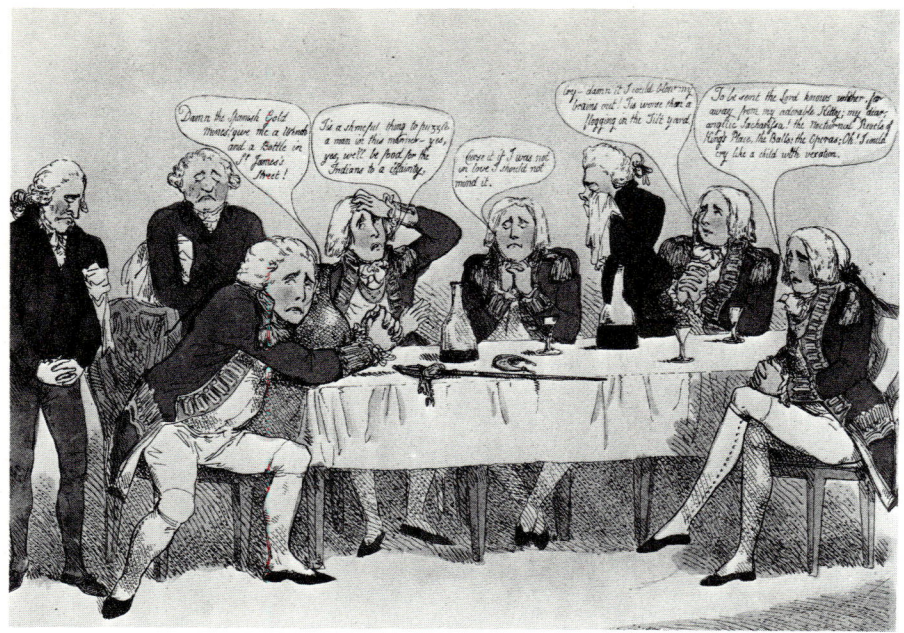

785

The Ensigns who heard him complain,
In shrugs to his shrug made reply;
And the Waiters, who felt for his pain,
Stood mournfully murmuring by.

"Ah me! what a pitiful plight,
To Spain or the Indies to roam!
What! send the white gaiters to fight,
Who look so divinely at home!
To think the battalions so gay,
Abroad on real service should rove!
Not to lounge the dull mornings away;
Nor to spend the soft ev'nings in love!

"Ah! why not like William the First,
Could not Billy to Scotia repair!
Rude valour for conflicts may thirst,
While beaux shou'd contend for the fair.
A Highlander's proper pursuit,
Is fighting, and such sort of things;
But with feathers it better will suit,
To attend upon wenches and kings.

"Thro' the Park we no longer shall stroll,
The children's sweet custard to eat;
No more two a-breast can we roll,
And jostle the cits in the street.
For this did I change from the line,
That in London I snugly might stay!
What an Irish promotion is mine,
To be sooner here than away!

"The danger is none of my care,
It is not the Dons that I dread!
But, ah! to be torn from the fair,
Ye subs, we had better be dead!
It is Billy that dooms us to range,
That he all our ranks may supply;
'Tis his to talk proudly and change,
It is our's to be draughted and die."

LC–USZ62–22434

786

The Ballance of Power. London. Published as ye Act directs, Jany. 17. 1781. [by R. Wilkinson, at No 58 in Cornhill.]
Mixed method 9¾ x 13¾ in.

A noble Britannia with the sword of justice weighs down the scale of power against the combined weight of Holland, France, Spain, and America. A poem at the bottom reads:

America, dup'd by a treacherous train,
  Now finds she's a Tool both to France and to Spain;

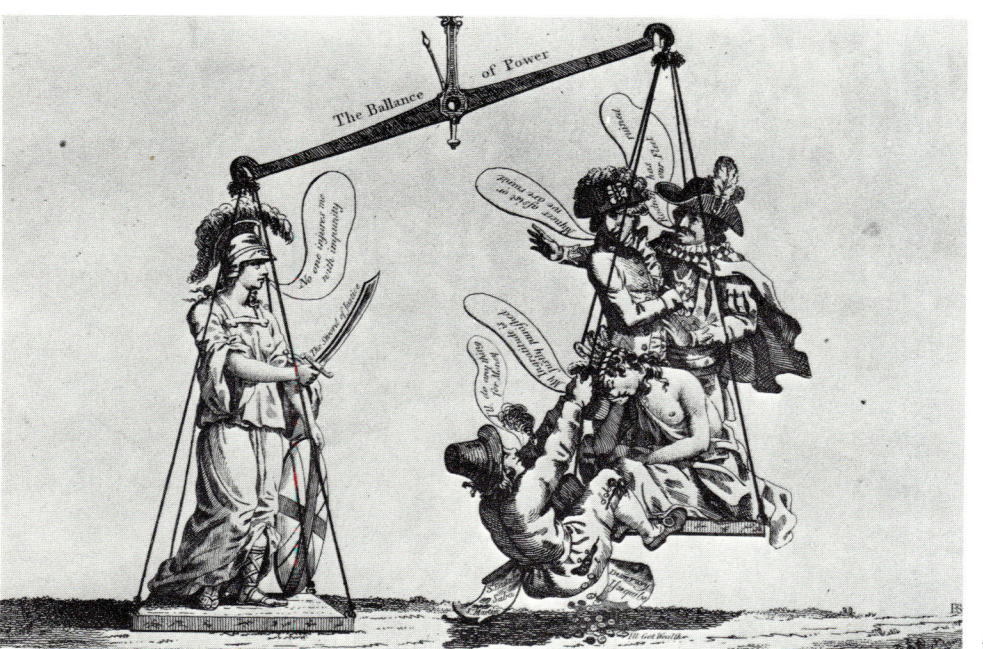

786

Yet all three united can't weigh down the Scale:
So the Dutchman jumps in with the hope to
  prevail.
Yet Britain will boldly their efforts withstand,
And bravely defy them by Sea and by Land:
The Frenchman She'll Drub, and the Spaniard
  She'll Beat,
While the Dutchman She'll Ruin by Seizing
  his Fleet:
Th' Americans too will with Britons Unite,
And each to the other be Mutual Delight.

Similar to item 762. CPPS 5827
LC–USZ62–1527

787
JACK ENGLAND Fighting the FOUR CONFEDERATES. Printed for Jno. Smith No. 35 Cheapside, Robt. Sayer & Jno. Bennett No. 53 Fleet Street, Jany. 20; 1781.
  Mixed method 6½ x 8 in. (image)

An English sailor prepares to fight the pathetic allies. "Yanky Doodle" dressed as an Indian lies on the ground moaning, "This fall has hurt my Back." "Monsieur Louis Baboon" vomits on the American saying, "Dem Jersey Pills have made a me Sick." A Spaniard, "Don Diego," has a bleeding eye, and a fat Dutchman puffs toward the English tar saying, "I have almost forgot how to fight." Below the title:

  To Arms you Brave Britons to Arms the
  Road to Renown Lyes before you.

The war in America seemed to be turning in Britain's favor at the time of this cartoon. Clinton took Charleston, S.C., on May 12, 1780, and Cornwallis defeated the Americans at Camden on August 16, 1780. The Spaniards had suffered defeat at Ft. Omoa on the coast of Honduras, and the French were repulsed at the Isle of Jersey. The Dutchman in this print represents a potential victim who is fat with wealth and no longer able to fight. CPPS 5828 LC–USZ62–1528

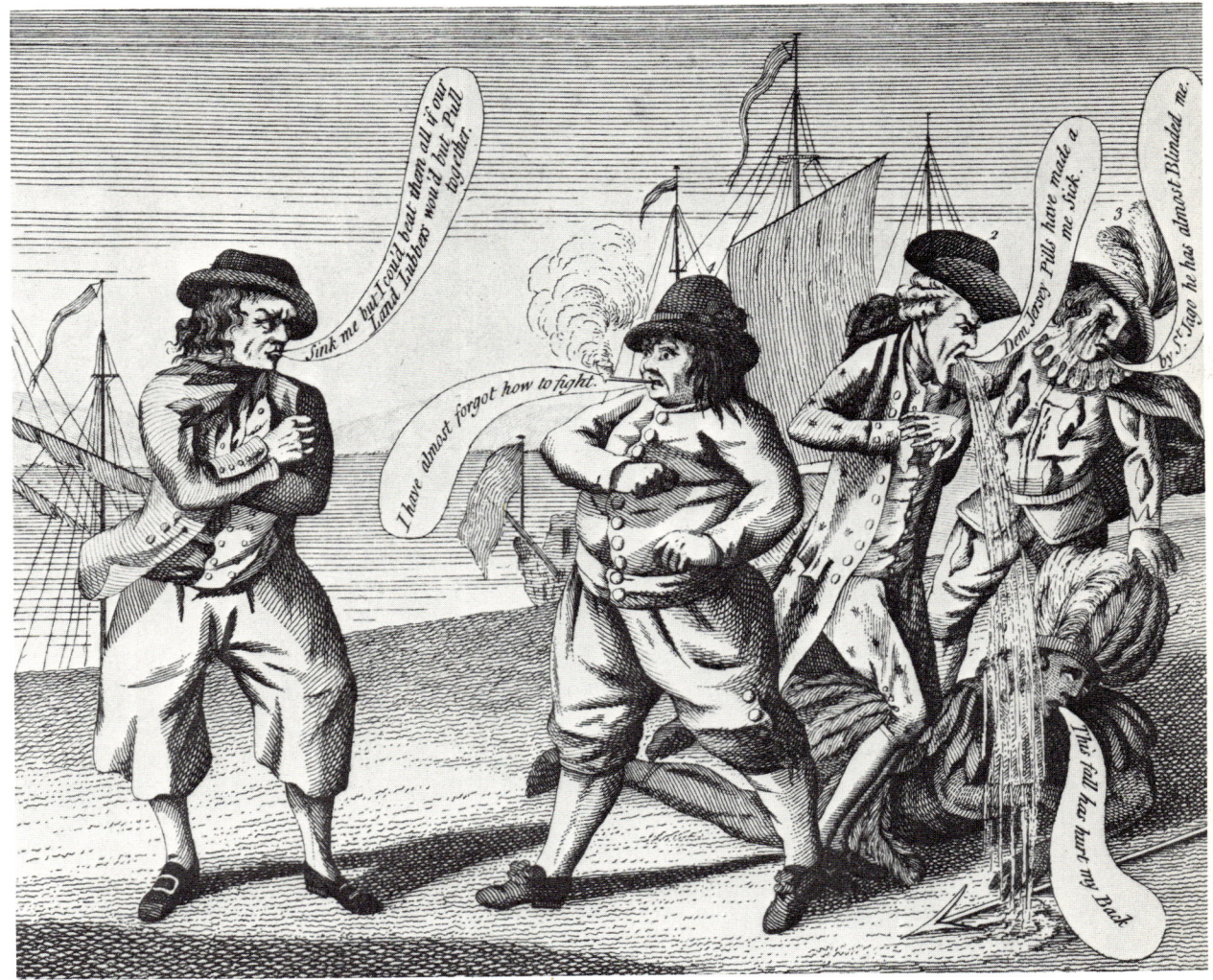

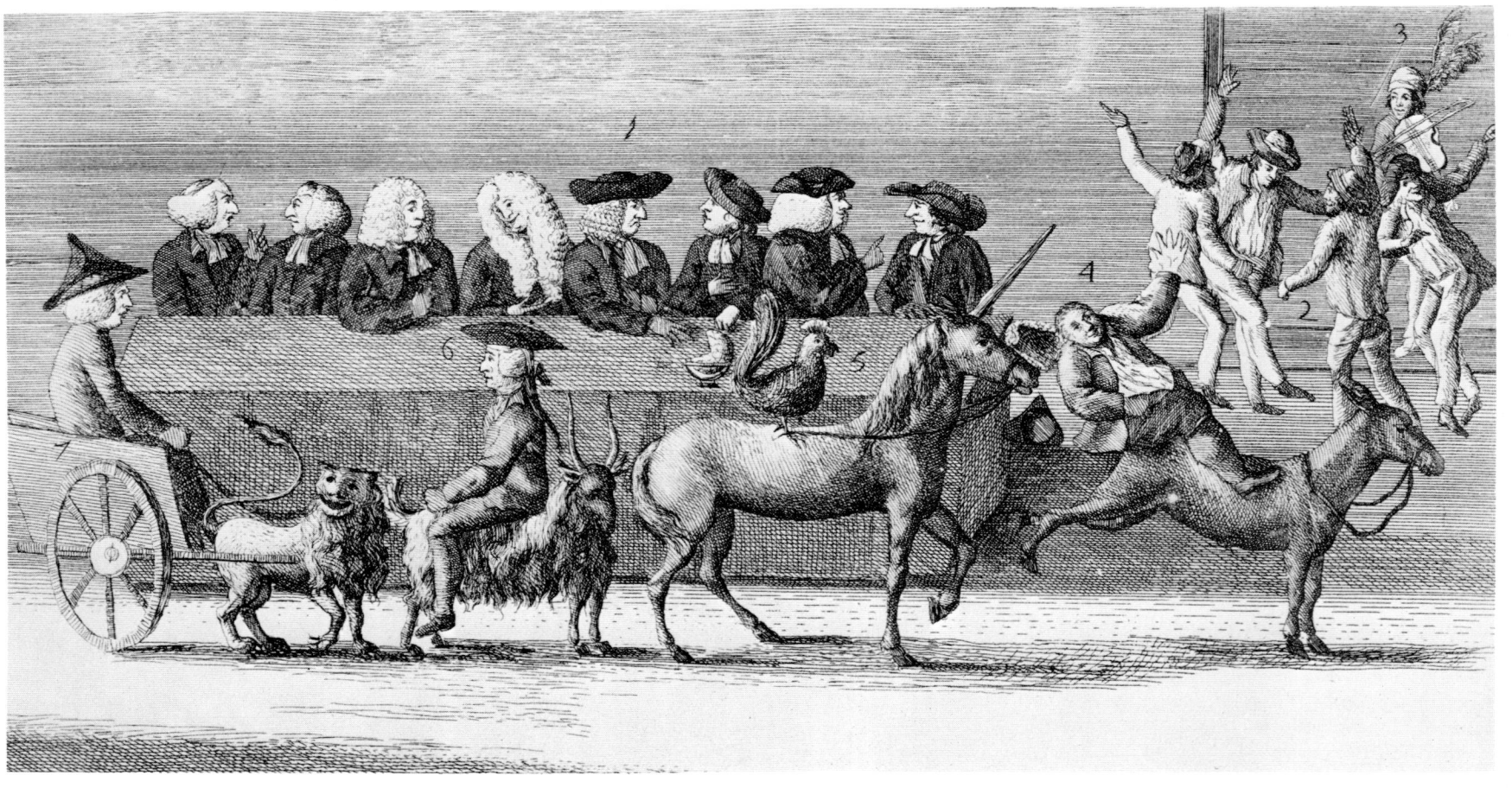

789

788

THE BUDGET. Published as the Act directs March 1, 1781 by W. Phelps.

Mixed method (hand colored) 7⅞ x 9¼ in. (image)

A beast with two heads, one horned, represents the British budget. Three headless men ride the back of the beast whose front rips at the breast of Britannia with a claw and whose back is the head of a dog or wolf which vomits empty purses at a group of Englishmen. Among casks and boxes of produce lie disbursement slips and a chest labeled "120,000 guineas for America." In the foreground dogs and savages devour food and a child. This cartoon pictures the suffering of the British people due to the Ministry's mismanagement of funds. CPPS 5834

789

ENGLISCH PRINTET. [English Print, 1781] Etching 6½ x 12¼ in.

Many things happen in this composite picture: 1. Lord North, seated with friends at a table, points to a globe with a large piece out of it and wants it for himself and his friends. 2. French sailors dance with joy at the safe arrival at Brest of a captured English convoy from St. Eustatius. 3. An American musician plays for the French sailors. 4. An Englishman is thrown by the American donkey. 5. The French cock rides the British unicorn. 6. An Englishman sits backward on the Spanish goat. 7. An Englishman sits in a cart drawn by the Dutch lion, but the lion is turning on him. CPPS 5839 LC–USZ62–45396

790

THE GIG. Wells del Pub. May 8 1781 by W. Wells, No 132, Fleet Street, London.
Mixed method 7⅛ x 9¾ in. (image)

Two British sailors with whips designated "Rodney" flog a Dutchman sitting in the base part of a top. The Dutchman says, "Mine Head be very Giddy indeed." Written on concentric circles on the top are: "Saba," "St. Eustatia," "St. Martin," "Demerary," "Issequibo," "Curass." Below "Tune Patriot Fair."

1
Long had the Artful, fly Mynhur,
To fill his Purse from year to year,
   Persue'd his Cunning Rig O:
America with France, and Spain,
He underhanded did sustain,
   And whipt his money Gig O.

2
For England, who had been his Friend,
And oft had promis'd he'd defend,
   He valued not a fig O:
He trifled with each just demand,
And Joind for gain a Rebel band,
   And thus kept up his Gig O.

3
Such Insolence no more to bear,
The English Trumpet sounds to War!
   And Vengeance rises big O:
Each Jolly Sailor cries away,
Our pastime let's no more delay,
   But whip the Dutchman's Gig O.

4
Brave Rodney with his hearty bands,
Eustatias Island soon Commands,
   Which makes him dance a Jig O:
And all must own he's Acted well,
The double fac'd Mynheer to quell,
   By flogging of his Gig O.

5
My Lads still raise your whips on high,
And all your Numerous Foes defy,
   Spain, Holland, or French Prig O:
They soon will sue again for Peace,
Your Glories every day increase,
   By flogging of their Gig O.

6
Then every Jolly hearty Soul,
Shall cheerful sing arround the Bowl,
   For none we care a fig O:
We'll beat the Dons, we'll humble France,

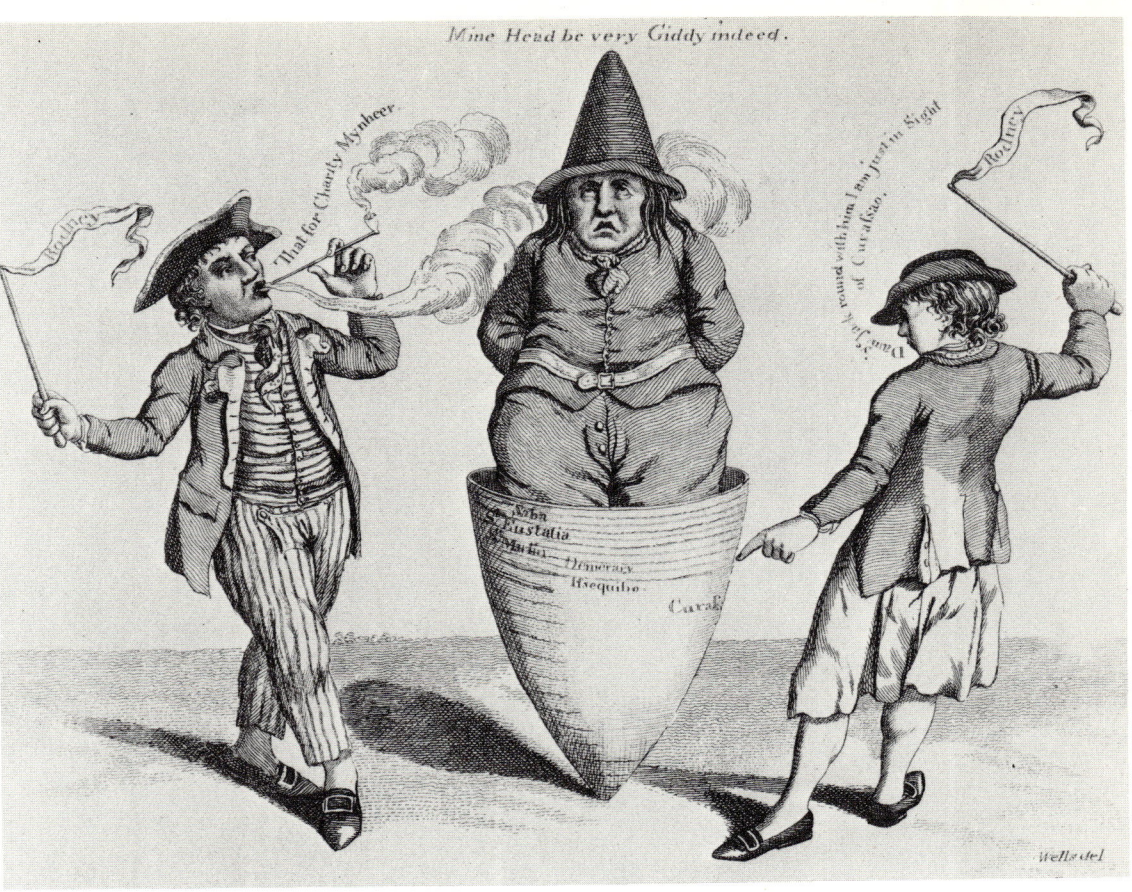

And make the heavy Dutchman dance,
   By flogging of his Gig O.

When Admiral Rodney learned that the Dutch had entered the war, he immediately conquered the Dutch colony of St. Eustatius, which had been a midway point for military supplies destined for America. St. Martin, Saba, Demerara (a part of Issequibo), and "Curass" (Curacao?) were other Dutch possessions in the Caribbean area. England looked to its navy for future victory and prosperity in these times. LC-USZ62-45476

791

The Late AUCTION at ST. EUSTATIA. by R_____ & V_____ 1781. Pub: by E. Hedges N 92. Cornhill London June 11.
Mixed method 9¾ x 13¾ in.

The cartoon represents Admiral Rodney and General Vaughan selling property and cargoes after their victory at St. Eustatius on February 3, 1781. Their delay was cited by many as a reason for the defeat of Cornwallis at Yorktown because too many ships remained during the auction, and some were diverted to carry

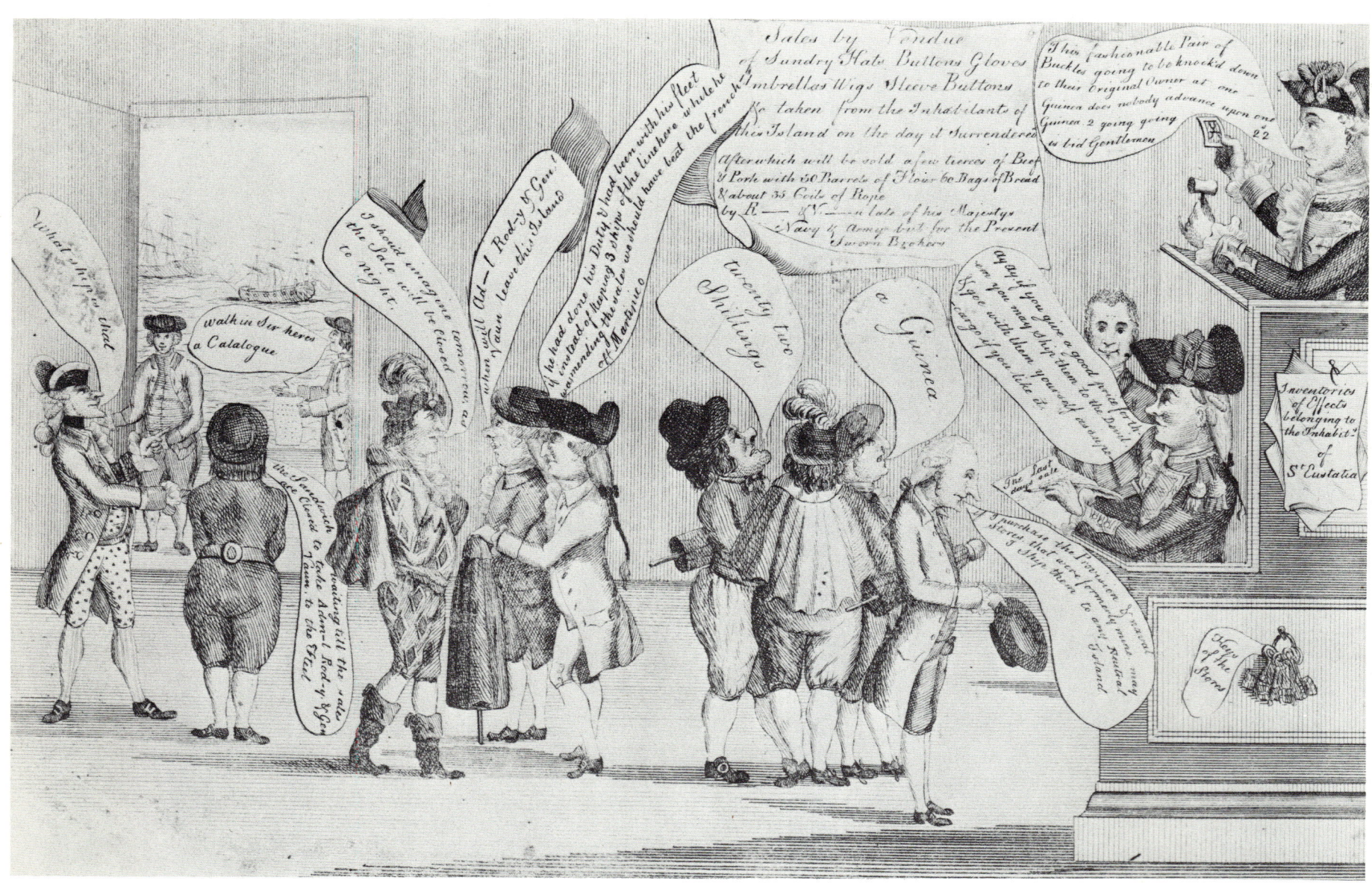

goods back to England. In the following April La Motte Piquet captured most of Rodney's convoy to England, and Rodney was embroiled in litigation over the affair for many years. CPPS 5842 LC–USZ62–45451

792
THE STATE NURSES. Pub by T. Colley Oct' 1, 1781 High Holborn.
Etching 7⅞ x 10⅞ in.

The British lion sleeps in a cradle, while four dogs representing Spain, France, Holland, and America bark without waking it. The dog designated America urinates on a paper inscribed "TEA ACT" and says, "Independence and no Taxation." Sandwich and Bute try to protect the sleeping lion. In the background George III hunts for stag, and Gibraltar is under siege. CPPS 5850 LC–USZ62–45452

793
DON VOLASEO. The Famous Spanish Partizan. Pub. by T. Colley Nov. 21. 1781. No. 257, high Holborn Sold by Cornell Bruton Street Bond Street.
Etching (hand colored) 9¾ x 13½ in.

A satire caricaturing Burke, who at this time opposed Admiral Rodney's action at St. Eustatius. This print accuses Burke of sympathy with the Spaniards and implies alliance with the Dutch, French, and Americans. CPPS 5854 LC–USZ62–45453

———— Another impression.

794
STATE COOKS' or THE DOWNFALL of the FISH KETTLE. Pubd. Decr. 10. 1781, by W. Wells No. 132 Fleet Street.
Etching (hand colored) 11¾ x 9 in.

George III has dropped a kettle of fish on the floor; each fish has the name of a Colony on it. Lord North commiserates with him. On the

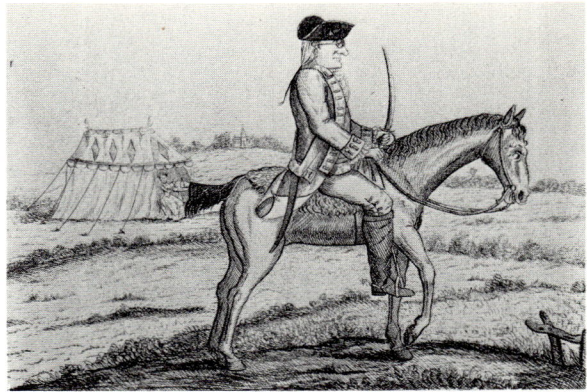
793

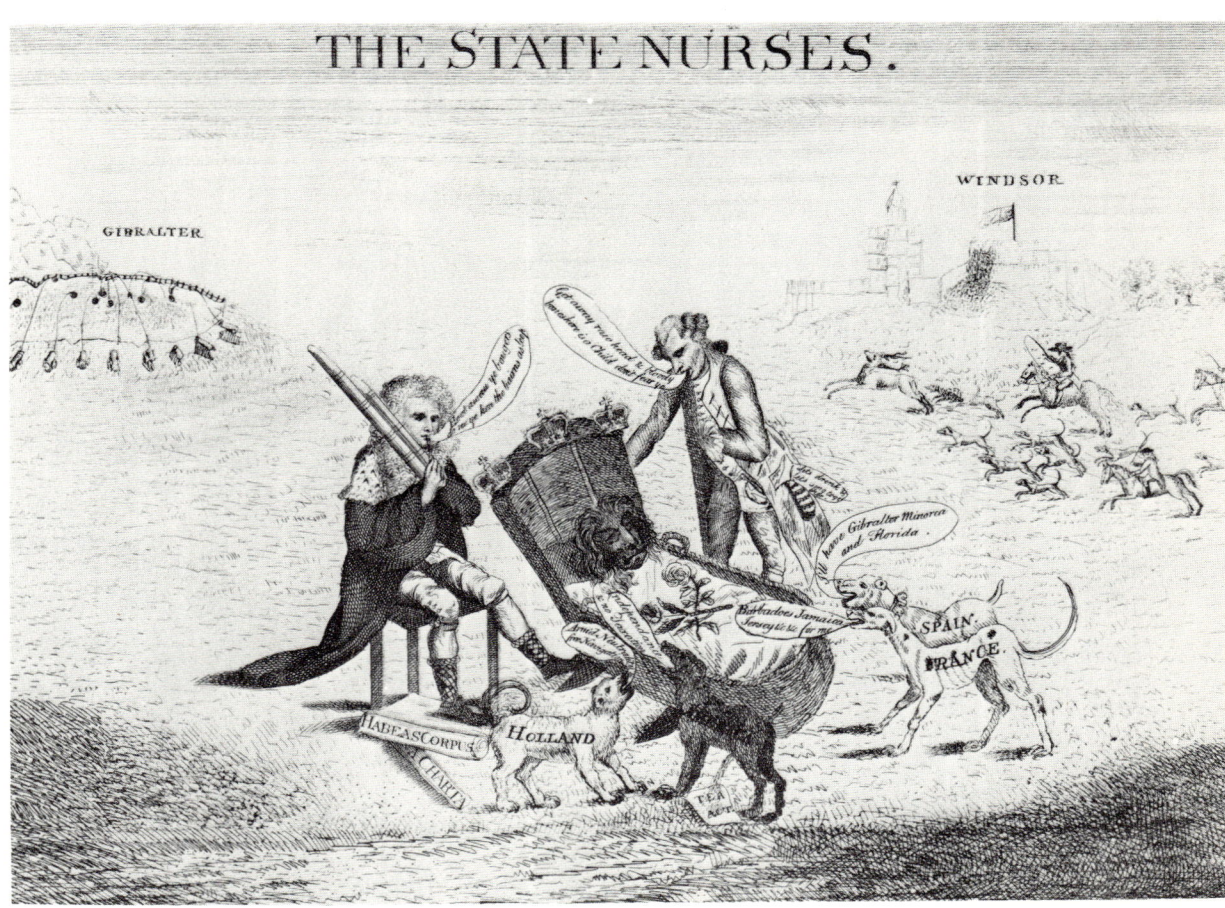
792

343

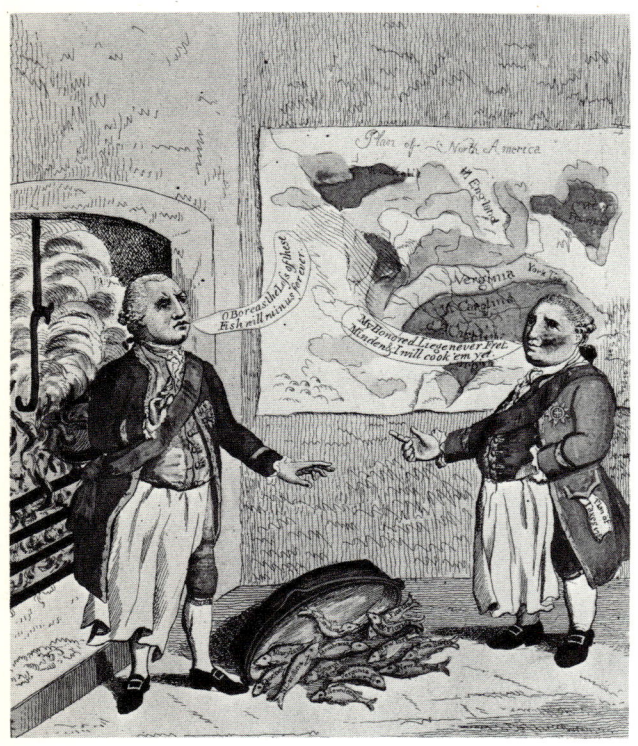

794

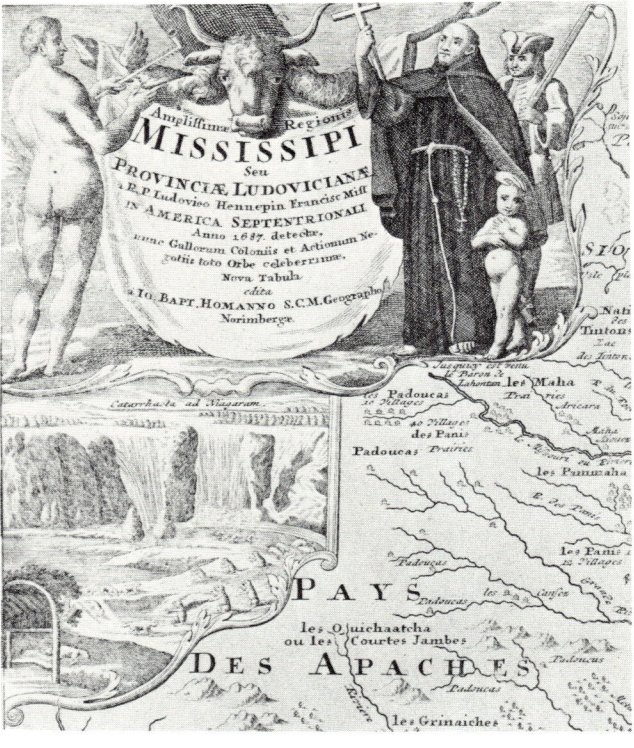

796

wall is a map of the Colonies. The King says, "O Boreas, the Loss of these Fish will ruin us forever." North in apron says, "My Honored Liege never Fret. Minden & I will cook 'em yet." In his pocket is a paper marked "Plan of Taxes 1782." Minden was a derogatory name for Lord George Germain who had disgraced himself at the Battle of Minden. This cartoon shows a reaction to the British defeat at Yorktown; news arrived in London on November 25, 1781. CPPS 5855 LC–USZ62–1529

795

[The inhabitants of America—A cartouche] 1746
  Etching 6¼ x 9¼ in. (image)

Pictures four Indians around the cartouche; in the background volcanoes explode. From a map entitled "Americae Mappa Generalis... Delineata ab Aug. Gottl. Boehmio...." In Homann, *Atlas Geographicvs Maior* (Norimbergae, 1759–81), no. 136.

796

[A French missionary, a soldier, an Indian, and a view of Niagara Falls, 1759–81]
  Etching 7¼ x 5¾ in. (image)

This continental picture sees the American West through symbols of its 17th- and early 18th-century history. French missionaries, noble savages, plenty of beaver, and the wonderful sight of Niagara Falls are combined in this cartouche to stir the adventurous heart of any geographer. From a map entitled "Ampliffimae regionis Mississipi... edita a Io. Bapt. Homanno...." In Homann, *Atlas Geographicvs Maior* (Norimbergae, 1759–81), no. 139. LC–USZ62–46086

797

[Indians and a bison—map ornament, 1759–81]
  Etching 6 x 4¾ in. (image)

An Indian man and woman stand near a bison. An opossum hangs by its tail from the top border, and a pelican stands in the foreground. On top two Indians pour water, representing the Mississippi River, from a cornucopia. From a map entitled "Ampliffimae regionis Mississipi...edita a Io. Bapt. Homanno...." In Homann, *Atlas Geographicvs Maior* (Norimbergae, 1759-81), no. 139.
LC-USZ62-46087

798

[An Indian, a European trader, and items of commerce 1759-81]
Etching 7½ x 6½ in. (image)

A European and an Indian trade amid items of commerce—rifles, skins, a saw, jewelry, etc. A ship's masts rise from behind the cartouche for this map entitled "Nova Anglia" in Homann, *Atlas Geographicvs Maior* (Norimbergae, 1759-81), no. 140.

799

[Two Europeans trade with five Indians—a cartouche, 1759-81]
Etching 11 x 10 in. (image)

The Europeans trade jewelry, clothing, and barrels for fish from the Indians. From a map entitled "Virginia Marylandia et Carolina in America Septentrionali...Ioh. Bapt. Homann." From Homann, *Atlas Geographicvs Maior* (Norimbergae, 1759-81), no. 143.
LC-USZ62-46088

800

[Two American Indians—a cartouche] 1781
Etching 2 x 2 in. (image)

Indians with grass skirts and feathered head gear decorate a map entitled "l'Amerique Septentrionale Divisee en ses Principaux Etats" in Laporte, *Atlas Moderne Portatif* (Paris, 1781), no. 23.

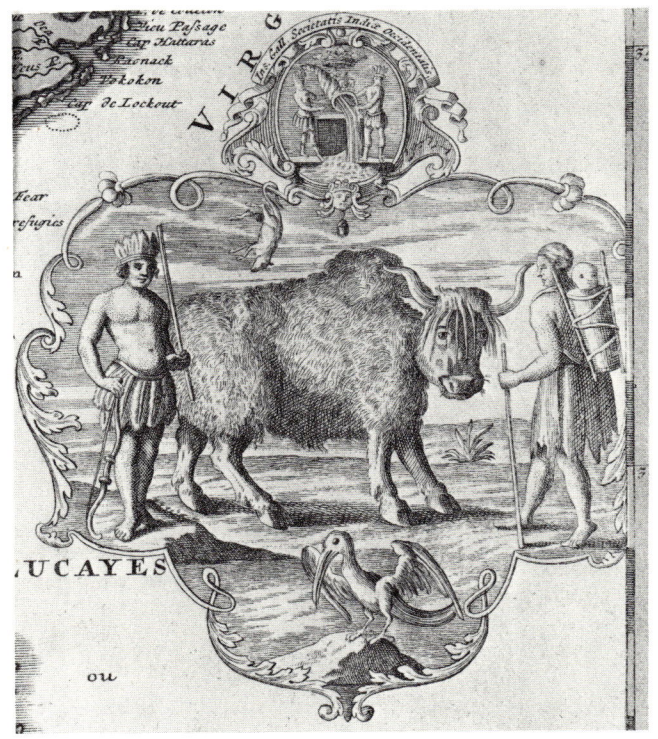

797

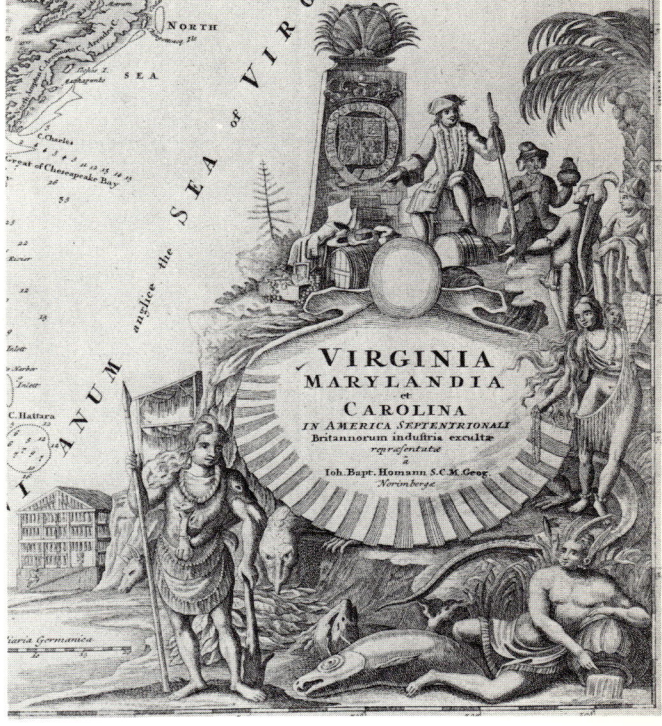

799

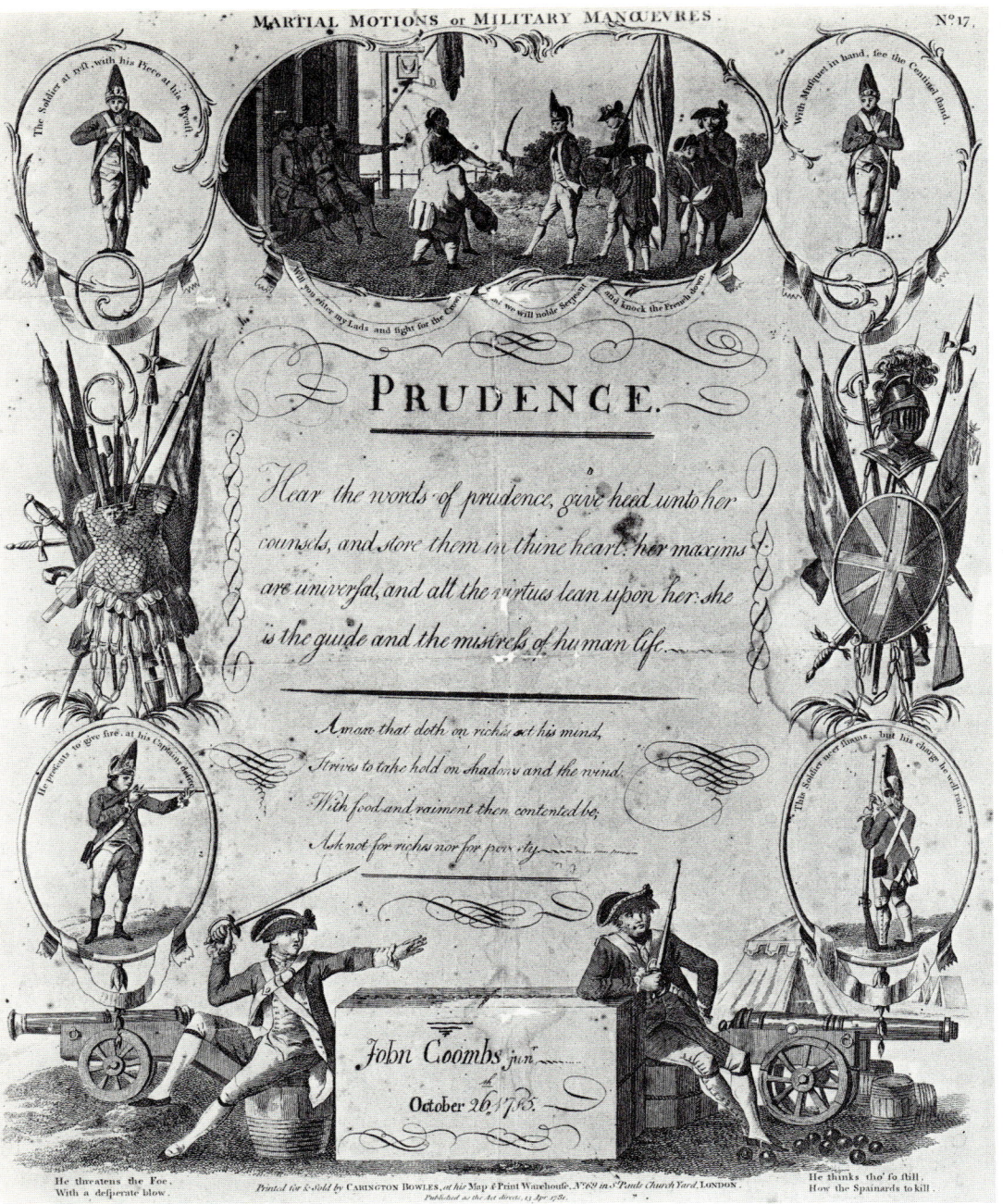

801

———Another impression. In Laporte, *Atlas ou Collection de Cartes Géographiques*... (Paris, 1787), no. 23.

801

MARTIAL MOTIONS OR MILITARY MANOUEVRES. PRUDENCE. Hear the words of prudence, give heed unto her counsels, and store them in thine heart; her maxims are universal, and all the virtues lean upon her: she is the guide and mistress of human life. Printed for & Sold by CARINGTON BOWLES, at his MAP & PRINT WAREHOUSE, No. 69 in St. Pauls Church Yard LONDON. Published as the Act directs 13 Apr. 1781.

Etching 17⅛ x 13¾ in.

This poster, expounding the prudence of enlistment, was used for recruiting soldiers in the war with France. Rhymed verses accompany pictures of British soldiers: "This soldier neer shams, but his charge he well rams." A short dialog says, "Will you enter my Lads and fight for the Crown? That we will noble serjeant and knock the French down." The bottom block has a soldier's name and date of enlistment in handwriting, "John Coombs junr. October 26, 1785." This poster was also used to recruit men for the war in the Colonies. Englishmen found more appeal in fighting the traditional enemies on the continent than in fighting the American colonists.
LC–USZ62–30533

802

[Yorktown] No. 2. [1781]
Mixed method 8½ x 11 in.

A Dutch print, sequel to item 781. An emaciated cow representing British commerce grazes on thistles representing the Scottish influences. Men representing France, Spain, and Holland have milked the cow. In the foreground John Bull kneels in prayer, while rats gnaw banknotes from a coffer, and the British

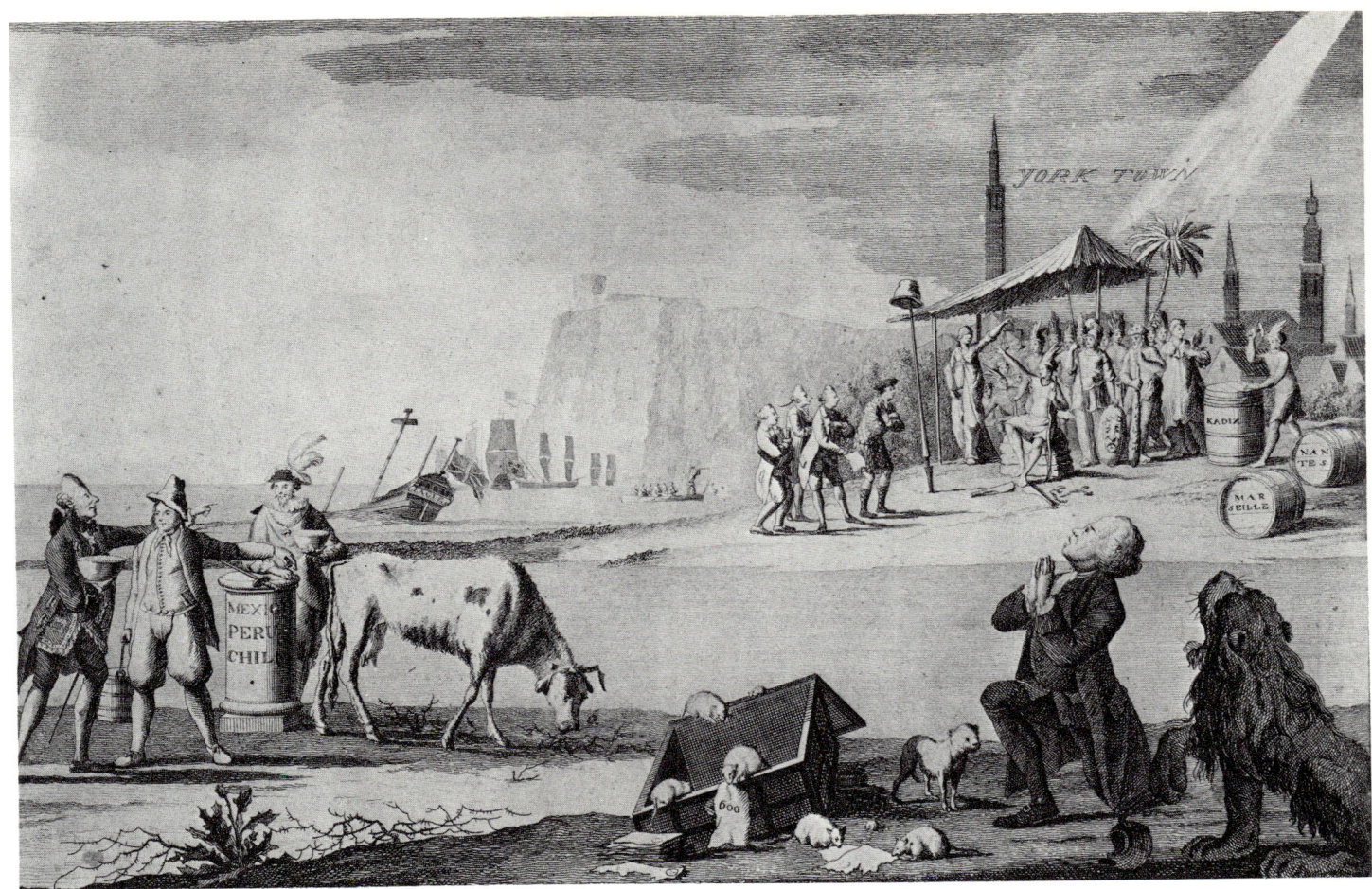

802

lion howls because he hurt his foot on a broken tea pot. In the background the surrender at Yorktown is represented by four Englishmen humbly approaching an American Indian who sits on a throne surrounded by Justice, Mars, and Hercules. At America's feet lie broken shackles and paddles, and in front of the throne a liberty cap rests on a lance. Another Indian prepares barrels for shipping to "Marseille, Nantes, Kadix." Out at sea Howe's flagship *Eagle* has sunk, while the French fleet sails.
CPPS 5859 LC–USZ62–17285

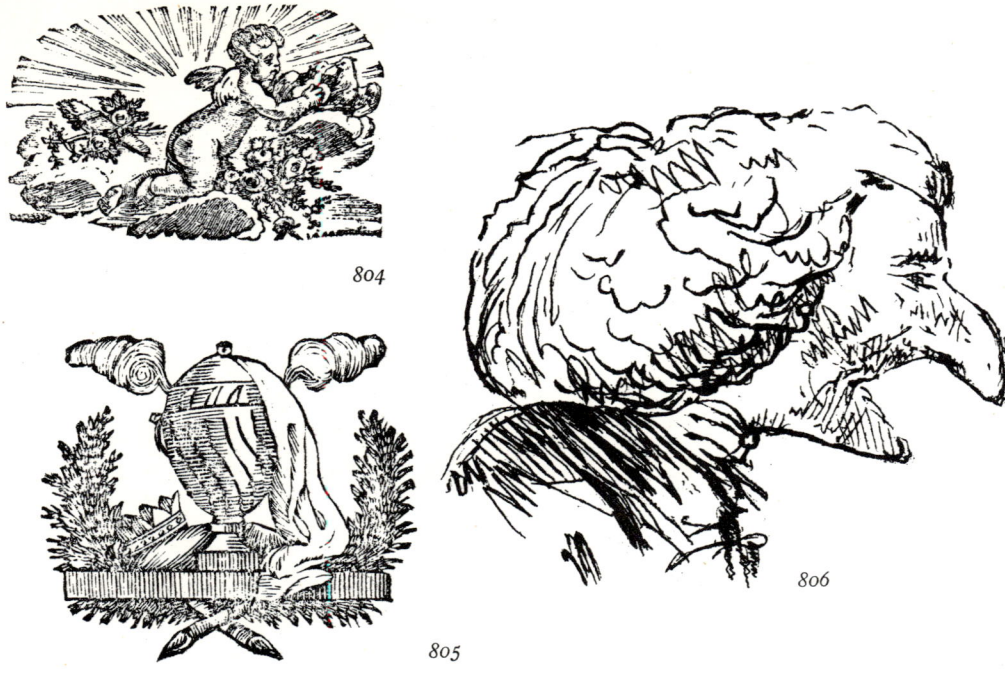

804

805

806

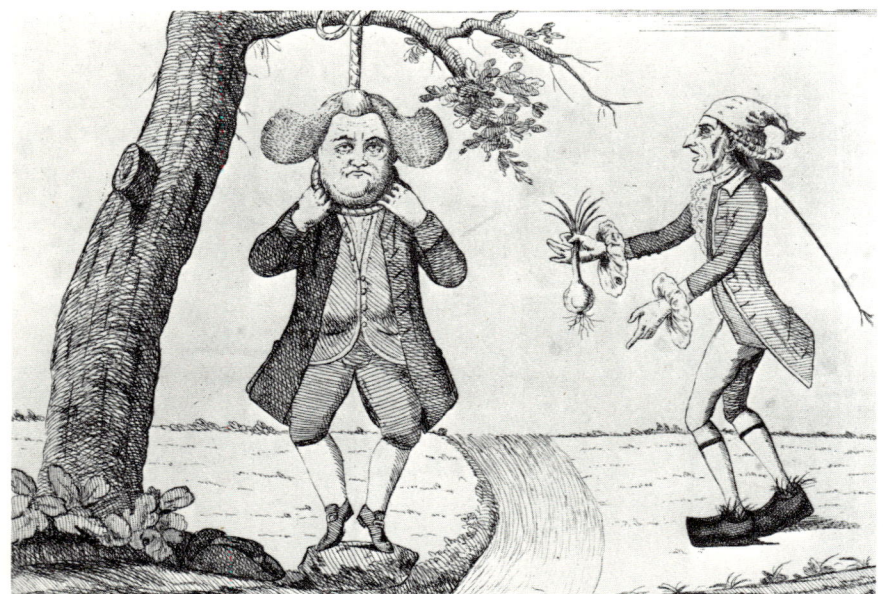

803

803

JOHN BULLS Alternative. [Pub. M. Darly? 1781]

Etching 6⅛ x 9 in.

John Bull with a noose around his neck stands on a rock. A Frenchman offers him a leek across a body of water. Probably refers to the alternative after Yorktown. CPPS 5860 LC–USZ62–45454

804

[A worried cherub holds a dove up to kiss another dove, 1781]

Woodcut 1¼ x 2 in. (image)

An allegorical book ornament from Hilliard d'Auberteuil, *Essais Historiques* (1781–82), p. 294. Refers to the hopes for reconciliation between the belligerents. LC–USZ62–45414

805

[A steaming urn about to explode—a book ornament, 1781]

Woodcut 1¾ x 2 in. (image)

Found in Hilliard d'Auberteuil, *Essais Historiques* (1781–82), p. x. Steaming tea pots and smoking bombs were often symbols of this war. See other allegories such as "The Tea-Tax-Tempest" (item 738) and "Orage Causé par l'impot sur le thé en Amerique" (item 739). LC–USZ62–45413

806

General Oglethorpe Publish'd as the Act Directs Jy. 13th. 1781. C.B. [Bretherton] Junr.

Etching 3⅞ x 3¾ in.

James Edward Oglethorpe (1696–1785) was best known as a philanthropist who founded Georgia in 1732 and as a general who defeated the Spanish in the battle at Ft. Frederica in the spring of 1742. At the time of this print he was an octogenarian, familiar with the London literati. He joined Burke and Boswell in arguing against Samuel Johnson's Tory views on the American war, and throughout the troubles with America, he strove to acquire the full rights of British citizens for Americans. At the news of Cornwallis' defeat at Yorktown he was discreetly quiet for a change. CPPS 5880 LC–USZ62–45455

807

THE COFFEE-HOUSE PATRIOTS; OR NEWS, FROM ST. EUSTATIA. H. BUNBURY Esqr. Delint. W. Dickinson Excudt. LONDON. Publish'd Octr. 15: 1781; by W. Dickinson No. 158 New Bond Street

Stipple 12⅝ x 14⅝ in.

Englishmen are amazed by the British victory at St. Eustatius. Many British merchants had used the port for trading with the enemy, and this print satirizes the lack of universal joy on the occasion. CPPS 5923 LC–USZ62–20401

808

[Cherubs imitate the times—title page ornament] J. Buys, inv. Reinr. Vinkeles, sculp. 1782

Mixed method 3¾ x 3¾ in. (image)

Three cherubs imitate Mercury, Neptune, and Liberty by holding their symbols. They stand around a monument with a globe on top and two inscriptions—one is draped in foliage reading, "Fides Mutua," and the other shows two clasped hands protruding from clouds holding two banners which read, "Concordia Res Parvae Crescunt" and "Qui Transtulit, Sustinet." On the ground are a scroll, a plaque, fasces, a tied bundle, and a cornucopia. From Loosjes, *Gedenkzuil, ter Gelegenheid der Vry-Verklaaring van Noord-America* (Amsterdam, 1782), title page.

809

THE ROYAL HUNT, or a PROSPECT of the YEAR 1782. South Briton fecit North Briton invt.

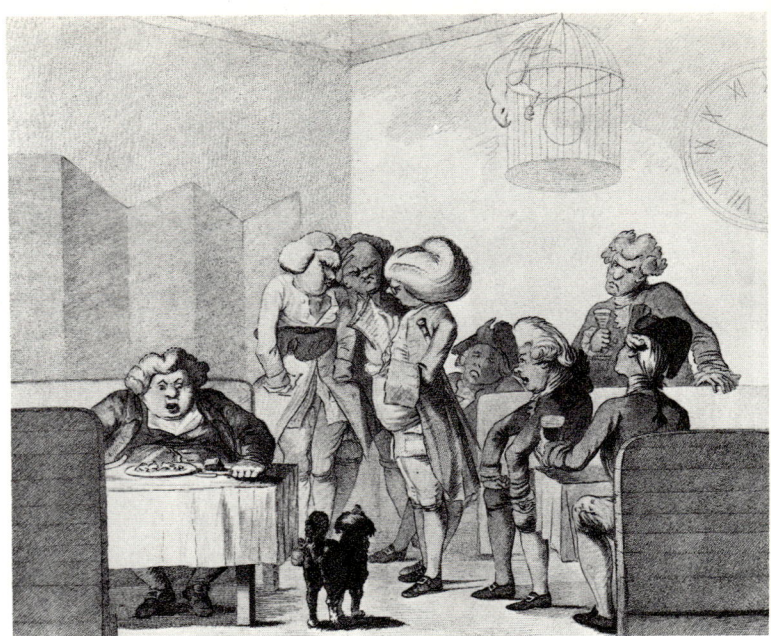
807

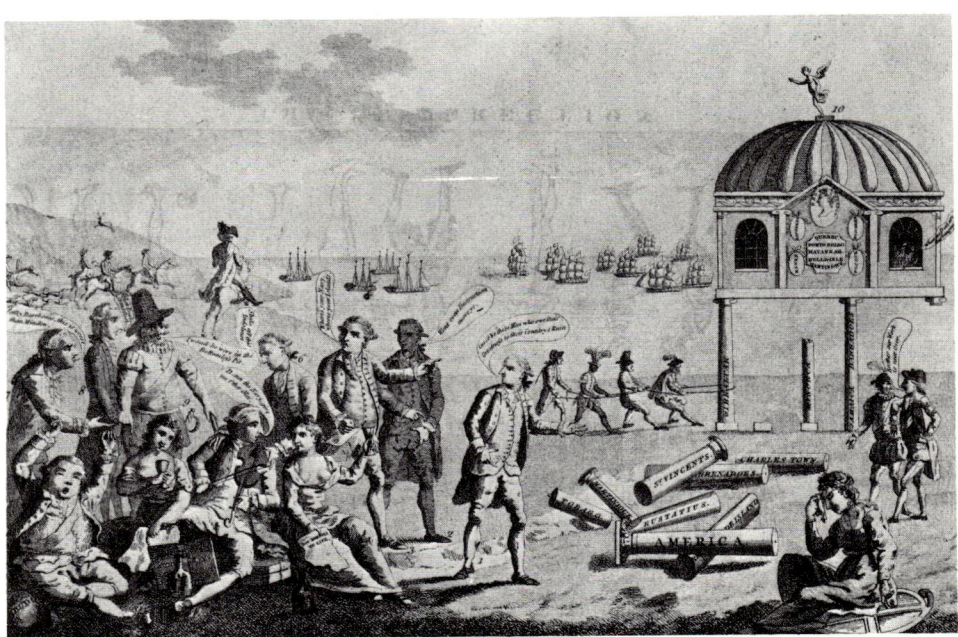
809

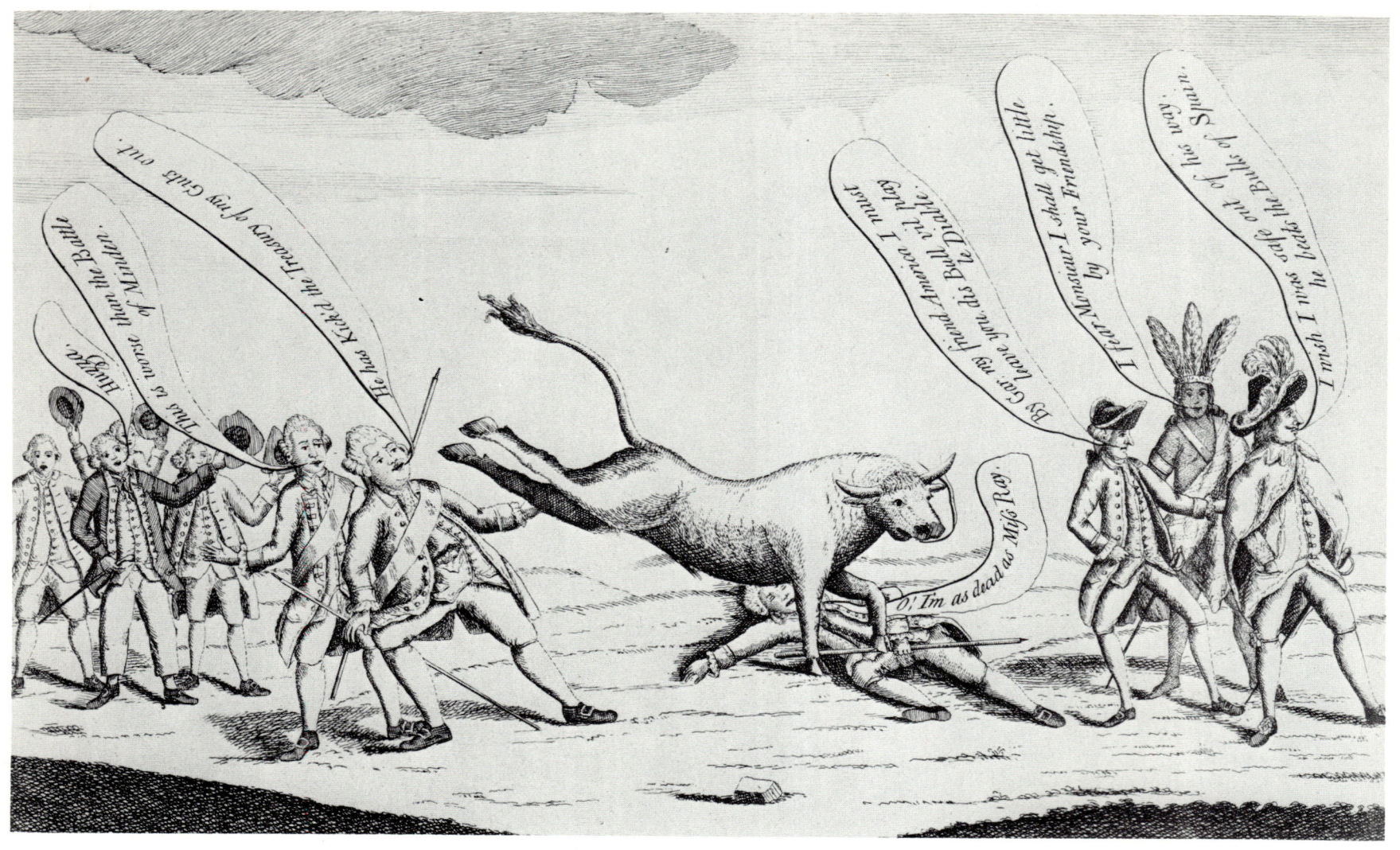

Published according to Act of Parliament by R. Owen, in Fleet Street to Feby. 16th. 1782. Mixed method 8½ x 12¾ in. (image)

Lord Sandwich between two courtesans carouses with North, Rigby, Amherst, and Germain. Looking on with disapproval are William Pitt (the younger), Fox, Burke, and Richmond; they point to a scene where a Frenchman, an American Indian, a Dutchman, and a Spaniard are pulling the pillars out from under the British Empire. Pillars representing "America," "Rhode Island," "Eustatius," "Tobago," "Martinique," "St. Vincents," "Grenadoes," and "Charles Town" are already fallen, while "Gibraltar," "Minorca," "Jamaica-Barbadoes" still stand. In the background George III hunts for stag, and a fleet of ships under sail attacks some unused ships. England could not mount a new offensive in America, and her resources were strained elsewhere. Although this cartoon shows indifference in the government, by this time George III and his ministers were very worried and were greatly offended by this satire. CPPS 5961 LC–USZ62–1530

810

The BULL OVER-DROVE; or the DRIVERS IN DANGER. London Publish'd as the Act directs Feby. 21, 1782 by I. Harris, Sweetings Alley Cornhill.

Mixed method 9¾ x 14 in.

A bull charges across the body of Sandwich before attacking France, America, and Spain. Behind the bull, Germain and North watch the attack, while British sailors cheer. Verses below read:

The State Drovers to madness, had drove the poor Bull,
Their Goads and their Tethers no longer can rule,
He Snorts Kicks and Tramples among the curst rout,
Who fall by his Fury or Stagger about.

O! may all such Drovers thus meet with their Fate.
Who Hamper, and Gall so, the Bull of the State.
May his Terror, thus fill them with fear, and dismay,
While the People all Chearfully Cry out, Huzza!

CPPS 5961. This print is a reissue of CPPS 5640 from 1780. LC–USZ62–45456

811

The CATCH SINGERS. Published as the Act Directs April ye 11–1782 by J Kendall Great Queen Street.

Etching 7½ x 7⅞ in.

Four men singing and drinking to celebrate their monetary gains from the war in America: Lord George Germain, Lord Richard Howe, Sir William Howe, and Lord North. See CPPS 5342 which estimates 1776 as the date of the copy in the British Museum. LC–USZ62–45458

812

The AMERICAN RATTLE SNAKE. [Gillray] Pubd. April 12th. 1782, by W. Humphrey, No. 227 Strand.

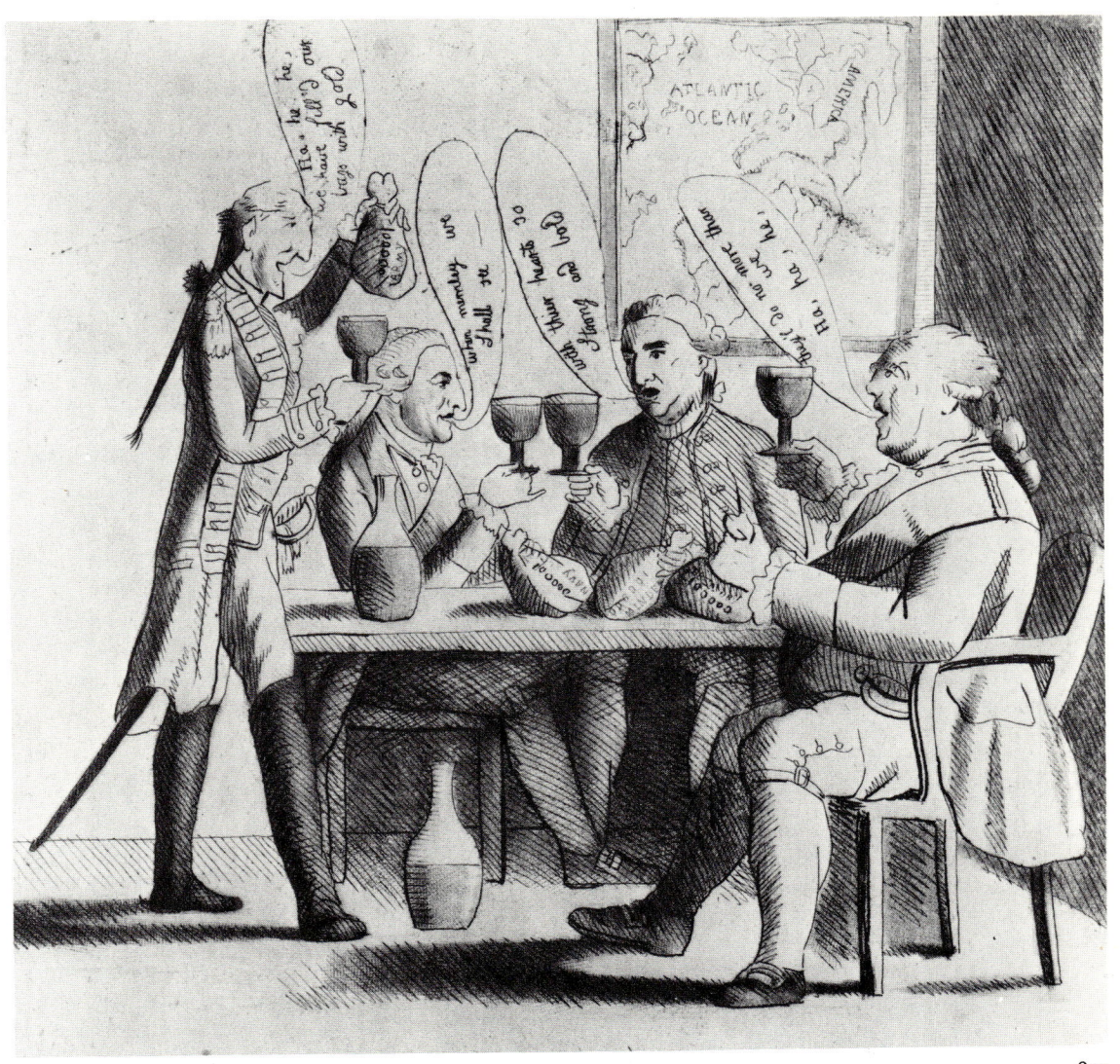

811

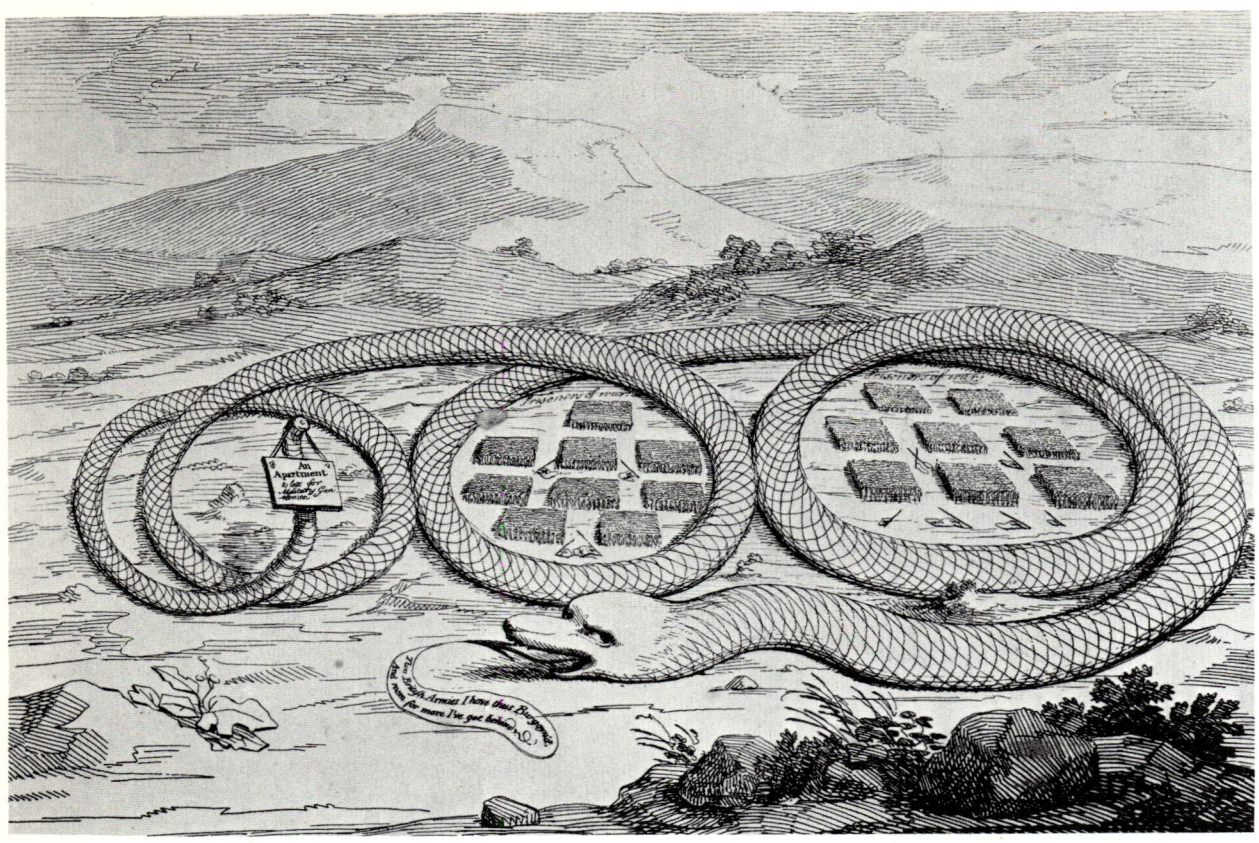

812

Etching 8½ x 12½ in. (image)

A rattlesnake, coiled around two British armies representing those of Burgoyne and Cornwallis, says, "Two British Armies I have thus Burgoyn'd And room for more I've got behind." On his tail is a sign reading, "An Apartment to lett for Military Gentlemen." Below some verse:

> Britons within the Yankeean Plains,
> Mind how ye March & Trench,
> The Serpent in the Congress reigns,
> As well as in the French.

CPPS 5973 LC–USZ62–1531

813

The POLITICAL MIRROR or an EXHIBITION of MINISTERS for April 1782. Razo Rezio inv. Crunk Fogo sculp.

Mixed method 5¾ x 9 in. (image)

The old ministers are driven into hell by the new ministers: Thurlow, Conway, Camden, Barré, Burke, Richmond, Rockingham, Fox, Wilkes, and Byng. Each makes a statement about his opposition in the past years, and General Conway says, "Your war in America I always condemned." This statement refers to his resolutions of February 22 for treating with the Americans and of February 27 for showing conquest to be impossible. The old ministers are Sandwich, Rigby, North, Mansfield, and Germain. Two devils welcome them to the pit. One holds a bottle to tempt Sandwich, and another grabs Germain. Above the two parties a winged angel flies with "The Mirror of Truth" to chase the old ministers away. Fleeing the scene is Bute riding on the back of a witch. CPPS 5982 LC–USZ62–45457

———— Another impression. In *The Westminster Magazine*, April 1782, p. 178.

814

WAR of POSTS T. Colley Fect. Pubd. by W. Richardson N.68 High Holborn London May 1, 1782.

Mixed method 9¾ x 13¾ in.

The new Ministry riding on posts as hobby horses, while the devil drives the old Ministry into hell. The new Ministry members are Pitt, Keppel, Conway, Burke, Fox, and Richmond. Old members are Nick, Sandwich, Amherst, North, and Mansfield. In the background a scaffold supports three hanging Secretaries of State: Stormont a Scot, Hillsborough an Irish peer, and George Germain of the Colonies. To the left of the Temple marked "Constitution" an American is giving another figure (probably John Bull) "Thirteen Stripes" with a lash. CPPS 5984 LC–USZ62–46093

815

PARADICE LOST. Publish'd May 10: 1782, by T.B. Freeman Strand.

Etching 9 x 13¼ in. (image)

Fox with a bunch of switches drives four of the old ministers out of the government. The figures are Bute, North, and probably Sandwich, Shelburne, or Germain. In the foreground a snake similar to the American rattlesnake in item 812 (CPPS 5973) looks on, while in the background a group of citizens enjoy the spectacle. LC–USZ62–45475

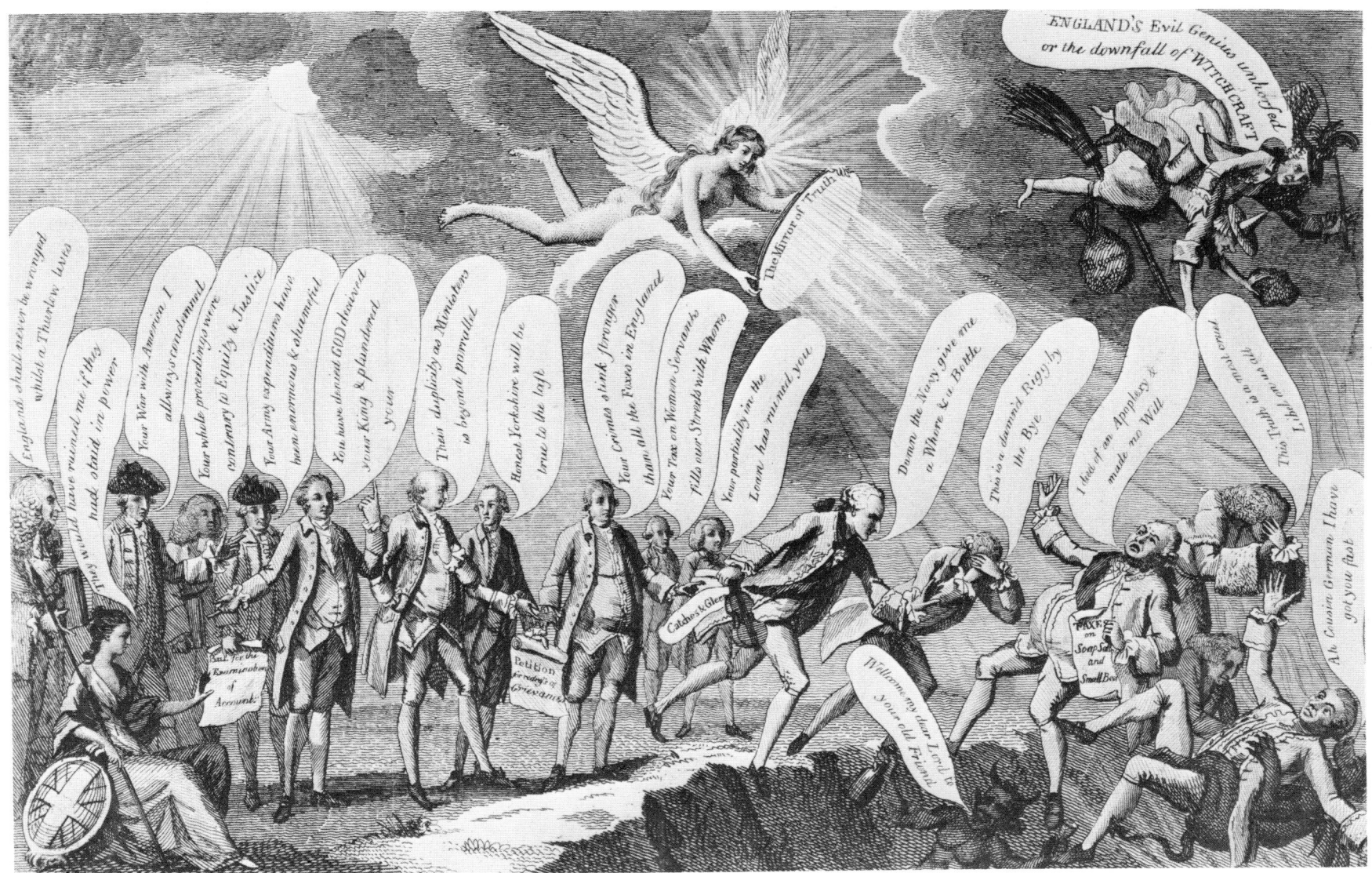

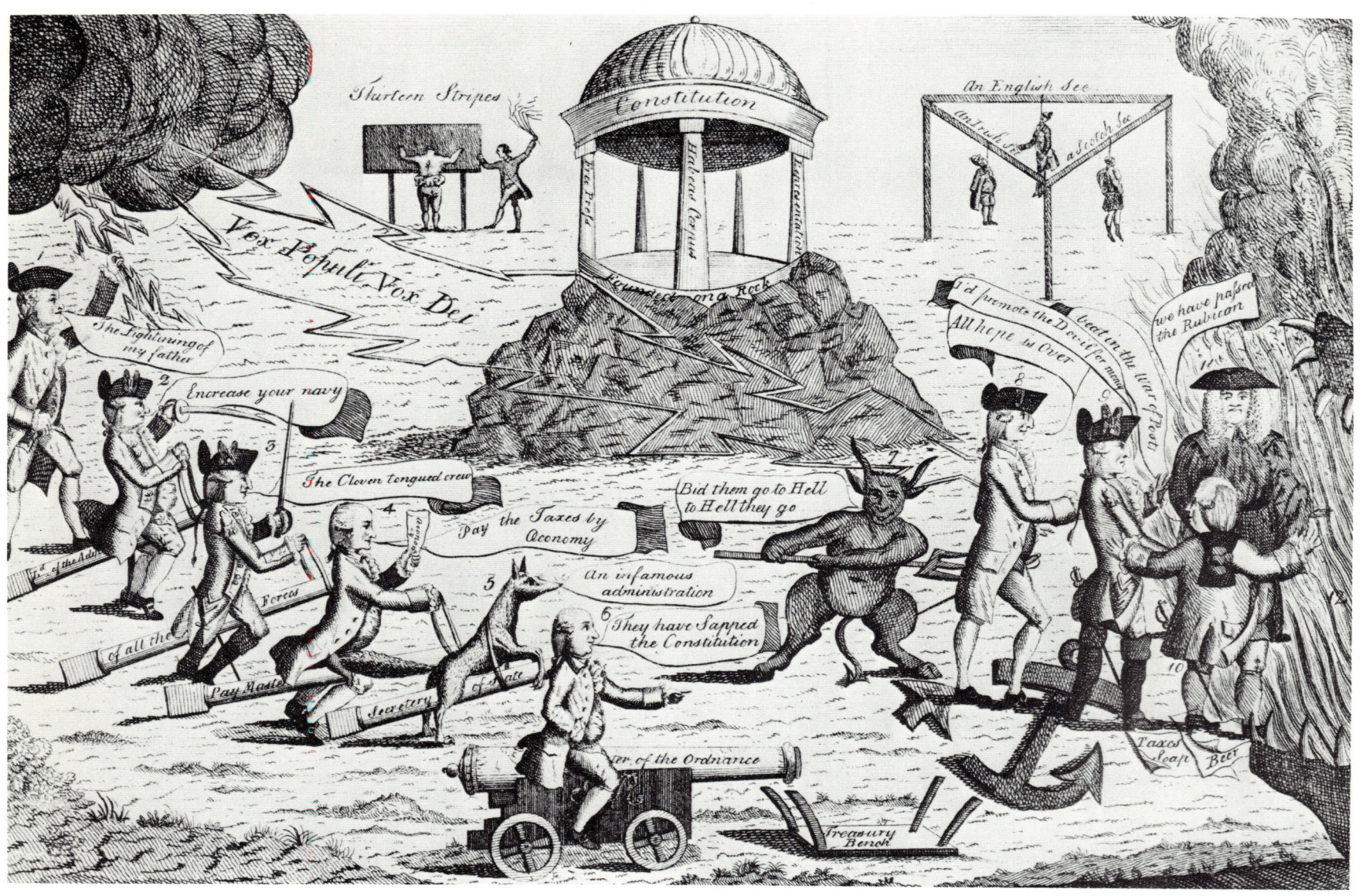

816

THE HOUR OF INSOLENCE We'll bring them at our feet! [1782?]

Pen and ink sketch 9⅝ x 13⅜ in. (image)

Lord North, other ministers, and two clergymen stand haughtily regarding a map of North America. LC–USZ62–45515

816a

THE HOUR OF HUMILIATION. How shall we repass the Rubicon. [1782?]

Pen and ink sketch 9⅝ x 13⅜ in. (image)

The same dejected ministers stand in front of the same map, while Lord North disappears into the background at the far right. On March 20, 1782, North resigned as chancellor of the exchequer and first lord of the treasury; some charge that he resigned to avoid an investigation into the conduct of the war.
LC–USZ62–45516

817

The late BOMBARDMENT of GOVERNMENT CASTLE. C. Goodnight Sculp. [Pubd May 1st 1782 by J. Barrow. Sold by E. Rich at the little Print Shop faceing Anderton's Coffee House Fleet Street. And at Mr Turners Frame maker and Print Seller, No 40. Snow hill]

Mixed method (hand colored) 9¾ x 13¾ in. (image)

The old Ministry in the King's castle and the new Ministry besieging it spit cannon balls at each other. Each missile is marked with a political issue. George III, Cornwall, North, Markham, and Germain are possible identities of the old Ministry. North says, "You plague us more than Congress." The new ministry representatives are Fox, Conway, Keppel, Burke, and Dunning. General Conway says, "Treat speedily with America." CPPS 5985
LC–USZ62–45477

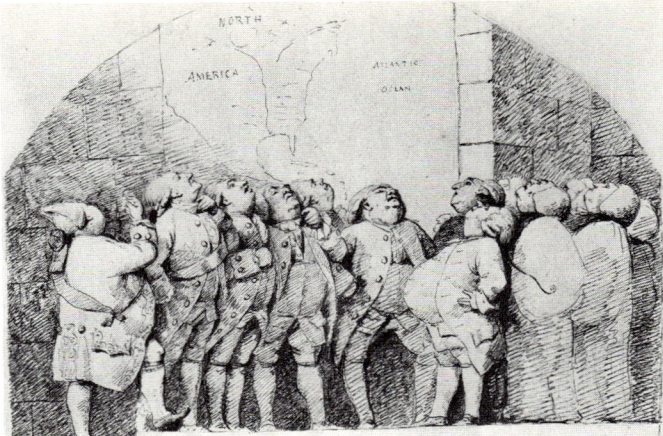
816

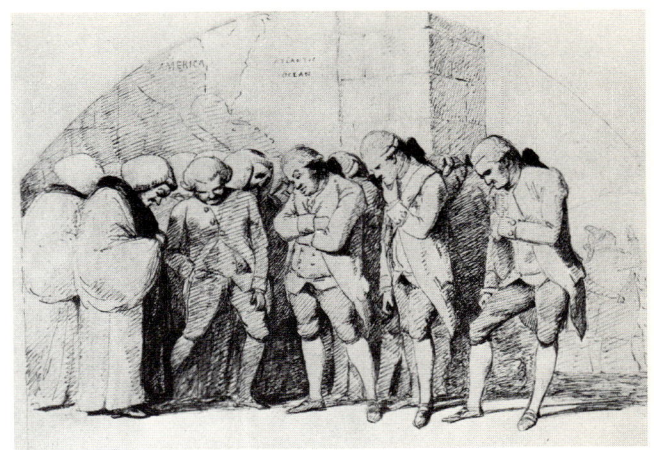
816a

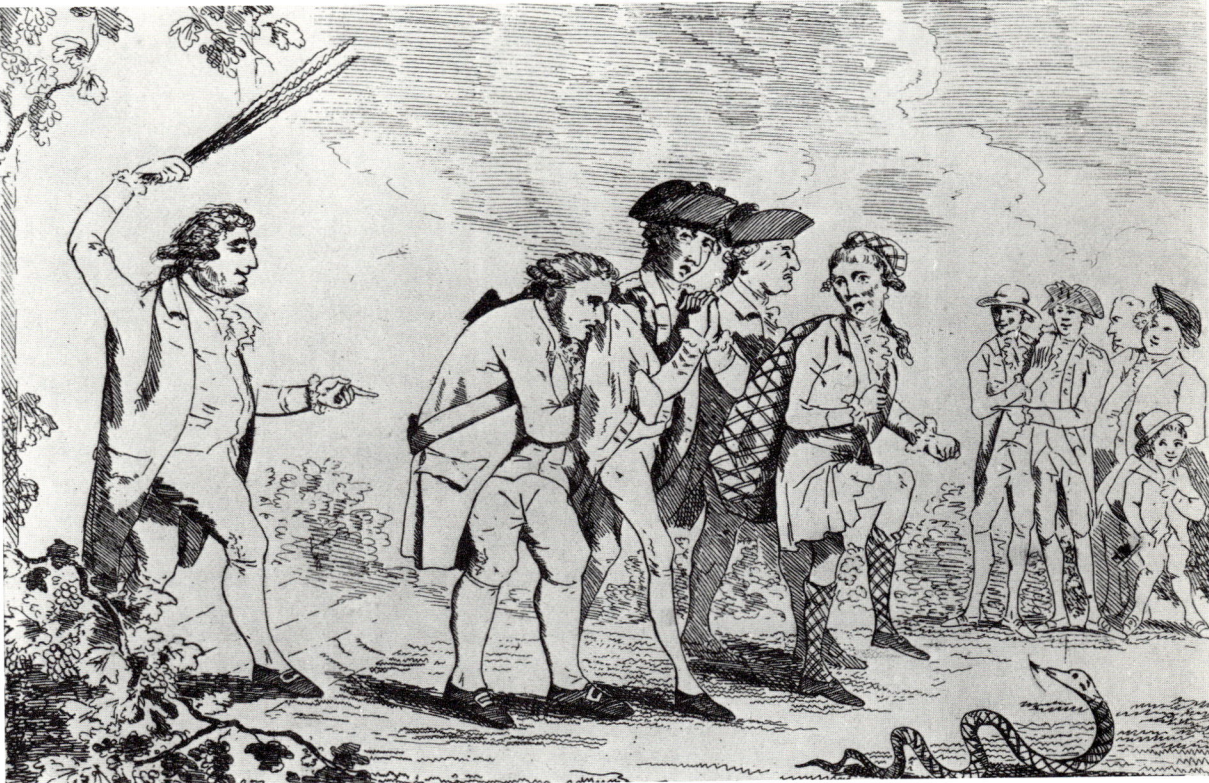
815

355

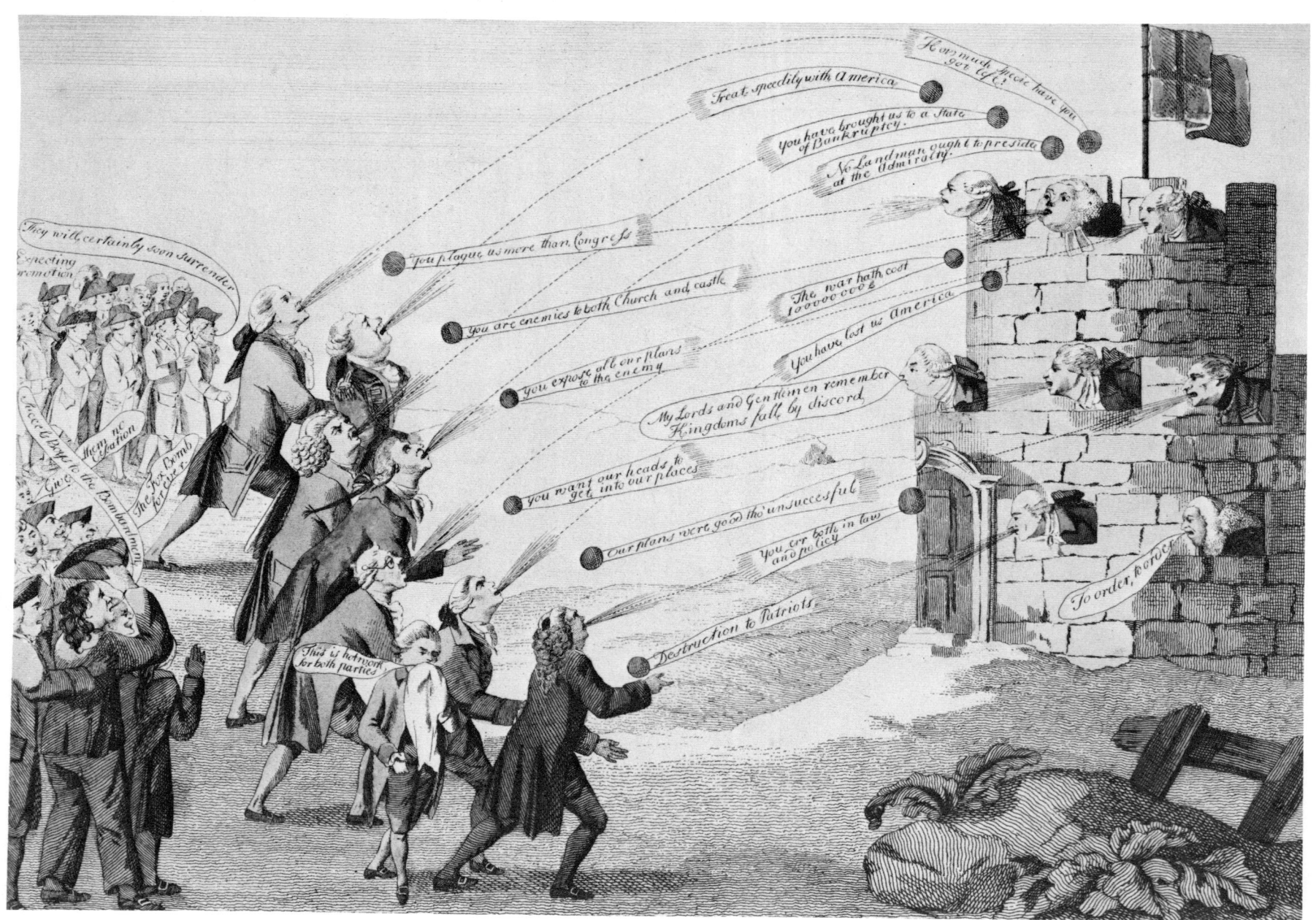

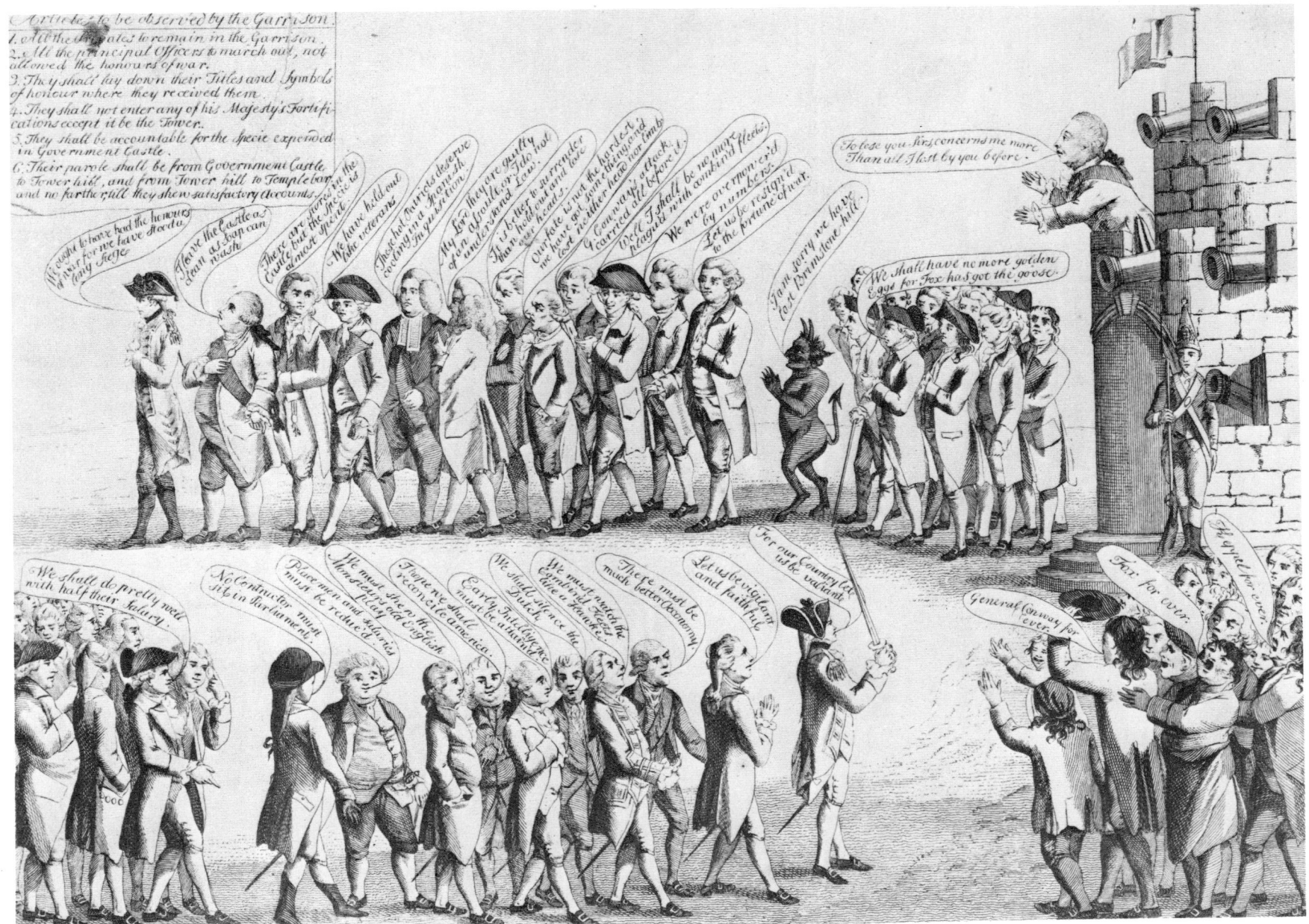

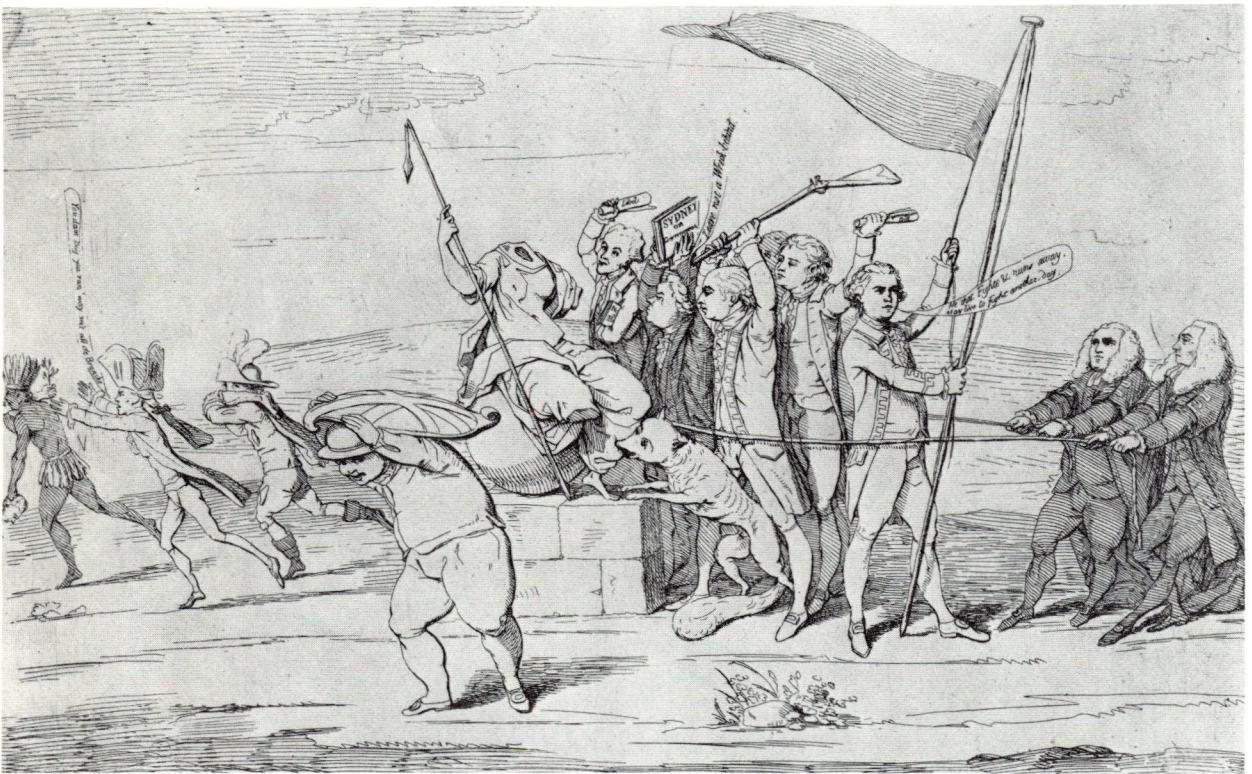
818

817a

THE SURRENDER of GOVERNMENT CASTLE, in March 1782, to the late besieging Minority. [Pubd according to Act of Parliament by J. Barrow, May ye 10th 1782. Sold by E. Rich, at the little Print Shop opposite Anderton's Coffee House Fleet Street.]

Mixed method 9⅞ x 13¾ in. (image)

The old ministers walk out of George III's castle, while the new ministers enter in the manner of a military victory procession. George III leans out of the castle and calls to his departing ministers, "To lose you Sirs, concerns me more Than all I lost by you before." Among the old ministers identified are Amherst, North, Germain, Markham, Mansfield, and Sandwich. A group of gentlemen watch the old Ministry leave and regret their loss. In the foreground, right, a crowd of commoners shout "General Conway for ever," "Fox for ever," and "Keppel for ever." The only identified member of the new Ministry is Keppel who says, "We must watch the Combin'd Fleets like a Hawke." Another says, "I hope we shall reconcile America." CPPS 5986 LC–USZ62–45459

818

BRITANIA'S ASSASSINATION. or⎯⎯⎯The Republican Amusement. [Gillray] Pubd. May 10th. 1782. by E. D'Archery St James Street.

Etching 10 x 14¼ in.

Members of the new Ministry, Fox (as a fox), Wilkes, Dunning, Richmond, Burke, and Keppel, dismantle a statue of Britannia. Thurlow and Mansfield attempt to keep the new ministers away by holding them within a rope. They represent the judiciary and the hope that the constitution and the laws will restrain Republican excesses. An American Indian, a Frenchman, a Spaniard, and a Dutchman run off with parts of the statue. CPPS 5987 LC–USZ62–45460

819

ANTICIPATION; or, the CONTRAST to the ROYAL HUNT. Publish'd May 16th. 1782. by Wm. Wells No 132 (opposite Salisbury Court) Fleet Street London. Britons fact.

Mixed method 8½ x 13½ in. (image)

A sequel to item 809 depicts the new Ministry restoring the British Empire, represented here by "the Temple of Fame." Conway sets the pillar "America" aright. "Charles Town" and "St. Vincents" are set aright also. "Eustatius" and "Rhode Island" are still on the ground, and "Tobago" is in place but not quite finished. "Gibraltar" and "Jamaica Barbadoes" still support the temple. Britannia holds an olive branch in the right foreground. Beside the temple an American Indian holding an olive branch is protected by a naval officer holding an olive branch and waving his sword at a kneeling Dutchman, while a Spaniard and Frenchman flee. Sir Guy Carleton shoots down an eagle from a window in the temple, and the eagle falls on the fleeing Frenchman. Sandwich is pictured as a balladsinger and North as a laundrywoman. Lord Rockingham plays oculist to George III, removing a film from his eyes. This action results in the King selling his hunting regalia and returning to matters of state. Lord Hertford is reluctant to surrender his keys of office, and Germain runs to him for sympathy. CPPS 5988 LC–USZ62–45461

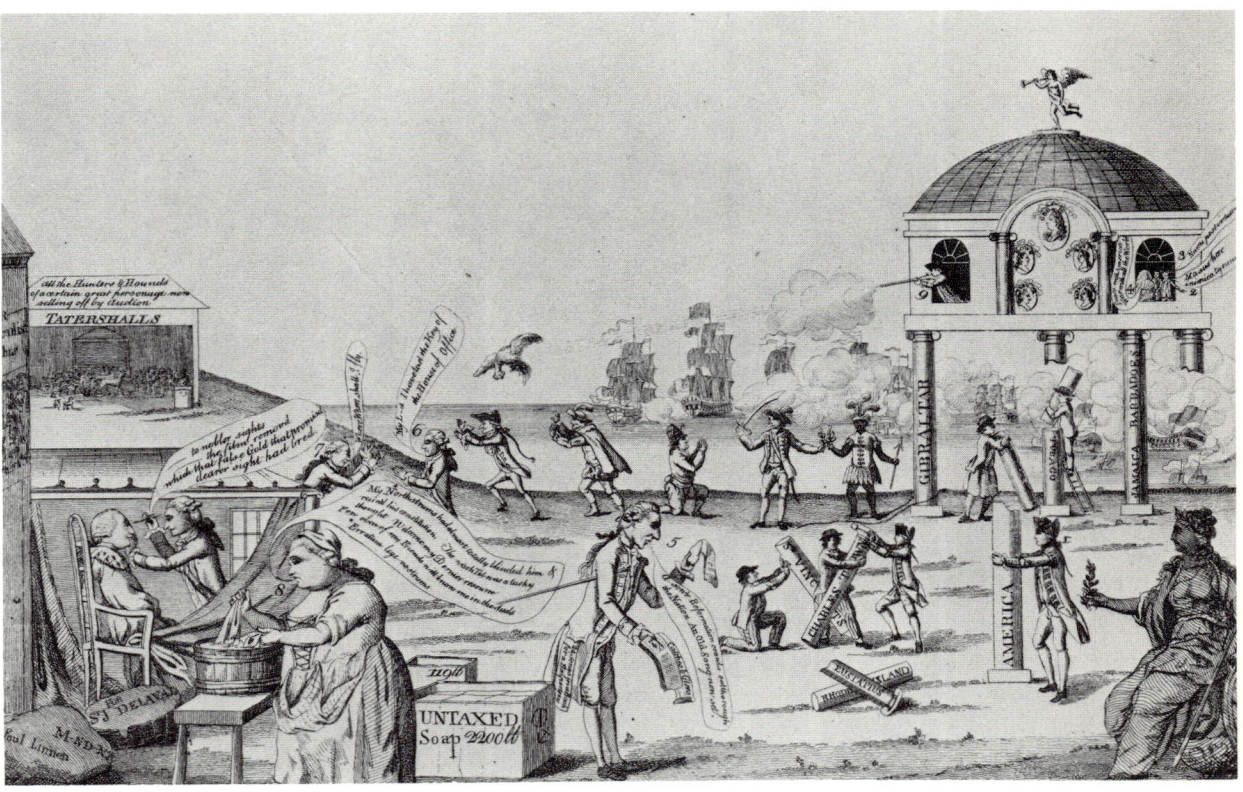

819

820

The RECONCILIATION between BRITANIA and her daughter AMERICA. Pub by T. Colley No. 5 Acorn Court Rolls Buildings Fetter Lane Old England Pub by W Richardson May 11, 1782 N. 68 High Holborn.

Etching 8 1/16 x 12 7/8 in. (image)

An American Indian with staff and liberty cap rushes to the arms of Britannia, while a Spaniard and a Frenchman try to pull America

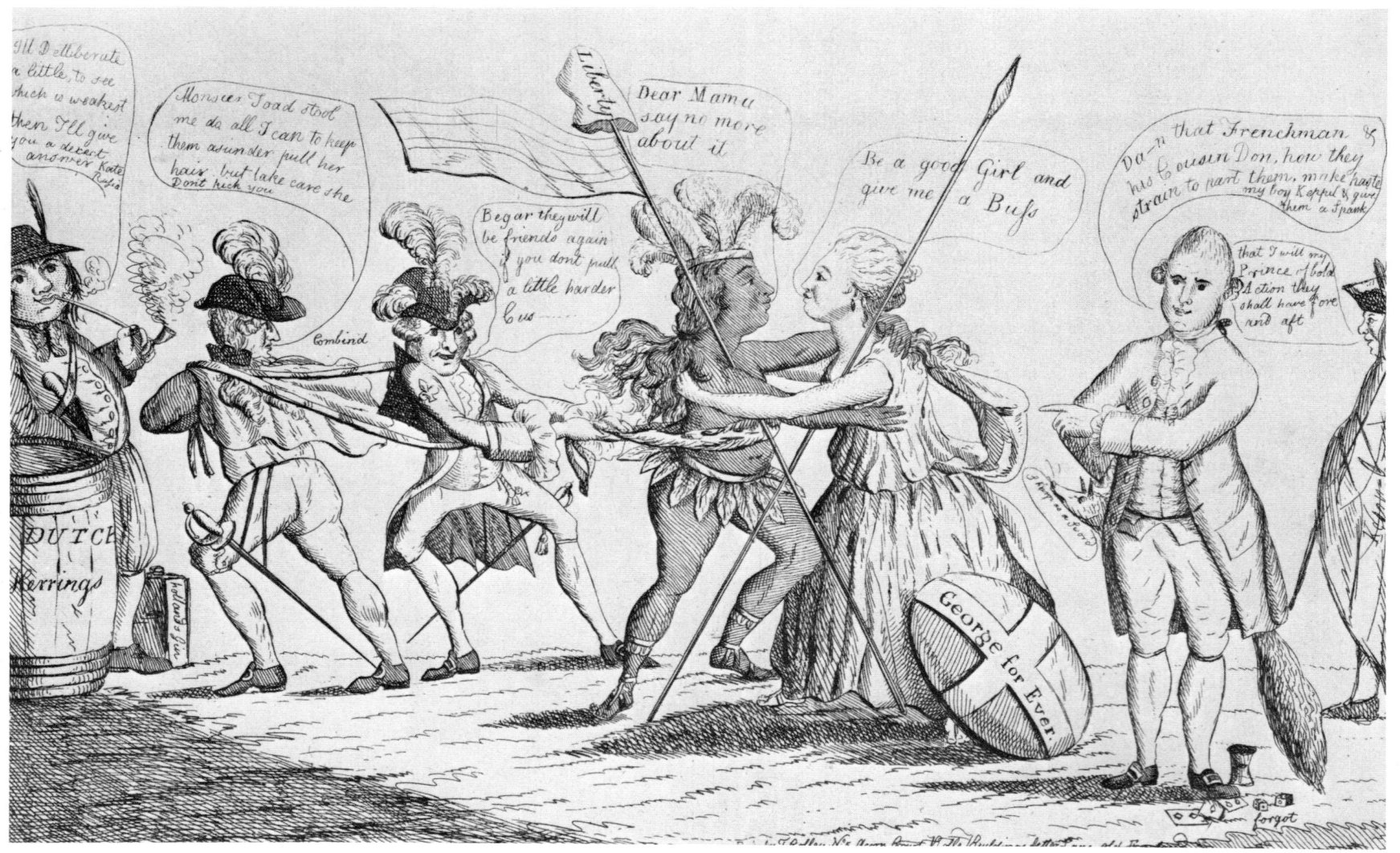

away. A Dutchman looks on saying, "I'll delliberate a little, to see which is weakest then I'll give you a direct answer Kate Russia." Fox and Keppel comment that the continental enemy should be punished. The artist of this cartoon seems uninformed about recent events. A chance for reconciliation between England and her former Colonies was very remote. The Dutchman could not consult with Catherine of Russia about participation in the Armed Neutrality League or the alliance with Spain and France because Holland and Britain were already at war. Beneath the print is a short poem:

1
A curse upon all Artifice
May Briton never thrive

2
While Roguish Minis—rs they keep
to Eat them up alive

3
By Lots they sell oh Dam—em Well
Each place we put our trust in

4
Cut them off short twill make good sport
Whilst honest men are thrust in.

CPPS 5989 LC–USZ62–1532

821

THE BRITISH LION engaging FOUR POWERS. Pubd. by J. Barrow June 14th. 1782. Sold by Richardson Print Seller, N.68 High Holborn.
Etching 9 x 14½ in.

The British lion faces a spaniel (Spain), a fighting cock (France), a rattlesnake (America), and a pug dog (Holland). From the corner nearest the lion a fox representing Charles Fox says, "I counsel your Majesty to give Monsieur the first gripe." Below a verse:

Behold the Dutch and Spanish Currs,
Perfidious Gallus in his Spurs.
And Rattlesnake with head upright,
The British Lion join to fight;
He scorns the Bark, the Hiss, the Crow,
That he's a Lion soon they'll know.

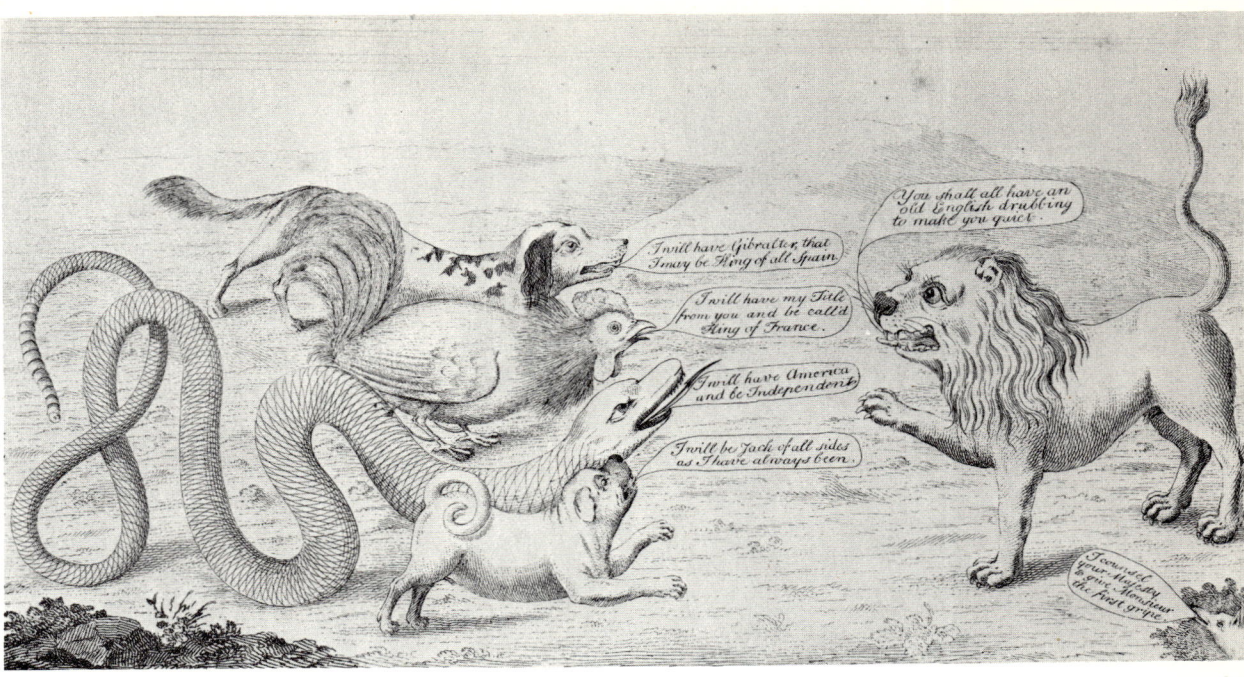

821

The spaniel says, "I will have Gibralter, that I may be King of all Spain." The cock says, "I will have my Title from you and be call'd King of France." The snake "will have America and be Independent" while the pug "will be Jack of all sides as I have always been." CPPS 6004 LC–USZ62–1533

822

THE STATE COOKS MAKING PEACE———PORRIDGE. Pubd. July 6th. 1782 by E. Hedges No 92 Cornhill.
Mixed method 9¾ x 13¾ in.

Keppel, Fox, Conway, perhaps Shelburne, and Richmond assemble a porridge of peace to offer the allies. An American Indian, a fat Dutchman, a skinny Frenchman, and a Spanish cavalier all avoid the offering. The American is closest to accepting but insists that his allies accompany him. The Dutchman has thrown his away, and the Frenchman says it is not good. The Spaniard will not consider it until he has Gibraltar. Below is a verse:

The State Cooks a making Peace____Porridge are found
Which they hand to our different Enimies round.
But they all seem averse, and will not hear Reason
And swear that it wants more Ingredients & Season,
Ah! what can the Cooks do in such a hard case?
If such folks will not eat tho! F-x has said grace.
Why give them what obstinate Children deserve
Beat them well, & if they wont eat it then let em Starve.

The new Ministry was faced with many dilemmas in its efforts to secure peace. It wanted to treat with America separately, but America had agreed to consult with the allies. Spain wished to continue the war until Gibraltar was hers, and thus America and France had

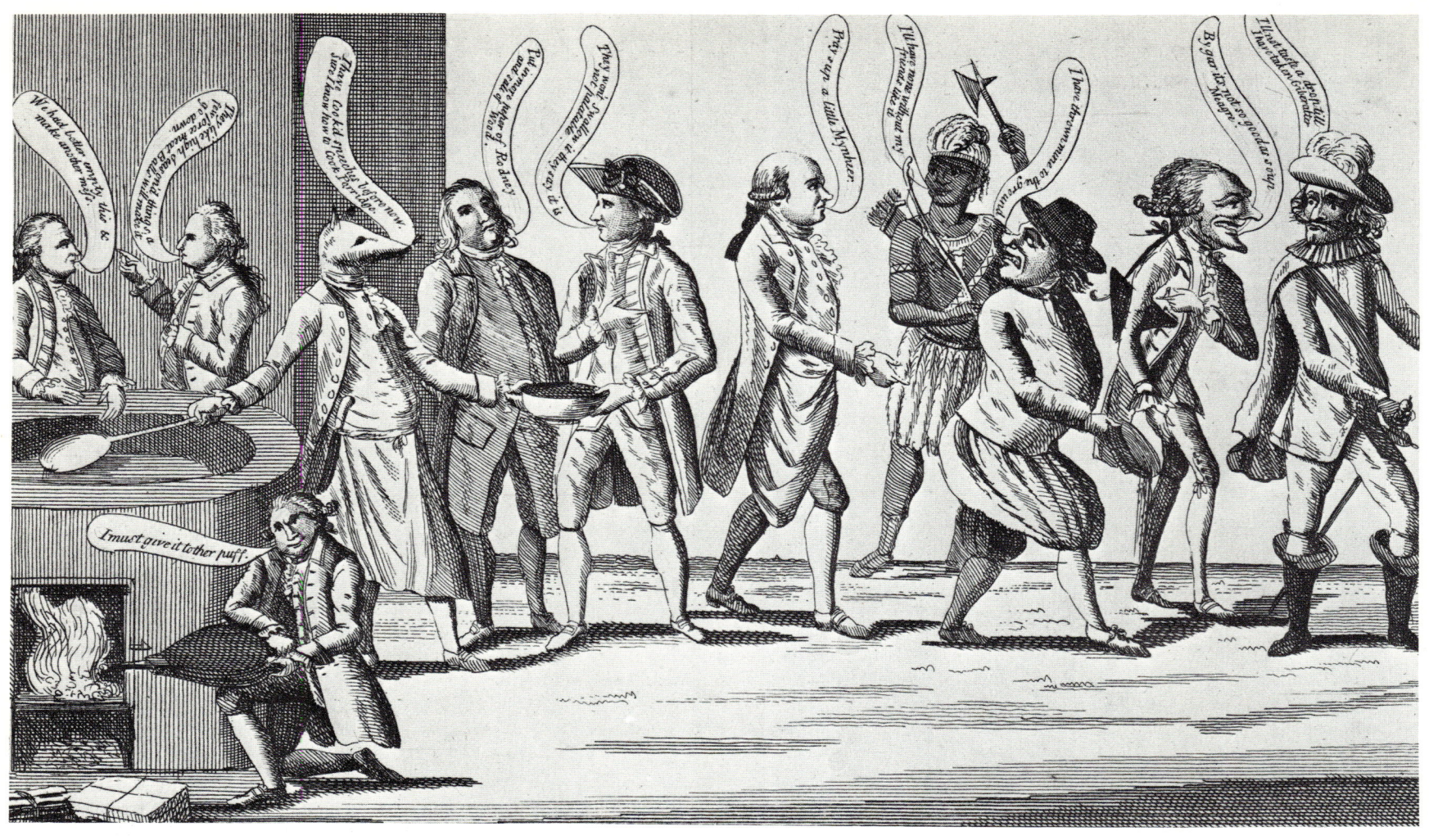

to wait for Spain. This cartoon predates October 5, 1782, when John Jay gave Richard Oswald a draft of the preliminary treaty which helped bring France and Spain into peace negotiations. It accurately shows America hesitating to follow the European allies when England is offering peace. CPPS 6009
LC–USZ62–1534

823

The HORRORS of WAR a VISION Or a Scene in the Tragedy of K: Richd: 3. London, Published as the Act directs, Decr. 1st, 1782, by D. Wilson.

Mixed method (hand colored) 8½ x 12½ in. (image)

Two British ministers see a vision of a maimed America, represented by an Indian woman with a knife in her breast, standing on a cloud interwoven with dead children, swords, knives, and bayonets. The two statesmen are North and probably Sandwich or Germain. Britannia looks on saying, "Oh I have drank of the deadly pois'ned cup administered by cor-

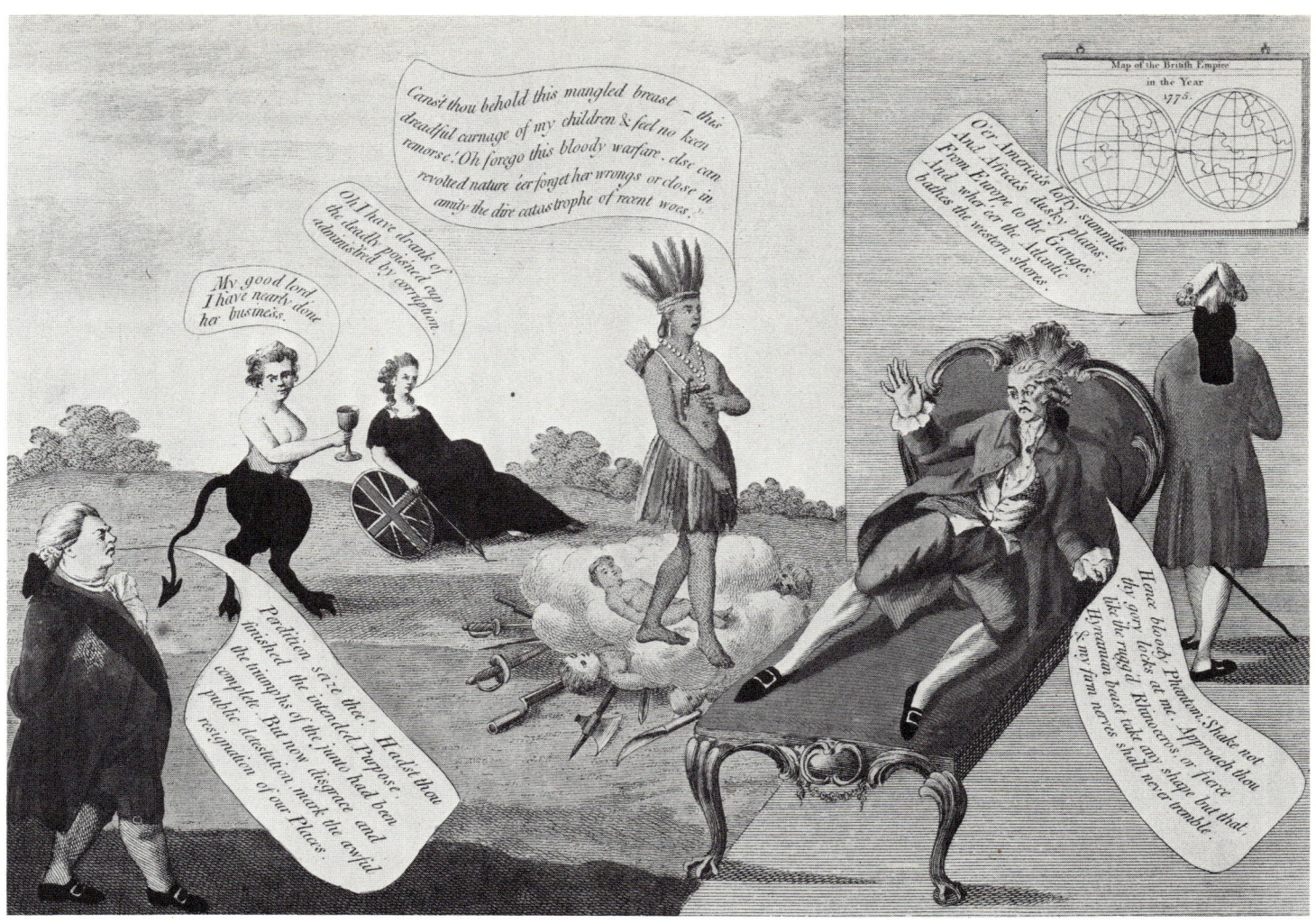

823

ruption." Concurrent with an end to the old Ministry and the end of hostilities in America, a large amount of literature concerning ministerial corruption and savage war tactics emerged in England. This cartoon is one of many which condemned the North Government. On Indian atrocities, see items 725 and 764. CPPS 6024 LC-USZ62-1537

824

The Habeas Corpus, or The Wild Geese flying away with Fox to America. No: 9 Pubd. by J. Barrow August. 27. 1782. No: 84 Dorset Street, Salisbury Court Fleet Street.

Etching (hand colored) 9⅞ x 13¾ in.

Seven geese fly Charles Fox, represented by a fox, to America because he favored recognition of America. The fox says, "I hope they will bear me safe to the dear Independent Congress." The Geese say: "To America he shall go for his heart is there," "My advice is to drop him in the Atlantic," "He is fitter to sit in Congress than in a British Parliament," "He bids fairer now to be the man in the moon than The

363

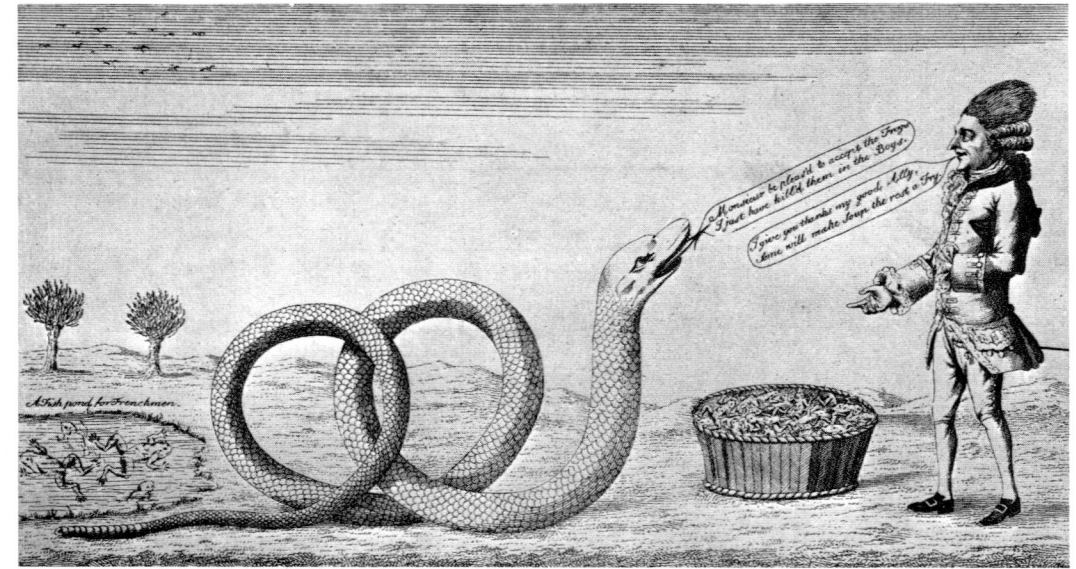

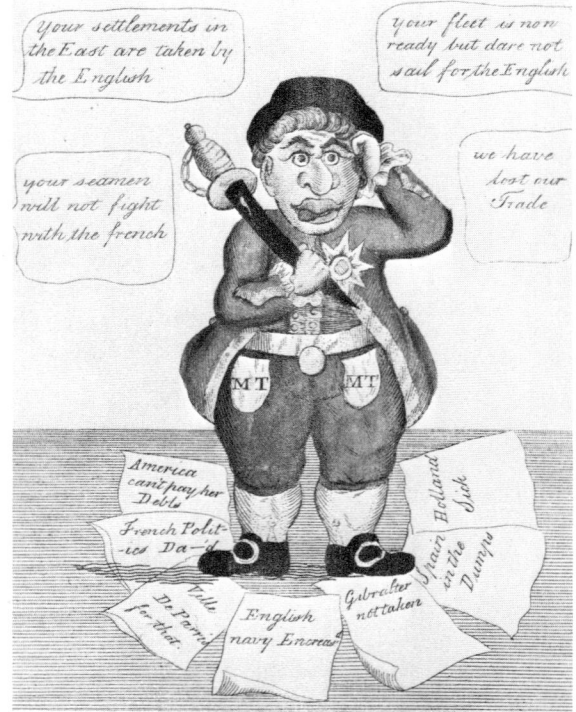

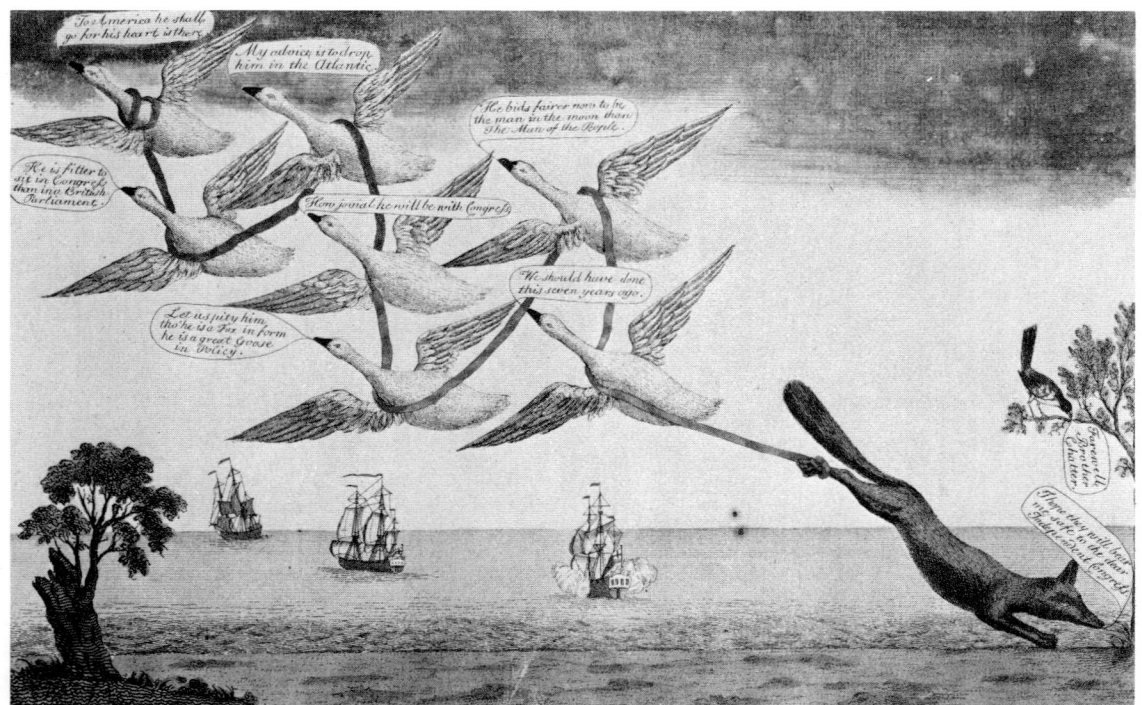

Man of the People," "How jovial he will be with Congress," "Let us pity him tho' he is a Fox in form he is a great Goose in Policy," and "We should have done this seven years ago." CPPS 6029 LC–USZ62–1535

825

PRINCE STADHOLD-R Resuming his Deliberation. Pub. by T. Colley Oct 24. 1782 London.
Etching (hand colored) 7⅝ x 6 in.

A British caricature of the problems besetting William V of Holland shows an ignorant-looking, fat man with empty pockets, holding a sword by the blade. Voices and messages tell him that the war is going badly for him, and one paper says that "America can't pay her Debts." CPPS 6038 LC–USZ62–45462

826

THE AMERICAN RATTLESNAKE presenting Monsieur his Ally a Dish of Frogs. No 10. Pubd by J Barrow. Novr. 8. 1782. N 84 Dorset Street, Salisbury Court, Fleet Street.
Etching 9¾ x 14½ in.

A plea to separate America and France, this print shows the American rattlesnake saying to a Frenchman, "Monsieur be pleas'd to accept the Frogs I just have kill'd them in the Bogs." Below a poem:

> O Britons be wise
> And part these Allies,
> Or drive them both into the Bogs;
> I think it is fit
> They both should submit
> To Old England, or live upon Frogs.

N.B. The Rattlesnake is a Character chosen by America.

CPPS 6039 LC–USZ62–1536

827

WONDERS WONDERS WONDERS & WONDERS. Dedicated to the Wonderfull Wonderfull Wonderer. Publish'd as the Act directs Novr. 9 1782 by I Langham print.

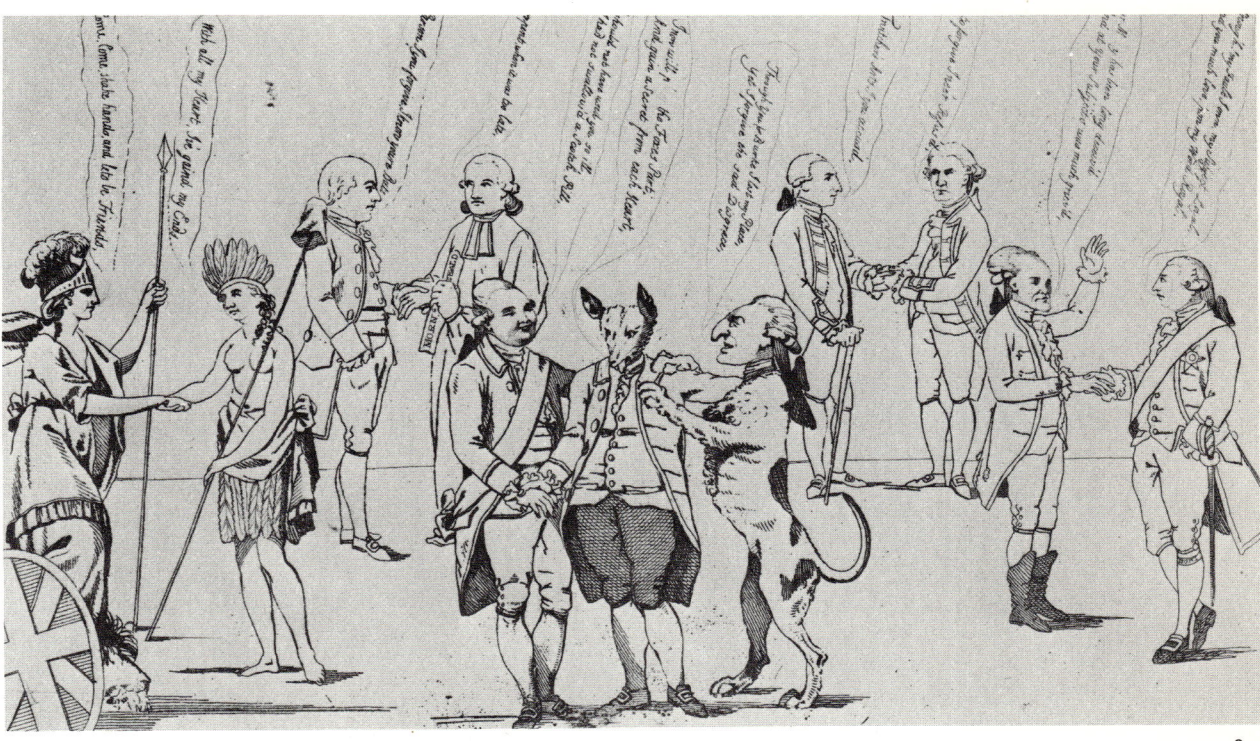

827

Etching (hand colored) 8¾ x 14½ in. (image)

Enemies stand improbably conversing together: Fox between Shelburne and Denbigh in the center, Britannia and America, Wilkes and George III, Richmond and Bate, Palliser and Keppel. An early impression of CPPS 6162.

———A later impression of the previous engraving. Dialog by the characters is filled in, and the imprint reads, "Sold by W Humphrey, 1783." Britannia says to America, "Come, Come, shake hands, and lets be Friends." The reply, "With all my Heart, I've gain'd my Ends." CPPS 6162
LC–USZ62–45466

828

LABOUR IN VAIN or let them tug & be Da__nd. Pub. by W. Richardson Novr 27. 1782 near

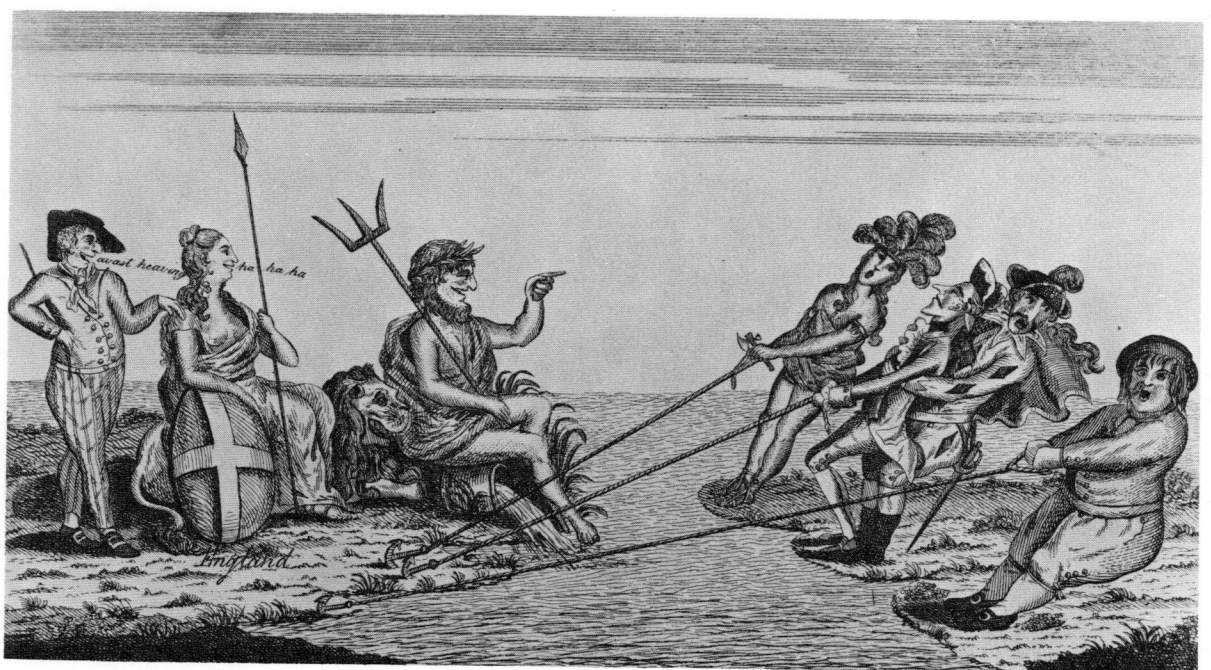

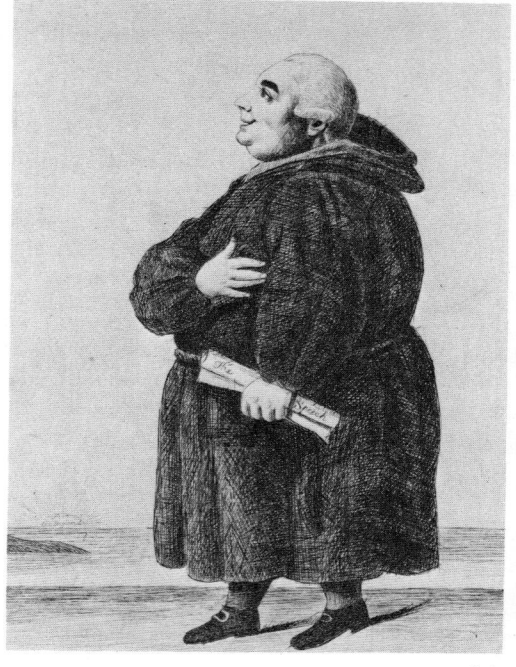

828

Surry Street Strand. Pub as the Act directs Nov: 27. 1782 by T. Colley. London.
Etching 7⅜ x 13¼ in. (image)

A tug of war in which a British sailor, Britannia, the English lion, and Neptune laugh at the four allies. An American Indian woman, a skinny Frenchman, a Spanish cavalier, and a fat Dutchman try to pull their lands toward England across a body of water. Below the picture a poem:

> Four Foes to old England have Wickedly Join'd
> To run with old England Away
> Old Neptune declares it is not to his mind
> And Brittania cries Stay you fools Stay.
>
> You may tug, & may tug, & strive all that you can
> And put your selves into great pain
> While Freedom & Honour is fixt on our Plan
> You will find it all Labour in Vain

Admiral Elliot had smashed the Spanish floating batteries at Gibraltar on September 13, 1782, and on October 14th, Admiral Howe ran the blockade and reinforced the garrison. The Spaniards lost all desire to continue the fight, and therefore the allies were all anxious to treat with England. CPPS 6040 LC–USZ62–34865

829

The Shell-born Jes__t. Ignatius Loyola Invt, Pubd, Decr. 18th, 1782.
Line engraving 7½ x 5¼ in.

On December 13, 1782, Shelburne refused to define the status of the former Colonies as stated in the treaty with America. He stands in monk's robes (thus the pun on jes__t, Jesuit), and in the background the setting sun is labeled "Poor Old England." CPPS 6045 LC–USZ62–45463

———— Another impression (poorly hand colored).

830

The BELLIGERENT PLENIPO'S. T: Colley, Fect: Pub by W Richardson N68 High Holborn. Decr. 8, 1782 as the Act Directs.
Mixed method (hand colored) 8½ x 12¾ in. (image)

Representatives of the five countries stand on five islands in the sea. George III with pieces of anatomy from his European rivals says, "I give them Independence." France with an arm missing says, "I must have Canada and Grenada for my Arm," a fat Dutchman says, "I insist on Eustatia & Ceylon for my foot," and a Spaniard says, "By Saint Anthony I must have Gibraltar for my Leg." An American Indian woman with staff, flag, liberty cap, and half of George III's crown stands on an island with pine trees smiling because "I have got all I wanted Empire!" CPPS 6051 LC–USZ62–1538 is the negative number for black-and-white prints.

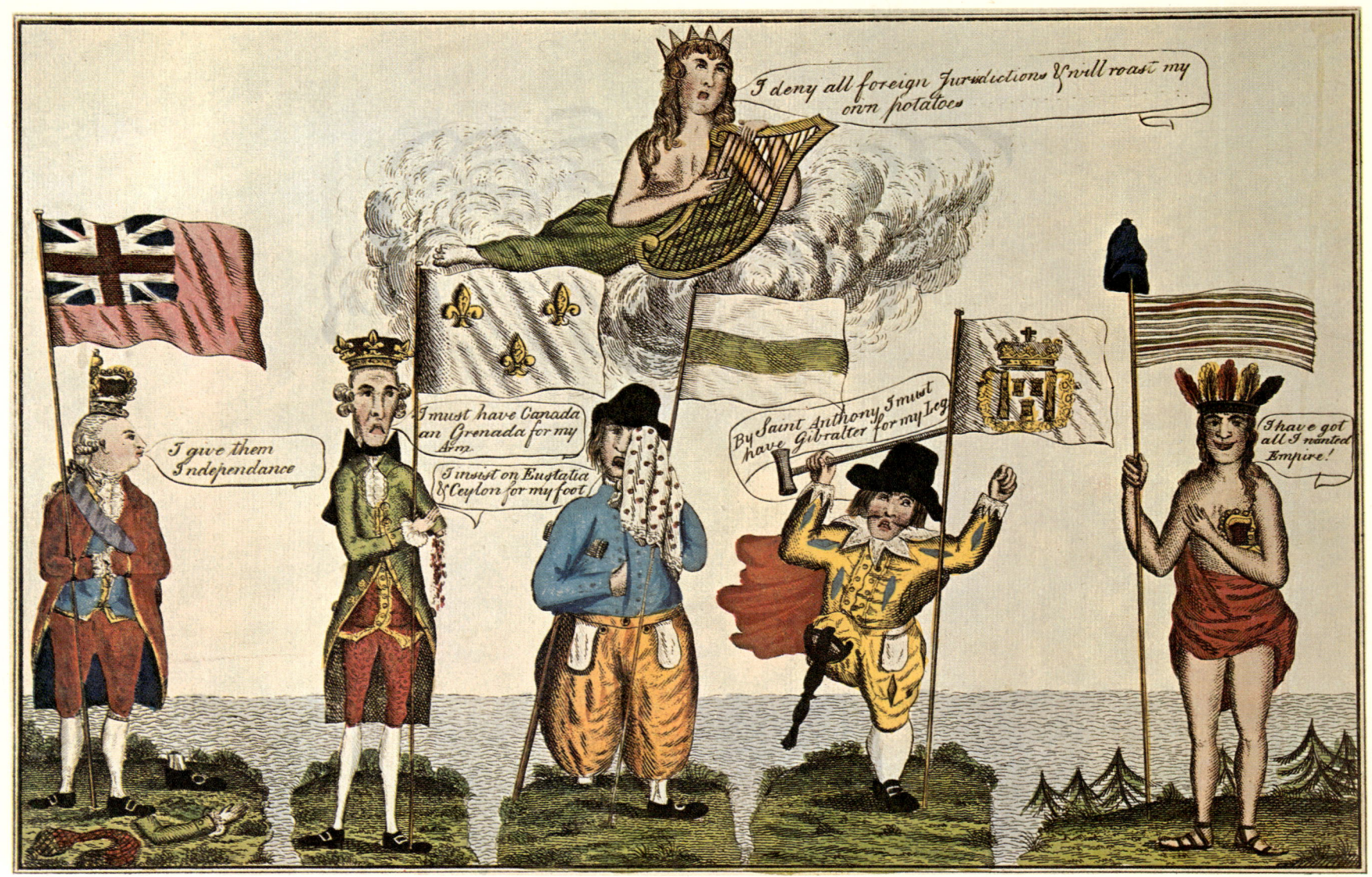

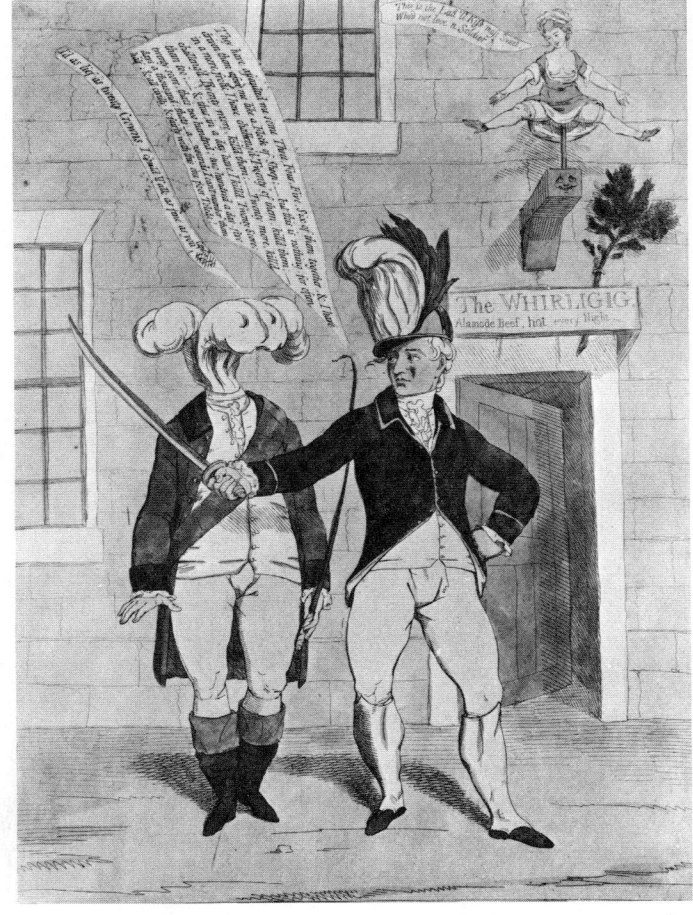

831

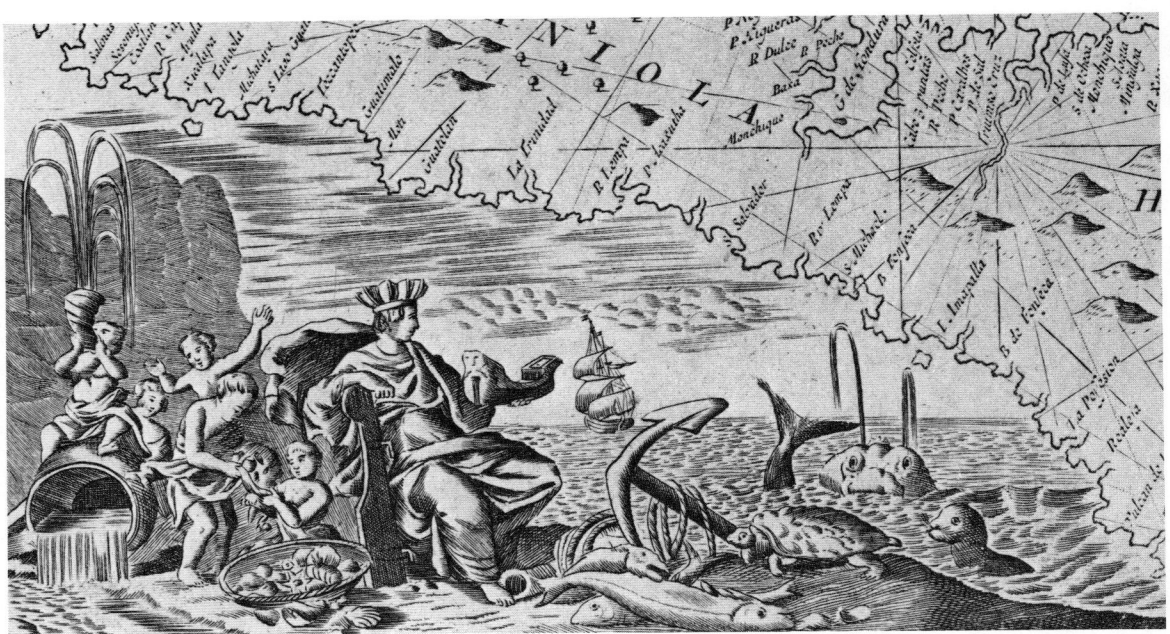

832

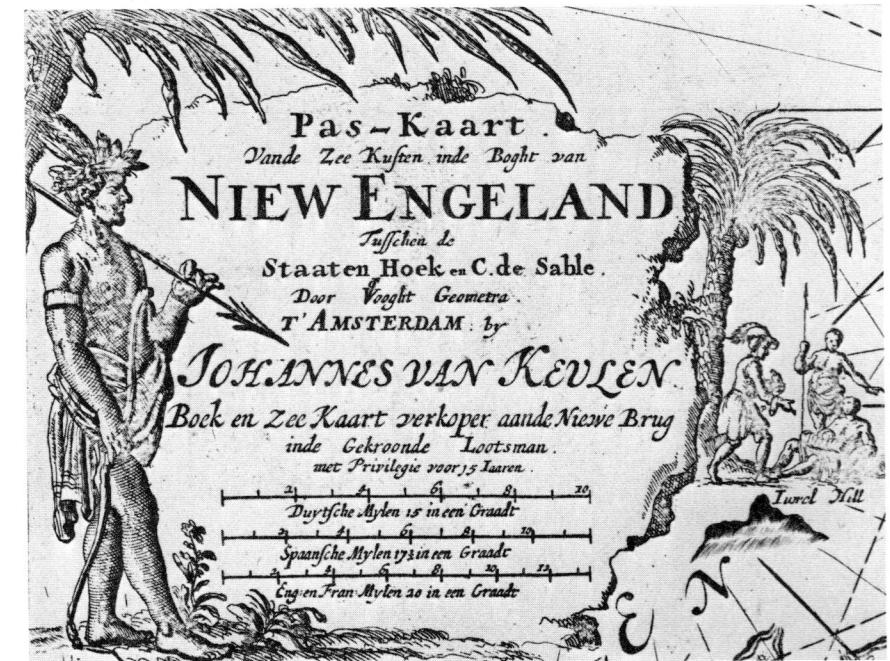

835

831

THE THUNDERER. [Pubd Augt 20th 1782 by Eh D'Achery St. James Street.]
Etching (hand colored) 12½ x 9 in. (image)
Col. Banastre Tarleton brags to the Prince of Wales about his war exploits in front of a bawdy house. CPPS 6116 LC–USZ62–45464

832

[An allegory describing America—a cartouche, 1782]
Etching 5 x 11 in. (image)
An American Indian watches an approaching ship. On a map of the West Indies in Voogt, *De Nieuwe Groote Lichtende Zee-Fakkel* (Amsterdam, 1782), no. 28. LC–USZ62–46082

833

[Two American Indians—a cartouche, 1782]
Etching 4¾ x 7 in. (image)
Two American Indians lean on a cartouche of a map of the Carolina shores in Voogt, *De Nieuwe Groote Lichtende Zee-Fakkel* (Amsterdam, 1782), no. 33.

834

[Two American Indians—a cartouche, 1782]
Etching 4 x 6½ in. (image)
Two Indians lean on a cartouche of a map of the Virginia coast in Voogt, *De Nieuwe Groote Lichtende Zee-Fakkel* (Amsterdam, 1782), no. 34. The man holds a banner, and the woman holds a parrot and an anchor.

835

[An American Indian with harpoon and two Indians with a European—a cartouche, 1782]
Etching 5 x 6½ in. (image)
A white man converses with two Indians under a palm tree, and a larger figure of an Indian with bow, arrows, and a feathered headdress faces right on a map of "Niew Engeland" in Voogt, *De Nieuwe Groote Lichtende Zee-Fakkel* (Amsterdam, 1782), no. 37. LC–USZ62–46083

836

[Indians and white men working together—a cartouche, 1782]
Etching 3 x 8 in. (image)
Two men work to secure a crate, and two others exchange money for goods. On a scale of distance used for a map entitled "Pas Caarte vande Noorder Zee culten van America" in Voogt, *De Nieuwe Groote Lichtende Zee-Fakkel* (Amsterdam, 1782), no. 42. LC–USZ62–46084

837

[Men hunting bears—a cartouche, 1782]
Etching 5 x 6 in. (image)
A man in furs with bow and arrow shoots a big bear with cubs. Two others with harpoons look around the cartouche of a map entitled "Pas Caarte vande Noorder Zee culten van America" in Voogt, *De Nieuwe Groote Lichtende Zee-Fakkel* (Amsterdam, 1782), no. 42.

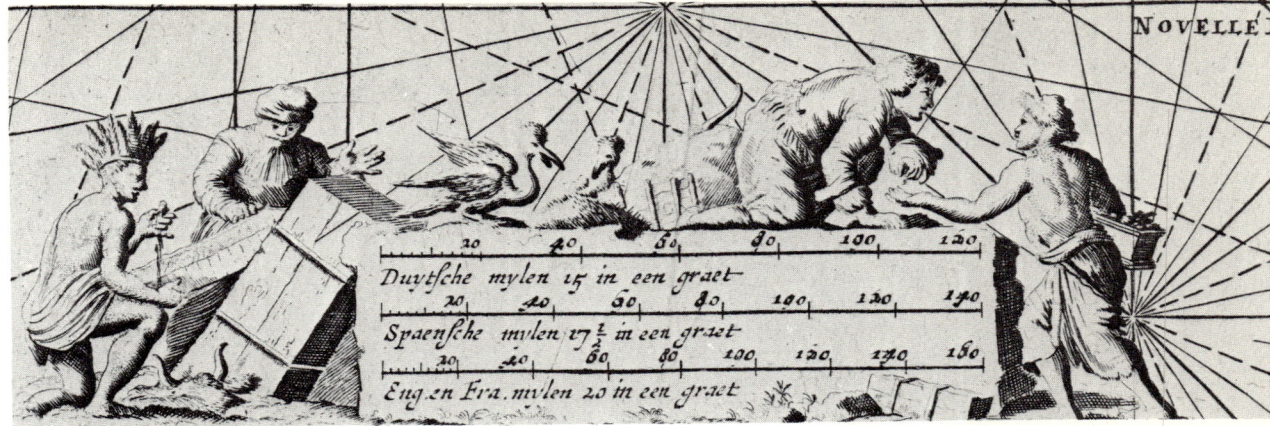
836

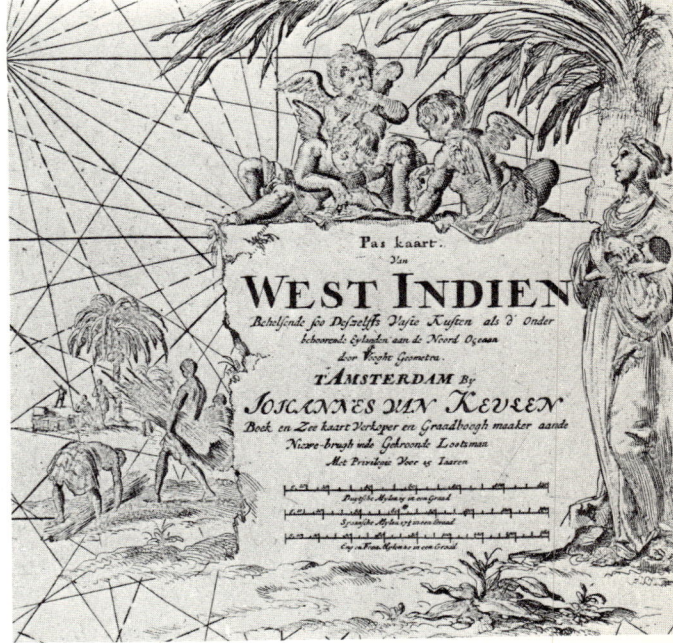
838

838

[Scene from the West Indies—a cartouche, Gerard Hulst van Keulen, 1782]
Etching 7½ x 7¾ in. (image)

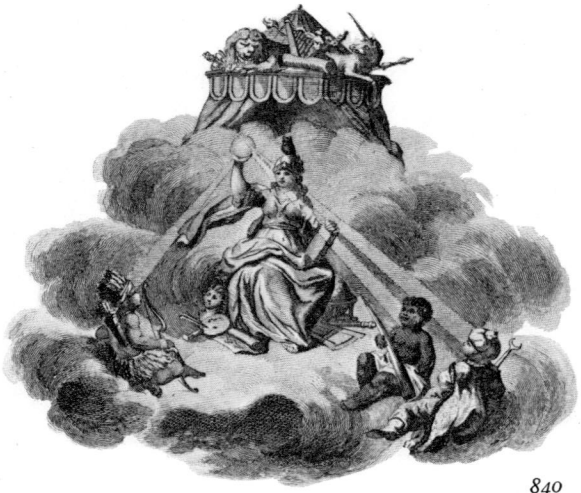

840

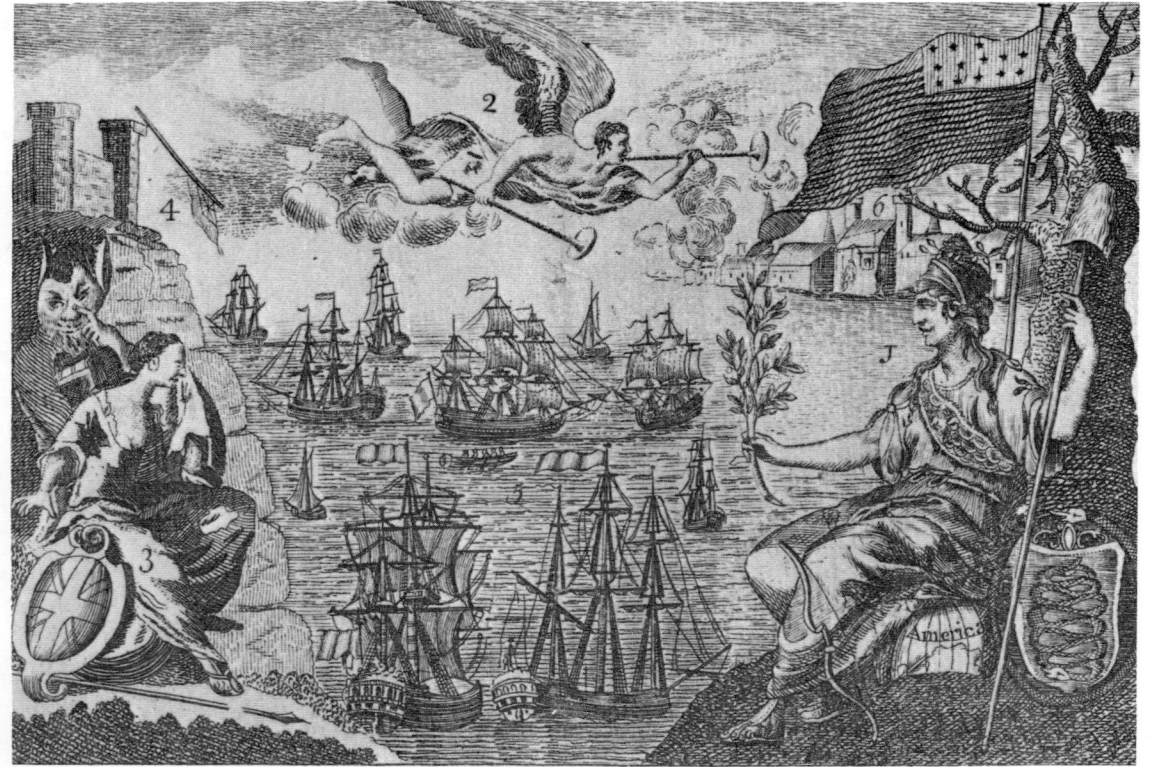

839

To the right of the title a woman nurses a child, cherubs play on top, and to the left, men harvest cane. On a map of the West Indies and shores of North and South America. From Voogt, *De Nieuwe Groote Lichtende Zee-Fakkel* (Amsterdam, 1782), no. 1. LC–USZ62–46081

839

AMERICA TRIUMPHANT and BRITANNIA in DISTRESS. [1782]

Etching 4⅝ x 6⅞ in. (image)

The "Explanation" below describes the print:

I America sitting on that quarter of the globe with the Flag of the United States displayed over her head; holding in one hand the Olive branch, inviting the ships of all nations to partake of her commerce; and in the other hand supporting the Cap of Liberty. II Fame proclaiming the joyous news to all the world. III Britannia weeping at the loss of the trade of America, attended with an evil genius. IV The British flag struck, on her strong Fortresses. V French, Spanish, Dutch, &c shipping in the harbours of America. VI A view of New-York, wherein is exhibited the Trator Arnold, taken with remorse for selling his country and Judas like hanging himself.

LC–USZ62–45922

──────── Another impression. In *Weatherwise's Town and Country Almanack*, 1782, frontispiece. Fielding, 1776

840

[Ornament for the title page of *The European Magazine* from 1782 until 1789] Seally Script. Bayly Sculpt.

Mixed method 3¾ x 3½ in. (image)

The goddess Europe sits on her throne and uses a lens to divert light down to an Indian, representing America, a Negro representing Africa, and a Turk representing Asia. The latter three continents are pictured as children and are seated at Europe's feet. LC–USZ62–45416

841

L'ANGLAIS CORRIGÉ COMME UN ENFANT. I. l'Anglais recevant la Correction de l'Amériquain, 2. demande grace a main jointe tendis qu'un Espagnol 3. lui tient la chemise un Français 4. se tenant le ventre a deux mains s'étouffe de rire 5. l'Hollandois se reposent tranquilement sur son commerce narque l'Anglois en lui montrant les cornes. [178?]

Etching (hand colored) 8½ x 10¾ in.

An American whips the naked buttocks of a fat Englishman with two bundles of switches, while a Frenchman, a Spaniard, and a Dutchman look on. LC–USZ62–17286

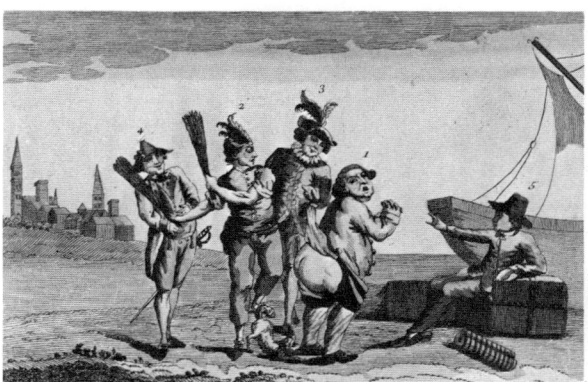
841

842

The Monument of Major André. Published as the Act directs by S A Cumberlege Jany: 1st: 1783 [1782]

Line engraving 6⅝ x 4¼ in. (image)

On top of the sepulcher Britannia weeps. On the sarcophagus a tableau portrays the capture of André and a messenger taking the note to Washington. From *The Universal Magazine*, December 1782, p. 329. LC–USZ62–45196

843

[An allegory of America at the close of War—a cartouche] Publish'd as the Act directs 2 Jan 1783]

Mixed method 14 x 12 in. (image)

America, in the attire of a goddess, looks at a youth. They are surrounded by scenes of American activity at the time: fishing, lumbering, weaving, domestic industries, and by many wild animals. From a map entitled "Bowles's New Map of North America and the West Indies, Exhibiting the British Empire therein with the Limits and Boundaries of the United States as also the Dominions Possessed in that Quarter by the Spaniards, the French & other European States . . . 1783" in G&M. LC–USZ62–46072

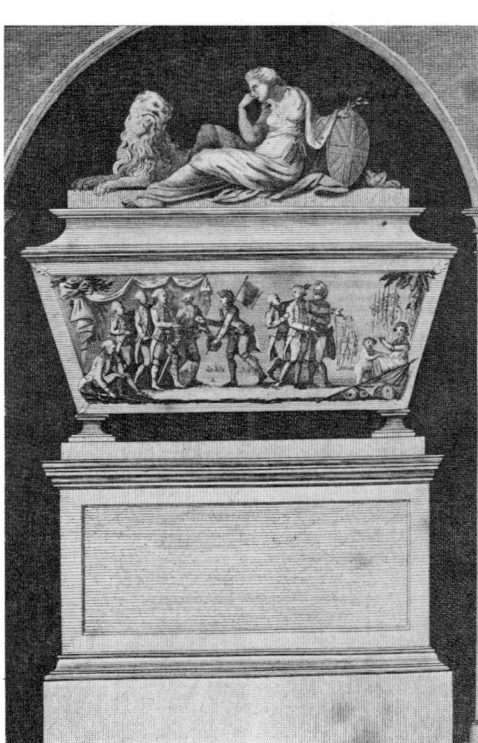
842

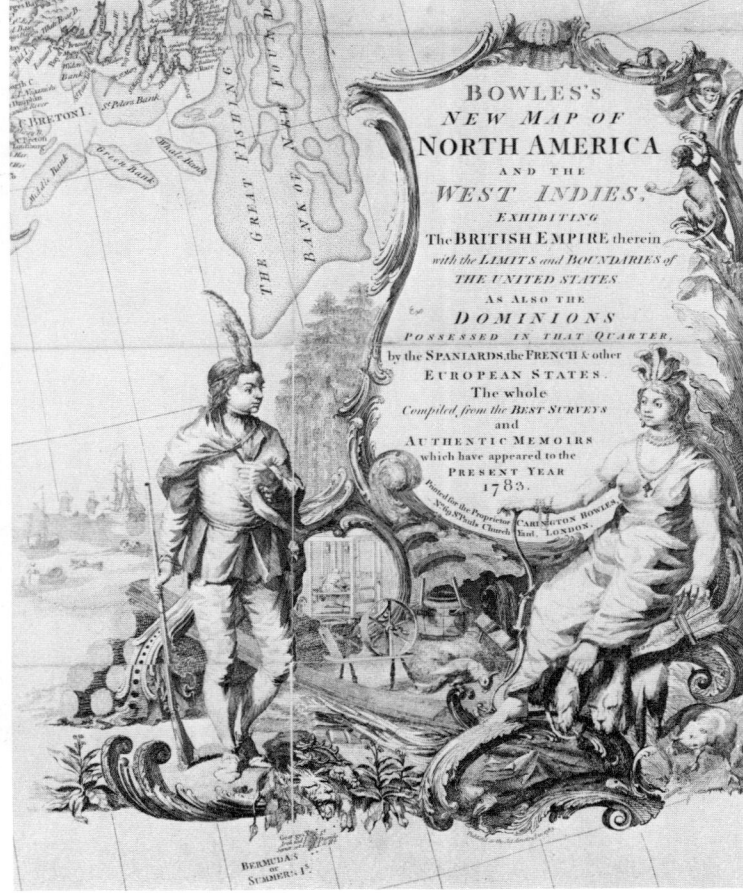
843

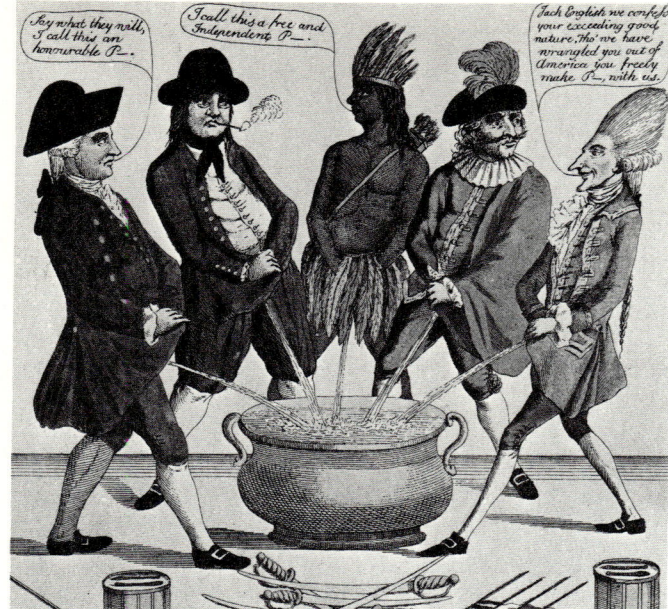

844

844

The General P___s, or Peace. Pubd by J. Barrow Jany 16th 1783 White Lion Bull Stairs Surry Side Black Friars Bridge.

Etching (hand colored) 8⅝ x 8¼ in. (image)

Five men urinate in a large pot. From left to right, an Englishman who says, "Say what they will, I call this an honourable p____," a Dutchman, an American Indian who says, "I call this a free and Independent P____," a Spaniard, and a Frenchman who says, "Jack English we confess your exceeding good nature, Tho' we have wrangled you out of America you freely make P____, with us." On the ground before the group lie five swords, two drums, and the respective flags of each country. Below some verse:

> Come all who love friendship, and wonder and see,
> The belligerent powers, like good neighbours agree,
> A little time past Sirs, who would have thought this,
> That they'd so soon come to a general P____?
>
> The wise politicians who differ in thought,
> Will fret at this friendship, and call it to nought,
> And blades that love war will be storming at this,
> But storm as they will, it's a general P____.
>
> A hundred hard millions in war we have spent,
> And America lost by all patriots consent,
> Yet let us be quiet, nor any one hiss,
> But rejoice at this hearty and general P____.
>
> Tis vain for to fret or growl at our lot,
> You see they're determin'd to fill us a pot,
> So now my brave Britons excuse me in this,
> That I for a Peace am oblig'd to write Piss.

LC–USZ62–1548

845

L____d Shel____, begging Monsieur to make Piss or P____e. Pubd. by J Barrow Jany. 21, 1783. White Lion Bull Stairs Surry Side Black Friars Bridge.

Etching 6 x 8½ in. (image)

Shelburne holds a chamber pot and asks a Frenchman, "Monsieur, be so obliging as to make piss with us." The cartoonist does not

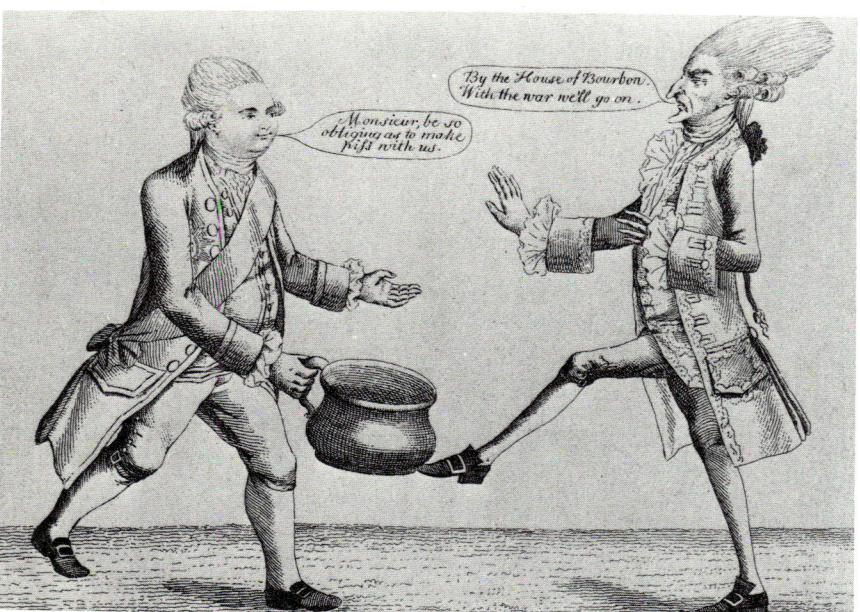

845

share Shelburne's desire for peace as indicated in the poem below:

> He's no heart of Oak
> But he's fit for a joke,
> That will ask of a Frenchman a peace;
> And such is our fate
> That we have of late
> Been degraded by puppies and geese.
>
> To Britons success,
> Against the Congress,
> On the Seas, and all over the plain;
> May they boldly advance,
> Make a Monkey of France,
> And asses of Holland and Spain.

When the Marquis of Rockingham died on July 1, 1782, Lord Shelburne became Prime Minister. His Government concluded the treaties with America, France, Spain, and Holland amid considerable protest from groups with varied interests. This cartoon plays mainly on English antipathy to France. The next (item 846) pleads the fate of the loyalists in America. CPPS 6168 LC–USZ62–45465

846

SHELB____NS SACRIFICE or the recommended Loyalists, a faithful representation of a Tragedy shortly to be performed on the Continent of America. Invented by Cruelty. Engraved by Dishonor. Pubd by E Dashery Febth. 10 1783 St. James Street.
Line engraving 9⅞ x 13¾ in.

Lord Shelburne smilingly watches America, personified by Indians, slaughter loyalists who were not protected by the treaty. A butcher weeps to see such bloodshed, and Britannia attacks Shelburne in anger. See CPPS 6171 LC–USZ62–1539

847

PEACE Porridge all hot. The best to be got. T. Colley Engd: [Pub. by W Richardson Feby 11. 1783 near Surry Street Strand.]
Etching 13¾ x 9¾ in.

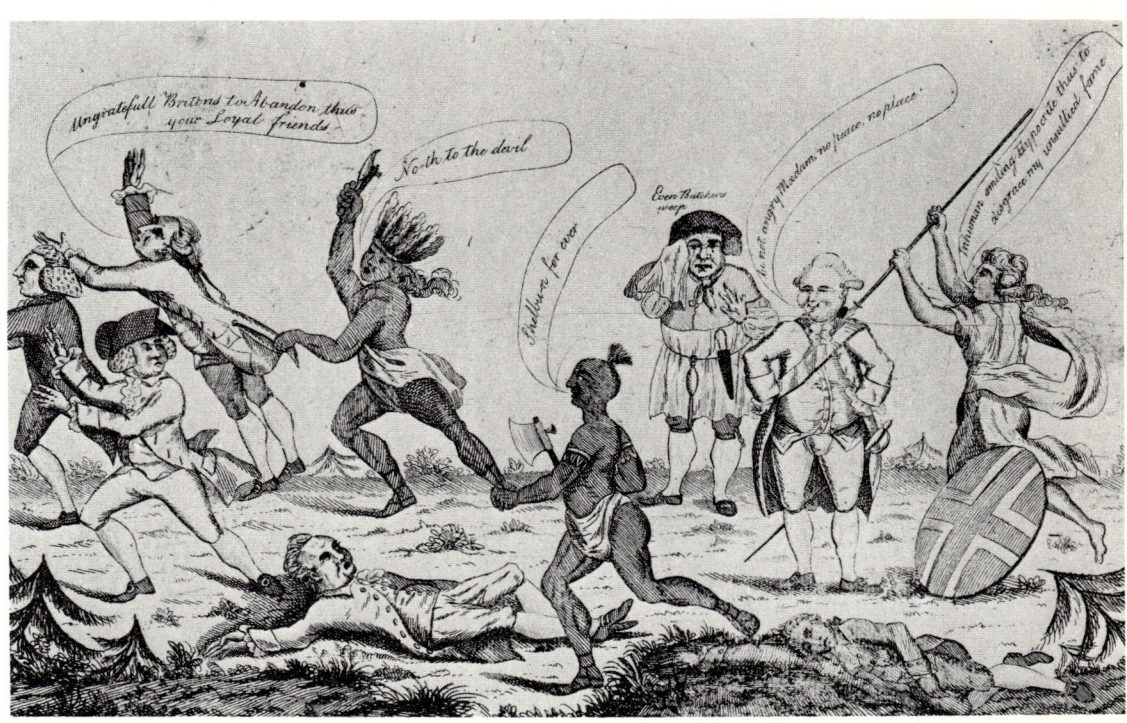
846

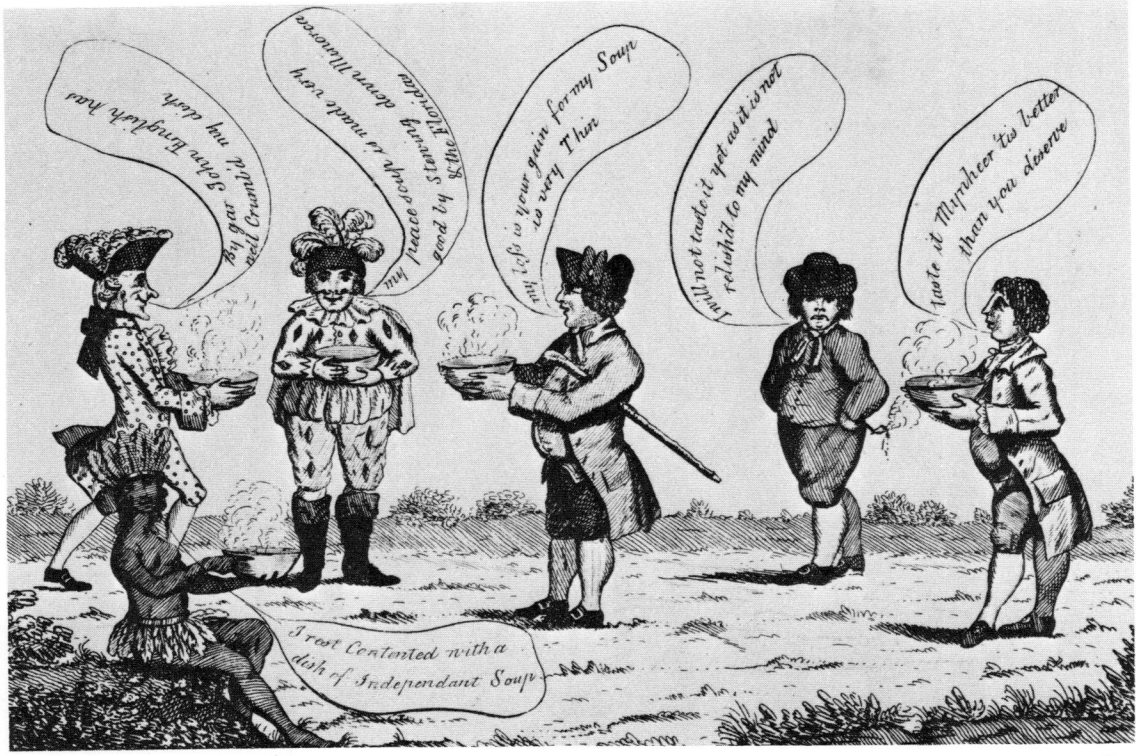

John Bull or an Englishman and his servant offer bowls of porridge to be shared in the peace. An American Indian woman says, "I rest Contented with a dish of Independant Soup." England says, "My loss is your gain for my Soup if very Thin," to which France replies "By gar John English has well Crumb'd my dish," and a Spaniard says, "My peace soup is made very good by Stewing down Minorca & the Floridas." The typically fat Dutchman says, "I will not taste it yet as it is not relish'd to my mind." Below are some verses:

SONG *Tune.* Roast Beef of Old England

The Frenchman & Spaniard are both Cock a hoop
With America too they have got such rich Soup
Yet a Blow or two more might have made them all Stoop.
  O' the rare Soup & the Cooks boys
  And O' the rare Cooks & the Soup

2
Their dishes, well crumb'd they have reason to Boast
The France & America have got the most
But England finds hers very thin to her cost
  O' the rare Soup &c

3
The Dutchman seems glouty, & is not in haste
The full flowing dish that's presented to taste
Let him sulk as he will he must take it at last
  O' the rare Soup & the Cooks &c

4
Belona has Smooth'd for the present her front
No longer in Blood & in dangers we hunt
Some are sorry—but many are very glad on't
  O' the rare Soup &c

5
Now plenty 'tis hop'd will return once again
And Commerce her sails widely Spread o'er the main
While Joy shall revisit each Nymp, & each Swain
  O' the rare Soup &c

6
The things have gone Cross for a long time Confest
Yet now to lament, is no more than a Jest
But as well as we can out of Bad make the best.
  O' the rare Soup &c

CPPS 6172 LC–USZ62–1541

848

A Political Concert; the Vocal parts By 1. Miss America, 2. Franklin, 3. F_x, 4. Kepp_ll, 5. Mrs. Britania, 6. Shelb_n, 7. Dun_i_g, 8. Benidick Rattle Snake. Colley Ingrad. Pub by W Richardson Feb: 18, 1783 near Surry St: Strand.

Line engraving 9¾ x 14 in.

America, as an Indian woman, and Britannia hold a pole with liberty cap atop; they sing: "Oh give me death or liberty, O give me &c." and "Brittons never, shall be Slaves" respectively. Franklin sings, "We'll return it untainted to heaven . . . ," and Fox says, "Give peace America with you & war with all the World." Keppel sings, "Then a cruising we will go . . ." and Shelburne, "Oh what a charming thing a battle, Oh &c &c." Dunning sings ". . . Oh what a Charming thing a Battle," and a snake sings, "Blood and plunder oh what a Charming thing a Battle." The snake represents Major André who joins in the chorus to remind those people favoring peace and independence for America that he died to preserve England's Colonies. Behind him is a crest with a ribbon reading, "Benidick Rattle Snakes Arms" over a picture of a devil playing a fiddle while sitting on top of a gallows. This protest against Shelburne's peace objects to the traitor Arnold retiring to England after hostilities when the hero André is dead. CPPS 6173 LC–USZ62–1542

849

Blessed are the PEACEMAKERS. Pub. by E Dachery Feby. 24 1783 St. James Street.

Etching 9⅞ x 13¾ in.

A Spaniard and a Frenchman lead George III and Shelburne up a hill to a house marked "Inquisition." A lean and lank-haired Yankee whips the Englishman with a scourge having 13 tails; he has captured a fat, surly Dutchman. CPPS 6174 LC–USZ62–45467

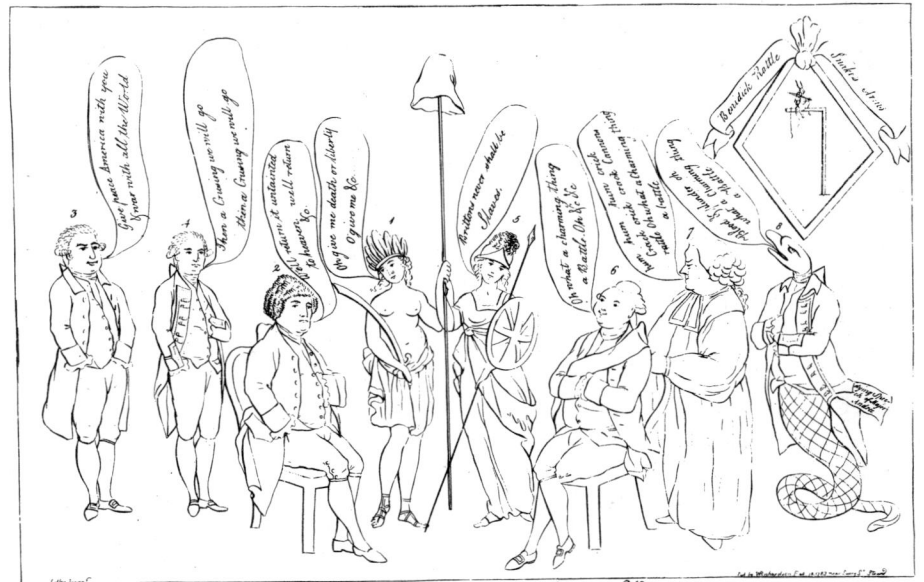

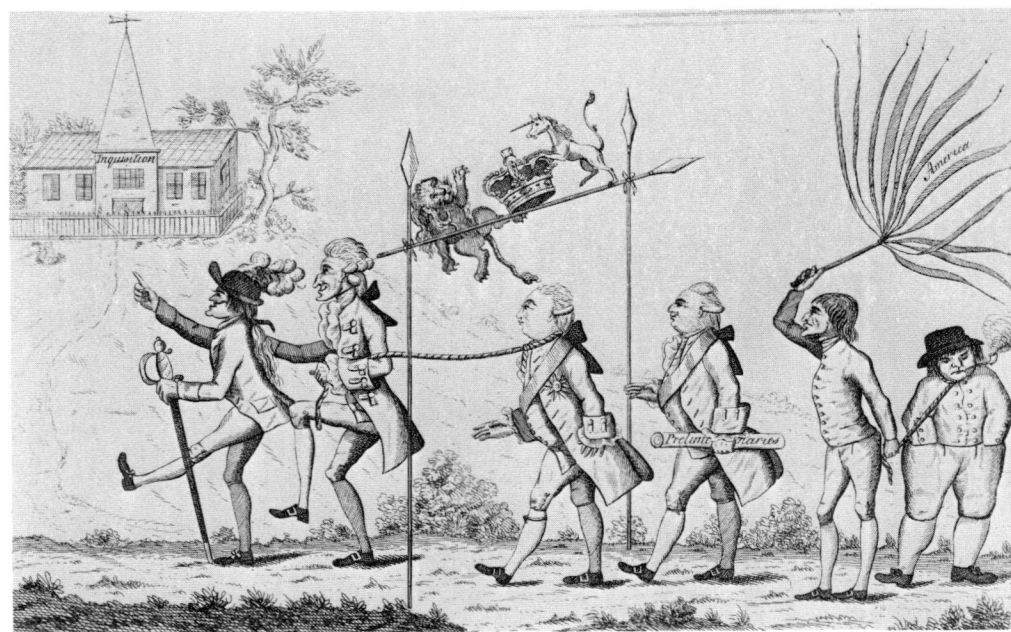

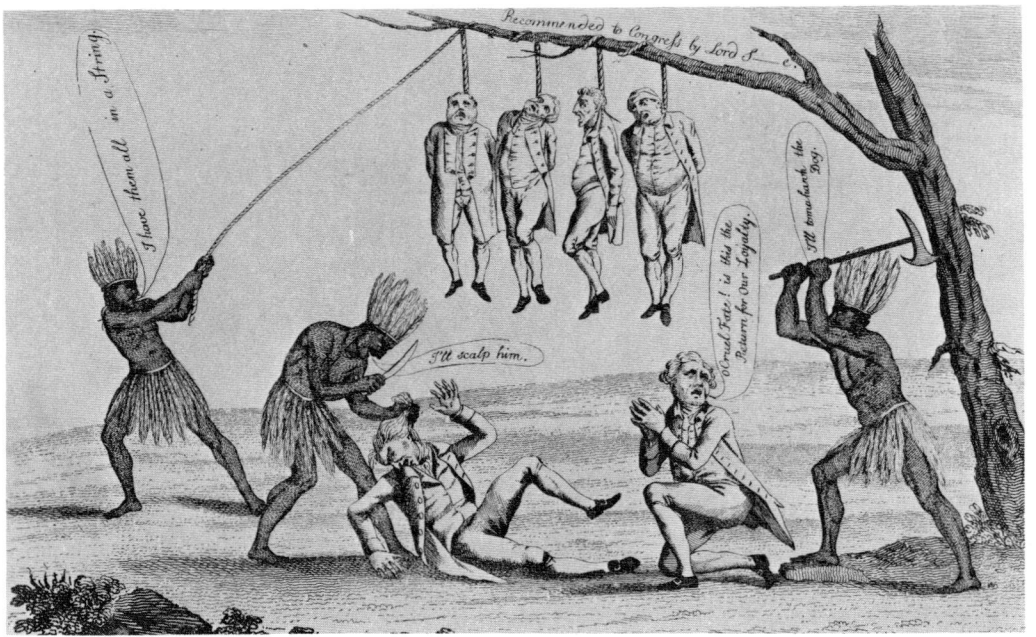

850

850

The SAVAGES let loose, OR The Cruel FATE of the LOYALISTS. Sold by W. Humphrey No. 227 Strand, [March 1783]

Mixed method 9¾ x 13¾ in.

Three American Indians, representing America, murder six loyalists. Above the loyalists hanging from a tree is inscribed "Recommended to Congress by Lord S_____e." which blames Shelburne for abandoning the loyalists to their fate. Below the print a couplet:

> Is this a Peace, when Loyalists must bleed?
> It is a Bloody Piece of work indeed.

CPPS 6182 LC–USZ62–1540

851

The TEA-TAX-TEMPEST. OR OLD TIME with his MAGICK-LANTHERN. Pubd. March 12, 1783. by W. Humphreys. N 227 Strand.

Mixed method 9¾ x 13¾ in.

A smaller version of CPPS 5490 and 5491. The most significant addition is the monolog given by Time who says:

There you see the little Hot Spit Fire Tea pot that has done all The Mischief—There you see the Old British Lion basking before the American Bon Fire whilst the French Cock is blowing up a Storm About his Ears to Destroy him and his young Welpes—There you See Miss America grasping at the Cap of Liberty—There you see The British Forces be yok'd and be cramp'd flying before the Congress Men—There you see the thirteen Stripes and Rattlesnake exalted—There you see the Stamp'd Paper help to Make the Pot Boil—There you see &, &, &.

CPPS 6190 LC–USZ62–1543

852

Mrs. General Washington, Bestowing thirteen Stripes on Britania. [March 1783]

Mixed method 6¼ x 4 in.

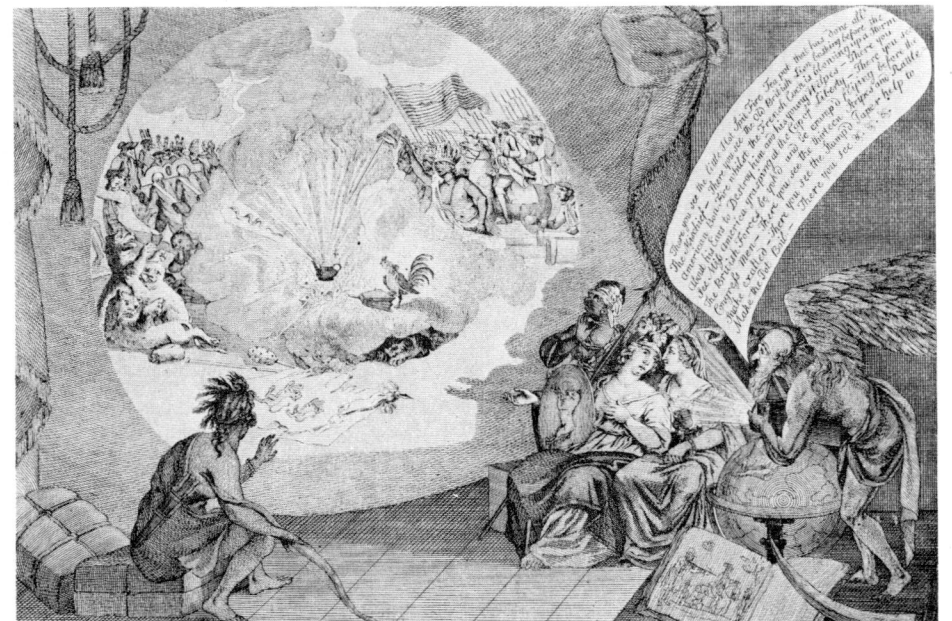

851

George Washington is represented in the dress of a woman, wearing a cockade in a tri-corner hat. He lashes Britannia using a whip with 13 lashes and says, "Parents Should not behave like Tyrants to their Children." Britannia says, "Is it thus my Children treat me." Behind Washington stand three men representing Holland, France, and Spain; they encourage Washington. The brief article which accompanies this cartoon cites a passage from *The Pennsylvania Gazette* of November 11, 1782, which states that "General Washington is actually discovered to be of the Female Sex." From *The Rambler's Magazine*, March 1783, p. 113–114. CPPS 6202 LC–USZ62–45484

853
The Only Booth in the Fair. PORTLAND & Co late Shelburne. I Boyne Invt & exct London Published as the Act directs No 2 Shoe Lane Fleet St April 9 1783.

Etching (hand colored) 11¾ x 9¾ in.

On April 2, 1783, the expected happened when the Shelburne Ministry was driven from office, and a coalition between Fox and North, former rivals, assumed power, with the Duke of Portland as Prime Minister. Fox wears a liberty cap with "Vox Populi" written on it and sits behind a barrier marked "American Letter Box." His image as a friend of the people and sympathetic listener to the Americans is about to be tarnished here because North offers him bribes in the style of the old Ministry. Fox had been accused of desiring power at any cost when he entered the coalition. Shelburne and Portland point to North indicating that he is less than honest. In front of the platform a sign reads, "Tricks on the cards by the noted Charly with many new Shuffles by the Rest of the Company." CPPS 6206

———Another impression (uncolored). Sold by W. Humphrey, 227 Strand. LC–USZ62–45468

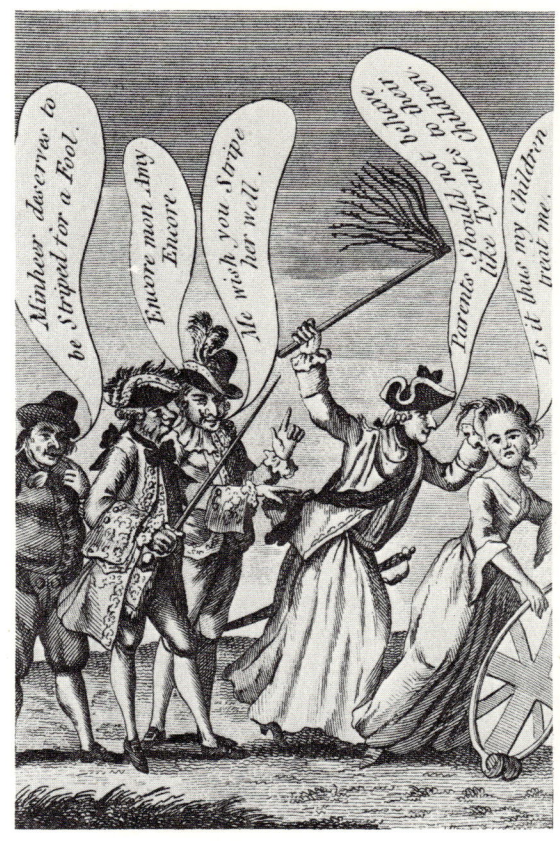

852

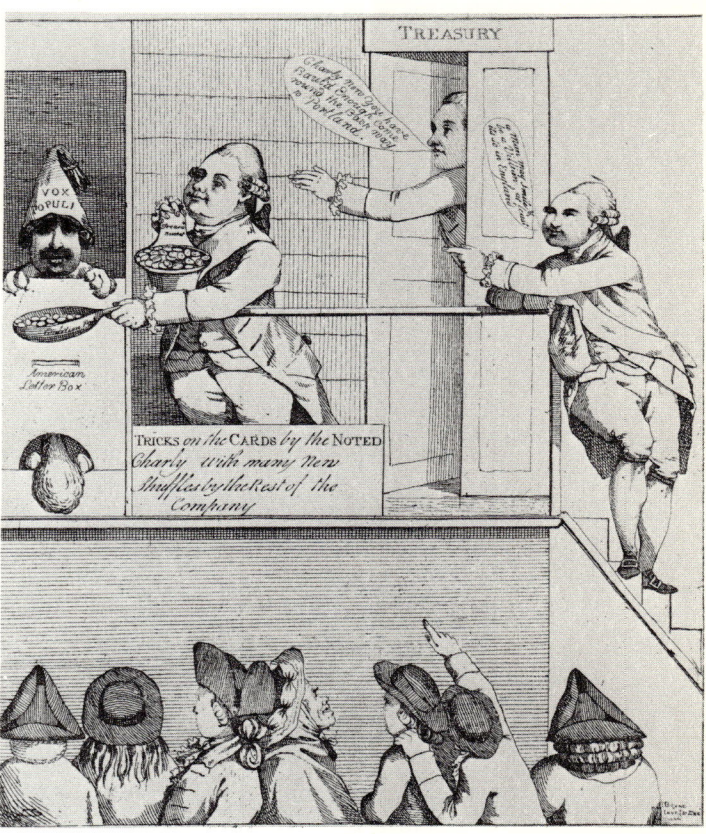

853

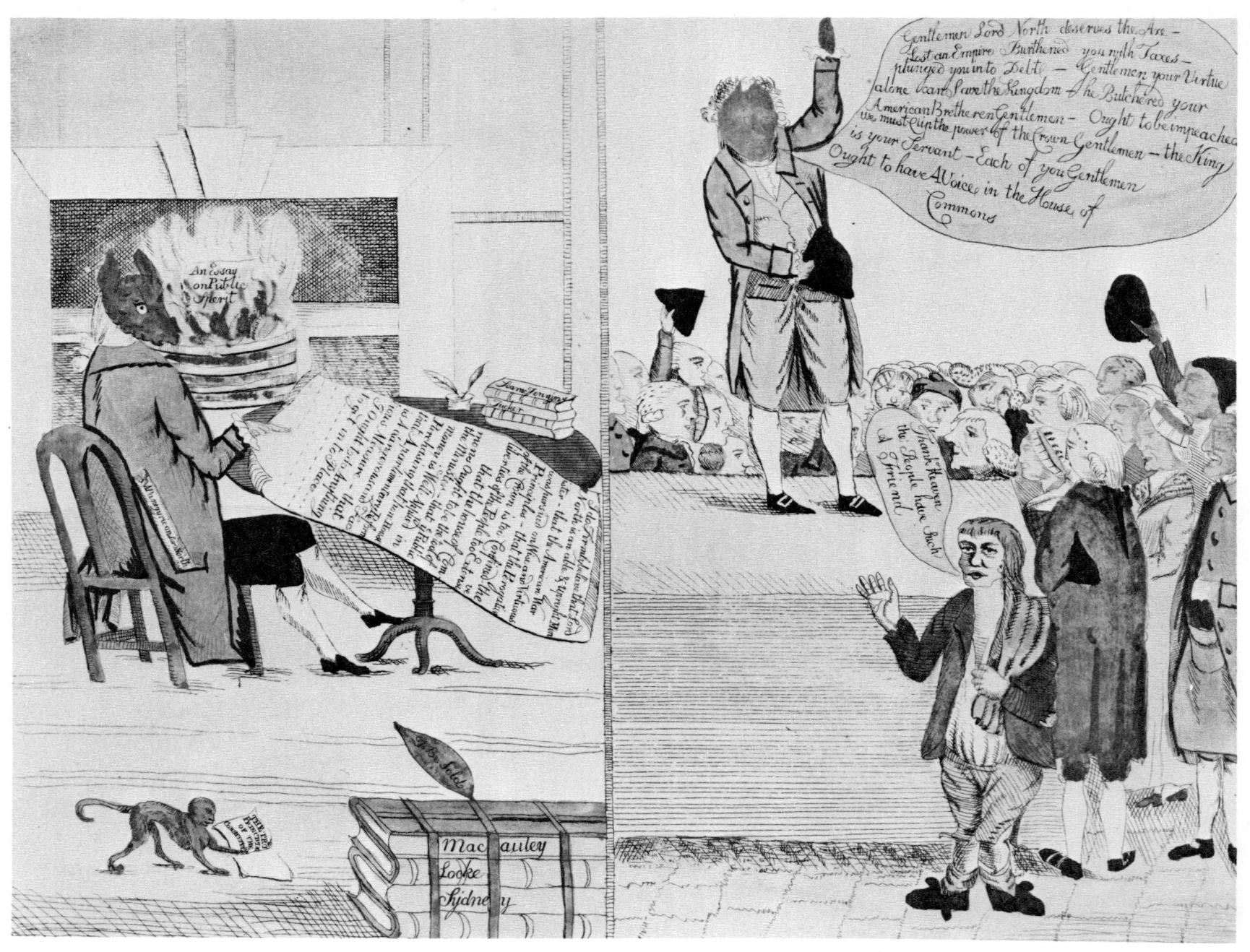

854

AN ANALYSIS OF MODERN PATRIOTISM Performed by Public Opinion & displayed by Public indignation. PH [erased] AW Sct. Pubd. Accorg to Act, Aprill ye 9 1783 by T Cornell Print Seller Bruton Street.

Etching (hand colored) 12⅛ x 9⅞ in.

Two pictures contrasting the works of Fox in and out of office. In office he supports the King, taxes, and the war with America; out of office he supports the populus action in Commons and condemns North's taxes and war with America. CPPS 6207 LC–USZ62–45469

855

THE TIMES, Anno. 1783. Pubd. Aprl. 14th 1783. by W. Humphrey, No. 227 Strand.

Etching (hand colored) 10 x 14 in.

John Bull throws up his hands saying, "'Tis lost! Irrevocably lost!" as the Devil flies away with a map designated "America." The Devil passes a gas which says, "Poor John Bull! Ha! Ha! Ha!" A Frenchman approaches Britain saying, "Ah, Ah, me Lord Angla, volez vous une pince de Snuff for de Diable will not give you back de Amerique." A fat Dutchman and a Spaniard watch the other two and military action at Gibraltar saying, "De Donder take you Monsieur, I think I have paid the Piper," and Spain says, "See Gibraltar! see Don Langara! by St. Anthony you have made me the Laughing Stock of Europe." CPPS 6210 LC–USZ62–1544

856

THE BLESSINGS OF PEACE. Publish'd according to Act of Parliament, by M. Smith in Fleet Street. April 16th. 1783.

Mixed method 10½ x 13⅛ in. (image)

George III confers with Fox, Richmond, Shelburne, Burke, Thurlow, Mansfield, Sheridan, North, Pitt, Nugent, Keppel, Ashburton, and Amherst about the state of the nation

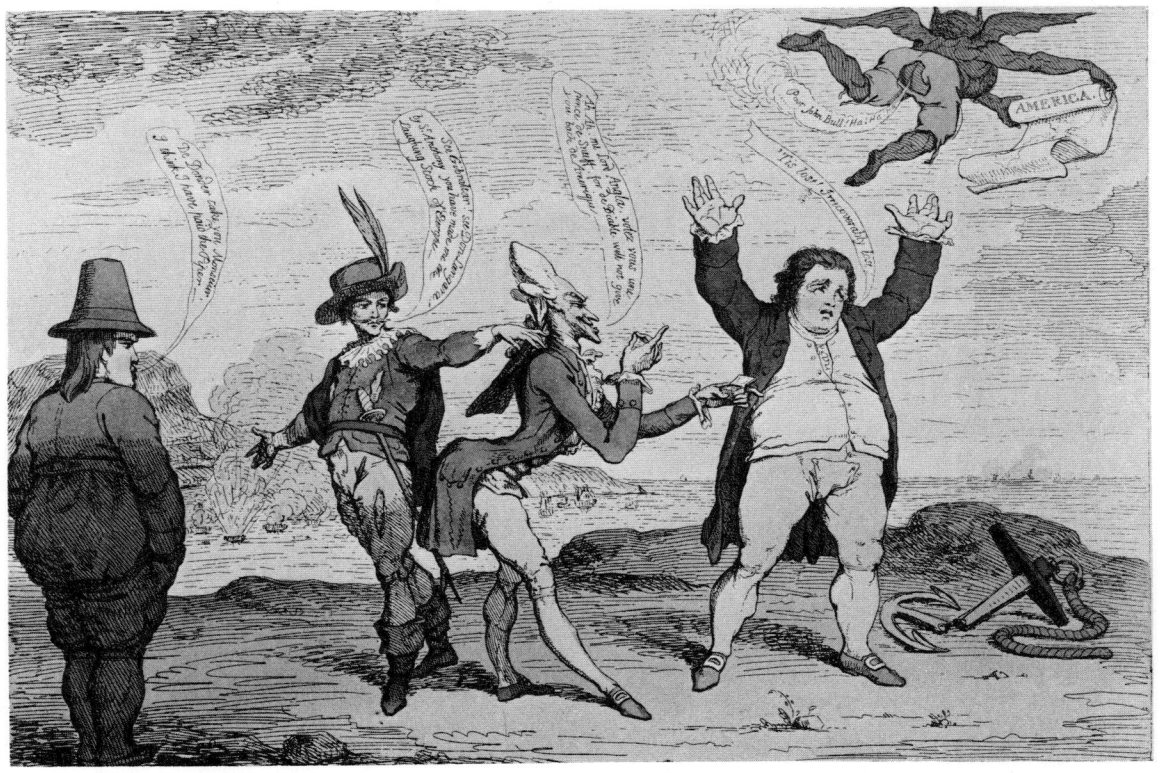

855

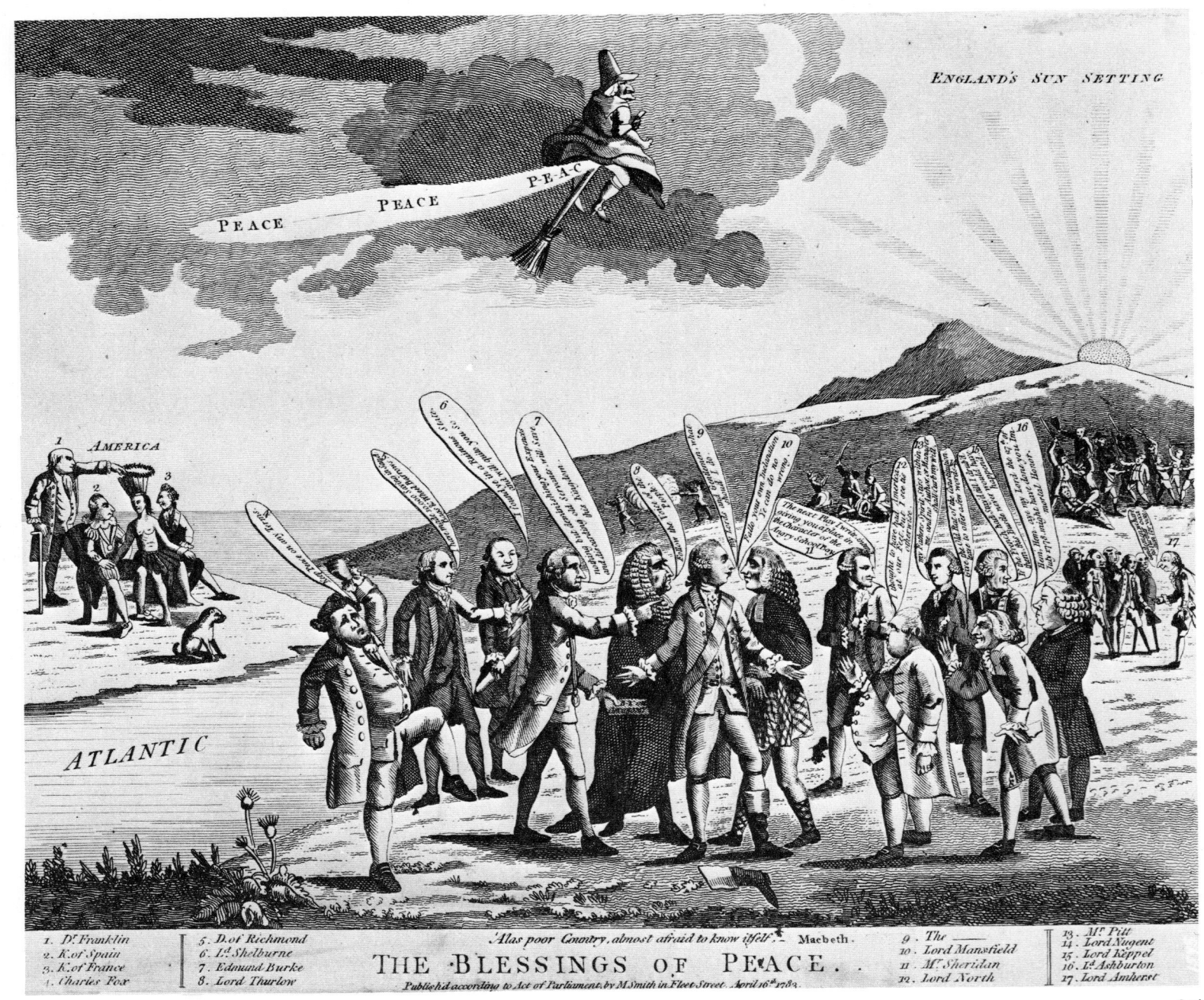

in 1783. In the background to the right sailors are rioting. Across a body of water designated "Atlantic," America, dressed as an Indian woman, receives the hands of Spain and France, while Franklin crowns her. A pug dog representing Holland sits nearby. Far in the distance England's sun is setting behind mountains. A quotation below the picture describes the feelings of the times:

Alas poor Country, almost afraid to know itself.—Macbeth

CPPS 6212 LC–USZ62–1545

857
Amusement for John Bull & his Cousin Paddy, or, the Gambols of the American Buffalo, in St. James's Street. Published 1st. May 1783, by I. Fielding, Pater-noster Row.
Mixed method 3½ x 6 in. (image)

A large buffalo, representing America, has created havoc on St. James Street. A woman peddler has fallen over and dropped fish and bread on the street, and English ministers rush to grab the goods. The ministers are Portland, Cavandish, North, Fox, Thurlow, Keppel, Shelburne, and Thomas Pitt (1737–1793) or possibly William Pitt. Fox recognizes the cause of the disturbance and says, "This American Buffalo, has occasioned glorious sport...." Shelburne claims that he will "share what I get among the Loyalists" in America. George III watches the entire scene and smiles. CPPS 6223 LC–USZ62–1546

858
The [ass]-headed and [cow-heart]-ed Ministry making the British [lion] give up the Pull. Pubd. by J. Barrow May 8 1783 White Lion Bull Stairs Side Black Friars Bridge.
Etching 9½ x 16 in.

A tug of war between the British lion and four animals: Spain (a spaniel), France (a cock), America (a rattlesnake), and Holland

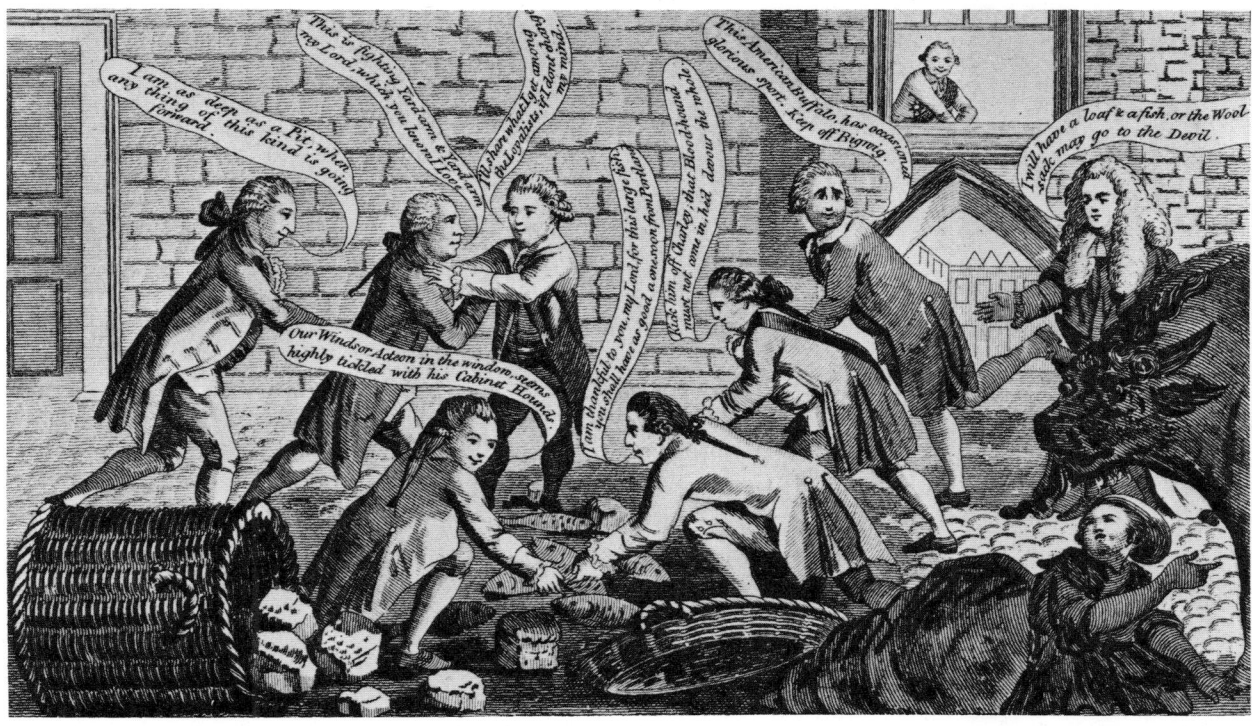

857

381

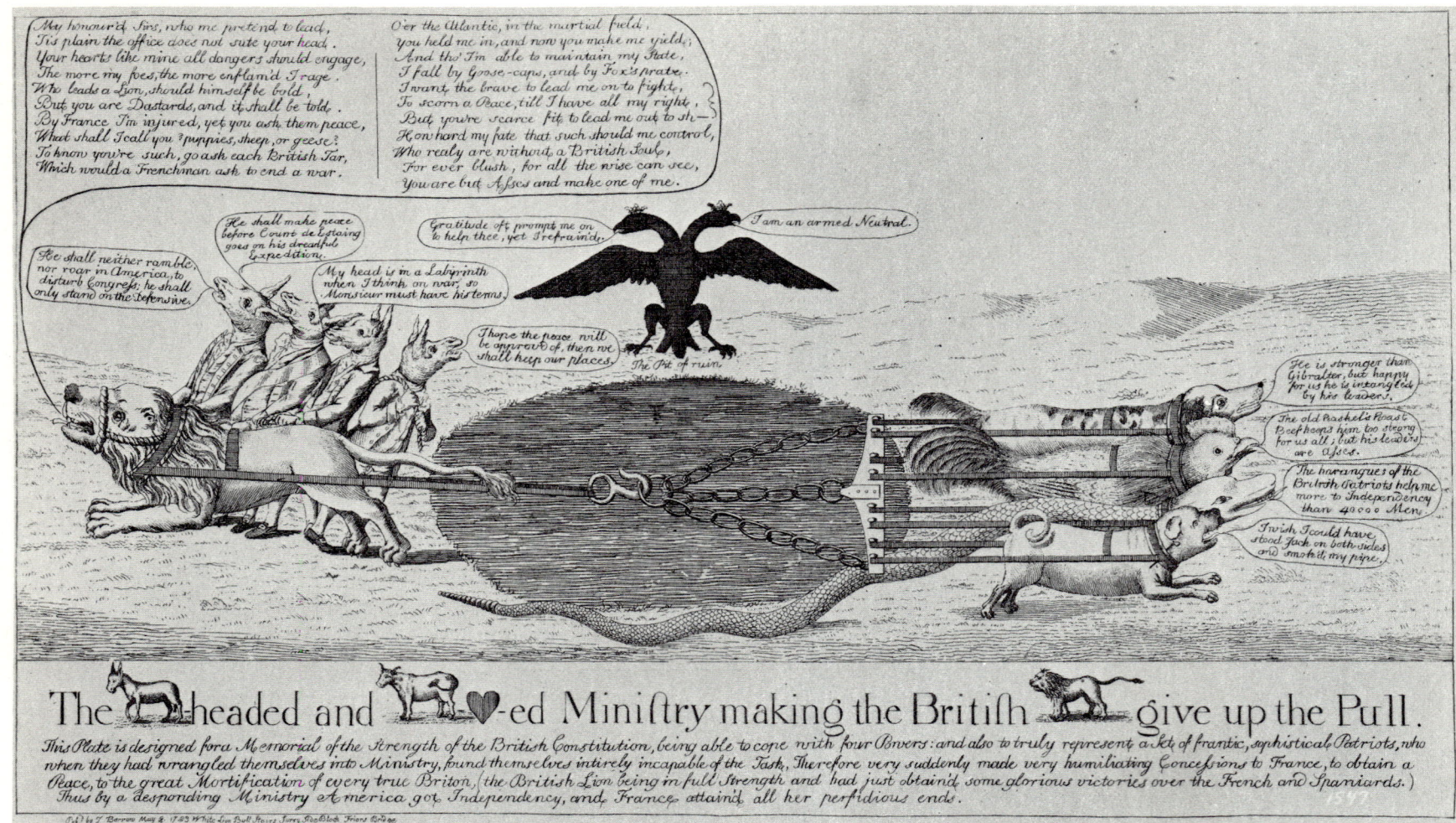

(a pug dog). The lion is holding his own, but four ministers with ass heads discourage the pull by alluding to problems with each enemy. One alluding to America says, "He shall neither ramble nor roar in America, to disturb Congress; he shall only stand on the Defensive." The American rattlesnake says, "The harangues of the British Patriots help me more to Independency than 40000 Men." The mud pit between the contestants is called "The Pit of ruin." The Russian double eagle says with one head to the allies, "I am an armed Neutral," and with the other head to the ministers, "Gratitude oft prompt me on to help thee, yet I refrain'd." The British lion recites a poem to the ministers—

> My honour'd Sirs, who me pretend to lead,
> Tis plain the office does not sute your head.
> Your hearts like mine all dangers should engage,
> The more my foes, the more enflam'd I rage.
> Who leads a Lion, should himself be bold,
> But you are Dastards, and it shall be told.
> By France I'm injured, yet you ask them peace,
> What shall I call you? puppies, sheep, or geese?
> To know you're such, go ask each British Tar,
> Which would a Frenchman ask to end a war.
> O'er the Atlantic, in the martial field,
> You held me in, and now you make me yield;
> And tho' I'm able to maintain my State,
> I fall by Goose-caps, and by Fox's prate.
> I want the brave to lead me on to fight,
> To scorn a Peace, till I have all my right,
> But you're scarce fit to lead me out to sh—
> How hard my fate that such should me control,
> Who realy are without a British Soul,
> For ever blush, for all the wise can see,
> You are but Asses and make one of me.

CPPS 6229 LC–USZ62–1547

859

"Oh fly," cries Peace, the Soul of Social Life. Stothard del. [Thomas?] Cook sculp. [July 1783]

Mixed method 5½ x 3⅝ in.

Assisted by a dark featured man with hydra-like hair, a youth approaches a pyramid with the names Lexington, Bunkers Hill, Saratoga, Brandywine, Guilford, and Camden engraved on it. The goddess Peace turns the youth away from American Revolution toward three other goddesses (one holding a staff with a liberty cap on top), and two cherubs sit on the ground reading books on astronomy, husbandry, and grammar. Below a short poem reads:

> "Oh fly," cries Peace, the Soul of Social Life,
> "Far from this Fiend of dire destructive Strife:
> "Ingenuous Youth, these Scenes attend no more,
> "But turn to Britain's once maternal Shore:
> "From Her fair Liberty's celestial Flame,
> "Religion, Language, Arts, & Commerce came."

From *The Universal Magazine of Knowledge and Pleasure*, 1783, frontispiece.
LC–USZ62–45560

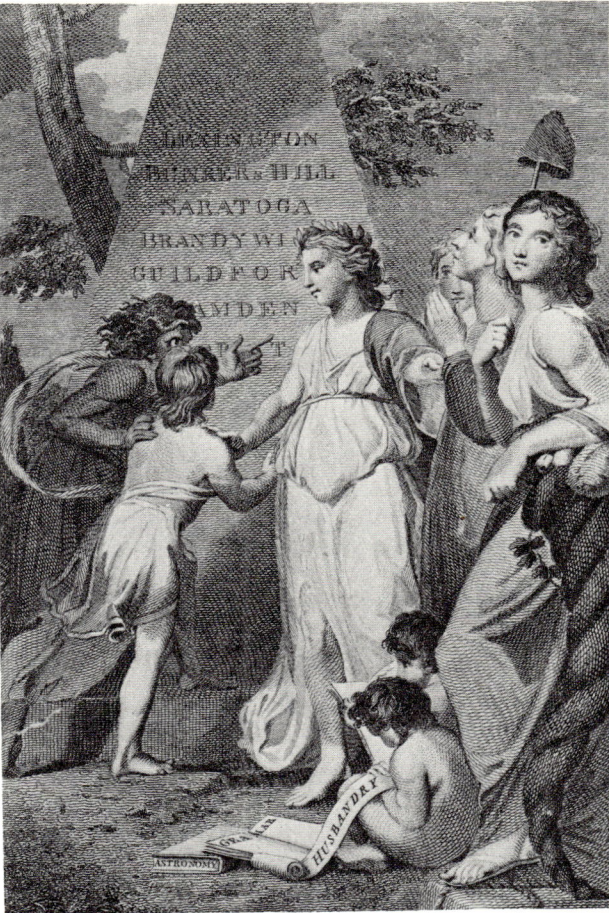

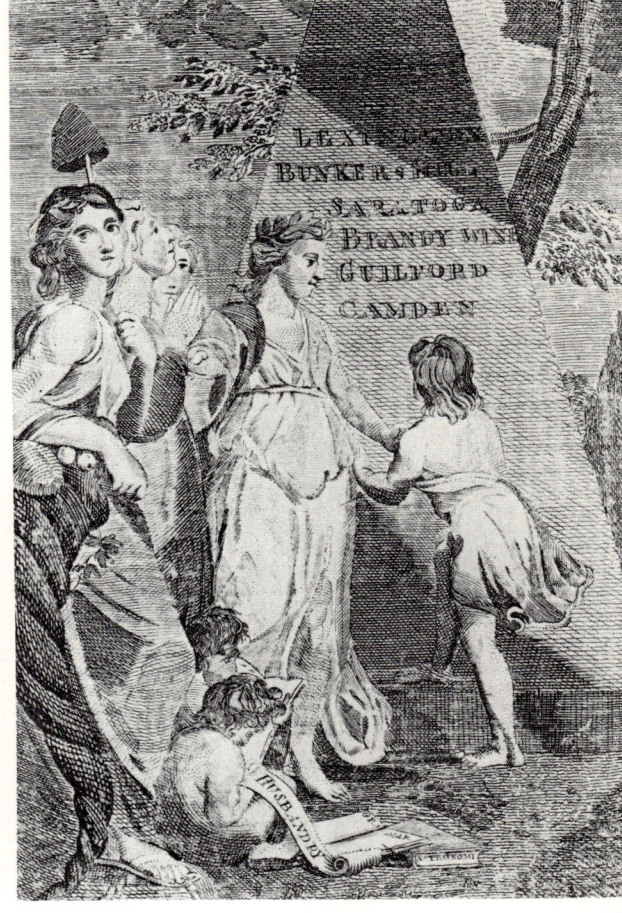

860

[Instruction of American youth] J. Norman Sc. [1783]

Mixed method 6½ x 4¼ in.

A youth approaches a pyramid with the names Lexington, Bunkers Hill, Saratoga, Brandywine, Guilford, and Camden engraved on it. He meets four muses dressed as Roman

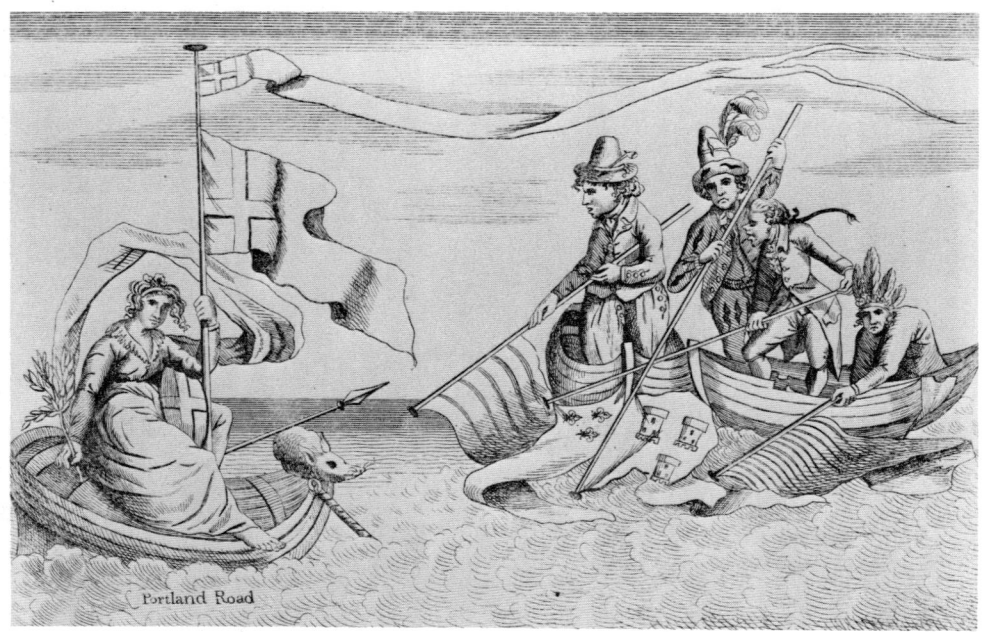

women. One holds a staff with a liberty cap on top. This frontispiece for *The Boston Magazine* of December 1783 is explained on p. 42:

> On a Pyramid are inscribed some of the principal Events of the late War between Great Britain and the United States of America. A youth representing the rising Generation of America, is reading the inscription.—Peace is supposed to remind him that while he retains a Remembrance of those important Events, yet, since the happy cessation of War, he ought to pay a close attention to *Religion*, *Liberty* and *Commerce*. On the ground are children studying the most useful Sciences. *Grammer*—which implies that we cultivate all Languages. *Astronomy*—necessary to navigation and Commerce. *Husbandry*—the source of *true* national wealth.

This engraving copies (and probably satirizes) the one in item 859, which appeared five months earlier in *The Universal Magazine of Knowledge and Pleasure* in England.
LC–USZ62–45279

861

DOMINION of the SEAS. BRITANNIA on board the FOX safe Moor'd in PORTLAND-road —— As Mistress of the Sea, she receives Homage from the whole World. NB A distinction contended for by our present Peace Makers. Pubd. by E. D'achery St. James's Street, Decr. 1st. 1783.
Etching 8¾ x 12 in.

Britannia in a small boat with a figurehead of a fox holds a shield, a banner of St. George, and an olive branch. The figurehead stands for Charles Fox, and the boat is riding in Portland Road which represents Lord Portland. The four allies in other small boats dip their flags in salute: Holland is a fat Dutchman, Spain a jester, France a gentleman with long pigtail, and America an Indian. CPPS 6274
LC–USZ62–45470

862

La Grande Bretagne mutilé. Das verstümmelte Britanien. Amsterdam [1783]
Mixed method 8¼ x 13¼ in.

Explanations are given in French and Ger-

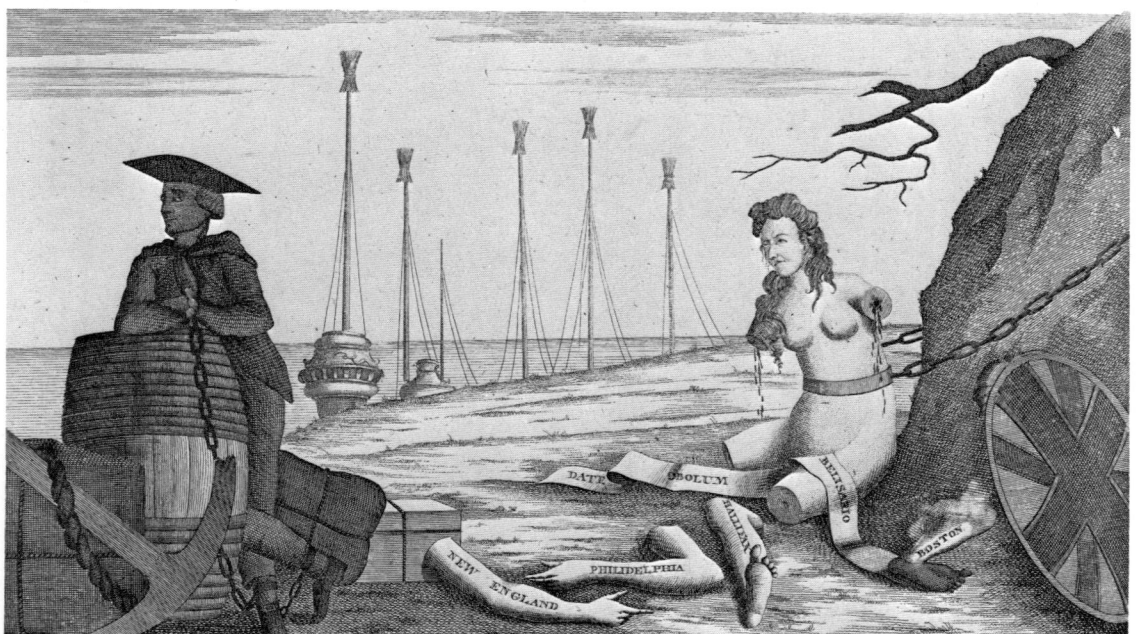

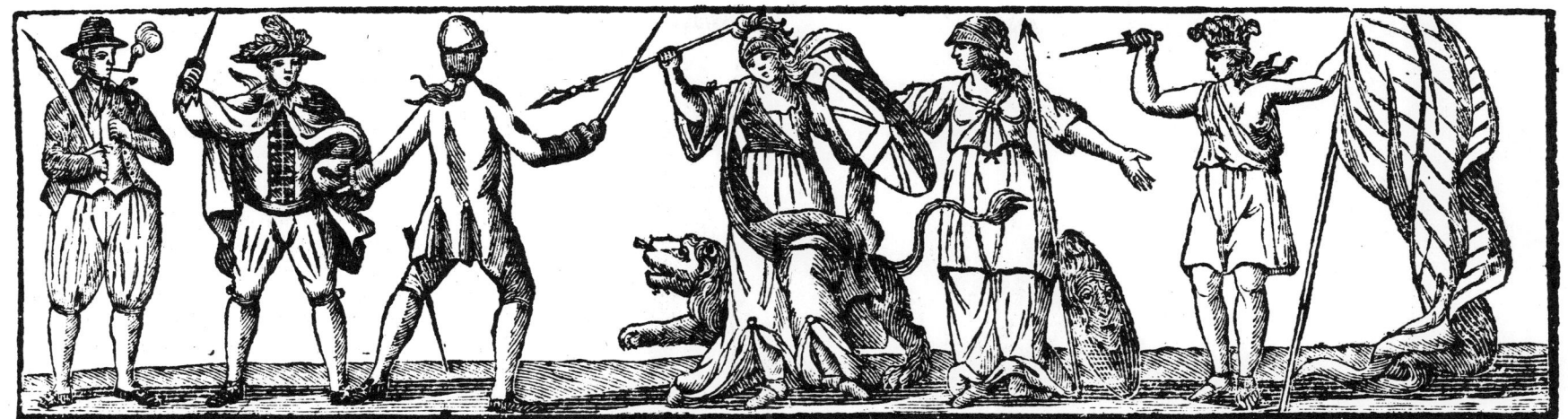

863

man. Britannia is dismembered and chained, her shield on the ground. Beside her lie limbs designated "New England," "Philidelphia," "Hallifax," and "Boston." A ribbon lying across her amputated legs reads, "Date Obolum Belisario." In the foreground to her right a sailor in chains is surrounded by bundles of commerce and looks out to sea. In the background ships are tied to the docks with broomsticks at their mastheads showing that they are for sale. This Dutch engraving repeats the theme of item 632 and shows that the British Empire and its commerce are badly damaged. LC–USZ62–15756

863

[Britannia attacked by her enemies, 1783?]
Woodcut 1⅞ x 7⅛ in. (image)

Britannia with shield and lance and backed by the British lion fights a Frenchman, a Spaniard, and a Dutchman. Another mythological figure with shield and spear indicates that America is behind her with a dagger. America is a woman with a feathered headdress and flag. Found in Barnard, *New and Complete History of England* as ornament for the Preface, p. iii. LC–USZ62–45541

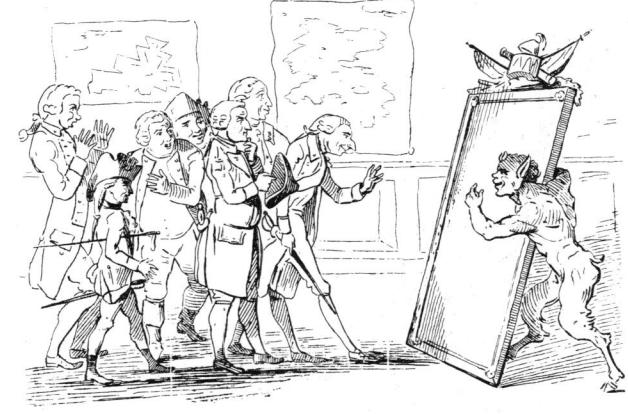

864

864

VELUTI IN SPECULUM. [1783]
Etching 4¾ x 6¼ in.

Seven British officers look into a mirror which a devil holds up for them. Their expressions range from smugness and pleasure to amazement and sadness. They are, from right to left, Amherst, Murray, Burgoyne, and perhaps Tarleton, Cornwallis, Clinton, and Sir William Howe. On the wall behind them hang maps of "America," "Montreal," and "Fort St. Philip." Grose's *Advice to the Officers of the British Army* (1783), for which this print is a frontispiece, is an often reprinted satirical manual on how an officer can achieve fame and fortune in the British Army through acts of deceit. It tells how to falsify reports to embellish one's stature and how to siphon off money from the common soldier's pay. The cartoon is particular to this edition. LC–USZ62–45521

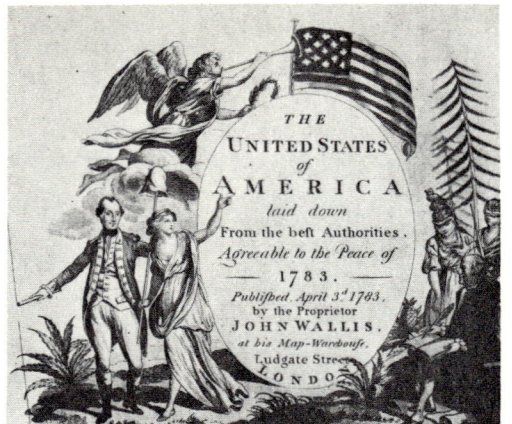

865

[America with her children and Commerce in the background—a cartouche] M. Brion de la Tour A Paris Chez Esnauts et Rapilly, rue St. Jacques, a la Ville de Coutances, Avec Priv. du Roi 1783.

Etching 6½ x 8½ in. (image)

America, as an Indian woman with feathered skirt and headdress, jewels, and fan, nurses two infants in a tropical landscape among lush foliage, a barking dog, and a pelican. Behind her a seaman moves a bound crate, and ships put out to sea. This sympathetic French portrayal of America sees the new nation in terms of peace and commerce. From a map entitled "Amérique Septentrionale, ou se remarquent les Etats Unis" in G&M.
LC–USZ62–46073

866

[Washington and Franklin founding the United States of America—a cartouche] 1783
Etching 6¼ x 7¼ in. (image)

A full portrait of Washington shows him leading Liberty. To the right, Franklin is writing in a book, accompanied by the goddesses Justice and probably Wisdom. On top Fame rides a cloud, and the American flag with 13 stars flies over the whole scene. From a map entitled "The United States of America laid down from the best Authorities, Agreeable to the Peace of 1783. Published April 3d. 1783 by the Proprietor John Wallis, at his Map-Warehouse, Ludgate Street, London." Phillips, *Maps*, p. 862. Negative in G&M.

867

[Iconography of Canada—a cartouche] 1783
Etching 8½ x 7½ in. (image)

Figures represent activities in Canada: priests baptize and preach, Indians climb around the middle of the cartouche, and a beaver, a duck, and some fish form the bottom.

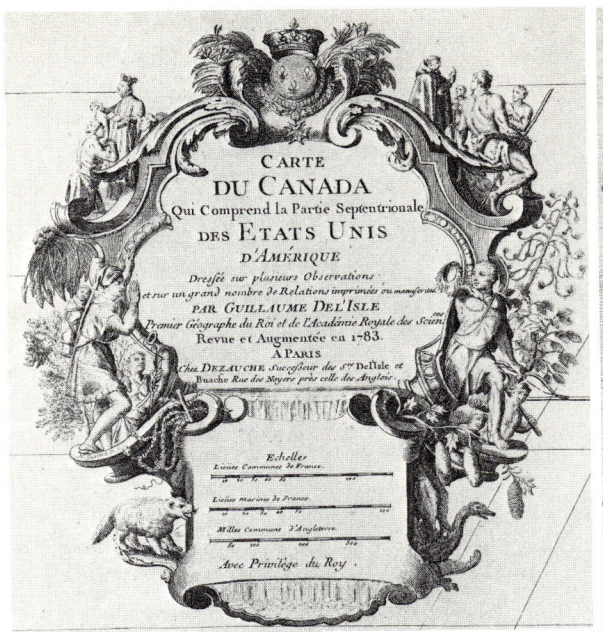

867

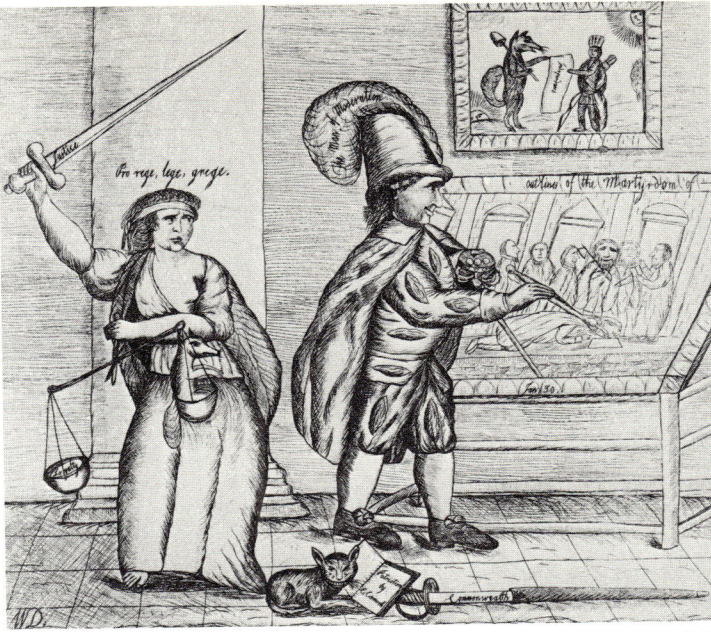

868

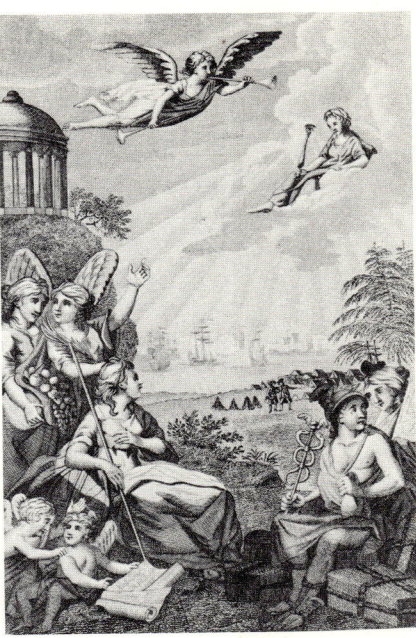

869

At the time this cartouche was printed, British and French influence and claims were still uncertain in the western territories of the new nation. From a map entitled "Carte du Canada Qui Comprend la Partie Septentrionale des Etats Unis d'Amérique." Guillaume de L'Isle, *Atlas Géographique et Universal*, v. 2 (Paris, 1784), no. 129. LC–USZ62–46092

868

THE HISTORICAL PAINTER. Pubd. as the Act directs, by J. Cattermoul, No. 376, Oxford Street, Feb. 10th. 1784.

Line engraving 9⅛ x 9⅛ in.

Charles Fox is compared to Cromwell who paints a picture of the execution of Charles I. On the wall behind the main action hangs a picture showing a fox with staff and liberty cap handing an American Indian a paper designated "Independence." CPPS 6408 LC–USZ62–45471

869

In the back Ground is Admiral Rodney's Engagement with Count De Grasse. Washington & Rochambeau's Advantage over the English Army, shews the Injustice, Fate & Uncertainty of War. The glorious Rays from Providence over Rodney's Fleet bring Peace and Plenty to Britannia. Fame sounds her praise & Genius & Commerce makes her Shine thro' the World. Publish'd as the Act directs Feby. 21st, 1784. Harrison, invt. Goldar del. et sc.

Etching 12¼ x 8 in.

Britannia sits with Mercury, Plenty, other gods, and cherubs, watching the scenes described by the title. From Rapin-Thoyras, *History of England*, v. 5 (London, 1789), frontispiece. LC–USZ62–45543

870

A NEW PANTOMINE. HARLEQUINE. Publish'd by E Hedges no 92 Cornhill Feby 25th 1784.

Etching 12¾ x 10¼ in.

Fox and North perform on a stage before an audience of their sympathizers. Fox holds a club over a bust of George III, and the crown and sceptre tied to a balloon float over the head. Fox passes a paper marked "Prerogative" to North, who is dressed as a huge bird. The Prince of Wales sits in a box to the left with his mistress Mrs. Mary Robinson and shouts "Bravo!" On the wall to the right is a map designated "Independent States of America." After the title is a simple etching of a fox running off with a goose.
CPPS 6424 LC–USZ62–45391

871

COALITION ARMS. Published by M. SMITH, March 8, 1784; and sold at No. 46, in Fleet Street.

Etching (hand colored) 7¾ x 11 in.

A coat of arms explaining the coalition

387

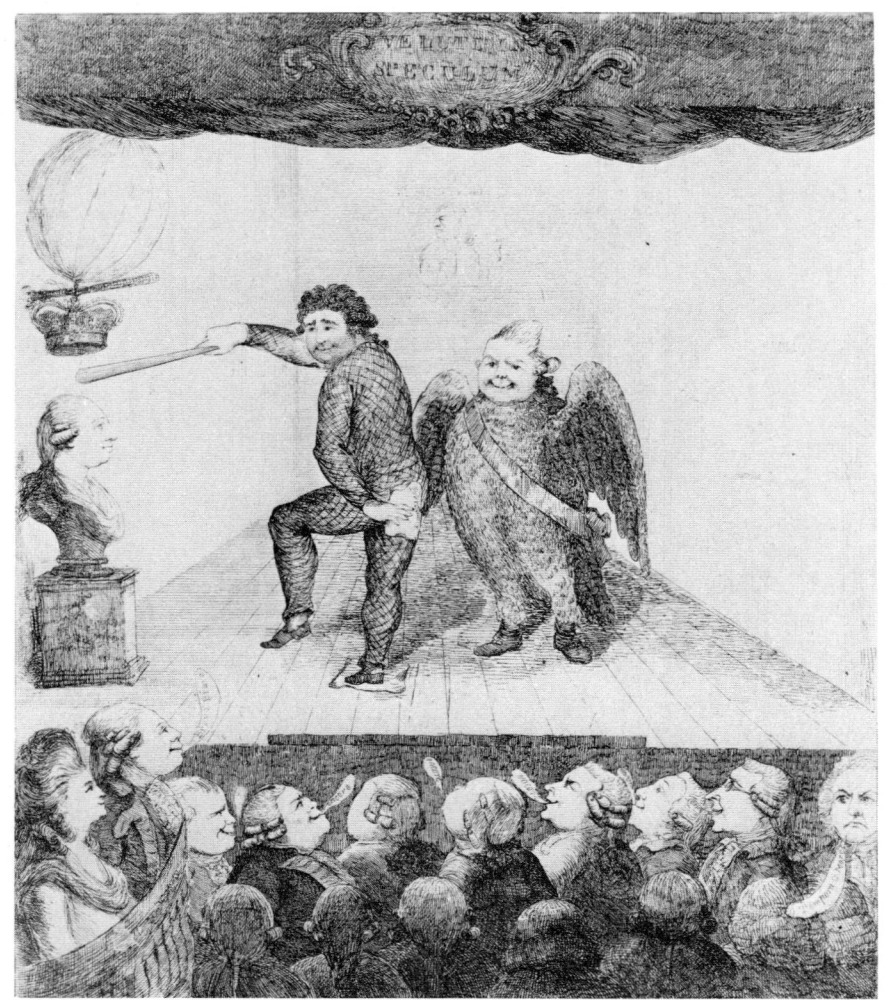

870

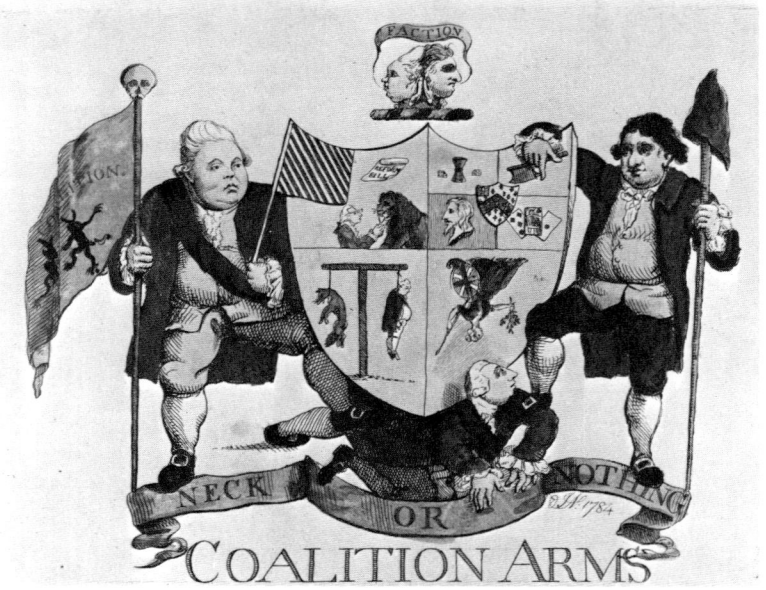

871

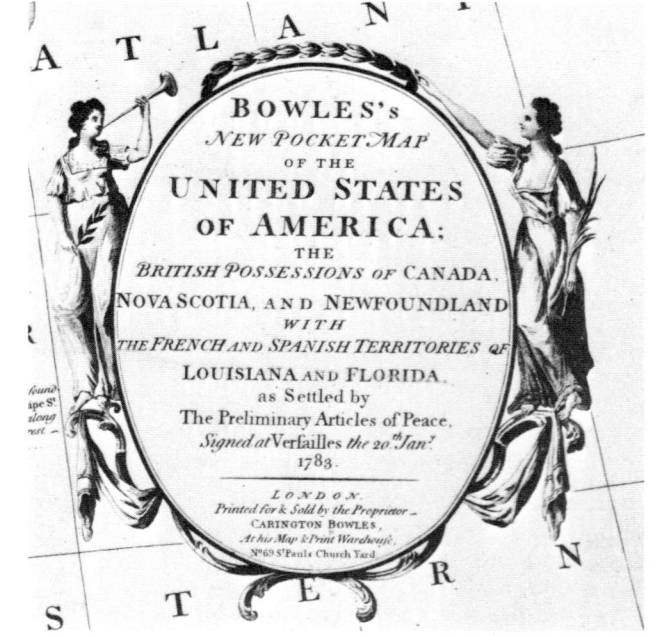

872

Government. North and Fox hold the arms of the new Government which pins George III to the ground. Fox's role as a Cromwell is expressed by the motto beneath inscribed "Neck or Nothing." In the quarters of the crest are two allusions to America. Upper left: an American flag held by North in a field with Burke pulling the lion's teeth and a paper designated Reform Bill. Lower right: Britannia upside down with olive branch in her hand refers to the frustrated reunion with America. CPPS 6441 LC–USZ62–30766

872
[The Blessings of Peace on America—a cartouche] LONDON. Printed for & Sold by . . . CARINGTON BOWLES, . . . No. 69 St. Paul's Church Yard 12 April 1784
 Mixed method 6 x 5½ in. (image)

Two beautiful women, probably Fame with her trumpet and Peace with her palm, decorate a cartouche for "Bowles New Pocket Map of the United States of America; the British Possessions of Canada, Nova Scotia, and Newfoundland with the French and Spanish Territories of Louisiana and Florida, as Settled by The Preliminary Articles of Peace, signed at Versailles the 20th Jany. 1783" in G&M Vault. Negative in G&M.

―――――――Another impression.

―――――――Another impression.

873
PRO BONO PUBLICO. THE POLITICAL CLUSTER in terrorem. WD. [Dent] Pubd. as the Act directs, by J. Brown, Rathbone Place, June 25th. 1784.
 Line engraving 14 x 9½ in.

A grape vine takes the shape of a gallows from which hangs a bunch of grapes resembling ministers. Fox, North, Burke, Keppel, Lee, Derby, Stormont, Cavendish, Portland, perhaps Carlisle, and House are the ripe grapes. Below them lie the "Trophies" of their political

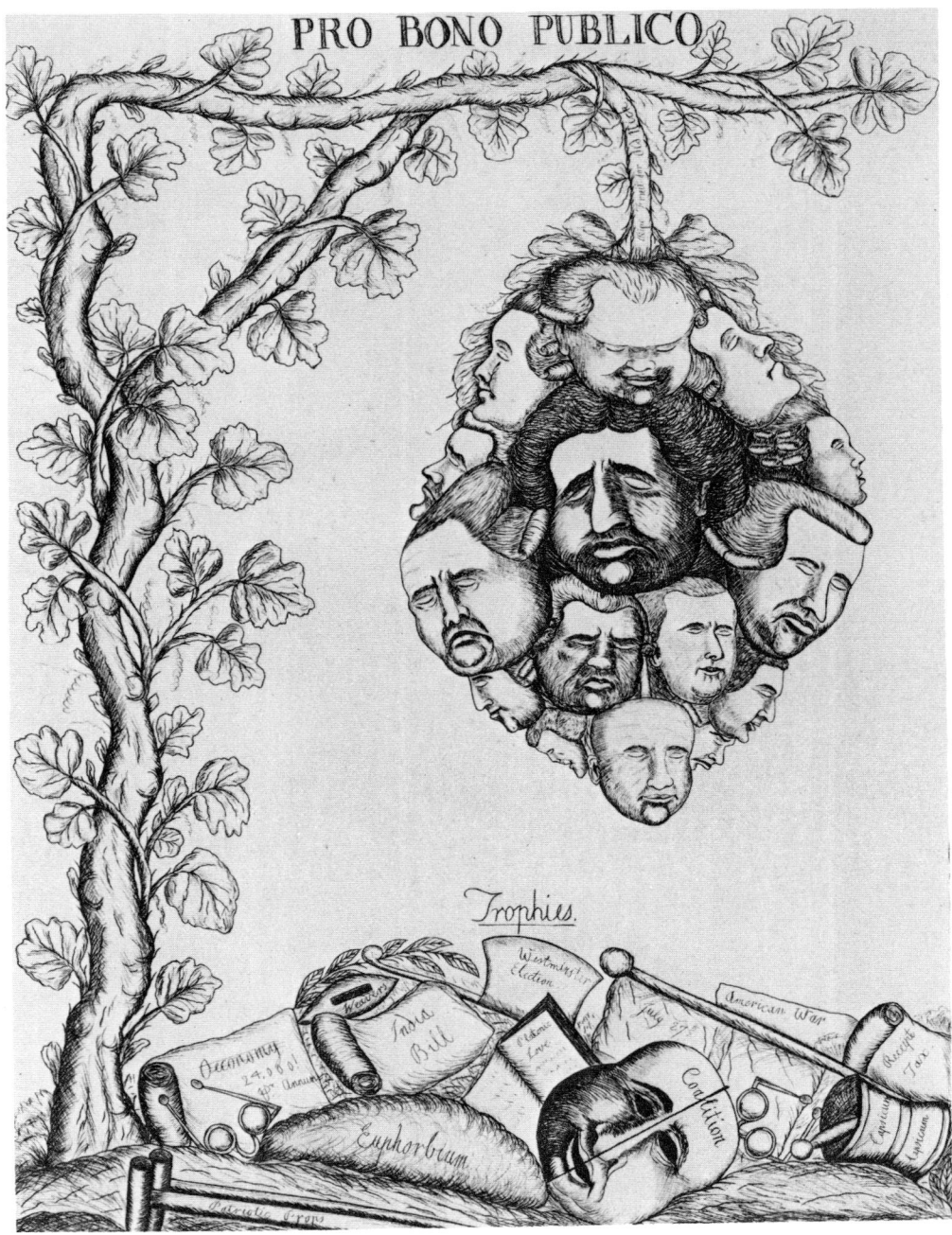

873

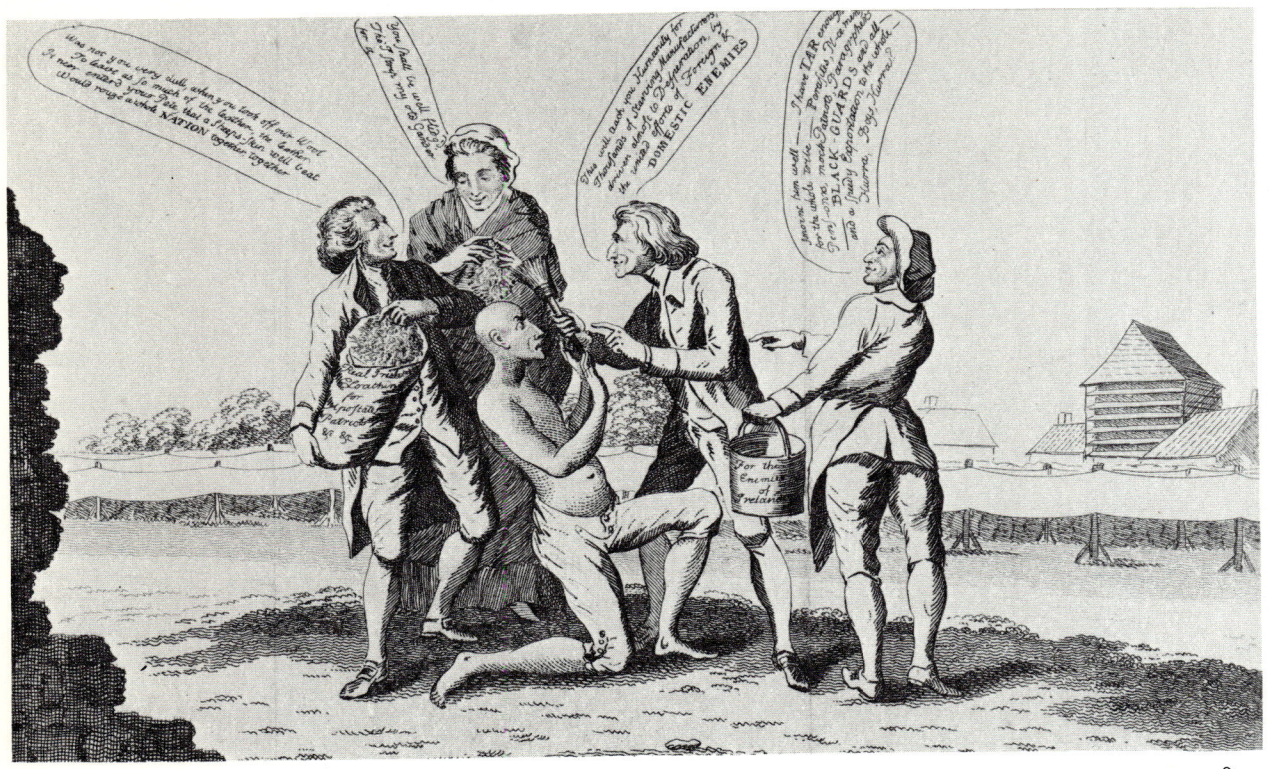

874

reign: "Oeconomy," "Euphorbium" (a scented fox tail), "India Bill," "Weavers," "Platonic Love" (claimed by Fox), "Westminster Election," "July 27th" (Battle of Ushant), "Coalition," "American War" (attributed to North), "Receipt Tax" (coalition measure dropped by Pitt), and "Patriotic Props." Throughout the remainder of Lord North's career in politics, cartoonists would label him as the man primarily responsible for losing the American Colonies. Cf. items 887, 893, and 896.
CPPS 6627 LC–USZ62–45472

874

TARRING AND FEATHERING The Reward of the Enemies of Ireland America Invent. Hibernia Fecit [August 1, 1784]
Mixed method 6⅛ x 10⅛ in. (image)

Fox and Sheridan tarring and feathering Pitt. The invention of the idea is ascribed to America on the opposite page: "The distressed Manufacturers of Ireland being drove to Desperation by the Rejection of protecting Duties, have adopted the example set them by their American Brethern of tarring and feathering such Persons as refuse to enter into a Non-importation and Non-consumption Agreement, judging that Measure the only Expedient to save this oppressed kingdom from Poverty and Wretchedness...." CPPS 6650
LC–USZ62–45474

———— Another impression. In *The Hibernian Magazine*, 1784, p. 345.

875

[American medals] D. Berger Sculp & Del. 1784
Mixed method 4¼ x 4½ in.

Four medals showing from left to right and top to bottom: 1) Liberty holding a shield with fleur-de-lis decoration protects the young Hercules (America) from an attacking lion (England); beneath are the dates 17 Oct. 1777 and

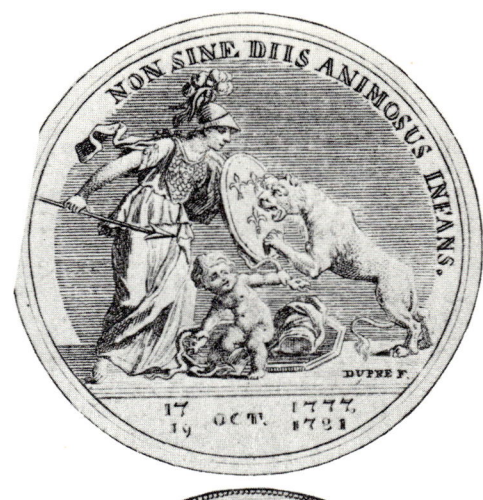
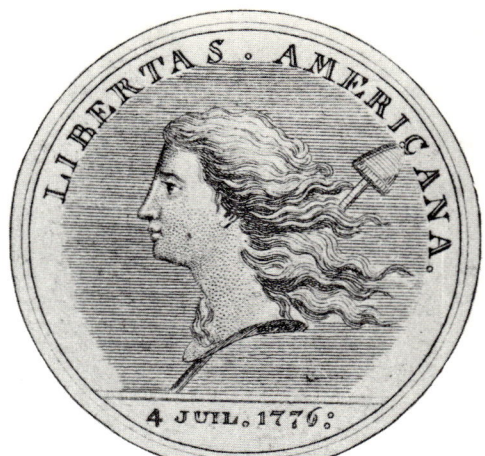
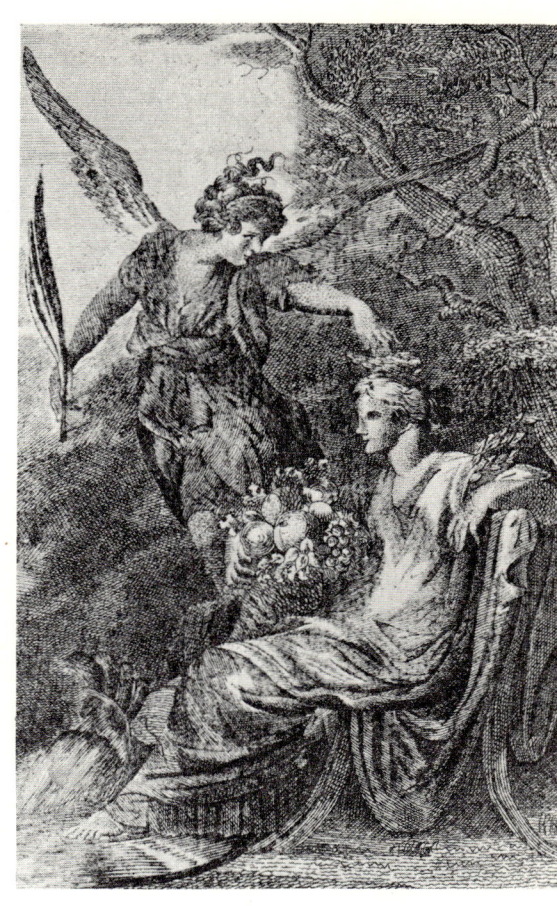

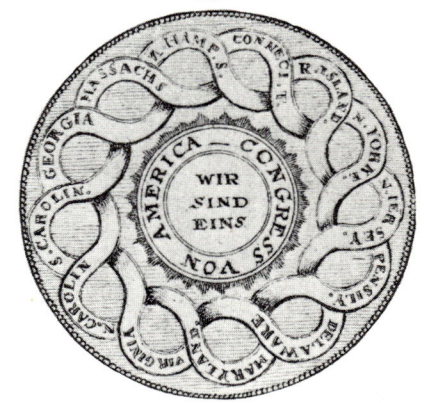
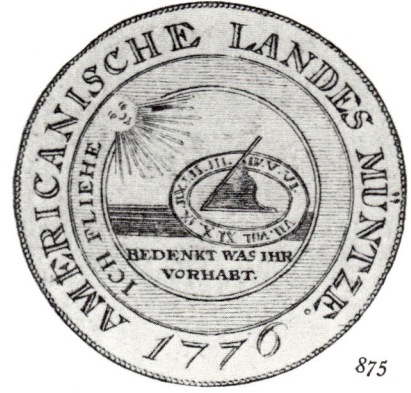

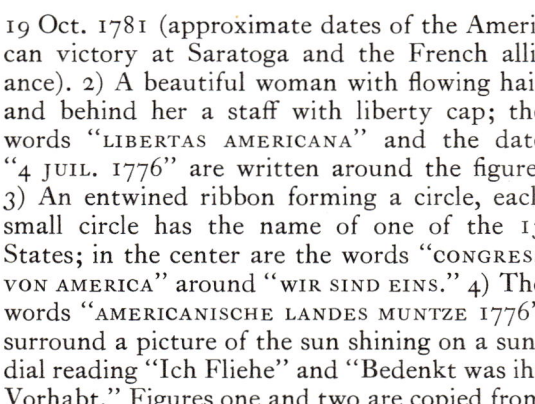
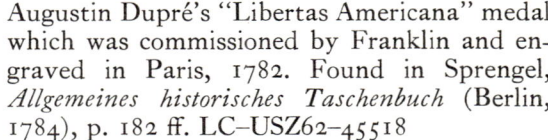

875   876

19 Oct. 1781 (approximate dates of the American victory at Saratoga and the French alliance). 2) A beautiful woman with flowing hair and behind her a staff with liberty cap; the words "LIBERTAS AMERICANA" and the date "4 JUIL. 1776" are written around the figure. 3) An entwined ribbon forming a circle, each small circle has the name of one of the 13 States; in the center are the words "CONGRESS VON AMERICA" around "WIR SIND EINS." 4) The words "AMERICANISCHE LANDES MUNTZE 1776" surround a picture of the sun shining on a sundial reading "Ich Fliehe" and "Bedenkt was ihr Vorhabt." Figures one and two are copied from

Augustin Dupré's "Libertas Americana" medal which was commissioned by Franklin and engraved in Paris, 1782. Found in Sprengel, *Allgemeines historisches Taschenbuch* (Berlin, 1784), p. 182 ff. LC–USZ62–45518

876

PEACE CROWNED BY VICTORY. J. NORMAN SC. [1784]
Mixed method 7¼ x 4 in.

A beautiful woman seated with a bountiful bowl of fruit and flowers receives a crown from a winged woman carrying a palm. Frontispiece

for *The Boston Magazine*, August 1784. Norman copied this piece from *The European Magazine*, 1783, frontispiece. LC–USZ62–45283

877

[Fox, Burke, and North] FRONTISPIECE [1784]
Etching 4½ x 4½ in. (image in oval)

Bust portraits caricaturing the coalition. The "Introduction" explains, "The Coalition formed between Lord North, the Right Honourable Charles James Fox, and Mr. Edmund Burke, haveing been justified under a pretence that the American war was the cause of their

391

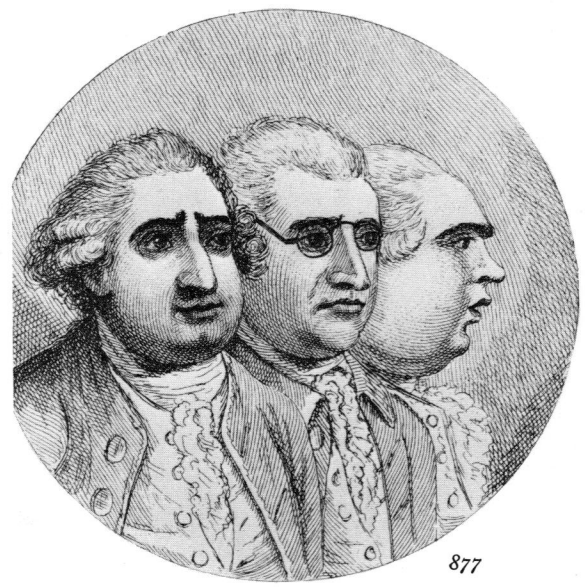

difference, and that when it was at an end, no reason any longer subsisted against their acting together in the service of their country, the following publication is submitted to the impartial and dispassionate reader, as at once the most direct and fairest means of exposing the futility of such a defince, and indeed of every argument in favour of so unnatural a junction." From Fox, *The Beauties of Fox, North, and Burke* (London, 1784), frontispiece.
LC–USZ62–45542

878
[A warship carries the seal of the United States—a cartouche] A Paris Chez Lattré Graveur du Roi Rue St. Jacques No. 20 1784
Etching 9½ x 9½ in. (image)

A sailor hangs national seals on the mast of a warship. The center seal is the American eagle with the E Pluribus Unum ribbon. The title of the map is "Carte des Etats-Unis de l'Amerique suivant le Traité de Paix de 1783. Dédiée et Présentée A. S. Excellence Mr. Benjamin

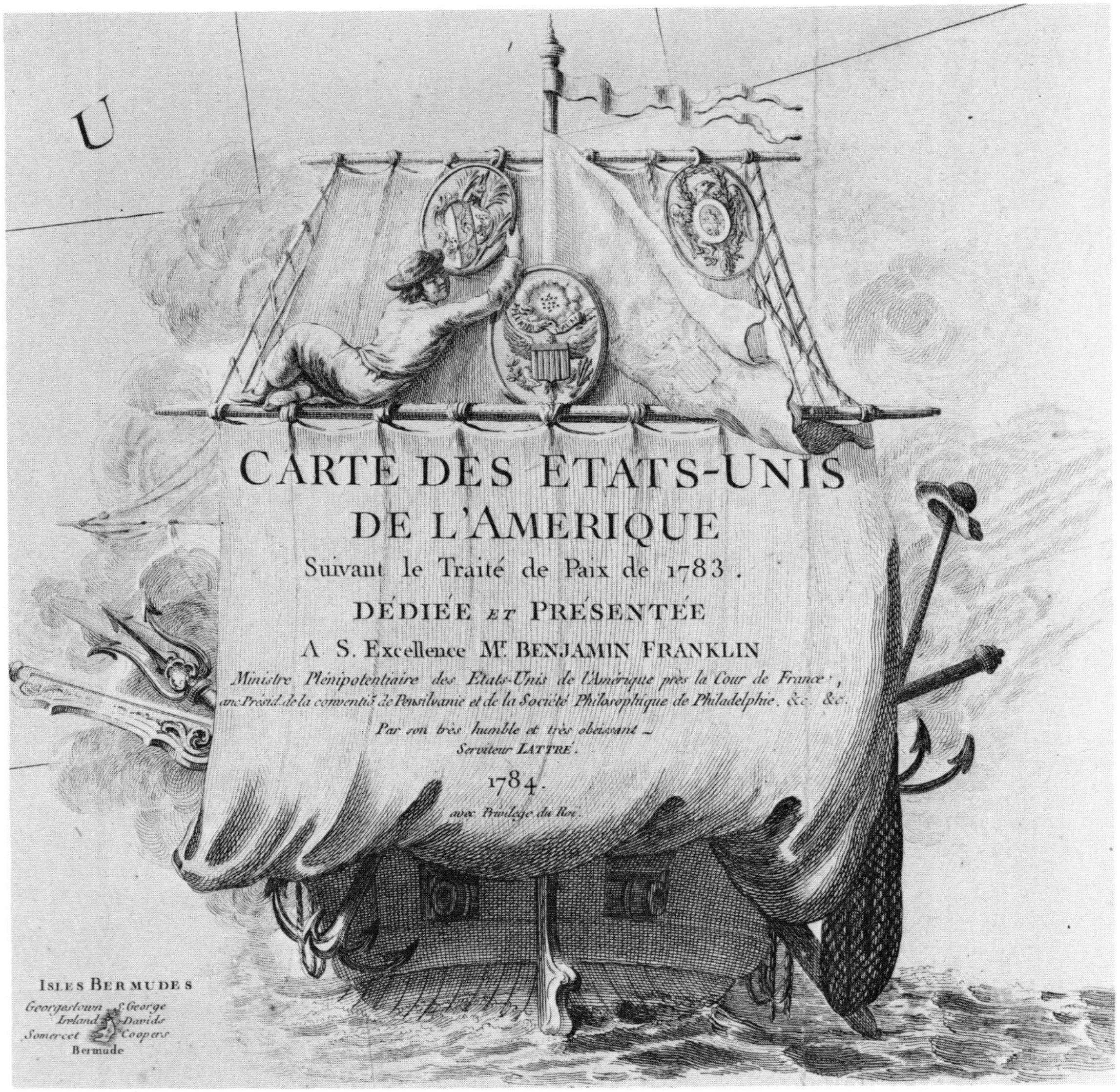

Franklin . . . Par son . . . Serviteur [Jean] Lattré. 1784" In G&M. LC–USZ62–46074

———Another impression.

879
[A French allegory on America—a cartouche] A Paris, chez Esnauts et Rapilly, rue St. Jacques, à la Ville de Coutances 1784 A.P.D.R.
Etching 7¼ x 8¾ in. (image)

On the left side a naval cannon is draped with an American flag and a Bourbon flag; on the right side a staff with liberty cap afixed is resting on a bush. From a map entitled "Carte des Etats-unis d'Amérique et du Cours du Mississipi; rédigée d'après différentes Cartes et Relations Anglaises, et les opérations de la derniere Guerre; avec les Nouvelles Limites Générales fixées par les articles préliminaires de paix, signés tant à Paris qu'à Versailles, le 30 9bre 1782 et le 20 Janr. 1783 . . . . Cette carte composée par le Sr. Brion de la Tour . . ." in G&M.

———Another impression.

880
The Hibernian Attempt. [April 1785]
Mixed method 4 x 6½ in.

George III, wearing half a crown, sits on his throne; a Negro with feathers in his hair and a striped flag runs from the throne with the other half of the crown. Pitt and Thurlow stand by the throne looking at the King, while an Irishman rides the British bull (John Bull), twisting its tail. From *The Rambler's Magazine*, April 1785, p. 141. CPPS 6787 LC–USZ62–45485

881
[The continents surround the goddess of geography] J. Buys inv. C. Bogerts sculp. 1785
Etching 4¾ x 8 in. (image)

The goddess of geography sits on a throne

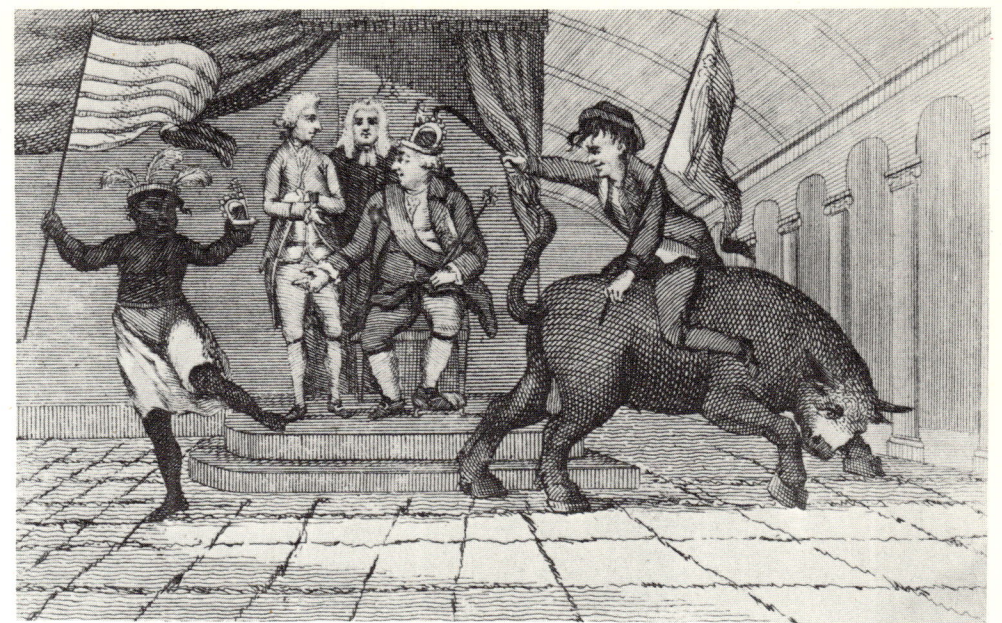

880

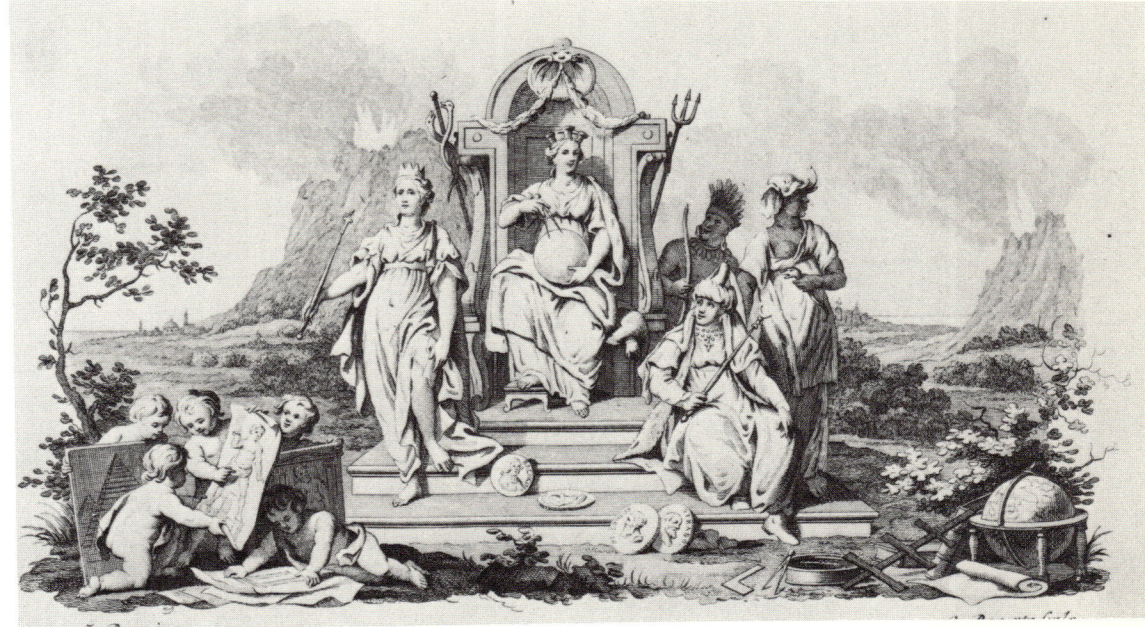

881

393

with a globe and compass in her hands; Europe, Asia, Africa, and America are by the throne, and nymphs play in the foreground. In the background is a wide expanse of landscape with two volcanoes. This allegory is from the title page of Bachiene, *Atlas* (Amsterdam, 1785). LC–USZ62–46090

882

While Commerce spreads her canvass o'er the main. [1786]
Etching 6⅜ x 3¾ in.

Columbia as a young Roman woman brings two children to Minerva who has a spear, books, and a globe. From a pedestal hangs a scroll reading "Independence the reward of Wisdom Fortitude and Perseverance." In the background a farmer plows a field, and ships set out to sea. Beneath is a poem:

> While Commerce spreads her canvas o'er the main,
> And Agriculture ploughs the grateful plain
> Minerva aids Columbia's rising race
> With arms to triumph and with arts to grace.

The advent of peace brought prosperity to America, and artists in the United States and Europe celebrated the new nation's commerce and agriculture. From *The Columbian Magazine, or Monthly Miscellany*, 1787, frontispiece. Fielding, 1841. LC–USZ62–30932

883

[Arms of the United States] Jas. Trenchard Sculp. [1786]
Etching 6⅜ x 4¼ in. (image)

"The Device of the Armorial Achievement, appertaining to the United States" is described as follows:

> CREST
> Over the head of the eagle, which appears above the escutcheon, a glory, *or*, breaking through a cloud proper, and surrounding thirteen stars, forming a constellation, argent, on an azure field.

In *The Columbian Magazine, or Monthly Miscellany*, September 1786, opposite p. 33. Stauffer, 3281. LC–USZ62–45508

884

THE REVERSE OF THE GREAT SEAL OF THE UNITED STATES. JT Sculp. [1786]
Etching 4½ x 7 in.

An explanation appears on the adjacent page:

> REVERSE
> A pyramid unfinished.—
> In the zenith, an eye in a triangle, surrounded with a glory, proper, Over the eye, the words—annuit coeptis: on the base of the pyramid, the numeral letters—M.DCC.LXXVI: and underneath the following motto or exergue—*Novus* ordo seclorum.

From *The Columbian Magazine, or Monthly Miscellany*, September 1786, opposite p. 51. Stauffer, 3282. LC–USZ62–45509

885

VENERATE THE PLOUGH. JT sculp. [1786]
Etching 2 x 2 in. (image)

Within a circle a man plowing with oxen is followed by America who carries a sheaf of grain and has a halo of 13 stars. This small picture is set into "The Plan of A Farm Yard" found in *The Columbian Magazine, or Monthly Miscellany*, October 1786, opposite p. 77. Stauffer, 3288. LC–USZ62–31153

886

THE POOR BLACKS GOING TO THEIR SETTLEMENT. [Dent] Pubd. as the Act directs for the proprietor by E. Macklew, No. 9, Haymarket, Jany 12th 1787, of [sic] may be had the new, very popular and comprehensive Print, entitled The French Treaty Reviewed &c &c
Etching 8½ x 15¼ in.

English ministers are caricatured as poor Negroes going to a settlement house. Burke, George Hanger (1751?–1824), and the Prince of Wales are already in the house, and Fox, North,

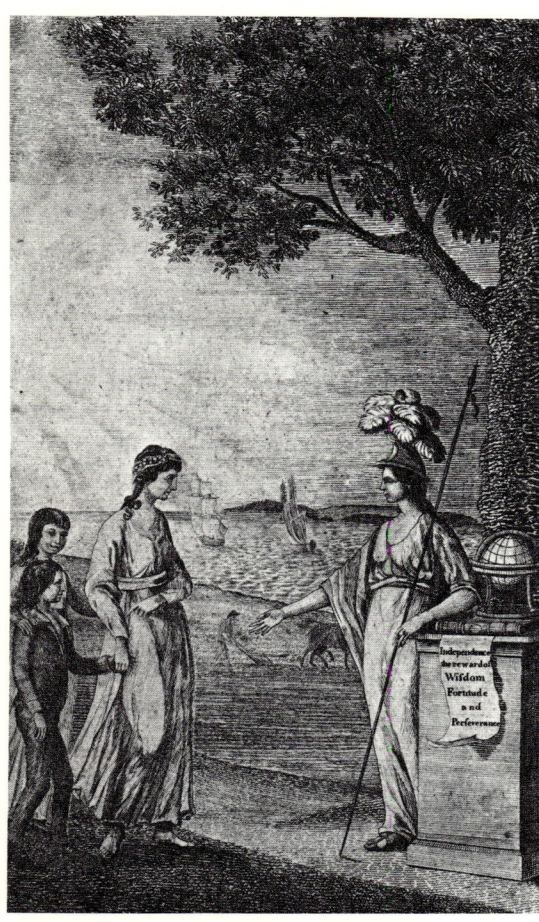

882

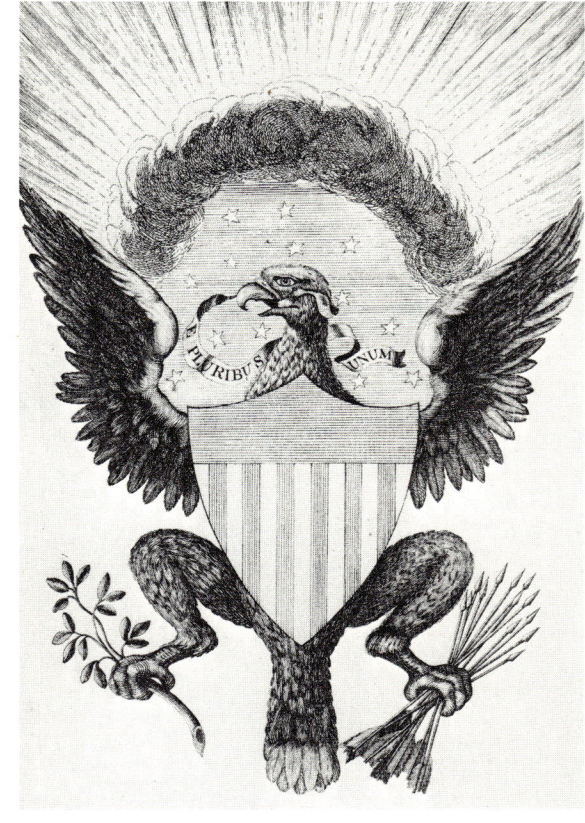

883

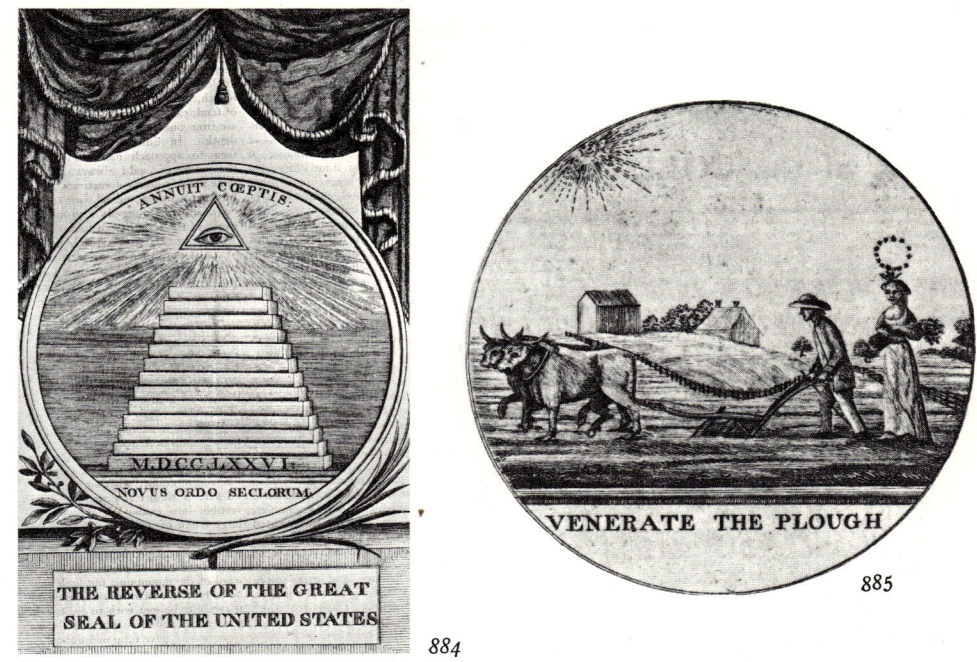

884

THE REVERSE OF THE GREAT SEAL OF THE UNITED STATES

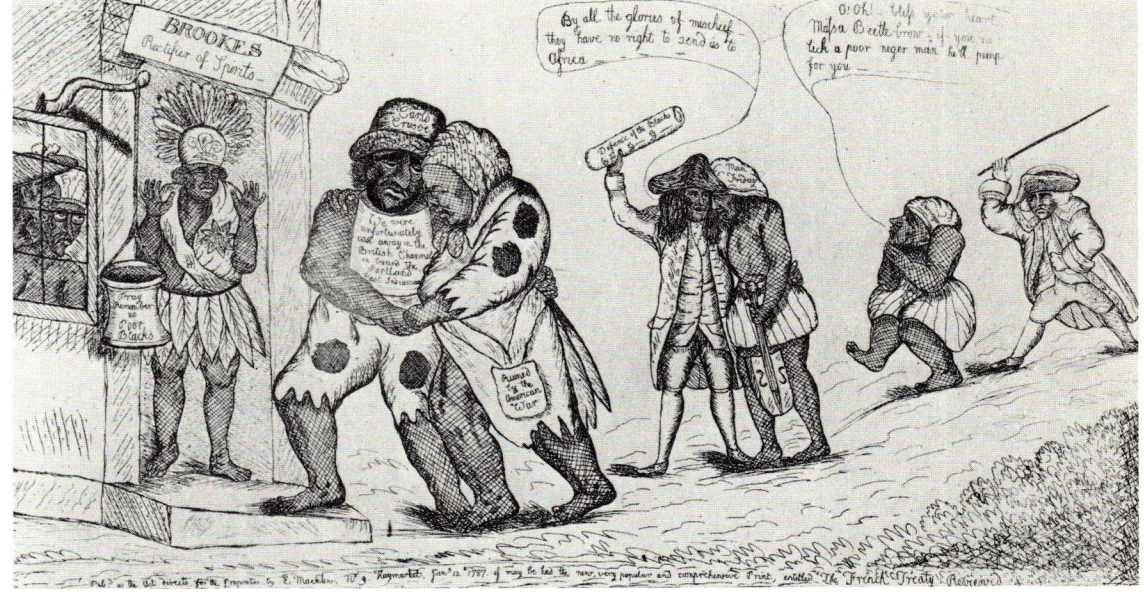

885

VENERATE THE PLOUGH

886

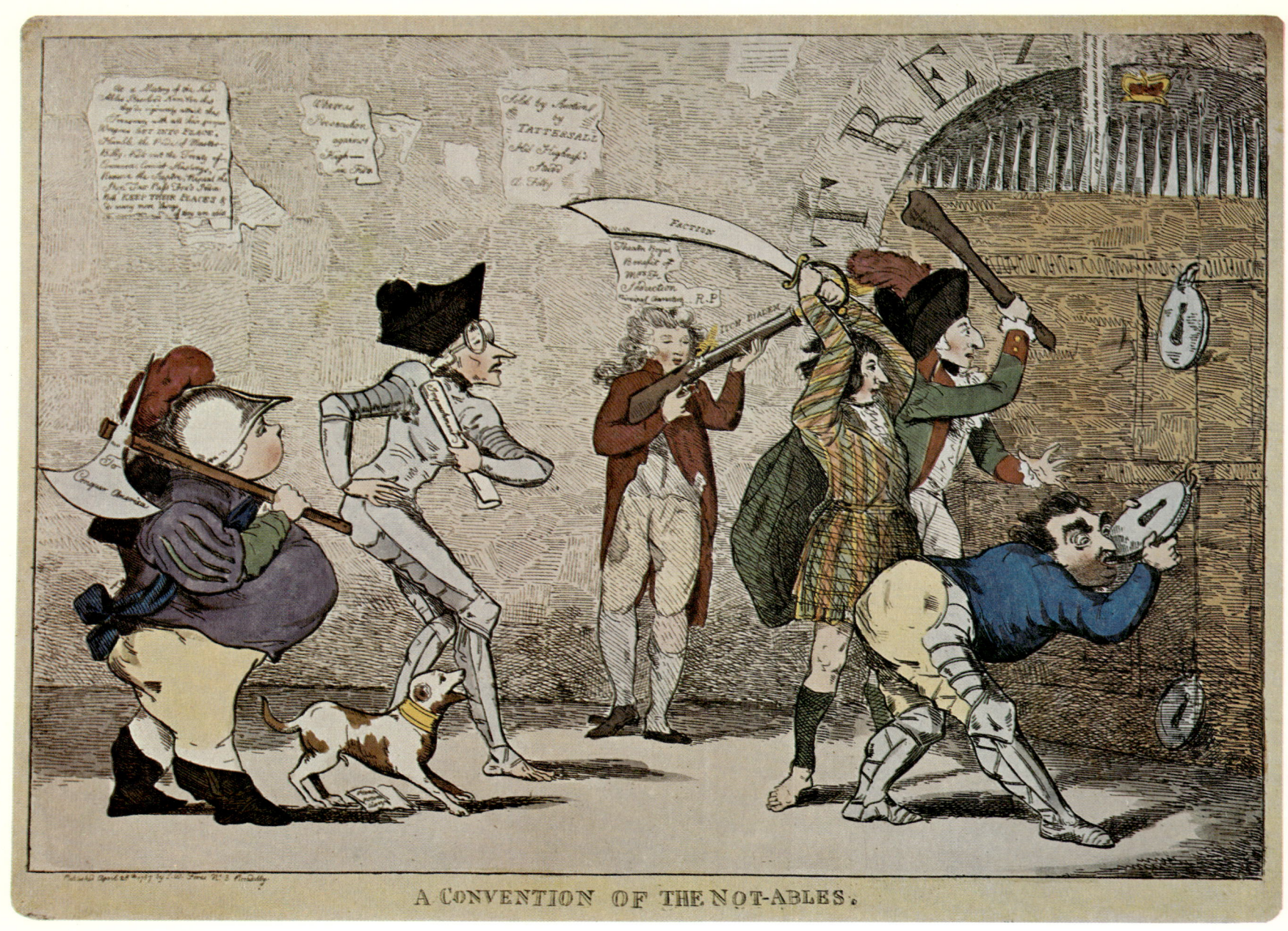

other Negroes, and perhaps Sheridan are walking toward the house with Lord George Gordon chasing them. From a ribbon around North's coat hangs a sign "Ruined by the American War." This cartoon satirizes the manner in which the Prince Regent and his friends settled the problem of freed Negroes in Sierra Leone and the attempted revolt in Newgate Prison raised by Gordon. CPPS 7127
LC–USZ62–45473

887

A CONVENTION OF THE NOT-ABLES. Published April 28th 1787 by S. W. Fores No 3 Piccadilly.
Etching (hand colored) 12 x 15½ in.

The Prince of Wales and his friends Fox, North, Burke, and Hanger try to beat down the door of the English treasury. North holds an ax designated "To Conquer America." This cartoon satirizes the efforts of the Prince Regent and his friends in their work with the Commercial Treaty of 1787, the Ship Tax, and the India Bill, among others. North's reputation as the man who was primarily responsible for losing America is still with him and reminds the reader that North had already impoverished Britain once. CPPS 7158

———Another impression (uncolored).

888

THE SICK PRINCE. [Gillray] Pubd. June 16. 1787. by S. W. Fores. No. 3 Piccadilly.
Etching (hand colored) 8⅝ x 10 in.

The Prince of Wales is on a deathbed with Thurlow, Pitt, and Richmond who want to kill him on one side and Britannia, Fox, Burke, North, and Sheridan who pray for his life on the other. The grim reaper has broken through a group of physicians and a naked, black savage in order to approach the bed. Above the deathbed is a scroll reading, "1800 Glory Conquest

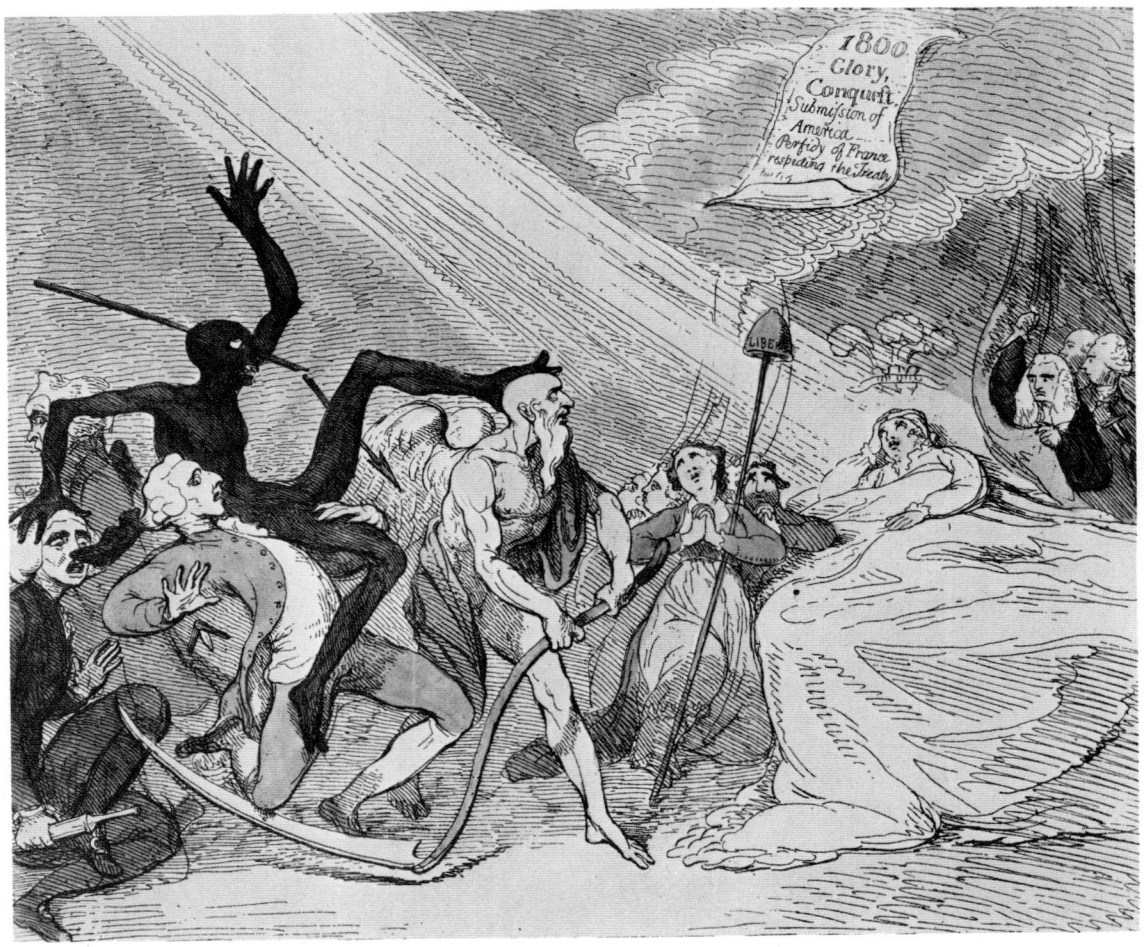

888

397

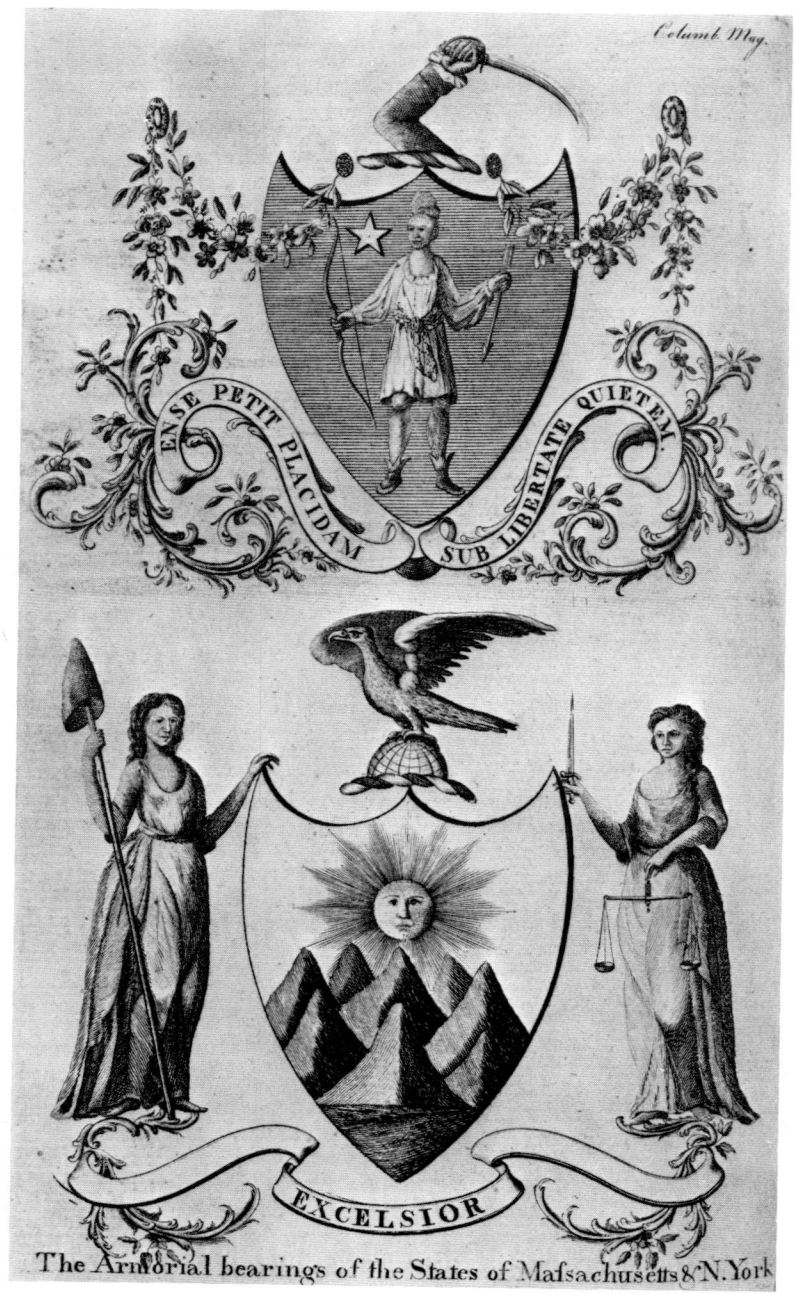

The Armorial bearings of the States of Massachusetts & N. York

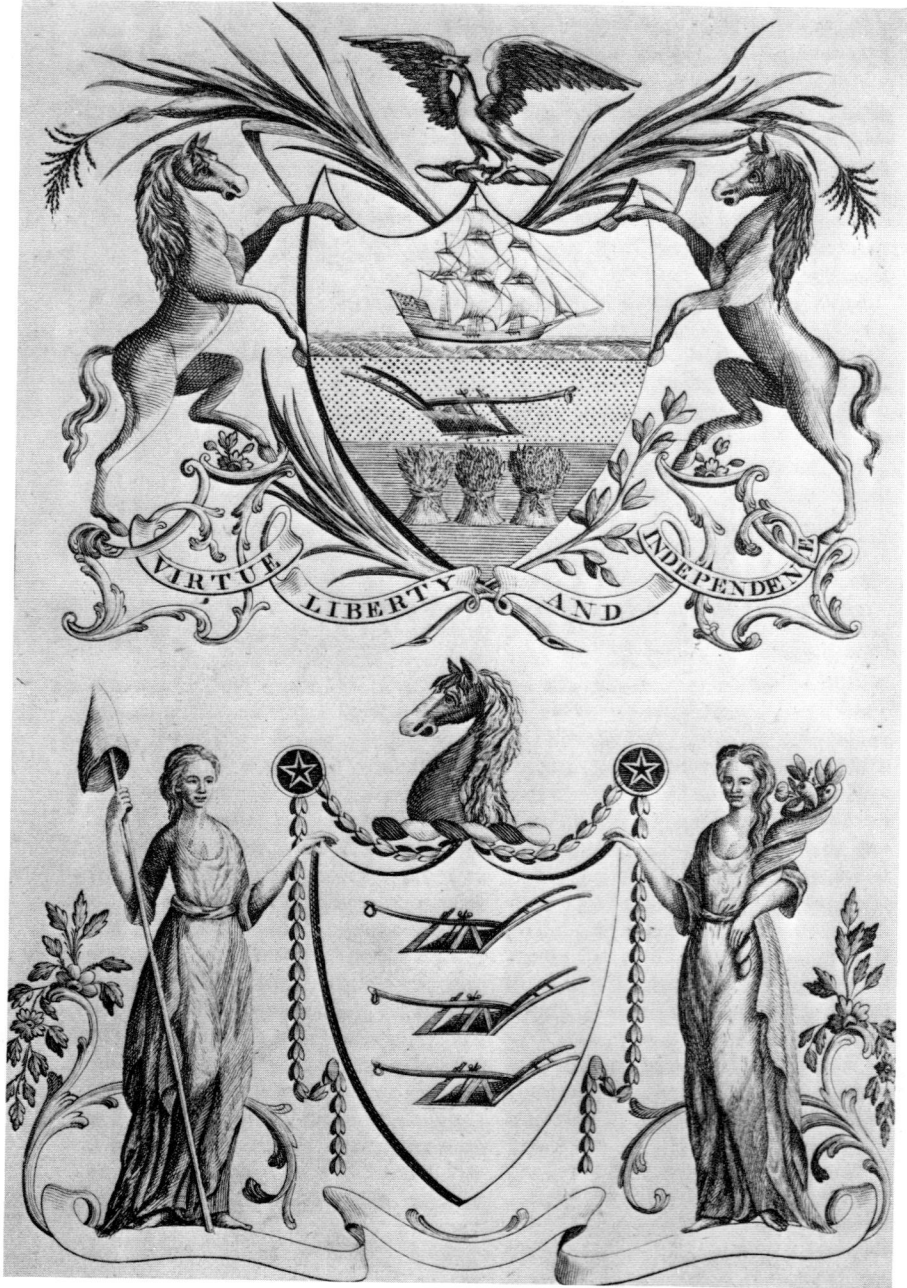

Submission of America—Perfidy of France respecting the Treaty." CPPS 7170
LC–USZ62–45563

———Another impression (uncolored).

889

The Armorial bearings of the States of Massachusetts & N. York. [Trenchard? 1787]
Etching 7¼ x 4⅜ in.

Descriptions read:

The Armorial Bearings of the State of Massachusetts

Sapphire, an Indian dressed in his shirt and mogossins, belted proper; in his right hand, a bow topaz; in his left, an arrow, its point towards the base; of the second, on the dexter side of the Indian's head, a star, pearl, for one of the United States of America.—Crest—On a wreath a dexter arm clothed and ruffed proper, grasping a broad sword, the pommel and hilt topaz, with this Motto, "ENSE PETIT PLACIDAM SUB LIBERTATE QUIETEM."

The Armorial Bearings of the State of New-York.

Argent, a sun rising over a hilly country proper.—Crest—An eagle soaring from a globe, proper; supported on the dexter side by Liberty, and on the finister by Justice.—Motto—"EXCELSIOR."

From *The Columbian Magazine*, October 1787, opposite p. 715. Stauffer, 3280.
LC–USZ62–45512

890

The Armonial Bearings of the States of Pennsylvania & New Jersey. [Trenchard? 1787]
Etching 6⅝ x 4⅝ in.

Descriptions read:

Armorial Bearing of the State of Pennsylvania.

Party surfess, argent and azure; on a fess, or, a plough proper: in chief, a ship under full sail in the sea proper; and in base three wheat sheaves; placed barways, or.—Crest—on a wreath, an eagle with his wings elevated, ready to soar aloft, proper.—Supporters—Two horses argent.—Motto—Virtue, Liberty and Independence.

Armorial Bearing of the State of New-Jersey.

Argent, three ploughs placed paleways proper.—Supporters—on the dexter side, Ceres, bearing Cornucopia; and on the finister side, the Genius of Liberty, holding a staff surmounted of the cap of liberty;—both figures in their proper habiliments.

From *The Columbian Magazine*, June 1787, opposite p. 491. Stauffer, 3279.
LC–USZ62–45511

891

REPRESENTATION of a COUNTY-CONVENTION for REDRESS of GRIEVANCE of COURTS. [1787]
Woodcut 3 x 5 in. (image)

Ten men sit around a table inside a large building. A short poem accompanies the picture:

> How blest is that Interpreter of Laws,
> Who rich and Poor make equal in a Cause!
> Who dares with steady hand the balance hold,
> And ne'er inclines it to one Side for Gold;
> Altho' in Rags, one Scale gives equal weight,
> Against the gilded Trappings of the Great.
> 'Tis such alone deserves our just Applause,
> And such alone gives Sanction to the LAWS.

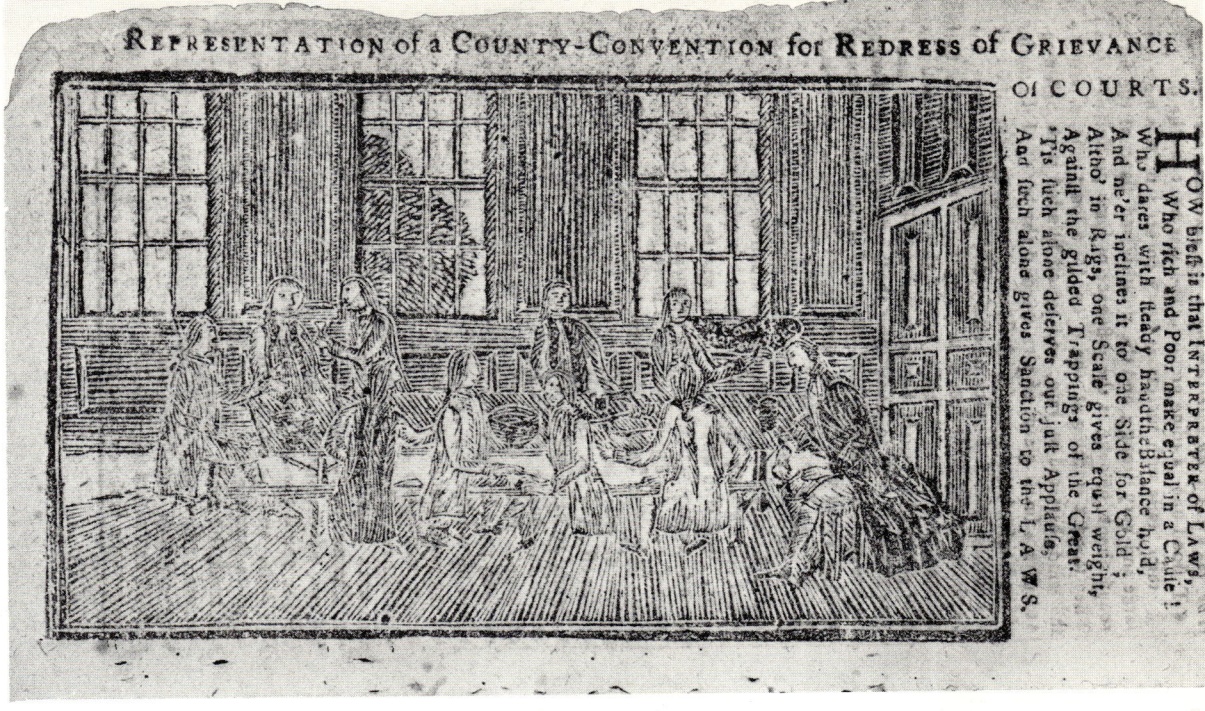

891

From *Bickerstaff's Genuine Boston Almanack*, 1787. LC–USZ62–45567

892

[Justice enthroned] 1787
Woodcut ¾ x ⅝ in. (image)

Justice sits on an obelisk with foliage in one hand and liberty cap on staff in the other. The picture was part of the masthead for *The Massachusetts Centinel* during the years 1787 to 1790. It symbolizes the motto on the masthead, "Uninfluenced by Party, we aim to be JUST." LC–USZ62–45588

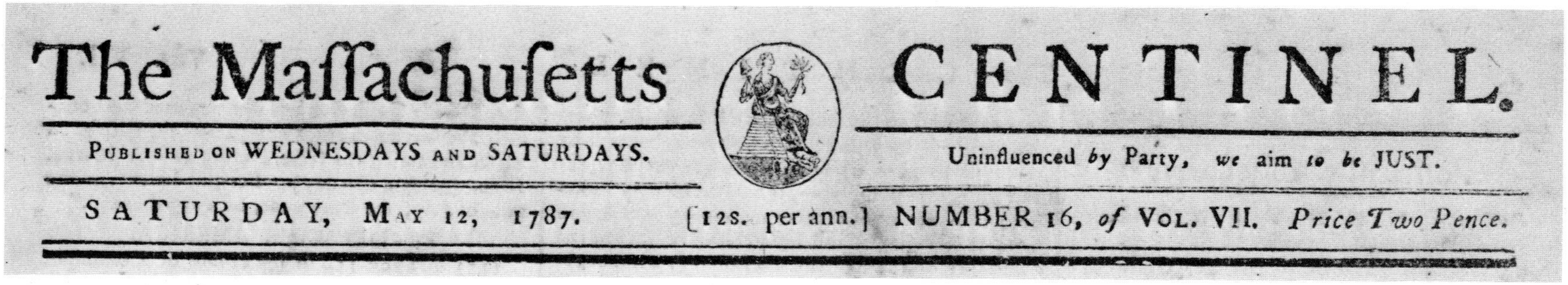

The Massachusetts CENTINEL.

PUBLISHED ON WEDNESDAYS AND SATURDAYS.   Uninfluenced by Party, we aim to be JUST.

SATURDAY, MAY 12, 1787.   [12s. per ann.] NUMBER 16, of VOL. VII. Price Two Pence.

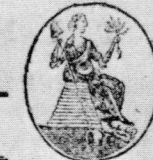

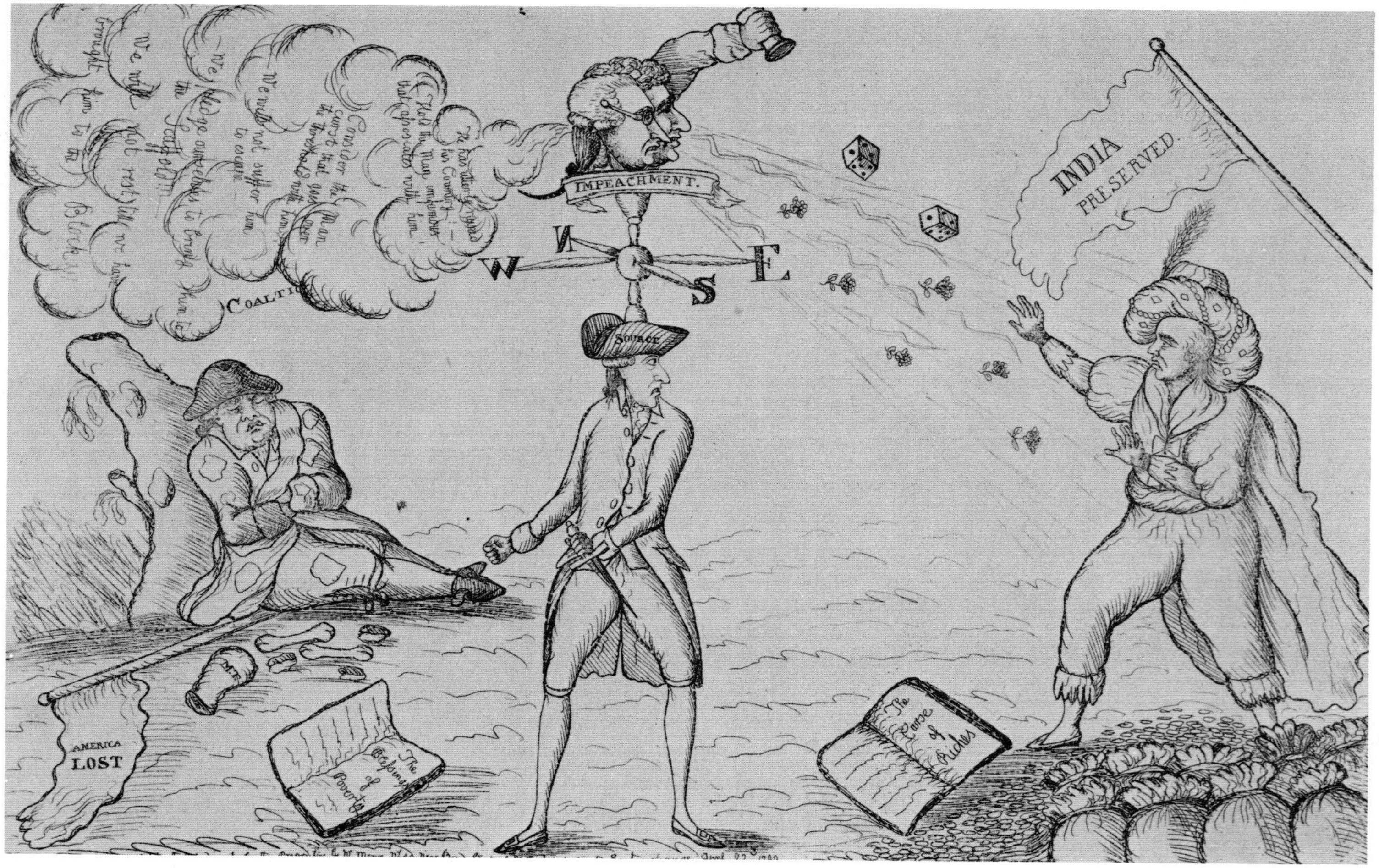

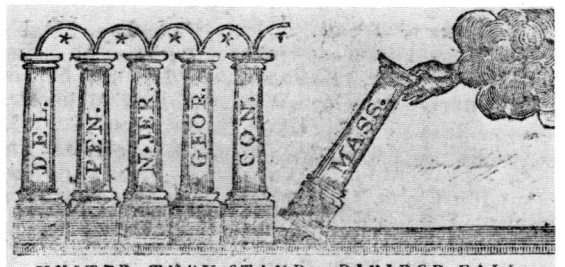

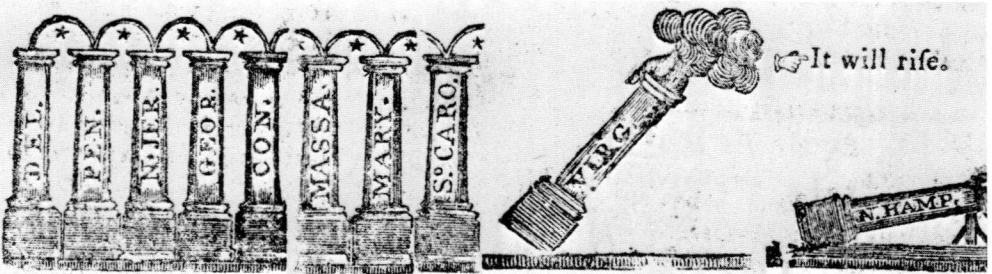

893

THUNDER, LIGHTNING and SMOKE, or, the WIND shifted from the NORTH to the EAST. Pubd as the Act directs for the proprietor by W Moore N48 New Bond Street & W. Dickie opposite Exeter change April 22 1788

Etching 9½ x 13¾ in.

On the extreme right Warren Hastings stands in turban and Indian garb amid money bags and under a banner which reads "India preserved." He stands against a blast of wind which comes from Burke and Fox whose heads are atop a weathervane, the shaft of which is a man designated "Source"—probably Philip Francis. Below the heads of Burke and Fox is a sign "Impeachment." Behind their heads is smoke with the following statements: "He has utterly ruined his Country," "Hold the man infamous that associates with him," "We will not suffer him to escape," "We pledge ourselves to bring him to the Scaffold," "We will not rest until we have brought him to the Block!!!" On the ground lies North with empty purse, naked bones, and a banner reading "America Lost" at his side. Once again North is pictured as politically ineffective after his loss of America even though poor health caused much of his decline. LC–USZ62–44842

894

THE FEDERAL PILLARS. [January 16, 1788 to August 2, 1788]

Woodcuts 1⅜ x 2⅝ in. and 1½ x 4½ in. (image)

A series of allegories which appears in *The Massachusetts Centinel* beginning January 16, 1788. The first shows five erect pillars representing the States of Delaware, Pennsylvania, New Jersey, Georgia, and Connecticut, all standing upright while a hand reaches from a cloud to set Massachusetts into line. Beneath the picture is the slogan "United They Stand—Divided Fall" (LC–USZ62–45589). In the issue of January 30, 1788, the same picture appears with the title "FEDERAL SUPERSTRUCTURE." On February 9, 1788, the Massachusetts column stands in place with an arch joining it to the other columns, and the title reads, "The GRAND FEDERAL EDIFACE." On the 13th of February New Hampshire appears and is still in the process of being erected when the convention in Maryland ratified the Constitution on May 7. On June 11, 1788, the South Carolina pillar stands upright, with Virginia and New Hampshire leaning; from this point the size of the pillars is larger (LC–USZ62–45590). By June 25, 1788, New Hampshire is up, and Virginia has a sign by it reading, "If it hath not—it will rise." Around the borders of this picture entitled "NINTH and the SUFFICIENT PILLAR" is the quotation, "The ratification of the Convention of nine States, shall be sufficient for the establishment of this Constitution. AR. vii." On July 5, 1788, Virginia is in place, and on August 2, 1788, New York is in place; North Carolina is swinging up, and a crumbled Rhode Island pillar has a sign reading "The foundation good—it may yet be SAVED." This is the last in a series of 11 pictures. LC–USZ62–45591

895

Behold! a Fabric now to Freedom rear'd. Trenchard Sculp. [1788]

Etching 5½ x 3⅞ in. (image)

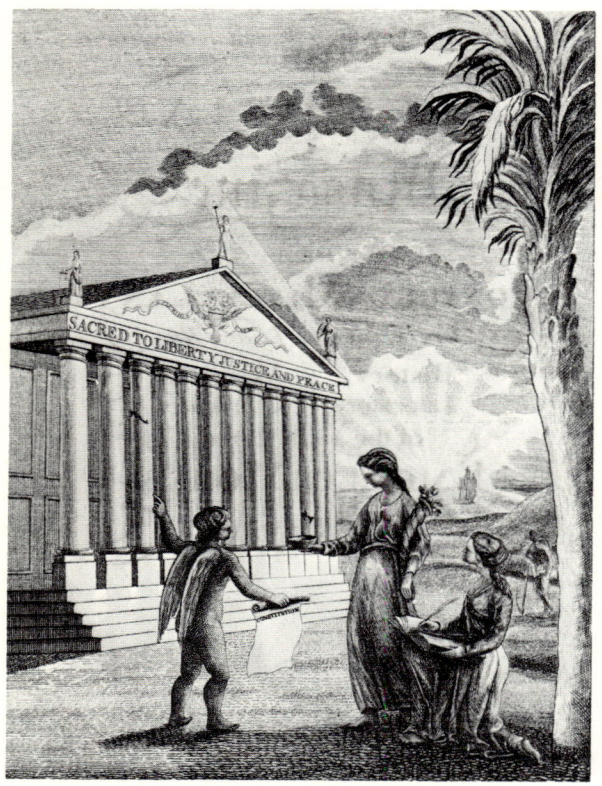 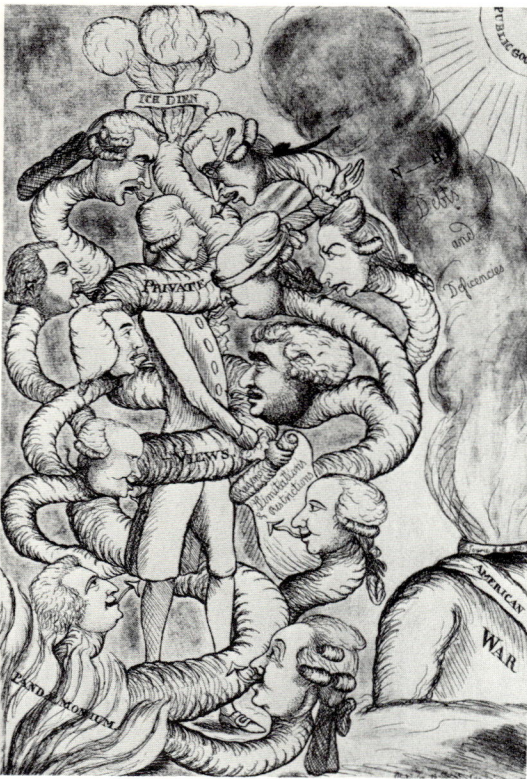

895 896

Concord approaches a temple with 13 pillars and the inscription "Sacred to Liberty Justice and Peace." The pediment is faced by an American eagle with ribbon reading "E Pluribus Unum." On top of the temple are statues of Freedom, with staff and liberty cap, Justice, with scales, and Peace, with a palm. Clio kneels beside Concord to inscribe the message delivered to her by Cupid who holds a copy of the Constitution. Below is a verse explanation.

> Behold! a Fabric now to Freedom rear'd,
> Approv'd by friends, and ev'n by Foes rever'd;
> Where Justice, too, and Peace, by us ador'd,
> Shall heal each Wrong, and keep ensheath'd the sword
> Approach then, Concord, fair Columbia's Son;
> And, faithful Clio write that 'WE ARE ONE'.

From *The Columbian Magazine, or Monthly Miscellany*, 1788, frontispiece. Fielding, 1707.
LC–USZ62–45513

896

THE MONSTROUS HYDRA, or VIRTUE INVULNERABLE. Sold by W Moore Oxford Street Pub by W Dent Jany 11th 1789
Mixed method 12¾ x 8¼ in.

The Prince of Wales surrounded by the heads of the Hydra representing Fox, North, Burke, and others. He holds a paper reading "Regency Limitations & Restrictions." Behind him the source of the hydra is in the lower left corner marked "Pandaemonium" from which grows the trunk of the monster designated "Private Views." On the lower right corner is another fire coming from a receptacle entitled "Source of all Evil" based on a foundation upon which is engraved "American War." The smoke from this fire designated "N___h's [North's] Debts and Deficencies" blocks out the light from the sun inscribed "Public Good."
LC–USZ62–30929

897

A Privy Council laying their Heads together, or Necessary business. Pubd. by W———

[name crossed out, but probably by W. Dent] Jany 6, 1789 Sold by W Moore Oxford Street.
Etching 6¾ x 10 in.

Pitt, Camden, and probably Thurlow sit in a privy together. William Pitt the Younger sits beneath a picture of himself while urinating on a fox. The picture is entitled "The Political Priapus Delineated by E. Burke." Pitt says, "Oh! must I lose my place." At his feet lies a bundle of carrots, representing the feathers of the Prince of Wales, with the banner reading "Ich Dien" as seen in "The Monstrous Hydra" (item 896). Camden sits under a crown which is being attacked by mice. These mice can represent such foreign trouble spots as America, Ireland, India, France, and Spain as well as many internal problems. At his feet is a banner reading, "Resolution to strain a Point." The next sitter, Thurlow, says, "Cruel, dam'd cruel case." A "Waxen Image" of Thurlow hangs on the wall above him with the Great Seal stuffed in its mouth. This cartoon on the Regency period uses the same theme of the necessary house found in item 692 on the "Necessary Politicians." The issue of America lost was still alive in British politics but was a less prominent concern than the immediate power struggle in Parliament and on the continent.

898
America! with Peace and Freedom blest.
[1789]
Mixed method 6 x 4⅛ in. (image)

America is a young woman enjoying the benefits of education once the war is over. Her shield rests by her side, and her staff and liberty cap lean against a tree behind her. She sits in the shade of a palm tree with books, a globe, a cornucopia, and bow with arrows. To her left a god with a lyre speaks with her while pointing to a statue of Fame on a small temple behind them. The god says,

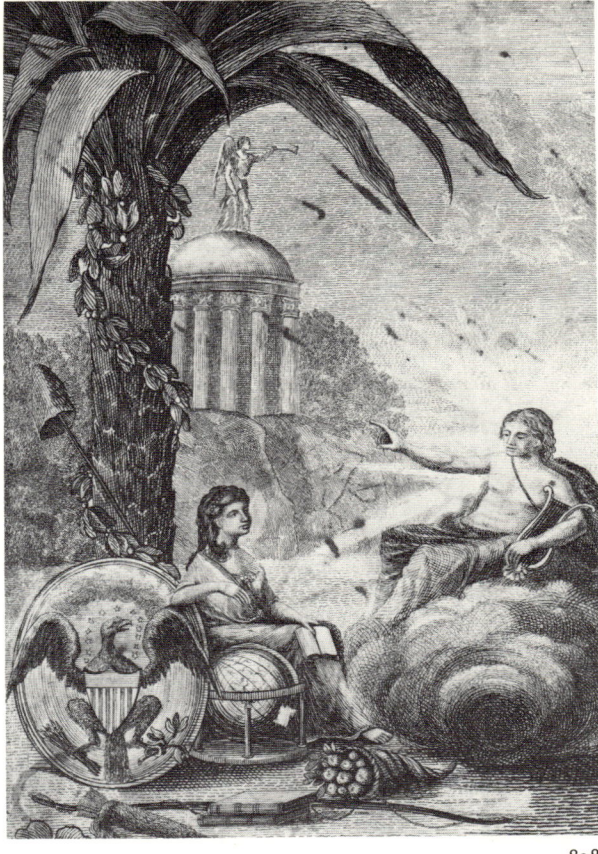
898

America! with Peace and Freedom blest,
Pant for true Fame, and scorn inglorious rest:
Science invites; urg'd by the Voice divine,
Exert thy self, 'till every Art be thine.

From *The Columbian Magazine, or Monthly Miscellany*, 1789, frontispiece.
LC-USZ62-45573

899
[Ornament for title page of *The Columbian Magazine* throughout the year 1789]
Woodcut 2½ x 3¼ in. (image)

An American eagle rests on a platform hold-

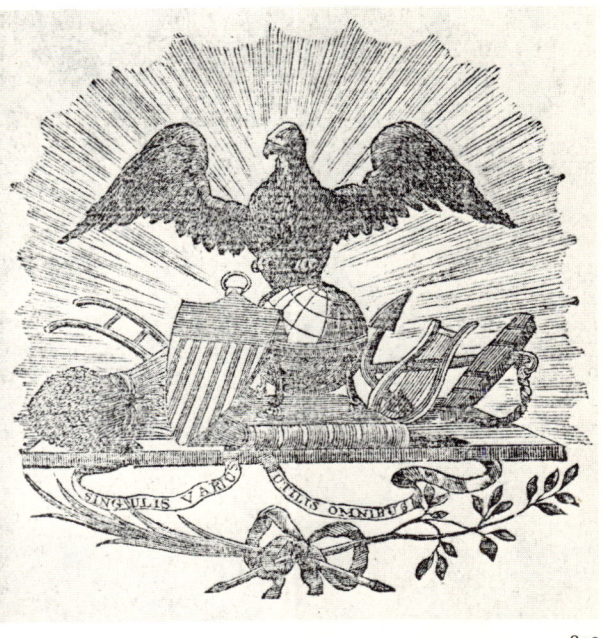
899

ing a plow, a sheaf of grain, the seal of the United States, a globe, a lyre, and a yoke. Beneath the platform is a ribbon reading "Singulis Varius Utilis Omnibus," and under the ribbon are a palm branch and an olive branch. Lines of radiating light rise from the entire vignette.
LC-USZ62-45574

900
[An Indian on the cartouche for "MAP for the INTERIOR TRAVELS through AMERICA, delineating the March of the Army."] T. Conder Sculpsit. [1789?]

403

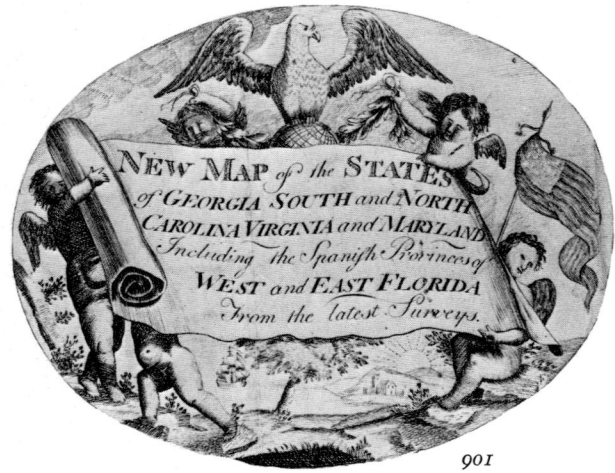

901

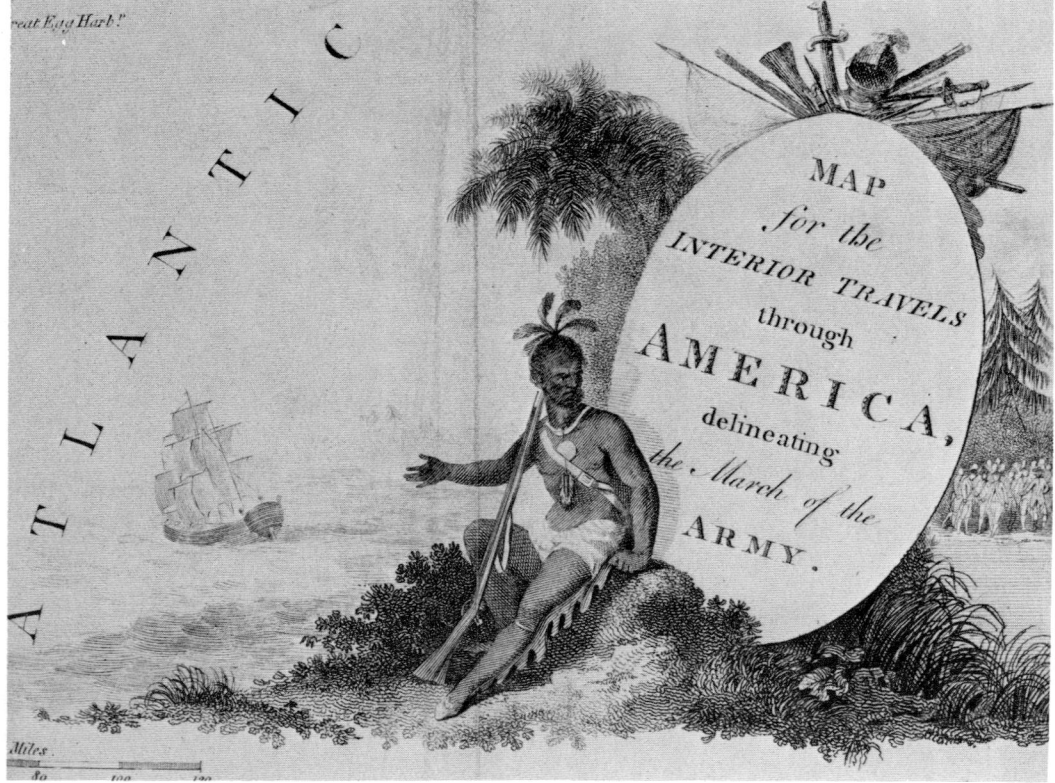

900

Etching 5 x 7 in. (image)

The Indian, with rifle, leggings, and ammunition belt, sits on a rock. In the background to the left a ship sails away, and to the right is a group of Europeans. From Anburey, *Travels Through the Interior Parts of America*, v. 1 (London, 1789), frontispiece. LC–USZ62–45544

901

[Cherubs celebrate the founding of the new nation—a cartouche] Cornelius Tiebout Sculp. N. York 1789

Etching 3¾ x 4¾ in. (image in oval)

Five cherubs hold up a scroll with the title "A New Map of the States of Georgia South and North Carolina Virginia and Maryland including the Spanish Provinces of West and East Florida from the latest surveys." On top an American eagle sits on a globe, the American flags flies on the right side, and underneath the scroll is a view of the sun shining on a small farm and a merchant ship. From Gordon, *The History of the Rise, Progress, and Establishment, of the Independence of the United States of America*, v. 1 (New York, 1789), frontispiece. LC–USZ62–45569

902

[Two women celebrate the birth of America among the family of nations] G. Gallager, del. Engrav'd by S. Hill. 1790

Mixed method 6½ x 4¼ in.

Two women stand by a globe on a pedestal. On the globe is written "America," "Europe," "Africa," and "Asia." Both women radiate purity and light, and one holds a staff with a liberty cap on top. At their feet is an open copy of Thomas Paine's *The Rights of Man* propped open by a palm. Lying discarded are keys, shackles, and a mask, while in the background a figure in armor and a haggish woman flee into darkness. They represent the retreating forces of war and discord before the new American

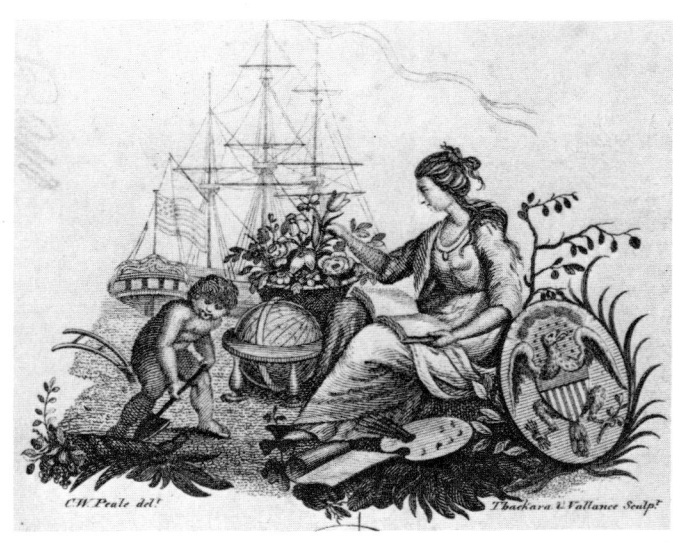

903

Nation. This allegory is from *The Massachusetts Magazine*, 1790. LC–USZ62–45522

903
[Title page ornament for *The Universal Asylum and Columbian Magazine*] C. W. Peale delt. Thackara & Vallance Sculpt. [1790]
Mixed method 2¾ x 3½ in. (image)

America sits enjoying the prosperity of peace. Her shield bearing the American eagle rests by her side. She is surrounded with symbols of culture: a scroll, a book, paint brushes and board, a globe, flowers, a child digging, a plow behind him, and an American ship in the background. *The Universal Asylum and Columbian Magazine*, January 1790, title page. Fielding, 1580. LC–USZ62–46096

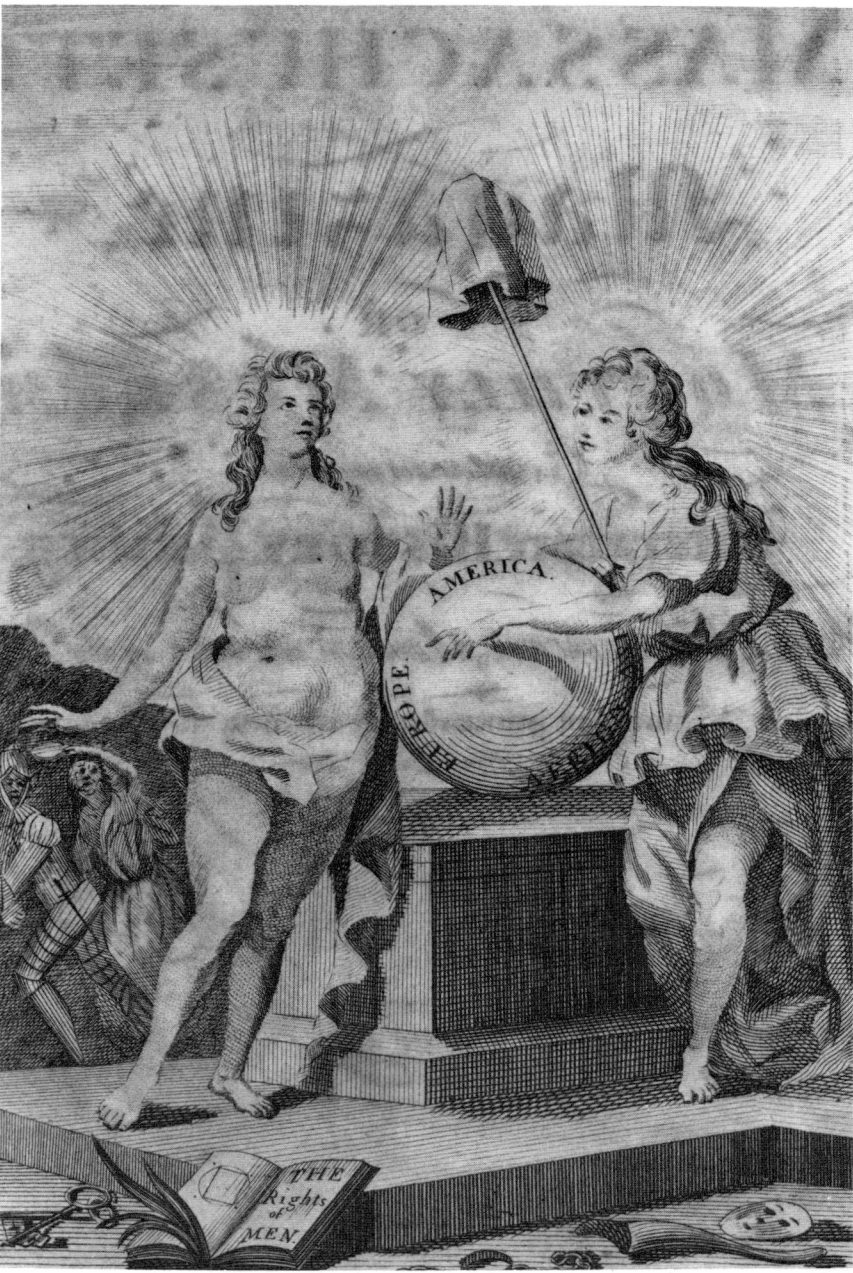

902

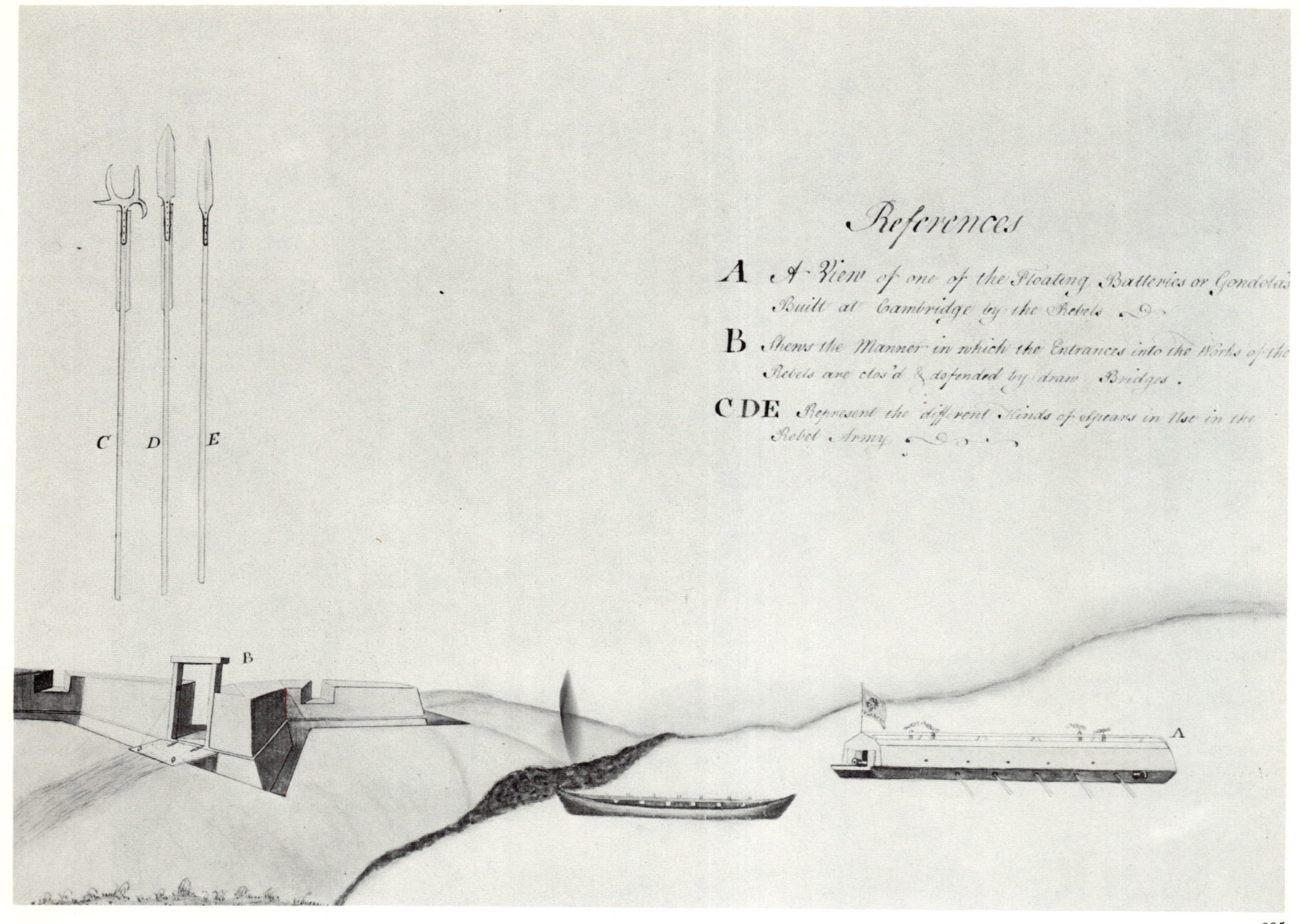

Chapter V

Weapons, Implements, and Fortifications

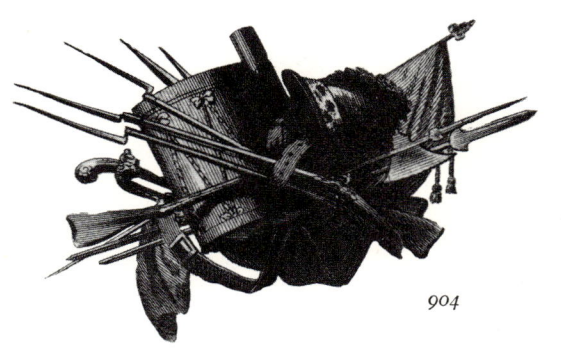

904

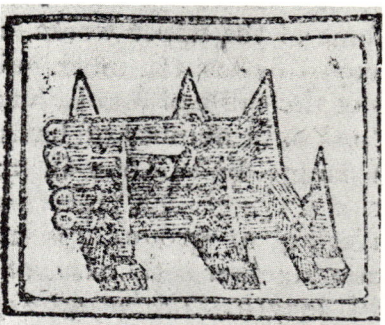

906

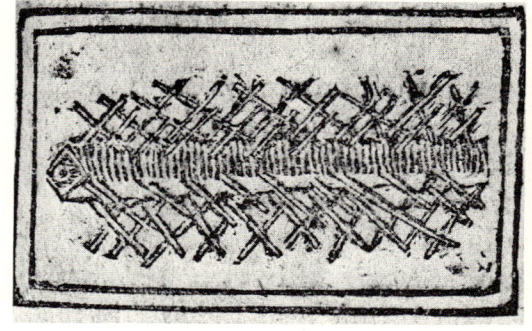

907

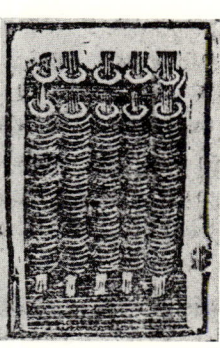

908

904
[Arms of the British Forces, 1785]
  Etching 2 x 3¼ in. (image)

Title page decoration for each volume of Andrews, *History of the War with America, France, Spain and Holland* (London, 1785). LC–USZ62–7975

905
[Armaments of the American rebels]
  Pen sketch with hand coloring 11½ x 16¼ in.

Charles Blaskowitz, a mapmaker with Howe's army, drew these sketches of patriot armaments used in the siege of Boston. The first two polearms at the left, a halberd and a spontoon, were used chiefly as symbols of rank. The third, a pike or trench spear, was thought to be effective against British bayonet attacks on fortified positions. In October 1775 two floating batteries like the one pictured here were ordered down the Charles River to fire into the enemy camp on Boston Common. One of the batteries was wrecked by the explosion of a cannon. LC–USZ62–45565

906
CHANDELIER, is a wooden frame, whereon are laid fascines or faggots, to cover the workmen while carrying on the approaches. [1776]
  Woodcut 1 x 1¼ in. (image)

Chandeliers were particularly useful on ground where digging was difficult. From Simes, *A New Military, Historical, and Explanatory Dictionary* (Philadelphia, 1776). LC–USZ62–45355

907
CHEVEAUX DE-FRIZE, large joints or beams, stuck full of wooden pins, armed with iron, to stop breaches, or to secure a passage of a camp against the enemy's cavalry. [1776]
  Woodcut 1 x 1⅝ in. (image)

A submarine version of chevaux de frise, attributed to Benjamin Franklin, was used in the Delaware River below Philadelphia and in the Hudson River below West Point. From Simes, *A New Military, Historical, and Explanatory Dictionary* (Philadelphia, 1776). LC–USZ62–45356

908
GABION, a cylinder basket, open at both ends, about three feet wide, and as much in height. They serve in sieges to carry on the approaches

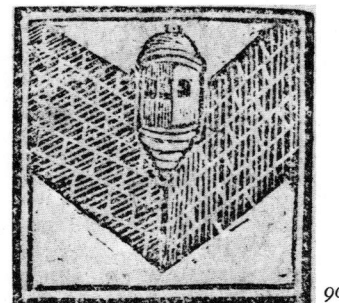

909

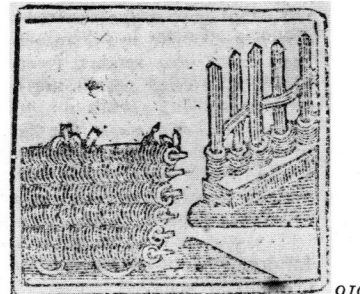

910

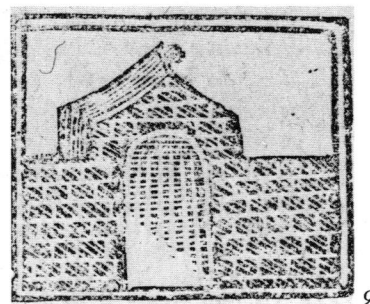

911

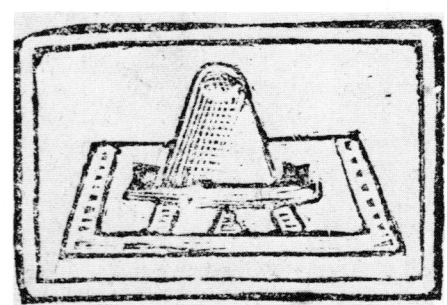

912

under cover, when they come pretty near the fortification. [1776]

Woodcut 1¼ x ¾ in. (image)

From Simes, *A New Military, Historical, and Explanatory Dictionary* (Philadelphia, 1776). LC-USZ62-45357

909

GUERRITTE, a fort or small tower of stone or wood, on the point of a bastion, or on the angles of the shoulder, to hold a sentry. [1776]

Woodcut 1⅛ x 1⅛ in. (image)

From Simes, *A New Military, Historical, and Explanatory Dictionary* (Philadelphia, 1776). LC-USZ62-45358

910

HURDLES, or clayes, made of branches or twigs, closely interwoven, are about five or six feet long, and three, or three and a half broad. Their use is to cover traverses, lodgements, caponeers, coffers, &c. and are covered over with earth, to secure them from the enemy's artificial fireworks. or stones which might be thrown upon them; they are also frequently used to cover marshy ground, or pass a fosse. [1776]

Woodcut 1½ x 1¾ in. (image)

From Simes, *A New Military, Historical, and Explanatory Dictionary* (Philadelphia, 1776). LC-USZ62-45359

911

ORGNES, thick long pieces of wood, pointed and shod with iron, clear one of another, hanging perpendicularly each by a particular rope or cord, over the gate of a strong place to be dropped in case of emergency. [1776]

Woodcut 1⅛ x 1¼ in. (image)

From Simes, *A New Military, Historical, and Explanatory Dictionary* (Philadelphia, 1776). LC-USZ62-45360

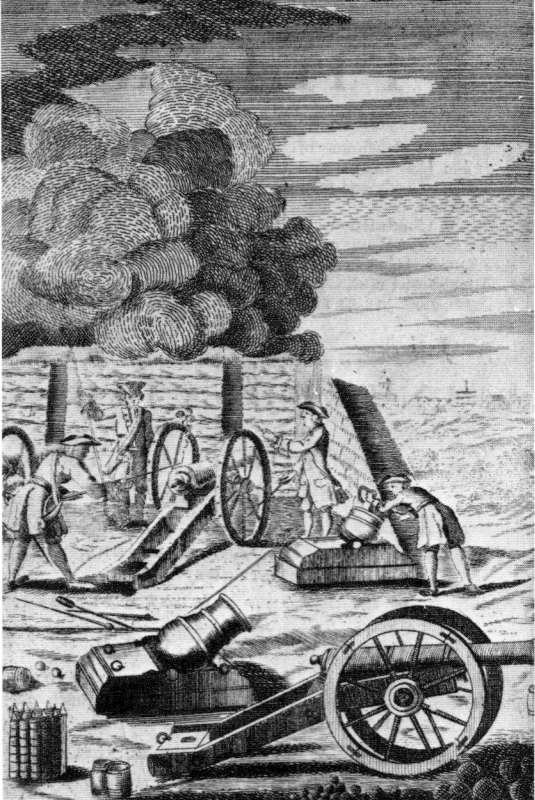

913

912

PETARD, a brass pot fixed upon a strong square plank, which has an iron hook to fix it against a gate or palisades. This pot is filled with powder; which, when fixed, breaks every thing about it; and thereby makes an opening to enter the place. [1776]

Woodcut ¾ x 1¼ in. (image)

From Simes, *A New Military, Historical, and Explanatory Dictionary* (Philadelphia, 1776). LC–USZ62–45361

913

[A variety of artillery pieces and other ordnance, John Norman, 1779]

Etching 6⅛ x 4 in. (image)

From Muller, *A Treatise of Artillery* (Philadelphia, 1779), frontispiece. LC–USZ62–45362

914

[Tools necessary to prove and load guns] PL IX. [John Norman, 1779]

Etching 6¼ x 7¼ in. (image)

This plate pictures wedge, priming iron, searcher, reliever, worm, ladle, sponge, searcher with one point, hand spike, and parts of wheels and axles. From Muller, *A Treatise of Artillery* (Philadelphia, 1779), p. 109. LC–USZ62–45363

915

Elevation of a Powder Cart [and] Plan of a Powder Cart. PL XIX [John Norman, 1779]

Etching 6⅛ x 7½ in. (image)

From Muller, *A Treatise of Artillery* (Philadelphia, 1779), p. 127. LC–USZ62–45364

916

Amunition Waggon XX [John Norman, 1779]

Etching 6⅝ x 12¾ in. (image)

This engraving also shows undercarriage and

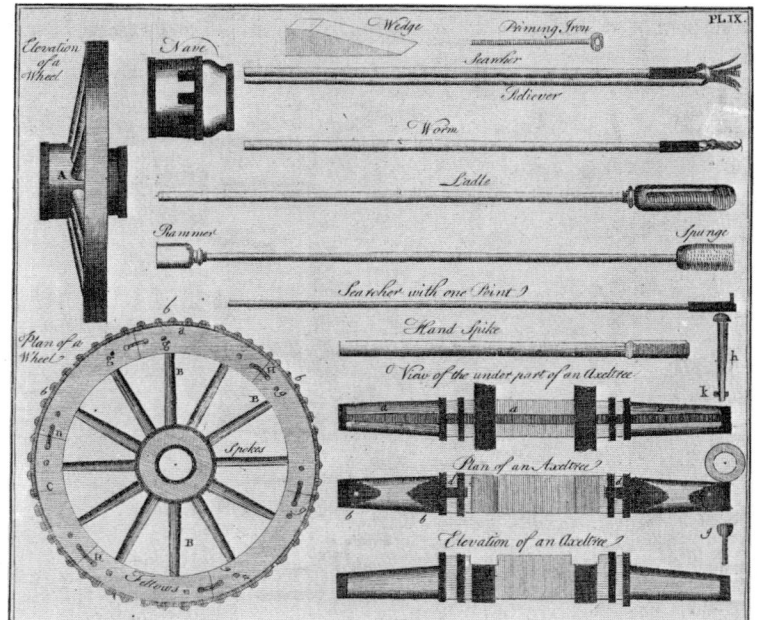

914

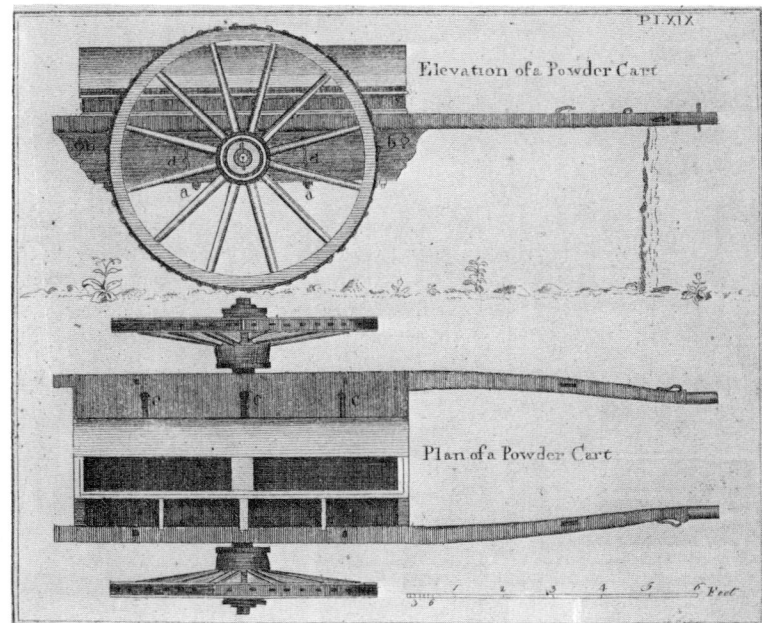

915

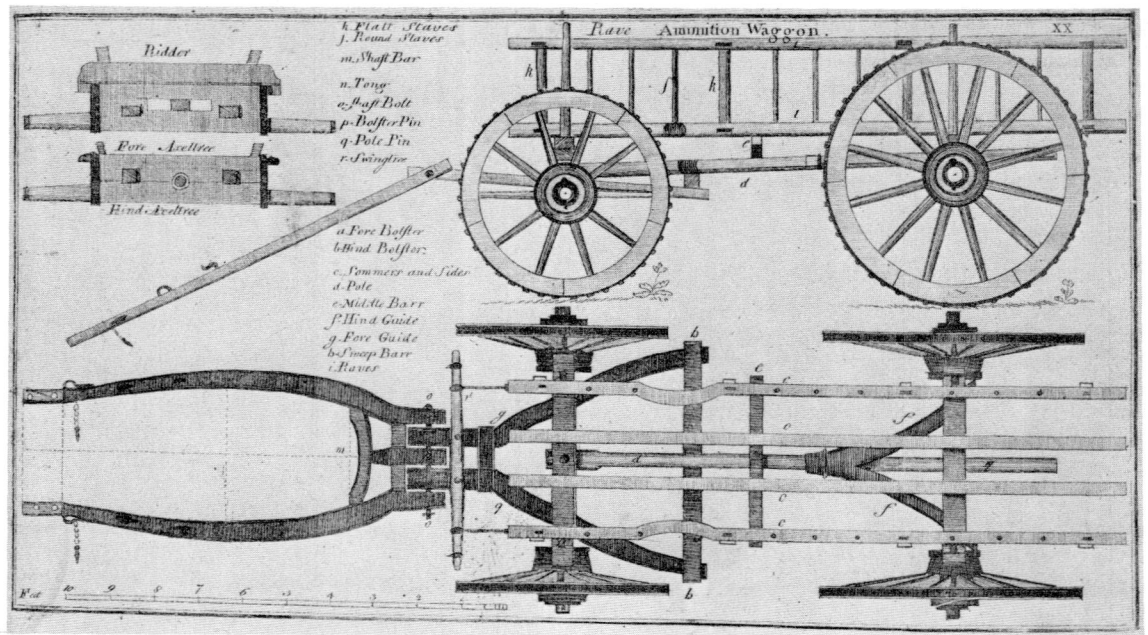

916

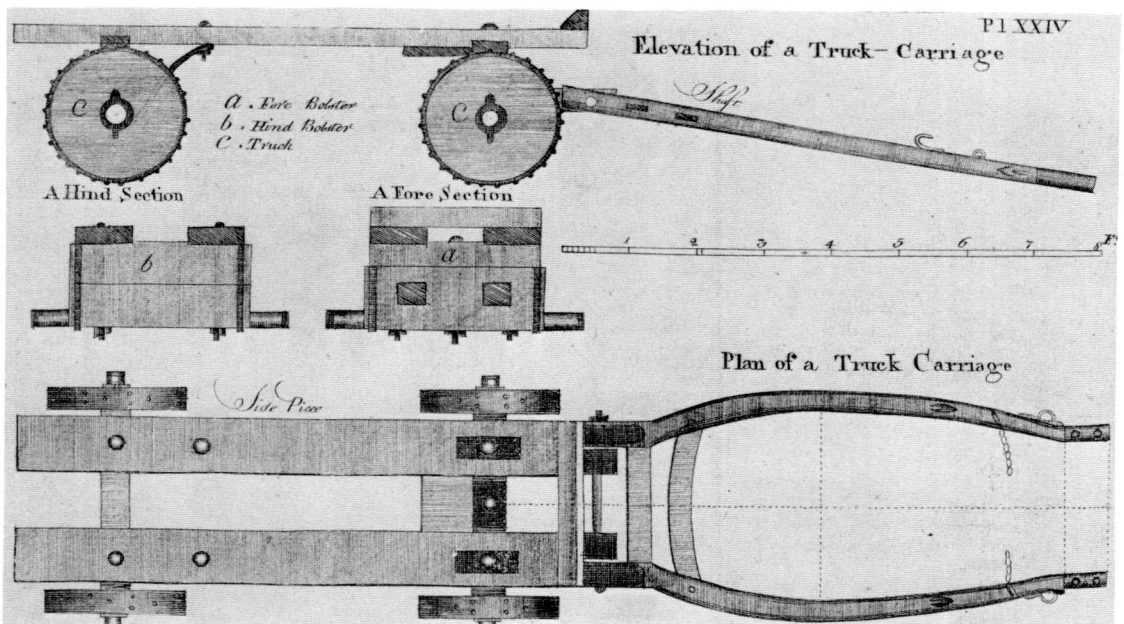

917

axles. From Muller, *A Treatise of Artillery* (Philadelphia, 1779), p. 128.
LC–USZ62–45365

917

Elevation of a Truck-Carriage [and] Plan of a Truck Carriage PL XXIV [John Norman]
Etching 5¾ x 10 in. (image)

From Muller, *A Treatise of Artillery* (Philadelphia, 1779), p. 137. LC–USZ62–45366

918

Pontoon Carraige [and] Pontoon. P XXVI [John Norman]
Etching 6 x 10½ in. (image)

From Muller, *A Treatise of Artillery* (Philadelphia, 1779), p. 140. LC–USZ62–45367

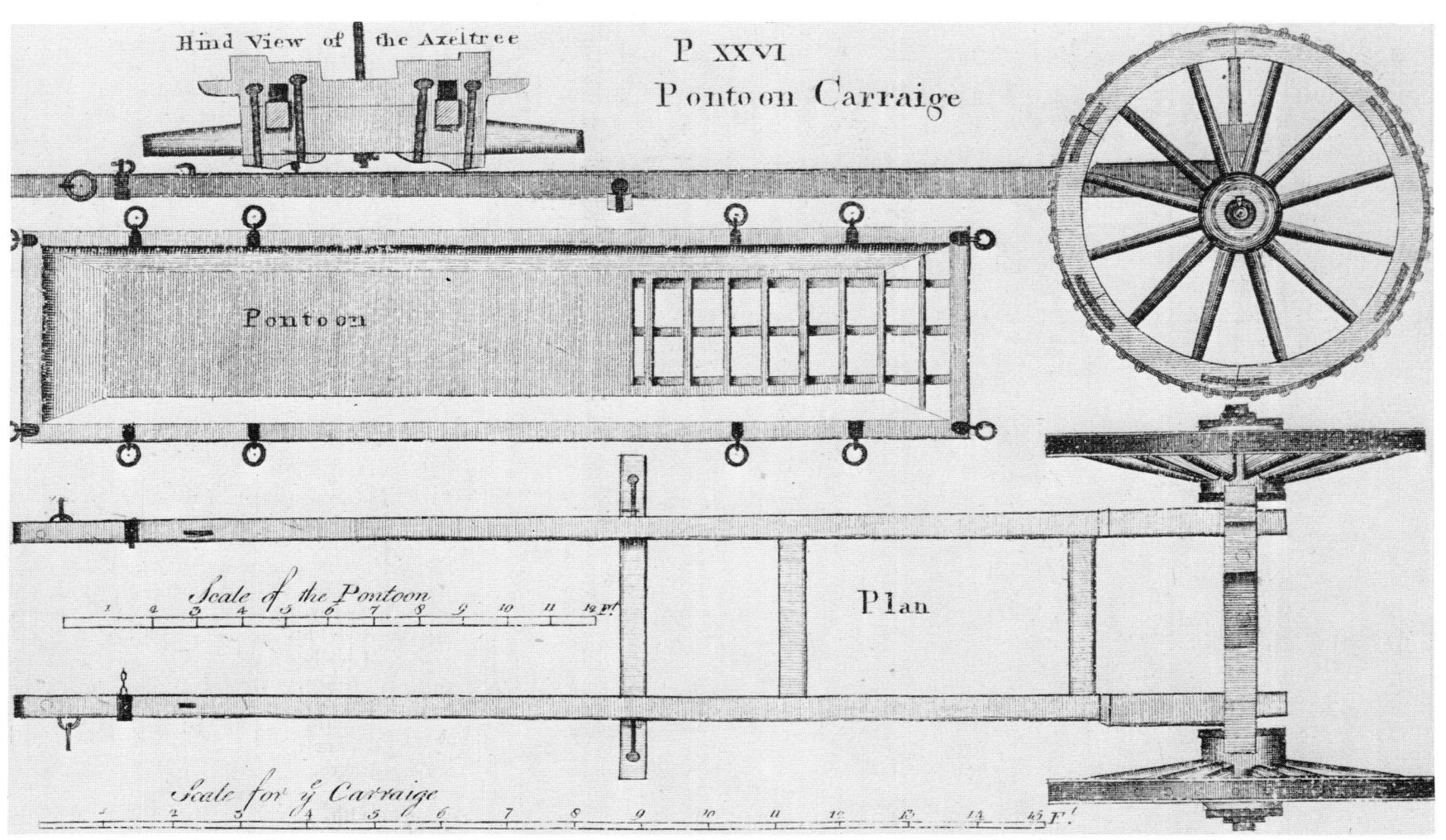

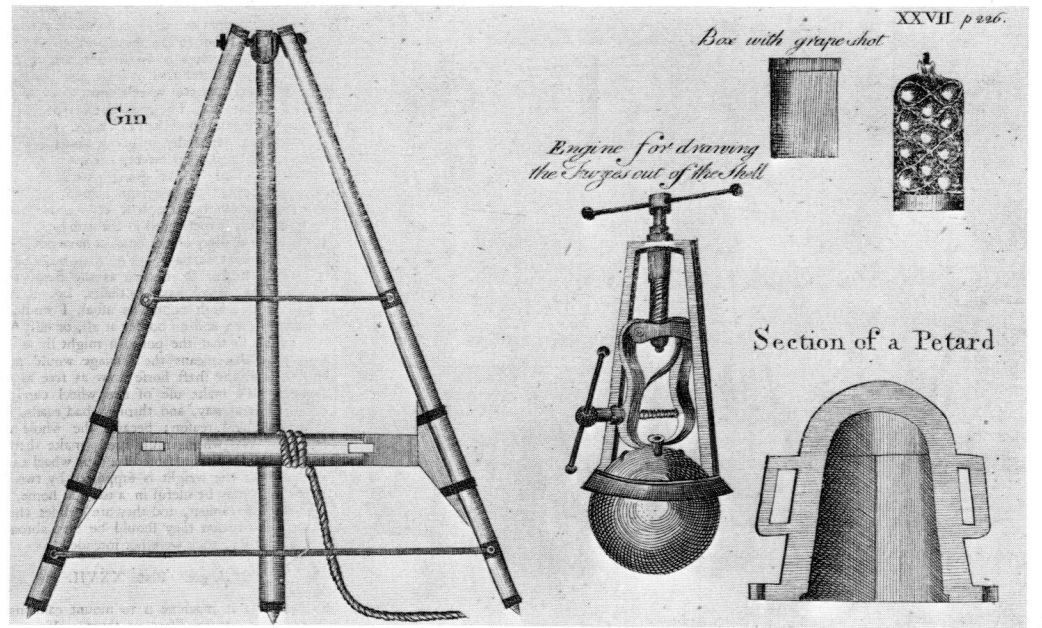

919

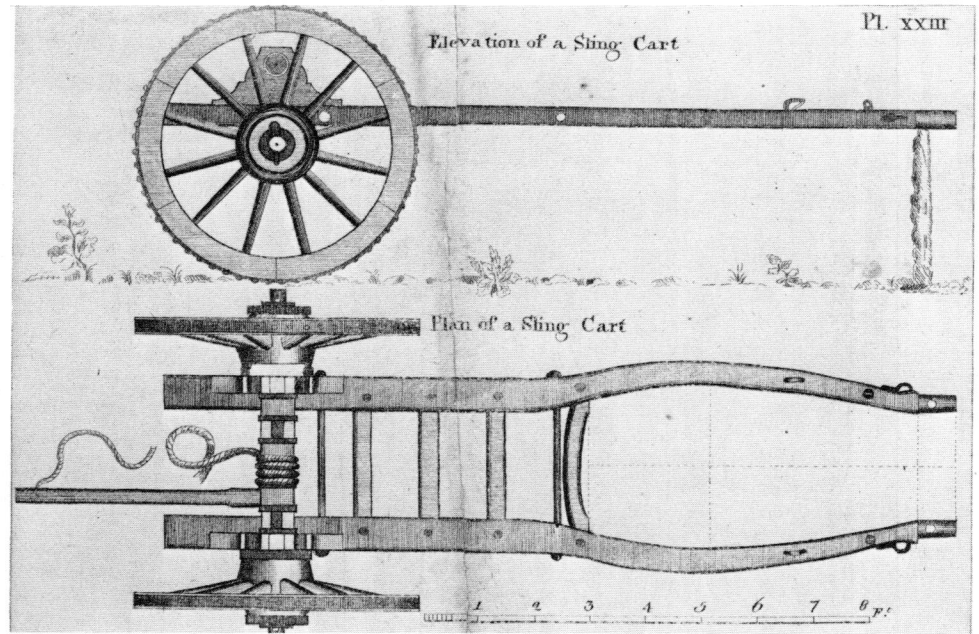

920

919
Gin Engine for drawing the Fuzes out of the Shell Box with grapeshot Section of a Petard XXVII [John Norman]
Etching 6½ x 10 in. (image)

From Muller, *A Treatise of Artillery* (Philadelphia, 1779), p. 143. LC–USZ62–45368

920
Elevation of a Sling Cart [and] Plan of a Sling Cart PL XXIII [John Norman]
Etching 6⅝ x 10 in. (image)

From Muller, *A Treatise of Artillery* (Philadelphia, 1779), p. 136. LC–USZ62–45369

921
The Section and Plan of a Block-house. [1789?]
Etching 10 x 7⅝ in.

Depicts cross section of the ground floor and upper story, designating the port holes for cannon, the loopholes for muskets, the door, the fireplaces, the ladder to the upper story, the sleeping platform, and the trap door. The officer's apartment and "holes made in the floor to fire upon the Enemy if they gain possession of the lower Apartment" are some of the features noted on the plan of the ground floor. From Anburey, *Travels Through the Interior Parts of America*, v. 1. (London, 1789), opposite p. 139. LC–USZ62–45546

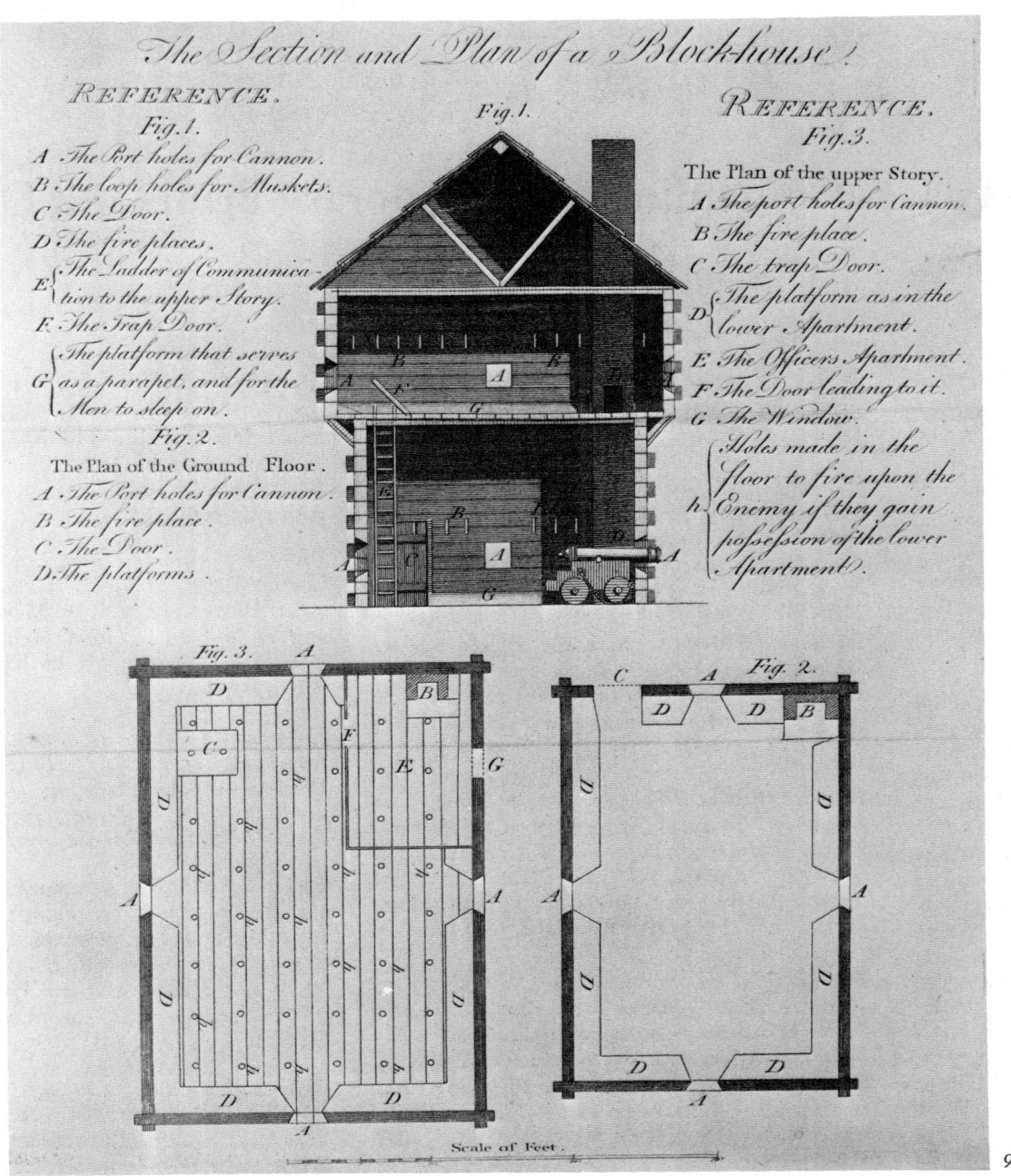

Appendix A

List of Books and Atlases Containing Contemporary Prints and Drawings

Ames, Nathaniel. *An Astronomical Diary; or Almanack For the Year of Our Lord Christ 1772: Being Bissextile or Leap-Year. Calculated for the Meridian of Boston, New-England, Lat. 42 25 North.* Boston, Nathaniel Ames, 1772. AY53.A8 RBC

[Anburey, Thomas]. *Travels Through the Interior Parts of America. In a Series of Letters. By an Officer.* 2 v. London, Printed for William Lane, Leadenhall-Street, 1789. E163.A53 1789 RBC

Andrews, John. *A Collection of Plans of the Capital Cities of Europe and Some Remarkable Cities in Asia, Africa, & America.* 2 v. London, J. Andrews, 1771. Phillips 5386 G1028.A28 1771 G&M

Andrews, John. *History of the War with America, France, Spain, and Holland; commencing in 1775 and ending in 1783.* 4 v. London, Published by his Majesty's Royal Licence and Authority. For John Fielding, Pater Noster Row; and John Jarvis in the Strand, 1785. E208.A56 RBC & shelf

The Annual Register; A Complete History of the Late War, or, Annual Register of Its Rise, Progress, and Events, in Europe, Asia, Africa, and America ... With ... Additions ... Taken from Capt. John Knox's Historical Journal of the War in America. 6th ed. Dublin, Printed by John Exshal, in Dame-Street, 1774. DD411.A5 1774

Atlante dell' America Contenente le Migliori Carte Geografiche, e Topografiche delle Principali Citta, Laghi, Fiumi, e Fortezze del Nuovo Mundo.... Livorno, G. T. Masi e Comp., 1777. Phillips 1167 G1100.A8 1777 G&M

Bachiene, Willem A. *Atlas, Tot Opheldering der Hedendaagsche Historie Beschreeven Door Gezelschap van Geleerde Mannen in Engeland.* te Amsterdam, M. Schalekamp, 1785. Phillips 657 G1015.B14 G&M

Barnard, Edward. *The New, Comprehensive and Complete History of England from the Earliest Period of Authentic Information to the Middle of the Year. MDCCLXXXIII.* London, Printed for the Author: and Published by Alex. Hogg at No 16, Pater-noster Row [1783]. DA30.B26

Bickerstaff's Boston Almanack, For the Year 1768; Being bissextile or leap Year. Calculated for the Meridian of Boston; but will answer without a sensible error for any part of New-England. Boston, Printed by Mein and Fleeming, and to be sold by John Mein at the London Bookstore, North-side of King-Street, 1768. AY53.B5 RBC

Bickerstaff's Boston Almanack, For the Year of our Lord 1769; Being the first Year after Leap Year. Boston, Printed by Mein and Fleeming, and to be sold by John Mein, at the London Bookstore, North-side of King-Street, 1769. AY53.B5 RBC

Bickerstaff's Boston Almanack. For the Year of Our Lord 1770; Being the second Year after Leap Year. Boston, Printed by Mein and Fleeming, and to be Sold by John Mein at the London Book-Store, North-side of King-Street, 1770. AY53.B5 RBC

Bickerstaff's Boston Almanack, For the Year of our Lord, 1772. Being Leap Year. Boston, Printed by John Fleeming, and to be Sold at his Shop in King Street, opposite the South-Door of the Town-House, 1772. AY53.B5 RBC

Bickerstaff's Boston Almanack. For the Year of our Redemption 1774; Being the Second after Leap-Year, The Fourteenth of the Reign of George III.... Boston, Printed and sold by Mills and Hicks, at their Printing-Office, in School-Street, next to Cromwell's Head Tavern, 1774. AY53.B5 RBC

Bickerstaff's Boston Almanack, For the Year of our Redemption 1777; Being the First after Leap-Year.... Boston, Printed and sold by John Boyle in Marlborough-Street, and Draper and

Phillips, one Door North of the Lamb-Tavern in Newbury-Street, 1777. AY53.B5 RBC

Bickerstaff's Boston Almanack, For the Year of our Redemption, 1778. Being the Second Year of American Independence. And the Second after Leap-Year. Calculated by Benjamin West, a Student in Astronomy, at Providence, and Author of this Almanack for twelve Years past, except those false Editions printed by Mycall, of Newbury, for 76 and by Boyle and Draper and Phillips, of Boston, for 77: The Author of this genuine Copy never had any Connexions with those Printers. Boston, Printed by E. Russell at his Printing Office late the Bell-Tavern, 1778. AY53.B5 RBC

Bickerstaff's Boston Almanack, for the Year of our Redemption, 1780. Being Bissextile or Leap-Year, and the Fourth of American Independence. Boston, Printed and Sold by Draper and Folsom, and John. Mycall, of Newbury, 1780. AY53.B5 RBC

Bickerstaff's Genuine Boston Almanack, 1787. AY53.B5

Bollan, William. *Continued Corruption, standing armies, and popular discontents considered; and the establishment of the English colonies in America, with various subsequent proceedings, and the Present Contest, examined, with Intent to promote their cordial and perpetual Union with their Mother-Country, for their mutual Honour, Comfort, Strength, and Safety.* London, Printed and sold by J. Almon, 1768. E211.B68 RBC

The Boston Gazette, and Weekly Republican Journal. From April 12, 1756 to April 5, 1779 was entitled *The Boston Gazette, and Country Journal.* American 18th-Century Newspapers

The Boston Magazine . . . containing, a collection of instructive and entertaining essays, in the various branches of useful, and polite literature. . . . Boston, Greenleaf and Freeman, North side of the Market, 1783. AP2.A2B7 RBC

[Brackenridge, Hugh Henry]. *The Battle of Bunkers-Hill. A Dramatic Piece of Five Acts, in Heroic Measure. By A Gentleman of Maryland.* Philadelphia, Printed and Sold by Robert Bell, in Third-Street, 1776. E241.B9B78

Brion de la Tour, Louis. *Atlas ecclesiastiques comprenant tous les eveches des quatre parties du monde . . .* Paris, Desnos, 1766. Phillips 80 G1015.B768 1766 G&M

Clarke, John. *An Impartial and Authentic Narrative of the Battle Fought on the 17th of June, 1775, between His Britannic Majesty's Troops and the American Provincial Army, on Bunker's Hill, near Charles Town, in New England.* London, Printed for the Author, and sold by J. Millan, Whitehall; J. Bew, in Pater-noster Row; and—Sewel, in Cornhill, 1775. E241.B9C485 RBC

Clouet, Jean Baptiste Louis. *Géographie Moderne avec Introduction. Ouvrage utile a tous ceux qui veulent se perfectionner dans cette Sciénce, on y trouve jusqu' aux notions les plus simples dont on a facilité l'intelligence par des Figures pour le mettre a la portée de tout le Monde, Chaque Carte a sur les marges l'explication de ce qu'elle renferme, la methode qu'on y suit a pour object de developper les connoissances qui tiennent a l'Histoire, ce qui rend cette Géographie tres interessant.* Paris, Clouet, 1780. Phillips 3519 G1015.C5 1780 G&M

Cockings, George. *The American War, A Poem; in Six Books.* London, Printed by W. Richardson for the Author, 1781. E295.C66 RBC

The Columbian Magazine, or Monthly Miscellany, Containing a View of the History, Literature, Manners & Characters of the Year. Philadelphia, Printed for T. Seddon, W. Spotswood, C. Cist, & J. Trenchard, 1787-90. AP2.A2U6 RBC

The Constitutions of the Several Independent States of America; The Declaration of Independence; The Articles of Confederation Between the Said States; The Treaties Between His Most Christian Majesty and the United States of America. Philadelphia Printed, London Reprinted with an Advertisement by J. L. DeLolme, For J. Walker, No. 44, in Pater-noster-Row, and J. Debrett, in Piccadilly, 1783. JK18 1783aa RBC

The Constitutions of the Several Independent States of America; The Declaration of Independence; and the Articles of Confederation between the Said States. To Which are now Added, the Declaration of Rights; the Non-importation Agreement; and the Petition of Congress to the King Delivered by Mr. Penn. 2d Ed. London, Printed for J. Stockdale, in Piccadilly, 1783. JK18 1783b RBC

Cowley, Charlotte. *The Ladies History of England; from the Descent of Julius Caesar, to the Summer of 1780.* London, Printed for the Proprietors; and Sold by S. Bladon, No. 13 in Pater-noster-Row, 1780. DA30.C875

Des Barres, Joseph Frederick Wallet. *The Atlantic Neptune, published for the use of the Royal Navy of Great Britain, by Joseph F. W. Des Barres . . . under the directions of the Right Honble. the Lords Commissioners of the Admiralty.* London, 1774-81. G1106.P5D4 G&M

copy	Phillips/LeGear No.
1	1198
2	1199

3	1200
4	1201
5	1202
6	1203
8	1205
9	3658
11	3655
12	3656
13	3657
14	3659
15	4473
16	4474
17	10323
18	10317
19	10320
20	10321

Des Barres, Joseph Frederick Wallet. *The Atlantic Neptune. The Sea Coast of Nova Scotia; exhibiting the diversities of the Coast, and face of the country near it: the banks, rocks, shoals, soundings, &c. together with remarks and directions for the conveniency of navigations and pilotage. Survey'd by order of the Right Honorable the Lords Commissioners of the Admiralty, by J. F. W. Des Barres.* 2 v. London, 1775–78. Phillips 1250 G&M Uncataloged

Drayton, John. *Memoirs of the American Revolution, from its Commencement to the Year 1776 inclusive: as relating to the State of South-Carolina: and occasionally refering to the states of North-Carolina and Georgia.* 2 v. Charleston, Printed by A. E. Miller, 1821. E263.S7D7 RBC

Dunn, Samuel. *A New Atlas of the Mundane System; or, of Geography and Cosmography: Describing the Heavens and the Earth, the distances, motions and magnitudes of the celestial bodies; the various empires, kingdoms, states, republics; and islands, throughout the known world.* London, Printed for R. Sayer and J. Bennett, 1778–[83]. Phillips 5990 G1015.D8 1783 G & M

DuSimitière, Pierre Eugene. *Portraits des Généraux, Ministres et Magistrats que se sont rendu célèbres dans la révolution des treize Etats-Unis de l'Amérique de Septentrional.* Paris, 1781. The plates from this volume are in the P&P portrait file.

DuSimitière, Pierre Eugene. *Portraits of the Generals, Ministers, Magistrates, Members of Congress and Others, Who Have Rendered Themselves Illustrious in the Revolution of the United States of North America.* London, Published by R. Wilkinson, No. 58. Cornhill, and J. Debrett, opposite Burlington-house, Piccadilly, 1783. E206.D97 RBC

Edes & Gill's North-American Almanack for the Year of our Lord 1769. Being the First after Bissextile or Leap-Year. Calculated for the Meridian of Boston, N. E. Latt. 42° 25′ North. Boston, Printed and Sold by Edes and Gill, in Queen-Street, [1769]. AY53.N6 RBC

Edes & Gill's North-American Almanack, and Massachusetts Register, For the Year 1770. Boston, Printed (upon Paper Manufactured in this Country) and Sold by Edes and Gill in Queen-Street; and T. & J. Fleet at the Heart and Crown in Cornhill, 1770. AY53.N6 RBC

The European Magazine, and London Review: Containing the Literature, History, Politics, Arts, Manners, & Amusements of the Age. By the Philological Society of London. v. 1–19 London, Printed for John Fielding No. 23 Pater Noster Row; John Debrett, opposite Burlington House, Picadilly; and John Sewell No. 32, Cornhill, 1782–90. AP4.E8

Extrait du Journal d'un Officier de la Marine de L'Escadre de M. Le Comte D'Estaing. 1782. E265.E96 RBC

Faden, William. *Atlas of Battles of the American Revolution, together with Maps shewing the Routes of the British and American Armies, Plans of Cities, Surveys of Harbors, &c., taken during that eventful period by Officers attached to the Royal Army.* London, Faden, 1770–93. [New York: collected by Bartlett & Welford, 1845?]

Phillips explains: "The original atlas published in London, 1793, was a collection of maps varying in number from seventeen to twenty-two, published at different times with this title. Bartlett & Welford purchased a large remainder of these maps and issued them with the above title-page. Their edition is distinguished by the broad letters with which the title is printed, and the omission of the place and date of publication. sf. Sabin's *Dictionary of Books Relating to America*. v. 1, p. 309." Since a reasonable doubt exists that these maps are restrikes, they are included in the checklist. Phillips 1337 G1201.S3F2 1845 G&M

Faden, William. *The North American Atlas, Selected from the Most Authentic Maps, Charts, Plans, &c. Hitherto Published.* London, W. Faden, 1777. Phillips 1207, 1208 G1105.F2, 1777, G1105.F2 1777a G&M

The Fall of Lucifer, an Elegaic Poem on the Infamous Defection of the Late General Arnold. Hartford, Printed by Hudson and Goodwin, 1781. PS700.A1F3 RBC

Fenning, Daniel. *Neue Erdbeschreibung von Amerika. Aus dem Englischen. Herausgegeben von August Ludwig Schlözer.* Gottingen und Leipzig: 1777. E143.F33

Force, Peter, collection. Ebenezer Hazard Papers, "American Stamp Act, 1765–1766." Manuscript Division

Fox, Charles James. *The Beauties of Fox, North, and Burke, selected from their Speeches, from the passing of the Quarter Act, in the Year*

1774, down to the Present Time. London, Printed for J. Stockdale, 1784. E211.F79 RBC

France. Depot des cartes et plans de la marine. *Neptune Americo-Septentrional Contenant les Cotes, Iles et Bancs, les Baies, Ports, et Mouillages, et les Sondes des Mers de cette-partie du Monde, depuis le Groenland inclusivement, jusques et compre le Golfe de Mexique . . . ou Recuil de Cartes Hydrographiques a l'usage des Vaisseaux du Roi.* Paris, 1778–80. Phillips 1211 G1106.P5S7 1780

The Gentlemen's Magazine: and Historical Chronicle. London, Printed by John Nichols, at Cicero's Head, Red Lion Passage, Fleet-Street; for David Henry, late of St. John's Gate. And sold by Eliz. Newberry, the Corner of St. Paul's Church Yard, Ludgate-Street, 1790. AP4.G3

Gillies, John. *Memoirs of the Life of the Reverend George Whitefield, M.A. Late Chaplain of the Right Honourable the Countess of Huntingdon . . . Comp. by the Rev. John Gillies . . . .* New York, Printed by Hodge and Shober, 1774. BX9225.W4G45 1774 RBC

Gordon, William. *The History of the Rise, Progress, and Establishment, of the Independence of the United States of America: Including an Account of the Late War; and of the Thirteen Colonies, from Their Origin to that Period.* 3 v. New York, Printed by Hodge, Allen, and Campbell, 1789. E208.G662 RBC

Grose, Francis. *Advice to the Officers of the British Army: with the Addition of Some Hints to the Drummer and Private Soldier.* London, Printed by W. Richardson, for G. Kearsley, in Fleet-street, 1783. U20.G8 1783 AC901.D8 vol. 523 RBC

The Hibernian Magazine or Compendium of Entertaining Knowledge Containing the Greatest Variety of the most Curious and Useful Subjects in every Branch of Polite Literature. Dublin, Printed by Thomas Walker at Cicero's Head No. 79 Dame Street, 1771–90. AP3.W3

Hilliard d'Auberteuil, Michel René. *Essais Historiques et Politiques sur les Anglo-Americains.* 4 v. Bruxelles, 1781–82. Title of the 2d part is *Essais Historiques et Politiques sur la Révolution de l'Amérique Septentrionale.* A Bruxelles et se trouve a Paris Chez l'Auteur, rue des Bons-Ensans-Saint-Honoré, 1782. E208.H63
  Cited as Hilliard d'Auberteuil, *Essais Historiques* (1781–82).

Hilliard d'Auberteuil, Michel René. *Essais Historiques et Politiques sur les Anglo-Americains. Tome Primier.* The title of the 2d volume is *Essais Historiques et Politiques sur la Revolution de l'Amerique Septentrionale.* Both have the imprint Bruxelles, 1782. E208.H64 RBC
  Cited as Hilliard d'Auberteuil, *Essais Historiques* (1782). Third volume is *Atlas* with maps and prints.

H-istoricus, P-oplicola, [pseud.]. *America pois'd in the Balance of Justice. In this Research, the Present Dissention between the Mother Country and her Colonies, is considered in a New Light, and supported by Arguments quite different from those held forth by the parliamentary Speakers, and polemical Writers, on either Side of the Question.* London, Printed for the Author, 1776. E211.H65 RBC

Homann, Erben. *Atlas Geographicvs Maior Exhibens Tellurem Seu Globum Terraqueum in Mappis Generalibus & Specialibus per Iohannem Baptistam Homannvm ejusque Heredes Editis.* 2 v. Norimbergae, curantibus Homannianis heredibus, 1759–81. Phillips 622 G1015 .H62 1781 G&M

An Impartial History of the War in America, Between Great Britain and the United States, from Its Commencement to the End of the War: Exhibiting a circumstantial, connected, and complete Account of the real Causes, Rise, and Progress of the War, interspersed with Anecdotes and Characters of the different Commanders, and Accounts of such Personages in Congress as Have distinguished themselves during the Contest. 3 v. Boston, Printed by Nathaniel Coverly and Robert Hodge, at their Office in Newbury-Street, 1781. E208.I36 RBC
  Copy 2 has 2 v.

An Impartial History of the War in America, between Great Britain and Her Colonies, from Its Commencement to the end of the Year 1779. Exhibiting a circumstantial, connected, and complete Account of the real Causes, Rise, and Progress of the War, interspersed with Anecdotes and Characters of the different Commanders, and Accounts of such Personages in Congress as have distinguished themselves during the Contest. London, Printed for R. Faulder, New Bond Street, 1780. E208.I34 RBC

An Impartial History of the War in America, Between Great Britain and Her Colonies, from Its Commencement to the end of the Year 1779. Exhibiting a circumstantial, connected, and complete Account of the real Causes, Rise, and Progress of the War, interspersed with Anecdotes and Characters of the different Commanders, and Accounts of such Personages in Congress as have distinguished themselves during the Contest. London & Carlisle, Printed for R. Faulder, Bookseller, New-Bond-Street; and J. Milliken, Bookseller, Carlyle, 1780. E208.I341 RBC

Jefferys, Thomas. *The American Atlas: or, a Geographical Description of the Whole Continent of America. Wherein are delineated at large, its several Regions, Countries, States, and*

Islands, and chiefly the British Colonies. London, R. Sayer & J. Bennett, 1775. Phillips 1165 G1100.J4 1775 G&M

Jefferys, Thomas. *Atlas des Indes Occidentales, ou Description Géo-hydrographique des Régions, des Cotes, des Isles, & des Mers, Connues sous le Nom d'Indes Occidentales, dans laquelle on trouve Réunis tous les Détails Géographiques & Nautiques qui Appartiennent à cette Partie de l'Amérique* .... Londres, R. Sayer & J. Bennett; Paris, Julien, 1777. Phillips 3943 G&M Uncataloged

Jefferys, Thomas. *A General Topography of North America and the West Indies. Being a Collection of all the Maps, Charts, Plans, and Particular Surveys, that have been published of that Part of the World, either in Europe or America.* London, for R. Sayer & T. Jefferys, 1768. Phillips 1196 G1105.J4 G&M

Jeffreys, Thomas. *The West-India Atlas: or, A Compendious Description of the West-Indies.* London, for R. Sayer & J. Bennett, 1775. Phillips 2699 G&M Uncataloged

Julien, Roch J. *Le Théatre du Monde Contenant les Cartes Générales et Particulieres des Empires, Royaumes et Etats qui le Composent.* 2 v. Paris, le Sr. Julien, 1768. Phillips 641 G1015.J8 1768 G&M

Kitchin, Thomas. *A General Atlas: or, Description at Large of the Whole Universe. Being a Collection of the Most Approved and Correctist Maps Hitherto Published.* London, R. Sayer and T. Jeffrys, 1773. Phillips 643 G1015.K55 1773 G&M

Knox, John, *comp. A New Collection of Voyages, Discoveries and Travels: Containing Whatever is Worthy of Notice, in Europe, Asia, Africa and America: In Respect to The Situation and Extent of Empires, Kingdoms, and Provinces; their Climates, Soil, Produce, &c. with the Manners and Customs of the several Inhabitants; their Government, Religion, Arts, Sciences, Manufactures, and Commerce.* London, Printed for J. Knox, near Southampton-Street, in the Strand, 1767. G160.K75

Korn, Christoph Heinrich. *Geschichte der Kriege in und ausser Europea, vom anfange des aufstandes der brittischen-kolonien in Nordamerikan.* Nürnberg, G. N. Raspe, 1776–84. E208.K84 RBC

Korn, Christoph Heinrich. *Geschichte der Kriege in und ausser Europa.* Nürnberg, Gabriel Nicolaus Raspe, 1777–78. E208.K84 Pts. 11–12 copy 2 RBC

Laporte, Joseph. *Atlas Moderne Portatif, composé de vingt-huit Cartes sur toutes les Parties du Globe Terrestre.* Paris, Chez Laporte, 1781. Phillips 654 G1015.L3 1781 G&M

Laporte, Joseph. *Atlas ou Collection de Cartes Géographiques pour l'Intelligence du Voyageur François; ou la Connoissance de l'Ancien et du Nouveau Monde.* Paris, Moutard, 1787. Phillips 662 G1015.L32

Le Rouge, George L. *Atlas Amériquain Septentrional Contenant les Details des Differentes Provinces, de ce Vaste Continent. Traduit des Cartes Levées par Ordre du Government Britannique.* Paris, Le Rouge, 1778–92. Phillips 1212 G1105.L4 1792 G&M

L'Isle, Guillaume de. *Atlas géographique et universal.* Paris, Dezauche, 1781 [1784]. Phillips 655 G1015.L575 1784 G&M

The London Magazine; or, Gentleman's Monthly Intelligencer. v. 34–59, 1765–90. London, Printed for R. Baldwin, at the Rose in Pater Noster Row. AP3.L7 RBC

Loosjes, Adriaan Pieterszoon. *Gedenkzuil, ter Gelegenheid der Vry-Verklaaring van Noord-America.* Amsterdam, W. Holtrop, 1782. E249 .L86 RBC

Lotter, Tobias C. *Atlas Géographique de Cent et Huit Cartes Générales et Spéciales par les Géographes Tobie Conrad Lotter, Matthieu Scutter, et Jan-Michel Probst, à Augsburg, et les Héritiers de Homan à Nurnberg.* Nürnberg, 1778. Phillips 3517 G1015.L7 1778

Lotter, Tobias C. *Atlas Novus Sive Tabulae Geographicae Totius Orbis Faciem, Partes, Imperia, Regna et Provincias Exhibentes Exactissima Cura Iuxta Recentissimas Observation* .... Augsburg, 1772? Phillips 3513 G1015.L73 1772 G&M

The Massachusetts Centinel. Boston, Published by Benjamin Russell, near the State-House, 1784–90. American 18th-Century Newspapers

The Massachusetts Magazine; or Monthly Museum. Containing the Literature, History, Politics, Art, Manners & Amusements of the Age. Boston, Printed by Isiah Thomas and Ebenezer T. Andrews, 1789–96. AP2.A2M4 RBC

The Massachusetts Spy or Thomas's Boston Journal. Boston, Printed by Isaiah Thomas, in Union-Street, 1770–75. American 18th-Century Newspapers

The Massachusetts Spy, Or, American Oracle of Liberty. Worcester (Massachusetts Bay), Printed by Isaiah Thomas, 1775–1804. American 18th-Century Newspapers

Morgan, J. Pierpont *and* David McN. Stauffer, *comps. Signers of the Declaration of Independence, July 4, 1776. Letters and Documents Collected by D. McN. Stauffer, 1876–1890, with additions by J. Pierpont Morgan, 1908.* Manuscript Division

Muller, John. *A Treatise of Artillery.* Philadelphia, Printed by Styner and Cist, . . . For John Norman, Engraver, 1779. UF144.M97 RBC

Besides a few pictures of ordnance, this book also contains many technical drawings of field equipment and parts.

Murray, James. *An Impartial History of the Present War in America; containing An Account of its Rise and Progress, The Political Springs thereof, with its Various Successes and Disappointments on Both Sides.* 2 v, London, Printed for R. Baldwin, No. 47, Pater-noster-Row; N. Frobisher, York; T. Robson, Side, Newcastle upon Tyne; Bayne and Mennons, Edinburgh; and Dunlop and Wilson, Glasgow, [1778]. E208.M983 RBC

Murray, James. *An Impartial History of the Present War in America; containing An Account of its Rise and Progress, the Political Springs thereof, with its various Successes and Disappointments, on Both Sides.* 2 v. Newcastle Upon Tyne, Printed for T. Robson, Head of the Groat Market, R. Baldwin, No. 47, Pater-noster-Row, London; N. Frobisher, York; C. Elliot, Edinburgh; and Dunlop and Wilson, Glasgow, [1780]. E208.M98 RBC

Murray, James. *An Impartial History of the War in America; from its first Commencement, to the Present Time; together With the Charters of the several Colonies, and other Authentic Information. Likewise the Rise, Progress, and Political Springs of the War now carrying on between Great-Britain, and the United Powers of France, Spain, Holland, and America; with a particular Account of the several Engagements both by Sea and Land.* Newcastle upon Tyne, Printed by and for T. Robson, Head of the Groat-Market; And sold by R. Baldwin, No. 47, Pater-noster-Row, London; N. Frobisher, York; C. Elliot, Edinburgh; and Dunlop and Wilson, Glasgow, [1782]. E208.M981 RBC

Ozanne, Pierre. [The Geography and Map Division has a collection of 23 original drawings made in 1778–79 when Ozanne accompanied the French fleet under D'Estaing to American water.] Ozanne Coll. G&M

Palairet, Jean. [*Collection of Maps.* London, C. Bowles & J. Bowles, 1755–71.] Phillips 4290 G1015.P23 1771

The Pennsylvania Journal and Weekly Advertiser. For October 24, 1765. Philadelphia, Printed and Sold by William Bradford, at the Sign of the Bible. American 18th-Century Newspapers

The Pennsylvania Magazine: or, American Monthly Museum. Philadelphia, Printed and Sold by R. Aitken, 1775–76. AP2.A2P4 RBC

The Pennsylvania Packet; and the General Advertiser. Philadelphia, Printed by John Dunlap at the Newest Printing-Office, in Market-Street, 1771–1773. American 18th-Century Newspapers

The Political Magazine and Parliamentary, Naval, Military, and Literary Journal. London, Printed for J. Bew, 1780–90. DA510.A2

Ponce, Nicolas. *Recueil d'estampes Representant les Differents Evenemens de la Guerre qui a Procure l'Independance aux Etats Unis de l'Amerique.* Paris, Ponce et Godefroy, 1784? E209.P65 RBC copy 1, E209.P65 RBC copy 3

Copy 3 is extra illustrated with the original wash drawings of plates 1–12 and 16, a pen-and-ink drawing of plate 13, two earlier states each of plates 1–13 and 16, and one each of plates 14 and 15. An extra wash drawing apparently designed for a title page but not lettered and not represented by an engraving is inserted before plate 1.

The Rambler's Magazine; or, the annals of Gallantry, Glee, Pleasure, and the Bon Ton; Calculated for the Entertainment of the Polite World; and to Furnish the Man of Pleasure with a most Delicious Banquet of Amorous, Bacchanalian, Whimsical, Humorous, Theatrical and Polite Entertainment. London, Printed for the Authors, 1783. AP3.R3 RBC

Rapin-Thoyras, Paul de. *The History of England, written originally in French by Rapin de Thoyras: translated into English, with additional notes; and continued from the Revolution to the accession of King George II, by N. Tindal. With the Reign of George II: by T. S. Smollett.* 5 v. in 1, London, J. Harrison, 1789. DA30.R2 1789 Rosenwald Coll.

Raymond, George Frederick. *A New, Universal and Impartial History of England, from the Earliest Authentic Records and most Genuine Historical Evidence, to the Spring of the Year MDCCLXXXIV.* London, Printed for J. Cooke, No. 17, Pater-noster-Row, 1784. DA30.R3

Reed, John. *Map of Philadelphia* [and] *An Explanation of the Map of the City and Liberties of Philadelphia.* Philadelphia, Printed for the Author, and sold by Mr. Nicholas Brooks, 1774. G&M Case 4G

Ripa, Cesare. *A Collection of Emblematical Figures, Moral and Instructive; Chiefly composed from the Iconology of Cavaliere Cesare Ripa, Perugino: Exhibiting the Elements and Celestial Bodies, Seasons· and Months of the Year, Hours of the Day and Night, Quarters of the World, the principal Rivers, the Four Ages, the Muses, the Senses, Arts, Sciences, Dispositions of the Mind, Virtues and Vices, as represented by the Ancient Egyptians, Greeks, Romans, and Modern Italians. Containing upwards of Four Hundred human Figures, engraved from* original Designs, with their Explanations; Illustrated by Variety of Authorities from Classical Authors: together with An Introductory Discourse on the Science of Iconology. The whole collected and arranged by George Richardson, architect.* London, Printed for the Editor, MDCCLXXVII. N7740.R515

The Rise, Progress, and Present State of the Dispute between the People of America and the Administration. By the Bishop of_____. [William Jackson, Bishop of Oxford, supposed author] London, Printed and sold by W. Bailey, 1776. E211.R59 RBC

Romans, Bernard. *A Concise Natural History of East and West Florida; Containing An Account of the natural Produce of all the Southern Part of British America, in the three Kingdoms of Nature, particularly the Animal and Vegetable.* New York, Printed for the Author, 1775. F314.R75 RBC

The Royal American Magazine; or, Universal Repository of Instruction and Amusement. Boston, Printed for I. Thomas, 1774–75. AP2.A2R6 RBC

Russell, William. *The History of America from Its Discovery by Columbus to the Conclusion of the Late War. With An Appendix Containing An Account of the Rise and Progress of the Present Unhappy Contest between Great Britain and her Colonies.* 2 v. London, Printed for Fielding and Walker, No. 20 Pater-noster-Row, 1778. E143.R96 copy 2 RBC

Sackville, George Sackville Germain. *Correspondance du Lord G. Germain avec les Généraux Clinton, Cornwallis & les Amiraux dans la Station de l'Amérique, avec Plusieurs Lettres Interceptees du Général Washington, du Marquis de la Fayette & de M. de Barras, chef d'escadre.* Berne, La Nouvelle Société Typographique, 1782. E237.S12 RBC

Santini, P. *Atlas universal dressé sur les meilleures Cartes Modernes.* 2 v. Venise, Remondini, 1776–84. Phillips 647 G1015.S34 1784 G&M

Scenographia Americana: or, A Collection of Views of North America and the West Indies. Neatly Engraved by Messrs. Sandby, Grignion, Rooker, Canot, Elliot, and Others; from Drawings taken on the Spot by Several Officers of the British Navy and Army. London, Printed for John Bowles, at No. 13, in Cornhill; Robert Sayer, at No. 53 Fleet-street; Thomas Jefferys, at the Corner of St. Martins Lane in the Strand; Carington Bowles, at No. 69, in St. Paul's Church-yard; and Henry Parker, at No. 82, in Cornhill. 1768. NE1714.S4 fol RBC

The Library of Congress owns the 1768 edition which was published jointly by Thomas Jefferys, Carrington Bowles, John Bowles, Robert Sayer, and Henry Parker. The original issue was published in 1760 by Thomas Jefferys.

A Short Narrative of The Horrid Massacre in Boston, Perpetrated In the Evening of the Fifth Day of March 1770, by Soldiers of the XXIX Regiment, Which, with the XIVth Regiment, were then Quartered There. With Some Observations on the State of Things Prior to that Catastrophe. Printed by Order of the Town of Boston, London, Re-printed for E. and C. Dilly, in the Poultry; and J. Almon, in Piccadilly, M.DCC.LXX. E211.A452 v. 4 no. 2 RBC

Simcoe. *A Journal of the Operations of the Queen's Rangers, From the End of the Year 1777 to the Conclusion of the Late American War.* Exeter, Printed for the Author, [1787]. E277.6 Q6S5 1787 RBC

Simes, Thomas. *A New Military, Historical, and Explanatory Dictionary: Including the Warriors Gazetteer of Places Remarkable for Sieges or Battles.* Philadelphia, Sold by Humphreys, Bell, and Aitken, 1776. U24.S6 RBC

Smith, William. *A Sermon on the Present Situation of American Affairs. Preached in Christ-Church, June 23, 1775, At the Request of the Officers of the Third Battalion of the City of Philadelphia, and the District of Southwark.* Philadelphia Printed, London Re-printed, a second time, For Edward and Charles Dilly, [1775]. E297.S662 RBC

Sprengel, Matthias Christian. *Allgemeines historisches Taschenbuch; oder Abriss der merkwurdigsten neuen Welt-begebenheiten enthaltend fur 1784 bie Geschichte der Revolution von Nord-America.* Berlin, Haude und Spener, 1784. E208.S75 RBC

Toplady, Augustus Montague. *An Old Fox Tarr'd and Feather'd. Occasioned by What is Called Mr. John Wesley's Calm Address to our American Colonys By an Hanoverian.* London, Printed for Mr. Lewis and Mr. Bell, 1775. E211.W48 RBC

The Town and Country Magazine; or Universal Repository of Knowledge, Instruction, and Entertainment. London, Printed for A. Hamilton; Junr. near St. John's-Gate, 1769–90. AP3.T6 RBC

An Universal History ... The Maps and Charts to the Modern Part of the Universal History. London, for T. Osborne, 1766. Phillips 639 G1015.U5 1766 G&M

The Universal Magazine of Knowledge and Pleasure. London, Pub. for J. Hinton, etc., 1765–90. AP3.U5 RBC

The United States Magazine: A Repository of History, Politics and Literature. v. 1, Jan.–Dec. 1779. Philadelphia, Printed by F. Bailey. AP2.A2U3 RBC

Voogt, Claes J. *De Nieuwe Groote Lichtende Zee-Fakkel Het Vierde Deel, Behelzende de Zee-*

Kusten van Guajana, Venezuela, Carthagena, Nova Costo-Rica, de Honduras, Yucatan, Mexico, Florida, Carolina, Virginia, Nieuw Nederland, Nieuw Engeland, Nieuw Vrankryk, Terre Neuve, en de Noorder Zee-Kusten van America, met de onderhoorende en tusschen leggende Eilanden. Amsterdam, G.H. van Keulen, 1782.

Phillips 1170 G1101.P5V5 1782 G&M

Weatherwise, Abraham. *Weatherwise's Town and Country Almanack For the Year of Our Lord, 1782.* Boston, Printed and Sold by Nathaniel Coverly and Robert Hodge, 1782. Almanac Coll. RBC

The Westminster Magazine or the Pantheon of Taste Containing a View of the History, Politics, Literature, Manners, Gallantry, and Fashions. London, Printed for John Walker, No. 20, Pater-noster Row, 1773–85. AP4.W4 RBC

Appendix B

Secondary Sources Cited in the Text

Baker, William S. *The Engraved Portraits of Washington.* Philadelphia, Lindsay & Baker, 1880. E312.43.B155

British Museum. Department of Prints and Drawings. *Catalogue of Political and Personal Satires.* v. 4, 1761–1770; v. 5, 1771–1783; v. 6, 1784–1792. London, Kegan Paul, 1883–1935. NE55.L7A3

Collection de Vinck. *See* Paris. Bibliothèque Nationale.

CPPS. *See* British Museum. Department of Prints and Drawings.

Fielding, Mantle. *American Engravers upon Copper and Steel: A Supplement to David McNeely Stauffer's American Engravers.* Philadelphia, Wickersham Press, 1917. NE505.S8

George, M. Dorothy. *See* British Museum. Department of Prints and Drawings.

Halsey, Richard Townley Haines. *The Boston Port Bill as Pictured by a Contemporary London Cartoonist.* New York, The Grolier Club, 1904. E215.8.H19 RBC

Hart, Charles H. *Catalogue of the Engraved Portraits of Washington.* New York, The Grolier Club, 1904. E312.43.H32

LeGear, Clara E. *See* U.S. Library of Congress. Geography & Map Division.

Lewis, Benjamin Morgan. *A Guide to Engravings in American Magazines 1741–1810.* New York, The New York Public Library, 1959. NE506.L4

Mulkearn, ed. *Topographical Description of the . . . United States.* See Pownall.

Paris. Bibliothèque Nationale. Department des Estampes. *Un Siecle d'histoire de France par l'estampe, 1770–1871; Collection de Vinck.* v. 1, Ancien Regime; v. 2, La Constituante. Paris, Imprimerie Nationale, 1909–29. NE55.P4V5

Phillips, Philip L. *See* U.S. Library of Congress. Geography & Map Division.

Pownall, Thomas. *Topographical Description of the Dominion of the United States.* Edited by Lois Mulkearn. Pittsburgh, University of Pittsburgh Press, 1949. E163.P88 1949

Richardson, Edgar P. "Charles Willson Peale's Engravings in the Year of National Crisis, 1787," *Winterthur Portfolio*, I:166–181, N9 .W52

Ristow, Walter William. comp. *A La Carte; Selected Papers on Maps and Atlases.* Washington, Library of Congress, 1972. GA231.R5

Sellers, Charles C. *Benjamin Franklin in Portraiture.* New Haven, Yale University Press, 1962. N7628.F7S4

Smith, John Chaloner. *British Mezzotinto Portraits; Being A Descriptive Catalogue of these Engravings from the Introduction of the Art to the Early Part of the Present Century*. 4 parts. London, Henry Sotheran & Co., 1878–82. NE265.S6

Stauffer, David M. *American Engravers upon Copper and Steel*. 2 v. New York, The Grolier Club, 1907. NE505.S8

Stokes, Isaac N. *The Iconography of Manhattan Island, 1498–1909*. 6 v. New York, R. H. Dodd, 1915–28. F128.37.S88

U.S. Library of Congress. Geography and Map Division. *A List of Geographical Atlases in the Library of Congress, with Bibliographical Notes*. Washington, D.C., U.S. Government Printing Office, 1909–63. Z6028.U5

    Cited as Phillips or LeGear, v. 1–4 compiled under the direction of Philip Lee Phillips; v. 5–6 by Clara E. LeGear; v. 7 in preparation.

U.S. Library of Congress. Geography and Map Division. *A List of Maps of America in the Library of Congress. Preceded by a List of Works Relating to Cartography*. Compiled by Philip L. Phillips. 2 v. Washington, U. S. Govt. Print. Off., 1901. Z6027.A5U5

    Cited as Phillips, *Maps*.

Wheat, Carl I. *Mapping the Transmississippi West, 1540–1861*. San Francisco, Institute of Historical Cartography, 1957. GA405.W5

Whitehill, Walter M. *Boston; A Topographical History*. Boston, Belknap Press, 1968. F73.3.W57

Index of Titles

Numbers in this index refer to entries, not to pages.

The Able Doctor, or America Swallowing the Bitter Draught, 664
The Accident in Lombard-Street Philada., 587
Admiral Byron, 21
Admiral Hughes, 128
Adml. Kempenfelt, 135
Admiral Keppel, 136–37
Admiral Parker, 164
[An allegory describing America—a cartouche], 832
[An allegory of America at the close of war—a cartouche], 843
[An allegory of Boston, 1769—a cartouche], 641
[An allegory on America during the 1770's—a cartouche], 661
[An allegory on New York—a cartouche], 694
[An Allegory on the British Colonies in North America—a cartouche], 708
[An allegory on the British Empire in North America—a cartouche], 699
[An allegory on the Mississippi Bubble—a cartouche], 722
The Allies.—Par Nobil Fratrum . . ., 764
The Alternative of Williams-Burg, 680
Amelia: or the faithless Briton, 344
America, 716
[America, 1771], 658
[America—a cartouche], 640
[America and two children—a cartouche], 634

America in Flames, 677
[America pois'd in the balance of justice, 1776], 705
America. To Perpetuate to Posterity the Memory of those Patriotic Heroes . . ., 761
America. To Those who wish to Sheathe the Desolating Sword of War . . ., 761
[America toe] her [Miss] taken [Moth]er, 731
America Triumphant and Britannia in Distress, 839
[America with gods and other continents watches the activities of Geography—title page], 777
[America with her children and commerce in the background—a cartouche], 865
America with Peace and Freedom blest, 898
The American General Lee taken Prisoner . . ., 270
[An American Indian points to a map of America—ornament from a title page], 659
[An American Indian warrior rests from the war—a cartouche], 718
[An American Indian with harpoon and two Indians with a European—a cartouche], 835
[American medals], 875
The American Rattle Snake, 812
The American Rattlesnake presenting Monsieur his Ally a Dish of Frogs, 826
Die Americaner machen das Corps des General Bourgoyne zu Gefangnen bey Saratoga . . ., 275

Die Americaner machen den Lord Cornwallis . . ., 327
Die Americaner wiedersetzen sich der Stempel-Acte, . . ., 243
Der Americanische Gener: Arnold, 10
1. Americanischer Scharffschutz oder Tager (Rifleman) 2. regulaire Infanterie von Pensylvanien, 241
Amerique, 631
The amiable Miss W__bb. [and] The intrepid Partizan, 198
Amunition Waggon, 916
Amusement for John Bull & his Cousin Paddy . . ., 857
An Analysis of Modern Patriotism Performed by Public Opinion & displayed by Public indignation, 854
L'Anglais Corrige Comme un Enfant . . ., 841
Les Anglois Molestes et Chatiees . . ., 756
Annapolis Royal, 453
Anticipation; or, the Contrast to the Royal Hunt, 819
Antisejanus . . ., 621
Appearance of the High Lands of Agameticus, N.E. with Penobscot Hills . . ., 485
Appearance of the Land from White Islands to St. Marys River . . ., 397
Appearance of the leading Mark over the bar [of Sandy Hook, with the lighthouse], 566
Appearance of the S:E: Point of Nova Scotia . . ., 404

Appearance of the Shore . . . to the Eastward of Halifax Harbor, 418
Appearance of the Shore to the Westward of Canso . . ., 402
Argus, 772
[Armaments of the American Rebels], 905
L'Armée française courant en Echiquier et Combattant les Vaisseaux . . ., 300
L'Armée françoise allant reconnoitre à St. Cristophe . . ., 301
L'Armee françoise Combattant L'Armée Angloise . . ., 297
L'Armée françoise courant en Echiquier pour Rejoindre L'Armée Angloise . . ., 299
L'Armée francoise faisant signal . . ., 298
L'Armée françoise Mouillée auprès de l'ance Molenieu dans L'isle de la Grenade . . ., 294
L'Armée françoise Mouillée auprès de l'Ance Molenieu [Point] dans l'isle de la Grenade . . ., 292
The Armorial bearings of the States of Massachusetts & N. York, 889
The Armorial Bearings of the States of Pennsylvania & New Jersey, 890
[Arms of the British Forces], 904
[Arms of the United States], 883
The [ass]-headed and [cow-heart]-ed Ministry making the British [lion] give up the Pull, 858
[Association meeting at York], 768
The Attack of the Fort on Sulivan's Island . . ., 260
Attaque de Brimstomhill . . ., 329
[An Attempt to Land a Bishop in America], 636
Avaunt ye troublers of a World's repose, 635

B. Franklin, L.L.D. F.R.S. Ambassador from the Congress of America to the Court of France, 68
B. Franklin, L.L.D. F.R.S. Born at Boston in New England, Jan. 6th, 1706. Died at Philadelphia, April 17th 1790. Eripuit Caelo Fulmen; Sceptrumque Tyrannis, 78
B. Franklin of Philadelphia, 57
B: Franklin of Philadelphia L.L.D. F.R.S., 58
La Balance du pouvoir . . ., 741

The Ballance of Power, 786
La Balle A Frappé son Amante, 323
The Beaver Islands . . ., 403
Behold! a Fabric now to Freedom rear'd, 895
The Belligerent Plenipo's, 830
Benjamin Franklin, 69, 73
Benjamin Franklin L.L.D. Envoy from the American Congress to the French Court, 65
Benjamin Franklin, L.L.D. F.R.S., 61, 70
Benjamin Franklin, L.L.D. F.R.S. One of the American Plenipotentiaries at the Court of France, 67
Benjamin Franklin Né a Boston, le 17 Janvier 1706, 79
Benjamin Franklin. Né à Boston, dans la nouvelle Angleterre le 17 Janvier 1706, 59
Benjamin Franklin. Né à Boston, dans la nouvelle Angleterre, le 17 Janv. 1706, 63
Benjamin Franklin. Né à Boston dans la Nouvelle Angleterre, le 17 Janvier 1706, 75
Benjamin Franklin. Né à Boston le 17. Janvier 1706. Eripuit coelo fulmen sceptrum que tyrannis, 74
[Benjamin Franklin] On l'a vu désarmer les Tirans et les Dieux, 77
Benyamin Franklin. gebohren 1706, 71
Berry Head, . . . & White Head Island . . ., 396
A Birds Eye View from part of Mount Pleasant A. to the Eastern Point of Long Island B__C., 605
The Birth-Day Ode . . ., 747
Blessed are the Peacemakers, 849
The Blessed Effects of Venality, 698
The Blessings of Peace, 856
[The Blessings of Peace on America—a cartouche], 872
The Bloody Massacre perpetrated in King Street . . ., 246
Bond Hollow bearing S.bE., 536
[Boston], 499
Boston Bay, 483
Boston Bay, the Light House bearing N.W.b.W. . . ., 486
Boston from Willis Creek, 500

Boston, seen between Castle Williams and Governors Island . . ., 484
The Bostonians in Distress, 673
The Bostonian's Paying the Excise-man, or Tarring & Feathering, 670
The Botching Taylor Cutting his Cloth to cover a Button, 754
The brave old [Tiyanoka] Hendrick the great Sachem or Chief of the Mohawk Indians, one of the Six Nations now in Alliance with, & Subject to the King of Great Britain, 111
Brigadier Genl. Arnold, 14
Bristol Neck Rhode Island 1765, 533
Britain, America, at length be Friends, 662
Britania and Her Daughter . . ., 766
Britania's Assassination, or_____The Republican Amusement, 818
[Britannia], 638
[Britannia attacked by her enemies], 863
[Britannia frees the dove of peace], 652
[Britannia toe] Amer[eye]ca, 730
The British Lion engaging Four Powers, 821
A British Sailor offering a Sword . . ., 311
Brittanias Ruin, 752
The Budget, 788
The Bull Over-Drove; or the Drivers in Danger, 810
The Bull Roasted: or the Political Cooks Serving their Customers, 765
Bunker's Hill on N. York Island, 548
Bunkers Hill or America's Head Dress, 697
By His Majestys Royal Letters Patent . . ., 784

Caduta di Niagara, 563
Cape Blowmedown, 461
Cape Blowmedown, open with Cape Split . . ., 459
Cape Poge bearing S 52° E . . ., 524
A. Cape Prospect bearing N: by E: distant 10½ Miles. B. Cape Sambro N:N:E: ¾ E: 14 Miles, 435
Cape Sable, 441
Cape Sable bearing N.E: by N: . . ., 439
Cape Sable bearing N.N.W. . . ., 438
Cape St. Mary . . ., 373

Cape Southampton . . ., 405
Cape Split, 462
Cape Spry N:N:E 1 Mile and ¼ distant. Beaver Isles E. by N. 10 Miles distant. Westermost Ledge of Pegasus Wing . . ., 408
Captain Asgill, 15
The Captivating Miss B_____. [and] The American Negotiator, 40
[Cartouche and ornament from a map . . .], 742
Castle William, 490, 492
The Catch Singers, 811
Chalbeate Spring near Saratoga, 562
Chandelier . . ., 906
Charles Gravier Comte de Vergennes Conseiller d'Etat Ordinaire, Ministre et Secretaire d' Etat et Chef du Conseil Royal des Finances, 203
Charles Henri Comte Destaing, Né le 24. Novembre 1729, 52
Charles Lee. Esqr. Americanischer General-Major, 148
Charles Lee Esqr. Major General of the American Forces, 150
Charles Lee, Esqr. Major General of the Continental-army in America, 147
Charles Lee, Esqr. Major General of the Continental-Army in America, 149
Charles Thompson Esqr. Secretary to Congress, 201
Charles-town [and] Fort-Sulivan [S.C.], 607
Chebucto Head . . ., 422
[Cherubs celebrate the founding of the new nation—a cartouche], 901
[Cherubs imitate the times—title page ornament], 808
The Chevalier D'_____n producing his Evidence against certain Persons, 649
Cheveaux de Frize . . ., 907
Chi Mi Vela é in Periglio e Chi Mi Svel, 715
[A Christian figure appears to an Indian—a cartouche], 633
The City Carriers, 647
The Closet . . ., 725
Coalition Arms, 871

The Coffee-House Patriots; or News, from St. Eustatia, 807
Colonel Arnold. Who Commanded the Provincial Troops sent against Quebec, through the Wilderness of Canada, and was Wounded in Storming that City, under General Montgomery, 9
Colonel Barre, 16
The Colonies Reduced. Its Companion, 632
The Colossus of the North . . ., 675
Combat Memorable entre le Pearson et Paul Jones, 310
The Commissioners, 728
The Commissioner's Interview with Congress, 729
Commodore Hopkins, 115
Commodore Hopkins, Commander in Chief of the American Fleet, 114
Commodore Hopkins. Commandeur en Chef der Amerj: Flotte, 116
Common-Wealth. The Colosus, 630
The Conference . . ., 643
The Conference between the Brothers How to get Rich, 711
Der Congress erklärt die 13 vereinigten Stâaten von Nord-America . . ., 261
The Congress or The Necessary Politicians, 692
Contemplez l'ouvrage de pouvoir arbitraire, 256
[A Continental soldier stands by broken pillars —a map ornament], 717
[The continents surround the goddess of geography], 881
A Convention of the Not-Ables, 887
The Council of the Rulers, & the Elders against the Tribe of ye Americanites, 676
Count De Grasse, 42
Count de Grasse, 43
Count de Grasse, the French Admiral, resigning his Sword . . ., 331
Count de Rochambeau French General of the Land Forces in America reviewing the French Troops, 776
Count DeGrasse, 44
The Courtiers Assembled, on hearing the News of the Death of the Rt. Honble. Wm. Beckford, 655
Crow Harbor . . ., 394
The Curious Zebra . . ., 737

Dartmouth Shore in the Harbor of Halifax, 414
David Wooster, Esqr. Commandr. bëy der Provincal. Armee in America, 236
David Wooster, Esqr. Commander in Chief of the Provincial Army against Quebec, 235
De Crillon, 41
De La Fayette, 141
The Death of Warren, 255
Debarquement des Troupes Engloises a Nouvelle Yorck . . ., 266
Dédié aux Milords de l'Amirauté Anglaise par un Membre du Congrés Américaine . . ., 727
The Defeat of the Spanish Fleet under Don Juan de Langara, by Sir George Brydges Rodney . . ., 313
A Design to represent the beginning and completion of an American Settlement or Farm . . ., 578
The desponding Hero of the Coldstream. A Military Madrigal, 785
D'Estaing, 53
Le Destin Molestant Les Anglois, 757
La Destruction de la Statue Royale . . ., 263
The Dissolution of P_____t, 671
D. Beniamin Fraencklin. Grand Commissaire plenipotentiare du Congres d'Amerique en France né à Boston 1706, en 17. Janvier, 60
Dr. Benjamin Franklin, 76
D. Benjamin Franklin, et vita inter Americanos acta, et magnis electricitatis periculis clarus, 66
Dr. Franklin, 62
Dr. Franklin. Coelis Eripuit Fulmen Sceptrumque Tyrannis, 72
Dr. Beniamin Franklin. gebohrn zu Boston den 17. Janrü. 1706, 64
Dr. Franklin erhält, als Gesandter des Americanischen FreyStaats . . ., 277

Dominion of the Seas . . ., 861
Don Volaseo, 793

E of Chatham, 172
E View of the City of New York, 546
Earl Mansfield, 155
The Earl of Shelburne, 189
Earl Temple, 199
An East Prospect of the City of Philadelphia . . ., 588
East View Hell Gate in the Province of New York, 544
An East View Montreal, in Canada . . ., 351
An East View of Gray's Ferry . . ., 345
An East View of Gray's Ferry, on the River Schuylkill, 582
An East View of the Meeting House in Hollis Street, Boston . . ., 517
The Eastern End of the Isle Sable . . ., 426
Edmund Burke Esqr, 19, 20
[Egmont Harbor—a distant view], 376
Die Einwohner von Boston wersen den englisch-ostindischen Thee ins Meer . . ., 248
Elevation of a Sling Cart [and] Plan of a Sling Cart, 920
Elevation of a Truck-Carriage [and] Plan of a Truck Carriage, 917
Elevation of Campus Martius, 579
Elevation of Powder Cart [and] Plan of a Powder Cart, 915
Elevation of the Commanding Officer's House [on Mud Island], 597
Elevations of State House [Philadelphia] . . ., 590
[Emblematical Print Adapted to the Times], 736
Encampment of the Convention Army . . ., 308
Ende der Feindseeligkeiten . . ., 343
Den Engelsman Op Zyn Uiterste . . ., 783
Englisch Printet, 789
The English Lion Dismember'd Or the Voice of the Public for an Enquiry into the Public Expenditure . . ., 767
The Englishman in Paris, 733

[Englishmen trade with Indians in a wilderness —a cartouche], 348.
The Entrance into Chisetcook Inlet . . ., 413
The Entrance of Boston Harbor , 487
Entrance of Egmont Harbor, 410
The Entrance of Havannah, from within the Harbour, 616
The Entrance of Keppel Harbor . . ., 411
Entrance of Keppel Harbour . . ., 406
The Entrace of Milford Haven . . ., 398
The Entrance of Mines Bason, 463
The Entrance of Port Bickerton . . ., 399
The Entrance of the River St. John, 472
L'Entré triumphale de troupes royales Nouvelle Yorck . . ., 267
L'Entrée au Port de Boston . . ., 488
Das Erste Bürger Blut . . ., 251
Die Erste förmliche Action zwischen den Americanern und Englandern bey Bunkers Hill . . ., 254
L'Escadre française mouillée à Boston . . ., 288
L'Escadre françoise entrant dans la Delaware . . ., 279
L'Escadre françoise entrant dans Newport . . ., 282
L'Escadre françoise mouillée devant New-york, 280
L'Escadre françoise sortant de la Méditerranée . . ., 278
Europe, Asia, Africa and America . . ., 724
The European Diligence, 750
[A European directs two Indians where to place their goods for barter—a cartouche], 743
The ever-memorable Peace-Makers Settling their Accounts, 648
An Extraordinary Gazette or the Disappointed Politicians, 735
Ezra Stiles S.T.D. L.L.D. President of Yale College, 191–92

The Fair American. [and] Old Nauticus, 122
The fair Virginian. [and] The devoted General, 18

Falls of Hinchinbroke River . . ., 412
[A farm at Egmont Harbor], 377
The Federal Pillars, 894
La Folie des Deux Partis . . ., 741
[Four coffins of men killed in the Boston Massacre], 654
[The Four Continents—a cartouche], 660
The f—x and h—d or Rival Candidates. . . ., 774
[Fox, Burke, and North], 877
[A fox in preacher's clothes—a caricature of John Wesley], 689
Frederick lord North, 162
Freedom, Peace, Plenty, all in vain advance, 780
[A French allegory on America—a cartouche], 879
[A French missionary, a soldier, an Indian, and a view of Niagara Falls]. 796
A Front View of the Lines taken from the advanced Post near Browns House, 505

G. Washington, 217
G. Washington, Generaal der Noord-Americaanen, 226
Gabion . . ., 908
The Gallant and Right Hon. Captain Lord Robert Manners Mortally Wounded . . ., 330
Gallant behavior of an English Sailor . . ., 312
Gay Head bearing N E ¼ E and Nomansland E ¼ S, 526
Gay Head bearing SE distant one Mile, 527
General Arnold, 12
Le General Arnold un des Chefs de l Armée Anglo-Americaine, 11
General Burgoyne, 17
General Carleton, 23
General Clinton, 28
General Eliott, 51
General Gage, 80
General Gates, 83, 88
Genl. George Washington, 210
General Green, 99
General Grey, 101
General Howe, 125, 127

General Howe Esqr. of the Conecticut and comander Army in America, 124
General Lee, 151
General Montgomery, 157
The General P____s, or Peace, 844
General Putnam, 177–78
General Reed, 181
General Reed. Member of Congress, President & Commander in chief of the State of Pennsylvania, 182
General Sir Guy Carleton, 24
General Sullivan, 196
Gen. Washington, 222
General Washington, 214–15, 223
1. General Washington. 2. General Gates. 3. Dr. Franklin. 4. Präsid Laurens. 5. Paul Jones, 221
Le General Washington. Ne Quid Detrimenti capiat Res publica, 229
1. General Washington's reitende Leibgarde. 2. die independent Company, Chef General Washington, 242
George Montgomery, Esqr Major General of the American Armies. Kill'd at Quebec Decr. 31st. 1775, 156
George the III, 93
George the IIId. King of Great Britain, France and Ireland, 91
George III. King of Great Britain &c, 92
[George Washington], 220
George Washington. Commandant en Chef des Armées des Etats-unis de l'Amerique, 211
George Washington. Commander in Chief of ye Armies of ye United States of America, 218
George Washington Eqer. Général en Chef de l'Armée Anglo-Amériquaine, nommé Dictateur par le Congrès en Fevrier 1777, 208
George Washington. Esqr. Americanischer Generalissimus, 207
George Washington, Esqr. General and Commander in Chief of the Continental Army in America, 206
Georges Washington, EQer. Général en chef de l'Armée Anglo-Amériquaine nommé Dictateur par le Congrès en Fevrier 1777, 212
George Whitefield. M.A., 232
The Gig, 790
Gin Engine . . ., 919
The Glorious Washington and Gates, 209
[The god Mars watches the goddess Fame unfurl a detailed map of New York and Pennsylvania—map ornament], 720
Governeer Morris Esqr. Member of Congress, 159
Grand Manan Island . . ., 468
Grand Passage in the Bay Fundy . . ., 448
La Grande Bretagne mutilé . . ., 862
The Great Financier, or British Economy for the Years 1763, 1764, 1765, 622
Guerritte . . ., 909
Guillaume Thomas Reynal, 183

H. Gates, 86
The Habeas Corpus, or The Wild Geese flying away with Fox to America, 824
Halifax in Nova Scotia, 423
The Harbour and part of the Town of Havannah, 616a
[Harmony Weeps for the Present Situation of American Affairs], 687
Heny. Laurens Esqr., 146
Henry Laurens Esqr. President of the American Congress 1778, 144
Hereabouts will be the Place to affix the Stamp, 619
Die Hessen, vom General Washington . . . zu Trenton . . ., 271
The Hibernian Attempt, 880
An Hieroglyphycal Epistle From [Britannia toe] Admiral [Rodney], 769
The High Lands of Haspotagoen . . ., 436
His Excel: G: Washington Esq: LLD. Late Commander in Chief of the Armies of the U.S. of America & President of the Convention of 1787, 224
His Excellency General Washington Commander in Chief of the united States of North America &c., 219
His Excy. George Washington Esqr. Captain General of all the American Forces, 216
His Excellency George Washington Esqr. Captain General of all the American Forces, 213
His Excellency Henry Laurens President of Congress, and Minister Plenipotentiary for treating of Peace with Grt. Britain, 145
His Excellency John Jay President of Congress & Minister Plenipotentiary from Congress at Madrid, 131
His Excy. John Adams, Esq., 1
His Excy. John Hancock, Esq: ——— Late President of the American Congress, 107
His Excy. Nathaniel Green Esq;—Major General of the American Army, 98
His Excellency S. Huntingdon President of Congress, 130
His Excy. William Heath, Esq. Major General in the American Army, 110
His Majesty King George the III. Contemplating a Medal of King Alfred, 90
The Historical Painter, 868
The Honle. Anthony Wayne, Esqr. Major General in the American Army, 231
The Honle. B. Lincoln, Esq. Major General in the American Army, 152
The Honble. Charles James Fox, 55, 56
The Honble Chas. James Fox, 54
The Honle. Henry Knox, Esqr. Major General of the Artillery in the American Army, 139
The Honle. Horatio Gates, Esqr. Major General in the American Army, 85
The Honble. Horatio Gates. Major General of the American Forces, 84
The Hon. James Otis, jun. Esq:, 163
The Honble. John Hancock, 105
The Hon. John Hancock, Esq; President of the Honourable the Continental Congress, 103
The Honble John Hancock of Boston in New England; President of the American Congress, 102
The Honble. Marquis LaFayette, Major General of the American Army, 140

The Honble. Samuel Adams, Esqr. First Delegate to Congress for Massachusetts, 3
The Hon; Sir Willm. Howe Kt. of the Bath. Commander in Chief of all his Majesty's Forces in America, 126
Hopsons Nose . . ., 407
Horatio Gates, Esqr. Major General of the American Forces, 82
The Horrors of War a Vision Or a Scene in the Tragedy of K: Richd: 3, 823
The Horse America throwing his Master . . ., 749
The Hour of Humiliation, 816a
The Hour of Insolence, 816
The House of Employment & Alms House, 593
Hugh, Earl Percy, 165–67
The Humble Petition of the Freeholders of the County of Middlesex, 646
Hurdles . . ., 910

[Iconography of Canada—a cartouche], 867
In the back Ground is Admiral Rodney's Engagement with Count De Grasse . . ., 869
Incendie de New-York, 269
[An Indian, A European trader, and items of commerce], 798
[An Indian and a frontiersman—a cartouche], 690
[An Indian Bows to Europe], 686
[An Indian on the cartouche for "Map for the Interior Travels through America . . ."], 900
An Indian Warrior Entering his Wigwam with a Scalp, 238
[Indians and a bison—map ornament], 797
[Indians and white men working together—a cartouche], 836
[The inhabitants of America—a cartouche], 795
[Instruction of American youth], 860
[Interior view of the fort on Mud Island], 598
Isle Haut and Cape Chegnecto, 464
The Isle Haut, bearing N.b.W. distant 3 Miles and Cape Chignecto . . ., 454
The Isle-Haute, bearing W.N.W. distant 2 Miles, 458

Israel Putnam. Esqr. General-Major der Americaner, 176
Israel Putnam, Eqer. Major Général des Troupes de Connecticut. Il commandoit en chef à l'affaire de Bunckershill près Boston le 17 Juin 1775, 179
Israel Putnam Esqr. Major General of the Connecticut Forces, and Commander in Chief at the Engagement on Bunckers-Hill Near Boston, 17 June 1775, 175

J. Dickenson, 46
J. Dickinson Esqr. Member of Congress & Author of Letters of a Farmer of Pennsylvania, 47
J. Hancock, 108
J. Reed, 180
Jack England Fighting the Four Confederates, 787
The Jail. Philada., 585
John Andre, Esqr. late Adjutant General of the British Forces in America, 7
John Bull Triumphant, 763
John Bulls Alternative, 803
John Hancock Esqr., 109
John Hancock, Esq: President of the American Congress, 106
John Hankock. Praesident des Americane Congresses, 104
John Malcom, 249
John Paul Jones, 133, 134
John Paul Jones. Commander of a Squadron in the Service of the Thirteen United States of North America, 132
John Wilkes, Esq;, 234
Joseph Thayendaneken The Mohawk Chief, 200
Journée de Lexington, 252
[Justice enthroned], 892

K. George II. crowned June 11, 1727. K. George III. crowned Oct. 25, 1760, 89
[Kings Bridge, New York], 555a

Labour in Vain or let them tug and be Da–nd, 828
Lady Harriet Ackland, 276
[La Fayette at Yorktown] Conclusion De La Campagne de 1781 en Virginie, 142
Landung einer Frauzösischen Hülfs-Armee in America . . ., 318
The Late Auction at St. Eustatia, 791
The late Bombardment of Government Castle, 817
[Liberty Conquers Tyranny], 688
Lt. Col. Tarleton, 197
Lieutenant Moody . . ., 314
The Light House on Sandy Hook, S.E. one Mile, 542
Light House S.E. 1 Mile distant, 415
Light House S.W.b.S. 1. Mile distant, 415
(a) Light House West 3° South 2½ Miles distant (b) Chebucto Head North 4° West distant 2 Miles (c) Citadel Hill, 416
Long Island open on the North Side of Nicks Mate Island, 501
Loon na werk 1780 . . ., 778
Lord Camden, 22
Lord Cornwallis, 34
Lord George Germaine, 94-95
Lord George Gordon, 96-97
The Lord God Omnipotent reigneth . . ., 642
Lord Hood, 113
Lord Howe, 119, 121
Lord Keppel, 138
Lord Loughborough, 153
Lord Robert Manners Mortally Wounded, 330
Lord Rodney, 185
Lord Shelburne, 188
L__d Shel__, begging Monsieur to make Piss or P__e, 845
Lord Thurlow, 202
Lord Viscount Howe, 118
Louisburg in North America . . ., 382

The Machine to go without Asses . . ., 651
Major André, von drey Americanern . . ., 315
Major General Arnold Wounded Dec 31–1775 at the attack of Quebec, 13

Major General Baron Steuben, 190
Major General David Wooster, 237
Major General Gates, 87
Majr. Genl. Greene, 100
Major-General John Sullivan, 195
Major General John Sullivan, A distinguished Officer in the Continental Army, 194
Major Genl. Joseph Warren Slain at the Battle of Bunker's Hill June 17th 1775, 204
Major Genl. Richd. Montgomery Slain in Storming Quebec Decbr. 31st 1775, 158
Major General Warren, 205
Major John Andre, Late Adjutant General to the British Army in North America, 8
Mal Lui Veut Mal Lui Tourne Dit le Bon Homme Richard, 782
De Man In't Hembd, of de Gefnuikte Hoogmoed. . . ., 779
The Manner in which the American Colonies Declared themselves Independant . . ., 262
Marital Motions or Military Manoeuvres . . ., 801
The Massacre perpetrated in King Street Boston . . ., 247
[Masthead for *The Massachusetts Spy*], 657
Mayjor General Amherst, 5
Mechios River near the Mills, 474
[Men hunting bears—a cartouche], 837
[Milford Haven. The Head of the Bay of Chedabucto], 393
[Minerva, the goddess of wisdom and war], 723
Miss Carolina Sulivan one of the obstinate daughters of America . . ., 701
Miss L_____n. [and] The Martial Lover, 168
Miss Sp__c__r. [and] The Pliant Premier, 160
Miss V_gh_n. [and] The American Hero, 123
Mr. Fitzherbert . . . Signing the Preliminary Articles of Peace . . ., 332
Mr. Trade & Family or the State of ye Nation . . ., 753
Mrs. C_____x. [and] The Steady Patriot, 50
Mrs. F_____g. [and] The lenient Commander, 81
Mrs. General Washington Bestowing thirteen Stripes on Britania, 852

Mrs. P_____t. [and] The Cautious Commander, 6
Mrs. W_____n. [and] The careful Commander, 25
The Mitred Minuet, 666
Le Mole St. Nicolas dans L'Ilse de St. Domingue . . ., 617
Moment de l'après midi du 11 Aoust 1778 . . ., 283
The Monstrous Hydra, or Virtue Invulnerable, 896
The Monument of Major André, 842
Mount Pleasant half way between the Cedars on the Hook & the Light House, 537
[A mountain landscape in Quebec—a cartouche], 356
Mud Forte [from] Province Island, 595

A N.b.E. View of the Fort on the Western end of Sulivan's Island . . ., 606
A N.W. View of the State House in Philadelphia taken 1778, 589
A N.W.b.N. View of Charles Town from on board the Bristol . . ., 611
The Narrows, (between Red and Yellow Hook, on Long Island, & the East Bluff of Staten Island,) bearing S.b.W., 543
Neu Jorck sive Neu Amsterdam, 550
The New Country Dance, as Danced at C****, 627
[A New Jersey scene—a cartouche], 565
A New Method of Macarony Making, as practised at Boston, 668
A New Pantomine. Harlequine, 870
New York, with the Entrance of the North and East Rivers, 541
News from America, or the Patriots in the Dumps, 703
The North Point of Grandmanan Island in the Bay Fundy . . ., 466
North Shore, 432
North Shore of Isle Sable . . ., 433
The North Star, 637
A North View of Castle William in the Harbour of Boston, 491

A North View of Pensacola, on the Island of Santa Rosa . . ., 613

O Qu'el d'estain . . ., 758
"Oh fly," cries Peace, the Soul of Social Life, 859
The Olive Rejectd. or the Yankees Revenge . . ., 732
The Only Booth in the Fair. Portland & Co late Shelburne, 853
[The oracle representing, Britannia, Hibernia, Scotia, & America . . .], 663
Orage causé par l'Impôt sur le Thé en Amérique, 739
Orgnes . . ., 911
[Ornament for the title page of *The European Magazine* from 1782 until 1789], 840
[Ornament for title page of *The Columbian Magazine* . . .], 899
The Ovens at the Entrance of Lunenburg Bay, 437

Paradice Lost, 815
The Parlmt. dissolvd, or, The Devil turn'd Fortune Teller, 672
Parrawankaw. [and] Dr. Squintum, 233
The Parricide. A Sketch of Modern Patriotism, 700
The Patriot . . ., 644
[A Patriot and a Tory wrestle for a pine tree flag—a cartouche], 706
[A Patriot and a Tory wrestle for a pine tree flag while an Indian watches—a cartouche], 707
The Patriotic American Farmer. J——n D-k-ns-n, Esq; Barrister at Law, 45
The Patriotick Barber of New York . . ., 679
Peace Crowned by Victory, 876
Peace Porridge all hot. The best to be got, 847
Pennsylvania Hospital, 591
A Perspective View of Montreal . . ., 350
Perspective View of the Country between Wilmington and the Delaware . . ., 594
A Perspective View of the Town and Fortifications of Montreal in Canada, 352

Petard . . ., 912
Philip Schuyler Esqr. Majr. Genl. in the American Service, 187
The Phoenix and the Rose . . ., 264
A Picturesque View of the State of the Nation for February 1778, 726
Plan du Combat de la Grenade gagné par Mr. Le Cte. d'Estaing sur l'Amiral Byron . . ., 295
Plymouth MDCXX, 674
A Political, Anatomical, Satirical, Lecture on Heads and No Heads . . ., 629
The Political Cartoon, for the Year 1775, 685
A Political Concert . . ., 848
Political Electricity; or, An Historical & Prophetical Print in the Year 1770, 656
A Political Lesson, 667
The Political Mirror or an Exhibition of Ministers for April 1782, 813
The Political Raree-Show: or a Picture of Parties and Politics, during and at the close of the Last Session of Parliament, 748
Pontoon Carriage [and Pontoon], 918
The Poor Blacks Going to Their Settlement, 886
Poor old England endeavoring to reclaim his wicked American Children, 709
[A Port Scene in South Carolina—a cartouche], 604
[A Port Scene in the South—a cartouche], 602
Prattle, 760
Précis de Cette Guerre, 303-7
Précis du Traité de Paix . . ., 333-42
Premiere Assemblée du Congrès, 250
Prerogatives Defeat or Liberties Triumph, 770
The Present State of Great Britain, 755
Prince Stadhold-r Resuming his Deliberation, 825
Prise de la Dominique, 287
Prise de l'Isle de la Grenade, 296
Prise de Pensacola, 319
Prise de Tabago, 321
A Privy Council, 751
A Privy Council Laying their Heads Together . . ., 897

Pro Bono Publico. The Political Cluster in terrorem, 873
[The products of Nova Scotia—a map ornament], 639
Prospect of the Paysaick Falls in New-Jersey, 569
Prospect von Quebec, 358
A Prospective View of the Town of Boston . . ., 245
Protestants, remember the Massacre of St. Bartholemews in Paris, & the burning of Martyrs in Smithfield, 704

Qualifying for a Campain, 710
Quebec, 359-60
Quebeck, 366

Ramea Isles on the S.W. Coast of Newfoundland . . ., 387
A Real American Rifle Man, 240
The Reconciliation between Britania and her daughter America, 820
Reddition de l'Armée Angloises . . ., 326
Reddition de l'Armée du Lord Cornwallis, 324
The Repeal, or the Funeral of Miss Ame-Stamp, 624
The Repeal. or the Funeral Procession, of Miss Americ-Stamp, 623
Representation du Feu Terrible a Nouvelle Yorck, 268
[Representation of a battle—a cartouche], 744
Representation of a County-Convention for Redress of Grievance of Courts, 891
[Representation of the American war—a cartouche], 759
Revd. Samuel Cooper D.D., 32
The Reverse of the Great Seal of the United States, 884
Review of the York Regiment . . . ., 740
Richd. Lord Viscount Howe Rear Admiral of the White and Commander in Chief of the Fleet in N. America, 120
Richtige Abbildung der den Americanischen Probinzialisten-belagerten und wiedereroberten Hauptstadt und Festung Boston in America . . ., 259
The Right Honble. Chas. Wolfran Cornwall Esq. Speaker of the House of Commons, 33
The R. Honble Earl of Dartmouth, 36
The Right Honble. Fredk. Earl of Carlisle, Lord Lieutt. of the Kingdom of Ireland, 27
The Right Honble. Lord Macartney, 154
The Right Honble. Lord North, 161
The Right Honble. The Earl of Hillsborough, 112
The Right Honourable The Marquis de la Fayette, Unanimously chosen Commandant of the National Guards, 143
The Rt. Hon. William Pitt, Chancellor of the Exchequer, 170
The Right Honourable William Pitt, Earl of Chatham, 169
Robert Hopkins. Esqr. Commodore of the American Sea Forces, 117
Robert Rogers. Commandeur der Americaner, 186
The Royal Hunt, or a Prospect of the Year 1782, 809

S. Deane, 37
S. Huntingdon, 129
S View of the City of New York, 545
S.E. George Washington. Général en Chef des Armées des Etats unis de l'Amérique, 228
S.E. Prospect from an Eminence near the Common, Boston, 511
A S.W. View of the Baptist Meeting House, Providence R.I., 532
A Sachem of the Abenakee Nation . . ., 244
St. Eustache une des Isles D'Antilles . . ., 320
St. Lucia in the West Indies taken Possession of . . ., 290
St. Mary's Bay, 375
Sambro Light-house, bearing west . . ., 420
Sambro Light-house, south-east . . ., 421
Samuel Adams Esq. One of the Delegates from the Province of Massachusetts-Bay to the

General Continental Congress of North America, 2
Sandy Point bearing W S W distant four Miles, 525
Sankoty Head, bearing S b W, distant 10 Miles, 528
Sankoty Head bearing SW when clear of the Shoals distant 4 Leagues, 529
Sta. Maria Island . . ., 388
Sarratoga, 274
Saulte de Niagara, 563a
Sauvage du NO. de la Louisiane, 239
The Savages let loose, Or The Cruel Fate of the Loyalists, 850
[Scene from the West Indies—a cartouche], 838
[A Scene in the British Colonies in North America—a cartouche], 719
[A Scene in the West Indies], 615
[A Scene on the Island of St. John—a cartouche], 721
The Scotch Butchery, 684
The Sea Fight between Keppel and D'Orvilliers, 281
Secretary Pitt, 171
The Section and Plan of a Block-house, 921
Shelb——ns Sacrifice or the recommended Loyalists, a faithful representation of a Tragedy shortly to be performed on the Continent of America, 846
The Shell–born Jes—t, 829
[Shirley Point open with Deer Island, Sailing into Boston Harbor], 531
The Sick Prince, 888
Siege du Fort S. Philippe, 328
The Siege of Rhode Island . . ., 286
Der Siegen Engeländer und der Streitende Americaner . . ., 693
Silas Dean, Esq., 39
Silas Deane Esqr. Commissioner from Congress in France, 38
[Silhouette of George Washington and bust profile of Benjamin Franklin], 225
Sr. George Bridges Rodney. . . . Admiral of the Blue & [Continental Fleet of his] Majesty's Ships sent to protect our Trade [in the] West Indies, 184
Sir Guy Carleton, 26
Sir Henry Clinton, 29
Sr. Henry Clinton, 31
Sir Henry Clinton, K. B. Commandant en Chef les Troupes de Sa Majesté Britannique dans l'Amérique, 30
Sir Jeffery Amherst. Knight of the most honorable Order of the Bath, Governor of Virginia, Colonel of His Majesty's 15th. and 60th. Regiments of Foot, Lieutenant, and Commander in Chief of His Majesty's Forces in North America from 1758 to 1764, 4
Sir Roger Curtis, 35
A Sketch of Mechios Mills, 475
[Slave workers in South Carolina and Georgia—a cartouche], 773
[A small cottage by the sea with barrels for merchandise stacked about it—a cartouche], 473
A Society of Patriotic Ladies, at Edenton in North Carolina, 681
Son mérite personnel l'emporte sur toutes les considérations, 258
A South East View of Christ's Church, 515
A South East View of the City of New York, in North America . . . ., 551
A South East View of the Great Town of Boston in New England in America, 496
South Entrance of Grand Passage, 374
The South Shore of Long Island . . ., 540
The South West Coast of Nova Scotia, 442–43
The South West Coast of Nova Scotia the Brazil Sunken Rock bearing E.b.S. ½ Mile, 440
A South West View of the City of New York, in North America . . ., 552
A South West View of the City of New York, Taken from the Governors Island at *, 549
The Southern Seal Isle . . ., 444
Spencers Island and the Entrance of Mines Bason, 463
The State Blacksmiths Forging fetters for the Americans, 696
The State Cooks Making Peace_____Porridge, 822
State Cooks or The Downfall of the Fish Kettle, 794
The State House, 592
The State Nurses, 792
The Statue, or the Adoration of the Wise-men of the West, 625
The Subtle Seducer. [and] The American Financier, 174
Suffrein, 193
Surprise de St. Eustache, 322
The Surrender of Earl Cornwallis . . ., 325
The Surrender of Government Castle . . ., 817

Take Your Choice, 702
The Takeing of Miss Mud I'land, 712
Tarring and Feathering . . ., 874
[Tarring and feathering], 669
The Tea-Tax-Tempest. or Old Time with his Magick Lanthern, 851
The Tea-Tax Tempest, or the Anglo-American Revolution . . ., 738
This is the Place to affix the Stamp, 619
The Thistle Reel, 682
Thunder, Lightning and Smoke, or, the Wind shifted from the North to the East, 893
The Thunderer, 831
The Times . . ., 650
The Times, Anno 1783, 855
[Title page ornament for *The Universal Asylum and Columbian Magazine*], 903
The Tomb-Stone, 620
Le Tombeau de Voltaire . . ., 745
[Tools necessary to prove and load guns], 914
The Town of Falmouth Burnt . . ., 257
The Triumph of America, 628
[Two American Indians—a cartouche], 713 800, 833–34
[Two Europeans trade with five Indians—a cartouche], 799
[Two women celebrate the birth of America . . .], 902

The Unfortunate Death of Major Andre . . ., 317

The unfortunate Major Andre offering his watch . . ., 316

The United States Magazine for January 1779, 746

Le Vaisseau le Lanquedoc, dématé . . ., 284
Le Vaisseau le Lanquedoc rematé . . ., 285
[A variety of artillery pieces and other ordnance], 913
Veduta di S. Eustachio, 618
Veluti in Speculum, 864
Venerate the Plough, 885
A Vieu of Plymouth, 771
A View from Bushongo Tavern 5 Miles from York Town on the Baltimore Road, 576
View from Charlestown 1773, 495
A View from Paulushook of Horsimus on the Jersey shore and part of York Island, 567
A View from the Camp at the East End of the Naked Sand Hills . . ., 434
View from The Green Woods towards Canaan and Salisbury, in Connecticut, 535
A View from the South Eastward of Halifax Harbor, 417
A View in America in 1778, 734
A View in Hudson's River of Pakepsey & the Catts-Kill Mountains, From Sopos Island in Hudson's River . . . ., 558
A View in Hudson's River of the Entrance of what is called the Topan Sea . . . ., 556
View of a pass over the South Mountain from York Town to Carlisle, 575
A View of a Swallow, or Pit, at Sinking Spring Valley, State of Pennsylvania, 572
[A View of an American River—a cartouche], 555
View of Annapolis Royal, 450
A View of Annapolis Royal, 453
A View of Bethlem, the Great Moravian Settlement in the Province of Pennsylvania . . ., 577
A View of Boston, 498

A View of Boston from Dorchester Neck, 503
[A View of Boston] 1 Mistic River 2 Charles-Town Point . . ., 494
A View of Boston taken on the Road to Dorchester, 497
View of Bunker's Hill, 510
A View of Campo Bello at the Entrance of Passamaquady Bay, 465
A View of Cape Baptist . . ., 456
[A View of Cape Cod], 530
View of Cape Egmont and Winter Rock . . ., 409
A View of Cape Rouge or Carouge . . ., 354
View of Cape Round bearing West . . ., 378
[A View of Castle William], 493
A View of Charles-Town, the Capital of South Carolina, 609
A View of Charles Town the Capital of South Carolina in North America, 610
View of Eden and Gascoyne Rivers . . ., 449
A View of Faneuil-Hall in Boston, Massachusetts, 514
A View of Fort Robertdeau, in Sinking-Spring Valley, State of Pennsylvania, 573
View of Fort William . . ., 489
[View of Fortifications Around Dorchester], 507
A View of Gaspe Bay . . ., 372
View of Gulliver's Hole, 452
[View of Hell Gate], 538
A View of Houses in the City of Albany, 561
A View of Louisburg, 390
A View of Louisbourg from the North East, 389
A View of Louisbourg Harbor, on the South Coast of the Island of Cape Breton . . ., 383
[A View of Milford Haven], 392
A View of Miramichi . . ., 371
View of Mud Island before it's Reduction 16th Novr. 1777 . . ., 599
A View of New Castle with the Fort and Light House on the Entrance of Pisquataqua River, 477
A View of New York . . ., 265
A View of Ohiopyle Falls, in Pennsylvania, 574
A View of Partridge Island . . ., 460

A View of Pensacola in West Florida . . ., 614
A View of Plaister Cliffs, in George's Bay, 381
View of Port George . . ., 379
A View of Port Hood . . ., 380
A View of Portsmouth, in New Hampshire . . ., 478
A View of Quebec from the Bason, 361
A View of Quebec from the South East, 362
A View of Quebec the Capital of Canada, in North America, 367
View of Roxbury from the advanc'd Guard Hous[e] at the Lines, 508
A view of St. John's, upon the River Sorell . . ., 349
View of the ancient Buildings belonging to Harvard-College, Cambridge, New England, 512
View of The Attack on Bunker's Hill . . ., 253
View of the Bridge over Charles River, 516
View of the Bridge over Mystic River & the Country adjacent from Bunker's Hill, 509
View of the British Fortress at Stoney-Point . . ., 309
A View of the City of Boston the Capital of New England, in North America . . ., 523
A View of the City of New York from Long Island, 547
A View of the City of Quebec, the Capital of Canada, taken from the Rock on Point Levi . . ., 368
A View of the City of Québec, the Capital of Canada, taken partly from Pointe des Peres . . ., 357
A View of the Coast at the Entrance of the River St. John . . ., 470
A View of the Coast of New-Hampshire to the Eastward of Mount Desart, 476
A View of the Cohoes or Great Falls of the Mohawk River taken from below, 560
View of the Colleges at Cambridge . . ., 513
A View of the Country towards Dorchester, taken from the advanced works on Boston Neck, 502
[A view of the countryside near Quebec—a cartouche], 355

View of the Court House in Salem Massachusetts, 482
A View of the East End of the Isle Sable . . ., 425
View of the Entrance into Annapolis Bason, 445
A View of the Entrance into St. Mary's River, 612
A View of the Entrance into the Bason of Mines . . ., 457
A View of the Entrance of Pasamaquady Bay, 471
A View of the Entrance of Petit Passage, 447
A View of the Entrance of Port Hood, 380
A View of the Entrance of the Gut of Annapolis Royal, 445
[View of the entrance to White Haven], 395
A View of the Fall of Montmorenci . . ., 369
View of the Falls of Niagara, 564
A View of the Falls on the Passaick . . ., 568
View of the Federal Ediface in New York, 554
A View of the Great Cohoes Falls, on the Mohawk River . . ., 559
A View of the Guard-House and Simsbury-Mines . . ., 534
A View of the Harbour of Boston taken from Fort Hill, 504
A View of the Highland of Neversunk . . ., 539
A View of the Lighthouse on Cape Henlopen . . ., 600
A View of the Lines thrown upon Boston Neck; by the Ministerial Army, 506
A View of the Natural Bridge in Virginia, 603
A View of the New Market from the Corner of Shippen & Second-Streets Philada., 586
View of the North Entrance of Grand Passage, 446
View of the North Entrance of Petit Passage, 451
A View of the North Shore of the Isle Sable . . ., 429
A View of the Obelisk erected under Liberty-Tree in Boston . . ., 626
A View of the Pierced Island . . ., 370
A View of the Plaister Cliffs, on the West Shore of Georges Bay, 381

A View of the Pulpit Rocks, between Huntingdon & Bald Eagle Valley, State of Pennsylvania, 571
View of the Rebel Fort and Works, on Mud Island . . ., 596
A View of the S.W. Shore of Cape Breton Island . . ., 386
A View of the Sea & Beach, from Mr. James Newbolds Plantation, near Indian River, 601
View of the Seat of his Excellency John Hancock Esqr. Boston . . ., 518
A View of the Shore to the Westward of Gabbarrus Bay . . ., 384
A View of the Shore Westward of the River St. John, 469
A View of the Town & Harbour of Halifax . . ., 424
View of the Town &c of Montreal, 353
[A View of the Town of Charles Town in South-Carolina from the South Shore of Ashley River], 608
View of the Triumphal Arch and Colonnade . . ., 347
View of the Triumphal Arch, and the manner of receiving General Washington . . ., 346
View of West Bank of the Hudson's River . . ., 272
A View on Schuylkill, near Philadelphia, 580
A View on the Schuylkill; with a SW. Prospect of Bush-Hill . . ., 581
A View Saw-Mill & Block House upon Fort Anne Creek . . ., 273
A View Taken from the Entrance Louisbourg Harbour, 391
A View taken from the Ridge of the N:E: Barr, the Isle Sable bearing W:12°S: distant, 428
A View taken from the South Side of the N:E: Barr . . ., 427
A View taken 4 Miles off shore, Halifax Harbor . . ., 419
A View taken in the Offing of Beaver Harbor . . ., 401
View taken off the Entrance of Beaver Harbor . . ., 400

View upon the Road from New-Windsor, towards, Morris Town, Jersey, 570
Virtual Representation, 683
Vuë de Boston. Prospect der König Strasse gegen das Land Thor . . ., 521
Vuë de Boston. Prospect des grossen Plazes gegen der alten Sud Kirche der Presbyterianer . . ., 522
Vuë de Boston. Prospect des Plazes vor dem Rath Haus . . ., 520
Vuë de Boston. Prospect von Boston gegen der Bucht am Hasen, 519
Vue de la basse Ville à Quebec . . ., 363
Vue de la Baye de Kings-town . . ., 291
Vue de la Nouvelle Yorck, 553
Vue de la Place Capitale a Quebeck . . ., 365
Vuë de la Rue Des Recolets de Quebeck . . ., 364
Vue de l'attaque de L'Isle de Ste. Lucie . . ., 289
Vue de la Ville de Savannah . . ., 302
Vue de l'entre de la Riviere de St. Mary Tiree de la carte de W: Fuller, 612
Vue de Philadelphia . . ., 584
Vuë de Salem . . ., 481
Vue du Fort et Ville de St. George . . ., 293
Vue du Port Philadelphie dans l'Amérique . . ., 583

W. H. Drayton, 48
W. H. Drayton Esqr. Member of Congress, 49
Die Wage der Mache . . ., 762
[The war in America—a cartouche], 714
War of Posts, 814
[A warship carries the seal of the United States—a cartouche], 878
Washington, 230
[Washington and Franklin founding the United States of America—a cartouche], 866
Washington. Généralissime des Americains, Libérateur des Etats-Unis. Contemporain et Ami du Général Lafayette, 227
Wegens de Staat der Engelsche Natie, in't Jaar 1778, 781
West End of the Isle of Sable . . ., 430
[West Point, New York], 557
West Shore of Richmond Isle . . ., 385

The Western Cliffs of Cape Dore, 455
Westminster Election. 1780, 775
What may be done Abroad. What is doing at Home, 645
When fell Debate & civil Wars shall cease, 678
While Commerce spreads her canvass o'er the main, 882

The Whitehall Pump, 665
Wide o'er the Ocean while Britannia reigns, 653
William Pitt. Il Faut Déclarer la Guerre a La France, 173
The Wise Men of Gotham and their Goose, 695
The Wolves, (a cluster of Isles) lying SE off the Entrance of Passamaquadi Bay, 467

Wonders Wonders Wonders & Wonders..., 827
Wreckers Den near the Pond on the Isle of Sable, 431

[Yorktown], 802

Selective Subject Index

Numbers in this index refer to entries, not to pages.

Abnaki Indians, 244
Abundance, 705
Academy of Newark, Del., mentioned, 594
Acteon, 606–7, 611
Aesopus, N.Y.; *see* Kingston
Africa, 724, 738–39, 754, 840, 851, 881
Agameticus, Highlands of, 485
Agriculture, 882, 885
Albany, N.Y., 561
Alligator, 658, 708, 713
Alms House, Phila., 593
Amelia Island, Fla., 612
America:
    as Benjamin Franklin, 745; as a buffalo, 857; as a burning city, 685; as a dog, 792; as a donkey, 789; as a fiddle player, 789; as a goose, 733; as an Indian child, 840; as an Indian man, 628, 649, 665, 672, 686, 718, 755, 757, 763, 767, 772, 787, 809, 818–19, 822, 832, 844, 846, 850, 861, 868; as an Indian woman, 622, 627, 631–32, 634, 640, 658, 660, 662, 664, 678, 700, 716, 724, 728, 731, 738–39, 759, 762, 765–66, 768, 777, 786, 802, 810, 820, 823, 827–28, 830, 843, 847–48, 851, 856, 863, 865, 881; as a Negro with feathered headdress, 880; as an old lady, 677; as a pillar, 637, 809, 819; as a rattlesnake, 3, 114, 211, 218, 345, 632, 657, 712, 735, 758, 812, 815, 821, 826, 851, 858; as a wheel, 651; as a white goddess, 620, 642, 691, 705, 715, 882, 898, 903; as a white man, 683, 736, 752, 770, 779, 781–82, 814, 841, 849, 859–60; as a young Roman woman, 882; as a zebra, 737
Americans, as young men, 783, 793
Ammunition wagon, 916
Anchor, 639, 707, 834
Angels, 642, 813
Anglican Church, 169, 515; mentioned, 666
Anglican influence, 623–24, 636, 666, 685, 710, 741, 816
Annapolis Basin, Nova Scotia, 445
Annapolis Royal, Nova Scotia, 450, 452–53; gut of, 447
Aphorism, 627
Argyle Head, Nova Scotia, 442
Armed Neutrality League, 750, 778–79, 820
"Articles of Capitulation," 84
Articles of Confederation, mentioned, 575
Ashley, 607
Ashley River, S.C., 611
Asia, personified, 724, 738–39, 840, 851, 881
Association of York, 767-68
Assunpink Creek, N.J., 346
Astrea, mentioned, 220
Atkins Wharf, Boston, 516

Bald Eagle Valley, Pa., 571–73
Bald Isle, Nova Scotia, 400–1, 403, 467
Ballad, 622
Baltimore Road, Chesapeake Bay, 576
Baptist Meeting House, Providence, R.I., 532
Barbershop, N.Y., 679
Barbadoes, W. I., 809, 819
Barrington Bay, Nova Scotia, 438
Basin of Mines, Nova Scotia, 449, 456–57, 463
Basking Ridge, N.J., 270
Basseterre, St. Kitts, W.I., 301, 329
Batteries, floating, 905
Battery, Phila., 588
Bay of Fundy, Nova Scotia, 448, 466, 470
Bayard's Mount, N.Y.; *see* Bunker's Hill
Beacon Hill, Boston, 494, 506
Beacon Street, Boston, 518
Bears, 751, 837
Beaver, 245
Beaver Harbor, Nova Scotia, 400–1
Beaver Islands, Nova Scotia, 403, 408
Beavers, 640, 674, 690, 694, 713, 796, 867
Beehive, 717
Belle Isle, 809
Bemis Heights, N.Y., 272
Berbice; *see* British Guiana
Berry Head, Nova Scotia, 396
Bethlehem, Pa., 577
Bill of Rights, 677, 754
Binney Isle, Nova Scotia, 379
Blacksmith's shop, 696
Blockhouse, 579, 921
Boar, 751
Bond Hollow, N.Y., 536
Bonetta, 245
Bonhomme Richard, 133, 310, 336

Boston and vicinity: evacuation of troops, 259, 697; in cartoons and allegories, 641, 652, 656, 664, 667, 683–84, 710, 725; landing of troops, 245, 642; mentioned, 17, 32, 165, 188, 481–82, 655, 760, 862, 905; views, 243, 249, 253, 288, 347, 483–523
Boston Massacre, 102, 246–47, 490, 654
Boston Petition, 664
Boston Port Bill, 16, 106–7, 481–82, 664, 671, 677, 702
Boston Tea Party, 248; mentioned, 664
Bowling Green, New York City, 263
Brandywine, Pa., Battle of, mentioned, 101, 142, 859–60
Brattle Square Church, mentioned, 32
Brazil Sunken Rock, Nova Scotia, 440
Bread, 773
Breed's Hill, Mass., 253, 510
Brest, France, 789
Brew House, N.Y., 552
Brimstone Hill, St. Kitts, 329
Brindley's house, R.I., 286
Bristol Neck, R.I., 533
Bristol, 607, 611
British Army: criticized, 710; mentioned, 270; officers, 864
British Empire, in cartoons, 645
British Guiana, 303–7, 790
British Navy, 294, 297–301; mentioned, 285, 292, 474
Broad Street, N.Y., 554
Browns House, 505
Buffalo, 797, 857
Bull, 751; as Britain, 810; *see also* John Bull
Bunker Hill, Mass., 253–56, 494, 509, 697; mentioned, 123, 175, 179, 859–60; possible view, 204
Bunker's Hill, N.Y., 548
Bushongo Tavern, Pa., 576

Cabbages, 711
Caduceus, 172
Cambridge, Mass., 255, 500, 510
Camden, S.C., Battle of, mentioned, 787, 859–60

Campo Bello, Nova Scotia, 465; Island, 468; Harbor, 471
Canaan, 535
Canada: invasion of, 194, 235; mentioned, 2, 4, 14, 88, 645, 666, 671, 830, 867; views, 348–472
Cannons, 697, 714
Canso, Nova Scotia, 379, 385, 402, 404; mentioned, 394
Cape Baptist, Nova Scotia, 456
Cape Blowmedown, Nova Scotia, 459–61
Cape Breton Island, Nova Scotia, 383–84, 386
Cape Chignecto, Nova Scotia, 454, 464
Cape Cod, Mass., 530
Cape Dore, Nova Scotia, 455
Cape Egmont, Nova Scotia, 409
Cape Henlopen, Del., 279; Lighthouse, 600
Cape Martingo, Nova Scotia, 395
Cape Negro, Nova Scotia, 440, 442
Cape Poge, Mass., 524
Cape Prospect, Nova Scotia, 435
Cape Rouge, Canada, 354
Cape Round, Prince Edward Island, 378
Cape Sable, Nova Scotia, 438–41, 443
Cape St. Vincent, W.I., 313
Cape Sambro, Nova Scotia, 435
Cape Southhampton, Nova Scotia, 405
Cape Split, Nova Scotia, 459, 462
Cape Spry, Nova Scotia, 408
Carénage, St. Lucia, W.I.; *see* Castries
The Carolinas, 604–11; mentioned, 98, 645
Carouge; *see* Cape Rouge
Carpenter's Hall, Phila., 250
Carpenter's Island, Delaware River, 596, 599
Castle Island, Boston Harbor, 484, 488, 491
Castle William, Boston Harbor, 484, 488–93
Castries, St. Lucia, W.I., 289–90
Cat, 758
Catholics: bishop, 702, 704; priest, 683
Catskill Mountains, N.Y., 558
Cedars, N.J., 566
Cedars, N.Y., 537
Ceylon, 830
Chalbeate Springs, N.Y., 562

Chandelier, 906
Chaos, personified, 55
Charles River, Mass., 516, 523; mentioned, 905
Charleston, S.C., 260, 606–11, 819; as a pillar, 809; mentioned, 28, 164, 774–75, 787
Charlestown, Mass., 253, 494–95; mentioned 17, 165, 516
Charlottesville, Va., 308
Chebucto Head, Nova Scotia, 416
Chedabucto Bay, Nova Scotia, 392–94, 398
Chelsea Hospital, England, 725
Cherubs, 640, 657, 686, 715, 724, 777, 804, 808, 838, 859–60, 901
Chesapeake Bay, 326; mentioned, 42, 113, 602
Chestnut Street, Phila., 589
Cheval-de-frise, 505, 907
Chisetcook Inlet, Nova Scotia, 413
Christ Church, Boston, 515
Christ Church, Phila., 588
Citadel Hill, Nova Scotia, 416
City Hall, N.Y., 551; *see also* Federal Hall
Civil liberties, 646, 702
Civil War, English, 623–24
Clergy, 816
Clio, 895
Coalition government, 870–71, 873, 877
Coat of arms, 871; of the United States, 883
Cock, as France; *see* France
Coconut, 640
Coffins, 654
Cohasset Point, Mass., 483
Cohoes Falls, N.Y., 559–60
Coldstream guard, 785
Commander in Chief's Guard, 242
Commerce: as a milk cow, 726, 781–82; in cartoons and allegories, 657, 743, 773, 862, 865, 869, 882, 897; personified, 473; temple of, 678
Commercial Treaty of 1787, 887
Conanicut Isle, R.I., 282
Concord, Mass., mentioned, 165
Concord, personified, 662, 761, 895
Congregational Church, Boston, 522
Connecticut, 534–35, 894; mentioned, 37, 235

Constitutional Convention, 224; mentioned, 590
Continental Army, 270; mentioned, 156, 181, 190, 242, 323, 573
Continental Congress, 250, 253, 261; mentioned, 1–3, 15, 37, 45, 48, 102, 106–7, 114, 129, 131–32, 144, 159, 174, 180, 187, 190, 194, 201, 240, 575, 590, 756, 824, 850; personified, 726, 729, 734, 756
Continental Navy, officer, 132
Convention Army, 308
Cooper River, S.C., 607, 611
Copp's Hill, Mass., 253, 494
Corn, 640, 759
Cornucopia, 662, 722, 797, 808, 890, 898
Coromandel Coast, India, 303–7
Corsica, 635
Court House, Philadelphia, 588
Courts, 891
Cow, representing England; see England
Cranberry Isle, Nova Scotia, 402
Crest of William Burnaby, 614
Crow Harbor, Nova Scotia, 394
Crown Point, N.Y., mentioned, 23, 760
Crucifixes, 764, 796
Culloden, Battle of, England, 620
Cumberland Island, Ga., 612
Cummins' Point, S.C., 611
Cupid, 234, 653, 895
Curass, 790
Customhouse, St. Eustatius, W.I., 618

Danbury Raid, Conn., mentioned, 235
Dartmouth Shore, Nova Scotia, 414
Death, 888
Declaration of Independence, 102, 229, 262
Deer Island, Boston Harbor, 531
Delaware, 45, 894; mentioned, 588
Delaware Bay, 279
Delaware River, 588, 595, 600, 743; mentioned, 584, 594, 599, 907
Demerara; see British Guiana
Denmark, personified, 778–79; mentioned, 750
Despotism: as a pillar, 702; as a road, 784

Devil, 620, 627, 629, 648, 666, 669, 672, 677, 682, 711, 725, 741, 813–14, 848, 855, 864
Discord, personified, 700, 775
Dog: as cur which dumps on England, 695, 781, 788, 792; as England, 778; as Lord Lincoln, 774
Dogger Bank, North Sea 303–7
Dominica, W.I., 287, 617
Dorchester Heights, Mass., 497, 502–3, 507, 511
Dorchester steeple, Mass., 507
Dove, 652, 731, 804
Drydock, 450
Duck, 867
Dutch; see also Holland
Dutch architecture, 561
Dutch Calvinist Church, Phila., 588
Dutch church, St. Eustatius, 618
Dutch Reformed Church, N.Y., 547, 550

Eagle, 35, 712, 726, 781, 802
Eagles, 69, 554, 727, 883, 889–90, 895, 899, 901–3
East Indies, 128, 193
East River, N.Y., 538, 541, 544
Eastern Isle, New Brunswick, 467
Economy, personified, 622
Eden River, Nova Scotia, 449
Edenton, N.C., 681
Egmont Harbor, Prince Edward Island, 376–77, 410
Electricity, 57, 62, 69, 656
Elizabeth, N.J., mentioned, 569
Elmira, N.Y., 194
England: as beggar woman, 752; as Britannia, 172, 234, 620, 622, 627–28, 632, 635, 637–38, 642, 651, 653, 655, 662, 664–65, 675, 678, 683, 698, 700, 705, 731, 736, 740, 750, 762, 766, 768–69, 772, 775, 780, 784, 786, 788, 813, 818, 820, 823, 827–28, 839, 842, 846, 852, 861–63, 869, 871, 888; as a bull, 880; see also John Bull; as a cat, 758; as a cow, 726, 781–82, 802; as a dog, 778; as an Englishman, 709, 755, 779, 781–83, 841, 844; as a lion, 661, 695, 700, 706–7, 726, 738, 758, 767, 781, 792, 802, 821, 828, 842, 851, 863, 871, 875; as a man on a donkey, 789; as a man on a horse, 667; as a sailor, 787, 828; as a wheel, 651
English Channel, 118, 310
English church, St. Eustatius, W.I., 618
Esopus Island, Hudson River, N.Y., 558
Essequibo; see British Guiana
Europe, personified, 686, 724, 738–39, 777, 840, 851, 881
Excise tax, mentioned, 670
Experiment, 607, 611
Export trade, mentioned, 479

Faction, personified, 55
Falcon, 253
Falmouth, Maine, 257
Fame, 220, 720, 746, 839, 866, 869, 872; temple of, 819
Fanal Point, N.Y., 279
Faneuil Hall, Boston, 514
Farms, 565, 576, 721, 885, 901
Fasces, 706–7, 808
Federal Hall, N.Y., 547, 554
Fire ships, 264
Fish and fishing, 639–40, 673–74, 719, 721, 794, 799, 867
Five Fathom Hole, Charleston Harbor, S.C., 611
Flags: American, 82, 114, 116, 147, 345, 491, 523, 706–7, 712, 731, 736, 830, 844, 851, 861, 863, 866, 871, 879, 880, 901; Dutch, 844; English, 136, 252, 349–50, 352, 360, 368, 523, 588, 615, 639, 844, 861; French, 749, 844, 861, 879; Spanish, 844, 861; Unknown, 179, 211, 230, 289, 330, 492, 697, 714; Pine Tree Flag, 706–7; Rattlesnake Flag, 114, 345, 712; Truce, 276
Flamborough Head, England, 310
Fleur-de-lis, 743, 749, 756, 780, 875
Float, 639
Floating battery, 905
Florida, 612–14; mentioned, 847
Fort at Havana, Cuba, W.I., 616

437

Fort at Oranjestad, St. Eustatius, W.I., 618
Fort at Pensacola, Fla., 613
Fort Campus Martius, Marietta, Ohio, 579
Fort Charles, St. Kitts, W.I., 329
Fort Frederica, battle at, mentioned, 806
Fort Hill, Boston, 496, 504
Fort Johnson, S.C., 607, 611
Fort La Cabaña, Havana, Cuba, W.I., mentioned, 616
Fort Mercer, Delaware River, mentioned, 693
Fort Mifflin, Delaware River, 596–99, 712; mentioned, 693
Fort Moultrie, Charleston Harbor, S.C.; see Fort Sullivan
Fort Omoa, Honduras, 311–12; mentioned, 787
Fort Robertdeau, Pa., 573
Fort Royal, Martinique, W.I., 333–42
Fort St. George; see St. George, Grenada, W.I.
Fort St. Johns, Canada, 349
Fort St. Philip, Minorca, 328, 864
Fort Sullivan, Charleston Harbor, S.C., 260, 605–7
Fort Trincomalee, 333–42
Fort William, Boston Harbor; see Castle William
Forts in Delaware River, mentioned, 599
Fox: as Henry Fox, Lord Holland, 627, 647–48, 655, 665; as C. J. Fox, 700, 741, 814, 818, 820–22, 824, 827, 853, 861, 868, 870, 873; as John Wesley, 689
France: as a cock, 736, 758, 789, 821, 851, 858; as a dog, 792; as a Frenchman, 622, 632, 664, 683, 698, 726–27, 733, 737, 741, 749–50, 752, 755, 762–63, 765–67, 778–79, 781–83, 786, 802–3, 809–10, 818–20, 822, 826, 828, 830, 841, 844–45, 847, 849, 852, 855–56, 861, 863; as French sailors, 789; as a sun, 756; mentioned, 1, 11, 43, 55, 61, 63, 91, 143, 183, 347, 678, 730, 757, 784, 793, 801, 845
Frederick, Md., mentioned, 308
Freedom, personified, 895
Freedom of the press, 646
Freehold, N.J., battle at, mentioned, 735

French Church, N.Y., 547, 551
French influence: alliance with America, 203, 229, 277, 720; army, 289, 296, 302, 318, 326, 328, 333–42; navy, 142, 278–85, 287–307, 321–26, 330, 331, 333–42; mentioned, 286, 333–42
Frenchman's Bay, N.H., 476
Frogs, 826
Fruit, 759
Furs, 348
Fury, 625

Gabion, 908
Gaff, 639
Galleys, 264
Gallows, 668, 680, 848, 873
Garbarus Bay, Nova Scotia, 382, 384
Garnet Head, Mass., 483
Gascoyne River, Nova Scotia, 449
Gaspee Bay, Canada, 370, 372
Geese, 695, 733, 824, 870
General Warrants, 620, 671
Genius, personified, 869
Geography, personified, 777, 881
Gay Head, Mass., 526–27
Georgia, 232, 612, 773, 894; mentioned, 689, 806
Germantown, Pa., 717
Germany: mentioned, 26, 757; mercenaries, 271, 725, 738
Gibraltar, 278, 762, 792, 809, 819, 830; mentioned, 51, 311, 645, 821–22, 828, 855
Gin, 919
Glasgow, 245, 253
Gloucester, Va., 325–26
Goat, 717, 751, 789
Goat Island, R.I., 282
Gondola, 905
Gordon Riots, mentioned, 96
Gouldsborough Harbor, N.H., 476
Governors' houses: New York, 550; Oranjestad, St. Eustatius, 618; Pensacola, 613
Governor's Island, Boston Harbor, Mass., 484
Grain, 885, 899

Granary, public, N.Y., 550
Grand Passage, Newfoundland, 374, 446, 448
Grandmanan Island, Nova Scotia, 466, 468
Grapes, 773, 873
Gray's Ferry, Pa., 345, 582
Great Awakening, 232
Green Island, S.C., 605
Green Woods, Conn., 535
Grenada, W.I., 292, 292–300, 809, 830; mentioned, 154, 193, 301
Grenadines, mentioned, 154
Greville Cove, New Brunswick, 469
Griffon, 657
Guerritte, 909
Guilford Courthouse, N.C., Battle of, mentioned, 859–60
Gulliver's Hole, Nova Scotia, 445, 452

Habeas corpus, 646
Hadley Beach, Nova Scotia, 392
Hairpiece, 697
Halberd, 905
Halifax, Nova Scotia, 411, 413–24; Lighthouse, 422; mentioned, 862
Hancock's House, Boston, 506; mentioned, 511
Hancock's Wharf, Boston, 496
Hand spike, 914
Hanover, Germany, mentioned, 645
Harlem River, N.Y., 544, 555a
Harmony, personified, 687
Hartford, Conn., 535
Harvard College, 512–13; mentioned, 32
Haspotagoen highlands, Nova Scotia, 436
Havana, W.I., 616–17
Head Harbor, New Brunswick, 471
Hector, 285
Hell; see Newgate
Hell Gate, N.Y., 538, 544
Hercules, 163, 234, 802, 875
Heroic Virtue, personified, 761
Hinchinbroke River, Nova Scotia, 412
Hog Island, Mass., 494, 611
Holden Chapel, Harvard College, 513
Holland: as a Dutchman, 632, 698, 726–27

750, 752, 755, 762–63, 765, 772, 778–79, 781–83, 786–87, 790, 802, 809, 818–20, 822, 825, 828, 830, 841, 844, 847, 849, 852, 855, 861, 863; as a lion, 789; as a pug dog, 792, 821, 856, 858; colonies, 193, 303–7, 322, 333–42, 618; mentioned, 128, 144, 757, 845; Navy, 278
Hollis Hall, Harvard College, 513
Hollis Street, Boston, 517
Honduras, Bay of, 311
Hopson's Nose, Nova Scotia, 407
Horses, 784, 890
Hospitals: Montreal, 351; Philadelphia, 591
Hotel Dieu, Quebec, 359
House of Employment, Phila., 593
Howland's Ferry, R.I., 282
Hudson Bay, Canada, 333–42
Hudson River, N.Y., 541, 551, 555a; mentioned, 907
Hudson River Valley and upper New York, 264, 276, 555–64
Hunting, 837
Huntingdon, Pa., 571
Hurdles, 910
Hydra, representing Fox, 896

Ignorance: as a road, 784; personified, 55
Independence Hall; see Statehouse, Phila.
India, 303–7; as a wheel, 651; mentioned, 645
India Bill, 873, 887
Indian Ocean, 333–42
Indian River, Del., 601
Indian Villages, 742
Indians: Bostonians disguised as, 248; captivity, 244; in cartoons and allegories, 4–5, 233, 622, 627–28, 631–34, 649, 658–60, 664–65, 672, 690, 693–94, 700, 707, 713, 718, 731, 738–39, 743, 757, 759, 761–66, 788, 795, 797–98, 800, 818–20, 822, 830, 832–37, 840, 867, 889, 900; in portraits, 111, 186, 200, 233, 238–39; in views, 272–73, 348–49, 364–65, 449, 604; mentioned, 88, 194, 233, 274, 534, 563, 573, 785; Mohawks, 111, 200; see also, America, personified

Indigo, 728, 757
Industry, personified, 761
Ireland: as a wheel, 651, as an Irishman, 770, 772, 880; mentioned, 55, 91, 106–7, 154, 199, 645; regiments from, 490; troubles in, 874
Iroquois, mentioned, 194, 563
Isis, 712
Isle Haut, Nova Scotia, 454, 458, 464
Isle of Jersey, England, mentioned, 787
Isle of Sable, Nova Scotia, 425–34

Jamaica, W.I., 809, 819; mentioned, 645, 655
James Island, S.C., 611
Jeddore highlands, Nova Scotia, 417
Jesuit's Church, Quebec, 351, 359
John Bull, 751, 755, 763, 802–3, 847, 855, 880
Justice, personified, 762, 802, 866, 889, 891–92, 895

Kent, England, mentioned, 81
Keppel Harbor, Nova Scotia, 406, 411
Keys, 902
King Street, Boston, 521
Kings Bridge, N.Y., 555
King's College, N.Y., 268, 551
Kingston, N.Y., 753
Kingston Bay, St. Vincent, W.I., 291
Kite, 656
Kops Hill; see Copp's Hill

Ladies of Edenton, N.C., 681
Ladle, 914
Lady William, 605
Lake Champlain, mentioned, 349; Battle of, metioned, 17
Lake George, N.Y., Battle at, 111
Lamb, 662
Lanceston, 245
Languedoc, 284–85, 288
Laurel, 234
Lead mining, mentioned, 573
Letters from a Farmer in Pennsylvania, 45, 47
Lexington, Mass., mentioned, 175, 859–60; Battle of, 251–52; mentioned, 860

"Lexington of the Sea," 474
Liberty, personified, 55, 635, 647, 657, 688, 703, 761, 784, 808, 859–60, 866, 889; mentioned 220
Liberty Cap, 11, 163, 179, 208, 211, 218, 234, 345, 635, 638, 642, 652, 657, 661, 674, 686, 690–91, 698, 702–3, 706, 728, 746, 752, 755, 759, 780, 802, 820, 830, 839, 848, 851, 853, 859–60, 868, 875, 879, 889–90, 892, 895, 898, 902
Liberty Tree, 114, 670, 673
Lighthouses: Boston, 486; Cape Henlopen, Del., 600; Halifax, Nova Scotia, 415–16, 419–21; Louisburg, Nova Scotia, 390–91; Sandy Hook, N.J., 537, 539, 542
Lightning; see electricity
Lilly, 291
Lincoln, England, 650
Lion, 661–62, 695, 700, 706–7, 713, 726, 738, 743, 758, 767, 775, 781, 792, 802, 821, 828, 842, 851, 863, 871, 875
Lively, 253, 291
Lizard, 658, 708, 713, 716
Les Loix de la Pensilvanie, 77
Lombard Street, Philadelphia, 587
London, 630, 647, 656
Long Island, Mass., 501
Long Island, N.Y., 540, 545, 552; Battle of, 265; Narrows, 543; mentioned, 703; Sound, 541
Long Island, S.C., 605–6
Long Wharf, Boston, 496
Lottery tickets, 675
Louisburg, Nova Scotia, 382–83, 389–91; mentioned, 372
Louisiana, 239, 303
Loyalist troops, 186, 194
Loyalists, 15, 39, 89, 149, 159, 268, 273, 534, 680, 846, 850
Lumbering, 349, 640, 843
Lunenburg Bay, Nova Scotia, 437
Lutheran Church, N.Y., 550
Lyre, 898–99

Machias River, Harbor, and Mills, Maine, 474–75
Madras, India, mentioned, 52
Madrid, Spain, 131
Magic lantern, 738–39, 851
Magna Carta, 55, 630, 651, 754, 775
Maine, 244, 474–75
Malden Bridge, 509
Manhattan Island, N.Y., 541
Manila, Philippines, mentioned, 648
Margaretta, 474
Marietta Territory, Ohio, 579
Market, Phila., 586
Mars, 720, 802; mentioned, 653
Marseillais, 285
Martin, 245
Martinique, W.I., 333–42, 809; mentioned, 113, 287, 321
Maryland, 45, 894
Mask, 902
Massachusetts, 481–531, 894; arms, 347, 889; Committee of Safety, 204; General Court, 482; mentioned, 2–3, 102, 163; Provincial Congress, 255, 482
Massachusetts Fishery Act, 702
Massachusetts Hall, Harvard College, 513
Medals, American, 875
Medford township, Mass., 509
Melons, 773
Mentor, 723
Meogenes Island, New Brunswick, 472
Mercury, 705, 742, 808, 869; mentioned, 172
Mermaid, 245, 279
Methodists, 233
Middle Dutch Church, N.Y., 547
Middle Passage, Newport, R.I., mentioned, 282
Middlesex, England, mentioned, 676
Middlesex Petition, 643–44, 646
Milford Haven, Nova Scotia, 392–93, 398
Miller River; *see* Wills Creek
Minden, Battle of, mentioned, 794
Minerva, 163, 234, 723
Mines Basin; *see* Basin of Mines

Minorca, 328, 809; mentioned, 847
Miramachi, Gulf of St. Lawrence, 371
Mirror, 3
Missionary, 796
Mississippi Bubble, 722
Mississippi River, 686, 722
Mobile, La., 303–7
Mohawk Indians, 111, 200
Mohawk River, N.Y., 559–60
Monkeys, 713
Monmouth, Battle of, 333–42; mentioned, 139, 539, 735
Montmorenci, Quebec, 369
Montreal, Canada, 350–53, 864
Moravians, 577
Morristown, N.J., mentioned, 570
Mortar, 691
Mt. Desart, N.H., 476
Mt. Pleasant, N.Y., 537, 605, 611; *see also* Bunker's Hill, N.Y.
Mt. Vernon, Va., mentioned, 346
Mud Island, Delaware River, 595–99, 712, 717
Mystic River, Mass., 494, 509

Naked Sand Hills, Nova Scotia, 425
Narragansett Bay, R.I., mentioned, 114
Narrows, Long Island, N.Y., 543
Natural Bridge, Va., 603
Negroes, 142, 215, 217, 230–31, 246–48, 271, 602, 604, 734, 738, 773, 880, 886, 888; punishment of, 673
Neptune, 686, 736, 775, 808, 828
Neversunk, Highland of, N.Y., 539
Nevis, W.I., mentioned, 329
New College, N.Y., 551
New Dutch Church, N.Y., 547
New England, 473–535, 632; mentioned, 21, 152, 862
New Hampshire, 476–80, 894; constitutional convention, 194; mentioned, 186
New Jersey, 565–70, 712, 743, 894; campaign, 194; crest of, 890; mentioned, 586
New Jersey Volunteers, 314
New Windsor, N.Y., mentioned, 570

New York City, 263, 541, 544–54, 630, 742, 839; evacuated by British, 343; fire, 268–69, 545–47, 549; harbor, 264; landing of British, 266–67; paupers' school, 268; stock market, 268
New York State, 536–64, 632, 710, 894; campaign, 194; crest, 889; mentioned, 23, 28, 52, 126, 279, 743; Provincial Congress, 156, 159
Newark, Del., mentioned, 594
Newbold's Plantation, Delaware River, 601
Newcastle, N.H., 477
Newfoundland, 373–75, 387
Newgate prison, Conn., 534; mentioned, 886
Newport, R.I., 282, 285–286, 317; mentioned, 193
Niagara Falls, N.Y., 563–64, 796
Nick, 814; *see also* Devil
Nix's Mate Island, Boston Harbor, 501
Noddles Island, Boston Harbor, 494
Nomans Land (island), Mass., 526
Nonconsumption agreement, 874
Nonimportation agreement, 874
Noodles Island; *see* Noddles Island
Norfolk, Va., 753
North America, mentioned, 645, 648
North Carolina, 894
North End Caucus, 204
North Meetinghouse, Portsmouth, N.H., 479
North River, N.Y.; *see* Hudson River
Northern Department, 187
Northumberland Fusiliers, 165
Nova Scotia, 379–424, 435–66; mentioned, 21, 639
Nutting Island, N.Y., 552

Ode, 747
Ohio River, 579
Old English Church, N.Y., 551
Old South Congregational Church, Boston, 522
Olive branch, 632, 638, 662, 723, 732, 819, 839, 871, 899
Omoa; *see* Ft. Omoa
Ontario, Canada, 200

Oranjestad, St. Eustatius, W.I., 618
Orgnes, 911
Otter, 348
Owl, 172

Paoli Massacre, Pa., mentioned, 231, 309
Paris, mentioned, 332
Parliament, 671–72, 675–76, 685, 698, 824; mentioned, 22, 33, 54–55, 155, 169, 173, 770
Parrot, 713, 834
Partridge Island, Nova Scotia, 460, 472
Passaic Falls, N.J., 568–69
Passaic River, N.J., 568–69
Passamaquady Bay, Nova Scotia, 465, 467, 471
Patriot, Pitt as, 629
Paulus Hook, N.J., 567
Peace, personified, 678, 761, 859–60, 872, 895; mentioned, 169, 903
Peace at Versailles, 332; mentioned, 333–42
Peace Commission, 723, 728–29, 737, 741, 802; mentioned, 43, 118; Washington's refusal, 229
Peerage, British, 629
Pegasus Wing, 408
Pelican, 797, 865
Penn family emblem, 691
Pennsylvania, 571–99, 632, 712, 717, 743, 894; crest of, 890; mentioned, 45, 308; Provincial Congress, 180
Pennsylvania Hospital, Phila., 591
Penobscot Hills, Mass., 485
Pensacola, Fla., 319, 613–14
Pensions, 630, 675
Petard, 912
Petit Manan Isle, N.H., 476
Petit Passage, Nova Scotia, 447, 451
Philadelphia, Pa., 583, 712, 726, 781–82; mentioned, 28, 74, 125, 131, 145, 575, 580, 582, 711, 735, 760, 862
Philadelphia Campaign, mentioned, 599, 693
Philip Inlet, Nova Scotia, 394
Phoenix, 264
Pierced Island, Gulf of St. Lawrence, 370
Pike, 691

Pilgrims, 674
Pine Tree Flag, 706–7
Pine trees, as symbol of America, 708, 830
Pisquataqua River, N.H., 477
Plains of Abraham, Quebec, 369
Pleasant River, N.H., 476
Plenty, personified, 761, 869
Plow, 706–7, 882, 885, 890, 899, 903
Plymouth, Mass., 674
Plymouth Harbor, Mass., 483
Poems, 45, 63, 89, 143, 149, 169, 246, 587, 635, 644, 653, 662, 678–79, 695, 727, 733, 746, 753, 763, 765, 786, 810, 812, 820–26, 828, 844–45, 850, 858–59, 882, 891, 898
Poland, mentioned, 149
Polly, mentioned, 474
Pontoon and Carriage, 918
Port Bickerton, Nova Scotia, 399
Port Campbell, Nova Scotia, 442
Port George, Nova Scotia, 379
Port Haldimand, Nova Scotia, 443
Port Hood, Nova Scotia, 380
Port Howe, Nova Scotia, 395
Portland, Maine; *see* Falmouth
Portsmouth, N.H., 478–80; mentioned, 52
Poughkeepsie, N.Y., 558
Powder barrel, 691
Powder cart, 915
Presbyterian Church: in New York, 547; in Philadelphia, 588
Priests, 867
Priming iron, 914
Prince Edward Island, 376–78
Princeton College, N.J., mentioned, 551
Prisons, 308, 314, 534, 550–51, 585
Privy, 692
Protecteur, 288
Protestants, 754
Providence, R.I., 532
Province Island, Delaware River, 595
Prussian Army, 190
Public good, as the sun, 896
Pug dog, as Holland; *see* Holland
Pulpit Rocks, Pa., 571

Pyramid, 702, 884
Quaker Meetinghouse, Phila., 588
Quakers, mentioned, 583
Quartering, 784
Quebec, 336
Quebec, 354–69, 683, 725; Battle of, 358; possible view, 9; mentioned, 2, 13, 16, 23, 156, 202, 235, 244, 350
Quebec Act, 666, 671, 677, 682, 702, 704
Queen's American Rangers, 186

Racoon, 565
Ramea Island, Nova Scotia, 387
Rams Head, Nova Scotia, 425, 429
Raree Show; *see* Vue d'Optique
Rats, 802
Rattlesnake, as symbol of America; *see* America
Rebus, 730, 731, 769
Recruiting poster, 801
Red Bank, Pa., 717
Red Hook, N.Y., 545
Reform Bill, 871
Reliever, 914
Renown, 284
Resolution, 330
Rhode Island, 532–33, 819, 894; as a pillar, 809; mentioned, 114
Rhode Island, Battle of, 286
Rice, 728, 757
Richelieu River, Canada; *see* Sorel
Richmond Isle, Nova Scotia, 385, 404
Ridgefield, Conn., mentioned, 14
The Rights of Man, 902
Robuste, 301
Rocky Bay, Nova Scotia, 419
Roebuck, 712
Roman Catholic Church, mentioned, 666
Roman church, St. Eustatius, 618
Romney, 245
Rooster, 172
Rose, 264
Roxbury, Mass., 508
Rum, 627

Russia, 750, 757, 779, 820
Rutgers House, N.Y., 546, 552

Saba, W.I., 790; mentioned, 322
Sailors, 862, 878
St. Christopher; *see* St. Kitts
St. Dominique, W.I., 287, 617
St. Eustatius, W.I., 320–22, 618, 789–90, 793, 807, 809, 819, 830; mentioned, 113, 184, 750
St. George, banner of, 861
St. George, Grenada, W.I., town and fort, 292–95, 297–98
St. George Cross, 234
St. George's Chapel, N.Y., 547, 549
St. James Palace, London, 647, 857
St. Johns, Canada, 349; mentioned, 9, 350
St. John River, New Brunswick, 469–70, 472
St. Kitts, W.I., 301, 329
St. Lawrence River and Gulf, 348–72
St. Lucia, W.I., 289–90
St. Maria Island, Nova Scotia, 388
St. Martin, W.I., 790; mentioned, 322
St. Mary's Bay, Nova Scotia, 452
St. Marys River, Ga., 612
St. Mary's River, Nova Scotia, 397
St. Nicolas Mole, Dominica, W.I., 617
St. Peter's Bay, Prince Edward Island, 378, 386
St. Sulpicius, Montreal, 351
St. Paul's Cathedral, London, 775
St. Paul's Chapel, N.Y., 547
St. Vincent, W.I., 291, 335, 809, 819
Saints, Battle of the, 184
Saints Passage, W.I., 330; Battle of, mentioned, 331
Sakonnet Passage, R.I., mentioned, 282
Salem, Mass., 481–82, 667
Salem Street, Boston, 515
Salisbury, Conn., 535
Salt works, Cape Henlopen, Del., 600
Sambro Lighthouse, Nova Scotia, 419–22
Sandwich Bay, Nova Scotia, 412
Sandy Cove, Nova Scotia, 445
Sandy Hook, N.Y., 280,
Sandy Hook Lighthouse, N.J., 566

Sandy Point, Mass., 525
Sankoty Head, Mass., 528–29
Santa Rosa Island, Fla., 613
Saratoga, N.Y., mentioned, 14, 17–18, 84, 88, 308, 859–60; Second Battle of, 272
Saratoga campaign, 272–76
Satyr, 55
Savannah, Ga., 302; mentioned, 52, 193
Scalping, 238–39, 764
Schuylkill River, Pa., 580–82; 588, mentioned, 584
Scipion, 342
Scotland, mentioned, 645
Scottish influences, 682, 684–85, 725, 755, 802; mentioned, 153
Seal of the United States, 878, 883–84, 899
Searcher, 914
Second River; *see* Passaic
Senegal, 245, 285; mentioned, 35
Sentry, 909
Serapis, 133, 310, 336
Seven Years' War, 169, 186, 203, 235, 244, 357, 563, 666
Sèvres medal, 78
Seymour and Molly, 323
Shackles, 902
Sheep, 688
Ship Tax, 887
Shipbuilding, 349, 366
Ships Stern Isle, N.H., 476
Shirley Point, Boston Harbor, Mass., 531
Shrewsbury shore, N.Y., 280
Shutes Folly, Charleston Harbor, S.C., 609
Sierra Leone, mentioned, 886
Simsbury Mines, Conn., 534
Sinking Spring Valley; *see* Bald Eagle Valley
Six Nations, 111
Skeletons, 623–25
Skull and crossbones, 177, 240, 619
Sling cart, 920
Snakes, 239, 565, 632; as envy, 234; as John André, 848; *see also* America, as a rattlesnake
Solebay, 607
Somerset, 253, 494, 712

Somerville, Mass., 500
Songs, 622, 627, 630, 766, 780, 785, 790, 847
Sons of Liberty, 201, 245, 680; mentioned, 623
Sorel River, Canada, 349
Sounding lead, 694
South Carolina, 604–11, 773, 894; mentioned, 50, 144
South Mountain, Pa., 575
South River, N.Y., 552
South Second Street Market, Phila., 586
Southern Seal Isle, Nova Scotia, 444
Spain: as a crest, 653; as a dog, 792, 821, 858; as a goat, 789; as a jester, 861; as a lion, 758; as a Spaniard, 622, 627, 632, 664, 698, 726, 741, 750, 752, 762–63, 765–67, 769, 778, 781–83, 786–87, 802, 809–10, 818–20, 822, 828, 830, 841, 844, 847, 849, 852, 855–56, 963; mentioned, 41, 53, 131, 678, 784, 793, 845
Spanish Army, 310–11, 328
Spanish fleet, 313, 319; officers, mentioned, 333–42
Spear, 691, 905
Spencer's Island, Nova Scotia, 463
Spontoon, 905
Spunge, 914
Squirrel, 565
Stamp Act, 22, 102, 155, 169, 188, 199, 243, 619–26, 650, 670, 679, 737, 851
Statehouse, Boston, 520; Philadelphia, 588–90, 592
Staten Island, N.Y., 543, 551–52
States, as pillars, 894–95
Stony Point, N.Y., 309; mentioned, 231
Suffolk Resolves, 204, 255
Sugar cane, 838
Sullivan's Island, S.C., 260, 605–7, 701
Sun, as the public good, 896
Surveying, 385, 431
Sweden, 778–79; mentioned, 750

Tappan, N.Y., 317
Tappan Sea, N.Y., 556
Tarring and feathering, 249, 668–70, 680, 874
Tarrytown, N.Y., 315

Taxes, 644; *see also* Stamp Act
Tea tax, 677, 681, 738, 792, 805, 851
Three Top Island, 395
Ticonderoga, N.Y., mentioned, 9, 18, 187
Time, Father, 738–39, 851, 888
Tiverton, R.I., mentioned, 282
Tobacco, 602, 625, 680, 727–28, 757
Tobago, W.I., 321, 809, 819; mentioned, 154
Toleration Act, mentioned, 689
Tomahawks, 238, 764
Toulon, France, 52
Trade, 348–49, 719, 728, 798–99, 836; mentioned, 583, 588, 601–2, 610, 643, 662, 779
Treaty of 1783, mentioned, 1, 366
Trenton, N.J., 271, 333–42, 346; mentioned, 98
Trinity Church, N.Y., 268, 545–47, 552
Trips's, R.I., 533
Truck-Carriage, 917
Truth, personified, 647; mirror of, 813
Tryal, 264
Tyranny, as a horse, 784

Unicorn, 789
U.S. Constitution, 187, 194, 894–95
Unity, mentioned, 474
Upper Bay, N.Y., 541
Urn, 805
Ushant, Battle at, 303–7

Vaillant, 288
Valley Forge, Pa., mentioned, 577
Venality, as a horse, 784
Versailles, France, 277; *see also* Peace at Versailles
Verses; *see* poems
Vice Admiralty Court at Halifax, 414
Vigilant, 712
Ville de Paris, mentioned, 331
Virginia, 603, 632, 680, 894; mentioned, 4, 18
Vue d'optique, 263, 266–68, 310, 320, 326, 364–66, 748, 771

Wall Street Presbyterian Church, N.Y., 547
Walnut Street Jail, Phila. 585
Wando River, S.C., 607, 611
Weavers, 625, 843, 873
Weazle, 291
Wedge, 914
West, the, 796
West Indies, 184, 287, 289–302, 320–22, 329–31, 333–42, 615–18, 754, 838; mentioned, 21, 26, 42, 52, 154, 164, 479, 583, 648, 713
West Point, N.Y., mentioned, 7, 314
Western Isles, Nova Scotia, 388
Westminster; *see* Parliament
Westminster Election, 873
Wheat, 639, 717, 890

Whigs, 54, 314; mentioned, 774
White Haven, Nova Scotia, 395
White Horse Isle, New Brunswick, 471
White Island, Nova Scotia, 397
White Plains, N.Y., mentioned, 186
Whitehead Island, Nova Scotia, 395–96
Wig, 701
Williamsburg Convention of 1774, 680
Winchester, Va., mentioned, 308
Winter Rock, Nova Scotia, 409
Wisdom, goddess of, 866
Witch, 813
Wolves, The, New Brunswick, 467
Worcester, Mass., 657
Worm, 914
Wrecker's Den, Nova Scotia, 431

Yale College, Conn., mentioned, 37, 191, 551
Yankee Doodle, 787
Yoke, 899
York, England, mentioned, 767
York, Pa., 575
Yorktown, campaign and battle, 142, 324–27; mentioned, 15, 28, 34, 42, 113, 139, 142, 184, 190, 197–98, 231, 791, 794, 802–3
Youghiogheny Falls, Pa., 574

Zebra, 737

Index of Artists

Numbers in this index refer to entries, not to pages.

Aitken, Robert, 690–91
Angus, William, 39, 43, 51, 93, 118, 141, 222
Annert, F. A., 488
Anville, Sr. d', 634

Barlow, 238, 272
Bartolozzi, F., 638
Basset, Andre, l'ainé, 263, 268, 553, 584
Bayly, 840
Beaurain, Chr. de, 631, 707, 720
Bedwell, 575
Benazech, Peter, 357, 371, 556
Berger, Daniel, 71, 221, 241–43, 248, 251, 254, 261, 271, 275, 277, 315, 318, 327, 343, 875
Bergmuller, 320
Bertaux or Berteaux, 287, 319
Berthalt, S., 777
Berthet, L. S., 173
Binet, L., 173
Birrell, 35, 41, 44, 113, 164
Blaskowitz, Charles, 905
Boehmio, Aug. Gottl., 795
Bogerts, C., 881
Bonnor, 653, 724
Bonnieu, 227
Bowan, Eman, 713
Bowen, Thos., 604

Boyne, I., 853
Bretherton, C., 806
Brion de la Tour, M., 718, 865, 879
Brompton, Richard, mentioned, 169
Bulfinch, C., 517
Bunbury, H., 807
Buys, J., 808, 881

C., J., 687
Caldnall, J., 639
Callet, 203
Campbell, mentioned, 207–8, 214
Canon, P., 740
Canot, P. C., 265, 351, 370, 382, 523, 551–52, 610
Carmontelle, Louis Carrogis de, 77
Carver, Captain, 355, 699
Carwitham, I., 496
Cathelin, Louis-Jacques, 74
Chamberlin, Mason, 58, 62; mentioned, 65
Chevillet, Juste, 63, 227
Chodowiecki, Daniel, 241–43, 248, 251, 254, 261, 271, 275, 277, 315, 318, 327, 343
Cipriani, G. B., 638
Cochin, Charles N., 59–61, 64, 66, 70, 76; mentioned, 67, 75, 745
Colley, T., 767, 814, 847–48
Coltellini, C., 715
Conder, 900
Cook, 8, 31, 332
Cook, J., 61, 70

Cook, James, 604
Cook, Thomas [?], 859
Cophius, Martin Gottfried, 659
Copley, J. S., 32, 144; mentioned, 3, 102, 146, 163
Corbutt, C., 727; mentioned, 114–16, 175, 194

D., P. E., 691
Darly, M., 315, 697, 728
Dawe, Philip, 673, 679–81
De L'Isle, 631
Denis, L., 759
Dent, 886
Des Barres, Joseph Frederick Wallet, 264, 362, 373–81, 383–472, 474–80, 483–87, 492–93, 497–505, 524–31, 536–43, 608, 616
Desrayes, Claude L., 75; (Desrais), 79, 212
D'Haisnc, 53
Dickinson, W., 807
Dixon, J., 667
Dodd, 8, 127
Doolittle, Amos, 192, 761
Dunn, Samuel, 699
Dupin, 11, 30, 179, 183, 208
Duplessis, Joseph, 63, 69, 73
Dupré, Augustin, 875
Du Simitière, Pierre Eugène, 37–39, 46–49, 86–87, 129–31, 145, 159, 180, 182, 190, 201, 219, 691; mentioned, 221

E., B. B.; *see* Ellis, B. B.

Eliot, J. B., 744
Elliot, Wm., 369, 559
Ellis, B. B., 38, 47, 49, 87, 130–31, 145, 159, 190, 201, 219

Faden, William, 565, 590, 719
Fauvel, 274
Feutry, poet, 63
Fiegl, 331
Filleul, Anne Rosalie, 74
Fisher, Edward, 58; mentioned, 169
Fittler, 310
Fogo, Crunk, 813
Fosseyeux, J. B., 134
Frentzel, G. F. J., 706
Fry, Joshua, 602
Fuller, W., 612

Gallager, G., 902
Gallaudet, Elisha, 232
Gauld, G., 614
Gibson, John, 713
Gillray, James, 315, 772, 818
Godefroy, Francois, 249–50, 252, 274, 287, 296, 324, 328
Goldar, John, 53, 73, 127, 138, 317, 869
Goodnight, C., 817
Gray, Henry, 260
Gray, W., 482
Green, Valentine, 144, 215
Grignion, Charles, 330
Guttenberg, Carl, 133, 738

Habermann, Francois Xav., 266–68, 363–65, 519, 521
Haid, J. Elias, 66
Halbou, Louis-Michel, 269, 323
Hamilton, 262, 270, 290, 311, 317, 325, 330
Hamilton, W., 716
Harrison, 869
Hawkins, 270
Heap, George, 588, 590
Hill, Samuel, 78, 143, 191, 482, 491, 509, 511, 513–14, 516, 518, 532, 564, 902; mentioned, 140

Hogarth, William, mentioned, 775
Holland, Captain Samuel, 362, 555, 721
Homanno, Jo. Bapt., 796–99
Howdell, Thomas, 265, 551–52

Ince, Captain, 382

Jackson, L., 717
James, Thomas, 605, 611
Jefferson, Peter, 602
Jefferys, Thomas, 555, 588
Jukes, F., 276

Keppel, Augustus, 736
Kitchin, Thomas, 473, 549
Koehler, G. Fredk., 51

L., J., 228
Lapi, Gio., 715
Lattre, Jean, 878
Lausan, 319
LeB., 228
Le Barbier, l'ainé, 250, 256, 269, 322, 324
Le Beau, Pierre Adrien, 75, 212
Le Gouaz, Yves-Marie, 617
LeGrand, 41
Leitch, Thos., 609
Leizelt, Balth. Frederic, 10, 366, 481, 553, 584
Le Mire, Noel, 142, 229
Leney, William, 187
L'Enfant, Pierre Charles, 557
Le Paon, L., 229, 328–29
LeRoy, Ta., 217
Lerpiniere, 310
Littleford, 102
Lodge, [John?], 253
Lotter, G. F., 661
Lotter, Matthew Albert, 590
Lotter, Tobias C., 550; (Tob. Conr. Lotteri), 742–43

M, 255
M., C., 745
McArdell, James, 57; mentioned, 58
Malcom, 585

Malpas, E., 716
Man, Thomas, 591–93
Manufacture Nationale de Sèvres, 68, 71, 78
Marillier, P. C., 322
Matraini, N., 618
Maverick, Peter R., 76
Mazell, Peter, 354, 372
Mellish, T., 610
Metz, 312, 330–32
Millar, 253
Miller, 35, 43–44, 113
Mitchell, John, 640
Molthrop, Reuben, 192
Montaland, Cite., 79
Montresor, John, 567, 596–99, 639; mentioned, 548
Moreau le Jeune, J. M., 134

Neé, François Denis, 77
Newton, James, 497
Nicole, Pierre, 596–98
Niquet, M., 302–6
Noble, 262
Norman, John, 1, 3, 32, 68, 72, 85, 98, 107, 110, 139–40, 146, 152, 158, 204–5, 216, 220, 231, 255, 257, 860, 876, 913–20
Notté, C. J., 133; mentioned, 221

O'Neale, 161
Ottaviani, J., 618
Ozanne, Jeanne-Françoise, 617
Ozanne, Marie-Jeanne, mentioned, 617
Ozanne, Nicolas, 617
Ozanne, Pierre, 278–80, 282–85, 288–89, 291–94, 297–302

Parson, T., 740
Patas, Jean-Baptiste, 256, 258, 707
Paton, Richard, 310
Patten, Thomas, 351
Peake, James, 578
Peale, Charles Willson, 224, 226, 345, 515, 582, 587, 589, 594, 903; mentioned, 100, 211, 213, 216, 220, 224, 227–29

Pelham, Henry, 247
Pelicier, J., 69, 108
Phillips, J., 755
Pierpont, W., 514
Pierre, Wm., 497, 500, 503
Pierrie, Wm.; see Pierre, Wm.
Pine, R. E., 761
Pollard, Robert, 17, 23, 67, 80, 91–92, 95, 101, 105, 115, 151, 162, 166, 276, 314, 330
Pomarede, D., 352
Ponce, Nicolas, 258, 319, 321–22, 329, 333–42
Pownall, Thomas, 523, 556, 558–60, 568, 578, 713
Prevost, B. L., 37, 46, 48, 86, 129, 180
Price, William, 496, 641
Probst, Ioh. Mich., 124, 149, 693
Pruneau, Noel, 211
Pugh, Mr., 523

R., R., 686
Ratzer, B., 549
Record, 312
Revere, Paul, 245–47, 626, 642, 652, 654, 657, 664, 666
Reynolds, Joshua, 4, 93; mentioned, 6, 19
Rezio, Razo, 813
Rhein, M., 722
Robert, Hubert[?], 633
Roberts, 367

Rogg, Gottfri., 722
Romans, Bernard, 506
Royce, 361

St. Aubin, Augustin de, rue de Mathurins, 59
Sandby, Paul, 371, 556, 558–59, 568, 578
Sauthier, C. J., 348
Scull, Nicholas, 588, 590, 717
Seally, 840
Serres, Dominic, 264, 613
Sharp, W., 218
Sherwin, J. K., mentioned, 169
Simpson, John, 754
Smart, 30
Smith, Saml., 609
Smither, James, 591–93
Smyth, Hervey, 354, 357, 369–72; mentioned, 357
Stothard, 859
Strutt, Joseph, 761

T., G. M., 563
Taylor, Isc., 687–88
Tchirikcow, Mrs., 631
Thackara, James, 575, 586, 903
Thomlinson, 147
Thornton, 290, 311, 325
Tiebout, Cornelius, 901

Trenchard, James, 100, 223, 344–46, 523, 535, 562, 576, 582–85, 589, 601, 889–90, 895
Trumbull, John, 215, 217

V., L., 745
Va de bon coeur, 727
Vallance, John, 517, 903
Vangelisti, Vincenzo, 203
Van Winter, P., 226
Vernet, 488, 583
Verney, 710
Vinkeles, Reinier, 226, 808
Voltaire, M. A., 758
Voysard, E., 714

W., A., 854
Walker, 193
Wallace, James, 264, 608
Watson, James, 4
Wells, J., 368
West, Benjamin, 113
Weyerman, Jacob Christoph, 659
Wilkinson, John (probably fictitious), 175
Will, John Martin, 9, 206, 762; mentioned, 235
William, 321
Williams, J., 725
Williams, W. A., 544
Wilson, Benjamin, 57; mentioned, 58

Index of Publishers

Numbers in this index refer to entries, not to pages.

Alibert Md. d'Estampes, au Palais Royal, 745
Almon, John, Piccadilly, 247, 702, 764
Ames, *Astronomical Diary; or Almanack*, 45
Anburey, *Travels Through the Interior Parts of America*, 238, 272–73, 308, 349, 900, 921
Andrews, *A Collection of Plans of the Capital Cities . . .*, 658
Andrews, *History of the War with America, France, Spain, and Holland*, 15, 31, 34–35, 41, 44, 51, 53, 73, 93, 99, 113, 121, 127–28, 135, 138, 141, 164, 167, 185, 193, 222, 904
The Annual Register, 5, 90, 118, 170–71, 352
Atlante dell' America, 359, 563, 618, 715
The Atlantic Neptune, 264, 362, 373–81, 383–472, 474–80, 483–87, 492–93, 497–505, 524–531, 536–43, 608, 616

Bachiene, *Atlas*, 881
Bakewell, Eliz., opposite Birchin Lane in Cornhill, 111
Barker, Henry, No. 82 in Cornhill, 351, 354, 357, 369–72, 382, 523, 551–52, 556, 558–59, 568, 577–78, 610
Barnard, *History of England*, 253, 270, 290, 311, 317, 325, 330, 863
Barrow, J., 817, 821; N. 84 Dorset Street, Salisbury Court, Fleet Street, 824, 826; White Lion Bull Stairs Surry Side Black Friars Bridge, 844–45, 858

Basset, André, l'ainé, Rue St. Jacques au coin de celle des Mathurins a Ste. Genevieve, 79, 263, 268, 553, 584, 759
Bennett, John, and Robert Sayer, No. 53 Fleet Street, 355, 615, 670, 673, 679–81, 699, 710, 787; *see also* Sayer, Robert
Bew, John, Paternoster Row, 24, 534
Bickerstaff *Boston Almanack*, 89, 103, 163, 169, 209, 234, 244, 309, 891
Bollan, *Continued Corruption . . .*, 638
The Boston Gazette, 652, 654
The Boston Magazine, 1, 32, 72, 146, 205, 220, 860, 876
Bowles, Carrington, No. 69 St. Pauls Church Yard, 351, 354, 357, 369–72, 382, 496, 523, 551–52, 556, 558–59, 568, 577–78, 610, 668, 801, 872; next the Chapter House in St. Pauls Church Yard, 634
Bowles, John, at No. 13 in Cornhill, 351, 354, 357, 369–72, 382, 523, 551–52, 556, 558–59, 568, 577–78, 610, 667; at the Black Horse in Cornhill, 634
Boydell, John, Cheapside, London, 310
Boyne, I., No. 2 Shoe Lane Fleet St., 853
Brackenridge, *The Battle of Bunkers-Hill*, 255
Bradford, William, 619
Brion de la Tour, *Atlas Ecclesiastique*, 631
Brown, J., Rathbone Place, 873
Byrne, G., No. 43 Fishamble Street, 160

Cattermoul, J., No. 376 Oxford Street, 868

Chereau, J., rue St. Jacques au desous de la Fontaine St. Severin au 2 Colonnes, 267
Ciseau, Nicolas, a Lyon a L'ensigne des armes de Bourges, 783
Clagget, Mr., Sugar Loaf Court, Fanchurch Building, London, 625
Clarke, *An Impartial and Authentic Narrative of the Battle*, 696
Clouet, *Géographie Moderne*, 777
Cochin, Charles N., aux Galleries du Louvre, 59
Cochin, C., Chev. de l'Ordre du Roi a Paris, 60
Cockings, *The American War*, 253
Colley, Thomas, No. 257 High Holborn, 792–93; No. 5 Acorn Court Rolls Building Fetters Lane Old England, 820, 828, 830
The Columbian Magazine, 100, 223, 225, 344–46, 512, 515–17, 523, 535, 554, 561–62, 569–76, 579–82, 586, 589, 594, 600–1, 882–85, 889–90, 895, 898–99, 903
Constitutions of the Several Independent States of America, 70, 218
"Corbutt"; *see* R. Purcell
Cornell, T., Bruton Street, Bond Street, 793, 854
Cowley, *Ladies History of England*, 281, 367
Cumberlege, S. A., at the Kings Arms, in Pater-noster Row, 56, 842

Darchery (or D'Archery, Darchey, Dashery, Dachery) Elizabeth, St. James Street, 770 818, 831, 846, 849, 861

Dareny, M. S., Opposite to the Kings Head Strand, 751
Darly, M., 39 Strand, 697, 709, 728–30, 760; M. Darly, 734, 803; Mary Darly, 39 Strand 701, 752
Debrett, J., Piccadilly, 43, 118
DeNeufville of Amsterdam, 215
Dennel, rue du Pt. Bourbon attent, 211
Dent, W., 897
Des Barres, Joseph Frederick Wallet, 264, 362, 373–81, 383–472, 474–80, 483–87, 492–93, 497–505, 524–31, 536–43, 608, 616
Dickie, W., opposite Exetor change, 893
Dickinson, W., No. 158 New Bond Street, 807
Dilly, E. and C., in the Poultry, 247
Drayton *Memoirs of the American Revolution*, 260
Dunn, *A New Atlas of the Mundane System*, 699
Dupin, house of, 11
Du Simitière, *Portraits*, 130–31, 145, 159, 182, 190, 201, 219

Edes & Gill, *North American Almanack*, 245, 624, 642
Esnauts et Rapilly, rue St. Jacques a la Ville de Coutances, 11, 30, 64, 133, 179, 212, 295, 714, 718, 865, 879
The European Magazine, 39, 43, 109, 118, 840
Ewart, T., in the Strand, 630
Extrait du Journal d'un Officier de la Marine, 52

Faden, William, *Atlas of Battles of the American Revolution*, 605–6, 611; *North American Atlas*, 348, 355, 549, 590, 612, 639, 674, 694, 713, 719, 721, 773; Faden, Wm., Corner of St. Martins Lane, Charing Cross, 348, 565, 605–6, 611, 773; Faden, W., successor to the late Mr. Jefferys Geographer to the King Charing Cross, 590; with Jefferys, Corner of St. Martins Lane, Charing Cross, 549, 694
The Fall of Lucifer, 12
Fenning, *Neue Erdbeschreibung von Amerika*, 360

Fielding, John, Pater noster Row, 15, 31, 34–35, 39, 41, 43–44, 51, 53, 73, 93, 99, 109, 113, 118, 121, 127, 128, 135, 138, 141, 164, 167, 185, 193, 222, 857
Fielding & Walker, Pater Noster Row, 29, 97, 748
Fores, S. W., No. 3 Piccadilly, 887
Fox, *The Beauties of Fox, North, and Burke*, 877
France, Depot des cartes et plans de la marine, *Neptune Americo-Septentrional*, 612
Freeman, T. B., Strand, 815

Gauld, G., 614
General Magazine, 696
The Gentlemen's Magazine, 286, 510
Gillies, *Memoirs of the Life of the Reverend George Whitefield*, 232
Gillman, W., Rochester, 676
Godefroy, Francois, rue de Francs-bourgeois, Port St. Michel, 249, 252, 287, 294, 302–6, 318–19, 321, 324, 328–29, 333–42
Gordon, *The History of the Rise, Progress, and Independence of the United States of America*, 901
Green, Valentine, N29 Newman Street, Oxford Street, London, 215
Grose, *Advice to the Officers of the British Army*, 864
Guttenberg, Carl, rue St. Hyacinthe la 2me porte par la place St. Michel, 133

H., Thom., a Londres, 59
Hamilton, A., Junr., near St. John's Gate, 6, 18, 123, 160, 168, 265; Fleet Street, 25, 40, 50, 81, 122, 174, 198
Harris, John, Sweetings Alley Cornhill, 765, 775, 810
Hart, Thomas, London, 9, 114, 195, 235; see also, H., Thom.
Hedges, E., No. 2, under the Royal Exchange Cornhill, 767; No. 92 Cornhill, 791, 822, 870
The Hibernian Magazine, 7, 27, 81, 96, 112, 123, 154, 156, 160, 198, 664, 666, 675, 677, 874; mentioned, 717

Hilliard-d'Auberteuil, *Essais Historiques*, 69, 108, 173, 217, 250, 256, 258, 269, 323, 804–5
Holland, W., 650
Homann, *Atlas Geographievs Maior*, 795–99
Humphrey, H., No. 18 New Bond Street, 760, 771
Humphrey, W., Gerrard Street Soho, 695; No. 227 Strand London, 750, 755, 763, 769, 812, 850–51, 853, 855

An Impartial History of the War in America (Boston), 68, 85, 98, 107, 110, 139–40, 152, 158, 204, 216, 231, 257
An Impartial History of the War in America (London), 2–3, 13, 65, 84, 106, 117, 120, 126, 150, 177, 213, 237, 240; mentioned, 717

Jefferys, Thomas, *The American Atlas*, 355, 555, 602, 674, 699, 713, 773; *Atlas des Indes Occidentales*, 615; *A General Topography of North America*, 555, 588, 602, 613, 674, 713, 773; *The West-India Atlas*, 615; the corner of St. Martin's Lane Strand, 351, 354, 357, 369–72, 382, 523, 551–52, 555–56, 558–59, 568, 577–78, 610, 614; Geographer to the King in the Strand, 612; Charing Cross, 588, 674; with Faden, Corner of St. Martins Lane, Charing Cross, 549, 694; *see also* Faden, William
Johnson, G., 737
Julien, *Le Théatre du Monde*, 633–34
Junius, 656

Kendall, J., Great Queen Street, 811
Kitchin, *General Atlas*, 713
Korn, *Geschichte der Kriege*, 10, 64, 104, 116, 148, 176, 186, 194, 207, 236, 358

Lane, William, Leadenhall Street, London, 272–73, 308, 349
Langham, I., 827
Laporte: *Atlas Moderne Portatif*, 800; *Atlas ou Collection de Cartes Géographiques*, 800

Lattré, Graveur du Roi, Rue St. Jacques No. 20, 878

Laurie, Robt., No. 17 Rosomonds Row. Clerkenwell, 768

Lavater, Johann, *Essai sur Physionomie*, 225

Le Camus Md. de Drap, 229

le Mire, Noel, à Paris, rue et porte St. Jacques, 229

Le Noir, Md. du Cabinet des Estampes du Roi au Louvre, 745

LeRay de Chaumont, 63

LeRouge, *Atlas Ameriquain Septentrional*, 356, 563, 674

L'Isle, *Atlas Géographique et Universal*, 239, 867

The London Magazine, 16, 22, 27, 33, 36, 42, 54, 94, 112, 136, 153–55, 161, 188, 200, 202, 544, 635, 647, 653, 662, 664, 666, 671, 675, 678, 682, 698, 703, 724, 736

Loosjes, *Gedenkzuil, ter Gelegenheid der Vry-Verklaaring van Noord-America*, 808

Lotter, *Atlas Géographique*, 550, 590, 660–61, 674, 722, 742–43; *Atlas Novus Sive Tabulae Geographicae*, 659–61

Macklew, E., No. 9 Haymarket, 886

Marks, J., on the pav'd stones St. Martin's Lane, 650

The Massachusetts Centinel, 892

The Massachusetts Magazine, 78, 143, 347, 482, 491, 509, 511, 513–14, 518, 532, 564, 902

Massachusetts Register, 1769, 642

The Massachusetts Spy, 657

Mills, I., No. 1 Ratcliff Row near the French Hospital Old Street, 766

Mitchell, P., North Audly St. Grosr Sqr, 775

Mondhare, Rue St. Jacques a la Ville de Caen, 744

Mondhare, rue St. Jean de Beauvais pres celle des Noyers, 326

Moore, W., W48 New Bond Street, 893; Oxford Street, 896

Morris, John, London, 82

Muller, *A Treatise of Artillery*, 913–20

Murray, *An Impartial History of the Present War in America*, 12, 17, 21, 23, 28, 67, 80, 91–92, 95, 101, 105, 115, 119, 125, 137, 151, 157, 162, 166, 178, 196, 214

Neé, François Denis, rue des Francs-Bourgeois, 77

New York Gazette, mentioned, 39

Owen, R., in Fleet Street, 809

Palairet [Collection of Maps], 634

Parker, H., in Cornhill, 604

Pennsylvania Chronicle, mentioned, 45

Pennsylvania Journal, 619

The Pennsylvania Magazine, 690–91

Phelps, W., 788

The Political Magazine, 24, 55, 534

The Political Register, 632, 645, 651

Pollard, Robert, No. 7 Braynes Row Spa Fields, 276, 313; No. 15 Braynes Row Spa Fields, 368

Ponce, *Receuil d'estampes*, 249, 252, 274, 287, 296, 303–7, 319, 321–22, 324, 328–29, 333–42

Ponce, Nicolas, rue St. Hiacinte, No. 19, 249, 252, 287, 296, 303–7, 319, 321–22, 324, 328–29, 333–42

P-oplicola H-istoricus, *America pois'd in the Balance of Justice*, 705

Porlier, graveur, editeur, rue des cinq Diamans, No. 8., 228

Portraits des Généraux, Ministres et Magistrats, 37, 46, 48, 86, 129, 180

Pridden, J., in Fleet Street, 627

Purcell, R., 9

The Rambler's Magazine, 852, 880

Rapin-Thoyras, *History of England*, 869

Raymond, *History of England*, 8, 312, 330–32

Reed, *Map of Philadelphia*, 591

Renegal, W., 772

Rich, E., little Print Shop facing Anderton's Coffee House Fleet Street, 817

Richardson, George, 716

Richardson, W., no. 68 High Holborn, 740, 814, 820–21, 830; near Surry Street Strand, 828, 847–48

Ripa, *A Collection of Emblematical Plates*, 716

The Rise, Progress, and Present State of the Dispute between the People of America and the Administration, 704

Rivington, mentioned, 39

Robson, T., Newcastle upon Tyne, 12, 17, 21, 23, 28, 67, 80, 83, 91–92, 95, 101, 105, 115, 119, 125, 137, 151, 157, 162, 166, 178, 196, 214

Roman, *Natural History of East and West Florida*, 686

Royal American Magazine, 664, 666

Russell, Ezekial, 45

Russell, J., No 7 Blewets Buildings Fetter Lane, London, 784

Russell, *History of America*, 19–20, 29, 62, 165, 172, 210, 361

Ryland and Bryer, at the King's Arms in Cornhill, 4

Sackville, *Correspondence du Lord G. Germain*, 208

Santini, P., *Atlas Universal*, 239

Sayer, Robert, at No. 53 Fleet Street, 351, 354, 357, 369–72, 382, 523, 551–52, 555–56, 558–59, 568, 577–78, 610; with John Bennett, 355, 615, 670, 673, 679–81, 699, 710, 787

Scenographia Americana, 265, 351, 354, 357, 369–72, 382, 523, 551–52, 556, 558–59, 568, 577–78, 610

Sewall, J., Cornhill, 43, 118

Shepherd, C., London, 102, 147, 175, 207; Lambeth Hill, Doctors Commons, 733

A Short Narrative of The Horrid Massacre in Boston, 247

"Signers Collection" of J. Pierpont Morgan, 59, 109

Simcoe, *A Journal of the Operations of the Queen's Rangers*, 555

Simes, *A New Military, Historical, and Explanatory Dictionary*, 906–12

Smith, Jno, No 35 Cheapside, 787

Smith, M., No. 46 Fleet Street, 856, 871; Long Acre near Drury Lane, 620, 625
Smith, W. *Sermon on the Present Situation of American Affairs*, 687–88
Sprengel, *Allgemeines Historisches Taschenbuch*, 221, 241–43, 248, 251, 254, 261, 271, 275, 277, 314, 318, 327, 343, 875
Stockdale, J., Bookseller, No. 181 opposite Burlington House Picadilly London, 144, 218

Terry, G., Paternoster Row, 672
Tomlinson, James, Oxford Street, 754
Toplady, *An Old Fox Tarr'd and Feather'd*, 689
The Town and Country Magazine, 6, 18, 25, 40, 50, 61, 81, 122–23, 160, 168, 174, 198, 233, 265, 313, 648, 677

The United States Magazine, 746
Universal Asylum and Columbian Magazine; see *Columbian Magazine*
An Universal History, The Maps & Charts, 473
The Universal Magazine, 14, 56, 189, 350, 585, 708, 780, 842, 859

Veridicus, 656
Voogt, *De Nieuwe Groote Lichtende Zee-Fakkel*, 832–38

Walker, J., 26; No. 20, Pater-noster Row, 197; No. 44 Pater-noster Row, 199
Walker, T., No. 79 Dame Street, 96, 160, 198
Wallis, John, Ludgate Street, London, 866
Weatherwise's Town and Country Almanack, 839

Wells, W., No. 132 Fleet Street, London, 790, 819
West, Benjamin (astronomer and almanac maker), 169, 209, 234, 244, 308, 891
The Westminster Magazine, 26, 88, 97, 181, 197, 199, 665, 700, 723, 726, 748
White, Wm., Angel Court, Westminster, 749
Wilkinson, R., No. 58 Cornhill, London, 38, 47, 49, 87, 130–31, 145, 159, 182, 190, 201, 219, 786
Will, J. M., 114, 147
Williams, W., Fleet Street, 711
Wilson, D., 823

Index of Persons

Numbers in this index refer to entries, not to pages.

Abingdon, Willoughby Bertie, 4th Earl of, 741
Acland, John Dyke, mentioned, 276
Acland, Lady Christian Henrietta Carolina (Lady Harriet), 276
Adams, 741
Adams, John, 1; mentioned, 201
Adams, Samuel, 2–3; mentioned, 201, 204
Alfred the Great, King of England, 90
Amherst, Jeffrey Amherst, 1st Baron, 4–6, 771, 809, 814, 817a, 856, 864
Amour, François Claude, *see* Bouillé, Marquis de
André, John, 7–8, 315–17, 842; mentioned, 14, 848
Antisejanus; *see* Scott, Dr. W.
Apsley, Henry Bathurst, 1st Baron, 665
Arnold, Benedict, 9–14, 839; as a snake, 848; mentioned, 7, 23, 160
Asgill, Charles, 15
Ashburton; *see* Dunning, John
Attucks, Crispus, 247, 654
Auckland, 1st Baron; *see* Eden, William
Augustus, Edward; *see* York, Duke of
Augustus, William; *see* Cumberland, Duke of

Barré, Isaac, 16, 626, 813
Barrington, Samuel, mentioned, 289

Bate, Henry, 827
Bathurst, Henry; *see* Apsley, 1st Baron
Beaumont, Charles de; *see* Éon, Chevalier d'
Beckford, William, 626, 643, 647, 649, 655
Bedford, John Russell, 4th Duke of, 620, 623–25, 645, 648, 655; as His Grace of Spital Fields, 623
Berainville, Chev. P. de, quoted, 143
Berkeley, Norborne; *see* Botetourt, Baron de
Bernard, Francis, mentioned, 245, 753
Bertie, Willoughby; *see* Abingdon, 4th Earl of
Blackstone, Sir William, quoted, 702
Blagge, John, 679
Blyfield, Amelia, 344
Blyfield, Horatio, 344
Boswell, James, mentioned, 200, 806
Botetourt, Norborne Berkeley, Baron de, statue of, 680
Bouillé, François Claude Amour, Marquis de, mentioned, 287, 321, 322, 329, 333
Brant, Joseph; *see* Thayendanegea
Bridinell, Rev., 276
Broome, mentioned, 679
Bulfinch, Charles, mentioned, 517
Burgoyne, John, 17–18, 725, 748, 812, 864; mentioned, 23, 82–83, 168, 272–74, 276, 308
Burke, Edmund, 19, 20, 741, 793, 809, 813–14, 817–18, 856, 871, 873, 877, 886–88, 893, 896; mentioned, 54, 144, 767, 806
Burnaby, William, mentioned, 614

Bute, John Stuart, 3d Earl of, 620, 623–24, 627, 629, 632, 637, 648–49, 651, 655–56, 664–66, 677, 682–85, 695–96, 702–4, 725, 729, 741, 751, 754, 763, 765, 770, 772, 784, 792, 813, 815; as Sejanus, 623; mentioned, 753
Byng, George, 813
Byron, John, 28; mentioned, 52, 283, 291, 295–96

Caesar, Julius, mentioned, 747
Caldwell, James, 247, 654
Calvin, John, mentioned, 636
Camden, Charles Pratt, 1st Earl of, 22, 626, 628, 665, 700, 741, 813; mentioned, 859–60, 897
Canterbury, Archbishop of; *see* Secker, Thomas
Carleton, Guy, 1st Lord Dorchester, 23–26, 819; mentioned, 200, 711
Carlisle, Frederick Howard, 5th Earl of, 27, 728–29, 737, 741, 873; mentioned, 144
Carr, Patrick, 247, 654
Castries, Armand-Charles-Augustin, Duc de; mentioned, 333–42
Catherine II, Queen of Russia, 745, 778; mentioned, 750
Cavendish, John, 857, 873
Cavendish-Bentinck, William Henry; *see* Portland, 3d Duke of
Charles I, King of England, 868; mentioned, 55
Charles II, King of England, mentioned, 584

451

Charles III, King of Spain, 645, 766; mentioned, 333
Charlotte Sophia, Queen of England, 626
Chatham, 1st Earl of; *see* Pitt, William
Clinton, George, mentioned, 570
Clinton, Sir Henry, 28–31, 735, 864; mentioned, 7, 14–15, 23, 34, 101, 334, 539, 774
Clinton, Thomas Pelham, 3d Duke of Newcastle, called Lord Lincoln, 774–75
Coetnempren, Armand Guy Simon de; *see* Kersaint, Comte de
Coleraine, 4th Baron of; *see* Hanger, George
Conway, Francis Seymour; *see* Hertford, 1st Earl of
Conway, Henry Seymour, 623–24, 626, 628, 813–14, 817, 819, 822
Cooper, Samuel, 32
Cornwall, Charles Wolfran, 33, 317
Cornwallis, Charles, 2d Earl of, 28, 34, 812, 864; mentioned, 98, 113, 184, 197, 324–27, 806
Crillon; *see* De Crillon-Mahon
Cromwell, Oliver, mentioned, 868, 871
Crozer, John, mentioned, 679
Cumberland, William Augustus, Duke of, 620
Curtis, Sir Roger, 35

D'Alais, mentioned, 303–7
D'Alembert, Jean Le Rond, 745
Dalrymple, John, mentioned, 311
D'Aranda, Comte, 332
Dartmouth, William Legge, 2d Earl of, 36, 626
Dawson, Captain, mentioned, 234
Deane, Silas, 37–40; mentioned, 144
De Berdt, Dennis, 626
De Crillon-Mahon, Louis de Berton des Balbes de Quiers, Duc, 41, 328; mentioned, 333
De Grasse, François Joseph Paul, Comte, 42–44, 321, 330; mentioned, 113, 184, 326, 869
Denbigh, Basil Feilding, 6th Earl of, 827
Derby, Edward Smith Stanley, 13th Earl of, 873

D'Estaing, Charles Hector, Comte, 52–53, 757; mentioned, 21, 42, 154, 193, 278, 279, 282–83, 285–86, 288–93, 295–96, 302, 333
Dickinson, John, 45–47; mentioned, 49
Doliscus, 344
Donaldson, Falconer; *see* Halifax, 2d Earl of
Dorchester, 1st Lord; *see* Carleton, Guy
Drayton, William Henry, 48–49; mentioned, 47
Du Bouexic, Louis Urbain; *see* Guichen, Comte de
Du Chaffault de Besné, Comte, mentioned, 333
Dunk, George Montagu; *see* Halifax, 2d Earl of
Dunmore, 4th Earl; *see* Murray, John
Dunning, John, 1st Baron Ashburton, 770, 817–18, 848, 856
Du Romain, Chevalier, mentioned, 291
Dyson, Jeremiah, 655

Eden, William, 1st Baron Auckland, 728–29, 737; mentioned, 27, 144
Effingham, Lady Maria, mentioned, 25
Effingham, Thomas Howard, 3d Earl of, 50, 741
Elderton, Reverend, mentioned, 510
Eliott, George Augustus, 1st Baron Heathfield, 51
Ellicott, Andrew, mentioned, 564
Elliot, John William, mentioned, 828
Éon, Charles de Beaumont, Chevalier d', 649

Faneuil, Peter, mentioned, 514
Feilding, Basil; *see* Denbigh, 6th Earl of
Feutry, Aimé Ambroise Joseph, 63
Finch-Hatton, Edward; *see* Winchilsea, 7th Earl of
Fitzherbert, Alleyne, 332
Fitzroy, Augustus Henry; *see* Grafton, 3d Duke of
Foote, Samuel, mentioned, 233
Fox, Charles James, 54–56, 700, 741, 774–75, 809, 813–15, 817–18, 820–22, 824, 827, 848, 853–54, 857, 861, 868, 870–71, 873–74, 886–88, 893, 896; mentioned, 19, 726
Fox, Henry; *see* Holland, 1st Baron of
Francis, Sir Philip, 893

Franklin, Benjamin, 57–79, 221, 225, 741, 745, 783, 848, 856, 866; mentioned, 1, 144, 160, 333, 656–57, 875, 878, 907
Franklin, Walter, mentioned, 679
Fraser, Simon, 684; funeral, 272; mentioned, 329
Frederick II, King of Prussia, 645; mentioned, 190
Fullarton, William, 770

Gage, Thomas, 80–81; mentioned, 23, 165, 245, 482, 664
Gálvez, Bernardo de Gálvez, Count de, 319, 333; mentioned, 303–7
Gates, Horatio, 82–88, 209, 221, 276, 333, 725; mentioned, 158, 160
Gawkee, Lord; *see* Temple, Richard Grenville, 1st Earl
George II, King of England, 89
George III, King of England, 89–93, 626–27, 629, 635, 644–47, 651, 665, 685, 696, 699, 702–4, 725, 741–42, 749, 753–54, 764–65, 772, 784, 792, 794, 809, 813, 817, 819, 827, 830, 849, 856–57, 870–71, 880; as an ass, 751; mentioned, 161, 189, 199, 202, 628, 672, 747, 854; statue of, 55, 263
George IV; *see* Prince of Wales
Germain, George Sackville, 94, 95, 626, 725, 741, 747, 754, 809–11, 813–15, 817, 817a, 819, 823; mentioned, 81, 101, 161, 302, 753, 794
Gibbs, James, mentioned, 532
Gloucester, Bishop of; *see* Warburton, William
Gordon, Lord George, 96–97, 741, 886
Grace of Spital Fields, His; *see* Bedford
Grafton, Augustus Henry Fitzroy, 3d Duke of, 623–24, 628, 637, 645, 651, 655, 700
Grandby, John Manners, Marquis of, 637; mentioned, 639
Graves, Samuel, mentioned, 257
Graves, Thomas, mentioned, 113
Gravier, Charles; *see* Vergennes, Comte de
Gray, George, mentioned, 582
Gray, Samuel, 247, 654
Greene, Nathanael, 98–100; mentioned, 231

Grenville, George, 620, 622–25, 737; as Mr. George Stamp, 623; mentioned, 199, 414
Grenville, George Nugent-Temple; see Temple, 2d Earl
Grenville, Richard; see Temple, 1st Earl
Grenville, Thomas, mentioned, 332
Grey, Charles Grey, 1st Earl, 101
Griffiths, Antony, mentioned, 679
Grimouard, Comte de, mentioned, 333–42
Guichen, Louis Urbain du Bouëxic, Comte de, 135; mentioned, 42
Guilford, 2d Earl of; see North, Frederick
Guillouet, Louis; see Orvilliers, Comte de

Halifax, George Montagu Dunk, 2d Earl of, 620, 623–25; as Falconer Donaldson, 623
Hamilton, Alexander, mentioned, 551
Hamilton, William, seat of, 581
Hancock, John, 102–9, 741; his home, 518; mentioned, 255, 516
Hanger, George, 4th Baron of Coleraine, 886–87
Harcourt, William, 270
Harley, Thomas, 643, 647
Harrington, 3d Earl; see Petersham, Viscount
Hastings, Warren, 893
Hayley, George, 700
Hayman, Francis, 627
Heath, William, 110
Heathfield, 1st Baron; see Eliott, George Augustus
Henley, Robert, 1st Earl of Northington, 627–28, 637
Hendrick (Tiyanoka), 111
Henry VI, King of England, 55
Hertford, Francis Seymour Conway, 1st Earl of, 637, 813, 817, 819; mentioned, 817a
Hill, Wills; see Hillsborough, 1st Earl
Hillsborough, Wills Hill, 1st Earl, 112, 636, 649, 655, 814
Holden, Samuel, mentioned, 513
Holland, Henry Fox, 1st Baron of, 627, 647–48, 651, 655, 665; mentioned, 54
Holme, Thomas, mentioned, 584
Hood, Samuel, 1st Viscount, 113, 184

Hopkins, Esek, 114–17, (called Robert Hopkins), 117
Hopkins, Robert; see Hopkins, Esek
Horne-Tooke; see Tooke, John Horne
House, Sam, 873
Howard, Frederick; see Carlisle, 5th Earl of
Howard, Thomas; see Effingham, 3d Earl of
Howe, Admiral Richard, Earl, 118–22, 629, 711–12, 726, 728, 802, 811; mentioned, 35, 51–52, 164, 282, 283, 285, 546, 781, 828
Howe, General William, 5th Viscount, 123–27, 629, 703, 711, 726, 728, 748, 811, 864; mentioned, 28, 80, 101, 165, 270, 596–99, 693
Hughes, Edward, 128; mentioned, 333–42
Huntington, Samuel, 129–30

James II, King of England, mentioned, 55
Jay, John, 131; mentioned, 1, 822
Jefferson, Thomas, mentioned, 764
Jenkinson, Elizabeth, mentioned, 33
Johnson, George, mentioned, 144
Johnson, Samuel, mentioned, 806
Johnstone, George, 728–29, 737, 741; mentioned, 144
Jones, John Paul, 132–34, 221, 336, 778, 783; mentioned, 309, 333

Kempenfelt, Richard, 135
Keppel, Augustus, Viscount, 136–38, 814, 817–18, 820, 822, 827, 848, 856–57, 873; mentioned, 280, 303–7, 736
Kersaint, Armand Guy Simon de Coetnempren, Comte de, 303–7
Knox, Henry, 139

Ladbroke, Sir Robert, 647; mentioned, 643
Lafayette, Marie Joseph Paul Yves Roch Gilbert du Motier, Marquis de, 140–43; mentioned, 52, 227, 230, 333
Lamb, John, mentioned, 679
La Motte-Piquet, 333; mentioned, 791
Landais, Pierre de, mentioned, 310
Langara, Don Juan de, mentioned, 313
La Perouse, Comte de, mentioned, 333–42

Laurens, Henry, 144–46, 221
Lavater, Johann Kaepar, mentioned, 226
Lee, Charles, 147–51; captured 270
Lee, Henry, mentioned, 567
Lee, John, 873
Legge, William; see Dartmouth, 2d Earl of
Lennox, Charles; see Richmond, 3d Duke of
Lincoln, Benjamin, 152, 325; mentioned, 302
Lincoln, Lord; see Clinton, Thomas Pelham
Livingston, Abraham, mentioned, 679
Locke, John, mentioned, 234, 636, 854
Loughborough, Alexander Wedderburn, 1st Baron, 153, 623–25, 684
Louis XV, King of France, 645
Louis XVI, King of France, 203, 766, 787; mentioned, 15, 144, 333
Loyola, Saint Ignatius of, mentioned, 829
Low, Cornelius, mentioned, 679
Lugg, William, 679
Luttrell, Henry Fownes, 644, 702
Luttrell, John, Capt., 311

Macartney, George, Baron, 154
McCrea, Jane, 725; mentioned, 274
McDougall, Alexander, mentioned, 679
Maitland, John, mentioned, 302
Malcom, John, 249, 668–70; mentioned, 692
Manners, John; see Granby, Marquis of
Manners, Robert, 330
Mansfield, David Murray, 2d Earl of; see Stormont, 7th Viscount
Mansfield, William Murray, 1st Earl of, 155, 637, 645, 651, 655, 664–65, 677, 682, 684–85, 696, 703, 725, 754, 763, 772, 813–14, 817a, 818, 856
Maria Theresa, Queen of Hungary and Bohemia, 645
Markham, William, Archbishop of York, 740, 817–17a
Maverick, Samuel, 247, 654
Mercer, Hugh, mentioned, 761
Micoud, de, 290
Montagu, John; see Sandwich, 4th Earl of
Montgomery, Richard, 156–58; death of 258; mentioned, 9, 23, 333, 349–50, 761

Moody, James, 314
Morris, Gouverneur, 159; mentioned, 551
[Morton, Perez?], 256
Moultrie, William, mentioned, 260
Mowat, Henry, 257
Murray, David; *see* Stormont, 7th Viscount
Murray, General James, 864; mentioned, 328, 371
Murray, John, 4th Earl Dunmore, mentioned, 753
Murray, William; *see* Mansfield, 1st Earl of
Musgrave, Dr. Samuel, 649

"Nelson" [Perez Morton?], 256
Newcastle; *see* Clinton, Thomas Pelham, 3d Duke
Newcastle, Thomas Pelham-Holles, 1st Duke of, 627
North, Frederick, 2d Earl of Guilford (Lord North), 160–62, 664–66, 672, 675–77, 682, 685, 696, 702–3, 732, 737, 741, 747, 763, 765, 767, 770, 789, 794, 809–11, 813–17a, 819, 823, 853, 856–57, 870–71, 873, 877, 886–88, 893, 896; mentioned, 16, 19, 33, 54, 94, 97, 112, 153, 199, 751, 753, 854
Northington, 1st Earl of; *see* Henley, Robert
Northumberland, 2d Duke of; *see* Percy, Hugh
Norton, Sir Fletcher, 625, 637, 655
Nugent, Robert, 1st Earl, 856

Oglethorpe, James Edward, 806
O'Hara, Charles, 324–25
Oronoco, Prince, of Africa, 745
Orvilliers, Louis Guillouet, Comte de, mentioned, 303–7, 280, 333
Oswald, Richard, mentioned, 822
Otis, James Jr., 163; mentioned, 234

Paine, Thomas, mentioned, 183
Palliser, Admiral Hugh, 827
Parker, Peter, 164; mentioned, 42, 260, 302, 605–6, 611
Parrawankaw, 233
Paul, François Joseph; *see* De Grasse, Comte
Paulding, John, 315

Peale, Angelica, mentioned, 587
Pearson, Richard, mentioned, 133, 309
Pelham-Holles, Thomas; *see* Newcastle, 1st Duke of
Penn, William, mentioned, 584, 588
Percy, Hugh, 2d Duke of Northumberland, 165–67
Petersham, Charles Stanhope, Viscount, 3d Earl Harrington, 168
Petty, William Fitzmaurice; *see* Shelburne, 2d Earl of
Pigot, Robert, mentioned, 286
Pitt, Thomas, 857
Pitt, William, 1st Earl of Chatham (1708–1778), 169–73, 623–24, 626–30, 637, 655, 700–1; mentioned, 22, 357, 692
Pitt, William (1759–1806), 809, 814, 856, 874, 880, 888; mentioned, 857, 873, 897
Pope, the (1779), 754
Portland, William Henry Cavendish-Bentinck, 3d Duke of, 853, 857, 861, 873
Pratt, Charles; *see* Camden, 1st Earl of
Prescott, William, mentioned, 175
Prevost, Augustine, mentioned, 302
Price, Richard, 174
Prince of Wales (later George IV, King of England), 627, 831, 886–88, 896
Putnam, Israel, 175–79; mentioned, 160, 204

Randolph, Peyton, mentioned, 250
Raynal, Guillaume-Thomas-François, 183
Reed, Joseph, 180–82
Richard III, King of England, mentioned, 823
Richmond, Charles Lennox, 3d Duke of, 741, 809, 813–14, 818, 822, 827, 856, 888
Rigby, Richard, 809, 813
Robinson, Mary (Mrs. Thomas), 870
Rochambeau, Jean Baptiste Donatien de Vimeur, Comte de, 324–26, 332–33, 776; mentioned, 52, 318
Rochford, William Henry Nassau Zuylestein, 4th Earl of, 637, 645
Rockingham, Charles Watson-Wentworth, 2d Marquis of, 623–24, 626–27, 813, 819; mentioned, 54, 199, 845

Rodney, George Brydges, 184–85, 762, 766, 769, 775, 791, 793; represented by a whip, 790; mentioned, 313, 320, 330, 790, 869
Rogers, Robert, 186
Rousseau, Jean Jacques, mentioned, 745
Rush, Benjamin, mentioned, 564
Russell, John; *see* Bedford, 4th Duke of

Sackville, George; *see* Germain, George Sackville
Sandwich, John Montagu, 4th Earl of, 620, 623–25, 655, 664–65, 696, 703, 741a, 747, 754, 792, 809–10, 813–15, 817a, 819, 823; as Jemmy Twitcher, 620, 623, 625
Schuyler, Philip John, 187
Scott, Dr. W., 620–21, 623–25; as Antisejanus, 620–21, 623
Sears, Isaac, mentioned, 679
Secker, Thomas, Archbishop of Canterbury, 636
Ségur, Louis Philippe, Comte de, mentioned, 333
Sejanus; *see* Bute
Shakespeare, quoted, 709, 856
Shelburne, William Fitzmaurice Petty, 2d Earl of, 188–89, 628, 815, 822, 827, 829, 845–46, 848–49, 853, 856–57; mentioned, 43, 850
Sheridan, Richard Brinsley, 856, 874, 886, 888
Shirley, Sir Thomas, mentioned, 329
Shuldham, Molyneux, 35
Sidney, Algernon, mentioned, 234, 636, 818, 854
Skene, Philip, 273
Spencer, Charlotte, 160
Squintum, Dr.; *see* Whitefield, George
Stamp, Mr. George; *see* Grenville
Stanhope, Charles; *see* Petersham, Viscount
Stanley, Edward Smith; *see* Derby, 13th Earl
Steuben, Baron Frederick William Augustus von, 190; mentioned, 557
Stiles, Ezra, 191–92
Stormont, David Murray, 7th Viscount, 814, 873
Stuart, Charles Edward, 754
Stuart, John; *see* Bute, 3d Earl of

Suffren Saint-Topez, Pierre André de, 193, mentioned, 282, 302, 303-7, 333
Sullivan, John, 194-96; mentioned, 286, 563

Tarleton, Banastre, 197-98, 831, 864
Temple, George Nugent-Temple-Grenville, 2d Earl, 199
Temple, Richard Grenville, 1st Earl, 627, 630, 655; as Lord Gawkee, 623; mentioned, 199
Thayendanegea (Joseph Brant), 200
Thomas, Isiah, mentioned, 657
Thomson, Charles, 201, 250
Thurlow, Edward Thurlow, 1st Baron, 202, 813, 818, 856-57, 880, 888; mentioned, 897
Thynne, Thomas; see Weymouth, 3d Viscount
Tiyanoka; see Hendrick
Tooke, John Horne, 649, 655, 677
Townshend, Charles, 626-28
Trecothick, Barlow, mentioned, 643, 647
Turner, Samuel, 647
Twitcher, Jemmy; see Sandwich

Van-Dyke, Francis, mentioned, 679
Van Wart, Isaac, 315
Van Zandt, Jacobus, mentioned, 679

Vaughan, Charlotte, 123
Vaughan, John, 791; mentioned, 753
Vergennes, Charles Gravier, Comte de, 203, 332; mentioned, 15, 333
Vredenburgh, Jacob, mentioned, 679

Warburton, William, Bishop of Gloucester, 623-24, 637; mentioned, 620
Ward, Artemas, 508
Warren, Joseph, 204-5; death of, 255-56; mentioned, 333, 761
Washington, George, 206-30, 324, 737, 756, 852, 866; at Trenton, 271; inauguration, 229, 345-47; mentioned, 110, 125, 140, 142, 152, 175, 180, 186-87, 190, 242, 280, 286, 325-26 333, 347, 507, 570, 693, 753, 842
Watons, Wentworth, Charles; see Rockingham, 2d Marquis of
Wayne, Anthony, 232, mentioned, 101, 309, 314
Wedderburn, Alexander; see Loughborough, 1st Baron
Wesley, John, 689
Weymouth, Thomas Thynne, 3d Viscount, 645, 655, 741
White, John, mentioned, 742

Whitefield, George, 232-33; as Dr. Squintum, 233
Wilkes, John, 234, 626-27, 629, 637, 644, 655-56, 665, 671, 675-77, 680, 692, 700, 703, 741, 813, 818, 827; mentioned, 22, 54, 199, 679, 702
William Henry, Prince of England, 313
William III, King of England, mentioned, 489
William V of Holland, 825
Williams, David, 315
Williams, Roger, mentioned, 532
Winchilsea, Edward Finch-Hatton, 7th Earl of, 627, 655
Wolfe, James: mentioned, 4, 6, 16, 357, 369, 371; residence at Gaspé Bay, 372
Wooster, David, 235-37; mentioned, 761

York, Archbishop of; see Markham, William
York, Edward Augustus, Duke of, 626
Yorke, Charles, 725
Young, James, 775

Zoutman, Admiral, mentioned, 303-7
Zuylestein, William Henry Nassau; see Rochford, 4th Earl of